Imperial
Vancouver Island

Other books by J. F. Bosher

The Single Duty Project: A Study of the Movement for a French Customs Union in the 18th Century, London (Athlone Press of the University of London), 1964, 215 pp., maps.

French Finances 1770-1795: From Business to Bureaucracy (Cambridge, Cambridge University Press, 1970), 370 pp. (repr. in soft cover, 2008)

The Canada Merchants, 1713-1763 (Oxford, Clarendon Press, 1987), 234 pp., two maps.

(Editor and contributor), *French Government and Society 1500-1850: Essays in Memory of Alfred Cobban* (London, Athlone Press, 1973), 326 pp.

The French Revolution (New York, W. W. Norton, 1988), LXI and 353 pp., eight maps; English edition (London, Weidenfeld and Nicolson, October 1989); paperback editions in London and New York, 1989.

Men and Ships in the Canada Trade, 1660-1760: A Biographical Dictionary (Ottawa Historic Sites & Monuments, Department of the Environment, 1992), 251 pages in quarto (also published in French).

Business and Religion in the Age of New France: Twenty-two Studies (1600-1760) (Toronto, Canadian Scholars' Press, 1994), 530 pp.

THE GAULLIST ATTACK ON CANADA, 1967-1997 (MONTRÉAL, McGILL-QUEEN'S UNIVERSITY PRESS, DÉCEMBRE 1998) 330 PP. (PAPERBACK EDITION, WITH CORRECTIONS AND A NEW PREFACE, MARCH 2000)

Imperial
Vancouver Island

Who Was Who, 1850-1950

J.F. Bosher

TO my brother and sisters:
Alan, Elisabeth, Avis, and Lorna

"We were everywhere received with 'Rule Britannia' and great demonstrations of Imperial patriotism . . . . Victoria is English with a splendid climate thrown in. Sentiment, vegetation, manners, all revive the best in England."
(Winston Churchill, September 1929)

Library of Congress Control Number:		2010903252
ISBN:	Hardcover	978-1-4500-5963-3
	Softcover	978-1-4500-5962-6
	Ebook	978-1-4500-5964-0

To order additional copies of this book, contact:
Xlibris Corporation
1-888-795-4274
www.Xlibris.com
Orders@Xlibris.com
71090

CONTENTS

PREFACE

If the twenty-first century did not find rambling Victorian titles intolerable, this book might have been called *Some Imperial Campaigners and their Friends on Vancouver Island from the Cariboo Goldrush and the Indian Mutiny to the Invasion from Mainland Canada after the Second World War, 1858-1958*. Settlements like Victoria, Nanaimo, Duncan and most of the rest were founded by sea from England, Scotland, and Ireland, not overland from Canada. In its first century of European occupation the Island was a haven for people from the British Isles, British India, the tropical colonies, and the frozen interior of North America. It was not part of Canada until 1871 and until 1866 it was a separate island colony, like Bermuda, Ceylon, Gibraltar, Hong Kong, Jamaica, Malta, or Singapore. Like them it naturally attracted Chinese, Japanese, Sikhs, and continental European immigrants. Victoria, protected by the Royal Navy at its Esquimalt station nearby, was founded in 1843 and developed as the main port on the west coast of British North America two generations before being overtaken by Vancouver on the mainland. Vancouver did not exist until 1886, when it suddenly sprang up like a mushroom where and when the Canadian Pacific Railway (C.P.R.) reached the Pacific Ocean at Burrard Inlet. A 75-mile sea voyage separated the two cities and Vancouver resembled Winnipeg and Toronto, with which it was linked by rail from its beginning, whereas Victoria, with Esquimalt naval station only three miles to the west, had characteristics in common with other island bases around the British Empire. Of course Canadians and Americans were also present but it is easy to forget that during the last Imperial century, before the Citizenship Act of 1947 and the Liberal Party's maple-leaf flag (1965), there was no Canadian nationality and at least half of Canada's population remained staunchly loyal to the Empire. Even attaching the Island to Imperial Canada was a constitutional act without social consequences for at least two generations. My family, who arrived from England a few at a time beginning in 1863, used to wonder when Canadians would notice this beautiful place, which was neither freezing in winter nor baking hot in summer, nor plagued by Canadian blackflies and mosquitoes. An age without natural gas or electricity was acutely sensitive to the difference.

The Island was visited during its Imperial century by many people who did not settle, such as the Inspector-General Overseas Forces. In the four years before the Great War (1914-18) this was General Sir Ian Hamilton (1853-1947). Much later, in 1935, he wrote the following brief letter to the Editor of *The Times* (London), who printed it on 27 April (p. 13) under the title, "Vancouver Island:"

> Sir,—During the four years of my tenure of the post of Inspector-General Overseas Forces it became my duty to visit every part of the world (except India, but including China) where even small detachments of our Regulars or Volunteers were in being. Knowing this, many British

officers on retirement have asked my advice as to the spot where they could best hope to keep happy and healthy themselves and to bring up happy and healthy families. I have always told them, the North Island of New Zealand or Vancouver Island.

I am, &c.,

Ian Hamilton.
1, Hyde Park Gardens, W.2, April 25

The cumulative effect of this kind of advertising over many years can only have been considerable.

The lives of 769 people who responded to such advertising are briefly summarized in this book. The information has been assembled over the past ten years from many sources and with the kind assistance of many people. This type of knowledge accumulates from a kind of historical gossip, intended to recognize the historic worth of Imperial soldiers, civil servants, engineers, and others too often ignored in an age hostile to what the world now disparages as "imperialism." The descendants of British families on Vancouver Island and elsewhere in Canada have been generous with their records, letters, photographs, and memories. My greatest debt is to John Palmer, son, grandson, and great-grandson of British officers in the Indian Army and the Indian Civil Service, who allowed me to read and copy from his great family collection and inquired among his relatives and friends in Victoria and Duncan for biographical details. Generous help of a similar kind came from Miss Margareta Greta Rice, living on Cedar Hill Road, Victoria; Miss Alison Maude at Fulford Harbour on Salt Spring Island; and in Vancouver city from Mrs. Giles Mackenzie *née* Rachel Jukes, daughter of *Major Andrew Henry Jukes (1885-1956) of the 9th Gurkha Rifles. Further information about the career of Major Jukes emerged from conversations with Sylvia Piddington, elder sister of my university contemporary and friend, Helen Piddington, and Helen also told me about their father, *Major Arthur Grosvenor Piddington (1878-1960), who fought the Great War in the British Army. I learned something of the Lake family from the late Lancelot Lake at his house at Lands End, near Swartz Bay, whence his wife Valerie, daughter of *Lieut.-Colonel Harold Lee-Wright, kindly sent me information about her own and her husband's family. Morgan Scott Ostler, daughter of *Colonel Gerald Bassett Scott (1875-1964), C.B., D.S.O., and sometime town councillor at Campbell River, north of Nanaimo, generously lent me the bulky records of her father's career in India and added her memories of family life and her father's activities in founding the Social Credit movement in Victoria in collaboration with Major A.H. Jukes. In adding my thanks to many individuals in the sources to certain entries I have tried to acknowledge others to whom my gratitude is due.

My brother and sisters have sent informative cuttings from newspapers on Vancouver Island for the past ten years. It was through the kindness of my sister in Oak Bay, Avis Rasmussen, that I contacted Mr. Bevan Gore-Langton, who at his house near Elk Lake told me something of his family and put me in touch with his cousins, John Roome at Maple Bay and Barry Roome at Cobble Hill, descendants of several British officers in the Indian Army. John Roome, who first informed me of the Brigadier Smeeton's career (and gave the Smeetons a cat) is still courteously waiting for something substantial in print! Avis also led me to several other descendants of Imperial families, notably the late Rona Murray, author of *Journey Back to Peshawar* (Victoria, 1993), who graciously brought out family records at her house in Metchosin. She was a daughter of *Major Robert George R. Murray (1888-1973), who retired to the Island after a career around the Empire in the 9th Gurkha Rifles and the Royal Flying Corps. In 2001 Avis and I managed to photograph houses, still identifiable, of the Murrays and other Imperial veterans who had settled between Mount Newton and Brentwood Bay.[1] Thanks also to Avis, I spent a sunny morning with Monica Oldham at her house in the Shoal Bay quarter of Victoria, where she was able to tell me about her family's life at Cobble Hill. Her sister Frances grew up to become the pharmacologist famous for warning the US government about the dangers of thalidomide, but their father, *Lieut.-Colonel Frank Trevor Oldham (1869-1960) was one of those public-spirited Imperials active on the Island for many years and in so many ways. Monica Oldham had also known the *Eardley-Wilmot and *Ravenhill families at Shawnigan Lake. Invited to lunch at the Union Club in Victoria by my lifelong friend, Reg Roy, professor at Victoria University, I met the author of a scholarly biography of William Lyon Mackenzie, Bill Rodney, who put me in touch with John Palmer and with descendants of *Major Orfeur Cavenagh (1885-1971), whose papers are kept at Victoria University. Professor Dorothy Gillian Thompson, my first Ph.D. student in French History, grew up in the Cowichan Valley near the *McLaughlin family of Indian-Army veterans and kindly led me to their descendant, Ian Roberts, on a horse farm at Port Perry, Ontario, who was generous with his collection of family papers when I paid him a visit.

Quite unexpected was the harvest of biographical information learned from friends and acquaintances in Ottawa. There I had access to more Rice papers through the kindness of Mr. Harington Rice, whom I met through Miss Greta Rice. In the New Edinburgh quarter of the city Commander and Mrs. Denis Forster introduced me to the late *Captain C.P. ("Pat") Nixon, R.C.N. (1917-2008), with whom my wife and I lunched almost every week until his death, and had the benefit of his memories of life in the British and Canadian navies as well as his childhood in Victoria and Esquimalt, his father having commanded the Officer's Training College at Royal Roads. Denis Forster, R.C.N., had taken Audrey, his English warbride, to visit a relative near Maple Bay soon after the Second World War, *Major Charles Leathley Armitage (1871-1951), one of the "Old Contemptibles" born in Gloucestershire, and she distinctly remembered Armitage returning to his house near Maple Bay from Duncan distressed by the news that "some damned Canadian is moving in next door!" Armitage quarrelled over water-rights with another neighbour, Mrs. Mainguy, grandmother of Admiral Dan Mainguy,

---

[1]   J.F. Bosher, "Vancouver Island in the Empire," *The Journal of Imperial and Commonwealth History*, vol. 33, no 3 (September 2005), pp. 349-68, SEE pp. 357-61.

another officer of the R.C.N. who retired to Ottawa, and who generously told me about his father, another admiral, and their family of emigrants from the Channel Islands. Dan kindly keeps the local Books-on-Beechwood shop stocked with the privately-published memoirs of the late Mrs. Jean Donald Gow, *Alongside The Navy 1910-1950: An Intimate Account* (Ottawa 1999). *Née* Jean Middleton Donald on 26 January 1903, daughter of *Colonel Dr. David and Mrs. Donald, she grew up at Esquimalt. I asked her on the telephone through her nurses on 12 March 2002 about her father's relationship with *Sir Charles Delmé-Radcliffe, both officers having served in Uganda in the 1890s and both retired to Victoria, B.C., in the 1930s. They were not friends, she said, one having been a civil officer and the other military.[2] During her time as an executive officer at the Canada Council, Audrey Forster met Mrs. Elizabeth Conlon, who responded to my questions with news and photographs of her father, *Brigadier Henry Herbert Montague Oliver (1897-1984), who had retired to Oak Bay, where she kindly showed me his house and more family records. She also gave me some of the papers of her father's friend, *Lieut.-Colonel Henry Shakespear Thuillier, who had fought on the North-West Frontier of India and lived his last years at Oak Bay in a small house on Beach Drive.

Relatives in England of certain Island families were generous with information and intelligently helpful in various way. David Waymouth, an officer retired from the Royal Navy, sent extracts from his mother's journal about the family life of the Harington Rice family. It was Jonathan Berry, my brother-in-law, who made searches in Nanaimo newspapers and put me in touch with Julia Candliss in Ealing, source of information about *Arthur Ward and family, sometime residents of Salt Spring Island. Flying officer (ret'd) H. Playfair, of Blackford House, near Yeovil in Somerst, with fond memories of his service with the R.A.F. at Patricia Bay in North Saanich, sent a photograph and notes on the Playfair family. At Brentwood Bay I spent an afternoon in May 2001 with Joan Playfair, as was, widow of Geoffrey Playfair, and their daughter, Judy White. They told me of Geoffrey Playfair, said to be the first casualty of the Second World War when an aircraft he was piloting for the R.A.F. was shot down on the English coast on 9 September 1939; and of his father, *Lieut.-Colonel Alan Playfair (1868-1952), veteran of the Indian Army, and produced a copy of his scholarly anthropological study, *The Garos* (London, 1909), written after his service in the hills of Assam as deputy-commissioner in eastern Bengal. I am indebted to David Page, editor of The Kipling Journal (London), for assistance in writing about Rudyard Kipling's visits to Vancouver Island and the Victoria Kipling Society there. The adventurous life of *Captain Henry Seymour-Biggs (1876-1952) emerged in letters kindly sent by his daughter Molly Jackson in Australia and from Ken Stofer, one of "Biggs' Boys" living in Oak Bay.

Newspapers in the nineteenth and twentieth centuries were less indiscreet than they are now but printed more and longer obituaries. Men of the armed forces

[2]   She died, aged 102, in Ottawa on 6 November 2005 (*Toronto Globe & Mail*, 9 November 2005, p. R15, obit.

were proudly celebrated by those generations. I have spent several years reading through microfilmed copies of the *Victoria Daily Colonist*, founded in 1858, of the *Cowichan Leader* (1912), the *Sidney and Gulf Islands Review* (1912), the *Victoria Daily Times*, and dipped continually into *The Times* (London) and other British, Canadian, and American newspapers accessible on the internet. Archivists and librarians were unfailingly helpful at the India Office Library, now at the British Library in London, the British National Archives at Kew (formerly Public Record Office), the Genealogical Society in its own building in London near the Barbican, and the Family Research Centre east of King's Cross Station (formerly census records at Somerset House on the Strand), unlike the smocked servingmen, who were as strangely difficult and obtuse as those in French archives, where I had worked on and off for forty years. Staff at County Record Offices in Hereford, Gloucestershire, Oxfordshire, and elsewhere in England went to endless trouble to answer questions and find records and photographs. My thanks are also due to staff members at the British Columbia Archives in Victoria and the City Archives at Duncan. I am grateful for research funds from York University which enabled me to keep my computer running and to buy books. The encouragement—sometimes sceptical—of scholarly friends, especially David Eltis, John Flint, Barry Gough, Harry Judge, and Reg Roy, has been stimulating. Most of all, I hardly know how to thank my wife, *née* Kathryn Cecil Berry, a loving companion who in the course of a busy life has commented with acute good sense during the past ten years on the stories condensed in this book.

A NOTE ON SOURCES

Most of the people in this book wrote about their lives with a modesty that was not false but based on their instinctive reserve and an assumption that it is bad form to talk about oneself, one's own doings, and achievements. Consequently, most of the truth about themselves and their families is not obvious and has to be discovered by research. Their revelations are like icebergs, fascinating to the eye but hinting at much more under the surface. What they wrote about each other tends to be similarly discreet, as they taught their children and expected of one another. In G. M. Young's famous Victorian proverb, "Servants talk about people; gentlefolk discuss things." The noble discretion of *The Times* in London, seldom breached except in reports of divorces, stands even today as a reproach to scurrilous gossip in the tabloid press. Five or six years of reading in back numbers of the *Victoria Daily Colonist* on microfilm convinced me that its editors were likewise discreet.

For an entirely different reason the sources for this book are also largely hidden. The Internet, one of the marvels of our time, offers more and more information, which remains accessible and need not be cited in support of every statement. This is fortunate because Internet addresses are not only rambling and ungainly, but also apt to disappear: "Oops, this link is broken!" too often greets the inquirer. I therefore cite the names of Internet authors, when possible, and trust that some sources online will be maintained come what may and need not be cited. The following may be found from any computer online and are rarely, if ever, acknowledged in this book:

(1) Births, marriages, and deaths in British Columbia are available, respecting only the law that personal information should not be disclosed until twenty years after a person's death. Thus, a death may be found up to within twenty years of the present, whereas a marriage or a birth will not be made public until the people concerned may be presumed dead. Otherwise, the only impediments are results of clerical errors and shortcomings. Clerks, the world over, seem incapable of coping with hyphenated names. The public sometimes filled out official forms so badly that clerks could not read them. For instance, the online recording of births, marriages, and deaths in British Columbia is a wonderfully useful service as a whole, but Alice, wife of *Colonel P. T. Rivett-Carnac, is recorded at her death as "Alice Revett Mar Cornac." Births, marriages, and deaths recorded in the British Isles from 1837 are too expensive in time and money for general use, but an index online indicates the year and quarterly date of these events and, more and more useful, family trees are being offered on the Internet.

(2) Canadian census records for Vancouver Island in 1881, 1891, and especially 1901 are generously offered online by universities on the Island, and authorities in Victoria provide increasing Internet sources. On the other

hand, I have cited British census records because extracting data from them is a tricky business. Six sets of census records—every ten years from 1841 to 1901—are online, but they record age and place of birth, not date of birth, and only at a price. Wives are invariably recorded without their maiden names, which can be difficult or impossible to discover. On the other hand, I have found British authorities at county record offices and elsewhere in Britain to be generous and friendly in response to inquiries, whether in person, by mail, or by e-mail. Various Internet chat lines are also useful. Genealogy must be one of the leading retirement hobbies throughout the Western world!

(3) For the Great War (1914-1919), the National Archives of Canada (NAC) offers online the essential two pages of records from the Canadian Expeditionary Force. These give place and date of birth, name of next of kin, previous military experience if any, religion, height, weight, colour of eyes and complexion, and identifying marks on the body. The limitations of this data are that some soldiers declared themselves to be older or younger than they were in order to get into the army and the recording clerks sometimes misspelled names. Some German names were crossed out and replaced by an anglicised version, apparently on the advice of the recruiting officers. The original files at the National Archives of Canada usually hold medical records and pay records not cited on the Internet. There is not yet an equivalent system for sailors, airmen, or civil servants.

Only brief entries—sometimes none at all—are given in this book for people already entered into the *Dictionary of Canadian Biography* or the *Dictionary of National Biography* because they are readily accessible and usually offer the best possible accounts with full lists of sources.

Some sources are abbreviated as follows:

Bateman, *The Great Landowners*—John Bateman, FRGS, *The Great Landowners of Great Britain and Ireland: A List of all Owners of Three Thousand Acres and Upwards; also One Thousand Three Hundred Owners of Two Thousand Acres and Upwards* (4th ed.; Harrison, 1883), 533 pp.

Begg, *History of British Columbia*—Alexander Begg (1825-1905), *History of British Columbia from its Earliest Discovery to the Present Time* (Toronto, William Briggs, 1894; facsimile edition, Toronto, McGraw-Hill-Ryerson, 1972), 568 pp.

Colonist—the *British Colonist* then the *Victoria Daily Colonist* (1858-1974), and finally the *Times-Colonist*. A searchable online version beginning in 2008 was too late to be used for this book.

DCB—*Dictionary of Canadian Biography*, (Toronto, University of Toronto Press, 1966 and following years, 14 vols. to the present) and online.

Duffus, *Beyond the Blue Bridge*—*Beyond the Blue Bridge: Stories from Esquimalt: History and Reminiscences compiled by The Esquimalt Silver Threads Writers Group*, ed. Maureen Duffus, (Victoria, Ventura Publishing, 1990), 189 pp.

Elliott, *Memories of the Chemainus Valley*—*Memories of the Chemainus Valley: A History of People: Saltair, Chemainus, Westholme, Crofton, Thetis, Kuper and Reid Islands*, ed., Gordon Elliott, (Victoria, Chemainus Valley Historical Society, 1978), 389 pp.

Gosnell, *The Year Book*—R.E. Gosnell, (1860-1931), *The Year Book of British Columbia, 1911-1914* (Victoria, British Columbia, Queen's Printer, 1897, revised in 1911 and 1914), 405 pp.

Howay and Gosnell, *British Columbia*—*British Columbia from the Earliest Times to the Present*, ed. Howay and Gosnell, (4 vols.; Vancouver, S.J. Clarke Publishing, 1914), vols III and IV consist of biographical notes and photos of some 1,350 men.

Hughes, *Shawnigan Lake, 1887-1967*—E.J. Hughes, Bruce Hutchison and Willard Ireland, *Green Branches and Fallen Leaves: The Story of a Community: Shawnigan Lake, 1887-1967* (Shawnigan Lake Confederation Centennial Celebrations Committee of 1966-67, 1967), 74 pp. in 4°

Kahn, *Salt Spring Island*—Charles Kahn, *Salt Spring: The Story of an Island* (Madeira Park, British Columbia, Harbour Publishing, 1998), 344 pp.

Longstaff, *Esquimalt Naval Base*—Major F. V. Longstaff, *Esquimalt Naval Base: A History of its Work and its Defences* (Victoria, B.C., The Victoria Book & Stationery Co. Ltd., 1941), 189 pp. + 7 plates.

Lugrin, *Pioneer Women*—N. de Bertrand Lugrin, *The Pioneer Women of Vancouver Island, 1843-1866* (Victoria, British Columbia, The Women's Canadian Club of Victoria, 1928), 312 pp.

MacFarlane—John M. MacFarlane, *Commissioned and Warrant Officers of the Royal Canadian Navy, 1910-1939* (Victoria, Maritime Museum of British Columbia Press, 1993), 71 pp.

Morgan, *Canadian Men and Women*—Henry James Morgan, *The Canadian Men and Women of the Time: A Hand-book of Canadian Biography of Living Characters* (2nd edn., Toronto, William Briggs, 1912), 1218 pp.

NAC, CEF—National Archives of Canada (Ottawa), Canadian Expeditionary Force.

Oxford DNB—Oxford Dictionary of National Biography (Oxford, Oxford University Press, 2004-2009) and online.

Pritchard, *Letters of Edmund Hope Verney—The Vancouver Island Letters of Edmund Hope Verney, 1862-65,* ed. Allan Pritchard (Vancouver, U.B.C. Press, 1996), 307 pp.

Riddick, *Who in British India—*John F. Riddick, *Who was Who in British India* (Westport, Conn., Greenwood Press, 1998), 445 pp.

Walbran, *B.C. Coast Names—*Captain John Thomas Walbran, RN, *British Columbia Coast Names, 1592-1906, Their Origin and History* (Ottawa, Government Printing Bureau, 1909; repr. Vancouver, J. J. Douglas Ltd., 1971), 546 pp.

Whitaker's—Whitaker's Naval and Military Directory and Indian Army List 1900 (London, Whitaker & Sons, 12 Warwick Lane, EC, 1900), 935 pp.

Who's Who in B.C.—Who's Who in British Columbia, 7 vols., 1930-48 (various BC editors and publishers in New Westminster, Vancouver City, and Victoria).

Williams, *The Story of St Peter's—*Williams, David Ricardo, *Pioneer Parish: The Story of St Peter's Quamichan* (Duncan, St Peter's Parish, 1991) 92 pp.

ABBREVIATIONS AND SYMBOLS

APM = Acting Provost Marshal or Assistant Provost Marshal

BC = British Columbia

BNA = British National Archives (Kew), formerly Public Record Office.

CB = Companion of The Most Honourable Order of the Bath (1725)

GCB = Knight Commander (KCB) and Companion (CB) of the Bath (1725)

CBE, (KBE) = Companion (Knight Comm'der) of the Order of the Br. Empire (1917)

CE = Civil Engineer

CEF = Canadian Expeditionary Force (in the Great War of 1914-1918)

CIE (KCIE) = Companion (Knight Comm'der) of the Order of the Indian Empire

CMG = Companion of the Order of St Michael and St George (1818)

KCMG = Knight Commander of the Order of St Michael and St George (1818)

GCMG = Knight Grand Cross of the Order of Saint Michael and Saint George (1818)

CO = Commanding Officer

CPR = Canadian Pacific Railway

CSI = Companion of the Most Exalted Order of the Star of India

CVO = Companion of the Royal Victorian Order (1896)

DCOR = Duke of Connaught's Own Rifles

DFC = Distinguished Flying Cross (1918)

DFM = Distinguished Flying Medal (1918)

DLS = Dominion Land Surveyor

DSC = Distinguished Service Cross (1901)

DSM = Distinguished Service Medal (1914)

DSO = Companion of the Distinguished Service Order (1886)

FRGS = Fellow of the Royal Geographical Society

GCVO = Knight Grand Cross of the Royal Victoria Order (1896)

GOC = General Officer Commanding

HBC = Hudson's Bay Company

HEIC = Honourable East India Company

HMS = His (her) Majesty's Ship

HQ = Headquarters

ICS = [British] Indian Civil Service

JP = Justice of the Peace

KCMG = Knight Commander of the Order of St Michael and St George (1818)

KG or LG = Knight of the Order of the Garter (1348)

MBE = Member of the Order of the British Empire (1917)

MC = Military Cross (28 December 1915)

MEF = Military Expeditionary Force

MEIC = Member of the Engineering Institute of Canada

MM = Military Medal (1916)
MP = Member of Parliament
MVO = Member of the Royal Victorian Order (1896)
NAC = National Archives of Canada in Ottawa
NLC = National Library of Canada in Ottawa
NWT = North West Territories
OBE = Officer of the Order of the British Empire (1917)
PA = political agent (in India)
PLS = Provincial Land Surveyor
PPCLI = Princess Patricia's Canadian Light Infantry
PWD = Public Works Department
RAF = Royal Air Force
RAMC = Royal Army Medical Corps
RCA = Royal Canadian Artillery
RCAF = Royal Canadian Air Force
RCN = Royal Canadian Navy
RCR = Royal Canadian Rifles
RFA = Royal Field Artillery
RFC = Royal Flying Corps
RMA = Royal Military Academy (at Sandhurst)
RMC = Royal Military College (1) Surrey (2) Kingston, Ont.
RN = Royal Navy
RCNWM Police = Royal Canadian North West Mounted Police
SPCK = Society for the Promotion of Christian Knowledge
TD = Territorial Decoration
VD = Volunteer Decoration
VI = Vancouver Island
YMCA = Young Men's Christian Association

INTRODUCTION

* A person with an entry in the A to Z pages below.

The lives of families migrating to Victoria, Esquimalt, Duncan, and other Island communities formed a social fabric binding Vancouver Island to the British Isles in the century 1850 to 1950. Personal correspondence and journeys back and forth reinforced the maritime links tying the Island to London, Bristol, Portsmouth, Glasgow and other British ports. In this and other ways the Island was like Bermuda, Bombay, Gibraltar, Hong Kong, Malta, St Helena, Singapore, Trincomalee (Ceylon), and other naval stations and ports around the empire. For a hundred years from the 1850s, the great age of the passenger liner, Imperial officers and their families arrived on the Island in ships from overseas or in coastal steamers from mainland North America. Many Imperials discovered the Island accidentally on their way home to England or Scotland across the Pacific Ocean from the Orient. Many others, such as Rudyard Kipling, I suspect, went to have a look in case they might decide to retire there. Kipling visited Victoria three times before deciding to settle in Sussex.[3]

For much of that century, Great Britain owned more ocean-going vessels than the rest of the world put together. Trans-Atlantic liners offered comfortable cabins for those who could afford them as well as the infamous huddled spaces on lower steerage decks for poorer emigrants. In words from one of Kipling's *Just So Stories* famously set to music by his contemporary, Edward German, soon after it was published in 1902,

> Yes, weekly from Southampton,
> Great steamers white and gold
> Go rolling down to Rio
> (Roll down, roll down to Rio!)

---

[3] J. F. Bosher, "Vancouver Island and the Kiplings," *The Kipling Journal* (London), vol. 83, no. 332 (June 2009), pp. 8-22.

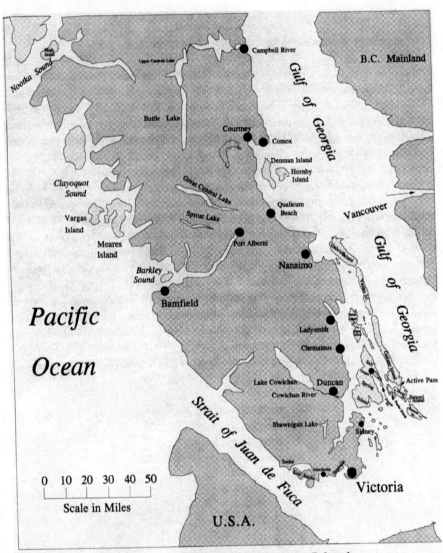

Nootka Sound

Upper Campbell Lake

● Campbell River

B.C. Mainland

Buttle Lake

Courtney ●
● Comox

Denman Island

Hornby Island

Clayoquot Sound

Great Central Lake

Vargas Island

Sproat Lake

Qualicum Beach ●

Meares Island

Port Alberni ●

Vancouver

Barkley Sound

Nanaimo ●

Gulf of Georgia

Gulf of Georgia

Bamfield ●

Pacific

Ladysmith ●

Ocean

Chemainus ●

Active Pass

Lake Cowichan
Cowichan River

Duncan ●

Shawnigan Lake

Sidney ●

Sooke
Metchosin

Victoria ●

Strait of Juan de Fuca

0	10	20	30	40	50

Scale in Miles

U.S.A.

The Southern Half of Vancouver Island
(The coastline is not accurate but only approximate.)

J.F. Bosher

Vancouver Island (South)

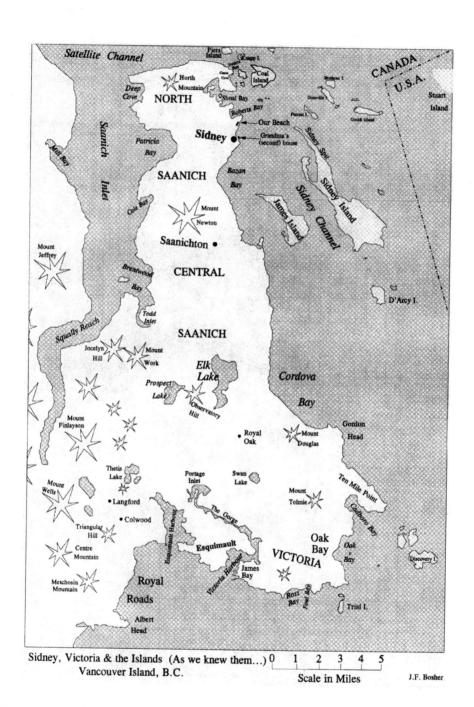

Sidney, Victoria & the Islands (As we knew them...)
Vancouver Island, B.C.

0   1   2   3   4   5
Scale in Miles

J.F. Bosher

Saanich Peninsula

Aerial View of Saanich Peninsula looking west

The Royal Navy had a station at Rio for many years to protect British shipping, and in the early 1860s Esquimalt was adopted as a station to replace Valparaiso on the coast of Chile.[4] Latin American ports were not as foreign then as they are now. The harbour at Valparaiso had been occupied in 1808 by the South America Station of the RN and served from 1837 as an early base for a new squadron as the navy gradually moved into the Pacific Ocean, east of the meridian 170_ West longitude, which is to say the half of that ocean off the western shores of South, Central, and North America.[5] The other half of the Pacific, west of the meridian 170_ West, began to be patrolled at about the same time by ships on the East Indies and China stations, which shared it from 1859 with the new Australia Station near Sydney.[6]

It is worth stressing that these naval advances into the Pacific Ocean from east and west, and the formation of the Pacific Squadron, were by no means parts of a concerted plan to take control of the region. They were partly exploratory and scientific, like the earlier voyages of captains James Cook and George Vancouver, and partly strategic, but only in the sense of being wary anticipations of foreign threats to British merchant shipping. The navy followed trade, and in the 1840s, British merchants settled in what Captain Cook had named the Sandwich Islands (Hawaii). *Richard William Janion was one of these before he moved to Victoria. Bases in the Pacific, like those in the Mediterranean and the southern oceans, were picked up one by one, sometimes reluctantly in the course of defensive arrangements, not in a strategy of grasping imperial ambitions.[7] Britain rarely, if ever, had such ambitions in Victorian times. Her investments in South America were immense, and when Argentina threatened to default on its loans in 1890, British forces might have taken control of the country if the government in London had not been still reeling from the consequences of having seized Egypt and the Sudan following Cairo's default on loans in 1882.[8] There was little desire to assume another such responsibility. Any national or concerted imperial strategy that might have been worked out would have been severely hampered, in any event,

---

[4]   Barry Gough, "Sea Power and South America," in Gough, *Britain, Canada and the North Pacific* (Aldershot, Hampshire, England, Ashgate Variorum, 2004), ch. xiii.

[5]   Barry Gough, *The Royal Navy and the Northwest Coast of North America, 1810-1914: A Study of British Maritime Ascendancy* (Vancouver, University of British Columbia Press, 1971), pp. 30, 243-5.

[6]   John Bach, *The Australia Station: A History of the Royal Navy in the South West Pacific, 1821-1913* (Kensington, NSW, Australia, New South Wales University Press, 1986), 260 pp.

[7]   W. P. Morrell, *Britain in the Pacific Islands* (Oxford, Clarendon Press, 1960), pp. 13-38; C. J. Lowe, *The Reluctant Imperialists: British Foreign Policy, 1878-1902* (Macmillan, 1967), 417 pp.; Sir Harry Luke, "The British Islands of the Pacific," in *The British Empire*, ed., Hector Bolitho (Batsford, 1947), pp. 218-19.

[8]   P. J. Cain and A. G. Hopkins, *British Imperialism 1688-2000* (2nd ed., Pearson Education Ltd., 2002), chapter 9, "Calling the New World into Existence: South America, 1815-1914."

by continual wrangling in London between a vigilant Treasury and the Admiralty, the War Office, the Colonial Office and the Foreign Office.[9]

As well as ships routinely stationed at Esquimalt, as at every station around the world, the RN had other vessels continually moving from one naval base to another in Victorian times. HMS *Sparrowhawk* arrived at Esquimalt on 28 October 1865 to find four other ships of the Royal Navy there, as well as a vessel of the U.S. Navy.[10] At least, one ship set out for Esquimalt each year, hoping to arrive before Queen Victoria's birthday celebrations on 24 May. It sailed (steamed from the 1890s) across the Atlantic to the Falkland Islands and around Cape Horn to Valparaiso, which was "nothing more than an English colony,"[11] a Chilean historian observed in 1880, stopping next perhaps at Callao, a lovely harbour near Lima, Peru, before moving northwards along the coast of California past—or perhaps visiting—San Francisco. During the summer, they would move about almost continually from Esquimalt to Alaska or to the Behring Sea and, in the autumn, visit Honolulu, then Tahiti, the Marquesas, and Easter Island, and so work back past the Galapagos Islands to a South American port where mails from home would have accumulated.[12] Valparaiso and Callao, stopping points on the way out to the Pacific North-West, were open to the Royal Navy as a result of vigorous British help in the struggle for Chilean and Peruvian independence from Spain early in the nineteenth century. This was in an old tradition, for British ships had attacked those parts of the Spanish Empire from time to time, beginning with Sir Francis Drake, who captured Valparaiso in 1578 and sacked Callao a few months later.

The freedom of these ports was part of an informal British empire in Spanish America marked also by investments, railways, engineering projects, and English-speaking settlements.[13] In its old Caribbean colonies and in taking over the Falkland Islands (more islands!) in 1832-1833, Britain was apparently ignoring the Monroe Doctrine by which the United States warned European nations in December 1823 to stay out of the Americas, but in the nineteenth century, London had no intention of seizing any Latin American country. Indeed, a team

---

9   Lance Edwin Davis and Robert A. Huttenback, *Mammon and the Pursuit of Empire: The Economics of British Imperialism, 1860-1912* (Abridged, ed., NY, Cambridge UP, 1988), pp. 112-21, "The Costs of Defending an Empire."

10 E. A. Porcher, *A Tour of Duty in the Pacific Northwest: E. A. Porcher and HMS* Sparrowhawk, *1865-1868,* ed., Dwight L. Smith (Fairbanks, Alaska, University of Alaska Press, 2000), p. 37. The four RN vessels were the *Sutlej,* the *Devastation,* the *Clio,* and the *Forward.*

11 Quoted in Cain and Hopkins, *British Imperialism, 1688-2000,* p. 268.

12 Major F. V. Longstaff, *Esquimalt Naval Base: A History of its Work and its Defences* (Victoria, BC, The Victoria Book & Stationery Co. Ltd., 1941), pp. 5-6. In 1887, the All Red Route between Britain and India via Hong Kong was inaugurated by the completion of the CPR to Port Moody and extended to what was to become the port of Vancouver.

13 John Darwin, *The Empire Project: The Rise and Fall of the British World-System, 1830-1970* (Cambridge University Press, 2009), pp. 135-141; Cain and Hopkins, *British Imperialism,* pp. 126, 258, 268, note 133; C. E. Carrington, *The British Overseas* (Cambridge, Cambridge University Press, 1950, pp. 1046-49.

of U.S. naval historians declared, at an international naval conference I attended at Greenwich in 1974, that any enforcement of the Monroe Doctrine depended on informal British assistance, a kind of naval "umbrella" maintained by the Royal Navy in 1823 and for many years.[14] After helping South American countries to win independence from Spain, Britain had no desire to do as the French Emperor Napoleon Bonaparte III did when he sent an army to seize control of Mexico in 1861 and persisted until defeated in 1867. It was as part of the British naval "umbrella" that Esquimalt was maintained.

The naval "umbrella" was a vital part of what John Darwin calls "the British world system" and that system is the real context of Vancouver Island's history—usually missing in Canadian historical writing.[15] The British government defended Vancouver Island as a separate British colony until 1866 and then decided to combine it with the newer colony of British Columbia founded in 1858. The Island was not a part of Canada until 1871, when London coaxed these combined colonies to join the Canadian Confederation. By then the Island's social character had been formed and it was attracting British officers and their friends from all over the British Empire for a variety of reasons discussed below. The Canadian Pacific Railway, which reached the coast in 1886, brought large numbers of British emigrants as well as Canadians. In the next few year others began to arrive by sea from the Orient on the "Empress" liners of the CPR's transpacific passenger fleet. Not until the Second World War (1939-46) did circumstances begin to discourage such immigrants. Not until after the war did the Island lose its British complexion with the arrival of more and more people from continental Canada.

A Canadian Continental Outlook

As people flooded in from east of the Rocky Mountains during and after the Second World War, they assumed a corollary right to Vancouver Island's history. Canadian historians tended to pick up the threads of the colony's story as though the founders were hardly worth bothering about. Salish and other tribes of aboriginals have always been able to say—though unfortunately not to write—"We knew the Island thousands of years before Captains Cook and Vancouver thought they had 'discovered' it." With just as much reason and in the same spirit, British historians might rewrite the Island's history as a part of the empire's expansion

---

[14] See also F. Thistlethwaite, "The United States and the Old World, 1794-1828," *New Cambridge Modern History*, vol. IX (Cambridge, Cambridge University Press, 1965), pp. 591-2.

[15] In writing about the Imperial context of Vancouver Island's history I have been guided by three great studies: John Darwin, *The Empire Project: The Rise and Fall of the British World System, 1830-1970* (Cambridge University Press, 2009), 800 pp.; P. J. Cain & A. G. Hopkins, *British Imperialism 1688-2000* (2nd edition, Longmans, 2002), 739 pp.; and Ronald Robinson & John Gallagher, *Africa and the Victorians: The Official Mind of Imperialism* (Macmillan, 1961), 491 pp., and their article "The Imperialism of Free Trade," *Economic History Review*, 2nd series, vol. VI, no. 1 (1953), pp. 1-15.

into the Pacific Ocean. The change in perspective would be substantial because the Island's past usually appears in Canadian history as if written by someone gazing across the continent from Montreal, Toronto, or Winnipeg. The view from the sea, the maritime story, as well as the Imperial story viewed from London or Victoria are usually absent or relegated to specialised or local studies, to articles in learned journals, and sometimes only to footnotes. Patriotic Canadians tend to regard the empire as foreign to their own national history, which is impoverished, even falsified, as a result. The British empire is a controversial subject in our time, as it was in Britain throughout the nineteenth century, but readers with broader horizons know that historical writing proceeds by an endless series of scholarly judgements, as if decided in a court of law. Precedents and traditions become established in history books as well as in law courts. Some general histories of the empire are written by witnesses for the prosecution, ready to blacken its memory as best they can. Others seem inclined to reflect the case for the defence, pointing out the empire's benefits in dauntingly cruel and corrupt parts of the world, and (as Gladstone hoped) "contributing to the general happiness of mankind."[16] Seekers after truth must make their way through many contradictions in historical writing.

Canadian perspectives have tended to be narrowly continental. They seldom reach out as far as the Island's British imperial context. Thus, Donald Creighton made a brief reference to "the British traders and explorers who came by the far easier sea route to grasp their share of the riches of Alaska seal and sea otter," but he buried it in a paragraph about the overland activities of the North West Company of Montreal and another on Canadian Confederation. A. R. M. Lower disposed of Captain Cook in an account of the continental explorations of Alexander Mackenzie, Simon Fraser, and David Thompson, all moving west from Canada, as if British Columbia were founded in the process. Lower read widely and reflected on world history in general but, passing quickly over the nineteenth century on the Pacific Coast and hustling British Columbia into Confederation, he wanted his readers to believe that by 1900, "there was already much difference between Vancouver Island as part of Canada and Newfoundland, a remote British colony."[17] Remote from where? And in what sense? Similarly, Edgar McInnis, in a chapter entitled "Dominion from Sea to Sea," forgot about the sea and only touched upon threats of American annexation and the financial difficulties drawing British Columbia into Confederation.[18] A similar silence about the Island's vital maritime and British Imperial origins mars a more recent study of the province

---

[16] For instance, Cain & Hopkins, *British Imperialism 1688-2000*.; Denis Judd, *Empire: The British Imperial Experience from 1765 to the Present* (HarperCollins Phoenix, 1996), 520 pp.; the quotation is in Darwin, *The Empire Project*, p. 146.

[17] A. R. M. Lower, *Colony to Nation: A History of Canada* (Toronto, Longmans, Green & Co., 1946), pp. 144-45, 404; in his study, *A Pattern for History* (Toronto, McClelland & Stewart, 1978), 381 pp., Lower's lofty, misty vision overlooked western Canada.

[18] Edgar McInnis, *Canada, a Political and Social History* (3rd ed., Toronto, Holt, Rinehart & Winston, 1969), pp. 316-17, 368-69.

by Brett McGillivray, who has devoted two pages to "First Nations, Claiming Back the Land" but none to the founding British.[19] More thorough and scholarly was Arthur S. Morton's chapter on "The Pacific Colonies, 1849-67," but it incorporated the Island's history even more firmly in a study of the Canadian west before British Columbia joined the Canadian Confederation.[20] Even the eagle eye of C. E. Carrington, a New Zealander by birth, was deflected by the specialised work on which he naturally depended for his quick summary of the British diaspora in the North-West Pacific. He put the Island's history in its Imperial context, but his sources led him to wrap it in a subchapter headed "Canadian Confederation, 1846-1867."[21] Special studies tend to convey a similar impression of narrowness by approaching Imperial loyalties in Canada as anomalous curiosities, as Carl Berger did in a much—cited scholarly study.[22]

A major event in Canadian national history, Confederation has been allowed to overshadow the Island's economic and social development, but the naval and diplomatic background has been similarly distorted. An official Canadian anthology of documents about Canadian relations with the United States went as far as omitting almost all references to BC and the Island in the years before they joined the Dominion in 1871.[23] It was silent about London's defensive negotiations with Spanish, Russian, and American authorities. The founding activities of the British, who established the Island colony and defended the Pacific Coast in general, have been all but excluded from this and most other histories of Canada. They were explicitly and indignantly excluded in the 1950s by Jean Bruchesi, who spoke for a part of the French Canadian population in resenting even the name British Columbia, *"qui aurait dû prendre alors le nom officiel de Colombie canadienne."*[24] In mentioning the province, Bruchesi preferred to call it simply "Colombie."[25] But he was thinking like many other Canadians, not only Québecois, when leaving the history of the British Empire in the Pacific region out of his country's history.

A continental view of the Island and its history also dominates the study of the Hudson's Bay Company, which pursued animal furs westwards across the prairies

---

[19]   Brett McGillivray, *Canada, A Nation of Regions* (Don Mills, Oxford University Press, 2009), ch. 10, "British Columbia, Canada's New Front Door," pp. 310-11.

[20]   Arthur S. Morton, *A History of the Canadian West to 1870-71* (Thomas Nelson & Sons Ltd., 1939), pp. 750-801, of which only pp. 750-68 treat the Island as a separate colony.

[21]   C. E. Carrington, *The British Overseas: Exploits of a Nation of Shopkeepers* (Cambridge, Cambridge University Press, 1950), pp. 549-52.

[22]   Carl Berger, *The Sense of Power: Studies in the Ideas of Canadian Imperialism, 1867-1914* (University of Toronto Press, 1970), 377 pp.

[23]   *Treaties and Agreements Affecting Canada in Force Between His Majesty and the United States of America, with Subsidiary Documents* (Ottawa, F.A. Acland, Printer to the King's Most Excellent Majesty, 1927.)

[24]   Jean Bruchesi, *Histoire du Canada* (nouvelle édition, Montréal, Éditions de Beauchemin, 1954, "Couronné par l'Académie française"), p. 544. Bruchesi's *Histoire* breathes hostility to the British overlords.

[25]   Bruchesi, *Histoire*, p. 380.

and over the Rocky Mountains to New Caledonia, as the territory was called until 20 August 1858, when Queen Victoria named it British Columbia.[26] In the years 1901-1914, the rail and passenger ferries to the Island, the Esquimalt and Nanaimo Railway, and the Canadian Pacific Navigation Company, including the transpacific passenger service, were all taken over by the CPR, but the history of that company has been written mainly as a continental story.[27] Not until the twenty-first century did Canadian scholars show a serious interest in the great maritime side of the HBC. Even then, two students of the company found themselves obliged to compile their own list of its ships, there being as yet no full and reliable account of early shipping to the Island.[28] Their careful work in this field was carried out against the prevailing Canadian bias. Ordinary readers must discover for themselves that not only did the HBC have a fleet of ships on the Pacific Coast, beginning with the *Columbia* and the more famous *Beaver*, which both reached the Columbia River from Gravesend in 1836, but there were also many private shipping ventures to the Island before it became a part of Canada.[29] It was the *Beaver*, which carried *Sir James Douglas several hundred miles north from Fort Vancouver on his historic voyage in spring 1843 to found Fort Victoria at the southern end of the Island.[30] Much detailed history has been written about later shipping at Victoria, Esquimalt, and elsewhere on the Island, as well as the worldwide role of British shipping in Victorian and Edwardian times, but no maritime equivalent to the standard continental history of Canada has ever appeared. Professor Barry Gough has been almost alone in pursuing the vital history of the Royal Navy in British Columbia. As for commercial shipping, few serious studies have added to the great compilation about maritime life on the north-west coast, which E. W. Wright published in 1895 at Portland, Oregon.[31] In short, the fundamental maritime aspect of Vancouver

[26]   John S. Galbraith, *The Hudson's Bay Company as an Imperial Factor, 1821-1869* (Toronto, University of Toronto Press, 1957), 500 pp.; E. E. Rich, *The History of the Hudson's Bay Company 1670-1870* (2 vols., The Hudson's Bay Record Society, 1959), vol. II (1763-1870), 974 pp.

[27]   John A. Eagle, *The Canadian Pacific Railway and the Development of Western Canada* (Montrel, McGill-Queen's University Press, 1989), 325 pp.; W. Kaye Lamb, *History of the Canadian Pacific Railway* (New York, Macmillan, 1977), 491 pp; John Murray Gibbon, *The Romantic History of the Canadian Pacific Railway: The Northwest Passage of Today* (New York, Tudor Publishing Co., 1937), 407 pp.

[28]   Judith Hudson Beattie and Helen M. Buss, eds., *Undelivered Letters to Hudson's Bay Company Men on the Northwest Coast of America, 1830-57* (Vancouver, UBC Press, 2003), pp. 408-415.

[29]   Derek Pethick, *S. S. Beaver: The Ship that Saved the West* (Vancouver, Mitchell Press Ltd., 1970), pp. 19-20 and *passim*.

[30]   Pethick, *S. S. Beaver*, pp. 45-46.

[31]   E. W. Wright, *Lewis & Dryden's marine history of the Pacific Northwest an illustrated review of the growth and development of the maritime industry, from the advent of the earliest navigators to the present time, with sketches and portraits of a number of well known marine men* (Portland,

Island, commercial, naval, and Imperial, is seldom allowed to intrude in Canadian accounts of British Columbia's history.

A maritime history of the north-west Pacific Coast is beyond the scope of this book, but something must be said about the need for it in explaining the origins and character of Vancouver Island. Barrie Gough's research into the history of the Royal Navy in that part of the world was all the more original because when he began to study the subject in England at King's College London, his PhD supervisor, Professor Gerald Graham, told him that the subject was not worth bothering about! Already something of a professional Canadian at King's College earlier, when I was there as assistant lecturer (1956-1959), Graham was an excellent senior scholar, but he grew up in Ontario and was typically ignorant of Pacific Coast history. As for commercial shipping, it still awaits its historian, though much incidental writing by W. Kaye Lamb and others has broached the subject. *Lloyd's Register*, compiled annually in London until 1873, offers tantalizing glimpses of what remains to be studied. The *Register* for the year beginning 1 July 1864, for example, lists twenty-two ships making the voyage from a British port to the Island in that year, most of them otherwise unknown. Their owners, captains, and passengers remain as obscure as if they lived on the moon.

Oregon, Lewis & Dryden Printing Co., 1895; repr. NY, Antiquarian Press, 1961; repr. Seattle, Washington, Superior Publishing Company, 1967) 494 pp.

Table II

Lloyd's Register of Ships Bound for Vancouver Island, 1 July 1864 to 30 June 1865				
Ship's	Captain	Tonnage	Owner	Home Port
Ashmore	Jenkins	430	Avery	Bristol
Friar	F. Chambers	565	Betts & Co.	Newcastle
Cyclone	J. Hossack	594	Cattock & Son	Aberdeen
Dusty Miller	J. Marks	596	J. Owen	Liverpool
Envoy	Fyffe	389	Tonge & Co.	Liverpool
Fairlight	W. Bush	588	Redfern & Co.	London
Windham	M. Young	864	McKenzie	London
Stephenson	Westlake	392	Westlake	Scarborough
Kaffir Chief	R. Griffin	187	W. Langton	London
Otter	Miller	275	HBC	London
Philippine	Davies	295	W. O. Young	London
Princess of Wales	Kingcome	583	HBC	London
Rising Sun	B. Bustin	824	Wright & Co.	St John
Rosedale	Phillips	459	Shepherd & Gourlay	London, Glasgow
Sea Nymph	Hppnh'm	256	Besant jr.	London
Vancouver	R. Peck	1101	W de Mttos	London

Source: *Lloyd's Register of British and Foreign Shipping. From 1st July, 1864, to the 30th June, 1865* (Cox and Wyman, Printers, 1864; repr. Gregg Press, 1964), no pagination.

In Canada, a continental approach to the Island's past, reinforced perhaps by a growing hostility to the British Empire, has blotted out the essential maritime past. At best, shipping between the British Isles and Vancouver Island has been reduced to a short chapter about the approach from the sea.[32] There has been an almost unconscious narrowing of the worldwide Imperial perspective of earlier times to a national one in which the central thread has been the history of a separate Canadian identity. In this, the Island's own history is missing. There is no mention, for instance, of the hydrographic surveys of shipping routes from England past the Falkland Islands, through the Strait of Magellan, and up the western coasts of South, Central, and North America and the Hawaiian Islands (before they were annexed to the American empire in 1897-1898). The route "around Cape Horn" for sailing ships was usually through the Strait of Magellan for steam—driven vessels. About 330 miles (530 km.) long and from 2½ to 15 miles (4-24 km) wide, usually beset by fog, heavy rain, violent westerly winds, and sudden squalls, the Strait of Magellan afforded too little room for tacking about. In any event, there had been sketch-maps and instructions for mariners but no full, reliable charts. Commercial shipping on this route was too risky until London produced new charts from the work of a five-year hydrographic expedition (1826-1831) under officers of the Royal Navy followed by another in 1866-1869 by the steamer HMS *Nassau* under *Captain (later Rear Admiral) Richard Charles Mayne as well as extensive surveys of waters around Vancouver Island.[33] Establishing and charting this trade route were considerable achievements. The great Pacific Ocean is anything but pacific, as Lady Harriet Dufferin, wife of a governor general, wrote on 13 August 1876 aboard HMS *Amethyst*: "The Pacific is even a nastier ocean than I imagined, very much nastier than the Atlantic."[34]

The Island in the Pax Britannica

By the time Victoria was founded, in 1843, the empire was faced with enemies different from those that had threatened the first British Empire. France was hostile to Great Britain throughout much of the nineteenth century, but it was no longer the threat it had been before the victories at Trafalgar (1805) and Waterloo (1815). Until then, it had always been ready to challenge British Imperial forces all over the world and had sent out an astonishing number of fleets to invade the British

---

[32]   Margaret Ormsby, *British Columbia, A History* (Vancouver, Macmillan, 1958), ch. 1.

[33]   Rear Admiral G. S. Ritchie, *The Admiralty Chart: British Naval Hydrography in the Nineteenth Century* (NY, Elsevier Publishing Co., 1967), ch. 12; *Proceedings of the Royal Geographical Society and Monthly Record of Geography*, New Monthly Series, Vol. 14, No. 7 (July 1892), pp. 473-474, by Admiral Sir George H. Richards, KCB, FRS.

[34]   The Marchiness of Dufferin and Ava, *My Canadian Journal 1872-8, Extracts from My Letters Home* (John Murray, 1891), p. 250. She added, "and the Captain's cabin [is] the least nice place one could possibly be in. The screw thumps and vibrates directly under it, and the pitching is longer, and in it one has to perfection that delightful sensation of being held in mid-air which is so very trying to the inner man."

Isles, beginning in 1689.[35] France gave up Canada to the British Empire in one of the seven wars often summarized as the "second Hundred Years' War" (1689-1815) and was ultimately defeated, its emperor imprisoned on a remote island in the south Atlantic. In the nineteenth century Romanov Russia posed a much greater threat to other remote islands on the north-west Pacific coast.

It might be fairer to describe the situation from the Russian point of view, because Captain Vitus Bering had discovered the northwest Pacific coast for St Petersburg as early as 1741, nearly half a century before the voyages of captains Cook and Vancouver. Russian forces having been established in Alaska for so long, British claims on the northwest coast of America posed a new threat to their sphere of influence. The HBC on the Island was in competition with the Russian American Company, founded in 1799 for trading out of Alaska. In short, Russia and Britain were rivals on the northwest coast and throughout the world from 1815, with the triumphant ending of their collaboration in resisting the assaults of Napoleonic France.[36] In 1821, Tsar Alexander I laid claim to the coast and its waters north of the fifty-first parallel in an effort to exclude British and American ships.[37] During the Crimean War (1854-1856), only a few years before the Cariboo gold rush of 1858, the British and Russian navies fought on the Black Sea, the Baltic Sea, the White Sea near the Arctic region, and in the North Pacific Ocean.[38] *Commander R. C. Mayne, visiting Esquimalt in 1857 aboard HMS *Hecate*, found "a Naval Hospital erected in 1854, when we were at war with Russia, to receive the wounded from Petropaulovski, and since that time continued in use."[39] At the time BC was formally established as a colony in 1858, Count Nikolai Ignatiev was leading a Russian mission to China in an effort to challenge British influence there. He had already succeeded in spreading Russian imperial power through large areas of central Asia. In a chapter entitled "The Great Russian Advance Begins," Peter Hopkirk summarizes the early history of Anglo-Russian rivalry in a large region

---

[35]   Lists of French and Spanish invasion fleets have been assembled in my *The French Revolution* (New York, W. W. Norton, 1987), p. 78, and "The Franco-Catholic Danger, 1880-1715," *History, the Journal of the Historical Association* (London), vol. 79, no. 255 (February 1994), pp. 20-23. Invasion plans of the revolutionary and Napoleonic governments are described in Édouard Desbrières, *Projets et tentatives de débarquement aux Îles Britanniques, 1793-1805* (5 vols., Paris, 1900-1902).

[36]   Barry Gough, "British-Russian Rivalry and the Search for the Northwest Passage in the Early 19th Century", *Polar Record*, vol. 23, no. 144 (September 1986), pp. 301-317.

[37]   Frederick Merk, *The Oregon Question: Essays in Anglo-American Diplomacy and Politics* (Cambridge, Mass, Harvard University Belknap Press, 1967), p. 129.

[38]   Barry Gough, *The Royal Navy and the North-West Coast of North America, 1810-1914* (Vancouver, UBC Press, 1971), chapter 5, "War with Russia in the Pacific, 1854-1856"; and for a more detailed account, Glyn Barratt, *Russian Shadows on the British Northwest Coast of North America, 1810-1890: A Study of Rejection of Defence Responsibilities* (Vancouver, U.B.C. Press, 1983), 196 pp.

[39]   R. C. Mayne, *Four Years in British Columbia and Vancouver Island* (John Murray, 1862), p. 25.

of north-eastern Asia across the Pacific Ocean opposite Vancouver Island.[40] In the same year that Fort Victoria was founded on the Island (1843), a mission from St Petersburg to Jerusalem revived a Russian presence in the Middle East that could be traced back to the fifth century AD, and from 1882, an Imperial Orthodox Palestine Society in Palestine strengthened Russian presence there at a time when the British government was supporting Turkey in its defence against Russian ambitions in that region.[41] London and St Petersburg had collaborated in the struggle against Napoleonic France and were to be allies again in the Triple Entente fighting against Germany in 1914-1917, but they were rivals around the globe for nearly a century between those great wars. The monumental Trans-Siberian Railway, which the Tsar opened at Vladivostok in 1891, was built in the course of Russian efforts to maintain power in the Pacific region.[42] Not until an Anglo-Russian treaty was signed in 1907 was there any noticeable mitigation of a rivalry that has come to be called "The Great Game," and even then their agreement was limited to little more than dividing Persia into two spheres of influence.

Governing authorities on the Island, alert to the Russian menace, made efforts to fortify Esquimalt and Victoria against attack in the 1850s and more seriously in 1878-1879.[43] The public were conscious of this danger because of reports from ships at the Esquimalt Station and the experienced reflections of retired naval and military personnel from the above-mentioned theatres of war. Many went to the Island and some, such as *John Bartlett, settled there permanently. Upon retiring, he settled in Victoria and at his death on 4 May 1914 had a grand public funeral managed by the British Campaigners Association with pallbearers who had served in the Baltic with him.[44] Other Island veterans of the Crimean War were *Captain George Rudlin, *Captain John Berkeley Michell, *Major John Wilson, *Peter Creeke Fernie, and *Brinkley Robinson.

In the Great Game with Russia, the Island counted for only a little, but it also played parts in other imperial games being played with the United States, Spain, and France. The threat of American annexation increased when, in 1867, Russia sold Alaska to the United States in an effort to create an antagonism between the two English-speaking powers.[45] Esquimalt offered the best harbour on the Pacific Ocean between San Francisco and Alaska, and the Island's geographical position

[40]   Peter Hopkirk, *The Great Game: On Secret Service in High Asia* (John Murray, 1990), pp. 297-98, chapter 23.

[41]   Derek Hopwood, *The Russian Presence in Syria and Palestine, 1843-1914: Church and Politics in the Near East* (Oxford, Clarendon Press, 1969), pp. 18-19, 96-122.

[42]   Harmon Tupper, *To the Great Ocean: Siberia and the Trans-Siberian Railway* (Secker & Warburg, 1965), chapter V.

[43]   Major F. V. Longstaff, *Esquimalt Naval Base: A History of its Work and its Defences* (Victoria, Privately Printed, 1941), pp. 15-18 (1850s); pp. 40-45, 122, 138-40 (1870s).

[44]   BC Archives, Minutes of the British Campaigners' Ass., 16 April 1914; *Colonist* 5 May 1914, p. 12; 8 May 1914, p. 7; see BC Archives, photo of the British Campaigners, 1913.

[45]   John S. Galbraith, *The Hudson's Bay Company as an Imperial Factor, 1821-1869* (Toronto, University of Toronto Press, 1957), pp. 171-74.

gave it a strategic importance as a base in the Pacific region during the scramble for territory in which the United States eventually went on to win Hawaii, the Philippines, Guam, and Wake. Much earlier, Captain Vancouver had made a treaty with the ruler of the Hawaiian Islands, which London named after Lord Sandwich, and King Liholiho had visited England (where he and his queen died in July 1824). The menace of American, French, and Russian interests in the Sandwich Islands, which had the best harbours in the central Pacific Ocean, prompted London to post a Captain Richard Charlton as consul at Honolulu as early as 1825.[46] A lively trade developed later with Victoria as well as San Francisco in which *Richard William Janion and Henry Rhodes (1823-1878), father of *Brigadier General Sir Godfrey Rhodes, were active. A growing number of American missionaries and other migrants at Honolulu and the fragility of British power so far away from home induced London to consent to Washington's control of Pearl Harbour from 1887 and its annexation of Hawaii a decade later.[47]

Vancouver Island was only a small part of the empire, but its geographical position lent it special value in the eyes of imaginative businessmen like *Sir Edward Watkin and statesmen like some of the secretaries of state for the colonies in London. It was for the Island's strategic importance, not its small patches of land or its fur trade, that London carried out the prickly and humiliating negotiations over the Oregon Boundary Treaty (15 June 1846), which divided the Oregon Territory between Britain and the United States along the forty-ninth parallel of latitude, and the Treaty of Washington (proclaimed on 4 July 1871), which settled several Anglo-American differences, including the quarrel over the San Juan Islands in the Strait of Georgia. All of this careful diplomacy had much to do with dangers from Russia, the development of an All-Red Route around the world, and the realization that concessions must be made to the United States in view of the difficulties in defending such a distant Island and its continental hinterland.[48]

Meanwhile, the Canadian government remained generally—some thought scandalously—indifferent to the dangers of attack on the Pacific coast. "Successive cabinets in Ottawa," writes a specialist on the Russian threat, "responded to these military realities by treating the defence of the Pacific coast at large as an Imperial responsibility and by declining to work with Britain."[49] An attack by British and French fleets on the port of Petropavlovsk on the Pacific Coast of Russia in 1854 was a failure; the Russians had a considerable navy and still held Alaska. Tension between London and St Petersburg in 1878 during a Russian war with Turkey caused

---

[46]   W. P. Morrell, *Britain in the Pacific Islands* (Oxford, Clarendon Press, 1960), pp. 64-65.

[47]   Barry Gough, *The Royal Navy and the Northwest Coast of North America, 1810-1914* (Vancouver, UBC Press, 1971), p. 232; Merze Tate, "Hawaii: A Symbol of Anglo-American Rapprochement," *Political Science Quarterly* (vol. LXXIX 1964), p. 574.

[48]   Gough, *The Royal Navy and the Northwest Coast*, pp. 50-83, 150-68; Frederick Merk, *The Oregon Question: Essays in Anglo-American Diplomacy and Politics* (Cambridge, Mass., Harvard University Belknap Press, 1967), pp. 139-78, 216-33, 255-308.

[49]   Glyn Barratt, *Russian Shadows on the British Northwest Coast of North America, 1810-1890: A Study of Rejection of Defence Responsibilities* (Vancouver, UBC Press, 1983), p. 143.

similar anxiety. The British Admiralty lent guns to Esquimalt then, and the Canadian government began to build defence works there at last. But Ottawa played little part in the Imperial defence of the Island and British Columbia. With a national capital nearly six hundred miles inland from the Atlantic Ocean at Halifax, Nova Scotia, and 2,200 miles from the Pacific coast, it was perhaps natural for Canadian governments to develop policies behind a continental horizon and a limited vision of international affairs. Only a British officer, *General (later Sir) Percy Lake, took any interest in expert reports brought back from the Russo-Japanese War (1904-1905) by *Captain (later Major General) H. C. Thacker, another British-born officer, who had spent seven months as the Canadian military representative in Manchuria and Japan at the request of the Earl of Dundonald, GOC, the Canadian Militia.[50] Thacker and Lake both eventually retired to Victoria.

The difference between Victoria and Ottawa is well illustrated by the story of Premier Richard McBride's purchase of two submarines in Seattle in 1914 with a cheque for $1,150,000 on the BC Treasury.[51] Men of the RN (not the RCN) sailed them home across the Strait of Juan de Fuca. This is a well-known incident in BC history, but some of its features are worth stressing in the present context. It was not McBride's duty to buy submarines or anything else for national defence, which was a federal matter under Section 91 of the BNA Act, but he took it upon himself to provide for the naval defence of his province against the menace of German attacks from the sea.

Like the Island's Imperial patriots in general, McBride knew that the Canadian government had long refused to contribute to the Royal Navy, had delayed too long before founding a naval service of its own, and was failing to give proper care to the Esquimalt naval station, including its dockyard, which the infant Naval Service of Canada had taken over in 1910. Although the naval establishment in Esquimalt then was ostensibly and constitutionally Canadian, its personnel were in fact almost entirely British Imperial. In addition to the above-mentioned officers, *Commander Eustace Downman Maude (1848-1930), RN, was acting commander of the RCN Voluntary Reserve from 4 August 1914.[52] At the head of the Hydrographic Survey was *Commander Phillip Cranstoun Musgrave (1863-1920) from Bedfordshire, who was nearing the end of a long career that began in the

[50] R. Guy C. Smith, ed., *As You Were!: Ex-Cadets Remember*, vol. I, 1876-1918 (Toronto?, RMC Club of Canada, 1884-1984, 1983), pp. 125-131; *Colonist*, 5 January 1905, p. 8. Maj. Gen. H. C. Thacker (1870-1953) was born at Poona, India and died in Victoria, BC.

[51] G. N. Tucker, *The Naval Service of Canada* (2 vols., Ottawa, King's Printer, 1952), pp. 284-7, 291-5; Roger Sarty, "'There will be Trouble in the North Pacific': The Defence of British Columbia in the Early Twentieth Century," *British Columbia Studies*, no. 61 (Spring 1984), pp. 18-26; James H. Hamilton, *Western Shores: Narratives of the Pacific Coast by James Kettle* (Vancouver, Progress Publishing Company Ltd., 1932, chapter 3, "Scaring off the German Cruisers"; Laura Authier, "Canada's Submarine Program: A Short History," *Resolution: The Journal of the Maritime Museum of British Columbia*, No. 55 (Winter 2001), pp. 3-5; 13-14.

[52] NAC, RG 9, II—F-10, Imperial Gratuities, vol. 304, file 12013-E.

RN.[53] *Major George Sisman (1876-1968), in the Royal Canadian Garrison Artillery at Esquimalt since 1906, was born at Sherborne, Dorset, and had spent twelve years in the British Army.[54] A considerable number of personnel lower in the hierarchy were also British-born, such as G. W. Morton-Mardell (1888-1951), an ex-naval rating from the RN, born in London, who had been working at the Esquimalt navy yard since 1900. McBride knew these and other naval officers on the Island who were experienced members or ex-members of the Royal Navy. They were the men he called on to act when Captain William Henry Logan (c. 1887-1955) of the London Salvage Association told him that he had learnt at the Union Club of two submarines being offered for sale by James Venne Paterson of the Seattle Construction and Dry Dock Company.[55] Chief among them were *Lieutenant Commander Bertram Edward Jones (c. 1890-1975), and Bernard Dodds Leitch Johnson (1878-1968), RCNVR, a mariner born at Birkenhead, England, and employed after the war as Lloyds's agent for BC; *Lieutenant Commander Adrian St Vincent Keyes (1882-1926) and Engineer Lieutenant Reginald Henry Wood (1870-?), a chief artificer engineer from Plymouth, Devon, "lent for duty under the Canadian government, for service in Esquimalt Dockyard," according to the official Navy List.[56] One of Wood's grandfathers had spent his life in the British Coast Guard Service.

These were the men who went to Seattle, inspected the submarines, hoisted the British flag on them, and sailed for Esquimalt. There, they were met by the superintendent of the dockyard, *George Phillips, a Londoner who had come to Esquimalt in 1898 as a representative of the British Admiralty and stayed on after 1910 to run the dockyard and train its Canadian staff. Contrary to rumours then and since, these submarines were not an insignificant addition to the forces at Esquimalt.[57] And defensive measures were soon justified when the German warship Emden was found to be prowling around the Pacific Ocean with intent to destroy trans-Pacific cable stations. However, when the Emden was sunk a few months later, it was by the action of an Australian cruiser, HMAS Sydney, Australia having established its own navy earlier

---

[53]   Colonist, 18 February 1920, p. 7, obit.

[54]   NAC, RG150, box 8952-37; Colonist, 30 November 1968, p. 24, obit.

[55]   The Navy League Annual, 1913-14, pp. 102-04, published in London by John Murray, described these submarines as the Antofagasta and the Iquique built for Chile on a model of the Electric Torpedo Co. of New York and waiting to be delivered.

[56]   Navy List, 1913, pp. 77c, 230, 399.

[57]   G. N. Tucker, The Naval Service of Canada (2 vols., Ottawa, King's Printer, 1952), pp. 284-7, 291-5; Roger Sarty, "'There will be Trouble in the North Pacific': The Defence of British Columbia in the Early Twentieth Century," British Columbia Studies, no. 61 (Spring 1984), pp. 18-26; James H. Hamilton, Western Shores: Narratives of the Pacific Coast by James Kettle (Vancouver, Progress Publishing Company Ltd., 1932, chapter 3, "Scaring off the German Cruisers"; Laura Authier, "Canada's Submarine Program: A Short History," Resolution: The Journal of the Maritime Museum of British Columbia, No. 55 (Winter 2001), pp. 3-5; 13-14.

in response to British appeals.[58] Observers in Victoria were acutely aware of Ottawa's complacency in counting on the British Empire and the United States for protection. Even as war was declared in August 1914, the usual Canadian view was still, in the words of a *Globe and Mail* heading, "So long as Britain Controls Seas Land Invasion of Canada Not Feared."[59] In 1935, a writer in the *Victoria Daily Colonist* thought it scandalous that Canadians were spending less *per capita* on defence than on postage stamps, that the British, *per capita*, were spending thirty times as much as Canadians, and that "our land, air and sea forces are almost insignificantly small."[60] *Captain Henry Forbes Angus, who chose to serve in a British regiment during the Great War, had already told BC school children, "It is the policy of Canada to keep [its] forces as small as possible ... We could hardly be attacked except in circumstances which would justify us in counting on the help of Great Britain, or the United States, or both. These countries both maintain relatively large and expensive armaments for the protection of their interests. It is on British forces that we rely for the protection of our citizens in foreign countries should such protection be necessary. The arrangement is very convenient."[61] He still held much the same caustic view when he was a professor at the University of BC in the late 1940s, and it was different from the thinking of his colleague in the Department of History, Professor F. H. Soward (1899-1985), an Ontarian whose lectures, seminars, and books, *Twenty-Five Troubled Years, 1918-1943* (1944) and *The Department of External Affairs and Canadian Autonomy, 1899-1939* (1965), expressed a Canadian national approach to the twentieth century.[62] I sat in their classes as an undergraduate student and knew them later as colleagues.

If we are to understand the people who are the subject of this book, we must focus on their attitudes to the world of their time and suspend the anachronistic Canadian patriotism of today, which will otherwise distort the Island's history. Many historians, including some Canadians, have already reached an understanding of the Island's Imperial perspective in the century 1850-1950. Canada's permanent forces seemed to be shamefully small, demoralized, and in a lamentable state in the 1890s: "The officers were either political appointees or former British officers who had stayed on when the garrisons left, often because they had married Canadian women."[63] A strong current of Canadian opinion held that "the Permanent Force

[58]   George Nicholson, *Vancouver Island's West Coast, 1762-1962* (Victoria, BC, Privately Published by George Nicholson, 950 Rockland Avenue, 1965), p. 137.

[59]   *Globe & Mail* (Toronto), 7 August 1914, p. 3.

[60]   *Colonist*, 10 February 1935, Sunday Magazine, p. 3, by Wilfred Eggleton.

[61]   H. F. Angus, *Citizenship in British Columbia, authorized for use in the schools of British Columbia* (Victoria, King's Printer, 1926), pp. 185-6.

[62]   *Empire and Nations: Essays in Honour of Frederic H. Soward*, ed., Harvey L. Dyck and H. Peter Krosby (Toronto, University of Toronto Press, 1969), pp. xiii, xv-xvi, 219-228. I sat in Soward's classes and seminars in the years 1949-50 and was one of his junior colleagues from 1959 to 1967 in response to his kind invitation.

[63]   Richard Arthur Preston, *Canada and "Imperial Defense": A Study of the Origins of the British Commonwealth's Defense Organization, 1867-1919* (Durham, NC, Duke University, 1967), pp. 184, chapter 7 and *passim*.

was at best a haven for loungers and at worst a threat to constitutional rule."[64] Until the end of the nineteenth century (we learn from a specialist in Imperial history), "Britain continued to formulate, execute and pay for the defence of her empire with virtually no support from the self-governing colonies."[65] Again and again, London tried, in vain, to persuade Ottawa to contribute to Imperial defence. "The British tried for years without success to collect some repayment of the funds they had spent to put down the Red River rebellion."[66] Ottawa's reluctance to contribute to Imperial defence was closely linked with its failure to keep abreast of what was really going on the world. "Prior to 1939," a specialist tells us, "[Canada] enjoyed no real tradition of strategic intelligence activity. Modern techniques for intelligence work, especially those developed since 1914 in the areas of wireless interception and code-breaking, were virtually unknown . . . Cryptographic innocence was, in September 1939, perhaps more complete in Ottawa than in the capital of any other belligerent power."[67] It was always London which gathered intelligence about aggressive movements around the world, responded to danger, took firm steps to meet it, and made the necessary decisions. The Canadian Department of External Affairs was not founded until 1909. Its historian unconsciously revealed Ottawa's insularity by writing that BC's first agent in London was appointed in 1901, making no reference whatever to Russia or Oregon and yet beginning his book with the dubious line, "Governments in Canada have always had to pay close attention to external relations . . ." [68] Early relations with Russia and the USA on the Pacific Coast were not on the map as he saw it.

Many patriotic Canadians of our time tend to see their country evolving by gradually asserting independence from the mother country: choosing to declare war on Germany slightly later than London, insisting on Canadian command of Canadian units during the Great War, repeatedly electing Prime Minister William Lyon Mackenzie King (1874-1950), grandson of the rebellious William Lyon Mackenzie (1795-1861), and resisting arrangements for a collective Imperial defence. But this is a narrow, one-sided view of what was happening in the early twentieth century.[69] As Ken McNaught expresses the result, "In the guise of

---

[64]   William Beahen, "A Citizens' Army: The Growth and Development of the Canadian Militia, 1904 to 1914," a Ph.D thesis, University of Ottawa, 1979, p. 141.

[65]   Brian Bond, ed., *Victorian Military Campaigns* (Hutchinson, 1967), p. 10.

[66]   Lance Edwin Davis and Robert A. Huttenback, *Mammon and the Pursuit of Empire: The Economics of British Imperialism, 1860-1912* (Abridged ed., NY, Cambridge UP, 1988), p. 120 and in general pp. 112-29.

[67]   Wesley Wark, "Cryptographic Innocence: The Origins of Signals Intelligence in Canada in the Second World War," *Journal of Contemporary History*, vol. 22 (1987), pp. 639-665, p. 639.

[68]   John Hilliker, *Canada's Department of External Affairs: The Early Years, 1909-1946* (vol. I, Montreal, McGill-Queen's University Press, 1990), pp. 3, 22.

[69]   Roger Sarty, *The Maritime Defence of Canada* (Toronto, The Canadian Institute of Strategic Studies, 1996), pp. 24, 47, 151, 187; C. P. Stacey, *Canada and the Age of Conflict: A History of Canadian External Policies* (2 vols.; Toronto, University of Toronto Press, 1981), vol.

independence, we went to war in 1939, just as we had twenty-five years before, in defence of policies in whose formation we had refused to participate."[70] In retrospect, the two terrible world wars of the twentieth century make nonsense of Ottawa's niggling concern to stress the differences between Canada and Britain when the international state of affairs warranted collaboration with London in maintaining strong professional armed forces. Seen in broader perspective, the survival of Canada owes less to the politics of Ottawa's jealous efforts to establish national independence than to London's willingness to observe events around the world, to alert Ottawa and other colonial capitals to danger, to send professional British officers to train Canadians in expectation of a war, and to lead in the defence against foreign enemies.

Most of the people in this book leaned towards London's views rather than Ottawa's. For example, *Lieutenant Colonel Charles Leonard Flick carried on a long quarrel with Ottawa and tended, like many others of his kind, to regard it as a regional capital, scarcely more important in world affairs than Delhi, Edinburgh, or even Victoria. *Captain John Thomas Walbran had difficulty remembering to report to Ottawa. He died before war against Germany was declared in 1914, but many Imperials in Canada, especially in BC, immediately reported to their regiments in or near London, the only capital city that counted for them. A large number of the 619,636 Canadian troops who went overseas in the Great War, especially the 37 percent of them born in the British Isles and many more who were their sons, thought of their proud Canadian identity as regional, not national. In this, they were like the Scots, the Welsh, the Yorkshiremen, the Channel Islanders, or the New Zealanders. It was mainly factions in Ottawa led by men like Colonel Sir Sam Hughes (1853-1921), who struggled to keep them separate as a national Canadian force. There were reasonable grounds then for Imperial patriotism, unfashionable though it may be in our time.

In view of Ottawa's policies, London learned with surprise during each of the two world wars that Canada was at last making a vigorous, effective, indeed heroic contribution in troops, funds, and equipment.[71] Any informed Islander would add that the Canadian Corps was commanded by an officer from Victoria, *General Sir Arthur William Currie, who had once taught school at Sidney in North Saanich and had befriended many British officers in Victoria who saw the world in an Imperial perspective. They might even add that Ottawa, following the opinion of an ex-cabinet minister, Sir Sam Hughes, had insulted Currie when he

---

II, is a good account of Canada's approach to the Second World War in what Colonel Stacey calls "The Mackenzie King Era." Unlike most other historians, Stacey had enough knowledge and experience to see both sides of these issues. See, for example, pp. 293-6 and 347-356.

[70] Kenneth McNaught, "From Colony to Satellite," in *An Independent Foreign Policy for Canada*, ed., Stephen Clarkson (Toronto, McClelland & Stewart, 1968), p. 175.

[71] J. L. Granatstein, *Canada's Army: Waging War and Keeping the Peace* (University of Toronto Press, 2002), p. 75; Desmond Morton, *A Peculiar Kind of Politics: Canada's Overseas Ministry in the First World War* (Toronto, 1982), *passim* on the extraordinary Sam Hughes.

arrived home from the war in 1919. Not until the Second World War was "the
peaceable kingdom" fully alive to dangers from abroad. By then, British Imperial
protection, so long taken for granted in Canada, was being quietly replaced by
American protection. President Roosevelt said in a speech at Kingston, Ontario,
as early as 18 August 1938, "The Dominion of Canada is part of the sisterhood of
the British Empire. I give to you assurance that the people of the United States
will not stand idly by if domination of Canadian soil is threatened by any other
empire."[72] To this day, Ottawa has never faced foreign aggression alone.[73] Thanks
to the British Empire, however, and later to the United States, Canada has never
been brutally occupied and plundered as Belgium, Denmark, France, Italy, The
Netherlands, Norway, Poland, and almost all other Continental countries have
been. And when Britain at last withdrew its forces and allowed the empire to
collapse, Ottawa automatically assumed that the United States would step into the
imperial breach as a new leader and protector ready to watch events around the
globe and to take difficult decisions. Most of the *dramatis personae* in the A to Z
part of this book would have agreed with some variant of this summary, doubtless
with qualifications of their own.

The Island's Attractions for Imperials

M ost of the 769 people with biographical entries in this book were born in
the British Isles or in India or in one of the colonies and went out to Vancouver
Island at sometime between the middle of the nineteenth century and the middle
of the twentieth. Most of them settled permanently, but some left after a few
years, and a few of the many visiting travellers are included here. A majority of the
British newcomers were soldiers, sailors, airmen, or civil servants who manned
and defended the British Empire at a time when Canada was a part of it. Their
families are mentioned with them, when possible, as are many of the businessmen,
clergymen, professionals, tradesmen, and shopkeepers with whom they mingled and
intermarried. It was not until after the Second World War (1939-1945), when the
empire was disintegrating, that the Island became well and truly a part of Canada.
Until then, its people showed unmistakable signs of their community's origins.

News of the Island's unusual charms soon spread around the empire. Already
during the 1880s, Victoria reminded *William Henry Barneby of Jersey or Guernsey:
"each house seemed to have a pretty flower-garden attached."[74] A visiting British
journalist in 1911 wrote, "As one crosses from Vancouver the beauty of the straits
prepares one a little for the beauty of the island which, so far as I saw it, has no bare

[72]   Quoted in C. P. Stacey, *The Military Problems of Canada: A Survey of Defence Policies and Strategic Conditions Past and Present* (Toronto, Ryerson Press for the CIIA, 1940), p. 29.
[73]   C. P. Stacey, *Memoirs of a Canadian Historian: A Date with History* (Ottawa, Deneau, 1982), p. 259: "Canada has never fought a war on her own, and probably never will. She has always fought as a junior partner in a large alliance."
[74]   W. H. Barneby, *Life and Labour in the Far, Far West, Being Notes of a Tour in the Western States,* British Columbia, Manitoba, and the North-West Territory (Cassell, 1884), p. 97.

or ugly places . . . Arriving at Victoria, I went straight through to Duncans [*sic*], and, looking from the train, was reminded by the greenness of the land, freshened by the delicate rain that was falling, of the mountainous parts of Ceylon."[75] To a lieutenant in the Royal Navy on his way around the world in HMS *Hood* during the mid-1920s, it seemed like "a non-tropical edition of Honolulu and one of the most delightful places we visited."[76] To Constance Bromley, an English journalist and an editor of a Calcutta periodical, the Island seemed like Kashmir. The Strait of Georgia made another English journalist, James Lumsden, think of the fjiord leading to Stockholm, and in 1926, Sir Henry Lunn (1859-1939) compared it to the Bay of Naples.[77] Governor General Lord Lansdowne, who visited in Autumn 1885, wrote to his mother, "If I had to live on this continent, I should pitch my tent here."[78] In 1888, a London firm of "Publishers in Ordinary to Her Majesty the Queen" published *A Sportsman's Eden* by *Clive Phillipps-Wolley, late British vice-consul at Kertch, in the form of twenty letters with a postscript. Letter XVII was written by his wife, who soon joined him in Victoria and there wrote ten pages describing the town, her Chinese servants, and many invitations to dances, picnics, tennis parties, and the theatre: "If only my husband would give up the world and all its pomps and vanities, I would be only too glad to live out the rest of my life in this land of sunshine and sea-breezes, doing all I could to tempt my friends at home to come and share my happy lot."[79] There they settled indeed for the rest of their lives and did work at attracting others from home, which in their case had been Dorset, where he was born at Wimborne, and Gloucestershire, where she was brought up at Clifton, an admiral's daughter, and they were recorded earlier in 1881 living with their first child at Morgan Hall in Fairford near Cirencester.[80]

It was such whiffs of enchantment that caused people like *Robert Florian Bernard Lechmere Guppy of the Indian Civil Service to buy, site unseen, a property on the remote west coast of the Island, where he rowed daily to his garden singing Greek songs he had learnt at Pembroke College, Oxford. At sometime in the late 1920s, *Colonel Gerald Bassett Scott met an enterprising estate agent from BC, who

---

[75] R. E. Vernede, *The Fair Dominion: A Record of Canadian Impressions* (Kegan Paul, Trench & Trubner & Co., 1911; New York, James Potts & Co., 1911; Toronto, William Briggs, 1911), p. 267. Robert Ernest Vernede (1875-1917), son of a solicitor born in Java and a mother born at Singapore, spent time on the Island in summer 1910.

[76] Instructor Lieutenant C. R. Benstead (MC, BA, RN), *Round the World with the Battle Cruisers* (Hurst & Blackett, 1924), p. 204.

[77] *Colonist*, 20 September 1918, p 7; James Lumsden, *Through Canada in Harvest Time: A Study of Life and Labour in the Golden West* (T. Fisher Unwin, 1903), p. 197; Sir Henry Simpson Lunn (1859-1939), *Round the World with a Dictaphone: A Record of Men and Movements in 1926* (Ernest Benn, 1927), p. 92.

[78] Ava, Marchioness of Dufferin, *My Canadian Journal 1872-8* (London, John Murray, 1891), chs. 15 and 16; Lord Newton, *Lord Lansdowne: A Biography* (Macmillan, 1929), pp. 34-40.

[79] Clive Phillipps-Wolley, *A Sportsman's Eden* (Richard Bentley & Son, 1888), p. 190.

[80] BNA, census records, 1881, RG 11/2557, pp. 14-15.

was travelling around India talking enthusiastically about ranching opportunities in the Kootenays, the Okanagan Valley, and Vancouver Island, and Colonel Scott was attracted to the Saanich Peninsula, where he could live as a gentleman farmer.[81] *Brigadier Miles Smeeton and his wife bought, site unseen, a farm in the forests on the wild west side of neighbouring Salt Spring Island. When they decided to leave, partly because London devalued the pound sterling in 1949, they bought a large yacht and sailed around the world for the next twenty years, writing to help pay expenses. A brass plate on the harbour wall opposite the Empress Hotel still marks their occasional visits to Victoria as they passed by.

A great many more Imperials arrived from India, but other British migrants to the Island might be described as "refugees" from the freezing winters, baking-hot summers, blackflies, and mosquitoes of continental Canada. As Karl Baedeker observed in the last line of his reputable guide to Canada, "Vancouver Island is almost free from the mosquito and the black fly, which are often troublesome on the mainland."[82] An arrival who would have known what Baedeker meant was *Major Charles Edmund Phipps, who retired to Victoria in 1899 from Cannington Manor, near the eastern border of what later became Saskatchewan, where he had been the Dominion Lands agent. Phipps was doubly a "refugee," belonging as he did to a family of ruined Protestant Irish landowners whom Queen Victoria supported by employing him and a sister in the Royal Household.[83] His two elder sisters died at Kensington Palace, and one of them, Harriet Lepel Phipps (1840-1922), was a maid of honour who became an unofficial secretary to the queen during the last twenty years of the reign while her brother was living in Cannington Manor on the Canadian prairies and later in Victoria on the Island. As the CPR pushed westwards in the early 1880s, Winnipeg became a centre of attraction in central Canada, somewhat like Chicago in the United States. The British and Imperial names of settlements west of Winnipeg are testimony to the memories and loyalties of early British settlers on the prairies: Barneby, Bengough, Ceylon, Khedive, Kipling, Stoughton, Wolseley, and many more, whence the original British settlers fled very early, leaving hardly a memory of their founding presence.

A good example is Grenfell, now in Saskatchewan, named after a remarkable English businessman, *Pascoe Du Pré Grenfell, who draws our attention because the town's pioneer Canadian historian gave no thought to him, much less his English origins.[84] Grenfell was not only a shareholder in the CPR Company, as she remarks, but also closely related to English railway financiers who were the principal

---

[81]   Notes and family documents kindly sent by a daughter, Morgan Scott-Ostler. See also J. F. Bosher, "Vancouver Island in the Empire," *The Journal of Imperial and Commonwealth History*, Vol. 33, No. 3 (September 2005), pp. 349-368, p. 358.

[82]   Karl Baedeker, *The Dominion of Canada with Newfoundland and an Excursion to Alaska* (Leipzig, Baedeker, 1907), p. 292.

[83]   K. D. Reynolds, *Aristocratic Women and Political Society in Victorian Britain* (Oxford, Clarendon, 1998), pp. 204. 207, 214.

[84]   A. I. Yule, *Grit and Growth: The Story of Grenfell* (Grenfell, Saskatchewan, Historical Committee, 1980), p. 70.

investors in Canadian railways. He came from a large family of Victorian notables, four of his father's sisters being the wives of George Carr Glyn (1797-1873), a notable banker active in Canadian financing; Charles Kingsley (1819-1875), the famous novelist; James Anthony Froude (1818-1894), the historian; and Rev. Sydney Godolphin Osborne (1808-1889), a remarkable philanthropist who went out to the Crimean War to help in the tasks undertaken by Florence Nightingale.[85] It may have been the Grenfell name that attracted other Imperial families to settle near the town in the early 1880s even before the railway had gone so far. Half a dozen of these families moved later to Vancouver Island and so gave the town a special interest in the Island's history as a refuge from continental Canada. Their stories are told below in notes on *Colonel William Belson, *Brigadier General Reginald John Gwynne, *Lieutenant Colonel Percy Henry Noel Lake, *Major General Charles Alexander Phipps Murison, a British officer by choice, not by birth, and *Charles Robert Tryon, son of an admiral in the RN. To these might be added Lake's younger brother, Sir Richard Stuart Lake (1860-1950), who became lieutenant governor of Saskatchewan soon after that province was formed in 1905. So many British families settling at one small place on the prairies and all eventually moving out to Victoria or near it are fair illustrations of the Island's function as a refuge for this kind of emigrant, the kind who first chose to live in Canada but found it unsatisfactory for one reason or another.

How closely all of these Grenfell families kept in touch after they moved to the Island would be difficult to discover now that most of that generation have died. Lance Lake remained silent on this subject. His aunt Mabel Belson and his father and uncle, the knighted Lake brothers, often passed by General Gwynne's place on the West Saanich Road, called "Ardmore Grange," as they drove between their houses in Victoria and their summer cottage with tennis courts at Deep Cove in North Saanich, close to where the Belsons lived. The Gwynnes too had lawn tennis courts; did they visit back and forth? If so, little sign of this remains, though the Belsons attended Holy Trinity Anglican Church facing the sea at Patricia Bay, a church generously patronized by the Gwynnes. Some of them lie buried in the churchyard there near the graves of my parents. It would be apparent to any soldier, however, that a "desk-walla" from Ottawa such as General Gwynne might have been separated by a great gulf from Imperial fighting officers like General Sir Percy Lake.

As its reputation grew, the Island had perhaps more than a normal share of eccentric gentlemen. *Captain Horatio John "Race" Robertson arrived from China, where he was born, with a large family and some Chinese servants who were seen occasionally pulling him through the streets of Victoria in a rickshaw. He bought Moresby Island, not far from Saanich, and tried to farm but was arrested when some of his Chinese nearly perished while trying to escape on a raft and

[85]   Roger Fulford, *Glyn's 1753-1953: Six Generations in Lombard Street* (Macmillan, 1953), p. 122; the biographies of all four of Grenfell's uncles-by-marriage in the *Oxford Dictionary of National Biography*; Mark Bostridge, *Florence Nightingale, the Woman and Her Legend* (Penguin Viking Books, 2008), pp. 219-20.

when he burnt down a native Indian village because the men did not turn up
for work.[86] *Robert Aubrey Meade, a minor nobleman's son who settled on a
homestead at Cowichan Lake after trying to grow coffee in Ceylon, lived alone in
his cabin, habitually drank champagne, disappeared periodically on some wild
adventure, and was called upon when any distinguished visitor came by because
he had the only evening dress in the region. Residents of the Sooke district, west
of Esquimalt, hardly knew what to make of Harald [sic] Charles Harvey Hewitt,
a Herefordshire gentleman's son schooled at Harrow, who built a house in 1912
and then went home to England, where he threw himself in front of the king's
horse during a race at Ascot on 19 June 1913, waving a revolver and a banner
of Suffragette colours, and was formally declared insane after recovering from
his injuries.[87] Somehow, he escaped back to his place at Sooke, where he kept a
snake pit, a bird sanctuary, and his own forest of ornamental trees, including an
English oak grown from an acorn he said he had taken from the King's Forest at
Buckingham Palace. After being arrested in 1920 during another trip to England
and tried for his Ascot adventure, he published a book discussing this adventure
in an effort to attract attention to "our public school system [which] is to blame
for the sequence of events which led to my becoming a 'long ticket' asylum case,
and I refer more particularly to the monastic system of sex segregation, which
causes sex inhibitions, shame, and the wreckage of lives."[88]

Officers from India and the British Isles

F or many British settlers and visitors, the Island seemed like an ideal
retreat, almost a Shangri-La, a haven from life in the outside world. It attracted
more and more Imperial soldiers and civil servants from India, where periodicals
discussed it in enthusiastic articles. On 6 January 1913, *The Pioneer* (pp. 3-4) of
Alahabad, capital of the United Provinces of Agra and Oudh, printed an article
by *Major John Harald [sic] Gore Palmer entitled, "Life in Vancouver Island,"
and on 8 October 1913 (pp. 7-8), another, "A Baltistan Holiday," in which he
mentioned earlier hunting expeditions on Vancouver Island. *The Pioneer* was one
of the best newspapers in India, according to a standard guidebook.[89] Palmer
evidently thought there were substantial compensations on the Island for all
the labour of building with wood, feeding and caring for chickens and livestock,
harnessing and unharnessing horses, clearing forested land and chopping wood,

---

[86] Peter Murray, *Homesteads and Snug Harbours: The Gulf Islands* (Victoria, Horsdal &
      Shubert, 1991), pp. 80-2.

[87] *The Times* (London), 20 June 1913, pp. 9-10; * *101 Historical Buildings of the Sooke Region*,
      ed., Raymond Vowles *et al* (Victoria, Sooke Region Historical Society, 1985), pp.
      146-8.

[88] Harald Hewitt, *From Harrow School to Herrison House Asylum: A Tragedy of Education* (C.
      W. Daniel, 1923), p. 6.

[89] *A Handbook for Travellers in India, Burma and Ceylon* (11th edition, John Murray, 1924),
      728 pp., p. 46.

gardening, cleaning, cooking, and other household chores. In the same years, another Indian Army veteran, *Colonel Sheridan Knowles Brownlow Rice, wrote "Vancouver Island" dated 27 August 1913 and "A Home for the Anglo-Indian," both published in *The Times of India Illustrated Weekly*.[90] They were leisurely rambling articles about conditions of life and personal experiences of Anglo-Indian visitors and settlers, mainly in the Cowichan Valley and Victoria, during the early years of the century.

Already, by 1912, the CPR Company was advertising its trans-Pacific service in newspapers at Calcutta and Bombay.[91] Since 1891, its "Empress" line of passenger ships had been sailing regularly between Vancouver and Yokohama, Japan, stopping at Victoria on the voyage in both directions. The *Victoria Daily Colonist* had announced as early as 15 September 1887 (p. 2) that Lord Salisbury, acting for the Imperial government, had agreed with Prime Minister John A. Macdonald upon a mail subsidy of $220,000 a year to the CPR for a bimonthly mail service between Hong Kong and Montreal by way of Victoria (there being no Vancouver to speak of at that time).[92] The CPR soon agreed to employ Royal Naval Reserve men as far as possible and to transport soldiers between England and the Orient at cost.[93] Praise of the Island never ceased to circulate around the empire. On 11 June 1918, there appeared a long article in *The Calcutta Empire*, written by Miss Constance Bromley, former editor of *The Looker On* of Calcutta: "Vancouver Island does not share the severe winters of Toronto, nor of Quebec, Montreal, and other Eastern cities, nor of the State of New York . . . Vancouver Island possesses easily the finest scenery you will find anywhere, and I speak from some knowledge of Kashmir, of China, Japan, Honolulu, San Francisco and other talked of places. In fact, the Island reminds one very forcibly of Kashmir, but being an Island has lovely coast scenery in addition . . . [etc.] I put in fourteen months there in 1912-13 and in all my travels I have yet to find a more beautiful city. Honolulu is beautiful, but the climate is too monotonous."[94]

---

[90] From a private collection of Rice family papers, thanks to the kindness of Miss M. G. Rice.

[91] *Bombay Gazette*, 10 January 1912 (a small daily with uncertain pagination); *Indian Planters Gazette & Sporting News*, 4 May 1912, pp. III and IV; *Times of India*, 1 May 1913, p. 1; 2 May 1913, pp. 1 and 2.

[92] This news was remembered in Victoria's official circles, as recorded in R. E. Gosnell (1860-1921), *The Year Book of British Columbia, 1911-1914* (Queen's Printer, 1897, revised in 1911 and 1914), p. 42.

[93] James H. Hamilton, *Western Shores: Narratives of the Pacific Coast by James Kettle* (Vancouver, Progress Publishing Company Ltd., 1932, pp. 172-3.

[94] Reprinted in the *Colonist*, 20 September 1918, p. 7. Her mother and two sisters were living in Victoria at that time. Others writing about the Island sometimes added that it had hardly any of the blackflies and mosquitoes, which infested mainland BC and the rest of Canada: see, for example, Ella Constance Sykes, *A Home-Help in Canada* (1912; 2nd ed., Smith, Elder & Co., 1915), 188-89, and a mosquito sketched on the title page of Edward Roper, *By Track and Trail: A Journey Through Canada* (W. H. Allen & Co., 1891),

In books, letters home, and by word of mouth, visitors and residents advertised the Island's benign climate, cheap land, excellent fishing and hunting, and growing Imperial settlements. A stream of visitors from the British Isles, some of them from substantial old families, wrote favourable impressions in their books of travel, published mainly in London.[95] "Is it indeed Victoria and Vancouver Island where we have arrived?" Lady Aberdeen wrote in 1893. "Has not the *Islander* lost her way, and brought us by a short route back to England, and landed at Torquay? The resemblance has almost a touch of the comical in it—the same scents, the same sort of greenness all round . . . the same moist feeling in the air, developing later on into a steady downpour. Then English voices and faces abound and English customs predominate . . ."[96] In 1908, another British traveller reported,

> Victoria is the most English town in Canada, being peculiarly so in all its characteristics, and being also more of a residential than a manufacturing city. Owing to its splendid climate and mild winters, it is chiefly inhabited by those who have retired from business, and have gone there to spend the rest of their days . . . The result is that Victoria, though a small city in comparison to Winnipeg, Montreal or Toronto, is relatively richer, and its shops in Government Street would be the envy of many a city with twice, or even three times, its population, while some of them would not be out of place in Bond Street.[97]

In 1910, a writer travelling as a journalist for a London weekly, *The Bystander*, sailed from Vancouver across the Strait of Georgia to Victoria and on to visit friends near "Duncan's" on Vancouver Island. "When I looked out of my window next morning," he wrote, "I almost believed myself to be back in England . . . All around the lake [Quamichan] were farms, belonging largely to Englishmen dairy-farming or fruit-farming, making use of science and co-operation, but not sacrificing beauty to utility . . . It should have been called New England, this beautiful country which has so many English people in it, which carries on so much of the English tradition and sentiment, and which has even the English pheasant."[98]

When a London publisher produced a popular book about *British America* at the turn of the century, the chapter on British Columbia was written by a member

---

455 pp., with remarks in chapters XVI, "Vancouver Island," and XXI, "Mosquito Time." Edward Roper (1833-1909) was a well-known English illustrator, landscape painter, and author.

[95]   See appendix infra, p. 812 "A Mixed Bag of Books before the Great War."

[96]   The Countess of Aberdeen, *Through Canada with a Kodak* (1893), ed., Marjory Harper (Toronto, University of Toronto Press, 1994), p. 146.

[97]   Basil Stewart, *The Land of the Maple Leaf, or Canada as I Saw it* (1908; Routledge, 1908), p. 64.

[98]   Robert Ernest Vernede (1875-1917), *The Fair Dominion: A Record of Canadian Impressions* (Kegan Paul, Trench & Trubner & Co., 1911; New York, James Potts & Co., 1911; Toronto, William Briggs, 1911), pp. 269-70.

of the Royal Colonial Institute who took a lively interest in encouraging emigration to the colonies. This was *William Saunders Sebright Green, who had lived in Victoria as a solicitor during the 1860s and recalled,

> In my humble opinion there was no pleasanter society to be found in any part of the British Empire than we had in the sixties. We had always ships of her Majesty's Navy in Esquimalt, and as the flagship of the admiral in the Pacific was always stationed [there] during a portion of every year, we had the advantage of a number of naval officers to assist us in our various sports and entertainments. A number of retired army officers were settled in our midst; a baronet carried on a dairy and garden farm, and his lady might be seen carrying her butter and eggs to market any day. There was no formality, no conventionality, but geniality, friendliness, and equality were the characteristics of our society.[99]

Such enthusiastic comments on the Island may have accounted for the arrival of more and more people like Mr Green. Curiosity brought some who merely visited but many remained in Victoria, on the Saanich Peninsula or in the Cowichan Valley and near it. Major J. H. G. Palmer's wife wrote in her journal, "About the end of 1925 Major-General and Mrs Eustace arrived from India and bought Mrs Innis-Node's place just beyond the Stokers on Quamichan Lake. It was curious how the news had gone around in India that a good place to retire to was Duncan, BC! I remember hearing that a long time before we thought of going to Duncan."[100] Her references were to a younger brother of Abraham "Bram" Stoker, author of *Dracula*, *Lieutenant Colonel Dr Richard Nugent Stoker, who settled at Cowichan Lake in 1898 after serving in the Afghan War (1878-1881), the Sikkim expedition (1888), and the Chitral Relief Force (1895-1902), and *Major General Alexander Henry Eustace, whose long career in India included command of the Kohat Independent Brigade on the Northwest Frontier (1915-1919) and later of the 2/12 Frontier Force Regiment (Second Sikhs). Mrs Palmer's "news" continued to go around India. An English Methodist missionary from Southern India, *Thomas Henry Maynard (c. 1865-1939), arrived in 1912 with his family of India-born children. In 1939 *Major General Sir Ernest Walker, erstwhile director of Medical Services in India but recently retired to a large property on the north shore of Quamichan Lake, wrote an article extolling the merits of the Island, such as its excellent private schools, and published it in the *Journal of the United Service Institution of India*.[101] Officers from the same regiments sometimes kept in touch: *Major Henry Napier Roome and *Colonel

[99] W.S. Sebright Green, "British Columbia" in *British America* (Kegan Paul, Trench & Trubner & Co., 1900), p. 165.

[100] Mrs Palmer, "Memoirs of an Old-Fashioned Grandmother," vol. II, 30, in a private collection, courtesy of John Palmer, a grandson. Her references were to CB, CBE, DSO, on whom see *Who Was Who*, 1929-1940, 420 and the *Cowichan Leader*, 16 March 1939, obit.

[101] Vol. 69 (1939), 523-4. For the Island's schools, see Jean Barman, *Growing Up British in British Columbia* (Vancouver, UBC Press, 1984), 215, note 50.

John Talbot both retired to the Cowichan Valley after serving together for some years in the Thirty-seventh Lancers (Baluch Horse). When Talbot died, Roome's brother, *Colonel Reginald Eckford Roome, who had served in another cavalry regiment in India, was a pallbearer at the funeral held at St Peter's Quamichan.[102] The Island naturally attracted many surveyors and engineers from the British Isles, such as *Captain Livingston W. N. Thompson, majors *Robert Lowe, *William Charles Merston, and *Alistair Irvine Robertson, and lieutenant colonels *Edward Gawlor Prior, *Charles Pearson Steer, and *M. R. Ten Broek. Several of these were born in India.

People from the Raj were at their most numerous on the Island between the end of the First World War and sometime in the years before and after 1947, when London granted India independence. No precision is possible on such a point but they and their influence appear in various organizations of that period. The British Imperial Campaigners' Association (BICA), founded in 1908 after a few false starts, at first enrolled mainly veterans of the Second South African [Boer] War (1899-1902) and the Riel Rebellion campaign (1885) but had among its founders *Dr George Gerald Potts, an Anglo-Irish ex-army surgeon, who read a paper based on personal experience, "The Outbreak and Final Collapse of the Indian Mutiny" on 21 February 1902 at Pioneer Hall, Broad Street, even before the BICA was properly organized.[103] The BICA was soon joined by such interesting figures as *Colonel Edmund Arthur Ponsonby Hobday, author of a remarkable book, *Sketches on Service in the Frontier Campaign of 1897-8* (London, James Bowden, 1898), about his long service in India, where he was born at Calcutta, and which shows the skill at drawing that British officers might learn at Sandhurst and Woolwich before the age of easy photography. Hobday was one of the association's vice-presidents and locally active in amateur theatricals, music, and the Natural History Society until, according to minutes of a BICA meeting on 19 November 1914, he was "promoted Brigadier-General and was ordered home [i.e., to England]. Applause."[104] His sons, also born in India, had found employment on the Island and played cricket there; nearly all soon joined British forces. For instance, Victor Maitland Hobday, born at Meerut, India, on 25 October 1894, enlisted in the CEF on 23 October 1914 but transferred overseas to the RFA and then to the West Yorkshires, where he was killed in battle on 7 June 1917. The *Colonist* described the family as "formerly of Victoria and Duncan."[105]

[102] Family papers and notes, courtesy of descendants of the Roome and Talbot families; *Vancouver Daily Province*, 23 April 1946, 22, obit.; *Cowichan Leader*, 25 April 1946, obit.; BNA, *Indian Army List*, January 1923, 527.

[103] BC Archives (Victoria) 74-A-79; Add MSS 381: *The Veterans' Association of Vancouver Island, Scrap Book.*

[104] BC Archives, 74-A-79; Add MSS 381: Minutes of the Imperial Campaigners' Association; *Colonist*, 20 February 1914, 3; *Who was Who*, vol. 3. In 1892, Hobday married Nora Pottinger (1866-1911), born in India, daughter of *General Brabazon Henry Pottinger (1840-1913), an officer who owned land in the Cowichan Valley.

[105] *Colonist*, 6 July 1917, p. 5, photo and obit.

In 1932, an India-Burma Society was founded in Victoria (stimulated perhaps by the example of a China-Japan Society formed in 1929) under the leadership of *Lieutenant General Sir Percy Henry Noel Lake and held its first meeting at the Glenshiel Hotel, owned by the society's secretary, *Captain Basil Ogilvie Breton. Breton too was born into one of those Imperial families with members active in the Raj. Exactly what drew him to the India-Burma Society is not clear, but he certainly shared that society's interest in promoting discussion of India and its politics and prospects from an Imperial point of view. In the society, they consorted with men like *Thomas Archdale Pope, who had spent his life employed in the Survey of India, and *Colonel Frederick Philip Smyly, an Anglo-Irish officer who had a long career in India and Africa. Some of the other three or four dozen members are more difficult to trace, such as Captain Henry Wilson N. Moorhouse, a shipping merchant's clerk from Birkenhead, Cheshire, who had served in the British Army during the war. He was then employed as vice-president of the Victoria and District Underwriters' Association, but left BC sometime later.[106] All these were attracted to the society by speakers such as the Second Marquess of Zetland, formerly Lord Ronaldsay, and *née* Laurence John Lumley Dundas (1876-1961), sent to Victoria in 1933 by the Council of Education directed from Winnipeg by that hardworking Imperialist, *Major Frederick John James Ney, who eventually settled on the Island and died in Nanaimo.[107]

The Kipling Society founded in Victoria in 1933, only three years before their hero's death, shows different links with India. It was unique in Canada and the first of only three Kipling societies outside England that were welcomed by the Kipling Society of London, which resisted all other attempts to form Kipling societies except for one in Australia and another in New Zealand.[108] Even more remarkable, it was founded and joined mainly by less-prominent citizens. The founder was an English baker from Epping, Essex, Alfred Edward Garbett Cornwell (c. 1875-1956), who constructed his own ovens at 1842 Oak Bay Avenue.[109] The parent society at first refused to sanction Mr Cornwell's organization, perhaps anxious about the uncertain dignity of a literary society founded by a tradesman, but he attracted a keen membership in Victoria. Reflecting that Kipling himself was certain to be delighted by such humble patronage and had professed love and admiration for Victoria—did they perhaps consult him?—the London society soon changed its mind. Mr Cornwell was able to preside over his Kipling Society until 1952 as a leading centre for some

---

[106] *Colonist*, 17 January 1933, 8; 23 April 1933, 3; 18 May 1934, 2; BNA, census records, 1881, England, RG 11/3955, 32-3; census, 1891, RG 12/3214, 23.

[107] James Sturgis and Margaret Bird, *Canada's Imperial Past: The Life of F. J. Ney, 1884-1973* (Edinburgh, University of Edinburgh Centre of Canadian Studies, 2000), 325 pp., *passim.*

[108] Notes from the *Kipling Journal* (London), courtesy of David Page, editor. The *Journal*, begun in 1927, kept in touch with the Victoria Kipling Society until the 1990s.

[109] *Colonist*, 14 January 1956, 21, obit.; 1891 census, England, RG 12/1363/8, p. 11, Alfred E. Corwell, "baker's assistant" aged sixteen, youngest son of Thomas J. Cornwell, a London baker.

of the empire's enthusiastic supporters who gathered at regular meetings, including an annual banquet, for toasts, recitations, readings, and singing.[110]

What might be called "the Kipling effect" was particularly strong on the Island. He visited in April 1892, arriving from Japan, and in the next few years, young *Robert William Service, future poet of the Klondike, began to amuse audiences by reciting Kipling's verses at Duncan while working on a farm in the Cowichan Valley. When Kipling made a second visit in October 1907, putting up in Victoria at the Oak Bay Hotel, he addressed the Canadian Club and attracted the biggest audience it had ever assembled.[111] His letters home expressed memories that must live in the hearts of most expatriate Islanders:

> There is a view, when the morning mists peel off the harbour where the steamers tie up, of the Houses of Parliament on one hand, and a huge hotel on the other, which as an example of cunningly fitted-in water-fronts and façades is worth a very long journey. The [Empress] hotel was just being finished . . .
>
> I tried honestly to render something of the colour, the gaiety, and the graciousness of the town and the island, but only found myself piling up unbelievable adjectives, and so let it go with a hundred other wonders . . . [112]

Soon after the First World War, Kipling befriended *Colonel Herbert Tom Goodland while they were both members of the Imperial War Graves Commission and so was linked again with Victoria, where Goodland had been living, though he was an Imperial veteran from Taunton, Somerset. Their friendship grew as Goodland helped the Kiplings in their search for the remains of their only son, killed on 27 September 1915, six weeks after his eighteenth birthday, fighting as a lieutenant in the Irish Guards.[113] Kipling left in his will, probated on 6 April 1936, a generous sum to the Prince of Wales Fairbridge Farm School for British orphans that had opened in 1935 on a thousand acres near Duncan.[114] This school and another like it in Australia had been built with public support and $30,000 from the British government, as a result of a campaign started by Kingsley Fairbridge (1885-1924), a British Rhodesian who went to England in 1909 as a Rhodes scholar and was troubled by the many homeless and orphaned

---

[110]   *Colonist*, 28 September 1933, 6; 31 December 1936, 2; 14 January 1956, 21, Cornwell's obit; 20 January 1939, p. 3; 29 December 1943, p. 18.

[111]   *Colonist*, 9 October 1907, 1; 10 October 1907, 1 and 3.

[112]   Rudyard Kipling, "Letters to the Family (1908)," in *Letters of Travel, 1892-1913* (New York, Doubleday, 1927), p. 178-180.

[113]   J. B. Hayward & Son, *Officers Died in the Great War, 1914-1919* (New Enlarged Ed., Polstead, Suffolk, J. B. Hayward & Son, 1988), p. 53; *The Independent* (London), Sunday 2 February 2007 10:51 column of Jonathan Brown.

[114]   *Colonist*, 7 April 1936, p. 2. It appears that the heirs were able to prevent this legacy from being actually paid.

children he saw there.[115] In August 1937, Colonel Goodland arranged for the Kipling Society to visit the school as a summer outing. They were met there by the headmaster, Colonel Harry Tremaine Logan, MC (1887-1971), a maritimer who had met Kingsley Fairbridge at Oxford University when they were both Rhodes scholars.[116] The success of this outing inspired the society to collect a set of Kipling's works to present to Fairbridge Farm School, and they held their annual picnic there again in August 1938.[117] According to a librarian in Duncan, who wrote an eloquent letter of praise for Kipling, the valley's general public besieged the town library for Kipling's books.[118] The Second World War gave the Victoria Kipling Society a new purpose. In February 1940, its monthly meeting received an appeal from the society in London for clothing and comforts for the crew of HMS *Kipling*, recently launched by the late poet's daughter, Mrs Bambridge, and the Victoria group responded in various ways, sending over seaboot stockings and an assortment of luxuries until the ship was sunk in the Mediterranean in 1942.[119]

Kipling's blend of romantic adventure and vigorous commonsense appealed to the general public all over the English-speaking world but particularly on the Island, where the Boy Scout movement, based on his writings about India, drew heavily on the leadership of Indian Army veterans. At its AGM in January 1936 the Scouts Association in Victoria appointed as its first vice-president *Lieutenant General Sir Percy Lake, who was to speak later to the Overseas League about "Why Britain has been able to conquer and govern India."[120] Among the dozen men elected to the Executive Council were five more officers who had served in India: *Major J. B. Hardinge, *Colonel J. S. Hodding, *Colonel F. T. Oldham, *Colonel B. A. M. Rice, and *Lieutenant Colonel A. B. Snow. In the Cowichan Valley, *Colonel Maxwell Edward Dopping-Hepenstal, an officer retired from the Gurkha Rifles, was the scoutmaster of the Quamichan Boy Scout Troop from 1926 until 1934 when he took charge as the district commissioner. Other stories about India besides Kipling's were read on the Island, notably those fanciful tales by *Mrs Lily Adams Beck, who wrote more than a book a year in Oak Bay during the 1920s, after travelling in the Orient. *Née* Elizabeth Louisa Moresby, she was named after her paternal grandmother, the India-born wife of Admiral of the Fleet *Sir Fairfax Moresby, and was all the more interesting because her father and grandfather had visited the Esquimalt Station in the course of their duties, so inspiring the naming of Moresby Island in the Gulf of Georgia.[121]

---

[115] *Colonist*, 21 August 1938, p. 6.

[116] NAC, RG 150, acc. 1992-93/166, CEF Box 5713-37; *Colonist*, 21 August 1938, p. 6

[117] *Colonist*, 27 August 1937, p. 3; 29 September 1937, p. 9; 21 August 1938, p. 6.

[118] *Colonist*, 10 May 1936, 28; 15 August 1937, 7.

[119] *Colonist*, 28 February 1940, p. 6; 24 November 1940, p. 5; 28 May 1941, p. 6; 27 November 1941, p. 2.

[120] *Colonist*, 31 January 1936, p. 5; 2 March 1937, p. 2.

[121] Walbran, *British Columbia Coast Names*, p. 342.

Officers of the Royal Navy posted at Esquimalt from the 1850s, in the course of their careers around the empire, were active in the social life of Victoria: parties, picnics, amateur theatricals, and cricket and tennis matches. Perhaps, the first Victoria Cricket Club was formed in September 1858 under the leadership of Thomas Harris, future mayor of the city (1862-1865), but the crew of HMS *Thetis*, including Lily Beck's father, the explorer Lieutenant John Moresby (1830-1922), defeated a local team at Beacon Hill on 29 May 1852.[122] Officers and men of HMS *Zealous* played several cricket matches in Victoria against other vessels in May and June 1870. "Victoria boasts a very good eleven, and our last match was against them," the officers recorded, "but they proved too strong, and beat us by ten wickets."[123] The president of the Victoria Cricket Club then was *Lieutenant Governor Joseph William Trutch, and its vice-president was Chief Justice Sir Matthew Baillie Begbie. In the early 1870s, members had to be gentlemen proposed by a club member in a letter to the secretary, but officers of the army and the navy on active service were automatically honorary members. This club insisted that the game should be played according to the rules of the Marylebone Cricket Club in London. Thirty years later, a new cricket club was organized on 17 March 1914 by the Civil Service Club in Victoria.[124]

---

[122] Derek Pethick, *Victoria: The Fort* (Vancouver, Mitchell Press Ltd, 1968), p. 197; Walbran, *British Columbia Coast Names*, pp. 342-3.

[123] *Our Journal in the Pacific, by the Officers of HMS Zealous*, ed., Lieutenant S. Eardley-Wilmot (Longmans, Green and Co., 1873) p. 39.

[124] *Victoria Daily Colonist* [hereafter *Colonist*], 18 March 1914, p. 9.

Sarah Taylor Marsden

Not only pensioned officers, but also wives, widows, and daughters of busy officials responded to news of the Island's merits. All too little can be gleaned from the records about most of the women whose devoted care and companionship was so fundamental in the lives of their men. Even their maiden names are often impossible to discover, not being recorded in census records. But ten years of studying the Island and its historical context leaves me with the impression that women's comparative absence from Imperial historical records in the century 1850-1960 was not a reflection of female weakness, much less of male contempt. It was a result of the privacy so prized in that age and so seldom honoured in our own. There is no disparagement of women in the story of the "bride ships," which carried some scores of women to the Island in the 1860s, including my great-aunt Sarah Taylor Marsden (1833-1916), future wife of *Captain William McCulloch, or in the work and circumstances of Ella Constance Sykes (1864-1939), who wrote to warn women, especially middle-class women, that if they took employment as "home helps," they would become drudges in most of western Canada, where conditions were harsh. Disguised as a gentlewoman employed as a "home help," she had been abused by most of the women she worked for, perhaps because their own lives were very hard. She concluded that emigrant gentlewomen could hope for a better life only on Vancouver Island, where families would be more likely to treat them as equals and include them in social and sporting events.[125]

Of course, the lives of some women are known well enough to be included in this book. *Evelyn Phethean, a public-spirited woman who died in Victoria, was the fourth daughter of Sir Montagu Frederick Ommanney, GCMG, KCB, ISO (1842-1925), permanent under-secretary of state for the Colonies (1900-1907), and moved to the Island from Winnipeg with her rancher husband in 1920. *Lady Mary Emily Swettenham, born Mary Copeland, daughter of the lord mayor of London, married Sir James Alexander Swettenham (1846-1933), who held high posts in Cyprus, Ceylon, Singapore, British Guiana, and Jamaica, but she died in Victoria, where she had been living at the Empress Hotel. Mary Lindesay (1836-1921), widow of Laurence Adamson, late Under Colonial Secretary for Cape Colony, was born at Fort Chunar, India, but buried in Saanich at Holy Trinity, Patricia Bay. *Miss Catherine Mary Sime, India-born daughter of Dr John Sime, CIE, LLD, LitD, of the Indian Educational Service and of Inchture, Perthshire, Scotland, had a career in Queen Alexandra's Military Nursing Service of India and was on active service in Mesopotamia and on hospital ships in the Persian Gulf before retiring to Maple Bay, where she had relatives. *Lady Evelyn Isabella Rose Hughes (c. 1868-1940), buried at Royal Oak Cemetery near Victoria, was born in India daughter of Colonel Ross Hutchinson and, in 1888, married Sir Walter Charleton Hughes (1850-1922), who was knighted for his work in the Indian Civil Service in Bombay. *Miss Mary Isabella Ingram had a distinguished Imperial career in India and elsewhere before settling at Victoria in Oak Bay.

---

[125] Ella Constance Sykes (1864-1939), *A Home-Help in Canada* (1912; 2nd ed., Smith, Elder & Co., 1915), pp. 147-151, 226-7.

Ordinary country folk also appreciated the Island's good features, as did my father's family and relations who migrated from rural Berkshire early in the twentieth century. Two decades earlier, a gardener from a Wiltshire village wrote from North Saanich on 20 April 1884 to his young nephew, a gardener's son in Sussex, who joined him on the Island later, after twelve years of service in the Royal Sussex Regiment:

> Dear Fred, . . . [Your friends] could not come to a better climate, a finer March month no one could wish. April is lovely, most of the ploughing and sowing is done. The fruit trees are in splendid bloom. The flowers are so gay, in fact nature itself seems to smile on this Island, but when you get into the interior of B.C. it is quite a different thing . . .
> I am, Dear Fred, Your affectionate Uncle, William Avons.[126]

In Avons's time, continental BC was a huge, rough territory, plagued with blackflies and mosquitoes like the rest of Canada, suitable for mineral prospecting, mining, and ranching, and with a population of pioneers and adventurers unaccustomed to the quiet, settled life of places like Duncan, Victoria, and nearby rural districts. To read a careful study like Marie Elliott's *Gold and Grand Dreams: Cariboo East in the Early Years* (Victoria, 2004) and follow the lives of the gold-seekers and gold commissioners mentioned in her pages is to learn that few of them were inclined to live in the quiet, domestic—some would say stuffy—fashion of people who settled in the Island communities. Exceptions to this statement can, of course, be found, and there were peaceful settlements of Imperial families in the Okanagan Valley and a few other settled parts of the provincial interior. But maintaining peace, order, and good government in the BC interior was exhausting. Philip Henry Hind (1832-1896) had a nervous breakdown and went to Australia for a change. Many others migrated to the USA or back to Britain. True, there were British emigrants like the banker *William Curtis Ward, who spent many years ranching in the interior of the province, but he eventually returned to England and untold numbers of others moved away or retired on the Island. Most of the men who settled at Walhachin, a model community for British gentlefolk founded in 1908 near Kamloops Lake by an enterprising American land surveyor, volunteered for service overseas in the Great War (1914-1918) and never returned.[127] One of the agents promoting Walhachin for the BC Development Association (London) was Ernest Edward Billinghurst (1864-1931), son of a bank manager in the Blackheath or Lewisham district of London, had an office at 54 Government Street, Victoria, where he died on 7 October 1931. Many of the differences between the Island and the mainland interior disappeared during the late twentieth century and are

---

[126] William Avons (1829-1905) to his nephew Frederick William Webber (1871-1940), National Archives of Canada [hereafter NAC], MG24. F 113, papers of the Shrapnel family, descendants of the famous British inventor of the exploding artillery shell, several of whom died in Victoria.

[127] Margaret A. Ormsby, *British Columbia, A History* ( ), pp. 376, 402.

now forgotten in our age of electricity, natural gas, heating oil, and motor traffic on paved roads, which have made life infinitely easier.

Once they reached the Island, people from the British Isles and Empire soon realized that their taste for a civilized country life could be satisfied even in Victoria, where large gardens near the sea were common and where beaches, rocky hills, and tumbled outcroppings guaranteed winding lanes, picturesque surroundings, and a scattering of parklike public terrain. Beacon Hill Park was developed formally on rocky land, but there were many patches of hilly ground left unowned and untended in Victoria before the Second World War. Its climate put the Island in what the Canadian government now classifies as zone 9, whereas no other part of the country has been so temperate, most of it, indeed, being in zones 3 and 4. Finding a climate like Devon or Hampshire, retired Imperials gardened assiduously, sometimes professionally. The Upland's development, north of Oak Bay, Victoria, was landscaped by *Frederick Street, born in Burma and a fellow of the Royal Horticultural Society. Among the pallbearers at Street's funeral was one of *Colonel A. E. P. Hobday's sons, born at Meermut, India, and working in Victoria as a landscape gardener when he enlisted in the CEF in 1914.

In fact, nearly all of the traceable professional gardeners on the Island who were not Chinese were born in Britain or somewhere else in the empire outside Canada: men such as *George Millett, a veteran of service in India, who worked at the Jubilee Hospital; Frederick Francis Saunders (1880-1934) from Reigate, Surrey, who kept the gardens of the Empress Hotel; and Thomas L. Lokier (1869-1970) from Bishop's Castle, Shropshire, who in his eighties established what became a public garden at the meeting of four streets in Oak Bay: Hamiota, Estevan, Musgrave, and Thompson. Lokier went out to Canada in 1880 and farmed for many years on a 160-acre homestead near Winnipeg and then on a ranch near Medicine Hat. When he moved to Victoria in 1940, he worked at first as a shipbuilder at HMC Dockyard in Esquimalt but was also active in the community. He joined the White Cane club of the Canadian National Institute for the Blind and, in 1957, began a campaign to persuade the federal government to provide a ferry to Vancouver Island as an extension of the trans-Canada highway. In retirement, he planted shrubs, flowers, and lawns and cared for this garden until he died on 11 February 1970, aged 101.[128] By then, the authorities in Oak Bay felt more or less obliged to provide for the maintenance of the Lokier Gardens, as they are still called.

Much of the labour in bigger gardens was done by Chinese immigrants, but the head gardeners were mainly English. When in 1920 my father, J. E. Bosher (1900-1991), arrived from Berkshire as a young man, he spent some months as head gardener at Hatley Park, Esquimalt, later adopted as Royal Roads Naval College, working for "old Mrs Dunsmuir," living in the coach house and directing the work of several competent Chinese labourers. Among my parents' gardening friends later were *Eric George Long and his wife Kathleen, who had gone to China in 1931 in the employ of the shipping firm, Butterfield & Swire. For ten years, Eric cared for wharves and ships at Shanghai, then Hankow, and finally Sottow. When

---

[128] *Colonist*, 12 February 1970, pp. 30 and 36.

Japanese forces invaded China, the Longs settled on the Island at Crofton, where they lovingly developed a large English garden. Old photos show them having tea with my parents on many occasions. They talked gardening endlessly, and when I visited Mrs Long in May 2001, then a widow aged ninety-six, she was still reminiscing about those days. On the walls of the house, among Chinese drawings and exotic engravings, were striking watercolours of peonies in the garden, which she had painted forty years earlier. I cite these family associations only because of my direct knowledge of them as examples of typical lives of the expatriate British population. Not all native Canadians had any understanding of the Island's Imperial population and its activities, but Bruce Hutchison (1901-1992), son of an English horticulturist born in Rome and educated at English public schools, acquired a journalist's grasp of Imperial history at Duncan, where he had worked during his summers as a youth, and he still saw in 1957 that although it was "in appearance like any other Canadian town, [it] still nourished the last remnants of a remarkable society, much publicized but seldom understood—English nobles, generals, admirals, fishermen, hunters, cricket-players, and pukka sahibs. Alas, they are near extinction."[129]

Exporting the Glorious Revolution of 1688-1689

Another aspect of Vancouver Island's difference from Canada is clear in census data about the population's religious affiliations. According to the census of 1921, Canada as a whole had 1,407,994 members of the Church of England comprising only 16 percent of the population, whereas Roman Catholics were 38.6 percent, more than twice as numerous. These proportions had evolved only a little since 1881, when 13.35 percent of Canadians had been Anglican and 41.43 percent Catholic.[130] In most parts of Canada, the Church of England ranked third in importance, according to Rev. Donald Fraser reporting to the Colonial Institute in 1877.[131] In BC, however, these proportions were reversed: Anglicans in 1921 were 30.7 percent of the population and Roman Catholics only 12.2 percent. A great many Irish Catholic peasants had emigrated to eastern Canada and Manitoba, as Lord Salisbury remarked publicly in 1886, but very few settled as far west as BC.[132] This religious contrast was even more marked on the Island. By 1921, more than 40 percent of the people in the city of Victoria were Anglican, and Roman Catholics there were only 6.3 percent. The remaining percentages being other Protestants—mainly Presbyterians and Methodists—these too were proportionally

---

[129]   Bruce Hutchison, *Canada, Tomorrow's Giant* (Toronto, Longmans, Green & Co., 1957), p. 320.

[130]   *Canadian Almanach and Miscellaneous Directory* (Toronto, Copp Clark, 1905), p. 335; *op. cit.*, 1926, p. 281.

[131]   Rev. Donald Fraser, D. D., "Canada: as I remember it, and as it is," *Proceedings of the Royal Colonial Institute*, vol. 8 (1876-77), p. 51.

[132]   Andrew Robert, *Salisbury, Victorian Titan* (Phoenix, 2000), pp. 384-5.

more numerous on the Island than in Canada as a whole.[133] The *Daily Colonist* in its own analysis of the 1921 census data proclaimed Victoria to be "the most Anglican city in Canada."[134] A Catholic writer confirmed this by denouncing "the WASPS of Victoria who held sway in society and religion."[135]

The religious composition of the Island outside of the capital was much the same. Few variations appear in particular districts where details are known. An analysis of the 450 people on Salt Spring Island, settled across a narrow strait from Cowichan, for example, shows a slightly higher Catholic population, according to *Rev. E. F. Wilson's survey in the 1890s: He counted eighty Catholics (18 percent), 220 Anglicans (49 percent), fifty Methodists (11 percent), thirty Presbyterians (7 percent), thirteen Lutherans (3 percent), three Congregationalists, two Greek Orthodox, and forty unknown.[136] There were also two members of the Salvation Army, a Protestant denomination which had appeared in Victoria in 1887 and, in five or six years, recruited a membership of about three hundred. But such variations make no significant change in the picture derived from census records. The Island, like Victoria, was overwhelmingly Protestant, with Anglicans being much the biggest single denomination, but with substantial numbers of Presbyterians and Methodists.

These contrasting proportions seem all the more impressive in analyses of particular occupations. Of 234 engineers of all sorts in the city in 1901, only seventeen were Catholic. There was only one Catholic among the twenty-one shipwrights registered as living in Victoria in 1901 and only twenty-one (11 percent) among the 193 ships' captains. Nor was this a recent development. The 1881 census for the whole Island shows, for instance, that only three of the forty-seven managers were Catholics; one of the thirty-seven contractors; and one of the twenty-two "agents." Among the thirty-two surveyors there in 1891, only one was Catholic, whereas there were eighteen Anglicans and seven Presbyterians (the rest included two Methodists, a Unitarian, a Jew, an agnostic, and an atheist).

---

[133] The Canadian Census of 1921.

[134] *Colonist*, 23 April 1933, p. 3.

[135] Patrick Jamieson, *Victoria, Demers to De Roo: 150 Years of Catholic History on Vancouver Island* (Victoria, Ekstasis Editions, 1997), p. 123.

[136] Charles Kahn, *Salt Spring: The Story of an Island* (Madeira Park, B.C., Harbour Publishing, 1998, p. 137.

Table I included two Methodists, a Unitarian, a Jew, an "agnostic" and an "atheist"). The

TABLE I

ANGLICANS AND ROMAN CATHOLICS ON VANCOUVER ISLAND								
Occupation	1881 Census (V.I.)			1891 Census (V.I.)			1901 Census (Victoria)		
	All	Angl	Cath	All	Anglican	Catholic	All	Anglican	Catholic
agents	22	7 (32%)	2 (9%)	141	65 (46%)	5 (4%)	112	46 (41%)	2 (2%)
bakers	32	11 (34%)	3 (9%)	68	30 (44%)	6 (9%)	57	17 (30%)	3 (5%)
bankers	8	7 (87%)	0	37	24 (65%)	2 (5%)	57	36 (63%)	0
carpenters	155	41 (26%)	13 (8%)	763	204 (27%)	59 (8%)	343	98 (29%)	14 (4%)
contractors	37	14 (38%)	1 (3%)	168	38 (23%)	6 (4%)	70	17 (24%)	6 (9%)
customs	0	0	0	14	6 (43%)	0	8	2 (25%)	1 (13%)
doctors	23	9 (39%)	0	47	23 (49%)	4 (9%)	34	14 (41%)	1 (3%)
engineers	43	17 (40%)	8 (19%)	186	82 (44%)	16 (9%)	234	90 (38%)	18 (8%)
farmers	855	313 (37%)	174 (20%)	1308	538 (41%)	180 (14%)	159	71 (45%)	12 (8%)
foremen	3	(2 Prots)	0	27	4 (15%)	5 (19%)	43	17 (40%)	2 (5%)
gentlemen	1	(Prot.)	0	37	24 (65%)	2 (5%)	27	16 (59%)	1 (4%)
innkeepers	83	27 (33%)	13 (16%)	132	47 (36%)	23 (17%	76	35 (46%)	11 (14%)
lawyers	23	16 (70%)	1 (4%)	51	35 (69%)	2 (4%)	67	45 (67%)	5 (7%)
managers	47	20 (43%)	3 (6%)	41	10 (24%)	1 (2%)	62	28 (45%)	5 (8%)
master mariners	25	4 (16%)	4 (16%)	71	22 (42%)	4 (6%)	167	42 (25%)	15 (9%)

merchants	97	17 (18%)	9 (9%)	55	11 (20%)	5 (9%)	222	56 (25%)	4 (2%)
miners	443	93 (21%)	47 (11%)	2111	385 (18%)	540 (26%)	167	52 (31%)	19 (11%)
policemen	23	7 (30%)	3 (13%)	31	16 (52%)	4 (13%)	27	9 (33%)	6 (22%)
shipwrights	20	7 (35%)	1 (5%)	24	8 (33%)	1 (4%)	21	14 (67%)	1 (5%)
surveyors	12	7 (58%)	0	32	18 (56%)	1 (3%)	13	8 (62%)	1 (8%)
teachers	82	35 (43%)	14 (17%)	143	60 (42%)	8 (6%)	169	70 (41%)	16 (10%)

Notes: (1) The census of 1901 is for Victoria only; the other two are for V.I. (2) The Reformed Episcopalians have not been counted with Anglicans. (3) All who were not Catholic may be assumed to be Protestant except for merchants, who were 18% Confucian in 1891 and 30% Confucian in 1901; Jews were rare and too few to affect the averages. (4) Presbyterians formed the second largest membership of most occupations, and in a few were more numerous than Anglicans. For instance, the Foremen in 1891 were 44% Presbyterian, which helps to explain the exceptional fall of Anglicans (15%) to fewer than Catholics (19%); similarly 50% of the miners were Anglican, Methodist, or Presbyterian. (5) The larger occupations (e.g. carpenters, farmers and miners) had a great variety of Protestants: Baptists, Congregationalists, Lutherans, Methodists, Reformed Episcopalians, Salvation Army, Unitarians, and others as well as Agnostics, Atheists and Spiritualists. (6) The 1881 census lists no customs personnel. (7) I assume that any errors of omission or transcription are random and therefore unlikely to affect general conclusions drawn from the figures.Source: databases compiled by Victoria University and Malaspina University College.

The proportions were similar for other professional and business groups.

The full significance of these proportions is apparent in their political effects. Of the forty mayors elected in Victoria during the hundred years beginning in 1862, half were Anglicans, one-quarter were Presbyterians, and the rest were mixed dissenting Protestants except for Lumley Franklin (c. 1820-1873) from Liverpool, who was Jewish.[137] No truly Roman Catholic premier of British Columbia was elected until December 1941 (John Hart, 1879-1957). The two Davie brothers elected earlier were Anglicans—and one of them a Freemason—who converted to Catholicism as adults under the influence of the high-Anglican Oxford Movement. None of the governors of the colony or the lieutenant governors of the province from 1871 until after the Second World War was Roman Catholic. Only after

---

[137] Valerie Green, *No Ordinary People: Victoria's Mayors since 1862* (Victoria, Beach Holme, 1992), *passim*, supplemented by census records of 1881, 1891, 1901 and many other sources of information about certain individuals.

the Second World War did fundamental changes begin to take place. In the meantime, the Catholic Church was, of course, protected and its faithful, including a few Imperial officers, were not molested. It seems to have been fairly treated with other religious minorities, as, for instance, when James Dunsmuir offered Catholic authorities land for building a church at Ladysmith on the same terms as the Anglicans, Methodists, and Presbyterians.[138] In the meantime, Vancouver Island and British Columbia were governed entirely by Protestant cabinets, civil servants, and lieutenant governors. For nearly a hundred years before the Second World War, a British emigrant to the Island, whether born in England, Scotland, Canada, India, or any other colony in the empire, found a religious environment recognisably similar to the one he had known at home. A scholarly student of the Island's schooling in colonial times found that the ideas and standards of educated British people prevailed throughout most of the nineteenth century.[139]

This Protestant environment was created in the British Isles immediately after the Glorious Revolution of 1688-1689, gradually modified, and carried out to every colony with soldiers, sailors, missionaries, merchants, and other emigrants. "Exporting the Revolution Settlement," in the apt phrase of P. J. Cain and A. G. Hopkins, had a religious side to it as well as the economic and social sides, which interested those two historians.[140] That religious settlement outlasted by at least half a century the political influences of 1688, which some historians of Victorian England tend to see as coming to an end in the 1880s.[141] But long before then, it had embraced a generous measure of toleration in a further revolution in 1827-1832. On 26 February 1828, by a parliamentary vote of 237 to 193, the Duke of Wellington's government freed Dissenters and Roman Catholics from the restrictions imposed since the 1660s by the Corporation and Test Acts. The next year, Parliament passed the Catholic Emancipation [or Relief] Act on 24 March 1829, which had royal assent on 13 April. Further steps in this liberal process were taken later, as in 1871 when the Universities Test Act removed the requirement that lawyers, teachers, preachers, etc., must take the oath and pass the religious tests. Jews likewise became full citizens by the Jewish Disabilities Removal Act (1845)

---

[138] Viola Johnson-Cull, ed., *Ladysmith's Colourful History* (Victoria, Ladysmith Historical Society, 1985), p. 227.

[139] Elsie Ina Watts, "Attitude of Parents toward the Development of Public Schooling in Victoria, B. C. during the Colonial Period," M.A. thesis, Simon Fraser Universisty, 1986, pp. 9, 108, 164ff. "Conclusion."

[140] P. J. Cain & A. G. Hopkins, *British Imperialism 1688-2000* (2nd ed., Pearson Education Ltd., 2002), pp. 87-100.

[141] K. D. Reynolds, *Aristocratic Women and Political Society in Victorian Britain* (Oxford, Clarendon, 1998), pp. 1-2; Jonathan Parry, *The Rise and Fall of Liberal Government in Victorian Britain* (New Haven, Yale University Press, 1993); Richard Price, "Historiography: Narrative and the Nineteenth Century," *Journal of British Studies*, vol. 35 (April 1996), pp. 220-256; Michael Barone, *Our First Revolution: The Remarkable British Upheaval That Inspired America's Founding Fathers* (New York, Three Rivers Press, 2007), 339 pp.

and the Jewish Relief Act (1858).[142] These measures, much earlier than in most European countries, formally restricted the privileged constitutional status of the established Church of England, but the public at large remained overwhelmingly Anglican. The quiet domination of the Anglican population was not to be altered in the main for several generations. In its modified form, the Revolution Settlement had become so permanently established by the early twentieth century and so far taken for granted that people who had lived in no other religious environment were hardly capable of explaining it or even recognising it for what it was.

Freemasonry had a cosmopolitan influence in that environment that was difficult to assess. This brotherhood developed in the nineteenth century as a major creative force, having spread earlier as hundreds of lodges were founded in towns and regiments offering "convivial society, moral and spiritual refinement, material assistance, and social advancement in all parts of the empire."[143] Men posted in Malaya were advised that "you can't get on in the East unless you're a mason."[144] A branch of the Grand Lodge of England, no. 783, was founded in Victoria on 19 March 1859, and by 1868, at least six Freemasons's lodges were active in the town, some based at St Andrew's Presbyterian Church, where the first pastor, Rev. Thomas Somerville, was Provincial Grand Chaplain of his lodge.[145] Meanwhile, in 1878, a prominent English architect and mining engineer, *John Teague, himself a Freemason, built an imposing "temple" on Douglas Street.[146] It was listed among the prominent buildings of Victoria in *Lovell's Gazeteer of British North America* (1881), which listed no such building in any other Canadian town.[147] By 1889, there were ten lodges of Freemasons in Victoria with a total membership

[142] Geoffrey Best, "The Constitutional Revolution, 1828-1832," *Theology*, vol. 52 (1959), pp. 226-34; Geoffrey Best, "The Protestant Constitution and its Supporters," *Transactions of the Royal Historical Society*, 5th series, vol. 8 (1958), pp. 107-27; J. C. D. Clark, *English Society 1688-1832: Ideology, Social Structure and Political Practice during the ancien régime* (Cambridge University Press, 1985), pp. 393-420; Rowan Strong, *Anglicanism and the British Empire c.1700-1850* (Oxford University Press, 2007), pp. 213, 284.

[143] Jessica L. Harland-Jacobs, *Builders of Empire: Freemasons and British Imperialism, 1717-1927* (Chapel Hill, The University of North Carolina Press, 2007), pp. 3, 282 and ch. 4, "Our First Duty as Britons."

[144] Margaret Shennan, *Out in the Midday Sun: The British in Malaya 1880-1960* (John Murray, 2000), pp. 136, 163.

[145] Pethick, *Victoria: The Fort*, p. 227, note 63; Matthew Macfie, *Vancouver Island and British Columbia: Their History, Resources and Prospects* (Longman, Green, 1865), p. 81; Alexander Begg, *History of British Columbia from its Earliest Discovery to the Present Time* (Toronto, William Briggs, 1894), p. 494.

[146] Martin Segger and Douglas Franklin, *Victoria, A Primer for Regional History in Architecture* (New York, A Pilgrim Guide to Historic Architecture, 1979), pp. 41 and 66-9. Teague was a Presbyterian who married Eliza Lazenby, twin sister of the Methodist Emma Lazenby, wife of David Spencer.

[147] *Lovell's Gazeteer of British North America containing the latest and most authentic descriptions of over 7,500 cities, towns, villages and places* (Montreal, John Lovell & Son, 1881), p. 431.

of 587 as well as a secret order of total abstainers, the "Good Templars" (1865), who were still active in Saanich when my maternal grandparents joined it soon after arriving from Manchester in 1912.[148]

After British Columbia became a province of Canada in 1871, five of the first seven premiers—to 1889—were Freemasons and one of them, G. A. Walkem, held the office twice for a total of six years; by 1918, seventeen premiers had governed the province, of whom ten had been Freemasons.[149] The first lodges in Victoria were organized by such prominent people as the HBC chief commissioner James Allan Grahame (1825-1905), the provincial registrar, and Attorney General Edward Graham Alston (1832-1873), and influential early businessmen like Robert Burnaby (1828-1878) and *Captain Joseph Johnson Southgate. The latter gained a contract to provision Imperial warships anchored in Esquimalt harbour and had the financial support of *Commander H. D. Lascelles, RN, for the general store he built in Victoria, where he also dealt in real estate and was elected to the provincial legislature in 1869.[150]

Some readers may interpret the Island's overwhelming Protestant character as the result of prejudice, but careful investigation shows that it resulted from a set of lingering old traditions, out of date by the twentieth century but originally based on experience. In the late seventeenth century, the British Isles were seriously threatened by the persecuting Catholic forces of France and Spain.[151] For four hundred years, tribunals of the Roman Catholic Inquisition in Portugal and Spain, with powerful bureaucratic and police support, had been officially working to destroy all "heresy" and all non-Catholic populations. The Inquisition was not suppressed in Portugal until 1821 and in Spain until 1834.[152] As late as the 1880s, *Rev. Walter Thomas Currie found that in Portugal, there were almost no non-Catholic churches and selling a Bible was a criminal offence. In France on and off from the mid-sixteenth century, thousands of Protestants (Huguenots) had been forced to flee to Britain, Holland, Switzerland, or (later) the United States. "It was perhaps significant," writes a specialist, "that one of the distinctive features of French Catholic persecution in the 1540s had been that those who were about to be burned had their tongues cut out first. If French Protestant crowds were militant, so were Catholic crowds, and they were generally more murderous;

---

[148] *History of the Ancient and Honorable Fraternity of Free and Accepted Masons and Concordant Orders*, ed., Henry Leonard Stillson, (Fraternity Publishing, 1892), pp. 204, 488, 893.

[149] They were McCreight, de Cosmos, Walkem, Beaven, A. E. B. Davie, Turner, Prior, McBride, Bowser, and Brewster.

[150] J. M. S. Careless, "The Business Community in the Early Development of Victoria, British Columbia," in *Canadian Business History: Selected Studies 1497-1971*, ed., David S. Macmillan (Toronto, McClelland & Stewart, 1972), pp. 104-124, see p. 110; *Colonist*, 2 February 1865; Fawcett, *Some Reminiscenses*, p. 62.

[151] J. F. Bosher, "The Franco-Catholic Danger, 1660-1715," *History: Journal of the Historical Association* (London), vol. 79 (February 1994), pp. 5-30.

[152] Toby Green, *Inquisition: The Reign of Fear* (Macmillan Pan Books, 2007), pp. xix,74-6, 150, 248-9, 310-11, 344-5.

where Protestants smashed images, Catholics butchered people."[153] The much-cited case of Michael Servetus, a Catholic burnt in France by Protestants on 27 October 1553, was almost unique, and there was never a Protestant equivalent to the massacre of Saint Bartholomew (August 1572) in Paris and other French cities. In the reigns of Louis XIII and XIV, men caught trying to escape from France were usually sent to be chained to huge oars in galley ships on the Mediterranean. Their wives and children were imprisoned in convents, and Catholic conversion was forced upon them. These painful events left long-lasting memories in many Protestants minds.

---

[153] Diarmaid MacCulloch, *Reformation: Europe's House Divided, 1490-1700* (Allen Lane, 2003), p. 308; *Calvinism in Europe, 1540-1620*, ed., Andrew Pettegree, Alastair Duke, and Gillian Lewis (Cambridge, Cambridge University Press, 1994), pp. 6, 16-17, 35, 100-3, 105-6, 108-11, 113-18, 250.

St Paul's Naval Church, Esquimalt

St Peter's Quamichan

The Island in the Second British Empire

Seen in an even broader perspective, the maritime history of the Pacific northwest leads inevitably to the events and personnel of a British Empire that had changed since the conquest of Canada in 1759-1763. The Empire was quite transformed by the time the Island colony began to grow in the 1840s and 1850s. The loss of the thirteen American colonies in the 1780s and the victories leading to the Treaty of Vienna in 1815 brought about fundamental reforms. Great religious movements sent missionaries out to the colonies and drove Parliament to abolish the slave trade (1807) and then slavery itself within the empire (1833). None of the famous earlier empires—Chinese, Egyptian, Greek, Spanish, Roman, or any other—had abolished slavery. Britain posted a squadron off the west coast of Africa to catch slave-ships and began to establish new naval stations around the globe for the defence of trading routes and the new colonies being reached by its merchants and investors: Singapore (1819), Aden (1839, the first addition to the empire in the reign of Queen Victoria), Hong Kong (1842), Sydney (Australia, 1859), and Esquimalt (1865) on Vancouver Island. These were added to earlier bases: Gibraltar seized in 1704, Bermuda held since 1767, Trincomalee (Ceylon 1795), Simonstown (1815) near Capetown, South Africa, and Malta in the Mediterranean Sea with its Grand Harbour at Valletta.[154] By the time James Douglas founded Victoria in 1843, the colony he was founding was an extension of what may be seen as a second British Empire.

The Admiralty evidently favoured islands. New naval stations—or potential stations, for some remained only convenient anchorages—were usually sited on islands or peninsulas and semi-islands, and in this, Esquimalt was typical. When in 1892 the father of *Major Ralph Sandwith Engledue urged the authorities to move the Esquimalt Station to a better site, he respected this preference by rejecting Burrard Inlet on the mainland near Vancouver City in favour of Barkley Sound on the Island's west coast.[155] Singapore was on a tiny island separated from Malaya by a narrow channel. Only a strip of sand linked Gibraltar to Spain, and the same was true of Aden near the mainland of what became the Yemen. Trincomalee was adopted on the island of Ceylon (now Sri Lanka), and even Bombay was an island when Portugal ceded it to England in 1661. Lest the Navy should need an extra island or two in an emergency, it took command of tiny places like Ascension and Tristan de Cunha in the South Atlantic Ocean, Diego Garcia in the Indian Ocean, a great scattering of islands around the Pacific Ocean, and eventually even crags like Rockall in the North Atlantic Ocean, where it was nothing more than a small barren rock, three hundred miles northeast of Scotland, in need of a warning beacon.

Simon Winchester discovered in the 1980s during a nostalgic tour of Imperial bases that "one of the more eccentric practices of the Empire was to decide that

---

[154]   J. Holland Rose, "The British Title to Malta," *The Indecisiveness of Modern War and Other Essays* (G. Bell & Sons Ltd., 1927), pp. 142-156.

[155]   *The Times* (London), 6 June 1892, p. 14, "Our Coaling Stations in the Northern Pacific."

certain of the more remote island colonies were not really countries at all, but ships."[156] Thus, Ascension Island joined the Cape squadron in 1816 as HMS *Ascension*, a tiny rock in the Grenadines became HMS *Diamond Rock*, and Tristan de Cunha was called HMS *Atlantic Isle*. The navy preferred to keep stores and installations at island bases because they could be defended on the sea, without the aid of land forces. A sobering glimpse of the Admiralty's reasoning was its disastrous failure to prepare Singapore for resisting a Japanese army, which attacked unexpectedly overland across Malaya and forced it to surrender on 15 February 1942.[157] When convenient islands were not to be had, the Admiralty preferred to retain sites on territories already firmly colonized. Halifax was chosen on the coast of Nova Scotia in 1748, nearly half a century after it became a part of the empire. Sierra Leone and Cape Colony were similarly secure by the time the navy began to invest in installations at Freetown and Simonstown (near Capetown). In a reciprocal strategic arrangement, of course, a naval base, whether in a colony or on an adjacent island, inevitably formed part of colonial defences. Thus, Esquimalt made Vancouver Island a fulcrum for the creation and defence of a second colony, British Columbia (1858) on the mainland. After joining the two colonies together in 1866, London pressed them to join the Canadian Confederation, which they did—with doubts and hesitation—in 1871.

---

[156] Simon Winchester, *The Sun Never Sets: Travels to the Remaining Outposts of the British Empire* (Hodder & Stoughton, 1985 as *Outposts*; New York, Prentice Hall, 1985), p. 115.

[157] W. David McIntyre, *The Rise and Fall of the Singapore Naval Base, 1919-1942* (Macmillan, 1979), 289 pp. *passim*.

Royal Navy Squadron at Esquimalt, 1870

The story of Canadian Confederation does not explain why the Island and BC were there to be confederated, and this is what is missing in most general accounts of Canadian history. What needs to be added is that as Great Britain recovered from the loss of what became the USA and developed its second Empire, it soon came to own nearly half of the world's ocean-going shipping. Between 1835 and 1845, an unrivalled network of British "mail lines" was formed across the seas of the world: The Peninsular and Oriental (P&O) Line from England to Egypt, India, and the Far East was established in 1837, the first year of Queen Victoria's reign; the Royal Mail Steam Packet Company to the West Indies and the east coast of South America in 1839 and, in the same year, the Cunard Line to North America; the Pacific Navigation Company (PSN) running on the west coast of South America between Panama, Chile, and Peru in 1840; and many smaller ones. Sir William McKinnon founded the British and India Steam Navigation Co. in 1862 with official, subsidised mail contracts for India, and in 1872, he opened a steamer service between Aden and Zanzibar.[158] In the 1860s, two British firms, Jardine, Matheson & Co. and Butterfield & Swire, ventured into trade with China and up the Yangtse River to the interior.[159] In 1865, a Glasgow firm founded the Irrawaddy Flotilla Company for inland steamship service, which grew into an immense fleet, with many ships, warehouses, dockyards, and mills around Burma.[160] The biggest and strongest firms began to take over lesser ones on an increasing scale after 1870 to form large-scale shipping enterprises.[161] By 1885, Indian newspapers were advertising many lines of steamships carrying passengers to and fro between India and western Europe: "Austro-Hungarian Lloyd's," "British India," "City," "Clan," "Ducal," "Hall," "Natal," "Star," all in addition to the famous old "P&O" Line.[162] The Blue Funnel Line, operated out of Singapore from 1890, soon had subsidiaries such as the Straits Steamship Company and was known throughout the Orient by 1902, when it extended its services to Vancouver Island.[163]

---

[158] P. J. Cain and A. G. Hopkins, *British Imperialism 1688-2000* (2nd ed., Pearson Education Ltd., 2002), pp. 294, 333; Peter Padfield, *Maritime Power and the Struggle for Freedom: Naval Campaigns that Shaped the Modern World, 1788-1851* (John Murray, 2003), pp. 370-1.

[159] Blake, Robert, *Jardine Matheson: Traders of the Far East* (Weidenfeld & Nicolson, 1999), 280 pp.

[160] Alister McCrae and Alan Prentice, *Irrawaddy Flotilla* (Paisley, James Paton Ltd., 1978), 195 pp.

[161] *China Trade and Empire: Jardine, Matheson & Co. and the Origins of British Rule in Hong Kong, 1827-1843*, ed., Alain Le Pichon (The British Academy, 2006), 626 pp.; Gordon H. Boyce, *Information, Mediation and Institutional Development: The Rise of Large-Scale Enterprise in British Shipping, 1870-1919* (Manchester UP, 1995), 346 pp.

[162] B. L., India Office, *The Pioneer* (Allalabad), 1 May 1885, p. 10; 7 May 1885, p. 10; 1 April 1890, p. 14; Boyd Cable, *A Hundred Year History of the P. & O. Peninsular and Oriental Steam Navigation Company* (Ivor Nicholson and Watson Ltd., 1937), chapters 1 and 2.

[163] Major F. V. Longstaff, *Esquimalt Naval Base: A History of its Work and its Defences* (Victoria, BC, The Victoria Book & Stationery Co. Ltd., 1941), p. 35.

The East Coast Mail Line, shuttling between Victoria, Nanaimo, Comox, and other places on Vancouver Island's protected inner waterways, must be seen in this context at a time when, according to *Edward Mallandaine's estimate in 1871, Comox, the Cowichan Valley, Chemainus, and Salt Spring Island taken all together had a population "for whites and natives" totalling no more than fourteen hundred.[164] The East Coast Mail Line was established in the 1860s by *Joseph Spratt, an enterprising blacksmith from Hampshire, who employed the steamers *Maude, Cariboo and Fly*, and *Wilson G. Hunt*, repairing and servicing them at the shipyard at the Albion Iron Works he had founded in Victoria in the early 1860s. Only a small enterprise in a remote part of the empire, Spratt's was nevertheless one of the British shipping companies that, collectively, were leading the world for three generations before the first of the Canadian Pacific Railway Company's mail steamers, the *Empress of India*, arrived at Victoria from Yokohama on 28 April 1891. This enterprise was capitalized at $500,000 secured in five thousand shares, on the initiative of *Captain John Irving, and looked superficially like a local Canadian enterprise. However, the business concern Irving was bringing to it had been developed by his Scottish father with new partners, including a brother-in-law, *R. P. Rithet, their common father-in-law, and *Alexander Munro, both emigrants from the British Isles. When the Canadian Pacific Navigation Company was founded in 1883, it bought Spratt's ships.[165]

Only two years earlier, in 1881, the CPR Company itself was founded in Montreal on the basis of British investments and guarantees, a conclusion Cain and Hopkins have confirmed from a huge scholarly literature.[166] Among the many signs of Imperial influence in the company were two shipments of rails, which arrived at Victoria from England by sea for building its extension to Esquimalt from the nearest convenient point for crossing from the mainland.[167] Steel rails might so easily have been bought in San Francisco. Many other such examples of half-concealed British enterprise could be cited. The argument is not that British companies were always successful or profitable—some, notably colonization companies, failed badly[168]—but that British funds and enterprise were major factors in the pioneering growth of western Canada in general and British Columbia in particular. Seeing

---

[164]   Edward Mallandaine, *First Victoria Directory*, fourth issue (Victoria, 1871), p. 56.

[165]   Irving sold the company to the CPR in 1901-1903, including fourteen ships. [See Robert D. Turner, *The Pacific Princesses: An Illustrated History of Canadian Pacific Railway's Princess Fleet on the Northwest Coast* (Victoria, Sono Nis, 1977), pp. 11, 37-9; Valerie Green, *No Ordinary People*, pp. 64ff.; N. R. Hacking and W. Kaye Lamb, *The Princess Story: A Century and a Half of West Coast Shipping* (Second ed., Vancouver, Mitchell Press, 1976), pp. 64, 77, 98-103, 338.

[166]   P. J. Cain and A. G. Hopkins, *British Imperialism 1688-2000* (2nd ed., Pearson Education Ltd., 2002), pp. 232-8. Supporting scholarship is duly cited in footnotes.

[167]   Don MacLachlan, "Esquimalt and the E. & N.," in Maureen Duffus, ed., *Beyond the Blue Bridge: Stories from Esquimalt: History and Reminiscences compiled by The Esquimalt Silver Threads Writers Group* (Victoria, Ventura Publishing, 1990), p. 69.

[168]   Paterons, *British Direct Investment*, pp. 46, 83.

all this development as useful in the empire, the British government offered the Canadian Pacific Navigation Company certain subsidies and monopolies as well as naval protection.[169] Shipping lines were not only protected by the Royal Navy, but also encouraged by its requirements in the moving of freight, passengers, and mails. So, for example, the Union Castle Company took over the Admiralty packet service from England to the Cape of Good Hope in 1857. By 1912, the CPR Company was advertising its trans-Pacific service in the newspapers of Calcutta and Bombay.[170] The navy's need for coaling stations had meanwhile encouraged the exploitation of coal mines on the Island at and near Nanaimo by the Dunsmuir family from Scotland aided by the investments of RN officers such as *Lieutenant Commander Horace Douglas Lascelles, who lies buried at Esquimalt.

Marine surveying and charting of the Island, as distinct from mere exploring, seem to have been first undertaken by Captain George Vancouver in the 1790s, and the first useful charts were among the thirteen published between 1789 and 1791 by Alexander Dalrymple (1737-1808), who was appointed in 1795 as the first hydrographer to the navy and devoted himself to the work. Little was added to these early surveys during the next few decades of warfare against France and post-war recovery, but in 1846-1847, two ships of the RN under Captain Henry Kellett (1806-1875) and Commander James Wood (1825-1860) sailed out to survey the Strait of Juan de Fuca, the harbours at Esquimalt and Victoria, and parts of the Gulf of Georgia.[171] As a result, several new charts of waters around the Island appeared among the many based on their work. This initiative reflected the greater attention given to colonies early in the second British Empire. The results of Russian and Spanish surveys had never been published and were difficult to obtain. Even less well known were such charts as Chinese explorers may have compiled in the fifteenth century.[172] Charts and other aids to navigation were urgently needed for shipping

---

[169] C. E. Carrington, *The British Overseas: Exploits of a Nation of Shopkeepers* (Cambridge University Press, 1950), pp. 463-9; J.H. Hamilton, "The 'All-Red Route,' 1893-1953," *B.C. Historical Quarterly*, vol. XX (1956), pp. 2-3.

[170] *Bombay Gazette*, 10 January 1912 (a small daily with uncertain pagination); *Indian Planters Gazette & Sporting News*, 4 May 1912, pp. III and IV; *Times of India*, 1 May 1913, p. 1; 2 May 1913, pp. 1 and 2.

[171] Rear Admiral D. W. Haslam (Hydrographer RN), "The British Contribution to the Hydrography of Canada," *From Leadline to Laser, Centennial Conference of the Canadian Hydrographic Service*, 5-8 April 1983 (Ottawa, Supply and Services Canada, 1983), pp. 24-25; Commander L. S. Dawson, RN, *Memoirs of Hydrography including Brief Biographies of the Principal Officers who have Served in H.M. Surveying Service between the years 1750 and 1885, compiled by Commander L. S. Dawson, R.N. in two parts* (Eastbourne, Henry W. Keay, The "Imperial Library," 1885), Part I (1750-1830), p. 17; G. S. Ritchie, *The Admiralty Chart: British Naval Hydrography in the Nineteenth Century* (NY, Elsevier Publishing Co., 1967), pp. 188-89; Howard T. Fry, "Alexander Dalrymple and Captain Cook: The Creative Interplay of Two Careers," in Robin Fisher and Hugh Johnston, eds., *Captain James Cook and his Times* (Vancouver, Douglas & McIntyre, 1979), pp. 42, 54-55.

[172] Gavin Menzies, *1421: the Year China Discovered the World* (Bantam Books, 2002), 650 pp.

to that quarter of the world governed from London, not least for the coastal waters east and south of the Island. As tides rise and fall, the sea races up and down twice a day, churning and boiling in narrow places like a river. A thorough charting of these waters began under one of the great successors to Dalrymple, Rear Admiral Sir Francis Beaufort (1774-1857) of the famous Beaufort Wind Scale, fourth official hydrographer in London. He had been selected for this post by Sir John Barrow (1764-1848), second secretary at the Admiralty, ancestor of *Francis John Barrow who emigrated to the Island early in the twentieth century. Surveying was continued by *Admiral Sir George Henry Richards in HMS *Plumper* and *Hecate* (1857-1863), Captain Daniel Pender in the *Beaver*, (1863-1871), and Commander Morris H. Smyth and his successors in the *Egeria* (1898-1910).

In 1830, Barrow and Beaufort took the lead in founding the Royal Geographical Society—which provided thereafter a lively audience for travellers—and in establishing a Scientific Branch of the Admiralty the next year to contain the Hydrographic Department, the Royal Observatory at Greenwich, the Cape Observatory, and the Nautical Almanach and Chronometer Offices, these last two being combined soon after.[173] Admiralty charts were on sale to the merchant fleets of the world from 1823, and by 1835 they were being printed at the Admiralty building in their modern form with standard abbreviations.[174] Barrow and Beaufort also sponsored the publication of the first *Admiralty Tide Tables* in 1833 and gradually extended them from ports in southern and western England to many parts of the empire overseas. In 1835, they arranged for a semi-official publication of weekly *Notices to Mariners* as a more useful successor to the *Nautical Magazine* and in 1849 the Admiralty published the first edition of *The Admiralty Manual of Scientific Enquiry* to engage British mariners in these great tasks of improvement.[175] This work was central to the history of the Pacific Northwest, but its character and significance are best seen in the context of several wider operations by the Royal Navy intended to make the seas of the world safe and free for all. Features of the *pax Britannica*, which followed the Napoleonic wars, these operations were assisted by technical and scientific improvements that, together with rearrangements in London, amounted to a kind of revolution transforming the empire in the 1840s and 1850s.

It was in this climate of Imperial projects and expectations that British people with experience in India first went to settle on Vancouver Island. Most of the early arrivals were employees of the East India Company (HEIC) who transferred to the Hudson's Bay Company (HBC) during the years before and after the Indian Mutiny (1857-1858). As it happened, the mutiny almost coincided with the Cariboo gold rush (1858-1859), which offered attractive prospects for men affected by the upheaval that

---

[173] G. S. Ritchie, *The Admiralty Chart*, pp. 192-96.

[174] Ritchie, *The Admiralty Chart*, p. 189. *Captain C. P. Nixon, RCN, often told me that he had found these charts still useful in conveying Lord Alexander, the last British-born governor general of Canada, up the BC coast in a destroyer after the Second World War.

[175] Ritchie, *The Admiralty Chart*, p. 198.

followed the British government's decision to take control of India by an act of 2 August 1858.[176] It was in 1858, the very year of the Cariboo gold rush, that *Captain Henry Wootton, who had been in the service of the HEIC, went to the Island and worked for many years as the first postmaster in Victoria. The transfer of employees, especially mariners, from the HEIC to the HBC seems to have taken place even earlier, perhaps through Sir John Henry Pelly (1777-1852), son of an HEIC captain and governor of the HBC in the years 1822-1852.[177] Pelly took an active interest in the Island, where a sawmill company depended on his son Albert Pelly & Co. as its agents in London; another son, General Sir Lewis Pelly (1825-1892), served in the Indian Army from 1841.[178] Was it Sir John Pelly who chartered the *Marquis of Bute* from the HEIC and sent her to Vancouver Island in 1854?[179] Captain David Home was in the service of the HEIC when the HBC appointed him master of the historic side-wheeler, SS *Beaver*, which he took to Victoria on her maiden voyage around Cape Horn in 1835-1836.[180] *Captain Herbert George Lewis began his career at sea in the East India trade but arrived in 1847 at Victoria as third officer of the barque *Cowlitz* and ended his career as government agent of marine and fisheries. Thomas James Skinner (1812-1889) made several voyages to Calcutta and Rangoon for the HEIC before the HBC hired him in 1853 to manage a farm on the Island.[181] When *Gilbert Malcolm Sproat arrived in 1860, he had been training to join the Indian Civil Service but decided instead to work for a firm of shipowners intent on procuring timber by building a sawmill at Alberni on the Island's west coast. *George Bohn Martin, who sailed to Victoria in 1862, was a naval seaman with a record of service for the HEIC at Poona, India, and he eventually married the daughter of another soldier in the Indian Army. *Captain James Gaudin was employed by the HEIC before joining the North American shipping service of the HBC in 1865. *Thomas Basil Humphreys from Liverpool claimed to have been a midshipman in the HEIC before going out to California and, in 1858, on to a political career in the Cariboo. It is more certain that *Henry Augustus Snow Morley from Nottingham had spent several years as a midshipman in the service of

---

[176] When Matthew Macfie reached Victoria in 1859, he thought the population was "not more than 1,500," and by 1865, he reckoned it at 5,500 (Macfie, *Vancouver Island and British Columbia: Their History and Prospects* (Longman Green, 1865; facsimile edition, Toronto, Coles Publishing Company, 1972), 73, 77 note.

[177] Walbran, *British Columbia Coast Names*. p. 377; *Fort Victoria Letters, 1846-1851*, Hartwell Bowsfield (Winnipeg, Hudson's Bay Record Society, 1979), see index entries, p. 270.

[178] *Fort Victoria Letters, 1846-1851*, ed., Hartwell Bowsfield (Winnipeg, Hudson's Bay Record Society, 1979), 8 n. 5; *The Times* (London), 23 April 1892, 11; *Proceedings of the Royal Geographical Society and Monthly Record of Geography*, New Monthly Series, vol. 14, no. 6 (June 1892), pp. 416-21, obit.

[179] *Colonist*, 6 August 1889, reporting McIntyre's second visit in command of another vessel.

[180] Pethick, *S. S. Beaver*, pp. 19-22, 27, 47; Walbran, *British Columbia Coast Names*, 244-5; Home drowned in the Columbia River on 12 February 1838.

[181] Valerie Green, *Above Stairs: Social Life in Upper-Class Victoria 1843-1918* (Victoria, Sono Nis Press, 1995), 33-44; *Comox News*, 2 June 1889, 1.

the HEIC when, about 1869, he went out to join an uncle in the Cowichan Valley, where he went to work for the HBC as an accountant.

Some who were not obviously employed by the HEIC also went from India to the Island: men such as *Alexander Caulfield Anderson, *John Alexander Andrew, *John Henry Pitts, *John Sebastien Helmcken, *Edward Hammond King, and *Major General Henry Spencer Palmer. A civil engineer from London, Thomas Alfred Bulkley with his wife Annette, had two children in India during the 1860s and two more on the Island at Nanaimo during the 1870s before returning to the south of England.[182] *Rev. Archdeacon William Sheldon Reece was born in India at Madras. Not the least of the officials with connections in India was capable young *Arthur Nonus Birch, whose father and older brother had long and distinguished careers in India. It is doubtful whether any other part of Canada had anything like so many Britons from the East Indies in this period.

Few if any of the above arrived at the Island directly from India by sea until after the CPR established its Trans-Pacific Empress Line of steamers in 1891, five years after its railway reached the Pacific coast. But there had been contacts with ports across the Pacific from the time of the famous exploratory visits of captains Cook and Vancouver in the eighteenth century. By careful research, historians in British Columbia from Judge F. W. Howay (1867-1943) to Professor Barry Gough have discovered a world of trading mariners selling the pelts of sea otters (*Enhydra lutris*) in Oriental and Indian ports from as early as 1786, when two Bombay-built ships, the *Experiment* and the *Captain Cook*, were dispatched from Bombay to the northwest Pacific coast by a group of merchants led by James Charles Stewart Strange (1753-1840), brother of a chief justice in the Supreme Court of Madras.[183] Eventually, the furs of seals as well as otters and other animals were traded. Contacts developed less with India than with China, Japan, and the Sandwich (or Hawaiian) Islands but were part of a network of trans-Pacific trade.

[182]   British National Archives at Kew (hereafter BNA), census records for 1871, RG 10/1247, 14; 1891, RG 12/967, 7; RG 12/62, 1, with thanks to Peter Goff, Dorothy Jones, and John Lewis of the Kingsclere, Hampshire, research group.

[183]   Barry Gough, "India-based Expeditions of Trade and Discovery in the North Pacific in the Late Eighteenth Century," *The Geographical Journal*, vol. 155 (2), (1989), 8-9; Gough, *Distant Dominion: Britain and the Northwest Coast of North America 1579-1809* (Vancouver, University of British Columbia Press, 1980), 50, 53, 57, 64-5, 68; Gough, *The Northwest Coast: British Navigation, Trade and Discoveries to 1812* (Vancouver, UBC Press, 1992), 67, 72, 77, 87-8, 91; F.W. Howay, "A List of Trading Vessels in the Maritime Fur Trade, 1785-1794," *The Royal Society of Canada, Transactions 1931*, section 2, 117-149; Vic Hopwood, "Sea Otter Fur Trade from Before the Mast," *B.C. Historical News*, vol. 37, no 1 (Winter 2003), 12-17; Bruce Watson, "Scots on the Coast Before Alexander Mackenzie," *B.C. Historical News*, vol. 37, no. 4 (Fall 2004), 17-20; Derek Pethick, *First Approaches to the Northwest Coast* (Vancouver, J. J. Douglas Ltd., 1976), ch. 5; Robert J. King, "'Bahía Botánica y Liqueyos': Alexandro Malaspina and British Designs in the Pacific," *Congresso Internazionale, nel bicentario della massima impresa di Alessandro Malaspina, tenutosi a Mulazzo, Castiglione del Terziere e Lerici dal 24 al 26 settembre 1993*.

Breakfast on Manoeuvres 1908
(Major A.H. Jukes, 9th Gurkha Rifles, on duty in India)

When in 1891 the CPR's Empress Line of passenger steamers began a regular shipping service between Vancouver and Japan, establishing regional headquarters at Hong Kong, more and more British people travelled to and from India by that route. The CPR advertised its "large, luxurious steamers" and "magnificent hotels" in such popular works as Murray's *Handbook for Travellers in India, Burma and Ceylon* and in the *Times of India*, a daily of Bombay, in *The Pioneer* (Allahabad), and severel other Indian papers.[184] In 1912, for instance, long and detailed advertisements appeared in the weekly *Indian Planters Gazette & Sporting News* (Calcutta) stressing the advantages of the "Canadian Pacific Railway Co.'s Royal Mail Steamship Line, The National Highway to Europe" and making a feature of its sailings "from Hongkong [*sic*] via Shanghai, Nagasaki (Inland Sea of Japan), Kobe, Yokohama, Victoria and Vancouver" on its "Empress" steamers.[185] It was competing with eight other shipping lines that sailed the other way around the world, through the Suez Canal and the Mediterranean Sea. The journey from India to England via the Pacific Ocean, Canada, and the Atlantic was almost twice as far, but the CPR was proud of its first-class rates, which included the cost of meals and births in sleeping cars while crossing Canada. It offered reduced rates to missionaries and officers sent out to Asia by the army, navy, and consular and civil services. More and more passengers chose the CPR's route, perhaps with a view to visiting Canada, and this was how many first reached the Island, which already had a reputation around the empire. As the *Western Morning News* of Plymouth, Devonshire, reported on 2 February 1907, "Victoria is the first and last port of call for steamers to and from China and Japan, as well as Honolulu and the Land of the Southern Cross. The Race Rocks light, a mere candlestick afloat, signals the steamer adieu with the Union Jack by day and flashes the broad rays of its light when dusk creeps on."[186]

Short Biographies, A to Z

Notes

The Queen's Medal was awarded during the second South African War, 1899-1902, until Queen Victoria died in January 1901 and thereafter it was the King's Medal that was awarded. Thus, the former is a mark of service early in the war and the latter of service near the war's end.

To save space and avoid repetition, initials of first and last names are used in these biographical notes and the names of some places must be understood as on the Island or else in Britain, unless otherwise specified. Thus, Ganges, for

---

[184] Murray's *A Handbook for Travellers in India, Burma and Ceylon* (John Murray, 11th edition, 1924), a full-page CPR advertisement in the unnumbered pages of the "Advertiser" at the back; microfilm of Indian newspapers in the British Library, India Office Collection.

[185] British Library, India Office Collection, *Indian Planters Gazette & Sporting News*, vol. LVII, no. 18 (4 May 1912), 2-4. Many of this paper's forty or so pages were filled with advertisements for sporting equipment, "punkah-proof lamps," and goods of all kinds.

[186] Proudly reprinted in the *Victoria Daily Colonist*, 2 February 1907, p. 11.

example, is to be taken as a small town on Salt Spring Island (and named after HMS *Ganges*), Ladysmith as a town north of Cowichan (named for the relief of Ladysmith in the South African War), and Victoria means Victoria, British Columbia, but Edinburgh is to be understood as the Scottish capital; London will mean London in England unless Ontario is specified; and Sydney is to be taken as Sydney, Australia, unless Nova Scotia is specified. Oak Bay refers to a part of Victoria. Jersey should be taken as one of the Channel Islands and Berkshire as an English county. However, Edmonton and Calgary are towns in Alberta, not the British towns they were named after, and Montreal is to be taken as Montreal, Quebec, rather than the little French town of that name.

Every book cited was published in London unless another place is mentioned.

* Has a biographical entry in this book.

ADDINGTON, Major Herbert Hiley (1859-1943). In 1896, according to Canadian census records, he went out to Vancouver Island and settled at Somenos in the Cowichan Valley, where he was a parishioner of St Peter's Anglican Church at Quamichan Lake, near Duncan, one of many British officers in retirement. He was unmarried and gave his profession as "Army." He appears there on a provincial voters' list in 1898. In August 1907, he was reported as staying in Victoria at the New England Hotel, and late in October that year, he passed through Victoria again on his way to England. He had apparently lived quietly at his place in Somenos for about ten years, but the next sign of his presence in the northwest was his arrival at San Francisco on 7 August 1925, coming from Papeete, Tahiti, in RMS *Tahiti*, a "ret'd Army Officer" aged sixty-six, "Tourist for Pleasure," destination Otaki, New Zealand. Other passenger lists show him arriving at Southampton on 24 June 1938 from Wellington, New Zealand, aboard the *Arama* (Shaw, Savill & Albion Company Ltd.) listed as a "ret'd Army Major" aged seventy-nine, giving Lloyd's Bank in London as a mailing address.

He was born on 12 March 1859 at Torquay, Devonshire, christened on 11 May, and the 1861 census found him, aged two, living with his family in East Teignmouth, Devon. His father, William Wells Addington, aged thirty-nine, was a magistrate born in Hertfordshire at "Scotsworth," Rickmansworth, and soon to inherit the family title as Third Viscount Sidmouth and to be succeeded in due time by HA's elder brother as Fourth Viscount. Their mother was *née* Georgiana Susan Pellew, daughter of the Very Rev. George Pellew, dean of Norwith, third son of the First Viscount Exmouth. Aged thirty-eight in 1861, she was born at Sutton, Yorkshire. HA had four sisters and two brothers, all older except one brother, Harold William Addington, aged eleven months, born at Dover, Kent. There were seven servants and a governess. HA was probably the "Henry H. Addington," aged twelve, born at Torquay, who is listed in the 1871 census as a pupil at a school in Littleham, Exmouth, Devon. Census-takers did not always report names and facts correcctly. I could find no entry for HA in the 1881 census, but he appears in 1891, aged thirty-two, as "Captain Royal Fusiliers," born at Torquay and living at "Manor House," Upottery, Devon (where his christening had been registered on 11 May 1859), with two domestic servants and a visitor, Thomas Mantell, "Prevost, Royal Fusiliers," born in Chelsea, London. Meanwhile, also in 1891, his elder brother, the heir to the title (likewise christened at Upottery), was living at Royston, Churchstanton, Devon, with a wife and four children born in New Zealand aged from two to eight, the wife being Ethel Mary Tonge, born in Norwich. They had five domestic servants with a gardener and family living next door in "Royston Lodge." In that same year, 1891, HA was dispatched to the north-west frontier of India with the Hazara Expedition, according to the reliable *Whitaker's Directory* (1900), and in 1898 he was promoted to major in the Third King's Royal Rifle Corps.

Although I find little else about HA's life, there is no lack of information about his elder brother, the Fourth Viscount Sidmouth, or their father, the Third Viscount. The latter died, aged eighty-nine, on 28 October 1913, having served for some years as an officer in the Royal Navy before entering the House of Commons as Member for Devizes and then the House of Lords, when he inherited the peerage at his father's death in 1864. He (HA's father) took a great interest in the Volunteer Force and the Franklin expedition in search of the North-West Passage in the early 1850s. He had even attended the farewell breakfast for Franklin at the house of Sir Robert Inglis, MP for Oxford University, held in 1845 at Bedford Terrace, another guest there being Monckton Milnes (1809-1885), poet, politician, supporter, disappointed suitor of Florence Nightingale, and later Lord Houghton, father of Lord Crewe. "On that occasion," *The Times* recalled, "Franklin took his fellow guests to the map after breakfast and pointed out the North-West Passage by which he would return 'in about two years' time.'" Was it his father's interest in the Franklin expedition that prompted HA to live on remote Vancouver Island in the Pacific North-West?

Sources: census 1861, England, RG 9/1400, p. 15; census 1891, RG 12/1671, p. 1; census 1891, RG 12/1873, p. 2; Canadian census, 1901, Cowichan (26 pp.); *Colonist*, 1 August 1907, p. 6; 20 October 1907, p. 8; *Whitaker's*, p. 13; Williams, *The Story of St Peter's*, p. 55; British Columbia Archives, Victoria, BC, *B.C. Voters List, 1898*; *The Times* (London), 29 October 1913, p. 11, obit.; 26 March 1915, p. 10, col. B, obit (brother's death).

AGNEW, Commander Ronald Ian (1895-1949). Born on 6 June 1895 in Toronto, he became a cadet at the Royal Naval College of Canada in Halifax, Nova Scotia, on 1 January 1911 and had a lifelong career in the Royal Canadian Navy, beginning even before that force had been properly established. Consequently, his training and much of his service was in the Royal Navy. Appointed as a midshipman on 15 January 1913, he served in HMCS *Niobe* in 1914 and again in 1915, in Ottawa and in Fisheries Service vessels during those years, in HMS *Drake* and HMS *Manners* both in 1916, in HMS *Princess Royal* (1917), in HMS *Pegasus* aircraft carrier (1919), in HMS *President* (1919), in HMS *Dryad* for a navigation course and at the Royal Naval College (1920), in HMCS *Patriot* as first lieutenant (1920), in HMCS *Aurora* as navigation officer (1920), in HMCS *Guelph* (1921), in HMS *Repulse* as assistant navigating officer (1924), in HMS *Hood* as assistant navigating officer (1924), in HMS *Dryad* (1925), in HMS *Weymouth* as navigating officer (1925), in HMS *Champion* (1926), in HMS *President* for a staff course (1930), in HMS *Renown* (1931), and in HMS *Atheling* in command (1943). In the course of these duties, he had served as a lieutenant with the North Russia Relief Force resisting the Bolshevik revolution (1919), at headquarters in Ottawa as intelligence officer (1923), as flag lieutenant to *Commodore Walter Hose at an Imperial Conference (1923), as lieutenant commander in charge of HMCS *Vancouver* from 1 March 1928 to 14 August 1928, and as commander of HMCS *Naden* and senior naval officer Esquimalt in 24 June 1931, and on 24 June 1931, he was appointed to take charge of the establishment at Esquimalt. After a short stint in Ottawa as naval staff officer from 27 May 1932, he became the commanding officer of HMCS *Saguenay* (River Class Destroyer-D179) from 3 May 1934 to 5 May 1936 and as commander (D) Eastern Division in 1934-36.

RA was decorated with the OBE on 10 August 1935 and named honorary ADC to the governor general in 1936, CO of the RCN Barracks in Halifax (1936) and then *Naden* (1938). RA was married and settled in Victoria, but he was not about to retire as the Second World War approached. From 4 December 1940 to 19 December 1941, he commanded HMCS *Prince Henry*, an armed merchant cruiser (F70), and promoted on 1 February 1942 to captain commanding Canadian ships and establishments in the United Kingdom (HMCS *Niobe*), then became CO of HMS *Atheling* (1943). The complicated position of Canadian naval staff in London and RA's part in it is explained by G. N. Tucker with his usual scrupulous care. RA was mentioned in despatches in 1943; he ended the war in temporary command of HMCS *Naden* (1945) and went on to serve as commodore and the Canadian naval member of the Joint Staff in Washington (1946) and again as senior Canadian liaison officer in London and CO of *Niobe* (1947).

On 15 October 1921, he married Eleanor Minna "Tony" Monteith in Oak Bay, Victoria. She was born there on 8 April 1897, daughter of William Monteith, a Scot who had migrated to the Island and become an insurance agent at Esquimalt, where the 1901 census of Victoria found him resident on Lampson Street with a family of which a son, *Roger George Monteith, was to fight as a major in Canadian forces during the Great War. Like so many Imperial officers, RA established his home near his wife's family, in a house at 1028 Linden Avenue, Victoria, though his duties left him little time to spend there. It was while serving in London that he died, aged fifty-four, on 22 March 1949 and was buried at sea in British waters from HMS *Finisterre*.

Sources: Royal Canadian Navy, official Internet site, "citations and biographies"; Longstaff, *Esquimalt Naval Base*, p. 79; Macfarlane, pp. 2-3; *Canada Gazette*, 10 August 1935, 9 January 1943; *London Gazette*, 1 January 1943; W. A. B. Douglas, "Conflict and Innovation in the Royal Canadian Navy, 1939-1945," in *Naval Warfare in the Twentieth Century*, ed., Gerald Jordan (Croom Helm, 1977), p. 217; Gilbert Norman Tucker, *The Naval Service of Canada* (2 vols., Ottawa, King's Printer, 1952), vol. II, chapter 16, "Liaison with the Admiralty"; Canadian census, 1901, Victoria, Esquimalt District (Monteith family).

ALDERSON, Henry Spencer (1874-1948). In 1911, he and his wife went to Canada, where he worked for a short time as a civil engineer with the CPR, and then they ranched in the West, first in the Fraser Valley and then in the Cowichan District, where they settled on Inverarity Road near Somenos Lake. There he lived for twenty-three years and died, aged seventy-three, on 8 March 1948 in Duncan. On 23 August 1958, his wife died there too aged eighty-two. They were buried in the churchyard at St Peter's Quamichan, like many others of their kind.

Born at Holdenby Rectory, Northamptonshire, son of Rev. Canon Frederick R. Cecil Alderson (1836-1907) of Peterborough (but born in Marylebone, London), he was living in March 1881 with his family at "The Vicarage" in Holdenby with his parents, three sisters, and a brother, as well as eight servants: governess, nurse, cook, parlourmaid, housemaid, scullery maid, nursery maid, and groom. They had not always lived in Holdenby as his eldest sister had been born at Ampthill, Bedfordshire. In 1881, both parents were aged forty-four, and his mother, Katherine Gwladys Alderson *née* Guest, was born in Glamorganshire, Wales, daughter of Sir John Josiah Guest (1785-1852) of "Cauford Manor," Wimborne, Dorset, and sister of Lord Wimborne. His other grandfather was Sir Edward Hall Alderson (1787-1857), a Baron of the Exchequeur, whose daughter, HA's aunt, had married the Marquis of Salisbury—a marriage Salisbury's father opposed—making HA a nephew of one of Queen Victoria's most distinguished prime ministers and a cousin of Sir Vere Brabazon Ponsonby, Ninth Earl of Bessborough (1880-1956), governor general of Canada in 1931-1935. With such a background, it is hardly surprising that gossips embroidered on it by, for instance, mistakenly identifying HA as a brother of General Edwin Alfred Hervey Alderson (1859-1927), who was in fact a cousin who served at Gibraltar, in Natal, and in the First Division, CEF, during the Great War.

HA attended Haileybury College in Hertfordshire, served an apprenticeship with an architect for four years, and then worked for seven years (1897-1904) in the Engineering Department of the London and South-Western Railway. The 1901 census found him, aged twenty-six, an "engineer's assistant" boarding in Wakefield St, London. He became assistant engineer on construction of the Exmouth & Salterton Railway and then temporary engineer in the roads and buildings branch of the Public Works Department in Punjab, India. This led on to the post of subdivisional officer in charge of all government roads and buildings at Jullundur, Punjab. In 1907-1910, he worked for the Rajputana Malwa Railway, finished constructing the 130 miles of the Phulera Rewari chord railway, and became assistant and acting executive engineer in charge of maintaining way and works at Phulera, Neemuch, Mhow, Sirsa, and Jaipur in Rajputana. In 1902, he married Julia Charlotte Moser, daughter of Henry Moser of London, and it may have been his wife who, like so many other wives, persuaded him to find other employment.

Sources: *Who's Who in B.C.*, 1933-1934, pp. 11-12; census 1881, England, RG 11/1563, pp. 9-10; census 1891, RG 12/1092, p. 25; census 1891, RG 12/750, p. 49 (father); census 1901, RG 13/46, p. 45; *Cowichan Leader*, 11 March 1948, obit.; C. V. Owen, "Alderson, Sir Edwin Alfred Hervey (1859-1927)," *Oxford DNB*.

ALEXANDER, Major General Ronald Okeden, CB, DSO (1888-1949), was born at Kandy, Ceylon, on 7 August 1888, son of J. A. Alexander, Ceylon Civil Service, and educated in Bedford, England. He began soldiering in 1907 by enlisting in the ranks of the Fifth Regiment NPAM (Black Watch). Canada being willing to grant a commission to many a soldier who would have remained a non-commissioned officer in Britain, Alexander emigrated in 1908 and became a lieutenant with the Third Regiment, now the Victoria Rifles of Canada. In 1910, he joined the Royal Canadian Regiment as a permanent force soldier and went with it to Bermuda in 1914. When he enlisted in the CEF on 5 November 1914, he declared himself a professional soldier, and his next of kin as J. A. Alexander of 24 Lawn Crescent, Kew Gardens, Surrey, England. He went overseas on 15 September 1915 as adjutant of the Twenty-fourth Regiment, CEF, and was promoted to the rank of lieutenant colonel after the battle of the Somme, with command of the regiment in France and Belgium; eventually, he joined the General Staff. He was admitted to the DSO on 1 January 1917, mentioned three times in despatches, promoted to brevet lieutenant colonel, and in 1946 awarded the United States Legion of Merit for "exceptionally meritorious conduct" in joint Canadian-U.S. preparations for Pacific Coast defences against Japanese aggression. At enlistment in 1914, he was diagnosed with varicose veins in both legs, and on 16 February 1917, a medical board said he had German measles, had been too long at the Front, and required a rest. By then, he had had spells in three hospitals, two in France and the Royal Free Hospital, Gray's Inn Road, London.

From 3 July to 3 October 1918, RA attended a Senior Staff Course at Cambridge, but was demobilized on 1 April 1919. In 1924, he became professor of tactics at RMC, Kingston, Ontario. Stationed at Winnipeg from 1928 to 1935, he went to Victoria as GOC in October 1940 with the rank of major general and in 1942 became supreme commander of Canada's west coast defences and inspector general for central Canada and in 1944-1945 inspector general for western Canada. While waiting in Victoria for his discharge from the army in 1946, he was active on the Red Cross Committee and the national clothing drive in aid of European children.

In 1917, RA married Gertrude Williams, daughter of Right Rev. Lennox Williams, D.D., and they had two sons and a daughter. One of their sons, Flight Lieutenant James Okeden Alexander, was shot down and killed during a mass raid over Rotterdam in August 1941, while serving in the RAF. When RA died on 27 July 1949 at the Veterans' Hospital after an illness of four years, he and his wife were living at 2551 Beach Drive, Oak Bay. Besides his wife, he left a son, Ronald Lennox Alexander, a married daughter in Toronto, and a brother in England, Wing Commander N. G. Alexander, MC. The funeral was at Christ Church Cathedral.
Sources: Alexander Papers, University of Victoria Special Collections, SC003; *Daily Colonist*, 29 July 1949, p. 15 and obit.; *Who Was Who*, 1941-50, p. 14; NAC, CEF papers, RG150, acc. 1992-93/166, box 82-9; R. C. Fetherstonhaugh, *The Royal Canadian Regiment, 1883-1933* (Fredericton, Centennial Print & Litho Ltd., 1981), pp. 202-4, 421; *Colonist*, 28 July 1949, p. 3, photo and obit.

ALLBURY, Henry Peatt (1885-1964). Born on 21 June 1885 in Kensington (or Tottenham?), London, son of Maria Allbury from Seaford, Sussex, and Alfred Allbury, a "nurseryman" born at Budswich, Sussex, in 1891, he was living, aged five, with his family at 4 Pemberton Place, Chalkuncle, Kent. He had two brothers and a sister. There was a "clothier" boarding with them and one servant. Ten years later, HA was employed as a solicitor's clerk and was living with his family in Kent at 3 Pemberton Place, Milton, near Settingham. His father was now a "gardener."

About 1900, he went out to farm on the Saanich Peninsula and on Sidney Island nearby. He called himself a "farmer" when he enlisted in the CEF, Thirtieth Battalion, on 23 November 1914. On returning after the war with the DSM, he moved to the Comox Valley, raised chickens and potatoes at first but then kept the Comox Plant Nursery at Grantham. For many years, he was connected with the Provincial Department of Ariculture in the Comox Valley and was often a judge at fairs and agricultural exhibits. When he retired, he moved at first to Victoria, but two months before he died, he went into a hospital at Comox. His wife Winifred, who had died earlier, was the second daughter of Canon J. W. Flinton (c. 1867-1938), a pioneer Anglican minister at Alberni, Comox, Saanich, and Salt Spring Island. HA died, aged seventy-eight, on 6 May 1964 at Comox, leaving a daughter at Grantham and three grandchildren.
Sources: NAC, CEF files, box 116-20, no. 77841; *Colonist*, 7 May 1964, p. 16, obit.; census 1891, England, RG 12/716, p. 24; census 1901, RG 13/810, p. 1.

ALLEN, Henry George (1874-1966). Born on 26 May 1874 at St Mary Newington in St Pancras, London, he trained in the British postal service and spent seventeen months in the Boer War with the Eighth City of London Rifles ("Post Office Rifles"). After the war, he remained there to help organize the South African postal service. Very young, he married Annie Mary Allen, and in 1910, they migrated to Manitoba. Shortly before the Great War, they moved west to Vancouver, where they lived at 1060 Georgia Street, and he was working as a bookkeeper when he enlisted in the Seventh Battalion, CEF, on 18 September 1914. His formal registration with regimental number 16506 was at Valcartier, Quebec.

After the war, he went into the Vancouver Postal Service but moved in 1936 to Cobble Hill on the Island, where he and his wife were active in St John's Anglican Church. She died, aged eighty-one, on 20 December 1954 at the hospital in Duncan, and he on 24 September 1966 in Saanich, probably at Resthaven Hospital. His age then given as ninety-five may have been an overestimate by about three years.
Sources: NAC, CEF files, box 98-24; *Colonist*, 22 December 1954, p. 6, obit.

ANDERSON, Alexander Caulfield (1814-1884). Born on 10 March 1814 near Calcutta, India, son of an indigo planter, and educated in England, he entered the service of the HBC in 1831 and, the next year, arrived at Fort Vancouver on the Columbia River. He assisted in 1833-1834 at the establishing of the trading post at Fort McLoughlin near Millbank Sound and another on the Stikine River.

In summer 1840, he had charge of Fort Nisqually, Puget Sound, where Anderson Island was later named after him, and in 1841-1848, he took charge of Fort Alexandria on the Fraser River, then followed John Lees in the Colville District. After serving as chief trader at Fort Vancouver on the Columbia River in 1851-1854, he retired from the HBC and in 1858 settled at Rosebank, Saanich, near Victoria, where he was known to be an Anglican and well regarded as one of the company's most intelligent and energetic officers.

In Victoria, AA became postmaster, first collector of customs for BC, and some years later was appointed commissioner for the settlement of the Indian land question. At his death, he was fisheries commissioner for BC. His last public services were (1) to collect and send edible fish to the International Fisheries Exhibition in London and (2) to choose a site for a salmon hatchery on a tributary of the Fraser River. On this last, the steamer he was in went aground and he was forced to spend the night on a sandbar without fire, blankets, or bedding. The night being damp and cold, he caught a fatal infection leading to his death on 9 May 1884 in Victoria. In 1838, he had married the eldest daughter of James Birnie of the HBC service in Oregon Territory, a lady who predeceased him by ten years; they were buried near one another in South Saanich, leaving several children and grandchildren. His mother was then still alive, aged ninety-two, and living at Georgian Bay, Ontario. AA wrote some of the best descriptive pages about BC (See *Colonist*, 10 May 1884). An Anderson Lake and Anderson Hill, as well as other places, were named after him.

Sources: W. Kaye Lamb, in the *DCB*; Alfred Stanley Deaville, *The Colonial Postal Systems and Postage Stamps of Vancouver Island and British Columbia, 1849-1871* (Victoria, C. F. Banfield, King's Printer, 1928), pp. 33, 43, 55-8, 66, 164, 166; Alexander Caulfield Anderson, *The Dominion at the West: A Brief Description of the Province of British Columbia, Its Climate and Resources* (Victoria, Richard Wolfenden, Government Printer, 1872) 112 pp. and appendices; Anderson, *A Brief Description of the Province of British Columbia* (1872) (Victoria, R. T. Williams, 1883), 33 pp.; Richard Somerset Mackie, "The Colonization of Vancouver Island, 1849-1858," *British Columbia Studies*, no. 96 (Winter 1992-1993), pp. 3-40, see p. 24; Walbran, *B.C. Coast Names*, pp. 20-1.

ANDREWS, Captain Hugh Bertram (1877-1947). Born on 2 November 1877 at "Marden Park," Godston, Surrey, second son of Arthur Andrews, "East India Merchant," and his wife Alice E. Andrews, he was recorded, aged three, by the 1881 census as resident with his family, including five elder sisters, in a lodging house at 4 Grand Parade, Eastbourne, Sussex. He served for eight years late in the nineteenth century with the "Imperial Army, Second Battalion, Twenty-third Royal Welsh Fusiliers" in China, India, Crete, and Egypt.

He then migrated to Canada where he became an accountant in the Dominion Customs Department at Victoria on 1 November 1911 and served until 31 March 1941, except for service overseas during the Great War. He joined a militia unit, like many others of his generation, and, when he enlisted in the CEF on 6 January 1916, was a member of the Fiftieth Gordon Highlanders, 6' 2½" tall and weighing

168 lbs., with medium complexion, hazel eyes, and brown hair. He was living with his wife, Winifred Courtney Andrews, at 1352 St Patrick St., had a young son, Cyril, and said he was a clerk and a member of the Church of England. He embarked at Halifax on 1 June 1916 with the Eighty-eighth Battalion, arrived at Liverpool on 8 June 1916, and transferred to the Twenty-ninth in which he was promoted to captain. After some time in France and England, he was returned to Canada on 18 October 1917 suffering bouts of malaria contracted during his earlier service in China and India. Discharged after the war, HA served in Victoria and Vancouver as a demobilization officer and then rejoined the Customs Department in Victoria. He lived with his wife and their two sons, Cyril and Francis, first at 1070 Davie Street, then at 1776 Beach Drive, Oak Bay, but when he died on 19 August 1947, aged sixty-nine, at Veterans' Hospital, they were living nearby at 2044 Granite Street. He had spent thirty-nine years in Victoria, thirty-three of them in the Customs Service. His wife and sons survived him.

Sources: NAC, RG150, CEF files, box 181-6; *Colonist,* 2 April 1941, p. 16; 21 August 1947, p. 7, obit.; census 1881, England, RG 11/1039, pp. 15-16.

ANGUS, Captain Henry Forbes (1891-1989). Born in Victoria on 19 April 1891, he attended Victoria High School, McGill University (thanks to funding by one of his wealthy relatives in business in Montreal), and qualified for a BA (1911), Hon. LLD (1949), at Balliol College, Oxford, BA (1913), Vinerian Law Scholarship (1914), and an MA (1919). He read law with Joseph Ricardo in London and was called to the Inner Temple Bar (1914) and to the Bar of British Columbia (1920). When the Great War began on 4 August 1914, he was in England and soon joined the British Army. He served successively as second lieutenant in the Wiltshire Regiment in India (1914-1916), as lieutenant in the Mesopotamia Campaign (1916-1919), and with the Thirty-fourth Indian Infantry Brigade from October 1918 to February 1919. There had been an interlude in 1917, when he was a staff captain attached to the Fourth Dorset Regiment (1917). At some stage, he was mentioned in despatches.

After the war, HA lectured in law at the "Khaki University," a temporary arrangement for returning war veterans at the University of British Columbia (UBC) in Vancouver and he then became assistant professor of economics. He rose thereafter to become head of the Department of Economics, Political Science, and Sociology in 1930. Such influence as he felt from his Unitarian mother and his father's Presbyterian family may have prepared him for a social-science approach to public life. Choosing to be an academic statesman rather than a scholar, HA was active in public affairs as, for instance, a member of the Royal Commission on Dominion-Provincial Relations (1841-1845) resulting in the Rowell-Sirois Report, as special assistant to the under-secretary of state for external affairs (1940-1945), as a member of the Royal Commission on Transport (1949), and as a member of the Canadian Social Science Research Council (1952-1956). Such activities and his administrative duties at the university left HA little time for scholarship, but he published *The Problem of Peaceful Change in the Pacific Area* (1937), *Canada and the Far East, 1940-1953* (1953), and articles as well as a book on Canadian-American relations.

A book he published in 1926, *Citizenship in British Columbia, authorized for use in the schools of British Columbia* (Victoria, King's Printer, 1926), affords some idea of his thinking in relation to the British Empire. On pages 185-86, he showed that, like so many in BC, he was acutely aware of Ottawa's complacency in counting on the British Empire and the United States for protection. "It is the policy of Canada to keep [its] forces as small as possible . . . We could hardly be attacked except in circumstances which would justify us in counting on the help of Great Britain, or the United States, or both. These countries both maintain relatively large and expensive armaments for the protection of their interests. It is on British forces that we rely for the protection of our citizens in foreign countries should such protection be necessary. The arrangement is very convenient." As a veteran of the British Imperial forces in India and Mesopotamia, he had had personal experience of what was at stake.

HA's family background shows strong British roots. His father, William Angus, was born at Bathgate, Linlithgow, West Lothian, in May 1841, and appears in the Scottish census taken in the following June, as the son of a "merchant grocer," Alexander Angus from Rafford, Morayshire, aged fifty, and his wife Margaret of Bathgate, aged forty. This couple, HA's grandparents, had seven older children, five of whom emigrated to Canada, as William HA's father did, but at different stages. William spent more than ten years in Salford, Lancashire, appearing there in 1871 as a salesman for a cotton manufacturing firm and sharing a dwelling at Pendleton with a much-older brother, Forrest Angus (1826-1919), and their sister Catherine (1836-1917), who kept house for them with the aid of a female servant. Forrest was working as "buyer to calico printers." It was in those years in Salford that Willliam met HA's mother, Mary Edith Dunckley, who was born there on 15 April 1850. They married in 1880, and the census for 1881 shows them a few months later living at 106 Eccles Road in Pendleton with a different female servant and William employed as a "spinner and manufacturer." About two years later, they emigrated to Victoria, where she gave birth to HA on 19 April 1891, and Canadian census records show all three of them a few weeks later living in the James Bay district. William died sometime during the next few years: the 1901 census records HA, aged ten, and his widowed mother living at 18 Stanley Avenue. Nearby on St Charles Street lived William's brother Forrest and three of their sisters, Jesse, Margaret (Margret?), and Katherine, who had emigrated together in 1887.

Staying in the latter household was a niece from Montreal, HA's cousin, Agnes Rhoda Angus, aged twenty-five, one of the six daughters born to Richard Bladworth Angus (1831-1922), a rich banker, financier, and philanthropist of Montreal. He was by far the most successful of the entire family of HA's future aunts and uncles living at Bathgate in 1841. He was probably the uncle who paid for HA's education, though HA may have earned the cost of his education by working in the long summers, as I and many other did. After some years of employment in the Manchester and Liverpool Bank, this uncle had gone out to Montreal in 1857 to work for the Bank of Montreal and risen up in its service, investing meanwhile in a joint-stock company with Donald Smith (the future Lord Strathcona) and

Smith's cousin, George Stephen (the future Baron Mount Stephen), so becoming one of the founding promoters of the Canadian Pacific Railway. Such an uncle must have loomed large in HA's mind.

In 1948-1951 as a boy at UBC, I attended some of HA's classes and remember him as a busy old person, austere, even bleak. This was doubtless unfair like most ideas the young have about their elders, as Professor Henry Mayo remarked when we recalled HA together in the countryside, south of Ottawa in the year 2001. Mayo liked and respected HA.

Sources: *Who's Who in B.C.*, e.g., 1947-1948, p. 4; *Who's Who in Canada*, 1958-1960, p. 24; Alexander Reford, in the DCB; Recollections of Henry Mayo, Ottawa, January 2001; census 1851, Scotland, CSSCT1851_173, p. 39, household 161; census 1841, Scotland, CSSCT1841_117-0174, p. 10; census 1871, England, RG 10/4011/33, p. 23; census 1881, RG 11/3942/94, p. 23; Morgan, *Canadian Men and Women*, pp. 28-9; *Canadian Who's Who*, vol. VIII (1958-1960), p. 24; H. F. Angus, *Citizenship in British Columbia, authorized for use in the schools of British Columbia* (Victoria, King's Printer, 1926), 296 pp.; H. F. Angus, ed., *Canada and Her Great Neighbour: Sociological Surveys of Opinions and Attitudes in Canada Concerning the United States* (Toronto, Ryerson Press; New Haven, Yale University Press, 1938), 451 pp.; Angus Family Papers, archives of the University of British Columbia (Vancouver); Donna McDonald, *Lord Strathcona: A Biography of Donald Alexander Smith* (Toronto, Dundurn Press, 1996 and 2002), pp. 132, 289, 299-300, 308-15, 350 and passim.

ANKETELL-JONES, Patrick Willoughby (1867-1932). He was born on 27 July 1867 on Mayo Island, Ireland, son of Henry Moutray Anketell-Jones and Caroline Diana Frances (*née* Carr-Lloyd) of Mayo and Bellview Park, Dublin, who had him educated as a cadet aboard the training ship HMS *Worcester*. He went on to join the Hooghli [*alias* Hooghly, Hooghley, or Hugli] Pilot Service at Calcutta, India, a branch or adjunct of the Royal Navy, which piloted ships through the shifting shoals in the 126 miles of the difficult river leading up from the Bay of Bengal to Calcutta. The importance of Calcutta [now Kolkata] as a leading Indian seaport, as well as the colonial capital until replaced by Delhi in 1911, conferred a major responsibility on the Hooghli Pilot Service. In 1922-1923, there were no fewer than fifty pilots, and that year, they escorted some 2,322 vessels totalling 11¼ million tons up and down the river. When PA joined the service in the 1880s, his senior officer was *Sherman Ransom, who also retired to the Island. But there was a considerable interval between their return home to the British Isles and their migration to the Cowichan Valley. In 1889 at St Peter's Church in Plymouth, PA married Miss Katherine Bluett, whose brother migrated later to Ontario and their two sisters to the Pacific coast. After leaving India, PA served as a JP on the bench in County Galway, busy for six years with the governing council, and for about fifteen years he farmed at Oughterard, County Galway. He spent five more years at Montreux, Switzerland, before moving in 1910 to Chemainus on the Island.

There, he bought a farm from Captain Conway, a Boer War veteran who had bought it earlier from a local pioneer, George Kersley. Like most educated British settlers—and many without formal education—PA was public-spirited and soon was active in the community. In 1911, he served as councillor for Chemainus Ward and in 1912 and 1913 was elected reeve of North Cowichan, first by a big majority and a second time by acclamation. He also served for several years as a director of the Cowichan Agricultural Society and for the two years 1915-1916, 1916-1917 was president of its board. For many years, too, he was a government representative on the Chemainus General Hospital Board. In 1915, he won a medal offered by the Canadian Bank of Commerce "for having the highest score in the 1915 Ladysmith Farmer's Institute and Oyster Harbour Women's Institute Exhibition." After his death, this medal found its way into the Duncan Museum, where it was stolen in September 2002. Again, like many others of his kind, PA won many prizes for his agricultural exhibits and very soon was recognized as an authority on field crops, fruits, and vegetables, particularly potatoes on which he became a specialist. He was soon in demand as a judge at agricultural shows in Vancouver and Victoria as well as smaller fairs throughout the province. In 1930, he judged at the winter show in Spokane, Washington State, and only ill health prevented him from doing the same the next year. He suffered from heart trouble and died, aged sixty-four, on 16 February 1932 while pruning fruit trees in his orchard. The *Vancouver Province* radio soon broadcast the news of his death to all parts of the province, "where his commanding and cheery personality had gained him many friends during his judging activities." His wife Katherine Anketell-Jones died, aged sixty-six, on 26 January 1936 at Ladysmith Hospital. They were survived by a son Edward M. Anketell-Jones and a daughter Aileen, both educated in Switzerland during the family's time there. On 3 June 1913, Aileen married Richard Cecil Mainguy (1886-1946), a BC land surveyor and brother of *Edmond Rollo Mainguy, and they made their home in Duncan. Her brother Edward was severely wounded in the Great War, married in 1921, and had two sons of whom one (Michael) served in the RCN for twenty-five years and then worked as an engineer in London with British Petroleum. A curious postscript to these notes comes from recollections of the late Captain Fred Frewer, ex-RCN, that the captain of a ship he once served on, perhaps HMS *Magnificent* but more probably the *Uganda*, bought a frock coast and a sword from Admiral (as he became) Rollo Mainguy, who had it from a cousin, P. W. Anketell-Jones. PA had worn them during his time in the Hooghly Pilot Service.

Sources: *Cowichan Leader*, 18 February 1932, obit.; 30 January 1936, obit.; *Cowichan Valley Citizen*, 1 September 2002, p. 2; Elliott, *Memories of the Chemainus Valley*, pp. 258-59; interview with Captain Frederick Frewer, RCN (retired) 6 December 2003; *A Handbook for Travellers in India, Burma and Ceylon* (London and Calcutta, John Murray, 1924), pp. 80-1 and 103-4; Pamela Kanwar, *Imperial Simla: The Political Culture of the Raj* (Delhi, Oxford University Press, 1990), 39-42; John M. MacFarlane, *Canada's Naval Aviators* (rev. ed., Shearwater, NS, Shearwater Aviation Museum, 1997), p. 6.

ANKETELL-JONES, Michael Willoughby (1923-2002?). Born in Victoria on 3 July 1923 (son of the above), he became a naval cadet in the RCN on 1 September

1941 and was trained at the King's Officer Training Establishment, then at the Royal Naval College Dartmouth (Special Entry RCN No. 55), and was gazetted as a midshipman (RCN) on 1 May 1942. He was at Royal Naval Engineering College for Training (1942), aboard HMS *Scourge* for training (1943), at RN Engineering College at Keyham (1944) and in HMS *Suffolk* for the Watchkeeping Certificate (1945).

After various other postings here listed, he was at HMC Dockyard, Esquimalt (1952), at NHQ Staff Ottawa (1954), at NHQ on Staff of Director General Ships as assistant chief of staff, Technical Services (1964). On 1 July 1964, he was promoted to captain RCN, and on 1 April 1969, he retired. For sometime thereafter, he worked for the British Petroleum Company, and after retiring again he became a sheep farmer in East Sussex, England.

Sources: John M. MacFarlane, *Canada's Naval Aviators* (rev. ed., Shearwater, NS, Shearwater Aviation Museum, 1997), p. 6.

ANSCOMB, Hon. Herbert Bertie (1892-1972). He was born on 23 February 1892 at Maidstone, Kent, where the census found him in 1901, aged nine, living at "Hove Villa," College Road, with his widowed father, an elder brother and sister and one domestic servant. His father, John Stake Anscomb, born in Sussex at Hove [or Brighton?], was a "road surveyor," though the 1871 census had recorded him as a "builder." HA's mother, Eliza Anscomb, born at Ardingly [or Linfield?], Sussex, had died during his early childhood. HA attended Maidstone Grammar School and then worked locally as a junior clerk until 1911, when he migrated to BC and worked as a clerk for the BC Electric Railway Co. Ltd. and later for various private companies. During the Great War, he served in the Royal Flying Corps.

In 1933, he was elected to the BC provincial legislature as independent member for Victoria but soon joined the Conservative Party and was re-elected in 1937 and 1941. He appeared to some, when contending for the party leadership after Dr F. P. Patterson in 1938 and R. L. Maitland in 1941, as "a gruff bulldog of a political infighter and a perennial candidate for the party leadership." During the coalition governments that Liberals and Conservatives formed as a bulwark against the socialist Canadian Commonwealth Federation in the years 1941-1952, HA served at different times as minister of mines, minister of trade and industry, and minister of finance. His political life ended with the victory of the Social Credit Party in 1952. For much of his time in Victoria, he was active in the Rotary Club, the Chamber of Commerce, the Publicity Bureau, and the Anglican Church. In 1925, he married Anne Maud Brooker of Victoria, and they lived in Oak Bay at 356 Newport Avenue. Mrs Anscomb died there, aged sixty-nine, on 8 May 1956 and HA, aged seventy-nine, on 12 November 1972.

Sources: census 1901, England, RG 13/767, p. 30; census 1871, RG 10/942, p. 4; *Who's Who in B.C.*, 1947-1948, p. 5; David J. Mitchell, *W.A.C. Bennet and the Rise of British Columbia* (Vancouver, Douglas & McIntyre, 1983), pp. 61, 69, 70, 73, 80, 84-101 passim, 140-1, 146, 148, 151, 154, 158, 159, 160, 162; *Margaret Ormsby, British Columbia, A History* (Toronto, Macmillan, 1958), pp. 457, 487.

ANTLE, Captain Rev. John (c. 1866-1949). He was born on the north-east coast of Newfoundland at Brigus, Conception Bay, two generations before Newfoundland became a province of Canada, and he died in the year it joined Confederation. After graduating at Queen's Theological College (1890) and becoming a minister in the Church of England two years later, he served in Newfoundland for five years and then followed his family to Washington State, immediately south of British Columbia.

The American Episcopal Church would not act on his suggestion for hospitals and a mission boat to serve the loggers and fishermen on the coast of Puget Sound, and in December 1899, the Anglican diocese of [British] Columbia asked him to organize a parish in the Fairview district, where he became the first vicar of Holy Trinity Church. With a boys' club he supervised there, he built a boat, the *Laverock*, for Sunday cruises. A few years later, he obtained a grant of $100 to survey the medical, social, and religious needs of settlers and loggers on the coasts and islands of the straits and inlets between Vancouver Island and the mainland. His conclusion was that a hospital mission ship, a circulating library, and a monthly magazine would all make a great deal of difference in those parts. After the inevitable opposition had been aired, the Missionary Society of the Church of England in Canada (MSCC) found funds for a mission ship, and in 1905, the *Columbia* was built in Vancouver with a dispensary, an emergency ward, a provision for a library, and a chapel. JA trained as an anaesthetist to assist a medical doctor who was hired—a man with mechanical skills—and before long, they were able to prompt authorities to build small hospitals at Rock Bay, Van Anda, and Alert Bay. When funds proved inadequate, JA travelled to eastern Canada, and to England, returning with $10,000 provided by the SPCK, the Women's Auxiliary, and other philanthropic bodies. A bigger vessel was envisaged, and the *Columbia II* was launched at New Westminster in 1910. The Columbia Coast Mission grew rapidly, adding a magazine, *The Log*, to its equipment.

At the age of seventy, about 1930, JA retired. In 1939, he went to England and there found a forty-eight-foot yacht called the *Reverie*, which had been built in Assam by *Henry Bertram Bayly, a tea planter, who was glad to exchange his yacht in England for a house Antle owned on the Island at Maple Bay. JA then sailed her adventurously out to the north-west coast for service with his various projects. She enabled him to live on Mayne Island, where he became the minister of its parish, but in 1948, aged eighty-one, he set sail for the West Indies. Like *Captain Eustace Downman Maude and for much the same reasons, he met such daunting difficulties that the Royal Vancouver Yacht Club sent two members to San Francisco to help him sail the *Reverie* home. He died at last, aged eighty-four, on 3 December 1949 in Vancouver city, but was buried at sea off Bowen Island.

Sources: Rev. L. Norman Tucker, *Western Canada* (Toronto, The Musson Book Co. Ltd., 1907), pp. 110-15 (photo); Frank A. Peake, *The Anglican Church in British Columbia* (Vancouver, Mitchell Press, 1959), pp. 132-5; *Colonist*, Sunday 4 May 1924, p. 13 (article by Vera Ashe); 13 April 1940, p. 6; 4 October 1940, p. 4; Anglican Archives in BC, the John Antle Collection, 4 cm of textual records dating from c. 1950; *Canadian Almanach*, 1909, p. 343; Donna McDonald, *Lord Strathcona: A*

Biography of Donald Alexander Smith (Toronto, Dundurn Press, 2002), pp. 455-6; Lukin Johnston, *Beyond the Rockies: Three Thousand Miles by Trail and Canoe Through Little-Known British Columbia* (J. M. Dent & Sons Ltd., 1929), pp. 59ff.

APPLETON, Colonel Henry (c. 1854-1929). Born in Manchester, son of a drysalter, he was educated for the Royal Engineers in which he was commissioned on 17 August 1874. He was promoted to captain on 17 August 1874, posted to the "Indian Establishment" on 25 October 1877, and appointed on 2 August 1878 to the Military Works Department, wherein he served at Mandalay with the Executive Engineers, third grade, from 21 December 1889. Meanwhile, he served in 1886-1887 as a "Mahsood Wuzaree Expert." HA went to Tibet in those early years, when few people did, and had time for big-game hunting there and for fraternizing with the Tibetans. His collections of mounted heads of large-game animals were famous and eventually displayed at museums in England and the United States.

After retiring from the Imperial Army, he went out directly to Victoria, arriving from the Orient on the *Empress of Japan* on 26 June 1907, and stayed with his brother, Frederick Appleton of "The Headlands," Gordon Head in Saanich. Early in August 1907, he boarded the *Princess May* to sail north, being interested in mining, and went hunting for big game in the Cassiar district with some friends, Mr and Mrs Conduitt, with whom he had once hunted in Burma. A misunderstanding arose later over the division of the costs for this expedition: a cook, guides, Hudson Bay Company stores, and other bills. Mr Conduitt thought HA had agreed to pay two-thirds of these costs, and Appleton insisted that his share ought to be only one-third. They eventually went to court in Victoria over this matter.

HA became a collector of Oriental prints, a recognized expert on them, and developed a notable collection of Hiroshige prints, which he showed publicly in Victoria and eventually sold to some of the famous Japanese print collectors of Chicago, Boston, New York, and London. He exhibited Japanese prints of the years 1760-1808 at the Alexandra Ballroom in Victoria on 10 March 1914. He also collected postage stamps, particularly Oriental stamps, and sold one of his collections for about $6,000. His interests and collections in the realm of art were marvellously varied. Cloisonné, Chinese laqueur work, Icelandic silver, Chinese porcelain, and other rare *objets d'art* were all gathered, and he was always willing to show them to others and to address the Island Arts and Crafts Society, who recognized him as an authority on many matters, particularly Oriental prints.

HA was also a serious botanist known throughout Western North America as a keen nature lover and advocate of wild-flower protection. He discovered and named several new varieties of which specimens were accepted by Kew Gardens in London, and his contributions to the Victoria Natural History Society's discussions were long remembered. He went often to the Sol Duc Olympic Mountains resort, and the American Geographical Society named a peak in the Olympic Range after him in recognition of his interest in the flora, fauna, and geography of that region. He published articles on these subjects in American magazines.

During the last seven years of his life HA lived at "Roccabella" in Victoria, but throughout his twenty-four years in Victoria he travelled abroad a good deal, adding to his collections of prints, postage stamps, and botanical specimens. When he died on 12 December 1929, aged seventy-five, his brother Frederick Appleton was living in California, and HA also left two nieces, Mrs Bertram Wood and Mrs Bruce Irving, and a cousin Francis Hawkins. Pallbearers at his funeral were *Lieutenant Colonel A. G. Wolley-Dod, *Major R. M. Greig, Cecil Chartres Pemberton (1864-1943), R. F. Taylor, E. B. Irving, and C. D. Stedman. He was buried in the Anglican part of Ross Bay Cemetery.

Sources: Notes from Captain T. W. J. Conolly, *Roll of Officers of the Corps of Royal Engineers from 1660 to 1898* (Chatham, Royal Engineers Institute, 1898) kindly sent by Ed de Santis; *Indian Army List,* July 1891, pp. 12, 194; *The Monthly Army List for May 1891*, p. 242; *Colonist*, 26 June 1907, p. 7; 4 August 1907, p. 4; 10 December 1907, p. 7; 6 March 1914, p. 7; 17 December 1929, p. 5; 13 December 1929, p. 5; 14 December 1929, p. 5; *Whitaker's*, p. 22; census 1861, England, RG 9/2762, p. 30; census 1871, RG 10/4063/15, p. 23.

ARGYLE, Thomas (c. 1838-1919). Born and brought up in Birmingham, Warwickshire, by an English father and a Scottish mother, he learned the gunsmith's trade, went to work for Chance Brothers of Birmingham, lighthouse builders, and then joined the Royal Engineers. The regiment dispatched him with a contingent of about 150 others around Cape Horn, aboard the vessel *Thames City*, to Vancouver Island, where they landed at Esquimalt on 12 April 1859. Unlike most of the contingent, who were set to make surveys and build roads and bridges in the interior of the colony, TA was kept as armourer and general smith at New Westminster, where he remained when the contingent returned to England. He met and in 1863 married Ellen Tufts, daughter of Samuel Tufts, descendants of a United Empire Loyalist family, who had settled at Halifax. The couple settled at first on land near New Westminster, where in 1871 TA received Crown grants totalling 155 acres, but in 1867, he was appointed keeper and Mrs Argyle, matron of the Race Rocks lighthouse, a few miles off Victoria.

This important lighthouse helped mariners to avoid Race Rocks, where many ships were wrecked, including the sailing vessel, *Nannette*, which the first mate, my great-uncle *Captain William McCullock (1827-1906), wrecked on those rocks on Christmas Eve 1860, shortly before the lighthouse was finished. When the province joined the Canadian Confederation in 1871, lighthouse administration passed from British colonial authorities to the Canadian Department of Marine and Fisheries, a prey to corrupt patronage, which cut TA's salary by 80 percent, burdened him with paying his assistants and buying his own supplies, and eventually dismissed Mrs Argyle. On 17 September 1874, TA rescued two men clinging to a makeshift raft and was arrested and fined $100 because they turned out to be deserters from HMS *Shah*. While diving for fish about 1885, however, he seems to have found gold sovereigns in a wreck and so managed better than he would have done on the tiny pension granted upon his retirement in 1888. He took his family to live on a farm at Rocky Point near Metchosin, a ten-room wooden farmhouse whence the children drove by horse and buggy to the Metchosin School. They led a simple but convivial life with neighbours and visitors, TA having a good singing voice, and in 1909, he attended a reunion of those Royal Engineers who, like him, had chosen to stay in British Columbia. The Argyles left two sons and three daughters when they died: Ellen Argyle, aged fifty-two, on 23 January 1917 and TA, aged eighty-one, on 14 March 1919.

Sources: Marion I. Helgeson, ed., *Footprints: Pioneer Families of the Metchosin District, South Vancouver Island, 1857-1900*, (Metchosin School Museum Society, . . .); Canadian census, VI, 1891; Frances M. Woodward, "The Influence of the Royal Engineers on the Development of British Columbia," *B.C. Studies*, vol. 24 (1974-1975), p. 39; Royal Engineers Living History Group, Internet site; Donald Graham, *Keepers of the Light: A History of British Columbia's Lighthouses and their Keepers* (Madeira Park, Harbour Publishing, 1985), pp. 22-30 and photo; "Total Loss of the British Bark *Nannette*," *The Daily British Colonist*, Victoria, BC, Sunday, 25 December 1860, vol. 5, no 11, p. 3.

ARMITAGE, Major Charles Leathley (1871-1951). He was born on 6 March 1871, at Cranton, Gloucestershire, son of Rev. Arthur Armitage and his wife Nona. Ten years before his birth, they were living at Petra Villa, Weston-super-Mare, with CA's paternal grandparents and five servants. In 1861, CA's grandfather, John Leathley Armitage, born in Leeds c. 1782, was "Magistrate, Deputy Lieutenant" at Weston-super-Mare and the grandmother Elizabeth came from near Thirsk, Yorkshire. CA had an elder sister, Emily Leathley Armitage, born in Yorkshire. Schooled in Bengeo, Hertfordshire. CA enlisted in the Liverpool Regiment in 1892 and was promoted to captain in 1900. In 1907, he transferred to the Sixth Battery, Worcestershire Regiment and served in France in 1914-1915. He was named to the DSO (*London Gazette*, 24 July 1915) for his part in assaults on the German lines at Richebourg and Festubert, and to the OBE (*London Gazette*, 3 June 1919). One of the "old contemptibles," he was served as chief constable at Southport from 1907 to 1919.

In that year, he migrated to an apple orchard at Salmon Arm, BC, and then to a property between Maple Bay and Quamichan Lake on the Island. He and his neighbour there, Mrs *Admiral Edmond Rollo Mainguy, quarrelled over water rights. A relative, Commander Denis Forster, and his wife Audrey of Ottawa remember visiting CA on the Island soon after the Second World War and hearing him complaining that "some damned Canadian is moving in next door." CA died, aged seventy-nine, on 17 September 1951 at Maple Bay.

Sources: census 1861, England, RG 9/1672, p. 21; census 1871, RG 10/2663, pp. 4 and 5; 1881, RG 11/1423, p. 61; *Who was Who*, vol. V, p. 35; interview with Commander Denis Forster, RCN (1916-2004), a relative born and brought up at Enderby, Okanagan; *Whitaker's*, p. 24; *Who was Who*, vol. V, p. 35.

ARMSTRONG, Charles Frederick Nesbitt (1858-1948). Known to family and friends as "Charlie" Armstrong, he was born on 25 January 1858 at Worthing, Sussex, sixth son of Sir Andrew Armstrong, First Baronet of Gallen Priory, King's

County, Ireland. His mother, Dame F. P. Armstrong, was born at Egham, Surrey. The family were originally from the Scottish border country and had moved to Ireland in the seventeenth century. Census-takers found CA, aged three, living with his family at "Glen Helen," Llanbobbig, Carnarvon, Wales, his father cited as "Baronet, Deputy Lieutenant, and Magistrate." With CA were several brothers and sisters, the four eldest born in Ireland: Edmund P. Armstrong, aged twenty-four, curate of Lullington-cum-Cotton, Mary A. E. Armstrong, aged twenty-three, Frances G. Armstrong, twenty, Constantia M. A. Armstrong, fourteen, Montague D'Oyly T. Armstrong, nine, and Agnes B. C. Armstrong, seven, the last two born in St Peter's Square, London. There were two domestic servants.

When he was sixteen or seventeen, CA went to sea as apprentice in a sailing ship, but came home after a year or two. When he next became restless, his family sent him out to Queensland, where he worked as a "jackaroo" on a cattle station, became known as a formidable boxing fighter, learned rough-riding, and became an excellent horseman. He drifted about Queensland and New South Wales, taking jobs as they offered but never very long. He eventually met Helen Porter ("Nellie") Mitchell, daughter of a rancher, and married her at St Ann's Presbyterian Church on 22 December 1882 when she was twenty-one. Her father David Mitchell was not in favour of the marriage but let her go ahead with it, and she soon had a child they named George Nesbitt Armstrong (1883-1971). But Nellie did not enjoy life as a housewife in the wilds of Queensland while CA was away working. She had already had some singing lessons and soon took to singing seriously at concerts. Eventually, she managed to take lessons in Europe with Charles Gounod and to join an opera company. She was fond of CA but formed a relationship with Louis Philippe Robert, duc d'Orléans, son of the comte de Paris, whom she met in 1890 and whose mistress she was for a long period. The timing of events is vague, but CA apparently turned up suddenly in Belgium, where there was a scene, and sometime later, he left her and George alone. In 1900, CA divorced Nellie in a Texas court, charging her with deserting him in 1894. Nellie suffered throughout her life from this scandal but had already become the world-famous soprano, Nellie Melba (1861-1931).

As for their son George, the courts awarded him to CA at the divorce. They lived a good deal on a ranch near Klamath Falls, Oregon, but when he was about twenty, George returned to his mother. CA settled down on Vancouver Island, just before the Great War, in a cottage with twenty acres at Shawnigan Lake. Nellie seems never to have called on him there, though some of her friends did, as also did George Nesbitt Armstrong and his wife, as well as their daughter Helen Pamela Fullerton Melba Armstrong (1918-?), who eventually married a son of the Second Baron Vestey, an English shipping magnate specializing in worldwide shipments of beef in cold-storage. In later years, CA joined the Union Club in Victoria and occasionally talked about his past life. According to *Captain C. P. Nixon, a relative, CA used to say at the club that *toast Melba* and *pêche Melba* were named after his wife, and the humour of this was that he was telling the truth! CA died, aged ninety, on 2 November 1948 at Oak Bay, Victoria, and his cremated remains were buried at Royal Oak Cemetery. When he left Shawnigan lake, his house there was purchased by *Frederick C. Mason-Hurley to gain access to the Lake from another house he had bought, and it became the Forest Inn, which, in 1939, was renamed Shawnigan Beach Hotel. CA was a close relative of *Nevill Alexander Drummond Armstrong and of *Commander Edward Atcherley Eckersall Nixon.

Sources: Interview with Captain C. P Nixon, Ottawa 18 March 2002; census 1861, England, RG 9/4342, p. 6; *Colonist*, 3 November 1948, p. 13 obit.; John Hetherington, *Melba: A Biography* (Faber & Faber, 1967), pp. 69, 94, 140, 229, 263-5 and passim.

Lt.—Col. N.A.D. Armstrong

ARMSTRONG, Lieutenant Colonel Nevill [sic] Alexandre Drummond (1874-1954). He was born on 18 April 1874 on Charlwood Street in Pimlico, London, son of Montague D'Oyly Fullerton Armstrong (born c. 1851 in Sloan Street, [or St Peter's Square?] London) and Florence Augusta Sophia Armstrong née Proby (born c. 1864 in Chiswick, London). NA appeared, aged six, in the 1881 census, living at No. 1 Norfolk Road, Littlehampton, Sussex, with his mother, Florence Augusta Armstrong, aged twenty-six, a brother Jack Proby Armstrong, aged two, born in Bayswater, London, and two sisters: Madalene R. Armstrong, aged seven, and Stella E. C. Armstrong, aged four, this last born at Castellemmare Di Stabia, near Naples. There was a servant girl, Emily Goddard, aged thirteen, born at Tarring, Sussex. Florence Armstrong was recorded as the head of this household, but as a wife rather than a widow, signifying that the father was simply absent. In 1891, when NA was sixteen, he was living with his family at "Belgrave House," Littlehampton, West Sussex (near Chichester), where his father was "living on own means."

NA's father was one of the younger of six sons born to Sir Andrew Armstrong, First Baronet of Gallen Priory, King's County, Ireland, descendant of a Scottish border family that had moved to Ireland in the seventeenth century, and his wife, Dame F. J. Armstrong (born c. 1813 at Egham, Surrey). The youngest of the six sons, NA's uncle, *Charles Frederick Nesbitt Armstrong (Charlie), was born at Worthing, Sussex, and became an adventurer who had the glory and the misfortune to marry the world-famous soprano known as Nellie Melba (1861-1931) on 22 December 1882 in Brisbane, Australia, before her musical career, when she was only a sugar manufacturer's young daughter named Helen Porter Mitchell.

NA became a roving adventurer, like his elders, joined in the gold rush to the Klondike in 1898, and spent many years hunting and guiding in the wilds of the north-west, where he met F. C. Selous (1851-1917), the famous hunter who eventually died fighting German forces in East Africa. NA had many adventures himself, which he related in two books: *Yukon Yesterdays: Thirty Years of Adventure in the Klondike. Personal memories of the famous Klondike Gold Rush* with fifty-four illustrations, two maps, and a photo of the author (London, John Long Ltd., 1936), 287 pp., and *After Big Game in the Upper Yukon* (John Long Ltd., 1937), 287 pp. with maps and many photos. NA retired to "West House," Shawnigan Lake, in 1905-1906 with his wife, Mary Anne Katherine Armstrong, (born c. 1875 in St George's Hanover Square, London) whom he had married on 1 January 1902. She was a daughter of Captain Andrew Charles Armstrong (employed in 1891 as "HM Inspector of Factories") and Alice Maria Murdoch. They had a daughter, Eileen Molly Nevill Armstrong (1903-1994), and took some part in local life. The *Cowichan Leader* reported on 12 June 1913 that "a committee consisting of Messrs N[evill] Armstrong, G. A. Cheeke, R. F. Springett, and *H. T. Ravenhill (hon. secretary-treasurer) have rented for the season the two wooden tennis courts recently built by Colonel Eardley-Wilmot. They will carry on the Shawnigan Lawn Tennis club and have arranged for club days on Wednesdays and Saturdays." At the end of April 1914, the Armstrongs attended a tea at "the newly formed Knockdrin Tennis Club. A large muster of members were present to enjoy the hospitality of *Colonel and Mrs Irton Eardley-Wilmot . . . The splendidly laid board courts were in excellent condition and had been repainted green, while the clubhouse looked very in smart in its suit of brown and green." NA was to live there for years at a time, between bouts of big-game hunting and military service, variously cited in BC directories as "retired" and "capitalist."

Reports in various sources of his military career are difficult to assemble as a coherent account. He had broken his right leg in 1907 and contracted pleurisy in 1912, but on 14 April 1916, the Canadian army declared him to be medically fit, 6" ¾" tall, with fair complexion, light blue eyes, dark hair, weighing (on discharge) 153 lbs., and an Anglican. This was in France, where he served in the Sixteenth Battalion, Fiftieth Highlanders of Canada from November 1914 to March 1915, having left Canada on 1 July with the Forty-eighth Battalion and reached France on 20 October but soon transferred to the Light Horse Battalion, the Sixteenth Battalion, Manitoba Regiment, as a lieutenant, then captain, and next to the Royal Staff College in England as a major until the general demobilization on 26 August 1920. The *Army List* for October 1915 (p. 1920f) shows him as Lieutenant N. A. D. Armstrong, Forty-eighth Canadian Battalion from 14 March 1915 (Overseas Contingent). In 1916-1918, he was commandant of the Canadian Corps, Sniping School in France, where he won admiration as the inventor of "the Armstrong carrier," a pack-saddle which was adopted by the British Army. Mentioned in despatches at least four times, on 1 June 1917, on 28 December 1917, on 31 December 1918, and on 11 July 1919 (once by Sir Douglas Haig), he was invested on 1 January 1919 in the OBE (Military Division) and at sometime became a fellow of the Royal Geographical Society.

Returning to Vancouver Island after the war, he soon divorced his wife, Mary Ann Katharine Armstrong (died 27 April 1954), whom he had married on 1 January 1902, and on 20 October 1920, she married John Butler Aitken, son of Rev. George and Mrs Aitken, who lived nearby. This did not discourage NA and his daughter from their activities in the community. In 1923, they held an "At Home" in the Shawnigan Lake A.A. hall where "badminton, bridge and mahjong were indulged in, together with many other attractive amusements, including fortune-telling by Miss Winn of Victoria, and conjuring tricks." A long list of guests attended, including the *Eardley-Wilmots, *Lieutenant Colonel H. H. B. Cunningham, *Commander and Mrs R. P. Kingscote, and the *Mason Hurleys. NA spent the summer of 1924 hunting for big game in northern BC and Alaska, as the *Cowichan Leader* reported on 23 October 1924: "Major Armstrong reports a very successful season. Game was wonderfully plentiful, he says, but the season was cold, snow coming very early. Coming out by way of White Horse, the steam boat was held up for some time by the immense number of caribou crossing the Yukon River." On 10 November 1925, he attended the third annual dinner of the Returned Veterans of Shawnigan Lake, and was present on other such occasions. Between the wars, NA spent much time writing his two books and also a series of articles about his experiences, particularly about the Battle of Amiens, published in April and May 1921 in the Sunday Third Section of *The Daily Colonist.* He signed them as "Chief Reconnaissance Officer, Canadian Corps."

When the Second World War began, NA was already employed as an instructor at a major small arms school in England, but in October 1941 *General George Pearkes engaged him to teach "Sniping, Observation and Scouting (SOS)" to the Canadian First Division in England. Pearkes had met and befriended him earlier in northern Canada and as head of an SOS school of the British Army during the Great War and commandant of a similar school there for the Canadian Corps. Records show NA on the staff of the National Rifle Association Wing (Bisley) of the Small Arms School from 5 January 1940, ranked as captain from 16 June 1940, temporary major under Major J. H. Mitchell (chief instructor), and himself instructor from January 1942. He was commandant of the Sniping School, Royal Marines Corps, between 1942 and 1945 with the rank of lieutenant colonel. He died, probably in England, on 21 November 1954.

Sources: NAC, CEF files, box 234-8; census 1861, England, RG 9/4342, p. 6; census 1871, England, RG 11/1120, p. 31; census 1881, RG11/1120/79, p. 31; census 1891, RG 12/838, p. 33; census 1891, RG 12/2521, p. 13; census 1901, RG 13/102, p. 24; *Henderson's Greater Victoria Directory and Vancouver Island Gazeteer*, 1912 and 1914, and Wrigley's BC Directory, 1918, 1919, etc., for Shawnigan Lake shows variously "Neville, A. D. Armstrong, capitalist" and "Armstrong, Neville A. D . . . retired"; PRO, *Army List* (monthly or quarterly volumes) for January 1942, pp. 1628a and 1927; and October 1915, p. 1920ff.; *Colonist*, 19 August 1917, p. 16; 2 February 1921, p. 8; 9 March 1921, p. 8; 19 August 1917, p. 16; 10 April 1921, Sunday, p. 18; 8 May 1921, Sunday, p. 19, Nevill A. D. Armstrong, "Battle of Amiens-Story of Engagement" (the final instalment); 11 November 1925, p. 13; 26 October 1941, p. 11; *Cowichan Leader*, 1910-1930 passim; interview with Captain C. P. Nixon, a relative, 18 March 2002; Hughes, *Shawnigan Lake, 1887-1967*, p. 57; John Hetherington, *Melba: A Biography* (Faber & Faber, 1967), 312 pp.; Jeffrey Richards, *Imperialism and Music: Britain 1876-1953* (Manchester University Press, 2002), 544 pp.

ASHBY, Lieutenant Dennis (1880-1943). Born on 16 October 1880 at Staines, Middlesex, and educated at St Dunstan's College, he went to South Africa and served in 1906 with Royston's Horse during the Zululand rebellion for which he held the medal and a clasp. The next year, he went to Canada with his brothers, L. A. (Jack) Ashby and Ralph Ashby, and arrived at Duncan on Easter Saturday. There, DA was employed building boats at Maple Bay, but when the war came, he enlisted in the Fiftieth Gordon Highlanders at Victoria on 11 January 1915, went overseas in the Thirtieth Battalion, CEF, and joined the Seventh Battalion in France in April 1915. He was wounded at Festubert, promoted to lieutenant in 1916 and transferred to the Fifty-fourth Battalion, wounded again on the Somme, and then served on the musketry staff until returning to Canada in September 1918. Much later, in 1942-1943, he served as an observer in the Aircraft Detection Corps, watching for enemy aircraft while employed at Cowichan flats as estate manager for W. E. Boeing of Seattle.

DA served the North Cowichan Council for many years as police commissioner and councillor. He became an outstanding naturalist, botanist, fisherman, and hunter in a community of such men, and his knowledge of ornithology gained him recognition in Dominion and other scientific circles. Friends knew him as "a man of rugged physical strength and rugged character as well. He was kindness itself. Yet he sailed into battle with all sail set and without a second thought, wherever he thought wrong was being done. With a brilliant brain and a most retentive memory, he had an extraordinary fund of general knowledge and also skill with his hands. We will remember him as a really good sportsman who always played the game, and as one who knew how it should be played. He was quite a character was Dennis. He will be missed by not a few." This letter to the *Daily Colonist* was signed JDG, whom John Palmer understands to be *Captain J. D. Groves, and he adds that one of Ashby's gifts to the public was a forty-two-foot stone cairn on Mt Prevost in Cowichan District, which DA designed, promoted, and supervised during its construction, as a memorial to the veterans of the Great War.

DA made many attachments. In 1921, he married Miss E. Maude Paitson and through her he had three brothers-in-law: E. W. Paitson, a former reeve, *R. W. Whittome, and C. R. Young Bazett. His wife survived him when he died in Duncan on 7 July 1943 and was buried at St Peter's Quamichan, with Rev. T. M. Hughes officiating. DA also left a son, Sergeant Pilot S. D. Ashby, who had gone to Britain at the age of seventeen under *Captain Henry Seymour-Biggs's sponsorship to join the RAF. After completing all his flying training at the advanced level, this son contracted TB and was an invalid for the rest of his life until he died aged sixty-nine.

Sources: Family information courtesy of John Palmer; CEF files, box 262-6; *Cowichan Leader*, 15 July 1943, obit.

ASHTON, Lieutenant General Ernest Charles (1873-1956), CB, CMG, VD, MD. He was born on 28 October 1873 in Brantford, Ontario, son of Rev. Robert Ashton, Church of England, principal of the Mohawk Institute, and Helen Margaret Ashton. They sent him to Trinity University and Medical College, where he qualified as a doctor in 1898. By the time he enlisted in Hamilton, Ontario, on 13 May 1915, he was an experienced physician but was already a lieutenant colonel with nineteen and a half years of service in the Dufferin Rifles and one and a half years of service in 32 Howitzer Battery CFA. The medics reported him as having a fair complexion, blue eyes, straw-coloured hair, "a stab wound on the front of the left thigh" and a "long scar" on his right ankle. He was an Anglican.

EA began his military career as a provisional second lieutenant in 1893 with the Dufferin Rifles of Canada but was a lieutenant by the end of the year and promoted to captain in 1896 and major in 1902. Five years later, he reached the rank of lieutenant colonel and was appointed CO of the Regiment for a five-year term. He transferred to the Reserve of Officers in 1912 and was gazetted the next year to organize and command a new Howitzer Battery. He was still in command of this Battery when the First World War was declared and was asked to organize the Thirty-sixth Battery of the CEF. In 1916, he became CO of the Canadian Militia and of the Reserve Canadian Brigades in England. An appointment as brigade commander of the Fifteenth Canadian Infantry Division followed the next year, along with the rank of brigadier general, and he returned to Canada to be temporary adjutant general with the rank of major general. His career never faltered as he moved up from district officer, commanding Military District No. 2 in 1930 to chief of the General Staff in the years 1935-1938, and on to special inspection duties in 1938-1939. Then came a special appointment to reorganize the Medical Services and to act as inspector general of Canadian Military Forces.

EA married Helen Margaret Weir (c. 1875-1960) in 1907, and they had a daughter. They retired to 1520 Despard Street, Victoria in February 1941, after his continuous service of forty-seven years. He lived quietly as a member of the Union Club and died, aged eighty-two, on 17 August 1956. She died, aged eighty-five, on 10 January 1960 in Oak Bay. He had been awarded the Order of the Bath (Companion), the Order of St Michael and St George (Companion), the Volunteer Officer's Decoration and, of course, the Colonial Forces Long Service Award. His final honour came posthumously in February 1994, when a new armouries building in Greater Victoria was named the Lieutenant-General E.C. Ashton Armoury.

Sources: NAC, CEF files, box 269-6; *Who's Who in B.C.*, 1947-1948, pp. 6-7; *Who was Who*, 1951-1960, p. 40; official regimental Web page, Internet.

AUDAIN, Colonel Guy Mortimer (1864-1940). He was born on 10 October 1864 in Cromac, Antrim, Ireland, son of Colonel John Willet Payne Audain and his wife Frances Cassidy. His father, who commanded the Bedfordshire Regiment (Sixteenth Foot), had him educated in Ireland and Switzerland and at RMC Sandhurst. In 1884, he joined the Suffolk Regiment in Cork, was posted to India, and, in 1890, transferred to the Hyderabad Contingent of the Indian Army. After many years in India, he took a long leave in 1901, returning home by way of Victoria, where he had a cousin, Robert Cassidy, QC, who introduced him to James Dunsmuir, the wealthy coal baron.

On 29 October 1901, GA married Dunsmuir's daughter Sara Byrd ("Byrdie") (1878-1925) in Victoria and took her to India. She hated life there for various reasons, and so they moved to Victoria in 1905 and in 1909-1911 built a house and estate they called "Ellora" in the lovely Pemberton Woods of the Fairfield district. Much of their estate was still visible when I wandered about in the 1930s, while visiting my cousins of the George Anstey family, who lived on the edge of Pemberton Woods. GA spoke fluently in the Indian language of the Sikh workmen on the estate, gardened enthusiastically, and lived as a "sportsman," hunting, shooting, fishing, and playing tennis with his father-in-law, James Dunsmuir, whom he befriended. While Dunsmuir was lieutenant governor of BC, Audain acted as his ADC, and when war broke out in 1914, he returned to England on the SS *Adriatic* and served at the Indian Military Depot and then as head of the Indian Section at the War Office. He and Byrdie travelled a good deal, and she died, of complications from kidney disease, in 1925 at Pau in south-western France, a town within sight of the Pyrenees and much visited by English people. GA continued to travel but in his seventies established a kind of home at Dinard in Brittany (France) with various friends. He died at last on 28 November 1940 in the Beverley Hills Hotel, Hollywood, leaving a son, James Guy Payne Audain, born in England at Bournemouth on 8 July 1903, who was schooled at Wellington College, Berkshire, and RMC Sandhurst, before enrolling in the British Army as a cavalry officer. James retired early to Victoria and died there, aged sixty-six, on 30 October 1970.

Sources: James Audain, *My Borrowed Life* (Sidney, Gray's Publishing, 1962), pp. 8-16, 31, 128; *Colonist*, 1 December 1940, p. 24, obit.; Terry Reksten, *The Dunsmuir Saga* (Vancouver, Douglas & McIntyre, 1991), pp. 237-43.

AUSTEN-LEIGH, Joan Honor (1920-2001). Born on 13 October 1920 in Victoria, daughter of *Lionel Arthur Austen-Leigh and Mrs Gertrude Austen-Leigh, *née* Evans, she was sent to school in England and in 1939 married *Denis Mason-Hurley. For twenty-five years, they ran the Shawnigan Beach Hotel and then moved to Victoria, where she became president of the Victoria Choral Society and, aged forty-eight, attended the University of Victoria. She took up "creative writing" at the University of British Columbia, took a master of fine arts degree in 1975, and went on to write several novels and plays. She was moved to these activities by knowing herself to be descended directly from Jane Austen's family and in 1979 joined with Jack Gray of New York in founding the Jane Austen Society of North America, which grew rapidly with thousands of members and branches in several countries. She also founded the society's journal, *Persuasions*, edited it for ten years, and became well known as a literary public speaker. Having inherited Jane Austen's writing desk, she and her daughters took it to London in 1999 and presented it to the British Library. In May 2001, she was made Honorary Doctor of Letters at Goucher College, Baltimore, which claims to have the biggest collection of Jane Austen's letters, memorabilia, and first editions.

So wide and deep is the literary heritage of Jane Austen that JA's activities are seldom noticed by the writers of our time. Claire Harman, for example, writes at length about what she calls the "Janeites" but approaches no nearer than JA's great-grandfather, James Edward Austen-Leigh (1798-1874), who generated some of the myths Harman seeks to dispel. "Part of the appeal of Janeism," she writes, "was its ingrained Englishness . . . .," which was not out of place on the Island. For her part, JA spent many happy days sailing around the Gulf of Georgia in the Mason-Hurley family's twenty-nine-foot sailboat, a cutter which they named *Elizabeth Bennett,* and wrote about her adventures in *Pacific Yachting* magazine. At the age of seventy-five, she took up the 'cello. When she died, aged nearly eighty-one, on 12 October 2001, she was survived by her son, Robert Mason Hurley, and three daughters: Freydis (Mrs Michael Welland), Tibbie (Mrs Robert Adams), and Damaris (Mrs Peter Brix) and their children. Her only surviving sister was living in England.

Sources: *Colonist*, 9 February 1917, p. 5; 8 July 1934, p. 11; 3 January 1940, p. 4: obit.; *Times-Colonist*, Sunday, 3 June 2001, p. D9, "The History of the Jane Austen Society"; 13 October 2001, May Brown, "Joan Austen-Leigh"; Joan Mason-Hurley, "Twenty-four Colonels on the West Arm Road"; *Raincoast Chronicles*, vol. pp. 52-61.; Deirdre Le Faye, *A Chronology of Jane Austen and her Family* (New York, Cambridge

University Press, 2006), 776 pp.; Hughes, *Shawnigan Lake, 1887-1967*, p. 71; Claire Harman, *Jane's Fame: How Jane Austen Conquered the World* (New York, Henry Holt & Co., 2009), pp. xx, 139.

AUSTEN-LEIGH, Lieutenant Lionel Arthur (1886-1960). He was born at Winterbourne, Gloucestershire, son of Rev. Arthur Henry Austen-Leigh (1835-1917), born at Speen, Berkshire, and his wife Mary Violet Hall-Say (1858-?), born at Swaffham, Norfolk. The 1891 census recorded him, aged four, living at "The Vicarage," High Street, Wargrave, East Berkshire, with his parents, four older sisters, and two brothers, one elder and the other younger. There were seven servants: a "lady help" (Alice Davison from Maidstone, Kent), nurse, cook, parlourmaid, schoolroom maid, housemaid, and kitchenmaid. Scholarly studies of the English novelist Jane Austen show that LA was directly descended from her family. In 1861, his father, then aged twenty-five, was "B.A. Fellow of St John's College, Oxford," and living at No. 1 Frogfirle just south of Alfriston in East Sussex with an aunt, Caroline Austen, aged fifty-five, and three of his brothers, the eldest of whom, Charles L. Austen-Leigh, aged twenty-eight and born at Tring, was the head of the household and a "Farmer, Comm. Clerk, House of Commons"; Spencer Austen-Leigh, aged twenty-seven, was "Farmer of 521 acres employs thirteen men and eight boys"; and Edward C. Austen-Leigh, aged twenty-one and born at Wargrave, was "Fellow of King's College, Cambridge." They had five servants, including a groom and his wife.

In 1871, LA's father was curate of Bray, Berkshire, and was living there at the vicarage with his father, LA's grandfather, James Edward Austen-Leigh, who was the vicar of Bray, then aged seventy-two and born in Hampshire. In that household in 1871 lived LA's aunt, Emma Cassandra Austen-Leigh, aged thirty-nine and born at Tring Park, Hertfordshire, and two of LA's uncles, both fellows of King's College, Cambridge, and both born at Wargrave: Edward Compton Austen-Leigh, "Assistant Master at Eton," and William Austen-Leigh, "Clerk in the House of Lords." The 1901 census found LA, aged fourteen, a schoolboy boarding at Rugby and his parents still at Wargrave with two of his sisters. It should be added that his mother, Violet Mary Hall-Say, had met his father at Bray, where in 1871 she was living, aged twelve, at Water Oakley, Minden Road, with her family. Her father, Richard Hall-Say, born in Liverpool, was a "magistrate" (recorded in 1891 as "J.P. for Berks. & Norfolk" but living in London) with six children and eleven servants plus a coachman and family next door. Like the Austen-Leighs, the Hall-Says were Anglicans.

In 1910, LA went out to live in Victoria and worked as a BC surveyor until the Great War, when he joined the RFA and fought in France with the British Expeditionary Force. In 1917, he was thought to be one of thirty-four BC surveyors in the army overseas. Upon his return to Victoria, he married Gertrude Evans, born c. 1891 at Broadford, Kent, and they had two daughters who were identified at his death, aged seventy-three, on 25 October 1960 in Ladysmith, as Mrs J. A. Peyman of Seasalter, Kent, and Mrs Denis Mason-Hurley of Shawnigan Lake, better known by her maiden name,*Joan Honor Austen-Leigh. LA was also survived by four sisters in England, but his wife had died, aged fifty-six, on 27 February 1953 in Victoria.

Sources: census 1861, England, RG 9/567, pp. 22-3; census 1871, RG 10/1299, p. 22; census 1891, RG 12/1001, p. 9; census 1901, RG 13/2918, p. 35; census 1901, England, RG 13/1156, p. 15; census 1871, RG 10/1299, pp. 10-11 (Hall-Say); census 1891, RG 12/104, p. 3 (Hall-Say); *Colonist*, 9 February 1917, p. 5; 28 October 1960, obit.; Deirdre Le Faye, *A Chronology of Jane Austen and her Family* (New York, Cambridge University Press, 2006), 776 pp.

AUSTIN, Brigadier-General John Gardiner (1872-1956). He was born in Barbados, a son of John Gardiner Austin, who had him educated privately and at RMC, Woolwich, where in 1891, he won the coveted Eardley-Wilmot silver bugle for outstanding prowess in sports; he excelled in the high jump, steeplechase, shot, and cricket. Even in retirement, he listed cricket and golf as his recreations. In 1891, he was commissioned in the Royal Artillery but transferred to the Army Ordnance Department in 1909 and served at the War Office and as director of Ordnance Services with the Commonwealth of Australia. He served in the South African War. In the Great War, he was on the staff of the First Australian Division at the landing and evacuation of Anzac during the difficult Gallipoli campaign and was mentioned in despatches and decorated with the CMG, the CB, and the *Croix de Guerre*. He became a brigadier in 1918 and served in 1926-1928 as inspector of Army Ordnance Services.

After retiring in 1928, he went to Victoria in January 1929, with his wife, settled at 1420 Beach Drive, Oak Bay, and turned to volunteer work with veterans' groups and the Red Cross. In November 1939, he became president of the Victoria Red Cross Society and worked at raising funds, for example by holding garden parties at Government House. He was a member of at least five clubs—I. Zingari, Free Foresters, Melbourne Cricket Ground, United Service Club, and Pall Mall Club (London SW)—and lived at 655 Island Road, Victoria, with his wife, Margaret Drew Moir, daughter of Rev. Charles Moir, MA, of Glasgow, and they had a son, John Gardiner Austin. The son and a sister, Mrs C. E. Yearwood, both in Victoria, survived his death on 2 November 1956, aged eighty-four, and there were also brothers and sisters in Barbadoes and England.
Sources: *Who's Who in B.C.*, 1933-4, p. 15; NAC, Immigration 1925-35; Captain F. G. Guggisberg (RE), *"The Shop," The Story of the Royal Military Academy* (1900; 2nd ed., Cassell & Company Ltd., 1902), p. 210; *Colonist*, 17 January 1937, p. 2; 27 April 1937, p. 3; 16 November 1939, p. 8; 7 August 1940, p. 4, L to E.; 4 Nov. 1956, p. 22, obit.

AXHORN, Ben (1864-1936). Born on 10 November 1864 at Tiverton, Devonshire, in a large family of lace makers, he went to sea very young on ships sailing to Australia and California. Having reached Victoria in 1889 on the bark *Tythonus*, he returned the next year and worked as a sealer for some years. From about 1900, he lived ashore and worked for the British-America Paint Company. He was an active member of the Sons of England and the Thermopylae Club. He died on 2 November 1936, aged seventy-two, leaving his widow and daughter at 457 Niagara Street (James Bay), and was buried at Colwood Burial Park.

Sources: *Colonist*, 3 November 1936, p. 10, obit.; census 1871, RG 10/2405, p. 28; Ursula Jupp, *Home Port Victoria* (Victoria, privately printed by Morriss Printing Co. Ltd., for 2254 Arbutus Road, 1967), 168 pp., see index.

BABBINGTON, Captain Hume Blackley (c. 1871-1934). He died in Saanich, aged sixty-three, a sea captain who had gone to the north-west Pacific coast forty-seven years earlier with his father and commanded vessels on that coast for many years. His father, famous in his day as captain of trans-Atlantic liners, was born in Liverpool and descended from a long family line of Irish gentry. The census-taker in 1881 found HB, aged nine, born at Liverpool, Lancashire, living in a school at 45 Nicholas Street, St Martins, Chester (Cheshire), headed by George Tinkler, aged thirty-seven, "Teacher of Classics, Mathematics & Sciences undergraduate London University," and his wife, Mrs Sarah J. Tinkler, with her three children. There were four other "scholars" in addition to Babington, and three servants (cook, nurse, and housemaid). HB spent many years at Prince Rupert, BC, and then settled at Brentwood Bay on Saanich Inlet, where he kept a repair shop for boat engines and hired out a fleet of small craft. He was a member of the Pacific Club, active in community affairs, and elected in 1933 as vice-president of the Associated Boards of Trade of Vancouver Island. He was well known as a breeder of angora rabbits. He died at Resthaven Hospital, North Saanich, leaving a sister and a niece.
Sources: *Colonist*, 23 October 1934, p. 3, obit.; census 1881, England, RG 11/3559, p. 4.

BAGSHAWE [Bagshaw], Edward Charles Bentinck (1856-1936). An English "refugee" from Manitoba, he settled at last in Victoria in the insurance and real-estate business and was active as a charter member of the British Campaigners' Association. He was born at Blatherwycke Hall, Northamptonshire, son and grandson of Anglican clergymen. He appears, aged fifteen, the youngest of three sons living with their family at Hove, near Brighton, Sussex, birthplace of their mother, Emma L. Bagshawe. Their father, Rev. Edward Bagshawe, aged forty-six, was identified as a "Resigned Clergyman, Annuitant" born at Bristock, Northamptonshire, and EB's elder brother Frederick, aged twenty-one, was an "Engine Fitter's Apprentice" born in Shropshire. In 1882, EB emigrated to Manitoba, where he farmed, but served with Bolton's Scouts in the Riel Rebellion Campaign of 1885. After some years, he found employment in life and fire insurance companies at Winnipeg. There, he married his wife, Frances Anne, and had several children of whom Edward Noel Bagshawe, born on 25 December 1894, worked as a clerk and then served as an officer in Canadian forces during the Great War.

In 1898, EB moved with his family to Vancouver and in 1899 to Victoria, where he went into the real-estate business and was district agent for the Federal Life Insurance Company at 39½ Langley Street. In 1901, they were living in Richardson Street, but towards the end of his thirty-seven years in Victoria, his address was 1405 Fernwood Road. He was one of the founders of the British Campaigners' Association in 1908 and was active in the Red Cross Society during the Great War.

When he died, aged seventy, on 18 May 1936, he left his widow, Frances Agnes Bagshawe, and ten children. His funeral was at St Matthias Anglican Church, the family being members of the Church of England, and he was buried in the family plot at the Ross Bay Cemetery. It was twelve years later, on 29 May 1948, that his wife died, aged eighty-three, in Victoria.

Sources: *Colonist,* 19 May 1936, pp. 3 and 16, obit.; *Victoria Daily Times,* 18 May 1936, pp. 1 and 16; 19 May 1936, p. 12; census 1851, England, HO/107/1745/137; census 1861, RG 9/1187, p. 12; census 1871, RG 10/3054, p. 2; census 1881, England, RG 11/1096, pp. 14-15; NAC, CEF files, box 338-26, regimental no. 77258.

BAILLIE-GROHMAN, William Adolf (1851-1921). Born at Gmunden, Upper Austria, at the north end of Lake Traunsee, he spent much of his life in England and elsewhere in the British Empire as a hunter and explorer. In this, he was breaking away from his wealthy Tirolean family, his grandfather, Adolf Grohman, a successful Viennese banker who had married an Irish beauty, Fanny Reid, who was a relative of the Duke of Wellington. Migrating to England was an extension of WB's boyhood wandering out from the family castle at Schloss Matzen near a branch of the Zillertal and the Inn Valley to hunt chamois and deer in the surrounding high alps. In England, he married Florence B. Nichalls, daughter of an active member of the London Stock Exchange who had investments in American railways. English census records for 1891 show this couple living at Cormongeon House in Nutfield, Surrey, with a son, a daughter, a cook, and a housemaid. WB was recorded as a Justice of the Peace.

However, the son, Harold Tom Baillie-Grohman, who grew up to become Rear Admiral Harold Tom Baillie-Grohman (16 January 1888-23 September 1978), was born in Victoria during their years in British Columbia. There, WB invested in the Kootenay Company Ltd. in the BC interior, registered in London, won concessions of 78,525 acres, built a sawmill, and promoted the Kootenay Valley in English journals to encourage emigration. He also spent about ten years in the 1870s and 1880s, working vigorously on an engineering project to divert the Kootenay River into the Columbia by way of a canal across Canal Flats. The canal was finished in July 1889 but local residents objected and after much altercation, the provincial government opposed the project. In earlier years, WB had hunted and explored in the Rocky Mountains, and he wrote books and articles about his adventures there, as well as his travels in the western United States and in Europe. WB befriended *W. H. Barneby and contributed a chapter to Barneby's first book, but must have met him again in 1888, both of them being in Victoria that year when Harold Baillie-Grohman was born there. WB engaged in pioneering activities much like what Barneby had in mind, investing in the Kootenay Valley in conjunction with his wife's father, Tom Nickalls. Mount Grohman, near Nelson, BC, was named for WB, who was a larger-than-life adventurer.

Sources: BNA, census 1891, RG 12/581, p. 10; census 1901, RG 13/94, p. 14; R. J. Welwood, "Baillie-Grohman's Diversion," *British Columbia Historical News,* vol. 36, no 4 (Fall 2003), pp. 6-11 (good on WB's engineering project; mistaken about his birthplace); Mabel Ellen Jordan, "The Kootenay Reclamation and

Colonization Scheme and William Adolph Baillie-Grohman," *B.C. Historical Quarterly,* vol. xx (1956), pp. 187-220; Mabel Ellen Jordan Collection, University of British Columbia, Special Collections (papers by and about the BG family); Wikipedia online encyclopedia; W. A. Baillie-Grohman, *Camps in the Rockies. Being a Narrative of Life on the Frontier, and Sport in the Rocky Mountains, with an Account of Cattle Ranches of the* West (Horace Cox, 1882), 438 pp.(mostly about western USA); W. A. Baillie-Grohman, *Fifteen Years' Sport and Life in the Hunting Grounds of Western America and British Columbia* (Horace Cox, 1900, repr. 1907), 403 pp.; W. A. Baillie-Grohman, *Tyrol & the Tyrolese. The people & the Land in their social, sporting and mountaineering aspects.*(1876, Longmans, Green & Co., 2nd ed., 1877), 278pp.

BAKER, Navigating Lieutenant Edgar Crow (1845-1920). He was born at Lambeth, Surrey, on 16 September 1845, son of Edward William Whitby Baker, attended the Royal Hospital School at Greenwich, and joined the Royal Navy in 1860. He was promoted eventually to navigating lieutenant aboard HMS *Niobe* and retired from the navy in 1878 and settled in Victoria, which he had visited while in the service. In 1872, he had travelled to Canada as an officer on half pay and in 1874 arrived in Victoria from Halifax as an employee. He was ambitious and had a valuable family connection with his first wife's uncle, Captain James Arnold Raymur, manager of a sawmill. Raymur's home in Victoria had a social life that was useful to EB. With his naval background, he fitted easily into life on the Pacific Coast and began by working as an agent in the Victoria office of the Hasting Saw Mill Company, which offered frequent contacts with local businessmen such as the grocers R. C. Janion, father of *Richard William Janion, and Henry Rhodes, father of *Brigadier General Sir Godfrey Rhodes, *R. P. Rithet, W. P. Sayward, *Joseph Spratt, and *J. H. Turner, a fellow Freemason and sometime mayor of Victoria. In 1878, EB returned from London with a capital sum gained by taking a lump payment as settlement by the Admiralty in place of his half pay.

He was shocked when his friend and partner F. J. Roscoe shot and killed himself in a suicide induced by hard times and threatened failures. EB was appointed grand secretary of the Masonic Order. At one time, he sold gunpowder with Captain R. G. Tatlow as a partner. EB was instrumental in the incorporation of the Victoria and Esquimalt Telephone Company on 3 May 1880, and by 6 May, telephone lines were working between Victoria and Esquimalt. He had a strong hold on the company. In August 1907, he and partners sold the Victoria Electric Illuminating Company to the London-based BC Electric Railway Co. for $19,607. In 1885, he and four partners formed the Esquimalt Water Works Company, incorporated in March. He became an accountant, notary, and conveyancer and served as accountant to the BC Provincial Treasury, as secretary to the BC Board of Trade, as superintendent of pilots, and as secretary to the Board of Pilot Commissioners. In 1882, he played a leading part in organizing the Victoria and Esquimalt Telephone Co. and worked as its managing director and secretary-treasurer until 1900, when the company merged with what became the BC Telephone Co. Ltd. He and R. B. McMicking introduced electric light in the city in 1886 under the name of Victoria Electric Company, which later merged with the BC Electric Co. Ltd. In

1882, EB was elected to the House of Commons as a Conservative member for Victoria, re-elected in 1887, but resigned after prorogation of the Third Session of the Sixth Parliament on 2 May 1889. Twenty years earlier, on 17 March 1869, he had married Frances Mary Jones, but it was his second wife who survived him when he died on 3 November 1920.

This was Marion Henrietta Crow-Baker, as she styled herself, daughter of John Greaves Clapham of Quebec, and she married EB in 1896 in Victoria. She led an active social life as a charter member of Towner Bay Country Club in North Saanich, a member of the Women's Canadian Club, the IODE, the Anglican Church, and the Oak Bay and Colwood Golf Clubs. She had no children but shared her house, "Sissinghurst" on Gorge Road, with a niece, Miss Jean Ross, daughter of Herbert G. Ross, of Vancouver. EB died, aged seventy-five, on 3 November 1920 in Victoria; she died there, too, aged eighty-three, on 5 January 1947.

Sources: J. K. Johnson, ed., *The Canadian Directory of Parliament, 1867-1967* (Ottawa, Public Archives, 1968), p. 18; *Who's Who in B.C., 1933-34*, p. 41; G. W. S. Brooks, "Edgar Crow Baker: An Entrepreneur in Early British Columbia," *B.C. Studies*, vol. 31 (1976), pp. 23-43.

BAKER, Lieutenant Reginald Steven (1904-1995). Born at Bath, Somerset, on 20 January 1904, he apprenticed as an electrician and became an electrical artificer in the RN on 15 July 1926, serving in turn aboard HMS *Defiance, Drake, Hood, Egmont, Glorious, Angelo, Vidette, Osprey, Rodney, Norfolk, Daedalus, Vernon,* and *Kestrel.* He transferred to the RCN (R) as a lieutenant with seniority from 15 October 1946. He retired on 15 February 1963, he died many years later in Victoria on 16 November 1995.

Sources: John M. MacFarlane, *Canada's Naval Aviators* (rev. ed., Shearwater, NS, Shearwater Aviation Museum, 1997), p. 15.

BAKER, Lieut.-Colonel Walter Way (1859-after 1916). He was born on 23 May 1859 in Bombay (or Karachi?), India, son of William Adolphus Baker (1834-1901), a major general, Royal Bombay Engineers (4 April 1834-29 August 1901). WB's mother, Jennie Lisette Henrietta Pockels, was daughter of a Dr Pockels of Brunswick, Germany (who died on 18 April 1870 at Mahablishwar, Bombay), and she married WB's father on 8 August 1858 at Karachi, India. After attending Clifton College in 1875-1876 and RMC, Woolwich, WB was commissioned as lieutenant in the Royal Engineers on 18 December 1878 and promoted to captain on 3 March 1889, to major on 31 December 1896, to lieutenant colonel on 25 September 1904 while serving at Mount Abu, Rajasthan, on the North-West Frontier, and to full colonel on 25 September 1909. He retired on an Indian Army pension on 9 April 1911 and was listed in 1912 with the Reserve of Officers, address c/o King & Co., Bombay, India.

His name crops up in a variety of sources: assisting Major W. H. Haydon, RE, to build a lighthouse on Manora Point near Karachi in 1889, serving at the War Office in 1896-1898, and living at 2 Park Place, Stoke Dameral, Devonport, in 1891 with his wife, Florence Catherine Acworth (born in 1865 at Rochester Kent), their three-year-old son Florian Baker, born at Woolwich, and three servants. She was a daughter of a Rochester solicitor, Brindley Acworth, and WB had married her on 24 April 1884 at Medway, Kent. In 1900, WB was in the Military Works Department in Punjab. The English census for 1901 shows them living at 23 Watts Avenue, Rochester, then with three children: Florian A. Baker, aged thirteen, born on 18 April 1887 at Satara, near Bombay, India; George B[rindley] Aufrère Baker, aged six, born in July 1893 at Bromley, Kent; and Phyllis May C Baker, aged two, born in April 1897 at "Satara, Rochester, Kent." They had a nurse and two servants. In due time, George attended Cheltenham College. WB was entered twice in the 1901 census, the second being as a visitor at his widowed father's home in Sussex at 1 Maze Hill Terrace, Hastings, with his sister Mabel T. Baker, then aged thirty-six and unmarried, born at Wargrave, Berkshire.

Another veteran of service in India, *C. G. Palmer, wrote in his family journal (pp. 69-70), after emigrating to the Cowichan Valley, "At last I met Colonel Baker, R.E., recently retired from Sup. Engr. in the Central Provinces in India who had known about me for several years. He had lived for a year at Crofton, Vancouver Island. According to him that island would give me all I sought; and my subsequent experience enables me to say he was not far wrong." In 1910, WB took his own family out to the Cowichan Valley, he then aged fifty-two, Florence, forty-five, and their three children—Florian, twenty-four, George, seventeen, and Phyllis, fourteen. The census-taker registered them as members of the Church of England and him as a "farmer." There was little sign of them thereafter. On 20 December 1916, Florian joined the Canadian Expeditionary Force in Victoria, claiming to have had experience in British Mounted Rifles and the CI Railway in India, survived the war, and died in Duncan, aged sixty, on 15 July 1947.

Phyllis May Baker married John Brearley in Vancouver city on 10 June 1922, scarcely three years before his death in Victoria on 8 February 1925. WB and Florence seem to have left the Island and died elsewhere at sometime between 1935 and 1943.

Sources: Palmer family collection (Victoria), "*The Book of the Palmers*," f. 69, courtesy of John Palmer; Canadian census 1911, NAC, RG 21, Statistics Canada, district no. 13, Nanaimo, BC, subdistrict 15, Comiaken; census 1881, England, RG 11/897, p. 4; census 1891, RG 12/1745, p. 20; census 1901, RG 13/723, p. 6; census 1901, RG 13/870, p. 33; NAC, CEF files, box 368-19; *Army List September 1898*, p. 447; *The Monthly Army List*, June 1907, p. 446; *The Quarterly Army List, October 1916*, p. 1963a (Indian Army); *The Royal Engineers Quarterly List*, October 1932, p. xxxi and October 1935, p. xxxv; notes from T. W. J. Conolly, *Roll of Officers of the Corps of Royal Engineers from 1660 to 1989* (The Royal Engineers Institute, Chatham, Kent, 1898), p. 56, courtesy of Ed de Santis; *Clifton College Annals and Register, 1862-1912* (J. W. Arrowsmith Ltd., Bristol, 1912), p. 104; *Cheltenham College Register, 1841-1910* (Bell & Sons Ltd., 1911), p. 687; E. W. C. Sandes, *The Military Engineer in India*, vol. II (Chatham, Kent, The Institution of Royal Engineers, 1935), p. 184; *Whitaker's*, p. 32; Marquis de Ruvigny and Raineval, Marquis of Ruvigny and Raineval Staff, *The Plantagenet Roll of the Royal Blood; The Isabel of Essex . . .*, "Walter Way Baker,

Lieut-Cpl., R.E., 6, 23 May 1859, m[arried] 24 Apr. 1884, Florence Emily Catherine, daughter of Brindley Acworth of Rochester, Solicitor . . ."

BARCLAY, Captain Thomas (1885-1937). Born at Mozuffarpur, India, on 17 April 1885, eldest son of J. B. Barclay of Skelbo, Scotland, and Behar, India, he was sent as a child to stay with his maternal grandparents at Yaxley, Huntingdonshire, where the census-taker found him, aged five, living in 1891 in a household with a cook, nurse, and housemaid. His maternal grandfather was Rev. Francis Hinde, "Clerk in Holy Orders," aged seventy-five and born there; his grandmother, Susan E. Hinde, aged sixty-seven, was born at Bath, Somerset, and they had an unmarried daughter there, TG's aunt Charlotte E. E. Hind, aged thirty-six, born at Sidmouth, Devon.

In due time, TB joined the Behar Light Horse in India but soon retired and went out to Koksilah, Vancouver Island, where he worked on a poultry farm and played cricket locally. A Canadian census-taker found him in 1911 at 1032 Fulton Street, Victoria, with his wife, Maud Florence M. Slater (born in June 1886), a sister of *Lieutenant Colonel A. F. M. Slater, and when on 6 June 1916 he joined the Canadian Expeditionary Force, he was already enrolled in the Eighty-eighth Victoria Fusiliers, but gave his address as Koksilah and his occupation as "rancher." Wounded in battle overseas and decorated with the MC, he transferred to the Thirteenth Field Ambulance.

Upon his return, the family settled at Metchosin, west of Victoria, where he was "ranching" still in 1925. He died there on 1 December 1937, leaving his wife and two sons as well as a stepson. He also had a brother living in India. At his funeral at St Mary's Anglican Church in Metchosin, the pallbearers were *Colonel R. C. Cooper, *Major R. G. H. Murray, *Captain O. Cox, M. Milne, R. Matthews, and *Private Gordon Charles Hartley. A pipe major played "The Flowers of the Forest," and the congregation sang "Oh God Our Help in Ages Past" and "Abide with Me." Much later, Mrs Barclay died, aged seventy-two, on 16 August 1959 in Victoria. **Sources:** NAC, RG150, CEF files, box 425-26; census 1891, England, RG 12/1954, p. 27; Canadian census, 1911, NAC, RG 31, Statistics Canada, district no. 13, subdistrict no. 12, Victoria; *Colonist*, 2 December 1937, pp. 5 and 16, obit.; *Cowichan Leader*, 9 December 1937, p. 7. obit.

BARKLEY, Captain Charles Edward (1829-1909). He was born in March 1829 at Leigh, Dorset, son of Mary Barkley and her husband, Rev. John Charles Barkley (c. 1800-?), who spent most of his life as vicar of Little Melton, Norfolk, and was the eldest son of Captain Charles William Barkley (1759-1832), CB's famous grandfather, an early mariner in the north-west Pacific Ocean, who gave his name to Barkley Sound on the Island's west coast. CB joined the Royal Navy, which kept him out of England for many years. His first appearance in the census records was in April 1871, when he was recorded as "Charles Barkley . . . Commander, R.N., Active List," living at Hapton Hall, Hapton, near Norwich, with his wife Harriet E. Barkley from Box, Wiltshire, and their two youngest children, Kate C. and Robert E. aged eight and two. Two elder daughters, Mary twelve and Florence eleven, were away boarding at a "Lady's Academy" in Heydon Road, Beech Grove, Aylsham, Norfolk. It is his wife's and children's names and dates which confirm that in 1881, he was the "Edward Barkley . . . Captain R.N. retired," aged fifty-two, living with them all (except Robert E. Barkley, then aged twelve) at Hill Farm, Garboldisham, Norfolk. They were employing a German governess and three servants.

When in 1887, CB took his family out to live on the Island they settled in the North Cowichan district at a place they called "Westholme." They lived there in retirement while their son *Robert Barkley farmed; and on 1 September 1897, their daughter Florence Annie Barkley married *Lieutenant Colonel George Edward Barnes. CB pottered on the farm, and when the railway began to deliver mail, he was the first to handle it. The postal authorities made him postmaster and established the post office at "Westholme," which soon gave its name to the settlement. He took a lively interest in Imperial affairs and became a keen member of the Victoria and Esquimalt branch of the Navy League when it was founded. "He was one of the most highly esteemed residents of the province," the editor of the *Daily Colonist* wrote at his death, "a fine type of English gentleman and sailor. Of late years he has not been very active but he at all times took the keenest interest in public affairs." He died, aged eighty, on 22 November 1909, when the house caught fire, and he, having at first escaped, went back in a desperate effort to find his copy of his grandmother Frances Barkley's account of her life with Captain Charles William Barkley. The Navy League made a point of expressing regret at his death during its AGM on 26 April 1910.

Sources: census 1871, England, RG 10/1837, p. 8; census 1881, RG 11/1972, p. 27; *Colonist*, 23 November 1909, p. 1, 3, 4; 27 April 1910, p. 2; Barry Gough, "Charles William Barkley," *Dictionary of Canadian Biography*, vol. VI, pp. 36-7; Walbran, *B.C. Coast Names*, p. 35; J. Richard Nokes, *Almost a Hero: The Voyages of John Meares, R. N., to China, Hawaii and the Northwest Coast* (Pullman, Washington, Washington State University Press, 1998), pp. 63, 78, 83, 180-2, 184; Elliott, *Memories of the Chemainus Valley*, pp. 93, 104.

BARKLEY, Captain Robert Edward (1868-1942). He was born at Folkstone, Kent, son of *Charles Edward Barkley and his wife Harriet E. Barkley and a great-grandson of the famous mariner Captain Charles William Barkley (1759-1832). The 1871 census found him, aged two, living at Hapton Hall, Hapton, Norfolk, with his parents and his sister, Kate C. Barkely, aged eight, born at Shurnep, Kent. There were four servants including two nurses, and the neighbours were "farmer's labourers." In 1887, RB's parents took him out to live in the north Cowichan district, where they farmed on a property they called "Westholme." He became a leader in agricultural circles, served on the executive committee of Cowichan Agricultural Society in 1912-12 and again in 1920-1930, on the executive of the Cowichan Creamery Association, and in 1903-1904 was elected second vice-president of the VI Flockmasters Association. In 1920, he joined its board of directors and served until 1934. He also joined the Cowichan Cricket and Sports Club, played tennis, squash, and polo, shot and hunted in the district, and owned several horses. In June 1915, he was commissioned in the Royal Marine Artillery and went to France with RMA Howitzer Brigade No. 15. He returned to Canada in April 1919 and, on being demobilized, was granted honorary rank of captain in the Royal Marines. When RB died, aged seventy-four, on 7 November 1942 in Duncan, he left his wife, Kate Evelyn Trotter, whom he had married on 17 April 1894, and a son, Captain E. T. Y. "Jim" Barkley, in the Imperial forces, last heard of serving in Singapore. Among the seventeen pallbearers at his funeral at St Peter's Quamichan were *Captain J. D. Groves, *Captain L. P. Foster, *C. W. Lonsdale, and J. Y. Copeman (Victoria), who attended as a representative of Union Club, Victoria.

Sources: *Cowichan Leader,* 12 November 1942, obit.; census 1871, England, RG 10/1837, p. 8; Canadian census 1891, VI; BC Directory, 1910, p. 674, for Westholme, "Barkley, Robert Edward, farmer"; 1922, p. 189, for Duncan.

BARNEBY, William Henry (1843-1914). Here is a Herefordshire squire who made two long journeys to BC during the 1880s, spent much time on the Island, and published a book in London about each visit. The first, *Life and Labour in the Far, Far West, Being Notes of a Tour in the Western States, British Columbia, Manitoba, and the North-West Territory* (Cassell, 1884), 432 pp., with maps, appendices, and an index, was the fruit of a journey across the United States during the spring and summer of 1883, reaching the Island by steamer from San Francisco. As he wrote in the preface, his purpose was "to collect as much information as possible, more especially as regards farming and emigration, in the hope of thus being able to assist those in England who might be thinking of seeking a new home across the Atlantic." With him went an old school friend whom he had known intimately all his life, Charles Meysey Bolton Clive (1842-83), born at Solihull, Warwickshire, educated at Harrow and Balliol, son of a prebendary of Hereford Cathedral and a resident of South Eaton Square, London, where he had lived with his wife, Lady Katherine Feilding (1842-82), a sister of the Eighth Earl of Denbigh. She had died only a few months earlier, leaving Clive with their five children and a desire for a change of air. The second of WB's companions, Captain Arthur Charles Mitchell (1847-1917), was the youngest of nine children born to a London merchant established in the neighbourhood of Marylebone. After military service in the Fourth Battalion of the Gloucestershire Regiment, he lived as a gentleman landowner first in Wiltshire at "The Ridge" and later at "High Grove," Tetbury, Gloucestershire, serving as a JP for that county and Wiltshire. He had been WB's brother-in-law since 1872, when he married Laura Harriet Hicks-Beach, one of Mrs Barneby's five sisters, and so was continually in touch with WB's circle of family and friends.

They sailed from Liverpool to New York on the White Star liner, SS *Germanic,* and travelled in leisurely fashion across the American west, stopping at St, Louis, Kansas City, Denver, Colorado Springs, Salt Lake City (taking great interest in what WB called "Mormonland"), and several parts of California, before sailing on a paddle-wheel steamer from San Francisco to Victoria, Vancouver Island. Their desire to encourage emigration to British North America made them pay special attention to the Canadian west, beginning at Victoria, which reminded them of

Jersey or Guernsey—"each house seemed to have a pretty flower-garden attached."
WB was "very pleased to find myself landed at Victoria, British Columbia, at last,
though it seems a long way from home, especially when one considers that a
letter takes nearly a month to reach England from here." Staying at the Driard
House Hotel, they met the travelling hunter W. A. * Baillie-Grohman, whose
acquaintance they had made on board the *Germanic*. He admired the Island as
much as they did but agreed to write a description of the Kootenay Lake district
for WB's forthcoming book.

WB made a second journey to the Island just after the town of Vancouver had
been founded as a coastal terminus for the new Canadian Pacific Railway, a trip
that took him on across the Pacific to Japan and eventually home through the Suez
Canal and the Mediterranean Sea. Not long after reaching home, he published
*The New Far West and the Old Far East: Being Notes of a Tour in North America, Japan,
Ceylon etc.* (E. Stanford, 1889), 316 pp. with a dedication to his wife's brother, Sir
Michael Hicks-Beach (1837-1916), then president of the Board of Trade.

WB was carrying letters of introduction to Justice *G. A. Walkem and
*Lieutenant Governor C. F. Cornwall, whose secretary, *Captain R. G. Tatlow, took
them to see the Hudson's Bay Company stores and to meet friends at the Union
Club, then only four years old. They had met Judge *Sir Henry Crease by chance on
the mainland and formed a friendship with him at their second meeting in Victoria.
On another day, they met Judge Matthew Begbie. They dined with *William Curtis
Ward to whom Mitchell had brought an introduction. They were soon invited into
several private houses, and foraging around the Island with various local people
as guides, they travelled out to Saanich and found an Indian to take them in his
canoe across Saanich Inlet to the Cowichan Valley, which impressed them as "one
of the best farming settlements on the island." There they met William Sutton, a
pioneer farmer and lumberman from Ontario, and Hon. William Smithe (1842-87)
from Northumberland, the premier of British Columbia who had been farming
for some years on three hundred acres in the Cowichan Valley. They regretted
having to leave Cowichan but hurried on to visit Nanaimo and the coaling station
at Departure Bay, admiring large arbutus trees on the way. WB liked the Island so
much that he bought a piece of property, lot 121 at Cordova Bay, and walking in
that district, he met John Tway from Jersey, Channel Islands, who talked to him
about local properties and their owners.

When WB admired the Island as the colony he would have chosen if he
had been obliged to emigrate, he was comparing it with the many parts of BC,
Manitoba, and the old NWT that he had already seen and intended to revisit.
The journey to Canada in 1883 was not his first. In the course of an earlier trip in
1881, he had not visited BC but, on the western prairies, had bought land three
miles from Otterburne Station, some thirty miles from Winnipeg, at a place he
called "Little Bredenbury." He had acquired it as an investor in the Midland of
Canada Railway, and during this second visit in July 1883, he and Mitchell waited
at Crookston, Minnesota, for a party of railway officials and Canadian members
of Parliament to join them on the way to visit this property. Among them were
a Scottish businessman and politician named Robert Jaffray (1832-1914) and

his colleague George Albertus Cox (1840-1914), both investors in the railway; Colonel Arthur T. H. Williams (1837-1886), MP for Port Hope, Conservative Whip in the Canadian House of Commons and soon to become a hero at the Battle of Batoche during the Riel Rebellion; and a brother of George Stephens, president of the Canadian Pacific Railway. These were all Canadians by birth or adoption who thought highly of the Winnipeg region, as did others with whom WB made acquaintance: McTavish of the Canadian Pacific Land Commission, Brydges of the HBC, and several prominent local settlers as well as businessmen and officials from Toronto. WB was grateful for their attentions and took careful note of all matters related to farming communities where emigrants might find employment. He recognized the agricultural merits of the prairies and saw that apart from Comox, Cowichan, and Saanich, there was little scope for serious farming on Vancouver Island. Few English visitors can have gone to more trouble to inform themselves, and this is why his personal preference for the Island is significant.

WB was so impressed with it that in 1888, he went out to the Island from England a second time, travelling on this occasion via the new transcontinental railway to Vancouver, then a tiny port recently founded on the mainland as coastal terminus of the Canadian Pacific Railway, and he continued on by steamer across the Strait of Georgia to Victoria. In his second book, *The New Far West and the Old Far East*, he recommended the creation of a trans-Pacific shipping line directly from Victoria to the Orient. He argued his case all the more forcefully because of his exasperation at finding that he could not sail to Japan except by way of San Francisco. Having travelled through Japan, which he found fascinating, and on through China and Ceylon, where he stayed with a relative, he also argued that the British government should establish closer relations with the Japanese.

At the same time, *The New Far West and the Old Far East* was intended to reinforce his first book by encouraging British emigrants to settle in western Canada. Again and even more clearly, he promoted the Island as the best part of Canada and an ideal place for gentlemen seeking a retreat. This was no shallow prejudice. WB's judgements about places and peoples had been formed in the course of much travel and observation. He and Arthur Mitchell had travelled together in Russia, Sweden, Norway, Denmark, and much of western Europe as well as North America. WB formed easy and pleasant relationships with a wide variety of people he met on his journeys, not excluding North-American Indians, Mormons, or others different from himself, and his broad acquaintanceship in the upper middle-classes beyond his own family is apparent in his writing, published and in manuscript. Born in London into a large circle of country gentlemen, he had lived in many parts of southern England and been welcomed particularly in the houses of relatives in Norfolk, Gloucestershire, Wiltshire, and Herefordshire, where he eventually lived with his wife and children at "Bredenbury Court" near Bromyard. His bachelor uncle Edmund Barneby gave him the Bredenbury estate as a wedding present, and he went to great trouble to improve and enlarge the place. It was *en connaissance de cause* that he wrote, "Had I to reside in the Colonies I should choose Victoria, for everything is purely English and the upper classes are as entirely so in manners and speech as anybody residing in England itself." [*The New Far West*, p. 133; *Life and Labour*, p. 401.]

It would be easy to criticize WB for what our age might describe as his "class-based" preferences and to denounce his social circles anachronistically for their wealth and privilege in the midst of much poverty. But family papers at the Herefordshire Record Office and the Bromyard and District Local History Society show the Barnebys to have been generous, conscientious, and public-spirited patrons of the people around them, continually working to improve schools, churches, charitable institutions, roads, and conditions of life generally. Mrs Barneby, *née* Alice May Hicks-Beach (1848-1933), founded the Herefordshire Nursing Association, presided over it for many years and was a member of the county education authority. One of the six sisters of Sir Michael Hicks-Beach, brought up at Coln St Aldwyn in the Cotswold hills of Gloucestershire, she inherited "the deep religious feeling, the strong sense of duty to the community, the calm judgment, and the powers of work," characteristic of a family in which "all became leaders in social enterprise." When she died early in 1933, aged eighty-four, at Longworth, one of the family's houses, a friend wrote of its spiritual quality, its spacious library where all gathered, "its bedrooms with their old chintzes and glowing fires; its long candle-lit dining table; its good cellar; and its many inmates, all busied in lesser or greater degree with cares for others in the outer world—it seemed immutable: and it has gone like a dream." [*The Times*, 2 February 1933, p. 25, obit.] It was from the home they kept at "Bredenbury Court" that WB ventured out twice in the 1880s to Vancouver Island as a visitor, thereby becoming the inspiration of those in his family circle who followed him across the world to Victoria.

During the next half century, a series of WB's relatives and friends went out to visit or settle permanently somewhere on the Island. Statements of their motives are lacking, but it is surely significant that they were not only related to WB in one way or another or to his wife's family, the Hicks-Beaches, but most of them were born in Gloucestershire or nearby, like the Barnebys themselves, whose estates were mainly in the neighbouring county of Herefordshire. Could Lieutenant John Henry Mitchell (1893-1925) not have known, when he retired from the Royal Navy to Comox in 1922, that his father had travelled out to the Island with WB in 1883? Could he not have been aware that his mother's older sister, Caroline Susan Elwes (1845-65), had married the great Michael Edward Hicks-Beach in 1864 a few months before her death? She was also a cousin of Lieutenant (later Admiral Sir) Arthur Bromley (1876-1961), RN, who married a daughter of James Dunsmuir, the Island's wealthy coal baron, in a grand wedding at Christ Church Cathedral in Victoria on 24 June 1904. A remarkable cluster of Gloucestershire and Herefordshire people on the Island suggests that common origins might draw people to follow one another out to a colony. Even Lieutenant Governor Clement Francis Cornwall (1836-1910), whom WB and his companions met in Victoria, was born at Ashcroft in Gloucestershire and his *aide-de-camp* Captain Robert Garnet Tatlow (1855-1910), an Anglo-Irish veteran of the RGA, had been schooled at Cheltenham College. At Departure Bay, they met a Gloucestershire farmer who came from a place WB knew. He was looking out for a farm to buy but had reached the conclusion that the Island was not a place for serious full-time farmers. It was better suited to independent or pensioned gentlemen who might be content with a small acreage. How could Edward Howe Hicks-Beach (1875-1967), RN, have met and married Alberta Louise Jaynes at a village on the Island in 1901 without some connection, either through his own family (he was a nephew of Sir Michael Hicks-Beach) or through another acquaintance in Gloucestershire, where the girl's parents were born? Her parents, William Penn Jaynes and Clara *née* Rhead, from Gloucester and Westbury-on-Severn respectively, had eloped to Ontario and moved on in the early 1870s to the Cowichan Valley. There, they had bought a grocery store—on a tip from John A. Macdonald, it is said—and had six children, including twelve-year-old Alberta Louise, by the time WB visited the Island in 1888. Together, they formed a family circle, and it was reinforced by friends, such as *William Baillie-Grohman, who contributed a chapter to WB's first book and who must have been on the Island during WB's second visit because his son Harold Baillie-Grohman was born in Victoria at about that time. Baillie-Grohman was already engaged in pioneering activities much like what WB had in mind, investing in the Kootenay Valley in conjunction with his wife's father, Tom Nickalls, a member of the London stock exchange.

Edward Howe Hicks-Beach applied to Victoria early in 1904 for a post as JP and stipendiary magistrate in the Skeena district of northern British Columbia and evidently held that post until 1909, probably longer. Young Cartwright, the mining engineer, met him at Hazelton, chief town in the Skeena Valley in October 1907. Upon retiring, Hicks-Beach and his wife almost certainly migrated to Oregon or California, where their two daughters married in due time. His famous uncle Sir Michael Hicks-Beach never visited the Island, and WB, the family's pioneering traveller, lived for most of his life in Herefordshire, with occasional visits to London, elsewhere in southern England, or on the continent. There is no way of knowing how many people were persuaded to visit the north-west Pacific coast as a result of their influence, but the number of those within their own family circles leaves a suggestive impression.

Sources: Herefordshire County Record Office, Hereford, Barneby family papers; Bromyard and District Local History Society, miscellaneous records; Worcestershire County Record Office, County Hall, Spetchley Road, Worcester, tel: 0195 763763, F99/131, "misc. papers of W. H. Barneby, including list of saloon passengers on S.S. *Parisian* for Quebec and Montreal, 1887"; W. H. Barneby, *Life and Labour in the Far, Far West, Being Notes of a Tour in the Western States, British Columbia, Manitoba and the North West Territory* (Cassell, 1884), 432 pp.; W. H. Barneby, *The New Far West and the Old Far East: Being Notes of a Tour in North America, Japan, Ceylon etc.* (E. Stanford, 1889), 316 pp.

BARNES, Lieutenant Commander George Barkley Fraser (1898-1985). He was born on 13 December 1898 at Esquimalt, son of *Lieutenant Colonel George Edward Barnes and grandson of *Captain C. E. Barkley. He became one of the eight Canadian midshipmen who graduated from the Royal Naval College of Canada in December 1916, after two and a half years there. The Great War being then in progress, he served as a midshipman aboard HMS *Leviathan* (1917), *Carnarvon* (1917), *Roxborough* (1917), *Minotaur* (1917), *Canada* (1918), and *Barham* (1919), by which time he was second lieutenant. In 1923, he was promoted to lieutenant in command of HMS *Armentiéres*, then HMS *Festubert* (1927), and became lieutenant commander (2 July 1928) in command of HMCS *Naden* (1929), *Champlain* (1930-1931). He retired in 1938 but was recalled for the Second World War in which he was on the staff of the commanding officer Pacific Coast as "Boom Defence Officer" (1939) and then, from 1 July 1942, as staff officer administration.

He and Captain A. P. Musgrave retired to VI where in 1983, GB, then aged eighty-three, was living at Crofton and Musgrave, aged 83, lived nearby. GB married one of the four daughters of Alexander Gillespie (1880-?) of the insurance and real-estate firm of Gillespie, Hart & Co., thus linking himself with a large clan of businessmen and soldiers including Jacob Hunter Todd, founder of the firm Messrs J. H. Todd & Sons Ltd., Dr J. W. Anderson of Hong Kong, and Lieutenant Colonel George Gaisford (Armoured Division, England). He died on 17 March 1985.
Sources: *As You Were! Ex-Cadets Remember*, ed., R. Guy C. Smith, No. 1877 (Ottawa; The RMC Club of Canada, 1884-1984, 1984), vol. I, 1876-1918, pp. 225-42; *MacFarlane*, p. 4; *Who's Who in B.C.*, vol. VI (1944-1946), p. 95.

BARNES, Lieutenant Colonel George Edward, CBE (1865-1928). He was born on 19 August 1865 in Edinburgh, son of George R. Barnes, Esq., MD, and joined the Royal Marine Artillery on 1 September 1883 as a probationary lieutenant. He was a captain from 1 September 1894, a major from 2 October 1905, and a full lieutenant colonel from 11 February 1919. He was put on the retired list at his own request on 1 September 1906, when the authorities also listed him among the Reserve of Marine officers. On 24 February (?) 1915, he was recalled for service in emergency, but, finally on 11 February 1919, "relegated to retired list on account of medical unfitness and granted substantive rank of lieutenant-colonel." The effort and study behind this dry list of promotions is evident in the list of examinations passed (or failed) in subjects like torpedoes, gunnery, arsenal, military equitation, and signalling, all the while aboard a series of ships. His record is peppered with approving remarks: "reliable," "zealous," "sound man," "good officer," etc.

Earlier, after some years at Greenwich Naval College and aboard ships at Hull and in the Channel, he was posted to submarine duties for the colonial service and then to South Africa, where the Second Boer War was in progress. To his King's Medal for South Africa were added clasps for Cape Colony, Orange Free State, and the Transvaal. In May 1902, he was seconded for three years as adjutant, Forfar and Kincardine Artillery Militia, which brought him appointment to the OBE, commander (Military Division). Under the heading "War Service" in his military record is listed: South Africa, 1900-1902, railway staff officer, Modden River, Kimberly, Vryburg, and Mafeking—in advance on Mafeking—February-June 1900 and later. His record as a railway staff officer in South Africa was marked "good knowledge of his work, very smart in the performance of his duties and very self-reliant." During the Great War, his name was brought to the notice of LCA for valuable services rendered in 1918.

At the appropriate place on his service record is the line, "Permission to reside in British Columbia on retirement." Early in his career, about 1893, he had been stationed for six years at Work Point Barracks, Esquimalt, to plan and lay loop mines as part of the naval station's defences. He found the Island attractive and on 1 September 1897 married Florence Annie Barkley, daughter of *Captain Charles Edward Barkley, RN, living in retirement at Westholme. Recalled for service in South Africa, Barnes eventually retired in 1906 on a small pension and took his wife and their son, born shortly before he was called away to South Africa, home on the *Empress of Britain*. They settled near her parents on a seaside property at Crofton, and on 14 February 1914, the *Victoria Daily Colonist* reported, "Major Barnes, late R.M.A., who was stationed here for six years when the Imperial forces garrisoned this port, came down specially from Crofton to renew his acquaintance with men who had served with him . . ." These were "some thirty ex-service men gathered at the Dallas Hotel . . . to establish in Victoria an Old Comrades Ass. for men who were in the R.N. or the Royal Marines." The Great War intervened but again he returned to what had become home. Among his friends there was *Major General G. R. Poole, who settled near him at Crofton, where they hunted and fished together. They also met *Robert Aubrey Meade, as Florence Annie Barnes wrote in a letter dated at Crofton 17 June 1912 and preserved at the Norfolk Record Office. It was addressed to "Mrs Meade" of Earsham, shortly after Meade's death, introducing herself thus: "My husband and I had the pleasure of meeting you & Captain [John] Meade [1812-1886, Robert Aubrey's Meade's older brother] when my cousin Mabel Raikes took us over to Earsham." She apologized for taking too long to answer a letter, saying that she had been away from home and busy with "a houseful of relations on a trip from England."

Their son, *George Barkley Fraser Barnes, was at school for a time with *Rollo Mainguy and *Philip Livingstone, three future officers together, at *P. T. Skrimshire's remarkable little British school near Quamichan Lake. They joined the Cowichan Valley Cadet Corps and spent summer 1913 in a camp at Sidney. GB took a keen interest in the Island's public affairs, attended meeting, and wrote letters to the newspapers. In a letter to the *Colonist* in April 1921, for instance, he denounced the members of the provincial legislative assembly for voting themselves salary increases and joined others like himself—Lieutenant *L. W. Huntington of the RNVR, *Mrs Moss, OBE, and others—in a meeting at the Duncan Opera House, where he said that "no Kaffir pow-wow would behave as disgracefully as the B.C. legislature." In another letter to the papers under the heading, "What is Sinn Fein?" he expressed the loathing of his kind for the republican Irish and recommended *Blackwoods Magazine* of November 1921 on the subject. Much of his concern was for the preservation of the Island's natural beauty, and he urged the need for a Canadian policy on natural resources. He died at last on 3 November 1928 and his wife on the following 30 September. Their graves are in the cemetery of the little Anglican Church on the old Island Highway where the road bridge crosses the Chemainus River and where they were married. They were survived by their son, his wife Daphne, and a daughter Heather.

Sources: BNA (PRO), ADM 196/62, page 100; Longstaff, *Esquimalt Naval Base*, p. 60, note 20; *Colonist*, 15 February 1914, p. 7; 2 February 1921, p. 8; 9 April 1921, p. 4; 5 May 1921, p. 9; 11 December 1921, p. 4: Letter to the Editor; 7 March 1925, p. 4; 2 October 1929, p. 14; 2 October 1929, p. 14, obit.; Norfolk Record Office (Norwich), MEA 11/110; Elliott, *Memories of the Chemainus Valley*, pp. 105-112, "(by) George Barkley Fraser Barnes."

BARRETT-LENNARD, Captain Charles Edward (1835-1874). An army officer, veteran of the Crimean War, who left a record of his voyage to the Island and around it, he was in Victoria from February to August 1860, for part of winter 1860-1861, and again in July 1861, altogether on that coast for two years. He signed the preface to his book at the Royal Thames Yacht Club, which shows him to have been an amateur mariner, even though his career was as an officer in the Fifth Dragoon Guards. He and a friend, Captain Napoleon FitzStubbs (1835-?), another army officer, took a twenty-ton yacht rigged as a cutter, the *Templar*, on the deck of a sailing vessel, the *Athelstan*, which carried them from England around the tip of South America and up to Victoria, capital of the colony of Vancouver Island. There they unloaded the *Templar* (a name showing that CB was almost certainly a Freemason) and sailed across to New Westminster at the mouth of the Fraser River, then the little capital of the separate, newer colony of British Columbia. (Not until 1866 were the two colonies combined as British Columbia.) After a short trip up and down the Fraser, they sailed past Burrard Inlet, then almost uninhabited, and continued northwards along the Strait of Georgia and around the Island, stopping from time to time to visit native tribes, which fascinated him, and settlements here and there, such as Nootka Sound on the Island's west coast.

CB wrote tantalizingly little about Victoria or Esquimalt in his book but was deeply interested in the Island and its development as a British colony. Its situation, he thought, "is admirably adapted for carrying on a trade with China, Japan, India, and Australia, and it is not too much to suppose that these colonies must become the great highway for traffic between the above-mentioned countries and England, in the event of the completion of this line of railroad [p. 181 ff.]." He was speculating that "the railway, now in progress between Halifax and Quebec" might be extended for several thousand miles westwards to the Pacific Coast. As everyone knows, this was not accomplished for another twenty years, and until then the city of Vancouver did not exist. CB refers continually to the Island as "Vancouver," knowing as he did that Fort Vancouver was several hundred miles south on the Columbia River. He spent time at San Francisco and was much concerned with the dangers he thought these two young British colonies faced from their near neighbour, the United States. He saw not only a threat of American expansive aggression, but also dangerous influences. His experience was that Americans were always ready to shoot or stab one another: "Acts of lawless violence are unhappily only too common in America [p. 250 ff.]." He was disgusted by the Yankee habit of "playing Poker and Euker, accompanied by drinking, smoking, and chewing . . . and spitting [p. 229]"; "the habit of indulging in frequent drinking at public bars, or liquoring, as the Americans term it, is a national vice . . . [p. 242]"; their "notoriously boastful disposition [p. 252]" and other objectionable characteristics. Of course, he also found much to admire in the United States. But he quoted an American friend, who told him, "Our liberty, equality, and fraternity, sir, are all moonshine, our boasted freedon is a snare and a delusion. My countrymen want [i.e., ought] to travel more, to correct their intolerable vanity and self-sufficiency [p. 253]."

CB lived most of his life as an English gentleman. Born at Rottingdean, Sussex, he appears in the 1851 census as a boy of fifteen living with several other boys at 40 Bloomsbury Place, Brighton, in the family of a Scottish tutor giving "Classes, Mathematical & General." It was in Brighton that he died at last, mourned by his children and many relatives, his first wife Fanny Darnell having died in April 1857 and his second, Ada Meredith Harris, in December 1873. As the fourth of five sons born to Sir Thomas Barrett-Lennard (1788-1856), CB did not inherit his father's baronetcy, which went to his oldest brother, Sir Thomas Barrett-Lennard (1826-1919). Did he talk about the Pacific Coast to his many relatives? One of his first cousins had a daughter who married a Canadian and died in Victoria, as did her husband. This was Georgina Boswell Barrett-Lennard (1882-1965), born at Peterborough, Ontario, and her husband, D'Arcy Everard Boulton (1876-1948), son of a Canadian senator, veteran of the South African War (1899-1902), born at Orillia, Ontario, who retired and died in Victoria. They had brought up their family on a farm at Russell, Manitoba, but a few of their children also moved to Victoria, including Commodore Angus George Boulton (1911-1992) of the Royal Canadian Navy. Some of the names these Canadian descendants gave their children show that they were aware of their English forebears.

Sources: Charles Edward Barrett-Lennard, *Travels in British Columbia, with the Narrative of a Yacht Voyage round Vancouver's Island* (Hurst & Blackett, successors to Henry Colburn, 13 Great Marlborough Street, 1862), 307 pp.; census 1851, England, HO, 107/16/4/4; Walbran, *B.C. Coast Names*, pp. 303-4; BC Geographical Names Office; BC Freemason website; New York Passenger Lists, T-715_318, p. 89 (FitzStubbs); *Colonist*, 19 October 1889 (letter by John Field); Christopher Bracken, *The Potlatch Papers: A Colonial Case History* (Chicago, University of Chicago, 1997), p. 114 (FitzStubbs).

Francis John Barrow
in the PCMR, 1940s

Francis John Barrow

BARROW, Francis John (1876-1944). He was born at Caterham, Surrey, third child of Alexander Maclean Barrow (1832-92) and Sarah Constance *née* Mallet, and the 1881 census found him, aged four, living at Harestone Valley, Dunedin, Caterham, with his parents, then aged forty-nine and forty-two. His father was a retired merchant born in Pimlico, Middlesex, and his mother born in Ireland. There was also a visiting cousin, his father's nephew, Frederick M. West, aged nineteen, born at Hawarden, Flint, Wales, "scholar at College for the blind," as well as four female servants, two of them nurses. Presumably, Barrow's older brothers were away at school. He studied mining at Camborne, Cornwall, and graduated as a mining engineer at Trinity College Cambridge. In 1901, he was "living on own means" at Camborne, Cornwall, as a boarder at 137 Fore Street in the house of an accountant, William J. Reeve and his wife, Sarah T. Reeve. He was certainly then attending the Camborne School of Mining. Others on the same census page were listed as "student mining school."

His health being delicate, in 1903, his parents sent him out to visit an older brother who had become a land surveyor in British Columbia. They spent several months on the Gulf Islands in the Straits of Georgia, and FB liked it so much that he returned there in 1905 and lived with his brother on Hill Island, not far from Sidney, to raise chickens in the hope of selling eggs. On 20 September 1906, he married a cultivated English girl, Amy Bradford, daughter of Sir John and Lady Bradford of Haywards Heath, Sussex, and they settled at first on Saturna Island and then on Shoal Harbour near Sidney, where they bought one of the old Brackman-Ker buildings that had earlier been part of a hotel, earlier still a grist mill. Mrs Barrow's private fortune enabled them to buy a boat, the *Toketie*, and to take long cruises northwards up the inner passage each year for three decades, broken only while he was serving as a private soldier during the Great War (1914-1918). But his wartime service was varied and unusual: Early in 1917, he enlisted in the Inland Water Transport Section of the Royal Engineers, who were recruiting men willing to work on rivers and lakes in Mesopotamia, Egypt, and elsewhere.

The brother who introduced FB to Saanich and the Gulf Islands was Captain Arthur Robert Maclean Barrow (c. 1867-1953), born in London, who went to BC in 1896 and in October 1899 qualified as a BC land surveyor. From time to time, A. R. M. Barrow and his wife Daisy used to visit FB in Saanich and on *Toketie*, and they too bought a boat, a small steamer called *Constance*, but from 1907 to 1910, this brother was busy laying out the townsite for Prince Rupert, BC. During those years, the Arthur Barrows lived at Prince Rupert in two tents on a raft substantial enough that Daisy had her grand piano with her. After that, they lived at Smithers, Johnson Landing in the Kootenays, in the Peace River district, and elsewhere in BC. But they family lived for long periods in Victoria, where on 26 April 1910, for instance, A. R. M. Barrow was elected to the committee of the Navy League, Victoria, and Esquimalt branch. He also died there, aged eighty-six, on 8 March 1953.

Meanwhile, FB attracts attention for three of his activities: first, his travels in Pacific Coast waters in search of native tribes, their petroglyphs and other Indian art on which he became a distinguished expert (as related by Beth Hill). He corresponded with anthropologists and wrote articles about Indian petroglyphs and pictographs. Secondly, his service overseas during the Great War, especially in the Inland Water Transport section of the Royal Engineers, deserves further investigation, as does his recognized expertise with a rifle, which qualified him to act as instructor and range officer in North Saanich during the Second World War. This was a third interesting feature of his life. As a boy, I met him at the three hundred-yard range we built in 1943 on Tatlow Road, off Horth Cross Road (now Wain's Road), when we were both members of the Pacific Coast Militia Rangers, a kind of home guard or militia composed of old soldiers and Boy Scouts. He is on the extreme right of a photograph of our unit taken in 1943, not long before he died at Sidney on 22 March 1944. So central was his part in that unit that the rifle range was named "Barrow's Range" after him. He was no doubt an old friend of that arch-sportsman *Lieutenant Colonel Lewis Carey, as he served as a pallbearer at Carey's funeral in January 1936 at St Stephen's Church, Mount Newton Crossroad, along with *Major Roger Monteith and others.

Sources: census 1871, England, RG 10/708, p. 8; census 1881, RG 11/804, p. 22; *Colonist*, 4 February 1917, p. 12; 28 March 1944, p. 5, obit.; 10 March 1953, p. 20, obit.; *The Sidney Review*, 10 June 1926, p. 4; Beth Hill, *Upcoast Summers* (Ganges, BC, Horsdal & Shubert, 1985), passim; FB, "Petroglyphs and Pictographs on the B.C. Coast," *The Canadian Geographical Journal*, vol. 24 (February 1942), pp. 94-101; John A. Whittaker, *Early Land Surveyors of British Columbia (P.L.S. Group)* (Victoria, BC, The Corporation of Land Surveyors of the Province of BC), 1990, pp. 9-11.

BARTLETT, John (1838-1914). Bartlett was born on 27 December 1838 at Shipton Gorge, Dorsetshire, and joined HMS *Victory* on 12 July 1853 as a boy of fifteen. He served on a long series of naval vessels: on HMS *Geyser*, he was present at the bombardment of Sveborg in the Baltic during the war with Russia and then was on HMS *Blenheim, St Jean d'Arc, Phantom, Scout Scatley*, and *Malacca*. Aboard HMS *Phaeton*, he was in the demonstration off Mexico at the time of the Emperor Maximilian and was on the Esquimalt Station later in HMS *Sutley* and *Malacca*. He was promoted to captain of the maintop before retiring on 27 December 1866, when he went to the Cariboo gold fields and mined for eight years. Bartlett retired to Victoria, died there on 4 May 1914, and was buried at Ross Bay Cemetery on 7 May in a coffin draped with the Union Jack on a gun carriage with sailors as pallbearers, a bugler to play last post, and followed by members of the British Campaigners Association, such as *Major John Wilson and *George Edwin Smith, who had served in the Baltic with him, Beaumont Thomas Frederick William Boggs (1863-1943), and Major Albert Edward Christie (1860-1954), D.S.O. They honoured him for his twenty-two years of service, for being present at the Indian Mutiny, and for being one of the oldest members of the Association, "always an active member of the Association, never absent from our meetings and always willing," etc. The association wrote a letter to his widow and three sons.

Sources: *BC Archives, Minutes of the British Campaigners' Ass.*, 16 April 1914; *Colonist* 5 May 1914, p. 12; 8 May 1914, p. 7; see *BC Archives*, photo of the British Campaigners, 1913.

BAXTER, Sergeant Andrew (c. 1840-1914). Born in Fifeshire, he joined the Ninety-second Gordon Highlanders and served with them for twenty-two years, of which sixteen and a half years overseas. Part of that time, he was in the company commanded by Major George Stuart White (1835-1812), who became Field Marshall Sir George White, VC, an Irish Orangeman like himself. AB served most actively in the Indian Mutiny campaign. Upon his retirement from the army, he went to Canada c. 1894 and in 1908 to Victoria where he died, aged seventy-four, on 2 April 1914, and was buried as a Seventh Day Adventist, with a military funeral. His coffin, draped in a Union Jack flag, was carried on a gun carriage, which was followed by a detachment of the British Campaigners (even though he had never joined that society), and by members of the Loyal Orange Lodge No. 1610. The pallbearers were W. J. Edwards, late RE and secretary of the British Campaigners; *Mr G. Edward Smith, late RN, a veteran of the Crimea, the Mutiny, and China; Mr F. J. Fleury of the Intelligence Department in South Africa; and Sergeant Bugler F. Mead of the Fiftieth Highlanders, who sounded the "last post" at the graveside. AB left a wife and six sons, three of them in Victoria.
Sources: *Colonist*, 4 April 1914, p. 10; 7 April 1914, p. 3, obit.

BAYLY, Henry Bertram (c. 1887-1940). Born at Stonehaven, Scotland, where his father, Henry B. Bayly, a Wiltshire man, owned property and married Rosanna, HB was apprenticed in his teens to a shipyard. In 1914, HB became a merchant seaman and served through the Great War as such. Then he became an engineer on a tea planter's estate in Assam near Pinsukia, eventually the manager, and there his son, Ian Bayly (my informant), was born c. 1927. But Ian knows nearly nothing about his parents' activities, as he was sent home to a boarding school in England where he lived from the age of three. He spent a few summers with his parents on a forty-eight-foot yacht they acquired and kept in England. This was because, according to common practice on tea plantations, his father had every fourth summer off. What Ian did not know was that HB built the yacht there in Assam, called her *Reverie*, and obtained special permission from the railway company to ship her to the coast and on to England, where he had her fitted out.

HB had a friend in India, and the two of them married sisters. One year, the friend and his wife returned to England by way of the Pacific Ocean, Canada, and the Atlantic and were much impressed on the way by the BC coast. In view of their favourable report, HB and family went to Victoria when he retired in 1937, sailing from India on a cargo liner across the Pacific, landing at Portland, Oregon, and taking a ferry from Seattle to Victoria. Ian remembers this because he was then ten years old. Looking for a place somewhere off in the country, they settled before long in a house at Maple Bay (on the point of the north or left-hand side of the bay), which had to be reached by boat from Maple Bay dock. They acquired the house from *Rev. John Antle in return for their yacht *Reverie*, which they had left in

England and which Antle then sailed adventurously across the Atlantic and around South America to the Island. Ian was sent to the provincial school in Duncan, where he recalls being cruelly teased for his English voice. He recalls knowing a neighbouring lady, Mrs Palmer, whose husband had been a medical doctor in India, and also knowing the Simes family at Maple Bay. In due time, Ian attended Royal Roads, joined the RCN, and became a naval architect at Greenwich.

He was therefore absent when HB died suddenly, aged fifty-three, of a stroke on 7 September 1940 at Duncan and was buried in a service in the chapel at the Royal Oak Crematorium, under Ven. Archdeacon A. de L. Nunns. A few years later, on 26 June 1944, Ian's maternal grandfather, Benjamin Armitage, died also at Duncan. His mother, HB's wife, *née* Gertrude Armitage, moved away from Maple Bay to Galiano Island, but died, aged eighty-eight, in Victoria on 16 January 1985, having first burnt the family photos and letters. Her funeral was held in the chapel at the Royal Oak Crematorium under Ven. Archdeacon Nunns. There had been four children of whom Ian was the oldest, the others being Conran, June, and Kathleen, all of whom had moved away.

Sources: Notes courtesy of a son, Ian Bayly, 179 Norwood Avenue, Pointe-Claire, Quebec, Canada H9R 1R3; tel. (514) 694-3443; *Cowichan Leader*, 12 September 1940, obit.

BAZETT, Major Lancelot Young (1891-?). He was born on 12 July 1891 in the Cowichan Valley, son of William Bazett (1861-1948) and Jane Rhys Katherine Gwynne Bazett (c. 1864-1936), who had bought a hundred-acre farm near Maple Bay in 1890 and, from their neighbours, stocked it with pure-bred Guernsey cows from Ontario. LB's father was one of the thirteen children born to a retired India civil servant, and the 1871 census recorded him, aged nine, living with his family at "Denmark House, Southeast Crescent," Reading, Berkshire. His father, LB's grandfather, Richard Young Bazett (c. 1811-?), appointed to the ICS in 1830, had married a much-younger woman from Cape Town, Cape of Good Hope, Mary Ann Bazett, aged thirty-four in 1871, and they already had six daughters ranging from Harriet, aged eighteen, down to Sibella (?) aged two, and five sons. Ten years later, the 1881 census found LB's father William Bazett, aged nineteen, still living with his family, now at 8 Castle Cresent in Reading, with a new brother, Seymour aged six, two visiting young women born in Madras, India, (Fanny Julia Eyre twenty-two and her sister Lucy A. Eyre twenty-one) with three servants. An older brother, LB's uncle Charles Bazett, aged nineteen, had become an "articled clerk in architect's office." About a year later, William Bazett went out "to learn farming" in Iowa, USA, later in Oregon, and after a few years moved to the Cowichan Valley. It is not clear where or when he married LB's mother, Jane Rhys Katherine Gwynne Bazett (c. 1864-1936), but they arrived from Oregon with two children, including Harold Mansel Bazett (c. 1888-1984), and soon had several more.

LB evidently followed in his grandfather's footsteps, perhaps because he was one of the remarkable generation of Cowichan boys who attended Quamichan Lake School kept in the years 1905-1925 by *P. T. Skrimshire. A number of boys, all from British families in or near the Cowichan Valley, were evidently inspired by

Skrimshire to distinguish themselves in Imperial forces later in life. LB joined the British Army or the Indian Army and was listed in 1935 as assistant commandant in Rajputana. When his mother died in 1936, he was still in India and his brother H. M. Bazett was in Burma, but in 1948, the year of his father's death, LB was mentioned as Major L. Y. Bazett on the Isle of Man. He did not return to settle on the Island, as did some of his uncles from Reading and his brothers.

Sources: *Cowichan Leader,* 29 January 1948, obit; *Colonist,* 9 May 1936, p. 16, obit.; *India List,* January 1884, p. 143; *India Office List,* 1935, p. 50; census 1861, England, RG 9/746, p. 88 (28?); census 1871, RG 10/1280, page 11; census 1881, RG 11/1301, p. 14; Livingston's *Fringe of the Clouds,* p. 15.

BEANLANDS, Rev. Canon Arthur John (1857-1917). A rector at Christ Church Cathedral in Victoria, he was born on 20 August 1857 in Durham and recorded in the 1881 census, aged twenty-three, as a son of Arthur Beanlands, aged fifty-eight, "M.A., City Magistrate, Civil Engineer & Mining Surveyor—Treasurer of Durham University," born at Bingley, Yorkshire. An old land-owning family of yeomen in the West Riding of Yorkshire, is how Burke's *Colonial Gentry* describes AB's family. His mother Jane Jowett, aged fifty-eight, was born at Wilsden, Yorkshire. No other children were mentioned then, but there were two servants and they all lived at Palace Green, a house in Cathedral Church Yard. AB's three sisters were born in the next few years. In 1884 in Kensington, AB married Laura Maud Hills, born on 1 October 1859 at Thanet, Kent, daughter of Walter Alfred Hills, a barrister of Ramsgate, Kent, and his wife Mary Anne Stubbs, sister of the bishop of Oxford.

According to the Canadian census for 1901, they emigrated to the Island almost immediately and in Victoria had four children: Dorothy Garnett Beanlands on 27 May 1887, Alison M. Beanlands on 11 May 1891, Angela M. Beanlands on 23 March 1895, and Bernard Paul Gascoigne Beanlands on 11 September 1897. They made their home at 24 Burdett Avenue, Victoria. Mrs Beanlands died, aged forty-three, on 21 June 1903 at Shawnigan Lake, where they probably had a summer cottage, like so many others in Victoria. In any event, about two years later, on 11 September 1905, AB married Sophia Theresa Pemberton (1869-1959) in Victoria, where he was then rector of Christ Church Cathedral. She was born in Victoria as a daughter of *Joseph Despard Pemberton and his wife Theresa Jane Despard Grautoff. In 1891, AB had published in Victoria a short book to encourage immigrants, in which he offered sound advice: For example, immigrants should be healthy, loyal, and ready for hard physical labour; this country does not welcome "the chronic grumbler or alien-hearted individual." He added sensible details about the limited prospects for large-scale farming near Victoria, Nanaimo, and indeed most of the Island.

AB's death is obscure, but he may have been living in Kent at Wickhurst Manor, Weald, Sevenoaks, when he died in 1917, two years before the death of his son Captain Bernard Paul Gascoigne Beanlands, aged twenty-three, in a flying accident on 8 May 1919 while serving in the RAF. Young Beanlands had brought down a number of enemy aircraft.

Sources: *Victoria Daily Times*, 27 September, p. 15; *Colonist*, 4 June 1921, p. 8; 11 June 1921, p. 8; census 1881, England, RG 11/4960, p. 26; *Canadian Almanach*, 1909, p. 343, Church of England; Canon Beanlands, *British Columbia as a Field for Emigration and Investment* (Victoria, R. Wolfenden, 1891), 60 pp.; Sir Bernard Burke, *A Genealogical and Heraldic History of the Colonial Gentry* (1891), pp. 414-16; *London Gazette* dated 18 January 1918; Richard Mackie, "Pemberton, Joseph Despard, engineer, surveyor, farmer, politician, JP, and businessman," *Dictionary of Canadian Biography*, (2000 University of Toronto Press, 2000); *London Gazette*, 18 January 1918; J. Horsfall Turner, *Ancient Bingley, Its History and Scenery* (Bingley, Yorkshire, Thomas Harris & Son for the author, 1897), p. 238.

BEAUMONT, Ernest Godfrey (1874-1967). He was born on 22 December 1874 in London, the youngest son of Lieutenant Colonel Godfrey Wentworth Beaumont of the Scots Guards and of Anna, daughter of Sir Edward Blackett, Sixth Baronet, and grandson of Captain Richard Beaumont, RN, and of his wife the Hon. Susan Hussey, daughter of Godfrey, Third Lord Macdonald of the Isles. EB attended Emmanuel College, Cambridge, from 1897, long enough to qualify for a BA. In 1911, he was attracted to Canada, where his parents had been quartered in the year 1863 with a Brigade of Guards sent out in connection with the *Trent* affair. In 1918, EB bought 160 acres on Discovery Island in the Gulf of Georgia, visible to the east from Oak Bay or Shoal Bay, and he settled there permanently. He was back in London, however, on 25 November 1920, when he married Constance Ida *née* Currie, widow of William Houston Long of Brighton and daughter of Archibald Hay Currie, British Consul at Nice (France), and his wife (EB's mother-in-law) Marion, daughter of Alban Thomas Gwynne of Monachty, Cardigan. The *Victoria Daily Colonist* reported a long list of distinguished guests.

EB was likewise absent from his island in 1924, when he went to Hong Kong and spent six months, building a Diesal motor cruiser, *Discovery Isle,* in which he later explored the waterways along the north-west Pacific coast between Glacier Bay (Alaska) and Olympia (Washington State). Generously public-spirited like so many of his kind, EB often took groups of young people out for pleasure trips in *Discovery Isle* and, in March 1962, was awarded a life membership in the Boys' Club of Greater Victoria in recognition of this hospitality. *Captain C. P "Pat" Nixon had fond memories of such trips during his boyhood in Victoria and Esquimalt. *Kyrle C. Symons had mixed memories, as he related in his book about St Michael's Boys' School: "At the kind invitation of Captain Beaumont, I took eleven boarders to visit him on Discovery Island, where he has a charming house. After a delightful day, we went on board his launch for the return; but unfortunately ran on a rock where, with the tide falling rapidly, we stuck. There was a small boat in which we got the boys to the beach one by one. There we stayed, marooned, till about 11 at night, rather cold and hungry and wondering if in time to come someone would find our bones bleaching there. However, on a last despairing walk around the Island, we saw a light and managed, by all yelling together, to rouse a Japanese fisherman who had come in for the night." He took them all to the Oak Bay boathouse for $1 a head.

On 24 January 1967, EB died, aged ninety-two, in Victoria. Some years earlier, his wife, Constance Ida H. Beaumont *née* Currie, had died there, aged seventy-eight, on 29 March 1952. She was no relation of *General Sir Arthur Currie, whose family name had been changed from "Curry" and "Corregon" earlier.

Sources: *Who's Who in B.C.*, 1933-1934, p. 19; *Colonist,* 4 January 1921, p. 9; 29 March 1962, p. 2 (photo); Kyrle C. Symons, *That Amazing Institution: The Story of St Michael's School, Victoria, B.C., from 1910-1948* (Victoria, Privately Printed, 1948?), pp. 43-44.

BEARD, Commander Charles Taschereau (1890-1948). Born in Ottawa on 30 July 1890, he went to England aged seventeen to join the Royal Navy and spent two years aboard the training ship *Conway* before transferring to the Royal Canadian Navy on 21 October 1910, when it could scarcely be called a navy, consisting mainly of fisheries patrol vessels. By the nature of his long career, in which he served with thirty different ships, British and Canadian, CB was one of the founders of the RCN. From 4 March 1909, he had been formally a member of the Royal Naval Reserve, and it was then that he first reached Esquimalt, aboard HMS *Algerine.* He served in *Niobe* (1910), *Dreadnought* (1911), *Lancaster* (1914), *Ramillies* (1919), and then mostly in the RCN. In 1922, he became senior naval officer at Esquimalt and the captain of *Naden.* He later held various posts at headquarters including director of Naval Reserves and also director of Naval Operations. In 1936, he was once again at *Naden* as commanding officer as well as commander of the dockyard.

He then retired from the RCN and represented Esquimalt as an MLA for six years. When the Second World War began, the RCN having been pitifully neglected, Ottawa was desperate to make the best of what there was. Beard was called out of retirement to take command of HMCS *Prince Robert,* a passenger vessel converted and commissioned in 1940 as an auxiliary cruiser. Her first mission was to join in a blockade off the Mexican coast attempting to bottle up enemy merchant raiders. On 25 September, CB was able to capture the *Weser* in international waters off Manzanillo and have her sailed back to Esquimalt. Ill health soon forced him to relinquish his command of HMCS *Prince Robert,* and he died in Esquimalt on 21 November 21, 1948.

Sources: *MacFarlane,* p. 5; files of Copyright ® 2000-2001 CFB Esquimalt Naval and Military Museum.

BEATLEY, Chief Petty Officer John James (1858-1944). Born on 23 April 1858 at Devonport near Plymouth, son of a Warrant Officer in the navy, he was recorded in the census of 1871 as living at 36 Bankwell Street, Plymouth, with his mother, Mary Ann Beatley, and an older sister working as "a laundress" to support her two daughters. He joined the RN in 1874, and in 1881, aged twenty-two, he was in the Armourer's crew aboard HMS *Northumberland.* He retired as a petty officer on 30 November 1898 after twenty-two years of service and eventually settled in Victoria at 3016 Donald Street. A Freemason and a member of the British Imperial Comrades Association, he died, aged eighty-six, on 31 January 1944.

Sources: *Colonist,* 11 February 1940, p. 17; 3 February 1944, p. 14, obit.; census 1871, England, RG 10/2113, p. 11; census 1881, RG 11/5635, p. 18.

BECK, Lily Adams (c. 1862-1931), *alias* E. Barrington, *alias* Louis Moresby, *alias* Lily Moresby Adams, became known as a prolific writer of mystical histories and fantasy novels with Oriental themes. She is widely believed to have been born c. 1862 as Elizabeth Louisa Moresby, daughter of a famous naval explorer, Admiral John Moresby (1832-1922), R.N., and therefore a granddaughter of *Admiral-of-the-Fleet Sir Fairfax Moresby, after whom Moresby Island in the Gulf of Georgia was named. Literary historians, and others such as Wikipedia online encyclopedia, accept this explanation of LB's identity and copy one another in the usual way, repeating that she travelled widely throughout Asia, dabbled in Theosophy, and, in her later years, became a novelist, publishing short stories at first in *The Atlantic Monthly, Asia* and the *Japanese Grassho.*

But her identity is uncertain. Nowhere does she appear in British census records with the rest of the family. An Elizabeth Louisa Moresby would be a plausible daughter for Admiral John Moresby because his own mother appears *inter alia* in census records for 1861 and 1871 as Eliza Louisa Moresby (1796-1874), born in London, wife of Sir Fairfax Moresby (1786-1877) his father. But Admiral Moresby's own children were recorded only in 1891 and only as four unmarried daughters: Ethel F. aged twenty-five, born at Southsea, Hampshire; Georgina aged twenty-three, born in Ireland; Hilda F. aged twenty-two, born in Ireland; and Gladys aged twenty, born in Ireland. Even the Oxford DNB mentions no other. They all lived in 1891 at "The Grange," Subdeanery, Chichester, South-West Sussex. At all events, LB went on to write novels such as *The Splendor of Asia* (1926) in which she attempted to interpret the life and teachings of the Buddha, and *The Glory of Egypt* (1926). Her romance entitled *The House of Fulfillment: The Romance of a Soul* (1927) touched upon the Indian philosophy of the Upanishads and supernatural phenomena.

After the Great War, perhaps in 1919, she settled in Victoria. In March 1925, she spoke to a large audience in Oak Bay in the hall attached to St Mary's Anglican Church on "How Clive Won India for the British Empire." In its Internet site, BC Bookworld declared her to be "the first prolific, female fantasy writer of Canada," absurdly naturalizing her, which she seemed to contradict by her origins and by dying in Kyoto, Japan, in 1931. No one is quite certain of dates or circumstances. *The Times* in London took the precaution of beginning its obituary with, "Our Ottawa correspondent telegraphs that Mrs L. Adams Beck, long a resident at Victoria, British Columbia . . . has died suddenly at Kyoto, Japan." She is said to have been a friend in England of Katharine Emma Maltwood, *née* Sapsworth (1878-1961), an artist, collector, and antiquarian, who in 1937-1938 migrated to Victoria and bought "The Thatch" in Royal Oak, formerly a restaurant, and there gathered a great collection of art and *objets d'art*, which is now kept by the University of Victoria as a museum. The two women had similar ideas and beliefs in the field of Oriental art and mysticism, and the collection at the museum has a complete set of Lily Adams Beck's novels. Local writing about Mrs Maltwood does not hazard a guess about LB's origins, seldom mentions the Moresby family, but describes the social set that surrounded her in the town during her years as a resident on Simcoe Street and/or Mountjoy Avenue.

In addition to books mentioned above, she is credited with *The Ninth Vibration and Other Stories* (1922; 4th printing 1926), *Dreams and Delights* (1922), *The Key of Dreams* (1922), *The Ladies* (1922) [pseud. E. Barrington], *The Perfume of the Rainbow* (1923), *The Chaste Diana* (1923) [pseud. E. Barrington], *The Treasure of Ho, A Romance,* (London: Collins, 1923), *The Divine Lady* (1924) [pseud. E. Barrington], *The Gallants* (1924) [pseud. E. Barrington], *The Ways of the Stars, A Romance of Reincarnation* (New York: Dodd, Mead, 1925), *Glorious Apollo* (1925) [pseud. E. Barrington], *The Exquisite Perdita* (1926) [pseud. E. Barrington], *The Thunderer* (1927) [pseud. E. Barrington], *Way of Power: Studies in the Occult* (1927), *The Empress of Hearts* (1928) [pseud. E. Barrington], *Captain Java* (1928) [pseud. E. Barrington], *The Story of Oriental Philosophy* (1928), *The Laughing Queen* (1929) [pseud. E. Barrington], *The Garden of Vision* (1929), *The Openers of the Gate, Stories of the Occult* (New York: Cosmopolitan, 1930) [including: "The Openers of the Gate," "Lord Killary," "How Felicity Came Home," "Waste Manor," "The Mystery of Iniquity," "Many Waters Cannot Quench Love," "The Horoscope," "The Thug," "Hell," "The Man Who Saw."] [pseud. E. Barrington], *Duel of the Queens* (1930) [pseud. L. Moresby], *The Irish Beauties* (1931) [pseud. L. Moresby], *The Joyous Story of Astrid* (1931) [pseud. L. Moresby], *Anne Boleyn* (1932) [pseud. L. Moresby], *The Great Romantic* (1932) [pseud. L. Moresby].
Sources: census 1861, England, RG 9/1382, p. 16; census 1871, RG 10/2047, p. 32; census 1891, RG 12/846, p. 5; *Colonist,* 8 February 1925, p. 13; 19 March 1925, p. 9; *The Times* (London), 8 January 1931, p. 14, obit.; *BC Archives,* GR 1304, BC Supreme Court (Victoria), Probate Files, BO 9275 [or B0 9275], for "Beck, Eliza Louise Moresby"; BC Bookworld, Author Bank, Internet site; Rosemary Alicia Brown, *Katharine Emma Maltwood, Artist 1878-1961* (Victoria, Sono Nis Press for the Maltwood Gallery, University of Victoria, 1981), pp. 36-37.

BEECH, Lieutenant Colonel Dr Lionel (c. 1850-1918). Born at Knockholt, Kent, he trained as a medical doctor at the Royal Sea Bathing Hospital (or Infirmary), where the census of 1871 found him working, aged twenty-one, as an "Officer, Dispenser" under the direction of George Horatio Chexfield. This small hospital was founded on 2 July 1791 by Dr John Coakley Lettsom to treat tuberculosis of the bones, lymph nodes, etc., and grew with bequests from several donors. LB went on to study and qualify at the London Hospital, where he was twice elected House Surgeon. In 1873 he entered the Indian Medical Service, being attached to the Thirty-eighth Native Artillery in Trichinopoly and later to the First Light Infantry at Secunderabad with which regiment he went through the Afghan War, 1879 and 1880, and received the War Medal. Then he worked as a civil surgeon at Bellary, India, during a famine and received the formal thanks of the government for his services. He also went to the Laccadive Islands on HMS *Kingfisher* on a leprosy commission and stayed there for three months. On 1 October 1892, he was promoted to surgeon lieutenant colonel.

In 1874, on first reaching India, LB married Ida M. McKee (1852-1931), born in Northampton daughter of Rev. James McKee, DD, chaplain in India and later vicar of Wymns Wold, Kent. When he retired from the IMS in 1893 or 1895, they went out to Manitoba, where he practised for eight or nine years, and then moved to Salt Spring Island. There at Ganges, they rented one of Harry Bullock's cottages in 1904 but soon bought a house and eight acres on Ganges Hill from Abraham Reid Bittancourt. After a while, LB found he had too much work for a retired doctor, so the community invited his son, Dr Alan Beech, then practising in Quesnel, BC, to join him. Thus relieved, LB launched a campaign to found a local hospital and by the end of 1913, with the help of a benevolent woman's group called The Guild of Sunshine, he had raised $3,000. The Gulf Islands (Cottage) Hospital was built in 1914 with two three-bed wards and added a third ward before the end of that year. When the hospital received $1,000 from the Lady Minto Fund, founded by the governor general's wife, it was renamed the Lady Minto Hospital and characteristically a retired soldier from the Royal Army Medical Corps, Corporal Newens, was appointed to manage it along with a matron or nurse. It was from LB's estate that the land for a nurses residence was purchased in 1935.

LB eventually retired from his Ganges practice and died, aged sixty-eight, on 16 December 1918 at Ganges, leaving his wife, a daughter, and five sons. In 1931, after both parents had died, the six children were recorded as *Sidney Percy Beech (c1877-1936), of Ganges Harbor, Dr Alan Beech and Stuart E. Beech of Salmon Arm, Gerard M. Beech of Winnipeg, and *Lieutenant Commander W. J. R. Beech, RCN, Ottawa.

Sources: census 1871, England, RG 10/993, p. 1; BL, India Office, *Indian Army List,* January 1905, p. 746; *Colonist,* 28 October 1931, p. 16; 17 December 1918, pp. 10 and 16, obit.; Kahn, *Salt Spring Island,* pp. 135, 157, 162, 202, 235; *Colonist,* 24 October 1931, p. 14, obit.; 28 October 1931, p. 16.

BEECH, Commander William James Robert (c. 1896-1975). He was born at Slindon, Sussex, in June 1895, son of *Lieutenant Colonel Lionel Beech, IMS, and arrived in Canada scarcely a year old. Brought up on Salt Spring Island, he attended University School, Victoria, and the Royal Naval College of Canada (1912-13). He served first in HMS *Berwick* (1913-1915) and then (1916-1921) in submarines of the RN in the English Channel and the North Sea and aboard HMS *Alecto.* In April 1918, he became lieutenant. After the Great War, he was posted to China with the first post-war flotilla to that station. In 1922, he served in the Royal Naval College of Canada and in 1923 aboard HMS *Versatile.* When preparations for Squadron Leader Stuart MacLaren's pioneering flight around the world were being made, Beech commanded HMCS *Thiepval,* a cruise to Japan via the Aleutian and Kurile Islands, arranging for refueling depots in 1924. Next, he was in command of HMCS *Patrician* in 1924-1926 and served on HMS *Repulse* in 1926-1928. He carried out a staff course at Royal Naval College, Greenwich, in 1921, and served on Naval HQ Staff at Ottawa in 1930-1931. In 1932-1933, he was executive officer at RCN Barracks, Esquimalt, and was promoted to commander in July 1923. On 4 September 1940, he succeeded *Commander V. G. Brodeur as CO at Esquimalt with command over naval forces on the Canadian Pacific

Coast. His last posting was as senior Canadian naval officer in London. One of his decorations was commander of the Legion of Merit (USA).

Mrs Beech, *née* Beatrice Wolfenden, was a daughter of A. R. Wolfenden of Victoria, and they had three children. When he retired, they settled in Victoria, where he died, aged seventy-nine, on 9 April 1975.

Sources: *Colonist*, 4 February 1934, p. 20; 31 August 1940, p. 2; 15 September 1940, p. 8; *MacFarlane*, pp. 5-6.

BEETON, Henry Coppinger (1827-1908). A major businessman in Victoria from the early 1860s, he lived there on and off for twenty years, played an interesting part in the Island's public and business life, and served as agent general for BC in London in 1893-1895. He was born on 15 May 1827 in London, son of Robert Henry Beeton, who was eventually one of the founders of the city's Commercial Gas Company (1867) and a director of other companies. HB's youth was in relatively humble circumstances: He appears in the 1851 census as a "warehouseman" aged twenty-three, born in St Pancras, London, but living at No. 1 Prospect Place near Mile End Road in Tower Hamlets with his father, a "Retired Publican," a widower aged fifty-three, born at Stowmarket, Suffolk. HB had a sister, Elizabeth M. Beeton, aged nineteen, also born in St Pancras, and keeping house with them was a maternal aunt, Mary S. Wigenson, evidently their mother's unmarried sister. In 1861, the aunt and the father, now a "House and Fund Holder," were still there, but HB, aged thirty-three, was married by then and living at No. 4, Belgrave Terrace in the Tower Hamlets (Hackney) quarter of London with his wife, Louisa *née* Ramie, aged twenty-eight, born in the Channel Islands at St Helier, Jersey. HB was described as "Commercial Clerk, Lace Trade," and they had three children born there: Louisa aged five, Florence three, and Arthur four months old, as well as two domestic servants. It must have been within the next year or two, after a period as senior partner in the firm of H. C. Beeton & Co. of London, that HB emigrated to Victoria and formed a partnership with *Lieutenant Colonel Hon. John Henry Turner. In 1884, they were the leading owners of the People's Steam Navigation Company, having acquired 27 percent of the shares, and at some stage, they took out a mortgage with the Bank of British Columbia to invest in the Oceanic Salmon Cannery.

There is no coherent biography but scattered references show much interesting activity and considerable to-ing and fro-ing between London and the Island. In 1871, HB, now aged forty-three, was living with Louisa at 108 Adelaide Road in Hampstead and identified as "Warehouseman in Wholesale Lace Warehouse," with three children: Henry R. Beeton, aged eighteen, "East India Merchant Clerk," born in Hackney; Louisa, aged fifteen; and Florence, aged thirteen. Ten years later, they had moved again, to 2 Adamson Road in Hampstead, where HB was described as "Merchant (Dry Goods)." Florence Beeton was still with them, now aged twenty-three, and their son Arthur C. Beeton was at home, now aged twenty and a "Merchant Clerk." They had a cook, a parlourmaid and a housemaid, and a visiting art student from St Heliers, Jersey. During HB's term as agent general for BC in London, he was also a special commissioner at an International

Fisheries Exhibition (1883) and an International Health Exhibition (1884), a royal commissioner of a Colonial and Indies Exhibition in South Kensington (1884 or 1886?), and doubtless busy promoting investments in BC as expected of an agent general. But by 1889, he was back in Victoria living in "Armadale," a house later occupied by Senator William John Macdonald (1832-1916). In 1897, he was promoting the British Yukon Company. But a Canadian reference work of 1898 cited his address as 33 Finsbury Circus, London. He certainly retired at sometime in the next few years to Axbridge, Weston-super-Mare in Somerset, where his wife died in 1906 and he on 14 June 1908, survived by one son and two daughters.

HB was known in Victoria to be a member of the Church of England, a believer in free trade, a Liberal in politics, an ardent admirer of W. E. Gladstone, but also a strong supporter of the movement for Imperial federation. Later in life, he became a Unitarian and served for a time as vice-president of the Wells Liberal Association not far from his retirement home.

Sources: *Victoria Daily Times*, 9 July 1908, p. 5, obit.; Morgan, *Canadian Men and Women*, p. 64; *Dominion Annual Register and Review for the 12th-20th Year of the Canadian Union*, ed., Henry J. Morgan (Toronto, Hunter, Rose & Co., 1885), p. 253; census 1851, England, HO197/1553, fol. 235; census 1861, RG 9/294, p. 8; census 1871, RG 10/194, p. 75; census 1881, RG 11/173, p. 28; Gosnell, *The Year Book*, p. 45; Gladys Young Blyth, *Salmon Canneries: British Columbia North Coast* (Lantzville, BC, Oolichan Books, 1991), p. 163; David Farrell, "*Keeping the Local Economy Afloat: Canadian Pacific Navigation and Shipowning in Victoria, 1883-1901*," *The Northern Mariner*, vol. VI, no. 1 (January 1996), pp. 35-44, see p. 38; Harry Gregson, *A History of Victoria, 1842-1970* (Victoria, Victoria Observer Publishing Co., 1970), pp. 110, 146-7, 150, 227.

BEEVOR-POTTS, Charles Herbert (1864-1953). A leading magistrate in Nanaimo, Vancouver Island, for a quarter of a century, he was born on 23 April 1864 at West Hoathley, Sussex, son of Dr Walter Jeffery Potts (1837-1898), and Julia Beevor (1833-1917). CB's paternal grandfather, George Potts (1807-1863), was elected Conservative member of Parliament for Barnstaple, Devonshire, in 1859 and lived (until his death on 20 December 1863) with all of his three wives (one at a time) at three addresses: Elm Grove, Dawlish, Devon; Trafalgar House, Barnstaple; and 29 Upper Seymout Street, Portman Square, in the west end of London, where he was born in Marylebone. George Potts was the second son of William Potts (CB's great-grandfather), who was born at Kelso, Roxburgh, Scotland, but seems to have settled in Devon with his wife Mary Bayly, daughter of William Bayly, Esq. of Baylys, Devon. In 1851, the census-taker found George Potts, aged forty-two, a "Gentleman" born in Marylebone, living at Elm Grove House, Dawlish, with his wife Ellen *née* Reed, aged twenty-seven, and her father, another "Gentleman" aged sixty-eight, along with George's two sons and four servants. The elder of the two sons was CB's father, then aged thirteen, was sent to Blundell's School, and went on to become a physician. CB's mother was a daughter of Sir Thomas Branthwaite Beevor, third baronet (1798-1879), who was born in Norfolk at Buckenham and died in Yarmouth, son of Sir Thomas

Beevor, second baronet (1753-1820), who lived at Hargham, Norfolk, and the title originated with the latter's father, Sir Thomas Beevor, who married Elizabeth Branthwaite in 1750. CB was the eldest surviving son of a family of nine or more children and educated at Great Berkhamsted Grammar School, Hertfordshire, articled to G. R. Dodd, solicitor in London, and admitted to practice as solicitor in England in 1888.

When he emigrated to the Island in 1889, his next brother, Ernest Edward Beevor-Potts (1866-1934—he tended to drop the Beevor in the name) had been living in Victoria for two years as a commercial salesman and ultimately settled in Oak Bay with his wife, Florence Annie Dempster. CB was admitted as solicitor in 1890, called to the Bar of BC in 1895, and soon became police magistrate for the city of Nanaimo, stipendiary magistrate for Nanaimo County, judge of the Small Debts Court, and juvenile judge. He remained in office at Nanaimo for more than twenty-five years. In 1893, he married Gertrude Mary Williams, daughter of Rev. W. H. Williams, MA, rector and rural dean of Portskewett, Monmouthshire, and they had three sons and two daughters. The family live in Nanaimo on Milton Street, later on Vancouver Avenue, and CB's office was on Commercial Street. He presided over the family, including other members who come out from England, until his death, aged eighty-eight, on 9 May 1953 in a Victoria Hospital. Mrs Beevor-Potts had died in Nanaimo, aged seventy-five, on 13 August 1944. Their relatives, children, and grandchildren settled on the Island and elsewhere in considerable numbers.

Sources: *Who's Who in B.C.*, 1937-1939, p. 169-170; 1942-1943, p. 39; 1944-1946, p. 14; census 1851, England, HO 107/1870/118/8; census 1871, RG 10/1059/128, pp. 9-10; census 1881, RG 11/1446/153, p. 1; *Handbook of the Court, the Peerage, and the House of Commons*, 12th year (P. S. King, 1862), p. 153; *Dod's Parliamentary Companion*, vol. 27, by Robert P. Dod *et al.* (Whittaker & Co., 1859), p. 269; Catherine W. Reilly, *Mid-Victorian Poetry, 1860-1879: An Annotated Biobibliography* (Mansell Publishing, 2000), p. 372; thePeerage.com (Internet)person pages 23430, 23445.

Sir Charles Alfred Bell

BELL, Sir Charles Alfred (1870-1945). When on 12 May 1939 he reached New York City *en route* to Victoria, having boarded the passenger liner *George Washington* at Southampton, he was thought to be the world's greatest expert on Tibet. He was certainly the author of several books and articles about Tibet, where he had spent some twenty years, and was planning to live in Victoria while writing a book about his friend the late Thirteenth Dalai Lama (1876-1933). Their friendship began in 1910, when the [British] government of India entrusted him with the Dalai Lama's care and protection during the first 2¼ years of an exile to escape the clutches of the Chinese government. There is a photograph of him with the Dalai Lama, taken in 1920-1921, in Melvyn C. Goldstein, *A History of Modern Tibet, 1913-1951* (1989), p. 55. CB's career and accomplishments as an officer in the ICS, beginning in 1889, are recounted by several authors, notably by Katherine Prior in the *Oxford Dictionary of National Biography* and by the authors of *Who was Who*, but his family background and his last six years and death in Victoria are less well known. When he registered at the Empress Hotel on 8 Jun 1939, he explained to curious news reporters that he had come "to escape from the confusion of England." There may also have been other reasons, such as loneliness following the death of his wife in 1936. She was Cashie Kerr Fernie, daughter of Jessie Kerr and her husband David Fernie (c. 1838-1903), a Scottish-born shipowner of Warrenside, Blundellsands, north-west of Liverpool, and she had been his companion for nearly a quarter of a century as well as the mother of his three children.

CB himself was born in Calcutta, India, on 31 October 1870, son of Annie Dumbell, born at Douglas on the Isle of Man, and her husband Henry Bell (c. 1832-?), an officer in the ICS, who was born at Uppingham, Rutland. When Henry Bell was eighteen, he was identified in the 1851 census, living at Uppingham as the second son, the third child, of John Bell (CB's grandfather), aged fifty-six, a medical doctor in general practice on the High Street with his wife, Catherine W. Bell, aged forty-nine, from a Staffordshire village, and their six children. They had a cook, a housemaid, and a general servant. The Bell family of physicians and surgeons were well established at Uppingham, where at least one member of the family had served at the great public school there. In 1875, when CB was five years old, his father was serving in the Bengal Civil Service (which he had joined in 1856) as a barrister-at-law, "Superintendant and Remembrancer of Legal Affairs, and Government Advocate," then "on sick furlough." In due time, he sent CB to Winchester and then New College, Oxford, whence the ICS sent him to Bengal in 1891 and, after nine years, to Darjeeling, which was where he became interested in Tibet. In March 1891, shortly before he left for Bengal, he was staying in South Kensington with his mother, then aged fifty, and two younger brothers. Their father Henry Bell was in India, and the birthplaces of the family offer a glimpse of their life, passing back and forth across the world. CB's brother George Henry Bell, aged sixteen, was born at Surbiton in the Surrey part of London, but the next brother, Claude John Bell, aged fourteen, was born at Calcutta like CB, and their cousin (their mother's niece), Mary A. Elliott, aged twenty-three, was born at Fateghar in the Punjab. Their household in South Kensington in 1891 had a cook, two butlers, and two lady's maids. Next door lived an elderly retired English "Indian Civil Servant" with a wife and daughters.

CB moved to Victoria, six years before his death, as an elderly celebrity, a fellow of the Royal Central Asian Society since 1921, a fellow of the Royal Geographical Society, and a winner of the Lawrence of Arabia Memorial Medal for his exotic travels and scholarly writing. He had served the ICS in Bengal, Bihar, and Orissa as assistant magistrate, district magistrate, settlement officer, and then district judge. He had conducted an exploratory mission in Bhutan in 1904 and a political mission to Bhutan in 1910, concluding a treaty by which the foreign relations of Bhutan were directed by the British government. CB was on political duty in Tibet, Bhutan, and Sikkim in 1904-1905 (watching from this perch Younghusband's expedition to Lhasa), 1906, 1908-1918, and 1920-1921 and was employed on the Tibet Conference between Great Britain, China, and Tibet in 1913-1914. He conducted a diplomatic Mission to Lhasa in 1920, remaining there on that occasion for eleven months. Heinrich Harrer (1912-2006), the Austrian traveller who became tutor to the young Fourteenth Dalai Lama, read CB's books with respect, and thought he was "a great champion of Tibetan independence" and "doubtless the first white man to come into contact with a Dalai Lama." In photographs, CB appears withdrawn and studious, far from the polo-playing Imperials of that age. When questioned in Victoria about his recreations, he replied, "Long travels and short walks." He soon moved into a house at 1420 Beach Drive, near *Brigadier General J. G. Austin and not far from *Sir Frederick Maze and *Sir Robert Erskine Holland, but it would be difficult to discover how much he had to do with them or with the other knighted Imperials in Victoria—*Sir Charles Delmé-Radcliffe, *Lieutenant General Sir Percy Lake, and the rest. He used a branch of the Royal Bank of Canada on Government Street as his postal address and probably buckled down in private to writing his *Portrait of the Dalai Lama* (Collins, 1946). He joined the Union Club but may have spent no more time there than at the Athenæum and East India Clubs, which he had joined after retiring to England in 1921 but left behind him in London. When he died, on 8 March 1945, Brigadier General Sir Percy Sykes, speaking in London to the Royal Central Asian Society, said, "With the death of Sir Charles Bell at Victoria, British Columbia, there passes off the stage the greatest authority on Tibet" and added that "he acquired a greater knowledge of the Tibetan language, literature, manners, and customs than any other Englishmen."

Among his publications were *English-Tibetan Colloquial Dictionary* (1905); *Grammar of Coloquial Tibetan* (1st edn., 1905; 2nd edn., Calcutta, The Bengal Secretariat Depot, 1919), 224 pp., and maps; 3rd edn., 1939); *Tibet, Past & Present* (Oxford University Press, 1924; second printing, 1926; cheap edition, 1927; first Indian Edition, New Delhi, 1990), 326 pp.; "The Dalai Lama; Lhasa 1921," *Journal of the Central Asian Society*, vol. XI (1924), pp. 36-50; "A Year [1920] in Lhasa," *The Geographical Journal*, vol. 63, no. 2 (February 1924), pp. 89-105, read to the society on 3 December 1923; *The People of Tibet* (Oxford, Clarendon Press, 1928), 319 pp., and 3 maps and 75 photos; "The North-Eastern Frontier of India," *Journal of the Central Asian Society*, vol. 17 (1930), pp. 221-31; *The Religion of Tibet* (Oxford, Clarendon Press, 1931), 235 pp; *Portrait of the Dalai Lama, The Life and Times of the Great Thirteenth* (Collins, 1946), 414 pp., two sketch-maps and 49 photos. His books went through several editions and some were translated into German.

Sources: Katherine Prior, "Sir Charles Alfred Bell (1870-1945)," *Oxford DNB*; census 1851, England, HO 107/2093/3 (Uppingham); census 1861, RG 9/1684/88, p. 5; census 1871, RG 10/2478/27, p. 11; census 1881, RG 11/3696, pp. 60-61; census, 1891, RG 12/32, p. 10; census 1901, RG 13/35, p. 50; *Colonist*, 9 June 1939, p. 2; *New York Passenger Lists, 1820-1957*, T-715_6328, p. 8; Riddick, *Who in British India*, p. 28; *Who was Who*, 1940-1950; *Journal of the Royal Central Asian Society*, 1945; Major General H. G. Hart, *The New Army List, Militia List, and Indian Civil Service List*, no. CXLV (John Murray, 1875), p. 476; Heinrich Harrer, *Seven Years in Tibet* (trans., Rupert Hart-Davis, 1953, repr. 1957), p. 288; Melvyn C. Goldstein, *A History of Modern Tibet, 1913-1951* (Berkeley, University of California Press, 1989), p. 55.

BELSON, Colonel William Harwood (1864-1964). He was born of English parents on 22 November 1864 at Malmsbury, Cape of Good Hope, South Africa, and migrated to Canada as a young man. In the census records for 1891, he is listed as an unmarried farm labourer aged twenty-seven, but he had already served in Lieutenant Colonel P. G. B. Lake's "Trenches Scouts" during the Riel Rebellion in 1886. Later, beginning in 1911, WB spent four years in the north-west with *Colonel Reginald John Gwynne's Sixteenth Light Horse and was attached (from 1912) to HQ Staff. His duties were to organize and inspect the Cadet Corps in the military district centred on Calgary, Alberta, but in 1914, he was sent to do the same in BC, replacing *Major A. B. Snow, who was at the same time transferred to the Maritime Provinces. WB was a guest of the British Campaigners' Association on 22 May 1914, when they met in Victoria to hear reminiscences about the Natal Rebellion of 1896, and on 27 May, he held the annual review of the Esquimalt school cadets at Macaulay Point.

The Belsons moved from Grenfell to Parksville, Vancouver Island, but on 11 November 1915, WB enlisted in Vancouver in the First Pioneer Battalion. He was then described as 5' 5½" tall, weighing 127 lbs., with "dark complexion, hazel eyes and dark hair." In 1916, he was sent to fight in France, where he was soon made ADC to his brother-in-law *Lieutenant General Percy Lake, but on 4 July 1917, he had an operation for "hemorrhoids and an anal fistula," which resulted in his being invalided and eventually sent back to Canada on the *Metagama*.

After the war, the Belsons went to live next to Sir Richard Stuart Lake on Chalet Road at Deep Cove, North Saanich. This was no doubt partly because Mrs Belson was Sir Richard Lake's sister Mabel Katherine Lake (1862-1940, born in Lancashire). They had met and married at Grenfell, Saskatchewan, where earlier "Major Belson, familiarly known as Billy, kept a butcher shop in the village in and around 1894, known as The Grenfell Cattle Company. We are told that his greatest success lay in the making of sausages." [Yule, *Grit and Growth*, p. 93] But butchering was only a resourceful soldier's occupation between two bouts of military service. He not only ran a meat business but was also active in the community and played cricket, polo, and tennis with the Lakes, the Gwynnes, and other local gentlemen. Mrs Belson was the first regent, and one of the founders, of the Grenfell Chapter of the IODE, the first IODE chapter in the province. With the wife of *Colonel R. J. Gwynne, she also organized a patriotic group called Children of the Empire.

In September 1917, WB was confirmed in his appointment at Victoria as local secretary for military organization throughout Military District No. 11 under the operation of the Military Service Act. Three or four weeks earlier, he had returned after more than a year of active service overseas. He left on the staff of *Lieutenant Colonel Arthur Edward Hodgins with the First Canadian Pioneer Corps and some months after reaching England he was attached to *Lieutenant General Sir Percy Lake's expeditionary force in Mesopotamia. On his way back to England, the liner on which he was travelling was torpedoed by a submarine, and he was one of the survivors picked up and taken to Malta. He finally reached England but illness contracted in the Middle East rendered him unfit for further active duty. He was eventually returned to Canada.

While WB was overseas, his wife Mabel Katherine (Lake) Belson had been living at Work Point Barracks in Esquimalt; in 1920, she was at 1048 Lyall St, Victoria, and city directories list them from 1925 as retired at Deep Cove. He played golf and joined the Union Club, and they maintained one of the useful tennis courts of the district. They also took part in local gala events at Deep Cove, often held at the Chalet with Major Bertram Taylor as judge in the boating competitions and WB in charge of the swimming along with Dr William Newton and *Major A. D. MacDonald.

Mrs Mabel Katherine (Lake) Belson died suddenly, aged seventy-seven, on 19 May 1940 at the family residence, "Harwood," Deep Cove, and was buried nearby at Holy Trinity Patricia Bay by *Rev. T. R. Lancaster. Born in Lancashire, the daughter of Lieutenant Colonel P. B. Lake and Margaret Lake, she had lived at Deep Cove for eighteen years during which she was prominent in the IODE, being a provincial councillor for many years, as well as active in the Allies' Chapter in Sidney. She left her husband, a daughter Katherine Clairmonde Belson (Mrs J. C. Burbidge) in Lahore, India, a son Percy William Belson (1900-1970) at Pender Harbour, BC, and two knighted brothers in Victoria. At her funeral, the pallbearers were Captain Cory Wood, Major H. Seale, *H. C. Layard, R. D. Harvey, M. J. Evans, and F. K. Herchmer.

Sources: NAC, RG150, CEF files, box 634-9; *Colonist*, 26 February 1914, p. 5; 23 May 1914, p. 3; 28 May 1914, p. 7; 26 September 1917, p. 5; 3 August 1934, p. 4; 21 May 1940, p. 5; *Who's Who in B.C.*, 1933-1934, pp. 101-102, 126; A. I. Yule, *Grit and Growth: The Story of Grenfell* (Grenfell, Saskatchewan, Historical Committee, 1980), pp. 92-93, 103; Nellie Horth, *North Saanich, Memories and Pioneers* (Sidney, Porthole Press Ltd., 1988), pp. 30, 58, 60, 66; *Sidney Review*, 17 February 1927, p. 6; 20 September 1928, p. 4; Major Charles Arkoll Boulton (1841-1899), *Reminiscences of the North-West Rebellions, with A Record of the Raising of Her Majesty's 100th Regiment in Canada and a Chapter on Canadian Social & Political Life* (Toronto, Grip Printing & Publishing Co., 1886), p. 501.

BENNETT, Colonel Charles Corbishly (1860-1944). Born on 14 January 1860 in York Township, Ontario, he became a professional soldier and was listed in the *Canadian Almanach*, 1902, as having served in the Sixth Regiment of Rifles as a major and adjutant and then been appointed as an officer in the Canadian Continent of the South African Constabulary. He served in the South African War

(1899-1902) and became a permanent force instructor of the Thirtieth Regiment of BC Horse, but when he enlisted in the Twenty-first Battalion at Kingston on 1 November 1914, he was on the "Asper Militia List, Canada." Embarking for overseas on 6 May 1915, he served mainly as a major at various places in England and France with the Fourth and Twenty-first Battalions and attached to Canadian Corps HQ. He was mentioned in despatches on 1 June 1917, became deputy assistant adjutant general, First Canadian Division on 9 February 1917, was brought to the notice of the secretary of state for war on 28 December 1917, and awarded the DSO (order LG 30450) on 1 January 1918. He was discharged on 1 October 1919 but was named assistant adjutant general and quartermaster general of the Island's military district before retiring from the permanent force in 1922 with the rank of colonel and the DSO and VC among his decorations. By then, he had spent nearly fifty years in militia and permanent forces.

    CB married Ethel May Read (1876-1948), widow of Rev. John William Laing (headmaster of Collegiate College, Victoria) on 22 February 1911 in Victoria and after the Great War, they retired to Victoria, where they lived on fashionable Rockland Avenue. They moved to Beach Drive and then (in 1937) to 1152 Fairfield Road. Like most soldiers, he suffered various injuries: His file contains medical records, for example, of a broken arm when he "tripped over some wire and fell," and in 1931, he had a surgical operation. The *Daily Colonist* published his photograph on the occasion of his eightieth birthday. After thirty-three years in Victoria, he died, aged eighty-five, on 13 May 1944 at St Joseph's Hospital, leaving his wife, three sons, and two daughters. He was buried at Royal Oak as an Anglican. Mrs. Bennett died, aged 82, on 29 May 1948 in Victoria.
Sources: NAC, RG150, box 643-43; *Canadian Almanach*, 1902, p. 152; *Colonist*, 11 December 1931, p. 8; 18 April 1937, p. 10; 16 January 1940, p. 9; 16 May 1944, p. 11, photo and obit.; Margaret A. Ormsby, *Coldstream—Nulli Secundus* (Vernon, Corporation of the District of Coldstream, 1990), p. 40.

    BERTING, Charles Bryan (1895-1968). Born on 11 December 1895 in Wimbledon, London, into a family of shipping clerks with a Dutch or Flemish background, he learned several foreign languages while working abroad for a trading firm during most of his life and is difficult to identify in archival records. Berting is not an English name, and in records of prisoners in 1916 interned at Ruhleben by German forces during the Great War, CB was cited as a young clerk from 59 rue Frédéric de Merode, Berchem, Antwerp. He is a good example of the restless, seaborne commercial people, characteristic of Victoria as an international port and making it different from towns of similar size in Ontario and the prairie provinces. By the time he settled on the Island in the late 1950s, there were many others like him in Vancouver, but when interviewed by the *Daily Colonist* at Christmas 1965, he was teaching school in Victoria. There he died, aged seventy-two, on 8 May 1968, leaving his wife Dorothy *née* Cousins, whom he had married in London about 1927, and their son, Bryan Sydney Berting, born in 1929 somewhere in Surrey but employed from 1956 as a BC land surveyor (licence no. 349). Dorothy, born about 1901, was the daughter of an Indian Army officer, possibly Samuel Cousins from Antrim, Ireland, who appears, aged sixty-three, in the 1901 census, retired in London in the Plumstead district near Woolwich. She had grown up in Simla and been trained as a nurse at the St George's Hospital in Bombay.

We know less about CB than about comparable figures such as *Joseph Boscowitz, but passenger records add to what the *Colonist* elicited from him. For many years, CB was posted on the eastern Caribbean island of St Vincent, which produced sugar, coffee, and tropical fruits. He sailed alone from St Vincent on a Royal Mail Steam Packet Company ship, the *Sannatian*, arriving in London on 9 February 1922, aged twenty-six, identified as a "clerk" with an address in Ealing. He was a "manager," aged thirty-four, by the time he sailed again to London, arriving from St Vincent on 7 February 1930 aboard the *Avelona Star*, a Blue Star liner from the Cape Verde Islands and giving an English address: 4 Stanley Villas, Amersham, Buckinghamshire. This time, he was with his wife Dorothy, aged twenty-nine, and their son Bryan Sydney, aged one. They were with him again in 1934 on a third voyage, arriving at Southampton this time on 23 October 1934 on the *Almanzora*, German East Africa Line, coming from Lisbon, and citing Portugal as their last country of permanent residence. Bryan Sydney was now six years old, and they gave their English address as c/o Hull, Blyth Ltd., 1 Lloyd's Avenue, London EC 3. According to what CB told the *Colonist*, they were living in Alexandria, Egypt, when the Second World War began in 1939 and had to escape overland to Port Said, whence they reached New York by sea. There is a puzzling record of their son, aged twelve, sailing from Liverpool to New York aboard the *Western Prince*, arriving on 10 August 1940 together with Eleanor Susan Berting, a "housewife" aged forty-four from Buckinghamshire whose last permanent residence was at Maidenhead, and two other children: Geraldine A Berting, twelve, and James F Berting, nine, both born in Berkshire. CB mentioned sailing from Port Said with two children, but the identity of the second is uncertain. We await further information. Dorothy disappears from the records after CB's death in Victoria.

Sources: *Colonist*, 25 December 1965, Sunday Section, full page by Vivienne Chadwick, "The Bertings have a Flair for Adventure"; christopherpaton@tiscali.co.uk, "The Ruhleben Story" (civilian internees or prisoners in WW I held at the Ruhlen concentration camp near Spandau, Germany); UK Incoming Passengers online, nos. 145330 and 149821; New York Passenger Lists, T—715_6488; BC land surveyors, numbered commissions under the Land Surveyor's Act (from 1905); census 1901, England, RG 3/571/155, p. 1 (Cousins); *Whitaker's*, p. 127 (Cousins).

BEST, Captain Victor Charles (1885-1979). Born on 6 September 1885 in London at 33 Bedford Square, St Giles, London, he was recorded in 1891, aged five, living there with his father, a widower then aged forty-nine, two brothers, Leonard Charles Best aged twenty-three and Edgar Best aged six, a sister Lilian Best aged twenty-one, and five servants: governess, cook, parlourmaid, housemaid, and kitchenmaid. His father Charles Best was a "Brewer Licensed Victualler" born in south-east Newington, London. Ten years later, in spring 1901, VB was a fifteen-year-old schoolboy at Laleham Preparatory School on the west side of Margate, Kent (now a school specializing in dyslexic pupils). He qualified as a veterinary surgeon, emigrated to the United States, where he lived for a time at Boston, Massachusetts, with his wife, Winifred Edith Best *née* Webster, and had at least one of their five sons: Frederick Webster Best (1894-?). They migrated later to Galiano Island, where VB was practising as a veterinary surgeon at the time he joined the Remount Depot of the CEF on 10 February 1916. After the Great War, about 1920, they moved with their family to Salt Spring Island, where they bought part of the old Tolson place south of Ganges and called it "The Alders." VB practised as the island's veterinary surgeon, assisted with the Boy Scouts and Wolf Cubs, and welcomed their sons from time to time. One of them, Gordon L. Best, attended Shawnigan Lake Boys School, Oak Bay High School, RMC, Kingston, Ontario, and then passed some time at Camp Borden before going to England in to join the RAF. He was a flying officer by the time he made a visit home from Shailah, Iraq, by way of New York in November 1934, and had spent a week or so with his brothers, Vincent and Norman Best *en route*. After serving in the Near East, Gordon L. Best was attached to the British Air Ministry for two years with the rank of wing commander, and in January 1941, he (and F. W. S. Turner, also of Salt Spring Island) was sent to Canada as a flying instructor under the terms of the British Commonwealth Air Training Plan. Another son Alan Best, of Reading, Berkshire, visited the parents at "The Alders" early in May 1936, and at the same time, the Bests had another visitor from Reading, Lieutenant Commander R. Coombe. When VB died, aged ninety-three, on 10 February 1979 at Ganges, he left his five sons—Norman, Allan, Gordon, Vincent, and Raymond—as well as twelve grandchildren and nine great-grandchildren.

Sources: NAC, CEF files, box 702-45; box 701-13; census 1891, England, RG 12/212, p. 25; census 1901, RG 13/823, p. 42; *Colonist*, 21 November 1934, p. 8; 1 May 1936, p. 7; 5 January 1941, p. 11; 13 February 1979, obit, p. 35; Kahn, *Salt Spring Island*, pp. 150, 234, 245.

BIDWELL, Commodore Roger Edward Shelford (1899-?). Born at Peterborough, England, on 14 September 1899, he appears in the 1901 census, aged one, living at the Grammar School, Peterborough, Park Road, with his schoolmaster father, Edward Bidwell, aged thirty-four, "Clergyman Church of England, schoolmaster," born at Shanton All Saints in Suffolk, and his mother Frances aged twenty-seven, born at Leamington, Warwickshire. He had two elder sisters, and they all lived in the school with other schoolmasters, pupils, and servants.

The family migrated to Canada, and in 1915, RB joined the Royal Naval College of Canada as a naval cadet, finished the course, and then qualified as a torpedo officer during a long course in England. He rose through the ranks to be a commodore in the Royal Canadian Naval Barracks at Esquimalt (1950), flag officer Atlantic Coast and senior officer in chief command (1951), and flag officer commanding the Canadian coronation review squadron (1953), and he retired at last on 1 June 1958.

Sources: *MacFarlane*, p. 6; census 1901, England, RG 13/1463, p. 31.

BIGGS, Major John Peter Mouat (1820-?). Several researchers speculate about him for their own purposes, according to their findings. Though reliable information about him is meagre, JB is worth recording as an Indian Army veteran arriving early on the Island. Records show him joining the Thirty-eighth Regiment, Madras Native Infantry, in 1836 and promoted to lieutenant on 8 October 1839 and to major on 20 October 1856 or 17 April 1857. The 1861 census for the Channel Islands records him, aged forty-one, as "Major retired HMEIS" born at Agra, India, living at 1 Paxton (Baxter?) Place, St Peter's Port, Guernsey, with his wife Sarah, aged twenty-six, born in Ireland, and four children: John W. Biggs, aged twelve, born at Nursingpore, India; Mary Biggs, nine, born at Hampatre (?), India; Jane Biggs, two, born at St Peter's Port, Guernsey; and Charles E. Biggs, eight months, born at St Peter's Port. With them lived JB's mother Barbara Biggs, sixty-eight, "Gent. Officer's Widow," born in England, and JB's sister-in-law, Margaret Forbes, thirty-six, born at Calcutta, India. The family had four domestic servants. Sarah must have been JB's second wife, unless she gave birth to John W. Biggs when she was fourteen years old. The equivalent census records for 1871 show no sign of JB or his family, but the Department of Lands & Works in Victoria recorded pre-emption of land in the Chemainus District on 10 February 1863 and the BC Archives (Victoria) also have correspondence with JB in that period. On 12 May 1863, Sir James Douglas appointed JB a Justice of the Peace for Chemainus and Salt Spring Island (separated by a narrow channel). He disappears thereafter from accessible sources. The widow Augusta Mouat Biggs recorded in 1891 census records with two children born in India, a third born locally, all living with three servants at Bideford, Devon, was probably the widow of Colonel James Andrews Mouat Biggs of the Bengal Army who had died at Cheltenham on 26 October 1887.
Sources: census 1861, Guernsey, Channel Islands, RG 9/4381/68, p. 17; India Office Library (in its own room in the British Library, London), *The East-India Register and Army List for 1853* (W. H. Allen, 1853), p. 89; *Indian Army and Indian Civil Service List*, 1860, p. 243, "*Madras Retired Officers*"; 1851; *op. cit.* for 1857, p. 106; *op. cit.* for 1860, p. 139; A. F. Flucke, "*Early Days on Saltspring Island*," *B.C. Historical Quarterly*, vol. XV (1951), p. 184, citing *The British Colonist*, 13 and 22 May 1863 and 24 October 1864; *BC Archives* (Victoria), GR-0766, box 3, folder 91, file 516, Chemainus District (Department of Lands and Works Pre-Emption Record for West-Coast Land, 1861-1886 ("J. Biggs; Major"); *BC Archives*, GR-1372, reel BO1309, file F149c, Colonial Correspondence with JB; Kahn, *Salt Spring Island*, p. 80; http:// hompi.sogang.ac.kr/ anthony/ Grigsby MaryTaylor.htm (no spaces; the story of Mary Taylor, a descendant).

BINNIE, Major Henry James (1867-1948). He was born in Windsor, Berkshire, on 1 January 1867 and followed in his father's and grandfather's footsteps by enlisting in the Life Guards; his grandfather had joined that unit from Linlithgow in 1821 and had received his commission from Earl Grey in 1848. HB spent twenty-one years in the First Life Guards, Royal Household Cavalry, noted for its discipline and traditions and entrusted with caring for the king's safety; recruits in it had to be not less than five feet eleven inches tall. He became paymaster-corporal-major in that regiment. On 25 October 1896 at All Saints, Notting Hill (London), he married Caroline Ann Plummer.

In 1906, he brought her to Canada and for seven years, they farmed at Elstow, Saskatchewan, but he also joined the militia. In the Great War, he enlisted on 7 July 1915 and was commissioned in the Twenty-ninth Light Horse. In 1916, he went overseas with the Sixty-fifth Battalion, but returned to Saskatchewan in 1919 after serving as an OC of demobilization. He retired in 1936, and they went to Victoria, which they had long planned to do. There they lived at 115 Leonard Street, near the sea, and then in Hampton Court.

Binnie's friends and relations were military: He was a friend of *Sir Arthur Currie, whom he first met in Winnipeg. His own son Stuart Harry Binnie, born in London in 1898, served with the Canadian army in the Great War. Among his collection of mementoes and photographs from his service in the Life Guards, he had, for instance, a photograph of Queen Victoria in 1897 attended by the Guards, including himself. Mrs Binnie remembered watching Queen Victoria's funeral from the top of Windsor Castle. In summer 1943, HB was honoured by the king "for long and meritorious service" in both the Royal Regiment and the Canadian Sixty-fifth Battalion. He died on 20 November 1948 in Victoria at St Joseph's Hospital. Mrs. Binnie died, aged 93, on 4 April 1966 in Victoria.
Sources: NAC, CEF files, RG150, box 738-12; *Colonist*, 22 August 1943, p. 3; 21 November 1948, p. 25, obit.

BIRCH, Arthur Nonus (1836-1914). Having served in the Colonial Office from 1855 as private secretary to Sir E. Bulwer Lytton, the Duke of Newcastle, and to Chichester Fortescue, he was appointed resident colonial secretary for BC in 1864 and acting governor in 1866-1867, on the Executive Council in Victoria until 1871. He did well in his post at Victoria and befriended such notables as *Colonel R. C. Moody, Judge Matthew Begbie (1819-1894), Arthur T. Bushby (1835-75), and Peter O'Reilly (c. 1829-1905). His next posts were at Penang as lieutenant governor (1871-1872) and in Ceylon as colonial secretary (1873-1876), leading on to higher employment and ultimately a knighthood. AB was indirectly a personal link with India because although he was himself born at Yoxford, Suffolk, his father was born in Calcutta about 1795 and his brother Ernest George Birch (1829-1909) had a career as a magistrate in India. The census recorded the family living in the High Street at Southwold near Norwich in 1851, when AB was fourteen years old, with two sisters: Louisa Rouse Birch, aged twenty-eight, born at Sibton, Suffolk, and Emily Elizabeth Birch, sixteen, born at Yoxford. Their parents were Rev. Henry Rouse Birch, fifty-six, "perpetual curate, Southwold," born in "Calcutta, Bengal," and his wife Lydia *née* Milford, a Londoner aged fifty-five. They had a cook and a housemaid. Another glimpse of AB's life appears in 1881 census records, where he appears as a twenty-four-year-old "Clerk in Colonial Office" staying at the King's Arms Hotel in Dorchester with Augustus Frederick Birch, aged thirty-four, born at Sibton, Suffolk, and his wife, Isabella Anne, aged twenty-four, born at Longchamp Hall, Pedistree, Suffolk. Augustus subsequently became vicar of Ellesborough, Buckinghamshire, and then vicar of Northchurch, Hertfordshire, with a large family and half a dozen servants.

Meanwhile, AB married Josephine Watts-Russell, born at Biggin, Oundle, Northamptonshire, where in 1891 they were living at Biggin Hall with three children, one of them aged fourteen born in Ceylon. With them lived Josephine's mother, Mary N. Watts-Russell, aged seventy-seven, born at Milford in Nottinghamshire, and five servants. AB was recorded as a banker. By 1901, Josephine had died and AB, still a banker, was living at 1 Old Burlington Street, St James Park, Westminster, with a daughter, Una C. Birch, aged twenty-four, and seven servants. Their neighbour at No. 2 was an "Assistant Clerk, Bank of England," with his household, and beyond him at No. 3 was a "Sub-agent, Bank of England." To how many people did AB talk about the Island before his death in London at 29 Grosvenor Place early in the Great War?

Sources: BNA (Kew), census 1851, England, HO 107/1803/10/847; census 1861, RG 9/1353, p. 16; census 1891, RG 12/1222, p. 12; census 1901, RG 13/97, p. 38; David Ricardo Williams, "The Man for a New Country," Sir Matthew Baillie Begbie (Sidney, Gray's Publishing Ltd., 1977), pp. 58-9, 67, 74-5, 88, 104, 185, 204-5; F. W. Howay, British Columbia from the Earliest Times to the Present (Vancouver, S. J. Clarke Publishing Company, 1914, pp. 194-95; The Times (London), 19 January 1909, p. 11, obit.; 2 November 1914, p. 5, obit.

BISCOE, Francis Ramsey Fraser (1884-1967). For about forty years, he was a successful real-estate agent in Victoria before spending his later years fishing at Crofton, north of the Cowichan Valley, and was living in Saanich at 4875 Cherry Tree Road shortly before he died. But he was born in India at Secunderabad, Travancore, son of William Fraser Biscoe and his wife Mary Alice née Crozier. His mother, too, was born in India, daughter of an officer in the civil service of Madras who retired to Lymington near Southampton. Of course, FB's parents sent him and his brothers and sisters to be schooled in the south of England. When they were not at school, they stayed at Lymington with friends of the family such as Captain Arthur Arnold of the First Madras Lancers, whose son Allan was born in India in the Neilgherry Hills. FB served for four years in the London Scottish Rifles before emigrating and recorded himself as a farmer when enlisting in the CEF at Victoria on 3 June 1918. On 23 January 1912, he had married Margaret Bluhm Carwithen at Sandwick on the Island and they had two children, Alice Fraser Biscoe and Reginald William Fraser Biscoe. But he had remarried after a divorce long before he died, aged eighty-three, on 27 December 1967 in Victoria and his second wife, Annie Ellen née Andrew, died aged eighty-nine, on 24 May 1977 at Comox.

Sources: Colonist, 29 December 1967, p. 18, obit.; NAC, CEF files, box 754-25, no. 2139979; census 1861, England, RG 9/664, p. 1; census 1891, RG 12/816, p. 40; census 1901, RG 13/1034, p. 2; BC Divorce Records, Internet, vol. 5, pp. 292, 296;

BISHOP, Captain Richard Preston (1884-1954). Born on 14 September 1884 at Starcross, Devon, a village on the right bank of the River Ex at its mouth, down the river from Exeter, he was recorded in the 1891 census as aged six, living at

"The Cottage," Kenton, Starcross, Devon, with his father, Richard P. Bishop, a fifty-seven year-old solicitor, his mother, Mary Alice Bishop, aged forty-three, born a British subject at Ligucira, Portugal, and four elder sisters. There were also three female servants. Ten years later, the family was still there, but three of the sisters were absent.

RB spent some years in the Royal Navy, but retired, migrated to BC in 1907, and was employed as a BC land surveyor. When the Great War began, he returned home and joined the thirty-first West Lancashire Regiment of the Royal Garrison Artillery; records of the CEF do not list him as serving with Canadian forces. He returned to the Island after the war, however, lived at Albert Head, and carried on working as a BC land surveyor for some years. With him by then was his wife, Vivien Oonah de Blois Green. By the time he died, aged sixty-nine, on 13 February 1954, he had spent forty-four years on the Island. During that time, he made a study of old charts, sailing directions, journals, etc., in order to write the history of Sir Francis Drake's voyage to the West Coast. The result was an article, "Drake's Course in the North Pacific," *British Columbia Historical Quarterly*, vol. 3 (1939), pp. 151-82.

Sources: census 1891, England, RG 12/1686, p. 16; census 1901, RG 13/2040, p. 5; Barry Gough, *Distant Dominion* (Vancouver, UBC Press, 1980), p. 13; *Colonist*, 9 February 1917, p. 5; 15 February 1954, p. 14, obit.

BLAND, James William (c. 1830-1894). He was born into an old English family, joined the Royal Navy, and served until 1850, when he retired to Callao, Peru, which he had visited in the navy. In 1859, he moved to Victoria, where he was employed as a marine engineer on board the *Beaver*, the *Maude*, and the *Otter*. His wife, Elizabeth was born in England on 12 January 1830 and died, aged 89, on 6 August 1918 in Victoria, having had ten children. Six survived, notably James William Bland (1853-1921) who was born at Callao, Peru, attended the Jessop School in Victoria and was appointed usher of the BC Supreme Court. JB died, aged sixty-four, on 17 March 1894 in Victoria, where his son of the same name died, aged sixty-two, on 24 February 1921.

Sources: R. E. Gosnell, *A History of British Columbia* (The Hill Binding Co., 1906), pp. 441-3.

BOGGS, Arthur Beaumont (1891-1915). He was born in Victoria on 28 July 1891, attended RMC, Kingston, Ontario, and took a commission in a unit of the Indian cavalry stationed at Dalhousie in the Punjab. His father, Thomas Frederick William Boggs, a big real-estate executive in Victoria, was born at Halifax, NS, on 5 August 1863 into a UEL family in the hardware business. AB had two sisters and a brother, the latter being Herbert Beaumont Boggs (1892-1915), who enlisted in the CEF at Valcartier, Quebec, on 24 September 1914 and was killed in action at Fleogsteete on 26 February 1915. The family lived at "Maplewood," 1133 Catherine St, Esquimalt, Victoria, and were Anglicans.

Sources: NAC, RG150, box 846-37; box 835-19; Howay and Gosnell, *British Columbia*, vol. IV, pp. 400-02, mainly about his father.

BOGGS, Theodore Harding (1882-1969). A professor of economics who was born in India and died on the Island at Ladysmith, he was a son of Canadian Baptist missionaries. His father, William Bambrick Boggs (1842-1913), was a Nova Scotian who became the secretary of the Canadian Baptist Foreign Mission Board, founded in 1832, and from January 1875 was active in a Christian mission to the Karens of Siam and then the Telugas at Bankok and elsewhere. Several years later, he married a fellow missionary, Flora Jane Eaton (1873-1823), at the British Consulate in Bankok and they spent much time in Southern India at Ongole in Andhra Pradesh. Their missionary work there is known from a diary he kept for many years. That is probably where TB was born on 26 January 1882, but he attended Acadia University (BA, 1902) and Yale University (BA, 1905; PhD, 1908). He taught economics, specializing in international trade, on which he wrote a book (1922), at a series of American universities and at the University of British Columbia in 1916-1930, where he was honoured with an LLD in 1930. On 23 June 1907, he married Muriel Evelyne Haley, and they had two children. After her death in Vancouver on 17 October 1919, he married Charlotte McGregor on 29 June 1938. In 1950, he travelled widely through Europe and retired to Ladysmith, where his recreations were motoring, tennis, golf, and the theatre. TB died, aged eighty-seven, on 10 June 1969 at Ladysmith. His wife did not die on the Island.
Sources: M. L. Orchard & K. S. McLaurin, *The Enterprise: The Jubilee Story of the Canadian Baptist Mission in India, 1874-1924* (Toronto, Canadian Baptist Foreign Mission Board, 1924), pp. 26, 36, 41 and passim; *The Canadian Who's Who, with which is incorporated Canadian Men and Women of the Time*, vol. viii, 1958-1960, (Toronto, Trans-Canada Press, 1960), p. 104.

BOND, Major James (c. 1863-1941). Born in England, he joined the Gloucester Regiment at the age of nineteen and served through the South African War, wherein he won medals for valour at the battles of Mafeking and Bloemfontein and was wounded. During the Great War, he drilled recruits for the 20th and 185th Battalions in Sydney, NS. He was also in the guard of honour during the Duke of Connaught's visit there, while the monument of King Edward VII was unveiled, and later during the Duke of Windsor's visit to Nanaimo as Prince of Wales. These occasions made a deep impression on him: "In respect for Queen Victoria," as the *Daily Colonist* put it, he wore his scarlet tunic, his Baden-Powell hat, and his medals at public functions in Nanaimo, and "he was known to thousands of British Columbians as the man who marshalled Empire Day celebrations there for the past twenty-three years." Among his prized possessions was "a velvet pansy which he clipped off a wreath in St George's Chapel sent to the funeral of the late Queen Victoria by the emperor of Germany."

He and his wife, Emily R. Bond, lived at Nanaimo, in a house on the Island Highway, for at least thirty years and had a son and two daughters. Married in Gloucester, England, they celebrated their fifty-seventh wedding anniversary on 21 September 1939, after thirty years' residence in Nanaimo. There he died, aged seventy-eight, in the first days of February 1941.
Sources: *Colonist*, 21 September 1939, p. 3; 5 February 1941, p. 3; *Nanaimo Free Press*, 5 February 1941, front page, obit.

BOOTHBY, Lieutenant Commander James R. (c. 1884-1915) He was killed, aged thirty-one, in battle on 3 May 1915 at Sari Bair (Dardanelles). Born in Scotland at Cupar Fife, he appears, aged eight, with his brother, Frederick L. M. Boothby, aged nine, staying with their great-grandmother, Charlotte Boothby, aged ninety-one, at 9 Warwick Place, Milverton, Warwickshire, where Charlotte died two years later. In the household were two of Charlotte's granddaughters and four servants. JB was schooled at Glenlamond, Scotland, and in 1900, he joined the artillery militia. Then he served in the South African War with the Twenty-fourth Imperial Yeomanry and won a medal with five clasps. He transferred to the Royal Scots and served with them in India. Returning to Scotland, he resigned his commission because of ill health and went to Vancouver Island, "where he resided with *F. H. Maitland-Dougall of Koksilah [his cousin] for two years." When the Great War began, he returned to Scotland and was commissioned in the armoured corps in which he was killed. He was well known in the Cowichan Valley as an outstanding sportsman. He was an extremely good horseman and a member of the Koksilah Polo Club. He also played golf and tennis. The news of his death came from his cousin, *F. H. Maitland-Dougall of Koksilah. His brother had meanwhile been trained at the Royal Naval College at Greenwich and joined the Royal Naval Flying Corps as a balloon pilot.
Sources: Colonist, 25 May 1915, p. 1, obit.; census 1891, RG 12/2473, p. 6.

BOTT, Lieutenant Colonel John Cecil Latham (1872-1926). He was born on 24 August 1872 at Devizes [or Marden], Wiltshire, and spent more than thirteen years in the Twentieth Hussars. In 1901, the census found him living in his widowed Irish mother's household at "Linden House," 5 College Lawn, Cheltenham, Gloucestershire, and identified as "Cecil Bott, single, aged twenty-eight, Lieut. 20th Hussars." Five of his sisters, all younger, were living there and the eldest of them, Kathleen Younghusband, with her husband, Leslie Younghusband, aged thirty-four, a captain in the Nineteenth Bengal Lancers born at Weston-super-Mare, Somerset, and their one-year-old son John, born in India. There were five servants: cook, nurse, parlourmaid, housemaid, and "between maid." While serving with his regiment in the South African War, he met a Canadian unit, which seems to have decided him to migrate to the Coldstream ranch near Vernon, BC, after the war. There he spent five years in the Thirtieth BC Horse, which was absorbed into the Second CMR wherein he was popular. He trained this unit and commanded them overseas in Flanders from spring 1915. The Victoria Daily Colonist printed a photo of him (10 May 1917, p. 5) when he was given command of the Sixteenth Reserve Battalion at Seaford, England. After the Great War, he returned to Coldstream, Vernon, which was a British community very much like those on the Saanich Peninsula and the Cowichan Valley. Early in 1926, he went to consult medical specialists at the Jubilee Hospital, Victoria, and there he died, aged fifty-three, on 21 May 1926, survived by his wife.
Sources: Colonist, 10 May 1917, p. 5; 22 May 1926, p. 5, obit.; census 1901, England, RG 13/2464, p. 2; Margaret A. Ormsby, Coldstream—Nulli Secundus (Vernon, Corporation of the District of Coldstream, 1990), 145 pp., pp. 32, 39, 41, 42.

BORRIE, Commander Geoffrey (c. 1897-1949). He was born at Stockton-on-Tees, Durham, son of William R. Borrie, a naval architect from Eston, Yorkshire, and his wife Ann, who was a native of Stockton. His grandfather, John Borrie, was a Scottish civil engineer who had settled at Southbank, Yorkshire. The 1901 census recorded GB, aged three, living at 8 Park Road, Stockton with his parents and one servant. He joined the Royal Navy, eventually transferred to the RCN, and served on both coasts of Canada. For a time during the Second World War, he was in charge at Prince Rupert but about 1934 retired to Victoria, where he joined the Naval Officers' Association and served as *aide-de-camp* at Government House. When he died, aged fifty-two, on 27 July 1949, he had been living with his wife Marjorie at 3350 Uplands Road, but he was found dead in his room at the Commercial Hotel in Duncan by a friend who noticed his car parked outside. He had been visiting people there. He was known to be suffering from heart disease and had a drug for it in his luggage.
Sources: census 1901, England, RG 13/4622, p. 1; census 1881, England, RG 11/4852, p. 33; *Colonist*, 28 July 1949, p. 21, obit; *Cowichan Leader*, 28 July 1949, obit.

BOSCOWITZ, Joseph (1835-1923). Head of a cosmopolitan family of fur merchants, he and his family have their place in this book as foreigners linking Vancouver Island with the British Isles. Whatever their loyalties, they lived in Victoria and London, doing business across the globe in an Imperial context. Their place in the empire was similar to that of *Richard William Janion, or of an enterprising American businessman, Cyrus West Field (1819-1892), who found that in order to lay a telegraph cable across the Atlantic Ocean, he had to go to England, the only country in the 1850s where he could find companies able and willing to produce and lay three thousand miles of seven-stranded copper wire covered with gutta-percha and armoured with iron wire. The United States was not yet sufficiently industrialized. Among many other people in a similar position were Paul Julius Reuter (1816-1899), founder of Reuters News Agency (1849), a native of Cassel, Germany, who opened his news office in London and became a naturalized British subject, and John James Audubon (1785-1851), the pioneering genius in American ornithology, who went to London when he wanted to publish his now-famous paintings of North American birds, though he was of American nationality and French extraction and education. Whatever their origins and motives, these people all found their venture capital, human support, and vital infrastructure in the British Empire.

Jewish fur buyers could be found in Bordeaux, La Rochelle, London, Paris, Rouen, and elsewhere throughout the seventeenth and eighteenth centuries, dealing in furs from Quebec and Russia, and no experienced European historian would be surprised to find equivalent families in Victoria when gold was discovered on the Upper Fraser River (1857) or even earlier. Jewish dealers were also attracted by the trade in furs of the pelagic seals that we used to see still swimming about the Gulf of Georgia during the 1930s and 1940s. JB was born in Bavaria, like another Victoria merchant with whom he was soon in business in

Victoria, George Pappenberger (1832-80), from Marktheidenfeld, Bavaria. Their wives were both from Philadelphia, where they had business connections, but Pappenberger had been in or near Victoria since 1857, drawn by the gold rush. There he and JB with other partners soon founded the Boscowitz Steamship Company with a fleet of "steam schooners" catching pelagic seals in the North Pacific and the Behring Sea in competition with Russian and American sealing companies. Their ships were commanded by such mariners as Captains Samuel Williams (1835-1914) from Norwich, James Douglas Warren (1837-?) from Prince Edward Island, and Bernard Leitch Johnson (1878-1968) from Birkenhead, near Liverpool, capable men who often shared in business ventures as well as commanding ships. A Birmingham emigrant, John Barnsley (1860-1924), who owned a sporting goods shop in Victoria during the 1880s, was later hired as manager of the Boscowitz Steamship Company until it was bought out in 1910 by the Union Steamship Company.

JB was in touch meanwhile with a relative in San Francisco, Leopold Boscowitz (1852-95), who traded in tobacco until he was drawn into the sealing business. Leopold made a fortune, retired to New York, and died there at 180 East 56th St, in June 1895 "from paralysis of the brain." Extending his trading circle in characteristic fashion, JB went to live in England, where the census of 1881 recorded him as a "fur merchant" living at Stoke, Guildford, with his wife Leah and their two daughters aged nine and eleven, both born in Victoria. By 1891, JB had acquired a house in Kensington, London, at 100 Cromwell Road, where Leah was then living with the daughters and seven servants, her "Husband Abroad." Ten years later, the family still owned 100 Cromwell Road, but it was inhabited by a relation, Jane Boscowitz, aged fifty-three, born in the USA but with two grown-up children from Victoria and ten domestic servants. Meanwhile, JB, Pappenberger, and their other partners were active as citizens in Victoria, assisting the fire brigade, and apparently well regarded in general. There were other such cosmopolitan traders in Victoria, as in every outpost of the empire around the globe.

Sources: *Colonist*, 11 September 1917, p. 11 photo and obit.; 21 March 1923, pp. 1 and 5, obit.; E. W. Wright, *Lewis and Dryden's Marine History of the Pacific Northwest* (Portland, Oregon, 1895), p. 304; Victoria City Archives (John Barnsley fonds.); *Colonist*, 12 April 1914, p. 10, obit.; *New York Times*, 7 June 1895, p. 5, obit.; census 1881, England, RG 11/777, p. 34; census 1891, RG 12/34, p. 20; *Times* (London), 1 Sept. 1921, p. 4, obit.; John Steele Gordon, *A Thread Across the Ocean: The Heroic Story of the Transatlantic Cable* (New York, Perennial, 2003), pp. 68, 83-7, 90-9, 122-5, 142-44; J. J. Audubon, *The Birds of America* (4 vols., Robert Havell, 1827-1838); *Ornithological Biography* (5 vols., 1831-1839); *A Synopsis of the Birds of North America* (1839); J. F. Bosher, *The Canada Merchants 1713-1763* (Oxford, Clarendon, 1987), pp. 32, 138, 181 (fur merchants).

BOURKE, Lieutenant Roland [Rowland] Richard Lane J. M. (1885-1958), VC. He was born on 28 November 1885 in London, and the census of 1891 found him there, aged five, with his family. His father, Isidore McWilliam Bourke, aged forty-eight, was a physician born in Dublin; his mother May Anne Bourke, aged thirty-four, was a Londoner; and he had three older brothers, all born in India: Henry Walter Laurie Bourke, aged seventeen, born at Calcutta; Isidore McWilliam Bourke, aged sixteen, born at "East Indies, Barent Square?"; John Joseph FitzDale Bourke, aged thirteen, born at "East Indies, Barrackpore." Then came two elder sisters, born in London, Winifred May Bourke, aged nine, and Matilda May Bourke, aged seven. It appears that their father had served for some years as an army surgeon, and he so appears in the 1881 census, aged thirty-nine, visiting a solicitor in Highbury, Islington, London.

RB migrated to Canada in 1903 as a young man, spent some time in the Yukon, then in farming on the lake shore at Nelson, BC. Early in the Great War, he was rejected by the Canadian services because of poor eyesight, and so he went to England and enlisted in the Royal Naval Volunteer Reserve. On 10 May 1918, during an assault on a German naval base at Ostend, he commanded a motor launch and twice forced his way into the harbour under terrible gunfire to rescue survivors of HMS *Vindictive*. For this, he won the Victoria Cross and was the only Canadian sailor so honoured. In 1919, he married and went with his wife on a lecture tour of Australia and New Zealand for the Navy League. After the war, they returned to his fruit farm near Nelson, BC, but, in 1932, moved to Victoria, where they lived at 1253 Lyall Street and he joined the staff of the naval dockyard. During the Second World War, he helped to organize the RCNVR (the "Gumboot Navy"), served in it through the war, and retired in 1950. After attending many events organized for winners of the Victoria Cross, he died in Esquimalt as a Roman Catholic aged seventy-two, the last of the RNVR's Victoria Cross winners, and was buried at Royal Oak, leaving his wife Linda and two sisters in Victoria, Mrs W. Louis and Mrs R. V. Venables.

Sources: *Colonist*, 31 August 1958, pp. 1 and 3, photo and obit.; census 1891, England, RG 12/31. p. 5; census 1881, RG 11/267, p. 11.

BOWEN-COLTHURST, Major John Colthurst (c. 1881-1965). He was born into the Anglo-Irish family of Sir George St John Colthurst (1850-1925), sixth baronet, who had inherited his title in 1878 and lived on 31,300 acres of the family estate in County Cork, where stood the famous Blarney Stone, part of the ruined Blarney Castle. After schooling, probably at Harrow, JB attended the RMA at Sandhurst. About 1900, he joined the Royal Irish Rifles and served in many campaigns around the empire: in the South African War in Orange Free State (March-April 1900), the Transvaal (June-November 1900), in Tibet around Gyantse with Colonel Francis Younghusband (1904), and in France early in the Great War. After serving at Mons in August 1914, he was severely wounded on the Aisne the following month, invalided home, and not returned to the front partly because of a medical board's report in March 1915 and partly owing to an adverse report by his commanding officer, Lieutenant Colonel W. D. Bird (later Major General Sir Wilkinson Dent Bird), who accused JB of attacking a German position on the Aisne without orders, thereby leading to a counterattack that resulted in the battalion suffering many casualties, including JB himself. Bird also accused him of breaking down during the fighting.

He denied these charges, arguing that Bird had a personal vendetta against him because of an argument the two men had had in 1914 after Bird had offered the regiment for service in Belfast to enforce Home-Rule legislation.

In 1916, JB was posted in Dublin, at Portobello Barracks, during an insurrection and became embroiled in a serious political and personal scandal when he shot and ordered the shooting of several men on 25 April, including three Irish journalists, Patrick Mackintyre, Thomas Dickson, and Francis Sheehy-Skeffington (1878-1916). The latter was a popular figure in Dublin, a Sinn Feiner, but also a notable champion of all sorts of minority causes and a pacifist. He had apparently gone into Dublin to help the wounded and to try to restrain his fellow citizens from looting. His widow took up the case, and a commission of inquiry was appointed. JB was tried, found guilty of murder but pronounced insane, and imprisoned in Broadmoor. In a letter about the incident, read at the court and published in *The Times*, JB argued that he had acted in what seemed at the time like an emergency under martial law in the expectation of attack by Sinn Fein and six hundred German prisoners of war released and armed by the Irish rebels. There had also been a rumour of Irish-American forces landing in Galway. Certainly, Irish terrorists had shot a great many British soldiers and others in a centuries-long tradition in which at least two of JB's own ancestors had been murdered in the seventeenth century. This view of the event may have induced British authorities to let JB use the insanity plea as a way out and to strengthen public suspicions of a cover-up. The case entered into the canon of British Imperial atrocities, as *The Times* declared in 1981. Whatever the reason, JB was soon released and emigrated to British Columbia with his wife and children. Mrs Bowen-Colthurst, *née* Rosalinda Lætitia Butler (1881-1940), was born at Seven Oaks, Kent, the youngest daughter of Lord Dunboyne, member of a very old Irish family whose family name was Butler, and among her brothers were Major General Leslie Butler of the Irish Guards, commanding the Devonshire Territorials, and Major General Theobald Butler, commanding the Royal Artillery in Bombay.

JB was not the only member of the family in British Columbia and probably not the first. Captain Richard St John Jefferyes Colthurst of the London Regiment, possibly a cousin and certainly a younger son of Sir George St John Bowen-Colthurst (1850-1925) of Blarney Castle, County Cork, lived near the Yukon boundary as a gold miner and trapper for many years before returning in 1936 to live in Essex at "Wakes" in the village of Colne. The Bowen-Colthursts may well have been in touch with him as they lived for about twenty years at Terrace on the Skeena River before settling in 1930 at Sooke, west of Victoria, in a house they called "Coolalta," later the Sooke Harbour Hotel. Their activities echoed in the local papers for the next thirty or forty years. In spring 1931, JB spent four months in Buenos Aires at the British Trades Exhibition; during the 1930s, he wrote caustic letters to the *Daily Colonist* about the BC game laws ("the Game Department has just appointed a game warden whose principal qualification was that he once mistook a farmer's black pig for a bear and shot it"). His wife was active in the Anglican Church, and in March 1933, he helped her to sponsor a reception for about fifty guests to hear a visiting team of the Oxford Group, an evangelical movement of Anglicans from Oxford and Cambridge colleges, founded by the U.S. evangelist Frank Buchman (1878-1961) and known from 1938 as "Moral Rearmament." JB also joined and spoke for the Social Credit movement as well as the Overseas League, which he addressed in March 1934 on "The British Empire, Past, Present, and Future" ("The two glories of the British Empire are Bibles and newspapers"). In 1939-1940, he made a tour of Northern China, returning across the Pacific on a Japanese liner. After his wife died in 1940, he moved to the Okanagan Valley, where he died, aged eighty-four, on 11 December 1965 in Penticton.

Sources: *Hart's Annual Army List*, 1913, p. 797, "*War Service of Active Officers*"; *The Times* (London), 25 August 1916, page 3, "*The Skeffington Inquiry*"; 28 December 1925, p. 6]: "*Death of Sir George Colthurst*"; 19 November 1938, p. 8, "*Alaska Highway*," 28 April 1981, p. 13, "*The Crime of Captain Colthurst*"; *Colonist*, 10 March 1933, p. 4; 23 March 1933, p. 9; 24 March 1933, p. 4; 22 December 1933, p. 10; 6 March 1934, p. 6; 27 November 1934, p. 4; 1 May 1940, p. 9; 2 August 1940, p. 10; *Whitaker's*, p. 119; Perceval Landon, *The Opening of Tibet: An Account of Lhasa and the Country and People of Central Tibet and of the Progress of the Mission Sent there by the English Government in the Year 1903-4* (New York, Doubleday, Page & Co., 1905), p. 457 lists him among the officers, misspelled as "*Lieut. J. C. Bourne Colthurst, Royal Irish Rifles*"; Keith Briant, *Oxford Limited* (New York, Farrar & Rinehart, 1938), chapter 6, "*The Oxford Group*."

BOYD, Lieutenant Colonel John Henry (1879-1971). He was born on 23 May 1879 at Mangalore, Madras Presidency, Southern India, son of John Ewart Edward Agincourt Boyd, Superintendant of Police (Indian Police), and grandson of Surgeon General David Boyd, Indian Medical Service. Educated at Bedford School and RMA Sandhurst, JB was found to be medically unfit for military service and articled to a firm of civil engineers. In 1899, he went to Ontario but soon returned, joined the British Army, and joined No. 3 Company, Twenty-seventh St Claire Borderers on an expedition to West Africa, where he saw service from Cape Coast Castle to Kumasi. JB took part in the famous Relief of Kumassi (1900-1901.) He spent the next year on the Gold Coast busy with public works and railways and then the five years, 1902-1907, in the mines survey there. When the Great War began, he was working on Nigerian railways but was sent home to serve in the Cameroons. Next, he was dispatched to Mesopotamia as "Lieut.-Colonel J. H. Boyd, O.B.E., R.E., Assistant Director" on the staff of the Inland Water Transport but from 1920 to 1929 became a lieutenant with the Colonial Service in Nigeria, busy again with public works and railways.

In Nigeria about 1910, JB befriended George Buchanan Simpson (c. 1886-1958), a civil servant in the postal administration born in Bedford, who retired to Cowichan Lake in 1914, and it was Simpson and his wife, a graduate of the Sorbonne, who induced JB and his wife Elizabeth to migrate to Cowichan Lake in 1919. The two families were neighbours for many years, and from 1921 to 1927, Simpson was local game warden and acting constable. For a while, the Boyds lived in Dr Stoker's house, then moved to a float house until they bought the old Oliver farm at Marble Bay, about eighty acres with pleasant sloping beaches facing Cowichan Lake, and lived there almost until JB's death. From 1933 to 1963, he was a leader in enlarging and improving local schools. In 1937, he agreed to serve as coroner for the Lake District and later that year was appointed stipendiary magistrate in the County of Nanaimo, judge of the Juvenile Court and the Small Debts Court, and coroner for BC offices he held for many years. At a meeting in October 1939 to establish a war-activities committee for Cowichan, he was named to an organizing committee. After the war, he served on the district school board as a trustee and secretary-treasurer, representing the community of Lake Cowichan. The Boyds were also active in the Parent-Teacher Association, the Kiwanis and Kinsmen's Clubs, the IODE, and the Anglican Church. Their three daughters, two of whom were born in BC, became teachers or nurses and married and had families. Perhaps, as a result of JB's recreations, which he listed as cricket, rugby football, and rowing, he lived past ninety-two and died on 30 July 1971. The J. H. Boyd Memorial Scholarship was founded in his memory.

Sources: *Who's Who in B.C.*, 1942-1943, p. 48; 1947-1948, p. 22; *The Daily Colonist*, 14 October 1939, p. 11; Lieutenant Colonel Leonard Joseph Hall, *The Inland Water Transport in Mesopotamia* (Constable, 1921), pp. 196-7; John F. T. Saywell, *Kaatza: The Chronicles of Cowichan Lake* (*Sidney, The Cowichan Lake District Centennial Committee*, 1967), pp. 63, 79, 98, 104-6, 169, 179, 193; *Colonist*, 1 August 1971, p. 23, obit.

BRADBROOKE, Brigadier General Gerard Renvoise (1896-1980). He was born at Bletchley, Buckinghamshire, son of William Bradbrooke, and was working as an unmarried labourer, an Anglican 5' 9" tall with fair complexion, blue eyes, and light hair, when he enlisted in the CEF at Winnipeg on 15 December 1914. His file is marked "Lieutenant," and his promotions came during the Second World War.

After that war he lived on Maple Bay Road in the Cowichan Valley, one of the many Imperials there, but later moved to Comox, where he took a large house that was later converted to a nursing home called "Glacier View." When he died, aged eighty-three, on 30 September 1980, leaving a son William and a grandson Nicholas in Tacoma, Washington, he was living in Victoria and had joined the Union Club.

Sources: *Recollections of John Palmer*; NAC, CEF files, RG150, box 990-29, regt. no. 81095; *Times-Colonist*, 2 October 1980, p. 54, obit.

BRAIDE, Colonel Reginald William (c. 1890-1968). Born in India, he was recorded in the British census of 1901 as a schoolboy boarding with other boys at 14 Alexandra Road, in the Foxhall Ward, Holy Trinity Southshore Parish, Blackpool, North Lancashire. The head of the household there was Frank Pennington, a schoolmaster, aged twenty-nine. Braide joined the South Lancashire Regiment and rose to the rank of colonel.

After the Great War, he migrated to Victoria, where he married Davida Ker (1898-1976) on 8 December 1925. They lived in Oak Bay until he died, aged seventy-eight, on 11 April 1968 and she, also aged seventy-eight, on 16 September 1976. She was a sister of two *Ker brothers, who fought in the Great War.

Sources: census 1901, England, RG 13/3974; *Victoria Daily Times*, 8 December 1925, p. 6, marriage; *Colonist*, 14 April 1968, p. 29, obit.

BRETON, Basil Ogilvie (1892-1969). In June 1924, the *Cowichan Leader* printed an advertisement for "B.O. Breton, Notary Public, Real Estate and Insurance Agent, Cobble Hill." On 23 October 1924, the *Cowichan Leader* reported, "Mr B. O. Breton came down from Lake Cowichan for the opening of the shooting season and is believed to have returned home with a heavy bag." The next sign of his presence on the Island was in Victoria in January 1933, when the local India-Burma Society advised prospective members to contact him as its secretary at the Glenshiel Hotel. According to the *Daily Colonist*, "Besides maintaining social fellowship between B.C. residents who have resided or served in India, Burma or Ceylon, and the Straits Settlements, the Society has an established connection with the European Association of India through which source the latest information regarding Indian affairs and politics is always available." The local India-Burma Society was a year old and planned to hold a general meeting on 16 January at the Glenshiel Hotel. The president of it was *Sir Percy Lake, and the guest speaker was to be the Marquess of Zetland, formerly Lord Ronaldsay. BB attended that meeting with his wife and their daughter Anne, mingling with about a score of others interested in Indian affairs. He was interested because as the *London Gazette* had announced on 1 January 1918, he had been an army cadet promoted on 26 September 1917 to second lieutenant for service in the Indian Army Reserve. In May 1934, he became assistant secretary of the India-Burma Society because *Sir Charles Delmé-Radcliffe had stepped in as secretary. The next bit of family news came in 1937, when the *Colonist* reported on 3 October that Miss Anne Breton, "daughter of Captain & Mrs B. O. Breton of the Glenshiel Hotel, is about to go to England with her uncle, Captain C. G. Breton R.N. (Retired) for about six months." Passenger lists show this uncle, Colin Guy Breton, a retired engineer commander of the RN, aged fifty-six, travelling from Vancouver on the *Canada*, vessel of the East Asiatic Company, with two nieces, Barbara Anne Breton, aged twenty-three, and Allison Margaret Breton, aged twenty-one. They arrived in London on 2 November 1937. I found no more news of BB until 13 September 1955, when he arrived in London on the *Empress of Australia* from Montreal, identified as a civil servant, aged sixty-two, from Antigua, British West Indies, making a two-month visit home to England, where he gave an address at Buckfastleigh, Devon.

BB was born on 30 November 1893 in Hampshire at Southsea or Portsmouth, son of an Anglo-Irish surgeon in the RN, Willliam Edward Breton (1850-?), born in Cork, Ireland. BB's mother, Alice Maud Breton, was born about 1857 to an English family in the Sandwich Islands (later Hawaii). The birthplaces of BB's brothers show a family moving around Britain and the empire. Two of them, Colin Guy and William D., were born at Sheerness, Kent, where the family was living in 1881 at 5 Naval Terrace and the remaining two, Douglas C. and Lawrence Duncan, were born in Cape Colony, South Africa. In 1901, BB, aged eight, was living with his family in Short Row, Portsmouth, his father serving there as a fleet surgeon, a rank he had held since 1895. Already a naval surgeon in 1871, his father had qualified further in 1874, then giving his address as 100 Patrick Street in Cork, Ireland, but in 1881-1882, perhaps earlier, was posted in Sheerness and in 1894 was staff surgeon aboard HMS *Superb*.

In 1913, most of the family emigrated to Alberta. Canadian Passenger Lists show the parents arriving at Quebec on 27 May 1913 from Liverpool on the *Teutonic*, identified in a list of British settlers. But when Lawrence Duncan Breton, an unmarried carpenter born on 28 September 1885 in Capetown, enlisted in the CEF at Edmonton, Alberta, on 3 November 1915, his mother was living at 65 Saxweimer Road in Southsea, Hampshire. As for BB, he was married by then and employed at Telfordville, Alberta, as a storekeeper. When he enlisted at Edmonton on 14 December 1915, he had had a fifteen-month officer's training course in England at Petersfield. He was described as 5' 10" tall, with a clear complexion, grey eyes, and brown hair. I found nothing further about him, but his brother Lawrence Duncan Breton died, aged seventy-nine, on 21 December 1965 on the Island at Campbell River.

Sources: NAC, CEF files, box 1046-18, regimental no. 811380; box 1046-65, regimental no. 155075; *Whitaker's*, p. 69 (father); *Cowichan Leader*, June 1924, advertisement; 23 October 1924, note; *Colonist* 10 January 1933, p. 8; 17 January 1933, p. 8; 18 May 1934, p. 2; 3 October 1937, p. 8; census 1881, England, RG 11/980 /96, p. 17; census 1901, PRO RG 13/999/141, p. 11; census 1901, RG 13/2114, p. 4 (Devonport, Tamar, Engineer Student College); UK Medical Registers, 1859-1959 online, 1875 (father); *Kelly's Directory for Kent*, 1882, p. 606 (father); UK Incoming Passenger Lists, 1878-1960 online, no. 3054/01; Canadian Passenger Lists online, T-4796 (parents); Supplement to the London Gazette, 1 January 1918, p. 100.

BREW, Chartres (1815-1870). A Protestant Irishman, in August 1858 he was recommended to the colonial secretary in London, Sir Edward Bulwer-Lytton, for the office of chief inspector of police to join the small staff of Governor James Douglas in policing the new gold colony of British Columbia at a salary of £500. He developed the Island's colonial police force on the model of the Irish Constabulary, and so it remained when the Island joined British Columbia in 1866 and Canada in 1871, until replaced by the Royal Canadian Mounted Police in 1950. CB preferred to hire British officers like himself in preference to local men, a preference that continued as a tradition long after his death. His activities for many years were among the miners and native tribes of the provincial interior, where he served *inter alia* as gold commissioner, but in October 1859, he became chief magistrate at New Westminster, in September 1862, acting treasurer of BC, and in 1864-1968 Douglas appointed him to the Legislative Council. When he died at Richfield, Cariboo, on 31 May 1870, he was mourned by his friend Judge Matthew Baillie Begbie and various family members who had come from Ireland to join him, notably his sister, Jane Augusta Brew, who kept house for him in Victoria even after she had married Augustus Frederick Pemberton (1809-1881) in 1861, a commissioner of police and uncle of *Joseph Despard Pemberton.

CB was born at Corofin, County Clare, Ireland, eldest son of the Honourable Tomkins Brew, stipendiary magistrate of Tuam, County Galway. At age twenty, he joined the volunteer British Legion, which went in 1835 to fight in the Carlist wars, and after enlisting in the Royal Irish Constabulary in 1840, he went off to the Crimean War as assistant commissary general. Returned to the constabulary in Ireland after the war, he was serving as inspector in the city of Cork when he was offered a post on the Island

Sources: M. A. Ormsby, "Some Irish figures in colonial days," BCHQ, XIV (1950), 61-82. (2000 University of Toronto/Université Laval); Margaret A. Ormsby, "Brew, Chartres," in the DCB; Colonist, 3 March 1968, Sunday, pp. 4 and 7, Cecil Clark, "Room with 10,000 Stories"; British Colonist (Victoria), 10 June 1865. Cariboo Sentinel (Barkerville, BC), 4 June 1870, 21 Sept. 1872; James K. Nesbitt, "Old Homes and Families," Colonist, [date?] Sunday section, p. 11; Colonist, 3 March 1968, Sunday, pp. 4 and 7, Cecil Clark, "Room with 10,000 Stories" [about the BC Police Force].

BROADWOOD, Captain John Henry (1881-1936). He was born on 15 March 1881 at Slaugham, Sussex, where the 1881 census recorded him, one month old, living at "The Hyde" with his family. His father, John A. Broadwood, then aged twenty-six, was born on the Isle of Man and living on "Income from Interest, No Profession," and his mother, Alice Broadwood, also aged twenty-six, had come from Ireland. JB had two elder sisters, Alice Kathleen Broadwood (the future Mrs Hedley-Peek), aged three, born at Crawley, Sussex, and Ethel aged one. They had nine servants: two nurses, a monthly nurse, a parlourmaid, a cook, two housemaids, a scullery maid, and a farm bailiff. Among the servants was also a visitor aged five, an upholsterer's apprentice aged fifteen, and his sister aged five. Ten years later, JB was living at Wainfleet House, Blackboy Hill, Bristol, a school headed by Rev. John Henry Wilkinson, clerk in Holy Orders, headmaster of a preparatory school with a long list of pupils. There seems to have been trouble in the family as the parents were living separately in 1901, the father resident in Wales with another wife. Meanwhile, JB joined the British Army, fought in the Duke of Cornwall's Light Infantry during the South African War and the Great War, and, after serving for thirty-five years, arrived, aged fifty, in Victoria on 1 August 1931. He settled in the suburb of Colwood and was joined on the Island by his two sisters, Mrs J. F. W. Lennard (*née* Ethel Broadwood), wife of a major in the British Army, and Mrs Alice Hedley-Peek (also *née* Broadwood). The latter had been recorded by the 1901 census as a visitor at the home of John Hedley, aged fifty-eight, a "medical practitioner" born at Ossington (?), Northumberland, and his wife, Mary E. (or C) Hedley, aged forty-seven, born in Doulais, Glamorganshire, and their three sons and one daughter. They had at that time two other visitors and five servants plus a Swiss governess.

These details help to make sense of a family event in May 1933. Late that month, the Lennard's daughter, JB's niece, married Thomas Sutherland Hartley at Holy Trinity Anglican Church, Patricia Bay, North Saanich, and it was JB who "gave her away," as the saying was. That church was chosen because the groom's parents, Captain and Mrs *Basil Shakespeare Hartley, lived at Deep Cove, a few miles north of the church. The wedding reception, with more than a hundred guests, was held two miles away in Sidney at the home of the bride's aunt, Mrs Hedley-Peek in Sidney. The young couple then went to Seattle for their honeymoon and then on to Bolivia, where the groom was manager of a mine. When JB died, aged fifty-five, on 8 July 1936 at Colwood, his sisters were both living there, and it was Alice Hedley-Peek who dealt with the funeral and postmortem details.

Sources: NAC, RG76-*immigration series* C-1, 1931, vol. 5, p. 162; *Colonist*, 26 May 1933, p. 8; 9 July 1936, pp. 5 and 16, obit.; 10 July 1936, p. 14, obit.; *The Times* (London, 19 January 1922, p. 4; census 1881, England, RG 11/1063, p. 19; census 1891, RG 12/1988, p. 3; census 1891, RG 12/1028, p. 36; census 1901, RG 13/5111, p. 5; census 1901, RG 13/4582, p. 25; NAC, RG76-*immigration series* C-1, 1931, vol. 5, p. 162.

BRODEUR, Victor Gabriel (1892-1976). He was born at Beloeil, Quebec, on 17 September 1892, one of the four sons of Emma Brodeur, *née* Brillon, and Hon. Louis-Philippe Brodeur, formerly minister of the navy and fisheries in Wilfrid Laurier's government and lieutenant governor of Quebec. His father had sponsored the bill creating the Canadian Navy and was, in fact, the first minister of the Royal Canadian Navy. VB was one of the first seven cadets to join the RCN when it was formed in 1909 and served on HMCS *Canada* (1909-1910) and the cruiser *Niobe* (1910-1911). Then he transferred to the Royal Navy for further training aboard HMS *Dreadnought* (1911-1913), was promoted to sub-lieutenant, attended a naval college in England (1913-14), and served on HMS *Berwick* on the West Indies Station (1913-1914) when she was involved in a Mexican revolution. Promoted to lieutenant (1915), he served on *Dreadnought* and *Caradoc* in the North Sea Fleet (1915-1917) and fought in an action against German light cruisers (October 1917) and in the Baltic Sea for action against the Bolshevik Russian fleet (1917-19). He specialized in gunnery and was the first Canadian naval officer to qualify as gunnery officer in the RN. He served as a staff officer at the Gunnery School in Devonport (1921-1922) and while there designed a gunnery model for which he was thanked by the Admiralty. There followed an appointment as naval staff officer in Ottawa charged with organizing the RCNVR (1922-1925). Further service in the RN and the RCN was followed by command of HMCS *Skeena* at Esquimalt (1931-2) and then commanded two Canadian destroyers sent to protect Imperial interests during a revolution at San Salvador (1932). He was posted as senior naval officer at the Esquimalt Station (1932-1934), and as commodore, then vice admiral, OC Pacific Coast, throughout most of the Second World War (1938-1940 and 1943-1947), serving in the interval as Canadian naval attaché in Washington (1940-1942). He was decorated with the OBE (June 1943) and the CB (January 1946), and in 1947, he retired with his wife to Vancouver.

He had married Doris Béatrice Fages (9 September 1915), and they had two children, Philippe (born in England, 1921) and Nigel (born at Victoria, 1932). Philippe became an officer in Canadian aviation; Nigel joined the navy and became an admiral, like his father. Two years after Mrs Brodeur died in London (1936), VB remarried Dorothy Whitfield at Bradford, England (2 June 1938). He was, of course, bilingual and thoroughly anglicized but warmly welcomed by the francophone group in Victoria. He and his wife gave much time to charity and church work in the two coastal towns. He died in Vancouver on 6 October 1976, his wife six weeks later, and both were buried there in the veteran's cemetery near Shaughnessy Hospital.

Sources: *The Canadian Who's Who* (Toronto, Trans-Canada Press, 1960), vol. VIII (1958-1960), pp. 130-1; *MacFarlane,* p. 8; John Greene, Marc Lapprand, Gérald Moreau, and Gérald Ricard, *French Presence in Victoria,* B.C., 1843-1991 (Victoria, L'Association historique francophone de Victoria, CB, 1991), pp. 169-71.

BROMLEY, Vice Admiral Sir Arthur, Eighth Baronet (1876-1961). He appears in this book because on 24 June 1904, he married Laura Mary "Maye" Dunsmuir (1884-1959), daughter of the Island's rich Scottish coal miner, James Dunsmuir, in a grand wedding at Victoria on 24 June 1904. She was born at Departure Bay near Nanaimo on 3 July 1884. They lived in London and at "Stoke Hall," East Stoke, Nottinghamshire, on the banks of the Trent River, but she often went home to the Island and died as Lady Bromley, the death of her husband's elder brother having left him as the Bromley family heir. A biographer of the Dunsmuir family thought her marriage was probably the most successful of all the Dunsmuir daughters' marriages. Shortly before the wedding, she met *Robert Aubrey Meade by chance while wandering about near Cowichan Lake.

AB was born on 8 August 1876, second son of Anne Bromley *née* Wilson and Sir Henry Bromley, fourth baronet (1816-95), and the 1881 census found him, aged four, at "Stoke Hall," East Stoke, Nottinghamshire, on the banks of the Trent River, with his grandfather, Sir Henry Bromley, second baronet, then aged sixty-four, "J. P. D. L. Bart," born in East Stoke, and his grandmother, Georgina Ellen Bromley, then aged fifty-four, born in Brighton. Also there were an elder brother, Maurice Bromley, aged five, born at Winthorpe, Nottinghamshire; a younger brother, Herbert Bromley, aged one, born at East Stoke; and twelve servants: footman, page, cook and housekeeper, lady's maid, kitchenmaid, housemaid, laundrymaid, scullery maid, nurse and lady's maid, two nursery maids, and schoolmistress. The neighbours lived in the "gardener's rooms" and other dwellings on the estate, evidently employed as gardeners, game keepers, and other retainers. A decade later, AB, aged fourteen, was a "Cadet Royal Navy" living at "Old Hall," Ashwell, Rutland, with his father, Henry Bromley, aged forty-one, "local J. P. living on own means," born at Kanrush (?), Carnarvonshire. With them were his father's wife, Adele Shipworth Bromley, aged forty-four, born at Wood End, Warwickshire; three brothers born in Nottinghamshire: Robert aged seventeen, Maurice aged fifteen, and Herbert aged eleven; a sister Esther Bromley aged nine, born in Rutland; and eight servants. His grandparents lived on meanwhile in "The Hall" at East Stoke, where in 1891, they had a visiting cousin, a sixty-five-year-old widow named Charlotte Shipworth born at Triningham, Buckinghamshire. A total of fourteen assorted grooms, game keepers, and other hands lived on the estate.

AB had a good career in the Royal Navy, was on the active list from 1892 to 1922, and rose to be a vice admiral superintending the Malta Dockyard (1906), with other responsibilities and when he retired with the rank of vice admiral, he was appointed Gentleman Usher to King George V and served under Elizabeth II until his death on 12 January 1961. He was twice decorated by the Royal Humane Society for saving life.

Sources: Terry Reksten, *The Dunsmuir Saga* (Vancouver, Douglas & McIntyre, 1991), pp. 241-2; census 1881, England, RG 11/3370, p. 1; census 1891, RG 12/2547, p. 6; census 1891, RG 12/2708, p. 1.

BROOKS, Major Allan Cecil (1869-1946). A soldier, naturalist, and distinguished ornithologist born in India, he lived much of his life on the Island and died at Comox. His father, William Edwin Brooks (1829-1899), was an engineer who began assisting his father (AB's grandfather) working out of Newcastle-on-Tyne on the Tyneside docks, but went to India in 1856 to work for the East India Railway. It was there, at Etawa, that AB was born on 15 February 1869, and he was named after Allan Octavian Hume (1829-1912), son of the Radical M. P. Joseph Hume who was a close friend of his father, a famous ornithologist, an official in the ICS, and known as the founder of the Indian National Congress, which held its first meeting in 1885. Both of these men collected bird specimens for the British Museum. As for AB, he had his early childhood in India but was sent home to England, aged four, and in 1881 his father moved to Milton, Ontario, then westward to Chilliwack, British Columbia. When AB's father died on 18 January 1899, it was at Mount Forrest, Milton, Ontario, but AB was already committed to BC, where he became a market hunter, big-game guide, naturalist, and bird painter. He was illustrating bird-books and selling his paintings more and more. He had learnt much taxidermy and all of the ornithologists' skills from his father's friends. As early as 1891, he was making collections and skinning specimens at the provincial museum in Victoria. In 1905, he bought a plot of land at Okanagan Landing and amused himself wandering around the coastal ranges of the Rocky Mountains. The Great War interrupted his life by breaking out while he was in England attending the National Rifle Match at Bisley in summer 1914 as a member of the Canadian team. He served as a major at the Second Army School of Scouting and in the British Expeditionary Force in France and was named to the Distinguished Service Order for conspicuous gallantry in operations of 2-3 September near Arras. A crack shot as well as a scout, in two days, he personally killed twenty of the enemy.

After the war, he went back to BC in April 1919 and was soon spending much time in the Okanagan Valley as well as at Comox with his friend Hamilton Mack Laing, collecting, painting, and ranging about. In 1920, he attended the annual meeting of the American Ornithologists' Union held in Washington DC and visited Louis Fuertes, the eminent American bird artist, at his home in Ithaca, New York State. By 1920, AB had become by far the best-known bird painter in Canada, but he was also a hunter particularly of predators of all kinds—hawks, crows, ravens, snakes, and many others—which he hated with a passion. He thought ideas about a divine balance in nature were all nonsense and did his best to protect birds and other victims of nature's predators.

In 1926 on 8 April, he married Marjorie Alston Holmes, a solicitor's daughter born in 1889 at Arundel, Sussex, who happened to be staying at Okanagan Landing. Their honeymoon trip was to Alert Bay, where he could collect surf birds, and the following year their son, Allan Cecil Brooks, was born in Vancouver City. They travelled a good deal together, sometimes separately, to New Zealand in 1931 and around the world in 1934-1935, but in 1928, they established a second home on the Island at Comox. They spent the winters of 1942 at Sooke, and he was in Comox in 1945, when he had his final illness and died, still working, on 3 January 1946. **Sources:** Richard Mackie, *Hamilton Mack Laing, Hunter-Naturalist* (Victoria, Sono Nis Press, 1985), 234 pp., pp. 83-4; Hamilton Mack Laing, *Allan Brooks, Artist-Naturalist* (Victoria, BC, Provincial Museum, 1979), 249 pp: *Colonist,* 28 October 1955, p. 18, obit.; Jean Webber, Internet files; G. Clifford Carl, "In Memoriam—Allan Brooks," *The Murrelet,* Jan.-Apr. 1946, p. 14; Hamilton M. Laing, "Allan Brooks, 1869-1946," *The Auk,* vol. 64, July 1947, p. 436; Allan Brooks, "In Memoriam: Charles de B. Green," *The Condor,* January 1930, pp. 9-11; Harry Harris, "An Appreciation of Allan Brooks, Zoological Artist: 1869-1946," *The Condor,* vol. 48, July-August 1946, p. 153; W. L. Dawson, "Allan Brooks: An Appreciation," *The Condor,* vol. XV, Mar.-Apr. 1913, p. 6; J. W. Wilkinson, "Allan Brooks: A Modern Audubon," Vancouver Sunday Province, 14 December 1930, p. 5; Allan Brooks, "Early Big-Game Conditions in the Mt Baker District, Washington," *The Murrelet,* Sept. 1930, pp. 65-67.

BROOME, Colonel Louis Egerton (1875-1951). On 25 March 1924, he and Commander Stuart MacLaren of the RAF took off at Calshot, England, in a valiant but unsuccessful attempt to fly eastwards around the world. When LB eventually retired to a farm on the Island in the Cowichan Valley, he was often called on to speak about the flight. On 7 May 1934, for instance, he lectured on it at Spencer's Dining Room in Victoria to forty or fifty people of the Overseas Club. He gave the same lecture to the Rotary Club at the Empress Hotel on 12 July and to the Gyro Club, also at the Empress, on 6 August. When the *Daily Colonist* interviewed him at home in 1940, he showed them a tiny crystal. "I am attached to that crystal," he said. "It was in the pocket of my flying coat when I crashed many years ago in the icy waters of the Behring Sea. The Japanese lady who gave it to me had told me there was trouble ahead but as long as I kept it near my heart I would not come to any serious harm. Well, here I am!" He had set it on a tiny table in a model house, carefully made and furnished, which he intended to exhibit at the YMCA Hobby Fair in Victoria on 5-6 April that year to raise funds for huts to shelter soldiers overseas. When asked why he built it, he said, "Well, I'm getting pretty old and I thought I would want something to play with in my second childhood." He had made most of the model house in his workshop using wood sent by friends from various parts of the world. "You ask me why I do it. Well, it's a mad, bad world outside these days, and I'm getting too old to do anything about it. Inside my workshop with my stove drawing well and the dog and a cat or two purring in front of it and fragrant smell of fresh-cut shavings of wood from far-off lands, all to me is peace—until it's time for the next news broadcast" (*Colonist*, 31 March 1940, p. 2). When he died, aged seventy-five, at the Jubilee Hospital, Victoria, on 10 March 1951, he left a daughter and a son, "Jack" Broome, late of the Royal Navy.

During the famous flight eastwards around the world, beginning on 25 March 1924, LB seems to have had two duties: First, he was to act as director of supplies travelling to Hakodate, Japan, aboard HMC minesweeper *Thiepval*, commanded by Lieutenant W. J. R. Beech, RCN, preparing depots of supplies along MacLaren's proposed route. The vessel returned to Esquimalt on 21 August after steaming ten thousand miles in northern waters and anchoring in the harbour of Petropavlovsk, in Avacha Bay on the east coast of Kamchatka, several times in July. Secondly, LB was to act as MacLaren's navigator in the flight from Japan across the North Pacific along the Aleutian Islands. It was hoped to do the entire journey in 292 flying hours, but the plane was forced down by fog and fell wrecked into the North Pacific. MacLaren and Broome were rescued, and their adventure was world famous in that generation. LB was made a member of the Royal Victorian Order (MVO).

Born on 20 April 1875 at Thurloe Square, London, he was the youngest son of Sir Frederick Napier Broome (1842-1896), a colonial governor who served in Natal, Mauritius (1880-1883), Western Australia (1883-1889), and Trinidad and was knighted in 1884. Lady Broome (c. 1831-1911), his mother, is known for her writing about New Zealand. Born in Jamaica as Mary Ann Stewart, she had first married George Robert Barker, an officer who was knighted in 1859 for his military service in India. As Lady Barker, she went to Bengal with her husband in 1860, but when he died in July 1861, she returned to England and in June 1865 married Frederick Napier Broome, eleven years her junior, with whom she spent a few years on a 9,700-acre sheep farm in New Zealand. Her writings, all based on her experiences, include *Station life in New Zealand* (1870) and *Station amusements in New Zealand* (1873) as well as stories for children and a cookery book based on her domestic life in New Zealand. Her father-in-law, LB's paternal grandfather, was rector of John the Baptist Church at the village of Kenley, Shropshire. The census of 1891 records "Louis E. Broome," aged fifteen, among the "scholars" at Winchester College, the famous public school, and he became a civil engineer. As such, he took various engineering posts beginning in 1900, chiefly in municipal engineering, dam design and construction, railway location and construction, and superintendence of floating equipment (dredges, tugs, dry docks, wharves)—most of this on the Panama Canal and for the U. S. government. He also acted as agent for Jardine, Matheson & Co. in carrying out engineering contracts with the Chinese government (railway location and surveys) at a salary of £1,000 per annum. He spoke fluent French and some Spanish. On 19 October 1916, he applied to join the British Army as an officer cadet with a temporary commission for the period of the war and was soon appointed as a lieutenant in the Inland Water Transport Section of the Royal Engineers. Promoted in 1917 to temporary captain and on 7 April 1919 to temporary lieutenant colonel, RE, he worked as one of the assistant directors of Railway Traffic (Class X) and had seniority from 8 February 1917. Later in 1919, he was attached to the Inter-Allied Commission at Berlin "and was engaged in repatriation of German prisoners in the

East." In April 1924, he owed Kodak Ltd., London, £3/15/6 and they were asking
the War Office where he was, but the last news they had of him was that he was in
Japan assisting in a plan to fly around the world.
Sources: PRO (London), WO339/ 76433; *Army List,* December 1919, p. 57f;
Colonist, 8 May 1934, p. 6; 5 August 1934, p. 5; 7 August 1934, p. 4; 31 March 1940,
p. 2; 13 March 1951, p. 19, obit; Longstaff, *Esquimalt Naval Base,* p. 88.

BROTCHIE, Captain William (1799-1859). A sea captain employed by the
Hudson's Bay Company to sail to Fort Vancouver on the Columbia River and later
to Victoria, he was born in Caithness, Scotland, son of David Brotchie, a mason
at Thurso, Caithness, and was first recorded as a seaman on the *Dryad,* sailing
on the long voyage from London to the Columbia River in 1830. In 1833-1834,
he was second mate on the *Ganymede* on a similar voyage and in 1834-1835 first
mate. He was captain of the *Cadboro* on the voyages of 1835-1838, of the *Nereide* in
a return voyage eastwards in 1838-1840, and of a round trip in 1940-1942. After
commanding the *Vancouver* from the Columbia to London in 1843-1844, he retired
because the company refused passage for his wife, though she had been allowed
to sail with him in 1840, 1844, and certain other years. In 1848, the Admiralty
and the company licensed him to cut spars on Vancouver Island, whereupon he
sailed for Victoria aboard the bark *Albion,* which in 1849 struck a reef off Dallas
Road, Victoria, a reef known thereafter as Brotchie Ledge. In 1850, he sailed to
the Island via Australia in business for the spar industry near Fort Rupert and was
busy until 1855, when he faced a failure.

It was at about that time that WB settled in Victoria. In 1858, Governor James
Douglas appointed him harbour master for the Island. He joined the Pioneer Cricket
Club but died at last on 28 February 1859 after a long illness. Contemporaries
described him as "a portly, good-natured, even-tempered man."
Sources: *Fort Victoria Letters, 1846-1851,* ed., Hartwell Bowsfield (Winnipeg,
Hudson's Bay Record Society, 1979), see index entry, p. 254; HBC archived files,
cited in Judith Hudson Beattie and Helen M. Buss, eds., *Undelivered Letters to
Hudson's Bay Company Men on the Northwest Coast of America,* 1830-57 (Vancouver,
UBC Press, 2003), pp. 123, 409-09, 412, 415; Derek Pethick, *Victoria: The Fort*
(Vancouver, Mitchell Press Ltd, 1968), pp. 205-6, citing *The Gazette,* 3 March 1859;
Walbran, B.C. Coast Names, pp. 64-5.

BROWN, Charles Henry (1886-1977). Born at Limassol, Cyprus, on 12 February
1886, he enlisted in the Royal Navy at Devonport, England, on 1 August 1910 as
a shipwright with HMS *Niobe.* He became a carpenter's mate on HMS *Excellent*
on 31 July 1912 and then a full carpenter on HMS *Victory* in 1913. After various
phases of service, he was a commissioned as a shipwright in the RCN on 15 April
1923 at Stadacona, then at Naden (1924), and later as shipwright commander
(1 July 1940) on the *Givenchy.* In 1942, he served on the staff of the supervising
engineer on the Pacific and retired on 4 July 1944 with the OBE. His death came
on 12 March 1977, aged ninety-one, in Victoria.
Sources: *National Archives* (PRO), London, ADM 188/520; *MacFarlane,* p. 9.

BRYANT, Lieutenant Colonel Jasper Mosley (1882-1937). He was born on 22 January 1882 at Newcastle-on-Tyne, youngest of the four sons of Edward R. Bryant, a merchant in the Spanish trade and is so recorded, aged nine, in the census of 1891 at Elswick, Newcastle-on-Tyne. He was commissioned as second lieutenant in the Royal Artillery on 18 August 1900 and was promoted to lieutenant on 28 June 1902 and served as lieutenant colonel from 3 December 1918 to 6 May 1920. In August 1920, he was recorded as a major serving in Mesopotamia with the Indian Army Ordnance Department but was on leave until 11 November 1920 with a home address of 189 Redland Road, Bristol. There he wrote asking for permission to retire and the Commander-in-Chief in India allowed him to do so on 12 November 1920 with the rank of lieutenant colonel.

On 19 October 1920, JB wrote from Bristol to the War Office, "Sir, Ref. Your etc. etc. I have the honour to inform you that I have secured a passage to Canada by S.S. 'Victorian' sailing 8 November 1920. My address after that will be c/o Bank of Montreal, Vancouver, B.C." He asked about pension arrangements and the reply on 27 October 1920 was "You will be eligible for retired pay at £273 a year under Army Order 324/19. When your retirement has appeared in the *London Gazette* instructions for the issue of retired pay will be given to the Assistant Paymaster General, Paymaster General's Office, Whitehall, S.W.1." As it turned out, the pension was reduced by 5½ percent and so amounted to only £258 a year. He ceased to be on the Reserve List of Officers in 1937 by virtue of his age (see *London Gazette*, 22 January 1937). As a result, his pension went down, but a document on file announces an increase on 1 August 1959 of from £357-14-0 to £400-13-0 a year. In 1956, he and his wife were living at Fulford Harbour, Salt Spring Island, BC, and in 1959 at Beaver Point, Ganges, where he died, aged seventy-eight, on 31 January 1960 and was buried at Royal Oak. It appears that he had migrated to Salt Spring Island in the wake of a cousin, Cecil Moxon Bryant (c. 1872-1937), who had settled there after a career as a mining engineer in Canada, where he had emigrated in 1897.
Sources: PRO, WO 374/10371; census 1891, England, RG 12/4197, p. 42; *The Social Register*, vol. 2, p. 93; *Colonist*, 2 February 1937, p. 5, obit.; 2 February 1960, p. 14, obit.

BUCK, Major Dr Arthur Herbert (1869-after 1947). He was born in 1869 at Cressage, Shropshire, son of John Henry Buck, a physician born in Norwich, and his wife Margaret from Sherbourne, Dorset. The 1871 census recorded them living in Cressage at Cressage Lodge with a cook, a housemaid, and a nursemaid, when AB was one year old. He had a brother, Edward John Buck, aged eight and a sister, Ellen Mary Buck, aged seven, both born in Norfolk. Educated at Uppingham and St Bartholomew's Hospital, London, he qualified as a physician and surgeon in 1892 (FRCS at Edinburgh, MRCS at England, LRCP at London) and was Brackenburg Surgical Scholar at St Bartholomew's, then joined the staff of the Royal Sussex County Hospital as consulting surgeon. In the Great War, it allotted 110 beds to military patients and AB had charge of one-third of these. He was also an honorary surgeon to the Larnach Hospital for officers. He was mobilized with his unit, 2nd East General Hospital, early in August 1914 and became surgeon-in-charge of Surgical Wards and Sections at Kitchener's Hospital. In 1915, he was appointed consultant for throat and ear cases in the Brighton area. In October 1918, a medical board judged him unfit for some unspecified reason, and he was directed to relinquish his commission—but granted the rank of major (ex. RAMC) on retirement. Long after the war, the War Office wrote to him c/o Barclay's Bank, Norwich (his address then in the *UK Medical Register*), saying that there was no employment for him in his military category.

He had married Lillian Maud Buck in 1914, and they had a son. In 1920, they sailed from Liverpool aboard the *Metagama*, arriving at St John, New Brunswick, on 20 April, and went across to the Island, where they were soon living on Third Street, Sidney, near my parents' house. In December 1921, their son John was badly, but not fatally, burned when his clothes caught fire. How long they remained in Sidney is unclear. They were still there in 1931, giving their mailing address to the *UK Medical Register* as c/o Barclay's Bank, Harpenden, Hertfordshire, but they certainly returned to England. Probably, the last documented address was cited in the *Register* as "Bathurst," Laurel Drive, Brundall, Norfolk, when AB was seventy-eight years old.

Sources: *Colonist*, 2 December 1921, p. 16; 12 January 1929, p. 18; BNA (formerly PRO), WO 374/10493 (several brief files from the War Office); *Who's Who in B.C.* 1931, p. 19; census 1871, England, RG 10/2761/44, p. 1; UK Medical Registers, 1895-1947; Kelly's Directories 1899-1916; Canadian Shipping Lists 1865-1935, T-14840 (*Metagama*, arriving 20 April 1920).

BULL, Captain John Augustus (1797-1860). He was born on 1 May 1797 at Lewisham, London, and had a career in the Royal Navy. During an assault on Russian vessels in the Gulf of Bothnia on 29 September 1855, in the Crimean War, "Second Master John Augustus Bull" of HMS *Firefly*, a 4,220-ton paddle vessel, played a leading part in capturing a barque and destroying two brigs, an action in which the enemy lost twenty-five men and many wounded; two British sailors were slightly wounded. In 1857-1860, he was captain of HMS *Plumper* and senior assistant surveyor on the Pacific coast under Captain Richards. Bull Passage, Lasqueti Island, was named after him. At Colwood on 7 February 1860, he married Emma Langford, third daughter of Justice Edward E. Langford, but he died suddenly later that year on 14 November at Esquimalt, soon after returning from the summer season's surveying on the coast. He had dined the previous evening with Dr Wallace of the RN hospital and was taken ill in the night. The *Colonist* reported, "A post-mortem showed an intense reddening of his stomach, but no sign of strain on any of his other organs. He was normally a healthy, sensible man." He was buried in the old cemetery, Quadra Street, Victoria.

Sources: *British National Archives* (PRO), ADM 188/ 690, no. J21731; *Life and Letters of the Late Sir Bartholomew James Sulivan*, K.C.B., 1810-1890, ed., Henry Norton Sulivan (John Murray, 1896), p. ?; Walbran, *B.C. Coast Names*, p. 71, citing the *Colonist*, 15 and 16 November 1860, obit.

BULL, Colonel Roland Osborne (1895-1972). He was born on 15 June 1895 in Winnipeg, son of Manlius Bull, a pioneer industrialist of the city, and his wife Mary née Nixon. After attending Kelvin Technical High School, Winnipeg, Trinity College School, Port Hope (1912-1913), and RMC, Kingston (1914), he joined the British Army, served in the Great War as second lieutenant in the RFA at Gallipoli and, on the Somme, won the MC for valour, and retired in 1919 with the rank of captain. In the Second World War, he served as a major in the VGC and then as commandant of Prisoner of War camps. He retired in 1944 with the rank of colonel and became town councillor at Oakville, Ontario, and a director of many companies: director and vice chairman, Gairdner & Co. Ltd.; director, Acadia-Atlantic Sugar Refineries Ltd., Davis Leather Co. Ltd., Great Northern Gas Utilities Ltd., and North Star Oil Ltd.; and a member of the Canadian Legion.

After a few years, he and his wife, Ruth Rushton Bull née Alexander, moved to Victoria, where he was active as a Conservative in politics and an Anglican, joined the Union Club and the Royal Victoria Yacht Club, and became well known as the founder of the Victoria Boys' Club on Yates Street. They moved at last to Sidney, where they gardened until he died, aged seventy-seven, on 15 November 1972 at Resthaven Hospital and was buried at Holy Trinity, Patricia Bay. He left his wife, a daughter Mary (Mrs P. Holman) at Sydney, Australia, two stepchildren, two sisters, and a brother, W. C. Bull of Winnipeg.
Sources: *Canadian Who's Who*, 1958-1960, pp. 148-9; *Social Register of Canada* (at the Ottawa Public Library), 1st ed., Montreal, 1958; *Colonist*, 16 November 1972, p. 64; 17 November, p. 11, photo, obit.

BULLEN, William Fitzherbert (1857-1921). He was born on 11 June 1857 near London, Ontario, son of W. F. and A. B. Bullen, and privately educated in eastern Canada. In 1878, aged twenty-one, he went out to Victoria and there in 1884 married Annie Amelia Bushby, daughter of Judge Bushby (1835-1875) and a granddaughter of Sir James Douglas. They lived on Esquimalt Road for forty-three years. He worked for some time at the Albion Iron Works but in 1893 went into shipbuilding and on the east side of Esquimalt harbour founded the BC Marine Railway, which repaired and cleaned ships both naval and commercial during the first decade of the twentieth century. He was its managing director for many years. The company built four ships for the Canadian Pacific Steamship Company, including the *Princess Beatrice*, launched in 1904, and the *Princess Maquinna*, launched in 1914 at about the time he sold the firm to Yarrows Ltd. in January 1914. He also repaired several warships. When he died in 1921, he was widely recognized as the founder of the BC shipbuilding industry. For himself and his family, he built a yacht, *I'll Away*, with eight berths, but in 1917, when it was evaluated at $5,000, he and his wife donated it to the Red Cross. He died, aged sixty-three, on 2 October 1921 in Esquimalt, leaving his son, William Fitzherbert Bullen, who died, aged twenty-two, on 30 March 1945 in Germany.
Sources: *Colonist*, 3 March 1917, p. 10; 3 October 1921, p. 1, obit.; Duffus, *Beyond the Blue Bridge*, pp. 51-8; Morgan, *Canadian Men and Women*, p. 168; Harry Gregson, *A History of Victoria, 1842-1970* (Vancouver, J. J. Douglas, 1970), p. 149.

BULLOCK-WEBSTER, William Howard (c. 1866-1945). An officer with Imperial origins serving in the BC Provincial Police Force from 1892, he later became a lawyer in Victoria, married there, and had a family. English census records of 1871 show him, aged four, living with his family and two servants at Tenby, Aberdovy in Wales. His mother, Julia *née* Price, then aged forty, was born there, and his father, Thomas, was born in Hendon (London) and identified as "Retired Officer, late Captain H.M. Indian Army," aged forty-eight. Ten years earlier, these parents were living in the Herefordshire village of Eaton Bishops, which is where WB and most of his brothers and sisters were born. However, an elder sister, Amelia Bullock-Webster, aged eleven in 1861, was born in the USA at Philadelphia, about a year after the parents' marriage in 1849 at the British Embassy in Paris. Evidently, the parents had gone to the United States soon after their marriage but returned to England in time for the next child, WB's sister Eliza Evelyn, to be born in Herefordshire about 1859. The 1881 census shows her, aged twenty-four, living with her widowed mother at Mornington Villa, Leckhampton near Cheltenham, Gloucestershire, Thomas having died in 1872. They had some private income as Julia, then aged fifty-five, was "independent" and Eliza Evelyn had "no occupation."

After attending Hereford Cathedral School, Sherborne School, and Trinity College, Cambridge, WB emigrated in 1886 to BC and pre-empted land in the continental interior at Keremeos with his brother Edward, born at Eaton Bishops two years before WB. Their mother Julia went out to stay with them, along with two of their sisters, from August 1894 to April 1896 and left a diary of her venture, as well as a number of watercolour paintings of life and nature around the homestead. Some of the paintings and the diary show that Thomas and Julia Bullock-Webster spent the years 1853-1855 in South Africa, where at Stellenbosch in August 1854, Julia gave birth to a son, Sydney Carlyon Bullock-Webster, and they were living at Cape Town in 1855. The diary reveals further that Thomas served at sometime as a deputy collector in the ICS at Sind, north of Bombay, and also that Julia had another son, George Russell Bullock-Webster (1858-1934), who became an Anglican minister. Neither he nor his brother Sydney Carlyon appears in any of the three census records of the family. From other sources, we learn that George Russell became a canon of Ely Cathedral, retired to Parkstone, Dorset, in 1932, and died there two years later. In June 1929, however, he sent to *The Times* some letters he had found "in an old bundle of family letters" written to his great-grandfather, John Purvis, FRS, by Sir Humphrey Davy. *The Times* printed three of them, one dated 29 August 1812 at Dunrobin Castle, which show that the two men had spent time together in Wales as friends with a common interest in natural science. Was this John Purvis one of Julia (Price) Bullock-Webster's grandfathers? The reverend canon's interest was scientific as much as personal, he being a student of microscopic plants and a fellow of both the Linnean Society and the Royal Microscopic Society.

Several local observers in BC naturally focus on Julia's diary and paintings, but WB had a lively career in the provincial constabulary, a force founded by Sir James Douglas early in the Island's history and eventually extended to enforce the law throughout the province. During the Klondike gold rush in the late 1890s, WB was chief constable at Glenora in the Cassiar district near the Yukon with eleven officers in his command posted at Lake Bennett, Teslin Lake, Echo Cove, Fort Simpson, and Port Essington. But in 1898, he was appointed stipendiary magistrate for the County of Nanaimo, which gave him jurisdiction over a wide area of the provincial northern interior, Nanaimo being relatively more important in the early years. On 18 September 1900, he married Marie E. F. de Bou of Victoria, formerly of New Brunswick, and they had two daughters of whom Barbara became a captain in the Canadian Women's Army Corps. Established later as a lawyer in Victoria, WB was evidently active in the Church of England: In June 1910, he signed a fund-raising letter to *The Times* (London), which also bore the signatures of a dozen others, including W. Burdett-Coutts, C. A. Carus-Wilson, R. Rhodes Bristow, *J. H. Turner, and William Ridley. WB died, aged seventy-eight, on 12 January 1945 in Victoria. His wife died, aged eighty-five, on 13 December 1954 in Oak Bay.

Sources: *Colonist*, 17 February 1934, p. 3; 13 January 1945, p. 5, obit; *The Times* (London), 27 June 1910, p. 5; 6 June 1929, p. 10, L to E; 20 February 1934, obit. (Rev. George Russell Bullock-Webster); census 1861, England, RG 9/1818/173, p. 7; census 1871,; census 1871, Wales, RG 10/5602/26, p. 11; census England, RG 11/2567/71, p. 3; census 1901, England, RG 13/1546, p. 5 (George Russell Bullock-Webster); Cecil Clark, *Tales of the British Columbia Provincial Police* (Sidney, BC, Gray's Publishing Ltd., 1971), p. 78; http://www.galleries. bc.ca/AGSO/ jbulweb.html, signed RHB.

BURBIDGE, John Cecil (1897-1980). Born at Ellborough-cum-Brough in East Yorkshire, the 1901 census found him, aged three, living in Brookside in that market town with a brother and two sisters, all older than he, and their parents, Howard D. Burbidge, aged forty-one, a "Manager, Corn Trade" born in Sheffield, and his wife, Eliza D. Burbidge, aged forty-one, born at Hull, Yorkshire. They employed a housemaid and a nurse. His paternal grandfather, John Burbidge, was an Anglican clergyman from London and vicar in a series of towns around the country. After his schooling, JB became a merchant in India/ Pakistan and then joined the Royal Flying Corps as a pilot in the Great War. He was wounded in action with the infantry on his eighteenth birthday, transferred later to the RFC, and learned to fly under the instructions of his brother Maurice. Another brother, Howard Churchill Burbidge, was killed in action in 1914-1918. It was somewhere in India that JB met his wife, Clairmonde Belson, daughter of *Colonel W. H. Belson and Mrs Mabel Belson *née* Lake, sister of Sir Percy and Sir Richard *Lake, and the Burbidges were at Lahore, India, at the time of Mrs Belson's death in Saanich in May 1940. They went back to India at the end of his service in the RAF but returned in 1947, when India became independent, to live at Ardmore, about eighteen miles north of Victoria. JB died, aged eighty-three, on 10 December 1980 in Sidney, survived by his wife at home and cousins in England. His brother, *Maurice Burbidge, had died in 1977.

Sources: Notes from Richard Lake, uncle of JB's wife; census 1861, England, RG 9/3468, p. 14; census 1891 RG 12/3915, p. 17; census 1901, RG 13/4460; *Colonist*, 21 May 1940, p. 5: obit. (Belson); *Times-Colonist*, 12 December 1980, p. 50, obit.

BURBIDGE, Captain Maurice (1896-1977). He was born on 15 April 1896 at Ellborough-cum-Brough in East Yorkshire. The 1901 census found him, aged five, living in Brookside in that market town with a younger brother and two sisters and their parents, Howard D. Burbidge, aged forty-one, a "Manager, Corn Trade" born in Sheffield, and his wife, Eliza D. Burbidge, aged forty-one, born at Hull, Yorkshire. They employed a housemaid and a nurse. His paternal grandfather, John Burbidge, was an Anglican clergyman from London and vicar in a series of towns around the country. He attended Pocklington School, founded in 1514 at West Green, Pocklington, East Yorkshire—once attended *inter alia* by William Wilberforce—and was then commissioned in the Royal Artillery, aged eighteen. During the Great War, he volunteered for the air observation service in France, learned to fly in a French *Caudron* with a top speed of fifty miles an hour, a stalling speed of about 40 mph, and no ailerons; he became an instructor after thirty-five hours of flying, transferred to the Royal Flying Corps, and spent the rest of the war as an instructor and bomber pilot, doing no artillery observation at all. In April 1917, the Gosport system of flying training was adopted and things improved a little. He joined a Handley-Page night-bomber squadron commanded by Trenchard, later Lord Trenchard, chief of air staff.

After the war, he stayed in the RAF. "When he was with 65 Squadron at Ford Junction, waiting to go out to India, a factory test pilot arrived with a D1110 to show the squadron's pilots how to fly this new machine . . . In 1925 the Fleet Air Arm of the Royal Navy was formed and about thirty-five naval and Royal Marine officers were sent to No. 1 Flying Training School of the R.A.F. at Netherhaven." He was a flight commander there. In 1928, he transferred to the reserve of officers and took a civilian pilot's license. It was then that he took the job of chief instructor of the Edmonton Flying Club, on the advice of Thomas Cowley, then RCAF liaison officer at the air ministry. He worked as chief instructor at Edmonton Flying Club from 1929 to 1940 and figures prominently in the club's early history. In December 1931, meanwhile, he was one of the pilots taking the first airmail from Edmonton to Fort McMurray, Chippewyan, Fort Smith, and Aklavik down the Mackenzie River. From 1940 to 1942, he was chief instructor at No. 16 elementary Flying Training School, which took over the Edmonton Flying Club, and in 1942, he went to Lethbridge as airport manager. A year later, he and Harry Hayter went to Costa Rica to join the staff of Transportes Aerios Centralano Americano, as operations manager of the Nicaragua-Panama section. Upon retiring to Victoria in 1953, MB accepted a "temporary" post as a master at St Michael's School but retired after six years because he developed an allergy to chalk dust. After that, he lived with his sisters Sybil and Lesley in semi-retirement "in a big rambling house on spacious grounds at Colwood," a western suburb of Victoria. There he died, aged ninety-one, on 2 September 1977.

Sources: G. E. Mortimer, "Aviator by Accident," *Victoria Daily Colonist*, 29 March 1959, *Sunday Magazine* pp. 2-3, a rambling, page-long article based on an interview; census 1901, England, RG 13/4460 [the name garbled as "Burbridge"]; various histories of the Edmonton Flying Club, founded in 1927; census 1901, England, RG 13/4460; census 1891, RG 12/3915, p. 17; census 1861, RG 9/3468, p. 14 (father).

BURNS, Thomas Fox (c. 1859-1939). Born in Winesgate, County Wicklow, Ireland, he joined the Wicklow Militia in 1877 but three years later enlisted in the Fifth Dragoon Guards at Rupert Lane, Liverpool. He soon volunteered for Egypt with the Fourth Dragoon Guards, received the Queen's Victoria Medal and Khedive Star in 1882, returned to England, and rejoined the Fifth Dragoon Guards at York. However, in 1884, he went again to Egypt, this time with the Kerry Camel Corps, and fought on the Nile in 1884 and 1886 for which he received the bar for the Nile and the bar for Abu Klea. In 1912, Burns retired to Victoria and lived there twenty-seven years, mainly at 54 Cadillac Avenue, Saanich, where he died on 6 February 1939 and had a funeral at St Andrew's Roman Catholic Cathedral, leaving his by his wife.

Sources: *Colonist,* 7 February 1939, p. 3, obit.

BURSEY, Sergeant George Butler (c. 1881-1937). Born at Ringwood, Hampshire, son of George B. Bursey, a carpenter, and his wife Mary, he was recorded there in 1881, aged two months, living with his family in Christchurch Street. In 1899, he enlisted in the Sixth Dragoon Guards in 1899 and spent three years in the South African War before being posted to India. There at Mhow, Central India, he transferred in 1907 to the army reserve, his army term having expired. He was then a sergeant, and after three years on reserve, he received a discharge in October 1911 and took up farming at Killarney, Manitoba, and then at Swift Current, Sask., before coming to Victoria in 1928. Bursey died, aged fifty-six, on 6 September 1937 in Victoria.

Sources: census 1881, England, RG 11 1198/20, page 2; *Colonist,* 16 September 1937, p. 2, obit.

BUTLER, Lieutenant Francis Algernon (1878-1936). He was born at Mentane in the south of France, eldest son of Captain John Bayfor Butler, RN, and Mrs Butler *née* Hon. Sybil Catherine Devereaux, and he was a grandnephew of Lord Tredegar, who led the charge of the Light Brigade during the Crimean War. His mother was born at 12 Portland Place, London, and there were noble relatives in the background: Before FB's birth, the 1871 census found his parents, aged thirty-eight and twenty-six, with their three-year-old son, Percy Butler born at Malta, and their daughter Nora Butler, born only three months earlier at West Nesson, Essex, all living at "Tregoyd Mansion" in Breconshire, South Wales, home of Mrs Butler's brother, Viscount Tregoyd, and his family. Twenty years later, she was a widow living at 21 Alexandra Road, Bedford, with her two sons: FB, then aged thirteen, and Humphrey Butler, aged ten. There were three servants. When FB was twenty, he joined the British Army in the South African War and went on to serve in 1902-1905 as superintendent of police in West Africa and Northern Nigeria, beginning while the high commissioner, Frederick Lugard, and his wife Flora Shaw were still there. In 1906, FB went to Canada and worked until 1914 as assistant superintendent of the government fish hatchery at Banff. When he enlisted on 2 March 1916 at Lethbridge, Alberta, he described his occupation as "Outside Civil Service." He claimed to have served for eleven years in the Fifth

British Middlesex Regiment, three years in the Cape Mounted Rifles, sixteen months in the Police in Northern Nigeria, and three months in the Eighty-second Battery. He was soon sent overseas in the CEF with the 113th Battalion. His wife was then Dorothy Jean Butler, living at PO Box 244, Banff, Alberta, but twelve years after he returned in 1919, they moved to Sidney, VI, and farmed on McTavish Cross Road at a place they called "Wendover." There he died, aged fifty-eight, of a heart attack on 20 June 1936, leaving his widow Dorothy and three daughters and his younger brother Humphrey then in the Federated Malay States. He was buried at Holy Trinity Anglican Church, Patricia Bay.

Sources: NAC, RG150, box 1343-8; *Saanich Peninsula and Gulf Island Review*, 24 June 1936, p. 3; *Colonist*, 24 June 1936, p. 4; 26 June 1936, p. 3, obit.; census 1871, England, RG [illegible], p. 2; census 1891, England, REG 12/1252, p. 20; for the West African, see Margery Perham, *Lugard: The Years of Authority, 1898-1945: The Second Part of the Life of Frederick Dealtry Lugard, Later Lord Luagrd of Abinger, P.C., G.C.M.G., C.B., D.S.O.* (Collins, 1960), part I.

BUTLER, Captain George Stephen (1834-1885). He was born at Solerton, Hampshire, and the census of 1851 found him living as a student of seventeen at the Royal Academy, Cold Harbour, in the parish of Alverstoke in Gosport. He joined the Seventeenth Regiment soon afterwards and fought in the Crimean War (1854-1856), wherein he was wounded at Sebastopol. According to his son Claude's account, much later at a meeting of the BC Historical Association, GB transferred for duty at Quebec in 1856 and went to the Cariboo to work as a miner in 1861. If this was correct, he must have gone home for a visit early that year, for in March 1861, he was found by the census, aged twenty-seven, already a "Retired Officer," living at Portchester vicarage, Hampshire, with an uncle, Rev. Charles R. Butler, vicar of Portchester, and three servants. Six years later, he went to Victoria, married there on 17 March 1868, and settled in Saanich, where his wife Fanny Catherine *née* Brett (1843-1920), a grocer's daughter from Portsea near his part of Hampshire, became the first woman school mistress in the district. She had the first piano there, too, and farmers came for miles to borrow it for dances, carting it off in horse-drawn wagons. GB died, aged fifty, on 7 November 1885 in South Saanich and was buried as an Anglican.

His widow Fanny lived on, and the 1901 census in the Victoria district found her, aged fifty-seven, living on a family farm in South Saanich, section 13, with her son Wilfred Stephen Butler (b. in BC in 1870), "farmer and gold miner," and his wife Virginia *née* Rey. Fanny's other sons were labourers on the farm: Claude (b. 22 October 1876), Hugh Arthur (b. 22 August 1873), and Geoffrey Thomas (b. 1 August 1877). With them were her several daughters: May (b. 17 November 1876), Gladys (b. 1 August 1879), a school teacher, Doris Victoria (b. 28 June 1881), and Rosalie Maud (b. 21 March 1889), who on 21 March 1889 had married Percy Fremlin Scharschmidt, collector of customs, born on 5 February 1892 at Comox. With this couple were their two young daughters, Daphne and Winifred, and two sons, Fanny's grandsons, Howard and Guy Hope Scharschmidt. The latter served

during the Great War as a lieutenant in the Sixty-seventh Battalion, CEF. Fanny, GB's widow, died aged sixty-eight on 15 November 1920, still in Saanich.
Sources: Records of St Stephen's Anglican Church, Saanichton; *Colonist*, 1 February 1936, p. 2; census 1851, England, HO 107/1660, f. 278; census 1861, RG 9/650, p. 5; census 1851, HO 107/1658, f. 252; Canadian census, 1901, Victoria and district.

BUTLER, Robert (1842-1917). Born in Manchester, he came from England on the *Thames City* with the Royal Engineers led by Colonel Wolfenden in the 1858-1863 period, remained behind when they left, and spent several years in the Cariboo and elsewhere in the interior. He was employed later by the King's Printer of the province and moved to Victoria with the printing establishment when the provincial capital was established there. He was a Freemason and a talented marksman in the Fifth Regiment, sent in 1876 to represent Victoria at Wimbledon, and complimented a few years later by the Marquis of Lorne, visiting the Island, for his skill in firing a 61-pounder muzzle-loading gun at Finlayson Point. He was believed to be the oldest civil servant in the province when he died, aged seventy-four, on 12 June 1917 in Victoria. He left his widow and six grown-up children.
Sources: Beth Hill, *Sappers: The Royal Engineers in British Columbia* (Ganges, BC, Horsdal & Shubert, 1987), p. 139; *Colonist*, 14 June 1917, p. 7, obit. and photo.

BUTTERS, Captain Ord Adams (1882-1971). He was born at Dumfermline, Fife, Scotland, son of Hugh Butters and his wife, Christina Adams, a Scottish couple who had married on 20 January 1876 at Beath, Fife, and lived near Dumferline at a place they called "Masterton." OB gave his permanent address as Broomfield, Dumferline, when on 12 March 1915, he applied for a temporary commission in the Regular Army "for the period of the war." Already, however, his address for correspondence was c/o Imperial Bank of Persia, 25 Fenchurch (Abchurch, etc.,?) Lane, London, EC. On the form, he answered a question about whether he could ride by writing, "I play polo and have done some hunting and racing." He had served previously in the "2 R.V.B. The Royal Scots, Edinburgh" and in the Fife and Forfar Yeomanry. When asked why he had resigned from that unit in October 1909, he replied, "Retired before leaving for Persia." With that experience behind him, he served in the Great War as a captain in the Wiltshire Regiment, then as assistant political officer in Mesopotamia and finally in Persia, where he commanded the Fourth Cavalry, South Persia Rifles, a force raised in 1916 and led by Percy Sykes. He was decorated with the OBE. After the war, he gave up his commission on 26 October 1920, joined (or rejoined?) the British Bank of the Middle East and was chief manager of it when he retired in 1939 and migrated to Victoria. He had spent about thirty years in Persia, and his wife Irene *née* Vanneman had been born there to a British family.

They lived for many years at 1476 Beach Drive, Oak Bay, and were inevitably called on to address audiences of people much like themselves. OB spoke, for instance, to the Overseas League about modern Iran on 3 February 1941 at the

Empress Hotel, and she did the same on 2 November 1942 concerning "The Intimate Life of the Persian People." In 1948, they were joined in Victoria by his niece and her husband, Major General R. P. L. Ranking, CB, CBE, MC, who arrived by ship from India and put up at the Clive Apartment Hotel, Oak Bay. Mrs Ranking, MBE, had served in 1942-1946 as senior commander of the Women's Auxiliary Corps in India. They came to see whether the Island might suit them in their retirement, but must have decided against it as nothing more was heard of them. The Island was beginning to lose its charm for such people after the Second World War, partly because it was less determinedly British and even more because the pound sterling was losing its exchange value and was seriously devalued in 1949. As for OB, when he died, aged eighty-eight, on 16 November 1971, he had lived in Victoria for thirty-two years.

Sources: PRO, WO 339/27043; *Colonist*, 4 October 1939, p. 6; 4 February 1941, p. 7; 3 November 1942, p. 4; 18 November 1971, p. 56, obit.; *Victoria Times*, 30/10/1940, p. 11; 27/11/1940, p. 11; 4/12/1942, p. 10; *Colonist* 30/10/1940, p. 13; 3/11/1942, p. 4; 11 February 1948, p. 6. For the South Persia Rifles, see Antony Wynn, *Persia in the Great Game: Sir Percy Sykes, Explorer, Consul, Spy* (John Murray, 2003), chapter 17.

CALCOTT, Frederick Septimus Berkeley (c. 1864-1917). He was born at Oundle, Northamptonshire, son of George Wallis Berkeley Calcott, a prominent surgeon born at Cheltenham, and his wife Annie Persia Calcott of Oundle. FC's uncle Rev. John W. C. B. Calcott was an Anglican minister born at Newcastle-on-Tyne. One of at least eight children, FC was away at school from an early age, attended Clifton College, and went into railway engineering. The 1891 census recorded him, aged twenty-seven, at Portland, Dorset, in the "District Verne Citadel" as "civil engineer, royal engineers department." For ten years, he was employed on the construction of the Cape to Cairo Railway from Mafeking to Bulawayo. He served in the South African War with Lieutenant Colonel Herbert Plumer's force, an irregular corps sometimes called the Matabeleland Relief Force, and was awarded the Queen's Medal with two clasps.

After that war, about 1905, he migrated to Cowichan Station in the Cowichan Valley, where he lived at "Woodhall" for twelve years and died, aged fifty-three, on 6 June 1917 at Essondale, leaving only his widow. There was no obituary mention of his many brothers and sisters in England.

Sources: *Cowichan Leader*, 14 June 1917, obit.; *Colonist*, 17 June 1917, p. 16, obit.; Lieut. Col. Herbert Plumer, *An Irregular Corps in Matabeleland* (Kegan Paul, Trench, Trübner & Co. Ltd., 1897), 251 pp.; census 1871, England, RG 10/1511, p. 11; census 1891, RG 12/1650, p. 29.

CAREY, Colonel Herbert Clement (1865-1948), CMG. He was born in Victoria in 1865, son of Joseph Westrop Carey (1832-1910), an Anglo-Irish land surveyor who had arrived in 1858 and served as mayor of Victoria in 1883-1884. After attending local schools and RMC, Kingston, HC was commissioned in 1884 in the Royal Engineers and served a long career in England, Halifax, Bermuda, and Hong Kong. After seven years at the War Office in London, he was posted to Ireland and later to Jamaica, where he was a lieutenant colonel until 1914. From 1914 to 1918, he was commander in Northern Ireland, twice mentioned in the *London Gazette* for meritorious service, and awarded the CMG. In retirement, he returned to Victoria, where he lived at 1737 Rockland Avenue with his wife, Kitty, and their daughter Ines, who married a Mr Mottershead. His mother, Caroline Louise Carey, had died, aged seventy, on 19 April 1899 in Victoria and his father, aged eighty-one, on 28 April 1910, having lived latterly at 318 Douglas Street. HC himself died, aged eighty-two, on 30 November.

Sources: *Colonist*, 9 June 1934, p. 8; 2 December 1948, p. 27.

Lt.—Col. Lewis Carey

CAREY, Lieutenant Colonel Lewis A. deVic (1871-1936). Born at St Martins on the island of Guernsey, he was recorded there, two months old in April 1971, living on Friquet Road with his family. His father, Adolphus Carey, born at St Martins, gave his occupation as "Secretariat" though the 1881 census listed him as a "Wine Merchant." LC's mother, Susan F. Carey, was born at Weymouth, England, and in 1871, he had two older sisters, though three brothers and another sister were added by 1881. There were four servants in 1871, plus a nurse in 1881. The family was Anglican, and he was schooled at Elizabeth College, Guernsey, and at Sherborne School in Dorset. He later said that he first came to Victoria at the age of nineteen but soon returned to England, and it was certainly he whom the 1891 census found boarding with a farmer and family at Whipton Barton, Heavitree (near Tiverton) in Devon. After training at Rhodesia House in 1894-1895, he was first commissioned in December 1899 in the Yorkshire Regiment but served through the South African War as a leader of mounted infantry from the Devon Imperial Yeomanry, Seventh Battalion, and reached the rank of lieutenant on 27 March 1901. He was at Druetdorp, Febanction, Weyvet, Orange River, Pretoria, and Diamond Hill and with Lord Frederick Roberts from Bloemfontein to Pretoria. Not retiring after the war, he went on to serve in the Matabele Rebellions (first in 1893 and second in 1895-1896), which gave him the opportunity to do much hunting, which he discussed later in his book, *My Gun and I: A Book of Shooting Memories* (P. Allan, 1933, 273 pp.). He was able to add, "I understand the Matabele language and can speak it reasonably well." After the South African War, he went back to live in Victoria, where in 1909-1910, perhaps longer, he found employment with the real-estate firm of Carey & Tunnard. He must have returned to England, however, possibly after the collapse of the property market in 1912-1913, because he re-enlisted with the Fifteenth Durham Light Infantry on the day Great Britain declared war in August 1914, giving his permanent address as "The Wolds, Tring, Hertfordshire." In August 1916, he was gazetted as second in command of the Eleventh APWD, rising to lieutenant colonel in October 1916. He was in the first battle of Mons, wounded at the battle of Loos, won the OBE, and, upon recovering, took command of a Welsh Regiment. Late in the war, he commanded a camp at Ripon with more than ten thousand men under him. In 1919, he got permission to go back to Vancouver Island, and at that time, his last address in England was No. 9, Lansdown Crescent, Bath. But earlier, he had lived for a time at "The Cottage," Marchington Hall, Marchington, Staffordshire.

On 17 July 1919, a medical board at Caxton House, London, granted LC six months sick leave with permission to proceed to BC on full pay. "I made arrangements with my bankers to forward same to Victoria every month," he wrote on 17 December to the Imperial Pension Office, Ottawa. "Since my arrival on October 16th last I have received no pay, but a few days ago I received a letter from the War Office stating that as I was not likely to be fit for General Service I must relinquish my commission. Now Sir, as I am entirely dependent on my pay, and have a wife and six children to provide for, and as it may be some considerable time before I receive my gratuity or pension, I respectfully ask if H.Q., Ottawa, will advance me monies . . . My gratuity amounts to £500, having served my country since September 1914 . . ." His family had joined him by then as the authorities had agreed in September 1919 "to provide passage for the wife, family and nurse of Lieut.-Colonel Vic-Carey at ordinary shipping rates." There is a series of letters written in 1926, and in all of them, LC had given his address either as Curtis Point, Sidney, BC, or Swartz Bay, Sidney, BC, these referring to the same place. He was paid a gratuity of £427.16.0 on 20 December 1919. The last letter on the file is a copy of one he wrote to the War Office on 8 November 1926: "Sir, About a year ago, I had the honour to write to you respecting my pension and also to inform you that the Pension Board at Ottawa were taking one-third of my pension unjustly and though I have written to them explaining their mistake they take no notice. I had hoped that some action through the War Office would have had some effect, but up to date the Ottawa Board still continue to unjustly deprive me of my pension. I also in my last letter drew your attention to the fact that my Pension was too small to keep myself and family and that I found it impossible to make both ends meet. I now again write to say that this condition still exists and had it not been for charity my family would have starved. I therefore hope Sir you will take immediate action and look into my very deplorable case."

To add to his small Imperial pension, he soon took to writing about the hunting and fishing he loved so much, and in 1921-1923, the *Daily Colonist* published a series of his articles. He wrote well, and many thought him a leading sportsman. "Having handled a gun since early youth," one of his admirers wrote, "he had shot game ranging from the lion and African buffalo to the local blue grouse. It is difficult for the hunter of today to emulate the exploits of Sir Samuel Baker, Gordon Cumming, [Frederick] Selous and other famous nimrods of the last century, but Colonel Carey comes as near to the feat as possible in his accounts of sport in Europe, Africa and North America. Along with Clive Phillipps-Wolley and Warburton Pike, Colonel Carey was one of the good English sportsmen who have made their home out here." Game birds in England, the west of Ireland, Germany, California, and France during the Great War, wolves and grizzly bears in BC, and even a murderous Kaffir in Rhodesia, all fell to his gun. He seems to have missed only India and Asia in general.

LC loved every aspect of hunting and fishing as sport, worried about industrial pollution of streams, suggested that fish hatcheries and nurseries be established at Elk Lake, and wrote about pheasants, their breeding and their enemies, as well as about dogs. "In every part of the world, wherever I have been, a dog has always been beside me . . . It goes without saying that we love our dogs next to our wives, and some of us more. Here in B.C. I have no hesitation in saying that we are more dependent on our dogs than in any other part of the globe." He even expressed sympathy with hostile farmers and remarked in an open "Letter to Shooters" (*Colonist*, 26 November 1924, p. 11): "By the way, did you hear of the "gentleman" who killed five tame turkeys and a white leghorn rooster in North Saanich last week? Why can't we get hold of him and kick him till his nose bleeds? Then lead him out with a ring through that member and make him pay the owner the value of the birds." He thought every boy should be brought up from his earliest youth to care for his gun, and he advised wearing woollen clothing because he had concluded after many years that there was no way to keep dry in that part of the world and one might as well be prepared to get soaked. But he thought the Island as a sportsman's paradise and recalled earlier events with pleasure: "I well remember March 25, 1910, the opening day of the season, going up to Duncan by the early train, which had a fair sprinkling of the right sort on board," etc. After his book of shooting memories, LC went on to write another called *The Wandering Angler*, probably based on articles to the *Colonist* and he was still revising it when he died.

LC appears in the 1901 census to have married at sometime in the middle 1890s and by 1901 had two daughters, Winsome and Joan, but his wife Mildred probably died, as he married again on 31 January 1906, at a time when his mother and his second wife both lived at 9 Lansdown Crescent in Bath. On the Island, they lived at various places in North and Central Saanich from 1924, but on 6 April 1929, their house burnt to the ground and they moved to 560 Rithet Street, Victoria, where he died, aged sixty-four, on 16 January 1936 and was buried at St Stephen's Church on Mount Newton Crossroad. He left his widow and two daughters Betty and Peggy, as well as a son Rex, well known as an amateur boxer, who died in Italy as a lieutenant in the PPCLI in December 1943. Pallbearers at LC's funeral were *Major Roger Monteith, *Francis John Barrow, Arthur Pitts (1889-1972), A. W. Perkins, George Buchanan Leckie-Ewing, and J. L. Tait. The *Colonist* wrote an editorial eulogy and J. W. Lowther published "An Appreciation," both of them speaking of his prowess as a hunter, a fisherman, a soldier, and an all-round sportsman with a sterling character.

Sources: PRO; WO 339 21750 (1915-1919), a file of correspondence, half an inch thick, concerning retirement and pension problems; Army List, January 1916, part 2, page 2461; *Colonist*, 15 May 1921, Sunday p. 19; 9 October 1921, Sunday p. 22; 23 January 1921, p. 18; 30 January 1921, p. 20; 15 May 1921, Sunday, p. 19; 26 November 1924, p. 11; 3 December 1924, p. 10; 16 December 1924, p. 10; 3 February 1929, p. 4, and 13 February 1929; 11 September 1929, p. 4; 6 April 1929, p. 2; 17 January 1936, pp. 1-2; 18 January 1936, p. 4; 19 January 1936, pp. 4 and 5; 22 December 1943, p. 11; census 1871, St Martins, Guernsey, RG 10/5768, p. 4; census 1881, St Andrews, Guernsey, RG 11/5630, p. 14; census 1891, England, RG 12/1680, p. 24; census 1901, RG 13/2023, p. 8.

CARTER, Wing Commander Albert (c. 1895-1956). Sometimes noted as "Canada's Pioneer Parachute Officer," he was born in Leeds, Yorkshire, and served in the Royal Flying Corps from 1917, establishing memorable jumping records with a parachute, sometimes from over twenty thousand feet without oxygen. At sometime between the world wars, he joined the RCAF and migrated with his wife Constance to Victoria, where they lived for fifteen years at 842 Selkirk Street. In the Second World War, he became senior administrative officer at the Patricia Bay Station in North Saanich. Next to his RCAF Station, there was an RAF station, which I remember well as it took over North Saanich High School during my first year there, and RAF officers graciously gave our Boy Scout Troop a weekly course in aircraft structure and maintenance. AC retired in 1943 from the RCAF after twenty-one years of service and died, aged sixty-one, on 8 November 1956, leaving his wife Constance at home and a sister in England. He is sometimes confused with another heroic Canadian Imperial flyer, Major Albert Desbrisay Carter (1892-1919) of the Royal Flying Corps.

Sources: *Colonist*, 11 November 1956, p. 9, obit.

CARTWRIGHT, Edward Rogers (1883-1975). Having returned home after working as a cowhand on the Okanagan Ranch of his elder brother, William Henry Cartwright (1881-1962), who eventually had a career as a BC land surveyor, EC sailed from Liverpool in April 1903 on *The Dominion* and took the CPR to Vancouver and on to Victoria, the entire voyage (excluding food) costing £28. He then spent some years employed on the Crofton family's 160-acre farm on Salt Spring Island, at the head of Ganges Harbour (now Harbour House Hotel). He had already qualified in mining engineering at the Camborne School of Mines, after some years at Radley, and next began to work as a mining engineer up the Skeena, Bulkley and Telkwa rivers, and also on Vancouver Island around Cowichan Bay. During the Great War, he served as an officer in the RE, went on to the army of occupation in Germany, and retired as a captain decorated with the CBE. On 6 April 1925, he landed at Victoria from the *Empress of Canada*, coming from Hong Kong, in the hope of picking up the threads of his life there again but was disappointed. There followed many years in various parts of the Orient, where he was employed by the Shell Oil Company and other firms. About 1958, he retired to "Willow Cottage" at Beaminster in Dorset, near the parish church, with his wife Frances Elizabeth and spent his time fishing, hunting, travelling abroad, and writing his memoirs.

EC was born on 31 March 1883 at Bampton Bryon, Herefordshire, the second of six children brought up in Radnorshire at "The Milebrook" near the River Terne on the five thousand acres of the Stonage Estate, which their father was managing for a cousin, Charles Coltman Rogers. EC's mother was from a wealthy family that "grew up thinking that nothing mattered except the Church and hunting," though they lost a great deal after the South African War. Her father (EC's grandfather) was one of the Poole Kings of Bristol involved in shipping to West Africa and appears in the 1881 census as William Thomas Poole King, aged seventy-four, born in Bristol, "African Merchant and Ship Owner," living at Avon Side, Clifton, Gloucestershire, with his wife Victoria M. L. King, aged sixty-one, born at Milverton in Somerset. Florence Mary King, aged thirty-six. One of their three grown-up sons (EC's uncles) was also an "Africa Merchant," and the other two were both "Timber Importers," one being also a shipowner and the other an accountant. The household had six servants. The 1891 census shows EC aged eight living at Standish House, Tewksbury, Gloucestershire, with his grandmother, Annie King, a widow aged fifty-nine, born in Hampshire at Stonehouse. In the household were her son and four daughters, all born at Brislington, Somerset, as well as some of her nieces and nephews and no fewer than thirteen servants: housekeeper, butler, valet, footman, two housemaids, a kitchenmaid, another maid, two laundresses, and three stablemen or grooms. EC's death was registered at Bridport, Dorset, in the last quarter of 1875, vol. 23, p. 454, and his wife's in the March quarter of 1976, vol. 18, p. 861. His memoirs are entertaining but reveal few precise details of his life and movements. I did not, for instance, discover when and where he was married.

Sources: Thanks to Dominic Thornton, Dorset History Centre, Bridport Road, Dorchester, for information about EC's death; E. R. Cartwright, *A Late Summer: The Memoirs of E.R. Cartwright*, C.B.E. (London, Caravel Press, 1964), 224 pp.; census 1881, England, RG11 2483/101, p. 4; census 1891, RG 12/2019, p. 12; census 1901, RG13/2355, p. 36; Canadian Passenger Lists 1865-1935, T-14881, arriving 6 April 1925 at Victoria from Hong Kong; UK Incoming Passenger Lists, no. 180091, arriving 23 January 1953; British Army Records, WW I online.

CAVENAGH, Major Orfeur (1885-1971). After retiring from the [British] Indian Army, he went out to Canada, joined the Alberta Provincial Police force but moved about 1927 to Cortez Island, where he built "Shalomar Lodge" as a holiday place, and then moved on to Sooke, west of Victoria, where in the 1930s, he kept "Glenairly," a farmhouse with six bedrooms, a billiard room, tennis court, and horses, which he worked in as sort of holiday camp. At some stage, he also had a dairy farm on the mainland. When he died, aged eighty-five, in Saanich, he left a son and a daughter.

He was born at York on 21 October 1885 (the NAC, CEF files Internet birth date 1895 is a misreading of the form) and named after his father, who was born in India about 1850 and retired as lieutenant colonel to "Clermont," Farnham, in Surrey. The census found the family living there in 1891. The mother, Caroline Cavenagh, then aged thirty-two and born in India, had also a daughter aged ten, Mabel N. Cavenagh, born at York, as well as a brother (OC's uncle), Arthur J. Colledge, aged twenty-seven and born in India, "living on his own means." They had a "Governess (school)," a male cook, and a groom. The 1901 census found young OC, then aged fifteen, on a list of students at Haileybury College, Great Amwell, Hertfordshire. When he enlisted at Valcartier on 23 September 1914, he was a "rancher," unmarried, his next of kin living at Steyning, Sussex, and he had had three years service in the Royal Garrison Artillery. He was 5' 9" tall, with fair complexion, blue eyes, fair hair, and tattoos: a rabbit on his left arm and on his right forearm a bulldog, a fox, and a bird. He served in Mesopotamia and, either before or after the Great War, in a cavalry unit of the Indian Army on the North-West Frontier and elsewhere, becoming a champion tent-pegger, according to family memory. Two earlier generations of the family had served in India, returning when possible to their home in England, which was "Moudlyn" at Steyning in Sussex. It served in the Great War as a hostel for Canadian soldiers. The outstanding member of the family was OC's grandfather, Major General Sir Orfeur Cavenagh (1820-1891), born at Hythe, Kent, and educated at Addiscombe, the East India Company School, who served for many years in India, then as lieutenant governor of the Straits Settlements from 8 April 1859 to 15 March 1867, and died on 7 July 1891 in England at Long Ditton; his offices in Singapore have been preserved, and a footbridge was named after him.

Sources: NAC, RG150, CEF files, box 1587-5; notes from his daughter and family papers at the University of Victoria, rare book room, including 13 MSS volumes of Major General Sir Orfeur's diaries; census 1891, England, RG 12/569, p. 19; census 1901, RG 13/1279; General Sir Orfeur Cavenagh, *Reminiscenses of an Indian Official* (W. H. Allen & Co., 1884), 372 pp; Captain Orfeur Cavenagh, *Rough Notes on the State of Nepal, Its Government, Army and Resources* [with a map], (Calcutta, Privately Printed, 1851), 264 pp. in 12_; *The Native Army in India: A Paper etc.* (1879), 22 pp.; F. Boase, *Modern English Biography*, 6 vols., 1892-1921; Riddick, *Who in British India*, p. 68.

CHAMBERS, Admiral Bertram Mordaunt (1866-1945). In the course of his lifelong career in the RN, he visited the Island more than once. The BC Archives, MS-2748, have his logbooks as midshipman; he cruised the BC coast in several RN vessels from October 1884 to September 1885, as he relates in his memoirs, *Salt Junk* (1927). "During the whole of our time at Esquimalt we used to lose a great many men by desertion; it was so easy to slip into one of the sound ferry boats and in an hour or two they could be in the [United] States, where desertion was not recognized as a crime" (p. 100). As for the Island, he loved it for the fishing and shooting it offered as well as the social life in Victoria. The careful reader of *Salt Junk* will be wary on two points: he usually refers to the Island as "Vancouver," trusting his readers to know that Vancouver City did not exist until 1886 and that when founded it was separated from Victoria by a sea voyage of some seventy-five miles. Secondly, he is companionable and his reminiscences about his family are relaxed and modest, but like icebergs, they show only what is on the surface.

Through his father, an English barrister named Charles Harcourt Chambers (1826-1876), born at Bombay, India, and his grandfather Charles Harcourt Chambers (1789-1828), a judge in the Supreme Court in India, BC descended from a brother of Sir Robert Chambers (1737-1803), a famous judge in India. Through his mother, Lucebella Hare, born *circa* 1824 near Torguay, Devon, BC descended from the great Stanley family of barons and baronets of Alderley in Cheshire. At Alderley on 24 September 1833, his maternal grandfather, Lieutenant Marcus Theodore Hare, RN (1796-1845), had married Lucy Anne Stanley (1798-1869), and their son, Captain Marcus Chambers, RN (1836-78), was "a loveable person" and an uncle whom BC liked. He was less fond of his humourless, snobbish "Aunt Hilda," Matilda Jane Tollemache, but as a child saw a good deal of her after his uncle married her on 17 June 1873. She was a niece of the Duke of Somerset and played a big role in the family after BC's father died. Before long, his widowed mother Lucebella made a second marriage with John Alexander Strong, a senior clerk at the Admiralty, and produced two stepbrothers, who both grew up to become Anglican clergymen. In the 1920s, one of them, Rev. Eustace Mordaunt Strong, held a living as vicar of a church at East Claydon, which was in the gift of *Captain Edmund Hope Verney's father, a curious connection. BC's family ramified in many directions with no lack of naval and military officers. For instance, his youngest sister, Ida Vere Maude Chambers (1874-1945), married Rear Admiral C. W. Winnington-Ingram (1856-1923), RN, thus making a link with another ramifying Imperial family.

It was in this setting that BC, aged fourteen, became a naval cadet on board the training ship HMS *Britannia*, embarking on a long career on the sea routes of the empire, as related in his book, *Salt Junk*. He was lent for a time to the Royal Australian Navy and listed in its official list dated 1 September 1912. At the time of the infamous explosion in the great harbour of Halifax, Nova Scotia, he had some authority there and played an important part in the aftermath, including the official inquiry, as J. G. Armstrong has recently explained. BC says characteristically little about his work at Halifax. On 11 July 1901 at St Jude's Church in South Kensington, he married Nora Annie Bertrand and the British Post Office directory for 1934 show them living in Chelsea at 1 Argyll Mansions, Beaufort Street. The National Portrait Gallery holds a portrait of him by Walter Stoneman (1919).

Sources: census 1871, RG 10/114/19, p. 29; census 1881, England, RG 11/2175, p. 10; John Griffiths Armstrong, *The Halifax Explosion and the Royal Canadian Navy* (Vancouver, UBC Press, 2002), pp. 22, 60-62-65, 67, 71, 91, 99, 189, 213 n.39; Admiral Bertram Mordaunt Chambers, *Salt Junk, Naval Reminiscences 1881-1906* (Constable, 1927), chs. xi, xxvi, and passim; T. H. Bowyer, "Chambers, Sir Robert (1737-1803), jurist and judge," *Oxford* DNB online; *The Gentleman's Magazine*, vol. 99, part I (1829), p. 566, obituary for Sir Charles Harcourt Chambers (1789-1828); Kelly's Directory, Buckinghamshire, 1928, p. 89; Riddick, *Who in British India*, p. 70 (father); C.E. Buckland, *A Dictionary of Indian Biography* (Swan, Sonenschein & Co., 1906); (repr. Westport, Conn., Greenwood Press, 1969), p. 78 (father).

CHAPMAN, Major Harold (1876-1917). Born at Goudhurst, Kent, on 23 November 1876, he attended Eton School, joined the Yorkshire Regiment, and then spent fifteen years in the British South African Police. He received the Queen's Medal and three bars for Transvaal, Relief of Mafeking, and Rhodesia and the King's Medal and two bars for 1901 and 1902. He migrated to the Island and settled at French Creek, Parksville, but early in the Great War returned to England and rejoined his old regiment in which he was wounded at Gallipoli in 1915. When he recovered in 1916, he resigned his commission in England, went home to French Creek, and enlisted at Vancouver as a private soldier in the CEF. Chapman then appeared as a tanned figure with a scar on his thigh, presumably from his wound at Gallipoli, and signed as an Anglican. He was sent overseas again, where he served in the 158th Battalion, and was killed in August 1917 by an exploding shell, leaving his wife, Irene L. Chapman.

Sources: NAC, RG 150 etc., box 1626-10; *Colonist*, 3 November 1917, p. 7, obit.

CHARLESWORTH, Second Lieutenant Alick Thomas Bentall (1893-1917). He was born on 16 January 1893 in Zanzibar, East Africa, son of a trading family. In 1871, more than twenty years before he was born, the census recorded his father, Alexander L. I. Charlesworth, aged four, born at Islington, Middlesex, living at 5 Crowland Terrace, Islington, in a large family headed by Thomas D. Charlesworth, aged forty-four, AC's grandfather, who was an "American Merchant" born at Great Yarmouth, Norfolk, and almost certainly in the "American corn trade" as the 1881 census mentioned. AC's grandmother, Margaret A. Charlesworth, was born in Scotland and had many other children. In 1881, AC's father was only thirteen, but his older brothers were already employed in the corn trade, the pharmaceuticals trade, or as commercial travellers, and we may surmise that it was trade that took AC's parents to Zanzibar at the time of his birth.

In 1909, he and his mother went out to the Island to join his father, who had gone there a year earlier. AC took employment as a surveyor in the Westholme district and lived for a time at "Craiglands," Metchosin. In October 1915, he married Elizabeth Rosina May Price of Salt Spring Island and a month later enlisted in the Canadian Army on 8 November in Victoria, leaving his wife at the Bell Apartments on Cook Street. His only military experience was eighteen months in the Officer's Training Corps at Christ's Hospital, London, but he went overseas with the Eighty-eighth Battalion, served for several months, and was then selected for a special training course for the Royal Flying Corps in England. It was while he was piloting an aircraft on 30 May 1917 that he was killed, aged twenty-four, at a time when his mother was a matron in charge of the nursing staff at the "R.N.D., Command Depot, Blandford."

Sources: NAC, CEF, box 1643-25; *Colonist*, 8 June 1917, p. 5, obit.; census 1871, England, RG 10/295, p. 45; census 1881, RG 11/249.

CHARTER, Lieutenant Richard Malet Boileau (1914-1941). Born in Duncan in 1914 to Hugh Malet Charter (c. 1886-1961) and his wife of Somenos in the Cowichan Valley, he attended St Aidan's School in Victoria and in 1926 was sent to Camberly School in England. His father, born at Southsea, Hampshire, had no military experience until—living at Duncan as a farmer—he enlisted at Victoria on 15 May 1916 as a private soldier to serve in the Great War. In 1927, the son enrolled in the Royal Naval College at Dartmouth, England, and graduated in 1932, served in the Mediterranean aboard HMS *Ramillies, Revenge,* and *Renown,* and in 1935 went to Greenwich College, London, for further training. RC was posted for a year to the destroyer HMS *Escort* taking refugees from the Spanish Civil War. From 1938 to 1941, he was stationed in China with the Yangtze River flotilla, serving most of the time on the upper river in HMS *Petrel.* On 10 January, he came home for a month's leave but was back in England on 11 March. When he was killed in 1941, he left his parents, a sister Diana, an aunt and uncle, Rev. and Mrs A. R. Fuller, in England at Sandringham, and aunts and uncles on the Island.

Sources: *Colonist*, 25 March 1941, p. 18; 26 March 1941, p. 5, obit., with photo; NAC, CEF files, box 1649-75, reg. no. 116943.

CHATTERTON, George Louis (1916-1983), MP. Born in South Africa on 16 January 1916, son of Henry B. Chatterton and Charlotte Van Zyl, he attended Boys' High School, Kimberly, SA, and Pretoria University and Cornell University, Ithaca, NY, and became an agrologist at Saanich, BC. He served overseas as a flying officer in the RCAF (1942-1946) and then became regional supervisor, Veteran's Land Act (1946-1961); director, Victoria and Vancouver Island Publicity Bureau

(1958-61); reeve and chairman of the Saanich Police Commission (1957-61); and president, Ass. of VI Municipalities 1960. He was elected to the House of Commons at a by-election on 29 May 1961, for Esquimalt-Saanich, and re-elected in 1962, 1963, and 1965, this as a Progressive Conservative. He died, aged sixty-seven, on 7 September 1983 in Vancouver City.

Sources: J. K. Johnson, ed., *The Canadian Directory of Parliament*, 1867-1967 (Ottawa, Public Archives, 1968), p. 114.

CHAWORTH-MUSTERS, William (1839-1906). The oldest son of Rev. William Musters Musters [*sic*], rector of Colwick and Westbridgford, Nottinghamshire, he took a commission as an ensign in the Ninety-sixth Regiment of Foot, which became later the Second Battalion of the Manchester Regiment. Very early in his career, he fell in love with a bricklayer's daughter, Lucy Byron (1840-78), probably a servant girl in one of his family's great houses, and when she became pregnant, he gave up his commission and they fled with a group of emigrants, travelling around Cape Horn to San Francisco, where their first child was born, and onto Vancouver Island. After landing at Victoria, they sailed to Comox in October 1862 aboard HMS *Grappler*, built a house, and lived as pioneer farmers for the next thirteen years, during which they were married in Victoria on 7 July 1867 at Christ Church Cathedral. Their life was no doubt very hard. Mrs Chaworth-Musters died soon after giving birth to a sixth child on 11 August 1878 and WC, broken-hearted, left the baby with a kind friend nearby, Mrs Margaret Carwithern, and took the other five children back to England. Two subsequent events linked the distinguished Chaworth-Musters family with the Island. The baby, a girl christened Lucy Sophia in memory of her mother at St Andrew's Anglican Church, grew up on the Island, eventually moved to Victoria, and on 14 August 1901 married a school teacher and militia soldier, the future *General Sir Arthur Currie, who was to be knighted in 1917 for his services as commander-in-chief of the Canadian Corps in the Great War. Her brother Harold Chaworth-Musters (1871-1942) went out from England to be present at the wedding. When Lady Lucy Sophia Currie died in July 1969, it was in Montreal, where her husband had been chancellor of McGill University. More than ten years earlier, however, during the 1950s, a family of one of her Chaworth-Musters cousins went out to settle in BC.

Sources: *Hart's Army List*, 1859, p. 337; Patrick T. A. Chaworth Musters, *The Musters: A Family Gathering* (Market Overton, Rutland, privately printed, 1998), pp. 100ff.; Richard Somerset Mackie, *The Wilderness Profound: Victorian Life on the Gulf of Georgia* (Victoria, Sono Nis Press, 1995), pp. 64-5, 83, 88, 92, 229; Daniel G. Dancocks, *Sir Arthur Currie: A Biography* (Toronto, Methuen, 1985), pp. 11 and 288; Edward Mallandaine, *First Victoria Directory*, fourth issue (Victoria, 1871), p. 56; A. M. J. Hyatt, General Sir Arthur Currie: A Military Biography (Toronto, University of Toronto Press, 1987), p. 7; Hugh M. Urquhart, *Arthur Currie: The Biography of a Great Canadian* (Toronto, Dent, 1950), p. 16. I am grateful to Mr and Mrs Robert Chaworth-Musters of Vancouver for information kindly given in March 2004 and to staff at the Nottingham County Record Office.

CHERRETT, William (1871-1904). He was born at 26 Burcham Street, Bromley, Kent, where the census of 1871 found him the day after his birth in the bosom of his family: his father, George Cherrett, aged twenty-six, a "joiner" born at Bluntford, Dorset; his mother, Mary Cherrett, aged twenty-three, born at Chester; and a four-year-old sister and a two-year-old brother. There were no servants, and the immediate neighbours were ropemakers and seamen. He enlisted very young as a bombardier in the Royal Garrison Artillery and was discharged from the regiment in 1903 at Singapore and set out for Victoria with a letter of introduction to Mr J. Martyn of Rithet Street. Before he could settle there, he was drowned, aged thirty-three, as a passenger on SS *Clallam*, which foundered on 8 January 1904 in a storm near Trial Island, off Victoria, on its way to Seattle, Washington. At a coroner's inquest, he was deemed a victim of manslaughter by Geo. Roberts (the ship's captain).
Sources: *Colonist*, 9 January 1904, p. 3; 10 January 1904, p. 1; 12 January 1904, p. 6; census 1871, England, RG 10/573/129, p. 9.

CHERRY, Cecil Robbins (c. 1884-1965). He was born at Windsor, Berkshire, where the 1891 census found him, aged six, living at 4 Alexander Terrace with his father, James W. Cherry, a "Solicitor, Managing Clerk," born at Newark, Nottinghamshire, and his mother, Mary M. Cherry, born at Packingham, Worcestershire. There were brothers and sisters all born at Windsor, Berks, but no servants either then or ten years later, when the family was living at 40 Grove Road, New Windsor, by which time his father had died, and CC was working as a bank clerk. In 1916, and doubtless earlier, he was living in Singapore as "Assistant" in Boustead & Co., 2 St Thomas Walk, a company of general merchants founded at Singapore in 1828 by Edward Boustead and with branches at Penang and elsewhere in Malaya. CC's name was on a "List of Qualified Jurors, Singapore." In time, he became president of the Harbour Board at Singapore and a member of the Legislative Council, and he and his wife were still there when Japanese forces attacked and seized the place during the Second World War. The Cherrys organized a St John's Ambulance Corps and otherwise helped in war work. The Japanese took CC prisoner, but his wife was killed when the ship carrying women and children away was shelled at sea by Japanese forces. CC already had a sister in Victoria, Mrs M. C. Ellis of 225 Oak Bay Avenue, and late in September 1943, she heard that he was still alive. What he did thereafter is not clear, but in 1961, he settled in Victoria, where four years later he died, aged eighty-one, on 17 September 1965, leaving his sister and younger relatives.
Sources: *Colonist*, 29 September 1943, p. 4; 18 September 1965, p. 22, obit.; census 1891, England, RG 12/1011, p. 19; census 1901, RG 13/1168, p. 39; Terry Foenander, "*List of Qualified Jurors, Singapore*, 1916," Part I.

CHESNAYE, Major Christian Purefoy (c. 1870-1943). Born at Simla, India, he served for many years in Africa as a senior official in North-east Rhodesia, and in the census records for 1901, he was recorded as "Magistrate Commissioner in N.E. Rhodesia," living at "Lachesnaye," Milton Road, Bournemouth, Hampshire, with his father, George Cochet Chesnaye, aged sixty-three, born in Ireland, a "Retired Surgeon Colonel of the Indian Army," his mother, Mary Chesnaye, aged sixty-three, born in Ireland, and three servants. At sometime, CC moved to California, but retired about 1940 to Victoria, where his wife died in February 1943 and he was living at the Windermere Hotel, Courtney Street, Victoria, when he died on 7 May 1943, aged seventy-three, leaving a daughter. His French name and that of the family house in Bournemouth, not to mention the family's Protestant religion, suggest that the Chesnayes may have descended from Huguenot refugees in Ireland. A village near La Rochelle in Saintonge, whence Huguenots fled abroad in the sixteenth to nineteenth centuries, was called La Chesnaye, and the name is not uncommon in Western France.

Sources: *Colonist*, 9 May 1943, p. 24; 11 May 1943, p. 16, obit.; census 1901, England, RG 13/1041, page 44; Riddick, *Who in British India*, p. 72 (grandfather).

CHRISTENSEN, Edward Victor August (c. 1864-?). His identity is not entirely clear. What seems certain is that ill health forced him to retire from the RN in 1898 and on 28 August 1915, he married Mary Ann Tibballs at Esquimalt on the Island. A year later, aged fifty-three, and declaring himself an Anglican, he joined the Royal Canadian Rifles on 18 July 1916, by pretending to be half a dozen years younger than he was. Then he tried to get to the battle front with that regiment but was obliged to return home to his family in Esquimalt because he was judged to be too old. As he spoke seven foreign languages (Arabic, Danish, French, German, Hindustani, Kanaka, and Swedish), he took comfort in thinking that he might be useful as an interpreter. On his wife's side, there were no fewer than forty relatives in khaki, thirty-six of whom were at the front, and by 1917, three of them had been killed in action.

We are less certain of his origins and earlier life. Born in Aulbory, Denmark, on 21 October, perhaps in 1864, he seems to have joined the Royal Indian Marine at Bombay on 24 May 1888 and, the next December, transferred to HMS *Boadicea* in which he served for ten years on the India Station of the RN. He was a petty officer in that period with various duties: For example, in 1889, he acted as interpreter to the Duke of Connaught and the Duke of Clarence during their visit to India. Later he did the same for Prince Nicholas, Czar of Russia, and Prince Rudolph of Austria. In the 1891 Indian Riot, he fought in Madras and Burma while Lord Kitchener was in charge of operations and Lord Curzon was viceroy. When that was over, he re-entered the naval service on HMS *Cossack* and, in the early 1890s, went with British forces to South Africa, where he took a hand in the Jameson Raid. He was wounded twice during that fighting.

Sources: *Colonist*, 27 January 1917, p. 5; NAC, CEF files, box 1697-28; http://canadiangre.web128.discountasp.net/searche . . . .

CHRISTIE, Major Albert Edward (1860-1954). He was born in Toronto, spent his youth in Bowmanville and Brantford, lived on the prairies before the CPR was built, traded with the tribes while living in their villages, and worked on the railway survey party. His military career began in the Riel Rebellion campaign (1885) in which he was wounded at the Battle of Batoche. In 1887-1889, he served in the Thirty-eighth Battalion of Dufferin Rifles as a captain and went to the South African War in Lord Strathcona's Horse, winning the Queen's Medal with four clasps for the Transvaal, Orange Free State, and two other campaigns. He spent 1907-1911 in the Sixteenth Light Horse Reserve while employed in the Union Bank of Canada at small towns on the prairies. In 1910, the bank posted him to manage the Victoria branch. When he enlisted at Victoria on 14 August 1915, he listed his employment as "Bank Manager" but was already living at Sixty-seventh Battery, CEF, Willows Camp, Victoria, while his wife, Mary Ludlow Christie (née Wetmore), remained in their house at 604 Linden Avenue. He had joined the Union and Pacific Clubs and was an Anglican and a Freemason. He left Victoria as second in command of the Sixty-seventh Battalion, Western Scots, but was invalided home from France after winning the DSO. After the war, he was active as secretary-treasurer of the British Campaigners Association. During the Second World War, his eldest son Charles was killed in Italy, serving with the PPCLI, but his second son, John, served with the RCAF and then became financial manager of the BC Power Commission. Christie died, aged ninety-three, on 3 July 1954 in Saanich; his funeral was held at Christ Church Cathedral.

Sources: NAC, CEF files, box 1699-3; *Colonist*, 29 January 1921, p. 9; 4 July 1954, p. 15: obit and photo; Brian A. Reid, *Our Little Army in the Field: The Canadians in South Africa*, 1899-1902 (St Catharines, Ont., Vanwell Publishing Ltd., 1996), p. 151.

CLARK, James Stewart (1850-1930). He was born at Troon, Ayrshire, and trained on the Clyde at the Charles Connell yard, famous in former years for building clippers engaged in the China tea trade. Later, he went to Barrow-in-Furness, Lancashire, where he became manager of the company best known as Vickers Sons & Maxim. There, the 1881 census found him, aged thirty, employed as "Manager in Shipbuilding Yard" and residing at 10 Storey Square with his wife, Jane Stirling Clark, aged forty, born in Parton, Cumberland. He had two stepchildren: Sarah Officer aged fourteen and John Officer aged eleven, both born in Scotland. Living with them, too, was his father, Stewart Clark, a widower, a "Retired Ship's Captain," aged seventy-one born in Scotland, and JC's sister, Mary Clark, aged thirty-two, likewise Scottish. There was one servant. Before long, JC was hired to build ships in Spain, where he worked for eight years and built three of the cruisers sunk later by the U.S. Navy in the battle of Santiago, Cuba (1898). After some years back in England as a consulting naval architect, he was engaged in 1896 by the Misubishi Company to found a steel shipbuilding industry in Japan. He stayed there for twelve years during which the Anglo-Japanese alliance was formed in 1902, and he built many steel liners and other vessels for Japanese shipping companies.

By the time he retired to the Island about 1908, he was widely known as an eminent naval architect and founder of the modern Japanese shipbuilding industry. His wife died, aged sixty-six, in Victoria on 16 February 1909, and on 3 April 1912, he married Florence D. Matheson in Vancouver. They settled at Quamichan Lake, but in 1916, he undertook to build wooden vessels in BC for the Imperial Munitions Board. In particular, he was in charge of producing two CGMM vessels, the *Canadian Winner* and *The Canadian Traveler*, at the Harbour Marine Company's yard. He died, aged eighty, on 13 January in Oak Bay, leaving his wife, who happened to be travelling in Britain, a son, Stewart G. Clark of Oak Bay, and two grandchildren.

Sources: *Colonist*, 15 January 1930, p. 5, obit.; census 1881, England, RG 11/4285, page 80.

CLARK, Lieutenant Colonel Robert Percy (1874-1932). He was born in London, St Pancras, but the 1881 census found him, aged six, living at 4 Paradise Place, Green Lanes, in Stoke Newington, with his family. He was the eldest son of Robert Clark, then aged forty-one, a "Feather Merchant," born at Walworth, Surrey, and Elizabeth F. Clark, aged thirty-five, from Camden Town. Ten years later, when he was sixteen and working as a "Stockbroker's Clerk," they had moved to 52 Poet's Road in Islington, where his father was employed as "Club Secretary" and his sister Florence L. Clark, aged eighteen, was a "Millinery Saleswoman." RC fought in the British Army during the South African War and then migrated to the Island. He was living at 2749 Olympus Willows, Victoria, when he joined the CEF as a staff captain on 25 September 1914 in Valcartier Camp. Then over forty with a wife, Mildred Hope Clark, he had been employed in Victoria as an "Agent." He had had four years in the "V.B. Royal Fusiliers; two years V.S.C. Royal Fusiliers; one year Royal Can.Rifles; three months I.M.R. Volunteers; eighteen months D.F.F.A.; six months K.L.H. and eight years 5th C.G.A." After going overseas in the first draft of the Fifth Regiment of Canadian Garrison Artillery, he was quickly promoted, appointed to command the Fourteenth Canadian Battalion, and then attached to the General Staff. Retiring with the rank of lieutenant colonel, he died, aged fifty-seven, on 8 April 1932 in Vancouver, and there his wife died, aged sixty-six, on 5 November 1951.

Sources: NAC, CEF files, box 1761-3, rank Brigadier-General; *Colonist*, 17 August 1917, p. 6; census 1891, England, RG 12/173, pp. 54-5; census 1881, RG 11/282, p. 2.

CLARKE, Captain Charles Edward (1854-1925). He was born on 10 November 1854 in Taunton, Devonshire, eldest son of Charles A. Clarke, merchant, who in 1868 apprenticed him to Ismay, Irmie & Co. of the White Star Steamship Company. At sometime in 1872-1874, he went out to BC, commanded several ships on the Pacific coast over the years, and in 1889 went seal hunting in the Bering Sea. Going ashore at last, he taught school at Metchosin for three years but was appointed harbour master and port warden for Victoria in 1894. The 1901 census found him there in that post, still unmarried and with a salary of $1,200 a year, but on 7 August 1906, he married Georgena [*sic*] Barbara Potts, daughter of *Dr George Gerald Potts of Victoria, in the Church of England. They lived at 1136 Summit Avenue until he died, aged seventy-three, on 28 November 1925. She survived him with their three children and died, aged seventy-five, on 30 August 1947 in Burnaby, BC.

Sources: *Colonist*, 29 November 1925, p. 5, obit.; Canadian census, 1901, Victoria.

CLAYTON, Lieutenant Colonel Henry Edward Gilbert (1867-1948). Born in "Hindostan," India, he was recorded in 1871, aged three, living with his parents at 4 Cedars Road, Clapham, Wandsworth, London, in his paternal grandmother's house. She was Jean Henrietta Clayton, a widowed "Annuitant," aged sixty-three, likewise born in India. His father, Edward Gilbert Clayton, aged twenty-nine, was a "Lieutenant Royal Engineers," born in "Hindostan," and his mother, Georgina E. S. Clayton, aged twenty-eight, was from Rufforth in Yorkshire. He had two India-born sisters aged five and two, and there were five servants: footman, ladies' maid, cook, nurse, and housemaid. In 1881, he was thirteen and living with his parents at 2 Anchor Gate Terrace, Portsea, where his father was a "Retired Major," employed at a government prison. With them lived a paternal uncle, Ernest W. Clayton, aged twenty-seven, a "Commercial Secretary," born in India, and his wife, Ellen N. Clayton from Clapham, Surrey. There were three servants, and a neighbour at 1 Anchor Gate Terrace was an Irish medical officer employed at the prison. In due time, HC joined the Royal Engineers and was commissioned in 1896 and listed in 1900 as Captain Henry Edward Gilbert Clayton, RE, commanding the Fifth Fortress Company at Portsmouth. His father was then recorded as "Hon. Major Edward Gilbert Clayton, late R. (Bengal E. Secretary & Inspector Prison Commission, Home Office, S.W. 31, Addison Gardens, W.)," who was born in 1841, had retired in 1880, and immediately found employment with the Home Office.

In 1921, HC retired to the Island with his wife and family. He was apparently less active in public affairs than some, but he wrote to the *Colonist* in June 1929 objecting to "Americanized News" and complaining about the small space in the paper given to cricket. Five years after moving to 909 Transit Road, Oak Bay, he died in Saanich, aged eighty, leaving his wife, two sons, and three daughters. His funeral was held at St Luke's Anglican Church, Cedar Hill.

Sources: *Colonist*, 1 June 1929, p. 4; 11 February 1948, p. 13, obit.; *Whitaker's*, p. 111; census 1871, England, RG 10/695, p. 15; census 1881, RG 11/1148, p. 2.

COCKBURN, Brigadier Clarence Beaufort (1892-1979). Born on 14 January 1892 in Hamilton, Ontario, son of a Scottish father, Lestock Cockburn (c. 1858-1942), and an English mother, Muriel Cockburn *née* Jacob (c. 1865-1947), he had a successful career in the British Army and then lived for many years in Victoria with his wife, Gladys Eveline Lewis (c. 1897-1976).

From their house at 261 King George Terrace overlooking the Strait of Juan de Fuca, he wrote to *The Times* in May 1957 warning that officers of the services without professional qualifications such as doctors or engineers should not migrate to Victoria, where "the prospects are grim for the retired officer without a profession or training for civil employment. Incidentally, the cost of living in Canada is extremely high, especially in Victoria, which is a most unsuitable place for the lower or middle bracket sterling pensioner without an adequate dollar income." Various profound changes had made settling on the Island in the post-war years much more difficult than before. Cockburn died, aged eighty-seven, on 2 March 1979 at the Royal Jubilee Hospital, leaving a married daughter, Joan F. H. Tremayne, a married sister, Isobel Bell-Irving, and nieces and nephews.

Sources: *Victoria Times*, 5 March 1979, p. 38 obit.; *The Times* (London) 8 May 1957, p. 11.

COCKBURN, Lieutenant Colonel Lestock Wilson Swanton (1885-1934). Born at Dawlish, Devon, on 16 August 1885, before the family emigrated to Canada, he attended RMC, Kingston, Ontario, and served for seventeen years in the RCA in Halifax, Kingston, and Victoria. In 1912, he went to England and qualified as a first-class instructor in gunnery. During the Great War, he served at Work Point Garrison and later went with the Canadian Expeditionary Force to Russian Siberia. There in Victoria, he married Aline Dorothy Wynne Day, on 9 August 1911, and when he enlisted in the CEF on 20 December 1918, giving his profession as "Major (Local Lt. Col.), R.C.A. (Perm. Force)," she was living with her parents, Mr and Mrs R. S. Day, at 1606 Rockland Avenue. In 1919, after the Great War, he was appointed commander of the Fifth Heavy Battery, RCA, at Victoria and so served until 1923. He turned to business for a while, and they went to live at Cowichan Station, then at Mill Bay. When he fell ill, he was treated by his father, Dr Lestock W. Cockburn (c. 1858-1942), until he died, aged forty-nine, on 4 October 1934 at the Jubilee Hospital, leaving a son, Peter, a daughter, Barbara, two brothers (one of whom may have been *Brigadier C. B. Cockburn), and a sister. His father died, aged eighty-four, on 12 September 1942 while resident at 2494 Windsor Road, Oak Bay.
Sources: NAC, CEF files; *Colonist*, 1 June 1934, p. 5, obit.; 5 October 1934, p. 5.

COCKLE, Captain John (1870-1917). Born at Whitehaven, Cumberland, he was recorded by the 1871 census, aged four months, living there at 35 Irish Street with his family. His father, William Cockle, then aged forty-eight, was a "Startler Horse Keeper," born in Hampton, Gloucester, and his mother, Mary, aged forty-three, was born at Antrim, Ireland. He already had several brothers and sisters including James Cockle, aged eighteen, employed as a "Railway stoker." They had a boarder from Ireland, James Killen, a cooper aged thirty, and there were several more boarders in the house a decade later, when he was ten. He went to sea in 1896 aboard ships of the Union Steamship Company on the Pacific Coast, became first mate on the *Cheslakee* in 1905, and took command of her in 1910 as she was ordered to relieve the *Cassiar* and the *Comore*. In January 1913, she left the Union dock with ninety-seven passengers and forty-five tons of freight, stopped briefly at Van Anda, left for Powell River in stormy seas, and sank when cargo shifted, causing her to list badly. Seven passengers who were too slow in reaching the deck drowned, but the rest were saved in lifeboats, and a court of enquiry in Victoria on 20 January 1913 blamed faults in the ship's construction—heavy superstructure—and praised JC and the pilot for their prompt action. After commanding other vessels, including the *Comox*, he was volunteered for service early in the Great War with sixty-four other employees of the Union Steamship Company. He (as #265378) and Captain Alfred E. Dickson joined the Inland Water Transport service of the Royal Engineers, and on 20 July 1917, JC died while navigating between Dover and French ports, leaving his wife, Hannah Bush Cockle, in Vancouver at 3465 Ontario Street. There she died, aged fifty-four, on 19 December 1928.

Sources: Gerald A. Rushton, *Whistle up the Inlet: The Union Steamship Story* (Vancouver, J. J. Douglas Ltd., 1974), pp. 55, 62, 67-9, 71; *Colonist*, 27 July 1917, p. 11, obit.; census 1871, England, RG 10/5253, p. 13; census 1881, RG 11/5185, p. 9; *Department of Veteran's Affairs*, Ottawa, Virtual Cemetery online.

CODVILLE, Colonel Francis Hillary MacDonnell (1889-1970). Born on 14 June 1889 in Ottawa, son of John James Codville, QC, and Edith Anna Lorrine MacDonnell of 443 Daly Avenue, he was schooled there and in Winnipeg before attending RMC, Kingston, and graduating in time to enlist in the CEF at Valcartier on 12 September 1914. He began the Great War with the Dragoons, but transferred to the PPCLI, and in 1920, he was posted to Work Point Barracks, Victoria, where he retired as lieutenant colonel in 1925 and bought the Egmont property of Walter Wray in Jarvis Inlet, including the post office. He immediately applied to divorce his wife, Marguerite Browne, whom he had married on 29 January 1916 at Sturgeon Creek, Manitoba, the correspondent being John Francis Dymoke Tanqueray, a civil engineer from London, and the marriage was dissolved on 18 October 1926. He then married an American school teacher, Icel Irene South (1901-1977), on 30 November in Vancouver, and in 1934, they moved to Maple Bay. In the meantime, he had become president and chairman of Codville Distributors Ltd. of Saskatchewan and Manitoba. During the Second World War, he was employed in Victoria as an army instructor, but he died at Maple Bay on 14 July 1970, leaving his widow, three sons, and three daughters. He was an Anglican and interested in the British Israelite movement, but his funeral was held privately at a funeral chapel in Duncan with friends and family members as pallbearers. His wife died, aged seventy-six, on 6 October 1977 in Duncan.

Sources: NAC, CEF files, box 1834-71; *Cowichan Leader*, 15 July 1970, obit.; BC Divorce Records, vol. 5, p. 156; Recollections courtesy of Monica Oldham; *Colonist*, 18 July 1970, p. 22, obit.; Betty C. Keller and Rosella M. Leslie, Bright Seas, *Pioneer Spirits: The Sunshine Coast* (Victoria, Horsdal & Schubart, 1996), pp. 92-3.

COLE, Major Coleridge Henry Tilyard [Tilleard?] (1885-?). He and his wife visited Victoria in July 1919 and promptly decided to settle there. They bought Princess Chikhmatoff's house in Oak Bay, 2031 Runneymede Avenue, one of their purposes being to live near their son, who was at Brentwood College in Saanich. According to my friend John Palmer, CC was probably a silent partner with Major Macbean in the Maple Bay Inn, a third partner being *Major A. B. Matthews. As a child, John Palmer used to play on the jetty at the Inn with Matthews's sons, Dennis and Peter, whenever their father was visiting Macbean there. However, CC and his wife moved away at sometime, and I failed to trace them further.

CC was born at Hove, Sussex, son of Edith Mary H. Cole (*née* Hutchison, in Germany, a British subject) and her husband, Charles John Cole, a solicitor born in Hampstead c. 1852. The 1881 census showed this father, aged twenty-eight, living with his parents (CC's paternal grandparents) at 17 Prince of Wales Terrace, London, and their three domestic servants; CC's grandfather was a "Queen's

Counsel," and his grandmother Georgiana was born in Gloucestershire. The 1891 census recorded CC, aged six, with his parents in Paddington (St Luke's parish) and in 1901, aged fifteen, he was staying as a visitor in Reigate, Surrey, at the house of a solicitor, Durand H. Cooper, aged thirty-five. His parents and two brothers were meanwhile still living in Hove at 22 Clarendon Terrance. From 8 December 1915 until 27 September 1922, CC served in the RFA, Thirtieth Brigade, giving his address as "Fairways," Allerton Avenue, Harrogate Road, Leeds. His service had taken him to India, France, and Mesopotamia, and he had risen from lieutenant to major. Meanwhile on 20 June 1920, he had married Dorothy C. MacAskie, either at St Mary's Church in Halifax, Nova Scotia, or at St George's Hanover Square, London (both cited, in different sources).

Sources: Recollections of John Palmer; *Colonist*, 7 July 1939, p. 6; census England, 1881, RG 11/23, p. 6; census 1891, RG 12/11, p. 51; census 1891, London, Paddington, St Luke's parish; census 1901, RG 13/625, p. 27; census 1901, RG 13/937, p. 35; BMD (UK), marriage 1920 at St George's Hanover Square, London.

COLEY, Arthur Altree (c. 1863-1941). Born at Wolverhampton, Staffordshire, he was the second of three sons, third of five children, born to Lucy Altree (born c. 1823 at Bilston, Staffordshire) and her husband Henry Coley (born c. 1823 in Wolverhampton), who probably married in 1848 at Alston, Warwickshire. The census-taker found AC, aged eighteen, living with the family and two domestic servants at Neachley Hall, South Donington, Shropshire, where his father was recorded as a "Manufacturer employing 80 pairs of hands." AC joined the Royal Horse Artillery and served in India as well as at home in England. Upon retiring, he went out to Vancouver Island and lived for many years at Metchosin, west of Victoria. At some stage, he moved to 3277 Linwood Avenue, Victoria, which was where he died, aged seventy-eight, on 25 April 1941, but he was buried in the churchyard at St Mary's, Metchosin and his wife was buried there too on 18 February 1964. She was Gertrude Emily Blackstaff, born in England, on 11 August 1883, who had emigrated to the Island with her parents in 1889, and had married AC in Victoria on 22 December 1907. Her parents had been pioneers, farming in a sparsely settled district, well, west of Victoria.

A letter AC wrote to the editor of the *Daily Colonist* in 1926 reveals that he was a British Israelite with bleak religious views: "The League of Nations will be, as it already is, a failure because it is built upon no foundation of righteousness. Great Britain in all sincerity is trying to erect a permanent structure upon a morass. There is clear guidance out of the present troubles, but it is being ignored even by the churches. The history of the British race past and present admits only of the explanation that we are Israel long lost to view, but disclosed in these days as bearing all the marks predicted in her. The immediate necessity is a general repentance and turning to God, who, faithful to the Covenent, has saved us from a thousand perils. Then with cleansed vision we shall know what we must do . . ." Gertrude was more than a match for AC, as she wrote a series of religious tracts that were published in London by the Covenenant Publishing Company: *The*

Abiding Kingdom (1931), *Out of this Danger* (2nd ed., 1950), *The Faith for the Present Need* (1952), and *The Divine Directive for Our Time* (1953).
Sources: census 1871, England, RG 10/2746, p. 3; census 1851, HO 107/1986/13; census 1841, HO 107/998/16/10 (Altree); Canadian census, 1901, for Island districts; E. E. Altree Coley, R. R. 1, L to E, in the *Colonist*, 7 April 1926, p. 6, "*League of Nations*"; *Colonist*, 27 April 1941, p. 6, obit.; *The Farmer's Magazine*, 3rd series, vol. 38 (July-December 2870), p. 137 (Henry Coley, Neachley Hall, newly elected.)

COLLARD, Lieutenant Colonel Charles Edwin (1868-1942). Born on 8 August 1868 at Alton Pancras, near Dorchester in Dorset, son of Rev. Edwin C. Collard, vicar of the parish, he served in the Royal Marine Light Infantry in the Portsmouth Division from 1 September 1887 to 31 March 1897 aboard HMS *Asia* and then HMS *Royal Arthur*, rising to lieutenant on 28 September 1889, assistant instructor musketry at sometime in 1895, and captain on 25 March 1897. He had qualified in Military Equitation at Canterbury in February 1892 and later earned a range-finding certificate at Aldershot. Seconded to the Uganda Rifles on 8 January 1898, he remained with them during the Sudanese Mutiny 1898-1899, for Special Service in South Africa from 21 May 1900 to 30 April 1901, and served next on the Staff of the Rand Rifles from 1 May 1901 to 30 September 1902. He was then appointed DAAG for musketry with the Transvaal Volunteers from 1 October 1902 to 31 March 1906, rising to major, Royal Marine Light Infantry (Chat. Dn) from 5 December 1905. He was major temporary lieutenant colonel, RM, aboard HMS *Ambitious* from 5 April 1918 to 20 April 1919, became a lieutenant colonel on 22 May 1919, and was at one time on Special Service for duty as CO of the Shetland Section, Royal Naval Reserve.

All the many marks and judgements of him on file in these stages were full of praise: "very good," "good and careful officer," "zealous, has tact and judgment, I recommend him for advancement," "great tact with men," "hard-working, thorough," etc. There is more about his splendid service with the Transvaal Volunteers. CC was placed on the retired list on 1 October 1909 at his own request, with a gratuity of £2,400 under Order-in-Council. Among his rewards and distinctions were the East Central Africa Medal, Uganda, forwarded on 15 June 1903; the SA Medal with four clasps (Cape Colony, Orange Free State, Transvaal, and Rhodesia); the King's SA Medal with clasps for SA, 1901 and 1902; a CB, military division; the RMLI; the Order of St Stanislas, second class (with sword), conferred by the Russian Government for distinguished serve in the Battle of Jutland; and the 1914 Star issued on 7 March 1919. Mentioned in despatches of the commander-in-chief, Grand Fleet, *London Gazette*, 15 September 1916, he "received an expression of their Lordships' appreciation 3 October 1918 re Organization of the Lookout system for the Shetland Island." A typed note on his file reads as follows: "Extract from a despatch from H.M. Special Commissioner for Uganda enclosing a report on an expedition into the Uzoma country, December 1899: I cannot conclude without expressing my appreciation of the way Captain Collard and his staff conducted the military part of the expedition, and would add a word of praise for the way in which his soldiers worked throughout the operations.

[signed], C. W. Hobloy [Hobley?], Civil Officer in charge of the Kavironde & Nandi Districts."

Pending repatriation to Canada, he was granted leave from 24 April 1919 and with his wife, Mary Hester, daughter of H. Ackeerman of South Africa (they were married on 17 December 1906), settled in the Cowichan Valley but took long trips back to England, as for instance, in the winter of 1928-1929. He joined the Union Club in Victoria and maintained a membership in the Sports Club, London. At the end of September 1921, CC left for Bulawayo, Rhodesia, for a long visit to his son. He and his wife were both registered on the voters' list for 1935 as residents at "The Garth," but he died somewhere outside BC on 19 August 1942, unnoticed by the Victoria papers and *The Times* of London.
Sources: BNA (PRO), ADM 196/62, p. 185; *Who Was Who*, 1941-1950, p. 236; *Who's Who in B.C.*, 1933-1934, pp. 36-7; *Colonist*, 1 October 1921, p. 8; 17 April 1929, p. 8; NAC, Election rolls for 1935, reel T4760.

COLLIE-MacNEIL, Major George William (1868-1937). Born on 5 May 1868 in Lancashire, he fought in the South African War in a British unit and in 1912 migrated to Alberta. When he enlisted in the First Canadian Mounted Rifles at Medicine Hat on 25 May 1915, he named his wife, Daisy Emma MacNeil, as his next of kin. He had had military experience in the Twenty-first Alberta Hussars. He was 6' tall, an Anglican, and gave his occupation as "gentleman." After the war, he settled with his wife and family at 2276 Cadboro Bay Road, Oak Bay, and died there, aged seventy-five, on 10 April 1937, leaving his wife, three sons, two daughters, all at home, and a brother, D. A. G. Collie-MacNeil, who was serving as British Consul at Guadalajara. Daisy Emma Collie-MacNeil died much later, aged seventy, on 19 October 1963 in Victoria. The name makes research difficult; few indexers can cope with it.
Sources: NAC, CEF files, box 7151-15; *Colonist*, 11 April 1937, p. 5; 13 April 1937, p. 6, obit.

COLLINS, Lieutenant Colonel George Atkins (1855-?). Born in India, son of John Charles Collins, surgeon major in the Bengal Army, and his wife Ann, he was christened on 29 October 1855 at Monghyr (?), West Bengal. The census-taker found him in 1871, aged fifteen, living with his family at 14 Priory Street, Cheltenham, Gloucestershire, and his father was reported as a widowed surgeon major, Bengal Army, born at Timsbury, Somerset, aged forty-eight. GC's brothers and sisters, all born in India, were William Edward Collins, aged seventeen, Laura Amelia Collins, thirteen, Arthur Hubert Collins, twelve, Gertrude Charlotte Collins, ten, and Charles Bury Collins, three. The father's sister-in-law, Sarah Bury, aged forty-seven, born in India, was also there, and they had four domestic servants. GC's father was married again, this time to Augusta Cerjat, born in Calcutta, and the 1881 census found them living at "Stanbridge House" in the hamlet of Slad, Panswick, Parliamentary Borough of Stroud, the father recorded as "Physician not practising, M.D. St Andrews, UMRC & LUC, Surgeon Major Indian Medical Service." They had a governess, cook, housemaid, and kitchenmaid, but GC was not there, having joined the Twelfth (Shekhowatter) Regiment of the Indian Army on 13 June 1874 as a lieutenant. In 1878, he had been awarded a medal for service in Afghanistan; in 1899, he had been posted at Ajmere; he was promoted to major in 1894; and in 1900, he was commandant of the Merwara Battalion. On 9 October 1880, he had married Elizabeth Fraser King, youngest daughter of the late George Mark King, Esq., of Baltinglass, Co. Wicklow, Ireland, this at Kingstown, Co. Dublin. Little had changed in the parental household at "Stanbridge House" by 1891, though GC's stepmother had had two children, Grace M. Collins, born at Cheltenham *circa* 1874 and Robert G. Collins, born in South Wales *circa* 1876.

GC retired on 2 January 1904 and took his wife out to Victoria, where they bought a house in Oak Bay on Foul Bay Road. There the Canadian census found them in 1911, but there is no sign of them thereafter. They may have returned to England when the Great War began in 1914.

Sources: Canadian census, 1911, Victoria; *Indian Army Quarterly List* for 1 January 1912, p. 666; census 1871, England, RG 10/2663, p. 6; census 1881, RG 11/2542, p. 33; census 1891, RG 12/2022, p. 6; *The Medical Times and Gazette, A Journal of Medical Science, Literature, Criticism, and News*, vol. 2 (9 October 1880), p. 445, marriage; IGI (Latter Day Saints); *Whitaker's*, p. 118.

COLLIS, Flight Lieutenant Douglas Percy (1887-1917). He was born on 9 May 1887 at Luton, Bedfordshire, son of Henry Percy Collis (c. 1861-1939) and Mary Claverhouse Collis (c. 1861-1939) [*sic*] and attended Horton School at Ickwell, just south of Northill, Bedfordshire. He and a sister, Elsie Dorothy Collis, born at Harpenden, Bedfordshire, were taken out to the Island by their parents early in the twentieth century, and the family was living at 126 Esquimalt Road, Victoria, when they both joined the CEF in the Great War. Elsie joined on 15 September 1915 as a "professional nurse" and much later, on 4 September 1928, married Harry Arthur Hunt in Strawberry Vale, BC. As for DC, he was employed as a "motor mechanic" when he enlisted on 15 May 1915 as a driver in the Canadian Army Medical Corps and went overseas in August 1915. In August 1916, he was gazetted as an officer in the Royal Flying Corps, despatched to France the following March, and was reported missing in August 1917. He soon turned up again and was home on leave in March 1919 with the rank of flight commander. After the war, he married his wife, Ida, and they had two sons and a daughter who had grown up by the time he died, aged seventy-eight, on 29 March 1966 in Victoria. They had lived for a time up the Island at Cumberland, but for many years since then at 3308 Kingsley Street. Mrs Collis died much later, aged eighty-three, on 12 October 1983. This family is elusive in the English census records.

Sources: NAC, CEF files, box 1886-33, no. 400091; *Colonist*, 25 August 1917, p. 6; 5 March 1919, p. 6; 5 May 1939, p. 14, obit.; 31 March 1966, p. 35, obit.; census 1871, England, RG 10/679, p. 24; census 1881, RG 11/633, p. 15; census 1891, RG 12/354, p. 18; census 1901, RG 13/1496, p. 18.

COLLISHAW, Air Commodore Raymond (1893-1976), CB 1941, DSO 1917 (and Bar 1918), OBE 1920 and 1946, DSC, and DFC. He was born in Nanaimo on 22 November 1893, the eldest of five children. His father, John Edward Collishaw, was born in Wales and (RC believed) grew up as the son of a hotel proprietor at Wrexham, Cheshire, near Liverpool. The father had gone adventuring in the gold fields of Australia and the Klondike but began working in Nanaimo as a coal miner circa 1891 and married Sarah, RC's mother, soon after that but not in BC. She declared her birth as in Wales about 1865. During RC's youth, his father went on working in the coal mines of Nanaimo between bouts of exploring for gold. As a young man, Collishaw served in 1908-1914 on ships of the Royal Canadian Fishery Protection Service, rising from cabin boy to qualified ships' master. When the Great War began, he attended Naval College and, after taking an RFC staff course, enrolled in the Royal Naval Air Service in 1915 and served as a patrol pilot on the English Channel and, in 1916-1918, as a squadron commander in France. The Canadian government, head buried firmly in the sand, had no airial force of any kind, but Canadians of British origin, like Collishaw, joined the RFC in large numbers. When the war ended, he was a lieutenant colonel holding second place among the pilots in the British Empire for the number of enemy planes destroyed (59-61) in wartime, had been mentioned four times in despatches, and been decorated with the DSC, DFC, and Bar. In 1919, he went on to serve in Egypt and, in 1919-1920, was commander of RAF Squadron 47 on the Russian Expedition of 1919-1920 in support of White Russian forces sent out in support of General Denikin with about two hundred officers and men, mostly veterans from the Western Front. This was, I think, in collaboration with the Dunsterforce, which crossed from Constantinople to the Black Sea and to Novorossisk. Collishaw then joined British forces in Northern Persia and in 1921-1923 went on to serve in Iraq as wing commander. He became Senior RAF officer on HMS *Courageous* in the British intervention between Arabs and Jews in Palestine during the years 1929-1932. A series of higher appointments followed: commander at Bircham Newton Station, England, 1932-1935; at RAF Station, Sudan, 1935-1936; at RAF Station, Heliopolis, 1936-1938; air officer commanding Egypt Group, RAF, 1939; air commodore, 1940. Early in the Second World War, his airial forces did much to hound Italian land and air forces out of the Western Desert in 1940-1941 and began the policy of destroying enemy planes on the ground with bombs set to explode on impact, which sprayed shrapnel over one thousand yards. Transferred to Halifax, NS, in 1941, he returned to England on special duties in 1941 and was promoted to air vice-marshal in 1942 in command of No. 14 Fighter Group with headquarters at Inverness and retired at that rank the next year. In London, he had long been a member of the Royal Air Force Club and gave his address as c/o RAFHQ, London.

He had married Juanita Eliza Trapp of New Westminster, and after the war, they settled in Vancouver, though he did not find this easy, as he had been abroad in uniform since 1908. At first, he took up placer mining in Barkerville, using high-pressure hoses to wash gold-bearing gravel and then spent two decades in various other mining ventures, particularly as president of Craigmont Mines Ltd. He died, aged eighty-two, on 29 February 1976 in North Vancouver.

Sources: Raymond Collishaw & R. V. Dodd, *Air Command: A Fighter Pilot's Story* (William Kimber, 1973), 256 pp. These memoirs set his record straight on a number of points missed or misrepresented in other accounts. Roy MacLaren, *Canadians in Russia 1918-1919* (Toronto, Macmillan, 1976), pp. 203-4; Appendix A., 228-242; *Canadian Who's Who*, vol. VIII (1958-60), p. 220; *Colonist*, 29 August 1941, p. 2; John MacFarlane & Robbie Hughes, *Canada's Naval Aviators* (rev. ed., Shearwater, Nova Scotia, Shearwater Aviation Museum Foundation, 1997), p. 66.

COLLISON, Venerable William Henry (1847-1922). An Anglican Irishman who devoted his life to missionary work among native tribes in northern BC, he was born on 12 November 1847 in County Armagh, schooled at Church of Ireland's Normal College and the Church Missionary College in Islington (London), and first taught at an industrial school in Cork. It was in London that he married Miss Marion Goodwin in 1873 and immediately took her halfway around the world under the auspices of the CMS to Victoria, where they arrived on 25 October 1873. Met there by *Dean Edward Cridge, who put them up, they were of his evangelical persuasion and inevitably embroiled in Cridge's quarrel with *Bishop George Hills, as was *Rev. William Duncan whom they joined at Metlakatla, BC, a few weeks later. WC began there as a layman, assistant to Duncan, working with the Zimshean (Tsimshian) tribes, but was ordained a few years later and went to the Haidas on the Queen Charlotte Islands, where he was the first missionary. It was as a pioneer that WC took the initiative in 1880 to open a mission to the Gitikshans in the northern interior of BC. Made an archdeacon in 1891, he worked in 1893-1894 as secretary to the North Pacific Mission, based at Metlakatla, for the Church Missionary Society and Bishop's Commissary. He mastered the Zimshean (Tsimshian), Haida, and Nishka languages well enough to translate hymns and prayers. His book, *A History of the B.C. Mission*, and his memoirs entitled *In the Wake of the War Canoes* (1915) are valuable records of their kind. Having had five sons and three daughters, his wife died in 1919 and he on 21 January 1922 at Kincolith (Gingolx), BC. Gail Edwards has written the most scholarly short biography.

Sources: Morgan, *Canadian Men and Women*, pp. 250-5; Gail Edwards, "Collison, William Henry, Church of England missionary and clergyman" in the DCB; Alexander Anderson, "*An official view of Metlakahtla*," Church Missionary Intelligencer and Record, [3rd] ser., 6 (1881): 50-52. "*Bishop Ridley and the North Pacific Mission*," Church Missionary Intelligencer and Record, [3rd] ser., 9 (1884): 165-67; of W. H. Collison, *In the Wake of the War Canoes* (Toronto, Musson Co., n.d. 1915[?]; Seeley Service & Co., 1915[?]), 352 pp.

COLLISTER, Captain Richard (1830-1908). He was born on the Isle of Man, son of William Collister of Corvalley, Howe, Port St Mary. The census-taker found him in 1861, aged thirty-one, living at 27 Sterling Street, Kirkdale, near Liverpool as a ship's carpenter, with his wife Elizabeth, aged twenty-seven, born there in Lancashire. They had a son, William H. R. Collister, aged three, and a daughter, Florence Victoria Collister, aged one, both born in Liverpool.

In 1876, they emigrated to Victoria, where they lived in the Johnson Street Ward of the town and later on Craigflower Road, and he was employed by the Canadian Federal Government for more than twenty years as "Steam Boat Inspector." He also worked for many years as a surveyor for the San Francisco Board of Marine underwriters and, in that capacity, inspected many lumber and coal vessels. They were both Methodists and appear in Canadian census records for 1891 and 1901, though his birthdate was misread as 12 December "1838" in the published version of the 1901 census. He died, aged seventy-nine, of heart failure on 25 October 1908 at Buffalo, New York, where he had gone to consult a heart specialist. His remains were returned for a funeral at Christ Church Cathedral and for burial in Victoria, with Canon Beanlands officiating. He was survived by his widow—until January 1923, when she died in Victoria—and by two sons and three daughters. William H[enry] R[ichard] Collister was employed by the Albion Ironworks, a boatbuilding firm, and eventually died, aged seventy-six, on 5 January 1935 in Vancouver City. The second son, John Richard Collister, who had married Elizabeth Cessford in Victoria on 12 February 1889, worked for the Victoria firm of John Barnsley & Co., and his employer Barnsley had married his sister, Elizabeth Jane Collister, in Victoria on 25 December 1887. The other two Collister daughters had also been married: Florence Victoria to Harry Groves Downer, who had taken her to live at Dawson City in the Yukon Territory, and Clara Mary had married Harry Oxenborough Miles in Victoria on 27 June 1895.

Sources: census 1861, England, RG 9/2721, p. 29; *Colonist*, 21 January 1923, p. 5, obit.; *The Manx Quarterly*, no. 6 (1909) Internet, citing the *Victoria Daily Times* of 27 October 1908.

COLVILLE OF CULROSS, Charles Alexander (1888-1945), Third Viscount and Thirteenth Baron (created 1609). He was born on 26 May 1888, eldest son of Charles Robert William Colville, Second Viscount, whom he succeeded in 1928. In 1904, he joined the Royal Navy as a midshipman, became a lieutenant in 1910 and a lieutenant commander in 1918, and served at the Battle of Jutland (1916) as a flag lieutenant (mentioned in despatches).

Already about 1914, he had taken a property facing on Saanich Inlet not far from Cole Bay and facing west across Saanich Inlet and stayed in Victoria while his new house was being built there; but he had to go off to the Great War before it was finished. After the war, he returned with the rank of commander and built up a country estate he called "Point Colville." In 1931, he married Kathleen Myrtle Gale, eldest daughter of his neighbour, *Brigadier General Henry Richmond Gale, CMG, of "Bardsey," Mount Newton, Saanichton, and they had a son. Their honeymoon was spent up Island at Qualicum Beach, and there his mother, Ruby, Viscountess Colville, visited from Britain about the same time. In May 1935, his sister, Hon. Mary Colville visited with a friend. Colville was a cultivated nobleman and spent much time, effort, and money in support of local cultural activities, particularly musical events. He was a patron of the Victoria Choral Union from its beginning in February 1935, and on 5 May 1936, they unanimously elected him president of it at their AGM in Memorial Hall; in their first year, they had staged Handel's *Messiah* and Brahms' *Requiem*. The *Colonist* reported on 6 December 1930, "A very charming form of musical entertainment was revived last night at the Empress Hotel when Edith Oliver, soprano, and Helen de Suzannet, mezzo-soprano, appeared in joint recital in aid of the Third Victoria (St Barnabas) Scouts and Cubs. The unusual feature of this was, of course, the duet work, a phase of the vocal art which has suffered neglect for many years . . . His Honor the Lieutenant-Governor and the Rt. Hon. Viscount Colville, the two distinguished patrons of the occasion, were present in person to join in the applause received by the two accomplished artists and their accompanist, Miss Dumbleton . . ." They sang such things as Léo Delibes, "Sous le dome épais," and Purcell's "Let us Wander." Boy Scouts acted as ushers and programme distributors at this event. Among Colville's many public services was generous attention to Shawnigan Lake Boys School of which he became one of the governors. Captain C. P. Nixon, who attended the school in those years, recalls that in 1944, having to refuel the destroyer HMCS *Chaudière*, which he commanded in the Atlantic and the English Channel, he was instructed to go to Fayal on Horta Island in the Azores. There he met Colville, who was serving as the resident British naval officer. When Nixon identified himself as a former student at the school and reminded Colville of meetings there during Lonsdale's term as headmaster, they had a long chat. Colville said, "Do you ever write to Lonsdale? Well, please ask him if he has ever heard of Horta etc., etc." Colville subsequently died in an air crash in March 1945. He had been a member of the United Service Club (London) and the Union Club (Victoria).

Sources: Captain C. P. Nixon, interview in Ottawa, 18 March 2002; *Colonist*, 4 August 1914, p. 6; 6 December 1930, p. 7; 16 June 1931, p. 8; 17 June 1931, p. 7; 6 May 1936, p. 6 with photo; 22 May 1936, p. 8; *Who's Who in B.C.*, 1933-1934, p. 37.

COLWELL, Flying Officer John (1916-?). He was born 14 December 1916 in Neemuch, Central India, son of Dr Harry Herbert Colwell (c. 1883-1977), a medical missionary who brought him in 1933 to the Island, where they settled on a farm near Nanaimo. He finished his schooling there and subsequently farmed with his father and sold eggs in Nanaimo. When the Second World War began, his father, who had served in the Great War, joined the Army Medical Corps and, in the post-war years, worked as a medical doctor aboard the *Thomas Crosby*, a missionary vessel serving the coastal communities. Meanwhile, the family moved to Jervis Street, Vancouver, though they also kept the farm. In 1940, JC joined the RCAF in which he trained at bases in Saskatchewan, excelled at mathematics and geometry and, in time, qualified as a navigator, an observer, and a pilot, and was promoted to sergeant. After further training at Rivers, Manitoba, he was posted overseas to Millom, Cumberland, for a one-month course before joining 405 Squadron at Topcliffe, Yorkshire, in September 1942. This was a Coastal Command squadron but was soon moved to Beaulieu, Hampshire, as a Bomber Command squadron. He flew on many bombing missions over enemy targets until 3 April

1943, when his plane drifted off course on the way to raid Essen and was shot down over Holland. Sympathetic but terrified, Dutch residents turned him in to German authorities, who put him in the prison camp Stalag Lut III. This was the camp where prisoners dug the famous tunnel for "the great escape," but being number 147 in line, JC was not one of the seventy-six who got away on the night of 24 March 1944.

He survived all the same and, after the war, retired to a dairy farm on the Island near Comox. His father, who had lived at Maple Bay for many years, died, aged ninety-four, on 5 February 1977 in Victoria. Besides his son, he left two married daughters in Victoria and his wife Annie, who died, aged ninety-five, on 18 November 1980. After many peaceful years, JC presented the diary he kept in the prison camp to the aviation museum at the Armed Forces base near Comox.
Sources: Dale McCartney, Assistant Curator, Comox Air Force Museum, e-mailed letter dated 28 August 2002 (thank you!); Rod Mickleburgh, "*Flier Donates Great Escape Journal to Museum*," Globe & Mail, 24 August 2002, p. A3; *Colonist*, 6 February 1977, p. 34, obit.

CONNELL, Colonel Arthur Reginald (1901-?). He was born on 16 March 1901, son of Rev. Canon Connell, Anglican rector of Clontarf, Dublin, Ireland, and schooled at Campbell College in Belfast. He joined the Indian Army on 21 November 1916 and had his first commission on 16 July 1920 in the Second Battalion, Fourth Gurkha Rifles, at the same time as John Masters, who mentioned him in one of his books. Connell was promoted to the rank of colonel on 16 July 1921 and became a company officer. In the course of his duties, he earned the Waziristan Medal. After six years in India, he retired from the army and emigrated to Canada. At sometime in the 1930s, he visited the Island and liked it so well that he moved there and found employment as a fisheries inspector on the BC coast. When the Second World War began, he was recalled to the Imperial forces and this time served in Burma as a major in the Fourth Inland Water Transport Group, a branch of the Royal Engineers. Most of Burma was in Japanese hands, and the British had to move troops and equipment across the strategic Chindwin River to a road the engineers had built if they were to reach Mandalay. To do this, they needed ramp cargo lighters, 15½ metres long and made of plywood. Two lighters were brought by road from Assam to Allied-held territory at Tamu on the banks of the Yu River, which runs into the Chindwin. Connell's task was to get the lighters onto the Chindwin River, which was very wide, in flood, and beset with rapids, snags, and rocks. At one point in the thirty-eight-kilometre voyage to the Chindwin, Major Connell conscripted four elephants to free the lighter from a sandbar. After ten days, the lighter reached the Chindwin. As a result, a brigade and its mules were able to cross the river to the engineer's road and carry on north to Tangdut, where three days later, the lighter was ferrying guns and vehicles of the Nineteenth Indian Division across the river and set them on their way to Mandalay. Connell rose to be a lieutenant colonel but partly owing to papers being lost or destroyed in the Government House fire of 15 April 1957, there was a delay of forty years after the war before he was belatedly awarded the

MBE for his services in Burma. The investiture was first arranged for sometime in 1950, but not until 20 September 1985 was he invested as a member of the Order of the British Empire. Michael Roberts, secretary to Lieutenant Governor Robert Rogers, read out his record.

The delay was also partly due to Connell's absence on a fishing voyage in the Queen Charlotte Islands in 1950. He and his wife, Patricia Angela Mary Brennan, Paddy Brennan's sister, who were married somewhere in Northern Ireland in 1941, had taken up fishing in a serious way. They spent about twenty years troll-fishing off the Goose Islands in a thirty-four-foot fishing boat and earned enough to spend winters at their house near Swartz Bay overlooking the patch of water one passes on the way to the Tsawassen ferry. The Goose Islands were about three hundred miles away by sea, quite a journey there and back each year for a middle-aged and then-elderly couple, and trolling is much harder work than gill-netting, but the Connells became accustomed to the work and fond of the life.

Sources: Notes from John Palmer, 17 August 2002 and 28 November 2002; *Arthur Connell's wartime diary of his service in Burma, 1943-1945* (38 pp. in MSS.); and a memoir he wrote about his time, riding the rods in Canada: "*Railroad Vagabonds*" (17 pp.); *Indian Army List*, April 1923, pp. 339 and 1311; *Times-Colonist*, 21 September 1985, p. D1 with photo.

CONNOLLY, Brigadier Charles Edward F. (1883-1949), DSO. Born a Roman Catholic at Enniskillen, County Fermang, Ireland, he served for fourteen years as a private soldier in the British Army Rifles Brigade in South Africa, Egypt, India, and the Sudan and in 1911, after retiring, went out to Canada. When the Great War began, he enlisted in Lord Strathcona's Horse at Valcartier on 25 September 1914 and was granted a commission on the field of battle, ending the war as a major in the Canadian Cavalry Brigade. On returning to Canada in 1919, he was appointed second in command of Strathcona's Horse and five years later commanded it as lieutenant colonel. In 1938 and 1939, he became assistant adjutant and quartermaster general of Military District No. 11 at its headquarters in Victoria and was stationed at Work Point. Late in 1939, he was posted to Calgary, where he succeeded General George Pearkes as officer commanding District 13 and then commanded District 6 (Halifax). When he died, aged sixty-six, on 28 September 1949, his address was 687 Falkland Rd., Victoria, and he left a wife and a son.

Sources: NAC, CEF files, RG150, box 1914-7; *Colonist*, 29 September 1949, p. 9; 30 September 1949, p. 19, obit.; *Times-Colonist*, 21-22 March 1982, p. 38, obit.

COMBE, Captain Harvey [Hervey?] Walter Henry Combe (1859-1922). Born in India on 14 September 1859, he settled in Victoria in 1881 and found employment as registrar of the Supreme Court of British Columbia. He led the movement to form the Victoria Golf Club, found and proposed the site on land owned by *Joseph Despard Pemberton (who donated it without charge), canvassed the town for members, and persuaded *Sir Richard Musgrave to act as chairman at the founding meeting held in the Temple Building on Fort Street on 7 November

1893. The club has a photograph of him. But the earliest documentary record of him that I could discover was an entry in English census records for 1881. He appeared, aged twenty, born in India, "son of a General in the Army" and visiting the household of Dudley W. Buckle, aged thirty-seven, "Captain Royal Artillery (retired)," his wife Georgina, aged twenty-seven, who lived with two young children and three servants in the High Street at Southover, Sussex. Buckle had served in the Afghan War of 1878-1880 and in the Curragh, Ireland.

By his family relationships, HC was a living embodiment of the empire, in some of its aspects. He was the eldest surviving son of Barbara Elizabeth *née* More-Molyneux (died 1916) and her husband Major General James John Combe (1821-1896), who had a career in the Indian Army, as did one of HC's uncles, Major General Boyce Albert Combe (1841-1920). Another uncle, Richard Henry Combe (1829-1900), was in the family brewing firm but living as a country gentleman, "magistrate, deputy-lieutenant" in Surrey at Pierrepont, Fensham, with a governess for the children and eleven domestic servants (1871). One of HC's brothers was Sir Lionel Combe (1861-1950), who commanded a brigade of the British Army during the Great War, and another was Sir Ralph Molyneux Combe (1872-1946), who became a barrister-at-law and was knighted in the course of his career as chief justice and attorney general of Nigeria. HC's paternal grandparents were Henrietta Anna *née* Church and her husband Charles James Fox Combe (1797-1875), who was named after Charles James Fox, a close friend of his father (HC's great-grandfather), who was Sir Edward Harvey Christian Combe (1752-1818), a successful brewer elected MP for London (1796-1817) and lord mayor of London (1799). This great-grandfather was also a warden of the Fishmonger's Company (1812-1814), a director of the Globe Insurance Company (after 1805) and the West India Dock Company (after 1811), and president of the Society for Prosecuting Felons (1817). His fortune was made in the brewing concern, which was ultimately associated with the names Whitbread and Watney Mann, etc. In 1806, he paid £30,000 for Cobham Park, an estate in Surrey, which became the Combe family seat until the 1930s. It had belonged to Jean-Louis Ligonier, First Earl Ligonier (1680-1770), a Huguenot refugee, commander-in-chief of the British Army at the time James Wolfe won Canada on the Plains of Abraham, and it was at Cobham Park that Ligonier had entertained William Pitt the Elder.

HC's grandfather being the youngest of five sons, Cobham Park passed through the hands of the senior lines of the family, but southern England had a remarkable sprinkling of his relatives. One of his forebears, a magistrate named Major Boyce Harvey Combe (1816-97), married into the family of Hercules Brabazon Brabazon [*sic*] (1821-1906), a renowned watercolour painter, and was asked by Brabazon to manage his estate at Oaklands, Sedlescombe, Surrey. One of his second cousins, Major Harvey Trewythen Brabazon Combe (1852-1924), an Etonian born at Florence, Italy, succeeded to the Brabazon estates but travelled a good deal in the Orient, leaving his wife to care for their two sons, who were both captains in the British Army during the Great War and one was killed near Hooge in November 1914. A first cousin once removed (i.e., of the previous generation) was Major General John Frederick Boyce Combe (1895-1967) CB, DSO, of the Eleventh

Hussars, so prominent in the Western Desert Campaign during the Second World War and famous in English post-war hunting and racing circles.

HC married Charlotte Margaret Wray (1862-1915), daughter of Rev. Henry Basil Brooke Wray and his wife Emily *née* Smith, who seem to have moved from England to Ontario. HC and Maggie (as he called her) had three surviving children: Harvey Brian Combe (1885-1950), Boyce Molyneux Combe (1894-1934), and Leonora Combe (1889-), who married Hew Patterson in Victoria on 29 October 1914. After Mrs Combe died on 15 January 1915, HC married Frances Gladys Tyrwhitt-Drake (1885-1959), a Victoria woman, on 22 May 1916. There is more to be learned about such interesting figures as HC.

Sources: Sir Bernard Burke, *Genealogical and Heraldic History of the Landed Gentry of Great Britain & Ireland* (vol. I; 1875), p. 268, "*Combe of Oaklands*"; census 1851, England, HO 107/1509/149; census 1861, RG 9/55/33, pp. 15-16; census 1871, RG 10/822/150, pp. 9-10; census 1881, RG 11/1071, p. 43; census 1891, RG 12/791, p. 2; Canadian census, 1901, Victoria; Canadian census, 1911, Canada, for Victoria; *Victoria Times*, 23 May 1916, p. 11, marriage; *Whitaker's*, p. 120; *The Times* (London), 8 January 1864, p. 10, col. A, obit.; 10 February 1903, p. 4, col. E; 5 February 1914, p. 11, col. F, obit; 15 June 1920, p. 19, col. C, obit.; 23 September 1922, p. 10, col. D, obit. (Brabazon); 9 January 1924, p. 17, col. A, obit; 14 July 1967, p. 10, col. F, obit.; 18 July 1967, p. 10, col. G, obit.; 21 July 1967, p. 10, col. G, obit.; R. G. Wilson, "*Combe, Harvey Christian* (1752-1818)," brewer, *Oxford* DNB, 2 pp.; Martin Hardie and Jessica Kilburn, "*Brabazon* (formerly Sharpe), Hercules Brabazon (1821-1906, watercolour painter," *Oxford* DNB, 4 pp.; Kelly's Post Office Directory of Essex, Herts., Middlesex, Kent, Surrey & Sussex, 1867, entry for Netherfield, a hamlet of Battle; Victoria Golf Club files.

COOPER, Lieutenant Colonel Richard Clive (1881-1940). He was born in Dublin, third son of William Alexander Cooper and Mary Ringland Ferguson, and the 1891 census found him, aged ten, living with them at 11 Cardigan Road, Richmond, Surrey. His father was a stockbroker from Wexford, Ireland, and his mother born in Dublin. With them were his brothers: Harry R., aged twelve, William J., eleven, and a sister Mary R., aged seven, all born in Dublin except Mary born there at Richmond. RC attended a grammar school briefly, but went to South Africa aged fifteen to enlist in the Rhodesian Volunteer Artillery. He served through the Matabele War in 1896-1897 and, in 1898, joined the British South African Police as a trooper and served through the South African War from the beginning until 1902, when he was discharged with the rank of sergeant. He received the Queen's Medal with five bars and the King's Medal with two. He then went through the East African Campaign, received the medal and a clasp, and was then employed in the Rhodesian Department of Agriculture.

In 1906, he went to Canada and, on 9 November, married Edith McSearle with whom he settled in BC at sometime in 1910. When the Great War began, he was employed as an accountant when he enlisted in Eighty-eighth Victoria Fusiliers at Valcartier on 17 September 1914. He was sent overseas in the Seventh Battalion, First Division, and promoted to major after the second battle of Ypres. As second in command of the battalion he fought at Ploegstreet, Fleurbaix, Flores, Festubert, Givenchy, and Messines, before being sent to England to take charge of a newly established Royal School of Infantry, formed for the training of Canadian officers at Shorncliffe. In 1916, he returned to Canada and held several appointments, including command of Shaughnessy Military Hospital in Vancouver. One of the battalion's few survivors, he was elected to the House of Commons in 1917 for Vancouver South and sat as a Unionist until the dissolution of the Thirteenth Parliament. He did not run in 1921 but worked in the investment business in Vancouver. He moved to Victoria, where on 6 December 1930, he made a second marriage with Dorothy May Langley, eldest daughter of *Major and Mrs W. H. Langley. When he died, aged fifty-nine, at the Royal Jubilee Hospital, on 10 March 1940 in Victoria, he left his wife and two daughters, Shelagh and Bridget. He had an Anglican funeral and was buried at Royal Oak.

Sources: census 1891, England, RG 12/619, p. 14; NAC, CEF files, box 1976-1937; *Colonist*, 12 April 1914, p. 14; 22 April 1917, p. 7; 12 March 1940, p. 3, obit.; *Times* (Victoria), 6 December 1930, p. 6; J. K. Johnson, ed., *The Canadian Directory of Parliament, 1867-1967* (Ottawa, Public Archives, 1968), p. 134.

COSTERTON, Captain Charles Ernest (1850-1927). He was born on 24 October 1850 at Eye, Suffolk, son of Harriet Costerton *née* Nayler, born at Eye, and her husband, Charles Fisher Costerton, magistrate, "district auditor," and "flax manufacturer," born near Great Yarmouth at South-town, Suffolk. In 1871, he was employing "100 hands or thereabouts" in a flax factory he owned in partnership with his father-in-law. That year, the census recorded CC as a "Secretary to Insurance Company," aged thirty, living with his parents and several brothers and sisters in the Ipswich Road, Scole, Norfolk, at "Scole House." Harriet Costerton was a widow, aged sixty, in 1891, still at "Scole House" but with her sister Louise Nayler, a visitor Helen Aylmer, one son Alfred, aged thirty-four, and six grown-up unmarried daughters. Meanwhile, CC went young to South Africa and joined the Natal Native Contingent in which he was promoted to captain and served through the Zulu War, "being present at the capture of Cetawayo." About 1892, he settled in the Vernon district of the Okanagan Valley and there, on 10 May 1893, married Gertrude Anna Perry. For about eleven years, he was employed in the BC civil service but, on retiring, lived from 1915 in Victoria at 448 Superior Street and was a member of the Army and Navy Veterans, Victoria Unit. At his death, aged seventy-six, on 31 December 1926, he left his widow and two daughters, one in Seattle and the other, Mrs H. H. Jones, in Victoria. His brother Clement F. Costerton was living at Vernon, and they had a brother and three sisters in England and another sister in China. CC was buried at Royal Oak Cemetery after a funeral at Christ Church Cathedral. Mrs Costerton died, aged sixty-six, on 6 October 1935 in Victoria.

Sources: census 1881, England, RG 11/1967, p. 8; census 1871, RG 10/1835, p. 8; census 1891, RG 12/1544, p. 10; *Colonist*, 2 January 1927, pp. 3 and 28, obit.

COTTLE, Joseph James (c. 1874-1937). Born in Devonshire, he joined the Imperial Army as a young man and served for ten years in India. On retiring

from the army, he migrated to Victoria, and except for a brief period away in the Yukon and service overseas during the Great War, he spent the rest of his life there. In 1917, he became deputy assessor at the Provincial Courthouse in Nanaimo, which became his home. He was one of the founders of the Great War Veterans Association, the first president elected for the Nanaimo branch, and was an active member of it until after it joined with other war veterans' societies to form the Canadian Legion of the BESL. He served as president of the Legion at Nanaimo until poor health obliged him to resign. He was also a prominent member of Nanaimo Aerie, No. 15, FOE. A great dog lover and a prominent judge of sporting and field dogs at shows, he was one of the founders of the Nanaimo Kennel Club specializing in sporting and field dogs, especially English Setters. He was one of the founders of the Nanaimo Kennel Club. Mr Cottle is survived by a brother and sister in England. When he died on 1 October 1937, it was in Kamloops, where he was on a three-week holiday. He left a brother and sister in England. At his funeral in St Paul's Anglican Church, Nanaimo, the pallbearers were all returned members of the "Trench Mortals," including Colonel D. R. Sargenant, Major W. W. R. Mitchell, V. C. Fawcett, and Captain Lionel Beevor-Potts.
Sources: *Nanaimo Daily Free Press*, Sat., 2 October 1937, p. 1; *Colonist*, 2 October 1937, p. 2, obit.

COVENTRY, Hon. Thomas George (1885-1972). The youngest of the six sons of the Ninth Earl of Coventry, twenty years younger than his oldest brother, he was elected Conservative Member of the Legislative Assembly of British Columbia for the Saanich district in 1924 by 1,433 votes, a huge majority as the Liberal Party candidate won only 912 votes and the Provincial Party member no more than 676. He sat in the Legislative Assembly in Victoria for four years during which time he was also manager of the Vancouver Island Racing Association on the Island, at a salary reported by the *Lethbridge Herald* as $5,600 a year, and was active in a movement to found a horse-racing park. In January 1925, he and his wife went back to England to join the thirty children and grandchildren celebrating the diamond wedding anniversary of his parents. In July 1929, the government sent him to London as overseas marketing representative on an annual salary of $4,000, and when his father died on 13 March 1930 (followed three days later by his mother), TC's share of the inheritance was £11,000. But he had debts and in a sudden reversal of fortune, in May 1934, his creditors assembled at Bankruptcy Building in London and declared him bankrupt. And for reasons unknown, he and his wife had divorced in 1930.

TC was one of the many extraordinary Imperial figures who found their way to the Island in the course of a complicated and adventurous life. Born in London on 25 August 1885, he appears, aged five, in census records for 1891 as much the youngest of five children living with their parents at Croome Court, Croome d'Abitot, Worcestershire, the ancestral seat of a noble family, which in mid-Victorian times held 13,021 acres in Worcestershire and 1,398 acres in Gloucestershire, totalling 14,419 acres, then worth £24,878. There were, in 1891, no fewer than twenty-seven domestic servants in the great house and more in other buildings on the estate. Ten years later, the census taker found TC, aged fifteen, at Eton. For some reasons, that can only be guessed at he did not follow any of the courses marked out for an earl's son but soon left school and spent six and a half years in the British Army. Then in 1907, he emigrated to Canada and joined the RCNWM Police, as did many other British gentlemen. After four and a half years service, he resigned and bought a farm near Castor in a grain-growing part of Alberta about a hundred miles east of Red Deer. A friendly neighbour, Rev. Martin W. Holdom (1884-1972), kept his own father in Buckinghamshire informed by long letters, now preserved at the Glenbow Archives in Calgary.

> I forgot to tell you [he wrote on 27 July 1910] about Coventry's wedding on the Monday [25 July]. Quite a nice few turned up to service in Church; the bride is quite a nice girl; dear old Holmes the shepherd who Jacques brought out from Sussex gave the bride away, there was lots of rice & shoes etc., we all adjurned [*sic*] to the ice cream parlour after the ceremony, and then the happy couple drove away in a buggy to Hildyard's old place for a four days honeymoon and so the Hon T. G. Coventry youngest son of the Earl of Coventry has been married, and that society organ the Castor Advance has a full account, "Constable T. G. Coventry R.N.W.M.P., son of Mr. & Mrs. Coventry Gloucestershire . . . England to Miss Mary Ward of Sussex Eng." Nobody here worries whether he was an Honourable or a Grave digger, as long as he is straight and a man. It is not what a man was, but what he is that counts in this country.

In February 1912, Holdom rode over to visit TC and reported, "He has retired from the RNWMP and bought land on the Paint Earth Creek, it is such a pretty place. When I rode up I found the Hon. T. G. Coventry cleaning wheat for seed in dirty old clothers. What would the dear Earl think? They were very please to see me and I stayed the night with them. Their little boy is growing splendidly."

Towards the end of June 1918, he was called up to join the Canadian Army and went off as a corporal, leaving Alice on the farm at Castor. The war ended four months later, and in a few years, they sold the farm and migrated to Victoria, where he moved in horse-racing circles and was elected to the provincial legislature, as recounted above. The financial disaster that overtook him was apparently caused by the BC government's decision in January 1934, during the economic depression of the time, to cancel his post in London. The newspapers reported what they knew of TC's financial affairs. It seems he lost a lot of money betting on horses and may have had earlier debts from his farming venture. He had borrowed from moneylenders since 1931. How he fared from 1934 until his death on 9 December 1972 is far from clear, but he probably found support or employment through members of the family. Most of his five brothers had died, but their children, his nephews and nieces, were legion. The Tenth Earl of Coventry, successor to his father, was TC's nephew, George William Reginald Victor (1900-1940), who was the eldest son of his eldest brother, and when the tenth earl was killed in battle early in the Second World War, it was his son, George William Coventry (1934-2002), who became the eleventh earl.

Sources: NAC, CEF files, RG150, accession 1992/93 166, box 2063-30; *Colonist*, 28 January 1925, p. 8; 18 March 1925, p. 1; census 1891, England RG12/2334, p. 17; census 1901, RG13/1342, p. 1; *A Preacher's Frontier: the Castor, Alberta, Letters of Rev. Martin W. Holdom 1909-1912*, ed., Paul Voisey (Calgary, Alberta, Historical Society of Alberta, 1996), 148 pp.; *Glenbow Archives* (Calgary, Alberta), M9004, Martin W. Holdom Letters, (letters dated at Castor, Alberta, 27 July, 8 August, 5 October, 7 November 1910, and 5 February 1912); *The Times* (London), 14 March 1930, p. 16, obit.; 24 May 1934, p. 9, col. B; 12 July 1934, p. 4, col. C; *The Lethbridge Herald* (Alberta), 11 July 1934, p. 5, col. F; *The Straits Times* (Singapore), 30 August 1929, p. 11; *Who was Who, vol. III* (1929-40), p. 294; Bateman, *The Great Landowners*, p. 108.

COVIL, Robert Percy (1884-1946). In 1911, he was recorded at Bamfield on the Island's west coast employed as an engineer with the trans-Pacific cable company. He was born in China in May 1884, and as his sister Lucy was born in China some five years earlier, the family must have lived there for at least that long. In 1901, he was living, aged twelve, with his family in Kent at 9 Durham Road, Beckenham. His father, Thomas Covil, aged fifty-three, was born in London at Woolwich and "living on his own means" and his mother, Ruby, aged fifty-two, came from York, where his brother Reginald, aged fifteen, was also born. Census records tell us that Thomas Covil was the son of an "Inspector of Waterman's Hall" in London, Richard S. Covil (RC's grandfather), who was born at Woolwich, and that the men of the family had earlier been employed as "watermen" and "lightermen."

RC claimed to have migrated to the Island in 1903. He married Blanche E. Porritt on 31 March 1913 in Vancouver City and died, aged fifty-nine, on 4 January 1946 in Nanaimo, where his wife died, aged eighty-four, on 20 July 1978.

Sources: census 1871, England, RG 10/486, p. 10; census 1961, RG 9/294, p. 43; census 1901, RG 13/687, p. 31 (81?); Canadian census, 1911 for Bamfield, BC; *Colonist*, 9 April 1910, p. 10.

COX, Major George Cecil Archer (1877-1933), MC. He was born in India, son of Colonel George Cox, and spent many years with the East India Railway as resident engineer and in other such posts. First commissioned as second lieutenant on 6 January 1904 at Delhi in the East Indian Railway Volunteer Rifles, he served in France with the Sixth Leicester Regiment during the Great War, was twice wounded and badly gassed, and awarded the MC.

In 1927, he retired to Victoria and, in 1933, was a member of the India-Burma Society there, with a house in Oak Bay on Carbury (Carberry) Gardens, leading uphill from the western end of Oak Bay Avenue. He died, aged fifty-five, on 29 January 1933 in the Jubilee Hospital, leaving his widow, a daughter (Mary Edith Cox), and a son, John Cecil Cox, at Trinity College School, Port Hope, Ontario. His funeral was at St Mary's Anglican Church, Oak Bay.

Sources: BL, India Office, *Indian Army List*, January 1905, p. 534]; *Colonist*, 17 January 1933, p. 8; 31 January 1933, p. 2, obit.

COX, Captain James Ernest Courtney, RN (c. 1874-1950). He was born at Portsea, Hampshire, son of Mary "Minnie" Cox, née Staney, and an absent sailor who died in the late 1880s. The 1891 census recorded JC as a "scholar," aged seventeen, living at 48 London Road, Portsea, with his widowed mother, his brother Desmond Cox, aged seven, and two sisters: Minnie B. Cox, aged twenty-two, and Alice M. Cox, aged five. They had a servant girl aged twenty. About a year later, JC joined the RN and was serving in the Indian Ocean as "Clerk" with seniority from 28 April 1892 aboard HMS *Brisk*, a twin-screw cruiser, third class, 1770 tons, 3500 horsepower, re-commissioned at Bombay 1 November 1891. In 1895, he was promoted to assistant paymaster and in 1900 was serving as such in Bermuda aboard HMS *Terror*. When he retired from the navy, he settled at Parksville, with a view over the sea, and used to have tea on Sundays with his neighbours, *Major and Mrs William Richard Wingfield-Digby and family. He died there, aged seventy-five, on 20 April 1950 at Parksville and was buried as an Anglican.

Sources: The Navy List, Corrected to The 20th December 1892 (HMSO, 1892), pp. 15, 206; *Whitaker's*, p. 129; notes and interview courtesy of Ronald Wingfield-Digby, Victoria, 12 May 2001; census 1871, England, RG 10/2130, p. 31 (mother); census 1881, RG 11/1141, p. 3; census 1891, RG 12/857, p. 3; census 1901, RG 13/5334, p. 1.

COX, Captain John G. (1843-1908). Born on 29 November 1843 in Nova Scotia to a family of mariners and shipowners, he was apprenticed on one of his father's ships and visited Victoria in 1882 while picking up a cargo of lumber for Peru. Two years later, he moved to Victoria and bought two sealing schooners, one for each of his younger brothers, Clarence Cox and William Cox. By 1892, he had become a partner in the firm of E. B. Marvin, a ship's chandler on Wharf Street, which controlled more than half of the sealing fleet. JC and James D. Warren were among the group of forty-six men who, in mid-June 1892, founded the Victoria Yacht Club under the patronage of *Colonel E. G. Prior, and JC was elected commodore. The 1901 census found him living with his wife Rebecca and their daughter Carlotta at 42 King's Road. He was still a ship chandler, but he soon became a Lloyd's agent in Victoria. They had a holiday at Cowichan Lake in August 1907, and he died, aged sixty-five, on 9 November 1908 in Victoria.

Sources: Terry Reksten, *A Century of Sailing, 1892-1992: A History of the Oldest Yacht Club on Canada's Pacific Coast* (Victoria, Orca Book Publishers, 1992), p. 7; *Colonist*, 28 August 1907, p. 6; Gosnell, *The Year Book*, p. 46.

CREASE, Lindley, K. C. (1867-1940). He was born in New Westminster on the BC mainland several years before Vancouver City was founded, scion of a scattered English family, which was in itself an example and an illustration of the Island's Imperial society during the century beginning about 1860. His father, Sir Henry Pering Pellew Crease (1823-1905), was called to the Bar in England in 1849 and in 1858 arrived on the Island, where he became the colony's first practising barrister.

Two years later, he was elected to represent Victoria in the Legislative Assembly, and in 1861, Governor James Douglas appointed him as the first attorney general, which he remained until 1870. In the years 1870-1895, he was a judge in the Supreme Court of BC. He was made a knight bachelor on 1 January 1896, the year he retired. The "Pellew" in his name was owing to his father (LC's grandfather), Captain Henry Crease, RN (1786-1862), having acted as tutor to Fleetwood Pellew, second son of Sir Edward Pellew, Viscount Exmouth, aboard HMS *Tonnant* in 1803. Until 1850, Captain Crease lived at "Ince Castle," Saltash, Cornwall, which is where LC's father was born. Also born there was a brother (LC's uncle), Major General John Frederick Crease (c. 1837-1907), who had a distinguished career in the British Marine Artillery.

LC was the fifth of the seven surviving children born to his mother, *née* Sarah Lindley (1826-1922), who has been remembered in Canada as a distinguished painter of flowers, plants, and landscapes. She married LC's father at Acton on 7 April 1853 and went out to the Island with him. The eldest of the three children of Dr John Lindley (1799-1865), she assisted her father in his work as assistant secretary to the garden of the Royal Horticultural Society at Chiswick, Middlesex, and the first professor of botany at University College, London. All three of Lindley's children became competent botanical artists but none worked with him so well or so fondly as Sarah, and she learnt a great deal from his student and artist-in-residence, Sarah Anne Drake (1803-1857), a talented flower-painter of whom she grew very fond. While helping his father at the family plant nursery during his youth, John Lindley befriended William Jackson Hooker (1785-1866), director of the Royal Botanic Gardens at Kew, and through him became assistant librarian at Sir Joseph Banks' library in Soho Square, London. As everyone knows, Banks (1743-1820) was the English naturalist who had sailed with Captain George Vancouver on the long voyage to the Island, which bears his name and brought home the first specimens of eucalyptus, acacia, mimosa, and an entire genus of plants now called *banksia*.

Sarah Lindley had a brother (LC's uncle), two years her junior, who grew up to become Sir Nathaniel Lindley (1828-1921), knighted in 1875. He went on from University College School and the college itself to become a justice at the Court of Common Pleas, then of the Queen's Bench, and finally a lord of appeal in Ordinary with a life peerage and the title Baron Lindley, author of famous books of jurisprudence. Of the four daughters and five sons born to him and his wife, *née* Sarah Katharine Teale, the best known was Sir Francis Oswald Lindley (1872-1950), who went from Winchester College and Magdalen College, Oxford, into the diplomatic service. He had a series of postings at embassies around the world—Vienna, Tehran, Cairo, Tokio, Sofia, and Petrograd—but like so many of his kind, he loved fishing, shooting, and hunting. This was probably in his mind when he stopped on his way home, ostensibly to visit his seven Crease cousins on the Island. There is not a word about them in the autobiographical book he published later, but he does mention fishing on Vancouver Island. He arrived at Victoria in April 1934 on the *Empress of Japan* after three years as British minister plenipotentiary to Japan. The *Daily Colonist* gave its usual careful attention to his visit. He spoke to a gathering of the Canadian and Kiwanis Clubs at the Empress Hotel. Five years LC's junior, he was the most prominent of LC's first cousins, and their meeting may have been brief and formal. Or was it friendly as a result of an acquaintanceship begun during the years of LC's schooling at Haileybury?

With such a family in his background—and foreground—is it any wonder that LC grew up with a strong sense of Imperial loyalty? He was on the executive of the British Empire Patriotic League along with *Brigadier General Robert Percy Clark, *Frank Victor Hobbs, and G. A. Okell (a Victoria city assessor who had emigrated from Lancashire), and he proposed the toast to the Empire at its first annual dinner, held at the Dominion Hotel in Victoria on 14 November 1921. A friend of *Colonel B. V. Layard, he was one of the pallbearers at Holy Trinity Church, Patricia Bay, when Layard was buried there on 30 December 1924. His fellow pallbearers on that occasion were *Colonel William Harwood Belson, *General R. J. Gwynne, *Colonel Cy Peck, and *Lieutenant Colonel Charles Bayard Messiter. He was, of course, a member of the Union Club and the Victoria Golf Club and prominent in the Conservative Party. As a senior partner in the family firm of Victoria barristers, Crease & Crease, LC may have looked like a big frog in a small pond, but his worldwide family gave him much to think about.

On 6 December 1937, his cousin Sir Francis Lindley's daughter, Mary Lindley, married Sir William Johnstone "Tony" Keswick (1903-1990), who was born in Japan and had been working as executive manager of the great old firm of Jardine, Matheson & Co. since 1934 at its head office in Shanghai. Keswick was also chairman of the Shanghai Muncipal Council, and as the aggressive Japanese empire advanced into China, threatening foreign interests all over the Far East and around the Pacific Ocean, there was great anxiety in British Columbia and California. I remember it well, as my father in North Saanich bought our first radio in order to hear news of events. Our predicament was all the more worrying because Ottawa and Washington DC seemed to be only dimly aware of threats to the Pacific Coast. It was in the full flood of this anxiety that LC died on 15 February 1940, before the Japanese attack on Pearl Harbour on 7 December 1941 brought the United States into the Second World War. Nor did he live to witness Keswick's career as a director of British Petroleum Ltd., director of the Bank of England, director of the Hudson's Bay Company, chief of staff to Duff Cooper as cabinet minister, a member of the British Shipping Mission to Washington, and on Field Marshal Montgomery's staff as a brigadier in the Twenty-first Army Group.

Sources: *Colonist*, 15 November 1921, p. 6; 31 December 1924, p. 5; 7 June 1931, p. 3; 25 April 1933, p. 7; 26 April 1933, p. 3; 20 April 1934, p. 10; 16 February 1940, p. 1: obit.; *Canadian Who's Who*, 1958-1960, p. 594 (Keswick); Richard Drayton, biogr. of John Lindsay, *Oxford* DCB; J. H. F. McEwen & Ian Nish, biogr. of Sir Francis Oswald Lindley, *Oxford* DCB; B. G. Gardiner, *"John Lindley," The Linnean, vol. 16* (1 January 2000), pp. 7-15; John Collins Francis & Henry Richard Fox Bourne, John Francis, Publisher of the Athenaeum, *A Literary Chronicle of Half a Century* (2 vols., vol. II, Richard Bentley & Son, 1888), pp. 185-87; G. Richardson, *"A Norfolk Network within The Royal Society,"* in Notes & Records of The Royal Society, vol. 56 (2002), pp. 28 and 32-39; *"Sarah Anne Drake, Botanical Illustrator,"* The Longham

Community Website, pp. 1-3; Sir Francis Lindley, *A Diplomat Off Duty* (Ernest Benn Ltd., 2nd ed., 1947), 200 pp.; Patrick O'Brian, Joseph Banks, *A Life* (Boston, Mass., David R. Godine, 1993), 328 pp.; Robert Blake, Jardine, Matheson: *Traders of the Far East* (Weidenfeld & Nicolson, 1999), pp. 230, 237, 246.

CRIDGE, Bishop Edward, BA (1817-1913). He was appointed in 1854 as chaplain and schoolmaster at the HBC fort at Victoria (succeeding Rev. R. J. Staines, who had arrived on 17 March 1840) and reached the Island on 1 April 1855 aboard the *Marquis of Bute* (leased from the Honourable East India Company), with his wife Mary *née* Winnelle from Boniford, Essex, whom he had married the previous year. EC himself was born at Bratton-Heming, Devonshire, on 17 December 1817, and was ordained in 1849 after attending St Peter's College, Cambridge (BA, 1848). His first appointments, before Victoria, were as deacon at Norwich Cathedral, then in London as curate at Christ Church, Stratford, but he also taught school in Devon at the Endowed Grammar School, South Molton. The HBC had built a small wooden church in Victoria, where the cathedral now stands and when the first version of the cathedral was built, he called it Christ Church after his London church. EC was the dean of that cathedral for many years. Early in his work, the Council of Vancouver Island appointed him to a committee charged with reporting on the state of schooling on the Island, and he became an informal superintendent of schools. He had grown up in a "low-church" evangelical tradition of Anglicanism rooted in the early Puritans, especially the Marian Exiles who fled to Geneva, Strassburg, and Frankfurt during the persecuting reign of "Bloody" Queen Mary (1853-1858) and there absorbed elements of continental Calvinist theology. Since Tudor times, Anglicanism had been a Christian compromise of Puritan ex-Calvinists and Anglo-Catholics in permanent opposition, like the government and the opposition in the House of Commons. EC went out to the Island in the spirit of the Colonial and Continental Church Society, which supported him and had Methodist feelings and objectives. When *Rev. George Hills, a "high-church" Anglican, was appointed bishop of [British] Columbia and arrived in January 1860, the controversy built into the Church of England was likely to flare up.

Quiet wrangling over several months gave way to open conflict on 5 December 1872, when Bishop Hills arranged a "high-church" consecration of Christ Church as a cathedral and *Archdeacon William Sheldon Reece preached a sermon that struck EC as advocating ritualism and "high-church" popishness. Apart from theological differences, Anglicans of the evangelical "low-church" tradition objected to the ceremonial, canticles, candles, vestments, and incense beloved of Roman Catholics and "high-church" Anglicans. EC believed that Bishop Hills and his followers were playing into the hands of Rome. Tactless and determined, he spoke out against these proceedings after the sermon, when he was expected merely to announce the number of the next hymn. Hills was not a very difficult or vindictive man, but such a public attack was intolerable and in 1874, EC was tried in courts both ecclesiastical and civil. Spellbound by these events, the Island's population divided into two camps; families were split over the issues. The ensuing quarrel seriously preoccupied the diocese, and a diocesan synod was formed in Victoria in 1875. After being defeated in both courts, EC formally left the cathedral and was followed by more than half of the congregation, some 250 leading parishioners supported by the *Victoria Daily Colonist.*

They found a temporary home in the Presbyterian Church with its Scottish form of Calvinism, acceptable in England since 1707, but EC soon got in touch with the Reformed Episcopalian Church in the United States, that is, the Anglican Church in the form adopted by Americans after their successful war of independence in the 1780s. The result was that in 1874, ED left the Church of England and became a bishop of the Reformed Episcopal Church, his diocese to include all of Canada and the United States west of the Rocky Mountains, triumphing to that extent over his old antagonist Bishop Hills. He also received an honorary DD at the Presbyterian Theological College, Montreal, for his services in the Protestant cause, formally awarded on 24 April 1895 at the hands of Rev. W. Leslie Clay of St Andrew's Presbyterian Church in Victoria. And he remained nearby as rector of a new Anglican church that was built for him in 1875 not far from Christ Church Cathedral on land donated by Sir James Douglas (ever a peacemaker) and called Church of Our Lord. EC served there as rector until 1908, when he suddenly became blind and had to retire. His wife Mary had died, aged seventy-eight, on 19 December 1905, but their family of nine children and his friends helped him through the next five years until his death, aged ninety-five, on 6 May 1913.

It is easy to portray EC as a pugnacious, opinionated cleric driven by faults in his character, but his friends preferred to see him as a courageous defender of the puritan, "low-church" tradition in the Church of England, determined to resist the looming influence of Rome. He expressed some of his ideas in a book he called *As it was in the Beginning, or, the Historic Principles Applied to the Mosaic Scriptures* (1900) published in the United States. As regards his influence on the Island, however, Canadian census records in 1901 and 1911 show that Reformed Episcopalians never grew in number and remained only a small minority of Anglicans. The American affiliation was inevitably distasteful to a loyal colony of the British Empire. Furthermore, a local revival of the age-old quarrel within the Anglican Church was itself likely to bring out the "least said soonest mended" instincts of many people, and I have to say that I was never made aware of the Cridge affair while boarding at Anglican Theological College on the campus of the University of British Columbia as an undergraduate in 1949-1950. More important, weathering gravestones in churchyards show that Imperial officers never ceased to gather loyally with the ambient population at St Peter's Quamichan near Duncan, at St Mark's at Ganges on Salt Spring Island, at St Stephen's in Saanich, and many other parish churches up and down the Island.

Sources: *Colonist* 11 September 1874, p. 3, "*Trial of the Very Rev'd Dean Cridge*"; Frank A. Peake, *The Anglican Church in British Columbia* (Vancouver, Mitchell Press, 1959), pp. 18ff., 76ff.; *Margaret Ormsby, British Columbia, A History*, p. 104; Edward Cridge, *As it was in the Beginning, or, the Historic Principles Applied to the Mosaic Scriptures* (Chicago, New York, Toronto, Fleming H. Revell Company, 1890); F. Henry Johnson, *A History of Public Education in British Columbia* (Vancouver, University of British Columbia Publications Centre, 1964), passim.

CROFTON, Alfred Gerald (1882-1942) and Ernest Alfred (1878-1961). Both residents of Salt Spring Island on what their kind liked to call "ranches" engaged in "mixed farming," these brothers were born Anglicans in Ireland, sons of Captain Hon. Francis George Crofton, RN (1838-1900)—youngest brother of Edward, Third Baron Crofton (1806-1869)—and his wife, Lady Georgina Paget (1809-1875). It was about 1897 that the two sons emigrated, like many other younger sons and younger sons' families. Shooting, fishing, and golf were what they did when they were not tending their small family farms. On 10 January 1901 in Victoria, EC married Mary Susanna Bullock (1870-1948), daughter of Rev. George Marten Bullock and sister of *Harry Wright Bullock. After her death there, aged seventy-nine, on 11 July 1948, he made a second marriage on 24 June 1949 with Grace Elizabeth Ward née Elkington, whose first husband, *Arthur Ward, had disappeared about 1920 in a small boat near Salt Spring, and this loving couple returned to England, where they lived and died at Sellack, a village in Herefordshire north-west of Ross-on-Wye: she on 30 March 1960 and he on 23 December 1961. Her brief obituary notice in *The Times* cited her birthplace as Salt Spring Island.

There, in the meantime, AC lived out his life with Frances Nona Wilson (1878-1951), whom he married on 17 September 1903. She was the ninth child of *Rev. E. F. Wilson. After having at least seven children, they died: he at Ganges on 3 October 1942, aged sixty, and she, aged seventy-three, on 19 January 1951, in Victoria, south of Ganges by some twenty-nine miles and a short ferry ride.

According to common knowledge in Victoria, the small coastal port of Crofton on Vancouver Island, north-west of Salt Spring Island and a short ferry ride away, was *not* named after this family but after a family called Croft.

Sources: *The Times* (London), 1 April 1960, p. 1, col. A, obit.; 28 December 1961, p. 1, col. A, obit.; *Who's Who in B.C*, 1933-34, p. 40; Kahn, *Salt Spring Island*, pp. 130-1, 157, 197, 265.

CROMPTON, Major John Arthur Philip (1871-1936). He was born on 22 June 1871 in Birmingham, fought in the British Army during the Second South African War (1899-1902), and then retired to BC as a lieutenant with the Queen's South African medal. When he enlisted in the Canadian Army in Victoria on 14 January 1915, he was a "rancher" at Creston, BC, where his wife, Mrs Florence Mary Crompton still was, but on a second "Officer's Declaration Paper," dated 15 November 1918, he gave his address as Pacific Club, Victoria, BC and his wife's as 2140 Empress St, Victoria. Retiring with the rank of major, he was employed as a school teacher and a music teacher and served a term as a school trustee. When Mrs Crompton died on 15 October 1934, they were living at 445 Constance Avenue, Esquimalt, and there he died, aged sixty-two, on 23 June 1936 and was buried as a Roman Catholic. In a posthumous public letter of appreciation, "An old friend" said that he had been straightforward and utterly sincere.

Sources: NAC, CEF files, box 2153-31; *Colonist*, 16 October 1934, p. 3, obit.; 24 June 1936, p. 4; 26 June 1936, p. 3; 28 June 1936, p. 4, obit.

CULLIN, Lieutenant Colonel Harold Joseph Rous (1875-1935). Born in Liverpool, son of a canon of the Church of England, he is recorded, aged six, in the 1881 census living with his family at Oughtrington Rectory. His father was then rector of Second Mediety, Lymm, Cheshire, and there was an elder brother, William H. A. Cullin, and an elder sister, Maude Ellen. He was educated at King's School, Canterbury, where he was an officer in the school cadet corps and good at cricket and athletics. He represented his school in gymnastics at Aldershot but also studied at the Sidney Cooper School of Art in Canterbury (1891-1893) and then with an architect, W. Stone, in London (1894-1895). Cullen was a member of the London Rifle Brigade in 1896-1898 and in 1899 became a lieutenant in the First London Royal Engineers. He studied at the School of Military Engineering in Chatham and, in January 1900, obtained a commission in the Thirty-eighth Field Company, Royal Engineers, and saw active service in Orange Free State and Cape Colony during the South African War. Shot in a leg and seriously ill, he was sent back to England in September 1900 with the Queen's Medal with three clasps and later became a captain and adjutant with the First London Royal Engineers, but retired in 1904 and emigrated to Canada.

Settling in Victoria, HC first worked in Samuel Maclure's office but, in May 1905, opened his own architectural practice. He was also bursar of the University School for several years after it was founded in 1906. On 5 August 1908, aged thirty-two, he married Frances Elizabeth Olive Bales, daughter of Charles Jacob and Frances Ann Bales, from Enderby, BC, this at Christ Church Cathedral. By 1916, according to army records, the Cullins had two daughters and a son, Alice Evelyn, aged six, Doris Olive, aged one, and Francis Rowland, aged four. The family lived at first on Cornwall St in a house HC had designed in 1912, but they soon moved on. HC remained active in the military and, on 8 September 1912, joined the newly formed Eighty-eighth Regiment, Victoria Fusiliers, as senior captain. He held a command in the civil aid force throughout the coal miners' strike on VI in 1913 and was stationed at Nanaimo for the first two months of the strike. At the same time, however, he was also a member of St Luke's Anglican Church. He was prominent throughout in the BC Society of Architects and served on both the Provincial Council and the Victoria Chapter Executive Council until 1914. By the time the Great War broke out in 1914, he had designed at least seven schools, mainly as architect by appointment to the Saanich School Board, notably Cedar Hill School, 1912, and its Manual Training Hall, 1913, and the eleven-room Tolmie School (now head office of the Greater Victoria School District No. 61). He also designed a number of houses in the Victoria district, such as one for the real-estate agent Roger G. Monteith, in 1913. In addition, he designed several commercial blocks and apartments.

He retired from his architectural practice in 1914 and worked full-time as commanding officer of the Eighty-eighth Victoria Fusiliers, being promoted to major and then to lieutenant colonel. In October 1915, Ottawa authorized him to recruit 1,050 men and to mobilize as an overseas battalion, so he issued an appeal for Victoria's unmarried men to join the regiment. In May 1916, the regiment left for Britain by train and troopship. As commander of the Eighty-eighth Battalion,

CEF, he was invalided out of the service in 1917 and retired on 6 September that year. In June 1918, he resumed his architectural practice and designed a residence in Oak Bay for *Francis Ashley Sparks, principal of St Aidan's School. Advised by his doctors to leave the coast, apparently as a result of ill health during the war, he moved to Kelowna where, in July 1919, he obtained a temporary appointment in the provincial civil service. Like many other returned soldiers, he had a very hard time making ends meet, but did design several buildings at Kelowna, notably a brick fire hall built in 1924. Late in 1925, he suffered a stroke, was unable to work for over two years, and returned with his family to Victoria. By 1933, he was listed in the Victoria City Directory as living in the Old Men's Home. At his death, he, Frances, and a daughter were living at the Menzies Nursing and Convalescent Home. He died on 12 August 1935 at the Royal Jubilee Hospital of bronchial pneumonia due to a cerebral haemorrhage and had a Masonic funeral and burial at Royal Oak, having been a lifelong member of the order.

Sources: Notes courtesy of Jennifer Nell Barr, Victoria, May 2001; *Colonist*, 8 September 1917, p. 7.

CUMMINS, George (1881-1914). He was born on 5 September 1881 in Shoreditch, London, and joined the Royal Navy as a young man. He served *inter alia* as an ordinary seaman aboard HMS *Shearwater* during the Somaliland campaign (1901-1903) and after the South African War retired to the Island. There he worked on various coastal craft and joined the British Campaigners' Assocation. When he died, aged thirty-three, at St Joseph's Hospital, Victoria, on 21 January 1914, the association took charge of his funeral for he would otherwise "have been buried as a pauper."

Sources: *National Archives* (PRO), London, PRO. ADM 188/347, no. 200193; *Minutes of the British Campaigners' Association, 1908-1935*, 19 February 1914; *Colonist* 22 January 1914, p. 7, obit.

CUNLIFFE, Lieutenant Colonel Walter Howell (1851-?). He was born in India on 4 October 1851 and sent to be schooled in England under the care of an India-born uncle, Rev. Henry Cunliffe (c. 1825-?), and his wife Mary, who lived at the vicarage, Shiffnal, Shropshire. The 1861 census found him, aged ten, living there with his elder sister Rosie Cunliffe and their uncle and aunt with six servants. On 14 September 1875, he married Gertrude Foster, daughter of William Fry Foster and his wife Caroline Cunliffe, born at Leamington, Warwick, and the 1881 census recorded them living at 65 Mill Road, Gillingham, Kent, with two servants, one of them a cook born in Canada. WC was then a captain in the Fifty-second Regiment, Oxford Light Infantry, and they had a daughter Gwynedd S. Cunliffe, aged four, born at Greasham, Hampshire. When he retired with the rank of lieutenant colonel, they went to live at "Wesgate," Countisbury, NW Devonshire, but he eventually migrated to Victoria.

This move may have been prompted by his wife's death, as he remarried in Victoria on 30 September 1914 at St Mary's Anglican Church in Oak Bay.

His new wife was Anne Catherine Meakin, eldest daughter of the late George Meakin of Callingwood Hall, Burton-on-Trent, and of Mrs Meakin of Victoria. Her brother, Reginald Abbotts Meakin (1888-1934) of the BC Horse, an Anglican from Dublin, gave her away. Living at 1118 Fairfield Road, WC became a scoutmaster and was serving in October 1914 as the district commissioner. They must have moved away in the next few years as their deaths were not recorded in BC.

Sources: *Colonist*, 25 October 1914, p. 6; *Victoria Daily Times*, 1 October 1914, p. 10; census 1861, England, RG 9/1854; census 1881, RG 11/890/81, p. 52; census 1901, RG 13/2145, p. 10.

CUNNINGHAM, Lieutenant Colonel Herbert Hugh Blair (1875-1939). He was born at Woolwich Arsenal, London, son of Major General J. P. Cunningham of the Twentieth Hussars, and the 1891 census records him, aged sixteen, as a "School Boy" at "Violet Lodge," 50 de Poys Avenue, Bedford, Parish of St Peter, Bedfordshire, living with his family: his father, John P. Cunningham, aged sixty-two, a "Lieut.-General Med. Dept Retired," born at St Nicholas, County Antrim, Ireland, and two younger brothers, aged twelve and nine. There was a housekeeper and a maid but no wife. The Cunninghams were an old and distinguished Anglo-Irish family, and after his education at Bedford School and London University, HC was commissioned in 1899 as lieutenant in the Sixth Royal Irish Rifles. He served in the South African War in the Natal Field Force in 1900, then as supply officer in Pilcher's Force, Transvaal, Orange Free State, and Cape Colony, and finally in charge of the barracks at Bloemfontein. In 1908-1910, he was employed organizing officer's training corps in Ireland but, in 1914, was sent to Egypt in the British Army of Occupation and then served in 1914-1916 with the Forty-second Division at Gallipoli, where he was promoted to captain. In the Sinai Peninsula in 1916-1917, HC was acting lieutenant colonel and sent next to France and Belgium in 1917-1918. He served on the HQ staff of the Ninth Army Corps, British Army on the Rhine, in 1919-1920, when he was promoted to lieutenant colonel. There followed appointments to the Third Lahore Division EEF in 1920, Palestine in 1920-1921, to HQ staff of the Fifty-third Division in Wales in 1921-1922, in the British Army of Occupation in Germany in 1922, and to the regular army reserve in 1922.

A few years after the Great War, he migrated to Victoria and, in 1930, was in the reserve of the Canadian militia. During the 1930s, HC took up the cause of old soldiers and, in 1937, helped to form a Victoria branch of the Corps of Commissionaires. There were already several thousand retired soldiers enrolled in British units of the Commissionaires. A Dominion Executive Council had been chartered in Montreal to establish branches in the main cities of Canada, and HC helped to organize the Victoria branch on 4 August 1937. A year later, the *Daily Colonist* printed a letter in which he wrote, "Just as the survivors of the old British Army remember their comrades of the heroic days of 1914, so do the originals of this Company remember their first commandant—*Brigadier-General Sir Charles Delmé-Radcliffe, K.C.M.G., then a sick man with his own days limited, yet who did not hesitate to devote his last days to furthering the cause of retired soldiers and sailors of the permanent forces as regular officers have invariably done in the past." Meanwhile, HC himself was active in other community work, for example, inviting the Women's Institute and others at Shawnigan to an at home in June 1925, and he was active in the Church of England as well as in his clubs, the Junior Naval and Military Club (London) and the British Public Schools Club of Victoria. He lived for a time at Shawnigan Lake, and later at 605 Courtney Street, Victoria, then at 1539 Richmond Road.

When HC died, aged sixty-three, on 26 January 1939, the funeral was at Christ Church Cathedral, and he was buried at the Military Cemetery in Esquimalt. A few days later, Lillian Wilson of 736 Craigflower Road, Victoria, wrote to the *Colonist*:

> I happened to call in to see [HC] just at a time when life to him was at its lowest ebb. I had just received a letter from England promising him a few shillings (charity) in response to his letter asking for even a meagre pension after his many years of service to his country. It seems he was entitled to nothing from Canada as he belonged to the British Army and to no pension from England as he was living in Canada. He had no means of returning to the Old Country so was dependent on kind hearts to give him help.
>
> Hoping to cheer, and perhaps to lift, his proud spirit, I asked to hear the story of the six war medals glittering on his uniform. Never before have I heard the story of such valor. The colonel told me that when he passed on to be with his old comrades once more that he wished no flowers to be sent. "Flowers should be for the living," were his words.

Sources: census England, 1891, RG 12/1248, p. 44; *Colonist*, 16 April 1937, p. 16; 2 August 1938 p. 4; 5 April 1925, p. 33; 28 January 1939, p. 14, 29 January 1939, p. 2 (with photo); 4 February 1939, p. 4; *Who's Who in B.C.*, 1931 p. 27 1933-1934, pp. 43-4.

CUPPAGE, Granville William Vernon (1867-1940). Born on 1 June 1867 in Dublin, Ireland, he was at an Anglican school in 1881 in Bulkington, Warwickshire, together with his brother Edmond (c. 1865-?). They were nephews of *Forbes George Vernon, their mother being his half-sister, Louisa Emily Vernon, which may have had something to do with their emigration. GC emigrated to Victoria and there married Marion Gwendoline Kane on 18 May 1898. In 1901, they were living at 14 Quebec Street, and he was working as a civil-service clerk on a salary of $1,140 a year. In 1903, he joined the Royal Victoria Yacht Club. When his wife took up with William Harrison Eudy in 1909, GC divorced her later that year, with effect from 21 December, and four days later married Edith Madeleine Reade (1884-1972) on Christmas Day. She was a daughter of *Frederick Murray Reade and thus a descendant of the famous Victorian novelist Charles Reade. Edith had a mind of her own and travelled a good deal by herself. In September 1951, aged seventy-four, then living at 2720 Somass Drive long after GC had died on 19 March 1940, she replied indignantly to a letter in the *Victoria Daily Colonist,*

> I believe myself only one of many Canadians of English origin to wonder how it occurs to Mr A. E. Newberry that the 1951 Englishman almost has to apologize for walking around. I have recently returned from the land of my birth, and you won't find anywhere a prouder and more confident people who have lived through their "finest hour" . . . Mr Newberry might read up a bit of BC history and discover that had it not been for the enterprise, foresight and sagacity of Englishmen, a Spanish flag might still be flying on Vancouver Island as it did at Nootka on the West Coast in 1789. He might consider the visit of Capt. James Cook, RN, to Nootka in 1778, and the assembly of the great British fleet at Spithead which challenged Spain's pretensions to the Pacific. He might remember the founding of Fort Victoria by the H.B.C. in 1843. He could then go on to 1849 when the Crown in London proclaimed the colony of Vancouver Island, to 1866 when British Columbia was united with Vancouver Island; and to confederation in 1871 as the bulwark against American expansion.

Edith Madeleine Cuppage, *née* Reade died, aged eighty-seven, on 26 February 1972 in Victoria.

Sources: census 1881, England, RG 11/3059, p. 5; census 1901, *Victoria; Colonist,* 20 September 1951, p. 4; *Terry Reksten, A Century of Sailing, 1892-1992: A History of the Oldest Yacht Club on Canada's Pacific Coast* (Victoria, Orca Book Publishing, 1992), p. 48; BC Divorce Records (Internet), vol. 2 (of 5), pp. 101, 102, 105.

Gen. Sir Arthur William Currie

CURRIE, General Sir Arthur William (1875-1933). Born into a Methodist family at Strathroy, Ontario, Currie took teacher's training but went out to BC in May 1894, before his final exams and when he was only nineteen years old. He stayed there with his great-aunt, Mrs Orlando Warner (*née* Jane Patterson), wife of a Victoria shipwright; they lived on Alston Street, overlooking the harbour. He arrived with some idea of making his way in the railway boom of the time, but turned his hand instead to teaching at Sidney for sixty dollars a month during the year 1995-1996. He had thirty pupils, aged six to eighteen years, and seems to have managed well enough. After only one year in Sidney, Currie moved back to Victoria in June 1896, took posts first at Victoria Boys' Central School, then at Victoria High School, and became a leading Freemason an active member of the Young Men's Liberal Association, and on 5 June 1897, he enlisted as a part-time soldier in the Fifth Regiment, Canadian Garrison Artillery. This entailed drilling on Saturday evenings at the Menzies Street Armouries, where my father later did the same. In 1900, Arthur Currie gave up teaching to become an insurance salesman in the firm of Matson and Coles. After *J. S. H. Matson quit the company in 1904 to take over *The Daily Colonist*, Currie was in charge, and five years later, during a property boom in Victoria, he joined RA Power in forming a real-estate firm in which he eventually lost heavily, as did some of his clients.

After a discouraging start, Currie enjoyed army life, became president of the BC Rifle Association (in 1905), rose to the rank of major in his militia unit, bought military textbooks from London, and spent much time in training courses taught by British army personnel at Esquimalt. An obvious choice for an army command, he led a Canadian brigade to England at the beginning of the Great War (1914-1918) and, by the end of it, had risen to the rank of general in charge of the Canadian forces. He was knighted in 1917 and in 1919 returned to Canada, but soon moved to Montreal, where he stayed for the rest of his life. Currie was a complicated person: tough, determined and uncompromising, a heavy smoker with stomach troubles, and inclined to colourful swearing. He came from a family that had faced difficult times: his grandparents were an Irish couple called Corrigan—he Roman Catholic and she Anglican—who were harried by the Catholic Church until they fled to Ontario, where they changed their name to "Curry" and became Methodists. It was Arthur Currie who changed the name again to "Currie."

Thereafter, two things stand out in a life too complicated to explain fully here: In 1920, Currie was appointed principal (i.e., president) of McGill University, a post he held for many years, and he responded to journalistic criticism of the loss of life in battles at which he had been the commander, by launching a successful lawsuit against a provincial journalist. The case was long and became famous during the late 1920s; for several weeks in 1928, indeed, it was the talk of the entire country. Some saw it as a struggle between common soldiers and the military establishment; others saw it as Currie's valiant defence of Canadian forces whose wartime record had been unfairly criticized and too quickly forgotten. However that may be, AC was a victim of slander during and after the Great War by the notorious cabinet minister in Ottawa, Sir Sam Hughes, (1853-1921), partly for personal reasons and partly because of his Imperial loyalties and connections. This last point has never been made clear.

AC was a favourite with the many British veterans who joined the Eighty-eighth Victoria Fusiliers of which he was the colonel in 1914. This unit had been organized earlier to supplement the Fifth Regiment CGA, which had hitherto been the only volunteer unit for home defence on the Island. When Currie said proudly in April 1914 that "no other regiment in the Dominion possesses the same number of medals for active service," he meant British medals awarded for service in the British or Indian armies. Seven of the eight officers he named on that occasion were born in the British Isles and had retired to Vancouver Island after serving around the empire with British forces: *Lieutenant Colonel J. A. Hall, *Captain H. J. Rous Cullen, *Captain Percy Byng Hall, DSO, *Captain Richard Clive, *Captain Moorhead, *Captain Paul Frederick Villiers, and *Captain William Glencairn Cunningham. The one born in Canada, *Captain Walter Bapty, was from an English family that had emigrated to London, Ontario. Bapty had become a physician after running away from home as a boy to join the Canadian contingent fighting in the Boer War. It is significant of his Imperial background that he was visited in Victoria by a British cousin, Major P. S. Bapty, a retired Indian army officer, hoping to retire to Victoria and travelling as a weapons specialist on an English rifle team that had just taken part in a shooting competition somewhere in Eastern Canada. Among this cousin's impeccable credentials as an Imperialist was his appointment as a reserve inspector of a police subdivision in England and as musketry officer for the Legion of Frontiersmen "throughout the world." There were other signs of AC as an Imperial. He was a sporting companion of *Captain Sir Charles Pigott Piers and wrote a preface for Piers's book of sporting memories, and he returned from India in 1931, full of praise for the British *raj* and its activities.

AC felt at home with the Island's British gentry, as did his wife, *née* Lucy Sophia Chaworth Musters (1875-1969), who was descended through her father from a county family of Nottinghamshire. She was the daughter of an English army officer who in the 1860s had fled to Vancouver Island together with the girl he loved, probably dismissed in disgrace for Victorian reasons by his gentlemanly parents, who lived on an estate near Nottingham. She seems to have been a bricklayer's daughter, perhaps a servant girl. After their long voyage around South America, they married in Christ Church Cathedral, Victoria, and tried pioneer farming up the Island, then largely virgin forest. They had several children. Then on 11 August 1878, only three years after AC's birth in Ontario, the children's mother (AC's future mother-in-law!) died giving birth to Lucy Sophia, and the baby's father, broken hearted, took their elder children back to England, leaving the baby with a kind neighbour, who informally adopted her. This was Jane Warner (1845-1911), *née* Patterson, an Anglo-Irish woman who had emigrated in 1852 and married Orlando Warner, a shipwright from Pugwash, Nova Scotia, and who turns out to have been AC's aunt! Thus, it may have seemed like destiny when AC met his aunt's adopted daughter while boarding in the Warner household, and they were married on 14 August 1901 in Victoria at St Saviour's Anglican Church. The Canadian census for 1901, compiled in the spring, shows the young couple, still unmarried, living on Alston Street with the widowed Jane Warner, Lucy recorded simply as a daughter, and AC as a boarder. Provincial vital-statistics records of the marriage, however, were in no doubt that it was "Lucy Sophia C. Musters" whom AC married (the clerks could never cope with hyphenated names.)

Sources: *Colonist,* 12 April 1914, p. 14; 17 April 1931, pp. 1-2, with photo; 30 August 1934, p. 5; *The Sidney and Gulf Islands Review,* 8 September 1927, p. 2; Howay and Gosnell, *British Columbia,* vol. IV, pp. 168-72, and photo; *The Sidney Review,* 8 September 1927, p. 2; Patrick T. A. Chaworth Musters, *The Musters: A Family Gathering* (Market Overton, Rutland, 1998), pp. 100ff.; BC Vital Statistics, B11368 GSU no. 1983525, marriage on 14 August 1901 in Victoria; Hugh M. Urquhart, *Arthur Currie: The Biography of a Great Canadian* (Toronto, Dent, 1950), 363 pp,; Daniel G. Dancocks, *Sir Arthur Currie: A Biography* (Toronto, Methuen, 1985), 332 pp.; A. M. J. Hyatt, *General Sir Arthur Currie: A Military Biography* (Toronto, University of Toronto Press, 1987), 178 pp.; and Robert J. Sharpe, *The Last Day, the Last Hour: The Currie Libel Trial* (Toronto, Carswell Co. for The Osgoode Society, 1988), 270 pp.; R. Craig Brown & Desmond Morton, *"The Embarrassing Apotheosis of a 'Great Canadian': Sir Arthur Currie's Personal Crisis in 1917,"* Canadian Historical Review, vol. LX, no 1 (1979), pp. 41-63.

CURRIE, Rev. Walter Thomas (1858-1915). A Canadian Congregational missionary who spent his last years on the Island, he was born in Toronto on 18 July 1858 and graduated at McGill University, Montreal, in 1885. Two professors had lasting influence on him: Sir William Dawson (1820-1899), with his deep scientific interests in geology and palaeontology, and Dr J. H. Stevenson. During his summers as a student, he worked for a blacksmith in rural Ontario in the best Canadian tradition and also learnt carpentry, cabinet-making, and the rudiments of building, all of which proved to be useful in his life as a Congregational missionary abroad. Even more useful (if one may put it thus) were his wives, Clara Wilkes from Brantford, Ontario, who went with him to Africa and died tragically in the interior of Angola in September 1886, and his second wife Amy Johnston, who had emigrated to Canada from Ireland on 25 December 1894.

It was with Clara that WC first travelled to Angola, a Portuguese colony, by way of Boston (Massachusetts), the British Isles, and Portugal. They landed in Angola on 4 June 1886 and worked there for the Canadian Congregational Foreign Missionary Society formed in 1881 with a good deal of help from an American society of Congregationalists already involved in a similar mission in another part of the country. Clara's death brought home to him the first of three great obstacles facing Christian missionaries in Africa: the diseases and physical hardships that threatened their lives. It was to WC's advantage that he had a year's medical training and quickly learnt to be an amateur healer, but his own health eventually broke down to the point where he was eventually forced to retire and so went to the Island. A second obstacle was the tribal habits of the natives in WC's life, the Ovimbundu and Umbundu trading peoples, who were strong, wealthy, and accustomed to trading in ivory, beeswax, and slaves, which called for a great deal of political skill and tact. They were long-distance traders moving about between the Equator and the Cape of Good Hope with great caravans of slaves. He faced a third difficulty in the determined Roman Catholic hostility to Protestant interferance in the Portuguese empire. The religious freedom he had grown up with in the British Empire was unknown in Portugal, where a man could be arrested for selling a Bible and where even the British Embassy Church had to be hidden away out of sight behind high walls. Harder to understand, perhaps, was a fourth obstacle: the hostility in Canada and the Western World generally of well-meaning but ignorant critics inclined to defend indefensible African cultures on social-scientific and Christian grounds ("who are we to tell Africans how they should live," etc.). WC faced all these troubles well enough in his biographers' opinions to rank with great missionaries of the past such as Livingston, Mackay, and Moffat. It was under the title "The David Livingstone of Canada" that the *Victoria Daily Colonist* printed a long article about his career in Angola.

John Butcher entitled the fifth chapter of his thesis about WC, "Defeated Hero: The 'Canadian Livingstone' Returns Home," which tells much about the obstacles to missionary work. After about twenty-five years of it, WC retired in 1911 to the Royal Oak district north of Victoria, where he and Amy settled in a house they called "Chissamba," the name of their Angolan mission. It was on the wooded, winding West Saanich Road where there were no tropical fevers, no slavers, and no hostile authorities. Amy had the strength and courage to develop the place as a fruit farm, with the help of a Chinese labourer, but WC was already an invalid and died, aged fifty-six, on 7 April 1915, after preaching deliriously in the Umbundu language for several days in his bed. His body was sent to Toronto and buried there in Mount Pleasant Cemetery on Yonge Street. Such was his and Amy's character, however, that on 23 May 1937, local people formally established a small park on the West Saanich Road, near Beaver Lake Road, with plaque and cairn as a memorial to them.

Sources: John C. Butcher, "*Canadian Missionaries and the Ovimbundu of Angola, 1885-1915*," MA thesis at Dalhousie University, 1975 (under the direction of my old friend and colleague, Dr John Flint, to whom I owe this reference); *Colonist*, 26 April 1926, Sunday, p. 28; Rev. Dr J. K. Unsworth, "*Saanich Resident Brought Light into African Night*," *Colonist*, 16 May 1937, p. 6; *Globe & Mail* (Toronto), 10 April 1915, p. 23; J. T. Tucker, *Currie of Chissamba (Herald of the Dawn)* (Toronto, The United Church of Canada, 1945), 180 pp., p. 10 and passim.

DALLAS, Alexander Grant (1821-82). A short biography in the *Dictionary of Canadian Biography*, by W. Kaye Lamb, sums up this interesting figure as seen from Ontario, but it leaves room for a note about his family on the Island and in the empire at large. AD went to Shanghai, where he lived next to the British Consulate as the first representative of the firm Jardine, Matheson, which had recently moved up from Canton, and he was one of only twenty-five British subjects there in December 1843. At a public meeting on 12 April 1853, he was much in favour of defensive steps against the troublesome Taiping forces, likely to attack from their headquarters in Nanking. These were revolutionary forces which General Charles

"Chinese" Gordon was later famous for defeating on behalf of Peking as well as London. We know from Lamb's careful article that the Hudson's Bay Company, to whose committee AD was elected in 1856, sent him on a mission of investigation to Victoria, where he arrived in May the next year. He had a decisive voice in the arrangements whereby the Island became a Crown Colony and James Douglas its first governor, and AD then became successor to Sir George Simpson, the company's chief representative in North America, who died on 7 September 1860. AD left for London on 24 March 1861 and on 31 December, he wrote a letter at the Reform Club (London) about "Vancouver's Island" and *The Times* printed it the next day. It was an urgent plea for Great Britain to take an interest in what he saw as a wonderfully promising Imperial outpost coming into focus as the only settlement near the Cariboo gold fields: "Provisions are as plentiful as gold, and cheaper than in any other country I know. The finest potatoes I ever saw were selling last winter in Victoria at 20 cents, or 10d. per 100lb. Flour and other necessaries were equally cheap and abundant . . . What is wanted is a line of English steamers from Panama to Victoria." He quoted a corroborating letter he had received from Victoria. Of course, AD was exaggerating the colony's merits, but his was an early voice in what was to become a chorus of approval for a remote colonial destination that was in many ways more like home than most—for the gentry at least. He had witnessed the effects on Victoria of the gold rush, which took the Island and the empire by storm in 1858, and on 9 March that year, he had married the third of Governor Douglas's nine daughters, a happy event in their uneasy relations.

On 3 February 1862, the company named AD governor of Rupert's Land, a vast prairie wilderness, where he spent many months laying the foundations for its organization as the NWT that were to be transferred to the Crown in 1869 and to form a constitutional bridge between British Columbia and Canada in 1871. He and his family were truly Imperial in their origins and activities, as can be seen in English census records, for example, in 1881. Then aged sixty, he was "late Governor of Rupert's Land," born in the West Indies, living at "Round Coppice," Iver, Buckinghamshire, with his wife, Jane *née* Douglas (1839-1909), a native of Fort Vancouver, Oregon Territory (on the Columbia River), although the census-takers persisted in believing her born in BC. A daughter of the late Governor Sir James Douglas (1803-77) and Lady Amelia Douglas, *née* Connolly (1812-1890), she and AD had with them at Iver three of their daughters and two sons, variously born in Kensington and Chelsea (London), Edinburgh, and Inverness. They had a governess and eight domestic servants. Less than a year later, AD died on 3 January 1882 in London at Trevor Terrace, Rutland Gate. *The Times* appears to have scarcely noticed his death. It printed only the shortest of obituary notices in the "deaths" column on 7 January, four days after the event. Perhaps, the confusing geography and complicated events of his career puzzled observers in Britain, but one of his sons, Alister Grant Dallas, born on 10 June 1866 in Victoria (where Jane was always glad to stay with her family), had a classic Indian Army career that stood out bold and clear in London. Two enthusiastic obituary accounts appeared in *The Times* after his death on 2 February 1931, relating how he rose to be a major general serving on the North-West Frontier of India, in the South African War, the Gallipoli Campaign, and in Egypt and Palestine, moving from the Sixteenth Lancers, to the Durham Light Infantry, the School of Musketry in South Africa, and the Fifty-third Division, frequently mentioned in dispatches, decorated with the CMG and the CB, and married to a daughter of Brigadier General H. F. Brooke of Ashbrooke, who had died in Afghanistan in action at Deh Khojah (16 August 1880). It is scarcely necessary to add that relatives of Sir James Douglas were big fish in the small Imperial pond of Victoria and AD and family were celebrated in the naming of Dallas Road, the main thoroughfare along the shore of the Strait of Juan de Fuca, facing south across the strait to the enchanting snowy Olympic Range in the State of Washington.

Sources: W. Kaye Lamb, "*Dallas, Alexander Grant, HBC administrator and businessman,*" DCB, vol. XI, pp. 230-31; *The Times* (London), 1 January 1862, p. 9, col. D, Letter to the Editor; 4 February 1931, p. 14, col. E, obit.; 12 February 1931, p. 14, col. F, obit. (Alister Grant Dallas); census 1871, RG 10/49/59, p. 29; census 1881, RG 11/1457/8, p. 9; *Whitaker's*, p. 140; Robert Blake, Jardine, Matheson: *Traders of the Far East* (Weidenfeld & Nicolson, 1999), pp. 125, 128; David Hodgkins, *The Second Railway King: The Life and Times of Sir Edward Watkin, 1819-1901* (Cardiff, Merton Priory Press, 2002), pp. 218, 233-34, 324.

DAVIDSON, Assistant Chief of Staff Geoffrey Huntley (c. 1915-1989). Born at Chengtoo, China, he became a naval cadet on 31 August 1934 aboard HMS *Frobisher* and a midshipman on 1 September 1935. He was then posted in succession on HMS *Royal Sovereign* (1935), *Victory, Revenge, Excellent,* and *Dryad*. In 1943, he was at Royal Roads, Esquimalt, but sent in 1944 to Gatineau (in command), NHQ, as director of naval training 1949 and other postings. After serving from 1959 at Hamilton on the staff of the commanding officer, naval divisions, and as assistant chief of staff, he retired on 5 July 1964 and died at Nanaimo on 24 March 1989.

Sources: *MacFarlane*, p. 16.

DAVIDSON, Captain Hugh James Alexander (1857-1933). Born at Nuperabad, India, son of General Alexander George Davidson, he started a long military career there but came to Canada with the Connaught Rangers in the 1880s, then joined the NW Mounted Police, served in Regiment 947 of the Kootenay Post's "D" Division as acting sergeant in "D" division, and was appointed inspector on 1 February 1889 at $1,400 a year. During the Riel Rebellions, he had been active, making a formal declaration on 30 May 1885 concerning the first shot fired at Duck Lake, Saskatchewan, in March 1885. He then raised a regiment at Pincher Creek, where he was living when the South African War broke out. He fought in South Africa in 1899-1902, returned to Canada with the Queen's Medal and four clasps, and, before 1914, organized the Seventy-ninth Cameron Highlanders in Winnipeg. He was too old to go overseas during the Great War but served as Registrar of Alien Enemies in Canada for four years. In 1930, he moved to 1042 Linden Avenue, Victoria, and there he died, aged seventy-six, on 26 September 1933, leaving his widow, four daughters, and a son Charles then at Yahk, BC. A Roman Catholic, he was buried at Ross Bay after a funeral at St Andrew's Cathedral.

Sources: NAC, R6657-0-7-E; *Colonist*, 28 September 1933, p. 3, obit.; *Civil Service List of Canada, 1908*, p. 23 (RNWM Police); Brian A. Reid, *Our Little Army in the Field: The Canadians in South Africa, 1899-1902* (St Catharines, Ont., Vanwell Publishing Ltd., 1996), p. 113.

DAY, John Edward (1862-1944). Born on 22 November 1862 at Gibraltar, he joined the RN at the age of fifteen and served on the Royal Yacht, *Victoria and Albert,* then on HMS *Triumph,* transporting troops to the Far East. In 1883, he went out to Victoria aboard HMS *Amphion,* and in 1892, he was there again on the *Warspite*. Discharged in Victoria as chief petty officer, he bought the Esquimalt Hotel and kept it until the RCN took it over in 1943. He then worked as manager of the Phoenix Brewing Company and was a member of the Navy League, the Naval Veterans Branch of the Canadian Legion, the British Imperial Comrades Association, one of the orders of Freemasonry, and the Odd Fellows. He loved lawn bowling and was past president of the Victoria Lawn Bowling Club. When he died, aged seventy-nine, on 30 January 1944, he left his wife and a nephew, Lieutenant Commander Ivan Day, of Victoria.

Sources: *National Archives* (PRO), London, ADM 188/138; *Colonist*, 11 February 1940, p. 17; 1 February 1944, p. 11, obit.

DEAN, John (1850-1943). He arrived in Victoria on 26 April 1884 but wandered off into the provincial mainland for several years, often on horseback, staking claims in hope of finding gold, working at construction projects, and saving his earnings. He began contracting to build, for instance, huge water tanks for the CPR in the Fraser River Canyon and then turned to speculating in property and, in April 1896, opened a real-estate office and mining brokerage at Rossland, BC. After becoming a JP, he was elected mayor on 15 January 1903 and worked hard for the town for some years until he grew tired of it and journeyed back to England and on from country to country around the world. About 1907, he returned to Victoria and took an interest in local politics. His name appears often in *The Victoria Daily Colonist:* advertising his real-estate office at 108 Government Street in March 1907, leading the cause in August 1909 for new water supplies from Gold Stream and the Malahat Range, reporting to the city council in June 1910 on his inspection of the property assessment rolls, and in many public causes.

On 2 October 1895, soon after his first arrival, JD had paid $375 for one hundred acres high up on Mount Newton in North Saanich, at a public auction. This was a speculation and soon seemed disappointingly remote, but now he built a cabin in a tiny valley at the mountain's top. On 9 December 1921, he gave eighty acres of this land to the Crown to be kept as a public park. His cabin and about twenty acres around it, he kept for himself, but on 26 August 1943, two days before JD's death, the province bought this too and set gangs of conscientious objectors (refusing military service in the Second World War) to building paths, guiding signs, picnic tables, fireplaces, and bridges over wet patches among the skunk cabbages (*Lysichiton americanus*). The whole hundred acres was preserved as a provincial park. My brother and I spent many a happy day there, sometimes among those conscientious objectors, and as Boy Scouts, we often spent nights in JD's cabin. It was furnished just as he left it, with an oak Morris chair, etc., and open to the Boy Scout Troop of *Freeman Foard King, who had befriended JD and encouraged him to donate it to the province. Appointed on 11 June 1934 to lead the North Saanich and Sidney Island Provincial Park Board, Freeman King watched over JD's cabin and the park with characteristic care.

JD was born on a farm in England at Stretton, Cheshire, on 17 December 1850, and it is said (though I could find no record of the event) that he came to public attention at the age of fourteen by winning the Royal Humane Society Medal for rescuing two younger boys from drowning in the River Mersey. In his early twenties, he decided to emigrate to North America and arrived at Halifax, Nova Scotia, aboard an Allen liner, *Leandinevian*, on 14 January 1873. He stayed for a while in Orillia, Ontario, with his uncle John Dean and then worked at various jobs in Toronto. Early in 1877, he took a steamer to Galveston, Texas, where he worked until 1882, when he returned to England to stay with his brother George, who had become a merchant in Manchester. A year later, he went back to Victoria, as related above. Like many self-taught people, JD had a range of original ideas and principles: For instance, he bought several burial plots in the Ross Bay Cemetery and generously buried some of his old friends there when they died. He himself was ultimately buried in the last of these plots. But long before then, he took part in politics, made several unsuccessful bids for the office of mayor in Victoria, and, in October 1927, addressed the Saanich Board of Trade in Brentwood Hall on "the very vexatious question of taxes." With very little formal schooling, he explored English literature, reading such works as John Milton's *Paradise Lost*, John Bunyan's *Pilgrim's Progress*, and a range of history books. Some of these were still in his cabin on Mount Newton when I used to stay there with Freeman King's Boy Scout troop before and during the Second World War. JD had died unmarried, aged ninety-two, on 28 March 1843.

Sources: Jarrett Thomas Teague, *Blessings in Plenty from John Dean: A Life and Park History* (Sidney, BC, privately published by the author, 1998), 59 pp., and sixty-one unnumbered pages of photographs, ISBN 0-9684453-0-6; Sidney Review, 6 October, p. 1; *Colonist*, 29 March 1907, p. 15; 25 August 1909, p. 4; 14 June 1910, p. 1; 5 December 1930, p. 6 (photo); T. W. Paterson, in *Cowichan Valley Citizen*, 23 September 2009.

DELMÉ-RADCLIFFE, Brigadier General Sir Charles, KCMG, CVO, 1909; CB, 1910; CMG, 1905 (1864-1937). He was born a son of Lieutenant Colonel Æmilius Charles Delmé-Radcliffe of Titchfield Abbey, Hants., who may have been the Charles Delmé-Radcliffe, "retired military officer," born at Hitchen, Hertfordshire, and staying at "Cams Hall," Fareham, Hampshire, in 1891 with a widowed uncle, Seymour R. Delmé, who was a landowner, aged eighty-three, born there and residing lavishly on an estate with stables, groom, footman, and gamekeeper but no women except six female domestic servants including a lady's maid. D-R was appointed in November 1893 as ADC to Major General Hopton commanding the infantry brigade at Gibraltar and served him for a year. He then joined the

Connaught Rangers in 1884, aged twenty, passed through the staff college at Camberley, and was posted to India as deputy assistant adjutant general (DAAG) of the North West District, where he served in 1895-1897. From 1898 to 1905, he was attached to the King's African Rifles in the Protectorate of Uganda, Kenya, and on the upper Nile River, where he commanded the British posts as captain and then as major and engaged in a series of operations that brought him to the attention of the Imperial authorities. Under his immediate superior, the remarkable and eccentric Sir Harry Johnston, he played a major part in what turned out to be a turning point in Uganda's history. Their main objective was to push the frontiers back towards Kenya and the Sudan in order to encompass large tracts of land as yet unclaimed by any European power, and this worried the Foreign Office. D-R is described by one historian as "a restless, ambitious man, who was an ideal tool for a policy of expansion. From the Nile stations he made a series of marches to the east, exploring the country, settling disputes, deposing and appointing chiefs and generally demonstrating British authority. He became a well-known and powerful figure especially among the Acholi, who gave him the name of 'Langa-Langa' (were-lion) because of his ability to cover great distances by night marches" (James Barber, p. 24). The order of events is not altogether clear, but early in 1901, he undertook a full-scale campaign in difficult, unknown country against mutinous African chiefs and, in four months, captured all but five of them, including the great Chief Mwanga, extended British authority to the Sudanese borders, and so assisted Johnston in a policy of Imperial expansion and development, which Lord Salisbury had not intended.

As commissioner of the Nile Province, D-R made explorations that were rewarded with the Murchison Award of the Royal Geographical Society. He shared Johnston's scientific and anthropological interests, sending him a pair of skulls of `rare wild dogs and reports about a fish "which chirrups like a bird," and otherwise contributing much to Johnston's polymathic two-volume study, *Uganda Protectorate* (1902). Delmé-Radcliffe is listed therein (p. 424) as an authority on one of the primates, *Colobus otoleucus*, and (vol. II, p. 774) as an authority on one of the Ungulata: *Cephalophus leucotis* and on *Hippotragus bakeris*. But the two fell out, and D-R wrote an angry letter to Lord Lugard when Johnston began to follow London's instructions by turning the administration of Uganda over to civil officers, who quarrelled with D-R. By coincidence, one of these was Lieutenant Colonel David Donald (1866-1936), MD, a Scottish physician who eventually retired to Vancouver Island at about the same time as D-R. According to Donald's daughter, Mrs Jean Gow, he was sent out with a commission from the Foreign Office to "to give medical aid to the natives of a vast region mainly, I think, around Lake Nyanza. The natives were dying of smallpox and my father was the first white man and the first doctor they had ever seen. After three years he contracted black water fever, so returned to England . . ." (Gow, 11-13, 17-24). On 16 March 2002, I telephoned Mrs Gow, then over one hundred years old and living in Ottawa, to ask whether her father had known D-R personally, and she replied that he had indeed but had disliked him as part of the antagonism of civil and military authorities in the region. However, from July 1902 to October 1904, D-R worked as the first British commissioner for delimitation of the Anglo-German Uganda Boundary, west of the Victoria Nyanza, and made surveys from the Indian Ocean to the border of the Congo Free State, which were completed towards the end of 1905.

In a complete change of scene during the years from 1906 to 1911, D-R served as Military Attaché in Rome, whence he visited Reggio, Calabria, immediately after the terrible earthquake of 4:21 a.m., 28 September 1908, in which 150,000 people died. Much later, in 1934, he related what he knew of this event at a meeting of the Overseas Club in Victoria at David Spencer's private dining room and again on 13 December 1934, at a meeting of the Men's Guild of Christ Church Cathedral. He had been charged with relief work organized with funds collected by the lord mayor of London. In 1911-1912, he served as a General Staff Officer First Grade, Western Command, and in 1914-1915 as Brigadier General Chief of Staff in the Third Army for Home Defence. There followed a series of duties as chief of the British Red Cross, as commissioner in the Balkans with the Greek forces (1912)—an appointment he owed to the influence of his father-in-law, Sir Frederick Treves, an eminent surgeon—as chief of British Military Mission, General Headquarters of the Italian Army in the Field (May 1915-August 1919), and as chief of British Military Mission, Klagenfurt, Austria (August 1919-March 1920), but he retired from the army at last in 1921.

D-R's career, as sketched above, kept him out of England for most of his life, and the lady he married on 3 July 1902 at All Soul's Church, Marylebone, refused to accompany him on most of his assignments. This was Lady Enid Margery Delmé-Radcliffe, née Treves, the only child of Sir Frederick Treves, and in November 1924, she filed for divorce from him on grounds of desertion. According to her account, reported in The Times, he stayed abroad longer than required and in general did not want to bother with her. D-R, for his part, explained that his means were limited, he would have liked to live on his family's Titchfield property, near Fareham, south-east of Southampton, but sold it for £182,000 to avoid paying high property taxes and lived abroad to escape from the burden of income taxes. In the last of The Times reports, the couple seem to have settled the differences between them and the case did not go to judgment, but D-R went to Victoria in 1931 to establish a branch of a company of which he was chairman, and she died in 1936.

Once established in Victoria, he spoke to many audiences about many subjects and was active in several fields of public interest. On 27 October 1931, he gave an illustrated address to surveyors and engineers in the board room of the Pemberton Building about "photogrammetric three-dimensional surveys from the air," which was a specialty of his company based in England and of which he was chairman. They had made such surveys on the continent of Europe and in Brazil and Argentina. He spoke about his adventures at the Gyro Club weekly luncheon at the Empress Hotel on 26 October 1941. Many of the members, hunters themselves, were thrilled by accounts of D-R's hunting exploits in India and Africa. In 1884, he shot a tigress in India that had terrified a village and killed a policemen and, on the upper Nile, had shot crocodiles and rampant elephants. On 21 December 1931, he addressed the Gyro Club about more of his adventures and, a month later, was warmly applauded again for what he had to say about the behaviour of animals and the native peoples he had seen and known in remote parts of the world. Like many Imperial hunters, he was keen on the "Preservation of Wild Life in the British Empire" and always willing to speak about the work of the Royal Society for the Preservation of Fauna in the British Empire, with which he had long been associated and which was one of 210 similar societies in Canada. D-R called on the members of the League to support their work. On 28 February 1933, he spoke to the Round Table Club, Victoria, about his survey work in India; on 7 March, it was "Africa" and to the Young People's Society at St Andrew's Presbyterian Church; and on 6 September, the Overseas Club again, this time about pre-war Europe and the origins of the Great War. He was guest speaker at the Alpine Club's twenty-eighth annual banquet on 26 March 1934, and told of his adventures climbing in the Himalayas.

As well as to public lectures, he gave his attention to certain clubs and good causes. He was especially active in organizing the Corps of Commissionaires. He was elected president of the Victoria India-Burma Society at the Glenshiel Hotel in the early 1930s and re-elected president in May 1934, also taking over the duties of secretary in place of B. O. Breton, who then became assistant secretary. A few weeks later, he wrote an open letter to the *Colonist,* thanking the Island Arts & Crafts Society and the National Gallery of Canada for sponsoring an "Exhibition of Water-Colours" at the Windermere Hotel, in fact 111 pictures from the Scottish Society of Painters in Watercolours. In November, he was promoting an entertainment at the Crystal Gardens, behind the Empress Hotel, to raise funds "In Aid of the Victorian Order of Nurses." At about the same time he was acting as hon. secretary of the local branch, National Council of Education, 6 Waldron Apartments, 837 Burdett Avenue, and advertizing a forthcoming lecture on "Explorers of the British Empire" by the traveller, hunter, and explorer, Sir Percy Sykes, whose arrival was to by airplane, courtesy of Major General E. C. Ashton, CMG, district officer commanding. Sykes was scheduled to speak to the Gyro Club, the United Services Institution, Victoria High School, and Shawnigan Lake Boys' School. It was as acting as hon. secretary, Victoria Branch, the Council of Education, too, that D-R advertised the visit of an internationally known organist and choirmaster, Dr Sydney H. Nicholson, from Westminster Abbey, who was "the world's leader in Boy Scout music—a special department of the Boy Scout movement. He is prepared to give lectures illustrated either with gramophone records or slides, but not to give organ recitals. Will be here from 30 November to 2 December (1934)." The Women's Association of Duncan United Church invited him in March 1936 to speak about Ethiopia; there seemed to be no end to the subjects he could discuss on the basis of his own experiences.

D-R had a private life with friends on the Island. Together with Sir Richard and Lady Lake, he attended a reception for Sir Ernest MacMillan at Government House on 8 May 1936. Sir Percy Lake, Sir Robert Holland, and Sir Charles Bell were also in his circle. And Admiral Dan Mainguy tells me that he befriended, and in a way courted, Mrs Admiral Rollo Mainguy, his grandmother, though not for long as he died in Victoria on 13 December 1937, while staying in a private nursing home at 3 Waldron Apartments, 837 Burdett Ave., having moved there from 1037 Richardson

Street. He was survived by a sister, Baroness von Ungern Sternberg, then living at Evanston, Illinois, and by a brother in England. D-R was given a monumental funeral at Christ Church Cathedral on 18 December 1937. Among the honorary pallbearers were Brigadier General Sir Percy Lake, Brigadier General D. J. MacDonald, Lieutenant Colonel C. E. Connolly, Commander C. T. Beard, RCN, Brigadier J. Sutherland Brown, Brigadier J. G. Austin, Colonel H. T. Goodland, Colonel J. S. Dennis, Colonel H. M. Urquhart, Colonel Eric Pepler, Captain H. H. Massey; Captain R. P. Bishop, Captain T. L. Thorpe-Doubble, RN (Retd), and G. C. L. Howell retired from the ICS. The active pallbearers were members of the Corps of Commissionaires under Colonel H. H. B. Cunningham. Fourteen cars followed the *cortège*, a bugler played last post; and a Union Jack flag was draped on the coffin.

He left various publications. On 8 May 1905, he read a paper, "Surveys and Studies in Uganda," to the Royal Geographical Society, which published it in two parts in their *The Geographical Journal*, vol. xxvi, no. 5 (November 1905), pp. 481-97 and no. 6 (December 1905), pp. 616-32. A splendid folding map was bound at the end of one of these volumes, and the whole is an account of his work, especially the triangulation surveys, observations, and studies of the tribes and other life. The main area was of the upper Nile from Lake Victoria on down. Part II (p. 491ff.) is "The Anglo-German Boundary Commission West of the Victoria Nyanza." D-R began work with it in July 1902, naming his colleagues and the German members with whom they had excellent relations. This paper is mainly a descriptive account of the country he traversed, and the people, animals, and flora in it.

Sources: *Who was Who*, vol. III (1929-1940), pp. 350-51; *The Times*, London, 1 November 1924, p. 4; 3 November 1924, p. 4; 4 November 1924, p. 5; 5 November 1924, p. 5; 14 December 1937, p. 18, obit.; census 1891, England, RG 12/882, page 1; James Barber, *Imperial Frontier: A Study of Relations Between the British and the Pastoral Tribes of North East Uganda* (Nairobi, East African Publishing House, 1968), chapter 3; Roland Oliver, *Sir Harry Johnston [1858-1927] and the Scramble for Africa* (Chatto & Windus, 1959), pp. 315-6; R. W. Beachey, A History of East Africa, 1592-1902 (I. B. Taurus, 1996), pp. 291, 376, 389-90; Sir Albert R. Cook, *Uganda Memoria*, 1897-1940 (Kampala, The Uganda Society, 1945), p. 154; *Who's Who in B.C.*, 1933-1934, p. 47; *Who was Who*, vol. III (1929-1940), pp. 350-51; Sir Harry Johnston, *The Uganda Protectorate* (2 vols. in 4o; Hutchinson & Co., 1902): vol. I, pp. 421, 424, vol. II, p. 774; *Colonist*, 25 October 1931, pp. 13 and 19; 27 October 1931, p. 3; 20 December 1931, p. 3; 22 January 1931, p. 3; 17 January 1933, p. 8; 26 February 1933, p. 3; 7 September 1933, p. 5; 23 February 1933, p. 5; 27 March 1934, p. 2; 18 May 1934, p. 2; 10 June 1934, p. 4; 2 September 1934, p. 8; 6 September 1934, p. 2; 6 November 1934, p. 4; 11 November 1934, p. 4; 23 November 1934, p. 4; 2 December 1934, p. 6; 4 December 1934, p. 6; 13 December 1934, p. 6; 2 April 1936, p. 7; 9 May 1936, p. 7; 14 December 1937, pp. 1 and 3; 19 December 1937, p. 5.

DENNIS, Colonel John Stoughton (1856-1938), CMG, CE, DTS. He was born at Weston, Ontario, near Toronto, son of Sarah Maria Dennis *née* Oliver, and named exactly like his father (1820-1885), who was a surveyor, militia officer, civil servant, entrepreneur, and deputy minister of the Interior, born in Kingston, Ontario, and the subject of an article in the *Dictionary of Canadian Biography*. Another source of confusion is that most sources give the son's birthdate as 27 October 1856, whereas he declared in 1919 on the legal Attestation Form of the Canadian Army that he was born on 22 October 1858. By this form, he enlisted in Vancouver, probably for the expeditionary force to Siberia, recording himself as a civil engineer and a colonel in the General Reserve. Was there some reason why he wished to appear two years younger than he was, or are other sources simply mistaken? In any event, he grew up in a prosperous, successful, attentive family who were Anglican, Conservative imperialists. He attended Trinity College School, then at Weston, as well as Upper Canada College and RMC, Kingston, Ontario. His activities in a long, busy life were mainly in three fields: engineering and surveying, soldiering, and encouraging British immigration.

In the seven years, 1872-1878, JD, at first only in his teens, spent long summers exploring and surveying in Manitoba and the NWT, sometimes with private engineers on contract and sometimes with civil servants, such as J. Lestock Reed, Dominion land surveyor. He qualified as both a land and topographical surveyor and, in 1878, was employed running a survey party to establish the fourth meridian in the NW Territories. The next year, then aged twenty-three, he was hired by the Hudson's Bay Company to plan towns, lay out building lots, take charge of construction, and install sewage systems in places such as Kenora (then Laval Portage), Prince Albert, and Winnipeg. In 1883, he opened his own office and went on with the same work at Brandon, Regina, and smaller places. He also worked on irrigation systems around Lethbridge and later the American Association of Irrigation Engineers elected him vice-president. From about 1885, he worked for the Department of the Interior as a topographical surveyor until 1897, when he was appointed chief engineer in the Public Works Department of the old NWT, and this led on to a promotion to chief commissioner in that department with headquarters at Regina. On 1 January 1902, the CPR engaged him, at first as superintendant and chief engineer of irrigation systems in western Canada, then as manager of the company's Department of Natural Resources, and finally as chief commissioner for Colonization and Development. He became sufficiently well known to be elected in 1917 as president of the Engineering Institute of Canada.

His first military experience was as commander of the Dominion Land Surveyors Intelligence Corps in the Riel Rebellion, a unit that also enrolled a younger surveyor, A. O. Wheeler, future founder of the Alpine Club of Canada. JD did not serve in the South African War and his service in the Great War was as representative on the British-Canadian Recruiting Mission in the United States, with the rank of lieutenant colonel, then full colonel. He was prominent, however, among the Canadians in two allied expeditionary forces dispatched to Vladivostok, Siberia, in 1918-1919, serving there first as commissioner of the Canadian Red Cross. As such, he made the astonishing recommendation, never acted upon, that Canada should take care of all former prisoners of war in western Siberia, whether Russian, German, or Austrian, of whom he reckoned about half a million were threatened by starvation and disease. His second assignment in Siberia was as a member of the Canadian Economic Mission in October 1918 (by Order-in-Council of 21 October 1918), and he crossed the Pacific in the *Madras*, arriving on 3 February 1919 at Vladivostok, where he became a good friend of Sir Charles Eliot, the British high commissioner. Battle-hardened officers probably thought of him as a "desk-walla," like *General R. J. Gwynne and others, but as chairman of the Corps of Commissionaires in Victoria during the 1930s, he worked hard on behalf of retired soldiers.

In 1882, JD's father established an enterprise with offices in England to offer advice and encouragement to prospective immigrants. It was close to his heart, and he called it Dennis, Sons and Co. As one of the sons, young JD, took up the colonizing enterprises of the CPR with enthusiasm. His lifelong concern to encourage British immigrants may be seen, for instance, in a talk he gave to the Overseas League in Victoria on 1 November 1937, only a few months before his death. He spoke urgently in favour of persuading the federal government to attract British people in order to keep Canada within the empire. "The most serious problem we are facing today," he said, "is to prevent the absorption of Canada by the United States of America."

One of the enterprises he assisted for this purpose, and with all his might, was the Prince of Wales Fairbridge Farm School in the Cowichan Valley, the only one in Canada. He was asked to choose a site for it and, in 1934, decided on the thousand-acre Pemberton estate at Cowichan Station, a couple of miles south of Duncan. The first children arrived from England in 1935. The original idea for the project and the movement to implement it must be credited to an English Rhodesian, Kingsley Fairbridge (1885-1924), who went to England in 1909 as a Rhodes scholar and devised a plan to help homeless boys and girls by means of residential farming schools to be established in growing British colonies. The first Fairbridge Farm School was established in Australia and the Vancouver Island School was the first in Canada. Most of the funds for it were raised in England during a drive sponsored by the Prince of Wales, who himself donated the first £1000 of the £60,000 required to build the school. Once launched, it drew the support of people in Canada, such as H. C. F. Cresswell of Montreal, one of JD's colleagues in the employ of the CPR Company, who attended the London meeting in 1934, and Captain James Cameron Dun-Waters (1864-1939), "laird of Fintry" in Scotland but born at Torquay, England, who went to Canada in 1910, and served during the Great War in the British Army in Gallipoli, Egypt, and France. Dun-Waters then developed a huge estate and cattle ranch on the western shores of Okanagan Lake and left it mainly to the Fairbridge Farm School. Rudyard Kipling, too, left a large bequest to the school in his will at his death in 1936, though his family managed to prevent the money from being paid. Meanwhile, the school's best friend in Canada, until he died in 1938, was JD then living at 1618 Rockland Avenue, Victoria. He had a hand in the appointment of other army officers as headmasters: Major Maurice Trew (c. 1891-?), a Cambridge graduate who served in the Coldstream Guards in 1916-1934, and

Colonel Harry Tremaine Logan (1887-1971) of the Seventy-second Seaforth Highlanders, a Nova Scotian Rhodes Scholar in 1908-1911, who met Kingsley Fairbridge at Oxford.

When JD died, a memorial stained glass window, made in England, was erected in the school chapel in his memory. The inscription read, "To the memory of Colonel J. S. Dennis, 1856-1938, friend and counsellor of the Prince of Wales Fairbridge Farm School. His colleagues, the president and officers of the CPR record their comradeship and esteem." The school had enemies as well as friends and apparently received no support from the provincial government, which closed it down in 1952. The memorial windows in the chapel were removed in 1976, to save them from vandals, and forgotten in the basement of Christ Church Cathedral for a quarter of a century. The school building, auditorium, staff homes, hospital, library, etc., formed the basis of a housing estate. JD had married the daughter of Robert Conroy of Aylmer, Quebec, and, at his death on 26 November 1938, left her and their daughter Eileen in Victoria. Three weeks earlier, he was visited in the Jubilee Hospital by J. B. Challies, president of the Engineering Institute of Canada, who was sent to present him with the Sir John Kennedy Gold Medal, the Institute's highest honour. Among the pallbearers at his funeral were *Lieutenant General Sir Percy Lake and *Major Cuthbert Holmes, surrounded by engineers and CPR colleagues from all over Canada.

Sources: NAC, RG150, box 2444-23, CEF files; *Colin Frederick Read, in the Dictionary of Canadian Biography, vol.?* (the father); Roy MacLaren, *Canadians in Russia 1918-1919* (Toronto, Macmillan, 1976), pp. 203-4; 228-42; Robert N. Murby, "*Canadian Economic Commission to Siberia, 1918-1919*," *Canadian Slavonic Papers,* vol. 11 (1969), pp.; *Colonist,* 2 November 1937, p. 3; 27 November 1938, pp. 1 and 3, obit. and photo; 29 November 1938, p. 3; 17 October 1939, p. 5, obit.; 9 November 1948, p. 6; Christina Martens, "*Society Tracks Down Chapel's Original Windows*," *Cowichan Valley Citizen,* 30 May 2001, pp. 1 and 9; Morgan, *Canadian Men and Women,* p. 317.

DENNY, Norah Creina (1885-1983). Co-founder in 1921 of Queen Margaret's School for Girls at Duncan, Vancouver Island, and its head mistress for many years, she was born at Wragby, Lincolnshire, son of Edmund Barry Denny (1860-1945), a physician and surgeon from Churchill, County Kerry in Ireland, and his wife, Emily Jane Barclay Denny *née* Allen (1858-1957), born in Dublin. The 1891 English census found ND, aged five, living with them in Lincolnshire at the Market Place, Wragby, Lindsey, her father aged thirty-six, her mother thirty-two, a sister Iris Deany aged two, and two brothers, Henry and Robert Edmund aged four and two, all born at Wragby, where their father had a medical practice and was a JP for Lincolnshire. With them was a paternal aunt, Elizabeth Denny, aged forty-seven, two lady nurses and five servants, including two grooms. Ten years later, in 1901, she had two more brothers, Thomas Hamilton, aged seven, and Arthur Dreoghel Gillingly, aged two, and with them was her maternal grandfather, Henry Colelough Allen, aged seventy-eight, born in Kilkenny. During the Great War, ND won recognition for service as a VAD nurse in England and France.

In 1919, she followed two brothers and an uncle, a medical doctor, who had migrated to the Island earlier, and on 4 April 1921, with Miss Dorothy Geoghegon of Duncan, she opened Queen Margaret's School for Girls. They were able to build a chapel for the school in 1934. CD had joined the Girl Guides in 1911 and in Duncan soon became a captain and commissioner of the movement. In 1963, after fifty years as headmistress of the school, she was formally welcomed as a Freeman of the city of Duncan. In retirement, she gardened, like so many around her, until 1 October 1983, when she died, aged ninety-eight, at Cowichan District Hospital in Duncan.

On 25 July 1928, less than ten years after her arrival, a first cousin of her father's died in Edmonton, Alberta, after a long career in the North-West Mounted Police. This was Sir Cecil Edward Denny, who was born at Shedfield, Hampshire, in 1850 and in 1921 inherited the sixth baronetcy and Tralee Castle in County Kerry, Ireland. As the NWMP did not have jurisdiction in BC until 1950, the province having its own older constabulary, he had no official duties in BC and it is doubtful whether they had anything much to do with one another. The relationship is interesting mainly for showing the baronetcy in CD's family background. But this cousin published two interesting books about the NWMP.

Sources: *Cowichan Leader*, 22 August 1962 and 3 August 1979; census 1891, England, RG 12/2597, p. 6; census 1901, RG 13/3068, p. 7; *Who's Who in B.C.*, 1942-1943, p. 97; 1944-1946, p. 68; Alan B. McCullough, *biography of Sir Cecil Edward Denny* (1850-1928), DCB online; Conrad Swan, *A King from Canada* (Stanhope, Weardale, County Durham, The Memoir Club, 2005), pp. 21-4.

D'ESTERRE, Sidney Burnaby Wood (1884-1969). Born at Plymouth (St Andrew's), Devonshire, on 7 April 1884, he was a son of James C. J. d'Esterre of Elmfield, Southampton, Hampshire, and his wife (SD's mother) Eleanor, both born in Bermuda. He appears, aged six, in 1891 census records living in the family at Kent House, Kent Road, Portsea, Portsmouth, his father, aged forty-one, "living on his own means," and his mother aged thirty-nine. There were three other children: James A. C. d'Esterre, aged ten, and born at Cape Colony, South Africa; Philip C. E. d'Esterre, eight, born in Plymouth; and Eleanor B. W. d'Esterre, two, born in Southampton. The family had four servants.

SD attended Marlborough College, left Oxford University with an MA, and, in 1912, went to Victoria, where he became a schoolmaster and a member of the Church of England. He joined the Eighty-eighth Victoria Fusiliers and, in 1914, enlisted in the Seventh Battalion and served overseas until 1919, when he returned to the Island and purchased the Elk Hotel at Comox about three years later. It was still under his management in 1932, and he lived there, though he had joined the Union Club and the British Public Schools Club in Victoria. He was still in Comox when he died, aged eighty-five, on 16 June 1969.

Sources: census 1901, England, RG 13/2784, p. 45; census 1891, RG 12/873, p. 12; CEF files, box 2480-8; *Who's Who in B.C.*, 1940-1941, p. 58.

DEVEREUX, John Walter Francis (1830-1906). Born on 15 August 1830 at Milford Haven, Pembroke, Wales, he went to sea, aged sixteen, and spent some years in the East India and Australia trades. At twenty-three, he had command of the *Bengal* and then worked as chief officer on mail ships, sailing between England and India. By 1863, he had saved enough to retire comfortably well off and retired the following year to Victoria with his family. He invested unwisely and went to sea again as captain of the government steamer, *Sir James Douglas*, until he was appointed superintendant of the Esquimalt graving dock in 1887. The 1901 census at Victoria recorded JD living next door to Thomas W. Paterson, contractor, and future premier of BC, at 76 Bay Street with his family: his wife, Mary Elizabeth Devereux (1840-1925), born in the West Indies; four daughters ranging in age from twenty to thirty-three; and two sons, Francis Algernon Devereux (1871-1960) and George Talbot Devereux (1875-1962). They had two Chinese servants, and there was also an absent older son, William Devereux, born c. 1863 in the West Indies shortly before JD and his wife went to Victoria. One of the daughters, Josephine Noble Devereux (1872-1961) married Andrew Tait Monteith (1859-1948), a Scottish stockbroker in Victoria. JD drowned accidentally, aged seventy-nine, on 25 May 1906 in Esquimalt harbour.
Sources: Barrie Humphrey, "*Malaspina's Lost Gallery*," in *Shale* (published by the Gabriola Historical and Museum Society, Gabriola Island), no. 10 (January 2005), pp. 3-23, see p. 17; Canadian census, 1901, Victoria;

DICKINSON, Lieutenant Commander Evelyn Roger Stirling (1896-1971). He was born on 6 July 1896 at Santa Fe, Argentine Republic, son of Alfred John Dickinson, and educated at Cheltenham School and at the Royal Naval Colleges in Osborne and Dartmouth. In 1909, he joined the Royal Navy as a cadet and, on 15 January 1914, went to sea as a midshipman. In October 1920, he retired with the rank of lieutenant. Between the wars, he worked for lumber companies in California and Northern Ontario, but on 2 September 1939, he was called for service as a lieutenant commander with the RCN, to which rank he had been promoted on 15 March 1926, and served as CO at HMCS *Naden III* Naval Training Establishment at Comox. In 1944, he was staff officer to the captain of HMC Dockyard at Esquimalt, and he reverted to the Royal Navy retired list on 17 April 1946. An Anglican, he had married Mary Birivkoff, daughter of Dmitri Birivkoff, in 1921, and they had two sons and four daughters. ED died, aged seventy-four, on 24 May 1971 in Saanich.
Sources: *Who's Who in B.C.*, 1942-1943, pp, 98-9; *MacFarlane*, p. 18.

DIGGLE, Lieutenant Wadham Neston (1848-1934). Born at Stokenham, Devon, on 13 January 1848, he joined the Royal Navy on 10 September 1861 and trained as a cadet in HMS *Britannia*. After leaving her on 17 December 1862, he served aboard HMS *Victory*, *Virago*, *Fisgard*, *Royal Adelaide*, and many others. Records show him as a lieutenant aboard *Crocodile* (1 August 1873 to 2 June 1874) and *Hector* (2 August 1874 to 7 July 1875). Particularly interesting was his earlier posting at Esquimalt on HMS *Grappler* when in the 1860s and 1870s, he invested some $5,000 in Hon. James Dunsmuir's coal-mining company at Wellington near Nanaimo, a venture in which Admiral Sir Arthur Farquhar and Captain Frederick Wilbraham Egerton were also interested for a short time. Dunsmuir eventually bought them out, and in this transaction, WD received about $750,000 for his interest in the venture, probably on 12 May 1883 when he sold his share in the Wellington colliery to Dunsmuir. When WD retired on 2 October 1879, he may have spent time at the Manor House, Bratton, Wiltshire, as the *Colonist* reported in an obituary, but the 1891 census recorded him, aged forty-three, "living on his own means" at 50 Westbourne Terrace in Paddington, London, with his wife, Lily J. Diggle, aged thirty-four, born in Paddington, and their three sons, Wadham H. Diggle, aged seven, Simard W. Diggle, aged six, and John N. Diggle, aged one month. Ten years later, they were living at 10 Chesham Street, St George, Hanover Square, Westminster, with five servants, and WD was listed as "retired Lt., R.N." He died, aged eighty-six, on 6 June 1934.

Sources: PRO; ADM 196/17, page 220; census 1891, England, RG12/13, page 15; census 1901, RG 13/84, p. 86; *Colonist*, 5 July 1934, p. 3: obit.; Gosnell, *The Year Book*, p. 39.

DIGGON, Harold Montague (1881-1955). Born on 29 July 1881 in England at Edmonton (Greater London), he was the third son of Philip Harold Diggon—born 1851 at Leigh, Kent (Greater London)—and Elizabeth Jane Symonds—born 1952 in Truro, Cornwall—who had married in Hammersmith, London, on 24 April 1869. During HD's childhood, the family moved from "Rowan Tree Cottages" in Hyde Side Road, Edmonton (a district full of plant nurseries), to Hackney, where their house in 1891 was at 1 Navarino Grove and in 1901 at 110 Graham Road. HD's father was an accountant recorded in 1891 as a "Shot Bow Manufacturer's Accountant," and in 1901 as a "Leather Merchant's Accountant" at a time when HD, aged nineteen, was employed as a "Printer's Compositor." HD had two older brothers, Albert and Roger Charles Diggon, and a younger brother, Horace Hamilton Diggon (born in Hammersmith in 1886), who went out to Toronto and there married Maggie Isabella Smith on 5 February 1910. During HD's childhood, the family in London had no servants, except one fifteen-year-old girl in 1991. Schooled in London, HD went in the course of his career from printing to journalism and publishing, collecting and selling books, and the stationery and office supply business. The only clue to his emigration is his military service, which may have encouraged him, like many others, to go abroad. He served with the Imperial Yeomanry in the second South African War (1898-1902), receiving both the King's and the Queen's medals. He was not yet on the Island when, in 1904, he married Lucy Ethel Hallett, daughter of Walter Hallett, born at Woodford, England.

Victoria proved to be full of opportunities for HD. He soon formed a partnership with a local businessman, Thomas Napier Hibben (1869-1930), who had inherited a printing & stationery office and bookshop on Government Street founded by his American father, who had arrived from San Francisco in 1858 during the gold rush. Hibben died, aged sixty-one, on 18 August 1930 in Seattle, Washington State. Long before then, HD and his wife had been able to move to "Highfields," 3606 Cadboro Bay Road. He joined the Canadian Legion (Pro Patria), the local Legion of Frontiersmen, the Union Club, the Royal Victoria Yacht Club, the AOF Sons of England, and the Kiwanis Club and held offices in the BPOE and the Royal Arcanum. He was a member of the Church of England and no doubt had the benefit, like many others, of membership in a local Freemason's lodge. He served variously on the City Council, the Police Commission, and the Board of School Trustees in the Saanich Municipality. When asked about his recreations, he replied, "Yachting, legerdemain, and gardening." HD died, aged seventy-three, on 20 April 1955 in Victoria, and his wife died there, aged eighty-seven, on 27 July 1971.

Sources: census 1881, England, RG 11/1389, p. 29; census 1891, RG 12/192, p. 24; census 1901, RG 13/223, p. 56; California Passengers and Crew Lists, 1893-1957; *Who's Who in B.C.*, 1947-48, *A Record of British Columbia Men and Women of Today*, ed., S. Maurice Carter (Vancouver, 1948), p. 59; *A History of the Book in Canada*, vol. 1 (1840-1918), ed., Yvan Lamonde, Patricia Fleming, and Fiona A. Black (Toronto, University of Toronto Press, 2004), p. 223.

DOBBIE, Captain George Staple (1889-1973). He was born in India, eldest son of *Colonel Herbert Hugh Dobbie, and spent his early childhood and holidays later at the family dwelling in the village of Merriott, Somerset, about four miles north of Crewkerne. There, the boys of the family and their only sister Annie played mostly at soldiers, marching around with the family pigs, Scyhlla and Charibdis. "Dolls were forbidden, and when one was discovered it was court-martialled and sentenced to be beheaded, if I remember correctly," one of them recalled many years later. Their mother died from appendicitis in her early thirties, having refused an operation, and their father being in India, the children's grandmother looked after them until he was able to return to England. A few years later he made a second marriage with a Miss Aimée Coke, "a charming Christian lady." By that time GD was at his first school, "Tyttenhanger Lodge" at Shenley, Barnet, Hertfordshire, where the census found him, aged eleven, and his brother *Archibald G. Dobbie, aged eight, in the care of the headmaster, Andrew H. Trollope. GD went on to Charterhouse, his father's old school, and then to Sandhurst, where he won a revolver as a pistol shooting prize and a silver tankard for the tug-of-war competition. He attended RMC at Camberley before being commissioned on 18 September 1909 as a Second Lieutenant in the Sherwood Forester's Regiment (Forty-fifth and Ninety-fifth).

From November 1909, he served with the First Battalion Secunderabad, at Deolali in India, but went to fight in the Great War as adjutant attached to the Sixth Dublin Fusiliers, Tenth Division, with which he was at Salonika in 1916 until he fell ill with dysentery and malaria. In 1917, he had a staff course at Cambridge and was then appointed brigade major in the Twenty-fifth Regiment Brigade in Ireland—"where I was highly reported upon by Brig.-Gen. Hon. L. J. P. Butler, C.B., D.S.O. of Irish Guards for efficient service," he recalled. Back briefly in France in 1918 attached to the Forty-sixth Infantry Brigade HQ, he soon went to Egypt with the regiment as adjutant, Second Battalion, in August 1919 and was active in battalion cricket and hockey. He took courses at the School of Musketry at Satara, India, a bombing course as early as 1914, a Staff Course at Cambridge in 1917, and an Adjutant's Special Drill Course at Wellington Barracks, London, in 1919. He was proficient at conversational French and learned Urdu to honours standard. His wife, Mildred, whom he married in 1915, almost died in Egypt. The medical officer thought she would not survive in Cairo or India, whither the regiment was about to proceed, and so Dobbie retired and left the regiment in Alexandria; on 16 August 1929, his name was removed even from the Regular Army Reserve. However, on 26 August 1939, he was listed with the South African Army's Reserve of officers, called up in the Second World War, and ordered to Bloemfontein with the Seventh Battalion Reserve Brigade as adjutant. He won the Military Cross.

When GD and Mildred went to Vancouver Island to join his parents and brothers, they settled in "The Hut," a small wooden house about two miles from Maple Bay, seven miles from Duncan, on land owned by his father Colonel H. H. Dobbie (q.v.). There GD fished, kept a few geese and chickens, and grew sweet peas for seed as a means of income. The seed, he sold to the Sutton, Dobbie, and Toogood seed firms in England. It seems the Dobbie Company was prepared to accept their seeds because of their family name. They lived near GD's sister Annie and her husband, *Colonel Sheridan Rice, and two other Rice families, who together sponsored a small Plymouth Brethren Assembly, at first in General Rice's house and later in a hall in Duncan. There was a strong tradition of Plymouth Brethren in the family, and as early as 1909, GD had had an experience of conversion during his first voyage out to India with the army. Upon coming into contact with missionaries on the Island, he and Mildred decided after a while to become missionaries themselves. In 1926, they went to St John, NB, and boarded the SS *Cariboo* (Elder Dempster Line) for South Africa, where they served the Presbyterian Church in the Africa Evangelical Band, at first in South Africa but later in the Belgian Congo. Eventually, he became principal of a training and Bible school for his mission in the Cape Town area. That is probably where he died.
Sources: Interviews, letters, and family records, courtesy of a granddaughter, Miss Margaretta Gretta Rice; census 1901, England, RG 13/1229, p. 7.

DOBBIE, Major Archibald Gordon (c. 1893-1975). Born the second son of *Colonel H. H. Dobbie, he spent his early childhood with his brothers and sister in a Somerset/Devonshire village but was in Canada when war broke out in 1914 and returned home to enlist in the King's Own Scottish Borderers. He remained in that regiment and was in Ireland with the Second Battalion during the troubles of 1922. He stayed with the Second Battalion through three years in Egypt and then went on with them to Hong Kong for three more years. He was adjutant of the battalion from 1925 to 1928, when he left the army, returned to Vancouver, where he remained. He went to Scotland later for a visit. The unit remembered him as tough, shy, and a loner but kind and forthright and impatient with fools. He was also known as a good all-round athlete. During the 1970s, his daughter Jean went to Scotland to visit regimental HQ at Berwick and met some of his friends.

His name was mistakenly inscribed on a cross in Merriott, Somerset, along with that of an even-younger brother who died in the Great War. In fact, AD survived the First World War, lived to the age of eighty-two, and died on 13 November 1975 in Saanich.

Sources: Interviews, letters, and family records, courtesy of a granddaughter, Miss Margaretta Gretta Rice; census 1901, England, RG 13/1229, page 7.

DOBBIE, Colonel Wallace Hugh (c. 1890-1952). He was late of the RCA, had commanded a heavy battery in the Great War, served variously at Halifax, Kingston, and Esquimalt between the wars, and was named to the DSO. He commanded the garrison at Sydney, NS, from September 1939 to his retirement in December 1945. He died aged sixty in the Veteran's Hospital on 18 January 1952 and was buried in a funeral at Christ Church Cathedral on 22 January, leaving his wife, Marguerite Josephine, at 1256 Judge Place, Saanich, a sister in Rhodesia, and several cousins. He seems to have belonged to the Church of England.

Sources: NAC, CEF files, box 2549-28; *Colonist*, 20 January 1952, p. 26, obit.

DOBBIE, Colonel Herbert Hugh (1859-1930). He was born in India at Cot, Outacamund, on 19 April 1859, son of Major General George Staple Dobbie (1819-1886) and called his own eldest son George Staple Dobbie. The family came originally from "the Stewartry of Kirkcudbright" and had many relatives, including General Sir William George Shedden Dobbie (1879-1964), famous for saving Malta in the Second World War; he once visited the Island during a speaking tour. HD's family, however, had established a family seat at Merriott in Somersetshire, about four miles north of Crewkerne. Dobbie attended Charterhouse School, where he was known as an athlete and excelled in cricket. According to a local newspaper reporting on the *Exmouth Week* on 9 September 1876, "Dobbie's bowling was really remarkable" in Exmouth vs. Plymouth and Exmouth vs. South Devon Rovers. His general athletic ability was all the more remarkable because he was a huge man, 6' 4" tall, and broad in proportion. According to *The Times* on 1 May 1878, the *London Gazette* of Tuesday 30 April 1878, reported of the "89th Foot [Royal Irish Fusiliers]—Gentleman Cadet H. H. Dobbie, from the Royal Military College, to be Second Lieutenant, in succession to Lieutenant E. G. Barrow, a Probationer for the Indian Staff Corps." (This last is in a long list of similar entries.) He joined the Indian Army on 29 May 1881 and served for twenty-six years, rising to lieutenant colonel on 1 May 1878, becoming second in command of the Thirtieth Punjab Infantry and, from 12 December 1901 to 12 December 1907, its commandant. During those years, he passed examinations in musketry, Hindustani, Persian, and Pushtu and fought on the North-West Frontier of India for long periods—in the expedition to Manipur in 1891, on campaign near Shebhadr in 1897-1898, then on the Samana River and in the Kurram Valley, at Tirah in 1897-1898, and in the Bazar Valley—and he was dispatched in 1899-1900 to deal with re-mounts in South Africa.

In 1900-1901, HD commanded the Thirtieth Punjabis Battalion in the China Expeditionary Force at Shan-hai-kwan. In two long letters written from Manchuria to his little daughter Annie (Gretta Rice's mother) in June and December 1902, he describes at great length a journey he and a surveyor took into interior China from Shan-hai-kwan, but says nothing about why he went. In 1904-1905, he was again in Manchuria on service and a photograph shows him in the centre of a group of seventeen dignitaries, mainly Chinese. An "international ensign" was flown at their meeting combining the Union Jack, the French tricolore, the Japanese flag, and a fourth flag showing a crown, possibly German, with a complex diagonal cross over the whole. It is entitled, "An international ensign combining the emblems of the six nations playing at Shan-hai-kwan." We know that an international shooting match was held at Shan-hai-kwan at which HD easily won the trophy, being chief musketry instructor, Eastern Command, India. Apparently, he left Vancouver and Victoria for Hong Kong on 7 May 1904 aboard the *Empress of India*, and his wife joined him at Shanghai on 7 December. They were at Shan-hai-kwan from 4 January 1905 until 5 July, sailed from China aboard SS *Dufferin* and rejoined the children at Merriott on 22 August. What was HD doing out there for fourteen months in 1904-1905? The occasion for his journey may have been the shooting match, but perhaps it also had something to do with preliminaries for the renewal of the Anglo-Japanese Treaty in September 1905 or the Treaty of Portsmouth (New Haven), which brought the Russo-Japanese War to an end on 5 September 1905.

HD had two wives: Margaret Ross Forlong Gordon (1861-1901), whom he married in 1887 and who was the daughter of Thomas Forlong Gordon, South Erins, Loch Fyne. After her death, he made a second marriage on 24 March 1904 with Aimée Pauline Coke (1845-1928), daughter of Colonel Coke of Trusley Manor, Derbyshire. Altogether, he had a daughter and five sons. Unable to afford to put his sons into British regiments, he decided they might have better opportunities in Canada. After a preliminary journey in 1910 to "scout around," he settled with the family in 1912 at a remote part of Maple Bay in a place they called "Sherwood," which had to be reached by boat. There the Dobbies had forty acres on the sea on a point of land looking into the bay and across from the Rice family. The colonel's huge bearded figure pulling a boat in all weathers from Maple Bay wharf to his home became a familiar sight. George Staple Dobbie, Archibald Gordon Dobbie, John Sheddon Dobbie—named after a relative, the General who was the heroic governor of Malta in the Second World War—and Herbert Dobbie and all settled or spent much time on the Island. Captain John Sheddon Dobbie and Second Lieutenant Herbert Dobbie were killed in the Great War, the former commemorated on the Tyne Cot Memorial in Belgium and the latter on the Thiepval Memorial in a French field near the villages of Beaumont Hamel and Pozières on road number D73, in the Somme about five kilometres from the village of Albert. Herbert had attended University School in Victoria (now called St Michael's University School) and excelled at many sports. The three younger sons all joined up in Canada and George returned. On 17 September 1912, soon after the family's arrival at Maple Bay, the only daughter, Annie Buchan Dobbie, married *Colonel Sheridan Knowles Brownlow Rice (1872-1936), whose family had likewise settled in and near the Cowichan Valley. She was to outlive them all, dying at last in 1952, aged 101.

The Dobbie family, like the Rices, were Plymouth Brethren, which was unusual among British officers on the Island, and HD, who had studied the Bible from his youth, used to read the New Testament easily in the original Greek. Retirement gave him leisure to pursue his studies. He had written articles for the *Times* of India, the *Field*, and *Blackwoods Magazine*. But his Christian faith was his greatest interest and the strongest feature of his character. He always showed a great willingness to help and encourage others and had a gift of inspiring love and affection among the people he met. About 1925, his wife having died, he went to live in Victoria at 1002 Vancouver Street and died there in 1930, aged seventy-two, on his birthday, 19 April.

Sources: Interviews and letters, courtesy of Margaretta Gretta Rice, and her pamphlet, *The Story of the Rice and Dobbie Families on Vancouver Island* (Victoria, privately printed, May 2001), 25 pp.; *Cowichan Leader*, 1 May 1930, obit.; *Army List*, October 1905, p. 2472 (War Service of Officers); *London Gazette* 22 June 1886 and 2 September 1887 and GGO 864 of 87; *Indian Army Lists*, January 1905, pp. 88, 256, 340, 659, 690 and 699; *The Borderer's Chronicle* (undated obit., by one JSE, who had met him in the army).

DOBBIE, Captain John Shedden (1894-1917). He was born at Landour, India, on 7 July 1894, the fourth son of Brevet Colonel H. H. Dobbie, Indian Army, and of Maple Bay, VI. He was schooled at Tyttenhanger Lodge, St Albans, England, and Weymouth College, Dorset. He came to Canada in 1911 and after a short time farming near Hespeler, Ontario, he entered Highfield College, Hamilton, in 1913, passed the entrance examinations for RMC, Kingston, but then entered the Bank of Montreal at Alberni, BC. In 1914, he enlisted in the Fiftieth Gordons and went overseas as sergeant in the Forty-eighth Canadian Infantry. In England, he received a commission in the Second Battalion, Gordon Highlanders, and went to France in July 1916. He was wounded in two places at the capture of Ginchy, 6 September 1916, and left on the battle field for dead. At night, he regained consciousness, found his way back to his men, and spent time recovering in the Fourth London General Hospital, England. Then he returned to the front and rejoined his battalion of Gordons in April 1917 and was again wounded but remained on duty continuously to the end. He was promoted to captain and was in command of his company at the capture of Broodseinde on 3 October, when his men reached their objective. On 5 October, he and others were killed in their dug-out by an explosive shell. A man of intense religious conviction, he was also an exceptional athlete and had played half-back for the Hamilton Tigers at Highfield College.

Sources: Sources for other Dobbie's, above; John B. Hayward, ed., *Officers Died in the Great War 1914-1919* (New ed., Polstead, Suffolk, J. B. Hayward & Son, 1988) p. 166.

DOLBEY, Major Dr Robert Valentine (c. 1878-1937), MS, FRGS. He was born in Sutton, Surrey, eldest son of Thomas Dolbey, "barrister-at-law, solicitor" from Montgomeryshire, Wales, and his wife Louisa Anne Dolbey from Shropshire. The census of 1891 found him, aged thirteen, the second of six children, living with their parents at "Strefford House" in Sutton. In his early twenties, he enlisted in the army and served in the South African War from 30 November 1900 to 31 May 1902, serving in the Transvaal, the Orange River Colony, and Cape Colony and returning to England with the Queen's Medal and four clasps. He immediately began a medical education in London and qualified as LRCP in 1902, MB in 1903, and MS in 1905. At sometime in the next few years, he moved to BC, where he practiced as a surgeon in Vancouver, residing at 709 Dunsmuir Street, and in Victoria, where he worked as an associate of Dr O. M. Jones. When the Great War broke out in 1914, RD was one of the many who returned to Britain to enlist in the Imperial forces. He served as a surgeon in the RAMC in France and then in East Africa under General Smuts until captured as a prisoner of war. Dolbey reached the rank of major by the time he published two books about his wartime experiences, one of them in the form of letters home, and a reviewer of the first book commented in the *Daily Colonist* in 1917, "This book will of course have a peculiar interest for the people of B.C. because Dr Dolbey's name was a very familiar one with us. He was in London attending the Congress of Surgeons of North America when the war broke out and at once enlisted." After the war, he took a medical post in Egypt and was employed for some years as professor of surgery at Cairo University. The *Colonist* reported his death, which occurred in November 1937 at Chelsworth Hall, Suffolk. He was commonly described by that time as "a Canadian doctor," though he was neither born nor educated in Canada and neither did he live most of his life there.

Sources: *Colonist*, 29 July 1917, Sunday, p. 15, *a review of Dolbey's A Regimental Surgeon in War and Prison* (John Murray, 1917), 248 pp; Dolbey, *Sketches of the East African Campaign* (John Murray, 1918), 219 pp.; *Colonist*, 4 December 1937, p. 6, obit.; *The Medical Register* (London, for the General Medical Council, 1915), p. 269; 1924, p. 303; *Geographical Journal*, vol. 52 (1918), p. 324; NAC, reel T6958, Active Militia, Military District No. 11, notes in a ledger; census 1891, England, RG 12/544, p. 8.

DONALD, Captain Colin Degge, (1899-1974). He was born 28 October 1899 on the Island at Chemainus, son of Harry Edwards Donald (1868-1965), who was born in London, south of the Thames, and died in Victoria, aged ninety-six, on 1 January 1965. The latter was a son of James Donald of Folkestone and his wife Ruth (CD's paternal grandparents). CD's father Harry had married Eleanor Wilmot Sitwell (CD's mother) on 9 August 1892 at St George's Anglican Church in Montreal, Quebec. She was born at Leamington, Warwickshire, and died, aged eighty-five, on 17 December 1955 in Victoria. She was a daughter of CD's maternal grandparents, Degge Wilmot Sitwell (1838-?), and his second wife, Rosamund Shuttleworth Holden. These details may help to discover how CD was related to *Lieutenant Colonel Dr David Donald, which he must have been, as the latter's daughter Jean Middleton Donald crossed the Atlantic from Southampton *en route* to Victoria in April 1930 together with CD and *Commander F. R. W. R. Gow, the husband she had recently married.

In any case, CD entered the Royal Naval College of Canada in 1914. He served in submarines of the Royal Navy during the Great War and in the Royal Canadian Navy during the Second World War. His career took him to HMS *Leviathan* (1917), HMS *Carnarvon* (1917), HMS *Roxborough* (1917), *Minotaur* (1917), *Ramilies* (1918), *Umpire* (1919), HM Submarine K-22 (1920), CH-14 (1921), and HM Submarine K-6 as navigation officer (1922). An outstanding sportsman, he was the heavyweight boxing champion of the RN Atlantic fleet at Gibraltar in 1923 and the next year was captain of the Victoria Rugby team. He went on to postings in command of HMS *Ypres* (1927), *Renown* (1929), *Champlain* (1930), *Naden* (1930), *Skeena* as executive officer (1932), and *Vancouver* in command (1934) and to the staff of the CO Pacific Coast as extended defence officer and CO Auxiliary Vessels based at Esquimalt and of the Fishermen's Reserve (1939). He commanded HMS *Ambler* (1940), *Givenchy* as naval officer in charge at Esquimalt (1945), *Givenchy* as captain, and HMC dockyard (Esquimalt) and King's harbour master and captain of the RCN Barracks, Esquimalt, and senior officer of Ships in Reserve (1945). Meanwhile, he was promoted to midshipman (2 February 1917), second lieutenant (2 February 1919), lieutenant (1 February 1921), lieutenant commander (1 February 1929), and naval officer in charge, Esquimalt (1945); *Givenchy* as captain of HMC dockyard (Esquimalt) and King's harbour master and captain of the RCN Barracks, Esquimalt, and senior officer of Ships in Reserve (1945).

On 16 February 1927, CD married Phyllis Joan Henderson at Christ Church Cathedral, the bishop of the Kootenay officiating because she was from Vernon, BC; they were attended by a guard of honour composed of officers from the naval barracks. They spent a short time at Coldstream Ranch in the Okanagan and then went to Halifax, where he was stationed. Later in the year, they went to England. He served with the RCN during the Second World War, beginning by commanding and organizing the Fishermen's Reserve from HMC motor vessel *Skidegate*. In 1948, he was one of the pallbearers at *Admiral Rowland Nugent's funeral in Duncan. He retired with the rank of captain and, in 1950, settled with his wife on Madrona Drive in Sidney, where he became an active member of the Sidney and Esquimalt branches of the Canadian Legion. When he died, aged seventy-four, at Resthaven Hospital on 7 September 1974, leaving his wife, a son, and a daughter, he was buried at Holy Trinity Anglican Church at Patricia Bay.

Sources: *Colonist*, 17 February 1927, p. 8; 8 September 1974, p. 26, obit.; Longstaff, *Esquimalt Naval Base*, p. 70; *MacFarlane*, p. 18; Canadian Passenger Lists, 1865-1935, T-14762.

DONALD, Lieutenant Colonel Dr David, MD (1866-1936). He was born to a Presbyterian family in Aberdeen, became a medical doctor, registered on 6 August 1892 with qualifications as LRCP and LRCS (Edinburgh, 1892), LFPS (Glasgow, 1892), and MDU (Durham, 1908). At Edinburgh, he had been a gold medalist. He joined the Imperial Army and served during the years 1897 to 1901 in the Somaliland and Uganda Campaigns. In Uganda, he was formally in the Indian Army and so paid, but had a special Foreign Office commission. His duty, his daughter recalled, was "to give medical aid to the natives of a vast region mainly,

I think, around Lake Nyanza. The natives were dying of smallpox and my father was the first white man and the first doctor they had ever seen. After three years he contracted black water fever, so returned to England." There he became deputy medical officer of health and school medical officer at Aldershot, Surrey, near the big army camp, until August 1910 when he and his family went to Canada aboard the *Empress of Ireland*. He had a private medical practice in Victoria and, in 1913-1914, was on the Board of School Trustees. When in August 1915 he joined the Fiftieth Gordon Highlanders at Valcartier as a medical officer in the CAMC, his wife, Bessie Donald, and their daughter Jean followed him to England and lived in a village on Salisbury Plain. At first, her address was c/o H. W. Gran, HalGarth Hall, Wintaton-on-Lyne. DD served in France, then in London as president of the Officers' Medical Board. In March 1915, he was put in command of the first Canadian hospital ship, *Letitia*, which was wrecked on rocks at Halifax, and then commanded the hospital ship, *Araguaya*, which travelled for ten months between Halifax and Liverpool. After another spell in France (twice mentioned in despatches), he was demobilized and returned to Victoria, where he served as medical health officer for Victoria schools for thirteen years, resided for some time at Langford, and retired at last in fall 1935. He had also been a life member of the St John's Ambulance Association of Canada and an Esquire of the Order of St John of Jerusalem. He died, aged seventy, on 2 February 1936 in Victoria, leaving a widow and a daughter, Jean Middleton Gow (1903-2005), wife of *Commander F. R. W. R. ("Peter") Gow, an intelligence officer in the RCN.

Mrs Gow, whose autobiography *Alongside* recounts interesting details of her father's life, was living, aged ninety-nine, in Ottawa while I was engaged in research for this book. On 16 March 2002, I inquired on the telephone whether her father had known Sir Charles Delmé-Radcliffe, as they had served in Uganda at the same time and had both retired later to Victoria. Her reply was that they were acquainted but were not friends because Delmé-Radcliffe was a soldier and DD, with a commission from the Foreign Office, was employed essentially as a civilian. Mrs Gow wrote several books, was a talented watercolourist, and employed for many years as a librarian, researcher, and an illustrator for Macmillan publishers. She died, aged 102, on 6 November 2005 in Ottawa.

Sources: NAC, CEF files RG150, box 2581-11; Jean Donald Gow, *Alongside The Navy 1910-1950: An Intimate Account* (Ottawa, JDG Press, 1999), pp. 11-13; 17-24 passim; *Colonist*, 4 February 1936, p. 2, obituary with photo; *The Medical Register* (London, for the General Medical Council, 1924, p. 304; *Globe & Mail* (Toronto), 9 November 2005, p. R15.

DOPPING-HEPENSTAL, Colonel Maxwell Edward (1872-1965), CBE 1919, DSO 1916. He was born in Ireland, third son of Colonel R. A. Dopping-Hepenstal of Derrycassan, Gravard, commanding officer of the Langford Militia, who sent him to be educated at King William's College, Isle of Man. After graduating at RMC, Sandhurst, he took a commission in the Thirty-sixth Battalion, Worcester Regiment, in 1892, serving mostly at Curragh in Ireland. He next spent some time with the Twenty-ninth Worcesters in the Central Province of India and in Burma, where he did some big-game shooting; there followed a year in Aden, where he played in the cricket eleven. When the Worcesters went home to England, he transferred to the Indian Staff Corps on 25 July 1896, because he thought he could not afford to live in England, and was at Raichore with the Fifth Infantry, Hyderabad Contingent, and engaged in the Tirah Campaign in 1897. After a while, he managed to transfer to the Third Gurkha Rifles with whom he went to Almora in the Himalayas, but soon transferred to the First KGO Gurkha Rifles, and served on the North-West Frontier in four separate campaigns against a variety of wild tribesmen, notably in Waziristan in 1901. There were, of course, interludes such as the durbar at Delhi in which King Edward VII was crowned emperor of India. MD learned the Hindustani and Gurkhali languages and with such facility that he was detached to Japan in 1907-1909 to become an interpreter in Japanese, Japan being an ally since 1902. Refusing a subsequent offer of a post as translator at the War Office, he returned to his regiment in India with the rank of major and was detailed with two other officers to organize a tiger-shoot for King George V, who was to visit the Maharajah of Nepal on the occasion of the last Delhi durbar. It was said that in nine and a half days, some thirty-nine tigers were shot, along with nineteen rhinos, a bear, and other game. The king himself shot twenty-one tigers and several rhinos.

MD was dispatched to France with the Indian Army in 1914 and, by 1917, had been wounded three times. For the rest of his life, he bore scars from a fire in a French farmhouse he entered in an effort to save some of his men trapped within. French authorities awarded him the *Croix de Guerre*. During the Great War, he also commanded the Second Battalion, First KGO Gurkha Rifles, fighting Turkish forces in Mesopotamia and badly wounded at Dujallah in the hills beyond Bagdad, was sent to the Bombay hospital organized by the forceful Lady Willingdon in the Gaekwar of Baroda's palace. "Years later," the *Daily Colonist* reported, "when Lady Willingdon visited Canada, Colonel Dopping-Hepenstal told her that he hadn't liked the purple pyjamas . . . which the patients at her hospital were made to wear." It was in Mesopotamia that MD won the DSO and the CBE and was confirmed as commander of the Second Battalion. After the war, he served in the Afghan Campaign in 1919, where a clasp was added to his India Medal, and was sent to preserve order in Amritsar when the Indian Congress Party was holding its meetings there. "With his Gurkhas and special police of doubtful loyalty, he managed to keep enormous sullen mobs in check," without suffering the disgrace brought upon Brigadier General R. E. Dyer (1864-1926) by what came to be called a massacre. (See Alfred Draper, *The Amritsar Massacre: Twilight of the Raj* (Buchan & Enright, 1981), 301 pp. and Arthur Swinson, *Six Minutes to Sunset: The Story of General Dyer and the Amritsar Affair* (Peter Davies, 1964), 216 pp.; and Major General Nigel Woodyat, *Under Ten Viceroys: The Reminiscences of a Gurkha* (Herbert Jenkins Ltd., 1922), pp. 282-6, 290.) Then, after another campaign, in 1921-1922, against tribesmen in Waziristan, MD retired in 1922.

Partly on the urging of a colleague, *Colonel Brinsley Rice, retired from the Sixth Gurkhas, MD went to live at "Lenamore," Stamps Road, near Duncan, Vancouver Island, with his brother and sister-in-law; they were all registered on the election rolls for Maple Bay in 1935. He joined the India-Burma Society in

Victoria and spent much time fishing, shooting, and gardening. At the annual fall fair of the Cowichan Agricultural Society in the 1930s, he won prizes for his Wealthy Apples, Crab Apples, Quinces, Nectarines, Clairgeau pears, and grapes. He also played cricket and, although he never married, enjoyed children and, for instance, managed the children's games at a Women's Auxiliary garden party held in the grounds of the St Peter's Rectory on 7 July 1933. Very active in the Boy Scout movement in Duncan, he revived the Quamichan Lake troop, eventually became district scout commissioner, and was one of the scoutmasters who (like my scoutmaster, *Freeman Foard King, another British soldier) brought senior scouts into the Pacific Coast Militia Rangers, a kind of home-guard guerrilla unit, during the Second World War. M. J. Ackonclose recalls him as "a nut-brown, spare little man, still retaining the deep tan received from his many years of soldiering in the British Army under the blazing sun of India. His inexhaustible energy more than made up for his lack of physical bulk. He worked hard with the Boy Scout movement in the valley, and became their highly respected commissioner." As a result of his long military career, he was tough, determined, good at Scouting, gently spoken, and used to being in charge. "He could outwalk most younger men." At the age of eighty-two and in declining health, he retired from active scouting but remained honorary commissioner—"a sort of commissioner emeritus." Many of his trophies and souvenirs were lost in a fire that destroyed his house between the wars, but he still had his collection of *kukris*, the famous Gurkha curved knives. MD died on 2 August 1965 and was buried in the churchyard of St Peter's Anglican Church, Quamichan Lake.

Sources: *Army List,* October 1915 (part 1), p. 399; *Who's Who in B.C.* e.g., 1947-1948, p. 60; *Who was Who,* vol. VI; NAC, Election rolls for 1935, reel T4760; *Colonist,* 20 September 1931, p. 24; 17 January 1933, p. 8; 8 July 1933, p. 8; *Colonist,* 24 October 1954, *Sunday Magazine,* pp. 1 and 8, G. E. Mortimer, *"This Weeks' Profile"; The Social Register, vol.* 2, p. 98; *Burke's Handbook to the Most Excellent Order of the British Empire,* ed., A. *Winton Thorpe* (The Burke Publishing Co. Ltd., 1921), p. 163; Muriel Jarvis Ackinclose, *Between Tzouhalem and Prevost: As I Remember Duncan* (Duncan, BC, Priority Printing Ltd., 2000), p. 99.

DOUGLAS, Sir James (1803-1877). Born at Demerara, British Guiana, he was the second son of a "Creole" lady who was the first wife of John Douglas, a merchant in Glasgow. They sent JD to school in Lanark, Scotland, where he seems to have had a good education in history, literature and public affairs, as well as business practices. After further instruction in French by a Huguenot tutor at Chester in England, he was apprenticed, aged sixteen, together with his elder brother Alexander, to the North-West Company based at Montreal. They left Liverpool on 7 May 1819 aboard the brig *Matthews* and on 6 August reached Fort William via Quebec. As it happened, the North-West Company was in mortal combat with the Hudson's Bay Company, which defeated its Canadian rival in 1821 and subsequently employed JD as a clerk at a series of fur-trading posts in the western part of the continent. In spring 1826, he visited the Pacific coast for the first time. The HBC had decided to supply New Caledonia, the future British Columbia, from

Fort Vancouver, built in 1824 on the north bank of the Columbia River, which was in touch with the British Isles by sea around the southern tip of South America. JD was sent north to help in opening the overland route from Fort Vancouver to Fort Alexandria on the upper Fraser River and Fort Okanagan at the junction of the Okanogan and Columbia rivers. As standard accounts relate, he founded Fort Victoria on the Island in 1843. He became the first governor of the colony of Vancouver Island until after it became part of British Columbia, then of Canada, and earned the respect in which he has usually been held.

Sources: John Adams, *Old Square-Toes and His Lady: The Life of James and Amelia Douglas* (Victoria, Horsdahl & Schubart, 2001), 243 pp.; *Fort Victoria Letters, 1846-1851*, ed., Hartwell Bowsfield (Winnipeg, Hudson's Bay Record Society, 1979), see index entry, pp. 256-58; Margaret A. Ormsby, in the DCB, vol. X, pp. 238-49 and online.

DUMBLETON, Henry (1821-1909). He and his family, born variously in England and Cape Colony, South Africa, swarmed into Victoria and district in 1886 and the following years. HD, born in Hampshire at Shirley, a western suburb of Southampton, and his wife, Clara Marion *née* Garcia, born on 1 May 1827 in the Cape of Good Hope, South Africa, lived with some of their daughters on Belcher Avenue, which from 1905 became the prosperous and fashionable Rockland Avenue, in a large house he called "Shirley" after his birthplace. Different sources cite different numbers for houses on Rockland Avenue and have to be treated with caution. The best source for viewing the family as a whole is the 1871 English census, which (supplemented from other sources) shows HD living as a "landowner" at Hall Grove, Windlesham, Bagshot, Surrey, with his wife Clara Marion *née* Garcia, born on 1 May 1827 in the Cape of Good Hope, South Africa. The birthplaces of their seven children show to-ing and fro-ing between England and South Africa: Ellen Annie, aged twenty-two, was born at the Cape; Clara Constance Augustas, eighteen, and Charles Douglas, sixteen, at Bagshot; and the youngest four at the Cape: Alice Beatrice, fourteen; Louis, nine; Alan Southey, seven; and Clara Eveline, five. Living with them was HD's brother Horatio Dumbleton, aged fifty-nine, born at Yately, Hampshire. They had a governess, eight domestic servants, and a coachman with family living next door, probably on the estate. Ten years later, the family was living at "Bromrylfe," Littleham, a suburb of Exmouth, Devon, but the children were elsewhere except for Ellen, Alice, and Clara Eveline. The governess and two of the servants had gone.

By 1901, three of HD's sons were living with their families at different addresses in Victoria or its vicinity. Next door to him on Rockland Avenue was Alan Southey Dumbleton (1863-1937), a solicitor, and his wife, Mabel C. Dumbleton, born in India on 3 May 1864, with their four daughters, born in Victoria in 1891-1896, the two youngest being twins. In the James Bay district, south of Victoria harbour, Henry Maurice Dumbleton (1847-1909), a civil engineer, was living at 6 Superior Street with three children and his wife, *née* Florence Mary Leneveu [often cited in error as "Leneven"], whom he had married on 4 January 1888 in Victoria. She was born there on 5 May 1870, daughter of David Leneveu, a prominent businessman who had arrived at Victoria from the island of Jersey (Channel Islands) by way of California and married Rachel, whom he had known earlier in England. Among the pallbearers when Leneveu was buried, aged sixty, in 1885, were such prominent citizens as Hon. J. W. Trutch and Sir Matthew Baillie Begbie. Meanwhile, Charles Douglas Dumbleton (1855-1928?) had taken a large forested property in the Highland District, northwest of Victoria and was living there as a "farmer" with his wife, Florence A. Dumbleton, who was born in Cape Colony on 26 January 1866 and died in Victoria on 2 March 1928. The eldest of their five children, Ernest, was born in Cape Colony on 19 February 1887; the second, Gladys, in California on 16 September 1891; and the rest on the Island. Unlike the rest of the family, who were Anglicans, Charles Douglas Dumbleton said he was a Baptist. HD died on 19 March 1909, but reports of his death in *The Times* (London) seem to be mistaken. Research into this branch of the Dumbleton family goes on, and there is more to be found.

Sources: census 1871, England, RG 10/806, pp. 3-4; census 1881, RG11/2138, p. 18; census 1881, RG11/2143/106, p. 3; census 1891, RG12/548, p. 6; *Colonist*, 20 March 1909, p. 6, courtesy of Leona Taylor; 21 November 1917, p. 18, obit.; 17 July 1927, p. (Ashdown-Green); 1 November 1925, Sunday, p. 36, obit.; 6 December 1930, p. 5, obit. (Holmes); 20 February 1936, p. 7, obit. (Horatio Dumbleton); 4 November 1952, obit. (Gerrard); NAC, CEF files, box 2721-79; Ruth H. Judson, "*Dumbleton and Leneveu Families*, 634 Michigan Street," in *Camas Chronicles of James Bay, Victoria, British Columbia* (Victoria, Camas Historical Group, 1978), pp. 109-10 (use with caution.)

   DUNBAR, Brigadier General James Secretan (1863-1951). Born in September 1863 in Quebec, son of James Dunbar, KC, DCL, he attended Quebec High School and Laval University and graduated with an MA in law, admitted to the Bar in 1886, and practised in Quebec until 1881, when he joined No 4 Company, Eighth Royal Rifles, as a private. He was promoted to lieutenant (1883), captain (1886), major (1893), lieutenant colonel (1900), colonel (1913), and brigadier general (May 1920). In 1887, he married Ida Temple, daughter of C. V. M. Temple, and they had a son, Lieutenant Colonel Bevan Dunbar, RCE, and a daughter, Mrs C. Hugo Raymont. JD retired to 1271 Monterey Avenue, Victoria, and spent his last years fishing, shooting, and gardening. When he died, aged eighty-seven, on 28 September 1951 in Saanich, he was buried as an Anglican.

Sources: NAC, CEF files, box 2725-33; *Who's Who in B.C.*, 1933-34, p. 54.

   DUNCAN, Major Charles Gordon Stewart (1873-1947). Born on 6 May 1873 either at Perth in Scotland or at Charlottetown, Prince Edward Island, he served for five years in the NWM Police and enlisted for South Africa in Lord Strathcona's Horse on 12 February 1900 at Victoria, giving his age as twenty-seven, his birthplace as "Scotland," his religion as Presbyterian, and his trade or calling as "N.W.M.P." As his next of kin, he named his mother, resident at "The Manse," Glendeson near Perth in Scotland. He was promoted to sergeant, wounded, invalided to England on 8 February 1901, returned to Canada, and discharged on 8 March 1901 with the Queen's Medal and clasps for Belfast, Orange Free State, and Natal. On 21 December 1901 in Victoria, he married Rachel Augusta V. Williams and found employment as an accountant. In spite of an old shrapnel wound incurred in South Africa, he enlisted for the Great War in the Fifth Regiment, Canadian Garrison Artillery in July 1916, recording his occupation as "Gentleman" and his religion as Presbyterian. He served in the Sixty-seventh Battalion as a lieutenant from 26 May 1915 and the Seventeenth Battalion as a captain from 24 June 1916. His wife, at the time of his enlistment, had a London address. She died, aged sixty-one, on 30 May 1931 in Vancouver but was buried in Victoria. His death at eighty-eight came in Vancouver on 3 April 1947. It is possible that two different men are being here confused, but if so, their lives and careers were almost identical.

Sources: NAC, RG 38, A-1-a, vol. 29, regimental no. 434 (reel T-2068; CEF files, RG150, box 2728-38; *Colonist*, 31 May 1931, p. 5, obit.

DUNCAN, William (1832-1918). A pioneer missionary born at Bishop Burton in east Yorkshire near Beverley, he was a determined evangelical layman who had the vigour and originality to establish a successful Anglican mission among the tribes at Metlakatla on the northern BC coast. His venture fascinated Sir Henry Wellcome (1863-1936), the American-born pharmaceutical magnate, founder of the Wellcome Foundation Ltd., who visited Victoria and Metlakatla before writing his study of it. A sympathetic contemporary account of WD and his work, with long quotations from his reports, was written by *Commander R. C. Mayne, RN in his *Four Years in British Columbia and Vancouver Island* (John Murray, 1862, ch. xii.). WD was assisted for some time by *W. H. Collison and both were in sympathy with *Dean Edward Cridge in his quarrel with *Bishop George Hills. When Hills brought his authority to bear, WD moved the Metlakatla community, lock stock and barrel, to a nearby site in Alaska, beyond Hills's jurisdiction. *Admiral B Mordaunt Chambers recalled "the dumpy little coaster *Boskowitz* [*Boscowitz*], carrying Mr Duncan, the missionary who had been the source of all the trouble" through the Seymour Narrows. Witnesses vary; point of view is everything! None of the above appears to have been so anxious about WD's personal illegitimacy as Jean Friesen writing in the *DCB*.

Sources: Jean Usher, *William Duncan of Metlakatla: A Victorian Missionary in British Columbia* (Ottawa, National Museum of Man, 1974), 163 pp.; Jean Friesen, in the DCB, vol. XIV, pp. 316-19; Henry Solomon Wellcome, *The Story of Metlakatla* (Saxon & Co., 1887), 483 pp.; *Colonist*, 27 July 1936, p. 3; Admiral Bertram Mordaunt Chambers, (1866-1918), *Salt Junk, Naval Reminiscences 1881-1906* (Constable, 1927), pp. 97-98.

DUNNE, Charles Walter (1863-1951). One of the many second or younger sons of landed families in England, he emigrated in 1890 to the Island, where he farmed at Chemainus, north of the Cowichan Valley. On 27 August 1896 at Metchosin, he married Annie Gertude Fisher (1874-1969), daughter of William and Elizabeth Fisher of Westholme, having boarded with the family for some time.

Their daughter, Dorothy Edith F. Dunne, born at Westholme on 25 June 1897, married *Major Francis Clavering Peere Williams-Freeman there on 19 June 1922. Two years later, her younger sister Gertrude Katherine Dunne (1902-?) married *Lieutenant General Gerald Robert Poole there on 3 September 1924. In due time, CD died, aged eighty-seven, on 22 December 1951 in Duncan, and Annie Gertrude Dunne died, aged ninety-five, on 6 May 1969 in North Cowichan.

Meanwhile, CD's elder brother, Thomas Russell Dunne (1861-1944), after schooling at Eton, had inherited the family estates of Bircher Hall and Gatley Park in Herefordshire and settled down to country life as a JP. It was Wellington College, not Eton, where CD had been schooled, followed by Corpus Christi College, Oxford, where he read classics. In 1881, the census recorded him, aged seventeen, as a "scholar" at RMC, Sandhurst. No doubt a career as a military officer was intended for him, but something intervened to make him emigrate. He may have failed, or the family's expectations may have been overwhelming. According to the 1871 census, his father, Thomas Dunne, born c. 1817 in London, was a "Gentleman J.P., extensive landowner proprietor," established at Bircher Hall, Yarpole, Herefordshire, and his mother Harriet, much younger, was born in India. They had a German governess and eight servants. The estate at Yarpole, a suburb of Leominster, had been purchased in 1679 by their forebears and many army officers had been born to the family in later generations, notably General John H. Dunne (1835-?). Among family friends was the famous gardener, Gertrude Jekyll (1843-1932). The family papers are held at the Herefordshire Record Office and the BNA at Kew.

Sources: *Alumni oxonienses*, Oxford Men online, matriculations 1880-1892, p. 179; census 1861, England, RG 9/1833, p. 2; census 1871, RG 10/2719, pp. 20-21; census 1881, RG 11/1320, p. 10; census 1891, RG 12/565, p. 44; census 1901, RG 13/620, p. 3; *Colonist*, 21 October 1937, p. 3, obit.

DUNSMUIR, James (1851-1920). See Clarence Karr in the DCB, vol. xiv, pp. 320-25.

DUNSMUIR, Robert (1825-1889). See Daniel T. Gallacher in the DCB, vol. xi, pp. 290-93.

DYKE, William (1867-1930), Born on 3 March 1867 at Bradford-on-Avon, Wiltshire, he is said to have run away from home, aged fourteen, to join the Royal Navy at Portsmouth as a cabin boy. The census-taker found him, however, aged fifteen in spring 1851, living with his family at "Canal Cottage," Bradford, Wiltshire. His father, also William, was a forty-four-year-old lock-keeper born at Alllington, Wiltshire, and his mother, Sarah, aged forty-two, was born at Horton (Wilts.). WD had four sisters and two brothers. Once in the RN, WD was assigned to HMS *Warspite* and in the following years travelled from one naval base to another, arriving at Esquimalt in 1891.

He liked Victoria so much that he took a discharge from the navy and worked as head steward at the Union Club from the time of his arrival until settling later at Crofton. There, he opened a store on Joan Avenue, attended the Presbyterian Church and on 30 April 1895 married a stonemason's daughter from Elgin, Scotland, who had arrived at Victoria at the same time with her family. He died, aged sixty-three, on 16 January 1930 at Crofton. Mrs Dyke, *née* Margaret Ann Brown, died aged seventy on 15 July 1941 in Burnaby, a suburb of Vancouver City.

Sources: census 1851, RG 11/2050, pp. 16-17; Elliott, *Memories of the Chemainus Valley*, pp. 155-60.

Knockdrin, Shawnigan Lake

Knockdrin, Ireland

EARDLEY-WILMOT, Colonel Irton (1859-1936). He was born on 8 April 1859 into a branch of an ancient Anglo-Irish family of Imperial officers with several branches and a family tree descending from Philippe le Hardi, king of France in the fourteenth century. IE's wife, Florence Levinge, was from another distinguished old family. The youngest son of Major General Frederick M. Eardley-Wilmot (1812-1877) and his wife Frances Augusta Pennington, IE was a grandson of Sir John Eardley-Wilmot (1783-1847) first baronet, MP for Warwick, who also served as governor of Van Diemen's Land. Family relationships ramble on and on. Through his maternal grandmother *née* Selina Jekyll (1798-1838), IE was distantly related even to Gertrude Jekyll (1843-1932), the famous English gardener.

After a career in Imperial forces, IE and his wife followed their son, Vere, to the Island, where they built a large house on a bluff overlooking Shawnigan Lake. "Vere went to Canada 3rd March 1910 (aged 24)," IE recalled later in a series of notes. "We sailed for Canada 24th May 1910. Bought 'Knockdrin,' Shawnigan Lake, Vancouver Island, 3rd September 1910. Left Shawnigan Lake for England 1st March 1911. Returned to live at 'Knockdrin' 17th October 1911." On 20 October 1910, even before that journey, IE joined the British Campaigners' Association in Victoria, later attended meetings of the Returned Veterans of Shawnigan Lake, became a JP, and, in 1917, was elected to the Duncan Board of Trade along with such men as *H. T. Ravenhill, H. B. Wingate White, W. H. Nott, Trevor Keene, and A. E. Brooke Wilkinson. In December 1912, and doubtless for some time earlier and on until the devastating economic collapse of 1913-1914, the Canada West Trust Company, Ltd. of Victoria and London listed him as its vice-president, the president being D. C. Reid. This was a company with a subscribed capital of $245,000 and an address in London at Whitehall House, 29/30, Charing Cross. IE was an active member of the Anglican Church, wrote letters to the newspapers in defence of Sunday observance, took up with the local British Israelites, and became a leader of the local Red Cross Society.

"Knockdrin" was less than a mile from Shawnigan Lake Boys' School and surrounded by a garden and a hundred acres of forest. During the 1920s, the family built a tea-house or pavilion and maintained two wooden tennis courts. Monica Oldham, a daughter of *Colonel F. T. Oldham, recalls that the men often held up their white tennis shorts with old school ties. The family had a happy social life with neighbours, including the "Twenty-four Colonels on the West Arm Road," recalled by the daughter-in-law of *Frederick Charles Mason-Hurley, who owned the Forest Inn, later the Shawnigan Lake Hotel. Family photographs show IE together with Florence and their son Vere Levinge Eardley-Wilmott and his wife and children. A small boy in one photo, IE's grandson Hugh (Vere's son) told me that although the family had lived in grand style, "Knockdrin" was seized by the government for back taxes when they finally left, an obvious sign of financial strain, though Hugh did not know the cause of it. Certainly, there were heavy expenses in sending Vere (1865-1965) to Wellington College, Berkshire, the Royal School of Mines, and the Imperial College of Science and Technology.

In 1850, a Captain F. W. M. Eardley-Wilmot had presented a silver bugle to the Royal Military Academy at Woolwich to be competed for annually, the winner of the greatest number of events to hold it for a year and have his name engraved on it. But in 1877, IE attended Sandhurst, not Woolwich, after entering Wellington College in 1872, aged thirteen, Dr Wrigley's at Clapham in 1875, and Oxford Military College in 1876. Family and service records afford a detailed, though sometimes confusing, summary of his career that is worth recording if only because such good sources are lacking for many other officers. We know that he spoke French, German, and eventually Hindustani. On leaving Sandhurst, he was almost immediately attached to the Seventy-fifth Regiment at Aldershot and then stationed with the Thirty-fourth Cumberland Regiment at Chaubrittia, NW Province of India, from 25 November 1878 to 25 November 1879, and at Raniket from 8 December 1879 to 25 November 1980. In 1881, IE was attached to the QMG's department for the purpose of making a military survey and report on the Northern Bengal State Railway, the Darjeeling Himalayan Railway, and the Kawmer Durlab Tramway for which he received a letter of thanks from the commander-in-chief dated 7 November 1883.

At Jhansi, he transferred to the Bengal Cavalry from 17 December 1882 to 12 August 1884, during which period he was on reconnaissance and survey duty in the Thansi district in February 1884. He was with the Eighteenth Bengal Cavalry at Nowshera from 24 August 1884 to 24 January 1885 and in England on furlough when the Russian war scare caused him to be recalled on 4 March 1885 and posted at Jhelum at the end of April. He won an extra certificate at the school of musketry at Chaugla Gulley in November 1887 and was at the cavalry exercise camp at Lawrencepur in December 1887 and in the garrison class at Naini Tal from April to September 1888. Then, until October, he was at Peshawar instructing signallers for the "Cabul Mission" and at Rawalpindi with a detached squadron from November 1888 to January 1889. An appointment on 13 May 1889 as AAG for musketry at Ambala-LaSaule followed a promotion to captain a fortnight earlier. There followed another series of postings and activities, but he was with the Kurram Field Force and the Tirah Expeditionary Force from August 1897 to February 1898, being present at the attack on Sadda on 16 September 1897. Promoted to major on 1 May 1898 (then aged thirty-nine), he moved about on more postings and then marched into Nowgong with the Eighth Bengal Lancers on 16 February 1903. In June 1904, he left the Eighteenth Bengal Lancers after twenty years of service and was offered a post as AAG of Northern Command at Murree but, on 1 September 1904, took an appointment as AAG Madras Command as chief instructor at the school of musketry and until December 1904 was at Bellary. From 1904 to 1908, he was at Maymyo and promoted to lieutenant colonel on 1 May 1904 and to substantive colonel by Lord Kitchener in May 1907. Serving meanwhile in 1906-1907 as chief instructor at the school of musketry at Maymyo, he left Burma for England on 10 May 1908 on furlough, pending retirement. He retired on 1 January 1910, having completed thirty-two years of service by the age of fifty-one.

This was by no means the first furlough, and there had been other interludes from time to time. He married Florence Levinge in Jhelum on 22 October 1885, when he was twenty-six, and they went on leave to England the following 28

February. Her family owned an estate in Ireland at Mullingar, County Westmeath. There, she had been brought up in "Knockdrin" castle of which her expert pencil sketch, showing tennis courts and other features, remained among the possessions they eventually took to Shawnigan Lake. They were staying at 31 Holles St, Merrion Square, Dublin, when on 29 October 1886, their son, Vere Levinge Eardley-Wilmot, was born. In the ensuing years, Florence sometimes lived with him wherever duty called but sometimes remained at home in England, where they were on furlough from 7 April to 17 November 1899, and in August 1901, he and Florence went off for two months to Muzaffarour (north central India). On 7 March 1902, he and A. M. Aikinson won the Punjab competition championship cup for lawn tennis doubles at Lahore. In June 1902, he was ill in hospital at Simla and, in August, went on two months' leave in Kashmir. They had another year of leave in 1903, beginning on 18 February. He wrote, "Florrie and I landed at Devonport on 12 June 1908. Stayed at Talbot Cottage, Carshalton." In 1909, they moved to Snaresbrook for him to accept, on 7 July, the post of governor of the Royal Merchant Seaman's Orphanage, but it was not enough to keep him there. The next year, they emigrated to Shawnigan Lake.

They left Shawnigan at last in 1932 as recorded in the colonel's notes: "Heart attack 14th September 1932. Florrie left 'Knockdrin' 17th October 1932. Florrie, Vere and I arrived in Ottawa on 7th November 1932 and lived with Vere at 55 Somerset Street West. We left Ottawa, 28th April 1933 and returned to Ottawa 14th October 1933 and moved into a flat at 61 Cartier Street. Left Ottawa 17 September 1935—arrived in London 29th September 1935, and moved into a flat at 194 Latymer Court, Hammersmith Road, W.6, on 23rd November 1935." IE died there on 17 July 1936, aged seventy-seven, and was buried at Ocklynge Cemetery, Eastbourne, Sussex, England. The son, Vere Levinge Eardley-Wilmot, worked in various parts of Canada as a surveyor, assayer, metalurgical engineer, and mill superintendent and served through the Great War in the First Canadian Pioneers and then the 252nd Tunnelling Company of Royal Engineers. His son, the elder of the colonel's two grandsons, John Vere Eardley-Wilmot, enlisted in the governor general's footguards, RCAC, Twenty-first Armed Regiment, and was killed in France, aged twenty-six, on 15 August 1944. "Knockdrin" survives as a bed-and-breakfast home on less than an acre under the name "Marifield," much altered by time and a fire in December 2002.

Sources: Letters to the author courtesy of Hugh Eardley-Wilmot, a grandson, dated 25 February 2003 at RR1, Norland, Ont., Canada K0M 2L0; notes from the family Bible; access to the foregoing and to the Eardley-Wilmot family tree courtesy of John Coles, Astrolabe Gallery, Ottawa; *Indian Army List*, January 1905, p. 88; *BC Archives, Minutes of the British Campaigners' Ass.*, 20 October 1910; *Colonist*, 18 February 1917, p. 4; 21 January 1921, p. 8; 17 May 1921, p. 4; 11 November 1925, p. 13; 19 September 1929, p. 8; *Canada* (London), vol. xxviii, no 362 (14 December 1912), p. x, advertisement; Hughes, *Shawnigan Lake, 1887-1967*, p. 51; *Victoria Times-Colonist*, 3 December 2002, pp. 1 and 2; Joan Mason-Hurley, "*Twenty-four Colonels on the West Arm Road,*" *Raincoast Chronicles*, vol. ?? pp. 52-61, p. 53; notes from Monica Oldham, F. T. Oldham's daughter, 511 Victoria St, Victoria, May 2001;

Captain F. G. Guggisberg (RE), *"The Shop": The Story of the Royal Military Academy* (1900; 2nd ed., Cassell & Company Ltd., 1902), pp. 52, 209.

EASTON, Lieutenant Archibald Philip Adair (1879-1932). He was born on 19 April 1879 in Sussex at Bognor (called Bognor Regis from 1929), son of Caroline Eliza Easton, and cited her as his next of kin at "Hillcrest," Duncan, when he enlisted in the Royal Canadian Dragoons at Shorncliffe on 12 September 1916. His father's name is not given in any of my sources but he was known to be a cousin of the Earl of Ypres and a godson of the Earl of Rosebery. The 1891 census listed AE, aged eleven, living in Baxted, Essex, as a visitor in the family of William L. Watts, an Anglican minister with five children and two servants, and after attending Uppingham School, he joined the British Army. The 1901 census recorded him as, aged twenty-one, a lieutenant in the militia boarding in a lodging house at Staines, Middlesex. He fought in the South African War (1899-1902) in the Lancashire Fusiliers and then with a commission in the Third Hussars. After that war, he went out to the Cowichan Valley and farmed until the Great War. About 1912, his father died and his mother and two sisters then joined him there. During the Great War, he seems to have moved from the Canadian unit he joined in 1916 to service as assistant gunnery officer on board HMS *New Zealand*. Many British officers from Canada, once overseas, transferred to British units.

After the war, he returned to the Island and in 1919 joined the Dominion Fisheries Service in which he became an inspector. He married Katharine Ann Woodward at Victoria on 18 December 1926, and they had two daughters. When he died, aged fifty-one, on 3 November 1932 at their home near Quamichan Lake, he left his family, including his mother, who died, aged ninety, on 8 June 1937, and the two sisters, one of whom was a Mrs Beresford. Three other sisters, all married, were living in England. He was buried locally as an Anglican, the active pallbearers being four petty officers of the RCN, but the honorary pallbearers were nearly all Cowichan men: Captain Arthur William Barton (1893-1968) and Messrs *H. S. Alderson, *R. W. Whittome, Thomas Pitt, Edwin Gunns, and (from Nanaimo) J. F. Tait. His wife died, aged eighty, on 2 September 1958 in Vancouver.
Sources: NAC, CEF files, box 2809-32 no. 15653; *Cowichan Leader*, 10 November 1932, obit.; census 1891, England, RG 12/1417, p. 3; census 1901, RG 13/1175, pp. 44-45.

EDWARDS, Sergeant Major William John (1868-1936). He was born in Tonbridge Wells, Kent, enlisted in the Royal Engineers as a very young man and served with them for twenty-four years in four major engagements of the South African War and then with the forces at Halifax, Nova Scotia, and Bermuda. At some time in 1904-1905, he was transferred to Esquimalt, where he and his wife Lydia lived at first in army quarters on Head Street at Work Point Barracks. Their children were christened at the garrison church, and the family befriended Scottish shipyard workers and other neighbours. WE was a keen fly-fisherman, a lifelong Freemason, and a member of the British Campaigners' Association. He served the city school board for twenty-six years as a "truant officer." When he died on

10 April 1936, leaving three sisters and two brothers in England, the family was living at 1762 Carrick Street, Victoria.
Sources: *Colonist*, 11 April 1936, pp. 1 and 8, obit.; Harriet (Edwards) Westby, "Family Life at Work Point Barracks," in Duffus, *Beyond the Blue Bridge*, pp. 80-1.

ELLIOTT, Brigadier General Gilbert Sullivan McDowell (1863-1937). He was born at Poonah, India, a descendant of the earls of Minto and a son of Colonel John McDowell Elliott of the Prince of Wales, Third Dragoon Guards, and his wife Mary. The family was living at Aldershot in 1871. GE graduated at RMC, Woolwich, and the School of Military Engineering, Chatham, joined the army in 1882, and served in India in 1884-1991 under General Sir Buchanan Scott. In 1897, he was sent to Asiatic Turkey for a year as military vice-consul at Var. There, his task was to keep the peace between Turkish and Armenian residents, and the FO was grateful for his services. He returned to Turkey as staff officer to the Macedonian Gendarmerie, and the sultan named him to the Imperial Ottoman Order of Osmanieh. He fought at Colenso and Spion Kop in the South African War under General Redvers Buller and, in 1901-1904, served as British commissioner on the Anglo-French Boundary of Niger and Chad and was active in the Kano-Sokoto campaign. There followed a term in 1906-1907 as British staff officer with the Macedonian Gendarmerie in the South African War, 1899-1900; Kano-Sokoto Campaign, 1903 (medal and clasp); made a colonel in 1911; and European War 1914-1919 (despatches, CBE). He was promoted to colonel in 1911 and retired from the army in 1920 with a range of decorations: Order of Osmanieh, second class; the Order of the White Eagle of Serbia, fourth class; the Queen's Medal and four clasps for South Africa; and the CBE.

According to Victoria and BC city directories, he and his wife Mary lived in Oak Bay at 2431 Currie Road, recently renamed after *General Sir Arthur Currie, for at least three years in 1923-1925, perhaps longer, and then moved back to England. There, he was a member of the United Services Club, London, and died at "Teviot House," Iver, Buckinghamshire, on 13 January 1937.
Sources: *Colonist*, 11 February 1937, p. 3; *Who was Who*, 1931-1940; census 1871, England, RG10/816, fol. 9, page 12; census 1891, England, RG 12/939, p. 4; Riddick, *Who in British India*, p. 117 (forebears).

ELLISON, Henry Lawrence (c. 1898-1956). Born in Clapham, London, son of William Richard Ellison, a "Military Clerk (Sgt. Major)" at Dictrict Red Barracks, Woolwich, and his wife Maud Agnes Lucy Ellison, he enlisted young in the army and had a long and distinguished war record. After a time at Ypres, he served in the RAF in France and Mesopotamia before being sent to Burma as a telephone construction engineer with the Imperial Army. After the Great War, he was involved in the Turkish-Greek war, landed at Constantinople on Christmas Day 1922, and, on retiring, settled in Gosport, England.

His elder brother, Ernest Thomas Ellison (1893-1979), had migrated earlier to Victoria, where he became well known as a gunsmith on Union Street. HE went to join him, sailing on the CPR vessel, *Melita* in March 1925, but soon settled on Lake Trail Road at Courtenay. He died, aged fifty-seven, on 14 July 1956 in Vancouver.

Sources: *Colonist,* 28 March 1925, p. 10; census 1901, England, RG 13/568; NAC, RG76, immigration, series C-1-c, 1925, vol. 2, microfilm reel T-14846.

ELLISON, Rev. William George Hollingsworth (1857-1929). Born in Stockholm, Sweden, son of Rev. William T. Ellison, Anglican chaplain at the British consulate in Gottenberg (Göteborg), he was recorded by the English census of 1871 living with his family at 17 Lodge Lane, Derby (Derbyshire). There his father, William T. M. Ellison, was "Vicar of St Michael's Derby," but born at Haugham, Sussex, and his mother, Jane Ellison, had been born a British subject in Rotterdam, Holland. With them were WE's two sisters Mary Anna (c. 1861-1944) and Cecilia J., both born in Sweden at Gottenberg, and the family had three servants. By 1881, the two daughters and their father were living in St John's Vicarage, Wandsworth, London, but Mrs Ellison had died and the father had remarried a certain Eleanor Edwards from Tutbury, Staffordshire, formerly employed as "Lady Superior" at the Diocesan Training College in Derby. WE was then studying theology in Lichfield, after taking a degree at Oxford University. In the next few years, he went as a chaplain to the British consulate at Genoa, then to Bombay, where he spent three years at a hospital and established a seamen's mission, as his sister Mary and his daughter Josephine recalled after his death. In Bombay, he met and married the secretary at the YMCA, Charlotte (1858-1928), who was born in India.

WE's health suffered in India, and on medical advice, the couple emigrated in 1888 to the Island. There, he was employed as naval chaplain to St Paul's Naval and Garrison Church at Esquimalt, where in June 1890, they had a daughter Josephine Eleanor Ellison. He also travelled by canoe to Sooke to hold services and was appointed later to St Mary's Church at Metchosin. There, he displeased the bishop of the diocese, Rt. Rev. W. W. Perrin, by speaking publicly against the South African War effort and by such irregularities as marrying a Chinese woman and a white man and lending his church for the burial of a Roman Catholic priest. Faced with criticism, he left the church and moved to the remote west-coast settlement of Port Renfrew, where he built a sawmill in the vain hope that roads would soon reach the settlement. He also wrote a book, *Settlers of Vancouver Island, A Tale for Emigrants* (1910). As Port Renfrew was not favoured with roads and there was no schooling for Josephine, the family tired of pioneering and returned for a few years to England, where WE worked as a "Church of England Emigration Chaplain." When his health began to suffer again, they moved back to Port Renfrew, but his daughter Josephine Eleanor, then aged nineteen, preferred Victoria, where she met Frederick Tyrell Godman (1875-1917) and married him in Esquimalt on 24 February 1910. He was a wealthy young man from a landowning family of Sussex, son of Major General Richard Temple Godman, a veteran of the Crimean War, schooled at Marlborough, and was visiting the Island while travelling on a world tour. This young couple were soon living on one of the family estates in Sussex, probably "Little Oathall" at Wivelsfield, a life that reminded Josephine of *Forsyte Saga.* After the Great War, she returned as a widow to Victoria, her husband having joined the Ninth Battalion of the Royal Sussex Regiment in the Great War and died on 12 October 1917 in a German prison camp at Holzminden.

Reunited in or near Victoria, they were a public-spirited family. Josephine was active in the Girl Guides and the Women's Institute. WE was active in the Anglican Church and joined the Anti-Vivisection Society and the Theosophical Society. After a few years, they were joined by WE's sister Mary Anna Ellison, who had become a teacher after attending private schools and St Hugh's College, Oxford. She had also taken up nursing in London, specializing in massage work. She wrote a *Manual on Massage,* which went through three editions and became a recognized textbook on the subject. She was employed by the Soldiers' Civil Re-establishment of BC and lived for many years in Victoria at 417 Vancouver Street. She lived long enough to record a few details of her brother's life in *Who's Who in British Columbia* (1933-1934). He died, aged seventy-one, on 2 May 1929 in Victoria, a few months after his wife's death there on 5 March 1928. It was nearly half a century later that their daughter Josephine Godman *née* Ellison (1890-1981) wrote a four-page note about the family, which was published after her death in a book she called *Footprints* (1983).

Sources: Marion I. Helgeson, ed., *Footprints: Pioneer Families of the Metchosin District, South Vancouver Island,* 1857-1900, (Victoria, Metchosin School Museum Society, 1983), pp. 92, 98-102; *Canadian Almanach,* 1902, p. 272; *Who's Who in BC,* 1933-1934, p. 56; Canadian census, Victoria, 1891; census 1871, England, RG 10/3561, pp. 5-6; census 1881, RG 11/2772, p. 28; census 1881, RG 11/659, p. 14; census 1891, RG 12/2879, p. 14; census 1851, HO, 197, 1711; census 1861, RG 9/1959, p. 2 (Eleanor Edwards); *Colonist,* 3 May 1929, p. 5; W. G. H. Ellison, *The Settlers of Vancouver Island, A Tale for Emigrants* (Arthur Chilver, 1910), 154 pp. (rare); *British National Archives* (Kew), GB/NNAF/P11451, papers of Major General Richard Temple Godman from the Crimean War.

ELLISTON, Lieutenant Peter (1877-1910). Born in Ipswich, son of a medical doctor there, he joined the Royal Garrison Artillery and was commissioned as a lieutenant on 3 April 1903. His unit, No. 58 Company (founded in 1886), was soon posted to Esquimalt, Vancouver Island. When Great Britain eventually gave up Esquimalt and withdrew its forces there, including fourteen Imperial officers, they left on 17 May 1906. But even then, a few remained behind and transferred to a new Canadian Garrison Artillery Company, No. 5, when it was formed under the command of *Colonel Josiah Greenwood Holmes. Chief among them were forty NCOs and men of No. 58 Company under PE's command. PE evidently intended to settle on the Island, like so many of his kind, but sad to say, he died there at Esquimalt on 1 August 1910.

The context of PE's brief career is worth summarizing for what it reveals of the Island's place in the empire. A Militia Council had been established in Ottawa on 17 November 1904 by the efforts of Sir Frederick Borden, on the recommendation of *Lieutenant General (later Sir) Percy N. H. Lake from the British Army, thus completing a cycle of changes begun in 1893. In 1905, Lake, chief of the General

Staff in Canada, brought Willoughby Garnons Gwatkin (1859-1925) over from England to be "director of operations and staff duties to develop plans and procedures for a militia that was becoming an army [Morton]." A few months later, Gwatkin brought out from England some 250 veterans from his old regiment, the Manchester Regiment, to join the Canadian Permanent Force being organized and he remained as Lake's assistant until 20 October 1909, when he returned to England. Two years later, however, Gwatkin returned to Ottawa as General Staff officer in charge of mobilization to prepare plans for war. At his request, an interdepartmental committee was formed to coordinate war planning under the chairmanship of Sir Joseph Pope.

These preparations ended when Ottawa began to neglect the forces and to rely on London in fundamental matters of foreign policy and defence. The election of 1911 brought Colonel Samuel Hughes (1853-1921) to the cabinet as minister of Militia. He was an Ontarian with a strong prejudice against British regulars and apparently set himself against all the above-mentioned preparations. Only Lake took any interest in expert reports brought back from the Russo-Japanese War (1904-1905) by *Captain (later Major General) Herbert Cyril Thacker, another British-born officer, who had spent seven months as the Canadian military representative in Manchuria and Japan at the request of the Earl of Dundonald, GOC, the Canadian Militia.

There was little response in Ottawa when in 1902, the Admiralty in London began to see German ambitions for what they turned out to be. Prime Minister Wilfrid Laurier's whole endeavour was to steer Canadian policy between Imperial loyalties and the refusal of Canadian nationalists to agree to expenditures on Imperial defence. After much consultation with London, neither he nor Prime Minister Sir Robert Borden, who succeeded him in the elections of September 1911, made useful contributions to Imperial naval defence. Federal authorities "emphasized Dominion autonomy rather than imperial integration," the naval historian Gilbert Tucker concluded. When the fear of war became a reality, "there was consequently no prospect that the Dominion could furnish substantial help towards winning the war at sea." It has to be added that Borden's Naval Aid Bill of 1912 had suffered badly from Liberal Party opposition, based on Quebec's shrill provincial attitudes. For several reasons, nearly all of them political, Ottawa dithered for more than a decade before 1914, focused mainly on defending its authority in matters of Canadian defence, and refused to spend what was needed to put Esquimalt and Halifax in reasonably defensive condition.

As early as 1912, Edgar Fawcett in Victoria was lamenting the decaying of the docks at Esquimalt, reduced to what he saw as "a small forest of worm-eaten piles. I could not but conjure up memories of the past, of Esquimalt's departed greatness, bustle and busy life. In 1858, and before my time, this was the B.C. headquarters of the San Francisco steamers, as well as the H.Q. of the navy. Of the latter there were always three or four vessels with nearly always a flagship, and such a ship!" He went on to observe in 1912 that only about every fourth house was occupied. "Oh! what desolation! What ruin and decay!" Jean Gow, daughter of a retired Scottish army doctor with a practice in Victoria, *Lieutenant Colonel Dr David

Donald, remembers efforts in 1911 "to bring an obsolete, grass-grown Dockyard to life again . . . [and how] the neglected relic of the old Royal Navy establishment in *Naden* was being reclaimed."

Meanwhile, indignant observers in Victoria went to some trouble and expense to prepare in response to the looming German menace. Ottawa, an inland capital well away from either ocean, was evidently inclined to do little about naval defence, but as a Canadian historian writes, "One brave pioneering light still burned in Victoria, B.C. A group of young men there started something akin to Britain's Royal Naval Volunteer Reserve with an unofficial blessing from the Minister (Tony German)." Among those active in these efforts was *George Phillips, who helped Premier Richard McBride in 1914 to shame Ottawa by buying two submarines in Seattle and sailing them over to Esquimalt. It was in the context leading to this drastic step that PE transferred from British to Canadian forces.

Sources: [British] Army List, October 1903, pp. 258, 305; census 1881, England, RG 11/1870, p. 77; census 1891, RG 12/1468, p. 34; Desmond Morton, "Gwatkin, Sir Willoughby Garnons, army officer," *Dictionary of Canadian Biography*, online; R. Guy C. Smith, ed., *As You Were!: Ex-Cadets Remember*, vol. I, 1876-1918 (Toronto? RMC Club of Canada, 1884-1984, 1983), pp. 125-31; Robert Craig Brown, "Hughes, Sir Samuel (1853-1921)," in the DCB online; Jean Donald Gow, *Alongside The Navy 1910-1950: An Intimate Account* (Ottawa, JDG Press, 1999), pp. 4-7; Edgar Fawcett, *Some Reminiscences of Old Victoria* (Toronto, William Briggs, 1912), pp. 127-8, ch. XIV, "Its Departed Glories, or Esquimalt Then and Now"; Barry Gough, *The Royal Navy and the Northwest Coast of North America 1810-1914* (Vancouver, University of British Columbia Press, 1971), pp. 239-42; G. N. Tucker, "*The Naval Policy of Sir Robert Borden, 1912-14*," *Canadian Historical Review*, vol. xxviii (March 1947), p. 30; Roger Sarty, *The Maritime Defence of Canada* (Toronto, The Canadian Institute of Strategic Studies, 1998), pp. 31-73; R. A. Preston, *Canada and "Imperial Defense": A Study of the Origins of the British Commonwealth's Defense Organization, 1867-1919* (Durham, NC, Duke University, 1967), pp. 200-2, 336-343; Commander Tony German, *The Sea is at Our Gates: The History of the Canadian Navy* (Toronto, McClelland & Stewart, 1990), p. 30.

ELWYN, Constable Thomas (c. 1837-1888). He was born in Ireland, eldest son of Lieutenant General Thomas Elwyn of the Royal Artillery, but his family, with its distinguished English military and naval tradition, was not Irish. His mother Anne was born c. 1816 at Carisbrooke, Isle of Wight, at the District Artillery Barrack, and his father, also born c. 1816, came from Sandwith, Kent. In 1881, these parents were living in retirement with a servant and a groom at "Clock House," Bromsgrove, Worcester. TE served in the Crimean War (1854-1856) as lieutenant in the Thirtieth Foot and, in 1858, joined in the gold rush to British Columbia. He arrived in Victoria on Christmas Day and his credentials were enough to win him a post in the police force being formed under Inspector *Chartres Brew. After five months as chief constable at Yale, he was appointed, on 8 June 1859, as assistant gold commissioner and stipendiary magistrate for the district of Lillooet and, ten years later, replaced Philip Henry Nind as gold commissioner and JP for the Cariboo district. His records at the BC Archives are an excellent source of information about the Cariboo region in his time. Promotions to government agent with the Western Union Telegraph expedition, and in 1868 to the Legislative Council in Victoria, led on to employment on the HBC steamer, *Otter*, and to deputy provincial secretary. On 4 October 1879, he married Rebecca, daughter of Captain William Henry McNeill, and they had two daughters. When TE died in Victoria, aged fifty-one, of "consumption," on 11 September 1888, he was survived by a younger brother serving as a lieutenant in the RN; another had been drowned when HMS *Slaney* foundered in the China seas. TE had insured his life for $12,000 so that his family—wife and a surviving daughter—were provided for.

Sources: Dorothy Blakey Smith, "Elwyn, Thomas, public servant," *Dictionary of Canadian Biography*, vol. XI, pp. 301-02; Marie Elliott, *Gold and Grand Dreams: Cariboo East in the Early Years* (Victoria, Horsdal & Shubert, 2004), pp. 35, 49 (photo), 59, 101; census 1871, England, RG 10/1670, p. 109; census 1881, RG 11/2939/52, p. 22; Lynne Stonier-Newman, Lynne, *Policing a Pioneer Province: The B.C. Provincial Police*, 1858-1950 (Madeira Park, BC, Harbour Publishing, 1991), pp. 17, 23; *Colonist*, 12 September 1888, p. 4, obit.

ELWORTHY, Lieutenant Frederick Barrington (1891-1957). He was born on 13 June 1891 in Victoria, son of Clara Emma Elworthy *née* Richardson in BC—daughter of George Richardson, who had arrived at Victoria in 1850—and her husband Frederick Elworthy (1854-1927). The latter was born at Taunton, Devonshire, on 13 November 1854, apprenticed in the dry goods trade in London, and, in 1872, went to India, where he managed a tea plantation. In 1886, he migrated to San Francisco as a tea merchant and then removed to Victoria in 1889 to work for Joshua Davies as auctioneer. In 1890-1914, he was employed as secretary of the British Columbia Board of Trade, and continued as city treasurer when in 1914, this board became the Victoria Chamber of Commerce. He was at the same time secretary of the Lumber Mills and Wholesale Grocers' Associations. Early in the century, he had helped with the negotiations for building the Empress Hotel. Elworthy senior died on 17 June 1927, his wife, FE's mother, having died two years earlier, leaving FE, two other sons, and a daughter. In 1901, the family was living at 144 Menzies Street in the James Bay district, but when FE joined the CEF on 18 September 1914, he cited his mother resident at 59 Menzies Street as his next of kin. He had been working as a bookkeeper and, having had three years in the RCA, was commissioned as lieutenant. After the Great War, he had married Violet Mary Wells on 15 November 1922 in Vancouver, and she died there, aged seventy-nine, on 4 September 1977.

His younger brother, Harold Barrington Elworthy (1901-1975), went to work in 1918 as an office boy for the BC Salvage Co., and went on to lay the foundation for a business empire by forming the Island Tug & Barge Co. Ltd. in 1925. It is said that he served later as president of the Bank of British Columbia, though this seems unlikely as that bank was absorbed by the Canadian Bank of Commerce in 1900. However, his company took over other towing firms, and he sold what had become a large business in 1960, but remained its chairman for twelve years and, after retiring, formed a new company, the Victoria Tug and Barge Co. Ltd. Active in causes like the Queen Alexandra Solarium and the University Development Board, he also took an interest in local history and heritage, became one of the governors of the University of Victoria, and founded the Princess Mary Restaurant in an old beached CPR liner. He died, aged seventy-three, on 15 June 1975. His wife, *née* Myrta Gladys McDonald, whom he married in Sidney on 4 November 1921, had died much earlier, aged forty-three, on 10 October 1940 in Vancouver.

Sources: City of Victoria Archives: Frederick Elworthy fonds—Location: 25 F 5, 36 E 3. PR 31; NAC, CEF files, box 2899-18; Canadian census, 1901, Victoria; Ruth H. Judson, "*The Elworthy Story,*" in *Camas Chronicles of James Bay, Victoria, British Columbia* (Victoria, Camas Historical Group, 1978), pp. 137-8.

EMBLETON, Charles Victor (1892-1964). He arrived at Halifax, Nova Scotia, on 6 June 1918, coming from Liverpool on the SS *Olympic* and made his way to Victoria. There he found employment and eventually moved up the Island to Campbell River, where he died, aged seventy-one, on 20 June 1964. But in 1942, he had been sufficiently well known to *Wilfred Henry Strickland Wardroper to serve as a pallbearer at his funeral in Duncan, along with *George Meredith Petch and other Anglicans. Unlike Wardroper, Petch and CE seem to have emigrated directly from the British Isles, without any intervening foreign residence, apparently as younger sons without prospects at home.

CE was born at Bournemouth, Hampshire, seventh child of a physician and surgeon, Dennis Cawood Embleton (1854-1900), and his wife, Eva Christina Jameson Waterlow, who lived an unsettled life, partly for professional reasons and partly for reasons of ill health. In 1880-1881, before CE's birth, they spent a couple of years on the island of Madeira at Funchal, where the father went to recuperate from illness but delivered lectures, *A Visit to Madeira in the Winter, 1880-81. Two Lectures etc.* (J and A. Churchill, 1882), 60 pp. CE's father died relatively young on 18 June 1900 at Swanage, Dorset, and in 1901, CE appears, aged eight, living with his widowed mother and three sisters in Ruislip, London, and with four domestic servants. But the father was born in Newcastle-on-Tyne, where his father, CE's grandfather, Dr Dennis Embleton (1910-1900), had been a noted and influential physician and surgeon, the first professor of medicine at what was to become the College of Medicine at Newcastle and physician to the Newcastle Infirmary (1853-1878). Admitted to the Royal College of Surgeons on 18 June 1834, the grandfather spent two years travelling on the European continent, attended medical courses in Paris, had a diploma from Pisa University, and took a serious interest in the local history and antiquarian past of Newcastle-on-Tyne. At his death on 12 November 1900, when CE was about seven years old, the archaeological and antiquarian society of which he was a member, published a long obituary notice. One might surmise that CE lacked the means or the inclination to live up to his distinguished forebears and emigrated to the Island as a way out. He died, unmarried and aged seventy-one, on 20 June 1964 at Campbell River.

Sources: census 1891, England, RG 12/901, p. 38; census 1901, RG 13/179, p. 22; Canadian Passenger Lines, T-4757 (arriving 6 June 1918), almost illegible;

The British Medical Journal, vol. 2 (2062), 7 July 1900, pp. 65-66, obit.; *The Medical Times and Gazette, vol. I* (26 March 1881), p. 365, "births"; *Archaeologia aeliana, or, Miscellaneous Tracts relation to Antiquity* (obituary read by F. W. Dandy on 28 November 1900); Dennis Embleton, *The History of the Medical School, afterwards the Durham College of Medicine at Newcastle-upon-Tyne for forty years, from 1832 to 1872* (Newcastle-upon-Tyne, A. Reid Sons & Co., 1890).

ENGLEDUE, Major Ralph Sandwith (1884-1970). Born in Darjeeling, India, where his father was posted, he was brought up in England, and during a career in the Indian Army, he married Dora Frances Crocker, daughter of T. E. Crocker of 33 Princes Gate, London SW, on 18 July 1907. In May 1923, they went to live in Victoria, and this was probably a result of his father's interest in the Island some thirty years before. Early in 1892, Colonel William John Engledue (1840-1906) and a certain Major William Clark submitted to the BC government a scheme for settling Scottish crofters on the Island's west coast, which they had evidently visited. They formed the Vancouver Island Development Syndicate (Ltd.), and John Robson (1824-1892), premier of BC (1889-1892), supported it shortly before he died. One of the father's ideas, as he wrote to *The Times* (London), was that the Esquimalt naval station was strategically in the wrong place and ought to be moved to "Barclay [i.e., Barkley] Sound" on the west coast of the Island. The whole scheme collapsed before the end of 1893 but probably encouraged RE, who doubtless heard about it in his youth, to go to the Island thirty years later. He and his wife lived for some years at "Linkleas," on Linkleas Avenue, Oak Bay, near the Victoria Golf Club, which they joined. They were Anglicans, and he became a sporting fisherman and joined the Union Club. But he kept his membership in the Junior Naval and Military Club, 96 Picadilly, London, and they moved back to England a few years later. RE died on 14 September 1970.

He was born into a prosperous middle-class Imperial family. The 1851 census shows his father, aged ten and born at Liverpool, living at home, which was then at Wilton House Crescent, Southampton, eldest son of John H. Engeldue (RE's grandfather), who was a forty-year-old "Agent to Peninsula & Oriental Company" and born in Portsmouth. His wife (RE's grandmother) Eliza P. Engledue, aged thirty, came from the West Indies. They employed five domestic servants, including a coachman. As an agent of the famous P&O Line of passenger ships, the grandfather had evidently been posted in Liverpool when RE's father was born. The father had a career in the Royal Engineers, was promoted to colonel in 1890, and, by 1900, had retired to Petersham Place in Byfleet, Surrey. He had evidently been serving in India at Darjeeling, where RE was born on 27 April 1884, and had the means to send RE to Wellington College, Berkshire, and on to RMC, Sandhurst. In 1901, when RE was sixteen, he and his own family were all living in Surrey in Petersham Place: two sons and two daughters with a governess and four servants—cook, parlourmaid, housemaid, and gardener with a wife and child, all living in. RE was *Gazetted* to the Second Border Regiment in Burma on 22

October 1902, transferred to the Eighty-ninth Punjabis, Indian Army, on 15 May 1904, and served during the Great War in Arabia, Egypt, Gallipoli, Mesopotamia, and North-West Frontier (India), with "Dunsterforce" in NW Persia, and in the defence of Baku on the Caspian Sea. His brave and effective activities at Galipoli are described in a book by Lieutenant Colonel P. G. Bamford, who concludes with the story of RE (then a captain) taking command of the battalion after the senior officers had all been either killed or transferred. Thrice wounded, thrice mentioned in dispatches, RE retired on 27 October 1920 and went out to the Island three years later.

Sources: *Who's Who in B.C.* 1933-4, p. 57; *Indian Army List,* January 1905; BL, India Office; *Indian Army List,* 1 January 1912, p. 148; *Colonist,* October 1929; census 1851, HO 107/1663/25, for Byfleet, Surrey (father); census 1901, RG 13/593, p. 6; Lieutenant Colonel Percy Geoffrey Bamford, DSO, 1st King George V's Own Battalion, *The Sikh Regiment, The 14th King George's Own Ferozepore Sikhs, 1846-1946* (Aldershot, Gale & Polden, 1948), 174 pp. passim; BNA, I 12020; John B. Hayward, ed., *Officers Died in the Great War 1914-1919* (New ed., Polstead, Suffolk, J. B. Hayward & Son, 1988) 286 pp., in 4o, pp. 276, 279, and 280; *The Times,* London, 1 April 1892, p. 15; Jill Wade, "' *The Gigantic Scheme': Crofter Immigration and Deep-Sea Fisheries Development for British Columbia,* 1887-93," B.C. Studies, no. 53 (special number, Spring 1982), pp. 28-44; *Whitaker's,* p. 176.

   EUSTACE, Major General Alexander Henry (1863-1939), CB, CBE, DSO. Born in Wynburg, South Africa, son of Colonel J. T. Eustace, he entered the British Army in 1885 and the Indian Army some years later. He served in the Black Mountain Expedition (1888-1891) as Field Intelligence Officer, First and Second Brigades, and was promoted to captain in 1896 and major in 1903. In 1903-1904, he was sent to Somaliland, East Africa, where he was mentioned in despatches and qualified for the DSO. Made lieutenant colonel in 1907 and colonel in 1911, he spent the Great War (1914-1918) on the North-West Frontier of India, commanding the Kohat Independent Brigade in 1915-1919. He was promoted to major general (1917), and commanded the Fifty-second Sikh (Frontier Force) in Afghanistan (1919) before retiring in 1920. The CB and CBE followed as well as honorary rank as colonel of the 2/12 Frontier Force Regiment (Second Sikhs).

   In 1924, AE moved to "The Garth," Cowichan, near Quamichan Lake, with his wife, Evelyn Mary, daughter of Samuel Stonestreet of Kimberley, South Africa, whom he had married in 1904. She died in 1927 when their only surviving son, John G. W. Eustace (1906-72), was serving in the ICS at Lahore. AE carried on until his death, aged seventy-five, on 11 March 1939, was active locally in the Canadian Legion and in cricket and the local sports club, and was willing to join Lieutenant Governor E. W. Hamber, *Admiral Rowland Nugent, and the provincial minister of agriculture, K. C. McDonald, in patronizing a dog show held by the Duncan Dog Club in August 1937. He was a staunch member of the British-Israel World Federation, vice-president of its Cowichan branch, and a pillar of St Peter's Quamichan Anglican Church, where Rev. T. M. Hughes found him to be a friend and ally: "He will be remembered by us as a man who was intensely loyal to the Church and Empire, both of which he served with unstinting devotion."

The parish gave him one of those grand military funerals of which it was then capable by virtue of its many Imperial residents. His coffin, covered with the Union Jack and his sword, cap and decorations, was carried out to a grave in the churchyard by six pallbearers, most of them soldiers, and accompanied by a dozen Imperial officers as honorary pallbearers, several from the Indian Army: *Major General Sir Ernest Walker, *Admiral Roland Nugent, *Colonel M. E. Dopping-Hepenstal, *Colonel A. F. M. Slater, *Lieutenant Colonel H. D. McLaughlin, *Major J. H. G. Palmer, *Major H. A. H. Rice, *Captain R. E. Barkley, Captain I. D. Mackenzie, and Mr Bateman Hope. Two more were still active and representing their units: *Major A. B. Slee, commanding officer, Sixty-second Field (Howitzer) Battery RCA, and Major *R. G. L. Parker, officer commanding "A" Company, Second Battalion (MG) Canadian Scottish Regiment. The Canadian Legion was there in force, and in that small wooden church full of people, choristers, and flowers, they all sang "Unto the Hills Around" and "Where the Light Forever Shineth" and the Ninetieth Psalm and threw poppies on the casket in the grave.

Sources: *Who's Who in B.C.* 1933-1934, p. 57; *Who Was Who*, 1929-1940, p. 420; *Who's Who*, 1952, p. 903; *Who was Who* 1971-1980, p. 251; *Cowichan Leader*, Thursday 16 March 1939, obit.; *Colonist*, 8 August 1937, p. 6; NAC, RG76, *immigration series* C-1-i, 1935, vol. 3, p. 82, microfilm reel T-14908; *Colonist*, 8 August 1937, p. 6.

FAIRBAIRN-WILSON, Major William (c. 1870-1955). He was born in Darjeeling, India, joined the Royal Engineers, and has to be distinguished from the William Fairbairn-Wilson who was born on 10 October 1880 at Banff, Banffshire, Scotland. WF enlisted in the CEF at Winnipeg on 1 February 1918, claiming long service in the Argyle and Sutherland Highlanders.

After the war, WF retired to Victoria, where he wrote occasionally to the *Daily Colonist* on Imperial issues. In 1930, for instance, he denounced Sir Stafford Cripps for working towards Indian national independence. "In his crusade against what, in his ignorance of reality, he called Imperialism, Sir Stafford urged nationalism for groups who had never formed a nation. He trained and encouraged a small minority to enslave a majority for the sake of the personal advantage of that minority. He was one of the hunters leading the pack to stop before the kill . . . Only those among us who are familiar with the true Indian mentality should be entrusted with the delicate task of mending the present condition of affairs, which threatens to get out of hand should words only be brought into action. The Indian masses are loyal, left to their own devices; they are well aware that the real Britain is their best friend, but it should be borne in mind that in the East more than anywhere else, a weak, vacillating ruler brings about his own destruction." When he died in Victoria on 25 October 1955, his funeral was at St Andrew's Presbyterian Church, contrary to a local newspaper report.

Sources: *Colonist*, 9 August 1930, p. 22; 26 October 1955, p. 18, obit.; NAC, CEF files, box 10483-27, reg. no. 3349116.

FAIRWEATHER, Staff Captain Neville Edward (c. 1876-1966). He was born in India at Mussoorie, a hill station in one of the outer ranges of the Himalayas, north of Dehra Dun, enlisted in the British Army, and served in South Africa and the Great War. The English census of 1901 found him living in London as an army captain. What he did during the 1920s is not clear, but he spent some time in Quebec and South Africa. By 1938, he was living in retirement in Victoria, at 1002 Carberry Gardens, and had joined the Imperial Campaigners' Association. Like many others, he had strong views on certain public issues and wrote colourful letters to local and other newspapers. These are easy to lampoon as the splutterings of an angry blimp, but they deserve careful attention as being forthright, entertaining expressions of views widely held at the time by a more-reticent Island public of British origin. In July 1937, he denounced the provincial state schools for their departures from British education as he knew it. He objected particularly to a schooling system that taught no religious or other high ideals and focussed narrowly on training in technical, professional, and executive skills. "Why not erect the sign of the dollar to worship at? It is quite elegant and should have a host of followers who are at present in this respect mentally cross-eyed." This was followed in October by a ferocious assault on the school curriculum for discouraging independence. "Jumbled like a bunch of cattle and graded in bunches, according to one's approximate abilities, how can individualism be produced? The real truth is that the inflated imaginations at the back of all this are of fungus growth who fool a bewildered public, educated to accept them as a godhead. Here is the danger of this international education, the preparation of the masses to accept some wonder man put forward by a clique of crooked gangsters." Mussolini, Hitler and Stalin, then active, were perhaps in his mind.

Much of what NF wrote was in defence of the British Empire and British leadership in the world. In February 1937, for instance, he thought the empire was being undermined by "insidious propaganda, universal brotherly love, gold bricks, and many other confidence tricks . . . Are we Britishers abroad, in the far-flung reaches of the British Empire, loyal to the code of our forefathers, and to the great heritage handed down to us by them? If we are, then why do some of our people entertain the Marxian theory, the Fascist theory, or any other non-British theory? . . . It is very easy to slip into being a follower of a peace-at-any-price policy . . . Has that apology for present-day British weakness, the League of Nations, got us anything but a tolerant contempt, rapidly becoming insufferable insolence? Universal peace is a wonderful thing, anyone will admit. But why Great Britain should turn herself into a European clown I, for one, cannot see. Every nation Britain has asked to co-operate with her in sacrificing something for the peace of the world has promptly ceased to be a member of the League of Nations." In that pre-war period, the philosopher R. G. Collingwood expressed a similar, if more dignified, exasperation in his memoirs. Canada's unpreparedness for the Second World War made NF so angry that in 1939, he became the president of a Defence of Canada League, using a postal-box number as an address. NF denounced the Liberal Party, the government of Mackenzie King, the readiness of the Canadian Army to refuse the services of experienced British officers, and what British people in general regarded as a muddled approach to the war. In May 1941, for instance, "No one but an ostrich, with its head in the sand to hide its blushes, would call our P.M., Mr King, particularly British-minded or most of his French-Canadian backers. To me he appears to have a mild De Valera complex." He praised the *Montreal Star* for a "British-mindedness" he thought comparable to that of the *Colonist.* "I have never been allowed, except in the *Montreal Star,* to enumerate a few of the acts of sabotage that followed conscription of manpower in Quebec during the last war. Evidently worse was feared by Mr [Mackenzie] King, and he was advised against asking Quebec to do its duty for the autonomy and benefits received under the British connection. It appears evident that, like Southern Ireland, French Canada wishes to be independent of the British Empire, though securing all the benefits from its protection." And in November 1942, under the heading, *Canada's Bureaucracy,* he writes, "Sir: Shades of Gilbert and Sullivan! . . . Besides our sensitive little bureaucracy there are two major choices—a shy, shrinking Conservative Party that does not want to hurt anybody's feelings, terrified to uproot the governmental bureaucratic machine and adopt a clear, straightforward British regime, and the C.C.F., with a mixed international complex, a chip on its shoulder and a rabid desire for power. Let us transpose the rabbit for the beaver as a public symbol. Poor Canada, what a set-up!"

NF died, aged eighty-seven, on 1 May 1966 at 5669 Sooke Road, leaving his wife Dorothy and a son, Geoffrey Neville Benson Fairweather in Canada and two daughters in London.

Sources: census 1861, England, RG 9 / 1472, p. 9 (NF's future mother); *British Library, Bengal Marriages,* vol. 137, fol. 97 [internet], James Fairweather married Annette M. D. Thorp in 1871 in Bengal; census, 1881, Jersey (St. Helier), RG 11 / 5615, p. 4; census 1901, England, RG 13 / 248, p. 6; *BC Archives, Minutes of the British Campaigners' Association,* 1908-1928, November 1935; *Colonist,* 12 February 1937, p. 13; 3 July 1937, p. 8; 1 October 1937, p. 4; 27 August 1939, p. 5; 17 March 1940, p. 11; 9 March 1941, p. 4; 30 May 1941, p. 4, 24 November 1942, p. 4; 3 May 1966, p. 23, obit.;

FALL, Squadron Leader [and Group Captain] Joseph Stuart Temple (1895-1988). He was born on 17 November 1895 at Hillbank in the Cowichan Valley, and brought up on a farm. His father, Harry Temple Fall (c. 1872-1931), was born at Tollerton, Dorset, one of three sons and three daughters born to a Yorkshire-born surgeon and his wife, Eliza Selina Fall from Lapminster, Hampshire. The 1881 census found this family living at Winfrith, Dorset, but ten years later, Henry Temple Fall, aged nineteen, was "a scholar" living at Weymouth College in Radipole, Dorset. At sometime in the 1890s, the three brothers went out to British Columbia, possibly in 1898 to the gold rush because two of them called themselves miners when they joined Canadian forces. One of these, JF's uncle Charles Slingsby Fall, joined Lord Strathcona's Horse on 10 February 1900, citing JF's father in Victoria as his next of kin, fought through the South African War on the body guard of the regiment's commander-in-chief, was awarded the Queen's Medal and clasps for Belfast, Orange Free State, and Natal, and took his discharge in South Africa, where he married and remained. When on 5 May 1916 the other uncle,

Joseph Fall, joined the 112th Battalion of the CEF as a lieutenant, he was working as a "mine superintendent" and living at 922 Burdette Avenue, Victoria. He, too, cited JF's father as his next of kin but living by then in the Cowichan Valley. There, JF attended the remarkable Quamichan Boys' School on the Maple Bay Road kept in the years 1905-1925 by *P. T. Skrimshire, who also taught such future Imperial worthies as *Air Marshal Sir Philip Livingston, *Admiral E. Rollo Mainguy, Dr Eric Elkington, *Major Lancelot Young Bazett, and *Captain Barkley Barnes.

On 23 August 1915, JF was accepted as a candidate for the Royal Naval Air Service (RNAS), went to Montreal and paid $350 to the Montreal School of Flying, but became impatient when he received no training. The money was refunded, and in November, he sailed to England and was appointed probationary flight sub-lieutenant on 26 January 1916. His movements thereafter were to Chingford (14 April 1916), to No. 3 Wing at Eastchurch (6 August 1916), to Dunkirk (1 February 1917), to No. 9 (N) Squadron (3 February 1917), to No. 3 (N) Squadron (28 February 1917), to No. 9 (N) Squadron (30 August 1917), and to No. 9 Group at Freiston (24 April 1918). In 1918, he transferred to the RAF as a captain and then a squadron leader and was posted to No. 4 Flying School (7 November 1918). In the war years, he flew almost entirely in Sopwith Camels and is credited by people who study these things in detail with shooting down, alone or in combination with colleagues, no fewer than thirty-six enemy aircraft of which eleven in the month of September 1917 alone. He was awarded the DSC with two bars. In 1936, he became a wing commander and, remaining in London, joined the Royal Aero Club and gave his address as c/o Bank of Montreal, London. During the Second World War, he served again in the RAF but, as a group captain, was mentioned in despatches on 11 June 1942 and, in 1943-4, was CO at the RCAF Station at Carberry. He retired in 1945 to Cobble Hill, where he lived until 1988.

Sources: W. R. Cumming, *"Joseph Stewart Temple Fall: The Man Who Refused to Die," Journal of the Canadian Aviation Historical Society,* Summer 1990; *Who's Who in B.C.* 1931, pp. 41-2; 1933-1934, p. 59; *Colonist,* 12 June 1917, p. 12; John M. MacFarlane, *Canada's Naval Aviators* (rev. ed., Shearwater, NS, Shearwater Aviation Museum, 1997), p. 103; Christopher Shores, Norman Franks & Russell Guest, *Above the Trenches* (Grub Street Publications, 1996); *London Gazette,* 23 May 1917 (DSO); census 1881, England, RG 11/2102, p. 9; census 1891, RG 12/1645, p. 3; NAC, CEF files, box 2985-36 (an uncle); *NAC, South African War,* RG 38, A-1-a, vol. 32, regimental no. 496 (an uncle).

FAWCETT, Captain Thomas Gordon (1895-1934). Born in Ottawa, he attended RMC at Kingston, Ontario, enlisted in the British Royal Engineers, and was promoted to captain in 1918. After serving in Gallipoli, India, and France during and after the Great War, he won the Military Cross and settled at 928 Selkirk Avenue, Victoria. There he joined the British Public Schools Club, the Legion, and the British Campaigners' Association. He died on 23 November 1934, leaving his mother and three brothers.

Sources: *Colonist,* 24 November 1934, p. 6, obit.; Army Lists.

FAWKES, Colonel Lionel Grimston (1849-1931). He was born on 2 May 1849 in Hertfordshire at a place variously reported as Hertford, Potter's Bar, and West Lodge near Barnet, though the family's old home was at "Farnley Hall" near Ottley, Yorkshire, where his father, Major Richard Fawkes, lived much as the family had done since the twelfth century. LF was schooled at Repton Blackheath Proprietary School and the RMA, Woolwich, before joining the Royal Artillery in 1869; he was to serve for thirty-one years. Early on, he "passed the staff college" and became a lieutenant (1 December 1870), captain (12 December 1880), major (21 July 1886), lieutenant colonel (3 February 1894), professor of military topography at RMA in Woolwich (16 April 1895), and a full colonel (16 April 1899). During his career, he served in the South African War (1899-1902) and in the West Indies, commanded the RGA at Clarence Barracks, Portsmouth (March 1900 to October 1901), and was brigade major of Artillery there under the Duke of Connaught's governorship. He was "one of the six officers who officiated as pallbearers at the funeral of the late Queen Victoria" (*Victoria Daily Colonist*, 25 August 1931, p. 1). Too old for the battle front in the Great War, he was on the staff of the School of Instruction at Fort Purbrook and in command of it in conjunction with Colonel Pearce, DSO. There he taught topography and gunnery, and the British National Archives at Kew (ADM7/953) has "Notes of a gunnery course at Shoeburyness prepared by L. G. Fawkes, 1877." In the *Army List* of 1906, Fawkes is listed under the heading of "Colonels on Full or Retired Pay or on a Pension."

LF devoted much time and effort to the cause of temperance. His sympathies were with evangelical Christianity, though he remained an Anglican. He also took great interest in missionary work at home and abroad. At Bedhampton, Hampshire, where he and Lady Constance Fawkes lived for twenty-two years, he acted as rector's warden at the parish church. He was the Bedhampton parish secretary for the Hampshire and Isle of Wight Band of Hope, on the Committee of the Portsmouth Labour Home, ruri-decanal secretary for the Church of England Temperance Society, and, for more than twenty years, the honorary secretary and treasurer of England for the Royal Artillery Temperance Society. He was local parish secretary to the Winchester Diocesan Conference and was on the Church of England Temperance Society Committee of the Winchester Diocesan Conference. For many years, he was treasurer of the Hampshire United Temperance Council, which merged eventually with the Christian Churches Social Union. He was manager and correspondent at the Council School and served as a member of the Ruri-Decanal Conference of Havant from its beginning. Under Canons Garbett and Wilson, he served at St Mary's Parish Church, Portsmouth, as treasurer of the Portsmouth Citizen's Union. He was a Justice of the Peace (JP) in the years 1911-1924 and attended the Petty Sessions and Brewster Sessions with faithful regularity. In 1924, he and Lady Fawkes sold "The Elms," their old mansion at Bedhampton, and crossed over to the Pacific Coast of British Columbia, arriving at Miner's Bay, Mayne Island, in the *Otter*, which sailed regularly between the islands in the Gulf of Georgia and Victoria.

On Mayne Island, Fawkes had bought a property including a big old house with thirty-five rooms, which they named "Culzean" after Culzean Castle in Ayrshire, where Lady Constance had spent her childhood. It stood among arbutus trees on the extreme northern point of Mayne Island. The big-game hunter Warburton Pike had built it in 1890, and since his time, it had been kept as a hotel by a Mr and Mrs Bennett and then purchased by *Commander Eustace Maude, RN (retd), and his family, who called it "Point Comfort." It was probably through Maude that the Fawkes learnt of the place, as his father, Sir George Maude, was the Queen's Equerry, a friend of the queen, and lived at Hampton Court, which might well have brought him into the same circles as those of the Fawkes family.

LF was an accomplished artist in watercolours and had served in Hampshire on the committees of the Fareham Arts and Crafts Society and as vice-president of the Hampshire and Isle of Wight Amateur Art Society. Some of his paintings hung in the Royal Military College at Sandhurst, and two others, including a portrait of Sir George Pollock, which used to hang in the National Gallery, London. On his walls at "The Elms" were such works as a signed portrait of Field Marshal Frederick Earl Roberts, who had sat in his study at "Englemere" for Fawkes to do the painting. LF had also done portraits of the Duke of Connaught, King George V, and (in 1880) the King's elder brother, the Duke of Clarence, a painting later presented to Queen Alexandra. Almost as soon as he arrived, LF exhibited two of his paintings at the Willows Exhibition held in Oak Bay by the Island Arts and Crafts Society. On the Gulf Islands and Vancouver Island, he painted and sketched many buildings and landscapes and also made notable copies of the works of the great English landscape artist, J. M. W. Turner. He had brought out with him at least two of Turner's own paintings inherited from a grandfather, Walter Ramsden Fawkes, who had been Turner's close friend and patron. They were what was left of the family's collection of Turner's kept at "Farnley Hall," originally one of the largest anywhere. LF willed his two remaining Turners to a niece, but soon after his death, Lady Constance lent these two paintings to the Vancouver Art Gallery for ten years, their man Jack Borradaile taking them under his arm wrapped in brown paper, on the *Princess Mary*. Not long after that, many of LF's own paintings—about four hundred of them—were lent to the BC Archives, which photographed them on microfilm and forgot about them. The archivists do not seem to know where they are or what became of them and were not interested, when I inquired, because LF was not a Canadian painter. The best collection I have seen was in the hands of Commander Maude's descendants on Salt Spring Island.

Lady Constance Eleanor Fawkes was the daughter of the Marquis of Ailsa, Scotland, a noblewoman in her own right and with a vigorous, no-nonsense turn of mind. She went about the island in gumboots and a small Ford truck and did the cooking in the house, though they had a housekeeper, a Mrs Hogben, and employed Jack Borradaile from Salt Spring Island to do practical work around the place. She used to weave on a loom and sew underwear for needy children in the east end of Vancouver. Sharing her husband's improving and charitable instincts, she organized the island's first fall fair at the Miners Bay Community Hall and helped to lend their place for benevolent money-raising events, with such games as croquet and clock golf on the lawn. The Fawkes were devout Anglicans, and LF used to read from the Bible and pray after breakfast. He was a founder of Mayne

Island's Sunday school and Lady Constance, with a small group of friends, used to go onto the wharf on boat-days with a portable organ to sing hymns. They led an active social life and had many visitors, including the lieutenant governor and other Island VIPs. In March 1931, they were visited by Deaconess Palliser, formerly of Deaconess Mildmay Home, London, who arrived on the *Aorangi* from Sydney, Australia. A watercolour of Lindley Crease's house, signed "The willow on which the Creases hang their hearts. To Lindley Crease from L. G. Fawkes, 21-6-1930," shows the Creases to have been good friends.

LF died, aged eighty-two, on 24 August 1931 at "Culzean" and was buried in the Island's little cemetery overlooking Active Pass. A memorial tablet soon appeared on the other side of the world in St Thomas Church at Bedhampton, Hampshire. Besides his widow, LF left two brothers: Rev. R. Fawkes of Poole, Dorset, and Judge A. Fawkes of Windsor. The fate of their two daughters recorded in the 1901 census is not clear. Lady Fawkes carried on at "Culzean," taking LF's place during his fatal illness to open the seventh annual exhibition and, in January 1933, entertaining some thirty guests to dinner for the fifteenth birthday of her grandson, Lawrence Kirby, who drowned near the Island not long afterwards. At her invitation, the Gulf Islands branch of the Canadian Legion held its meeting at "Culzean" in August 1938 at which *captains R. B. Longridge and McIntosh spoke. She died, aged ninety-one, on 24 October 1946, leaving her entire estate to Jack Borradaile, including George III silverware, Dresden china, and French furniture, but taxes took $45,000 from the estate and left little for him and his wife. He sold "Culzean" in 1946 for $13,500, and twelve years later, it was torn down.

Sources: *Hart's Annual Army List*, 1915, pp. 41 and 166; *Kelly's Handbook* etc. 1917, p. 551; his address was "The Elms," Bedhampton, Havant; *Kelly's Handbook to the Titled, Landed and Official Classes*, vol. 53 (1927), p. 634; newspaper cuttings (undated) from England kept at the BC Archives and kindly sent to me by my sister Elisabeth. For Fawkes's army career, I have used these cuttings and also the notes kindly sent by Mr Stephen Phillips, senior librarian, Aldershot Library, Berkshire, England, on 2 November 2000; census 1871, England, RG 10/780, p. 1; census 1901, RG 13/1008, p. 1; census 1901, RG 13/1307, p. 12; *Colonist*, 16 August 1929, p. 3; 4 March 1931, p. 8; 12 May 1931, p. 8; 4 January 1933, p. 11; 12 May 1931, p. 8; 18 August 1931, p. 16; 25 August 1931, p. 1; 3 August 1938, p. 4; James Hamilton, Turner (New York, Random House, 1997), pp. 50-5, 111-115, 150-8, 171-2, 205, 224-7, 232-5, 272-5; *National Archives*, Kew, ADM7/953, "Notes of a gunnery course at Shoeburyness prepared by L. G. Fawkes, 1877"; Jack Borradaile, *Lady of Culzean* (Privately printed, n.d.), 91 pp.; Peter Murray, *Homesteads and Snug Harbours: The Gulf Islands* (Victoria, Horsdal & Shubert, 1991), pp. 25-8;

FELL, James (1821-1890). Born in 1821 at Muncaster Head in Cumberland, he went into business in London in 1841 but moved in a few months to Liverpool, where he traded in tea and wine and was briefly a shipowner until about 1861, when he went to Victoria. Captain Walbran put his emigration date as 1858, but JF appears in the 1861 census living in Great James Street, Liverpool, with his wife Sarah *née*

Thornton. She was born there, and they were living in her elderly widowed father's house, he having been a grocer. There is no mistaking their identity.

In Victoria, JF went into partnership with John Finlayson to launch a spice and coffee business, later a general grocery trade. In 1868, the partnership was dissolved, and JF carried on alone but incorporated in January 1895 as "Fell & Co. Ltd." with $75,000 in capital in $100 shares owned by James F. Fell, Martha T. Fell, Thornton Fell, Jessie T. Morley, and Henry Moss. In the Canadian census of 1891, JF is listed as a grocer, but in 1898 he registered an auxiliary screw-propelled steamer of sixty-four tons, listing his occupation as "merchant" on the registry. He was still in business in Walbran's time and prominent in public life. Active in politics, he was a strong supporter of free trade and stood, unsuccessfully, as a candidate for the House of Commons in 1882. For fourteen years, he was a member of the School Board and was one of the organizers of the first Mechanics' Institute as well as a trustee of it. He was also a trustee of the Royal Jubilee Hospital, a member of the St George' Society, and a founder and sometime president of the BC Benevolent Society. A man with his own views on life, he was unorthodox enough in the early 1880s to be president of the Spiritualist Society. Victoria was English enough to enjoy eccentricity and elected him mayor of the city: He served in 1885-1887 as successor to *Robert Paterson Rithet. His daughter, Jessie Thornton Fell, married *Henry Augustus Snow Morley. JF died, aged seventy, on 8 December 1890, and Sarah Jane died, eighty-three, on 6 February 1942, both in Oak Bay.

Sources: Valerie Green, *No Ordinary People: Victoria's Mayors Since 1862* (Victoria, Beach Holme, 1992), pp. 102-5; Walbran, *B.C. Coast Names*, p. 177; David Farrell, "Keeping the Local Economy Afloat: Canadian Pacific Navigation and Shipowning in Victoria, 1883-1901," *The Northern Mariner*, vol. VI, no. 1 (January 1996), p. 40; census 1851, England, HO 107/2174. 42/74; census 1861, England, RG 9/2679, p. 25; *Colonist*, 4 January 1895, p. 5; 3 October 1936, obit. and photo of H. A. S. Morley.

FERNIE, Peter Creeke (1830-1915). Born at Allonbury, Huntingdonshire, grandson of a surgeon in the Black Watch who had served with Wellington in the Peninsula War, Fernie was educated as an architect but ran away from home in 1848 and enlisted in "C" Battery of the Royal Horse Artillery. He served in the Crimean War as a sergeant, saw the charges of the Heavy Brigade and the Light Brigade, and himself took part in actions at Alma, Inkerman, Balaclava, and Sebastopol. He was sent on the *Marlborough* to India for the Mutiny, wherein he fought at Allahabad under Sir Hope Grant and saw much hand-to-hand fighting. In 1861, he was discharged from the army at Woolwich, having served fourteen years with the Royal Horse Artillery, and went out to BC in the gold rush by the Colon-Aspinwall route. He tried prospecting on the Stikine River and Wild Horse Creek, spent three years at Nanaimo working for the Vancouver Coal Co., and then joined a brother on a cattle ranch in the Kootenays. Next, he bought a large tract of land in south Saanich near Keating, where a cement plant was to be built in 1915, but sold it in 1908 and went to live at 137 Government Street, Victoria.

When he died, aged eighty-five, on 3 October 1915, he left a brother, William Fernie, at 2227 Oak Bay Avenue, and two sisters in England. He had been a member of the Odd Fellows. He was the oldest member of the British Campaigners' Association and buried with full military honours: His coffin was mounted on a gun carriage drawn by six horses, with six sergeants of the Fifth Regiment acting as bearers, while the band of the fifth attended in a body. The Sixty-seventh Overseas Battalion under Colonel Lorne Ross and the Thirty-first British Columbia Horse under Major Heursemeule were present. A firing party under the command of C. S. M. Maynard of the Eighty-eighth Victoria Fusiliers gave a saluting volley as the coffin was lowered into a grave at the Ross Bay Cemetery.
Sources: *Minutes of the British Campaigners' Association*, 19 September 1915; *Colonist*, 5 October 1915, pp. 1 and 7: photo.

FitzHENRY, Major Claude Brittain (1862-?). He was born in Litherland, Waterloo, a north-western suburb of Liverpool, son of an Irish physician, Edward H. FitzHenry, "M. D. Glasgow, M.N.C.S. England," and Mary Bower FitzHenry born in Liverpool. The 1871 census found him there, aged eight, living with his parents and four servants at 1 Esplanade. Ten years, later he was a lieutenant in the Wexford Militia, boarding at 21 Lexham Gardens, London, where most of the boarders were recorded as "scholars." He fought in the Sudan in 1884-1885 and received a medal with two clasps. He became a commissioned officer in 1891 and went on to serve in South Africa in 1896, for which he had another medal. In 1898-1900, and probably longer, he was a captain in the Seventh Hussars serving as an instructor at the RMC, Sandhurst.

At sometime before the Great War, he emigrated to Cobble Hill, south of Duncan, and was one of several Imperial officers and others who contributed to a patriotic fund in November 1914 and submitted a number of resolutions at a meeting of the Shawnigan Farmer's Institute. He was listed in an Island directory as a "retired Major." There being no local record of his death, perhaps he returned to the British Isles on the occasion of the war, as did many other Imperials.
Sources: census England, 1871, RG 10/3838, p. 1; census 1881, RG11 0051/67, page 5; census 1861, RG 9/2725, p. 15; *Whitaker's*, p. 189; *Colonist*, 29 November 1914, p. 18; *Henderson's Greater Victoria Directory and Vancouver Island Gazeteer*, 1914, for Cobble Hill.

FitzWILLIAM, William, Viscount Milton (1839-1877). The most extraordinary "overlander" of all, he and his friend and doctor, Walter Butler Cheadle (1835-1910), walked across Canada to the Island in 1862-1863 and visited Victoria twice, in September and November 1863. They also went to Nanaimo and the San Juan Islands aboard HM gunboat *Forward* at the invitation of *Captain H. D. Lascelles and then returned to England *via* San Francisco, the Isthmus of Panama, and on SS *China* to Liverpool, arriving there on 5 March 1864. They aroused much interest in the British Isles by lecturing widely on their journey, and their book about it went through nine editions by 1891. Having visited the San Juan Islands with men of the Royal Navy, they believed that London ought to insist on having the international boundary drawn so as to put those islands in BC, and WF published an early account of this quarrel with the United States. He was deliberately arguing against "the anti-colonial party in this country" (p. 4), deeply anxious about the Island's fate, already talking about a transcontinental railway as an Imperial link with the Orient (pp. 6, 11, 12, etc.), and indignant about Willliam Henry Seward (1801-72) visiting the Island and boasting that it would soon become American territory (p. 446).

The facts of WF's life and adventures need to be told because he has been widely ignored and sometimes sneered at in Canada, for the usual reasons of democratic inverted snobbery (e.g., by R. T. Wright in *Overlanders* (1985 and 2000). He was the eldest of twelve children of the Sixth Earl Fitzwilliam (1815-1902) and legally the heir to the title and to the family's great estate in Yorkshire: Wentworth Woodhouse, with "the most enormous private house I have ever beheld," as written by James Lees-Milne, visiting in 1946 on behalf of the National Trust. "Strange to think that until 1939 one man lived in the whole of it." That man was the eighth earl and grandson of WF, and Lees-Milne could hardly have been unaware of the mystery surrounding the family and the estate, a mystery best explained by Catherine Bailey, who cleared it up by careful research.

Various members of the family tried to prevent WF from inheriting title and property by claiming that he was an illegitimate impostor, apparently because he was epileptic in an age when epilepsy was widely thought to be an intolerable satanic curse. They had some success in concealing his malady as well as their reasons for dishonestly rejecting him and his son as illegitimate. The first amazing feature of his life was that he married Laura Maria Theresa Beauclerk (1849-86) on 10 August 1867 and then took her to the remote HBC trading post at Fort William on Lake Superior, where on 25 July 1872, she gave birth to a son at Pointe de Meuron nearby amid a wild but kindly frontier community of Indians and trappers. The child's birthplace became part of his name: William Charles de Meuron, Seventh Earl Fitzwilliam (1872-1943), whom the family called Billy. After an attempt at public life and a parliamentary career, WF and his wife seem to have gone to live in Virginia under an assumed name. WF went at last to France and died in Rouen on 20 January 1877. The family then turned its hostility against the Canadian-born Billy, who was sufficiently tough, clever, and lucky to win the struggle and so came into his inheritance. But the estate was cursed by the huge coal beds upon which it stood and upon which the family's wealth depended, as well as a troubled community of coal miners. Catherine Bailey makes a fascinating tale of all this.

James Lees-Milne, visiting in May 1946, thought the family and its unique property were hounded by the Labour Government, which "as an act of sheer class-war vindictiveness . . . decided in 1946 to destroy the park of this magnificent house, seat of the Earls Fitzwilliam, by carrying out open-cast coal-mining there." He admired surviving bits of magnificence in the great house but was saddened by its decay and by the chaos left by official bulldozers—"worse than French battlefields after D-day."

Sources: William Fitzwilliam, Viscount Milton (1839-1877), and Dr Walter Butler Cheadle (1835-1910), *The North-West Passage by Land. Being the narrative of an expedition from the Atlantic to the Pacific with the view of exploring a route across the continent to British Columbia through British territory, by one of the northern passes in the Rocky Mountains* (Cassell, Petter, and Galpin, June 1865), 397 pp., with two maps and twenty-three engraved pictures; Viscount Milton, *A History of the San Juan Water Boundary Question as Affecting the Division of Territory Between Great Britain and the United States* (Cassel, Petter, and Galpin, 1869), 446 pp., with maps; Barry M. Gough, *The Royal Navy and the Northwest Coast of North America, 1810-1914* (Vancouver, University of British Columbia Press, 1971), notes on pp. 151 and 167; Catherine Bailey, *Black Diamonds: The Rise and Fall of an English Dynasty* (Viking Bks, 2007; Penguin Bks, 2008), 518 pp.; Walter B. Cheadle, *Cheadle's Journal of Trip Across Canada 1862-1863,* ed., A. G. Doughty and Gustave Lanctot (Edmonton, M. G. Hurtig, 1971), 311 pp.; Michael Shaw Bond, *Way Out West: On the Trail of an Errant Ancestor* (Toronto, McClelland & Stewart, 2001), 247 pp. Bailey's study is scholarly and wide-ranging; the other two are without indexes or full notes and otherwise deficient, though they have their points of interest. Useful and scholarly (though outdated) notes on Viscount Milton's life appear in V. G. Hopwood's summary life in the *Dictionary of Canadian Biography*, vol. X (1972), pp. 699-700; *The Daily Free Press* (Winnipeg), 16 February 1877, "Death of Lord Milton"; J. T. Ward, "*The Earls Fitzwilliam and the Wentworth Woodhouse Estate in the Nineteenth Century,*" *Bulletin of Economic Research*, vol. 12, no 1 (1960), pp. 19-27; James Lees-Milne, *Some Country Houses and their Owners* (1975; Penguin Books, 2009), pp. 132-33.

FLEMING, Captain Charles Morton Colderwood (1894-1942). Born in Glasgow, son of Mr and Mrs Samuel Fleming, he attended Glasgow Royal Technical College but, in his early teens, became a cadet with Smith & Sons, shipowners. He was sailing on the China coast when the Great War began but went immediately home to England via Shanghai and soon joined the Royal Naval Reserve. From 1915, he was at sea on naval vessels in the Mediterranean and elsewhere and was aboard the armed merchant ship, *Marmora* when she was torpedoed south of Land's End. He was one of those rescued by a passing patrol boat. His first cableship was the *Mackay-Bennett*, which he joined in Glasgow in 1920 to work for the Commercial Cable Company. He served the Atlantic cables aboard her for several years and then went to the *Marie Louise Mackay*, operating out of Plymouth and Halifax, NS, being moved back and forth between these two ports.

While he was serving as chief officer on the *John W. Mackay*, he obtained an appointment in 1927 as captain of the cableship *Restorer* stationed in Victoria. This post took him thousands of miles around the Pacific Ocean repairing cables in the Guam Islands and other remote places. He joined the Canadian Club and United Services Institution of Vancouver Island and as recreations loved fishing and shooting and the activities of the Alpine Club of Canada, and the Automobile Clubs of BC and Canada. He married Phyllis May Slocombe, daughter of Albert George Slocombe of Bridgewater, Somerset, and they lived with their son Charles at Ten Mile Point and later at 1244 Victoria Avenue, Oak Bay, where he died, aged forty-seven, on 14 February 1942. He was survived by his wife and son as well as two sisters and his brother Samuel in Scotland. He was buried as a Presbyterian at Royal Oak Cemetery.

Sources: *Who's Who in B.C.*, 1933-34, pp. 61-62, with photo; *Colonist*, 15 February 1942, p. 3, obit.

FLICK, Lieutenant Colonel Charles Leonard (1870-1948). He was born at Halesworth, Suffolk, son of Richard William and Charlotte Flick, "The Holt," Melton, Woodbridge, Suffolk, and educated at Bracondale Boarding School in Norwich, Yarmouth Grammar School, and Felsted School, Dunmow, Suffolk. His first active service was in Rhodesia (1896). In the South African War (1899-1902), he fought with the South African Light Horse in Natal (1899), the relief of Ladysmith, including actions at Colenso (December 1899), and then at Spion Kop, Vaal Kranz, Tugela Heights, Pieters Hill, Orange Free State, Laing's Nek, and the Eastern Transvaal. He was mentioned in despatches by General Sir Arthur Buller (*London Gazette* 8 February 1901) and awarded the Queen's Medal with six clasps and the King's Medal with two clasps. Professional soldier that he was, he studied the three phases of the Battle of Paardeberg, which had lasted for ten days, and in Victoria was able to describe it to the British Campaigners' Association as their guest speaker on 19 February 1914, though he had missed the battle himself, much to his regret, by being away with Buller's Force in Natal.

After the South African War, he was briefly in Rhodesia with the Imperial Yeomanry, but emigrated in 1903 to Merritt, BC, where he kept a general store. There, he raised and organized the Thirty-first BC Horse in April 1911 and, after a Militia Staff Course in 1913, was gazetted its commanding officer. He was able to recruit eight officers who had seen active war service and to bring the regiment to a high state of efficiency. It attended annual camps at Vernon, BC, where it distinguished itself with fine field work and good horsemanship. In August 1914, CF had the regiment mobilized to full strength at once and all were disappointed when they were not allowed to go overseas as a unit. About a hundred officers and men were absorbed into Lord Strathcona's Horse at Winnipeg and sent to England with the First Canadian Division. CF himself was seconded in March 1915 to the Twelfth Royal Fusiliers, Seventy-third Brigade; in 1915, he commanded the Seventh Battalion, Essex Regiment, in Gallipoli, where he was wounded and awarded the CMG; and in 1916-1919, he commanded the Sixth Battalion, Devon Regiment, in Mesopotamia. In 1918, he served as GOC of Euphrates Defences in 1918. Sent next to India during the Indian riots of 1919, he raised, organized, and commanded No. 2 Special Battalion, was then employed on the North-West Frontier, and retired at last, having been honoured with the CBE (1918), and the VD.

In May 1920, he returned to Canada, this time to Mayne Island in the Gulf of Georgia, but until 1924, he commanded the old BC Horse, soon to be revived as a militia unit, the Fifth Cavalry BC Horse. He had trained many distinguished officers, such as Colonel H. H. Matthews, CMG, DSO, who in 1935 was the commandant of the RMC at Kingston, Ontario, and in post-war parades of

ex-servicemen, he appeared proudly in the old yellow and blue uniform of the
BC Horse. He retired in 1929 and joined the Royal Victoria Yacht Club and the
Pacific Club (Victoria), but was serving as chairman of the Mayne Island school
district in 1941 when appointed as registrar of enemy aliens and reporting officer
for Japanese residents on the Gulf Islands. Contrary to what some would expect of
an Imperial officer, he defended the Japanese on the islands against the suspicious
hostility of others, arguing as he had been doing since 1938 that there was no
evidence of them working for Japan.

Apart from such employment, he focussed for the rest of his life on three
principal aspects of military life. First, he was always ready to respond to any call
on his time or knowledge and to speak in public. On 29 June 1920, he addressed
the Kiwanis Club on his experiences and observations, sailing from England to
Gallipoli via Gibraltar and Malta and Alexandria during the Gallipoli Campaign.
In January 1921, he was serving as the first president of the Pacific Coast Officers'
Association, affiliated to the Officers' Association of London, "formed to assist
disabled officers and the dependents of officers who were killed, or died of
wounds, or sickness during the German War," and he secured the patronage of
his friend, *General Sir Arthur Currie, for the local branch. On 12 April 1921, he
spoke again to the Kiwanis Club, this time to denounce the officials ("mossbacks"
and "cobwebs") who secured sinecures through political influence in Ottawa,
obtained pensions, and prevented efficient administration of the militia. Many
similar speeches and letters followed over the years.

Here was another of CF's major preoccupations. He became a vociferous and
determined critic of the federal government and its policies. In speeches and
letters about political favouritism, he worried the federal government enough
that W. Foran, secretary of the Civil Service Commission, wrote a long defensive
letter to the *Colonist* at the end of September 1921. Moving on to military matters,
CF wrote letters and pamphlets explaining how badly Canada had organized the
army before and during the Great War. There was much to be said on this subject,
and he knew whereof he wrote, particularly about the activities of the eccentric
minister of defence, Hon. Sam Hughes, who had much to answer for. (See, for
instance, Ronald G. Haycock, *Sam Hughes: The Public Career of a Controversial
Canada, 1885-1916*, Ottawa, Canadian War Museum and Wilfred Laurier U. P.,
1986, chapters 9-15.) CF thought the administration had wasted money on too
many expensive and useless political appointments while he had had to spend
his own money to look after the BC Horse. Many other critics agreed with him,
and as early as February 1938, a high military official in Ottawa had written to
tell him that nobody in Ottawa was interested in the defence of Canada, except
for the patronage the militia afforded. A few veterans were speaking out in
Parliament but having no effect. It was Canadian political culture in general
that incurred the wrath of CF and his friends. In May 1921, he attacked the
provincial legislature for raising its own salaries when funds were needed for
hospitals, schools, and the militia. He was the first speaker on the subject at
a large gathering in the Pantages Theatre, Victoria, on Sunday afternoon, 29

May 1921. During the 1930s, his attacks were concentrated on official delays in organizing for a war that he, like so many of his kind, anticipated and he was anxious to meet the trouble head on, not by appeals to the League of Nations or other peaceful overtures. He kept abreast of military science, read French and British journals on the subject, and was an early advocate of the armoured tank. In retrospect, it would be difficult to disagree with him. In the early years of the Second World War, he was also vociferously indignant at the anti-British propaganda he saw widespread in Canada. By 1942, however, he had concluded that preparations for the Second World War had been speedier and more efficient than for the Great War.

In a third line of activity, CF wrote and spoke at length about his own wartime experiences, especially in Mesopotamia. The earliest of these memoirs were long articles to the *Daily Colonist*, usually printed in its Sunday supplement. Perhaps, a list of his publications is the most economical way of conveying the tenor of his principal writings, which were clear, often pungent, and evidently the work of an educated officer.

(1) *Twelve Months with General Buller in South Africa* (Robinson, Pickering, and Hunt, 1902?), 80 pp.

(2) *"Just What Happened": A Diary of the Mobilization of the Canadian Militia, 1914* (Privately Printed, 1917), 99 pp. [British Library 9081 e 28]

(3) *The Record of the 6th Devons in the Great War of 1914-19* (n.d., n.p.)

(4) *A Canadian in Gallipoli* (n.d., n.p.)

(5) *A Short History of the 31st British Columbia Horse* [with portraits] (Victoria, BC, J. Parker Buckle, 1922), 39 pp. [British Library 08821. b. 50]

(6) *Colonist*, 20 February 1921, Sunday p. 18, "Bagdad under Arab and Turkish Rule." A learned synopsis of history since the seventh century with a description of the city, where he had evidently spent much time.

(7) *Colonist*, 27 February 1921, Sunday, p. 18, "When I was a King" (Flick was temporarily the ruler of the place and treated as king by the population. He describes travelling with a military escort through the villages and the countryside and his many encounters with various local authorities and others. "On reflection," he wrote, "one wonders who has the better part—the free Bedouin, with his magnificent stature, his splendid health, his roving life in a genial climate, his frugal meals, and little thought for any sumptuous clothing—or the stunted, half-starved citizens of the modern cities of Europe and America, with the wages of slaves for their work and the picture palace for their amusement."

(8) *Colonist*, 27 March 1921, Sunday, p. 18, "Messenger of the Desert" (The dramatic tale of how Major Leachman, disguised as a Kurds, brought the British commander of the Devon Regiment a message, saved or relieved the town and fort of Nasiriyeh, and fooled the German commander Von Presser, who was captured with all of his private papers.)

(9) *Colonist*, 3 April 1921, Sunday, p. 19, "Islam in Mesopotamia."

(10) *Colonist*, 29 May 1921, Sunday, p. 19, "When I was a King—A Command Performance" (At Shattra, he ordered a command performance at the local native theatre, and here describes it in dramatic detail.)

(11) *Colonist*, 5 June 1921, p. 9, "Training of Disabled Soldiers" (A voluntary workshop organized at 714 Fort Street to help train disabled soldiers.)

It must be said that there are puzzling entries in the census records. Was CF the Charles L. Flick, aged one, whom the census of 1871 found together with a brother and sister, likewise babies, all born at Halesworth, Suffolk, and living with Robert Howard, aged fifty-five, an "Agricultural Labourer?" Was he the Charles L. Flick, aged twenty-one, born at Halesworth, Suffolk, whom the 1891 census recorded as a "Wholesale Draper's Assistant" at St Vedast Foster, London, and who in 1901 was living with his parents at 12 Pembury Road, Tottenham, and employed as a clerk? Those parents were, indeed, Richard W. Flick, aged sixty, employed as a "Wine & Spirit Merchant & Farmer" born at Sax Mundham, Suffolk, and the mother Charlotte Flick, aged fifty-four, born at Chichester, Sussex. When CF died, aged seventy-seven, on 8 February 1948 in Saanich, he left a son, a daughter, and his widow, *née* Marie Lydia Laura Milward, youngest daughter of Joseph Milward, Skeleton Lake, Muskoka, Canada, whom he had married in 1904.

Sources: NAC, reel T.6958, "*Active Militia with Service Before World War 1,*" notes in a ledger; *Colonist*, 20 February 1914, p. 3; 16 January 1921, p. 14; 29 January 1921, p. 5; 20 February 1921, Sunday p. 18; 27 February 1921, Sunday, p. 18; 3 April 1921, p. 1; 3 April 1921, Sunday, p. 19; 13 April 1921, p. 5; 13 May 1921, p. 14; 29 May 1921, Sunday, p. 19; 31 May 1921, p. 5; 26 June 1921, p. 18; 5 June 1921, p. 9; 30 September 1921, p. 4; 2 October 1921, p. 14; 10 October 1937, p. 4; 30 October 1937, p. 4; 25 January 1938, p. 4; 1 February 1939, p. 4; 2 February 1940, p. 4; 2 May 1940, p. 4; 7 May 1941, p. 4; 16 May 1940, p. 4; 20 June 1940, p. 4; 10 April 1941, p. 10; 3 June 1941, p. 4; 29 August 1941, p. 4; 10 February 1948, p. 13, obit.; 12 February 1948, p. 4, "*An Appreciation*" by Major F. V. Longstaff, 50 King George Terrace; *Victoria Times*, 10 February 1948, p. 16, obit.

FOOT, Captain Edwin Cunningham (1862-?). He was born at Worthing, Sussex, on 4 December 1862, son of Rev. Cunningham Noel Foot, rector of Dogmersfield, Hampshire, and his wife, Sophia Maria Foot. In 1871, the census found ECF and his four brothers living at the rectory in Dogmerfield with their parents, a governess, and three servants, but in 1881, he was living, aged eighteen, at Worthing with a seventy-year-old great-uncle, Robert Williams, a retired London magistrate whose wife Emily was an "Earl's daughter." There were other relatives in the house and no fewer than eleven servants.

In the course of his career, as reported in the *Daily Colonist*, EF took a diploma at the Forestry College of Nancy, France, gained a good working knowledge of French, and was elected a fellow of the Royal Geographical Society in 1912 for his charts of the water supply and reports of the trade routes in unexplored regions of Abyssinia, the El Wady Desert, and the Italian Somaliland. He compiled a dictionary of the Galla Language for the British Foreign Office. When he enlisted at Fernie, BC, on 27 March 1916 as a lieutenant in the 225th Battalion, he had been employed in Victoria, where he lived with his wife (Eveline Mabel Foot) at 227 Menzies Street, on the staff of the Forestry Branch, Department of Lands. The *Colonist* said he served as a lieutenant in a New Zealand military unit and qualified as captain in the Bangalore Rifle Volunteers, at Madras, India, but EF declared on his enlistment form that he had no military experience.

Sources: NAC, CEF files, box 3175-29; census 1871, England, RG 10 /1229, p. 5; census 1881, RG 11/1095; *Colonist*, 21 January 1917, p. 5, photo.

FORDYCE, Colonel Henry Lawrence Dingwall (1867-?). He was born on 12 July 1867 in Bayswater, London, son of Major General Sir John Fordyce (1806-1877) of the Royal Horse Artillery and his third wife, Phoebe Graham. She was born in Mehidpore, Bengal, daughter of James Graham, surgeon in the Bengal Army. The Fordyces had married in India in 1847, but in 1871, HF was living with his mother, then aged forty-four, "wife of Major General John Fordyce, Commissioner of Shirland Division of the Army in Bengal." With them was an elder brother, Arthur L. D. Fordyce, born at Ferozepore, Bengal, then eighteen, and they had one servant, a nurse. The census of 1881 found Dame Phoebe Fordyce, a widow aged fifty-four, living at 47 Penywern Road, Kensington, London, with her daughter, Sidney Agnes Fordyce, aged twenty-four, born in India, and two servants. HF attended Wellington College, Sandhurst, and was commissioned in the Royal Artillery on 16 February 1887. On 28 June 1889, he was appointed to the Indian Army and on 19 June 1891 to Supply & Transport Corps, which took him to Jubbulpore in 1903 and to many parts of India over the next twenty years. In June 1923, he and his wife and two daughters, Joan and Monica, arrived from Jersey, Channel Islands, and bought a property on Marchmont Road, Duncan, from Mr H. C. Mann. Mrs Fordyce and her daughters were planning to visit England shortly. Duncan town directory shows the family living near Duncan c. 1926 and the last sign of the family there was a marriage at Quamichan on 7 June 1927 of Sidney Dingwall Fordyce and Ian Napier Roome, a couple who soon returned to Britain.

There were several branches of the Fordyce family. For instance, a first cousin of HF's father, Major Robert Dingwall-Fordyce (1875-1935), served with the Militia Battalion of the Gordons and then went through the South African War in the Royal Scots Greys, took part in the relief of Kimberley, and was invalided home after being wounded at Paardeberg. Home for him was Brucklay Castle, Aberdeenshire, inherited from his father, where he took a great interest in the Boy Scout movement and was a staunch member of the East Aberdeenshire Unionist Association.

Sources: census 1871, England, RG 10/177; census 1881, RG 11/49, p. 41; India Office List, October 1910; *Indian Army List,* January 1905, p. 45; October 1910; *Cowichan Leader,* 30 August 1923; *The Times,* London, 20 November 1935, p. 9; Riddick, *Who in British India,* p. 129 (father).

FORREST, Colin Murray (c. 1884-1941). Born in Scotland, he spent thirty years in China in the service of Butterfield and Swire and, in 1934, retired to Victoria, where he lived as the owner of Tweedsmuir Mansions (Park Blvd.) and The Coffee Cup on Government Street. He organized a scheme to build the Cathay Apartment Hotel, and he it was who built the Royal Oak Inn, a landmark north of Victoria for many years. When the Second World War broke out, he sold the Inn and went to Vancouver, where he died, aged fifty-seven, on 26 February 1941, leaving a widow, a daughter, and two sons: Collin Peter Forrest (born in Canton) in the army and Ian Forrest at Shawnigan Lake School.
Sources: *Colonist*, 13 October 1940, p. 24: photo; 1 March 1941, p. 6, obit.

FOWLER, David (c. 1859-1937). He was born eldest son of Thomas Fowler, agricultural labourer, and his wife Hannah, at Dunnington, Yorkshire, where the 1871 census found him, aged twelve, living with them at Common End with three younger brothers and four sisters. His nearest brother, Charles, aged nine, emigrated much later to the United States, where he settled at Portland, Oregon. In the meantime, DF joined the Royal Marines and, by 1891, was a corporal living at 17 Admiralty Street, East Stonehouse, Devon, with a wife, Alice M. M. Fowler, from Stoke Dameral, Devon, who was a "Tailoress." With them was a niece, Ethel Crocker, born in Portland, Oregon (?). The 1901 census listed the three of them living still at East Stonehouse but in the "District Royal Marines" surrounded by other sergeants and drum majors of the marines and their families. DW served in the marines for twenty years, in the South African War with the Plymouth Division, and then retired on a pension.

In 1908, he moved to Victoria, where he became a prominent Freemason and was hired by the Esquimalt Waterworks Company. Five years later, he left to become private secretary to Joseph Austin Sayward (c. 1863-1934), a pioneer lumberman and businessman of Victoria, for whom he supervised the management of the Sayward Block on Douglas St When Sayward died early in 1934, DF retired to live on his pensions at his home at 417 Henry St When he died, aged seventy-eight, on 31 March 1937 while visiting his brother Charles Fowler in Portland, Oregon, he left a sister and brother in Portland and four sisters and two brothers in England. His wife must have died earlier in England, but in Victoria, he left Ethel, whom they had apparently adopted. She died there, aged seventy-six, on 27 January 1959.
Sources: *Colonist*, 17 April 1937, p. 2, obit. and photo; census 1871, England, RG 10/ 4755, p. 23; census 1891, RG 12/1739, p. 19; census 1901, England, RG 13/2105, p. 5.

FOX, John (c. 1866-1954). Born in London, he joined the British Civil Service and went to Ceylon as an accountant in 1900 to reorganize the postal system. He became assistant postmaster general there and later spent two years in Malta reorganizing its post office. Like others with similar colonial careers, he wanted to retire outside the British Isles and, in 1923, went with his family to the Cowichan Valley, where he bought the imThurn's property on Maple Bay Road near *Major J. H. G. Palmer's place. With them were the Fox's daughter-in-law, Ena Timarcheff, who had recently arrived from the Far East. She and her mother were White Russians who had fled across Siberia to Harbin, Manchuria, where she found employment in a Canadian bank. "They bought a piece of land on Richards Trail," Mrs Palmer recalled, "a picturesque lane that ran from the opposite shore of Quamichan Lake several miles to Westholme, and were chicken farming . . . we used to hear stories about her brother, who had been an officer in the Imperial Russian Army, and his heroic rescue of Russian aristocrats; some called him another Scarlet Pimpernell." After thirty-one years, JF died, aged eighty-eight, at Queen's Daughters Hospital, Duncan, leaving his wife, Edith Mary Fox, two grandsons, John Ernest Fox (Duncan) and Lieutenant Alexander Edward Fox, RCNAS, Portage La Prairie, and other relatives. He had outlived his two sons. Major Palmer was honorary pallbearer at the funeral in St Peter's Quamichan, where the hymn chosen was "Fight the Good Fight."

Sources: *Cowichan Leader*, 28 January 1954, obit.; Mrs J. H. G. Palmer, "*Memoirs of an Old-Fashioned Grandmother*," 1920s, part II, pp. 16-17, in private family papers.

FOXWELL, Captain Caleb Henry (c. 1879-1942). As a retired British officer, he went out to Victoria in the early 1920s and found employment on the staff of the Empress Hotel. He joined the Union Club, next door to the hotel, the Trail Riders of the Canadian Rockies, and the Alpine Club of Canada, still headed by *A. O. Wheeler in Sidney, because one of his hobbies was mountain-climbing. CF was one of the group that made the first ascent of Mt Robson and had various other achievements.

He was useful to the hotel for the same reason that as an officer in the Royal Welch Fusiliers, he showed an aptitude for running the officers' mess in Cairo; he was the son of a wine merchant. He appears, aged eleven, in the 1881 census living with his family in London at 147 Edgeware Road. Unusually and rather perversely, the men and boys in the family recorded only their initials, but the family is unmistakeable. CF had six sisters and a brother, and their father, A. W. Foxwell, aged forty-four, was a "Wine Merchant" born in Birmingham, son of a draper. Their mother was a Londoner born in the St Pancras district. Ten years later, CF was employed as a "shipping clerk" and was boarding at 12 Rochester Street, not far from home, together with an elder brother, Alfred Foxwell, who was a "dock clerk." CF enlisted as soon as the Great War broke out and, by the end of 1914, had been commissioned in the Royal Welch Fusiliers for meritorious service in the field. When his unit was dispatched to Cairo, he was asked to take charge of the officers' mess, but growing tired of this, he joined a force that was rounding up the Senussi tribe in the Egyptian desert. They were sent next to Imbros in the Dardanelles, where he was one of the survivors, and at Tenedos, an old fortified town in Asia Minor, one of his jobs was to search the harems and households for weapons. He was reported to be dead after an air raid in autumn 1916 at Salica but was recovered wounded and invalided home to England. He spent the last years of the war at the War Office. After living in Victoria throughout the interwar years, he died there at last, aged seventy-two, on

31 August 1942, leaving his wife, Frances Kathleen, who died, aged seventy-two, on 21 June 1956.

Sources: *Colonist*, 11 September 1921, p. 5; *Who's Who in B.C.*, 1937-1939, pp. 38-9; vol. VII (1947-48), pp. 72-3; census 1881, England RG 11/16, p. 4; census 1891, RG 12/14/89, p. 21; *Who was Who*, vol. 5 (1951-1960), p. 390; *The Daily Colonist*, 2 September 1925, p. 8; 13 June 1933, p. 5; 25 June 1933, p. 1; 29 August 1941, p. 1 (photo).

"Bardsey", Brig. Gen. Gale's house, Corner of the west Saanich Road and
Mount Newton Cross Road

GALE, Brigadier General Henry Richmond (1866-1930). He was born 16 April 1866 at Sidbury, Devonshire, eldest son of Henry Richmond H. Gale (died 1913), JP, and his wife Emma, of "Bardsea Hall," near Ulverston, on the Lancashire coast near the Lake District. The 1881 census found him, aged fourteen, living with them in "Bardsea Hall," his father recorded as "Justice of the Peace for Lancashire, Farmer of two hundred acres. Employing two men." His sister Eleanor Mabel does not seem to have played much part in his life, but the nearest in age of his two brothers, Edmund William, then aged twelve, was at a boarding school at Applethwaite, Windermere. HG was schooled at Harrow and RMA, Woolwich. After serving in the South African War 1899-1902 (King's and Queen's medals; CMG) and in India, he was commissioned in 1910 as lieutenant colonel in the Royal Engineers, became chief engineer in 1916 and assistant director of works 1916, and retired in 1919 as brigadier general. He was named CMG (1916) and FRGS. In 1903, he married Kathleen Jane Villiers-Stuart (1873-1958), eldest daughter of Lieutenant Colonel Henry J. R. Villiers-Stuart, DL of Castletown County Kilkenny (but born in London) and they had three daughters.

The Gales went to Vancouver Island in 1918 or 1919 and settled in Saanich on the south-west side of Mount Newton on a property they called "Bardsey" after his father's estate. They built a charming manor house in a Tudor style amid the Douglas firs and arbutus trees, where it was still when I photographed it in 2001. "Although he lived a retired life," the *Colonist* reported at his death, "he was well known in the community as a man of versatile interests, and a great lover of the out-of-doors, one of his favorite pastimes during his earlier residence here being walking and climbing." He used to walk in the woods and fields with a friendly neighbour, *Lord Colville of Culross, who married his daughter Kathleen Myrtle a few months after his death. Very soon, on 2 July 1931, their daughter Lois Margaret married Dr Ronald Scott-Moncrieff, son of *Lieutenant Colonel William Emsley Scott-Moncrieff, and in 1948, Ethne Evelyn Mary (1912-1997) married *Major E. Rex Gibson, a retired Imperial soldier teaching school at Oak Bay. These marriages were celebrated nearby at St Stephen's Church on the West Saanich Road looking out at the Malahat mountains over Saanich Inlet. HG died, aged sixty-four, on 28 July 1930 and was buried in the churchyard at St Stephen's. In January 1933, Mrs, Gale and Ethne attended a meeting of the India-Burma Society in Victoria.
Sources: *Who's Who in B.C.* 1933-1934, p. 199; *Colonist*, 30 July 1930, pp. 5 and 18, obit.; 17 January 1933, p. 8; *Colonist*, 10 December 1952, p. 12; census 1871, England, RG 10/2043, p. 8; census 1881, RG 11/4282, p. 1; census 1881, RG 11/5206, p. 82.

GALLOWAY, Frederick William (c. 1881-1974). Born in Aberdeenshire, where his father was a Presbyterian minister in a rural parish, he came from a long line of Scottish covenanters. He had an adventurous turn of mind, attended RMA at Woolwich, where he was later proud to say that he had won "the higher riding certificate," and entered the Indian Police Force. He landed at Bombay in November 1901 and was sent out on plague duty in a rural district. The service took him to various parts of India, but he spent most of his twenty-two years there in the Himalayas or on the North-West Frontier. Promotion came slowly. He applied himself to writing articles for *The Tatler, Truth (Queer Stories), Chambers Journal, Wide World Magazine,* and *The Scottish Field.* In 1908-1909, the *Boys' Own Annual* published an article of his, "The Indian Police," in a series with the general heading, "What Shall I be?" It is an early account of his service with descriptions of life in the Indian Police, advice about the process of joining it, and five photographs. At one time, he applied to the Colonial Office for a post and was offered one in Lagos, which he turned down. He soon became an enthusiastic hunter, as autobiographical pages written in retirement show, and shot leopards, tigers, elephants, crocodiles, deer, antelopes, and birds of all kinds. "My grandfather . . . arrived in Canada complete with a panther skin," his granddaughter writes. "He was mortally offended when my grandmother tried to get rid of it at an I.O.D.E. rummage sale, and he bought it back." But he also thought a great deal about life and people in India and wrote long, thoughtful paragraphs on the issues of Indian independence. He strongly objected to the post-1918 policy of the British government, which was already giving way to the self-rule movement, and accordingly resigned at last about 1922 or 1923 and returned to England, so sacrificing a promotion to his principles. During one of his furloughs home, he had married Edith Annie Smith (c. 1884-1953), also from Aberdeen, and they had two children. Looking at an atlas to find a part of the British Empire, which "would be best for ourselves and a family growing up," they decided on British Columbia, where they arrived in the early 1920s.

They lived briefly in North Vancouver and Courtenay but soon settled at Duncan, where he practiced law from about 1930, having used long furloughs during his career to read law in London at the Middle Temple. One of his son's friends at Duncan Grammar School and Cowichan High School, who worked for a time at the Court House in Duncan, recalls that Galloway "had a large black Labrador named 'Major' and when he went in to work, and back after lunch, he used to hang onto the dog's tail and with the command 'up Major' the dog would pull him up the long flight of stairs to his second-floor office. Both parties seemed to enjoy this performance." The eldest son, Angus Frederick Galloway (c. 1915-1940), born in Kafauli, a police station in the Himalayas, grew up to became a brilliant cadet at RMC, Kingston, Ontario, won the Governor General's Medal and the Lieutenant Governor's Medal, and, after two years at Cambridge and some training at Chatham, took a commission in the Royal Engineers. He died, aged twenty-five, on 31 May 1940, serving with the Fifty-ninth Field Company at Lapanne, France. Mrs Galloway, who took an MA at the University of Aberdeen, had a strong influence on their children and was very active in Red Cross work during the war in the Cowichan Chapter of the IODE of which she was regent for several years. Two daughters married clergymen and a grand daughter, Margaret Horsefield, has published a fascinating illustrated study of a pioneering lady on the Island's west coast, Ada Annie Rae-Arthur, better known as "Cougar Annie."

Sources: F. W. Galloway, "*Life in the Indian Police,*" a typescript of c. 112 pp., courtesy of a granddaughter, Margaret Horsefield; letter from Margaret Horsefield, 18

December 2001; *Boys' Own Annual*, 1908-1909, pp. 126-8, F. W. Galloway, "*The Indian Police*" under the general heading, "What Shall I be?" 3 pp.; notes from John Palmer, 15 January 2002, p. 1; *Colonist*, 17 July 1940, p. 3, obit.; Margaret Horsefield, *Cougar Annie's Garden* (Nanaimo, BC, Salal Books, 1999), 260 pp. in 4o.

GANN, Herbert (1878-1959). He was born on 1 August 1878 at Whitstable-on-Sea, Kent, son of George Herbert Gann, a shipowner who was listed in the *Canterbury & Vicinity Directory*, 1889, as a Whitstable "Carrier by Water." The family was evidently well established in that district. The 1881 census found HG, aged two, living with his parents and four sisters in Joy Lane, Seasalter, near Whitstable, but in 1891, he and six sisters, all born at Whitstable, were living at "The Elms," Greenwich, London, with their widowed mother, Emma J. Gann.

Apprenticed young to a shipyard at Teignmouth, Devon, he then moved out to Vancouver Island, where he farmed on Wilkinson Road in South Saanich. He joined the Canadian Expeditionary Force on 3 September 1915 as a private soldier without military experience. At that time, he and his wife, Mrs Edith Florence Gann, were living at Colquitz Avenue, Victoria, and he gave his occupation as "yacht builder." They were Anglicans. After the war in which he served in the Sixty-seventh Battalion, he found employment at Yarrows Shipyard and then with the Rodd Brothers marina at Canoe Cove in North Saanich. Mrs Gann died, aged sixty-seven, on 23 March 1948 in Victoria, and HG died, aged eighty, on 31 March 1959 in Saanich.

Sources: NAC, CEF files, box 3395-38; census 1881, England, RG 11/965, p. 1; census 1891, RG 12/512, p. 9; *Canterbury & Vicinity Directory*, 1889, listing Whitstable; Terry Reksten, *A Century of Sailing, 1892-1992: A History of the Oldest Yacht Club on Canada's Pacific Coast* (Victoria, Orca Book Publishing, 1992), pp. 121-2.

GARTSIDE-SPAIGHT, Brigadier General Cavendish Walter (1857-?). He was born on 17 February 1857 at Derry Castle, Killaloe, Ireland, which in due course he inherited. First commissioned in the British Army on 29 November 1876, he had a busy career around the empire and, from 29 November 1900, was on the list of officers in reserve. He was living at Duncan in 1921 and 1922, possibly longer, and had a connection with other families in the district because in 1922, his daughter, Irene, married Hon. Evelyn Arthur Grenville Temple-Gore-Langton (1884-1972), son of William Stephen Temple-Gore-Langton, Fourth Earl of Stowe and of Helen Mabel Montgomery. Several members of the *Temple-Gore-Langton family lived at Shawnigan Lake, in Victoria, and elsewhere on the Island. CG attended St Peter's Quamichan in the early 1920s and, at the Cowichan Fall Fair and Exhibition in September 1921, won second prize for his photographs of "six farm scenes" as well as the first prize for his sunflower plants. He soon disappeared, however, and seems to have settled elsewhere.

Sources: *Army List*, October 1910, pp. 2010b and 2546; Williams, *The Story of St Peter's*, p. 55; *Colonist*, 17 September 1921, p. 14.

GAUDIN, Captain James (c. 1839-1913). Born in the Channel Islands at St Martins, Jersey, he became a master mariner and sailed to Victoria, where he was

employed by the Hudson's Bay Company as captain of the *Lady Lampson* and, as such on 6 February 1973, married Agnes Anderson (1849-?), born at Colville, BC, daughter of *Alexander Caulfield Anderson. Their honeymoon trip home to Jersey was by way of Cape Horn. He sailed back and forth, but Agnes seems to have lived much of her early married life on Jersey, if the births of their children there c. 1873, c. 1876, and c. 1880 are any guide. By 1881, only the second, Mabel Agnes Gaudin, had been born in Victoria (c. 1875). In the late 1870, he bought land on Craigflower Road, Victoria, and built a house and garden he called "Illa Villa" after his ancestral property at St Saviour, Jersey. He became owner and skipper of a Clipper, *Rover of the Seas*, in July 1878 and sailed her for ten years after which he took the post of Victoria harbour pilot. Soon after that, he joined the Marine and Fisheries Service as master of the *Sir James Douglas*. In 1892, having given up command of the *Quadra*, he became commissioner of wrecks, examiner of masters and mates, and marine agent in command of a scattered crew of lighthouse keepers for two decades. He took an interest in public affairs during those years and, for instance, in April 1910, was elected to the committee of the Victoria and Esquimalt Branch of the Navy League. When he died, aged seventy-four, on 12 January 1913 at Oak Bay, his successor as marine agent was Captain Edward Livingstone Robertson. His wife died in May 1929, leaving him with their son and three daughters, including Mabel Agnes, who had married *James S. Harvey of Knapp Island on 8 November 1899.
Sources: census 1881, England, RG 11/5617, p. 5; *Colonist*, 27 April 1910, p. 2, "*Growth of Navy League in Province*"; 21 May 1929, p. 5; Donald Graham, *Keepers of the Light: A History of British Columbia's Lighthouses and their Keepers* (Madeira Park, Harbour Publishing, 1985), pp. (see index p. 268 for c. 60 entries).

GEAKE, Harry James, RN (1850-1930). He joined the Royal Navy in his youth and served in China during an early Chinese War and then in the Egyptian Campaign of 1882; from 1888 to 1906, he was posted at Esquimalt. When the British government turned Esquimalt naval base over to the Canadian government, Geake retired and worked for a number of years on the BC coast as a marine engineer. He joined the British Campaigners' Association on 28 September 1911. Then he went home to England and died, aged eighty, on 16 June 1930 at Westcliff-on-Sea in Sussex.
Sources: *Colonist*, 8 July 1930, p. 5, obit. and photo; *BC Archives, Minutes of the British Campaigners' Ass.*, 1907-1935, 28 September 1911; but see BC Vital Statistics, entry for 7 January 1946.

GERRARD, Major Frederick Wernham (1887-1974). Born on 25 November 1887 at Auchindoir, Aberdeenshire, son of M. G. Gerrard, MA, PhD, he attended the University of Aberdeen and there was chosen as a cadet for the Police Training School in India and served in the Indian Police in 1908-1929. He was seconded to the Indian Army in 1915-1921, fighting with the 116 Mahrattas at first on the North-West Frontier and in 1916-1923 in Mesopotamia. There, he joined the Civil Administration as assistant commissioner of police in Basra on 5 July 1916, in Nasiriya on 1 January 1917, in Baghdad on 1 April as inspector general of police, and in Basra again from 1 October. He was created CIE in the Birthday Honours List of 1920, retired from military service with the rank of major in 1921, and, two years later, returned to police duty in India. In 1928, the authorities chose him to investigate and reorganize the police at Aden and the next year at Shanghai. Arriving in China on 28 May 1929, he served as commissioner of the Shanghai police from 7 October 1929 to 1938 and succeeded in carrying out his mandate to reorganize that force in order to make it less corrupt and more effective in ending the wave of armed robberies that overtook the city in the years 1924-1930, a difficult task in which he was supported by the Watch Committee of the Shanghai Municipal Council. In June 1938, he resigned, his service recognized by the award of the CIE, and embarked on the *Empress of Japan* for Vancouver Island, the home of his wife, Dorothea Ursula, daughter of G. H. Teague, whom he had married in London in November 1928.

They settled at 1601 Ross Street, Victoria, BC, where he died on 14 March 1974. No satisfactory local obituary informs us about his life in retirement because the employees of both Victoria newspapers were on strike at the time of FWG's death.

Sources: Robert Bickers, *Empire Made Me: An Englishman Adrift in Shanghai* (Allen Lane, 2003), pp. 187, 197, 198, 302; notes kindly sent by Dr Robert Bickers, Bristol University, 9 October 2003; Sir Arnold Wilson, *Loyalties: Mesopotamia*, vol. II, p. 367; *Colonist*, 18 June 1938, p. 3, photo; *Who was Who*, 1971-1980, p. 294, obit.; *Men of Shanghai and North China: A Standard Biographical Reference Work. ed.*, George F. Nellist (Shanghai, Oriental Press, 1933), p. 148.

GERRARD, Major Halford Dumergue (1855-1925). Born on 5 July 1855, he was commissioned in the British Army on 29 April 1874, transferred to the Indian Staff Corps, and served in Burma in 1885-1886. He was promoted to major on 29 April 1894 and retired next day. In September 1882 at St Thomas in Devonshire, he had married Alice Beatrice, third daughter of Henry Dumbleton of "Hall Grove," Bagshot, England, and of "Rocklands," Victoria. Upon his retirement, this couple retired to Victoria, but HG was then appointed British vice-consul at San Diego, California, where they lived until his death at the end of October 1925. Mrs Gerrard then moved to join her family in Victoria, where she died, aged ninety-seven, on Trafalgar Day in 1952, as *The Colonist* remarked with its still-customary Imperial sensibility.

Sources: *India Army List*, January 1907, p. 706; *Colonist*, 1 November 1925 (Sunday), p. 36, obit.; 4 November 1952, obit.; *Whitaker's*, p. 206.

GIBBS, Captain James (c. 1868-1941). Born in London, he served for forty years with the China Navigation Company, sailing out of Shanghai, and retired about 1931 to Vancouver Island. There, he lived with his wife on Daisy Avenue at Marigold, a few miles from Victoria, until his death, aged seventy-three, on 17 September 1941. He was buried at Royal Oak as an Anglican.

Sources: *Colonist*, 18 September 1941, p. 5, obit.

GIBSON, Major Reginald Evelyn "Rex" (1892-1957). Born on 7 November 1892 at Hatfield Peveril, Essex, he had an interesting family background. His father, Edward Gibson (1837-1914), was born at Great Malvern in Gloucestershire, attended Marlborough School in Wiltshire, became a prosperous merchant in the Russia trade, and spent many years in a circle of British merchants at St Petersburg. There on 30 November 1867, a quarter-century before RG's birth, he married the first of his two wives, Mary Isabel Wylie (1849-1886), the fourth child (eldest daughter) of George Wiley (1808-1884), a merchant at St Petersburg, and his wife Mary Cattley (1820-1900), who had married there on 21 June 1839. Mary Cattley was a daughter of Robert Cattley (born 1787 at York—died 18 April 1859 at Chepstow) and Frances "Fanny" Moberley (1789-1872, born and died at St Petersburg), who had married on 3 June 1815 at St Petersburg. Though born in Russia, Mary Isabel Gibson, née Wiley, appears in the English census for 1881 living in Essex with her husband, RG's father, and their children at "Skreens" Park, Roxwell, four and a half miles west of Chelmsford. There were two daughters and three sons ranging in age from nine years to eight months. Mary Isabel died, aged thirty-six, on 8 May 1886, and two or three years later, Edward Gibson made a second marriage with a much-younger woman, Violet, born c. 1863 at Richmond, Ireland. The 1891 census recorded her and Edward living at "Crix Mansion" near Hatfield Peveril, northeast of Chelmsford, with two of his first wife's children, grown up by then, notably Henry Gibson, aged twenty-nine and working as "merchant's clerk," perhaps for his father. Violet also had a child of her own, RG's older brother Douglas Gibson, aged three. RG was born the next year and appears, aged eight, at "Crix Mansion" in the 1901 census together with his parents, two half-sisters, and a younger sister Evelyn G. Gibson, born, like him, at Hatfield Peveril. RG's father, Edward Gibson, was now described as a "Timber Merchant." At "Skreens" in 1881, they had ten servants, and at "Crix Mansion" in 1891 and 1901, there were six—a Swiss governess, parlourmaid, two housemaids, kitchenmaid, and nursemaid—which says something about RG's childhood. He was sent to Mowden Preparatory School and Sherborne School and, at sixteen, went to work in a private bank in Paris belonging to his family. It was later absorbed by Lloyds Bank, and after the Great War, he served with Lloyds Bank in Cologne and Antwerp. As a result, he spoke fluent French and German. In September 1914, he enlisted in the Royal Artillery and was commissioned in November. He served at Ypres, the Somme, and Cambrai and, in January 1917, was appointed staff captain, RA, Third Corps. He was thrice mentioned in despatches and won the Military Cross.

In July 1926, he went out to Canada and began farming the next year at Winterburn, near Edmonton. Before going to Canada, he had climbed a little in Switzerland, for example, up the Jungfrau in January 1925, and he soon took to climbing and exploring in the Rocky Mountains. In 1930, he joined the Alpine Club of Canada and was active in it for the next eighteen years, climbing, skiing, and serving on the executive of the Club. He developed a passionate love for the mountains and made over two hundred climbs, including many first ascents, a climbing record "probably unsurpassed by any amateur climber in Canada," according to an obituary notice in the *Canadian Alpine Journal*. When fighting began in the Second World War, he joined the RCA in February 1941, and in 1942, he was Canadian military representative with the U.S. Army's Mount McKinley expedition to test cold weather equipment. He was injured during this expedition and discharged from the army with a pension, but the army took him back in 1943 as an instructor at the Little Yoho Military Camp, where members of the Alpine Club gave instruction in mountaineering to an army group. In winter 1943-1944, he helped in the Lovat Scout training in Jasper Park and was promoted to major.

It was in the Alpine Club that he met and, in 1948, married Miss Ethne Evelyn Mary Gale (1912-1997), daughter of *Brigadier General Henry Richmond Gale of "Bardsey," Mt Newton Cross Road in Saanich, a woman who had graduated as a member of the Alpine Club in 1936 and become a keen mountaineer. They soon left the Edmonton farm and moved to Saanichton, where they had a daughter Kathleen. There, RG became an enthusiastic sailor and fisherman. "His home in Saanichton showed many evidences of his skill as a carpenter. With an axe he was an expert and many will remember his demonstrations of how to split firewood at numerous camps." Keenly interested and active in astronomy, he would sit up for hours to see an eclipse of the moon. He was deeply religious and gave impressive sermons at camp services on Alpine Club expeditions. In a tragic accident during the night of 18-19 August 1957, he died as a result of a fall while climbing Mount Howson (2,759 metres high), in the Rocky Mountains between Terrace and Smithers. The Club was shocked. John Wheeler, grandson of its founder, admired RG: "[He] was one of the most outstanding Canadian mountaineers between the wars. He was my mountaineering mentor when I was a youngster, when we made climbs together from 1940 to 1943 inclusive. He was godfather to my eldest daughter, Kathleen. Ethne and Rex lived at 'Bardsey,' the Gale house near Saanichton, from 1948 until 1957. After Rex died Ethne moved to a house on Radcliffe Lane in Victoria, where she spent the rest of her life." John Wheeler and his wife used to visit RG's widow and daughter, Ethne and Kathleen Gibson, at 659 Radcliffe Lane, but when Ethne died on 11 May 1997, she was buried at St Stephen's Church, on the West Saanich Road near "Bardsey."

Sources: Interviews and correspondence with John Wheeler, esp. his letter to the author, 10 July 2001; *Canadian Alpine Journal*, vol. 41 (1958), pp. 111-114; *Uprope: Newsletter of the Potomac Apalachian Trail Club, Mountaineering Section*, vol. 4, no 2 (Fall 200), obit. of Donald Hubbard (1900-2000), who was with EG in the fatal mountaineering accident.

GIFFORD, Hon. Maurice Raymond (1859-1910). Organizer of the Imperial Campaigners' Association in Victoria, he was born at Ampney Park, Cirencester, Gloucestershire, fourth son of the Second Baron Gifford and Hon. Frederica, daughter of Baron Fitzhardinge. MG was educated on HMS *Worcester* and HMS *Greenhithe* and was employed in 1876-1882 as an officer in the Mercantile Marine Service. In 1882, he served as "galloper" for Mr G. Lagden, special correspondent for the *Daily Telegraph*, on the Egyptian Campaign, and, in 1885, fought in the Riel Rebellion Campaign, Canada, under General Middleton (medal and clasp).

One of Gifford's three brothers, Lord Gifford, "a leading member of the English Establishment," was deeply involved in business investments in the Bechuanaland Exploring and Exploiting Company along with George Cawston, a company that eventually amalgamated with Cecil Rhodes enterprises in the British South Africa Company. In 1890, MG went out to Africa and, in 1893, served as a scout in Salisbury's Column in the Matabele Campaign (medal), raising and commanding "A" and "B" Troop, "Gifford's Horse," in the Matabele Rebellion of 1896. He was severely wounded, his arm amputated at the shoulder on 6 April, and in that month, the queen made him CMG in recognition of services in Matabeland. Later, he received the Jubilee Decoration, being in command of the Rhodesian Horse in the procession of 22 June 1897. Three months later, he married Marguerite Thorold, eldest daughter of Captain Cecil Thorold of Boothby Hall, Grantham, Lincolnshire; they had a son and three daughters. He joined the Kimberley Mounted Corps in 1900, one-armed as he was, and served on Colonel Mahon's staff at the relief of Mafeking (medal and three clasps).

At sometime in 1907, MG went out to Victoria where, as the *Colonist* reported, "Since arriving in B.C., the Hon Mr Gifford has met a great many old comrades of these wars, and others who served in the same." In that spirit of leadership so strong in many people of his social class and profession, he invited the veterans of the Egyptian War (1882), the North-West Rebellion (1885), the Matabele War (1893), the Matabele War (1896), and the South African War (1899-1902) to meet in Victoria on 8 November 1907. His purpose, as a notice in the *Colonist* declared, was to organize an Imperial veterans' society and interested men were invited to send their names and addresses to A. J. Goward, BC Electric Railway Co. Ltd., Victoria. "The Committee in charge of arrangements is providing a little programme and other entertainment." The result was the Imperial Campaigners' Association, which flourished on the Island until supplanted between the wars, like several other early societies of veterans, by the Royal Canadian Legion. MG then retired with his wife to her late father's house, Boothby Hall, Grantham, where he went out hunting and shooting and was to be found at Arthur's Club or Orleans Clubs when in London. He died on 2 July 1910 at the house of a physician in Hoddesdon, Hertfordshire, where his cigarette set fire to "some petrol which he had been using to clean spots from his trousers."

Sources: *Who was Who*, 1897-1916; *Colonist*, 5 November 1907, p. 6; *The Times* (London), 4 July 1910, p. 9, col. E, obit.; John S. Galbraith, "*Origins of the British South Africa Company*," in *Perspectives of Empire: Essays Presented to Gerald S. Graham*, ed., John E. Flint and Glyndwr Williams (Longman; NY, Barnes & Noble, 1973), pp. 150-169; Antony Thomas, *Rhodes* (BBC Books, 1996), pp. 190, 208.

GLOSSOP, Major Francis Edward (1866-1931). He was born in Twickenham, Middlesex, son of Rev. George G. P. Glossop (born c. 1828 at Isleworth) of "Amyand House," vicar of Twickenham, and his wife Eliza M. Glossop, who in 1871 were living there with five children and six servants. As a young man, he took a commission in the Leicestershire Regiment and had a long career in the British Army in the Burma campaign, in which he was wounded, in the South African War, and in the

Great War. During the latter, he was on staff in England as an expert in musketry. After the war, he returned to the Okanagan Valley, BC, where he had first gone about 1911 with his wife, Ellen Sabine Glossop, but about 1928, they moved to Mill Bay, Vancouver Island, where he was active in St John's Anglican Church, Cobble Hill, and served as a representative at the Synod meeting in 1929. He was buried at that church, his coffin draped with the Union Jack, when he died in December 1931. Among the pallbearers were four other officers: *Captain C. G. D. Sprot, *Captain A. D. Welstead, *Captain J. N. Hughes, and Captain A. B. James.

The Glossops were a substantial middling family of Twickenham and Isleworth, adjoining villages in Middlesex, west of London across the Thames from Kew Gardens, on an estate held by descendants of Charles I and in the hands of the Dukes of Northumberland during FG's childhood. At "Silver Hall," Isleworth, FG had a cousin, Walter Herbert Newland Glossop (1864-1918), whose father, Francis H. N. Glossop (born c. 1816), was a JP and "barrister not in practice." The names of the dwellings in which the two cousins grew up have survived on the map in Silver Street, Isleworth, and Amyand Park, Twickenham. WHNG emigrated in 1905 to the Okanagan Valley, where he bought fifteen acres in the Long Lake Subdivision, and in 1906 became a director of the Kettle Valley Irrigated Fruit Lands Company, which promoted the sale of three thousand acres of land between Midway and Rock Creek. He was there to welcome his cousin FEG a few years later. When WHNG enlisted on 21 April 1916 as a major in the 225th Bn., CEF, he gave his address as "Kettle Valley." Before 1905, he had survived for six years in the Suffolk Regiment, mainly in India, but he was killed in France, aged fifty-three, on 1 April 1918. He was survived by the wife he had married at Rock Creek on 1 December 1913, Margaret Harriet *née* Stirling, and a son, Francis Walter Andrew Glossop, who was killed, aged twenty-eight, serving with the Queen's Own Cameron Highlanders of Canada near the end of the Second World War on 30 March 1945, leaving his widowed mother and his wife, Beatrice Glossop.

Sources: census 1871, England, RG 10/1315, p. 45; census 1871, RG 10/1312; *Colonist*, 5 June 1929, p. 18; 13 December 1931, p. 24, obit; NAC, CEF files, box 3589-13; *Cowichan Leader*, 17 December 1931, obit.; Margaret A. Ormsby, *Coldstream—Nulli Secundus* (Vernon, Corporation of the District of Coldstream, 1990), p. 35; *Whitaker's*, p. 210.

GODFREY, Commodore Valentine Stuart (1898-1968). He was born on 14 August 1898 in Wandsworth, Surrey, a suburb of London, son of Emmeline Godfrey (*née* Stuart), born in Ireland, and Ernest H. Godfrey, born in Northampton, whom the 1901 census recorded as "Secretary to the Central Chamber of Agriculture." VG was then eight years old, had a sister Eveline M. Godfrey aged four, and they lived with one servant at 38a Earlsfield Road in Wandsworth. He attended prep school at Bedford, but came to Canada with his parents in 1908 and attended Ashbury College Ottawa, and the Royal Naval College of Canada at Halifax in 1913-1916. During the Great War, he joined the RN and served in aboard HMS *Cumberland* (1915-1916) and HMS *Benbow* (1927), being promoted to lieutenant (1920) and lieutenant commander (1927). In that year, he transferred to the RCN in which he rose to acting commodore (1937), captain (1943), and commodore (1947). In 1932-1934, he commanded the destroyer HMCS *Champlain* and, between 1925 and 1941, was inspector of naval ordnance in Halifax. During the Second World War, he commanded HMCS *Prince David* (1941-1942), was chief of staff to naval member at Washington DC (May 1943), and duties of naval member to end of that year, and, in June 1944, commanded HMCS *Prince Henry* and the landing ships of the first group "J" force while they landed in Normandy and went on to southern France. He fought in Greece, was twice mentioned in despatches, became chief of staff to the CO on the Pacific Coast (1945-1947), naval member, Canadian Joint Staff, Washington (1947-1949), and commodore, Newfoundland, 1949-1952, and was awarded the OBE. He enjoyed fishing, shooting, golf, and membership in the Army and Navy Club. His home was at 1004 Terrace Avenue, Victoria. He died an Anglican, aged sixty-nine, on 25 April 1968 in Victoria.

Sources: *Canadian Who's Who,* 1958-1960, p. 424; census 1901, England, RG 13/486, p. 18.

GOOD, Captain Henry Berkeley (1830-1887). Born on 27 September 1830 at Hockerton, Nottinghamshire, son of Rev. H. Good, vicar of Winbourne Minster, he joined the Canadian Rifles in 1850, became a lieutenant in 1852, and was sent to Calcutta. In 1857, he returned to England on two years' leave, but was immediately recalled for the Indian Mutiny as adjutant of Kuroachee Depot. In 1861, he was sent with the Seventieth Regiment to New Zealand, where he stayed until 1863, when he was ordered home and honoured with a promotion to captain without purchase. In 1864, he exchanged into the First Battalion of the Twenty-fourth Regiment.

In 1858, he married Eliza Lambert, daughter of John Lambert, Esq., of St Finnan's County, Galway. In 1866, they moved out to Victoria, where he was employed by the Inland Revenue Department and where, as *The Daily British Colonist* put it at his death, "his genial manner has made him universally liked and respected till now bidden to answer the roll call which none shall gainsay or resist." At his death in Victoria, aged fifty-seven, on 10 May 1887, he left his wife, three sons, and four daughters.

Sources: *Colonist,* 11 May 1887, p. 4, obit.; R. E. Gosnell (1860-1921), *The Year Book,* p. 41.

GOODE, Lieutenant Colonel Stuart (1869-1964). Born in England, he was first commissioned on 24 April 1889 and had regimental rank on 10 December 1890 in the Bedfordshire Regiment, which sailed to India from Malta, arriving at Rawalpindi in 1891. In the next thirteen years, he served with the Isazai Expedition in 1892, with the Chitral Relief Force under Sir Robert Low in 1895, and with the First Battalion of the Bedfordshire Regiment, including the storming of the Malakand Pass and an engagement near Khar (medal with clasp). On 22 November 1890, he became a lieutenant and on 25 June 1898 a captain. In 1900, he was noted as a captain in the First Bedfordshire stationed at Mooltan, India. After many years in India, he retired with the rank of lieutenant colonel to

Victoria, where he lived for many more years at 1230 Belmont Avenue until his death, aged ninety-four, on 19 November 1964. Among his friends was Colonel G. B. Scott, whose daughter recalls that SG used to walk out to visit them at their place in Royal Oak.

Sources: Notes, documents, and letter kindly sent by Mrs Morgan Scott-Ostler; *Indian Army List*, July 1891, p. 219; *Hart's Annual Army Register*, 1902, pp. 251 and 251b; *Whitaker's*, p. 212; *Colonist*, 21 November 1964, p. 22, obit.

GOODLAND, Colonel Herbert Tom, CD, DSO (1874-1956). Retiring in 1928 from the Imperial War Graves Commission and previous service as an officer in the Royal Berkshires, the Tenth and Sixteenth Irish Divisions, and the Royal Munster Fusiliers, he settled in Victoria as deputy sergeant at arms in the provincial legislature and was soon well known in many circles on the Island. He was an active Freemason, joined the Rotary Club and the Pro Patria Branch of the Canadian Legion, and became president of the Canadian Club and the United Services Institution. In October 1929, he gave an illustrated lecture to the Society of St George on "The War Graves of the British Empire (France and Belgium)" and repeated it in Duncan on 30 April 1930. On Saturday, 7 November 1931, he was in charge of the street sale of Remembrance Day poppies in Victoria and spoke to various groups on the subject. His first wife, Ethel Haill *née* Hawkins (1877-1930), having died in Oak Bay, where they lived at "Westways" in the Uplands Estate, he married Marjorie Kathleen Ryall on 16 June 1931 at St Luke's Anglican Church in Cedar Hill district, the church he attended regularly. They had a honeymoon in Banff, Alberta, and, on 23 February 1933, were "noticed" at tea at the Empress Hotel by the *Daily Colonist*. They were guests at Government House on 2 May 1933 at a dinner for a visiting historian from England, Philip Guedalla. In 1933, HG was chairman of the Victoria branch of the Council of Education, which had been founded and directed in Winnipeg by *Major Frederick John James Ney, and he chaired the January meeting at which the Marquess of Zetland spoke about Lord Curzon and his achievements in India. In 1936, he and his wife spent several months in England and he went with other Great War veterans to the unveiling of the Vimy Memorial in France. On 12 February 1943, Goodland gave an address, "Silent Cities of the Empire," to the United Service Institution at its annual dinner at Prince Rupert House, Victoria; in this, he was assisted by *Major Frederick Victor Longstaff, who showed slides of military cemeteries overseas (the "silent cities"). It was on the Saanich side of suburban Victoria that HG died, aged eighty-one, on 13 August 1956, but I could find no reference to the second Mrs Goodland's death.

HG was born in Taunton, Somerset, third son of a Taunton coal merchant, Charles J. Goodland, and his wife Kate, who was born in Canada at Montreal. They appear in the 1881 census living at 30 Bridge Street, HG aged six, his parents aged thirty-five and thirty-four, his four brothers aged ten, eight, four, and two, and a sister aged three. There were two domestic servants. Ten years later, HG was a boarder, aged sixteen, at Hart House School in Tregony, Cornwall, but the following year, he emigrated to Canada and worked on farms in Manitoba and in

BC at Chilliwack on the coastal mainland, where in 1908, he became the manager of the Chilliwack Canning and Preserving Company and, by 1912, was an alderman of the town. Two years earlier, he had helped to form Chilliwack's "D" Company of the 104th Regiment and he soon enlisted in Alberta in the 101st Regiment of Edmonton Fusiliers. He happened to be in England when Britain declared war on Germany (8 August 1914) and immediately enlisted the Royal Munster Fusiliers, affiliated with his two Canadian units, and was put into its Sixth Battalion then stationed in Ireland at Curragh, which did not offend his Freemason's instincts. Among his war decorations were the DSO, the White Eagle of Serbia and the French *Médaille de la Reconnaissance.*

His file at the War Office, fortunately one of those still intact after the destruction of many others in German bombing raids, shows details of his war service ending with his appointment to the Imperial War Graves Commission on 1 September 1919 with the rank of colonel. He soon became the commission's deputy controller and, as such, spent thirteen years in charge of constructing British and Imperial war cemeteries and memorials. One of the most interesting tasks in those years was to guide and assist Rudyard Kipling and his wife in their anxious search for their sons' fate on the battlefield of Loos during the war, and HG became a good friend of the Kiplings. When Kipling died early in 1936, HG wrote an obituary "Appreciation," which the *Daily Colonist* printed in its Sunday supplement on 19 January (p. 17). There followed a close association between the Kipling Society in Victoria, which promptly invited HG to speak to them about his friend and their hero. But HG had wide interests and sympathies. He also wrote for the *Colonist* an article about the "Columbia Coast Medical Mission," which the *Colonist* published on 7 February 1937. When pressed to name his recreations, he mentioned motoring and golf, but they rarely diverted his attention from public causes. On the Imperial War Graves Commission, he had struggled to impose a certain equality of memorials, preventing the wealthy from building monuments that would overshadow the humble gravestones of the poor.

Sources: *Colonist*, 26 September 1929, p. 5; 27 December 1930, p. 7; 1 May 1931, p. 7; 17 June 1931, p. 8; 25 October 1931, p. 5; 17 January 1933, p. 2; 15 March 1933, p. 6; 3 May 1933, p. 8; 24 February 1933, p. 2; 28 January 1936, p. 5; 19 June 1936, p. 2; 20 November 1936, p. 8 with photo; 7 February 1937, p. 5; 7 June 1939, p. 4; 31 January 1940, p. 2; 3 April 1941, p. 11; 13 February 1943, p. 5; BNA (formerly PRO) at Kew, WO 339/10632; *Who was Who*, vol. 5 (1951-1960), p. 433; census 1881, England, RG 11/2368, p. 4; census 1891, RG 12/1826, p. 1; David Gilmour, *The Long Recessional: The Imperial Life of Rudyard Kipling* (New York, Farrar, Straus and Giroux, 2002), pp. 279-282; Chilliwack, BC, War Memorial online; J. F. Bosher, "*Vancouver Island and the Kiplings,*" *The Kipling Journal* (London), vol. 83, no. 332 (June 2009), pp. 8-22.

GOODWIN, Frank (1857-1934). Born on 5 November 1857 in Mereworth, Kent, he was living there at "Smartswell" in 1871 with his widowed mother Louisa Goodwin, "Landowner and Farmer," aged thirty-nine, born in Margate, Kent, his older brother Sidney H. Goodwin, aged seventeen, and his four sisters:

Emma L. Goodwin, aged fifteen, Ada Goodwin, aged eleven, Annie Goodwin, aged ten, and Florence Goodwin, aged seven, all born at Mereworth. They had a governess and a general servant. Census records show his brother in 1881 as heir to the family farm of sixty acres, employing nine men and a boy, growing hops and fruits in 1891, but away at Ramsay, Huntingdonshire, in 1901, he employed a farm manager and potato merchant with a wife, three children, and a domestic servant.

As the younger son, FG went to South Africa in 1876 with the Union Steamship Company and served with a Capetown unit in the Basuto campaign in 1880-1881 (medal and bar). Two years, later he returned to England but soon went out to Canada "in search of adventure." He enlisted in the RCNWM Police and served in the Riel Rebellion Campaign (1885). Invalided out of that force, he worked for the CPR until 1893 and took up farming and government service in Swift Current and Lethbridge, North-West Territories, until he retired in November 1924 and soon went out to Victoria. There, he was known as a Freemason and a member of the Army and Navy Veterans. When he died, aged seventy-six, on 11 October 1934, he had been staying at the Ritz Hotel, Fort Street, Victoria, and was survived by his widow and family in the East.

Sources: *Colonist,* 12 October 1934, p. 6, obit.; census 1871, England, RG 10/918, p. 13; census 1881, RG 11/902, p. 9; census 1891, RG 12/670, p. 21; census 1901, RG 13/1470, p. 10.

GOOLDEN, Commander Massey (c. 1888-1971). He was born in Paddington, London, where the 1891 census recorded him, aged three, living at 11 Southwick Place, St John's Parish, South Paddington, with his father Edwin R. Goolden, "solicitor," aged forty, and his mother, Eva Sophia Goolden, aged thirty, from Chudleigh in Devon. MG had an elder sister and was the second of four sons, all born in London except Francis Hugh W. Goolden, aged five, born at Sandown on the Isle of Wight. There were four servants. Ten years later, MG, aged thirteen, was living as a student at Bradfield Gollege in Berkshire, directed by Rev. Herbert Branston Gray. He joined the Royal Navy on 15 April 1907, attended a naval college in 1908, and was promoted to lieutenant on 31 December 1909. Thereafter, he was posted to HMS *Dominion* (1911), to *Prince of Wales* (1914), and, on loan, to the RCN, acting as CO at Stadacona and as senior naval officer at Halifax (1925). He retired with the rank of captain in the RN but was recalled for service in the Second World War and had a career leading to naval officer in charge at Esquimalt (1942). He reverted to the RN retired list on 1 March 1944 and was then appointed to the RN service at Washington DC and retired with the Distinguished Service Cross. Reflections in his diary in January 1944 suggest that he may have determined to remain in the Royal Navy because of trouble he had witnessed in the Royal Canadian Navy: "No two senior officers trust each other; they are always striving to get ahead of each other, they have less loyalty amongst themselves than they have from us [British officers]; if only they could see that and not be always under the impression that we want to usurp their jobs. The 'Nelles' episode brings some of this out into the open. The minister (a veritable politician) has too much power and the [Naval] Board does not really function as such . . . Everything is done below board and not above." The "Nelles episode," which he referred to, was the cunning and politically motivated replacement of Vice Admiral Percy W. Nelles by Vice Admiral George C. Jones. After retiring from the navy, MG settled in Victoria, and when he died in Saanich, aged eighty-three, on 8 July 1971 and was buried in a service at St Paul's Esquimalt, he left his wife Alix, two daughters, and a stepdaughter.

Sources: *MacFarlane*, p. 25; *Colonist*, 10 July 1971, p. 26, obit.; census England, 1891, RG 12/14, p. 10; census 1901, RG 13/1141, p. 6; Lieut. Richard Oliver Mayne, *"Keeping up with the Jones's: Admiralship, Culture, and Careerism in the Royal Canadian Navy,* 1911-1936," (Internet, Canadian Forces Leadership Institute, Queen's University, September 2002), pp. 27, 30-2.

GORDON, Captain James Urquhart (c. 1866-1941). Born in Aberdeen, Scotland, he appears, aged four, in the Scottish census of 1871, the fourth of five children living with their mother at 10 Old Machar, Aberdeen. He went to sea, rose to be a ship's captain, and "sailed the seven seas for forty years before coming to Victoria ten years ago to make his home," according to the *Daily Colonist* in November 1941. He lived at the Bessborough Apartments and was a Freemason and, from 1931, an active member of the China-Japan Society. He was elected to the executive of the Red Cross in Victoria in February 1935 at the same meeting, which elected *Sir Richard Lake as its president. When JG died, aged seventy-five, on 10 November 1941, the Freemasons took charge of his funeral. He left only a niece in Scotland.

Sources: *Colonist*, 23 February 1935, p. 6; 13 November 1941, p. 5, obit.; census 1871, Scotland, Roll CSSCT 1871-35, Old Machar, Aberdeen.

GORE-LANGTON family. At least six men from various branches of this remarkable old West-country clan went out to the Island and several died there. Many branches of the Gore and Langton families went on living separate lives, but the combined branches of the two families formed themselves in 1783 when a Colonel William Gore (1760-1847), son of Edward Gore and Barbara Browne, married a Bridget Langton, daughter of Joseph Langton, and the children they had at "Park House, Newton Park, in Somerset, a few miles west of Bath, took the name Gore-Langton, probably for the usual reason that the Langtons made a transfer or inheritance of property contingent on preservation of the family name. One of the sons Colonel Gore had, by his second wife, Mary Browne, also took the name Gore-Langton. This was William Henry Gore-Langton (1802-1875), two of whose grandsons emigrated to the Island: Gerald Wentworth Gore-Langton (c. 1885-1937) and Montague Vernon Gore-Langton (c. 1887-1915), who grew up together mainly at "Padbury Lodge," a manor house on a Buckinghamshire estate where the census of 1891 recorded them as boys with their family and nine domestic servants. Their elder brother inheriting the estate, these two went out to the Island to make their way and settled in the Cowichan Valley before the Great War. Both returned to England early in the war to serve as lieutenants: Gerald Wentworth Gore-Langton in the Thirteenth/Eighteenth Hussars in which he was soon awarded the MC and the *Légion d'honneur* for distinguished service in the field and later (1919) the DSO and Montague Vernon Gore-Langton, who was decorated for gallantry on 10 August 1915 at Cuinchy, France, in the First Battalion, Irish Guards, and was killed in action the following November. The surviving brother, Gerald Wentworth Gore-Langton, did not return to Canada either but, in 1925, married Geraldine Isobel Nicholas, *née* Glazebrook, widow of Captain J. R. Nicholas and younger daughter of W. Glazebrook. Gerald Wentworth Gore-Langton retired in 1927 to his wife's house, "The Lowe," Wellesbourne, Warwickshire, where he died on 22 May 1937.

Three of their distant cousins, however, brothers who descended four generations from Colonel William Gore's first marriage, followed a similar course and did return to the Island after the Great War. These were Robert Lancelot Gore-Langton (1885-1948), Captain Norman Eric Gore-Langton (1886-1970), and Richard Gerald Gore-Langton (1892-1978), all of whom married and lived out their retired lives on the Island. As young men, they were among the officers attending the Shawnigan Farmer's Institute when it met at Cobble Hill on 25 November 1914 to raise money for the patriotic fund. On 22 December 1914, Robert Lancelot Gore-Langton married Winifreda Lillian Margaret Nixon, daughter of Captain Arthur G. Nixon of the Rifle Brigade, and he was living near Vancouver when he died, aged sixty-two, on 26 January 1948. Captain Norman Eric Gore-Langton married Irene Monica Greaves-Banning (c. 1886-?) from Lynn, Cheshire, daughter of Major Arthur C. Greaves-Banning, at St Peter's Anglican Church, Quamichan, on 18 August 1914, almost two years before joining the 143rd Battalion of the Canadian Expeditionary Force at Victoria on 25 May 1916. He was then enrolled as an officer because he had already served in 1904-1910 as a lieutenant in the Sixth Dragoon Guards of the Imperial Army. His brother Richard Gerald came out before the war and, after serving through the war years in the Royal Navy, married Laura Edith P. Bevan on 2 June 1925. That marriage ended in a divorce, and in 1936, he married Doreen Audrey Davies with whom he brought up four children on a large farm in Saanich, where Gore-Langton Road commemorates the family's presence.

The three brothers cited above were grandsons of William Henry Powell Gore-Langton (1824-1873) and Lady Eliza Mary Grenville (died 1879) of "Hatch House," Hatch Beauchamp, near Taunton in Somerset, where their father, Henry Powell Gore-Langton (1854-1913) was a JP and where they passed most of their childhood. Many an Imperial officer lived in "Hatch House" before and after the Gore-Langtons, not least Brigadier Andrew Hamilton Gault (1882-1958), DSO, EC, CN, a famous Canadian soldier from Montreal, who married the niece of an earlier owner. Gault was a proud Imperialist, who fought in the South African War and founded Princess Patricia's Canadian Light Infantry, the last regiment to be raised in the empire by a private citizen. The Gaults lived on the estate from 1923, after his retirement from the army. In 1931, he bought the property and gave it to his wife. Churchwarden and benefactor of the surrounding communities, he served as Conservative MP for Taunton from 1922 to 1935 and was made a Freeman of the Borough. Memorials to him and to the Gore-Langton owners are prominent among the many that decorate the local church.

At least one other member of the family, Lieutenant Commander Evelyn Arthur Grenville Temple-Gore-Langton (1884-1972), became a citizen of Vancouver Island. Like the three "Hatch House" brothers, he descended four generations from Colonel William Gore's first marriage. A native of Bournemouth, Hampshire, he was the youngest of the eight children of William Stephen Temple-Gore-Langton, Earl Temple (1847-1902), who died at Cairo on 28 March 1902, and his wife, Helen Mabel Montgomery (1854-1919), daughter of Graham Montgomery and Alice Hope-Johnstone. He was brought up at "Park House," Newton St Loe, Somerset, where in 1891, the census found him, aged six, together with his family and their sixteen domestic servants. Coming out to the Island after the Great War in which he served in the Royal Navy, Lieutenant Commander E. A. G. T. Gore-Langton married Irene Maria L. Gartside-Spaight at St Peter's Quamichan near Duncan on 25 April 1922. She was a daughter of Brigadier General Cavendish Walter Gartside-Spaight (1857-?), an Anglo-Irish soldier who lived in the Cowichan Valley for some years after the Great War. Ten years later, E. A. G. T. Gore-Langton was still there and attended the funeral of Colonel John Talbot as a pallbearer at St Peter's Quamichan on 13 April 1932, but he moved away before his own death, as did his wife and father-in-law.
Sources: *Burke's Peerage & Baronetage*, ed., Charles Mosley (106th ed., 1999), vol. II, pp. 560, 2796-99; Victoria City Archives; census 1891, England, RG 12/1155, p. 2; census 1891, RG 12/1944, p. 8; census 1891, RG 12/4372, p. 31; census 1901, RG 13/1367, p. 7; census 1901, RG 13/2274, p. 6; NAC, CEF, RG 150, box 3656-34; *Who was Who*, vol. III, p. 534; *The National Gazetteer of Great Britain and Ireland* (1868); *Colonist*, 29 November 1914, p. 18; 6 October 1915, p. 5; 12 April 1968, p. 24, obit.; 7 May 1970, p. 45, obit.; *Victoria Daily Times*, 4 November 1915, p. 3; David J. Bercusson, *The Patricias: The Proud History of a Fighting Regiment* (Toronto, Stoddart, 2001), pp. 19-24, 33-4, 49, 121-5, 130-5, 141, 236-7, 281-2

GORNALL, Robert William (1875-1932). Born in London (Lambeth, Surrey) in 1875, in 1891 he was a boy of fifteen employed as a groom at Harrow-on-the Hill, where he lived with his family at 4 Crown Street. His mother Matilda Gornall and his father, John R. Gornall, a tailor, were also born at Lambeth, Surrey, and RG had a sister and three younger brothers, one of them a tailor's apprentice.
About 1910, he went out to Victoria and, on 26 May 1916, enlisted in the First O/S/ Canadian Pioneers, having been a sergeant in the Fifth CGA for the previous five years while working as an electrical engineer and living with his wife at 2640 Roseberry Avenue. But there had been military service earlier: the British Imperial Campaigners recorded him on 20 May 1915 as a private in the First Cameron Highlanders, SAC, who had fought in the Nile Campaign, Egypt, in 1898, and in South Africa in 1899-1902, holder of the Queen's and King's medals, the Kedive's medal, and the Egypt medal. On the enlistment form in 1916, regimental number 490676, he gave his birthdate as 13 June 1878, making his age forty-eight years and eleven months, three years younger than in fact he was, either to qualify for the CEF or perhaps, like many others, he could not always remember how old he was. After twenty-two years in Victoria (minus the years of the Great War), he died there on 8 September 1932.

Sources: census 1891, England, RG 12/1039, p. 29; NAC, CEF files, box 3660-18; *Colonist*, 9 September 1932, pp. 3 and 16, obit.

GOSSET, Major General William Driscoll (1822-1899). Printed sources make him out to be a Londoner born on 13 April 1822, but he declared to the census-takers in 1871 and 1881 that he was born in Ireland. Trained as a gentleman cadet at RMC, Woolwich, he was commissioned in the Royal Engineers and sent to make surveys in Ceylon, where in time, he became surveyor general. On his return to England, the colonial secretary, Sir Edward Bulwer Lytton, sent him and his wife, Helen Dorothea Gosset (born in Datchet, Buckinghamshire), to serve as colonial treasurer in British Columbia, where they arrived on Christmas Day 1858. He was expected to perform other duties in that small expanding colony, such as postmaster from 13 June 1859, but was heartily disliked by some of his contemporaries, such as the prominent merchant Robert Burnaby (1828-1878). WG was inclined to insist on administrative standards he had known elsewhere, soon quarrelled with Governor James Douglas, and so in September 1862, they returned to England, ostensibly on sick leave. There, they remained and his career prospered. He became a fellow of the Royal Society of Edinburgh and, by 1871, was living at "Mill Hill House," Woolwich, (St John's Parish), as colonel in command of the Royal Engineers at the Royal Military College.

The birthplaces of their children, as recorded in 1871, marked some of their geographical movements: Ernest aged thirteen, born at Colombo, Ceylon; Percy aged ten, born in Middlesex; and Helen aged seven and Lilian five, both born at Stoke, Devonshire. Gosset's niece, Mary Gossett, aged twenty-six, came from Northam, Devonshire. They had eight servants, including a "soldier pensioner" working as groom. Ten years later, the census-taker found him at "Sandfields," Mortlake, Surrey—where many Anglo-Irish families went—living as a retired major general with his son Percy, "undergraduate at Oxford," and three daughters, including Maria, aged twenty-two, born on Vancouver Island, perhaps away at school when the census was taken in 1871. His wife had died, aged forty-nine, in Kensington, London, in June 1879, and it was not far away, in Fulham, that he died, aged seventy-seven, in June 1899.

Sources: census 1871, England, RG 10/785; census 1881, England, RG 11/846; Victoria Numismatic Society, publications and Internet files; John Adams, *Old Square-Toes and His Lady* (Victoria, Horsdahl & Schubart, 2001), p. 133; Margaret A. Ormsby, *British Columbia: A History* (Toronto, Macmillan, 1958), pp. 157, 172, 177; Alfred Stanley Deaville, *The Colonial Postal Systems and Postage Stamps of Vancouver Island and British Columbia, 1849-1871* (Victoria, C. F. Banfield, King's Printer, 1928), pp. 56-181 passim.

GOW, Commander Francis Robert Williams Roberts "Peter" (c. 1899-1942). Born in Halifax, Nova Scotia, he enrolled in 1914 as a cadet at the Royal Naval College of Canada, and his career developed rapidly, as might be expected during the Great War. He became a midshipman on 2 February 1917, a sub-lieutenant on 1 February 1917, was at Naden in Esquimalt as district intelligence officer in 1923, and staff officer to the senior naval officer RCN at HMCS *Stadacona* in 1931 and died aged forty-three on 8 November 1942 on service at sea in an aircraft crash. He had served aboard HMS *Leviathan* (1917), HMS *Carnarvon* (1917), *Roxborough* (1917), *Minotaur* (1917), *Ramillies* (1918), *Patrician* (1926), HMS *Queen Elizabeth* (1927), HMS *Champion* (1928) and *Venture* (1942). At Greenwich, London, he had married Jean Middleton Gow (1903-2005) early in August 1929.

Born at Aldershot, Berkshire, daughter of *Dr Colonel David Donald and his wife, she had been taken out to Esquimalt, where her father was posted, and spent her early years at the Dockyard and around the naval station generally. In the course of her life, she became an illustrator, librarian, researcher, and writer for the CBC and an accomplished author. In 1930, a few months after their marriage, she and FG sailed from Southampton in SS *Calgaric*, together with her brother, *Captain Colin Degge Donald, born at Chemainus on the Island. The two men were then aged thirty, and Jean was twenty-seven. When I began research for this book, she was living, aged nearly one hundred, in a retirement home in the New Edinburgh district of Ottawa, where I telephoned to ask about her father's relationship with *Sir Charles Delmé-Radcliffe, both having served the empire in Uganda at about the same time and reached Victoria in the 1930s. She died, aged 102.
Sources: *Toronto Globe & Mail*, 9 November 2005, p. R15, obit.; *Victoria Daily Times* 23 August 1929, p. 6; *MacFarlane*, p. 25; Canadian Passenger Lists, 1865-1935, T-14762; NAC, DND, Virtual Cemetry online.

GRANT, Captain Walter Colquhoun (1822-1861). Born in Edinburgh to a military family, he heard in 1848, while at RMA, Sandhurst, that Vancouver Island was to be granted to the Hudson's Bay Company. When financial losses forced him to give up his officer's career, he bought land in the new colony and became the first independent settler there.

Landing at Victoria on 11 August 1849, he set about founding a settlement at Sooke, twenty-five miles to the northwest. He stayed for only about four years and three months because he was short of funds, not very experienced or committed, and ultimately daunted—like many others before and since—by the many tasks of pioneering life, even in that benign climate. Nor was he always on good terms with the governor, the local tribes, and others he had to deal with. He is remembered with sympathy for importing the yellow Scottish broom, which now brightens many parts of southern Vancouver Island and for his somewhat erratic efforts to establish himself in the wilderness. Upon returning to England, he joined the army on 30 November 1855 as a cornet and, from 29 March 1859, held the rank of captain in the Queen's Regiment of Dragoon Guards. He served during the Crimean War as lieutenant colonel of a Turkish cavalry unit and, when he died some years later, aged thirty-nine, was brigade major at Lucknow in central India, still thinking of returning to the Island but only in some official capacity.
Sources: Army List, 1860-1861, p. 228; Army List, 1857-1858, p. 197; Barry M. Gough, "Grant, Walter Colquhoun, soldier and settler," *Dictionary of Canadian Biography* Online; Willard E. Ireland, "*Capt. Walter Colquhoun Grant, Vancouver Island's First Independent Settler*," *B.C.H.Q.*, vol. 18 (January-April 1953), pp. 87-125;

Fort Victoria Letters, 1846-1851, Hartwell Bowfield (Winnipeg, Hudson's Bay Record Society, 1979), see index entry, p. 262.

GRAY, John Frederick (1864-1939). Born somewhere between Sheffield and Chesterfield, Derbyshire, he joined the British Army and was [Lord] Robert Baden-Powell's batman during the tribal uprisings in Afghanistan in 1880-1881. They marched with the Thirteenth Hussars all the way to Lucknow, India, which took a year and eight months. He served through the Great War and retired in 1919 to 802 Blanshard Street, Victoria, where he was delighted to meet his former officer, Lord Baden-Powell, during one of his visits to the Island. After twenty years, JG died and the Anglican Church, of which he was a member, buried him in the family plot at Ross Bay Cemetery.
Sources: *Colonist,* 23 May 1937, p. 5; 5 November 1939, p. 3, obit.

GRAY, John Herbert (c. 1878-1965). Declaring himself born on 10 December 1880 at Jonchard [Jorhat?], Assam, India, and living as a farmer with his wife "Gladys R. Kfrax" at "Courland," Crescent Road, Tove Bay, Victoria [now called Gonzales Bay], JG was an Anglican who signed on to the 143rd Battalion, CEF, as a lieutenant on 23 May 1916. He was already a militia member of it and had some years of experience in the (1) Artists Rifles (2) the East Kent Yeomanry in South Africa and (3) the Northumberland Yeomanry in which he had served in three wars.

Jorhat, in upper Assam, is near Sibsagar, a few miles south of the Brahmaputra River and not far northwest of Burma. In the twentieth century, the district has been busy with tea plantations and their study and development, but Murray's *Handbook, India, Burma & Ceylon* (1924) for tourists said almost nothing about Assam and offered not even a map of it. JG returned from the Great War, and after about fifty years' residence near Victoria, he died, aged eighty-seven, at 3409 West Saanich Road.
Sources: NAC, CEF files, box 3757-47; *Colonist,* 29 July 1965, p. 31, obit.

GRAY-DONALD, Lieutenant Colonel George (1855-1927). Born in Scotland at Kincardine-on-Forth on 14 April 1855, son of Thomas Donald (1823-1882), a shipwright, and his wife Euphemia Gray (1827-95), GG became an engineer and led an adventurous life in many parts of the world. By the time he reached Victoria, where he spent the five years (1910-1915), he had worked and fought in India, China, Hong Kong, Egypt, Greece, and elsewhere, and with a gift for languages, he spoke, Arabic, Turkish, and several European languages. He and his family first reached Canada on SS *Lake Manitoba,* arriving at St John, NB, in 1906 and going on the a quarter-section of land near Calgary, where they tried to ranch in the years 1906-1910. He had married Adelaide Mary Redford (1865-1944) on 7 January 1890 at St Peter's Church, Tynemouth, Northumberland, and they had three children, Nigel Gray-Donald (1891-1918), Erceldoune Gray-Donald (1900-1993), and Uarda Gray-Donald, a daughter born about 1900 or 1901. The family recalls that he joined the

CEF, transferred to the Royal Engineers, and never returned to Victoria. His family left, too, but one son, Erceldoune, settled eventually in Montreal, so founding the Canadian branch of the family. GG is included here because of his leading role in the local squadron of the Legion of Frontiersmen. In 1912, he was living at "Caraigellachie," 2315 Bowker Avenue, Victoria, and the Legion's organizing secretary, J. W. Fairlie, at 409 Belmont House, reported, *inter alia*, "Mr Gray-Donald is accustomed to command, having been in charge of the Transportation Department in the Sudan, and also his connection with us gives us a desirable prestige in the city . . . We have had weekly parades from the first meeting, which have consisted of foot drills, mounted drills, and lectures, the men showing great interest. E. Gray Donald was elected Trumpeter, he having travelled over China to England and out to Victoria, and, although a boy, is a true 'frontiersman' who rides splendidly." Two years later, on 31 March 1914, local newspapers reported that the Executive Committee was looking for new members, inviting interested men to join by getting in touch with GG, the Victoria commander, at sub-unit headquarters, 409 Belmont House. There was to be a mounted parade in the Horse Show Building, Victoria, at 8:00 p.m. on a Friday in April 1914. "Members requiring mounts, please notify the secretary on or before 1 April. Uniforms can now be ordered from F.G. Gowan, Government Street, Regimental tailor. [signed] G. Gray Donald, Commander." In July, the *Daily Colonist* reported that the Legion of Frontiersmen "has now a membership all over the world of 10,000, all of whom are registered in London." Six of them led by GG acted as scouts for two detachments of the Fiftieth Highlanders in competitive manoeuvres on 1 July that year. GG remained in the British Army after the Great War and died at last in action, on 21 December 1927 at the Mount of Olives in Palestine. His wife died in June 1944 at Quebec City, not far from her son Erceldoune in Montreal.

Sources: Erceldoune Donald Gray-Donald (1900-?), "*Notes Biographical, Historical and Reminiscent*," (1990), typescript in the Gray-Donald family collection, kindly lent to me by a grandson Trent Gray-Donald (Ottawa) in December 2008; Canadian Passenger Lists 1865-1935, T-507, arriving 23 March 1906; *British Army List*, Nov. 1916, p. 808d; *BC Archives*, MS-0677 (Longstaff Papers), vol. 410, file 391; *Colonist*, 28 March 1962, pp. 11 and 16, obit.; *Colonist*, 31 March 1914, p. 2; *Colonist*, 14 April 1914, p. 12; *Colonist*, 3 July 1914, p. 7.

GREEN, William Saunders Sebright (1830-1906). He lived in Victoria as a solicitor during the 1860s. Though his identity is difficult to establish, the forename "Sebright" appearing only later, WG was born at Buckden, a small village in the St Neots district of Huntingdonshire (part of Cambridgeshire since 1974), son of Frances Green (c. 1810-?) and her husband John George Green (1788-?). In census records for 1851, WG's father appears as a fifty-year-old widower living at Buckden in the High Street, "Captain Army, Gentleman Usher to the Queen & in the Commission of the Peace, Farmer of 170 acres [employing] 4 Labourers." By 1851, WG, still only William S. Green aged twenty-one, had an elder brother, Francis Green, aged twenty-eight, born at Christchurch, Hampshire, and two sisters, Margaret Green, aged thirty-one, born in Dublin, and Frances C. Green, twenty-four, born at Buckden. There were three domestic servants and three "visitors": Eliza and Sophia Price, aged twenty-six and twenty-four, born at Gloucester, and Francis Sace, nineteen, a "farm pupil," born at Ingthorpe, Yorkshire.

By March 1859, when WG was married at Bishopton by Rev. W. Cassidy, vicar of Grindon, assisted by Rev. G. Green, vicar of Bishop Auckland, he was reported as "W. S. Sebright, 4th son of Captain Green of Buckden, Huntingdonshire, Esq., Stockton-upon-Tees." The name "Sebright-Green" was established by the time WG died, when BMD (UK) cited the name in its hyphenated form. However, WG was no longer at Buckden in 1861, when census records showed the rest of the family much as in 1851, though his brother Frank Green, aged thirty-eight, born at Harpit, Hampshire, was "landowner & farming own land 150 acres" along with his son (WG's nephew), John G. Green, aged five, born at Wentworth, Surrey. With them was their paternal aunt, Margaret Maltby, seventy-six, a "Gentlewoman Fundholder" born in Buckden. There were four domestic servants. WG's father was still there in 1881, aged ninety-two, but the next British census in which WG himself appeared was in 1901. He was then living as a solicitor at 42 Grove End Road, St Marylebone, London, with his wife, Matilda J. Green, aged forty-five and born in Cheltenham. With them, there were two stepsons: Frances K. S. Hosali, "Daughter of M. J. Green," aged twenty-three, born in St Marylebone; and Kina M. Hosali, aged two, ditto. They had one servant.

WG and his wife went out to Victoria at sometime in the early 1860s, and he worked there as a solicitor for some ten or twelve years, in partnership with Elisha Oscar Crosby and George Pearkes. Had there been some sort of family trouble over his marriage? The terminal dates of his time on the Island are vague, but signs of his activity are unmistakable. When in April 1866 Henry Norton Tooby from Gloucester cut his own throat fatally with a razor, WG was one of the chief mourners at the funeral at Christ Church Cathedral. On 9 February 1869, his wife gave birth to a daughter. In 1870, he reported for the government in a publication printed in Victoria, *Debate on the Subject of Confederation with Canada* (Victoria, 1870, legislative council). More satisfying is his own recollection in his contribution to a volume entitled *British America,* published in 1900 by the London publisher, Kegan Paul, Trench, Trübner & Co. WG cited as "W. S. Sebright Green, F.R.C.I., F.R.S.I. (*late of British Columbia*)": "In my humble opinion there was no pleasanter society to be found in any part of the British Empire than we had in Victoria in the sixties. We had always ships of her Majesty's Navy at Esquimalt, and as the flagship of the admiral in the Pacific was always stationed at Esquimalt during a portion of every year, we had the advantage of a number of naval officers to assist us in our various sports and entertainments. A number of retired army officers were settled in our midst; a baronet carried on a dairy and garden farm, and his lady might be seen carrying her butter and eggs to market any day. There was no formality, no conventionality, but geniality, friendliness, and equality were the characteristics of our society."

WG had become a member of the Royal Colonial Institute. As such, he wrote a long letter to the editor of *The Times* in September 1895, about colonization, with much mention of Australia as a gold colony and a proposal to found a colonization society to assist emigrant settlers. In the same year, he published a fourteen-page pamphlet, *Colonization and Expansion of the Empire* (1895), and he read a paper to the RCI on 26 November 1895 entitled, "Why Should Not the Law Students have a classified examination?" WG's first wife must have died at sometime in the 1890s, as he married again in 1901 in London at St George's Hanover Square. He died at last in 1906 at his home in the Paddington quarter of London's west end.

WG's nephew, John George Green (junior) and his wife Florence Mary, who had carried on the Buckden estate and then moved to St Mark's Lodge, Cambridge, had two of their sons killed in the Great War: Lieutenant Alan Edward Green, who died on 13 October 1915 somewhere near Loos. And Captain John Leslie Green, VC, of the RAMC, Fifth Battalion Sherwood Foresters (Notts & Derby Reg't), who was killed on 1 July 1916, aged twenty-six.

Sources: Malton Messenger, 9 April 1859 [Internet site by Bab Sanders]; Royal British Legion Internet site, Buckden, Roll of Honour; census 1841, England, HO 107/453/2, p. 31; census 1851, HO 107/1750, /18/89; census 1861, RG 9/981, p. 14; census 1871, RG 10/1524, pp. 18-19; census 1881, RG 11/1611, p. 7; census 1891, RG 12/1242, p. 4; census 1901, RG 13/119, p. 20; census 1901, RG 13/1479, p. 5; WG, *The Times* (London), 13 September 1895, p. 14, L to E; WG, FRCI, FRSI (late of British Columbia), *"British Columbia" in British America* (Kegan Paul, Trench, Trübner & Co. Ltd., 1900), pp. 153-171, see p. 165; WG, *"Why Should Not the Law Students have a classified examination?"* WG published a fourteen-page pamphlet, *Colonzation and Expansion of the Empire* (1895); George Browne and William Saunders Sebright Green, *The practice of the Court for divorce and matrimonial causes; containing the acts of 1857 and 1858, the rules and orders; with practical directions applicable to the conduct of any suit; with an appendix of new precedents, drawn in accordance with the authorized forms* (London: V & R Stevens and G. S. Norton, 1858), 76 p.

GREENHOUSE, Major Frank Stewart (1885-1988). Born on 24 December 1885 at Upton Park, Chester, Cheshire, he was living in 1891 at 24 Poole House, Newton, Chester, with his parents, six brothers and sisters, and two servants. His father, Charles Greenhouse, from Norton, Radnorshire, was then a forty-four-year-old "Bank Manager of [the] North and South Wales Bank, Chester." Ten years later, the census found FG, aged fifteen, living at Mostyn House School, a preparatory school at The Parade, Parksgate, Neston, Cheshire, and on 18 January 1905, after attending the RMA, Sandhurst, he was commissioned in the British Army. Three months later, he was promoted to lieutenant and soon dispatched to India, where he joined the Ninety-fourth Infantry and eventually commanded the Third Division, Southern Army, Staffs, and Troops, Fifth (MHDW), Division at Baroda. In the meantime, his career as an Indian Army officer took him to Afghanistan, Mesopotamia (from 8 December 1916), and Persia (Iran), where he served in the South Persia Rifles organized to protect British oil installations near the Persian

Gulf during the Great War. The Anglo-Persian Oil Company had been formed on 14 April 1909 with an initial capital of £2,000,000 with Lord Strathcona as chairman and William Knox D'Arcy as a director. This was in response to the discovery in the middle of 1908, by D'Arcy and the Burmah Oil Company, of commercial quantities of petroleum at Masjid-i-Sulaiman in Persia, which the Persian government signed over to Britain. Among the issues at stake were supplies of petroleum for fuelling the Royal Navy, which Admiral John Fisher had committed in 1904 to adopting oil-driven engines, and the maintenance of British influence in that south-western zone of Persia, arranged in 1907 with Russia, which claimed control of a northern zone near the southern frontier of its own expanding empire.

After the war, the Anglo-Persian Oil Company hired FG to manage their office at Teheran and there he lived for several years. Late in July 1938, however, he arrived in Victoria and put up at the Old Charming Inn, 1420 Beach Drive, Oak Bay, in order to marry Ruth Elizabeth Phillips at the Garrison Church, Esquimalt. She was a daughter of George Phillips, who lived with his wife and children in Oak Bay and had come out from England in 1894 to take the post of civil manager of the dry dock at Esquimalt. FG identified himself at that time as resident at "Eversley," Lyndhurst, Hampshire, where he and his bride travelled to visit his mother Mary Greenhouse, but Adelaide Ellis gathered later that he had come out to join his brother at Sproat Lake. The Second World War soon broke out and the Greenhouses stayed in England, where he served in the Home Guard, and they had three children. After the war, the family went back to the Island and lived at Mill Bay. He took an active part in community affairs, helped to organize the Community League, and served for a time as its vice-president. They sent their son John to school in England; what became of Andrew is not clear, but Anne died, aged eleven, on 9 October 1957, and Mrs Greenhouse died two years later on 9 November 1959, aged only fifty-two. They had moved by then to Victoria, where FG lived on and became a founding member of St Phillip's Anglican Church. It was there that his funeral was held when he died in 1988, aged almost 103.

Sources: *Indian Army List*, October 1910, pp. 27, 153a, and 399; census 1891, England, RG 12/2867, p. 11; census 1901, RG 13/3381, p. 4; Adelaide Ellis, *Along the Mill Bay Road* (Cobble Hill, Fir Grove Publishing, 1990), p, 37; *Colonist*, 31 July 1938, p. 8; 4 August 1938, p. 8; Sir Arnold Wilson, *Loyalties: Mesopotamia 1917-1920 A Personal and Historical Record* (2 vols., Oxford UP, 1931), vol. II, p. 373; Benjamin Shwadran, *The Middle East, Oil and the Great Powers* (3rd edn., New York, John Wiley & Sons, 1973), pp. 17, 25-28; Antony Wynn, *Persia in the Great Game: Sir Percy Sykes, Explorer, Consul, Spy* (John Murray, 2003), chapter 17, "South Persia Rifles."

GREEN-WILKINSON, Brigadier General Louis [Lewis?] Frederic (1865-1950). He was the eldest son of Lieutenant General Frederick Green-Wilkinson, CB (1825-1913), a distinguished Imperial officer who sent him to Wellington College and the RMC at Sandhurst, Berkshire. In 1886, LG joined the Rifle Brigade and saw active service in Burma (1886 and 1888), in the Dongola Expedition (1896), in the Nile Expedition (1897), and throughout the Second South African War

(1899-1902), in which he took part in the relief of Ladysmith. From 1906 to 1907, he acted as private secretary to the Duke of Connaught, who was then Inspector General of the Forces. On 18 May 1904, he married Sarah May Trench (1873-1934), daughter of Hon. Frederic Sydney Charles Trench and Lady Anne Le Poer Trench.

In 1908, he retired from the army and they took up poultry farming on Salt Spring Island, almost next door to William Lawrence Hamilton and family at "Dromore" on the waterfront at Fulford Harbour. The Canadian census for 1911 shows them there with two daughters, Sheelah Adrienne Sarah and Oonah Anne, aged five and four, and several boarders. At that time, his parents were living in London SW at 19 St George's Square, his father a member of the Carlton Club and the Army and Navy Club. But his father died in 1913 shortly before LG returned home for the 1914-1918 war, taking command of the 166th and 148th Infantry Brigades. In July 1917, the *Daily Colonist* reported that LG and his family were living temporarily in Scotland at Fort William, where he had been in charge of the Tay defences since returning from France. He was mentioned in dispatches, awarded the DSO in 1917, the *Légion d'Honneur*, and then inducted as a companion of the Order of St Michael and St George.

On 28 November 1955, their daughter Sheelah Adrienne Sarah Green-Wilkinson married Dudley Oliver Trench, Fifth Baron Ashtown, son of Frederic Oliver Trench, Third Baron Ashtown, and Violet Grace Cosby. LG had died five years earlier, on 11 April 1950, in London, where he and his wife had returned in their declining years, the girls having left home.

Sources: *The Times* (London), 12 April 1950, page 8, obit.; *Burke's Peerage and Baronetage*, 106th edn., vol. I, pp. 129-130; Queen's Royal Surrey Regimental Association Internet site; *Who was Who*, 1897-1916, pp. 294-5, about his father; *Colonist*, 5 July 1917, p. 4; 31 July 1917, p. 4; Canadian census, 1911, *Salt Spring Island*; BC Directory for 1921, pp. 208-9; Heather Asplin at hometown.co.uk/ heatherasplin/Lg 300998.html, marriage.

GREENWOOD, Major Arthur Alexander (1920-?), PhD, FCIS, FRSA, FSCA, FR, Econ.S., P.Adm. He was born on 8 March 1920 at Corby Glen, Lincolnshire, son of Dr Augustus Charles Greenwood, physician and surgeon, and Constance Elfrida Thomson Greenwood *née* Dick. They were not a local family: Dr Greenwood was born c. 1872 at Newark, Nottinghamshire, and his wife c. 1875 at Brighton, Sussex. AG recalls that in the years 1896-1898, his father was *locum tenens* at Bristol to the famous cricketer, Dr W. G. Grace, and, after returning from service in the Great War, played himself as captain of Corbey Glen Cricket Club for many years.

AG was schooled at Oakham School and Sidney Sussex College, Cambridge University (PhD, 1987). He married (1) Betty Doreen Westrop, daughter of Brigadier Sidney Albert Westrop (20 July 1946) and (2) Shirley Knowles-Fitton, daughter of Wing Commander Alec Knowles-Fitton (16 September 1976) and had two children, Jane Alexandra Greenwood and Nicholas Alexander Westrop Greenwood. In 1939, he joined the Royal Lincolnshire Regiment as second lieutenant, captain (1942), and major (1953) and served in Norway, Iceland, India, and Burma. In 1942-1945, he was ADC to Field Marshal Sir Claude Auckinleck and much later wrote a biography of him. Staying in the army after the war, he was GSO2 (Int.), Middle East in 1951-1953, chief instructor of School of Military Intelligence, UK, in 1954-1956, and then retired from the army. In 1959-1975, he worked as a member of the London Stock Exchange; founder and director, Allied City Shared Trust PLC (1964-1973); chair, Lincolnshire Chickens Ltd. (1963-1987), Alderney Offshore Services Ltd. (1976-80), and British North Channel Company Ltd. (1976-1980); and director of Longy Investment Trust Ltd. (1976-1980) and other companies.

Having saved enough to live comfortably, he emigrated to Vancouver Island in 1980 in the wake of his three sisters, who had gone out to join a friend from Lincolnshire, Miss Norah Creina Denny (1885-1983), born on 3 August 1885, daughter of Emily Barclary Allen (1858-1957) and her husband Edmund Barry Denny (1860-1945), LRCS, JP for Lincolnshire, when in 1921, she founded Queen Margaret's School at Duncan. "My father, a doctor, was very strict," AG writes, "and so my sisters were glad for a job out of the U.K. My mother joined them after W.W. 2 and paid for me to come out on holiday in 1947 when I was a captain in my county regiment—The Royal Lincolns. I vowed some day to join my family and my 1st cousin Lieut.-Colonel Kemble Greenwood, M.B., B.S., F.R.C.P. who retired early from the R.A.M.C. to live on Vancouver Island and became a rich dermatologist. He was doing an exchange with the U.S.A. army & visited my sisters and then decided to retire early. The Army H.Q. at the War Office were furious of course! After serving twenty years in the Army I was granted a 'Golden bowler' in 1959 after twenty years service. A pension for life at thirty-nine as a major and then a bonus £6,000 to leave early! Only a Socialist Government could be so generous (under Harold Wilson)! First I had to make some money as I wished to educate my two children as I was educated. I looked at Lloyds (insurance) then at the College of Arms (no money) then at the Stock Exchange (lots of money). So I joined the London Stock Exchange and bought my membership. Within three years I was earning a full general's pay and after four years more than Prime Minister Thatcher. So in 1980 I emigrated (via Alder in the Channel Islands) to Vancouver Island. My two sisters (one had died, also my mother) and cousin met us at Victoria. I have never returned to the U.K." AG became a citizen in 1983 and found employment as lecturer in Genealogy at Malaspina College (1984-1993). During his civil life, he became a Freeman of the city of London (11 April 1960), president of Old Oakhamian Club (1960-1961), liveryman of Worshipful Company of Pattenmakers (1965), founder and member of Alderney Rotary Club, Channel Islands (1979), vice-president of Reform Party of Canada (1994-1995), and a member of the Authors Society, the Society of Genealogists, the Heraldry Society, the Heraldry Society of Canada, the Association of Professional Genealogists, and the Church of England. He published: *A Brief History of the 4th Battalion; The Royal Lincolnshire Regiment* (1949); *The Greenwood Tree in Three Continents* (1988); *Field-Marshal Auchlinlech, A Biography of Field-Marshal Sir Claude Auchinleck, G.C.B., G.C.I.E., C.S.I., D.S.O., O.B.E., LL.D., by his former A.D.C.* (Witton le Wear, Durham, 1990), 338 pp.; *The Greenwood Family Formerly of Haddenham, England,* (1996); and many articles on genealogy. He found time for golf, shooting, and membership in three clubs: Carlton (UK), Union (Victoria, BC), and The Pilgrims.

AG had an uncle, Lieutenant Colonel Arthur Rowland Greenwood (c. 1873-?), whose career in the RAMC took him to India, whence he returned home to England in 1908. He met and married Edith Grace Sharland, niece of another Indian Army officer, *Colonel A. A. Sharland, who lived in Victoria, in "Queenswood House" near Telegraph Bay, in the years 1929-1934, and this couple's only son, Lieutenant Colonel Kemble Greenwood (1919-2002), retired ultimately to the Cowichan Valley. The complex social history of Imperial campaigners and how they influenced each other's movements has yet to be pieced together.

Sources: *Letter to the author from Major A. A. Greenwood*, 1419, Madrona Drive, Nanoose Bay, BC, Canada V9P 9C9 dated 16 and 28 February 2003; Alexander Greenwood, *Field-Marshal Auchinleck: A Biography of Field-Marshal Sir Claude Auchinleck, G.C.B., G.C.I.E., C.S.I., D.S.O., O.B.E., LL.D., by his former A.D.C.* (Witton le Wear, Durham, 1990), 338 pp.; census 1901, England, RG 13/3023, p. 18; census 1901, RG 13/592, p. 30; 1891, RG 12/761, p. 40; *Canadian Who's Who*, 1998, p. 493; *Who's Who in B.C.*, 1947-48, p. 57 (Norah Creina Denny).

GREER, Colonel Horace Charles (1884-1974). Born September 1884 at Kildare, Ireland, son of Colonel James Greer, he was schooled at St Joseph's College and Wimbledon College. He obtained a commission in the Third Hussars (1905) and was promoted to lieutenant (1910), captain (1913), and brevet colonel (1918). In the Great War, he served overseas with the First Canadian Division (1914-1919), in AA and QMG No. 10 (1921-1925), as director of supplies and transport, MD No. 10 (1925-1930), and as DS and TO Headquarters Ottawa (1930-1931). Then he went to Victoria as DS and TO No. 11, 1931 with his wife, Margarette Tomney of St John, NB. They lived at 1394 Esquimalt Road with their son and four daughters. He died, aged eighty-nine, on 11 November 1974 in Victoria.

Sources: *Who's Who in B.C.*, 1933-1934, p. 73; vol. VI (1944-1946), p. 100; NAC, CEF files, box 3803-36.

GREIG, Major Robert Moore (1883-1956). Born on 7 November 1883 in Wimbledon, Surrey, son of Robert Greig (c. 1842-?), aged forty-nine, a Curate, Church of England (born at Bramshot, Hampshire), and Elizabeth S. Greig (c. 1854-?), born at Salisbury, Wiltshire), he was living in 1891, aged seven, with the family at 36 Tavistock Street, St Peter, Bedford. In 1901, they were living at 62 Beaconsfield Street, Bedford St Paul, Bedfordshire. There were several children in the family and one general servant. He was commissioned as second lieutenant in the British Army on 19 August 1903, appointed to the Indian Army, Forty-second Regiment, on 7 November 1904, and, in a few days, made a Double Company or "Wing Officer."

After many years in India, he retired to Victoria in 1929. His wife Ethel died in April 1955 and he, aged seventy-two, on 15 November 1956, leaving a daughter in Portland, Oregon, and two brothers in England. His funeral was at Christ Church Cathedral.

Sources: *Indian Army List,* January 1905, pp. 147a, 353; October 1910, pp. 152, 353; census 1891, England, RG 12/1249, p. 3; census 1901, England, RG 13/1489, p. 37; *Colonist,* 22 November 1956, p. 25, obit.

GREIG, Colonel William Best, OBE (1870-1941). He was born at sea in the Indian Ocean in March 1870 to Captain John G. Greig and on his father's ship. Schooled at Brentwood College, Essex, at Stratford-on-Avon and at Sandhurst, where he graduated in 1891, he joined the Royal North Lancashire Forty-seventh Regiment and after a year transferred to the Twenty-second Madras Infantry, and then again to the Eighty-seventh Punjab Infantry. After losing a leg in some battle, he was invalided out of the Indian Army and retired in 1908 to Qualicum Beach, Vancouver Island, where he was one of the earliest white settlers. "He had forty (40) acres," a local historian tells us, "above where De Greek had his farm, encompassing the south end of the golf course, the south side of West Crescent, and the north side of Hoy Lake Road. He and his brother lived on the second floor of his barn, which would have stood on the north side of Hoy Lake Road. He sold his farm to the Merchants Trust and Trading Company, which built the Qualicum Beach Hotel. The hotel was built just north of where this barn stood." His handicap does not seem to have prevented him from rejoining his regiment at Woolwich in 1914 and, after serving in India for the second time (1914-1920), returned to the Island, where he lived at Englishman's River near Parksville. On 19 March 1927, he married Elizabeth Ann Macdonald of Picton (?-1954). Twelve years later, they moved to Arbutus Road, Gordon Head, Victoria, where they could attend meetings of the India-Burma Society. His time there was brief; he died, aged seventy-one, in Victoria on 9 July 1941 and was buried at Royal Oak after a funeral at St Michael and All Angel's Church, West Saanich Road. Mrs Macdonald lived on until 1954.

Sources: *Who's Who in B.C.* 1931, p. 45; *Colonist,* 17 January 1933, p. 8; 10 July 1941, p. 3, obit.; Brad C. Wylie, *Qualicum Beach: A History of Vancouver Island's Best Kept Secrets* (Qualicum Beach Historical & Museum Society, 1992), pp. 30-31.

GRENFELL, Pascoe Du Pré (1828-1896). Variously mentioned as an "American Merchant" or a "copper merchant," he has an entry herein only because the town of Grenfell, Saskatchewan, was named after him as an investor in the CPR, and Grenfell was where half a dozen Island families first settled in Canada. Not until 1905, well after the CPR had reached the Pacific coast, were the provinces of Saskatchewan and Alberta created out of the southern NWT. It was even later that the family of *Lieutenant General Sir Percy Lake, for instance, moved to the Island. They, like several other British families, had settled first at Grenfell in the 1880s because the transcontinental railway being built by the CPR Company had reached that far and was selling off the corridor of land granted in its contract with the Crown signed in Ottawa (21 October 1880). GP signed on behalf of Morton, Rose & Co. as well as for himself.

So far as is known, GP never went to the Island but was indirectly involved in its history by investing heavily in the CPR. Furthermore, he is an example of the many British capitalists whose funds made the CPR possible and so helped to keep Canada and the Island within the British Empire. Another investor who signed the original CPR contract was Richard Bladworth Angus (1831-1922), a Scot whose nephew, *Henry Forbes Angus, was born in Victoria. But the story of these capitalists is not simple. Some of them invested heavily in the United States, whose early industrial development was indeed largely carried out with British capital, while others such as *Sir Edward Watkin (who did visit the Island) made patriotic efforts to further the empire's interests and thought of the CPR as part of an "All-Red Route," a way of reaching across to India, Hong Kong, and the Far East.

GP spent his life in London and Buckinghamshire, but he and others like him brought the American, British, and Latin parts of the Americas to the attention of the investing public in London. He was related to several great families. His wife, Sophia Grenfell (1833-1898), daughter of Admiral John Pascoe Grenfell (1800-1869) from another branch of the ramifying Grenfell family, was born in Montevideo, as was her brother, Vice Admiral Sir Harry Tremenheere Grenfell (1845-1906). GP's aunt Emily (1805-1875) married into a branch of the great Osborne family. In 1898, one of GP's sons, Lieutenant Colonel Cecil Alfred Grenfell (1864-1924), married Lady Lilian Maud (1873-1951), daughter of George Spencer-Churchill, Eighth Duke of Marlborough, which of course made a link with Winston Churchill.

Sources: W. Kaye Lamb, *History of the Canadian Pacific Railway* (New York, Macmillan, 1977), pp. 71-72; Andrew Smith, *British Businessmen and Canadian Confederation: Constitution-Making in an Era of Anglo-Globalization* (Montreal, McGill-Queen's UP, 2008), 229 pp.

GRIGG, Major Edward W. (c. 1877-1941). Born at Liskeard, Cornwall, England, where his father, also Edward W. Grigg (c. 1833-?) was a farmer, he served with the Somersetshire Light Infantry in India and, in 1910, went to live on the Island, where he lived near Duncan for fifteen years and a short time at Port Washington, Mayne Island. He rejoined his regiment during the Great War and, in 1919, retired to Duncan. There, he was interested in sporting events and, in September 1921, refereed boxing bouts held on a stage erected at a Great War Veterans' Association sports day. The judge on this occasion was C. M. Lonsdale, headmaster at Shawnigan Lake Boys' School. In 1939, EWG and his wife moved to Victoria, where they lived at the Sussex Apartment Hotel, and he died there on 5 April 1941, aged sixty-four, and was buried at Royal Oak, leaving his wife and two sisters in England.

Sources: *Colonist*, 7 September 1921, p. 10; 6 April 1941, p. 5, obit.; census 1891, England, RG 12/1808, p. 7; census 1901, England, RG 13/2026, p. 27.

GRIGGS, Captain Quartermaster Thomas Henry (1884-1972). He was born at Bedford on 22 July 1884, son of Thomas Griggs, hotel proprietor, and schooled at Bedford Public School and at the Military School of Dispensing and Compounding, Aldershot. Obtaining a commission in the RAMC, he served in 1901-1908 (Queen's Medal with five clasps). After the war, he moved to Canada and, when he enlisted at Valcartier in the Great War on 24 September 1914, had tattoos on his chest, right arm, and right leg. He served overseas with the First Canadian Field Ambulance, First Division, from 1914 to December 1915 as dispenser of medicines, and from 1915 to August 1919 as captain quartermaster, Twenty-first Field Ambulance, Seventh Division, Imperial forces. This service took him to France, Belgium, and Italy. He was mentioned in despatches three times and awarded "11th June Special Medal, Asiage Plateau," 1914-1915 Star, and British War and Victory Medals. He remained in the army after the war and, in March 1921, joined the permanent force as district dispenser. In 1928, he was awarded Long Service and Good Conduct Medals.

About 1922, he moved to North Saanich with his wife, Mary Gwendoline Nicholls, daughter of G. Nicholls of Lichfield, England, whom he had married in 1908. They lived for thirty-seven years at 1850 Dean Park Road, where Mrs Griggs died in 1938. Their one daughter, Gwendoline Mary, born in Malta in 1911, eventually married Arthur E. Fido of North Saanich. THG lived there or nearby for some fifty years during which he was an active Freemason for forty-two years and also registered with the Institute of Applied Sciences, Chicago, as an associate member. He was buried at St Stephen's Church, southwest of Mount Newton.

Sources: NAC, CEF files, box 3843-19, regimental no. 32927; *Who's Who in B.C.*, 1933-4, pp. 71-2; *Colonist*, 11 April 1972, p. 25, obit.

GROVES, Major James Douglas (1882-1960). Born on 5 August 1882 at 6 Rivington Place, Cromwell Street, Stretford, Lancashire, he was a son of Anna Eva Groves *née* Marsland and her husband, James Grimble Groves, a cashier who became a J.P, D.L., and M.P. They sent JG to be schooled at Rossall and then Christ College, Cambridge, but the family at large were in the brewing business and wealthy. Rather than go into the family business he obtained a commission in the Cambridge University military training corps (1900-1901) and served for ten years in the 2/1 Derbyshire Yeomanry until October 1910, when he retired as a second lieutenant. Then, still avoiding the family brewing business, he emigrated to the Island in 1910 and settled at Westholme in a "picturesquely-situated residence" not far from Duncan. There he developed a small but successful sheep farm. He also rode about in the hills and hunted down the cougars who preyed on his sheep, often with Arthur Holman who shot altogether about 300 cougars. JG strongly supported the Cowichan District Riding Club, the Boy Scouts, the Royal Canaduan Sea Cadet Corps (managed by *Admiral Rollo Mainguy) and arranged for the sea cadets's barracks at Maple Bay. In England he had married Mary Millicent Walker, daughter of Thomas Walker, barrister, and they had two sons.

In 1915 JG returned to England, rejoined the Derbyshire Yeomanry as a captain, and fought on the Western Front in France with the Sherwood Foresters, Notts and Derby Regiment. Recovering from a wound, he served as a musketry instructor somewhere in Kent until returning to the battle-front, where he was wounded again at Lens on Dominion Day 1917. The *Victoria Daily Colonist* reported in August 1917 that he was in Fishmonger's Hall Hospital in London, where his wife and sons were visiting him. He was discharged as medically unfit on 3 January 1919 and the family returned to Westholme. The B.C. Directory for 1922, p. 1142, listed him as "Groves, J.D., farmer," and in 1933-34 his recreations were fishing, shooting, riding, boxing, motor boating, and hunting. He was breeding sheep and winning prizes for his pedigree flock of Shropshires with forty registered ewes. He was a member of the United Sports Club (London), the Union Club (Victoria), the Cowichan Country Club, the Canadian Legion, and the Anglican Church. He was the first president of the Great War Veterans' Association and active in founding the Legion memorial to Cowichan war dead on the top of Mount Prevost. The family had strong links with England, travelled there often, and JG as a Conservative was interested in the politics of both countries. Their youngest son, Jocelyn James Douglas Groves, joined the Royal Engineers and on 3 December 1937 married the daughter of another British officer at St. Mary's Church, Alverstoke in Hampshire. When JG's wife died in 1956 he donated a stained-glass window in her memory for the west end of All Saints Church at Westholme. There he was buried when he died, aged 77, in Duncan at King's Daughters Hospital on 18 January 1960. His elder son was then identified as Lieut.-Colonel James I. Groves of Cloe-Henley Manor, Whitechurch, England.

Sources: *Cowichan Leader*, 6 February 1960, obit.; 9 December 1937, p. 7; BNA (PRO), WO 374/29639; Letter from John Palmer, 15 January 2002, p. 4; *Who's Who in B.C.*, 1933-34, p. 72; Elliott, *Memories of the Chemainus Valley*, p. 73; *Colonist*, 19 August 1917, p. 16.

GRUCHY, William Charles Rich de (1888-1941). Born in County Kerry, Ireland, son of Charles A. de Gruchy, who was a "shipwright pensioner" born at St Heliers on the island of Jersey, he was only circumstantially Irish as his paternal family were Jerseymen and his mother, Clara de Gruchy, was born at Devonport, Devonshire. It was there that the 1901 census found WG, aged thirteen, living at 10 Millton Cove with his parents, an elder sister, and two younger brothers but no servants. In 1910, WG joined the Royal Navy at Devonport and sailed to Halifax, Nova Scotia, in the old ship which became HMCS *Niobe*. He transferred to the Royal Canadian Navy, a pioneer in those early days, and in 1914, he was transferred to Victoria. There, he served in 1914-1918 as chief carpenter's mate in HMCS *Rainbow* and then as chief shipwright in HMCS *Dockyard* at Esquimalt, and a foreman shipwright from 1939.

For twenty-seven years, he lived in or near Victoria, perhaps longest at 1703 Albert Avenue. He joined the Royal Victoria Yacht Club, the Naval Veterans' Branch of the Canadian Legion, and the Army and Navy Veterans, Victoria Unit No. 12. When he died, aged fifty-three, on 11 March 1941, he left his widow, a son, a sister, and brother in the England and was buried as an Anglican at Royal Oak.

Sources: census 1901, England, RG 13/2108, p. 24; *Colonist*, 15 March 1941, p. 3, obit.

GUPPY, Robert Florian Bernard Lechmere (1882-1976). He was born in Trinidad, seventh of the eight children of Robert John Lechmere Guppy (1836-1916) and employed as Chief Schools Inspector but better known as an explorer and naturalist for whom *poecilia reticulata*, the popular pet tropical fish, was named Guppy. RG's mother, Alice Rostant, was born at New Orleans the daughter of a French-Creole family with a sugar plantation in Trinidad. RG was schooled at Queen's Royal College, Trinidad, and Pembroke College, Oxford, where he was a rowing blue with the Pembroke College Boat Club and generally athletic. In 1903, he won firsts in the quarter-mile race, the 100-yards dash, the 120-yards hurdle, and the broad jump. In 1905, he passed the ICS exams and then took an examination in horsemanship. At Oxford, he had met Ethel Winnifred Guest (c. 1884-1953) from Slough, daughter of Walter Guest, an engineering supervisor with the Great Western Railway and also an artist, a calligrapher, and an inventor, who had descended from Isambard Kingdom Brunel (1806-1859), the famous builder of bridges and mammoth ships. They married on 1 December 1906 and, a week later, sailed for India, where he went on to serve as a magistrate and sub-collector of taxes in the state of Madras, travelling around from village to village, often living in tents while his family took refuge in a hill station. A keen and talented officer, RG became proficient in several Indian languages and progressed well in the service. Mrs Guppy was not well, however, and seems to have been threatened by hostile Indians and somehow been poisoned. In 1920, they decided to leave India. They had read about Vancouver Island in the *London Illustrated News* and responded to an encouraging letter from the postmaster at Port Alberni, on the west coast, by purchasing a property near Tofino, sight unseen. With five children by then, the elder ones born in England and accustomed to being sent there to school and the youngest, aged two, born at Kodiakanal, Madras Presidency, the move was a serious matter.

They reached Victoria in summer 1921, with all their belonging including a tiger skin, the gun that had shot the tiger, and Mrs Guppy's evening dresses, and sailed on up the west coast to Tofino in the CPR's *Princess Maquinna.* RG soon found that he would need the ICS pension for which he would have to serve three more years to make up a total of twenty. He left his wife with the children there at Tofino and went back to India, whence he returned in January 1925. He had leave coming to him so that his retirement from the ICS was dated April 1926. To satisfy his dream of a small farm in pleasant seaside surroundings, he then bought two small islands near Tofino and spent much time on them, clearing land and planting gardens. He reached them by rowing a small boat, and Mrs Guest refused to go with him, their five children being a handful for a woman now without servants. The children remembered him pulling out to his islands across the inlet, singing songs in ancient Greek, like the rowing blue from Oxford he had once been. Restless like his forebears, RG eventually went off adventuring, spent some time in Balize, and later went to Cayman Brac, where he died in 1976 at the age of ninety-four.

Sources: Letter from Anthony Guppy (a son), 16 March 2002; Anthony Guppy, *The Tofino Kid: From India to this Wild Coast* (Nanaimo, privately published, 2000), pp. 15, 19-21, 55, 58, 75-6, 160; *India Office List*, 1919, p. 632; NAC, Immigration records 1925-35: RG76, series C-1-1 1925, vol. 1, page 1; reel T-14881.

GURNEY, Captain Arthur Broughton (1878-1962). He was born in Chelsea, London, on 20 December 1878, son of Rhoda Gurney (c. 1846-?) and her husband

Rev. Arthur F. Gurney (c. 1848-?), who was "Minister, Bournemouth Baptist Church & Barrister at Law, not practicing" when the 1881 census found the family living in Christchurch at "Heatherside," Moorland Road. After attending King William's College, Isle of Man, where they probably lived at one stage, a sister having been born there, he trained as a marine engineer and joined the British Army.

AG went to the Island before the Great War and, when he enlisted as a lieutenant on 8 July 1917 in Vancouver, was employed as a marine engineer at Parksville with a wife named Anna Maria. He signed as an Anglican and claimed to have had eighteen years of military service, both active and reserve. Upon his return at the war's end, they moved to Mayne Island, but when he died, aged eighty-four, on 22 December 1962, he was at Coquitlam.

Sources: NAC, CEF files, box 3891-10; census 1881, England, RG 11/1194; census 1891, RG 12/4690; Mary Elliott, *Mayne Island and the Outer Gulf Islands: A History* (Mayne Island, Gulf Islands Press, 1984), p. 54.

GWYNNE, Brigadier General Reginald John (1863-1942). Born in London on 16 September 1863, son of James Eglinton Anderson Gwynne, JP, FSA, and Mary Earle "May" Gwynne *née* Purvis (1840-?), he was brought up on the family estate at Folkington Manor, Postgate, Sussex, and sent to Eton and Pembroke College, Oxford. His father had been a civil engineer and two elder brothers followed in his footsteps, but in 1885, RG emigrated to Canada. There, he had relatives, notably Hon. John Wellington Gwynne (1814-1902), an Irish-born lawyer who had emigrated to Canada in 1832 and become a railway promoter and a believer in Confederation, whom Prime Minister John A. Macdonald had appointed to the Supreme Court of Canada on 14 January 1879. Exactly why young RG emigrated or what he did during his first two years in Canada is not clear but in a letter of 20 January 1888 applying to join the Royal North-West Mounted Police, he added a PS: "I may add that I know the country almost 'by heart' between Whitewood and Indian Head [now in Saskatchewan], having lived there for two years and hunted with foxhounds round there." The address he gave was "C/o Messrs Mitchell & Bucknell, 'Millwood,' Binscarth, Manitoba," which is near the present border with Saskatchewan. Before joining the RNWM Police, he wrote and obtained the support of Prime Minister John A. Macdonald and one of the RNWM Police commissioners in Ottawa, Frederick White, to whom Chief Justice J. W. Gwynne had appealed for support on RG's behalf.

As a result, on 30 January 1888, White wrote to a fellow commissioner at Regina:

> My Dear Herchmer,
>
> I send you herewith correspondence with Mr Reginald Gwynne respecting the arrangements of himself and a friend named Flindt.
>
> I am afraid Gwynne will not make a contented Policeman for five years, but being a man of good physique and education and without faults except a want of steady application to any particular calling, I suppose there can be no objection to engaging him and his friend.

The Hon. Mr Justice Gwynne, one of the Judges of the Supreme Court, came to my office a short time ago on behalf of Gwynne, and although I did my best to dissuade him from encouraging the applicant, he said he thought it was the best thing that could be done for him.

Yours etc.,

Fred*k* White

RG took his oath of allegiance and signed on for five years on 11 February 1888, but served, as it turned out, for no more than 220 days. An experienced horseman who had practised shooting at Oxford, he was then a slim young man, 5' 11" tall, weighing 160 lbs., with blue eyes and fair hair (Medical Report dated 10 February 1888). But he suffered an injury after only a few weeks, purchased his discharge for $159 with effect from 20 September 1888, and promptly regretted that he had not applied instead to be invalided out of the service, which would then have paid his medical bills.

In 1894, RG married Mary Mayall Taylor (1872-1957), born a daughter of a Justice of the Peace at Oldham, Lancashire, and destined to outlive him by fifteen years. According to the 1901 census records, they then had two daughters, Evelyn Violet Gwynne (born 29 January 1895) and Betty Gwyn Gwynne (born 20 April 1899). Betty died, aged seven, of a ruptured appendix, and in St Michael and All Angels Anglican Church at Grenfell were installed—"oak standard lights (later altered to electric) were a gift . . . by General R. G. Gwynne, C.M.G. in memory of Betty Gwyn Gwynne." Long before then, RG had been appointed deputy sheriff at Grenfell, a kind of overseer or manager of the town, and it was he who sponsored its wide tree-lined streets and pleasant urban appearance. Canadian historians with their characteristic inverted snobbery tend to mock him as "an Englishman who had vainly tried to succeed as a Saskatchewan country squire," but in fact, he was one of a community of similar people there who tried to organise the kind of life their families had in England: They played cricket, hunted coyotes with hounds as a substitute for fox-hunting, and supported an Anglican church, as did their wives and children. With him in this were *the Lake brothers, the *Murisons, and others described by A. I. Yule in *Grit and Growth*.

On 1 April 1907, RG enlisted in the army at Grenfell and soon obtained the rank of major in the Sixteenth Light Horse, at its headquarters in Regina. He had some influence in the formation of this regiment, which was entrusted to him, to *W. H. Belson, and to a Major Wright. The next year, on 22 April 1908, RG was appointed to command it as lieutenant colonel and resigned his civic posts. He took several courses of training, wrote a manual, *Explanation and Details for Movements in Cavalry Training* (1909), and, on 27 November 1911, became officer commanding the Seventh Cavalry Brigade. As the Great War approached, he was appointed organizer and inspector, Cadet Corps, Military District No. 10 (1 January 1912), and the war minister, Sam Hughes (1853-1921), soon made him director of Cadet Services at Militia Headquarters in Ottawa. There he remained throughout the war, rising to brigadier general, acting deputy adjutant general, and was decorated with the CMG. On the day he retired, 30 June 1920, the adjutant general sent him a long letter of thanks and praise in affectionate terms. Fighting soldiers tend to despise such officers as "desk-wallas," but there can be no doubt that such men were needed at HQ in Ottawa.

After the war, RG and family moved with much pleasure to a small country estate they called "Ardmore Grange" on the West Saanich Road, two or three miles from Sidney on Vancouver Island. There, Mrs Gwynne wrote a history of Holy Trinity Church, Patricia Bay, (where the Gwynnes and their daughter are now all buried) with a short account of the early years in Saanich:

> We were new comers to Vancouver Island in 1920. The real estate agents had taken us in hand to show us desirable places to make our future home. The Saanich Peninsula was a happy hunting ground; there were many spots where we willingly would have settled, the difficulty was to decide—which? Time and again in these house-hunting expeditions we passed a little white church. It was ideally situated at the junction of two roads, overlooking Patricia Bay, a part of lovely, almost landlocked Saanich Inlet. The walls of the little church were weather-stained and rather shabby, nevertheless it attracted us and one day we asked our driver to stop the car that we might go inside. The interior was very plain and simple, the walls in places stained with damp, but there was clear evidence of loving care; it was clean and neat; there was a beautiful red frontal on the Altar; the brass cross was brightly polished in spite of the sea air which soon tarnishes brass; the flowers in the vases were fresh and sweet; there was, even in the empty church, an atmosphere of reverence and devotion. We felt that we were at home and made welcome even before we found a house to live in. We settled eventually within two miles of the little church and for fifteen years it has been our spiritual home.

The Gwynne family had always been Anglicans, and their services to Holy Trinity, Patricia Bay, began upon their arrival. In mid-January 1922, RG and Mrs Gwynne were both re-elected to the Holy Trinity Church committee, and the general was also elected lay delegate to the Synod. In October 1926, he was appointed chairman of the North Saanich Committee for the new Cathedral in Victoria and authorized to receive subscriptions to the building fund. For at least ten years during the incumbencies of Rev. T. M. Hughes and Rev. T. R. Lancaster, RG was a church warden. On 27 June 1929, *The Sidney Review* (p. 4) published a letter from him and the other warden, Guy F. Pownell, explaining that Holy Trinity had legal title to its graveyard: "Any burials which have taken place in the past, in Holy Trinity Churchyard, of people, other than those of the Anglican Faith, have been by the courtesy of the Anglican Church." As well as their regular financial contributions, the Gwynnes donated a "white and gold burse and veil" woven by Mrs Gwynne in 1935, a "purple pall" made by Mrs Gwynne in 1940, and wiring for electric light, which the family gave in memory of General Gwynne, after he was buried in the church's graveyard on 22 March 1942; he had died two days before. In 1959, Miss Evelyn Gwynne gave "a violet lectern and pulpit hangings" in memory of her mother, who had been buried there in 1957.

The family had a busy social life in North Saanich for more than twenty years. Much of it was essentially community work, such as the children's party they held at "Ardmore Grange" on 6 January 1929 for the Holy Trinity Sunday School of which Mrs Gwynne was the superintendent. But RG also joined the Union Club in Victoria. For some years, he rode a horse into Sidney to collect his mail and do other business. They had a grass tennis court where the North Saanich Tennis Tournament was held in October 1930 and in other years. They also had what Nellie Horth describes as "a first-class croquet lawn" and were next door to the fifty-acre Ardmore Golf Club when it opened in 1933.

Evelyn Gwynne became a lifelong friend of my mother. The Lancashire origins of Mrs Gwynne, born at Oldham, were enough to create a certain bond with the Simister and Marsden families irrespective of social differences, and from 1920 when she was still only seventeen, my mother had much to do with Evelyn Gwynne through the church. She played tennis on the Gwynne's court from time to time and later was often a guest at "Ardmore Grange," as they called it. I remember being taken there as a small boy during the 1930s. RG and Mrs Gwynne were already old and only smiled distantly, but I recall Miss Gwynne as one of the many friendly, jolly English people who inhabited North Saanich in those years. We have in our collection a hymnal presented to Evelyn at Christmas 1907, a "Prize for diligence" at St Michael and All Angels Sunday School at Grenfell, Saskatchewan: William Henry Monk (Professor of Vocal Music in King's College London), ed., *Hymns Ancient and Modern for Use in the Services of the Church, with Accompanying Tunes* (London, William Clowes & Sons Ltd., 1906), 514 pp. In middle age, Evelyn gave it in friendship to my mother and my sister Avis kept it when my mother's books were being disposed of in February 1999. The Gwynnes and my parents all lie buried near one another now in the churchyard at Holy Trinity, Patricia Bay, with others of their kind. Theirs was a world of lively, friendly, charitable, often musical social circles based on a common view of the Island as a part of the British Empire.

Sources: NAC, RG18, vol. 3376, SF 2079. All references to RG's brief RNWM Police career are in the same file; NAC, T 6552, census records for the "Town of Grenfell"; NAC, RG24, file 1295; Annie Ida Amy Yule, *Grit and Growth: the Story of Grenfell* (Regina, Monarch Press, 1967), pp. 51, 86, 103; A. N. Reid, "*Local Government in the North-West Territories*," (III, "The Villages"), *Saskatchewan History*, vol. 4 (Spring 1951), pp. 49-50; R. G. Haycock, Sam Hughes: *The Public Career of a Controversial Canadian*, 1885-1916 (Kitchener, Ont., Wilfrid Laurier University Press, 1986), p. 140; Desmond Morton, "The Cadet Movement in the Moment of Canadian Militarism, 1909-1914," *Journal of Canadian Studies*, vol. 13 (summer 1978), p. 65; *Who's Who in B.C.*, 1940-41, pp. 87-88; Mary Maynall Gwynne (1873-1957), *A History of Holy Trinity Church, Patricia Bay, North Saanich, B.C.*, ed., A. L. C. Atkinson (Sidney, BC, 1967), 20 pp. [a typescript, originally published as an article on 29 May 1935, updated by Evelyn Gwynne, and at the National Library of Canada, Ottawa, Stacks

BX5613 P3G9]; *The Canadian Who's Who*, 1938-1939, p. 292; *The Quarterly Militia List*, passim; Canadian War Museum, Ottawa, photograph album (of Adjutants General) no. 19910051-007 with a photograph and career summary of General Gwynne; Nell Horth, *North Saanich, Memories and Pioneers* (Sidney, Porthole Press Ltd., 1988), p. 30 [ISBN 0-919931-12-X]; *Victoria Daily Colonist*, 22 March 1942, p. 3; *Montreal Gazette*, 23 March 1942, p. 14; *The Sidney and Gulf Islands Review*, 12 January 1922; 21 October 1926, p. 3; 27 June 1929, p. 4.

HAFFENDEN. See Wilson-Haffenden

HAGGARD, Lieutenant Colonel Andrew Charles Parker (1854-1923). He was born at Bradenham, Norfolk, on 7 February 1854, fifth son and seventh child of ten born to William Meybohm Rider Haggard and his wife Ella, daughter and co-heiress of Bazett Doveton, EICS He attended Westminster School and joined the Twenty-fifth Regiment (King's Own Borderers) in 1873. For about twenty years, he served in India, Aden, and especially Egypt, where he became a staff officer in 1882, during the conquest of that country, and soon transferred to the Egyptian Army. The memoirs he published in 1896 under the title *Crescent and Star* tell a rollicking tale of adventure and comradeship in a tone perhaps *de rigueur* among young officers, but his special service on the Red Sea Littoral took him into the bloody Battle of Tamai in 1884 (mentioned in despatches) and put him in command of the First Battalion Egyptian Army (Fourth Class Osmanieh) facing the forces of Osman Digna in 1884-1885. In 1885, he went on reconnaissance to Hasbeen in operations again at Suakim and on a Special Recruiting Commission with Brigadier General Yusuf Pasha Schudi to investigate abuses of the Egyptian conscription service. In 1885-1886, he commanded the First Egyptian Battalion in operations on the Nile, including the battle of Ginness on the frontier (despatches, medal and star, several clasps, DSO, third class Medjidie).

A generation later, on 31 May 1914, he published in the *Victoria Daily Colonist* (p. 15) a long letter in answer to the question, "What troops took part in the battle of El Teb?" He had himself taken part and named other officers. He wrote, "My late friend, Valentine Baker Pasha, [who] was seriously defeated owing to the cowardice of the worn-out and ill-paid force of the old Egyptian army, which he commanded. The second battle [of El Teb] was fought on Leap Year's Day 1884. While I was myself left to defend the town of Suakin with some of the mutinous blacks and superannuated Egyptians of Arabi Pasha's former army, which had escaped from the massacre under Baker and Colonel Sartorius, a force sailed down the Red Sea to Iringitat in ships escorted by H.M.S. *Sphyx*, H.M.S. *Carysfort*, and H.M.S. *Euryalus*, the flagship of the late Admiral Sir W. Hewett, V.C. Valentine Baker, who had, in the first battle of Teb, received a bullet in his cheekbone, and was burning for revenge on the followers of Osman Digna, accompanied this force as a volunteer. By reference to my book *Under Crescent and Star*, published by Blackwood some years since, and compiled from records I had kept of the war, I find that under Sir Gerald Graham, V.C., there served as staff Colonels Sir Redvers Buller, Herbert Stewart Clery, Wauchope, Tayulor, of the 19th Hussars, and 'Keggy' Slade, the last two being, like myself, on Sir Evelyn Wood's staff as raisers and commanders of the new Egyptian army; Colonel Ardagh of the Royal Engineers, the intelligence office, while, as independent officers, who had fought under Baker, were Captain Harvey, late of the Black Watch, and one or two more, including Colonel Burnaby as a volunteer. That old war dog, Sir William Hewett, who was determined to see the fun himself, went in command of the naval brigade, with which were also present Commanders Crawford-Caffin of the *Sphynx*, and others . . . ," etc.

Early in 1899, AH moved—perhaps fled—to the United States, pursued by his creditors. He was undoubtedly facing a financial crisis, as his younger brother, Sir H. Rider Haggard, hints in his memoirs, but there may also have been a personal scandal of the kind that Victorians and Edwardians were loath to discuss in print. In 1906, he married Ethel Fowler (c. 1865-?), born in New Brunswick and widow of one Edward Fowler. Sources make no mention, however, of the fact that AH was already living with her five years earlier at "Whitestock Hall," Colton, North Lonsdale, Lancaster. No doubt he was a "retired lieut.-colonel in the Indian Army," as they told the census-taker there in 1901. But was he, as they said, her cousin and a widower? In 1891, he had been recorded as a married officer living in the south of England without his wife. True, his dwelling then was a military institution of some kind, but sources say nothing of his first wife.

In 1907, the Haggards retired to the Cowichan Valley, Vancouver Island, where they stayed at the Riverside Hotel and then moved into a log house on the river with his collection of Sudanese and Egyptian brassware and Oriental *objets d'art*. He fished, hunted, and wrote more than two dozen books of poetry, historical fiction, and popular history, including three historical novels about Henry IV (1589-1610) of France and his times. These never won him even a tiny fraction of the fame enjoyed by his younger brother, Rider Haggard, author of *King Solomon's Mines* (1885), *She* (1887), and many more. But his articles on sport and travel published by *Blackwoods Magazine, The Field,* and the *Victoria Daily Colonist* would interest any biographer. In 1905, for instance, his short article, "The Land of Olive-Oil," in *Chambers's Journal,* shows that he knew Lucca and other places in Tuscany. As for his social circles on the Island, local sources that portray him as pompous and arrogant can hardly be taken seriously, as they are inclined to say such things about Englishmen in general. The Haggards had many friends and stayed in Sidney with Rev. and Mrs T. C. Desbarres in summer 1918, not long before their final departure. Even critics mention the "Haggard fishing fly" for which AH became locally famous, and he had much to do with the establishment of the hatchery for sporting fish established on Lake Cowichan in 1910 by the Dominion Government. On 11 March 1914, the *Daily Colonist* printed a long and influential letter from Haggard, "A Threatened Danger," warning that the Cowichan River was about to be ruined by the Canadian Power & Land Co. of Vancouver, which had applied to divert its water to produce electricity. He was co-founder of a Veteran's Club of British Columbia in 1915.

The next year brought a visit by Rider Haggard, who reached Victoria from Australia in the course of a tour around the empire, asking governments for grants of land to demobilized Imperial troops after the war. The Rider Haggards had once planned to move to the Island themselves. That was many years earlier when, in April 1881, they decided they would have to leave their South African farm, but they gave up the idea when their sailor brother, John G. "Jack" Haggard, told derogatory stories about the Island, which he had visited in the Royal Navy. The criticism was premature, and the Rider Haggards may have regretted their decision because after visiting AH, Rider thought the Cowichan Valley and Victoria were among the loveliest places in the world. These two brothers were fond of one another, and all his life, Rider carried a pocketknife that Andrew had given him when they were boys together in England. It was Rider who wrote to tell Andrew that their nephew Mark, son of their brother Bayett Haggard, had died heroically with the King's Own Scottish Borderers in 1914: "Poor Mark has gone. The King both telegraphed and telephoned to Julia (his mother) expressing his thanks and sorrow." Right after the war, in 1919, the Haggards sold their house at Cowichan to James Dunsmuir and returned to England, where he died on 13 May 1923 at St Leonards on the East Sussex coast. Mrs Haggard lived to a great age and died at last in 1957.

Sources: *The Times* (London), 12 September 1882, p. 4; 5 January 1892, p. 2; 27 April 1896, p. 15; 16 May 1923, p. 16, obit.; 21 May 1923, p. 11; *Who was Who*, vol. II (1916-1928), pp. 448-9; A. C. P. Haggard, *Crescent and Star* (Edinburgh & London, Blackwoods, 1896, 1898 and 1899 editions), 406 pp.; H. Rider Haggard, *The Days of My Life: An Autobiography* (2 vols., Longmans, Green & Co., 1926) at Carleton Univ., and also *The Private Diaries of Sir H. Rider Haggard, 1914-1925*, ed., D. S. Higgins (Cassell, 1980); and D. S. Higgins, *Rider Haggard: The Great Storyteller* (Cassell, 1981), 266 pp.; Lilias Rider Haggard, *The Cloak That I Left: A Biography of the author Henry Rider Haggard*, K.B.E., by his daughter (Hodder and Stoughton, 1951), pp. 109-110; census 1891, England, RG 12/1742, p. ?; census 1901, RG 13/4002, p. 6; *Colonist*, Sunday 15 September 1907, p. 17; March 1914, p. 11; 12 August 1914, p. 7; 18 October 1914, p. 15; 13 July 1918, p. 12; Lynne Bowen, *Those Lake People: Stories of Cowichan Lake* (Vancouver, Douglas & McIntyre, 1995), pp. 15-18, 25; *Who was Who*, vol. II (1916-1928), pp. 448-9; *Chambers's Journal*, (Edinburgh) vol. VIII (Dec. 1904-Nov. 1905), pp. 577-580; John F. T. Saywell, *Kaatza: The Chronicles of Cowichan Lake* (Sidney, The Cowichan Lake District Centennial Committee, 1967), p. 46.

HAIG-BROWN, Roderick Langmere (1908-1976). Hyphenated here and in most current sources, the name has no hyphen in British census and other records. It was usual to add another name to distinguish a Brown or Smith family. RH was born on 21 February 1908 at Lancing, Sussex, son of Violet Mary *née* Pope, a prosperous solicitor's daughter, and her husband, Lieutenant Colonel Alan Roderick Haig-Brown, DSO (1877-1918), who was teaching at Lancing, a public school in that scattered Sussex village. Ten years earlier, RH's father was recorded in the census as a schoolmaster at Charterhouse, the famous public school at Godalming, Surrey, where he was born, his father (RH's grandfather) being the headmaster, then aged seventy-seven. When RH was ten years old, his father was killed fighting in France with the British Army. His memory was a strong influence on RH, but the most powerful figure in the family was RH's grandfather, Rev. William Haig-Brown (1823-1907), headmaster of Charterhouse for more than thirty years. Born on 3 December 1823, this grandfather qualified at Pembroke College, Cambridge, and played a big part in the life of RH and Charterhouse until his retirement in 1897 and death on 11 January 1907. In 1879, he published a history of the great school. Census records there in 1901 show the headmaster-grandfather, aged seventy-seven, born in Bromley, a suburb of London; his wife Annie Marion, sixty-five, born at Peckham, Surrey; Alan Roderick Haig Brown, schoolmaster aged twenty-three, still single and born at Godalming, Surrey; an elder sister (RH's aunt) Alice Mary Haig Brown, thirty-seven; followed by seven domestic servants.

Troubled, as the family was, by the death of his father, RH was expelled from Charterhouse for various absences, and after some years with a tutor, he went out to work in lumbercamps in northern Washington State and on Vancouver Island. His later story is well told elsewhere. After returning home to see his mother, he settled on the Island, married Ann Elmore from Seattle, and lived for the rest of his life at Campbell River in a house they called "Above Tide." He loved fishing, hunting, and the Island's natural terrain, and worked as a writer and conservationist. In time, he became a stipendiary magistrate and a public figure. As Mrs Morgan Scott-Ostler writes, he was not a popular person and ordinary Canadian citizens tended to see him as an outsider. It is worth stressing that the people in this book would have recognized him as one of themselves. If he had not won a certain renown for his writing, his behaviour, personal habits, clothing, and voice might have caused the prejudiced muddle-heads of the country to describe him as a "remittance man." Many another so-called "remittance man" was similarly capable and public-spirited.

Sources: census 1861, England, RG 9/437, pp. 2-3; census 1881, RG 11/779, p. 25; census 1881, RG 11/2110, p. 28 (Pope); census 1901, RG 13/248, p. 1; notes by Morgan Scott-Ostler; *Canadian Who's Who*, 1958-60, p. 463; Valerie Haig-Brown, *Deep Currents: Roderick and Ann Haig-Brown* (Victoria, Orca Book Publishers, 1997), 216 pp.; *To Know a River: A Haig-Brown Reader*, edited by Valerie Haig-Brown, the author's daughter, with an introduction by Thomas McGuane (1996); Anthony Robertson, *Above Tide Reflections on Roderick Haig-Brown* (Madeira Park, BC, Harbour Publishing, 1984); E. Bennett Metcalfe, *The Life of Roderick Langmere Haig-Brown: A Man of Some Importance* (Seattle & Vancouver, James W. Wood Publishing, 1985), 238 pp.

HAINES, Arthur Edward (1881-1935). Born on 5 March 1881 in Kent, he was living as a teamster at 1803 Chambers St, Victoria, with his wife, Mabel Annie Haines, and one child, when he enlisted in the Canadian Army at Victoria on 7 September 1915. He excelled at gymnastics and was a sports instructor. He was already a veteran soldier, having spent two years in the West Kent Regiment, five years in the Royal Horse Artillery, and five years in the Army Veterinary Service, and had crossed flags over a horseshoe tattooed on his left forearm as well as a scar on his right eye. He had fought through the South African War with British forces, and when overseas in the Great War, he transferred to the Fifty-fourth Battalion. Mentioned twice in despatches, he won the MC and, at his death, the *Colonist's* praise for "a splendid

military career." After a total of twenty-five years in Victoria, he died there, aged fifty-four, at 634 Speed Avenue, leaving his wife and two sons.
Sources: NAC, CEF files, box 3923-40, regimental no. 102409; *Colonist*, 22 February 1935, p. 3, obit.

HALE, Alfred Henry (1863-1938). Born at Bristol [or Bedminster?], Gloucestershire, he was recorded as aged three in 1871, living with his family at Colyer, Poplar Cottage, Huntspill [*sic*], Somerset. His father, Richard Hale, aged forty-five, was a sea captain born in a Gloucestershire village, and his mother Mary Ann Hale, aged forty-four so born also. He had an elder brother, Charles Hale, who at age twelve was already listed as a sailor. Ten years later, AH was recorded as an "apprentice engineer fitter," and in July 1884, he joined the RN. He served in several ships and was in the crew of one that went out to Esquimalt in April 1892. Nearly twenty years later, in 1911, he returned to Canada and in 1914 went to the Torpedo Department at the Royal Naval College. In 1922, he was made a torpedo instructor in the RCN and in 1927 a Torpedo Artificer, and in 1930, he transferred to ASO Department. He retired in 1933 and lived at 931 Esquimalt Road with his wife, a son, and five daughters, who survived him when he died, aged seventy-five, on 8 November 1938 and was buried at St Paul's Garrison Church.
Sources: *Colonist*, 10 November 1938, p. 15, obit.; census 1871, England, RG 10/2389, p. 28; census 1881, RG 11/2418, p. 27.

HALHED, Richmond Beauchamp (1857-1947). He was a second cousin of Lord Baden-Powell (1857-1941), founder of the Boys Scout movement, their grandfathers having been sons of a London merchant, David Powell (1725-1810), and his wife Lætitia Clark (1741-1801). During BP's visit to the Island in April 1923, he stayed with the Halhed family in their little house next to the sea at Chemainus, where they had a governess, Miss Allison, and a concrete tennis court. The two men happened to be the same age, had much in common, and were friendly enough that whenever BP visited the Island, he stayed with them. On a later visit, he brought Lady BP to visit the Halheds. Biographers of the famous man seem unaware of the Halhed relationship. By the 1920s, BP's mother was long dead and he had outgrown his mother's anxiety over the suitability of his acquaintances. He had consulted a wide variety of men while preparing to found the Boy Scout movement. Besides, RH had relatives in Imperial service in India and was named for one of his forebears, Edward Halhed Beauchamp (1815-1885), a distinguished captain in the Royal Navy. RH was also visited by Lord Willingdon, governor general of Canada in 1926-1931, a keen supporter of the Boy Scouts and a friend of BP.
RH was born at Harbledown in Kent, near Canterbury, on 3 June 1857, second son and fifth child of a barrister-at-law with an estate of sixty acres, Francis Halhed (1804-1880), born at Yately House, Hampshire, and his wife, Mary Ann Powell (1819-1899), from London. Census records in 1861 and 1871 show them all living in Harbledown at "The Limes" in the London Road, RH aged three and thirteen. He was educated as an engineer. On 8 August 1882, he married Gertude Ellen Fielding (1858-1928), whose mother was a Spencer

Chapman, and the young couple immediately sailed to Sydney, Australia, arriving on 17 October 1882 *en route* to New Zealand. There at Auckland, they had three children in 1883-1887 and then returned home and migrated to Vancouver Island, where they were settled at Shawnigan Lake in time to have a fourth child there on 24 October 1890. RH was soon recruited by the Provincial Police Force and posted to Chemainus. BP's own military and policing background prepared him to take a lively interest in the BC Provincial Police, which was a constabulary, different from the Royal Canadian Mounted Police. Founded by Sir James Douglas when the Island was still a separate colony, it adapted to each change in the Island's status, becoming the province's police force after 1871 and it was not replaced by the RCMP until 1950. They collaborated with the Royal Navy in maintaining peace and safety on the Island and throughout the province. That adult equivalent to the Boy Scouts, the Legion of Frontiersmen, of which RH was an ideal member on the Island, could only have interested BP, who had kept a watch on *Roger Pocock's activities. Mrs Halhed died, aged seventy, on 20 September 1928 at Chemainus and RH himself, aged eighty-nine, on 24 May 1947, some six years after BP.

Sources: census 1851, England, HO 107/1577/129/16; census 1851, HO 107/1656/39 (Beauchamp); census 1861, RG 9/517, p. 17; census 1871, RG 10/904, pp. 24-25; Elliott, *Memories of the Chemainus Valley*, pp. 229-240; The Halhed Family Genealogical Website, http://www.halhed.com/; Tim Jeal, Baden-Powell (1989; Pimlico Press, 1995), pp. 374-82, 627-29; Robert Baden-Powell, *Scouting for Boys: A Handbook for Instruction in Good Citizenship*, ed., Elleke Boehmer (Oxford, Oxford University Press, 2004), Introduction.

HALL, Frank Addison (1879-1943). Born at Hemel Hempstead, Hertfordshire, son of Charles Addison Hall, he went to Alberta about 1898 and spent some time "ranching" as a "cowboy" before enlisting on 6 February 1900 at Calgary in Lord Strathcona's Horse. He cited his next of kin as his father, Charles A. Hall, living in 1900 at 48 Abbott Road, Southport, and in 1901 at Monaco, California. After serving in the South African War with Lord Strathcona's Horse, he transferred to the Second Canadian Mounted Rifles and eventually received the Queen's Medal with clasps for Belfast, Natal, South Africa 1901, and South Africa 1902. Upon returning to Canada, he moved to the BC coast but returned to England early in the Great War and was commissioned in the Territorial RASC. He served with the Fifty-third Welsh Division in Mesopotamia, Palestine, and France and also with the army of occupation in Germany.

After the war, he returned once again to Canada and moved in 1922 to Cowichan, where he worked on government geodetic surveys and was for some years a surveyor's assistant to Mr J. B. Green at Tzouhalem. A keen sportsman, he played badminton until he fell ill and died, aged sixty-three, on 6 February 1943 at Duncan. He was survived by his wife (*née* Ainslie Willock) and two young daughters, his mother, and a brother, Lloyd Hall in England. An Anglican, he was buried at St. Peter's Quamichan by Rev. Canon T. M. Hughes. Among the pallbearers were *Major H. A. H. Rice, *Captain J. D. Groves, and H. E. Donald.

Sources: NAC, RG 38, A-1-a, vol. 42 (reel T-2072), South African War; *Cowichan Leader*, 11 February 1943.

HALL, Lieutenant Colonel John Albert (1868-1932). Born in Manchester [or Blackpool?] on 24 August 1868, son of Mary Jane Hall, *née* Borthwick, and Robert Hall, a "Woollen Manufacturer's Agent" born in Salford, he was recorded in the 1871 census as a two-year-old living with his parents in Warrington Road, Cheadle Morely, Cheshire. With them were his maternal grandparents, John Borthwick, aged sixty-eight, "Formerly Turner & Fitter" born at Disley, Derbyshire, and Marion Borthwick, aged sixty-seven, born in Salford. In 1881, the family, now with a daughter, were living on River Hill, Ashton-upon-Mersey. He was sent to English public schools, where he excelled at chemistry and mathematics, became a gold medalist in chemistry at Owen College, Manchester, and was hired as a lecturer in chemistry at Manchester Polytechnic School. Later, he did research at the Creighton Aniline Works.

During the early 1890s, he and two friends from college days, Frederick Moore and J. W. Fisher, decided to emigrate and tossed a coin to see which of the colonies they would go to. Their choice fell on Canada, and in 1893, they went to the Island, where they soon established the Victoria Chemical Works, which grew into a large enterprise with a factory at the outer wharf. They remained with the firm until it merged with Canadian Explosives Ltd., which became Canadian Industries Ltd., and built a larger plant on James Island in the Gulf of Georgia, off the coast of Saanich. (Thanks to an uncle, a war veteran on the permanent staff there, I spent the summer of 1950, making dynamite at the James Island plant.) The census recorded JH in 1901 as a "Chemical Works Proprietor" living in Castlewood St, Victoria, with his wife, Anne Hall (*née* Gatenby), born on 25 October 1868, in Derbyshire. They were Anglicans and employed a Chinese servant, who declared himself an agnostic born on 24 November 1884 in China. In October 1899, JH joined the Fifth CGA, at first as honorary lieutenant quartermaster but was promoted to captain in August 1901 and eighteen months later became lieutenant colonel in command. This was only three years and four months since his first appointment. Next, he worked in Victoria for several years to bring the Eighty-eighth Fusiliers into existence and was appointed their commanding officer when they were established on 3 September 1912. When disturbances broke out in 1913 among the miners at Nanaimo, he was appointed to command the Civil Aid Force, assisted by a detachment at Ladysmith under command of the future *General Sir Arthur Currie and other detachments at Cumberland and Wellington nearby. When he joined the CEF at Victoria on 8 November 1914, he recorded his occupation as "Gentleman." At that time, he and his wife were Anglicans living at "'Longtowe,' Esquimalt, Thaburn PO."

He no sooner arrived in England with the Thirtieth Battalion in 1915 than his long experience in the explosives business as manager of Victoria Chemical Works brought him to the attention of the War Office. After a short time in France, he was appointed to the explosives committee at Whitehall and was soon employed by the Ministry of Munitions as a member of the Imperial Munitions

Board and became inspector of all munitions plants in Great Britain. He also did much research work at Whitechapel for the Munitions Board, and later in the war, his duties also took in all of the munitions plants in Canada. By the time he arrived back in Victoria at the end of 1917, to spend a week as a guest of the Union Club, he had also been training troops at Shorncliffe. After the war, they lived at "Longstone," 1211 Old Esquimalt Road near Lampson Street, and spent the summers at a cottage they bought at Shawnigan Lake. Mrs Hall's unmarried sister came out to stay with them. At JH's death on 18 May 1932, the *Daily Colonist* recalled his founding of the Victoria Chemical Company many years earlier: "The death of Colonel Hall severs the last link with this old chemical company, which was the first to be established in B.C. and among the first to be established in Canada. Mr Moore and Mr Fisher pre-deceased Colonel Hall, whose knowledge of chemistry and mathematics won for him an enviable record in the realm of science. Colonel Hall was quoted quite frequently and extensively by Lunge, the noted German chemist, in his many works, which are accepted as textbooks to the chemical industry. Colonel Hall is quoted particularly on matters dealing with sulphuric acid and alkali, these two chemicals having an important part in the study of heavy chemicals." His funeral and his wife's later were at St Paul's Garrison Church, Esquimalt.

Sources: NAC, CEF files, box 3946-39; census 1871, England, RG 10/3666; census 1881, RG 11/3504, p. 19; *Colonist*, 2 January 1917, p. 5; 14 April 1917, p. 5; 19 October 1921, p. 8; 19 May 1932, pp. 1 and 2 and 18, obit.; 1 September 1937, p 12; *Sunday Islander*, 10 April 1988.

HALL, Major Percy Byng (1880-1964). He was born on 29 June 1880 at Murree, India, son of Elizabeth (Goldney) Hall and General Charles Henry Hall, a native of Basingstoke who commanded an infantry regiment in India for thirty-eight years and retired in 1885 as commissioner of Lahore with the rank of general. General Hall returned to England but died in Germany in 1893 and his wife in 1912. PH's paternal grandfather, Charles Hall of Basingstoke, had married an Austrian woman and served as British attaché to the court of Wurtemberg. After attending Wellington College, Berkshire, and RMC, Sandhurst, PH was commissioned, aged eighteen, in the Derbyshire Regiment (Sixth Yeomanry Brigade) and became a lieutenant on 16 October 1895. On 25 April 1901, he transferred as lieutenant to the Thirty-fourth Sikh Pioneers and was stationed in the Punjab for eight and a half years, with excursions such as a campaign in China in 1900, under General Sir Garret O'Moore Creagh (1848-1943), in which he was awarded the DSO. On 1 November 1905 in Lahore, India, he married Miss Muriel O'Callaghan, daughter of Sir Francis O'Callaghan (1839-1909) of County Cork, Ireland, who was a railway engineer widely known for having built the Attock bridge in India, the Khojak tunnel in Baluchistan, and the Uganda Railway. In August 1906, PH and his wife went to Canada and ranched in Alberta for a year.

In 1907, they moved Shawnigan Lake but the next year settled in Victoria, where he formed a partnership with Arthur Hereward Floyer (c. 1858-1933) to sell real estate and insurance, specializing in property at Port Edward, some twelve

miles south of the mouth of the Skeena River, now the historic site of an early salmon cannery. He was also manager of Anglo-British Columbia Securities Ltd. and perhaps other businesses. They had three children: Percy Byng Hall (born 17 April 1907), Maureen Hall (born 27 May 1910), and Desmond Hall (born in December 1912). PH joined the Conservative Party and the Union Club. He liked hunting, boating, amateur theatricals, and music. They lived on St Patrick's Street in Oak Bay and were popular socially in the city. When the Great War began, he was a major in the Eighty-eighth Fusiliers, formed in Victoria in autumn 1912, and seems to have remained there as a training officer. Already in the previous summer, he had led nineteen men in field manoeuvres and "fought a rearguard action," the *Colonist* reported, "against the whole of the 72nd Highlanders along the side of Elk Lake [eight miles north of Victoria] so successfully that they were obliged to choose another route for their advance on Victoria." In old age, they moved to Ganges, Salt Spring Island, where Muriel (O'Callaghan) Hall died, aged seventy-four, on 25 April 1954, and PH died, aged eighty-four, on 7 May 1964.
Sources: Howay and Gosnell, *British Columbia*, vol. V, pp. 98-9; Lieutenant Colonel E. W. C. Sandes, *The Military Engineer in India* (2 vols.; Chatham, Royal Engineers Institution, 1933 and 1935), vol. II, pp. 86, 130, 145, and 153; Army Lists; *Colonist*, 12 April 1914, p. 14.

HALSTED [Halstead], Gunner Arthur R. (1883-1917). Born on 15 November 1883 at Burnley, Lancashire, he was living at 537 Rithet Street, James Bay, Victoria, with his wife Nora when he enlisted in the 103rd Battalion on 8 December 1915 in Victoria. He was an Anglican with a ruddy complexion, blue eyes, and brown hair. He had been working as a clerk, but had fought in the South African War, spending four years in the RFA, two years in the Lancashire Infantry, and three years in the South African Constabulary. He fought at Mafeking when he was only seventeen years old. During the Great War, he went overseas in 1916 as company sergeant major in the Canadian 103rd Battalion, but gave up a sergeant major's stripe in order to rejoin the artillery as a gunner. Soon after going to France, he was wounded and died on 22 July 1917, serving with the Ninth Brigade, CFA. He was survived by his widow and two children.
Sources: NAC, CEF files, box 3966-35, regimental no. 706127; *Colonist*, 2 August 1917, p. 7, photo and obit.

HAMILTON, Captain Andrew (1843-1933). Born at Coombe-Raleigh, Devonshire, son of Major Alexander Duke Hamilton, who had served at the battle of Waterloo (1815), he attended Dr Burney's Royal Naval School at Gosport and joined the Thirty-first Regiment as an ensign. He served at Gibraltar, in South Africa, and in India at the close of the Mutiny. He first went to Canada in 1883 from Kelvindon, Essex, where he had been living after retiring from the army. After two years at the western end of the CPR, somewhere on the prairies, he took his wife and youngest sons to Victoria, where except for a period of farming at Agassiz, he lived for the rest of his life. For nearly fifteen years, he wrote articles for *The Canadian Gazette* and was a strong supporter of the Reformed Episcopal Church.

He died, aged ninety-three, on 21 February 1933, leaving four sons, including Captain Anthony Hamilton, DSO, of Sussex. At his funeral, the pallbearers included Lieutenant Colonel C. B. Schreiber, Captain P. W. de P. Taylor, and *Major D. V. Porteous.
Sources: *Colonist*, 12 November 1929, p. 11; 22 February 1933, p. 3; 24 February 1933, p. 2, obit.

HAMILTON, Major Andrew Victor (1883-1940). He was born in Chelsea, London, in July 1883, son of John F. Hamilton (c. 1839-?), born in Streatham, Surrey. The father was recorded in 1871 as a "Merchant, East India" and in 1881 as "China & Japan merchant." The census of 1891 recorded AM as, aged seven, born in Chelsea, London, but living with his two sisters and mother Alice M. Hamilton (c. 1845-?), born at Winchester, Hampshire, all as "boarders" at Gore Court Mansion, Otham near Maidstone, Kent, the house of William S. Forster, aged fifty-seven, a "Solicitor practicing in London (farmer here)" with wife and five children. AH's father was absent. There were eight servants. Ten years later, AH, still single, was a "Steam Engine Maker Fitter" boarding at 6 Milton Road, Swindon, Wiltshire, the home of Zacharia Peskett, aged fifty-five, "Railway clerk, Loco Works" (born at Horsham, Sussex), and his wife Annie (aged fifty-seven, born in Swindon, Wilts.) and their two daughters and a son, who was also a "Steam Engine Maker Fitter," doubtless one of AH's colleagues.

Early in the twentieth century, AH moved to the Island where in 1906-1916, he was employed in railway and power development and other construction projects. He married Winifred Maud Mckeard in Victoria on 12 July 1909, and on 1 December 1916, he and his wife Winifred were living at 449 Moss Street, Victoria, when he was commissioned as lieutenant in the Eighty-eighth Victoria Fusiliers. They were Anglicans, and he described his occupation as "Manufacturer." He transferred later to the Third Battalion of the Canadian Machine Gun Corps and fought in France until December 1918, when he was invalided home, and the following June became assistant purchasing agent for BC. In 1928, he transferred to the traffic division of the Department of Public works as an inspector in Vancouver. In 1933, he became chief purchasing agent for that department and held this post until his death, aged fifty-seven, on 27 September 1940 in Victoria. The funeral was at St Mary's Anglican Church, Oak Bay. He left his widow and three daughters at home, 1397 St David Street, Oak Bay.
Sources: NAC, CEF files box 3976-16; *Colonist*, 29 September 1940, p. 6, obit.; census 1871, England, RG 10/1145, p. 57; census 1881, RG 11/76, p. 31; census 1891, RG 12/685, p. 4; census 1901, RG 13/1907, p. 11.

HAMILTON, William John Lawrence (1859-1946). Soon after his arrival on the Island in 1891, he settled nearby on Salt Spring Island on sixty-six acres of waterfront at Isabella Point near Fulford Harbour with his wife, Caroline Louisa Hayward (1860-1932), and their four English children; they then produced seven more. WH hardly merits the patronizing terms in which local authors describe him, evidently prompted by the inverted snobbery Canadians so often apply to people with English gentlemanly backgrounds. He was an electrical engineer born on 13 March 1859 at Kilcronaghan, County Londonderry, son of Archdeacon Edward James Hamilton, and nephew of a former Viceroy of India; their family tree stretched back to 912 AD, their ancestors having come over with William the Conqueror. The head of the house in 1944 was Lord Holm Patrick, and their names were on the Plantagenet roll of the Blood Royal. WH was himself educated at Uppingham School at Armagh and the Royal School of Mines. He became manager of the Maxim-Weston Company of London. He descended from the great Lawrence family of officers from the Indian Army and the ICS through his aunt Catherine Harriette Hamilton (1820-1917), who had married the Right Honourable Sir John Laird Mair Lawrence (1811-1879), Baron Lawrence of the Punjab and Grateley, governor general and viceroy of India. Apart from inventing an incandescent light bulb, which he sold to the Edison Corporation, Hamilton lived quietly on his island property, which he called "Dromore" after the family estate in Ireland, and cared for his farm and family, a demanding task because some of the children were born blind. But he may have been not quite what he seemed.

Census records suggest that they were social "refugees," like certain others on the Island, seeking a new life free from family expectations or reproaches. They had married in 1884 in Marylebone, London. In 1891, shortly before emigrating, they were living in London at 14 Somerset Road, Ealing, with their four eldest children, variously born at Herne Bay (Kent), Portrush (Ireland), and Ealing. WH's identity is clear as an Irish-born electrical engineer, but Caroline L. born at Andover, Hampshire, on 21 November 1860, figures in the 1881 census records as a cook employed in the household of a Marylebone dairyman and family and, in 1871, at Andover as the ten-year-old daughter of a widowed "needlewoman," Elizabeth Hayward, from Bagshot, Surrey, who was recorded in 1861 at Andover as the wife of a coal dealer with a several children and a new-born daughter named Caroline. That baby seems to be the Caroline Louisa (Hayward) Hamilton, who died, aged seventy-one, on 9 January 1932 at Fulford Harbour, wife of WH, who died, aged eighty-seven, on 16 May 1946 in Ganges, both on Salt Spring Island. **Sources:** Kahn, *Salt Spring Island*, pp. 115-16; *Who's Who in B.C.*, vol. VI (1944-46), pp. 105-106; *Colonist*, 17 May 1946, p. 10, obit.; *Who was Who*, 1897-1916, p. 416; BNA, census 1881, England, RG 11/642, p. 14; census 1861, RG 9/715, pp. 7-8; census 1871, RG 10/1243, p. 44; census 1881, RG 11/146, p. 35; census 1891, RG 12/1029, p. 10.

HAMLEY, Thomas Wymond Ogilvie (1818-1907). He was born on 30 December 1818 in Bodmin, Cornwall, third son of Vice Admiral William Hamley, RN, who had distinguished himself serving as a Flag lieutenant at the battle of Zara (1808). TH served briefly in the RN but soon retired to enter the Imperial Civil Service and, after some years in Somerset House, was appointed the first collector of customs for the mainland colony of British Columbia, still separate from Vancouver Island. There was no port on the mainland, and he arrived at Esquimalt on 12 April 1859 aboard the *Thames* with Captain Luward and 125 Royal Engineers sent to equip the new mainland colony with roads, bridges, and the other infrastructure of a British colony. Also on board were Colonel Richard Wolfenden (1836-1911) and Robert Butler (1842-1917), both employed later as printers in the provincial civil service. Another major figure in the colony's early life, Peter O'Reilly (1829-1905), who became a lifelong friend, arrived the same day on another ship. They began their careers together at the capital, New Westminster, and when, in 1866, the two Pacific Coast colonies were joined together, they moved in due time with the government to Victoria. TH sat in the Legislative Council in 1864-1871, and when, in 1871, British Columbia became part of Canada, he remained collector of customs. On his staff at various times were the journalist and memorialist, Edgar Fawcett (c. 1846-1923), a civil engineer, William Atkins (1846-1923), and a clerk, John Newbury (1863-1934), all active in the customs service and in Victoria after he retired in 1889. He lived alone, except for servants, at his house on Burdette Street, corner of Victoria Crescent, and when he died in 1907, he left only nephews and nieces in England and one relative in Canada, Mrs Justice Irving.

His willingness to serve in that remote colony may have had something to do with a shipmate in the navy, the future Admiral Sir Algernon Lyons, having visited Esquimalt earlier. TH always said he obtained his post through the influence of his younger brother, Edward, who had just returned from China and was having some success as a writer. But other brothers, too, became prominent figures in their time. The eldest, William, served the Royal Engineers in Syria in 1849 and in the Baltic expeditions of 1854-1855, rising to become a major general. The second died a colonel in the Royal Marine Light Infantry. The fourth son was the well-known General Sir Edward Bruce Hamley (1824-93). Edgar Fawcett, who knew Hamley well, wrote, "Mr Hamley was the last of three brothers, and all of us have heard of the youngest, Sir Edward, the hero of Tel-el-Kebir, who, with his eldest brother, were generals in the British army. Sir Edward was a noted tactician, and it was through this he became the hero of Tel-el-Kebir. He was also prominent in the Imperial Parliament as a speaker. The elder brother I heard little of from him, but I know he was very proud of his younger brother. The late collector was in early life in the British civil service, and subsequently joined the navy, and served on the China stations." TH died, aged eighty-eight, on 15 January 1907 in Victoria.

Sources: Edgar Fawcett, *Some Reminiscences of Old Victoria* (Toronto, William Briggs, 1912), pp. 111-12; Alfred Stanley Deaville, *The Colonial Postal Systems and Postage Stamps of Vancouver Island and British Columbia*, 1849-1871 (Victoria, C. F. Banfield, King's Printer, 1928), pp. 56, 66; Charles William Wilson, *Mapping the Frontier: Charles Wilson's Diary of the Survey of the 49th Parallel, 1858-1862, While Secretary of the British Boundary Commission*, ed., George F. G. Stanley (Toronto, Macmillan, 1970), p. 86n.; Margaret A. Ormsby, *British Columbia: A History* (Toronto, Macmillan, 1958), p. 157; *The Times* (London), 15 August 1893, obit. for General Sir Edward Bruce Hamley.

HANKIN, Commander Phillip James (1836-?). Born on 30 May 1836 at Stanstead, Hertfordshire, he was the fifth of the fourteen children of Daniel and Elizabeth Dorothy (née Potter) Hankin. He joined the Royal Navy and went to the Island in 1857 aboard HMS *Plumper* and again later in HMS *Hecate*. In 1864, he resigned with the rank of commander and returned to Victoria, where he was employed at first as a junior clerk in the colonial secretary's office but rose to become superintendent of police, governor of Victoria Jail, and then colonial secretary of BC. On August 3, 1865, he married Isabella Gertrude Nagle, born in New Zealand, fourth daughter of *Captain Jeremiah Nagle. When the Island and BC were joined together in 1866, he lost his posts and returned to England, whence he was sent to serve the colonial service in British Honduras and Sierra Leone. In 1869, he was appointed colonial secretary in BC and returned to the colony until 1871, when the new Canadian federal administration damaged his career prospects and he went back once more to England to work as private secretary to the Duke of Buckingham. In 1901, the census found him, a "retired Commander, R.N." with his wife Isabel, aged fifty-three, living in a lodging house at The Strand, Hyde, Isle of Wight. His memoirs are in Victoria at the BC Archives.

Sources: census 1901, England, RG 13/1025, p. 42; Lindsay Elms internat site; W. George Shelton, ed., *British Columbia & Confederation* (Victoria, University of Victoria, 1967), p. 161; Pritchard, *Letters of Edmund Hope Verney*, p. 286 n.3.

HARBORD [alias Harbourd], Captain Montague Dodgson (c. 1856-1941). He was born at Wisbech, Cambridgeshire, a handsome Georgian town in the fens, son of William and Sarah Harbord. His identity is confusing, even uncertain, and warrants recording details. The 1871 census found him, aged six, living with his family at "Chase Side," Edmonton, Middlesex (London), his father, aged thirty-three, being an "Annuitant" born at Liverpool, and his mother, aged thirty-one, born at the tiny village of Belleau in Lincolnshire. He had a sister Constance Ellen, aged four, born at Brayloft, Lincolnshire, and two locally born brothers, Albert "Bertie" and Horace, aged three years and ten months. In 1881, the father was absent, the mother was listed as a "Retired Farmer's Wife," and they lived at 185 Eastgate, Louth, on the eastern side of the Lincolnshire wolds, where MH, aged sixteen, was employed as a "sailor." The other children were recorded as Bertie Gordon aged twelve, Horace Mann eleven, Florence Harriet six, and Edith Henrietta four, the latter two now recorded as born at Plaistow, Essex. Constance Ellen was away at school in Southchurch. The father, William Harbord, died in the late 1880s, and 1891 found his widow Sarah, aged fifty-nine, "living on own means" at 32 Altima Street, Stralding, Lincolnshire, with Constance E., Edith H., and a new nine-year-old son, Reginald C. Harbord, born at Louth. The 1901 census recorded MH, aged thirty-six, as an "Estate Agent-Auct[ioneer]" living alone at "Belleau House, Norton, Derbyshire," now in the southern suburbs of Sheffield, just north of the Derbyshire border. In March 1902, he married his wife Elizabeth

According to five reports in the *Daily Colonist* in 1936-1941, MH became a master mariner and commanded sailing vessels all over the world, presumably in the years between the censuses of 1881 and 1901. At one time, he worked in the Rand gold mines in Johannesburg and took part in an expedition against the Matabele's in 1896. He migrated with his wife to Victoria c. 1916 and, in 1919, formed the Chalbert Shipyards, where he "superintended the building of wooden schooners on the Industrial Reserve." Active in veterans' circles, he even had an army friend, *Major Alastair Irvine Robertson, die in his house in 1934 and often attended gatherings of the British Campaigner's Association. He was present at a dinner on 28 November 1935 where "fifty veterans of campaigns in Canada, India, South Africa, Egypt and Europe gathered at the British Campaigners' Association annual dinner" under the presidency of *Colonel Lorne Ross with talks, toasts, communal singing, and piano solos. When in 1940 some four or five hundred young men wanted to form a unit to help Finland in its battles with Russia, MH offered to train and lead them. He was at the association's luncheon at Speedie's Café on 28 May 1941 to celebrate Paardeberg Day and its annual dinner at Spencer's Dining Room the next November, where he spoke about the Matabele expedition. In old age, he used to broadcast stories of his travels and adventures, and he was active in the Conservative Party. While living at 1115 Mears Street, his wife Elizabeth died, aged seventy-four, on 28 June 1939 and he, aged eighty-four, on 28 May 1941. They were buried as Roman Catholics. His death certificate, filled out by a friend, is tinged with doubts about the facts of his life and gives his date of birth as "1856 (?)," his birth place as "England," and his time spent as a master mariner as "possibly over forty years."

Sources: *Colonist*, 1 March 1936, p. 5; 22 November 1936, p. 3; 16 February 1940, p. 6; 29 May 1941, p. 13, obit.; census England, 1871, RG 10/1342, p. 44; census 1871, RG 10/330, p. 37; census 1891, RG 12/2562, pp. 4-5; census 1901, RG 13/4347, p. 25; English Civil Registration, Ecclesall Bierlow District, *Derbyshire West Riding of Yorkshire*, vol. 9c, page 507.

HARDINGE, Major John Bayley (1890-1965). Born 18 February 1890 in Shropshire, he was a son of Rev. John Bayley Hardinge (born at Touge, Shropshire) and his wife Sophia (born in Oxford). His own family is elusive, but the 1891 census recorded his paternal grandparents living at Stafford House, Market Drayton, Shropshire: the grandfather, Rev. John W. H. Hardinge, "Retired clerk in Holy Orders-Clergy," and the grandmother, Catherine A. Hardinge, both born at Walton, Lancashire. Also in the house were four of Hardinge's cousins and their parents: Edward Lloyd, "Major, Indian Cavalry," aged forty-two, born in India; his wife, Mary R. Lloyd, (evidently a daughter of the resident grandparents), aged thirty-three, born in Leamington, Warwickshire; Hugh S. Lloyd, aged eleven, born in Sydenham, Kent; Irene C. Lloyd, aged nine, born in Camberley, Surrey; Edward R. Lloyd, aged eight, born in Camberley, Surrey; and Robin H. Lloyd, aged seven, born in Market Drayton. They had a French governess and two housemaids. The various birthplaces of these children show the instability of the family's life, and JH, after attending Hartford House School and Winchester College, may have found it easy to move as a teenager to Canada, where he arrived in 1907. In 1914, he joined the Machine Corps and rose during the Great War to lieutenant (1916) and major (1917). He returned to Canada in 1919 with the MC, the DSO, and the *Croix de Guerre* and became a director of the Portlock Company (1925) and a JP in Saskatchewan.

In 1923, JH married Hazel, daughter of Edward Stanley of Victoria, where they moved in 1927 and lived at 1057 Richmond Avenue, later at 999 Beach Drive, Oak Bay. An additional reason for moving to the Island was that JH's elder brother, Henry Tetlow Hardinge (c. 1880-1955), had settled on a farm near Duncan in the Cowichan Valley. H. T. Hardinge was born in Odiham, Hampshire, a village about halfway between Aldershot and Basingstoke, while their father was "Curate of Winchfield" nearby. JH was soon elected to the executive of the Canadian Manufacturers' Association, Island branch (22 February 1933). He took up yachting, joined the British Public Schools Club, and became a scoutmaster. He proposed a toast to "The King" at the celebration of Lord Baden-Powell's birthday in February 1933, an occasion on which *Freeman Foard King, scoutmaster in Sidney, gave the toast "To B-P." Again, it was Freeman King who seconded JH's nomination as Conservative candidate in the Island riding the following June in preparation for a forthcoming provincial election. JH was nominated by *Spencer Percival of Pender Island, and following Percival's example, he began to write to the local press on Imperial and other public affairs. "I can only say," he told the voters, "far as I am personally concerned, that I have only one political faith, and that faith is a supreme confidence in the common sense of the people who, once they stop to think, will do the right thing." Notwithstanding the support of G. H. Watson, manager of the Sidney [Lumber] Mills, and people like my parents who invariably voted Conservative, the people did the wrong thing and defeated JH at the polls. He then took up the cause of retired Imperial soldiers like himself and became first vice-president, Imperial Veterans' Association, Victoria and Island branch. "There are 200,000 ex-Imperials residing in Canada," he wrote to the *Colonist*, in 1937, "40,000 in B.C. and 7,000 on the south end of Vancouver Island . . . The public generally classify all veterans as 'returned men,' little realizing the vast difference in treatment received by the Canadian veteran and the Imperial. The Canadian government has been most generous to the Canadian soldier and sailor and the existing Canadian Pension Act is sufficiently flexible to make it human. The British Government on the other hand, for centuries has been notorious for the scandalous treatment it hands out to its ex-soldiers and sailors." He cited examples. In December 1838, he was one of the pallbearers in December 1939 at the funeral of Colonel Arthur Henry Morris, CMG, DSO, and as commander of the veteran guard during a visit by the governor general on 30 March 1941, he shook hands with the Earl of Athlone. JH died, aged seventy-three, on 13 January 1965 in Vancouver.
Sources: *Who's Who in B.C.*, 1933-4, p. 74; census 1891, England, RG 12/2128, p. 4; *Colonist*, 8 April 1931, p. 8; 22 February 1933, p. 6; 26 February 1933, p. 7; 5 March 1933, p. 4; 15 July 1933, p. 2; 21 September 1937, p. 4; 23 July 1938, p. 4; 30 March 1941, pp. 1 and 11; John F. T. Saywell, *Kaatza: The Chronicles of Cowichan Lake* (Sidney, The Cowichan Lake District Centennial Committee, 1967), pp. 58, 65, citing the *Duncan Leader*, of 15 July 1915; Riddick, *Who in British India*, p. 161 (forebears).

HARRIS, Lieutenant Colonel Alexis Ernest (1883-1944). Born at Boston Massachusetts on 20 November 1883, son of Ernest A. Harris, civil engineer, he attended schools in Ottawa and RMC, Kingston, Ontario, and joined the Fifth

Heavy Battery, RCA. Promotion followed to lieutenant (August 1905), captain (1910), major (1915), lieutenant colonel (1918), and then deputy commandant Royal Canadian School of Artillery at Work Point, Esquimalt. In 1915-1919, he served in the British West Indies 1915-1919, and there his wife, *née* Leila Ione Wadmore, was living at Vigu, [Vigne?], Castries, St Lucia, British West Indies, when he joined the Canadian army on 16 March 1915 at Quebec as a major. She was a daughter of *Colonel Robinson Lyndhurst Wadmore of the RCE, and he had married her on 25 January 1911 in Victoria, where Wadmore was then posted as commandant of Military District No. 11. They eventually had four sons.

In 1921, after the Great War, they went to live in Victoria and, after being recalled for duty in Halifax, retired at last in October 1933 to their former house at 766 Esquimalt Road. AH was by then part of an extended family of Imperial soldiers. In January 1943, his wife's sister, Mrs Horace Westmorland, wife of *Colonel Horace Westmorland, came to visit them. The Westmorlands had married there in Victoria on 25 June 1913, and their son, Captain H. Lyndhurst Westmorland, was by then serving in the Fourteenth Punjab (Pathan) Indian Army and fighting in Libya and elsewhere. On 30 September 1944, AH died at the Jubilee Hospital, leaving his widow as well as three sons: Lieutenant C. E. Harris, Corporal Dennis Harris, and Ian Harris.

Sources: *Who's Who in B.C.*, 1944-1946, p. 107; NAC, CEF files, box 4081-24, lieutenant colonel; *Colonist*, 24 January 1943, p. 7; 8 October 1933, p. 22; 1 October 1944, p. 2, obit.

HARRIS, John (c. 1876-1934). He was born c. 1876 at "Meadowend," Sandford, Devonshire, where his mother Eliza was also born. His father, George Harris from Knowston nearby, was a country labourer, as he was himself as a teenager at Creditor, Devon, when he joined the Devonshire Regiment. After several campaigns on the North-West Frontier of India, including one at Tirah, and in the South African War, wherein he was present at the sige of Ladysmith, he retired about 1912 to Victoria. There he lived for twenty-two years during which worked at the post office and was a member of the Imperial Campaigners' Association. When he died, he was living at 2647 Forbes Street with his wife Mabel and two sons; the funeral was at St Alban's Anglican Church. Three sisters and a brother still lived in England.

Sources: BC Archives, "*Minutes of the British Campaigners' Association*, 1908-1928"; census 1891, England, RG 12/1760, p. 5; census 1881, RG 11/2231; *Colonist*, 18 March 1934, p. 3, obit.

HARRISON, Lieutenant Colonel Thomas Elliott (1862-1939). He was born 14 June 1862, son of T. E. Harrison (1808-1888) of Whitburn, Sunderland-on-Wear, a well-known engineer who built the Firth of Forth Bridge in Scotland. TH was schooled at Eton and Trinity College Cambridge; in 1893-1899, he was master of the East Galway Hounds. During the South African War, he fought in the First Royal Dragoons and commanded the Fourth Battalion of Imperial Yeomanry (despatches, DSO, and both medals) and, in the Great War, served with General Allenby in Egypt. In 1890, he married Daisy Wright (died 1920), youngest daughter of William Wright of Saxelly Park, Melton Mowbray, and they had two sons, Charles Harrison and Colonel Ralph Harrison, who was drowned in England in 1937.

About 1920, they retired to Victoria where he was the first president of the Public Schools Club, which later became the Empire Club, and remained a member for the rest of his life. For many years "until his hearing failed," he also attended meetings of the Overseas League. At his death on 3 March 1939, he was living at 1054 Princess Avenue.

Sources: *Who was Who*, vol. 3, p. 601; *Colonist*, 4 March 1939, pp. 3 and 14; 7 March 1939, p. 14, obit.; 8 March 1939, p. 5.

HARTLEY, Instructor Commodore Basil Shakespeare (c. 1867-1946). He was born in Dolting, Somerset, son of Rev. T. S. Hartley, born in Tottenham, Middlesex, and his wife Mary from Lincolnshire. The 1871 census recorded BH, aged four, living with his family in Church Street, Sutton, Cambridgeshire, where his father was the local curate. BH had four older sisters, and there was a servant. Ten years later, he was a fourteen-year-old "scholar" in the RN training ship, *Britannia*, and on 14 June 1892, he became a naval instructor; the 1901 census recorded him, aged thirty-five, as a "Naval Instructor" still (or again?) aboard the *Britannia*. The RN lent him to the RCN in 1910, and he served aboard the training ship *Niobe* until 1914, when he was appointed director of studies at the Royal Naval College of Canada when it was first established. After the Halifax explosion on 6 December 1917, he moved with the college to Kingston, Ontario, and then to the new college establishment at Esquimalt. He settled with his wife and family at 677 St Patrick Street, Victoria, and remained there in retirement when the Dominion government closed the college in 1922. Later, they moved to Deep Cove on Saanich Inlet about twenty miles north of Victoria and were, of course, present at Holy Trinity Anglican Church, Patricia Bay, a mile or two south of Deep Cove, when their son Thomas Sutherland Hartley married Joyce Mowat Lennard in May 1933. She was the daughter of Major J. F. W. Lennard of London and Mrs Lennard of Deep Cove. The bride's uncle, *Captain J. H. Broadwood, gave her away and her aunt, Mrs Hedley Peek, held the wedding reception at her house in Sidney. A hundred guests assembled for the occasion. The young couple honeymooned in Seattle and then went to Bolivia, where the groom was the manager of a mine. When BH died, aged seventy-nine, in Victoria, he was survived by his wife and two sons, Captain T. S. Hartley and Rev. Basil Hartley.

Sources: *MacFarlane*, p. 29; *Colonist*, 26 May 1933, p. 8; 5 or 6 April 1946, obit.; census 1871, England, RG 10/1929, p. 19; census 1881, RG 11/480, p. 71; census 1901, RG 13/2080, p. 1.

HARTLEY, Charles (1865-1935). After the Great War (1914-1918), he went to live in Victoria at 430 St Patrick Street in the Foul Bay district. There he was active at St Matthew's Anglican Church and joined the Overseas League, which was very active between the wars. On 14 December 1931, about sixty members of the league assembled to hear him speak about India and also (according to the habits of that time) to be entertained by a piano recital and amusing recitations by Miss Ora Pearson. CH died, aged sixty-nine, on 26 January 1935 and was buried after a funeral at St Matthew's Church.

He was born on 12 February 1865 at Beccles, Suffolk, son of Rev. Alfred Hartley, vicar of Steeple Ashton, and his wife Ann. The 1871 census recorded him there, aged six, in "Vicarage House" with his parents, a stepsister Elizabeth Knubley aged seventeen, born in Cumberland, as well as an eight-year-old brother Henry A. Hartley and a sister Lorina aged three. He attended Fauconberg Grammar School in Beccles and then Malborough College (1879-1883), where the 1881 census recorded him aged sixteen on a long list of teenaged boys. Next, he was at Magdalen College, Cambridge, where he graduated BA (1887), wrangler, second-class Tripos, MA, and became captain of Magdalen College Cricket Team. There followed a long career as a teacher of languages, mainly classical, beginning as classics master at Cathedral School, Worcester. He moved on to teach as "modern language and classical master" at Christ College, Brecon, where the 1891 census found him boarding in the house of an elderly widow at 12 Bridge Street, St David. After a period as professor of languages at Malborough College, he went out to Colombo, Ceylon, where in September 1896, he joined the staff of Royal College as lecturer in modern languages and English. He became acting principal (October 1897 to August 1898), acting principal assistant (April 1902 to January 1903), principal on a salary of Rs. 9,600 per annum (23 June 1903 to May 1919), assistant censor in Ceylon (1915), and acting director of public instruction (1910). In his years at Royal College, Ceylon, he made a reputation for three activities: for arranging to have the college moved in 1913 to the healthier and more agreeable surroundings of Cinnamon Garden; for encouraging sports, especially cricket, which he played seldom but well, and yachting in his boat, *Fiona*, and as a lecturer and honorary secretary of the Colombo Sailing Cub; and for his firm but strict principalship of the college. In 1897, he once caned the entire upper sixth form; but between 1908 and 1916, he defended the college against efforts in some quarters to have it abolished. He was later fondly remembered for his eccentricities. Silent and determined, he travelled nearly everywhere on a bicycle dressed "in Cannanore suit and faded green tie, a Shakespearan collar, white shoes and a crumpled hat, ('a monstrosity of the hatters art')."

Sources: *Records of Royal College, Colombo, Ceylon; Thacker's Indian Directory for 1912,* the resident's list, p. 144; *Colonist,* 15 December 1931, p. 8; 27 January 1935, p. 20, obit.; census 1871, England, RG 10/1929, p. 4; census 1881, RG 11/2038, p. 11; census 1891, RG 12/4570, p. 4.

HARTLEY, Gordon Charles (1878-1957). Born on 7 February 1878 at Kennington (or Walworth), Surrey in Greater London, he was the eldest son of Annie Louise Hartley, born in the Kent Road, and her husband Charles Hartley, a wine merchant born in Westminster, London. The census-taker found them in 1881: GH aged three and a younger brother Frank Hartley, aged three months, living at 14 Percy Lane in Lambeth, London. Ten years later, he was boarding at East London Industrial Institute School in Lewisham (headmaster, James

Cartwright), where he learned to be a carpenter. GH served in the Royal Navy for five years as a mechanic, first class, and then married in 1902 at Lewisham and took his wife out to Victoria, where their address was Maywood Post Office. They had two children by 11 May 1915, when he enlisted in the Thirteenth Field Ambulance, Canadian Army Medical Corps, in Vernon, BC. He was 5' 8½" tall, with brown eyes, black hair, and a tattoo on his left forearm. A member of the Church of England, upon his return from overseas, he lived quietly with his family, serving *inter alia* as a pallbearer at the funeral of *Captain Thomas Barclay in Metchosin, west of Victoria. He died, aged seventy-eight, on 29 December 1957 still in Victoria. Mrs Mary Hartley died there, aged eighty-five, on 6 October 1965.

Sources: census 1881, England, RG 11/622, p. 5; census 1891, RG 12/522, p. 2 (of 7); NAC, CEF files, box 4124-56, regimental no. 524601.

HATCHER, Regimental Sergeant Major Frank (1866-1941). Born on 14 December 1866 at Kingsombourne, Hampshire, the younger of two sons of Thomas Hatcher, a bricklayer, and his wife Sarah, FH joined the Royal Marine Artillery, aged eighteen, and later claimed to have visited every major port in the empire. He reached Victoria on 28 March 1894 with the first contingent of Imperial troops, and after serving at Work Point for six years, he left the permanent force and in 1901 joined the local Fifth Regiment, CGA. He served in it for sixteen years, as a sergeant for eleven of them and drum major for the last five. In 1913, he was chosen for the Canadian team going to shoot at Bisley. By the time he enlisted on 1 January 1916 in the CEF, he had retired from the service, worked for a while in the Circulation Department of the *Colonist*, and was employed as a "License Inspector" for Victoria, living meanwhile at 1622 North Pembroke Street, Victoria, with his wife Alice and their three children. Being almost too old for military service, he lied about his age, stating it as forty-three and his birth date as 14 December 1872. His hair was turning grey, and he had a tattoo on his left forearm, but his eyes were still blue and his complexion "fresh." After only a few months overseas with the Tenth Ammunition Column, Colonel F. A. Robertson had promoted him to quartermaster sergeant and recommended him on 28 October 1916 for the Distinguished Conduct Medal for courage and devotion on the Somme. French authorities awarded him the *Médaille militaire*. He retired at last in 1924 and settled in Victoria at 1616 Myrtle Avenue, where he died on 2 January 1941 and was buried as an Anglican at the Colwood Burial Park in a military funeral with a guard of honour.

Sources: NAC, CEF files, RG 150, box 4151-27, regimental no. 313897; census 1871, England, RG 10/1206, p. 29; *Colonist*, 18 January 1917, p. 5; 14 March 1917, p. 5; 3 January 1941, p. 3; 5 January 1941, p. 3, obit and photo; 7 January 1941, p. 2.

HAYWARD, Harold Blackney (1880-1966). He was born on 28 December 1880 at Aldershot, Hampshire, son of Major General H. B. Hayward, and the family's restless Imperial life can be traced in the birthplaces of five daughters: Thayatmyer, Burma; Port Blair, Andeman Islands; Sutton-at-Home, Kent; Crayford, Kent; and

Aldershot, Hampshire. HH attended a school in St Leonards, Hastings, East Sussex, went on to Tonbridge School, and then worked for four years as a member of the London Stock Exchange. After that, he spent two years in Malaya planting rubber, but in 1908, he went to Duncan, VI, and was working as "Club Secretary" and a member of the militia when he enlisted at Valcartier on 23 September 1914. He had a toe missing from his left foot and tattoos on his forearms. He mentioned his father as his next of kin, then living at Grayforest, Kent, England. Sent overseas with the Gordon Highlanders (later called the Sixteenth Battalion), he was wounded and taken prisoner by the Germans, exchanged to Switzerland in 1917, and discharged in 1919. He then returned to Duncan and took up farming but, in 1921, was appointed vendor at the government liquor store there. While in Switzerland in 1918, he had married Aileen C. Macbean, who was born at Hong Kong daughter of W. Macbean of Hampshire, and they settled with a son and a daughter on the Maple Bay Road. After her death, aged forty-seven, on 15 May 1941, he married again. He was a keen member of the Cowichan Cricket Club (in 1912-1913 was wicketkeeper for BC against the Australians), attended St Peter's Anglican Quamichan, and spent his time gardening, fishing, and boating. He died on 6 January 1966, aged eighty-five, at the King's Daughters Hospital, Duncan, leaving his second wife Betty and two sons—Commander Robin Hayward (Halifax) and A. B. David Hayward (Dartmouth, NB)—and two daughters. He was buried at St Peter's Quamichan.

Sources: NAC, CEF files, box 4198-8, regimental no. 28633; *Who's Who in B.C.*, 1933-1934, pp. 76-7; vol. V, (1942-1943), p. 145; vol. VI (1944-1946), pp. 111-112; census 1881, England, RG 11/785, p. 1; census 1891, RG 12/765, p. 49; *Cowichan Leader*, 12 January 1966, obit.; *Colonist*, 16 May 1941, p. 5, obit.

HAYWARD, Major William Henry (1867-1932). Born on 23 October 1867 at Dover, Kent, he appears there, aged three, in the 1871 census, living at 16 Maison View Road with his brother Frederick G. Hayward, aged two, and their parents. The father, Henry Hayward, aged twenty-eight, was an "Auctioneer & Surveyor" born at Dover and their mother, Marianne Hayward, aged twenty-five, was born at Mapledurham, Oxfordshire. They had a general servant and a nurse. Ten years later, these two brothers were boarding at Barrows School, Borden, Kent. WH went on to Sutton Valence Grammar School, Dover College, and the Crystal Palace School of Engineering, where he took the Colonial Course. He spent some eighteen months in Scotland and married a Scottish lady, Jeannie, some four years older than himself and in 1886, they emigrated to Æmilia County, Virginia, where they had a daughter, Violet, on 28 September 1887, and he spent eight years tobacco planting and farming.

In 1894, they all emigrated to the Island, where they lived for a year in Victoria and then bought part of the Glengarry Farm at Metchosin. In 1897, Queen Victoria's Jubilee year, he gave a large painting of the queen as a prize for school children in the district. The BC census found them in March 1901 still farming there, employing three servants, all Anglicans like themselves. But a few months earlier, WH had been elected as a Conservative MPP to hold one of the two seats for Esquimalt in the Provincial Legislature, but after a dissolution in June 1903 and the redistribution of seats, when Esquimalt was reduced to one member, he decided not to run again. An invitation to visit E. B. McKay at Duncan in 1903 led him to buy the Skinner estate at Quamichan Lake, where they arranged a home they called "Erleigh" and where, in 1907 and 1909, he contested the election as Conservative candidate for the Cowichan seat and defeated his Liberal opponent, John N. Evans. A strong, fluent, public speaker, chosen as deputy speaker for two sessions of the Legislature, WH held the seat until 1918 and was appointed, in 1912, as chairman of the Royal Commission on Agriculture, which caused him to travel in Europe and the British Isles. His principal interest was in agriculture, and so he assisted the Cowichan Creamery, led the way in obtaining the lease of the grounds for the Cowichan Agricultural Society, and worked hard for the good of the Cowichan Valley.

After some experience in the Seventy-second Regiment, Lord Strathcona's Horse, WH became military paymaster of the First Canadian Pioneers, joined the CEF as a major at Winnipeg on 11 November 1915, and was in England in time for a medical examination at Hounslow on 21 December. He was sent to the battle front in France early in 1916, but was re-elected at home on the Island later that year as MPP, defeating K. F. Duncan, who subsequently enlisted in the CAMC. On leave of absence early in 1917, WH spoke in aid of the Red Cross and other war causes at Duncan, Seattle, Victoria, Vancouver, and other centres, and also attended sessions of the Legislature. At the end of March, a crowd of several hundred listened to him speak at the Princess Theatre, Victoria, in aid of the Red Cross. He had become a notable public figure on the Island, and his activities were frequently reported in the local press, occasionally with his photograph. Early in May, he was elected honorary president of the Duncan Lawn Tennis Club while his friend W. H. Elkington presided over the South Cowichan Lawn Tennis Club. But he returned to London that summer, attached to the Canadian Pay Office, and became chairman of the advisory committee dealing with irregular cases. At that time, he was promoted to major. In 1918, he resigned his seat in the Legislature, was demobilized late in 1919, but remained in London's Hendon district, where his wife and daughter joined him early in 1920. For eleven years, he worked in the CPR's immigration and colonization branch, making several visits to the Island, but he died, aged eighty, on 7 February 1932.

Sources: *Colonist*, 15 February 1917, p. 5; 27 March 1917, p. 7; 28 March 1917, p. 9; 6 May 1917, p. 20; *Victoria Daily Times*, 8 February 1932, p. 1; *Cowichan Leader*, 8 February 1932, obit. and photo; NAC, CEF files, box 4199-49; census 1881, England, RG 11/972, p. 17; census 1871, RG 10/1006, p. 1; Ronald J. Weir, "Major William Henry Hayward," in Marion I. Helgeson, ed., *Footprints: Pioneer Families of the Metchosin District, South Vancouver Island*, 1857-1900 (Victoria, Metchosin School Museum Society, 1983), pp. 139-143.

HENDERSON, Richard (1854-1945). He was born in April 1854 at sea near South America, son of John Henderson of Glasgow and St Andrews. The only evident census record of him in England was in 1901, when he was living in

Cheshire at Overleasom, Brentwood Stables, Bidaton near Wirral, with his wife
and children. He was then aged forty-six and employed as a shipowner, and his
wife, Hildegarde, daughter of Henry Oelrichs of New York, whom he had married
in 1887, had been born in Caunstaat, Germany. Their daughter Julia, aged nine,
had been born in New York and their son Malcolm in Birkenhead, Cheshire, but
they were to have two more children. There was a visitor, Helen Bell, from Glasgow,
aged twenty, and eight servants. The neighbours on both sides were coachmen
with their families. In the meantime, RH became chairman of the Anchor Line
Steam Ship Company (1899-1912), a member of the Mersey Docks and Harbour
Board (1900-1917), a trustee of the Rangoon Railway Co. (1903-1923), and deputy
chairman at Liverpool of the London and Globe Insurance Company (from 1907)
Clubs: Constitutional and Western (Glasgow).

At sometime before 1925, they went out to the Island and took a large house
at 348 Foul Bay Road, Victoria, where RH listed music, golf, and motoring as his
recreations. He retained memberships in the Constitutional Club and the Western
Club of Glasgow. He died, aged ninety, on 24 February 1945 in Victoria. His wife
there, aged 85, on 18 September 1948.
Sources: *Who's Who in B.C.*, 1933-34, p. 78; *Colonist*, 25 February 1945, obit.; census
1901, England, RG 13/3400, p. 6.

HENEAGE, Major Alfred René (1858-1946). He was born in Chelsea, London,
to a noble Lincolnshire family whose home was "Hainton Hall," Lincolnshire,
but the 1861 census recorded him, aged two, living with his family at "Tags End
House," Great Gaddesden, Hertfordshire. His father, Edward Heneage, aged
fifty-eight, was "Deputy lieutenant for Lincolnshire" born in London and his
mother, Renée C. L. Heneage, aged thirty-three, was born in Chelsea. He had two
elder brothers also born in Chelsea—Windsor R. Heneage, aged six, and Hugh
E. F. Heneage, aged four—and a younger brother, Everard H. F. Heneage, aged
seven months, born at Great Gaddesden. There were two visitors: a widowed uncle,
George F. Heneage, aged sixty, MP for Lincolnshire, born in Marylebone, London,
and the father's unmarried lady cousin, Frances A. Hoare, aged thirty-eight, born
in Marylebone. There were eleven servants, including three listed as visitors: a
lady's maid, a footman, and a groom. The farms and cottages all around probably
belonged to the estate. At sometime in the following decade, AH was orphaned
with two brothers and a sister. While they were away at school, "Hainton Hall,"
an immense estate that filled eleven pages of the 1871 census, was in the hands
of relatives, Edward Heneage, a landowner and infantry captain, aged thirty-one
and born there, and his wife, Lady Eleanor C. Heneage, aged twenty-six and born
at Connamore near Cork, Ireland, together with two sons, two daughters, and
a long list of servants and retainers. AH attended the Royal Military College at
Sandhurst and went on to serve from 1882 in the Egyptian Expedition. He was
wounded fighting at the battle of Tel-el-Kebir. In the 1891 census, he was recorded
as a captain in the Fifth Dragoon Guards, aged thirty-two, based at Aldershot
under Colonel J. B. B. Dickson. In 1899-1902, he served with the Tenth Hussars
in the South African War in operations in Natal (1899-1900), at Lombard's Kop,

in the defence of Ladysmith, including the sortie of 7 December 1899, and in the action of 6 January 1900 in the Transvaal, east and west of Pretoria, in Natal in 1900, and was mentioned in despatches in the *London Gazette* on 10 September 1901. He was awarded the DSO, the Queen's Medal with three clasps, and the King's Medal with two clasps. He also had a tour of service in India.

In 1904, AH retired to the Island of which he may have heard from a relative, Vice Admiral Algernon Charles Fiaschi Heneage (1845-1915), who spent some time in the late 1880s in command of the naval station at Esquimalt. At all events, AH bought seventy-six acres of waterfront property on the west side of Thetis Island, facing Chemainus. He returned to England and persuaded his sister Eveline Mary Heneage, then over forty years old, to come out to keep house for him. She had been at art college and stayed with the Hoare family cousins, bankers and landowners, notably in 1891 at Wavenda in Buckinghamshire. The brother and sister lived on Thetis Island in two primitive cottages on the beach while clearing and construction was being done for a place they called "Heneage House." There they lived almost for the rest of their lives. AH bought a motorboat for the short run across to Chemainus, and when it broke down, he would be rescued by others, customarily neighbourly in those early years. Eveline grew lavender, distilled it as lavender water, and sold it in bottles imported from Italy. They enjoyed as much social life as they could of the kind they were used to and attended events at Government House in Victoria, such as a grand ball held on 31 January 1907. It was reported that on one of their visits to a garden party at Government House in Victoria, she wore a hat decorated with feathers she had gathered from chickens at home. They were Anglicans and arranged for a minister to travel from Chemainus once a month for services, which they held in an upstairs bedroom or a downstairs storeroom. When AH died, aged eighty-eight, in a Chemainus hospital on 3 May 1946, he left the property to the Church of England, which developed it as an active summer centre called Camp Columbia. Eveline then moved into a nursing home in Victoria, where she died, aged ninety, in 1952.

AH had an elder brother and a younger. The latter, Rev. Hon. Thomas Robert Heneage (c. 1877-1967), joined him on the Island but went to England when the Great War began in August 1914 to offer his services as an army chaplain. Not being accepted, he returned on the SS *Megantic* and settled in Vancouver City. He inherited the family property and the title as Lord Heneage when the eldest of the brothers died in 1954, but being seventy-six years old then, and deaf to boot, he refused the inheritance and remained in Vancouver, where he died, aged ninety, on 19 February 1967.

Sources: *Hart's Annual Army List,* 1915, p. 1499; *BC Archives, Minutes of the British Campaigners' Ass.,* 19 November 1909; *Colonist,* 1 February 1907, p. 8; 3 November 1914, p. 5; 1 February 1907, p. 8; 5 May 1946, p. 14, obit.; 7 May 1946, p. 3; *BC Archives,* "Minutes of the British Campaigners' Ass.," 19 November 1909; census 1871, England, RG 10/3406; census 1871, RG 10/1338, p. 8; census 1881, RG 11/8264, page 1; census 1891, RG 12/566, p. 1; census 1891, RG 12/1150, p. 14; Peter Murray, *Homesteads and Snug Harbours: The Gulf Islands* (Victoria, Horsdal & Shubert, 1991), pp. 125-6; Longstaff, *Esquimalt Naval Base,* pp. 27, 124.

HEPBURN, Harold Frankland (1887-1968). Born in 1887 in London, England, schooled at Eastbourne College in 1904, he was on the office staff of Apollinaris Brunnen Actien, Geselchaft, Neunaha in Germany, and also was employed by Lloyd's of London and the London office of the Antofagasta, Chile and Bolivia Railway. About 1910, he went to Canada, worked at first in a real-estate firm at Kamloops, BC, and then became a partner in Griffiths & Co. Ltd. of Victoria, a director of the BC Bond Corporation, and manager of the Victoria office of C. M. Oliver & Co. Ltd. During the Great War, he served, in 1914, with the BC Horse internment operations at Vernon, BC, but, in 1915-1918, was in the Eleventh Canadian Machine Gun Regiment of the CEF and, in 1918, transferred to the RAF. After the war, from 1919, he returned to Victoria and worked once more in a series of business and government offices: with the Canadian Pension Commission; as vice-president and secretary of Henley, Hepburn & Co. Ltd., stock brokers and bond dealers, real estate, and insurance; as a member of the BC Royalty Dealers Association and the BC Bond Dealers Association; and others.

His office was at 737 Fort Street. In 1915, he had married Nellie Howe Stratt, daughter of Charles E. Stratt of Kamloops, BC, and they lived at 1028 Chamberlain Street and then at 643 Beach Drive, Oak Bay. He joined the Union Club, the Victoria Golf Club of which he became captain, and the Colwood Park Racing Association of which he was steward, and he played golf, tennis, and polo. When he died, aged eighty, on 1 December 1968, he was buried at Royal Oak as an Anglican. His wife had died there earlier, aged eighty-five, on 18 September 1948.

Sources: *Colonist*, 3 December 1968, p. 22, obit.; *Who's Who in B.C.*, 1942-1943, pp. 147-8.

HERITAGE, Captain Henry ("Harry") (1871-1940). Born on 23 July 1871 in Warwick, he enlisted in the Sixteenth Queen's Own Lancers and spent many years with this famous cavalry regiment in India. He later became instructional officer to the United Provinces White Horse, with HQ in Cawnpore. On retiring, he went to the Island and farmed at Comox but later moved to Vancouver to be instructional officer for the Sixth Regiment, DCOR. When he enlisted in Vancouver on 18 January 1916, he was employed as "Warrant Officer" and living at 620 Beatty Street, Vancouver, with his wife, Adelaide Heritage. By that time he had been in the Sixth Regiment, DCOR, for eight years but recorded nothing on the form about previous service in India.

Sent overseas in 1916 with the Fifty-seventh Battalion, he was wounded in France and, on returning, served as an army supervisor at William Head. Upon his discharge, he joined the Federal Civil Service from which he retired in 1934. He wrote about military affairs to the newspapers and was a founder of the Twenty-One Club and of an Imperial veterans' organization open to veterans of twenty-one years of service or more. His wife died, aged seventy, on 13 January 1935, and he followed, aged seventy-three, on 18 November 1940, leaving two daughters and a son. They were buried as Roman Catholics.

Sources: NAC, CEF files, box 4290-4, lieutenant; *Colonist*, 19 November 1940, p. 3, obit.

HICKEY, Major Robert Hume Fayrer (c. 1861-1929). He was born in India, eldest son of Major Robert J. F. Hickey (c. 1827-?) of the 101st Foot, who served in India but was born "in the Western Islands" of Scotland. In 1871, the family was living at Lidford, Devon, seven and a half miles south of Tavistock, in the "Governor's House (Dartmoor Prison)," where the father was governor of the prison. They had several servants. The mother, Mary Taylor Hickey (c. 1834-?), was born in Ireland. Two sisters, Mary E. J. Hickey aged thirteen and Isabella K. J. Hickey aged eleven, were born in "East Indies" as was one of his five brothers, Walter R. J. Hickey, aged eight. The other four younger brothers, aged two to six, were born at Chatham (Kent) or Portland (Dorset), showing that the family had left India when RH was about four years old. In 1881, RH was still in Lidford at home but had more young brothers and sisters and was recorded as a "Commercial Clerk, unemployed." There was only one "General Servant." Shortly after that, he obtained a commission in the army and served in India until about 1892, when he retired to Parksville, VI, where he lived for the next thirty-seven years. He does not seem to have been related to three other Hickey families, all engineers or mariners, who lived in Victoria at that time, all from Newfoundland, Eastern Canada, or the USA.

On 25 June 1893, he married Charlotte Emily Reeves (c. 1874-1942) in Nanaimo, who may have come from Ireland, and they had several children. The best known is Charles Robert Reeves, born at French Creek on 10 September 1897, who spent two years as a student at the Nanaimo General Hospital and then enlisted in the CMR on 17 March 1916 in Victoria, describing himself as an unmarried farmer. Overseas, he soon transferred to the Royal Naval Air Service. A talented fighter pilot, he became a flight commander, shot down many enemy planes in France, and was listed in the *London Gazette* on 3 August and 2 November 1918 as receiving the DFC and Bar. He was himself shot down and killed on 3 October that year and was awarded the DSO. His father RH died, aged sixty-eight, on 22 December 1929 at home in Parksville, leaving a widow, two sons, and four daughters, including Janet Hume Hickey, who had married Archdeacon Henry Alexander Collison of Duncan. Mrs Hickey died, aged sixty-eight, on 7 January 1942.
Sources: census 1871, England, RG 10/2144; census 1881, RG 11/818, p. 45; *Hart's Army List*, 1881, p. 557; *Colonist*, 14 September 1918, p. 11; 15 September 1918, p. 18; 21 December 1929, p. 19, obit.; *London Gazette*, 3 August and 2 November 1918; John M. MacFarlane, *Canada's Naval Aviators* (rev. ed., Shearwater, NS, Shearwater Aviation Museum, 1997), p. 150.

HILL, Francis Charles (c. 1874-1915). Born in India, the census-taker found him in 1881, aged seven, living in the army camp at Aldershot in the Aldershot "Huts" with his parents: his father, Francis Charles Hill, aged forty-five, born in Scotland in 1835, was "Lieutenant-Colonel Commanding 56th Reg't" who had fought in the Crimean War, and his mother, Frances D. Hill, aged thirty-three, born in Ireland. He had two brothers, Arthur Hacket Hill, aged ten, born in Ireland, and Rowley Richard Hill, aged four, born in India, and one sister, Alice Helen Hill, aged five, born in India. There was also a visitor, John William Huckisson

[Huchison?], a major brevet lieutenant colonel born in Ceylon. There was no mention of servants, but his parents were able to send him to Westward Ho! School and Dover College. He also travelled widely and lived in Australia for several years before settling in the Cowichan Valley in 1909 with his parents, who lived in or near Duncan at "The Pompadours."

There FH owned property in Duncan, as well as a few acres at Qualicum Beach. A clever artist, he painted watercolours that won prizes at local exhibits, and he was said to be a keen sportsman. FH enlisted in a BC infantry unit soon after war was declared in 1914 and died, aged forty-one, in battle on the western front on 24 April 1915. He was ultimately buried at Ypres, Belgium. His parents had returned to England by then and were living at "Glenariff," Hythe, Kent, his father recorded as "late of the 2nd Battalion Essex Regiment."

Sources: census 1881, England, RG 11/1252, p. 1; NAC, RG 150, Accession 1992-93/166, box 4348-4, Regimental Number 16776; *Colonist*, 25 January 1917, p. 5, obit.; *Whitaker's*, p. 257; Veterans's Affairs, Canadian Virtual [Internet] War Museum.

HILLS, Bishop George (1816-1895). The first bishop of [British] Columbia, he was appointed with the invaluable financial support of Angela Georgina Burdett-Coutts (1814-1906) and headed the Anglican Church in BC in the years 1860-1892. The Island being viewed in London as the site of a remote naval station in the Pacific Northwest, it was perhaps natural to appoint a bishop with strong Imperial connections. GH's father, Rear Admiral George Hills, RN (died 1852), had married GH's mother Diana Hammersley (1783-1854), who was the daughter of a senior partner of Cox & Co., bankers and army agents at Craig's Court in Whitehall, named Charles Hammersley (1782-1862). She gave birth to GH on 26 June 1816 at Eythorne, Kent, about six miles north of Dover. Educated at King William's College, Isle of Man, and at Durham University, he was ordained on 6 December 1840, served at Great Yarmouth and other parishes in the north of England, and had been a canon of Norwich Cathedral for about nine years when he was appointed bishop of [British] Columbia in 1859. Durham University had awarded him an honorary DD.

Only three years after they reached Victoria in January 1860, Bishop Hills and his wife were visited by one of his first cousins, Lieutenant (later Sir) Edmund Hope Verney (1838-1910), RN, who arrived for a three-year posting at Esquimalt as commander of HMS *Grappler*, and the Hills had many other naval relatives. At Victoria, the empire did not look as secure in the 1860s as it does in retrospect. In 1851, only a few years before the bishop and his party went to Victoria, Napoleon's nephew had established himself by a *coup d'état* in Paris as Emperor Napoleon III and by defeating Mazzini and Garibaldi in Rome as the defender of the papacy, *fille aînée de l'église*, as of old. So established as a semi-autocratic emperor, in 1853, Napoleon III sent Admiral Febvrier des Pointes on an aggressive mission into the Pacific Ocean, and in 1855, he dispatched a corvette, *La Capricieuse*, to Quebec to see whether something might be done to revive the French loyalties of Quebec's population, which was known to be pleased at the reconciliation of Paris and Rome.

Next, in 1861, a few months after Bishop Hills reached Victoria, the emperor dispatched a large French force across the Atlantic to capture Mexico City in an effort to establish an explicitly Catholic regime under Archduke Maximilian. This extraordinary venture was successful at first and only defeated by Mexican forces in 1867 with American assistance. Meanwhile, Napoleon's client Pope Pius IX, still defended in Rome by French troops, published a notorious Syllabus of [Eighty] Errors on 8 December 1864 denouncing Protestantism as well as most modern thinking. Six years later, on 13 July 1870, a Vatican Council reinforced this sweeping denunciation of the modern world by a document entitled *Pastor æternus*, which declared Pius IX to be authoritative and infallible in such matters. By then, as if to support Papal claims, France had 56,500 priests, more numerous and dynamic than at any time since the French Revolution. The dangers inherent in these developments were eventually removed by the failure of Napoleon III's projects, the collapse of the Second French Empire in the Franco-Prussian War (1870-1871), and the Catholic Church's defeat and disgrace in France as a result of the famous Dreyfus Case (1894-1905). People with objective knowledge of all this history can only see these events as revealing a long tradition of French and Spanish Catholic hostility to the British Empire and the rest of the Protestant world.

GH arrived in Victoria in January 1860, scarcely two years after the gold rush of 1858 had brought the swelling population and chaos usual in such events. After about five years, he returned home to England to raise funds and took the opportunity to acquire a clergyman's most valuable asset, a wife. She was Maria Philadelphia Louisa King, daughter of Vice Admiral Sir Richard King. They married on 4 January 1865 but had had no children by the time of her death. In addition to the social chaos of a frontier society, they had also to deal with the evangelical, puritanical, "low-church" Protestant régime already established in Victoria by *Dean Edward Cridge, who had been established as dean of Christ Church Cathedral since 1854. Cridge and GH were soon waging a struggle well known in the Church of England, which, unlike the Roman Catholic Church, has comprised two religious traditions ever since Tudor times. The "low-church" tradition stems from the Marian Exiles who fled to Geneva and Strasbourg during the reign of "Bloody" Queen Mary (1553-1558), absorbed Calvinist doctrine, and returned to England with Queen Elizabeth I (1558-1603). The policy of Elizabeth's government was to reconcile the Calvinism of the returning exiles with the Catholic theology of the Church of England, thought to have been altered only by eliminating the authority of the Roman Papacy, urging the clergy to marry, and making a few theological and liturgical reforms. Details were neatly and eloquently stated in the Thirty-Nine Articles (1563) reprinted in the *Book of Common Prayer*, used in Anglican churches the world over. The effect was to create a quiet struggle throughout the Church of England that resembles the parliamentary struggle and endless debate in the House of Commons between the government and HM Loyal Opposition. Thus, the Anglican community at the University of Toronto has been quietly divided between Wycliffe College and Trinity College.

GH was neither intolerant nor unreasonable, though the twenty-first century is inevitably inclined to think him so. He did not try to "establish" his church as it was in England, with land grants, tithes, and a patronizing overlordship in the parishes. He realized that the aristocratic associations of the Church of England were not suitable in a country held together, as one miner told him, by "gold, gambling, whisky, and women." But he had strong sympathies with the Oxford Movement of his time and had "high-church" views—"spiky" was the word used by theological students at Anglican Theological College at the University of British Columbia when I boarded there as a non-theolog in 1949-1950. He opposed the non-sectarian schooling being gradually established in his time as a detestable American innovation. He held a widely shared view that the empire was best served by a church led by a social élite with authority in an ordered society and so was bound to clash with the egalitarian, puritanical, social-welfare approach of clergymen like Edward Cridge. Many on the Island, both clergy and laity, shared his views.

On 5 December 1872, GH arranged a "high-church" consecration of Christ Church as a cathedral and *Archdeacon William Sheldon Reece (born in India) preached a sermon that struck Dean Cridge as advocating "ritualism" and high-church popishness. Tactless and determined, Cridge spoke out forthwith against these proceedings after the sermon, when he was expected merely to announce the number of the next hymn. After being defeated in fascinating trials held at courts ecclesiastical and civil, Cridge left the cathedral and was followed by more than half of the congregation, some 250 leading parishioners, and supported by the *Victoria Daily Colonist*. They attended Presbyterian churches for a time but eventually joined the American Reformed Episcopalian Church of which Cridge became a bishop and built their own church, appropriately lower down the cathedral hill. The two sides in this astonishing split in the Anglican community—a veritable earthquake—attacked one another with nothing more than words, in the best parliamentary tradition, peaceable behaviour that was uncommon outside the empire.

Mrs Hills died, aged sixty-five, in Victoria on 30 April 1888, and GH retired home to England, where he died in Parham, Suffolk, on 10 December 1895. He had been a vigorous, hard-working bishop, walking about remote parts of his diocese to hold services and encourage the clergy, taking a practical interest in the indigenous tribes, recruiting more clergy in England, and providing for schools. He named Angela College for girls (1866) after his patron, Angela Burdett-Coutts, and promoted the Boys' Collegiate School and residential schools for native pupils, such as All Hallows' Indian Girls' School (1884), founded on the mainland at Yale by Anglican sisters from Norfolk, England. It was to him that a Catholic priest, *Jules Xavier Willmar, applied to serve the Church of England as a missionary. A variety of Anglican foundations in England had funded his activities. It is perhaps testimony to his leadership and perhaps to his ecclesiastical cause that by 1901, as recorded in Canadian census records, "Episcopalians" had become a small minority on the Island and throughout the province whereas people registered as "C. of E." were much the most numerous religious body. Some 42 percent of people in Victoria were Anglican; Roman Catholics were scarcely 6 percent. [see Table I, p . 61]

Sources: Jean Friesen, biogr. in the DCB; *John Adams, Ross Bay Cemetery* (revised ed., Victoria, Sono Nono Press, Heritage Architectural Guides, Victoria, 1998), p. 13;

Walter Noble Sage, "The early days of the Church of England on the Pacific Slope 1579-1879," *Journal of the Canadian Church Historical Society*, vol. 2, no. 1 (1953), pp. 1-17; George Hills, *No Better Land: The 1860 Diaries of the Anglican Colonial Bishop*, ed., Roberta L. Bagshaw (Victoria, Sono Nis Press, 1996), 307 pp.; W. P. Morrell, *Britain in the Pacific Islands* (Oxford, Clarendon Press, 1960), pp. 102; Pierre Renouvin, *Histoire des relations internationales* (8 vols., Paris, Hachette, 1954), vol. V, pp. 346-350; Eveline Bossé, *La Capricieuse à Québec en 1853: les premières retrouvailles de la France et du Canada* (Montréal, Éditions de la Presse, 1984), passim; *The Papal Encyclicals in their Historical Context*, ed., Anne Fremantle (New York, Mentor, 1956), pp. 143-152; Roger Price, *A Social History of Nineteenth-Century France* (Hutchinson, 1987), p. 262.

HIRSCH, Major John (1864-1932). He declared on his enlistment forms in the South African War and the Great War that he was born on 29 February 1864 at Dinting, Derbyshire, which was a part of Glossop, itself a suburb of Manchester. The only plausible John Hirsch in the census records for 1871 and 1881, however, was born at Liverpool, one of the many children of Hermann Hirsch (c. 1823-?), a widowed merchant born at Teterow, Mecklemburg, Germany. JH came to Canada later in 1881, attended Guelph Agricultural College intent on farming, but soon went to California as a placer miner. Refusing to renounce his British citizenship, he returned to Canada, served in the Guelph Battery in 1885-1886, and then settled at Cowichan Lake, VI. After working on survey parties here and there, he passed surveyor's exams in April 1892 and articled to C. E. Perry with whom he worked at Nelson, BC. By 8 February 1900, when he enlisted in Lord Strathcona's Horse at Nelson, BC, for service in the South African War, he described himself as a civil engineer. At the end of the war, he was discharged on 13 January 1901, eventually held the Mons Star and the Queen's Medal and a clasp for Natal and the King's Medal, but immediately transferred to the South African Constabulary as a lieutenant. He went surveying and engineering with A. E. Hodgins (q.v.) on the Imperial Military Railways, qualified in October 1902 to survey in Orange River Colony, and spent many months in Bloomfontein.

At sometime in 1904, he returned to the Island, surveyed timber on its west coast, but, on 19 September 1906, married Miss Marie Estelle Aikman of Victoria and soon settled on a farm in Cowichan Valley. He opened a surveyor's office in Duncan, later took H. M. Clague as a partner, and joined the Eighty-eighth Regiment of Fusiliers, but on 8 November 1914, he joined the army in Victoria and went overseas in February 1915 as machine gun officer with the Thirtieth Battalion. He was eventually invalided home and appointed assistant provost marshal with the rank of major, for Military District No. 1 with headquarters in London, Ontario. He was demobilized in 1919 and settled in Victoria in failing health. He died in Vancouver on 23 March 1932, and his wife died there, too, on 26 December 1947. They were buried as Anglicans.

Sources: John A. Whittaker, ed., *Early Land Surveyors of British Columbia* (P.L.S. Group) (Victoria, Corporation of BC Land Surveyors, 1990), pp. 69-70, with photo; NAC, RG 38, A-1-a, vol. 47 (South African War Service records); RG 9, II-A-5, vols.

14 and 15 (Medals Register); CEF files, RG 150, box 4387-9; census 1871, England, RG 10/3489; census 1881, RG 11/3940.

HOBBS, Frank Victor (c. 1855-1959). After six years on the Island's west coast "in timber operations" and selling kitchen utensils at Port Renfrew, he moved to Cadboro Bay near Victoria in 1908, built a house, planted a cherry orchard, and served as postmaster there in 1914-1929. He had broad interests and was intensely loyal to the empire. As early as 1901, he took his wife and small daughter home to England, where they stayed with relatives while he bicycled around continental Europe with a German friend. One of his fondest memories was watching Queen Victoria's funeral procession in January 1901 while his small daughter sat on one of the golden paws of the lions at the base of Nelson's Column. He joined the Navy League and was elected to its committee in April 1910.

FH was born at Bruton, Somerset, where the 1871 census shows him, aged eight, with his brother Edwin, aged four, living with their mother Priscilla, aged forty-one, and their father Joseph, a "carpenter journeyman," aged forty, and three boarders—a "drainer" with a wife and a "pipelayer." In 1881, FH was himself boarding at the local gasworks, where he worked as a stoker. He and his brother Edwin were trying to farm when in 1889, they gave up and ventured out to the Island. FH spent the first summer on the west coast, working on the telegraph line then being laid. That fall, he went to Nanaimo and bought a piece of land from the Esquimalt and Nanaimo Railway, which later turned out to be the site of a coal mine. Edwin worked meanwhile at the court house in Victoria and turned to farming in the Cadboro Bay district, and while delivering milk to the Jubilee Hospital in Oak Bay, he met and married a hospital cook, Eliza Hix, on 20 November 1895, and they had three children. On 12 August 1906, Edwin died, aged forty, when a horse crushed him against a tree. More fortunate or more capable, FH began to sell off his land to British immigrants at $1,000 an acre and, in 1915, bought a store, where he opened a post office. He became a Freemason, a Grand Master of the Grand Orange Lodge of BC, was elected to the Saanich Municipal Council and the School Board, became a JP, and was a public figure in the district with a strong hand in building the Cadboro Bay school and Frank Hobbs School, which opened in 1951. Before he died in Victoria, aged ninety-six, on 5 April 1959, he was delighted to learn that a grandson had graduated at the University of BC, taken an MA at the University of Toronto, and become a professional meteorologist and a lieutenant commander in HMCS *Bonaventure*.

Sources: *Colonist*, 27 April 1910, p. 2; 18 December 1929, p. 1; census 1871, England, RG 10/2427, p. 24; census 1881, RG 11/2399/55, p. 19; Ursula Jupp, *Cadboro: A Ship, A Bay, A Sea-Monster*, 1842-1958 (Victoria, Jay Editions, 1988), pp. 29, 33 (Chapter 5, "The Hobbs Family"), 34, 35, 52; *Canadian Almanach*, 1926, p. 542.

HOBDAY, Colonel Edmund Arthur Ponsonby (1859-1931). Born in Calcutta, India on 17 May 1859, son of Lieutenant Colonel Thomas F. Hobday, Bengal Staff Corps, and Louisa E. Hobday, he attended Temple Grove, Eastsheen, Wimbledon School, and the Royal Military Academy, Woolwich. In 1879, he obtained a commission as lieutenant in the RFA and served as adjutant to the Royal Horse Artillery, Dublin, in 1884-1887; ADC to the commander-in-chief in India (Lord Roberts) in 1888-1889; captain of "N" Battery, RHA, in 1893-1896; and on the Army Staff (SSO) at Mooltan and Rawalpindi, 1896. Among the campaigns he took part in was the Punjab Frontier Campaign, 1897-1898; the Malakand Relief Column as staff officer, 1897; the relief of Chakdarra; and Operations in Upper Swat (action at Landaka), Bajour (night attack of Nawagai), Mohmand Country, and Buner (Action of the Tanga Pass) as DAAG First Brigade Malakand Field Force (in which he was mentioned four times in despatches, medal, and two clasps). He went on to serve as DAAG, Army Staff, Punjab Command 1896-1900; commander of the One-hundredth Battery RFA in 1901-1904; and commander of the First Brigade, RFA at Rawalpindi, 1905-1910. Meanwhile, in 1881, his widowed mother, Louisa E. Hobday, aged fifty-eight, born in Calcutta, India, was living in Paddington with her late husband's sister, Henrietta N. Hobday, aged sixty-three, born at Edgbaston, Warwickshire, like her brother. EH was particularly skilled at sketching and painting, taught at military college to all officers, and published a book reminiscent of his service in India, *Sketches on Service in the Frontier Campaign of 1897-8* (James Bowden, 1898), 159 pp.

In about 1910, EH retired to Vancouver Island, where the Canadian census found him the next year, aged fifty-two, already naturalized and farming near Duncan with his wife Nora *née* Pottinger, born in India, aged forty-four, together with three small children, all born in India: twin brothers Rupert and Victor, aged sixteen, born in October 1895, and Jocelyn, aged twelve, born in September 1898. They were living next door to Charles and Harriet *Bazett and family. Before long, EH moved the family to Victoria. In 1914, he was a member of the Victoria Natural History Society, president of the Victoria Amateur Dramatic Society, and a vice-president of the British Campaigners' Association. At that association's "smoking party" on 19 February 1914 at the AOF hall, Broad Street, he proposed the health of the guest speaker, *Colonel Charles Flick, in a speech in which he stressed that "the South African campaign was an Imperial campaign and testified to the solidarity which prevailed throughout the Empire. Volunteer corps from India, Burmah, Africa itself, Canada, as well as from the British Isles, came forward." On 19 November 1914, the British Campaigner's Association announced that he had been "promoted Brigadier-General and was ordered home [i.e., to England]. Applause." Two days later, the *Daily Colonist* reported that he had gone. In England, he raised the 104th Brigade, RFA, and went to France in 1915 with the Twenty-third Division but in April 1916 joined the Sixteenth Division AC and served until demobilized in April 1919. He was mentioned twice in despatches and decorated with the CMG (1915), Star, and General Service and Victory medals.

When he died, at Southsea, on 2 June 1931, the *Colonist* recollected that "Colonel Hobday was a resident of Victoria for a number of years before the war, and during his stay here he made a wide circle of friends. Prior to his death he had practically lost his sight, which was a great blow to him, as he was unable to continue his painting, which was one of his achievements." He also enjoyed music and, like many other officers, played cricket as long as he could. In Victoria, he had been a member of the Union Club and in London of the Army and Navy Club. He was remembered in Victoria partly because of the three sons he had in India by his wife, Nora Pottinger, daughter of Lieutenant General Brabazon Henry Pottinger (1840-1913) of the Royal Artillery. One son, Captain Victor Maitland Hobday, was known in Victoria and Duncan as an architect before enlisting and was killed in 1917, serving overseas in the West Yorkshire Regiment. His twin brother, Captain Rupert Edmond Hobday, was working as a landscape gardener in Victoria before joining the Royal Scots Fusiliers in 1914, and after the war, he settled in England. The youngest son, Joscelyn Arthur Hobday, attended Collegiate School in Victoria, returned after the war, and lived there until 19 October 1971 when he died, aged seventy-two, in Saanich. All three Hobday brothers had been members of various city cricket teams.

Sources: *Who was Who*, vol. 1, 1897-1916, p. 572; census 1871, England, RG 10/23, p. 27; *Colonist*, 20 February 1914, p. 3; 24 March 1914, p. 7; 21 November 1914, p. 11; 7 June 1931, p. 5, obit; 6 July 1917, p. 5, photo and obit.; *BC Archives*, "*Minutes of the British Campaigners' Association*", 19 November 1914; NAC, CEF files, box 4399-53; NAC, CEF files, box 4400-2; John B. Hayward, ed., *Officers Died in the Great War 1914-1919* (New ed., Polstead, Suffolk, J. B. Hayward & Son, 1988), 286 pp., in 4o, p. 81.

HOBSON, Lieutenant Colonel James (1896-1979). Born in England, he joined the Indian Army after the Great War and in 1922 transferred to the police force in Scinde and Bombay, wherein he served for twenty-one years and rose to the rank of deputy commissioner of police. He visited Victoria in 1940 when his wife and two sons made their home there, and on 12 May 1941, he spoke at a luncheon meeting of the Gyro Club on "The India Police," saying (for instance) that that force had been entirely British until 1922 when men from certain Indian families were admitted to it. Among the guests at this lecture was Bruce Hutchison, Canadian journalist and writer. Hobson arrived at Victoria again on 2 August 1943 on a nine-month medical leave and with the hope of making his home in Canada after the war. He was by then deputy commissioner of the Bombay City Police. On 5 August 1943, he addressed 130 men at the Rotary Club in the Empress Hotel on his experiences; on 4 October 1943, he spoke to the Overseas League on "Some Experiences of an Officer in the Indian Police," with Sir Robert Holland in the chair; and on 14 October 1943, he spoke to the Lions Club at Spencer's Dining Room about crime in Bombay. After settling in Victoria, he died there, aged eighty-three, on 8 May 1979.

Sources: *Colonist*, 11 May 1941, p. 3; 13 May 1941, p. 11; 5 August 1943, p. 11; 5 October 1943, p. 6; 15 October 1943, p. 3.

HOCKING, Captain and Major Norman Penrose (1876-1956). Born on 31 March 1876 at Swansea, Wales, he was recorded by the 1881 census living at "The Royal Fort, Bristol St Michael, Gloucestershire" with his mother, Sarah J. Hocking, aged thirty-nine, together with four brothers and a sister. There are strong indications in the various census records that his father was Henry Hocking, recorded in 1871 as "Assayer of the farm of Penrose & Hocking" and living in Swansea, at a time when Sarah, the wife and mother, was staying in the household of a banker's clerk in Bristol. In 1891, she was listed as a widow living with all of the children, but later that year, NH, aged fifteen, joined a windjammer and so began a career of twelve years at sea. He made several voyages to Africa and India, where he lived long enough to learn to speak Hindustani, and eventually came to command a China coaster. After that, he spent four and a half years on inland waterways in Burma and South Africa. In 1908, presumably back in England, he joined the Legion of Frontiersmen recently founded under the inspiration of *Roger Pocock and remained interested in it after moving to the Island in 1912.

He formed a launch service at Deep Cove, North Saanich, with two brothers, John and Llewellyn Hocking. In the Great War, he enlisted at Victoria on 17 November 1915, first in the Gordon Highlanders but then overseas with the Eighty-eighth Fusiliers of Victoria. He had been living at Deep Cove with his wife, Bertha Hocking, and recorded his occupation as "master mariner." His religion, he said, was Unitarian. At sometime late in the Great War, he was recruited, or transferred, into the Inland Water Transport of the Royal Engineers at a time in 1917 when they were desperately trying to turn the tables on the Turkish forces, which had defeated and humiliated a British army at Kut-el-Amara. He was an expert in the marine movement of supplies, became deputy assistant director on the staff in Mesopotamia with the rank of major, and was mentioned twice in despatches and awarded the OBE, mainly for skill and daring in the South Pacific. The citation mentioned that he had been in the merchant marine through three wars, including the Boer War, when he served aboard troop transports. After the war, he ran the mail boat out of Port Alberni for Stone Brothers, then kept a store at Rivers Inlet for a time but returned to the sea as master of freighters and deep-sea representative of the Canadian Government Mercantile Service Guild and master of freighters in the Canadian Government Mercantile Marine until it disbanded. During the Second World War, he took over the Brentwood-Mill Bay ferry until 1946. Still in the Legion of Frontiersmen, he was active in the Island squadron, and hoping to organize a sub-unit out in Deep Cove. When he died, aged eighty, at St Joseph's Hospital in Victoria on 9 September 1956, he was survived by a son William Hocking of Victoria and a daughter, Mrs Stan Clarke of Sidney.

Sources: NAC, CEF, RG150, box 4403-38; Lieutenant Colonel Leonard Joseph Hall, *The Inland Water Transport in Mesopotamia* (Constable, 1921), p. 201; *Saanich Peninsula and Gulf Islands Review*, 12 September 1956, pp. 1 and 4, obit.; *Colonist*, 11 September 1956, p. 7, obit.; *BC Archives*, Longstaff Papers, MS-0677, vol. 438; census 1871, England, RG 10/2568, p. 5; census 1871, RG 10/2568, p. 5; census 1871, RG 10/5456, p. 5; census 1891, RG 12/1964, p. 14.

HODDING, Colonel James Sweet (1867-1930). He was born at Bellary, India, son of Major George C. Hodding (c. 1835-?), Indian Army (born in Marylebone, London), and of Ellen A. Hodding, aged twenty-seven (born in Madras, India). In 1871, they were living at 8 St George's Road, Hampstead, and JH had two brothers, William H. Hodding six and John G. Hodding one, both born in the "East Indies." With them too was his father's brother William Hodding, aged twenty-two, "Merchant naval service P&O" born in Marylebone, London. They had three servants. By 1891, the father was "Colonel H.M. Madras Staff Corps" boarding at Westford House, Dodderhill, Droitwich, Worcestershire, along with his wife and two of their children, and by 1901, the mother was a widow living in Kent with her sister and one son, Charles Hodding, working as a clerk, while another son, William Henry Hodding, had become a "Manager [of] Turkish Baths" in Torquay, Devon. Meanwhile, JH had obtained a commission in the Second Royal Fusiliers and was serving in India, where he was to remain until retiring with the rank of major on 1 March 1908. Most of his twenty years in the army was spent on the North-West Frontier of India and in South Africa.

In 1909, he moved to Duncan, VI, where he lived on Kenneth Street with his wife, Alice Mary (Smyth) Hodding, whom he had married at Southsea on 7 April 1896. He wrote to the War Office as soon as the Great War broke out, was briefly enrolled in the British Columbia Horse [from 19 to 28 October 1914], but then went overseas and served as a major in the Thirteenth Battalion of the Royal Fusiliers (RF) from 16 November 1914, the Fifteenth Battalion RF from 20 July 1915, and the Sixty-ninth Punjabis, Indian Army, from 12 October 1915 when they went to Egypt on 5 October 1915, but he was invalided home from Mesopotamia via Aden on 17 March 1916. Upon recovering, he was back in the Fifteenth RF from 30 September 1916; the Second RF from 25 June 1917; the Fifth RF from 5 March 1918; and the 174th P. O. W. Company in France from 23 November 1918. These details show how an officer could be moved about from unit to unit. JH returned to Duncan after the war, played cricket, tennis and cards, and spent much time as a member of the British Campaigners' Association and the Canadian Legion when it was founded later and a leader of the Boy Scouts. His interest in the Scouts may have been prompted by Lord Baden-Powell to whom he is said to have been related and who visited Duncan more than once during JH's eighteen years there. When struck down by a heart attack on 6 March 1930, he was buried at Ste Anne's cemetery at Tzouhalem nearby, being a Roman Catholic, and the funeral was held at St Edward's RC Church with a Boy Scout guard of honour, thirty members of the Legion, and pallbearers both military and civilian. He was survived by his wife and one son, Trumpeter Aubry Vyvian Hodding (c. 1900-1971), the other, James Douglas Hodding (c. 1899-1916) having died serving in France during the Great War. The trumpeter son had served in the trenches in France, too, until the authorities discovered that he was under aged and sent him home. Mrs Hodding died, aged ninety-six, on 27 May 1967 in Victoria.

Sources: NAC, RG9 series II-F-10, *Imperial War Gratuities*, vol. 134; *Colonist*, 10 June 1917, p. 19; 30 July 1929, p. 11; 7 March 1930, p. 14, obit.; *Cowichan Leader*, 10 August 1916; 17 July 1919, p. 1; 18 March 1930, p. 10; NAC, CEF files, RG 150, box 4405-21; *BC Archives*, "*Minutes of the British Campaigners' Ass.*," 19 February 1920; a note at the Cowichan Valley Museum (Duncan) says that Hodding was a relative of Lord Baden-Powell.

HODGINS, Lieutenant Colonel Arthur Edward, MEIC (1861-1939). He was born in Toronto on 15 April 1861, son of Maria Burgoyne Hodgins, *née* Scobie, and Hon. Thomas Hodgins, KC, LLD, judge of the Admiralty Division of the Supreme Court, and attended Upper Canada College (Toronto) and RMC (Kingston) in 1878-1882. An outstanding cadet, he was sent with the artillery team representing Canada at Shoeburyness in 1881 and promoted to lieutenant on 27 June 1882. During the years 1882-1900, he was employed by the CPR Company as a civil engineer on the prairies and in the Rocky Mountains and on its other rail branches in the state of Maine, USA, and elsewhere. Next, he was a divisional engineer on the construction of the Inter-Oceanic Railway of Vera Cruz, Mexico (1889-1890), and in charge of surveys for straightening the River Don through Toronto. Meanwhile, in 1897-1903, he served as secretary of the Dominion of Canada Rifle Association. When the South African War broke out in 1899, he was busy with railway engineering and designing the Hall Mines Smelter and some of the principal buildings in the town of Nelson, BC, but was also OC of the Nelson company of the Rocky Mountain Rangers, founded in 1897, which joined the Royal Canadian Regiment and went to South Africa with the First Canadian Contingent. As a lieutenant in it, he was attached to the staff of the director of Railways, Sir Percy Girouard, RE, and was in the actions at Paardeberg and Bloemfontein. He rose to the rank of major in charge of constructing military railways in the Transvaal and Orange Free State and went on to serve after the war as superintendent engineer of the Central South African Railways. On returning to Canada in 1904, he worked as District Engineer in charge of the location and construction of the Grand Trunk Pacific Railway from Kenora to Winnipeg and on to Lake Nipegon, some five hundred miles.

In October 1907, he visited Victoria with a view to settling there and, being known already, was interviewed by a reporter of *The Daily Colonist.* Two years later, he retired to the Island, where he and his wife, Rose Mary Heathcote of Shawhill, Wiltshire, daughter of Thomas J. Heathcote, JP, lived for some years at Duncan and where he was appointed assistant public works engineer for Vancouver Island in April 1914. That posting was brief as he went off to the Great War as OC, First Canadian Pioneer Battalion, which he organized and recruited in Victoria and which served overseas in the First Canadian Division. He then served as assistant director of Light Railways and Roads for the Third and Fourth Armies. After fourteen months, he was invalided home and, in 1919-1924, was attached to the Provincial Department of Public Works as district engineer for the roads and bridges of Vancouver Island. When he died, aged seventy-eight, on 18 December 1939, he and his wife were living at 1471 Fairfield Road, Victoria, and he was a member of the Union Club. He was survived by a son in Vancouver, another in Victoria, and a daughter, Mrs Walter Edmonds in Southern Rhodesia. He also left a brother, *Lieutenant Colonel C. R. Hodgins, who was one of his pallbearers together with *General James Secretan Dunbar, *Colonel C. C. Bennett, *Colonel H. C. Carey, Major F. W. Gregg, *Lieutenant Colonel W. H. Belson, Captain Cory-Wood, Captain G. H. Bevan-Pritchard, Lieutenant W. Winkle, and Sergeant Major W. Stone. The Canadian Legion was represented by *Lieutenant General Sir Percy Lake.

Sources: NAC, RG9, microfilm reel T6957; *Colonist,* 22 October 1907, p. 7; 19 April 1914, p. 3; 19 December 1939, p. 5; 22 December 1939, p. 3, obit.; notes from Donald Luxton; *Who's Who in B.C.* 1933-1934, p. 84; Henry James Morgan, *Men and Women of the Time: A Hand-book of Canadian Biography of Living Characters* (2nd edn., Toronto, William Briggs, 1912), p. 538; *Report of the Proceedings of the Dominion of Canada Rifle Association,* Ottawa, R. J. Taylor, 1905, p. ix; Brian A. Reid, *Our Little Army in the Field: The Canadians in South Africa,* 1899-1902 (St Catharines, Ontario, Vanwell Publishing Ltd., 1996), p. 109; R. C. Fetherstonhaugh, *The Royal Canadian Regiment,* 1883-1933 (Fredericton, Centennial Print & Litho Ltd., 1981), pp. 87, 129, 140.

HODGINS, Lieutenant Arthur Wilfred Marrable (1894-1945). Born in February 1894 in Sunderland, England, son of Colonel C. R. Hodgins of Colwood, BC, he attended Westword Ho!, United Service College, and RMC, Woolwich, where he was schooled as a mining engineer. In 1914, he joined the Artists' Rifles, then the Royal Garrison Artillery, and, by 1916, was serving in the Anti-Aircraft Corps. Sir John Wakefield, lord mayor of London, presented him with a gold medal for bringing down the Zeppelin L15 flying over London. In 1918, he served in France with a unit of heavy artillery. After the war, he worked for a time at Pueblo, Colorado, in the Colorado Fuel and Iron Works, but visited Canada in 1930 and decided to settle on the Island at Qualicum Beach, not many miles north of his father and his uncle, *Lieutenant Colonel Arthur Edward Hodgins. Like so many others, he spent his time, playing golf, fishing, hunting, and as a member of the Church of England. He died at last, aged fifty-one, on 23 November 1945 in Saanich.
Sources: *Who's Who in B.C.* 1933-1934, pp. 84-5.

HODGINS, Lieutenant Colonel Charles Richard (1863-1940). He was born in January 1863 in Toronto, third son of an Anglo-Irish lawyer, Hon. Thomas Hodgins, a judge of the Admiralty Division of the Supreme Court, and attended Upper Canada College (Toronto) and RMC (Kingston, Ontario). In June 1885, he entered the Royal Artillery as lieutenant and a year later qualified as instructor, School of Army Signals, at Aldershot. His career then developed in the British Mountain Artillery on the Black Mountain Expedition on the North-West Frontier of India (1888), in Burma (1890); as assistant superintendent of Ordinance Factories at Kirkee, Bombay, and Cawnpore, India; as adjutant volunteer artillery, England (1894-1899); and as major and OC in the Royal Artillery on the west coast of Africa (January 1900-1903). In 1903, he qualified at the Army Ordnance College, Woolwich, and was appointed to the Royal Arsenal, Woolwich, then as chief ordnance officer at Royal Dockyard, Woolwich (1904), on the African west coast (1905), in the Straits Settlement at Singapore (1906), and in Ceylon (1909), and as ADC to the governor and commander-in-chief in Sierra Leone (1901). He had meanwhile risen in the Royal Artillery to captain (1894), major (1904), lieutenant colonel AOD (1914), and lieutenant colonel RA (1917), and he raised the 120th Siege Battery, RA, in 1916 and served with them in France. During the Somme campaign, he suffered shell shock and was invalided to England. Thereafter, he served as lieutenant colonel commanding the Siege Training Brigade at Bordon, England (1917-1918).

He had married Aimée Gertrude Burgess (?-1938), eldest daughter of Colonel H. M. Burgess, RA, on 17 January 1891, and they had four sons, all of whom were with him in the Great War. One had been killed and the other three wounded. After the war, he and his wife settled at Colwood, VI, a suburb of Victoria, and about 1930, he joined the India-Burma Society. This brought him into close contact with *Lieutenant General Sir Percy Lake, who had founded the society, and *Sir Charles Delmé-Radcliffe, one of its strongest supporters, and in May 1934, he was elected to its managing committee. He died, aged seventy-seven, on 24 February 1940 in Victoria. Mrs Hodgins had died earlier, but he was survived by his sons: Major Richard Hodgins in England, Captain J. N. M. Hodgins at Qualicum Beach, P. R. Hodgins of the Canadian Scottish Regiment, and A. W. M. Hodgins then in Peru.

Sources: *Who's Who in B.C.* 1933-4, p. 85; *Colonist*, 26 June 1929, p. 4; 18 May 1934, p. 2; 17 August 1938, p. 3, and 3 July 1929, p. 4; 16 August 1938, p. 12; 25 February 1940, p. 3: obit.; for C.R. Hodgins's father see *Appleton's Cyclopedia of American Biography*, ed., James Grant Wilson and John Fiske (6 vols., New York: D. Appleton and Company, 1887-1889), ed., Stanley L. Klos, 1999.

HODGINS, Captain John Noel Miles (1897-1972). Born on 15 January 1897 at Dover, Kent, son of *Colonel Charles Richard Hodgins of Colwood, BC, he attended Westward Ho! United Services College and R.M.C., Woolwich. In 1915, he obtained a commission in India with the Royal Garrison Artillery, but transferred to the Queen's Own Corps of Guides, Frontier Force, on the North-West Frontier of India. He went with them to Palestine and Mesopotamia, was badly wounded in 1918, and retired in 1922. The next year, he moved to Qualicum Beach, VI, another of the keen anglers living there and went in 1928 to South Africa, where on 4 June 1929, he married Dorothy Gardner Williams, third daughter of Gardner Williams, managing director of De Beers Consolidated, South Africa. Returning to Canada with her in 1929, he lived at "Mera Koi" in Qualicum Beach and took up golf, fishing, big-game hunting, and attending the Anglican Church. After many years, he died, aged seventy-five, on 30 June 1972 in Victoria, and his widow died a few months later on 28 December 1972 in North Vancouver.

Sources: *Who's Who in B.C.* 1933-1934, pp. 85-6; 1942-1943, pp. 151-2.

HOEY, Major Charles Ferguson (1914-1944), VC. He was born in Duncan, VI, grandson of a distinguished British Army officer, Major General Charles Rudyerd Simpson (1856-1948), whose daughter Mary Simpson (c. 1890-1976) married an Irish Presbyterian, Ferguson Hoey (c. 1890-1961), and went with him to Vancouver Island about 1909. She, CH's mother, appears, aged one, in the 1891 census living with her family in Kensington at 52 Argyle Road, a district of army officers, solicitors, and civil servants. Her father, then a "Captain Lincolnshire Regiment," was born a barrister's son in Bloomsbury, his wife Leonora at Bromley, Kent, and the children, CH's aunts and uncle, in or near London. Before the Great War, she and Ferguson Hoey tried raising poultry in the Cowichan Valley; but then in the 1920s, he joined the real-state firm of J. H. Whittome & Co., wherein he rose from bookkeeper to director. Active members of the Duncan Tennis Club, the Hoeys lived at 745 Wharncliffe Road with their three children of whom CH, the eldest, intended from childhood to be a British soldier. He attended Duncan Grammar School and then RMC at Sandhurst, after which, aged twenty, he joined the Lincolnshire Regiment in which his maternal grandfather had served. When war broke out in 1939, he was stationed in India and he died on 16 February 1944 in Burma at Maungdaw during an assault on a Japanese machine-gun position. He was one of only two Canadians who were awarded the Victoria Cross in the war with Japan, and his mother accepted it at a ceremony in January 1945. In Duncan, a 160-acre park was named in his honour in 1945. It is three and a half miles east of Cowichan Lake Village, with the Cowichan River running through it, and is still owned by the Crown.

Sources: Tom Henry, *Small City in a Big Valley: The Story of Duncan* (in 4_, Madeira Park, BC, Harbour Publishing, 1999), pp. 130-1; *Colonist*, 1 December 1959, p. 16; census 1891, England, RG 12/20, p. 36; census 1861, RG 9/166, p. 25.

HOLLAND, Sir Robert Erskine (1873-1965). Born in London on 29 June 1873, he was the second son of Sir Thomas Erskine Holland, KC, a distinguished London jurist, and attended Winchester College and Oriel College, Oxford. Called to the Bar at Lincoln's Inn, he joined the ICS in 1893 and, in 1895-1925, served mainly in the political department, as secretary to the Board of Revenue at Madras and later as British consul at Muscat. He was on political duty with the Mesopotamia Field Force from 1 November 1915 to sometime in 1917 (mentioned in despatches). From 22 December 1919 to 7 August 1925, he was chief commissioner of the north-western Indian province of Ajmer-Merwara, rose to be agent to the governor general in Rajputana, and until 1931 was a member of the secretary of state's Council of India. In this work, he played a part in the Imperial suzerainty of the Indian princes, in negotiating with them, and in forming British policy. In 1919, he was on the codification committee appointed by the government of India to standardize political practice. As agent to the governor general (AGG) in the Great War years and later, he was astute enough to play a vital role in supervising the princes and in dealing with difficult Imperial relations with them. He turned out to have a sound view in opposing the British policy of non-interference in the princely states of India and played a major part in the secretary of state's council. Leaving this council in July 1931, he then practised law for some time until appointed as judicial adviser to the government of Siam (Thailand) and a judge of the Supreme Court.

He arrived at Victoria from the Orient on 4 May 1936 on the *Empress of Russia* and stopped at "Vines" with his old friend, *Major A. H. Jukes for a few days during which he spoke to the *Daily Colonist* about the state of affairs in Siam, where he had been an official adviser for the previous three years. His intention, he said, was to spend some weeks in North America and then go on to London, where he planned to resume his practice as a barrister, but in October 1937, he was evidently still in Victoria. In what turned out to be the first of many public appearances, he spoke to the Overseas League at David Spencer's Tearoom on the afternoon of 4 October 1937 about the life, customs, and present position of Siam. He said that Japanese influence had grown in Siam. They had captured 70 percent of its trade and had opened banks. It was following Japanese advice that the Siamese government got rid of foreign advisers, but many Chinese had moved into the country, too. He was formally thanked by *Captain T. L. Thorpe-Doubble and was ready to speak again on this subject on 22 November 1937, this time to the Gyro Club at the Empress Hotel, where he was introduced by *Major H. Cuthbert Holmes. In March 1938, he spoke in Toronto to the Empire Club of Canada on "Changing India." Such public activities became a regular part of his life: He was a leader in the local branches of the Navy League, the Overseas League—which elected him chairman on 8 January 1940 at the Empress Hotel—and other Imperial organizations. In what was evidently a kind of retirement, he found a house he called "The Cottage," almost on the beach at 1131 Beach Drive, Oak Bay, south of the Oak Bay Beach Hotel. He bought a yacht and sailed about the Gulf of Georgia, Saanich Inlet, and other sheltered seas east of the Island.

In August 1940, British authorities suddenly called upon him to serve again in India and he left on 6 September. However, Victoria had become "home" by then, though he maintained his membership in the Athenæum Club, and he returned in 1942 to live in Oak Bay for the rest of his life. Peering through the discretion of Imperial society at that time, which tended to live by the Victorian principle that "servants talk about people, gentlefolk about things," the historian may surmise that RH was one of those for whom the Island offered a refuge from family troubles in England. In 1910, he had married Anne Crow, daughter of Francis E. Crow, but he brought with him to Victoria a charming lady known only as Frieda. It is Frieda, indeed, and not Mrs Holland who appears lounging at "Vines" in a photograph together with RH, Mrs Editha Jukes, and her son John, a picture snapped almost certainly by *Major A. H. Jukes. One can only guess at the reason for their tense, anxious expressions. However that may be, RH resumed lecturing widely in Canada and the United States on questions relating to India, the Far East, and Pacific relations. In 1943, he gave a series of seven talks on the CBC entitled *Post-War Pacific* in which he reviewed the history and prevailing situation of each part of the Pacific region. On 18 August 1943, he was the guest speaker at a meeting of the Kipling Society held in a Victoria garden, and on 7 October, he spoke on "Loyalties" to the Lions Club at a lunch at Spencer's Dining Room, explaining *inter alia* that without British rule in India, the war effort there would have collapsed. On 10 October 1943, the *Daily Colonist* (p. 4) published a long letter to the editor under the heading "India Described" and followed it on 9 November (p. 4) with an article RH wrote, "Famine in India is Outlined." He was engaged in raising funds for famine relief, promoting a movement in Victoria to send such funds to India, and so wrote to the *Colonist* to tell the public of a London fund, officially sponsored, to manage an Empire wide programme for India relief. In its summer 1947 number, the *International Journal* published an article he entitled "Union of India."

RH did not restrict his interests to India: on 24 March 1948, he spoke to the White Cane Club at Prince Robert House in Victoria about "The Peril of Palestine," having made a close study of the Palestine issue. He thought that if Russian troops were landed there, another world war might ensue. It was his opinion, too, that "the partition scheme was wrong from the first . . . it constituted a violation of Charter principles, it was against the principle of self-determination, it was against righteousness and justice." Like many other Imperial officers and civil servants, RH put no faith in the United Nations as it was constituted after the Second World War. Its "cold and barren philosophy" and its secular objectives appalled him. Abandoning the Christian framework was, in his opinion, losing the baby with the bathwater. In a page-long article entitled "UN Can't Keep Peace," which the *Colonist* published on 16 December 1956 in its Sunday Magazine (p. 4), he wrote, "An unbridgeable gulf separates Eastern and Western nations at present . . . Men will fight and die, if they must, for an idea, but social upheaval and conflict will not be cured by arming unconvinced levies or by mustering nations. No contingent will be effective unless the men composing it feel that the cause for which they are fighting is such as to inspire devotion and sacrifice." The gist of his argument was that the UN would be wholly incapable of preventing future wars, and its failures during the past half-century have certainly proved the soundness of his views. Sir Robert Erskine Holland, KCIE (1925), CIE (1917), CSI (1921), CVO (1922), VD (1920), MA, died aged ninety-two on 30 September 1965 in Victoria.

Sources: *Who was Who* (London), 1961-1970, p. 541; Riddick, *Who in British India*, p. 177; *Empire Club of Canada: Addresses . . .* in 1937-1938 (Toronto, Printers Guild, 1938), pp. 271-287; *Colonist*, 5 May 1936, p. 14; 5 October 1937, p. 13; 4 October 1939, p. 6; 9 January 1940, p. 4; 4 August 1940, p. 6; 29 August 1940, p. 2; 2 February 1943, p. 16; 19 August 1943, p. 7; 8 October 1943, p. 8; 10 October 1943, p. 4; 9 November 1943, p. 4; 14 November 1943, p. 4; 25 March 1948; 16 December 1956, *Sunday Magazine*, p. 4 (photo); *Post-War Pacific: Seven Talks by Sir Robert Holland over the C.B.C.*, 1943, 36 pp.; *International Journal*, vol. 2 (summer 1947), pp. 187-199; S. R. Ashton, *British Policy Towards the Indian States, 1905-1939* (Curzon Press, 1982), pp. 57, 71ff., 79ff., 94, 129, 180, 198; Sir Arnold Wilson (a friend and colleague), *Loyalties: Mesopotamia: A Personal and Historical Record*, (2 vols., Oxford, Oxford University Press, 1931), vol. I, pp. 102, 104; vol. II, p. 374; British Library, India Office Papers, Younghusband collection of photographs, photo 448/10 (86) and (87); notes and photograph courtesy of Mrs Rachel (Jukes) Mackenzie.

HOLLINS, Major Christopher Wordsworth (1893-1945). He was born on 28 May 1893 at Tufnell Park, London, son of Priscilla Anna Hollins and Rev. William Tyndale Hollins (born in Gloucester) and grandson of Rev. James Hollins (born in Birmingham). He spent four years in an officer's training course, went to Canada in 1910, and settled at Lloydminster, Saskatchewan. Being six feet, two inches tall, he joined the Canadian Army in Winnipeg on 18 December 1914 and served overseas as warrant officer and lieutenant in the Thirty-second Battalion and the Fifth Canadian Infantry Battalion. After the war, he went farming and ranching from 1919, married Elfrieda Hollins, and, in 1940, moved to Parksville, VI. Descended from a line of Anglican ministers, he became a Freemason and a member of the AF and AM, in the Greenstreet Branch of the Canadian Legion,

BESL. In 1940, he became a lieutenant in the original Saskatchewan Company of Veterans Guard of Canada and rose to be captain and adjutant and then major, commanding No. 29 Active Company. In that service, he was killed, aged fifty-one, on 5 April 1945 and buried at Parksville in St Anne's churchyard.
Sources: *Who's Who in B.C.*, 1942-1943, p. 153; NAC, CEF files, RG 150, box 4448-2; census 1871, England, RG 10/2526, p. 1; census 1881, RG 11/3110; census 1891, RG 12/1694, p. 20; census 1901, RG 13/466, p. 5; Department of Veterans' Affairs, "Virtual Cemetery" online.

HOLME, Major Harold Leopold (1879-1931). Born on 20 January 1879 in Naples, Italy, he joined the British Army and won the DSO for some distinguished action in battle. His army file in London, however, is a record of medical and emotional troubles. In December 1910, he had a nervous breakdown, which a medical board said was due to overwork and reading for the Staff College. He was granted leave to visit relatives in Italy, but in 1912, he suffered another nervous breakdown, this time in Hong Kong. Early in 1913, he sprained an ankle while skating, went on leave to India, and returned well. In April 1916, he fractured a shoulder and was in hospital again. Late in 1917, he contracted a serious ear infection while at Aden and went on three months' home leave, reaching England on 14 February 1918 by a series of vessels. Later that year, he had an attack of influenza while in Italy. In August 1920, he was living at Exmouth, Devon, on leave until 20 September 1920, when he decided to retire.

He wrote to the War Office (WO) on 10 August 1920 about his plans: "I propose to leave for Canada on 22 October 1920 . . . as I am taking steps to get married and settle in Canada . . ." He asked about retirement arrangements, pay, etc., and said that his address would be c/o the Bank of Montreal, Victoria, Vancouver Island. The WO gave its approval on 25 August 1920. HH married Eva Cordelis Eveline Basden, born at Weybridge, Surrey, and by 1 January 1921, they were living at Cowichan Station, VI, where, on 20 October next, they had a son christened John Lawrence Basden Holme. Not content with things in the Cowichan Valley, on 14 June 1922, they proposed to live nearer to Victoria, but a year later, HH wrote to tell the WO that he was returning to England in July 1923 on SS *Andania* and proposed to live in Switzerland. Was this OK? It was, but Switzerland evidently did not suit him either, as he wrote from Les Avants, sur/Montreuse on 4 March 1924 to ask the WO whether he might have a promotion to lieutenant colonel. He pointed out that he had a total of twenty-five years and five months of military service of which twenty-two years and a month had been in the Regular Army. The WO refused on the grounds that no promotions were permitted in his category. He then went to live with his in-laws "C/o F. G. Basden, Esq., Moorlands, Exmouth, Devon."

The file was silent for six years, but in 1930, a firm of London solicitors, Chamberlayne, Keene & Co., wrote to tell the WO they were worried about Holme's wife as this officer had had a nervous breakdown and returned to London. "It would appear from our instructions," they continued, "that the cause or the result of the breakdown, is that the Officer has received or purports to have received messages from spirits giving warnings of impending catastrophes to the British Empire and India, and in consequence of such warnings had given instructions to his Bankers, Messrs Cox and King's Branch of Lloyds to realize all his securities and send the proceeds abroad. We are taking proceedings on behalf of the Officer's wife for the protection of the Officer's Estate and we are instructed to ask you to afford such assistance as you may be able in connection with the Officer's Pension . . . (to prevent it being sent abroad, and please treat all this in the greatest confidence)." Involved in this legal proceeding to stop Holme from taking away all the family's funds were his wife, his brother, Richard Henry Holme, a retired banker living at 28 Fitz George Avenue, London, and HH's two sons (a second, Norman Alexander Holme) having been born in the intervening years. This consortium had evidently wrested control of the family's affairs from what the solicitors referred to as "the patient."

Within a few weeks, HH turned up in Victoria, and on 5 August 1931, the *Daily Colonist* reported, "While a wife with her two children in England anxiously awaits word from her husband, Major Harold L. Holme, D.S.O., police here are investigating the possibility that clothing found last Saturday on the Dallas Road waterfront may mark the tragic end of a brilliant military career." He was said to have retired from the Royal Artillery in 1920 after serving in Malta, Bombay, Aden, Hong Kong, and Poland and to have come back to Victoria on holiday with the intention of returning to England on 12 August. He was known to have heart trouble and observed to swim daily in the early morning. Local authorities concluded that he had drowned, aged fifty-four, on 1 August 1931 in the icy tide waters of the Strait of Juan de Fuca.

Sources: PRO (London), WO 339/5939; *Colonist*, 14 January 1921, p. 8; 5 August 1931, p. 2.

HOLMES, Rev. David (1837-1915). He was born in Bolingbroke, Lincolnshire, on 7 September 1837, attended Holton Holgate School and, in 1865, matriculated at St Augustine's College, Canterbury. In 1867, he went to BC via the Panama and San Francisco, was ordained by *Bishop George Hills, spent several years at Yale, Hope, and Chiliwack mainly among the native tribes, but, in 1873, was assigned to duty on the Island at Cowichan. This was a large pastorate extending north to Nanaimo, and he rode around it on horseback, living meanwhile at Duncan. In Chemainus, he took over from *Rev. Archdeacon William Sheldon Reece, whose parsonage was then at Quamichan. DH immediately began to build three churches, one at Quamichan, another at the Chemainus River, and a third at Westholme (this latter completed on 7 August 1880, chiefly out of funds from the SPCK). In 1871, DH married Susan Abercrombie Nagle, daughter of *Captain Jeremiah and Catherine Nagle of Victoria, and they had six children of whom Isabella married Captain Roberts of Kuper Island and Susan Isabel Holmes married a son of Rev. R. J. Roberts on 14 May 1904. Canadian census records show the family living on the Island, and there, DH and his wife died at Duncan, he, aged seventy-eight, on 19 October 1915 and she, aged eighty, on 24 January 1921.

Sources: Elliott, *Memories of the Chemainus Valley*, pp. 97-101;

HOLMES, Major Henry Cuthbert (1890-1968). Born in December 1890 at Bellary, India, son of William Cuthbert Holmes, BA, of the ICS, who in 1912 brought his family to live at Millstream, near Victoria, VI, and then in the town itself. After attending the Royal Naval School at Dartmouth and Balliol College, Oxford, HH became a barrister. But during the Great War, he served in France with the Twenty-ninth Lancers, the Irish Guards, and on the Supreme Council. In 1917, after two years overseas, he was wounded and sent home on leave, staying with Mrs C. M. Dumbleton of 1750 Rockland Avenue and predicting at length in the *Daily Colonist* that the Allies would be in Germany by 1918. During that leave, he married Philippa Despard Pemberton, daughter of F. B. Pemberton, JP, BCLS; they had three sons and two daughters. After the war, he qualified as a barrister at the Middle Temple, London, and returned to Victoria as—in the course of a long career—president of Pemberton & Son Ltd. (real estate) and director of the Durable Mat Company of Canada, Victoria Properties Ltd., Pacific North-West Real Estate Association (past vice-president), and the Canadian Committee of National Real Estate Associations, a governor of Brentwood College (Saanich), chairman of the National Council of Education, Victoria Branch, and active in the University Extension Association of Victoria, the Victoria Branch of the Canadian Institute of International Affairs, the United Service Institution, and the Corps of Commissionaires Council. In 1927-1928, he was an Alderman in the city of Victoria. He had an office at 625 Fort Street and resided at 336 Newport Avenue, Oak Bay. Such was his social position that he was at the head table with Randolph Churchill, Major John Churchill, *et al.* in September 1929 when Winston Churchill dined at the Empress Hotel on 5 September 1929 and was called on to express formal thanks when in May 1933 the historian Philip Guedalla, one of his classmates at Oxford, spoke to the Men's Canadian Club. He was able to maintain his membership in London clubs such as the Guards and Vincents, as well as the Victoria Gyro Club and the Automobile Club (BC). The family was Anglican. It seems natural that such a man should be, as he was, a leader in the group of Victoria gentlemen who founded Brentwood College. Notable among his children was his eldest son, Lieutenant Colonel W. D. C. Holmes (1922-2000), who served overseas with the Royal Engineers during the Second World War. HH died, aged seventy-seven, on 23 May 1968 in Victoria.

Sources: *Who's Who in B.C.* 1942-1943, p. 153; vol. VI (1944-1946), p. 120; 1947-1948, p. 98; *Colonist*, 28 March 1917, p. 5; 6 September 1929, p. 2; 3 May 1933, p. 3; 5 March 2000, p. D12, obit.; Jean Barman, *Growing up British in British Columbia: Boys in Private School* (Vancouver, UBC Press, 1984), p. 36.

HOLMES, Lieutenant Colonel Josiah Greenwood (1845-1928). Born on 10 November 1845c at St Catharine's, Ontario, where his family had settled on coming from England in 1835, he was a son of Josiah H. Holmes, a native of Grantham, Lincolnshire. He attended Grantham Academy and upon his return to Canada joined the Nineteenth Militia Regiment, St Catharines Garrison Artillery.

He was with them during the defence against the Fenian raids in the Niagara Peninsula (1866 and 1870). In 1871, he took a commission in the permanent force as a lieutenant in "A" Battery, Canadian School of Gunnery, and later the RCA, formed when Imperial forces were withdrawn from everywhere in Canada except Halifax and Esquimalt. In 1878, he won first prize offered by the Dominion Artillery Association for an essay entitled "The organization, equipment and localization of artillery for the Dominion of Canada." After twelve years, he reached the rank of lieutenant colonel and was sent in 1883 to Esquimalt to organize the coast defences, with the rank of acting deputy adjutant general, and led an expedition against the Skeena Indians in 1888. After a posting in 1893 to Winnipeg and then London, Ontario, where he was DOC from 1898 to 1901, he was entrusted again with the military district directed from Esquimalt until his retirement in 1909.

In 1870, he had married Elizabeth, daughter of William Kew of Beamsville, Ontario, and they now lived for a time at "Wolston," 620 Andrew Street, Victoria, but more permanently in Oak Bay at 1003 Carberry Gardens. When Mrs Holmes died in 1926 and he on 13 May 1928, funerals were held at St Mary's Anglican Church, Oak Bay. They were survived by three daughters and two sons, Colonel W. J. H. Holmes, DSO of Victoria, and Mr H. A. Holmes of the Canadian Bank of Commerce head office in Toronto.

Sources: Longstaff, *Esquimalt Naval Base*, pp. 149-150; *Colonist*, 15 May 1928, pp. 1-2, obit., and photo; J. C. Berezowski, *"A Window into History,"* *Times-Colonist Islander*, 5 December 2004, p. D9; Morgan, *Canadian Men and Women*, p. 543.

HOLMES, Terence Charles (1906-2000). He was born in Victoria in 1906, the youngest of William Cuthbert Holmes's five children by his wife, Clara Evelyn Dumbleton. The family lived at "Rocklands," the house that Rocklands Avenue was named after, but also spent long periods at a log cabin in the Highlands, now known as the "Pike House." In consequence, TH spent little time at school but learned English from his father and French from his mother. He articled as a BC Land Surveyor, aged seventeen, and graduated in 1925. As such, he spent many years surveying west of the Chilcotin Valley, on triangulation surveys of the Coast Range and south of Telegraph Creek. He enrolled at Victoria College in 1927, at the University of BC in 1928, qualified as a mining engineer in 1933, and took a doctoral degree in geology at the universities of Minnesota and Chicago, which led him ultimately to the post of chief geologist and chief engineer in Canada. Meanwhile, he and his wife Irene, whom he met while an undergraduate in Vancouver, brought up four boys in South Porcupine, BC. He became a leader in the Boy Scouts, on the local school board and the church building committee, and in other community work and played tennis, golf, and curling. When he retired, they settled in North Saanich. He published two books: *The Forces that Drive Subsurface Geologic Processes* (1998) and *A Thinker* [memoirs] (2000). He died at home on 28 April 2000 and was buried at Holy Trinity Anglican Church, Patricia Bay.

Sources: *Oak Bay Star, a local Oak Bay weekly*, 10 May 2000.

HOLMES, William Cuthbert (1874-1930). He was born on 20 November 1874 at 67 Eccles Street, Dublin, youngest son of Charles Holmes, and was educated privately and at Trinity College, Dublin. As a member of a distinguished Anglo-Irish family of sailors and notables headed by Lord Heytesbury, he entered the ICS, passing twenty-third in his year. He was not a robust person but went out to India in 1877 and rose as a magistrate to the eminence of a judge's office and "was known as the justest judge in India," according to a family tradition. A charming person interested in human affairs and history, in 1890, he married a lady with musical, literary, and artistic tastes, Miss Clara Evelyn Dumbleton (c. 1866-1926), of Hall Grove, Bagshot, Berkshire, daughter of Henry Dumbleton of a prominent landowning family at Shirley, a suburb of Southampton, and his wife Clara Marion Dumbleton (born at Cape Town, South Africa). During the long furloughs granted to ICS officers, he visited a variety of places with a view to retiring somewhere outside Ireland, having concluded that Irish republican terrorism rule would soon render the country unfit for families like his. He spent time in Australia, the southern France, Switzerland, the Black Forest in Germany, and the Isle of Wight.

When at last he retired in 1902, after twenty-five years of service, it was to Vancouver Island that he took his family. The Dumbleton family may have influenced that decision as they had already settled in Victoria at a place they called "Rockland" for which Rockland Avenue was named. WH and his family lived in Victoria but had a cabin in the Highland district at Pike Lake, where he could indulge his fondness for riding, walking, and mountaineering and for much longer in the year than anywhere else in Canada. He was too old to serve in the Great War, though he tried to do so, but took a keen interest in it and contributed generously to war charities. His eldest son landed in France with the Twenty-ninth Lancers, transferred to the Irish Guards, was severely wounded on the Somme, and retired in 1921 after serving with the Supreme War Council. The youngest son, one of the brilliant junior officers of the Canadian Contingent, was killed in June 1916. His daughter Lona Beatrice, who married H. C. Bridges in April 1923, devoted herself to her father during a long illness that led to his death in Victoria on 5 December 1930.

Sources: *Colonist*, 6 December 1930, p. 5, obit.; Ruth H. Judson, "*Dumbleton and Leneveu Families*, 634 Michigan [St]," in *Camas Chronicles of James Bay, Victoria, British Columbia* (Victoria, Camas Historical Group, 1978), pp. 109-110.

HOLMES, Lieutenant Colonel William Desmond Charles (1922-2000). The eldest son of Major Henry Cuthbert Holmes and Phillippa Despard Holmes, *née* Pemberton, he was born in Victoria, attended Brentwood College, Saanich, which his father had helped to found, and was an outstanding sportsman in rugby, soccer, and cricket and a champion marksman. In 1939, aged seventeen, he drove across Canada on a motorcycle to attend RMC, Kingston, Ontario, and won the Sword of Honour at his graduation. His success brought him a commission in the Royal Engineers in which he served in the Second World War with the

J.F. Bosher

Eighth Army in North Africa, at the Anzio Beachhead, as a paratrooper at the Battle of Arnhem, and at various parts of Europe. In 1950, he volunteered for service in Korea and was awarded the Military Cross for his part in the battle of the Imjin River. In 1952-1954, he served as British Liaison Officer in Fort Belvoir, Virginia, USA, and, in 1957-1961, was seconded to the Public Works Office in Nigeria, where he constructed the Uba-Bama Road in a remote northern part of the country. He served as CRE Operations in Aden at the start of the Radfan War in 1963.

He retired from the Royal Engineers in 1966 and rejoined his wife, Patricia Leslie Siddens, and the five children they had had since their marriage in 1947. The family firm of Pemberton, Holmes Ltd., a leading real-estate company on the Island, was glad to employ him, and he was particularly good at managing properties in the Metchosin district. He was successful for many years, but the harsh life of his war years had put strains on his health and he died of cancer on 3 March 2000.

Sources: *Times-Colonist*, 5 March 2000, p. D12, obit.

HOLMES, William Dumbleton (1893-1916). Born on 10 June 1893 in Mangalore, India, son of William Cuthbert Holmes, he was commissioned as lieutenant in the Eighty-eighth Regiment, Victoria Fusiliers, and joined the CEF as such on 11 January 1915 in Victoria. He was quickly promoted to captain and was killed in battle, aged twenty-three, on 13 June 1916 and buried in Belgium. Recommended for the Victoria Cross when first under fire, he was awarded the DSO in November 1915 and the MC on 1 January 1916.

Sources: NAC, CEF files, RG 150, box 4465-5; *Department of Veteran's Affairs*, "Virtual Cemetery".

HOLMES, Lieutenant Colonel William Josiah Hartley Holmes (1871-1954). Born on 28 May 1871 at St Catharines, Ontario, son of *Lieutenant Colonel J. G. Holmes, he became a civil engineer and joined the Canadian Militia in 1891. As a result, he was granted a commission in the CEF when he joined it on 2 August 1915, citing his father, then living at Carberry Gardens, Oak Bay, as his next of kin. Army doctors at Shorncliffe, which he reached at the end of August, declared him fit, though he was over forty-four years old and his legs were scarred by operations for varicose veins. He was one of the many surveyors from the Island who joined the army during the Great War—at least thirty-four of them by February 1917. He was by then OC of the Third Canadian Pioneer Battalion, and there was speculation later that year that this unit might become part of the Railway Construction Division. WH survived the war and lived until 10 July 1954, when he died, aged eighty-one, in Saanich. At the beginning of 1925, his son, Lieutenant William Montague Hartley Holmes (c. 1900-1925), had been accidentally shot to death in Halifax.

Sources: NAC, CEF files, RG 150, box 4465-27; *Colonist*, 9 February 1917, p. 5; 3 June 1917, p. 10; 2 January 1925, p. 1.

HOPKINSON, William Charles (1878-1914). Some believe that he was born in 1878 in Yorkshire, but R. J. Popplewell, a specialist in the intelligence operations WH was caught up in, believes he was born and brought up in India. Certainly, the English census records for 1881 and 1891 show no such person. His father was killed at Kabul in 1879, and in 1901-1907, WH served in the Indian Police, having grown up familiar with several Indian languages. After visiting British Columbia during a long leave in 1907-1909, he was hired by the Canadian Department of the Interior to investigate a conspiracy of Sikhs to foment a revolution against British rule in India. An organization calling itself "Ghadr" was gathering funds, men, and weapons on the Pacific coast of Canada and the United States and planning secret shipments to India. From 1908 to 1914, WH worked undercover, building up a system of informers within the Sikh community and keeping in touch with the British police in India. He was prominent in the affair of the *Kom agata Maru*, which tried to land Sikh passengers illegally at Vancouver in July 1914. This affair, which whipped the Vancouver Sikh community into a frenzy "and gave a great fillip to the Ghadr Party," led to several assassinations. "On 21 October 1914 WH was waiting outside the court room at Victoria to testify in favour of his friend [Bela Singh, who had shot some Sikh assassins threatening him in the temple at Vancouver] when a Sikh named Mewa Singh shot him at point-blank range in the chest." WH died there and then, but the assassin was caught and British authorities foiled the conspiracy against India. Some questions about his life remain unanswered, but Popplewell's is the most convincing history of the affair in general.
Sources: Richard J. Popplewell, *Intelligence and Imperial Defence: British Intelligence and the Defence of the Indian Empire, 1904-1924* (Frank Cass, 1995), pp. 151-3 and passim.

HOSE, Vice Admiral Walter (1875-1965). Born on 2 October 1875 aboard the P&O Steamer, *Surat* in the Indian Ocean off Ceylon, he was a son of the archbishop of Singapore, Rev. George F. Hose (born in Cambridge about 1839), and Emily Harriet Hose (born about 1849 at Knightsbridge, Devonshire). By 1881, when the family was living at Dunstable, Bedfordshire, his sister and a brother had been born at Singapore, another brother in "Malacca Straits Settlement, India," and a third at Addlestone, Surrey. WH became a naval cadet on 15 January 1890 aboard HMS *Britannia* and had a long career that took him several times to the China station, to Crete during the Turko-Greek War in 1897, to Venezuela in 1904 aboard HMS *Charybdis* to frighten the president who had imprisoned the crew of a British ship and failed to pay debts to British firms, and to Newfoundland and many other parts of the empire. After taking the War Staff course at Greenwich and other courses at the Military Staff College, Camberley, he was promoted to commander in 1908 and commanded, in turn, HMS *Tweed, Ringdove, Kale, Redbreast,* and *Jason.* In 1911, he was lent to the RCN and, in June that year, took command of HMCS *Rainbow* for almost the next six years. His wife, whom he married in 1905, was from St John's Newfoundland, and as early as 1909, he was corresponding with Admiral Kingsmill about the possibility of service in the Canadian Naval Service. In 1912, he resigned from the RN in order to remain in the RCN and was given increasing responsibilities and promotions until he retired at last on 30 June 1934. In summer 1917, he became captain of Patrols on the east coast, then senior naval officer at Halifax, in 1920, assistant director of the Naval Service, and, in January 1921, succeeded Admiral Kingsmill as the director. Having been decorated with the CBE, he retired at last to England and died there in June 1965. His importance to Vancouver Island was as an officer of the Royal Navy in the high command, which determined Esquimalt's future almost from the time Canada took control of it in 1910.

Sources: Longstaff, *Esquimalt Naval Base,* pp. 161-3; Gilbert Norman Tucker, *The Naval Service of Canada* (2 vols., Ottawa, King's Printer, 1952), vol. I, pp. 151-2, 277-8, 354; *MacFarlane,* pp. 32-3; census 1881, England, RG 11/1646; census 1891, RG 12/1715, p. 8; RG 12/1710, List of the Officers, Crew, Royal Marines and of all other persons not on board on the night of 5 April 1891.

HOSKINS, Stephen Hamilton (1869-1959). A gentleman farmer living in the Cowichan Valley near Duncan, he was born in May 1869 at Ware, Hertfordshire, at "Fanham's Hall," son of Edward Hamilton Hoskins, shipping merchant. His mother, Hannah Ann *née* O'Brien at Hoddesdon, Hertfordshire, was one of the seven children of Rear Admiral Donat Henchy O'Brien (1785-1857) from County Clare in Ireland and his wife Hannah (SH's grandmother), youngest daughter of John Walmsley of Castle Mere in Lancashire. The family believed that the rear admiral's book, *My Adventure During the Late War* (1839), had inspired Frederick Marryat's popular story, *Peter Simple* (1834), but this seems doubtful. In 1881, SH, aged eleven, was living in Rose Valley, Hoddesdon, with his widowed mother and several brothers and sisters, including a clerk and a sailor. They had a governess, a cook, and a housemaid, but there were no signs of the wealth characteristic of the successful shipping merchant. Thirty years earlier, in 1851, SH's mother had lived in a household with a butler, footman, groom, lady's maid, cook, kitchenmaid, and housemaid. After attending St Catherine's School in Broxbourne, SH taught school in the years 1885-1890 and then emigrated to the Assiniboia part of Manitoba, where he farmed for four years before moving on to BC in 1894.

In 1896-1898, he was a special police constable in the Islands District, and then appointed constable in 1898, he transferred to Victoria (1900) and on to East Kootenay (1902) and Kimberley (1905-1910). Hired in the town of Nelson as assessor and collector, keeping mining records, etc., in 1913, he was appointed government agent, gold commissioner, and stipendiary magistrate at Hazelton. There followed transfers to Smithers (1918), Anyox (1931), and Duncan (1932), where he settled in Berkley Street with his wife, Margaret Hilda Ward, whom he had married at Fernie in 1903, and their three sons. She was the third daughter of Rev. Philip Gordon Ward, vicar of Braughing, Hertfordshire. SH died, aged eighty-nine, on 18 August 1959 in Duncan, where his wife died, aged eighty-eight, on 28 February 1967.

Sources: *Who's Who in B.C.,* (1933-1934), p. 87; (1937-1939), p. 61; vol. V (1942-1943), pp. 154-5; 1940-1941, pp. 103-04; VI (1944-1946), pp. 121-2; 1947-1948, p. 100; census 1881, England, RG 11/1399, p. 30; BNA, census, 1861, RG 9/805, p. 3;

BNA, census 1851, HO 107/1705/50; O'Brien, *My Adventure During the Late War: A Narrative of Shipwreck, Captivity, Escapses from French Prisons, and Sea Service in 1804-1814*, (Henry Colburn, 1839), 402 and 493 pp. with maps and illustrations; *Oxford DCB*, "O'Brien, Donat Henchy (1785-1857)."

HOUGHTON, Lieutenant Colonel Charles Frederick (1839-1898). Born on 27 April 1839 into an Anglo-Irish family in County Tipperary, he held a commission from 1855 to 1863 in the Imperial Army: as ensign Fifty-seventh Regiment from 1 May 1855, as lieutenant 26 February 1856, served in the Crimean War from 1853 to March 1856, as lieutenant Fifth Regiment of Infantry from 2 February 1858, as lieutenant in the Twentieth Regiment of Foot from 31 March 1858, and as captain from 5 March 1861. On 30 June 1863, he sold his commission and went to Victoria with *Forbes George Vernon and a letter of introduction to Governor James Douglas. They soon settled in the Okanagan Valley, and CH was elected federal MP for Yale and Kootenay in winter 1871-1872. When an office was created for deputy adjutant general (DAG) in the province he was commissioned on 21 March 1873 as lieutenant colonel in the Militia and first DAG in BC. Part of his job was to train the Militia, and he served thus until 31 March 1881, when he was moved to Winnipeg and in 1888 to Montreal. There he retired but soon moved back to Victoria. One reason for this was that on 27 March 1879, he had married Marion Dunsmuir (1854-1892), daughter of the wealthy and influential Hon. Robert Dunsmuir. He died in Victoria shortly before the South African War and was buried at Ross Bay "under a three-tiered marble tombstone."
Sources: Longstaff, *Esquimalt Naval Base*, pp. 36, 44, 45, 58 n. 5, 138; J. K. Johnson, ed., *The Canadian Directory of Parliament, 1867-1967* (Ottawa, Public Archives, 1968), p. 278; Major Charles Arkoll Boulton (1841-1899), *Reminiscences of the North-West Rebellions, with A Record of the Raising of Her Majesty's 100th Regiment in Canada and a Chapter on Canadian Social & Political Life* (Toronto, Grip Printing & Publishing Co., 1886), p. 499; John Adams, *Ross Bay Cemetery* (revised ed., Victoria, Sono Nono Press, Heritage Architectural Guides, Victoria, 1998), p. 12.

HOULGATE, Henry Laurie (1876-1945). Born on 9 August 1976 at Whitehaven, Cumberland, son of William Houlgate, a Yorkshire bank manager and his Scottish wife Anne, he became a mining engineer and was working in Calgary, Alberta, when he enlisted in the Second Canadian Mounted Rifles on 5 January 1900. His father, brothers, and sisters were then still at Whitehaven though his mother had died more than ten years earlier. As HH's Queen's Medal shows, with its four clasps for Johannesberg, Diamond Hill, Cape Colony, and Orange Free State, he fought in the South African War but took his discharge on 14 November 1900 with the intention of settling there. At sometime in the next few years, he became assistant resident in Northern Nigeria and went "up country" to the remote town of Sokoto. He left Africa well before the Great War, married Clara Evans at Victoria on 26 August 1912, and was working as an engineer when he enlisted in the CEF at Pond Farm Camp on 8 December 1914. By that time, he had a brother living in Vancouver, as well as his wife in Victoria, and after the Great War, this couple settled on Mayne Island, where they lived on his army pension and wages from employment by the post office. "From 1926 to 1945," Marie Elliott tells us, "H. L. Houlgate trundled the mail from the wharf to the post office by wheelbarrow." They both died in Vancouver, however, he aged sixty-nine on 16 April 1945 and she aged sixty-six the following 19 December.

Sources: NAC, CEF files, box 4529-77; NAC, RG 38, A-1-a, vol. 49, reel T-2073; census 1881, England, RG 11/5186, p. 1; census 1891, RG 12/4314, p. 1; Marie Elliott, *Mayne Island & The Outer Gulf Islands: A History* (Gulf Islands Press, Mayne Island, BC, 1984), pp. 54 and 64

HOWELL, Gerard Charles Lisle (1875-?). From the early 1930s until after the Second World War, he lived with his family in Esquimalt as a retired officer from the ICS. Born on 16 March 1875 at Dhera Ghazi Khan in the Punjab, son of Lieutenant Colonel Horace Howell and his wife Ella, he attended Lancing School in Sussex and Christ Church, Oxford (MA) and qualified for the ICS in 1899. He served for some years as assistant commissioner and deputy commissioner, Punjab Frontier Province, then as director of Fisheries in the Punjab, but left India in time to join the Machine-Gun Corps (Cavalry) in France in 1916-1918 during the Great War. Though gassed at the battle of the Somme, he was able to work after the war as organizing secretary of the British Trawlers Federation, secretary of the British Fisheries Society, and on the Fisheries Research Advisory Committee to the Development Commission.

In the course of that career, he moved to Victoria with his wife, Cicely Johnson, daughter of Matthew Warton Johnson, whom he had married in 1901. They lived at 464 Lampson Street with their two sons; he maintained his membership in the East India United Service Club, and the Fly Fishers Club and remained a Roman Catholic. He wrote *Ocean Research and the Great Fisheries* (Oxford, Clarendon Press, 1921) and *Rudiments of Ski-running* (Chateau d'Oea). Mrs Howell died on 25 November 1928, but I find no sign of his death. He is recorded, however, arriving in London on 30 May 1939 aboard a Furness Line passenger ship, *Pacific Ranger*, giving a forwarding address as c/o Neish, Howell, and Haldane, 47 Watling Street, London EC 4.

Sources: *Who's Who in B.C.*, 1933-1934, p. 88; (1937-1939), pp. 62-63; vol. V (1942-1943), p. 156; vol. VI (1944-1946), p. 122; census 1891, England, RG 12/824 (Lancing School); UK Passenger Lists online, 1878-1960, no. 161291, arriving in London from Vancouver on 30 May 1939.

HOWLAND, Colonel Gilbert (1882-1960). He was born on 12 September 1882 at Putney, Surrey, eldest son of Bradfield Howland from Great Dunmow in Essex, a fishmonger's manager with several children and three domestic servants. In 1871, the father, aged eighteen, had been a lithographer's apprentice boarding with a school principal and singing teacher, and the census of 1881 had registered him as a lithographer with a wife, Anna, from Brompton, London. Whatever it was that induced him to become a fishmonger, he had begun life with other thoughts and ambitions. His son, GH became an electrician, joined the First City of London Royal Victoria Garrison Artillery, spent six years in the South African Constabulary, and then moved to western Canada. When he enlisted in the Canadian Army on 9 February 1916, he was working as an electrician in Lethbridge, Alberta, but married to Gertrude Annie Howland of 1748, 30th Avenue East, Vancouver, BC. They had two boys and a girl. He was granted a commission in the army because he had spent several years in the 101st Regiment, Edmonton Fusiliers, in addition to his service in South Africa. Sent overseas as a major with the Sixty-third Battalion, CEF—113th Battalion Lethbridge Highlanders—he arrived in France in 1917 with the Thirty-eighth Battalion and later with the Forty-ninth Battalion, First Edmonton Regiment.

After the war, he returned to Edmonton, Alberta, but by 1933 when the CPR Tennis Club elected him president, he had moved to Victoria. His wife died, aged fifty-five, on 26 April 1940, and ten years later, he was living at 32 Paddon Street with a second wife, Phyllis, and working as a storekeeper for Ramsay Machinery Company. By 1957, they had moved to 3749 Quadra Street and GH had been active for several years in the BC Indian Arts and Welfare Society in which he had followed *Alice Ravenhill as president. They moved at last to 2094 Brighton Avenue, Oak Bay, and by then, he was recording his birthplace as Richmond—up the Thames from Putney. When he died, aged seventy-seven, on 12 May 1960, he was buried at Royal Oak after a funeral at Christ Church Cathedral and was survived by two daughters, his sons Bradfield and Christopher, and his widow, as well as his younger brother, Norman Anderson Howland (1882-1978) living on Salt Spring Island. Canada was kind to men like Howland, but they usually made good use of their opportunities and lived as public-spirited citizens.
Sources: NAC, CEF files, RG 150, acc. 1992-1993/166, box 4561-6; *Colonist*, 28 March 1933, p. 6; 23 January 1952, p. 16; 14 May 1960, p. 16 obit.; census 1871, England, RG 10/684, p. 27; census 1881, RG 11/661; census 1891, RG 12/452, p. 35; census England, 1901, RG 13/432; *B.C. Directory, 1950-1951*; 1957, Victoria.

HUGHES, Lady Evelyn Isabella Rose (c. 1868-1940). In 1939-1940, she lived at the Windermere Hotel in Victoria and then at "Beachcroft" on Cook Street. This entry is for who she was—another Imperial on the Island—rather than anything she did. She was born at Poona, India, eldest daughter of Colonel Henry Stephen Hutchinson of the Bengal Staff Corps and later the ICS. The family appears in the 1871 census, when she was two-years old, living in Gloucestershire near Bristol at "Redland House," Westbury-on-Tayon, home of her paternal grandmother, Elizabeth H. Hutchinson, aged fifty-one, and born in Calcutta. Her father, aged thirty, was born in Camden Town (London), but her mother, aged twenty-one, was born in India at Simla. With them in that household were her father's sisters, two of them born at Cheltenham and the other in France, and they had seven servants. Ten years later, when she was twelve, her father was away in India and she lived with her mother in Christchurch, Bournemouth, at No. 2 Elbana, Holdenhurst. With them was her brother, Leslie Hutchinson, aged eight, born at Clifton, Somerset, and a sister Mabel, aged eight, born in India at "Maliableshnar." They had a governess and one servant. In 1888, EH married Sir Walter Charleton Hughes (1850-1922), who was knighted for his work at Bombay in the Indian Public Works

Department. He had also been secretary to the Government of Bombay, PWD (1887-1892), chairman of the Board of Trustees for the Port of Bombay (1892-1898 and 1900-1910), as well as chairman of the Bombay Improvement Trust 1898-1900. When he retired, they lived in London, where he died on 30 March 1922. They had three children of whom a daughter lived in London as Mrs Clifford Norton, but their son, soon after his father's death, emigrated to Seattle, Washington State, USA, a short ferry ride across the Strait of Juan de Fuca from Victoria.

They had named him Layard Launcelot Hughes when he was born in India at Poona on 31 October 1892 and, on naturalization papers drawn up in Seattle in 1925, declared himself to be a "fruit merchant." Within a few months, on 6 June 1926, he married Isabella Catherine, a Scottish woman born in Glasgow on 30 June 1885, and she likewise became a naturalized American citizen. They both filled out a printed naturalization form, which read, in part, "It is my bona fide intention to renounce forever all allegiance and fidelity to any foreign prince, potentate, or sovereignty, and particularly to [written by hand] *George V, King of Great Britain & Ireland*, of whom I am now a subject . . . I am not an anarchist; I am not a polygamist nor a believer in the practice of polygamy." It was to visit this son and daughter-in-law that EH retired to Victoria, and it was during a stay with them in Seattle that she died on 27 October 1940. Her remains were returned to Victoria for burial at Royal Oak Cemetery.

Her son, Layard Launcelot Hughes, died, aged eighty, at Baltimore, Maryland, in October 1872. The 1901 English census affords a glimpse of him as a nine-year-old boy living with brothers and sisters in Hampshire with his maternal grandmother at "Ganesh Khind," in Grafton St Mary's, Pokedown, St James, Bournemouth. They had a Swiss governess, a cook, and a parlourmaid.

Sources: *Colonist*, 29 October 1940, p. 3, obit.; *Who was Who*, vol. II (1916-1928), p. 529; census 1871, England, RG10/2569, p. 19; census 1881, RG 11/1194, p. 39; census 1901, RG 13/1037, p. 4; *U.S. Naturalization Records*, series M1542, drawn up by the Dictrict Court for the Western District of Washington State, at Seattle, in 1925 and 1936.

HUGHES, Captain Jasper Nicholls (1872-?). In 1920, he and his wife went to the Island, where they bought an acre of land at Mill Bay, on the west side of Mill Bay Road, and kept a cow or two, sold milk and butter, and built a house of stone quarried nearby. Their house was still standing in 1990, but near the Thrifty Shopping Centre, which made it vulnerable to "development." Born in Wales at Langherne, Carmarthenshire, son of the Anglican rector there, he had spent several years as a tea planter in India and there married Mabel Alise, six years his junior, who was born in Madras. He had served in the First World War as an officer in the Labour Corps. In April 1932, they gave their last permanent address as Cobble Hill (near Mill Bay) when landing at San Pedro, California, from SS *Pacific Exporter*. They disappear from view thereafter, settling perhaps in the United States.

Sources: Adelaide Ellis, *Along the Mill Bay Road* (Cobble Hill, Fir Grove Publishing, 1990), p. 33; census 1881, Wales, RG 11/5469/18, p. 11; census 1891, RG 12/369, p. 16 (Guy's Hospital, London).

HUMPHREYS, Major Arthur Seldon (1880-?). Born in England in 1880, son of George Beauchamp Humphreys, a solicitor, he joined the Imperial Yeomanry and, in 1901-1902, served in South Africa in the Royal Army Service Corps, receiving the Queen's Medal with five clasps. In 1914, he was promoted to major and served in the Great War, winning the DSO and being mentioned in despatches. On the quay at Le Havre, he met Kathleen Euphemia Dunsmuir (1891-1941), James Dunsmuir's daughter from Victoria, who was running a soup kitchen for the troops, and married her in London on 20 October 1915. When poor health obliged him to retire from the army in 1917, they went out to Victoria, where he served as ADC to several lieutenant governors. With the family's ample resources in Victoria, they lived at "Westover" in the Rockland quarter until 1929, when he retired again, and they built a house in Oak Bay at 1456 Beach Drive, near where they had lived briefly in 1920-1921. He became a pillar of the Union Club—though he kept a membership in such London clubs as Boodles and the United Services—and they had a son and three daughters. As a lively and socially ambitious member of a leading family, however, Mrs Humphreys entertained on a lavish scale, decided to become a Hollywood actress, and began to find her husband boring and obstructive. He was persuaded to move to Shanghai in 1930 "with an annuity that paid him £20 a month and the promise of a further £300 to start a business" (Reksten, p. 252). A new owner of the house in Oak Bay turned it into "The Small Charming Hotel." Mrs Humphrey's career in movies, begun at forty years of age, did not flourish even after the ill-fated Island firm of Commonwealth Productions was launched on her ample credit, and she was in great distress by the time she was killed in a London air raid on 8 March 1941. What became of AH in Shanghai?

Sources: *Who's Who in B.C.*, 1933-1934, p. 91; *Colonist*, 18 June 1921, p. 8; 30 September 1932, p. 8; 11 February 1934, p. 8; Terry Reksten, *The Dunsmuir Saga* (Vancouver, Douglas & McIntyre, 1991), pp. 250-6; James Audain, *From Coalmine to Castle: The Story of the Dunsmuirs of Vancouver Island* (NY, Pageant Press, 1955), pp. 185-6, 210-211.

HUMPHREYS, Thomas Basil (c. 1840-1890). Born in England and schooled at Walton-on-the Hill (near Liverpool), "he claimed to have served in the East India Company, first as a cadet and later as a midshipman" (*Colonist*, 19 August 1951). He was provincial secretary and minister of mines in 1878-1882.

He married Caroline Watkins on 3 November 1873 in Victoria; she died on 28 October 1926; he died, aged fifty, on 26 August 1890 in Victoria.

Sources: Jean (Foote) Humphreys, "*The Hon. Thomas Basil Humphreys: A Controversial Contributor to Change in Early B.C. Politics*," in *British Columbia Historical News*, no. 35, no. 3 (summer 2002), pp. 9-15; *Colonist*, 19 August 1951; Victoria census 1901.

HUNT, Lieutenant Colonel Archibald William (1893-1956). Born on 4 July 1910 at Aldershot, Hampshire, probably a soldier's son, he went to Halifax, Nova Scotia in 1910 and worked as a painter, leaving his widowed mother living at 204 Victoria Road, Edmonton, London. He enlisted in the Canadian Army at Halifax on 23 August 1915, served overseas with the Royal Canadian Regiment, won the Military Medal at Ypres, and was mentioned in despatches on the Somme. Wounded at Vimy in 1917, he recovered in time to serve with the Canadian continent in Siberia in 1918-1819 and was then appointed to the PPCLI at London, Ontario, There he became an expert marksman and was sent to shoot at Bisley with the Canadian team in 1925, 1935, 1936, and 1937. In the Second World War, he was commissioned as a general staff officer at HQ Military District 10 (Winnipeg) and was awarded the OBE. He was invalided out of the army in 1946, retired to Victoria, but continued to shoot as a member of the Victoria District Rifle Association and to help in training servicemen and cadets. Some of his men went to shoot at Bisley in their turn, where he continued his interest in shooting. Living as he did at 637 Beach Drive, Oak Bay, he could walk to the Royal Victoria Golf Club and joined the Seniors Golf Association. He died on 14 December 1956 at the Veteran's Hospital, leaving his wife, Marjorie, and three daughters, three sisters in England, and a brother and sister in Rhodesia. An Anglican, he had a funeral at Christ Church Cathedral, where among the pallbearers were Brigadier W. G. Colquhoun, Brigadier G. R. Bradbroke, Colonel R. L. Mitchell, Lieutenant Colonel J. H. Carvosso, Lieutenant Colonel W. E. Stone, Lieutenant Colonel J. N. Edgar, and * Lieutenant Colonel M. R. Ten Broeke.

Sources: NAC, CEF files, RG 150, box 4617-32; *Colonist*, 15 December 1956, p. 30, obit.; 16 December 1956, p. 15, photo and obit.; R. C. Fetherstonhaugh, *The Royal Canadian Regiment, 1883-1933* (Fredericton, Centennial Print & Litho Ltd., 1981), pp. 233, 252.

HUNTER, Major Hugh Blackburn, MC (1880-1956). He was born in Kelso, Scotland, and served from November 1898 to 31 March 1908 in the Queen's Edinburgh Rifle Volunteer Brigade of Royal Scots. From 1 July 1910 to 31 May 1913, he served as a lieutenant, then captain in the ASC (T), but resigned to go to Canada. When he returned in 1915 to volunteer for service in the Great War, one of his commanding officers commended him as "one of my best supply officers . . . he has the Aldershot supply Certificate with a high percentage of marks and has the work at his finger ends. I was sorry to lose [him] when business took him to Canada. He went on a year's leave first and then resigned on a suggestion by me because his staying on blocked the appointment of other officers. Captain Hunter has now come back for patriotic reasons to serve his country and I hope he may get a position for which he is eminently fitted." He won the MC in the course of the war.

He was back in Canada after working as an employee, then as manager of the Victoria branch of the Huron & Erie Mortgage Corporation and the Canada Trust Company. During his twenty-five years with them, he joined the Union Club but devoted most of his spare time to leading Boy Scouts. For many years, he was the district scoutmaster. Early in January 1936, he was the guest at a Christmas party held at the disused railway station that served as a meeting hall for the First Sidney Boy Scout Troop, including four boys I knew as a child: Gilbert Baal, Bruce Baker, Robert Deildal, and Roy Tutte. When he died, aged seventy-five, on 30 October

1956, he left only two cousins in California, but his funeral at Christ Church Cathedral, Victoria, was attended by large contingents of Scouts.
Sources: PRO (London), WO339/24433; *Colonist*, 14 October 1934, p. 14; 31 October 1956, obit.; 1 November 1956, p. 26, obit.

HUNTINGTON, Lionel Welby (1884-?). He was born on 22 October 1884 at Darwen, Lancashire, the youngest son of Emily Louisa *née* King, a Londoner from Camberwell, and William Balle Huntington (c. 1849-?), a paper maker born at Mitcham, Surrey. Living at Darwen in "Woodlands Cottage" in 1891, there were also two older sisters and seven servants: a cook, three housemaids, a scullery maid, a dustman, and a governess. After attending Eton and Trinity College, Cambridge, LH went out to BC in 1910 but returned to England to serve throughout the Great War as an officer in the RNVR. He trained as a signals officer, and his service, as detailed in the British National Archives, PRO, ADM 337/118, page 57, was mainly with the Tenth Cruiser Squadron in HMS *Pembroke III, Teutonic,* and *Armadale Castle.* He was sent to Egypt and the Dardanelles, where he was wounded while working with armoured cars and sent to Malta Hospital. While on leave during the war, he had stayed at Powyke Court, Worcester, and "The Boynes," Upton-on-Severn, Worcester, and in 1922, his father's addresses were 143 Picadilly, London, and Blackmore Park, Hanley Swan, Worcestershire. When LH was demobilized on 6 February 1919, however, he gave his address as "Blackmore Farm," Somenos, Vancouver Island.

He became a public-spirited citizen of the Cowichan Valley, active in many ways. On 3 May 1921, he was chairman of a Cowichan district meeting at the Duncan Opera House packed with people indignant that the provincial legislature had raised MLA's salaries. The meeting was addressed by *Mrs Colonel Claude "Maggy" Moss, OBE, *Lieutenant Colonel G. E. Barnes, *Mr Ruscombe Poole, and Mr H. P. Tooker. Drawing on his experiences in Africa, Colonel Barnes declared that no Kaffir pow-wow would behave as disgracefully as the BC legislature. Mr Huntington said he was born in Lancashire, where the public took the view that what Lancashire thinks today is what England will think tomorrow and believed that the people of Cowichan might likewise carry the provincial public with them. In July that summer, LH and his sister travelled down the Cowichan River from Cowichan Lake to Duncan with a party in an Indian canoe, and in September, he won second prize for six perennials he displayed at the Duncan Exhibition.

On 3 August 1922, he married Elizabeth, daughter of J. P. Roberts of Vancouver, and they eventually had three sons. She was soon active in the IODE and, in 1925, offered her house for meetings of the *Sir Clive Phillipps-Wolley chapter of Cowichan Station nearby. Funds for the village library and the IODE were raised by dances, parties, and teas held at the Huntington's house. So supported, that chapter of the IODE had the courage to go on record as opposed to vulgar comic strips for children. LH was a member of the Union Club (Victoria), the Windham Club (London), and the Jericho Country Club (Vancouver), but at sometime in the 1920s, they settled on a property of some sixty-eight acres near Cherry Point on Cowichan Bay, which they called "Lambourne" and LH soon became vice-president of the Vancouver Island Horticultural Association and president of its Cowichan branch. He evidently intended to develop his property in the manner of an English country estate and had a water tower built and supplied by a Petter motor pump designed by the Petter brothers from England, who spent much time on the Island. To lay out the grounds, LH hired half a dozen labourers together with my father, J. E. Bosher (1900-1991), to direct them as head gardener. Dad, who in the early 1920s had managed the garden for old Mrs Dunsmuir in Esquimalt at what later became Royal Roads Naval College, had grown up in the gardener's cottage on an estate near Bracknell, Berkshire, where my grandfather had been head gardener, producing vegetables, fruits, and flowers for the resident owner. One of the immediate tasks was to lay out tennis courts as LH was keen on lawn tennis, having played for Cambridge University in his student days. He was also fond of fishing, shooting, and squash and was active in the Church of England. Bill Dennis of Delta, BC, whose father seems to have had a longer association with LH, recalls, "My dad was the butler, the gentleman's gentleman and executive assistant to that master of the household . . . I could always tell where Mr Huntington had been by the odor of those Egyptian cigarettes 'Abdullah' which he always smoked." Many years after my own father had left about 1931 to work in the Plant Pathology Laboratory on the Dominion Experimental Station in North Saanich, LH sold "Lambourne" and it was eventually turned into an inn and later still subdivided for use as a housing development. When I visited it in 2001, the coach house in which my parents and I had lived during the first year of my life in 1929-1930 was still recognizable from old photographs, but the main house had burnt down. What became of the Huntington family, I could not discover.

Sources: *Who's Who in B.C.*, 1931, pp. 49-50; PRO, ADM 337/118, page 57; census 1871, England, RG 10/293, p. 22; census, 1891, RG12/3412, p. 49; *Cowichan Leader*, 10 August 1922, p. 5; *Colonist*, 5 May 1921, p. 9; 9 July 1921, p. 13; 17 September 1921, p. 14; 8 April 1925, p. 16; 16 December 1925, p. 7; 19 December 1925, p. 7; Bill Dennis, of Delta, BC, "*The Butler of Lambourne*," an undated memo at the Cowichan Valley Museum, Duncan, 6 pp.; *Cowichan Valley Citizen*, 26 April 2000, p. 14.

HUTCHINSON, Francis George (c. 1876-1937). Born at Kendal, Westmorland, son of Annie and Francis Hutchinson (c. 1854-?), a domestic gardener, he was working with his father when the 1891 census found them living at 17 Swan Street, West Derby, Lancashire. His younger brother was already employed as a plumber. The next year, FH joined the East Yorkshire Regiment of Light Infantry and served in it and the Somerset Regiment for thirteen years in Egypt, Burma, and India, mainly the latter. He returned to England in 1906 and transferred to the Oxford and Buckingham Light Infantry but, after marrying, retired in 1911 with the intention of emigrating. They travelled through the United States and settled in BC, where he was employed for five years by the Canadian Consolidated Mining and Smelting Co. On 22 October 1918, he joined the police force in Victoria and worked as city constable until the end of 1934, living meanwhile at 1163 Chapman Street. He died, aged sixty-one, on April 1937, leaving his widow at home and a younger sister in Liverpool.

Sources: census 1891, England, RG 12/2999, p. 33; *Colonist,* 1 November 1934, p. 5; 20 April 1937, p. 5, obit., and photo.

INGRAM, Miss Mary Isabella "Molly" (1908-1994). She was born in London, daughter of Isabella Ann Ingram, *née* Sime (c. 1882-1927), and her husband, who was a son of Colonel Matthew J. T. Ingram. She was taken to Lahore, now in Pakistan, when she was about six months old, and for some mysterious reason, her father went off to Canada a few months later, leaving her and her mother to fend for themselves. As it happened, the mother's parents, John Sime and his wife, Ann Metcalf Sime, were living comfortably at Lahore, where he was a distinguished director of public instruction for the Punjab and where they had other children, MI's aunts and uncles. She became fluent in that form of Urdu known as "Hindustani" and in due time was sent to be schooled at Cheltenham Ladies' College in England, St James' Secretarial College, Grosvenor Place, London, and Switzerland, where she became fluent in French. When her mother's health failed, they moved to Singapore (1938), where she joined MI5, a branch of the Intelligence Service, in April 1939 and was soon serving as personal assistant to the defence security officer. A week before Singapore fell to the Japanese (on 7 Feb. 1942), she and her mother escaped to India on a French ship, zigzagging all the way to avoid the enemy, and in April 1942, she found employment with Special Force 136, which was directed to sabotage Japanese forces in all occupied territories. Her next assignment was as an intelligence officer with Lord Mountbatten's HQ staff in New Delhi, then as a staff captain with the Chief Engineer's Branch in charge of transport and accommodation, and finally in the Far Eastern Bureau, the only woman admitted to high-level meetings. Her medals included the 1939-1945 Star, the Burma Star, and the Home Defence Medal, as well as the 125th Canadian Silver Anniversary Medal.

When India was granted independence and partitioned in August 1947, she and her mother went home to England by the route across the Pacific, Canada, and the Atlantic so they could visit MI's aunt, Susan Emily Palmer, *née* Sime, and her family. This aunt, her mother's younger sister, had married *Major J. H. G. Palmer of the Indian Army, who had taken his family to Duncan, VI, some years earlier in order to join his parents. They were *Charles George Palmer of the ICS and his wife Annie Isabella Palmer, *née* Porter, who had started the whole family transfer by moving from India to the Island in 1910. But it was the Sime sisters who were the essential nucleus of the clan, for a third sister, Miss Catherine Mary Sime (1875-1945), moved to the Cowichan Valley in 1926. Furthermore, C. G. Palmer and Ann Metcalf Sime, *née* Palmer, were brother and sister, the children of General Henry Palmer (1807-1892), who was born and died at Mussoorie, India. Through her Palmer, Sime, and Ingram forebears, MI was related to several old Scottish, English, and Irish families. Her Ingram grandfather was at one time master general of the Royal Ordnance Corps. Dr John Sime, CIE, LLD, LitD, of the Indian Educational Service was born at Inchture, Perthshire, Scotland. Indirectly, she was even related to *Maréchal* Edmé Patrice Maurice MacMahon, second president of the Third French Republic. When the Sime sisters met, after many years, in Duncan and Victoria in 1947, MI and her mother decided to settle nearby, all the more because they did not look forward to the troubles of housing and rationing in post-war England. They bought a house in Oak Bay at Newport and Orchard Streets, which allowed the two sisters, who had not seen one another since 1922, to spend time together. When in 1958 Palmer's parents were too old for their rural place in Duncan, they bought a house on Deal Street, which was only five house away from "Aunt Isa and Molly" by way of back lanes. They were all the happier to be together because they had lost their three brothers, all killed or died on service before the Great War, in West Africa, Somaliland, or India. And their sister Kate had died in 1945. Among other things, Molly Ingram made a close study of the Amritsar Affair (1919) and spoke about it because she thought the situation had been falsely reported and General R. E. H. Dyer had been unjustly treated as a result of it.

In Victoria, she worked for twenty years as the chief researcher with the Department of Vital Statistics and enjoyed gardening at their house in Oak Bay. Beginning in 1971, she worked for the Monarchist League and, after a meeting with John Aimers, became Victoria chairman. By her charm, hard work, and wide acquaintanceship, she increased the membership from 33 to 216 by 1974. She had met members of the royal family on various occasions. "I got all sorts of war medals," she told a *Colonist* reporter, "but I wasn't in uniform. I've met Prince Charles several times . . . [Lord Louis Mountbatten] was absolutely fantastic, the most glamorous person I ever met. He had a gorgeous speaking voice and was terribly good looking. I sat next to him at a dinner in London for Winston Churchill in about 1960 and saw him again at Buckingham Palace three weeks before he died."

Sources: Notes 6 and 17 August 2002 and family papers, courtesy of John Palmer, her first cousin; census 1881, England, RG 11/1346; census 1901, RG 13/492, p. 8; Joanne Jones, "Miss Molly Ingram," *Oak Bay Star*, 23 October 1974; Grania Litwin, "Monarchy Molly has Enjoyed Royal Career," *Times-Colonist*, 25 November 1989; Barnett Singer, "Molly Ingram's Memories of Imperial India," *The Islander*, *Times-Colonist*, Sunday, 29-30 July 1984, p. 8; Grania Litwin, "Monarchy Molly has Enjoyed Royal Career," *Times-Colonist*, 25 November 1989.

IRVING, Lieutenant Colonel Lennox (1863-1938). Born on 16 May 1863 at Pembroke, Ontario, son of Andrew Irving, registrar of the County of Renfrew, and Mary C. Irving, youngest daughter of Dr Cannon, a surgeon in the Royal Navy, he was brought up a Presbyterian, schooled in Pembroke and at Queen's University (BA), where he became captain of the university Football Club. After serving as secretary of the Pembroke Library Board, he was called to the Ontario Bar in 1900. He attended RMC, Kingston, and was gazetted lieutenant, Forty-second Regiment (1883), captain (1887), major (1898), and lieutenant colonel (1901), and retired (1908) with long-service decorations. During the

Great War, he joined the CEF at Renfrew, Ontario, on 17 July 1916 and was appointed a year later as second in command of the 240th Overseas Battalion, CEF, Lanark and Renfrew, and went overseas with them. Attached to the Thirty-eighth Battalion Royal Ottawa Regiment in France, he was appointed one of the representatives under the MSA. After the war, he and his wife, Grace Barnet, daughter of A. Barnet of Renfrew, lived in Victoria at 515 Foul Bay Road. He died, aged seventy-five, on 10 November 1938 in Victoria and was buried as a Presbyterian.

Sources: *Who's Who in B.C.*, 1942-1943, p. 161; NAC, CEF files, box 4715-41; Morgan, *Canadian Men and Women*, p. 569.

IZARD, Edward Whitaker (c. 1888-1978). He was born at Wisbech, Cambridgeshire, second son of Rev. Arthur Izard, Anglican vicar of St Augustine's Church there, and his wife Susannah E. Izard, both born in London. The 1891 and 1901 censuses list his elder brothers and sisters as Theodore A., Lily Jane, Margaret, Constance, and Annie M. and his younger ones as Mary C. and Henry. By 1901, when EI was thirteen, the family had moved to the rectory at Slindon in the Chichester district of Sussex, where the father was rector of the parish. In 1906, EI went to work for Yarrows, shipbuilders, as a pupil at their new Clydesdale plant, where he learnt to design and test marine turbines, then a new technology. He did so well that Norman Yarrow chose him to work as assistant manager at Esquimalt when Yarrow was sent there by his father, Alfred Yarrow, to manage the shipyard purchased from *W. F. Bullen in 1914. He and *Norman Yarrow worked together filling the many orders for ships needed during the Great War, between the wars, and on through the Second World War. EI carried on at general manager after the yard was sold to Wallace Shipyards in 1946. He retired from the shipyard at last in 1957 and died, aged ninety, on 22 June 1978 in Victoria. Among his activities in Victoria, where he lived, was as a bell-ringer at Christ Church Cathedral. So long and faithfully did he serve that his name was inscribed on a treble bell in the cathedral tower:

> IN MEMORIAM, EDWARD W. IZARD When ye hear my voice abroad Come ye to church to serve the Lord (1983)

Sources: Duffus, *Beyond the Blue Bridge*, pp. 52-3; census 1891, England, RG 12/1305, pp. 24-5; census, 1901, RG 13/964, p. 13; Christ Church Cathedral, Victoria, bell and bell-ringer's register.

JACKSON, William (c. 1879-1958). Born in Glasgow, he joined the British Army and fought in the South African War (1899-1902) as a trooper with the Sixteenth Company, Fifth Imperial Yeomanry. He was wounded when his horse fell on him and was not fit to serve in the Great War. For many years, he lived at Regina but moved in 1946 to Victoria, where he lived with his wife and family at 1125 Empress Avenue, then at 2650 Quadra Street. Like so many others, he took part in the fiftieth anniversary celebrations of the South African War in 1949. He died, aged seventy-nine, on 4 August 1958, leaving his wife Rose, a son, Harry, and three daughters.

Sources: *Colonist*, 16 August 1949, p. 23; 5 August 1958, p. 18, obit.

JANION, Richard William (c. 1852-1889). Born at Honolulu, when Hawaii was still called the Sandwich Islands, he was a son of Richard Charles Janion (born c. 1813) of Rocksavage, Cheshire, and his wife Donnitel Rodriquez born *circa* 1832 in Santiago Chile. They all belonged to a large cosmopolitan family of merchants engaged in a three-way trade between Honolulu, Liverpool, and Victoria. There are uncertainties and contradictions in surviving accounts of this larger family, but English census records for 1871 show RJ, aged eighteen, living with his family at "The Grove," Halewood, Much Woolton, Lancashire, very near Liverpool, with seven domestic servants including a coachman and a gardener. He had there and then a young brother, Habert [or Robert Mellor?] Janion, aged eight, born in Liverpool, and five sisters, whose birthplaces are revealing: Mathilda Isabel Janion, aged twenty, was born at Honolulu; Ellen Mary Janion, seventeen, was born at Santiago, Chile, like her mother; and Emelia Vida Janion, fifteen, was born in Liverpool, as were Constance L. Janion, twelve, and Gertrude Rose Janion, ten. Not far away in 1871, at "Westwood," Alderley Road in Chorley, Lancashire, was a paternal uncle, Joseph Janion, a solicitor aged forty-eight, born at Rocksavage, living with his wife Charlotte, aged thirty-two and born a British subject in Gibraltar. They had seven children.

Ten years later, in 1881, RJ was recorded in Liverpool as a twenty-nine-year-old "merchant, insurance agent and vice-consul for the Sandwich Islands" living at 5 Livingston Avenue, Toxteth Park, part of Liverpool, with a wife, two sons, a daughter, and two nieces. He had married Annie Isabel Rhodes (c. 1851-1920) at St John's Anglican Church in Victoria on 29 April 1875, she being a daughter of Henry Rhodes (c. 1823-1878) and his wife Sophia Harriet Cape (1831-1899) from Ceylon. We know some of this from BC divorce records later in which Sophia Harriet petitioned a BC court for a divorce, RW having gone off to San Francisco, California, where in due time he was to die in January 1889. Sophia Harriet (Cape) Janion died much later on 12 November 1920 in Victoria, where her parents likewise died, her mother on 30 April 1899 and her father on 8 November 1878. Meanwhile, in 1881 at Toxteth Park, Lancashire, RJ and his wife had with them a son Henry Cheshyre Janion, born in Victoria on 20 March 1877, a second son Richard Cheshyre Janion, born at Gateacre, Liverpool, on 4 April 1878, a daughter Beatrice Constance Janion born at Gateacre, Liverpool, who was destined to wed an Irish-born insurance agent named John H. Poff in Victoria on 29 April 1902. And while RJ and his family were at Toxteth Park in 1881, his parents and his sisters were still at "Grove House," Much Woolton, as before. The trail of birthplaces and marriage places shows the family's movements in the course of their commerce. There are also signs of further relationships: The two nieces staying with RJ and his wife in 1881 were named Briggs, but to follow all hares is to get lost in confusion.

Sources for the history of Honolulu show that in April 1845, RJ's uncle, Robert Cheshire [Cheshyre?] Janion (after whom RJ gave his sons the name

"Cheshyre") formed a partnership with a pair of Liverpool merchants, James and John Starkey. In the years 1845-1851, Honolulu had on Ka'ahumanu Street the trading firm of Starkey, Janion & Company with its own fleet of sailing vessels in which to export Hawaiian sugar and products of the whaling fishery and acting as agents for the Northern Assurance Company of London. Descendants of the Starkeys found their way later to Victoria, but after 1851, Robert Cheshire Janion returned to Liverpool, leaving various partners at Honolulu. The Janions were active at Honolulu for many years.

Half a century later, in 1901, the Canadian census for Victoria showed RJ's family resident at 204 Yates Street, with a store on Store Street near the large red-brick Janion Hotel, which may or may not have been built by one of the family—sources disagree about the Janion Hotel's origins. In time, it became the headquarters of the Esquimalt—Nanaimo Railway. The Janions had been in business with Henry Rhodes *père* (1823-1878) at Victoria from the late 1850s, and they had opened an office in Portland, Oregon. Annie Isabel (Rhodes) Janion, who had first turned up in Victoria in 1860 and married there in 1875, was now "a retired lady," and her sons were "commission agents" and "salesmen" or employed at the Albion Ironworks and her daughters were "stenographers" or married ladies. Their aunt Sophia Edith Janion (c. 1859-1902), RJ's sister, had married George Anthony Walkem (1834-1908), an Irish-born barrister who had served as attorney general of the province and a politician who had been elected premier in 1878. In 1906, in Victoria, Richard Cheshyre Janion (1878-1944) married Anna Elizabeth Brownrigg (c. 1871-1949), probably descended from Sir Henry John Brownrigg (1798-1873), a chief inspector of the Royal Irish Constabulary, and his wife Lady Elizabeth Cooke (died 23 January 1880). In 1901, Henry "Harry" Rhodes *fils* (1857-1931) and his wife Marion Begnall (c. 1861-1955) had a four-year-old son, *Godfrey Dean Rhodes, who was destined to have a remarkable career around the empire as a railway engineer.

Sources: Edward Greaney, "Hawaii's Big Six, A Cyclical Saga," reprinted from *The Encyclopedia of Hawaii*, a 1976 Bicentennial Project, by permission of The University of Hawaii Press); Danda Humphreys, *Building Victoria: Men, Myths, and Mortar* (Surrey, BC, Heritage House Publishing, 2004), pp. 52-4; Geoffrey Castle and Barry F. King, *Victoria Landmarks* (Victoria, Amity Press, 1985), pp. 62-63; census 1871, England, RC 10/3855, p. 25; census 1871, RG 10/3679; census 1871, RG 10/4410, p. 9; census 1881, RG 11/3651, p. 63; census 1881, RG 11/3651, p. 63; census 1881, RG 11/3721; census 1891, RG 12/876, p. 28; 1891, RG 12/3008, p. 25; census 1901, RG 13/989, p. 36; census 1901, RG 13/3509, p. 7; BC Divorces, online, vol. I, page 058, petitioner: wife; S. W. Jackman, *Portraits of the Premiers: An Informal History of British Columbia* (Sidney, Gray's Publishing Ltd., 1969), pp. 31-40; *Fort Victoria Letters*, 1846-1851, Hartwell Bowfield (Winnipeg, Hudson's Bay Record Society, 1979), see index entries, pp. 263 and 271 (Sandwich Islands).

JARVIS, Lieutenant Colonel Arthur Murray (1863-1930). He was born on 6 April 1863 in Toronto and, very young, began ranching and farming in the NWT. On 25 June 1880, he joined the RCNWM Police and, by the time he joined the army on 27 June 1915 at Shorncliffe, claimed to have served for thirty-one years. He received a medal at Fort Selkirk, Yukon, on 11 July 1902 for service in the North-West Rebellion of 1885. Promoted to inspector on 16 May 1893 and to stipendiary magistrate in BC in 1899, he went to fight in the South African War. The Grand Recorder, AOUW, Winnipeg, listed him with members of the Ancient Order of United Workmen who went to South Africa, and Medal Registers show that he was a major in Lord Strathcona's Horse entitled to the Belfast, Orange Free State, and Natal Campaign clasps to the Queen's South Africa Medal. Was it by taking leave from the police that he took part in so many military events? On 30 June 1911, he retired on a pension of $1,178 a year. In the Great War, he served as a lieutenant colonel on the Second Division HQ Staff of the CEF in Canada, Britain, and France, was mentioned in despatches four times, and received the CMG, the CBE, the 1914-1915 Star, and the British War and Victory Medals. After a period as assistant provost marshal, he was struck off strength on 13 October 1919 with the general demobilization.

He retired to the Island with his wife Gertrude Mary Jarvis, who soon began to complain of him being in bad health, in bad temper, and inclined to troublesome behaviour. In 1924, when they were living in Sidney on Marine Drive, he had a row with a neighbour, a Mr A. Miller, who had treated Gertrude's dog as a stray. She seems to have moved to Patricia Bay, on the other side of the Saanich Peninsula, whence she wrote to the commissioners of the RCMP in Ottawa on 17 November 1925, "Since the war, Col. Jarvis has been in a bad mental condition; [but] his family refusing to see this . . .," seems to think the trouble is her fault. In the files of correspondence about him, Mrs Jarvis mentions that her cousins, *Brigadier General H. C. Nanton and his sister, widow of John Davidson Clark, are trying to help her in dealing with her husband—a situation unlikely to soothe an angry man. The quarrel ended on 5 April 1930 when he died in Montreal during a visit there and was buried as an Anglican.
Sources: NAC, CEF files, RG 150, acc. 1992-93/166, box 4794-60; NAC, RG18, series G, vol. 82, file 385-93, part 2, promotion; NAC, Record Group 9, II A5, volume 14, page 102, reel C-1-12; NAC, RG 9, II A5, vol. 12, p. 61; *Sidney Review*, 1 May 1924, p. 5; 8 May 1924, p. 6; Brian A. Reid, *Our Little Army in the Field: The Canadians in South Africa*, 1899-1902 (St Catharines, Ont., Vanwell Publishing Ltd., 1996), p. 150; *Colonist*, 17 April 1937, p. 2, obit., for Mrs Clark.

JAYNES, William Penn (1846-?). Born near Gloucester, youngest of three brothers born to Edwin and Charlotte Jaynes, who had a timber business in London, WJ secretly married in 1870 the teenaged daughter, Clara Rhead (1851-1941), born at Newnham, Gloucestershire, to William Rhead, a civil engineer, and his wife Catherine. The fuss upon the discovery of this marriage caused them flee away to Ontario in disgrace. Advised, it is said, by John A. Macdonald, MP for Victoria at the time, they moved out later to the Cowichan Valley. There they kept a store near the Quamichan Indian Reserve and were among the founders of Duncan nearby, where they opened another shop. Canadian census records for 1881 show WJ as a "merchant" there. He may have been assisted by one of his brothers, such as Percy Franklin Jaynes (1851-1920), who inherited the family estate at Larhkay Villa, Huccleote, Gloucestershire, or Thomas Edwyn Jaynes, who became a solicitor at St Michael's Parish, Gloucester. In any event, on 26 November 1894, their daughter Clara Florence Jaynes (c. 1862-1968) married *J. H. Whittome, a successful real-estate and insurance agent in Duncan, and on 2 September 1903, a much-younger daughter, Alberta Louise Jaynes (1879-1946), married Edward Howe Hicks-Beach (1875-1967).

A third brother, William Franklin Jaynes, later migrated to BC, where he became a magistrate at Hazelton in the Skeena River Valley and married Rosetta Isabella Hicks at Dewdney on 29 July 1908. The family's ramifications might be traced even further.

Clara (Rhead) Jaynes died, aged eighty-eight, at Duncan on 29 September 1941, and Clara Florence (Jaynes) Whittome died, aged ninety-five, on 4 September 1968 in North Cowichan, but I find no sign of HJ's death there or anywhere else.
Sources: census 1851. England, HO/107/1962; census 1861, RG 9/1763, pp. 13-14; census 1871, RG 10/2615, p. 41; Tom Henry, *Small City in a Big Valley: The Story of Duncan* (in 4_, Madeira Park, BC, Harbour Publishing, 1999), pp. 34-5; E. R. Cartwright, *A Late Summer: The Memoirs of E.R. Cartwright*, C.B.E. (Caravel Press, 1964), p. 51.

JEPSON, Lieutenant Henry (1845-1921). Born on 31 October 1845 in Lancashire, he joined the army very young and served for thirty-two years, mainly in India, often on the North-West Frontier, though one of his sons was born at Aden in the Persian Gulf. HJ advanced slowly in the Indian Army through the ranks of non-commissioned officers until 2 July 1884, when he became one of the honorary commissioned and warrant officers, a "Conductor" in the Ordnance Department at Bombay. After retiring to England, he and his wife, Ellen "Fanny," moved out to the Island in 1914 to join their three sons, "Fred, Harry and John," two of whom were partners in a bookstore at Nanaimo.

One of these, Lieutenant Henry Rothwell Jepson, born on 6 May 1880 at Aden, had served for three years with the Twelfth Lancers in the South African War and described himself as a "merchant" when he joined the Eleventh CMR on 29 September 1915 at Vernon, BC. Sent to France, he transferred to Lieutenant Colonel W. N. Winsby's Forty-seventh Battalion, was wounded at Vimy Ridge, and died on 5 August 1917 in hospital at Boulogne. His younger brother, Michael John A. Jepson, born on 19 March 1889 at Poona, Bombay Presidency, India, was working in Nanaimo as a sailor at the time he enlisted in the Canadian Army in Victoria. He had no earlier military experience. He died on 4 September 1918 and was buried at New Westminster.

HJ himself died, aged seventy-five, at home at 225 Vancouver Street, Nanaimo, leaving his widow and one son, Frederick. The pallbearers at his funeral in St Paul's Church, Nanaimo, were all ex-sergeants of the British Army, and they buried him with a Union Jack on the casket. Ellen Jepson died, aged ninety-three, on 27 March

1951, but their remaining son, Frederick (c. 1882-1978), lived at Nanaimo until 12 February 1978 when he was ninety-six.

Sources: *Indian Army List*, July 1891, p. 500; *Colonist*, 16 May 1917, p. 5; 31 March 1921, p. 9, obit.; 9 August 1917, p. 4; *Nanaimo Daily Free Press*, 25 March 1921, front page, obit.; NAC, CEF files, box 4828-48 and box 4829-2, regimental no. 75609.

JOHNSON, Captain George (1842-1930). Born in 1842 at Hilswick, Shetland Islands, he went to sea in 1854 and earned a master's certificate, issued by the Board of Trade in 1870. He sailed the seas for sixty years during which he visited most ports of the world and had many adventures. He once saw Florence Nightingale at work during the Crimean War.

Settling at last in Victoria, he took employment as skipper of the SS *Iroquois* but on 10 April 1911, the day she capsized off Sidney, he refused to take her out because he thought her unfit and it was Captain Albert Sears who was in command. GJ kept the Esquimalt Light House for nine years and, in December 1929, was interviewed, aged eighty-seven, for the *Daily Colonist* as a grand-old mariner. When he died, aged eighty-nine, at the Jubilee Hospital, he had been living in Victoria for thirty-five years, mainly at 615 Constance Avenue, Esquimalt, but his three daughters were in California.

Sources: *Colonist*, 25 December 1929, p. 18; 24 December 1930, p. 5, obit.; Fred Rogers, *Shipwrecks of British Columbia* (Vancouver & McIntyre, 1973), pp. 96-8.

JOHNSTON, Major Edwyn Harry Lukin (1887-1933). He was editor at Duncan of *The Cowichan Leader* in 1911-1913, then city editor of the *Victoria Daily Colonist* until 1915, when he went overseas as a soldier. Born in Surbiton, Surrey, on 8 August 1887, he appears, aged three, in census records of 1891, living with his family at "Manor House," Cheriton, Kent, attended by a nurse, a governess, a housemaid, and a cook. His mother, Ellen J. Johnston, *née* Lukin, aged twenty-nine, and his father, Rev. Robert E. Johnston, "Clerk in Holy Orders, Tutor," aged thirty-two, were both Londoners. EJ had an elder brother, Robert V. L. Johnston, aged five, and staying with them was their maternal grandfather, Robert H. Lukin, a widower aged sixty-four and a "Barrister at Law, living on own means," born at Southampton. There were four boarders in the house including two teenaged girls. Ten years later, aged thirteen, EJ was recorded in census records as a student boarding with many other boys at Junior King's School, Archbishop's Palace, Canterbury.

In 1906, he went out to Canada and had a very rough time of it, as he told his son Derek in later years, until joining the staff of *The Vancouver Province* and then moving onto the Island. There at Somenos in the Cowichan Valley, he married Miss Bertha May Court at St Mary's Anglican Church on 18 April 1912. She was born in Kent at Canterbury. When he enlisted as a lieutenant in the Eighty-eighth Victoria Fusiliers on 12 January 1916, he had been living in Canada for almost ten years and in Victoria with his wife for the last three. What befell him during the next twelve months was reported at length, with a photograph, by the *Victoria Daily Colonist*, as befitted one of their reporters away in the war. After a course at

Shorncliffe, he was transferred to the Canadian Machine Gun Depot and asked to serve as an instructor. But he preferred to go to France and so transferred to the Sixteenth Scottish. There follows a long description in his own words of life at the front under fire: "I had a long talk with *General [Arthur] Currie on Tuesday. He looks older, but very fit and is very highly thought of. He told me that Major Pym, late of the 88th, was serving as subaltern in the 7th. Funnily enough, today I was at the main dressing station and who should be there but the old Major. He is better, but this sort of life is hard on a man of his years." He went on to mention several BC officers and men he had recently met or heard of in France. Overseas in 1917, he became staff captain "intelligence" with the Nineteenth Canadian Infantry Brigade and was promoted to deputy assistant adjutant general the same year at Witley Camp; he was promoted to major on 2 December 1918. During the war, he was at Vimy Ridge (1917), Passchendaele (November 1917), Avions (June 1917), Hill 70 (August 1917), and Amiens (August 1918) and mentioned in dispatches on 1 January 1919.

In March 1919, after the war, he rejoined the *Vancouver Province* as a reporter and, a few months later, interviewed Lord Jellicoe, who was spending some time on the Pacific Coast before going on to New Zealand as its new governor general. Jellicoe's purpose was to report to London on harbour conditions and other naval matters to be ready in case of a war in the Pacific. When EJ turned out to know enough about the coast to give him useful information, Jellicoe spoke to him openly about what he was doing but urged him not to print what he said or repeat it to others. More than a year later, EJ received a photograph of Jellicoe in uniform signed, "A memento of unbroken confidences." It was therefore with intense interest that EJ went to report on the famous Washington Naval Conference of 1922 and also travelled up the BC coast with U.S. President Harding. In 1928, he was made European reporter of the Southam Newspapers with HQ in London, which pleased him immensely. He loved the British Isles as his three books show and felt a deep affinity with the British people. This must have been evident to Lord Jellicoe and to Marie, Lady Willingdon, wife of a visiting governor general, when she met EJ at Qualicum. "And there," she wrote in a preface to his book, *Down English Lanes* (1933), "—as always when English men and women meet far from Home—we talked of England and its atmosphere surrounded us." In 1926-1928, EJ was glad to send his son, Derek Lukin Johnston, to Shawnigan Lake Boys' School, with its English headmaster, *C. W. Lonsdale, whose first years in BC had been as hard and difficult as his own. EJ's end was mysterious. Just after interviewing Chancellor Adolf Hitler in November 1933 in Germany, he disappeared on the short voyage from Hook in Holland to Parkston Quay in England.

Sources: census 1891, England, RG 12/751, p. 46; census 1901, RG 13/796, p. 8; *National Archives of Canada*, Ottawa, CEF files, box 4862-7; *Colonist*, 7 January 1917, p. 10; 19 November 1933, pp. 1 and 2; 12 May 1936, p. 4 (Willingdon); *The Times* (London), 23 November 1935, p. 16; R. H. Milne and Lucille Kocurek, eds., *Shawnigan and the War* (Duncan, BC, Solitaire Press Ltd., 1990), pp. 149-152; EJ, *In England Today* (J. M. Dent; NY, E. P. Dutton, 1931), 214 pp.; EJ, *Down English*

Lanes (Heath Cranton, 1933) 204 pp.; and EJ, *Beyond the Rockies: Three Thousand Miles by Trail and Canoe with 52 illustrations and a map* (J. M. Dent, 1929), 212 pp.

JOHNSTON, Paymaster Captain William John Cochrane (c. 1877-1938). Born in Creetown, near Edinburgh, he joined the Royal Navy early in the 1890s and served at first as assistant clerk on HMS *Victory*. The English census of 1901 recorded him, aged twenty-three, born in Scotland, employed as "Assistant Paymaster" on HMS *Prince George*, then at Gibraltar, and commanded by Commander Sydney R. Fremantle. WJ served thereafter in various other ships, for example, *Royal Sovereign* in the Channel fleet and in HMS *Powerful* at Australia, South Africa, and China, and at least twice in the East Indies. He retired to Victoria in 1930 and, for the last seven years of his life, served the Canadian Legion as secretary of the Naval Veterans' Branch, No. 42, Canadian Legion. He was also a member of the Navy League. He was a quiet, retiring person and generally friendly. When he died in 1938, he left his wife, a son, and a daughter.
Sources: *Colonist*, 27 November 1938, p. 5, obit., and photo; census 1901, England, RG 13/5330, p. 2; *Whitaker's*, p. 287.

JONES, Colonel Arthur William (1851-1934). Born on 23 May 1851 at Branxton, Northumberland, he attended Edinburgh Academy and, in 1873, settled in Victoria, where he ran a real-estate and insurance business at Broad and Broughton Streets, later at 72 Fort Street, and, in 1901, was living at 72 Cook Street. Like so many others of his generation, he was devoted to life in local militia units and held responsible posts. For twenty years, he was a staff officer in charge of the Army Ordnance Corps and Army Service Corps at Work Point, and from 1903, he was in charge of the Imperial garrison's stores in Esquimalt. When Canada took over Esquimalt from the Royal Navy in 1905, he was paymaster for Military District No. 11. He retired in December 1906 and was replaced by Captain W. F. C. Sullivan from Quebec. In retirement, AJ and his wife, Emma *née* Loewen (1872-?), daughter of a German immigrant brewer, lived at 1160 Rockland Avenue. Her sister Laura later married an attorney general of the province, *R. H. Pooley, whose family connections and house in Esquimalt, "Fernhill" on Lampson Street, hospitable to officers of the Royal Navy stationed there, gave the Pooleys social prominence. AJ was a charter member of the Union Club, one of the oldest members of the Victoria Golf Club, and president of it in 1920-1924, characteristically dressed in tweeds, with a tweed cap and the small military mustache of that generation. He died, aged eighty-three, on 15 May 1934, survived only by his widow who held a private funeral.
Sources: Canadian census, 1901, Victoria; *Colonist*, 1 December 1906, p. 3; 25 March 1921, p. 8; 16 May 1934, p. 3: obit., and photo.

JONES, Lieutenant Commander Bertram Edwin (c. 1891-1975). He was born at Bromley, Kent, where the 1891 census recorded him, aged three months, living at 4 Queen's Cottage with his family. His father, Daniel Jones, aged thirty-six, was a police constable born at St Clements, Oxford, and his mother, Annie E. Jones, aged thirty-six, was born at Stepney, London. He had two elder brothers: Harry D.

Jones, then aged seven, born at Lewisham, Kent; and Arthur Charles Jones, aged four, born at Bromley. There were no domestic servants, and the neighbours were a coachman on one side and a gardener on the other. Ten years later, the family was living in Sidney Lane, Bareby, Yorkshire, and BJ had a young brother, Alick George Jones, aged four, born at Hemingbrough, Yorkshire. BJ joined the Royal Navy in which he served for a number of years in the submarine service and rose to become captain of submarine C28.

Upon retiring, he went to live in British Columbia and reported at Esquimalt when the Great War began in case he might be needed. As it turned out, he was soon called on to sail two new submarines from Seattle to Esquimalt. They were purchased for $1,150,000 from the Seattle Construction and Dry Dock Company, which had built them for the government of Chile, but was willing to sell them to the government of British Columbia. The idea and the decision grew out of a meeting on 29 July 1914 at the Union Club in which Henry B. Thompston, B. F. Barnard, *Captain W. H. Logan—representative of the London Salvage Association—and J. V. Paterson, president of the Seattle builders, were discussing the dangers of German attack from the sea. Premier Sir Richard McBride took the initiative by sending Logan to inspect the submarines at Seattle and conferring with the naval authorities at Esquimalt. The Admiralty in London, consulted by Sir Robert Borden, advised going ahead with this purchase, and so BJ led a couple of small crews to pick up these vessels at Esquimalt and brought them back on the night of 4-5 August. He commanded one of them, and other was under Lieutenant Bernard Leitch Johnson of the Royal Naval Canadian Volunteer Reserve. The whole operation was supervised by Lieutenant Henry Byng Pilcher, RN, acting senior naval officer at Esquimalt, and by *Lieutenant Commander Keyes, who happened to be at Esquimalt. He was a brother of Admiral Sir Roger Keyes, RN. BJ died, aged eighty-four, on 9 November 1975 at Coquitlam, BC.

Sources: Gilbert Norman Tucker, *The Naval Service of Canada* (2 vols., Ottawa, King's Printer, 1952), vol. I, pp. 286-7, 291-2; James H. Hamilton, *Western Shores: Narratives of the Pacific Coast by James Kettle* (Vancouver, Progress Publishing Company Ltd., 1932), chapter 3, "*Scaring off the German Cruisers,*" pp. 44-5 and passim; Marc Milner, "The Birth of the Submarine Service," *Legion Magazine*, May/June 2005; census 1891, England, RG 12/628, p. 20; census 1901, RG 13/4429, p. 7.

JONES, James McNab (1849-1918). Born in Ireland, a Presbyterian, on 24 August 1849, he went to Canada in 1864 and, when he joined the British Campaigners' Association in October 1917, was credited with having fought in the Egyptian campaign in 1882 with the Canadian *voyageurs*, and against the Fenian Raid of 1866 with the Manitoba Contingent. In the voters list of 1898, he was listed as a miner living on Quadra Street and, in 1901, as a house painter at 113 Chatham Street, Victoria, with his wife, Fanny Moore Jones (1854-1934). He died, aged seventy, on 5 April 1918 in Victoria.

Sources: *Minutes of the British Campaigners' Association,* which he joined in October 1917; BC Voter's List 1898, Sessional Papers of the BC Government, 1899; Canadian census, Vancouver Island, 1891; Canadian census, 1901, Victoria.

JONES, William Henry (1879-1953), JP. Born on 9 February 1879 in Manchester, son of Robert Henry Jones, a retired naval officer, he was educated in England and joined the Third King's Own Hussars wherein he served for six years. In 1901, he married Henriette Gard, daughter of Joseph Northmore Gard, and they had four sons and a daughter. But in 1907, they moved to Nanaimo, VI. From 1910, he served there as a school trustee for twenty-seven years; from 1912, as an insurance agent for twenty-five years; from 1925, as a JP for fifteen years; from 1939, as a coroner; and from May 1945, as stipendiary magistrate and judge of the Small Debts Court. He was also active in the AF and AM, the Kiwanis Club, the Canadian Legion, the Knights of Pythias, and the Church of England. When he died in 1953, he was survived by his wife Henriette Gard, daughter of Joseph Northmore Gard, whom he had married in 1901, and some of their five children. They had lived at 412 Wakesiah Avenue, Nanaimo.
Sources: *Who's Who in B.C.*, 1953, p. 45.

JUKES, Major Andrew Henry (1885-1956). He was born on 11 November 1885 at Brandon, Manitoba, son of Andrew Jukes (1857-1922) of St Catharines, Ontario, who was in turn the son of Augustus Louis Jukes, AJ's grandfather, who had gone out from England in 1836. Another son, AJ's younger brother, Arthur Ewart Jukes (1887-1954), was born on 12 October 1887 also at Brandon, and the two brothers have sometimes been confused because both served as majors during the Great War. Their careers were different, however, as the younger brother, Major A. E. Jukes, served in the Seventy-second Canadian Seaforth Highlanders and spent the rest of his life as a businessman and financier in Vancouver, whereas AJ served in the (British) Indian Army and lived most of his life thereafter on the Island. A further source of confusion is that their paternal grandfather, Augustus Louis Jukes (1821-1905), was born in India, leading some to the erroneous conclusion that AJ of the Indian Army was also born there. This grandfather, son of Andrew and Georgina Jukes, qualified as a medical doctor in Toronto and then practised as a physician for more than thirty years at St Catharines, Ontario. In 1848, he married Phoebe Adams (c. 1832-1897), and they had seven children of whom the fifth was Andrew (c. 1857-1922), father of the two majors. Grandfather A. L. Jukes has his own place in history as the senior surgeon in the North-West Mounted Police, and he happened to be entrusted with Louis Riel's medical care when Riel was captured in 1885. Dr Jukes developed a certain respect for Riel, whom he declared to be sane rather than the contrary, as some thought.

AJ attended RMC at Kingston, Ontario, and, on 22 June 1905, accepted one of the commissions in the Indian Army, which the British government then offered each year to RMC graduates. For the first nine months, he was attached to the Dorset Regiment. After that, he served with the Royal Irish Fusiliers and other Imperial regiments and was appointed ADC to General Campbell at Delhi during the Durbar of 1912. By February 1914, he was serving in the Ninth Gurkhas at Dhera Dun and expecting to be promoted to captain of its Second Battalion. He spent much of the Great War on the Suez Canal, then on the North-West Frontier of India at Kohat and Thal, where his unit still was in April 1919, when the Afghan War broke out. He kept diaries throughout his years of service and photographs of military life, mainly on the North-West Frontier. Honoured with the DSO and granted a period of training at the famous Staff College in Camberley, west of London, he remained in the Ninth Gurkhas until 1929, when he retired to twenty-three acres in Saanich about fifteen miles north of Victoria on a small extension of Mount Newton Cross Road running from the West Saanich Road down to the sea near Brentwood Bay. He bought it from a *Captain William Randall McDonnell Parr, ex-Royal Irish Rifles, who lived on an adjoining property, and there were several other retired Imperials nearby, mostly Anglicans in the rural parish of St Stephen. On this place, which he called "Vines," AHR had an orchard and developed a species of seedless black grapes, which he sold to the Saanich Cooperative Winery in which he invested. He was sick of war and anxious to live a quiet rural life with his wife, Miss Editha Maud Goward (c. 1893-1975), who was born at Calcutta, daughter of an English couple, Maud and Edwin Goward. The latter was in an import-export business in India but settled eventually at "The Glen," Heathfield, Sussex. Maud Goward's sister Hilda married Hugh Langdail, who was in the Anglo-Iranian Oil Company working mainly in Bombay and elsewhere in India but settled near his wife's parents at "Heathfield House." AJ married Editha on 10 February 1914 at Barrackpore, a suburb of Calcutta. They had a son while still in India and two daughters later in Canada. The family fished for salmon and grilse on Saanich Inlet and enjoyed those lovely sheltered waters in a sailboat they called *Ivanoe*. AJ had been diagnosed with a fatal malaria but, in these happy surroundings, lived a healthy life for many years.

He had an interesting circle of relatives and friends, such as the Bell-Irving family and the Vancouver branch of his own family; a colleague from the Ninth Gurkhas, *Major Robert George Robin Murray (1888-1973), who settled almost next door; *Sir Robert Irskine Holland, who settled in Oak Bay after the Second World War perhaps as a result of seeing the Island with his friend Frieda as guests of the Jukes family in May 1936; and Major General Sir William L. O. Twiss, KCIE, CB, CBE, MC (1878-1962), GOC, in Burma in 1937-1939, who visited from India and England in July 1938. Mrs Jukes was related to A. T. Gower of the BC Electric Company, and others in the Gower family said to have interests in Anglo-Iranian Oil. A thoughtful, independent person given to wide reading, AJ was troubled by the economic depression of the early 1930s and attracted by the ideas of Major Clifford Hugh (1879-1952), a Scottish civil engineer and the founder of the Social Credit Movement, who had served in the Royal Flying Corps during the Great War. developed his economic theories from 1919 in articles in the journal *New Age*, edited by A. R. Orage, and in books such as *Credit-Power and Democracy* (1920) and *Social Credit* (1924), which went through several editions. Socialists hated his doctrines, the British Labour Party formally rejected them in 1922, and the next year, some Canadian admirers invited Douglas to Ottawa, where he expounded his ideas to the House of Commons' committee on banking and commerce. AJ launched a social credit movement on the Island with friends such as *Colonel Gerald Bassett Scott, also retired from the Indian Army, apparently with the intention of stimulating public interest in Major Douglas's ideas rather than following Alberta's version of Social Credit based on Premier Aberhardt's Christian fundamentalism. He wrote often to the local press and spoke more and more in public. Well ahead of his time, in February 1948, he told a public meeting at Deep Cove, North Saanich, "The real fight to free the individual from the growing oppressive power of government is never mentioned either by Liberal or C.C.F. candidates . . . [they,] Cameron and Winch ought to go to Russia to find out why Stalin lives in a country called 'The Union of Soviet Socialist Republics.'" It was too soon—only three years after the Second World War—to make Canadian socialists and Liberals see the terrible evils of Soviet Russia he was already aware of.

A series of troubles induced AJ to leave "The Vines" on a wild adventure that was ultimately fatal. In March 1940, he stood for election as a candidate for "New Democracy" in the Nanaimo riding but was defeated. He clashed with a group of politicians, mainly from Vancouver, who had little interest in the theory of Social Credit but wanted to do in BC what Aberhardt had done in Alberta. This "bloc of blockheads," as he called them, won the provincial elections in 1952. When Mrs Jukes objected to her house and life being filled obsessively with the papers, people, and activities of the Social Credit Movement, AJ retreated to an outbuilding, but not satisfied, she went off to Vancouver. At sometime in 1954 or 1955, he cashed his investments in the Saanich Winery and with his secretary, Sylvia Piddington, an Imperial officer's daughter who sympathized with his predicament, bought a fifty-one-foot ketch in England, *Dawn Star*, in which they sailed around the Mediterranean Sea for several months. It was an idyllic voyage except that he had serious trouble with his teeth, and they stopped at Gibraltar to see a dentist. As they headed home across the Atlantic late in 1956, following the time-honoured southerly route to take advantage of the trade winds, his health grew worse and they stopped at the Canary Islands, where he died in hospital at Las Palmas on 6 December. Sylvia Piddington and John Jukes, the eldest son who flew over, hired a Spanish crew to sail *Dawn Star* to Florida, where the family commandeered her. Discreet and sensible as usual, the *Daily Colonist* published a short report untainted by the gossip, which the escapade had provoked in Victoria. AJ was the founder of Social Credit on the Island and an interesting figure, who deserves a more intelligent, sympathetic, and informed biographical record than has yet been written.

Sources: Notes, private archives, and interviews, courtesy of Mrs Rachel (Jukes) McKenzie, 24 May 2003; *Indian Army List*, October 1910, pp. 446 and 1530; Lieutenant Colonel Frederick Sinclair Poynder, *The 9th Gurkha Rifles*, 1817-1936 (The Royal United Service Institution, 1937), pp. 170, 171, 260; *Colonist*, 15 February 1914, p. 7; 5 May 1936, p. 14; 28 July 1938, p. 4; 9 March 1940, p. 2: photo; 18 December 1943, p. 4; 4 May 1946, p. 4; 12 February 1948, p. 3; 13 December 1956, p. 25: Photo and obit.; David J. Mitchell, *W.A.C. Bennett and the Rise of British Columbia* (Vancouver, Douglas & McIntyre, 1983), 464 pp, pp. 120-121; RG 150, acc. 1992-1993/166, CEF, box 4989-21; *Glenbow Archives*, Calgary, Alberta.

KEANE, Rupert Cameron (c. 1881-1966). Born in Ceylon, he lived there for many years in the service of both the government of Ceylon and that of the Federated Malay States. During the Great War, he fought in France, Germany, and

Belgium with Imperial forces and then worked as director of the War Pensioners of Canada and a member of the Army, Navy, and Air Force Veterans Association. In Victoria, he lived for thirty-three years with his wife, Florence Mary Keane, mainly at 3 Chown Place, and died in Saanich, aged eighty-five, on 31 January 1966. She died there, aged ninety-five, on 18 September 1968.
Sources: *Colonist*, 12 September 1931, p. 4; 1 February 1966, p. 24, obit.

KENNAIRD, Captain Harold George (c. 1894-1960). Born at Greenwich, London, he was recorded in the 1901 census as aged seven and living with his family at 12 Delafield Road, Charlton, Greenwich, London. His father, Herbert E. Kennaird, then aged thirty-four, was a "Waterman, Barge" born at Greenwich, and his mother Lucy Kennaird, aged thirty-five, was also from Greenwich. His brothers and sisters were Richard twelve, Robert eleven, Bertie six, and Lucy three, and there was a visitor, Adelaide Kennaird, aged twenty-one, and also a "nurse monthly" aged twenty-three. HK went to sea very young on merchant ships but served through the Great War as an officer in the Royal Navy.

After the war, he went out to the Pacific Coast, where he sailed for many years as captain of a small tramp steamer, the *Cascade*. In 1924, he and some friends converted her into a diesel-powered car ferry on the half-hour run between Brentwood Bay and Mill Bay. Renamed MV *Brentwood*, she shuttled traffic across Saanich Inlet for many more years under his command, thus saving passengers from driving over the Malahat. She was replaced in time by the more-modern MV *Mill Bay*, and soon after the Second World War, HK retired with his family to 8725 Patricia Bay Road, where they bought a farm from L. G. Thomas and raised ducks, pheasants, and guinea fowl for sale. We occasionally bought a duck there during my childhood, and I recall HK's cheery greeting. Early in 1959, they sold the farm to Walter G. Cullimore of Victoria, who ran the farm with HK as his adviser. HK died, aged sixty-six, in Sidney on 22 April 1960, leaving his wife Marjorie, a son John, as well as two brothers and three sisters in England. One of the sisters was married as Lady Bettesworth of Monte Carlo.
Sources: *Saanich Peninsula and Gulf Islands Review*, 27 April 1960, p. 12 obit.; *Colonist*, 8 March 1959, p. 12; 24 April 1960, p. 21, obit.; census 1901, England, RG 13/563, p. 13.

KENNEDY, Captain Sir Arthur Edward (1809-1883). He was born on 5 April 1809 in County Down, Ireland, and spent twenty years in the British Army. Then he became a colonial official and served in Sierra Leone and Western Australia before being appointed as the third and last governor of Vancouver Island as an independent colony. Arriving there in March 1864, he sponsored mining explorations on the Island and made a good start but soon quarrelled with the Island's Colonial Assembly over the cost of postal services and a movement to press for the union of the Island with the newer mainland colony of British Columbia. He returned to England, was knighted, and went on to serve as colonial governor in West Africa, Hong Kong, and Queensland. In 1883, on a return voyage from Australia to England with his daughter, he died between Aden and Suez and was buried at sea. She arrived safely but alone in England and was met by her brother-in-law, the Fourth Earl of Clanwilliam, a naval officer and husband of Elizabeth Henrietta *née* Kennedy. The earl was a second cousin of *Robert Aubrey Meade, who settled on the Island about 1889.

Sources: Matthew Macfie, *Vancouver Island and British Columbia: Their History and Prospects* (Longman Green, 1865), pp. 155-6; Alfred Stanley Deaville, *The Colonial Postal Systems and Postage Stamps of Vancouver Island and British Columbia, 1849-1871* (Victoria, C. F. Banfield, King's Printer, 1928), p. 97; *The Times* (London), 21 June 1883, p. 5; *The Reminiscences of Doctor John Sebastien Helmcken*, ed., Dorothy Blakey Smith (Vancouver, University of BC Press, 1975), pp. 213-214n.

KENT, Lieutenant Lionel Braund (1878-1943). Born on 7 September 1878 at Old Charlton, Southwark, on the Thames near Woolwich, he was the son of Richard Horatio Couch Kent, a barrister-at-law and member of Lincoln's Inn, whom the English censuses of 1881 and 1891 recorded as Horace Kent, born about 1856 at New Cross, Kent, and his wife Elizabeth Hearn Kent *née* Braund, born the same year as her husband but in Belgravia, Middlesex (London). LK was schooled at Oxford High School and London University, where he studied law.

The family moved to South Africa, and he went with them, but after some years moved to Victoria in 1910 and married Katherine Pearson Milner there on 2 December 1911. When he enlisted on 31 March 1915, he was established as a broker resident at 4 Linden Apartments and a member of the Eighty-eighth Volunteer Force. In the Eighteenth Canadian Battalion at first, he transferred overseas to the Twenty-eighth Battalion, Sixth Brigade, Second Canadian Division, and was wounded and evacuated. When he recovered, he transferred to the Imperial Army as second lieutenant in the Third Battalion, York and Lancaster Regiment. Again in France, this time in the Sixteenth Brigade, Sixth Division, he was wounded a second time and a document on his War Office file shows that he arrived from France at Dover on a hospital ship with wounds to his left leg. By 22 April 1918, he had had five operations, was applying for a wound gratuity, and was deemed fit only for home service. He received the MC for gallantry, but his superior officer, Lieutenant Colonel St J. Blunt, would not recommend a promotion. In 1919, he retired back to Victoria, where he was active in the Pacific Club, the Union Club, the Victoria Golf Club, and St Mary's Anglican Church, Oak Bay.

Correctly anticipating another war with Germany, as did so many of his kind, he wrote to Right Hon. Leslie Hoare Belisha, PC, MP, Secretary of State for War (London), on 28 September 1938:

> Sir: In view of the very critical situation now existing in Europe and the apparent determination of Germany to force a conflict in which England will be involved, I have the honour to approach you with the request that my name be restored to the list of Reserve of Officers . . . Having fully recovered from my wounds . . . I am fully fit and in the best of health . . . I may be called upon to serve in any capacity in the

critical struggle in which the Empire may become involved. I may say
that I am an Englishman born and educated in England and have been
many years in South Africa and Canada.

The War Office politely refused on the grounds that he was over age. His wife
had died on 13 January 1935 in Oak Bay, where they lived, and he died on 23
April 1943, leaving his father and a sister in Johannesburg, South Africa; and two
brothers in England reported to be both distinguished.
Sources: BNA (PRO), WO 339/70088; *London Gazette,* 3 February 1919; NAC, CEF
files, box 5104-5; *Colonist,* 27 April 1943, obit.; census 1881, England, RG 11/1030;
census 1891, RG 12/522, p. 38; census 1901, RG 13/603, p. 27.

KENT, Lieutenant Colonel Marshall Aubrey (1891-1978): Born on 8 September
1891 in Victoria, he was the son of Charles Herbert Kent (1862-?), who had arrived
from Manchester in 1865 as a baby and, on 13 July 1886, married Georgina Seymour
Waitt, MK's mother. In 1901, the father was employed as manager of M. W. Waitt
& Co., booksellers and stationers, and was living with his family at 243 Yates Street,
Victoria. MK became a "merchant," probably in the family business, but in 1909
joined the Fifth Regiment, CGA, and so was able to join the Canadian Army on 1
January 1916 with a lieutenant's commission. He served in France with an artillery
unit, until demobilized in 1919 but carried on in the reserve army with the rank of
lieutenant colonel, employed meanwhile as president of the firm of Kent-Roach,
electrical dealers of Victoria. Between the wars, he lived at 641 Yates Street and
was active in the community as a Boy Scout leader and "a sportsman" by which that
generation meant a fisherman and hunter. In 1925, he argued publicly against the
provincial game laws that seemed intended "to exterminate birds and animals."
He began the Second World War as GSO at Petawawa Camp, Ontario, and was
transferred in May 1943 to the staff of the Officer Selection and Appraisal Centre
at Chilliwack, BC in charge of its artillery section. After the war, he lived in Oak
Bay and was active in public affairs until his death there on 23 February 1978.
Sources: NAC, CEF files, box 5104-7; *Colonist,* 18 December 1925, p. 15; 18
December 1925, p. 15; 5 November 1948, p. 1; 4 January 1949, p. 1; 11 January
1949, p. 3; 5 June 1949, p. 2 Magazine; 2 December 1951; *Victoria Daily Times* 22
May 1943, p. 15; 30 March 1926, p. 4; 6 January 1949, p. 4.

KER, Colonel Bernard Russell (1897-1981). He was born on 14 June 1897 in
Victoria, son of David Russell Ker, who sent him to Haileybury College in England
and RMC, Kingston, Ontario. During the Great War, in 1914-1919, he served in
France with the RFA and was decorated with the OBE, but he was with the RCA in
Canada and Europe during the Second World War. Between the wars, he worked
as a director, later as president, of the real-estate firm of Ker, Stephenson Ltd.,
Victoria, and for the Pacific Coyle Navigation Co. Ltd. of Vancouver. In Victoria,
his office was at 909 Government Street. He married Marie Louise Durand and
had three daughters, and they lived on Rockland Avenue at 1470 and then 1826.
He spent time shooting, fishing, and playing golf, but served as chairman of the

Board of Governors of University School, Victoria, and in other public-spirited activities. He died, aged eighty-three, on 4 June 1981 in Victoria, predeceased by his brother *Major R. H. B. Ker and their sister, Laura Davida Ker, who married *Colonel Reginald William Braide.
Sources: *Canadian Who's Who* 1958-60, p. 590; *Who's Who in B.C.*, 1947-1948, p. 115; Canadian census, 1901, Victoria.

KER, Major Robert Gordon (1885-1974). He was born on 6 February 1885 at Abu Road Station, Rajputana, India, and was sent to Ebor School on Dorset Road, Bexhill, Sussex, where the 1901 census recorded him, aged sixteen. The name "Ebor" derives from Eboricum, the Roman name for York, though the headmaster of this school, Arthur J. H. Brown, was a Londoner and his wife was Irish. At sometime before the Great War, RK and his wife, Janet Maud Ker, moved to Victoria, where they lived at 107 Wellington Avenue and he worked as an accountant. When he joined the CEF on 25 April 1917, he was already in the Fiftieth Gordon Highlanders and was immediately commissioned as a lieutenant. He returned to Victoria after the war, but when he died, aged eighty-nine, on 11 June 1974, he was in Vancouver.
Sources: NAC, CEF files, box 5109-38; census 1901, England, RG 13/874, p. 16.

KER, Major Robert Henry Brackman (1895-1976). He was born on 26 March 1895 in Victoria, son of Laura Agnes (Heisterman) Ker (c. 1875-1937) and David Russell Ker (1862-1923), a merchant who was also born there and who sent him to University School, Victoria, and Haileybury College, England. RK cited three and a half years (1910-1913) in the Haileybury Officer's Corps as military experience when he joined the Fiftieth Gordon Highlanders as a lieutenant early in the Great War and went overseas with the Eighty-fourth Battalion, CEF. Transferring to the Royal Flying Corps, he won his wings in December 1915 and served in France with twenty-four and forty-one squadrons before being was posted to Camp Borden, Ontario, in May 1917, to command a training squadron of the RFC. When it became the RAF in 1918, he was promoted to major.

On retiring from the forces, he had a long career with his father's flour-milling firm in and around Victoria and in other companies on the Pacific Coast. In 1920-1924, he was ADC to the lieutenant governor of BC and served as Dominion director, Air Cadet League of Canada, JP for the province of BC, president of Victoria Chamber of Commerce, and chairman of the Victoria Community Chest Campaigns and in other such public-spirited tasks. In 1923, he married Helen Maud Nation, from Ontario. They soon had a son and a daughter with whom they lived in Shasta Place. RK was a member of the Church of England, the Union Club, and the Victoria Golf Club, and was fond of photography. When he died, aged eighty, on 20 October 1976, he left his wife, his brother *Bernard Russell Ker, and his sister Laura, wife of *Colonel Reginald William Braide.
Sources: NAC, CEF files, box 5109-40; *Who's Who in B.C.*, 1947-1948, pp. 115-6; 1953, p. 47; Canadian census, 1901, Victoria.

KEYES, Captain Adrian St Vincent (1882-1926). He was born in India, son of Sir Charles Patton Keyes (1823-1896), officer in the Madras (Indian) Army, and Catherine J. Keyes, née Norman, sister of Field Marshal Sir Henry Norman, Indian Army; she was born in Calcutta to a mother (Charlotte Norman) born in New York. These were long-serving Imperial families in India and around the empire. AK's brother Lieutenant Charles Valentine Keyes (1876-1901), for instance, was killed on 25 June 1901 while serving in Nigeria with the Corps of Guides. The 1891 census found AK, aged eight, living with his mother, his maternal grandmother, and two sisters at "Thorncliffe Lodge" in Cheriton on the Kentish coast. There were six servants: nurse, lady's maid, cook, parlourmaid, and two housemaids. His father and his older brothers, including the future famous Admiral Sir Roger John Brownlow Keyes (1872-1945), First Baron Keyes, were away on service. AK became a naval cadet in 1895 and a midshipman on 15 May 1898 and became one of the earliest submarine officers in the Royal Navy. Having served in 1903 in one of the original RN "Holland" boats, he eventually commanded two submarines himself, as well as the submarine tender, HMS *Onyx*. He retired from the RN in 1909, decorated with the CBE, DSO, and the MID and, when the Great War began, was working in Toronto for the Temiskaming and Ontario Northern Railway.

The order of events in his wartime career are not clear, but the facts seem to be that in 1914, he took a commission in the RCN and was stationed at Esquimalt, probably aboard one of the British ships recently turned over to the RCN, and was therefore at hand when *Premier Sir Richard McBride, on his own initiative, paid $1,150,000 cash for two submarines from Seattle, originally intended for the Chilean government. McBride later persuaded Ottawa to adopt them for the RCN, but in the meantime, they arrived at Esquimalt immediately on 5 August 1914, manned by another British-trained submariner, *Lieutenant Commander Bertram E. Jones, RN. So secret was this transaction that gunners at the coast battery nearly fired on them, there being much anxiety on the coast about German ships known to be off the coast. The next day, AK was appointed OC, Submarines in the RCN, and on 1 October next named "O.C., H.M.C.S. *Shearwater* and Submarine Flotilla." Later in the war, he was recalled to the RN, served in the Dardanelles Campaign and was present at the landing of the expeditionary forces at Gallipoli as naval officer in charge of "Y" beach. He rose in the service, was appointed in 1918 to the staff of the commander-in-chief at Portsmouth, and retired in 1919 as lieutenant commander. He died on 6 October 1926.

Sources: census 1891, England, RG 12/751, p. 1; census 1881, RG/11/148, p. 38; Marc Milner, "The Birth of the Submarine Service," *Legion Magazine* (Ottawa), May/June 2005; *MacFarlane*, p. 37; James H. Hamilton (Capt. Kettle), *Western Shores: Narratives of the Pacific Coast* (Vancouver, Progress Publishing, 1932), chapter III, "*Scaring off the German Cruisers*"; Cecil Aspinall-Oglander, *Roger Keyes* (Hogarth Press, 1951), chapter 1 and pp. 152-3, 161.

KING, Charles Henry (1855-?). He was born on 15 April 1855 in Birmingham, Warwickshire, son of Joseph and Elizabeth (Rawlins) King, who were farmers, and he went to sea as a teenager for four years with an uncle who was captain of a ship.

He then sailed to South America, where he worked as a timekeeper at a silver mine in Peru. During a revolution there in 1873, he was seized by the rebels, managed to escape by swimming a river, went to Panama, walked across the Isthmus, and took passage to New York. After some years there, he sailed to India, where he joined the police force at Madras and rose to the rank of second-class inspector. The authorities sent him to Rangoon in Burma to serve on the frontier as police inspector during one of the frequent periods of unrest there. About the year 1879, he took six months' leave of absence in England and then resigned in order to seek further adventures. In South America once more and thence to the state of Texas, he fought as a scout with the Eighth Cavalry during the Apache Indian War. He went next to San Diego, where he bought a schooner for fishing and trading on the Pacific coast of California and Mexico.

After selling his schooner in San Francisco, he joined the crew of a sealing schooner, the *Mary Ellen,* from Victoria, BC, commanded by Alex McLean, whom Jack London had described as the leading character of his famous novel, *The Sea Wolf.* They made several sealing trips after which CK took employment on other schooners, such as the *Vancouver Belle* when it was captured by the Russians and came very near being sent to Siberia. He was freed six months later, and after one last sealing trip in 1893 on the CD *Rand,* he spent seven years in the cannery business on the Fraser River as net foreman and another seven years in charge of the isolation hospital near Victoria. Eventually, he bought a launch for casual hunting, prospecting, and whatever came to hand. His adventurous life came to an end when he happened to fall and suffer a serious injury. On 4 September 1893, he married Annie Nicholas, daughter of an English couple, James and Annie Nicholas, and went to live at 975 North Park Street, Victoria, where he joined the Sons of England, the Church of England, the Conservative Party, and sports clubs. Perhaps, his wife had changed him, as the Victoria census of 1901 had identified him as a Methodist employed as "Net foreman in a cannery." His old habits soon returned, however, for he evidently moved on and died somewhere else.

Sources: Canadian census 1901, Victoria; Howay and Gosnell, *British Columbia,* vol. IV, pp. 932-3.

KING, Captain Edward Hammond (1832-1861). A colourful figure for a few years on the Island, his short life is well summarized in the *DCB* by my old friend and teacher, Syd Pettit. EK is listed here as one of many officers in the Imperial forces who retreated to the Island after serving in India and China. He was born at Stoke Damerel, Devonshire, son of Major John King of the Twenty-first Fusiliers and his wife Anne Robinson. In 1851, EK enlisted in the Ninety-fourth Regiment as an ensign and, having been promoted to paymaster of the Fifty-ninth Regiment, was invalided home on 16 October 1857. He spent a few months as a superintendent in the Welsh Constabulary and, in 1859, migrated to the Island with his family.

EK had married Harriett Nice Holmes on 14 September 1854. Disappointed in his hopes for a post as a police officer or an accountant on the Island, he went into printing and publishing. A libel case in which he was embroiled led him to assault a barrister, Edward Graham Alston (1832-1873), and Chief Justice David Cameron sentenced him to a month's imprisonment. When Governor James Douglas pardoned him in response to a citizen's petition, EK interested the government sufficiently to be sent as a special constable to investigate the wreck of the *Florencia* on the Island's west coast on 31 December 1860. During the return journey, he stopped at Dodger Cove in Barkley Sound and there he died on 7 March 1861 from gunshot wounds in a hunting accident. He was survived by his widow, two daughters, and a son. Such was the public interest in his mysterious death that the island on which he died was later named Edward King Island.

Sources: Sydney G. Pettit, "*King, Edward Hammond* (1832-1861), soldier, printer, and publisher," *DCB* vol. IX, pp. 428-29; Madge Wolfenden, "*The early government gazettes*," *BCHQ*, XVII (1943), 171-90; Walbran, *B.C. Coast Names*, pp. 285-6.

Freeman and Elsie King

KING, Freeman Foard (1891-1975). Renowned in the Victoria district in his middle age as a naturalist and Boy Scout Commissioner, he had emigrated to Canada from Sussex in 1910, aged nineteen, and farmed in Saskatchewan. He was born on 8 August 1891 at Tillington, a village about a mile west of Petworth, Sussex, eldest son of Foard King, a farm manager, himself the son of Edmund G. King (FK's grandfather), who in 1881 had farmed 930 acres, employing twenty-five men and nine boys, all this in the same district of Sussex. The last quarter of the nineteenth century brought hard times to much of the English countryside, partly because of a free-trade policy that allowed the importation of cheaper Canadian wheat. It was to the wheat country that FK emigrated. He described himself as a farmer when he enlisted in the CEF at Saskatoon on 24 December 1914 and arrived in England aboard SS *California* on 3 December 1915 with the Ninth Canadian Mounted Rifles. He took courses in physical training and bayonet fighting, but for three years of that war, he served with the British Red Cross because "ankylosis of the great toe on the right foot and lung trouble" rendered him unfit to fight in France. He was sent back to Canada on 23 February 1918 and discharged on 28 May while living at Perdue, Saskatchewan. Meanwhile, on 28 October 1916, he had married Elsie Grace Culver (1895-1985) at Folkstone, Kent, while on leave in England. After the war, they tried farming on a homestead at Perdue, Saskatchewan, but it proved too discouraging and in 1923, they moved to the Island, where they felt more at home.

On the Island, FK found employment at the lumber mill in Sidney, eighteen miles north of Victoria, and in January 1931, his family moved into a house on Third Street, two hundred yards from the three acres to which my parents had moved in 1930. At the mill, Freeman worked for some years as a saw filer, a planerman, and a tallyman. When the mill closed in 1934, he went up the Island and, in 1937, joined the BC Forest Service as a ranger at Campbell River to fight the dangerous forest fire that broke out in June 1938 north of Upper Campbell Lake. Public-spirited, like so many of their kind, FK, his wife, and their family of three girls devoted themselves in North Saanich to the Boy Scouts, Girl Guides and the junior branches, the Wolf Cubs, and Brownies. For about twenty years during the 1930s and 1940s, before he became established in Victoria, FK was an outstanding scoutmaster in Sidney. This was what mattered to FK most. Many years earlier, aged sixteen at home in England, he had formed the First West Sussex troop and persuaded the Reverend Arthur Newman to be its scoutmaster. On first moving to Saskatchean, he had founded and supported Boy Scout troops before the First World War at Saskatoon, Redbury, Prince Albert, and Raddison.

In Sidney, his wife and daughters ran the Wolf Cub pack when my brother and I were small boys, and we spent half a dozen years in FK's troop of Scouts during the 1930s and 1940s. An old unused railway station south of Beacon Avenue was adapted as a Scout hall. We admired him, and he went to much trouble to involve the troop in village activities, turning us out, for instance, for Armistice parades on 11 November each year and putting on demonstrations on Sidney sports days. Meanwhile, Mrs King was a Girl Guide Commissioner for many years and, in 1929, was president of the Sidney Parent-Teacher's Association. We were often at their house for one reason or another. Army doctors in 1914 described FK as 5' 11" tall, with a fair complexion and blue eyes, but he was a tense, watchful Englishman, very fit, with a beak nose and a dramatic sense of life, always ready to take charge in emergencies. Somehow, it was he who first learnt of the disastrous disappearance of an RCAF vessel, the *BC Star* on which an uncle of mine was lost, and came to tell my father and go with him to tell my widowed aunt, who had two young children. At Edith Whiting's wedding on 26 May 1934 (a daughter tells me), FK posted four Boy Scouts at the Whiting's house to protect the wedding gifts while the couple were away being married at St Andrew's Church. Late in November 1936, he and one of his scouts, John Gurton, worked heroically in relays for twelve hours in an effort to keep a patient at Resthaven alive by artificial respiration, there being no mechanical respirator, this at the request of Dr H. G. Burden. The patient was Sundar Singh, a Sikh, who nevertheless died that evening of the "creeping paralysis" that had moved up his body. FK took those of us who became King's Scouts into the Pacific Coast Militia Rangers in 1943, when Japanese forces were invading the Aleution Islands, Singapore, Hong Kong, and other British places in the Pacific Ocean, and we were expecting an invasion of the Island, all the more because of the large communities of Japanese immigrants in the province. Much to my boyish delight, we were issued Winchester 30/30 carbines and ammunition and practised weekly at Barrow's Range (named after *Francis John Barrow) on Tapping Road near Deep Cove, North Saanich, occasionally with Sten sub-machine guns. FK led expeditions into the Island's forests to learn how to live in them, discovering what was edible and how to deal with bears and cougars and practising in the use of knives, axes, first aid, and in splicing and knotting ropes.

Each summer, FK organized a camp for troops from the Island in general, and several put up tents on Miss Moses's farm at Deep Cove, which I well remember. In spring 1943, FK was delighted to become Boy Scout Field Commissioner for Greater Victoria, and by 1949, the Kings had moved to 541 McKennzie Avenue in Victoria. By 1951, he was executive commissioner in the district. In that capacity, he built Camp Barnard at Sooke and brought new vigour to the Boy Scout movement as a whole. Meanwhile, his wife and their daughters, Grace, Gwen, and Kathleen, were giving faithful help with the Scouts and ran the Guides, Cubs, and Brownies. When FK moved to Victoria, he began to make a name for himself as a naturalist, what we might now call an environmentalist. Not only did he have much to do with inducing *John Dean to donate his 170 acres of parkland to the province, but he also persuaded his shy bachelor friend, Thomas Francis, to do the same with his extensive acreage on the West Saanich Road, about twenty minutes' drive from Victoria. These two parks are now called each after its original owner. In 1971, FK became an official park naturalist in BC by special Order-in-Council. The following year $5,000 was raised by public subscription for a present on his eighty-first birthday, formally given by *General G. R. Pearkes at a testimonial dinner attended by 250 people. Not long after that, the municipality of Saanich presented him with $1,000 and conferred "the Freedom of the municipality" upon him. When FK died on 26 September 1875, Mrs King returned to Sidney, where my mother met her from time to time. There she died on 16 November 1985.

Sources: *The Sidney Review*, 30 April 1925, p. 6; Avis Walton, "*The Kings of Victoria*"; *Colonist*, 24 May 1929, p. 8; 4 January 1931, p. 7; 24 November 1936, p. 5; 4 May 1975, pp. 5, 6, and 15; NAC, RG150, Acc 1992-1993/166, G106, vol. 5164, regimental no. 114516; census 1861, England, RG 9/622, p. 2; census 1871, RG 10/1103, p. 19; census 1881, RG 11. 1113, p. 28; census 1891, RG 12/847, p. 14; census 1901, RG 13/955, p. 22; *Victoria Sunday Times Magazine*, 4 August 1951, pp. 6-7; notes from Pat King, Edith (Whiting) Moore's daughter, dated 12 January 2000; E. D. Ward-Harris, "*Freeman King*," *Beautiful British Columbia*, winter 1973, p. 44 (with photos); John Shaw, ed., *Nature Rambles with Freeman King* (Victoria, *Colonist* Printers Ltd., no date, (1982?), 70 pp. but no page numbers; see "Introduction."

KING, Herbert Percy (c. 1867-1946). Born in Madras, India, he described himself as "steel manufacturer" in Madras, aged 56, when he arrived in Victoria on 14 September 1918 aboard the *Suwa Maru* coming from Shanghai. His entries were similar when he reached Canada on 17 June 1923 in the *Empress of Canada* with his wife Agnes and again when they landed in Vancouver from Shanghai on 14 June 1926 aboard the *Empress of Russia*. He had lived in India and China for many years, and seems to have been one of the travellers who "discovered" the Island during his many ocean voyages. Once settled in Victoria, he joined the China-Japan Society and was elected to its managing committee during its second annual meeting held in the Oak Bay Beach Hotel on 15 October 1931. *Ernest Alfred Mountford Williams was in the chair and among some two dozen members present were H. B. Darnell (1865-1950), who had lived for some years at Peking (Beijing), *Captain James Urquhart Gordon, Mr and Mrs *Colin Henry Rutherford, *Captain Percy Vernon-Jackson, and Captain and Mrs *A. D. S. Powell. For several years HK and his wife Agnes had been living in a house they had bought at 2824 Burdick Avenue, Oak Bay. HK died, aged seventy-nine, on 3 May 1946 in Victoria. HK is easily confused with a Percy Herbert King, who was born in Brighton c. 1885 and died at Prince Rupert, BC. In 1964.

Sources: *Colonist*, 17 October 1931, p. 8; 5 May 1946, obit.; Canadian Passenger Lists online, T-4874, arriving 14 September 1918; T-14885, arriving 14 June 1926; Canada, Ocean Arrivals online, arriving 17 June 1923.

KINGSCOTE, Commander Robert Pringle (c. 1884-?). Born in Australia, almost certainly descended from the age-old Kingscote family of officers, gentlemen, and public servants, he was sent to England as a boy and became a naval cadet on 15 January 1900. Promoted to midshipman on 15 May 1900, he was found, aged sixteen, by the 1901 census, serving aboard HMS *Warspite*. On 15 May 1903, he was promoted to second lieutenant on the training ship *Good Hope*, an armoured cruiser and flagship of the First Cruiser Squadron, and, on 31 December 1905, became a lieutenant on HMS *Drake*, an armoured cruiser and flagship of the Second Cruiser Squadron Atlantic Fleet. There followed further promotions to lieutenant commander (1907) and in 1939, fifteen years after retiring from the RN, he transferred to the RCN with seniority from 31 December 1913 and was then

posted at HMCS *Naden* as sports officer at the Esquimalt barracks with the rank of commander. For two years, he was executive officer at *Naden* and CO at the time when naval training was moved from *Naden* to the east coast. He retired in 1944 as acting captain and worked with the Rainbow Sea Scouts with a special interest in boxing, having been finalist in the British army and navy boxing championships in 1907 and 1908 and heavyweight champion of the Grand Fleet in 1915. When the *Colonist* sponsored the first Vancouver Island Golden Gloves Championships in 1948, he was one of a committee of three in charge of the event. He also spent much time with the youngsters at the Esquimalt Boxing Club. He and his wife decided in 1950 to live in New Zealand, where his mother lived at Hawkes Bay, and they departed on 16 February.
Sources: census 1901, England, RG 13/5335, p. 3; *Colonist*, 16 February 1950, p. 17; *Macfarlane*, p. 38.

KINGSLEY, Commander Harry (1900-1976). Born at Shanghai, China, in September 1900, he became a cadet at Royal Naval College of Canada in 1916. In 1941, after a naval career here detailed, he became a commander in charge of HMCS *Skeena* and in 1947 senior officer in the reserve fleet on the west coast, and then commander of the dockyard and King's Harbour Master at Esquimalt. He retired on 21 November 1950 and died, aged seventy-six, on 7 March 1976 in Victoria.
Sources: *MacFarlane*, p. 38.

KIRKENDALE, Captain George (c. 1871-1945). Born in Hamilton, Ontario, he went to Victoria in 1892 and lived in the James Bay district on San Juan Avenue, then at 49 Oswego Street, and finally at 648 Dallas Road. On 4 February 1907, he was appointed shipping master and, three days later, married Margaret Florence Hart, who had arrived at James Bay from England, aged seven, in 1889. They had three sons, and the family attended the James Bay Methodist Church. Upon the death of the Harbour Master *Captain C. E. Clarke, GK took his post and worked at both jobs concurrently until 1942, when he retired. When he died, aged seventy-three, on 9 January 1945 it was said that he had lived in Victoria for fifty-three years, had been well known in shipping circles, and had taken part "in a search for pirate treasure believed to have been buried on Cocos Island." Mrs Kirkendale died, aged eighty-one, on 26 January 1963, leaving her sons, David, John, and George. The latter had worked for eight years at Hafer Machine Shop and then spent twenty-five years in the RCN from which he retired to Canoe Cove, North Saanich, in 1960.
Sources: Jean Mason, "George Kirkendale," in *Camas Chronicles of James Bay, Victoria, British Columbia* (Victoria, Camas Historical Group, 1978), p. 124; *Colonist*, 10 January 1945, obit.; 29 January 1963, obit.

KITCHING, Major General George (1910-1999), CBE (1945), DSO (1943). He was born on 19 September 1910 in Canton, China, son of George Charlesworth Kitching and Florence Dagmar Rowe Kitching. His father was employed at Shameen, near Canton, as manager of a British business firm, A. S. Watson Ltd., dealing in a wide variety of merchandise including pharmaceuticals, liquor, and soft drinks. The Kitchings lived in a house adjoining the Watson warehouse and factory, where GK and his elder brother Hugh had a happy childhood. Early in 1916, G. C. Kitching took his family to live in Victoria as a convenient place to wait for the passing of dangerous warlords, then rampant in southern China. They rented a house in Rupert Street between Humboldt and Beacon Hill Park. "To Hugh and me," George writes, "the park and the shoreline on its western limits were a paradise. In 1916 the park was largely wild and unspoiled and we used it to the full, accompanied by a number of other children who lived in the area. We stayed in Victoria for about nine months during which we visited Toronto." After trying and failing to arrange safe passage to England, the family returned to Shameen and the two sons were sent to a boarding school in Wei-Hai-Wei. There about twenty of the eighty boys were White Russian refugees from the Bolshevic revolution. After a year or so there, the boys were taken to live in England, at first at their mother's family home in Somersham, Huntingdonshire, but they were soon enrolled at Cranleigh School, Surrey. Their father served meanwhile as a captain in the British Army, which sent him on 18 February 1920 to Nasiriya, Mesopotamia. In due time, GK attended RMC, Sandhurst, and was commissioned in the Gloucestershire Regiment and served in 1930-1938 in Singapore, Malaya, and India.

During the Second World War, he had a career in the Canadian Army: in the Royal Canadian Regiment in 1939-1940; as GSO III, HQ First Canadian Division in 1941; at Staff College in 1941-1942; as GSO II, HQ First Canadian Corps in 1942; as lieutenant colonel commanding the Loyal Edmonton Regiment in 1942; as GSO I First Canadian Division in 1943; as brigadier commanding Eleventh Canadian Infantry Brigade in 1943-1944; GOC Fourth Canadian Armoured Division (acting major general) in 1944; mentioned in despatches in 1944; BGS and C of S First Canadian Corps, 1944-1945; on returning from overseas in August 1945 was appointed Vice-QMG at NDHQ; was in Washington DC National War College in 1947-1948; was brigadier general, staff (plans) army HQ in 1948-1951; subsequently commandant of Canadian Staff College and commander in the BC area; appointed vice-chief of the General Staff, Ottawa in 1956 and later chairman of the Canadian Joint Staff in London; as GOC Central Command in 1962-1965; commissioner in Ontario Pavilion, Expo 70 at Osaka, Japan; chairman of the LCBO in 1970-1976; colonel commandant of the RC Infantry Corps in 1974-1978; president of the National Council, Duke of Edinburgh's Award in Canada in 1967-1970; Legion of Merit (US); commander, Order of Orange Nassau (Netherlands); commander of the Military Order of Italy; member of the Institute of International Affairs; chairman of the Gurkha Welfare Appeal (Canada) in 1974-1977; patron of Old Fort York in 1975 and Sir Edmund Hilary Foundation; patron of Pearson College; and honorary president of the Pro Patria Branch No. 31 of the Royal Cdn. Legion in 1985-1988. In October 1946, he married Audrey Katherine Calhoun, and they had a son George and a daughter Katherine. They lived at 3434 Bonair Place, Victoria, where he gardened, collected postage stamps, and attended the Anglican Church.

Sources: *Canadian Who's Who*, 1997, p. 662; Major General George Kitching (1910-1999), *Mud and Green Fields: The Memoirs of Major-General George Charlesworth*

Kitching (St Catharines, Ont., Vanwell Publishing Ltd., 1993), pp. 15-16; Sir Arnold Wilson, *Loyalties . . . Mesopotamia*, p. 375.

KITTO, Dora Frances Eales (1873-1949). For many years the president of the Victoria branch of the SPCA and a contributor to the *Victoria Daily Colonist*, she is also believed to have been the founder of the first Anti-Vivisection Society in Canada. She was born on 25 January 1873 at Slough, Buckinghamshire, daughter of Francis Bowyer Kitto (1842-1906) and his wife Lavinia Mary *née* Tilly (1842-1926), who in 1868 had married there, where Lavinia was born, and where DK's father was employed as a "corn merchant." In 1881, the census found DK, aged eight, living with her family near Slough in the High Street at Upton Chalvey, but ten years earlier, her father had been a London bookseller in Islington, where he was born. His parents (DK's grandparents) were Dr John Kitto (1804-1854), DD, a Plymouth stonemason's son, and a Londoner, Annabella Fenwick (1810-1897), who were married on 21 September 1833 at Christ Church, Newgate Street, London, and had ten children. Dr John Kitto joined the Church Missionary Society (1823) and spent several years circulating its tracts in Malta, Turkey, Egypt, and Russia. Author of *The Pictorial Bible* (1840), *The History of Palestine* (1853), *The Lost Senses: Deafness and Blindness* (1845), and much similar writing that went through various editions, he lived in Woking, Berkshire, during the 1840s, then in London at Camden Town, and died in Wurtemberg, Germany, where he seems to have studied. This extraordinary Anglican writer and teacher influenced the lives of his children, DK's uncles and aunts. One son became the vicar of St Martin-in-the-Fields, London, and another, Edmund Spencer Kitto (1840-1906), was employed in London as a "wholesale stationery manager" and married Joanna Inglis Weir (1844-1932), who was born in India near Madras, daughter of Robert Dundas Weir. DK's father, the fifth of the ten children, in 1867 took over the publication of *Friend*, an Anglican periodical, and devoted himself to the literary and Christian education of his children.

There were six of them when, at sometime in the late 1880s, he and Lavinia took them out to live in Victoria. In 1901, they were living together at 69 Belcher Street with one Chinese domestic servant, the father and son employed as "assayers" and the daughters as schoolteachers or "tutors." They dispersed after their parents died, he on 17 July 1906 and she on 31 July 1926. DK's younger brother, Alec John Kitto (1876-1916), became a lawyer in Vancouver, joined the RC Field Artillery in the Great War, and was killed at the Somme on 16 September 1916. An elder sister, Margaret Elizabeth Kitto (1871-1925) became known as an artist, painter of historical scenes. DK herself lived for a time at 957 Southgate Street, and when she died, aged seventy-six, on 14 April 1949, she was living at St Ann Street. She wrote articles for the *Daily Colonist*, usually printed in its Sunday supplement: "Sketches from the Life and Reign of Queen Victoria, 1819 to 1901" (1931) and "Our British Heritage" (1941). Aware of efforts in the Victoria district to import and protect English songbirds, she recalled in one of her articles the first time she had heard a nightingale at home in England:

My first experience of hearing this favourite song-bird was when, as a small child, I was brought out of doors on a moonlit night to hear a nightingale singing in the garden. It was a typical old-fashioned, luxuriant English garden, with nothing very regular about it. In fact, it was distinctly irregular in design, and therein lay its charm! The songs of birds were ever heard there and the nightingale was partial to the locality. Birds and animals that decided to adopt this environment as their own were never molested . . . When we speak of English birds, the skylark, blackbird, thrush, nightingale, linnet and finch, and many another whose liquid notes are but a memory, we seem to hear them again at their happiest and best, and it is a memory that we would tenderly preserve.

Sources: *Colonist*, 24 May 1931, Sunday, p. 3; 29 June 1941, Sunday p. 2; *Colonist*, 31 May 1933, p. 4; 15 April 1949, p. 19, obit.; Canadian census, 1901, Victoria; W. H. K. Wright, *West-Country Poets: Their Lives and Work* (Elliot Stock, 1895), pp. 48-51; John Kitto, DD, *The History of Palestine from the Patriarchal Age to the Present* (Edinburgh, Adam & Charles Black, 1853), 426 pp; http: www. members.ii net. net. au/~kjstew/ KITTO onename study.htm [no spaces].

KNIGHT, Henry George (c. 1873-1962). Born on 12 February 1872 at Eling, Hampshire, probably the son of a village constable, he joined the Third Battalion of the Grenadier Guards and served for six years, including those of the South African War. He was in engagements at Paardeberg (1900), under the command of Lord Roberts when Pretoria was invaded, and in the escort for Commander Cronje during the time when four thousand prisoners of all nationalities were marched for twenty miles to the Modder River. Later, he rejoined his own battalion in a march on Bloemfontein. He was awarded no fewer than seven bars to his Queen's and King's medals. At sometime before the Great War, he moved to Victoria, where he was living as a "rancher" with his wife, Clara, at 681 Transit Road, Oak Bay, Victoria, when he enlisted in the No. 11 Detachment of Military Police, CEF, on 21 January 1918. After the war, he lived for twenty years in Victoria and died, aged eighty-nine, on 23 August 1962 in Saanich.
Sources: NAC, CEF files; *Colonist*, 2 March 1940, p. 5.

KNIGHT, Lieutenant Commander John Harry (c. 1880-1958). Born at Alverstoke near Portsmouth, he was the eldest son of Henry P. Knight, a "Lieutenant Railway Engineer" and his wife Sarah. The 1881 census found him, aged five, living in Park Road, Hythe St Leonard, Kent, with two brothers and a nineteen-year-old "2nd Lieutenant Essex Rifle Militia" born in India. JK became a cadet in the RN, had a normal career, and retired as a lieutenant commander. Then, with seniority dated 19 December 1910, he joined the Canadian hydrographic survey in 1914 and, on loan from the RN to the RCN in 1914, was posted to HMCS *Rainbow* and in command of it in 1917. Retired from the RCN, he was mobilized for the Second

World War and, in 1940, appointed as navigation instructor at Stone Frigate and then Royal Roads. He died, aged seventy-seven, on 6 December 1958 in Saanich.
Sources: *MacFarlane*, p. 38; census 1881, England, RG 11/1014, p. 51.

KNIGHT, Robert Ivan (1901-?). He was born on 29 November 1901 in Calcutta, India, son of George William Knight, CIE, director of public instruction in Bengal, and grandson of the founder of the *Calcutta Statesman*. He was schooled at Oundle in Northamptonshire and Sidney Sussex College, Cambridge, spending vacations with relatives at "The Poplars," Frimley, near Camberley in Surrey: Captain Henry Raleigh Knight (c. 1856-?) of the Buffs Regiment and his family. Poor eyesight discouraged him, and in 1925, he migrated to the Island to help a cousin work a chicken farm at Errington near Parksville. After obtaining a teacher's diploma at the University of British Columbia, he spent the years 1927-1929, teaching at Shawnigan Lake School as assistant master. In 1933, he suffered a bout of rheumatic fever while he was an honours student in physics at the University of British Columbia. In 1935, he founded Qualicum Beach School with assistance from Aubrey Dashwood Muskett and two uncles then living at Eastbourne, Sussex. As headmaster, RK directed it along the lines he had learnt at Oundle, a firmly Anglican school established in 1556 by the Grocers' Company with the motto *God Grant Grace* and the objective of preparing Christian gentlemen for university. He was said, in fun, to believe in "the seven Cs": Christianity, classics, cricket, cadet corps, cold baths, courtesy, and corporal punishment. Most of his pupils were boarders from central or northern districts of the Island. He was president of the Canadian Club at Qualicum Beach, active in the Anglican community there, and played tennis and golf. In 1970, he closed the school and later deposited its papers and his own at the *BC Archives* (Add. Mss. 1327).
Sources: Patrick A. Dunae, ed., "The Homeroom," Malaspina History Department website; *Who's Who in B.C.*, vol. V (1942-1943), p. 180; 1947-1948, p. 119; Jean Barman, *Growing up British in British Columbia*, p. 111; *The Ubyssey* (University of British Columbia), vol. XVI (29 September 1933), p. 4; census 1891, England, RG 12/565, p. 8; census 1901, RG 13/609, p. 40.

KNIGHT, William (c. 1866-1934). He was born in Hampshire, became a civil engineer, and was employed for more than forty years by the British engineering firm of Sir John Jackson on its projects in Africa, Singapore, and other places at home and abroad. Sir John Jackson (1851-1919) was a Yorkshireman educated at York and the University of Edinburgh, who trained as a civil engineer and became one of the biggest contractors for public works. Among his company's contracts was the last section of the Manchester Ship Canal; Dover harbour; the foundations of Tower Bridge; the Admiralty Docks at Kayham, Devonport; the Admiralty Harbour at Simon's Bay, Cape of Good Hope; Singapore harbour; the great railway across the Andes from Arica on the Pacific Coast to La Paz, capital of Bolivia; and the great barrage dam in Iraq across the Euphrates at Hindia, near Babylon. In 1913, the firm sent WK out to Victoria to supervise the construction in 1914-1918 of the Ogden Point Breakwater, protecting the harbour from heavy seas. He had it constructed of huge granite blocks, projecting into the Strait of Georgia off Dallas Road. WK settled at last in Victoria near his breakwater at 137 Dallas Road and died, aged sixty-eight, on 13 July 1934, leaving his widow and a daughter, as well as two sons in Singapore.

Sources: *Colonist*, 15 July 1934, p. 5, obit.; *Who was Who*, 1916-1928, p. 546; W. David, *The Rise and Fall of the Singapore Naval Base*, 1919-1942 (Macmillan, 1979), pp. 67, 86, 102, 135-6.

KNOCKER, Major Arthur Gerald (1874-1963). He was born on 17 September 1874 at Dover, Kent, son of a solicitor, Edward W. N. Knocker and his wife Clara C. Knocker, born in Belgium. Aged eight in 1881, AK was living with his three brothers and two sisters in Castle Hill House, Dover St James, Kent, together with their parents as well as their father's brother, also a solicitor, and five servants: butler, cook, nurse, housemaid, and undernurse, all women except the butler. After attending Dover College, he served with the Royal Irish Fusiliers through the South African War. He took part in operations in Natal, the relief of Ladysmith including the action at Colenso, and Tugela Heights (14-27 February 1900); was slightly wounded at Pieters Hill; fought in the Transvaal in May and June 1900 and east of Pretoria from July to 29 November 1900; and in actions at Reit Vlei and Belfast. After a spell in Cape Colony, north of Orange River, he was again in the Transvaal for nine months from 30 November 1900 and yet again from November 1901 to 31 May 1902. But in September and October 1901, he was sent to the Zululand frontier of Natal and on staff as assistant provost marshal. He was mentioned in despatches in the *London Gazette* on 10 September 1901 and won the Queen's Medal and four clasps as well as the King's Medal with two clasps. After several post-war years in India, he retired in 1913 to Cowichan Station, VI, where his elder brother, Captain Lionel Chantrell Knocker (c. 1872-1955) was living (having fought through the Great War in the Cheshire Regiment) but went back to join his old regiment when the Great War broke out. His service therein was mainly in Egypt.

He returned to Cowichan Station, after the war, with his wife, Violet Constance Knocker (c. 1885-1957), born in Tasmania, and they lived on Dingwall Road. Until she died in February 1957, she was a devoted member of St Andrew's Anglican Church, Cowichan Station, sometime president of the Women's Guild, a canvasser for the Red Cross, and active supporter of the SPCA. He was secretary and groundsman of the South Cowichan Lawn Tennis Club for many years and was also postmaster at Cowichan Station for four years in the 1930s. Lionel Chantrell Knocker died, aged eighty-two, on 23 June 1955 in Duncan. When AK died in King's Daughters Hospital, Duncan, on 2 March 1963, he left a stepson, Donald De Wintern Douglas of Victoria, and a sister-in-law, Lionel's widow on Riverside Road, with whom he had made his home since 1957.

Sources: *Hart's Annual Army List*, 1913, p. 1446, "War Services—Retired List"; census 1881, England, RG 11/ 1001/92, p. 18; census 1901, RG 13/2605, p. 26; BNA, WO 339/46944 (Lionel Chantrell Knocker); *Cowichan Leader*, 7 February 1957, p. 8, obit.; 6 March 1963, p. 8, obit.

KOECHLIN, Marcel Charles (1874-1953). An English tea planter in southern India, he eventually migrated to the Island, where he lived at Duncan with his wife, Barbara Florence *née* Martin (born at Stoney Stanton, Leicestershire), and there they both lived for the rest of their lives. I do not have all the details, but he was born a British subject at Le Havre, France, joined King Edward's Horse, regimental no. 649, on 8 September 1914 in London, aged thirty-nine years and ten months, was promoted to sergeant on 15 September 1915, and served in France through the Great War until 23 August 1917, when he was evacuated to England with some illness (rheumatic ostitis?). On 16 November 1918, he was transferred to a reserve unit. In the official Army Pensions Records is a statement that he "has gone" to Trivandrum, India, which was near the south-western tip of the subcontinent and became the capital of Kerala. Mrs Koechlin appears, aged six, in census records for 1891 as one of the three daughters of Rev. John Martin, aged forty-two (born at Cold Overton, Leicestershire), living at "Charley Hall," Leicestershire, her mother being Sophia Constance Martin, aged forty-two, both parents born in Leicestershire. There was a visitor, a boarder, and seven servants.

MK and his wife sailed to Tacoma, Washington State, aboard the *Europa*, landing on 26 March 1932, giving their address as Duncan, BC, and his occupation as "planter" at Trivandrum, India. Immediately above them on the passenger list—probably travelling with them—were *General Cavendish Walter Gartside-Spaight and his wife Louisa Donna Cavendish-Spaight. All this offers only a glimpse of their lives, which ended, MK's, aged seventy-eight, on 3 December 1953 in Oak Bay, and his wife's, aged eighty-five, on 29 September 1969 in North Cowichan (almost certainly at Duncan).

Sources: BNA (Kew), WO 364, British Army Pension Records 1914-20; U.S. Passenger and Crew Lists, 1893-1957; census 1891, England, RG 12/2514, p. 5 (Martin).

Lt. Gen.Sir Percy Henry Noël Lake

Sir Percy Lake's house

LAKE, LIEUTENANT GENERAL SIR PERCY HENRY NOËL (1855-1940).

I. Personal and Family Life

He was born at Tenby, Wales, on 29 June 1855, son of Lieutenant Colonel Percy Godfrey Botfield Lake (1829-1899), whose life must be summarized as part of his own background. Born into an English family, the father attended Cheltenham School when it was quite new and was commissioned, aged sixteen, in the Eighty-first Regiment but transferred to the Fifty-fourth, the one hundredth, the Second West India Regiment, and finally the One Hundredth Royal Canadian Regiment, the first British regiment to be raised outside Great Britain. Of his brothers, PL's uncles, one was dean of Durham Cathedral for twenty-five years and two others died serving as Imperial officers, one at Gibraltar and the other of cholera at Calcutta. PL's father was stationed in turn on the island of Jersey; at Kingston, Ontario; Quebec City; and Trinidad, Demerara, Jamaica, and Santa Lucia (as private secretary of the lieutenant governor). He retired and, at last in 1884, after several efforts to settle, joined his younger son Richard Stuart Lake (1860-1950) at Grenfell in the NWT, together with his wife, the mother of this family, Margaret Lake *née* Phillips (1830-1908), born to an English family at Quebec. PL did not go with them because he was in school at Uppingham and, then in August 1873, gazetted to the Fifty-ninth Foot Regiment (later the Second Battalion, East Lancashire Regiment.) He visited whenever he could.

At Grenfell, in what was to become eastern Saskatchewan, the Lakes built a large farmhouse they called *Winmarleigh Grange* and, with several other families like themselves, enjoyed a country life as English as could be managed. They farmed, hunted, played polo and tennis, rode to hounds in pursuit of coyotes, and organized a cricket eleven, amateur theatricals, the Anglican parish of St Michael and All Angels, and a militia unit to face the troubles of the Riel Rebellion. When the province of Saskatchewan was formed in 1905, Richard Lake became its first lieutenant governor, and in 1910, he married Dorothy Marion Schreiber Fletcher, youngest daughter of James Fletcher, LLD, of Ottawa. A sister, Mabel Lake, married *William Harwood Belson, an immigrant from an English family at Malmsbury, Cape of Good Hope, who served briefly in 1916 as ADC to PL. Early in 1921, these families moved to Victoria, where Sir Richard Lake (as he had become after the

Great War, along with the other lieutenant governors of the provinces) was already a leader in the provincial Red Cross Society, and PL joined them in September with his wife, Hester Fanny Woodyer (1852-), daughter of a Victorian architect, Henry Woodyer (1816-1896) of Grafham Hall near Guildford, Surrey, whom he had married in 1891. PL had first visited the Island on an inspection tour in 1907. The Belsons lived at Deep Cove, North Saanich, near a summer cottage on Chalet Road taken by Mrs Belson's two brothers. The latter, both knighted by then, lived in Oak Bay, the Sir Richard Lakes at 1280 Newport Avenue from 1923, and the Sir Percy Lakes at 1004 Terrace Avenue, Oak Bay, from 1925. Both families were active at St Mary's Anglican Church and in other ways, though it is difficult to distinguished one Lady Lake from the other in the many newspaper references to their leadership, donations, and public appearances. It is certain, however, that Lady Hester Fanny Lake died, aged 93, on 3 December 1945 in Victoria.

II. Career before the Great War

PL spent almost fifty years in military service around the empire, rising in the British Army from captain (1883-1891) to major (1891-1899), lieutenant colonel (1899-1902), brigadier general (1904-1905), major general (1905), and lieutenant general. He fought in the Afghan War (1878-1879) as assistant field engineer with the Afghanistan Field Force, passed through Staff College with honours (1884), served in the Sudan Campaign (1885) attached to the Intelligence Department, and earned medals in several engagements. In 1888-1890, he was with General Intelligence at Army HQ and in 1891-1892 was secretary to Lord Wantage's Committee on the terms of service in the army.

He had long and satisfactory assignments in Canada. Did his Canadian mother and his family's migration to Canada predispose him to get along in Ottawa better than most senior British officers posted there? Whatever the reason, he was tactful and shrewd enough to establish friendly relations in Canadian military circles and won the confidence of the federal government, though it must be said that he was one of the professional soldiers who did not agree with the controversial Canadian War Minister, Sir Sam Hughes (1853-1921). It would be interesting to discover what his relations were with Lieutenant Colonel (later Brigadier General) *Reginald John Gwynne (1863-1942, q.v.), a neighbour of his family at Grenfell, Saskatchewan, whom Hughes appointed in 1912 as organizer and inspector of the Cadet Corps, Military District No. 10, then director of Cadet Services at Militia Headquarters in Ottawa. After the Great War, the Gwynnes, like the Lakes, settled on the Island, where the latter drove past the Gwynne's house at Ardmore on the West Saanich Road on the way to and from the cottage at Deep Cove. However that may be, PL became quartermaster general in the Canadian Militia (1893-1898) and then assistant quartermaster general in charge of the Mobilization Branch at Army HQ in Ottawa (1899-1904). Next, after a spell in India as chief staff officer, Southern Command (1904), he served as chief of the General Staff, Canadian Militia (1904-1908)—that is, the Canadian Army at the time—and inspector general of Canadian forces and chief military adviser to the Minister of Militia

(1908-1910). It was typical of him to be active in Ottawa in many directions. On 1 March 1905, he spoke at the Annual General Meeting of the Rifle Association. On 6 April 1907, at his insistence and in the face of a general Canadian indifference, he arranged for Colonel Herbert Cyril Thacker (1870-1953) to speak at St George's Hall, Ottawa, about what he had learnt as Canadian attaché with the Japanese forces in Manchuria during the Russo-Japanese War (1904-1905) and to repeat the talk at RMC, Kingston, Ontario, two days later. In 1909, PL warned the country that Canada should prepare to resist invasion on the Pacific Coast, and this was remembered thirty years later in Victoria. Meanwhile, he wrote several reports, which show a keen mind and independent judgement. A good example is his *Report Upon the Best Method of Giving Effect to the Recommendations of General Sir John French, G.C.B., G.C.V.O., Regarding the Canadian Militia*, 1 George V, Sessional Paper No 35b A 1911 (Ottawa, King's Printer, 1910), 16 pp., bound together with French's own report on the Canadian forces.

In London as well as Ottawa, Lake was recognized as an outstanding soldier and so accumulated a great many honours and decorations: Companion of the Bath (1902), Commander of the Bath (1916), Companion of St Michael and St George (1905), Knight Commander of St George (1908), Knight Chairman of the Board of Visitors for RMC, Kingston, Ont. (1906-1908), member of the General Staff of the Empire (1907), and president of Ottawa's Minto Skating Club (1910). From 1913 to 1920, he was honorary colonel of the East Lancashire Regiment. In 1923, the Royal Central Asian Society elected him a fellow. On 11 January 1936, the Premier of BC presented him with "a patron's emblem of the Old Contemptibles' Association" at a rugby game between teams from the RCN and New Westminster. But this is to get ahead of events, particularly a devastating turn of events in Mesopotamia.

III. Mesopotamia

On 19 January 1916, PL was sent from India, where he had been chief of the General Staff (1911-1916), to succeed General Sir John Nixon (1857-1921) at Basra as GOC of the war against Turkish forces in Mesopotamia. The appointment was made by the (British) Indian government in Delhi to which that part of the empire had been assigned, and may have resulted from PL's careful study of Mesopotamian defence in the years 1911-1915. He had recommended improving military transport by land and water, but his recommendations had not been implemented and there was now no longer enough time to make these improvements. His appointment came too late to make up for earlier negligence by his predecessors. Chief among these were General Sir Beauchamp Duff (1855-1918), commander-in-chief in India, "a desk officer who had never commanded so much as a regiment and who owed his appointment to his service as Kitchener's Chief of Staff. Having to combine the duties of C-in-C with the advisory role of the former Military Member [of the Viceroy's council], Duff remained at the Viceroy's side at Simla during the campaign. He did not go to the operational headquarters at Basra; he did not even visit Bombay, where the troops embarked and whence the wounded returned, nor did he station any member of his staff there to find out what was going on" (Davd Gilmour, *Curzon*, pp. 477-8, 489-90). But the double duty had fallen to the inexperienced and negligent Duff as a direct result of Lord Kitchener's earlier insistence on removing the Military Member. Once installed as commander-in-chief, however, Duff had been protected from his critics by Sir Charles Hardinge, who had insisted on keeping him at Simla and had impeded efforts by more far-seeing officers who, like PL, had wanted to make better preparations for the forces in Mesopotamia.

As a result, PL's predecessors in Basra and the officers who now answered to him, notably Major General Charles Vere Townsend (1861-1924), had underestimated the strength of the Turkish armies in Mesopotamia fortified by their German allies, as well as the need for inland water transport. Consequently, the Tigris Corps led by Lieutenant General Sir Fenton John Aylmer (1862-1935) and then Lieutenant General Sir George Frederick Gorringe (1868-1945) was unable to relieve Townsend's army besieged at Kut-el-Amara since 3 December 1915. After a desperate resistance, during which PL tried to send relieving forces from Amar aboard the nine-hundred-ton river steamer, HMS *Julnar*, and Lord Kitchener ordered Townsend to offer money as a bribe to Halil Pasha using T. E. Lawrence in the negotiations, Townsend was forced to surrender on 29 April. This was one of the worst military disasters in British history, all the more because the Turks starved and abused the defeated army and put them through a murderous death-march to prison camps in Turkey. As commander-in-chief, PL was at first held responsible and removed, though he must have known, as a post-war inquiry reported on 26 June 1917, that nobody in his position could have saved Kut from the misjudgements of his predecessors at Basra and his superiors at Delhi. According to Roger Ford, informed authorities blamed Sir John Nixon, Lord Hardinge, Sir Beauchamp Duff, Sir George Barrow, and Austen Chamberlain, in that order. The unwritten law of the British officer, "never complain, never explain," prevented PL from speaking out, and his nephew, Lancelot Charles Lake (1924-2003), with whom I spent an afternoon at his home in North Saanich, either knew nothing about the affair or, like PL himself, was determined to say nothing. Too many historians (e.g., Briton Cooper Busch, *Britain, India, and the Arabs, 1914-1921*, Berkeley, Univ. of California Press, 1971, 522 pp., p. 111, and even the informed and careful Ronald Millar, *Death of an Army: The Siege of Kut, 1915-1916*, Boston, Houghton Mifflin Company, 1970, pp. 285ff., 288) have misrepresented the causes of the disaster by concluding that the subsequent British victories at Kut and Baghdad in March 1917 were results of superior generalship by PL's successor, Sir Stanley Maude. Certainly, Maude was a capable officer, but he was also in fact the beneficiary of improvements in river transport already set in motion by PL. Missing in most accounts of the campaign is the large-scale, though late, activity of the Inland Water Transport section of the Royal Engineers, which recruited boatmen and navigators around the empire, even on Vancouver Island, but following orders that had been issued too late to avert the Kut disaster. PL had recommended them years earlier and been overruled.

IV. Founding the Royal Canadian Legion

PL retired from the army on 29 November 1919, moved to Victoria in September 1921, and began almost immediately to work towards a unified organization of war veterans. The British Legion had been founded early that summer in response to the urging of Douglas, Earl Haig, commander-in-chief of all British armies including the Canadians. On 2 June, a group in Victoria known as the Veterans of France had put forward what was probably the first detailed plan for amalgamating ex-servicemen's organizations in Canada. They proposed what they called "The Canadian Legion" to unite all who had served in France, in Britain, or in any of the Imperial campaigns of the past and to offer associate membership for veterans who had served only in Canada. On the Island, as elsewhere in Canada, putting this idea into effect was difficult in the face of the competing loyalties—based on regimental camaraderie—of the many existing veterans' groups with names such as Amputations Club, Army and Navy Veterans, British Campaigners' Association, British Campaigners' Legion of Frontiersmen, British Imperial Comrades Association, Gallipoli Veterans Association of Vancouver Island, Grand Army of United Veterans, Great War Veterans Association, Imperial Veterans Association, North-West Field Force Association, Old Comrades Association, Pacific Coast Officers' Association, Red Chevron Society, Returned Veterans of Shawnigan Lake, and Veterans Club of BC. Four years later, no agreement had been reached, and on 28 August 1925, PL published a long letter entitled "Earl Haig's Proposals" ending with an appeal to all veterans to attend a public meeting on 1 September at Christ Church Cathedral hall, Victoria. He organized it, chaired it, and was elected to lead a "unity committee" of seven officers at a Dominion-wide conference in Winnipeg on 25 November. Characteristically of Victoria, four members of that committee were English-born and two of the three Canadians were born in Victoria to British families and had attended British public schools (Haileybury and Loretto). A few days before setting out for Winnipeg, PL explained the issues again at a mass meeting at the Chamber of Commerce in Victoria, chaired by *Colonel Cy Peck, VC. The Victoria committee played such a leading part at the Winnipeg conference that PL was elected by acclamation to serve as the first Dominion president of the newly created Canadian Legion of the British Empire Service League.

Returning home, he spoke again and again over the ensuing years to Legion branches that quickly formed in towns all over the Island and the province. In November 1929, the Pro Patria Branch of the Legion made him a life member "for his great service to the veterans of the Empire." He spoke about many matters as well as wartime reminiscences, the Legion's objectives, and the red poppies campaign. For instance, at the annual convention of the BC Branches of the Canadian Legion held in May 1929, "Sir Percy deplored the fact that in B.C. the teaching of the Bible in the schools was not permitted." On 1 March 1937, he spoke to the Overseas League about "Why Britain has been able to conquer and govern India" and argued that the only reason why 160,000 British people were able to rule 350,000,000 Indians was the unconscious effect of the English Bible, which had imposed certain habits of conduct that won the trust and acceptance of most of the native population most of the time. PL had spent fifteen years in India and spoke about it at Saint Augustine's Hall, Deep Cove, on 3 April 1933, under the auspices of the Allies Chapter, IODE, and he served that year as president of the India-Burma Society (Victoria), which he and others had founded in 1932. Deeply interested in Imperial problems, he spoke on "England and Egypt" to the IODE in Victoria on 26 March 1925. He made himself useful in the United Service Club and the Church of England and in November 1939 agreed to act as one of the directors of the Victoria Boys' Brass Band, which had been founded about twenty years before by one C. H. Rowles. He went to London with others in July 1933 on behalf of the British Empire Service League to press the minister of pensions on behalf of British veterans. In January 1936, he and his brother, Sir Richard, attended a commemorative service for George V at Shawnigan Lake School for Boys. A few days later, he was elected first vice-president of the Victoria Boy Scouts' Association. PL was sadly missed throughout the Island and abroad when he died, aged eighty-five, in Victoria on 17 November 1940 and was buried at Royal Oak.

Sources: The best biography to date is J. F. Cummins's, *"Lieutenant-General Sir Percy Lake and Some Chapters of Canadian and Indian History," Canadian Defence Quarterly,* vol. III, no 3 (April 1926), pp. 244-256. It was the principal source of a four-page biography in *National Encyclopedia of Canadian Biography,* ed., Jessie Edgar Middleton and W. Scott Downs (Toronto, Dominion Publishing Co. Ltd., 1937), pp. 1-4, with photo. Good summaries are in the *Dictionary of National Biography,* twentieth-century supplement, vol. II, p. 2738; Longstaff, *Esquimalt Naval Base,* appendix C, pp. 153-160, and *Who's Who in B.C.,* 1933-1934, p. 101 and 1937-1939, pp. 78-79. The family in Grenfell figures in Annie Ida Amy Yule, *Grit and Growth: the Story of Grenfell* (Regina, Monarch Press, 1967), pp. 50, 85-6 and J. K. Johnson, ed., *The Canadian Directory of Parliament,* 1867-1967 (Ottawa, Public Archives of Canada, 1968), p. 316; Riddick, *Who's Who in India,* p. 208. Among the many English census records of the family, PL appears, aged five, *en famille* at 21 West Cliff, Preston in Lancashire, in census 1861, RG. 9/3129, p. 56; aged fifteen at Uppingham in census 1871, RG 10/3301, p. 36; aged twenty-five at an army base in census 1881, RG 11/785/93, p. 3; and aged forty-five in Chelsea with wife, mother, and two servants in census 1901, RG 13/77/198, p. 59. Various internet sites sketch the background of PL's wife, Hester Fanny Woodyer, daughter of a distinguished Victorian architect.

For PL's pre-war career, see *Indian Planters Gazette & Sporting News,* 4 May 1912; *Report of the Proceedings of the Dominion of Canada Rifle Association,* Ottawa, R. J. Taylor, 1905, pp. 117, 129-130; Colonel Percy N. Lake, *Report Upon the Best Method of Giving Effect to the Recommendations of General Sir John French, G.C.B., G.C.V.O., Regarding the Canadian Militia,* 1 George V, Sessional Paper No 35b A 1911 (Ottawa, King's Printer, 1910), 16 pp.; Desmond Morton, *The Canadian General: Sir William Otter* (Toronto, Hakkert, 1974), pp. 147, 235-6 (photo), 292-9, 304-7, 322-3; Richard

Arthur Preston, *Canada's RMC: A History of the Royal Military College* (University of Toronto Press for the RMC, 1969), pp. 201-2.

Details of PL's activities in the Great War are in these sources: Brigadier General F. J. Moberley, ed., *The Campaign in Mesopotamia, 1914-1918* (3 vols.; HMSO, 1923-1925), Vol. I, pp. 58, 73, 179-81, 195-6, 383, Vol. II, pp. 9-10, 31, 45, 264, 276-7, 282-3, 278-282, 357-8, 565-6, and Vol. III, p. 444; Lieutenant Colonel Leonard Joseph Hall, *The Inland Water Transport in Mesopotamia* (Constable, 1921), 253 pp.; David Gilmour, *Curzon* (John Murray, 1994), pp. 477-84; 489-90; Major R. Evans, *A Brief Outline of the Campaign in Mesopotamia 1914-1918* (Sifton Praed & Co. Ltd., 1926), 135 pp. with folding tables; four black-and-white folding maps in end-pocket; Roger Ford, *Eden to Armageddon: World War I in the Middle East* (Weidenfeld & Nicolson, 2009), pp. 50-62, 93, weak on the water-transport issue; Ronald Millar, *Death of an Army: The Siege of Kut, 1915-1916* (Boston, Houghton Mifflin Company, 1970), pp. 152-8, 163-8; 206; 215-6; 226; 238; 246-7; 251-3; 258; 260; 283-5; 288; Edmund Dane, *British Campaigns in the Nearer East 1914-1918* (Hodder & Stoughton, 1918), pp. 135, 151 and 258; Sir Arnold Wilson, *Loyalties: Mesopotamia, A Personal and Historical Record* (OUP, 1931), passim, Gertrude Bell, *The Letters of Gertrude Bell*, ed., Lady Bell, DBE (2 vols., Ernest Benn Ltd., 1927), vol. I, p. 371; Vol. II, pp. 504-541; and Briton Cooper Busch, *Britain, India, and the Arabs, 1914-1921* (Berkeley, Univ. of California Press, 1971), 522 pp., p. 111.

For PL's life in retirement, see *Colonist*, 2 June 1907, p. 2; 3 June 1921, p. 9; 10 September 1921, p. 8; 27 March 1925, p. 9; 28 August 1925, p. 4; 2 September 1925, p. 3; 21 November 1925, p. 1; 28 November 1925, p. 1; 10 May 1929, p. 6; 13 November 1929, p. 5; 17 January 1933, p. 8; 17 January 1933, p. 8; 27 July 1933, p. 7; 24 April 1934, p. 6; 12 September 1934, p. 4: L to E, Lieutenant Colonel F. W. L. Moore, "Be Prepared"; 28 January 1936, p. 9; 17 February 1939, p. 4; 2 November 1939, p. 4; *Sidney & Gulf Islands Review*, 29 March 1933; *Wrigley's Vancouver—Victoria and B.C. Directory*, from 1925; Clifford H. Bowering, *Service: The Story of the Canadian Legion, 1925-1960* (Ottawa, Dominion Command, Canadian Legion, 1960), pp. xxvi, 17-18, 24, 26, 32, 37, 39-41, 46, 51, 53-4, 61-3, 125, 185, 235.

LANCASTER, Rev. Thomas Reed (1900-1951). An Anglican minister on the Island in and near Sidney in the years 1936-1941, he arrived from Manitoba, where he had served in churches since emigrating from the north of England in 1921. With him went his wife, Anita *née* Allardyce, born at North Battleford, Saskatchewan, whom he had met and married somewhere on the prairies. He was at first an assistant at Christ Church Cathedral in Victoria. They lived later and for several years next door to my family in Sidney near Roberts Bay, while he was rector at St Andrews Church, successor to Rev. T. M. Hughes, and their two children, John and Susan, were born there. My father was the rector's warden at St Andrews and our two families became friendly. I am still in touch with Susan, who in due time grew up, married Roger Ferguson, and lived many years in Portland, Oregon. I lost touch with John who grew up to follow his father into the church. A sensitive, kind, and cultivated man, TL was immensely helpful to my family and we grew to love him.

Not only did he draft my brother and me into the St Andrews church choir and enlist us to ring the chimes—which he procured for St Andrews from the cathedral when it replaced them with bells—but he also had something to do with my having one of the vacant student rooms at Anglican Theological College on the campus of the University of British Columbia (Vancouver) in 1949-1951. There were other acts of kindness for my brother and sisters. In 1941, he joined the RCAF and became chaplain to the Western Command. After the Second World War, he was assigned to parishes in the BC interior, and in August 1949, returning from a summer's work on the trail crew in Kootenay National Park, I spent a night with TL and his wife in Nelson, BC. When I arrived, Mrs Lancaster played a joke on TL by having me pretend to be a beggar asking for help. It was a sad day when he died, aged fifty, on 16 July 1951 in Penticton, BC. His widow soon settled in Victoria, remained in touch with my parents, and was thus a link with John and Susan.

TL was born at Dean in Cumberland. He appears, aged nine months, in the 1901 census, the youngest of five children living with their widowed mother, Mary, aged forty-one, keeper of the Bee Hive Inn at Deensdale, Cumberland. His three brothers and one sister, all born at Lamplugh, Cumberland, allow us to trace the family to the 1891 census. It shows TL's eldest brother, John, and their mother Mary living at Kirkland, Lamplugh, with Mary's husband, their father. He was William Lancaster, an "Iron Ore Miner" aged thirty-eight, born at Lamplugh. Earlier census records suggest that William had had a troubled life. In 1881, he was living alone with his unmarried mother, aged sixty, at Relton near Lamplugh, and in 1871 and 1861, he and his mother were keeping house for her cousin, an "Iron Ore Miner" named William Wood, also unmarried. Their livelihood evidently came from the iron mining industry for which Lamplugh was noted. The town was north of the Lake District, eight miles south of Cockermouth and nine miles east of the little port of Whitehaven.
Sources: Notes courtesy of Susan (Lancaster) Ferguson, a daughter; census 1901, England, RG 13/4882, p. 8; census 1891, RG 12/4312, p. 29; census 1881, RG 11/5184, p. 34; census 1871, RG 10/5252, p. 22; census 1861, RG 9/3945, p. 4; *Colonist*, 1 May 1936, p. 13; 24 July 1951, p. 5, obit and photo; *Saanich Peninsula and Gulf Islands Review*, vol. 39, no. 29 (18 July 1951), p. 1, obit.

LANG, Albert Veysey (1879-1940). He was born on 14 November 1879 at Newport, Monmouthshire, served in the Imperial Yeomanry in the South African War and was living as an married "builder" at RMD No. 3, Cary Road, Victoria, when he enlisted on 13 March 1917. He had married Gertrude Mary Burridge (c. 1879-1973) on 3 June 1915 at Central Park. She was born at Bristol, daughter of a "produce broker," Edward Burridge, and his wife Henrietta, who in 1891 were living at Garston, Lancashire, and by then had three sons, Mrs Lang's younger brothers (also a cook and a nurse). The family moved out to Canada, where the parents were living at 54 Ruby Street, Winnipeg, when the youngest son, Arthur John Burridge, born at Liverpool on 28 June 1886, enlisted in Vancouver on 9 November 1914. He was then an electrician with no military experience. The two elder Burridge sons, Mrs Lang's brothers, served in the RAF. AL died, aged sixty-one, on 5 July 1940 at his home, "Morello," Carey Road, Saanich, leaving his wife, a son, and a daughter at home; three brothers and three sisters all in England; and his Burridge brothers-in-law on the Island. Gertude Mary Lang, *née* Burridge, died much later, aged ninety-four, on 23 November 1973 in Victoria.

Sources: NAC, CEF files box 5368-3; NAC, CEF files, box 1313-6; census 1881, England, RG 11/2483; census 1891, RG 12/3005, p. 30; *Colonist*, 7 July 1940, p. 5, obit.

LANGLEY, Hon. Alfred John (1820-1896). He went to Victoria in 1858, year of the Cariboo gold rush, and founded the wholesale drug firm of Langley & Co. in partnership with his brother James Langley, who died in November 1895. The gold rush in California in 1849 had attracted them to San Francisco, and there they had founded the Langley & Michaels Company, which grew to be one of the largest pharmaceutical firms in the city. Born in Lichfield, Staffordshire, on 15 October 1820, AL went first to Nova Scotia when he was young along with his brother James, with whom he subsequently rushed off to both western gold fields.

In Victoria, the governor James Douglas soon appointed AL to the Legislative Council and in 1862 sent him to London as commissioner for the colony during the great exhibition of that year. Interested in public affairs, he advertised the colony in London and did what he could to attract investments to the Island as well as to other parts of British North America. It was while he was in London that year that he arranged for the publication of a short book he had written earlier, *A Glance at British Columbia and Vancouver Island* (1862). On 13 October 1862, he attended a meeting of the British North American Association at a London tavern chaired by R. W. Crawford, who had shipping interests. Also present were London bankers, businessmen, and members of Parliament, as well as several men from Canada, including "Hon. A. T. Galt, late finance minister of Canada." It appears that the British North America Association had been formed several months earlier, on 31 January 1862, at the same place under the same chairman, to discuss railways proposed for Ontario and the Maritime Provinces. AL reported that he was offered a knighthood that year but felt he should decline and return to Victoria. When he did so, it was with a wife, Mary Edwin (born in Dublin) whom he had married while in England that year. His pharmaceutical firm grew over the years at 31 Yates Street, and he founded a branch of it in the new town of Vancouver, which suddenly appeared in 1887 where the Canadian Pacific Railway reached the coast. AL and his wife made their home in Victoria on Fairfield Road at "The Maples" and there brought up several children as Reformed Episcopalians. Mrs Langley died in 1876, but AL lived for another twenty years. He died, aged seventy-five, on 9 April 1896, survived by two daughters and three sons, notably *William Henry Langley, a barrister, and Dr A. F. Langley. If the several other Langleys on the Island were related to AL, the relationship is not obvious.

Sources: *Colonist*, 10 April 1896, p. 5, obit.; *The Times* (London), 14 August 1862, p. 7, col. E; A. J. Langley, *A Glance at British Columbia and Vancouver Island* (R. Hardwicke, 1862), 44 pp.; Gosnell, *The Year Book*, p. 362.

LANGLEY, Sergeant William Harold (1876-1946). He was born on 14 August 1879 at New Ferry, Cheshire, where the census recorded him, aged five, living with his grandparents at 7 Grove Road, Lower Bebington, New Ferry, the grandfather working as a gardener and his wife and daughters as dressmakers. Ten years later, WL, aged fifteen, was a "soap stamper" still living with them. He enlisted in the Grenadier Guards, served for five years and then another two years in the 104th Regiment, fought through the South African War, and then migrated to BC. When he enlisted in the CEF on 23 September 1914 at Valcartier, he was working as an "engineer" and his wife, Gertrude Blanche Langley, was living at Hazel Court, Chilliwack, BC. They lived on in BC after the war and a daughter married Kenneth Castley of Cowichan Lake. WL died, aged seventy, on 22 May 1946 near Duncan when he drove off the road at Lloyd's Hill, Westholme, and hit a fallen tree, which went through the windshield. He had been on his way to visit the Castleys at Lake Cowichan. Most references to "W. H. Langley" in BC during his lifetime were not to him but to *Major William Henry Langley.
Sources: NAC, CEF files box 5379-36; census 1881, England, RG 11/3571, p. 17; census 1891, RG 12/2874, p. 18; *Cowichan Leader*, 30 May 1946, obit.

LANGLEY, Major William Henry (1868-1951). He was born on 13 February 1868 in Victoria, one of the three sons of Hon. Alfred John Langley (1820-1896), a native of Lichfield, Staffordshire, who had migrated to Nova Scotia, then in 1849 to California, where he had founded a wholesale pharmaceuticals company, Langley & Michaels. In 1858, he followed the gold rush to Victoria, where he and his brother James established a similar company, Langley & Co., which soon became the town's biggest pharmaceutical firm, ultimately with a branch in Vancouver. WL's mother, Mary Edwin Langley, died soon after his birth in 1868. Twenty years later, WL's father died on 9 April 1896 leaving two daughters and three sons, notably a Dr A. F. Langley and WL, who had been accepted by the BC Bar in 1890 after attending Trinity College School, Port Hope, Ontario, and the Inns of Court in London. The 1901 census in Victoria found WL, aged thirty-three, established as a barrister at 233 Fort Street, and on 3 January 1906, he married Gladys Annie Mona Baiss, daughter of J. S. Baiss.

After serving in the ranks of the Fifth Regiment of Canadian Garrison Artillery in 1887-1890, he went on as a commissioned officer in 1890-1896 and joined the CEF as a captain on 23 October 1915. He was sent overseas with the Sixty-second Battalion, promoted to major in August, and transferred to the Twenty-ninth Battalion and First Division Signals. Returning to Victoria in 1918, he was appointed officer in charge of War Service Gratuities until demobilized in 1919. They were living at 645 Foul Bay Road in 1915 but now moved to 2657 Cavendish Road and later to 1031 Terrace Avenue, Oak Bay, with his barrister's office at 625 Fort Street. He began to take a lively interest in public affairs and on 9 January 1921 published an article in the *Daily Colonist* entitled "Vancouver Island as a Crown Colony with Free Trade." He thought of the Island as "the England of the Pacific," which needed, for geographical and economic reasons, to be able to direct its own destiny. In 1922, he became clerk of the house in the BC legislature. He was active in veterans' circles and, for instance, was one of those who proposed a toast at a concert held by the Army and Navy Veterans Association to celebrate the formal opening of their new premises on 12 April 1924. His eldest daughter married *Lieutenant Colonel Richard Clive Cooper on 6 December 1930 in Victoria, and her sister Mona went to London in September 1938 to take up a post with the Empire Parliamentary Association of Westminster Hall. A keen yachtsman throughout his adult life, he was a staunch member of the Royal Victoria Yacht Club, served for a time as its commodore, sailed out of Oak Bay in his yacht *Viola*, and achieved a certain renown in 1933 when he and his wife sighted the famous local sea-monster, *Cadborosaurus*, near Chatham Island, about three miles from Oak Bay. Others had seen it at the same time, and all judged it to be a huge creature about eighty feet long, moving along the sea in loops like a monstrous snake. He died, aged eighty-two, on 22 February 1951 in Victoria, leaving his wife, a son, and three daughters, and was buried as an Anglican.

Sources: NAC, CEF files, box 5379-37; *Who's Who in B.C.*, 1937-38-39, p. 80; *Colonist*, 9 January 1921, p. 12; 4 September 1938, p. 7; 5 May 1940, Sunday Section, pp. 1 and 3; *Victoria Daily Times*, 6 December 1930, p. 6; 5 October 1933, p. 1; Terry Reksten, *A Century of Sailing, 1892-1992: A History of the Oldest Yacht Club on Canada's Pacific Coast* (Victoria, Orca Book Publishing, 1992), pp. 19-20, 35, 37, 39, 46, 60, 62, 83, 91, 106, 117, 129-130, 143, 217; Ursula Jupp, *Cadboro: A Ship, A Bay, A Sea-Monster, 1842-1958* (Victoria, Jay Editions, 1988), 71 pp.;

LASCELLES, Lieutenant Commander Hon. Horace Douglas (1835-1869). He was born in 1835, seventh son of Henry, Third Earl of Harewood (1797-1857), of "Harewood House," a stately home built in 1759 near Leeds, Yorkshire. HL joined the Royal Navy in 1848 and in 1860 arrived at the Esquimalt Station as first lieutenant on HMS *Topaze*. From 1862 to 15 June 1865, he commanded the station as lieutenant commander of HM gunboat *Forward* and led several punitive expeditions against native tribes. He also invested in real estate and by investing became one of the proprietors of the Harewood Coal Mining Company, when it hired Robert Dunsmuir to manage operations at their mine near Esquimalt. Upon his retirement with the rank of commander, he returned to Victoria, where he died nearby at Esquimalt on 15 June 1869 and was buried in the naval cemetery next day, the same day that Governor Frederick Seymour (1820-1869) was buried there. Lascelles Mountain was named after his father.

HL's grandnephew, the sixth earl, faced after the Second World War with 75 percent death duties, considered offering the house to the National Trust, and in November 1947, James Lees-Milne was entertained there by the earl's wife, HRH Victoria Alexandra Windsor, sister of George VI, with this in view. He liked her but thought she was naive when she said that whatever happened, the family must not emigrate or desert the country—did Lees-Milne know that the earl's granduncle had died at Esquimalt? The rooms in Harewood House struck him as "superb and the long gallery one of the noblest apartments I have seen in an English house." The National Trust did not, as it turned out, acquire the house, but it survived under other auspices.

Sources: Walbran, *B.C. Coast Names*, p. 301; Paul M. Koroscil, *British Columbia: Settlement History* (Vancouver, Department of Geography, Simon Fraser University, 2000), pp. 4-8; Koroscil, "Robert Dunsmuir: A Portrait of a Western Capitalist," in *Canadian Frontier*, eds., Gordon Stewart and Brian Antonson (Richmond, BC, 1978), p. 17; James Audain, *Alexander Dunsmuir's Dilemma* (Vancouver, 1964), p. 23; James Lees-Milne, *Some Country Houses and their Owners* (1975; Penguin Books, 2009), pp. 99-104.

LAUNDRY, George Herbert (c. 1879-1960). Born at Port Isaac, Cornwall, he served as a trooper in the South African Constabulary, and in 1901 the census record found him working as an able seaman aged twenty-two aboard the sailing schooner *Amy*, then at Fowy. He retired later to the Island, married Elizabeth Mary Rowland on 21 July 1926 at Fulford Harbour, Salt Spring Island, and died, aged eighty-one, on 30 January 1960 in Saanich.
Sources: census 1901, England, RG 13/2209, p. 72; Records of St Stephen's Church, Mt Newton Cross Road, VI.

LAWS, Lieutenant Colonel Henry William (1876-1954), CMG (1919), DSO (1915). Born in London in 1876, son of Richard William Laws, he became a mining engineer and in 1902-1903 worked in West Africa as chief mining manager and engineer of the Niger Company. He led three prospecting expeditions into Bauchai Province, where he found the rich alluvial tin deposits in the Garra Mountains of the Badiko District. When these were developed, they became an important part of Nigeria's economy, and he moved the company's headquarters from Naraguta to Jos. There he built a bungalow he called "Tudun Wada," which later became a residence for the governor of Nigeria. HL was a member of the Institute of Mining and Metallurgy. In August 1914, he joined the Royal Naval Division and took part in the Antwerp Expedition. Later, in Gallipoli, he raised a tunnelling company called the Eighth Corps Mining Company for underground defence of the trenches, and later he commanded similar forces in France. Decorated for these services, he retired about 1930 to Saanich with his wife, Grace Margaret Laws, *née* Davidson, daughter of Thomas Davidson of Tulloch. They lived at 2410 Queenswood Drive, where he spent more than twenty years gardening, motoring, and building and altering his houses. When he died, aged seventy-seven, on 19 December 1954, the funeral was at Christ Church Cathedral and he left his wife, a son, a granddaughter, and two sisters in England.
Sources: *Who was Who*, 1951-1960, p. 642; Jennifer Nell Barr, *Saanich Heritage Structures: An Inventory* (Victoria, 1991), p. 16; *Colonist*, 21 December 1954, p. 22, obit.

LAYARD, Lieutenant Colonel Brownlow Villiers (1838-1924). He was born on 3 January 1838 at Riversdale, near Dublin, to an Anglo Irish branch of a family thought to have been Huguenot refugees from Montpellier. A better-known branch included civil servants and army officers in Ceylon, notably Sir Austen Henry Layard (1817-1894), distinguished diplomat, archaeologist, and son of

Henry P. J. Layard of the Ceylon Civil Service. BL obtained a commission in the Ninth Regiment of Foot and served as ensign and lieutenant from February 1855 to 27 December 1862. Then he "sold out and re-entered the Army in 1863," in order to join his father's regiment, the Twenty-eighth Foot Battalion of the First Gloucester Regiment, known later as the Gloucesters. With them and later with the West Indian Regiment, he was stationed at Hong Kong, in Sierra Leone (October 1863 to August 1865), the West Indies (August 1865 to May 1870), and in Malta as aide-de-camp to the staff of the governor (May 1872 to January 1875). By January 1875, after a few years in England (March to October 1863, May 1870 to May 1872), he had served on full pay for nine years and 156 days and on half pay for two years and 144 days. He retired with the rank of lieutenant colonel in 1882 and on 4 November 1882 married Clara Lattey, daughter of Robert John Lattey, JP. After living for some time in Ireland, they migrated in 1906 to a property on the south shore of the Booth Canal near Vesuvius Bay at the north end of Salt Spring Island, where their two sons, *Arthur Raymond and *Henry Camville Layard, had been farming for several months. Their first house was a pre-cut, packaged wooden house purchased in New Westminster and barged over to Booth Bay, where they called it "Riversdale" after a place in Ireland. They occasionally visited Victoria, which could be reached by road or rail from North Cowichan after a short crossing to Crofton or from the south end of Salt Spring Island by way of the Saanich Peninsula or by sea on small coastal steamers. These sometimes served the Gulf Islands better than they do now. On 22 December 1907, the *Colonist* (p. 18) reported "Colonel and Mrs B. V. Layard of Vesuvius Bay are at the Balmoral [Hotel, Victoria] for a few days." But to shorten the journey, the family moved in 1915 to Deep Cove, North Saanich.

What prompted this move was the outbreak of the Great War, which aroused deep feelings of anxiety and Imperial loyalty expressed, for instance, in a letter from BL printed in the *Colonist* on 5 November 1914:

> Sir—I would suggest that various localities should make an alphabetical roll of the name and place of birth of the men who have volunteered for the service of Great Britain and the cause the British Dominions represent, viz. Justice between man and man, and to prevent the weak being trampled on by the iron heel of the bully.
>
> In time, perhaps sooner than we think—the God of Battles may be pleased to end this bloody and uncalled for war—we hope to welcome back the victors to their various homes, but many will go to Christ in the trenches, or be lost on the stricken field, their burial place unknown until the day when land and sea will give up their dead. It therefore now behoves us, whilst it is still day, to record the names of all, so that in a few years our descendants may know `who stood for God and right', as we know today in England in the village rolls who stood up against the Armada.
>
> Offering my suggestion for what it is worth.

His sons all soon qualified for the roll of volunteer he was recommending.

At Deep Cove, BL was a keen and fair-minded observer of public affairs. Late in April 1917, he wrote again to the *Colonist* in opposition to a suggestion for a cannery at Cowichan Bay on the other side of Saanich Inlet. He thought it would be monstrous to deplete the fish stocks and ruin the fishing there while the young men were away at the war. "Remember, Cowichan and all the Inlet . . . feeds the Indians, who might starve as far as the alien speculator cares." He died, aged eighty-five, on 27 December 1924 and was buried in the churchyard of Holy Trinity (Anglican), Patricia Bay, leaving his widow and three sons, the least known of them reported in the *Colonist* obituary as "Commander C. B. Layard, D.S.O., serving aboard H.M.S. *Cyclops* at Malta." Among the pallbearers were *Lieutenant Colonel Charles Bayard Messiter, *Lieutenant Colonel Cyrus Wesley Peck, *Lieutenant Colonel William Harwood Belson, *Brigadier General Reginald John Gwynne, and Lindley Crease (1867-1940).

Sources: Notes dated 1 January 1875, kindly sent to me by Mrs Geraldine Layard, who recalled that her late husband, one of BL's sons, obtained documents at the regimental museum in Gloucestershire; notes from Camville Layard Jr, grandson of Colonel B. V. Layard; Kahn, *Salt Spring Island*, pp. 153, 157; *Colonist*, 22 December 1907, p. 18; 5 November 1914, p. 4; 27 April 1917, p. 9; 30 December 1924, obit., 31 December, p. 5; Thomas K. Ovanin, *Island Heritage Buildings: A Selection of Heritage Buildings in the Islands Trust Area* (Victoria, Island Trust, 1984), p. 18.

LAYARD, Group Captain and Major Arthur Raymond (c. 1889-1967). Born at Ryde on the Isle of Wight, son of *Lieutenant Colonel Brownlow Villiers Layard and his wife, Clara Layard *née* Lattey (c. 1851-1945), he was a younger brother of *Henry Camville Layard. In 1905 or 1906, these two brothers came out to farm at the north end of Salt Spring Island and were joined there soon afterwards by their parents. AL served in the Royal Flying Corps in the Great War. After the war, he and his brother returned to Deep Cove, where they opened a machine shop and marina in the south corner of Deep Cove, next to what is now the government wharf, a friendly place that I well remember from my childhood. They also built four houses in the area: one for their parents, one each for themselves, and a fourth for their mother's sister, Mary Lattey, who had also emigrated from England. But they maintained strong friendships on Salt Spring Island and spent much time there. In February 1931, for instance, they spent a weekend as guests of their relative, N. W. Wilson of "Barnsbury" on Salt Spring Island, and were active in the Salt Spring Island Conservative Association during the 1930s. At some time in the middle 1930s, they bought a house at Rainbow Beach, "Rainbow Beach Camp," where they lived for long periods and welcomed members of the family from Deep Cove and friends such as the architect, *Major Karl Branwhite Spurgin, ex-British Army, and his wife. They organized a tennis tournament in August 1939 with a shooting gallery on the side run by *Captain V. C. Best; another neighbouring officer, *Colonel A. B. Snow, presented trophies to the local Cubs. AL was alert to public affairs, was elected to committee of the Salt Spring Island Development Association, and wrote to the Victoria newspapers in May 1928 under the heading

"Where credit is due" to correct a couple of U.S. reports crediting Americans with certain deeds, which had, in fact, been British. In the Second World War, he enlisted in the RCAF, served mainly at Trenton, and retired with the rank of group captain. Many missed him when he died, aged seventy-eight, on 5 April 1967 at Ganges.

Sources: Notes courtesy of Camville Layard and Mrs Geraldine Layard dated 15 August and 2 October 2000; *Colonist*, 15 May 1928, p. 4, L to E; 4 January 1929, p. 8; 17 February 1931, p. 6; 24 May 1933, p. 15; 12 August 1934, p. 10; 22 May 1936, p. 7; 15 November 1936, p. 12; 15 August 1939, p. 7; 6 February 1940, p. 9;

LAYARD, Henry Camville (c. 1886-1960). Born at Rochester, Kent, son of *Lieutenant Colonel Brownlow Villiers Layard, in 1905 he went out to the north end of Salt Spring Island with his brother *A. R. Layard and farmed (or "ranched" as the term then was) until the Great War. Early in the war, on 10 October 1914, while still at their island home and before enlisting, HL married Constance Langford Frances Pellew (1887-1979), descendant of a distinguished English family which counted among their ancestors Admiral Edward Pellew, First Viscount Exmouth (1757-1833), who already had a connection with Vancouver Island, having been godfather of the pioneering attorney general, Sir Henry Pering Pellew Crease (1853-1905). HL enlisted in the RNVR on 2 July 1916, embarked on 7 July 1916 to go overseas from Montreal to Liverpool on SS *Grampian*, at the expense of the British government, and served mostly in the North Atlantic and the Mediterranean on HMS *Hermine*, *HMML 408*, HMS *Catania*, then *Hermine* again. At last on 15 February 1919, he embarked as a passenger on SS *Canada* at Liverpool for the voyage to what had become home. We know all this from his post-war application for a British War Gratuity, which brought him 120 pounds sterling.

After the war, he and his brother A. R. Layard opened a machine shop and marine in the south corner of the Cove, next to what is now the government wharf. HL and his wife were active in the life of the neighbourhood and the peninsula. They also spent much time on Salt Spring Island, like the rest of the family. At the annual concert and dance of the Island's Choral Society in April 1937, for instance, "Mrs C. H. Layard rendered, in her usual effective manner, two violin solos: Bach's *Air*, and a Russian melody." I recall HL serving during the Second World War as a cheerful member of the North Saanich branch of the Pacific Coast Militia Rangers, a kind of home guard of elderly men and a few Boy Scouts; he was active in our weekly target practice on a three-hundred-yard rifle range that the PCMR built on Tapping Road, Deep Cove. HL died, aged seventy-three, on 30 October 1960 in Sidney and Mrs. Constance Layard, aged ninety-two, on 9 October 1979 in North Saanich.

Sources: Notes from Camville Layard Jr, grandson of Colonel B. V. Layard; census 1901, England, RG 13/1025, p. 26; BNA, RG 9 series II-F-10 (British War Gratuities): vol. 160 file no. 10775-H-32; Kahn, *Salt Spring Island*, pp. 153, 157; Thomas K. Ovanin, *Island Heritage Buildings: A Selection of Heritage Buildings in the Islands Trust Area* (Victoria, Island Trust, 1984), p. 18; *Colonist*, 30 April 1937, p. 3.

LAYBORN, Captain Algernon Thomas B. (c. 1871-1957). He was born at "Byways," Broadstairs, Kent, as was his brother, Lieutenant Colonel Sidney Picton Layborn (c. 1865-1940). They were sons of Thomas R. Layborn, a "Licensed Victualler," and his wife Charlotte. The 1871 census found them living at home at 9 Northfleet, Gravesend; the 1881 census found them at "The Grammar School," Aspenden (near Buntingford), along with another brother named Percival Layborn, aged eleven. In 1891, AL was living as a "licensed Vict. Manager" in Finsbury Park, London, with his widowed father, and in 1901, Sidney Picton Layborn was a captain in the army boarding at the Albemarle Hotel, Brighton, Sussex, and recorded for some unexplained reason as born in Australia. From 1898 to 1907, the latter served in the Royal Canadian Rifles and in the South African War and won the Queen's Medal and five clasps. They both settled in Victoria, where AL lived for a time at 2065 Oak Bay Avenue and died there, aged eighty-six, on 24 October 1957, leaving his wife Laura, a son, and a daughter. SL went back to England and died there, aged seventy in 1940.
Sources: *Colonist*, 5 January 1940, p. 6, obit.; 26 October 1957, p. 18, obit.; census 1871, England, RG 10/895, p. 25; census 1881, RG 11/1409; census 1901, RG 13/921, p. 18 (13?); Brian A. Reid, *Our Little Army in the Field: The Canadians in South Africa*, 1899-1902 (St Catharines, Ont., Vanwell Publishing Ltd., 1996), pp. 46, 152; R. C. Fetherstonhaugh, *The Royal Canadian Regiment*, 1883-1933 (Fredericton, Centennial Print & Litho Ltd., 1981), pp. 59, 87, 417.

LEACOCK, Henry William (c. 1874-1956). He was born in Islington, London, son of Fannie Eliza Leacock and her husband Henry Leacock, an "Under Registrar at Royal Academy," and at sixteen, he joined the Honourable Artillery Company. The 1891 census found him as a private in the Royal Marines posted at Shannon. After ten years of service, he retired as a sergeant major, joined the City of London Imperial Volunteers for the South African War, and came away with the Queen's Medal and three bars. In the Great War, he became a sergeant in the Twenty-third Anti-Tank Battery, RCA, by lying about his age as being forty-four and ended the war as regimental sergeant major in the First Brigade Canadian Field Artillery. After the war, he became government storekeeper at Banff National Park for twenty-six years and retired in 1942 though he went on to serve for another ten years in the Corps of Commissionaires at Victoria. When he died in Victoria in September 1956, leaving his wife and four sons, he was a freeman of the city of London.
Sources: NAC, CEF files, box 5483-47; *Colonist*, 11 September 1956, p. 5, obit., and photo; census 1881, England, RG 11/277, p. 23; census 1891, RG 12/1743; census 1901, RG 13/5332.

LEADER, Lieutenant Colonel Lionel Frederick (1870-?). Born in 1870 in County Cork, Ireland, son of Captain Henry Leader, he was schooled at Tenby, Pembrokeshire, and at Winchester House. He was commissioned in the King's Regiment (1891), became a major (1908), and a lieutenant colonel (1920). The 1901 English census found him, already an infantry captain, living at 7 Greenkeys Road, Toxtell Park, Liverpool, with his wife Mabel, born in Manchester, and a two-year-old son, Eustace. During the Great War, he served in Africa (1915), Mesopotamia (1916), and France (1916-1918). Badly wounded in Mesopotamia, he retired in 1922 to a place on Gibbins Road, Duncan, VI, where he joined the Cowichan Country Club and lived a quiet life, though he travelled back to Britain in 1926-1927 and returned on the CPR vessel, *Montcalm*. He was apparently not well settled on the Island, as he stayed a while in 1934 at the James Bay Hotel and then disappeared.

Sources: *Who's Who in B.C.* 1933-1934, p. 107; *Colonist*, 19 May 1934, p. 8; census 1881, Wales, RG 11/6409, pp. 38-39; census 1901, England, RG 13/3436, p. 11; NAC, RG76, *immigration series* C-1-c, 1927, vol. 1, p. 26, microfilm reel T-14848.

LEECH, Peter John (c. 1827-1899), RE. Born to an Anglo-Irish family of Dublin, he joined the Royal Engineers and served in the Crimean War and in Egypt before being sent to BC with the Royal Engineers in 1859. When they left in 1863, he was one of the many who remained and was active in a variety of occupations before settling at Esquimalt as a telegraph clerk and postmaster. In the 1881 census, he was recorded as a surveyor's assistant living in the Metchosin and Esquimalt district, and the 1891 census marked him as a Unitarian. He had many adventures while surveying northern BC, laid out Bella Coola townsite, managed a Hudson's Bay store, and became city engineer of Victoria. As lieutenant and astronomer, he accompanied the Vancouver Island Exploring Expedition led by Dr Robert Brown, a government agent, in 1864. The Leech River in the Sooke district was named after him when about $100,000 in gold was taken from it.

Then he joined a party sent to survey the route for the overland telegraph line, which was intended to reach across British Columbia, Alaska, Siberia, and Russia to the European capitals. This work was abandoned on the successful completion of the second Atlantic cable. Leech was later city engineer of Victoria and took part in many important works throughout the province. In 1873, he married Mary Macdonald, one of four sisters who arrived on the bride ship, *Tynemouth*, and Mrs Leech became well known as the organist in Rev. Edward Cridge's Reformed Episcopal Church. They lived near Beacon Hill Park in an ugly two-storey house they called "Avalon" on a site where the Goodacre Towers apartment was built later. He died, aged seventy-three, on 6 June 1899 in Victoria.

Sources: Beth Hill, *Sappers: The Royal Engineers in British Columbia* (Ganges, BC, Horsdal & Shubert, 1987), pp. 137-9; Harry Gregson, *A History of Victoria, 1842-1970* (Victoria, Victoria Observer Publishing Co., 1970), p. 58-9; Walbran, *B.C. Coast Names*, p. 303; Canadian census, 1881 and 1891 for BC.

LEARY, Captain Charles Sidney (1883-1950?). He was born on 2 November 1883 at "Hurkhurst" [Hawkhurst] in Kent, northwest of Tunbridge, son of an Irish father, Rev. H. C. Leary (Anglican) and an English mother, who took him to Canada in 1890. As a young man, he worked in London, Ontario, as an editor. Moving to BC, he went into the lumbering business at Nakusp, where he joined the militia, the 102nd RMR at Kamloops. When he signed up for the CEF at New

Westminster on 17 January 1917 as a lieutenant in the 225th Battalion, CEF, he was working at Nakusp as a "lumber contractor." He was Anglican. His next of kin was a friend, as he had no relatives. He served from 5 January to 12 August 1916 in the 105th Rocky Mountain Rangers, from 12 August 1916 to 1 February 1917 in the 225th Battalion, and from 14 February to 1 May 1917 in the Sixteenth Reserve Battalion. From November 1917 to October 1918, he was serving in the Royal Canadian Forestry Corps as a member of the Technical Board of Examiners whose duty it was to examine all officers and men as to their technical qualifications, this at Windsor and Virginia Water for the director of Timber Operations. Then he was sent to Egypt on a special mission, but his ship, SS *Aragon*, was torpedoed and sunk on the way. Soon after arriving in Egypt on 9 January 1918, he was sent to Cyprus by Brigadier General E. V. Paul "with special instructions regarding the possible exploitation of the forests of Cyprus." Eventually, it was decided to do nothing about those forests and so he returned to Egypt. Then, as General Paul writes, "I directed him to proceed to G.H.Q., 1st Echelon, Palestine on the 20th April 1918 to interview Brigadier General Davis, D.S.T., regarding the firewood question and difficulty of water transport etc. On return to Cairo and pending provision of a passage to England, he carried out temporary duty as consultant in R.E. Timber Park, Port Said." Paul goes on to praise his work, all this in a letter of 3 June 1918.

While applying for a gratuity in 1920, CL was living at the Brett Hospital, Banff, and then at Calgary. In a long undated letter to the assistant adjutant general, Calgary, he explained his wartime service, adding to the above that "in November 1917 General McDougal, chief of the Forestry Corps, selected me to proceed on special mission to Egypt, with the Egyptian Expeditionary Force, on behalf of the British War Office . . . incidentally, I was torpedoed and sunk twice before reaching Alexandria. In June 1918, having completed the work laid out for me, I was recalled home and was again torpedoed off Malta, but not sunk. On reporting to General McDougal, London . . . I was sent to operate a proposition in the North of Scotland." In October 1918, he was sent to the First Canadian Reserve Battalion, Seaford, to serve a probationary period of one month. His purpose was to go to fight in France, but he never managed this and seems to have lost a rank in the attempt. After that, he was briefly in the First Reserve Battalion, Seaford, he was discharged as medically unfit, his health having suffered from his wartime hardships. At first, he went to Calgary but then retired to Victoria with his wife, Florence Jordan, whom he married at Nakusp on 29 December 1922. An Anglican, he was in the Knights of Pythias, the Canadian Legion, and the Union Club (Victoria), was elected to the BC Legislature for Kaslo-Slocan in 1924, re-elected several times, for example, in 1937 and 1945, became Liberal Party whip, and served at Victoria as minister of public works and railways early in the Second World War. Some sources say he died at Nakusp in 1950 but his death does not appear in BC official records.

Sources: *Colonist*, 6 December 1939, pp. 1-2; NAC, CEF records in RG 150, Box 5490-22; NAC, RG 9 series II-F-10 (British War Gratuities), Vol. 297, file no. 10792-C-119; census 1891, England, RG 12/695, p. 40.

LEE-WRIGHT, Lieutenant Colonel Harold (1882-1952). Born in Paddington, London, son of Lee Wright, a solicitor from Cape Town, South Africa, who in 1881 was already living in Kensington at 35 St Charles Square, he was recorded in the 1891 census as eight years old and living with his parents at 57 Waldgrove Road, Twickenham, Middlesex. His father was then described as a "Colonial Solicitor, Secretary to Public Companies," aged forty, and his mother was Helena Lee-Wright, aged twenty-six, born at Birkenhead, Cheshire. They had two servants. After schooling at St Paul's School, Hammersmith, he attended the Royal Military Academy, Woolwich, where the 1901 census recorded him as a "Gent. Cadet" while his parents were at 7 Metbury (Melbury) Mansion Flats, Kensington, London, with a cook and a parlourmaid. He emerged at the top of his class, therefore was able to choose his corps, and was commissioned in the Royal Engineers on 2 August 1902. After passing through the School of Military Engineering at Chatham, he went to Fort Monckton, Gosport, where he was trained in submarine mining. In spring 1905, he was sent to Sheerness for a course in the Brennan Torpedo, after which he was posted to 30 (Submarine Mining) Company at Plymouth. A year later, his unit was redesignated: "Fortress Company RE." In April 1906, he was posted on loan to Halifax, Nova Scotia, and in March 1907 to Victoria, BC, where he stayed for a year. While there, stationed at Work Point Barracks, he took part in the opening of the legislature and is to be seen in a photograph standing on the steps with Lieutenant Governor James Dunsmuir and many others. In April 1908, he was posted to 22 Fortress Company RE on the Isle of Wight, then attended a three-month advanced course at the SME, Chatham, in 1910 and on 15 October that year was appointed adjutant to the London District Telegraph Company RE (Army Troops), Westminster. In 1916, he joined the Expeditionary Force in France where he took troops to the battle of the Somme. In November 1916, he went to General Byng's Third Army Staff and was promoted to acting lieutenant colonel. About two months before the armistice, he left France and went to the Signal Service Training Centre at Maresfield, where he remained in a lieutenant colonel's appointment until February 1920. He was twice mentioned in despatches and was awarded the DSO. Back in England in 1919, he became OC of a demobilisation unit in Bedford, where his troops were called in to cope with riots in Luton. In 1920, he transferred to the Royal Corps of Signals and from 1923 to 1925 commanded the Rhine Signal Company in Cologne, Germany. In 1925, he was OC of Signals Company in Crowborough, Sussex, and his last appointment was as lieutenant colonel commanding the Depot Battalion from which he retired on 20 November 1929.

He then moved with his family to London, where he had been appointed chief engineer of the Racecourse Betting Control Board, which was setting up a public automatic system for placing bets. The board went out for bids to various manufacturers and received quotes on betting machines based on mechanical, hydraulic, pneumatic, and electrical devices. The device they chose was proposed by the British Telephone Company for an electrical system called the Totalisator (or "Tote" as it was soon named). As there were many race courses that had only a couple of meets a year, a portable device was needed as well as permanent installations at the larger race courses. Colonel Lee-Wright supervised the process from beginning to end in order to install the new machines throughout Britain, and this took four years. He then retired permanently and took his family to live on a boat in Cornwall.

HL had always wanted, however, to return to Canada, where he had so much enjoyed his time as a young man. He planned to go in 1936 but fell ill and was not able to come out with the family until March 1939. They then went to Victoria and built a small house at Deep Cove in North Saanich. It was there that Lancelot Lake met and married HL's daughter Valerie. When the Second World War broke out, CL offered his services and was appointed to the UK Technical Mission, which involved testing artillery at the gun-proving range in Hamilton, Ontario. Accordingly, he and his wife moved to Hamilton in March 1942, but unfortunately, after eighteen months, he became seriously ill and had to return to Deep Cove. While there, he served with the Pacific Coast Militia Rangers and took part in setting up communications for air raid and enemy-landing precautions. He managed to acquire some old army telephones, perhaps through his old army cronies at Work Point Barracks, and his daughters recalls that he ran a line from his house on Chalet Road all along Tatlow Road and up the side of Cloake Hill to Francis Barber-Starkey's house. Meanwhile, his daughter Valerie stayed for a time in Ontario working in the British Admiralty Technical Mission Offices in Ottawa. She remembers later a "mock disaster exercise in 1942, when we anticipated a Japanese invasion such as had occurred all around the Pacific Ocean littoral, in which my mother and other women manned the Deep Cove community hall stocked with pillows, blankets, crockery, canned food etc., and I was in a van (don't know who drove it) with Gilbert Baal . . . and Grace Meares, a teenage girl who lived on the West Saanich Road down the hill near Tatlow Road. The van was supposed to be the ambulance, and we were the stretcher bearers." Gilbert Baal worked in the drug store on Beacon Avenue, Sidney, kept by his father (an immigrant from the Channel Islands). Grace Meares was ahead of her time in behaving as a kind of high school female commando who used to drill a company of girl cadets during my years at the school. CL died, aged seventy, on 1 December 1952 and was buried at Holy Trinity Anglican Church, Patricia Bay.

Sources: Notes and documents kindly sent by Mrs Valerie Lake, *née* Lee-Wright, in August 2000; census 1881, England, RG 11/41, p. 37; census 1891, RG 12/1027, p. 28; census 1901, RG 13/569, p. 48; census 1901, RG 13/22, p. 12.

LEGGE-WILLIS, Arthur Elwyn (1869-1951). He was born at Peshawar, India (now in Pakistan), son of Colonel James Legge-Willis of the Indian Army. The 1881 census recorded him, aged nine, as a student at "Westholme," Titchfield near Fareham, under a headmistress called Jane Jeffries. In 1905, he and his wife Edith O. Legge-Willis settled in the Okanagan Valley, BC, where he worked for many years as manager of a fruit farm. During the Great War, they lived for a time on Thetis Island but in 1919 went to Victoria, where they lived at 2810 Tudor Road, Saanich. He was prominent in amateur theatricals, and they attended an Anglican church. He died at the Jubilee Hospital, aged eighty-two, on 21 August

1951, leaving his wife, a daughter in England, Mrs H. K. Leghorn, and a son John William Arthur Legge-Willis.

This son, born on 16 September 1898 at Herne Bay, Kent, went to Canada at an early age with his parents and was a wireless operator by the time he enlisted on 22 April 1916 in Victoria. With 195 days as a member of the RCGA, he soon had a commission as lieutenant.

Sources: NAC, CEF files, box 10421-27; census 1881, England, RG 11/1170, p. 3; *Colonist*, 23 August 1951, pp. 16 and 22, obit.

LEIGHTON, Captain Arthur (1880-1953). He was born on 5 January 1880 at Wakefield, Yorkshire, son of Robert L. Leighton, "M.A. (Oxon) Master of Grammar School and born at Broughton, Lancashire, and Mary E. A. Leighton from Wakefield. The 1881 census found him, aged one, living with them, a younger brother, and a sister, and there were four teenaged boys in the house as "scholars," as well as a cook, a laundress, and two nurses. Ten years later, the family was larger, with five sons and two daughters, living at "Master's Ho," 65 Elton Road, Bristol.

He moved to Manitoba, where he worked as a farmhand until 1902, when he enlisted in the Second Canadian Mounted Rifles and served in the South African War. Upon returning, he took up law at the University of Manitoba and was called to the Bar in 1908. Shortly after that, he married Alice Sophia Wright (1887-?), born at Britannia, Ontario, and in 1912, they moved to the Island, where he practised law at Nanaimo. In 1915, he went to Vancouver to enlist in the Seventy-second Seaforth Highlanders, Second Canadian Infantry Brigade, with a commission as lieutenant and was later promoted to captain. His wife followed him to England in 1916 and worked as a volunteer at St Dunstan's Hostel for Blind Soldiers and Sailors. Arthur was wounded in the knee and spent some time in England recovering before returning to France. In 1919, they returned to Nanaimo where Arthur went on practicing law and Alice worked in many charitable societies. For forty-one years, he was a well-known lawyer at Nanaimo and Departure Bay, eventually senior partner in the firm of Leighton, Meaken & Weir. He died, aged seventy-two, on 1 August 1953 at Essondale and she, aged seventy-two, on 24 July 1959 at Nanaimo.

Sources: Alice and Arthur Leighton Collection of photographs and 125 letters at Malaspina College, Nanaimo, BC; NAC, CEF files, box 5557-25; census 1881, England, RG 11/4576, p. 49; census 1891, RG 12/1964, pp. 14-15; *Colonist*, 4 August 1953, p. 6, obit.

LEWIS, Captain Herbert George (1828-1905). Born on 2 January 1828 at Aspeden, Hertfordshire, he attended Cheltenham College but at age sixteen became a midshipman in the East India trade and made many voyages to India and China. In 1846, he was employed as Third officer of the barque *Cowlitz*, Captain Weynton, and arrived at Victoria in spring 1847. Leaving his vessel in Victoria, he was for a time stationed at Fort Simpson, but then returned to England. He returned to Victoria as Second officer on the HBC chartered barque, *Tory*, on her voyage to Victoria and thence home via China in 1850-1852. Next he was appointed

First officer of the HBC steamer *Otter* leaving England for the Pacific Coast in January 1853. On arriving at Victoria, he and the ship were put into coastal service with the *Beaver* and Lewis commanded various HBC ships in the next few years, notably the *Otter* and the *Labouchère*. Between 1854 and 1870, he often acted as pilot and interpreter on British naval ships, navigating the difficult inland passages on the coast, which was not well known then. In 1869, he visited England, where he married Mary Langford, daughter of Captain Edward E. Langford (1809-1895), a Brighton man who had spent several years as bailiff of Colwood Farm for the Puget Sound Agricultural Company, a subsidiary of the HBC Back at Victoria, HL and his wife lived at 114 Belville Street and acquired much property in and around the city. He stayed with the HBC until 1883 and was employed as agent in the Marine and Fisheries Department of Canada from April 1887 to September 1892. He worked thereafter as shipping master in Victoria until his death. His office was on a wharf at James Bay, His wife died on 17 May 1903 and he, aged seventy-seven, on 30 March 1905.

Sources: R. E. Gosnell, A *History of British Columbia* (The Hill Binding Co., 1906), 783 pp. in 4_, pp. 318-319; Canadian census, Victoria, 1901; Walbran, *B.C. Coast Names*, pp. 304-5.

LEWIS, James (c. 1828-1922). He was born at Cardiff, South Wales, and the 1851 census found him, aged thirty-two, living at Hull as "R. N. Able Seaman" with his wife Mary, aged thirty-five, a bookbinder. They had a daughter, aged fourteen then, and two more daughters and two sons later. He served through the Crimean War (1854-1856) and in actions in the Baltic Sea and also had a medal for taking part in the battle at Sevastopol. When he retired from the sea about 1870, he took his wife and daughter to the Island and settled at Nanaimo, where he became a charter member of the local lodge of the Ancient Order of Foresters and took an interest in local affairs. He is to be seen in a photograph of the oldest members of the British Campaigners' Association (1913). He died, aged ninety-four, on 9 January 1922, leaving his sons James and William and three daughters, all married.

Sources: *Nanaimo Free Press*, Monday 9 January 1922, obit.; census 1861, England, RG 9/3591, p. 12.

LEY, Captain Richard Halse (1881-1961). He was born on 1 September 1881 in South Kensington, London, one of the twin sons of Lieutenant Colonel Hugh Halse Ley (c. 1851-1906), a native of Helston, Cornwall, and his wife Edith Harriet Blagdon Hale (of the Hales of Bradely, Gloucestershire). The 1891 census found him, aged nine, living at 10 Kemmerton Road, Beckenham, Kent, with them, his twin brother Lindsay H. Ley, and his sister Victoria E. J. Ley, aged nine, born at Cottle, Wiltshire. An elder brother was already away at school and in due time became Lieutenant Colonel Arthur Edwin Hale Ley (1879-1963), OBE of the Royal Deccan Horse (Indian Army). A great uncle, Colonel John Morgan Ley (1794-1864), had served in the Madras Horse Artillery and had a son (Edwin Ley) who founded an Australian branch of the family. In 1891, RL and family had three servants. His father, aged thirty-nine, was then "London Manager to Gonzalez, Bryant Co. Sherry Shippers, Major 3rd Light Infantry" and was recorded in 1901 as a "Director of Schweppes" living with the family in Mornington Road, Bournemouth. By then, RL had attended Sherborne School, Dorset, and was finishing a course in London at Crystal Palace Engineering School. In 1901, he went to BC and worked until 1907 as an assayer at Hall Mines Smelter, Nelson, BC. In 1907, he married Jessie Marcia Blakeman and worked in 1907-1912 in the Mining and Customs Assayer Office and in 1912-1915 as sales agent for the Giant Powder Company. His wife died in childbirth in 1909 and when he joined the Eighty-eighth Battalion of the CEF on 6 January 1916, he named his sister Mrs Joan Bovill as his next of kin. He was living then at Willows Camp, Victoria, but later that year, he married Therese Janet Mesher. He served overseas during the Great War, at first as captain and adjutant of the Eighty-eighth Battalion, CEF, and First Reserve Battalion. He transferred to the Twenty-ninth Balloon Section of the RFC/RAF and in 1915-1919 served in Palestine, where he was twice mentioned in despatches.

His assaying job was not kept for him, and after the war, he and the family moved in 1921 to Victoria, where he became a controller of the Liquor Board of BC with offices in Victoria. They lived at various addresses, notably the Hampton Court Apts. on Cook Street. The children were sent to boarding school: John to various schools ending up at Shawnigan Lake in 1934 whence he joined the Navy in 1941 and went to Dartmouth and Sage was schooled at St Christopher's until sent to Strathcona Lodge School for Girls at Shawnigan (1936-1941). There were distant relatives in Victoria, such as Cecil Ley, a second cousin of RL's father, who was a master at St Michael's School in Victoria. RL died, aged seventy-nine, on 16 March 1961 in Victoria.

Sources: Notes courtesy of Mrs Sage German (a daughter), 8 Baldwin Street, Port Hope, Ontario, 11 February 2005; *Who's Who in B.C.*, 1933-34, p. 107; vol. V (1942-1943), p. 191; NAC, CEF files, box 5633-28; *Colonist*, 18 March 1961, p. 15, obit.; census 1891, England, RG 12/625, p. [illegible]; census 1901, RG 13/1041, p. 40.

LIDDIARD, Albert (1868-1951). Born probably on 24 October 1868 in Hammersmith, Middlesex, son of Charles Liddiard, "laundryman," and his wife Emily, "laundress," he was found by the 1881 census, aged twelve, living at 54 Junction Terrace, Acton, with them and his brother Horace Liddiard, aged fourteen, born at Hammersmith. They had a sister Clara Liddiard, aged twenty-one, a "Laundress," along with younger brothers and sisters. Their neighbours were a costermonger and a labourer. Evidently, AL and his brother Horace both crossed the Atlantic. Twenty years later, in 1901, Horace and his wife (a laundress) were living in Acton with their nine-year-old son born "in America." Meanwhile, AL served for twelve years with the British Army—the "14th ROH" (Regiment of Horse?)—in which he fought through the South African War.

Then he settled in Victoria, where he was working as a plasterer when he enlisted there in the CEF on 16 November 1914, citing his brother Horace, of

25 Leith Road, South Acton, London, as his next of kin. His age of eighty-four was cited at his death in August 1951 and details in the 1881 census together show that he lied about his age, as many did, when he enlisted, claiming to be thirty-eight and born in 1876. On returning after the Great War, he lived at 2251 Cadboro Bay Road, attended an Anglican Church and the Army, Navy, and Air Force Veterans Association, died aged eighty-four on 25 August 1951, and was buried at Colwood.

Sources: NAC, CEF files, box 5638-14; *Colonist*, 29 August 1951, p. 13, obit.; census 1881, England, RG 11/1355; census 1901, RG 13/1203, p. 41.

LIDDIARD, Thomas (1855-1929). Born at Aldbourne, Wiltshire, where he was living at "The Butts" in 1871, aged fourteen, with his mother "Eliza Pearce," aged fifty-six, who had remarried George Pearce, a sixty-nine-year-old "Carpenter employing one boy." The boy was TL, already recorded as a carpenter. His brother James, aged sixteen, was "a bricklayer's labourer," and there was a sister, Ann Liddiard, aged eighteen. The census recorded these children as "wife's son" or "wife's daughter." There were several other Liddiard families living in Aldbourne. The following year, 1882, TL joined the First Royal Sussex Regiment and served in the Egyptian campaign under Lord Wolseley. In 1893, he went to Canada, spent two years in Montreal, some time in Sacramento, California, and settled in Victoria in 1902; there he was a member of the Sons of St George and of the British Campaigners Association; he worked for some years as timekeeper *on construction work*. After living here for twenty-seven years, he died on 16 July 1929, leaving his widow, a son, and a niece, and was buried at Royal Oak.

Sources: *Colonist*, 17 July 1929, p. 5, obit.; census 1871, England, RG 10/1256, p. 11.

LIGHTBODY, Colonel James (1880-1947). Born in Glasgow, Scotland, he became a timber merchant there, prominent and successful enough to be made a JP and a Freeman Burgess of the city. He became a yachtsman on the Clyde and joined a territorial regiment in 1898. During the Great War, he was commissioned as a gunnery officer in the famous Fifty-second Lowland Division in which he served in Palestine under General Edmund Allenby, who mentioned him in despatches. JL's service also took him to France, Egypt, and Syria, and then he commanded a unit of brigade artillery with the Fifty-third Welsh Division. After the armistice (1918), he was in charge of demobilizing the Egyptian Expeditionary Force and did not return to civil life until September 1920. He was decorated with the DSO and the TD.

As a timber merchant, he had often visited Canada and in 1921 he and his wife, Ethel Tyner Lightbody, moved to 2040 Granite Street, Oak Bay, Victoria, to carry on as a timber exporter and to make their home. Early in the Second World War, he commanded an officers' voluntary training association in the Bay Street armouries composed of ex-officers from the Great War, and when the popular patriotic singer Gracie Fields visited a military hospital at Esquimalt in December 1941, she met and joked with him there. JL retired in August 1943 as auxiliary services officer, Pacific Command. After twenty-five years' residence in Victoria, he died, aged sixty-seven, on 9 December 1947 in Saanich, known as a member of the Union Club and the Canadian Legion, past president of the United Services Institution, past commodore of the former West Bay Corinthian Yacht Club at Esquimalt, and still a member of the Royal Clyde Yacht Club. Mrs Lightbody had died, aged fifty-four, in 1935 in Oak Bay, but he left six nephews in Glasgow and two stepdaughters in Vancouver.

Sources: *Colonist*, 4 October 1921, p. 8; 15 May 1936, p. 5; 18 December 1941, p. 7; 12 August 1943, p. 11; 10 December 1947, pp. 1 and 15, obit., and photo.

LINDSAY, Colonel Frederick Archibald (1876-1938). He was born in Dundee, Scotland, schooled in Perth, and then spent a number of years on a bush station in Australia, where he became a border rider, cattle driver, and big-game hunter. He fought in the South African War and then in East Africa and stayed in Uganda to hunt big game. After spending some years in Dundee and London in the distillery business, he served as an officer in the British Army during the Great War. After the war, he spent time in western Canada and arrived in Victoria in March 1925 on a Canada-wide tour. He stayed at the Empress Hotel and addressed the Chamber of Commerce on 20 March.

Having decided to settle in Victoria, he brought his wife, Helen A. A. Lindsay whom he had married in Edinburgh in 1905, out from Perth, and they were soon active in the life of the city and the Island in general. In June 1934, he was made honorary colonel of the Second Battalion (MG), Canadian Scottish Regiment, which included units at Sooke, Duncan, Nanaimo, and on Salt Spring Island. A member of the Junior Constitutional Club of London and the Royal Automobile Club, he also joined the Union Club (Victoria), became a director of the Queen Alexandra Solarium, the Sunshine Inn, and other charities, took a lively interest in the local division of the Navy League, and was its president in 1932-1938. For four years, he was commodore of the Royal Victoria Yacht Club. He cruised the waters of the Gulf in his yacht, *Eileen*, and bought a summer house on Julia Island in the Gulf of Georgia. When four Vancouver youths were seen breaking and entering the house on 24 June 1938, they were taken for trial at Ganges, Salt Spring Island. FL died, aged sixty-two, on 9 November 1938 in Victoria, leaving his wife and two daughters, who held his funeral at St Andrews Presbyterian Church.

Sources: *Colonist*, 19 March 1925, p. 3; 3 June 1934, p. 3; 21 July 1938, p. 3; 23 July 1938, p. 3; 10 November 1938, pp. 1, 4 and 5, obit., and photo; *Terry Reksten, A Century of Sailing, 1892-1992: A History of the Oldest Yacht Club on Canada's Pacific Coast* (Victoria, Orca Book Publishing, 1992), pp. 105, 112, 116, 120, 124-5, 162.

LINDSELL, Colonel Robert Frederick. (1856-1914). Born at Biggleswade, Bedfordshire, home of several Lindsell families, he was a son of Charles Samuel Lindsell, "J. P. Banker, Brewer and Landowner," also born in Biggleswade, and his wife, Annie Lindsell, *née* Harding, born at Solihull, Warwickshire. RL seems to have been the eldest of five children and was away at school in 1871 when the census found his family and their seven servants living at "Holme House," Biggleswade.

These parents had married on 17 January 1854. RL joined the British Army and commanded the Second Gloucestershire Regiment in the South African War, taking an active part in Mitchener's Kopje at Paardeberg and winning the CD. In 1900, he was officially listed as a lieutenant colonel commanding the Second Gloucesters at Aldershot. In 1913, after some years in retirement, he visited *Major Lorne Ross and *Captain Gerrard at Cowichan and then went up the coast to Hagansburg, near Bella Coola, where two of his sons were living on a large farm he had bought for them. There he went fishing on 8 April 1914 and disappeared. He had been planning to return to England in June but disappeared at Bella Coola. He had recently stayed with his sons at the Norwegian village of Hagansborg, where he had bought them a large farm. On 8 April, he went fishing for trout on the Bella Coola River and did not return. The alarm was raised when he failed to appear at the home of Mr S. Le C. Grant, where he was making his temporary residence, or at any of the neighbours. He was planning to return to England in June. Constable Broughton searched fruitlessly for him, and his son, Gerald Charles Huntingdon Lindsell, offered $150 for him or his remains. Local fishermen eventually found his body, and it was assumed that he had been swept off his feet in trying to cross the river and carried under one of the logjams, numerous in the spring season. He was buried in a coffin draped with the Union Jack in the presence of a large crowd of local people. This was about the time he had been planning to return to England, probably to stay with his brother, C. T. Lindsell, a "gentleman farmer" at Turry Grange, Bedfordshire.

RL's son, Gerald Charles Huntingdon Lindsell, was born on 23 February 1883 at Portsmouth, served in 1902-1907 as a lieutenant in the Lincolnshire Territorial Regiment, and then went out to BC, where he joined the 102nd Rocky Mountain Rangers. On 5 May 1909, he married Adeline Chrystal *née* Travers and was living with here at 1115 Mears Street, Victoria, on 13 March 1916 when he was commissioned in the 143rd Battalion, CEF. He was an Anglican and gave his occupation as "Gentleman." During his time on the farm at Hagansborg, he published a pamphlet, *The Grey Geese* (Toronto, W. H. Aptd, 1931), 18 pp. He did not die in BC.

Sources: *Colonist*, 9 May 1914, p. 7; 2 July 1914, p. 6; 2 July 1914, p. 6; *Bella Coola Courier*, Saturday, 11 April 1914; 20 June 1914; census 1871, England, RG 10/1550, p. 41; census 1881, RG 11/1630, p. 29; census 1881, RG 11/1629/98; NAC, CEF files box 5657-40; *Whitaker's*, p. 320.

LISTER, Colonel Frederick (1879-1944). Born in 1879 in Lincolnshire, a son of yeoman parents, he went out to South Africa in 1896 and became a trooper in the Bechuanaland Border Police with which he served in the Matabele rebellion (1896-1897). Later, he joined the British South African Company's police in Rhodesia and served through the South African War. In 1903, he went to Ontario but moved in 1907 to BC, where he worked in logging camps and sawmills. In the Great War, he was commissioned in the 102nd Battalion, CEF, went overseas under Lieutenant Colonel John W. Warden, rose to the rank of colonel, and won the MC. He died, aged sixty-five, on 22 December 1944 at "Camp Lister."

Sources: *Colonist*, 31 January 1917, p. 5; 12 December 1924, p. 14.

LITTLE, Hugh Islip (1874-1940). He was born on 31 January 1879 at Aylsham, Norfolk, and the 1891 census found him living with a farmer at St Andrew Schethdale (?), Norfolk, as a "Farm Pupil" together with a nineteen-year-old journalist. In 1893, he went out to the Island with two brothers and was known in Victoria as a sportsman, playing cricket and on a rugby team of which *A. T. Goward was captain. He served in the South African War with the Canadian Mounted Rifles and retired with the Queen's Medal and three clasps. He then became a big-game hunter and hunting guide in northern BC, and when he later joined the Saanich Police Force as one of its first constables, his home was known for its many heads, horns, and other trophies. In 1914, he became chief constable and on resigning in 1918 worked for more than twenty years as caretaker at the Dominion Observatory on Little Saanich Mountain. He died, aged sixty-six, on 14 October 1940, leaving his wife and a son.

Sources: NAC, RG 38 A-1-a, vol. 60 (T-2076), *Colonist*, 16 October 1940, p. 3; 19 October 1940, p. 2, obit.; census 1891, England, RG 12/1489, p. 1.

LIVINGSTON, Air Marshal Sir Philip Clermont (1893-1982). He was born on 2 March 1893 in the Cowichan Valley, only son of Clermont Livingston (c. 1850-1907) and his second wife, the first, Mary Ellen Livingston *née* Clark of Walthamstow, Essex, having died in 1889. When in 1881 the census recorded his father with his first wife resident at 10 Forest Rise, Walthamstow, he was employed as a "Ship Insurance Agent." Thirty years earlier, the 1851 census had found the father five months old and resident at his birthplace, 10 Stamford Hill, Stoke Newington, with his parents, PL's paternal grandparents, Jasper Livingston, who was a shipowner born in Jamaica c. 1815, and his wife Mary, a Londoner. PL describes his father as a conscientious, pious lover of country life, never happy in the London trading firm of Livingston, Briggs & Co., and enchanted by a book about British Columbia purchased by chance at Liverpool Street Station on his way home to Epping. When the firm failed in 1891, he took his family to a ten-acre farm they called "Clevelands" on the Island between the Cowichan and Koksilah rivers, where PL was born. There, PL was recorded in the Canadian census of 1901 with his two half-brothers and three half-sisters. He reviews his childhood in his memoirs, but says nothing about the marriage of his half-sister, Louisa Muriel Monteith Livingston (1881-1972), to *Edward Christopher Musgrave in Victoria on 9 October 1901. That same year, the father became manager of the Tyee Copper Company, based in London, which had offices in Duncan, a mining claim on Mount Sicker, ten miles away, and by 1905 a smelter at Ladysmith. The copper seam suddenly ran out in 1907, and PL's father died on 20 October. PL's widowed mother, an Essex farmer's daughter trained as a nurse, carried on bravely for a couple of years at the centre of what had become a busy social life. "We always seemed to have a house full," PL recalled. "There were whist parties, for which the big, square drawing-room was opened. Robert W. Service, the Canadian poet, was frequently at these. He worked at

Corfield's Farm, adjoining ours, and served in the store and the post office. Then there were young neighbours who crowded in after tennis at the club, under the shadow of Tzouhalem." At ten, PL had entered *Percy Truscott Skrimshire's remarkable Quamichan School, four miles away, and the Livingstons attended St Peter's Church at Quamichan. With much determination and courage, PL's mother took him to London at the age of sixteen to be educated and trained as a doctor and managed to arrange for him to attend Jesus College, Cambridge, and a London hospital. He became an eye specialist and published papers on vision and its science.

In 1916, he joined the Royal Navy and spent the years 1915-1917 as a naval doctor at sea, then 1917-1919 at a London hospital, and after the war joined the RAF as a medical officer. He was posted to Iraq and India and generally moved around the empire. His memoirs, *Fringe of the Clouds*, tells the story of his RAF career. In August 1945, he was sent to visit hospitals in San Francisco and took the opportunity to visit the Island, where he was met in Victoria by his old friend Eric Elkington. They drove to Duncan and called on their old teacher, *Percy Truscott Skrimshire, and perhaps it was that visit which prompted him to retire to Maple later. He had married Lorna Crespin, eldest daughter of C. W. Legassicke Crespin, in London on 8 July 1920, and they had two sons, Clermont and Michael. When he died, aged fifty-seven, on 13 February 1982 at Maple Bay, he was buried at St Peter's Quamichan near the graves of his parents, his mother's ashes having been sent over from Kensington when she died there in 1929. His name at the end of his life was followed by the letters KBE (1950), CBE (1946), CB (1948), AFC (1942), FRCS, FRCSE, LRCP, DPH, and DOMS.

Sources: *Who was Who*, vol. VIII, p. 452; Air Marshal Sir Philip Livingston, *Fringe of the Clouds* [memoirs] (Johnson Publications Ltd., 1962), pp. 11-14, 19, 97, 122, 213; Williams, *The Story of St Peter's*, p. 65; census 1851, England, HO 107/1503/128/14; census 1881, RG 11/1732, p. 12; census 1881, RG 11/991, p. 8 (Jasper Livingston); census 1891, RG 12/815, p. 12.

LLOYD, Captain Hugh Salisbury (1879-1914). He was born at Sydenham, eldest son of Colonel Edward Lloyd, Punjab Cavalry, born in India, and Mary R. Lloyd *née* Hardinge in Leamington, Warwick. In 1891, the census-taker found HSL, aged eleven, living with his family at his maternal grandfather's place, "Stafford House," Drayton-in-Wales, near the town of Market Drayton in Shropshire, the grandfather being John W. Hardinge, aged seventy-three, a "retired clerk in Holy Orders" born at Walton, Lancashire. HSL had a brother, Edward A. Lloyd, aged eight and a sister, Irene C. Lloyd, aged nine, both born at Camberley, Surrey. There were a "French governess (school)" and two housemaids. In 1897, HSL was gazetted to the Royal Marine Light Infantry and went on to serve in Central Africa attached to the King's African Rifles and on the West and East coasts of Africa. He served also as ADC to the governor of Uganda and as such was appointed to assist Winston Churchill, then secretary of state for the colonies, on tour of that colony. HSL became a superb shot and won the Prince of Wales Cup at Bisley and other trophies. As a marine, he was also on naval duty and, as it happened, served two years under Captain V. A. Stanley (as he then was) on HMS *Royal Arthur* when she was stationed at Esquimalt.

As soon as he retired from the RMLI, he went to settle in Victoria, where he arrived in March 1913. He had at one time been in charge of the Imperial Government Survey of the Uganda boundary line and now set out to qualify as a surveyor in BC. After passing examinations, he was attached to *Colonel W. J. H. Holmes and worked under him in summer 1913 in the Strathcona Park survey up the Island. Early in 1914, he joined the recently formed Fiftieth Gordon Highlanders as a captain, but died suddenly, aged thirty-five, on 26 April at St Joseph's Hospital as a result of an appendectomy. He was survived by his wife Hilda *née* Squire of Thurleston, Devonshire, whom he had married in 1903, their son and two daughters, and his parents, then living at Culver House, Bedford, as well as his two sisters and two brothers. One brother was then a commander in the RN on the China Station and the other an army captain. HSL was buried with a military funeral at Christ Church Cathedral. Among the pallbearers were Captain J. F. Foulkes, Major W. C. Angus, both of the Fifth Regiment, *Captain F. V. Longstaff, Corps of Guides, *Colonel W. J. H. Holmes, Lieutenant Colonel W. H. Coy, Major Lorne Ross, Major G. B. Hughes (son of Hon. Sam Hughes, federal cabinet minister), and Major P. T. Riddell. Many other officers of Victoria attended, including *Captain B. H. Tyrwhitt-Drake, *Captain W. H. Bullock-Webster, *Lieutenant Colonel Arthur W. Currie, and a group from the Marine Old Comrades Association, notably Major Barnes, RMA.
Sources: *Colonist*, 28 April 1914, p. 7; 30 April 1914, p. 7, obit.; census 1891, England, RG 12/2128, p. 4.

LLOYD, Captain Robert William Henry (c. 1868-1940). He was born in Wales and went to sea as a young man, with initial training on the River Mersey. He had many adventures during his seventeen or so voyages around the world in sailing vessels, including thirteen times around Cape Horn. In 1893, for instance, he was the only survivor of the *Bessarabia*, which turned over and sank in heavy seas. In the years 1893-1898, he served as second mate on five ships, but when the Second South African War began in 1899, he joined the Cape Mounted Police.

In 1909, he went out to BC and settled at first in the Okanagan Valley. Returning to the coast a few years later, he took command of the *Clansman* and other coastal vessels. During the Great War, he was skipper of a small boat sailing in the dangerous waters of the English Channel. He returned to the Pacific Coast after the war, resumed his old employment, and made many trips to all parts of the coast, including journeys up the Courtenay River. He was well known in the Comox Valley for thirty-one years and retired to a farm on the Lake Trail Road about 1931. When he died there, aged seventy, on 14 January 1940, he left only his wife, who lived on there. He was buried at St Andrew's Anglican Church, Sandwick, under auspices of Courtenay Branch Canadian Legion.
Sources: *Colonist*, 16 January 1940, p. 14, obit.; *Comox District Free Press*, Thursday, January 18, 1940, p. 1.

LONG, Eric George (1902-1980). Harbour Master in 1947-1980 at Crofton on the Island, where he was also superintendent of the Osborne Bay wharf owned by the Hillcrest Company, he was born in the Surrey part of London on 12 August 1902 and apprenticed in his youth to the Blue Funnel Line. He was in their service from 25 September 1918 to 24 May 1928 and then joined the China Navigation Company (a subsidiary of Butterfield & Swire). To repeat in detail, he served as able seaman from 10 March 1923 to 15 June 1923 and was seconded as third mate for the *Compagnie generale transatlantique* from 28 March 1924 to 26 February 1925 and second mate for them from 26 February 1925 to 1 July 1925. On 24 May 1928, he became second officer on ships of the China Navigation Company from 24 May 1928, obtained his first mate's certificate on 14 February 1930 (No. 4752 Hong Kong), and was chief officer from 29 April 1932. He was on furlough to England from 30 December 1930 to 30 April 1931—"special leave." From 26 July 1934 to 3 May 1935, he was away on leave, suffering from sunstroke. Again on leave from April 1935 to 20 January 1936, he was in England, and from 14 December 1940 to 13 June 1941, he was "on long leave" in Canada. During much of his service time, his will was registered with Kingsbury and Turner, 369/7 Brixton Road, London SW9, and his next of kin was recorded as Lionel Durbar Long, c/o "The Stag," London.

When he suffered some physical defect (poor eyesight?), he was posted ashore in various Chinese towns: at Hong Kong from 17 October 1932 to 11 February 1934 in the "Preventive Department," at Shanghai from 16 February 1934 to 16 April 1935 as No 3 godown superintendent (acting), at Hankow from 20 January 1936 to 20 December 1936 as No. 2 godown superintendent, at Swatow from 28 December 1936 to 1 April 1938 as godown superintendent, at Shanghai again from 4 April 1938 to 31 January 1939 as godown superintendent (No. 2 Peking), at Shanghai still from 1 February 1939 to November 1940 as godown superintendent (Watung), and there still from April 1940 to 14 December 1940. In spring 1931, he married Kathleen Ashford at Wandsworth, London, and they went off to China where she recalled living for ten years at Shanghai, then at Hankow, and finally at Sottow. He was employed by the British firm of Butterfield & Swire to care for wharves, and the company provided the family with a house there. Eventually, they had a daughter Leila and two sons.

Early in the Second World War, they took six months' leave, intending to go to Australia but went instead to Canada when their ship was redirected as a result of the war. They could not then return to China and settled at first, in January 1941, at Penticton, BC. There they roomed with a family who had lost their farm for debt, apparently as a result of drought. This seems to have been an unhappy period, and early in 1945, the Longs moved to Sidney, Vancouver Island, where they lived in a series of rented houses, mainly on Mills Road. According to Mrs Long, my parents helped them in various ways and became fast friends. After three years in which they built a house on Second St, Eric Long got a job at Crofton as superintendent of the Osborne Bay wharf owned by the Hillcrest Company and also as harbour master. Crofton was their home from late in 1947. But EL may have visited the Island many years earlier in the course of his career at sea.

Among their friends and neighbours nearby were *Captain James Harrison "Harry" Worsley (1890-1975), known to his friends as "Binks," whose second wife was a cousin of Kathleen Long's, and Francis Augustus "Frank" Considine, who had commanded the local militia unit. Considine was born in Ireland. He and his brother St John Considine married sisters and in the early 1920s emigrated to Maple Bay, near Duncan, where they had a chicken and fox farm. The Considine brothers played on the Victoria cricket team against visitors such as the Hollywood team on which David Niven, Errol Flynn, and other British actors used to play. As it happened, my father had known Worsley and Considine in the Sixteenth Battalion of the Canadian Scottish Reserve Regiment, and I have a wartime photograph of them together with a fourth soldier called Vaughan Pritchard whom I have not yet identified. My parents visited the Longs quite often, meeting "Binks" Worsley and the Considines at the same time, and were evidently fond of all three families. Binks died on 22 December 1975 at Chemainus, and EL died, aged eighty-six, on 19 November 1988 at hospital in Duncan.

In April that year, the Longs attended my parents' golden wedding celebration at the little house on Foul Bay Road, Victoria, where they had moved in 1986. I did not meet them then—because I remained perversely in the kitchen, according to Mrs Long—but my wife and I visited them at Crofton on a sunny afternoon early in March 2000. Then a widow of ninety-six, she and her daughter Leila graciously received us with tea, sandwiches, answers to my many questions, and the loan of two photographs showing my parents with them and the Worsleys on a similar occasion long ago. Kathleen Long was a talented painter, and many gorgeous garden scenes, flowers, and shrubs hung on her walls.

Sources: Information from two visits to Mrs Kathleen Long and her daughter Leila at Crofton; School of Oriental and African Studies (London), Swire Papers, JSSIII 7/2, Box A10; New York Passenger Lists, 1820-1957, T-715_2607, p. 167; *Ladysmith Chemainus Chronicle*, 4 May 1967, p. 17; 13 December 1972, p. 6; NAC, T4760, Elections rolls for 1935 (Considine).

LONGRIDGE, Captain Robert Begbie (c. 1885-1970). Born at Knutsford, Cheshire, he was found, aged six, by the 1891 census-taker, living with his family in Chester at "Kilrie" in the London Road. His father, Robert C. Longridge, aged forty-one, was "Assoc. M.I.C.E. Manager of a Company" born at Bedlington, Northumberland. His mother, Mary R. Longridge, aged thirty-five, was Scottish. He had seven sisters and was then the only boy in the family. There were six servants: lady nurse, lady housekeeper, housemaid, cook, nurse, undernurse. Ten years later, RL was boarding, aged sixteen, Aldenham School, Elstree, Hertfordshire, headmaster Rev. Alfred Hands Cooke, MA (Cantab.). In 1912, he went out to BC and farmed near Kamloops. During the Great War, he left on 6 August 1914 and returned to England to serve with the Sixteenth Lancers and then the RAF. He was back in BC on 1 July 1919 and in 1936 moved to the Island, where he settled on Stamps Road near Duncan. There he was active in the Canadian Legion, served at one time as the first vice-president of its BC Command, and ran in the Nanaimo federal riding as a Conservative candidate. He died, aged eighty-five, on 28 December 1970 in Victoria.

Sources: *Colonist,* 6 September 1938, p. 4; census 1891, England, RG 12/2828, p. 3; census 1901, England, RG 13/1314, p. [illegible]; R. J. Evans, *The History of Aldenham School* (1599-1969) (Old Aldenhamian Society, 1969), passim.

LONGSTAFF,
Major Frederick Victor
(1879-1961),
A MANY-SIDED FIGURE IN VICTORIA.

I. Family and early life
II. Mountaineering
III. Military service
IV. Maritime interests
V. Public-spirited activities

I. Family and early Life

He was born on 15 June 1879 at Ilkley, Yorkshire, son of Lieutenant Colonel Llewellyn Wood Longstaff (1841-1918), OBE, and Mary Lydia Longstaff, *née* Sawyer, who had four sons and three daughters. FL.'s elder brother Dr Tom George Longstaff (1875-1964) became a well-known traveller, explorer, and alpinist and was chief medical officer and naturalist on the Mt Everest expedition in 1922. Their father had travelled a great deal, been an active member of the Royal Geographical Society, and helped to finance Scott's first Antarctic expedition, as a result of which Scott named an Arctic mountain "Mt Longstaff." Their maternal grandfather Thomas W. Sawyer of Southampton had been sent to Canada in the winter of 1861-1862 with the Second Scots Guards to resist the Fenian invasion from the USA. FL's parents lived most of their lives at "Ridgelands," Wimbledon, but when his father died his mother went to live with her daughter Kate at "Garden House," Ightham, Kent. FL kept in touch with this sister, Mrs A. F. Wedgwood, whose husband was killed in the Great War. Six months after their mother died on 3 April 1933, aged eighty-eight, Kate visited him in Victoria with "the Misses Wedgwood" and he held a luncheon for them at the Forrest Inn, Shawnigan Lake. That was thirty years after he had first visited the Island in 1903 during a mountaineering expedition to Glacier in the Rockies with his father, brother Tom, and sister Kate.

II. Mountaineering

Mountaineering was at the centre of his and his family's life. He took up photography in order to record the places and people encountered on mountaineering expeditions and as early as 1896 became a fellow of the Royal Geographical Society. In September 1910, his brother Tom joined *A. O. Wheeler in leading an expedition into the Spillimacheen Mountains, a minor range of the Selkirks, and Tom became famous later for his exploits in Greenland and

444

the Himalayas. FL joined the Alpine Club of Canada in 1911, only five years after Wheeler and others founded it, and it was in the life of that club that he met his future wife, Jennie Long McCulloch, who joined in 1912. She was a daughter of W. F. McCulloch, a government assayer in Victoria, and they were married in March 1921 at Christ Church Cathedral, Victoria, with another club member,*F. B. Mitchell of Sidney, as best man. The bride received an heirloom broach of sapphires and amethysts and was taken off on the afternoon boat for Vancouver, thence to Igtham, Kent, to visit his widowed mother (source of that heirloom broach) and to honeymoon in France. Much of their married life was spent in mountain ranges of the province: the Island's mountainous west coast in 1925 aboard the CPR *Maquinna* with a party of forty-five from the Victoria Chamber of Commerce, the Bridge River icefield in 1931, the club's camp in Paradise Valley with the Wheelers in July 1933, a pack-pony trip through the Chilcotin country to Bella Coola in 1938, and many more. On 23 January 1914, the *Colonist* printed a long letter in which he recommended avoiding duplication of geographical names. On 7 February 1929, it printed an open letter to the president of the CPR in which he protested against regulations preventing the public from visiting Glacier National Park, which he had "known and loved since 1903." FL was always writing to local papers about some issue of public interest.

III. Military service

Mountaineering is a summer sport and various military activities took more of FL's time and attention. By training he was an architect, though he came away from Eton and Cambridge University with a diploma in agriculture, and soon after moving to Victoria before the Great War, he worked with Colonel Ridgeway-Wilson, architect of St John's Church and Christ Church Cathedral. But while at Cambridge, he joined the 2/5th Battalion, East Surrey Regiment, on 11 October 1899 and was commissioned as lieutenant on 11 April 1906 and thereafter rose to captain (28 March 1907) and major (1 December 1914). From 2 February 1912 to 29 August 1914, he held a temporary commission in the Active Militia of Canada, attached to the Corps of Guides, but was asked to resign on 22 March 1915. According to a medical report that year, he had never recovered from an attack of pleurisy and influenza in April 1914 and "attacks of mental and physical depression render him unable to undergo sustained physical exertion. He has a flabby heart evidenced by his pallor and small feeble pulse." Meanwhile, he was already active as a staff officer in the Legion of Frontiersmen and worked at 6 Adam Street, Adelphi, its headquarters in London throughout the war. When he returned to Victoria in 1919, it was as an officer in the Legion detailed to recruit and organize squadrons in BC and bearing a letter of 24 April 1918 signed by Lieutenant Colonel E. R. Johnson, a retired staff officer from India then in his middle seventies:

> Major Frederick Victor Longstaff, a member of the Executive Council and Staff Officer for overseas, has given invaluable assistance as Intelligence Officer in the collection of information from all overseas

commands, and has drawn up schemes for the administration and grouping of units in every part of the Empire. In addition, he has spent much time in the distribution of Legion news, its collection and editing. [He also gave generous financial donations to the Legion on several occasions].

Three months later, however, he received another letter from Lieutenant Colonel Johnson filled with alarm that the Legion was being taken over by Colonel D. P. Driscoll, who was treating the Legion "as a source of revenue to himself" and was openly hostile to him and FL. Perhaps, they were thinking of the Legion as a gentleman's voluntary corps, and Driscoll was expecting to draw an officer's salary. Perhaps, his three-year absence fighting in Africa made him impatient of these "desk-wallas." Whatever the reason, a quarrel developed and early in April 1919, FL received a blunt, angry letter from Colonel Driscoll accusing him of disloyalty and of unwarranted opposition to himself. The Victoria squadron of Frontiersmen stopped meeting in the early 1920s, though it revived in the Second World War.

IV. Maritime interests

A boating disaster near Victoria in 1934 resulted in the formation of a Victoria Lifeboat Association, and FL played a leading part in its founding. "For over twelve years," he remarked in January that year, "I have been making a study of life saving on the West Coast of Vancouver Island and have much material on the subject. As I represent the Royal Lifeboat Institution on the Pacific Coast of Canada, the head office has supplied me with a copy of its regulations for 1926 and the Board of Trade description of the rocket apparatus . . . I have an alphabetical list of shipping disasters which go back to 1858 and a wreck chart compiled by the late Captain J. T. Walbran . . ." The several founding meetings were reported in the *Daily Colonist* that year, and FL's frequent letters to the editor were really notices of the new association's activities and instructions to the public. Ten years later, he was still writing in the same way. "This letter," he wrote in 23 January 1935, "is the twenty-sixth of the series being issued with the authority of the Directors of the Vancouver Island Lifeboat Association." As a public-spirited British officer, he was naturally inspired by the Royal National Lifeboat Institution, founded in a London tavern on 4 March 1824 by a group of volunteers led by the Archbishop of Canterbury, Manners Sutton, who was responding to an appeal by Lieutenant Colonel Sir William Hillary, a resident of the Isle of Man distressed by the many tragic wrecks he witnessed there. This, probably the world's first lifeboat organization, was dramatized and encouraged in 1838 by the legendary rescue of people on a doomed ship by eighteen-year-old Grace Darling, who became a heroine throughout the empire. FL was also a hard-working supporters of the Connaught Seamen's Institute, modelled on the British Seamen's Homes at ports around the empire, proposed in Victoria as early as 1908 by Rev. E. W. Matthews, general secretary of the British Sailor's Society, and opened at last in November 1914 on the corner of superior and St Oswego Streets, where it was formally dedicated by the Anglican bishop of the diocese. It is not surprising that FL was a founding member of the Thermopylae Club (1932) for retired mariners, a lifelong supporter of the Navy League from sometime in the 1890s, the conscience and organizer of Trafalgar Day celebrations in Victoria, and the author of what was for many years the only history of the Esquimalt Station of the Royal Navy. Much of his considerable body of writing on these and other matters he did at his home, "Seabank," 50 King George Terrace, on a hillside where he could keep an eye on the Strait of Juan de Fuca.

V. Public-spirited activities

FL engaged in a wide range of public duties, apparently driven by serious Christian commitments. For many years, he was Vestry Clerk and Registrar of the Sunday School at Christ Church Cathedral, Victoria. He, as much as anyone, founded and led the First Victoria Company of the Boys' Brigade in 1940, having written an article entitled "Christian Manliness" to promote it early in December 1939. Boys aged twelve to seventeen were invited to join at St Andrew's Presbyterian Church Hall, Mrs [Colonel] *F. W. L. Moore undertook to play the piano for hymns and physical training, and its volunteer officers were soon "receiving up-to-date instruction in the Boys' Brigade system of training from Major F. V. Longstaff," who had been inspecting and reporting on the companies of the Vancouver and District Battalion. Lest FL should be suspected of excessive piety and good works, let us hasten to add that he was a life member of the National Rifle Association and urged men and boys to learn to shoot at home or in community halls, etc. He joined the Royal United Service Institution of Whitehall, London, and from 1933 was Dominion organizing secretary of the Incorporated Soldiers', Sailors', and Airmen's Help Society based at 122 Brompton Road, London SW 3. As such, in November 1939, he wrote to *The Daily Colonist,* 16 November 1939 (p. 4): "Sir—A memorandum containing knitting directions for gloves, mittens, wristlets, pullovers, seaboot stockings, scarves and Balaclava helmets, has just been received by me, as Dominion organizing secretary . . . The Admiralty is hoping that women will knit garments by the thousands to keep sailors warm this winter . . ." In February 1925, he was the guest speaker at the Victoria and Vancouver Island Branch of the Canadian Author's Association and over the years often addressed the Victoria Branch of the BC Historical Society. When in November 1939 that association held its AGM at the Empress Hotel, 148 members attended and FL was the convenor of its maritime committee.

His many articles show detailed research into Imperial and local naval history, the growth of Christ Church Cathedral, and many aspect of the province's past, but always with wide horizons. For example, in the July 1929 number of the *Canadian Defence Quarterly,* he published an article on HMS *Ganges,* launched at Bombay in 1821, which came to Esquimalt in June 1857 and gave its name to the town of Ganges on Salt Spring Island. He collected an interesting library of five thousand volumes, many pamphlets, and photographs, which he ultimately bequeathed to the BC Provincial Archives. After his death, the archives drew up a twenty-five-page list of the correspondence, notes, and other private papers he left to them, in addition to articles such as "Christ Church Cathedral," *Colonist*, 8 March 1953, Sunday Section, p. 11 (an entire page); "Notes on the Early History of the Pacific Station and the Inception of the Esquimalt Royal Naval Establishment," in *Canadian Defence Quarterly*, vol. III (1926), pp. 309-318; "Captain George Vancouver, 1792-1942: A Study in Commemorative Place-names," *B.C. Historical Quarterly*, vol. 6 (April 1942), pp. 77-94; "Centenary of the Pacific Station, 1837-1937," *B.C. Historical Quarterly*, vol. 8 (April 1944); "Eight Rainbows," *B.C. Historical Quarterly*, vol. 8 (April 1944), pp. 107-110; "Story of the Swiss Guides in Canada," *Canadian Alpine Journal*, vol. 28 (1942-1943), pp. 189-197; "Swiss Guides in Canada: Further Notes," *Canadian Alpine Journal*, vol. 29 (1944-5), pp. 49-52; and "War Service of the Cruiser *Uganda*," *Daily Colonist*, 2 November 1952, Sunday, p. 7. "In my diary of 1903," he wrote, "I find an entry under date of Monday August 17, 'went on SS *Princess Victoria* on her trial trip in the Sound.' I remember I went with my father and I talked with Captain Walbran who took the figures on which he computed her speed. The invitation card sent to my father by Captain Troup is now in the B.C. Archives. On April 29, 1925, I went out on the *Princess Louise* to meet the first *Marguerite* when she arrived. I also remember when the *Princess Alice* arrived in 1911, and the *Adelaide* in 1910, and they were the last [CPR] Coast steamers to come round Cape Horn, as the Panama Canal was first used in 1914."

FL died, aged eighty-one, on 4 October 1961 in Victoria.

Sources: *Canadian Who's Who*, 1958-1960, pp. 660-1; *BC Archives*, MS-0677 (FL's Papers); PRO, WO 374/42857; *Colonist*, 23 January 1914, p. 10; 31 March 1921, p. 8; 2 September 1925, p. 2; 21 October 1921, p. 4; 19 March 1925, p. 4; 30 August 1925, p. 4; 30 December 1925, p. 4; 7 February 1929, p. 4; 7 February 1925, p. 8; 2 August 1931, p. 8; 27 July 1933, p. 3; 19 January 1934, p. 4; 27 October 1937, p. 4; 11 March 1939, *Sunday Supplement*, p. 3; 7 September 1939, p. 4; 8 September 1939, p. 9; 4 October 1939, p. 4; 16 November 1939, pp. 4 and 11; 17 November 1939, p. 3; 16 November 1939, p. 4; 9 December 1939, p. 4; 11 March 1939, *Sunday Supplement*, p. 3; 7 September 1939, p. 4; 8 September 1939, p. 9; 4 October 1939, p. 4; 16 November 1939, pp. 4 and 11; 17 November 1939, p. 3; 21 May 1933, p. 26; 4 January 1940, p. 9; Muriel Aylard, "Major Frederick Victor Longstaff," in *Canadian Alpine Journal*, vol. 45 (May 1962), pp. 165-6, a reference I owe to the kindness of Dr John Wheeler; Longstaff, *Esquimalt Naval Base*, passim; Ursula Jupp, Home Port Victoria (Victoria, privately printed by Morriss Printing Co. Ltd., for 2254 Arbutus Road, 1967), pp. 57 and 116; A. O. Wheeler, *The Selkirk Mountains: A Guide for Mountain Pilgrims and Climbers* (Winnipeg, privately published, 1912), pp. 31 and 139; PRO, WO 374/42857; Canadian Defence Quarterly, July 1929; Riddick, *Who in British India*, p. 218 (brother); Tom Longstaff, *This My Voyage* (John Murray, 1950), 324 pp. and photos; Colin Wells, *Who's Who in British Climbing* (Buxton, Derbyshire, The Climbing Company, 2008), pp. 287-88. I am most grateful to Dr John Wheeler for friendly information, useful pointers, and many corrections.

LONSDALE, Christopher Windley (1886-1952). Headmaster and founder of Shawnigan Lake School, Vancouver Island, he was born on 1 February 1886 at Thornthwaite, Cumberland, son of Canon Henry and Mrs Jane Lonsdale of Arlaw Banks, Barnard Castle, County Durham. His father was born at Macclesfield, Cheshire, and his mother at Nottingham, where she was a daughter of William Windley. The 1891 census found CL, aged five, living at "The Vicarage," St Cuthberts Without, Cumberland, where his father was then the vicar. We know that CL was educated at Westminster School, and indeed, the 1901 census found him there, aged fifteen, boarding at 2 Little Dean Yard, Westminster, whence he went on to study at Durham University. He held a commission in the British Army for a short time. After travelling in India and Japan, he went to BC in 1907. After some very hard and discouraging years, which he spoke about much later to *E. H. L. Johnston's son, he was able to settle at Duncan in 1909 and farm there on part of the old Holmes estate. He was soon coaching local pupils and early in 1912 "he started at Shawnigan Lake what has developed into one of the premier private schools in Canada," as the *Cowichan Leader* declared at his death forty years later. It was the opinion of at least two former pupils, *Captain C. P. "Pat" Nixon and the Ottawa portrait painter, Robert Hyndman, that CL established the school single-handed, though with support by well-wishers and his unmarried sisters, Mabel and K. Ella Lonsdale. What support he had from his wife, *née* Lucy French (1886-?), whom he married in Vancouver on 17 August 1912, seems uncertain. According to several passenger lists, she travelled almost continually from about 1915 until well after CL's death, often with their daughter Elizabeth and sometimes with their son Robert.

CL had a devoted following, including *Percy Truscott Skrimshire, who had kept a boys' school at Quamichan Lake from 1905 but closed it down in 1925 and joined the staff of Shawnigan Lake School. On 13 February 1928, the school, then with 112 boys, became a foundation owning itself and administered by a board of governors. It should be stressed at this point that CL was also a governor of the former Strathcona Lodge School for girls and had been appointed a JP. Known as a keen shot, a judge of working dogs, he was also interested in all games and played most of them. In Victoria, he was a member of the Union Club and carried weight in the Private School Association. He had two nephews on the Island, Christopher E. Lonsdale at Shawnigan Lake School and Cedric Lonsdale in Chemainus.

CL died at Penticton on Sunday 3 August 1952 at 6:15 a.m., and his funeral was held at St Ann's Church (C of E), French Creek, near Parksville. He died on his way to visit C. W. Twite, an old colleague at Vernon, but was compelled to go into hospital at Penticton. His body was returned to Parksville and buried there in French Creek Cemetery. His sisters were then back in England, and his wife did not die on the Island.

Sources: census 1891, England RG 12/4287, p. 16; census 1901, RG 13/94, p. 7; notes from Captain C. P. Nixon; *Cowichan Leader*, 7 August 1952, p. 1, obit.; *Cowichan Leader*, 6 March 1958, p. 3; R. H. Milne and Lucille Kocurek, eds., *Shawnigan and the War* (Duncan, BC, Solitaire Press Ltd., 1990), pp. 149-152; UK Incoming Passenger Lists, 1865-1935 (a dozen arrivals); Canadian Passenger Lists, 1865-1935 (ten arrivals).

LORDEN, Chief Petty Officer Henry "Harry" (c. 1863-1948), RN. Born at Hoo, Kent, he was recorded, aged eight, in the 1871 census, living "near Hoo Mill" with his father, Joseph Lorden, aged fifty, an agricultural labourer born at Cooling, Kent, his mother Frances Lorden, aged forty-seven, from Halstow, Kent, and four sisters, two elder and two younger. There were no servants and the neighbours were labourers and a "washerwoman." The 1881 census revealed an elder brother, William Lorden, aged twenty-seven, who was a "Private H.M. 1st Class Army Reserve" born at Cooling, and HL, aged eighteen, was employed as a "Bricklayer's labourer." Later that year, he joined the Royal Navy as a stoker and qualified as a diver, and in 1882, he was on one of the ships that bombarded Alexandria. Two years later, he was aboard a ship in the Persian Gulf, hunting down slaving ships and freeing the slaves. In 1890, after a four-year posting to the China station, he was sent to Esquimalt on board HMS *Espiègle* and then HMS *Daphne*. By that time, he had qualified as a diving instructor and was next employed for four years as instructor at Chatham Dockyard. At sometime in the early 1890s, he married and the 1901 census found him living at 42 Adelaide Road, Gillingham, Kent, with his wife, Emma Lorden, from Blackfriars, London, both aged thirty-eight, with an eight-year-old daughter, Hilda, and a five-year-old son, Harold, both born there at Gillingham. He was still a "Stoker, R. Navy" and the neighbours were shipwrights, painters, carpenters, and draper's assistants.

After the Great War, they retired with the family to Victoria, where Mrs Lorden died, aged seventy-one, on 21 September 1933. By 1941, HL and a daughter were living in 1941 at 727 Wilson Street, where he gardened assiduously and was a member of the Naval Veteran's Branch No. 41 of the Canadian Legion. His adventures in the RN were told in an article with a photograph, by W. I. Fletcher, in *The Daily Colonist*, Sunday section, 27 April 1941 (p. 3). When he died, aged eighty-five, on 29 April 1948, he was the oldest member of his Naval Veteran's Branch and a Freemason belonging to the Victoria-Columbia Lodge, AF and AM, No. 1. Besides his daughter at home, he left a son Harold in Seattle and another daughter.
Sources: census 1871, England, RG 10/901, p. 47; census 1881, RG 11/884, p. 7; census 1901, RG 13/737, p. 10; *Colonist*, Sunday section, 27 April 1941, p. 3; 1 May 1948, p. 10, obit.

LOWDEN, Robert S. (1875-1940). Born on 5 January 1875 at Partick near Glasgow, he enlisted with the Seaforth Highlanders in 1893, trained at Aldershot until 1895, and then served in India, Malta, and Crete. As a sergeant major in 1897, he entered the National Field Force and the next year went with Kitchener on the expedition up the Nile to Khartoum. He was in the battle of Khartoum and the battle of Atbara and won the Egyptian Sudan Medal and the British Sudan Medal. In the South African War, he won both the Queen's and the King's medals with a total of five bars. He had served for twelve years.

Then he came to Alberta, where he married, joined the militia—the Nineteenth Alberta Dragoons—and worked as a grocer until 1914, when he enlisted on 25 November for service overseas. As RSM of his battalion in France, he won the Mons Star. Early in 1936, he moved to a house on Lagoon Road, Esquimalt, where he died on 14 January 1940, aged sixty-five, a veteran of four campaigns with Imperial forces and three years in the Canadian Army. He lived mainly alone, and not being well known after only four years in the town, he was cited mistakenly by the local papers without his middle initial and as aged sixty-two. He was survived by a daughter in Alberta.

Sources: NAC, CEF files, box 5765-19; *Colonist*, 18 January 1940, p. 3, obit.

LOWE, Major Robert (1882-1955). Born on 1 April 1882 at Coupar Angus, Perthshire, only son of Dr John Lowe, he attended George Watson's College and later joined the Royal Horse Guards (the Blues) and was several times on escort duty with King Edward VII. Early in the 1900s, he went to Winnipeg and then on to the Pacific coast, where he worked as an engineer and surveyor. He travelled over much of BC on foot and horseback and was well known in the north and the Cariboo. He helped to locate the centre line for the PGE railway along Anderson Lake and walked from Fort Fraser to Smithers over the right of way for the Canadian National Railway before rails were laid. On one expedition, he walked over the Nass Glacier and on another went in from Bella Coola, up the valley and over the mountains to the Chilcotin with a pack-train. He went home when the Second World War began, was commissioned in the Scottish Horse, and served for six years in the Near East, Palestine, and Egypt, where he was awarded the Order of the Nile.

When he returned to BC, he married Bertha Mabel Robinson on 18 August 1928 in Vancouver, and they lived for a while at Burns Lake and Penticton before going to Duncan, where he worked on the housing project at Cowichan Lake and then settled on Alington Road. At the Cobble Hill Fair in September 1934, he won prizes for his runner beans, sheaf of wheat, and field pumpkins. He died, aged seventy-two, on 6 March 1955 and was buried in a funeral at St Peter's Quamichan taken by his grandson, Rev. John Lowe. He was survived by his widow and five daughters: Miss Una at home, Mrs John Bazett (Duncan), Mrs Brian Davies (Duncan), Miss Anne (McGill), and Miss Marjorie (RCAF, St Johns, Quebec).

Sources: NAC, CEF files, box 5769-13; *Cowichan Leader*, 6 March 1955, obit.; *Colonist*, 8 September 1934: the twenty-sixth annual Cobble Hill Fair.

LYLE, David (c. 1867-1942). Born in London, he joined the Royal Engineers as a young man and specialized in fortifications, barracks, and roads. He spent five years in Malta and another five on the island of Jersey and was then sent to North China as foreman of works. Arriving in China in 1907, he designed the line of blockhouses for the British and American sections from Peking to Shan-Hai-Kwan in 1910 during the Sun Yat Sen revolution in China. These blockhouses were built in accord with the Boxer uprising settlement, whereby foreign nations were allowed free passage at all times from Peking to the sea, in order to evacuate their legation staffs if necessary. In 1912, he returned to England to take a course in architecture, joined the Royal Institute of British Architects, and then returned to China, aged fifty-three, to practise his profession, arriving at St John, New Brunswick, from Liverpool on 11 April 1921 as a passenger aboard the *Corsican*.

In 1926, he retired with the rank of sergeant major and, embarking on the *President Jackson* at Kobe, Japan, reached Victoria on 29 April 1926 with his wife, Ann. She was an English woman aged forty-four, born at Winston, Cheshire, and he was then fifty-nine. They settled at a place in Saanich he called "Pangridge." In 1940, the prime minister in Ottawa was "deeply touched" to receive DL's personal treasures, including a gold watch, some jewels, a box of medals, and Freemasonry insignia, as a contribution to the war effort. There was a covering letter in which DL asked, "Could your Minister for War arrange for me to have a rifle and say, 100 rounds of ammunition, so that I could sit on my verandah and watch for and shoot parashooters. I am seventy-three years old and can't run about much." He died, aged seventy-five, at the Jubilee Hospital on 29 September 1942.
Sources: *Colonist,* 17 August 1940, p. 2; 30 September 1942, p. 3, obit.; T-14843; New York Passenger Lists, 1820-1957, M237_615, p. 9; Canadian Passenger Lists 1865-1935, T-1488.

McARTHUR, James (c. 1841-1921). Born in Scotland, he served for thirty-two years in the Royal Engineers, stationed variously at Malta, Bermuda, Halifax, and Ireland, and then took his discharge and Long Service Medal. He went to Canada, joined the Canadian Army, and lived in or near Victoria from 1895 and from 1900 was foreman at Work Point Barracks. Altogether, he spent fifty-three years in the Imperial and Canadian forces. Some months after being injured by a streetcar, he died, aged eighty, on 26 May 1921 at his home at 905 Esquimalt Road, leaving four sons and a daughter. He was buried as a Roman Catholic but with a volley fired off by a military firing party. The pallbearers were quartermaster sergeants R. D. Mylerea, J. T. Eastie, and T. Jones, sergeant majors T. E. Charles and J. A. Gillan, and Company Sergeant-Major M. T. Sullivan.
Sources: *Colonist,* 27 May 1921, p. 7, obit; 31 May 1921, p. 7.

MACBEAN, Major Ronald Eden (1890-1954). On 20 April 1922, he took over the Maple Bay Inn at Maple Bay, one of the two seaways in and out of the Cowichan Valley (the other being Cowichan Bay), and managed it for many years through the 1920s and 1930s, although, when it burnt down on 1 August 1946, it was owned by Mr and Mrs Archie Seymour. Already on 15 August 1923, British Army records showed RM's address (pardonably truncated) as "The Maple Inn, Royal Mail Delivery no. 1, Duncan." As the *Cowichan Leader* reported, "African spears and unique implements of war are found around the lounge, while the back entrance door, which also leads into the lounge, has a panelled effect . . . the whole building is lit by electric light." RM was a handsome, convivial man with a good singing voice, having been a Westminster Choir boy in his youth, and was one of the soloists at concerts in Duncan. He had a silent partner in owning the inn: Major Lancelot Arthur Shuldham Cole, born in India on 11 April 1891, son of Rev. Theodore Edward Fortescue Cole and his wife Eleanor Marie Shuldham, daughter of Colonel Arthur James Shuldham (1823-1905) of the Inniskillin Fusiliers. These two majors had been friends and colleagues during the Great War, and both had substantial families with distinguished forebears. RM's mother, Annie Caroline Ann *née* Fisher, was a second cousin of Prime Minister Sir Anthony Eden (1897-1977), their common ancestors being Sir Frederick Morton Eden (1766-1809) and his wife Anne Smith, who had married in 1792. It is perhaps more interesting that RM also had a great-uncle, *Captain Charles Edward Barrett-Lennard, who visited the Island earlier, sailed around it, and wrote a book about his expedition.

RM was born in Edinburgh on 19 July 1890, elder son of Captain William Alleyne Macbean of the Royal Garrison Artillery, who was posted to Esquimalt in the 1890s and still there with his family in 1900, according to *Whitakeer's Naval and Military Directory*. There is no lack of documentation showing RM's identity, and the I. G. Macbean he recorded as his next of kin when enlisting in Victoria was his younger brother, Ian Gordon Maclean, with whom he had been at school in Windsor, Berkshire, in early youth and who had become a marine engineer. RM's war service began on 8 December 1914 when, aged twenty-four, he enlisted in Victoria at Willows Camp, declaring himself to be an Anglican "rancher" with no previous military experience. On service overseas later, he transferred to a British unit and in 1917 won the MC "for conspicuous gallantry and devotion to duty when leading the advance party of a raid. When held up by strong enemy covering parties . . . he led a bayonet charge against the enemy, accounting for their leader with his revolver . . . a fine example of dash and determination." Long before he died, aged sixty-three, on 14 December 1954 in Vancouver, his father had been recalled from Esquimalt with the RN in 1906.

Sources: John Palmer, letter to the author, 28 June 2002; NAC, CEF files, box 6589-53, regimental no. 107406; *Cowichan Leader*, 25 May 1922; *Whitaker's*, p. 331; Muriel Jarvis Ackinclose, *Between Tzouhalem and Prevost: As I Remember Duncan* (Duncan, BC, Priority Printing Ltd., 2000), pp. 22, 25, 53; *Supplement to the London Gazette*, 27 September 1917, p. 9577; British Army World War I Medal Roll Cards 1914-1920 online; http://www.william1.co.uk/t36.htm.

McCALLUM, Arthur Edward (1836-1899). Incomplete and confusing sources suggest the following, which, however, remains open to correction: AM was born on 10 September 1836 in Russia to Charles and Margaretta McCallum and christened on 19 June 1839 at St Luke's, Chelsea, London. He married Rosa Warren on 22 January 1867 at St Mary-le-Bone, Middlesex (London), and the 1881 census found them at 30 Denmark Villas, Hove, Sussex, where he was recorded as a retired captain in the Ninety-first Regiment, aged forty-four, born [christened on 19 June 1839?] at Chelsea and she as a "Lady" born in London. They then had a son, Arthur, aged thirteen, born at Fort George, New Brunswick, and there were two servants.

AM and Rosa emigrated to Vancouver Island where the 1991 census found them living in two of fourteen rooms of a wooden house in Esquimalt. He was recorded as an "agnostic" retired officer born in Russia to a Scottish father and a Welsh mother, she as aged forty-seven and an Anglican with two English parents. Their son was not there, and the English census of 1901 found an Edward A. McCallum, aged twenty-seven, an unmarried mechanical engineer born in Russia and living as a boarder at 57 Yarburgh Street, Moss Side, Lancashire. AM died, aged sixty-two,

J.F. Bosher

on 11 April 1899 in Victoria. Rosa McCallum died, aged eighty-three, on 3 October 1923 in Esquimalt. Was Lieutenant Arthur Howard Kirkman McCallum, who was born on 22 April 1896 in South Cowichan, a relative of theirs? When the latter joined the Fiftieth Regiment, GH of C on 9 February 1916 in Victoria, he was an Anglican "Officer of Active Milita," living at 1826 Hampshire Road, Victoria, with Mary Frances McCallum *née* Mackenzie, whom he had married in Victoria on 21 December 1915.

Sources: Canadian census 1891, Vancouver Island; census 1881, England, RG 11/1098, p. 11; census, 1901, RG 13/3709, p. 12; NAC, CEF files box 6606-46.

McCULLOCH, Captain William (1827-1906). He reached Victoria as first mate aboard a sailing vessel, the *Nannette* [*sic*], on Christmas Eve 1860, when she ran aground and was wrecked on Race Rocks before she could enter the harbour. The Race-Rocks lighthouse was not yet active. The local population were delighted to retrieve her cargo of gin before she sank into deep water. The story of this wreck was reported in the *Daily British Colonist* on 25 December 1860 (pp. 1-3) under the heading "Total Loss of the British Bark Nannette," and retold several times later. WM was born on 12 May 1827, a Presbyterian in North Ireland, and had a long career at sea before taking the *Nannette* around South America to Victoria, but once there, he married and settled permanently on Michigan Street in the James Bay quarter. Edgar Fawcett, editor of the *Victoria Colonist*, remembered him in 1912 as one of his friends in the Wesleyan Methodist Church nearby, where WM accompanied his very-determined wife, brought up as a Methodist. A portrait sketch of him and a summary of his sailing career as a sea captain on the BC coast are in E. W. Wright, ed., *Lewis & Dryden's Marine History of the Pacific Northwest. An Illustrated Review of the Growth . . . etc.* (1895), p. 97, and Appendix 4. He was listed in *Henderson's British Columbia Gazeteer* (1882-1883) as captain of the Hudson Bay Company's steamer *Otter* in 1885 and again in 1887 as captain of the steamer *Amelia*.

On 3 March 1864, he married my great-aunt, Sarah Taylor Marsden (1833-1916), who was the first of our family to emigrate and always known in the family as "Aunt McCulloch." The third child of Samuel Marsden and Hannah Brierley and a sister of our great-grandfather George Marsden (1827-1910), Aunt McCulloch was born on 17 April 1833 at Chorley, northwest of Manchester, into a large working family centred on Manchester and Salford. The "Taylor" in her name was in memory of her uncle, Rev. James Marsden (1797-1874), an enthusiastic Methodist. Family lore says that she came to Victoria around the Horn on a sailing vessel and married the ship's captain. But this is only partly true, like most lore in most families. She married McCulloch certainly, but he was not the captain of *The Robert Lowe*, one of the famous "bride ships" in which she travelled. It was a Captain Congalton who brought the ship to Victoria. Precisely why Aunt McCulloch sailed to the Island is nowhere recorded, and it would be interesting to know because she was one of only 118 emigrants who went from Britain to British Columbia in 1863, whereas fourteen thousand left for New Zealand, twenty thousand for Victoria (Australia), ten thousand for Queensland, and seventeen thousand for Canada. The family believed that at nearly thirty years of age, Aunt McCulloch had no prospect of marriage at home and so responded to advertisements by the Female Middle-Class Emigration Society.

The secretary of that society, Susan Rye (1829-1903), wrote to *The Times* on 12 September 1962, "My forty women are to start in the *Robert Lowe* next Monday, and as further funds are required I shall be obliged by contributions being sent at once to me here; or to the treasurer, Mr William Cunliffe Brooks, Bank, Manchester." She had concluded an earlier letter, sent from Manchester, with regrets that she had not the space to write—"about the miseries of Manchester, and what I believe emigration will also do for a few of the unemployed factory girls." The whole enterprise of "bride ships" to the Island was assisted by the bishops of Oxford and London and the lord mayor of London, who had formed the British Columbia Emigration Society "for the purpose of encouraging the emigration of respectable, industrious women to the colony as a step towards supplying wives for the miners and others, and establishing a solid basis of colonial existence." Prominent in the BC Emigration Society was the philanthropic Baroness [Angela] Burdett-Coutts (1814-1906). As a result of their efforts and Susan Rye's arrangements for the selection of the women and their voyage, Sarah Taylor Marsden sailed from Liverpool on the *Robert Lowe*—the second "bride ship" of that period—one of thirty-eight women carefully chaperoned by *Rev. William Sheldon Reece and not allowed to mingle with the other passengers. Another of the prospective "brides" was Emma Lazenby (1842-19340, who in 1867 married David Spencer (1837-1920), the Welsh founding owner of Spencer's Deparment Store on Government Street. When the *Robert Lowe* arrived at Esquimalt early in January 1863, its female passengers, ferried to Victoria, were met by a welcoming committee headed by the mayor's wife, with a thousand curious spectators watching from behind them.

The colony on Vancouver Island had been discussed in *The Times* (London) and advertized occasionally in Britain. Various reports were published in the years around 1860, chiefly because of the excitement over the gold rush of 1858. Sarah, then nearly thirty years old, evidently responded to appeals of the kind published in London, only two years after her arrival, by Matthew Macfie in his *Vancouver Island and British Columbia: Their History, Resources and Prospects* (London, 1865, pp. 496-97):

> Respectable females, neither afraid nor ashamed to work as domestic servants, are greatly in demand. Strong and active young women, qualified to serve as efficient cooks and housemaids, would have no difficulty in obtaining £4 to £5 per month and board. So much is the want of this class felt, that if 500 girls of good character and industrious habits could be sent out in detachments of fifty in each vessel, and at intervals of a month, they would be absorbed almost immediately on their arrival. But the presence of this sex is as urgently required on social and moral grounds. There are many well-disposed single men prospering in the various trades and professions, who are anxious to adopt the country as their home. But the scope for selecting wives is so limited that they feel compelled to go to California in search of their interesting object, and

not unfrequently are they tempted to remain on American soil—their
industry as producers and expenditure as consumers being lost to the
colonies. There is no territory on the globe presenting to unmarried
virtuous females such opportunities of entering that state upon which
every right-minded woman cannot but look with approval.

This proved to be true in Sarah Taylor Marsden's case, as she was married in
Victoria on 3 March 1864, scarcely a year after her arrival. Some visitors, such as
Duncan Macdonald, described British Columbia as "an inhospitable wilderness,"
but Aunt McCulloch took an optimistic view, which turned out to be justified. She
and the rest of the thirty-eight women passengers were undoubtedly "respectable,"
but not much more, according to the naval officer who ferried them from the
Robert Lowe over to Victoria. "This afternoon," he wrote to his father on 12 January
1863, "I took them all round to Victoria in the ship [HMS *Grappler*] and landed
them there. They are evidently of a lower class than those who came out in the
Tynemouth, and perhaps better suited for the colony on the whole."
　　Nearly twenty years later, in 1884, when WM was employed as master of SS
Amelia, the McCullochs appear in the records living at 125 Michigan Street in the
James Bay district on a point of land between the Inner Harbour (James Bay)
and the Outer Harbour on the Strait of Juan de Fuca. When I visited in 1997,
the original house was no longer there, having been replaced by a larger one
occupying the two lots formerly numbered 125 and 127 Michigan St. In 1889,
a city directory lists their son George as a clerk in the Post Office, but by 1894,
George had "a candy factory" at 30 Government St, which is between the Dallas
Road and Battery St near Holland Point. George's "factory" was probably a shop
where he and his wife sold home-made sweets.
　　According to census records for 1891, several other Marsdens were then
living with the McCullochs at 125 Michigan Street: Harry (1866-1924), his wife
Minerva *née* Livesay (1867-1908), Taylor (1864-1932) and his wife Elizabeth Ellen
née Willett (1863-1931), all born in England. The Taylor Marsdens also had two
children with them: Harry aged three, born in England, and Amy (1891-1967)
aged one, born on the Island at Nanaimo. In 1893, the elder Harry Marsden was at
a different address, but he and his brother Taylor were both still in Victoria. They
were working as "cornice makers" and later as "tinplate workers." In the census
records, they and their families all declared themselves to be Baptists, which is
interesting as the McCullochs were both practicing Wesleyan Methodists. None of
these visiting Marsdens was still in Victoria in 1894, according to the city directory
for that year; my mother recalled hearing that they returned to England because
their wives did not like Victoria.
　　Amy Marsden (1891-1967), my mother's Nanaimo-born first cousin, married
George Stanfield Blake (1876-1940) and kept in touch with my mother's family.
I recall meeting her on one of her visits from England to Victoria, a vigorous,
warm-hearted old lady much like my grandmother. She was widowed in 1940 when
George Blake, a geologist, was murdered by marauding Arabs while surveying or
prospecting in Palestine. Her father and uncle, Taylor and Harry Marsden, were

Aunt McCulloch's nephews, sons of her brother George Marsden and of Mary Anne Rodgers, George's second wife. In March 1953, one of Aunt McCulloch's grandsons, son of Amy (Marsden) Blake, emigrated with his wife and small son Rodney on the *Empress of France*, bringing his large yacht *Shona* over by steamer and train. This was Geoffrey Blake (1918-2001), a naval architect who came out to work for the RCN at Esquimalt. He, his wife Mary, and their three children, including Sara and Simon born after their arrival in Victoria, lived in their yacht near Victoria for some years, then at 755 Lampson St, Esquimalt, and Geoffrey built a small sailing cabin cruiser, *Snowflake*, in which they cruised the Gulf of Georgia. About 1966, they moved to Ottawa.

With the death of my parents' generation, contact with Marsdens in England dwindled, though Amy (Marsden) Blake's daughters, Joan and Barbara, both married in England, were warmly hospitable when I visited them in the 1950s and again in 1992. Barbara's husband, John King (1920-1998), spent much of his working life as the city engineer at Slough in Berkshire. But I must end these rambling notes. My excuse for them is that WM's family life is relatively familiar and an example of the vast fabric of social life that used to tie the Island more firmly to the empire than to Canada.

Sources: *The Daily British Colonist*, 25 December 1860 (vol. 5, no 11), p. 3; Pritchard, *Letters of Edmund Hope Verney*, p. 114; Jacques Marc, ed., *Historic Shipwrecks of Southern Vancouver Island* (Victoria, The BC Heritage Trust, August 1990), pp. 28-31, with a short bibliography; Fred Rogers, *Shipwrecks of British Columbia* (Vancouver, J. J. Douglas Ltd., 1973), pp. 81-3; *The Times* (London), 12 September 1862, p. 8, col. D; *The Times* (London), 5 September 1862, p. 8, col. F; Marion Diamond, *Emigration and Empire: The Life of Maria S. Rye* (Taylor and Francis, 1999), 304 pp.; Duncan George Forbes Macdonald, *British Columbia and Vancouver's Island Comprising . . .* (Longman Green, 1862), pp. 393 ff.; Matthew Macfie, *Vancouver Island and British Columbia: Their History and Prospects* (Longman Green, 1865), 574 pp.; Joseph Despard Pemberton, *Facts and Figures Relating to Vancouver Island and British Columbia, Showing What to Expect and How to Get There, with Illustrative Maps* (Longman Green, 1860); Alexander Rattray, *Vancouver Island and British Columbia* (Smith Elder, 1862), 182 pp.; BC Archives, NW 325.711 R4B4: Barbara L. Riber, "The Robert Lowe," a typed article based on newspaper reports of the time. The Robert Lowe left Gravesend on 18 September 1862 and arrived in Victoria 114 days later on 12 January 1863, having not touched land once on the voyage; Lugrin, *Pioneer Women*, pp. 101, 147 and see Chapter XI, "The Bride Ships"; *The Sidney & Gulf Islands Review*, 9 November 1916, p. 2, obit.; Lyn Gough, *Wise as Serpents: Five Women and an Organization that Changed British Columbia* (Victoria, Swan Lake Publications, 1988), p. 21 (Emma Lazenby); Newton Henry Chittenden, *Travels in British Columbia* (Victoria, 1882; reprinted by Gordon Soules Book Publishers Ltd., 1984), p. 71; Edgar Fawcett, *Some Reminiscences of Old Victoria* (Toronto, William Briggs, 1912), 294 pp., p. 294; George Scott, *Memorials of James Marsden, of Oldham and Dewsbury, who for fifty-seven years served his generation as a missionary collector, Sunday school teacher, class leader, local preacher, and visitor of the sick and dying* (London, Hamilton, Adams & Co., Paternoster Row, sold also at 66, Paternoster Row, Leeds: H. W. Walker Briggate, 1874), 151 pp.

McADAM, William Alexander (1889-1961). The last of the nine agents general for BC in London during the century before 1960, he was acting agent general in 1934-1941 and full agent general in 1941-1958. He first went out to the province in 1910 to work in Vancouver City for the Canadian Bank of Commerce, but it was at Duncan on the Island that, on 15 April 1914, he married Inez (1885-1964), daughter of William Chalmers Duncan (1836-1919), born at Sarnia, Ontario, and founder of the town of Duncan. Its founding was a result of Duncan and his neighbours stopping the train on the newly built railway in August 1886 and offering his land for a station that had not been on the original plan. It may be that many Imperials settled at and near Duncan as a result of WM and Inez talking enthusiastically about it in London in the course of his work as agent general.

WM was born in Manchester on 19 December 1889, son of John and Margaret F. McAdam, and, after attending Hulme Grammar School, was employed by the British Linen Bank at Edinburgh in 1905-1910. Having reached BC in 1910, he became publicity and industrial commissioner for the city of Victoria in 1919 and the BC government in 1922, which appointed him assistant deputy minister of finance. He was transferred to London in 1923 as secretary to the agent general for BC, who at the time was Frederick Coate Wade (1860-1924), KC, agent general in 1918-1924. In London, WM was ultimately decorated with the CMG and joined the East India Club, the Sports Club, the Rotary Club, and the Royal Automobile Society. He retired in 1958 to the Island, where he lived in the Cowichan Valley, mailing address PO Box 755, Duncan. He was back in England in October 1960, living at Oatlands Park, near Weybridge, Surrey, and died, aged seventy-one, at Walton-on-Thames Hospital, leaving his widow, a son, and a daughter. Inez returned to the Island, where she had been born on 1 October 1885, and died, aged seventy-eight, on 30 January 1964 at Langford.

Sources: *The Times*, London, 6 July 1961, p. 25, obit.; *Who's Who*, 1944, p. 1706; *Who was Who*, 1961-70.

McCUTCHAN, Lieutenant Edward Head (1882-1931). Born on 20 December 1882 in Rangoon, Burma, he served for three years in the British South African Police and three years in the Natal Police. At sometime before the Great War, he moved to Port Arthur, Ontario, where he was living with his wife, Maude Hannah McCutchan, and was commissioned as a lieutenant in the Ninety-fourth Overseas Battalion of the CEF on 8 January 1916 at Port Arthur and transferred later to the Fifty-eighth Battalion.

In 1929, they moved to 1760 Landsdowne Road, Victoria, where they attended St Luke's Anglican Church at Cedar Hill and he was active as a Freemason. After eighteen months in Victoria, he died, aged forty-nine, leaving his widow, two sons, a daughter, his mother, Hon. Mrs Verker of Camberley, England, a brother, Lieutenant Commander D. R. McCutchan in Malta, and a sister, Mrs Gladys Matthews, in Dublin, Ireland.

Sources: NAC, CEF files RG150, box 6684-3; *Colonist*, 22 April 1931, p. 16, obit.

MACDONALD, Major Alastair Douglas (1875-1948). He was born in Victoria, son of Catherine Balfour Reid Macdonald, who in 1857 had married W. J. Macdonald of "Armadale," Victoria, one of the first mayors of the town, originally from Valley North, Uist, and Glendale, Isle of Skye, who was named a senator of the Dominion of Canada. In the Great War, AM served overseas in the Royal Artillery and after the war bought farming land from Alex McDonald of North Saanich, who appears to have been no relation. He called his farm "Duntulm" and raised Jersey cows for many years, winning prizes such as the Jersey Roll of Honour in August 1943 awarded to "Seagull," who produced more than 4,000 lbs of butterfat in the year. Success and his distinguished family background gave him the wherewithal for travelling and politics. In Autumn 1925, he went to England and then joined the North-west Saanich Conservative Association, which elected him to its executive committee along with *Captain MacGregor McIntosh and J. M. Copithorne. In 1933, he was president of the North Saanich Board of Trade, which had been incorporated the previous year, and managed to have wild carrot classified as "a noxious weed." He was one of the delegates from Saanich at the annual convention of the Island's Associated Boards of Trade held at Saanichton 5-7 July 1933. A year later, he, *Colonel W. H. Belson, and Dr William Newton judged the swimming competitions at a big gala event at the Chalet, Deep Cove, for North Saanich Community Day. After the royal visit to Victoria in May 1939, he wrote a letter to the *Colonist* suggesting that in future, war veterans ought to have preference in presentations to the king and queen.

AM had a number of interesting military friends and relations. His eldest brother, *Lieutenant Colonel Reginald James Macdonald, RA, DSO, *Croix de Guerre*, has his own entry in this book. Another brother, the family's second son, attended Collegiate School in Victoria and then joined the naval training ship, HMS *Britannia* at Portsmouth. This was *Captain W. B. Macdonald, DSO, who had a career in the Royal Navy that took him to China during the Boxer Rebellion and as commanding officer of the Suez Canal defences forces during the Great War. He acted later as liaison and naval transport under General Allenby in Palestine (DSO and was mentioned in dispatches). In August 1937, he died serving in some capacity in Germany. These brothers had a cousin, Brigadier General Blakeney, CMG, DSO, RE, who visited AM in May 1934, arriving from Asia on the *Empress of Canada*, and put up in Oak Bay at the Beach Hotel. He had spent many years in Egypt and Africa, had become a crusading member of the British-Israel Federation, and had taken to giving public lectures. Interviewed at the hotel, he said there was a sinister force behind the financial chaos in the world today. In the next few days, he lectured on the economic situation of the world and on the probability of war. "We must all realize that democracy has failed," he said. "It has become so corrupt that a change is imperative." This was a widespread idea in the depression years of the 1930s, which encouraged the fascist and communist movements that were so successful at the time. AM died, aged seventy-three, on 9 January 1948 in Sidney and was mourned *inter alia* by the elders in my family, who were old friends.

Sources: *Colonist*, 27 September 1925, p. 8; 9 May 1931, p. 3; 24 February 1933, p. 7; 12 May 1933, p. 2; 7 July 1933, pp. 1 and 6; 19 May 1934, p. 8; and 25 May

1934, pp. 1 and 3; 3 August 1934, p. 4; 12 September 1934, p. 7; 1 and 3; 5 August 1937, p. 3; 7 August 1937, p. 6, obit and photo; 2 August 1939, p. 4; 15 August 1943, Sunday, p. 6.

MACDONALD, Lieutenant Colonel Reginald James (1867-1951). He was born in Victoria, eldest son of Senator *W. J. Macdonald of "Armadale," Victoria, and brother of *Major A. D. Macdonald of "Duntulm," North Saanich, of *Captain William Balfour Macdonald, and of Miss Macdonald, Clive Drive, Victoria. He was educated privately and at RMC, Kingston, Ontario, where he passed out first and was awarded a cadetship at the Royal Military Academy, Woolwich. In 1887, he was commissioned in the Royal Artillery and, after a period of regimental service, was went on to serve as an inspector of Warlike Stores for six years ending in 1900. Posted then home to Esquimalt as a captain for about five years, he returned to England in 1905 and qualified as an instructor in gunnery on the Long Gunnery Staff Course. Then he was seconded for service with the Royal Malta Artillery and remained on Malta until war broke out in 1914. Then he held the Central Fire Command. In 1916, he was in command of the Seventy-third Heavy Brigade of Artillery in France and with the British Salonica Expeditionary Force, this until 1917 when he caught malaria and was invalided home. He was mentioned in despatches and received the DSO, the Serbian Order of Karageorge (with swords), the Greek Military Cross, and the Greek Military Medal.

He married Mary Schofield, daughter of A. T. Schofield, MD—with whom he settled at "One Oak," Camberley, Surrey—and had a son. He liked fishing and golf and joined the Army and Navy Club in London. More unusual, he also had a military artist's talent for watercolour sketches of military regalia. Early in his career, he became an authority on military uniforms and a painter of military figures based on careful historical research. He illustrated and published a book, *The History of the Dress of the Regiment of the Royal Artillery 1625-1897* (Henry Sotheran & Co., 1899), xvi and 131 pp., with twenty-four coloured plates and many drawings, and he painted pictures of many regiments, which were widely hung in regimental messes and museums. In 1934, he produced a series of thirty watercolour sketches of the old uniforms of the Royal Scots for the Princess Royal, who was the regiment's colonel-in-chief. The queen and the Prince of Wales then ordered sketches to be made for them. His designs for the plaques, commemorating the Highland regiments, were accepted for the Scottish War Memorial at Edinburgh. When he died, aged eighty-four, at Camberley on 28 September 1951, his friends remembered him as courteous, witty, and amusing with caricatures of people casually drawn for fun.

Sources: *Who's Who* 1935, p. 2093; *As You Were! Ex-Cadets Remember*, ed., R. Guy C. Smith, No. 1877 (Ottawa; The RMC Club of Canada, 1884-1984, 1984), vol. I, 1876-1918, pp. 147-8; *Colonist*, 12 September 1934, p. 7.

MACDONALD, Captain William Balfour (1870-1937), RN, DSO. Born in Victoria on 19 June 1870, he was the second son of *Senator W. J. Macdonald of "Armadale," Victoria, and brother of *Major A. D. Macdonald of "Duntulm," North Saanich. He attended Collegiate School and then joined the naval training ship,

HMS *Britannia* at Portsmouth. He rose from midshipman (15 November 1886) to acting sub-lieutenant (14 November 1889), sub-lieutenant (14 February 1890), lieutenant (30 June 1892), commander (31 December 1904), acting captain (28 October 1915), and captain (retd) (1 June 1920). In the course of his career, he served in China during the Boxer Rebellion and at many other places and in 1907-1910 was flag commander to the commander-in-chief at Portsmouth. He was captain of HMCS *Niobe* at the inauguration of the Canadian Navy in 1910. In the Great War, he was in charge of the Suez Canal defence forces and later acted as liaison and naval transport officer under General Edmund Allenby in Palestine. He was named to the Order of the Nile (third Class) and the DSO. His service was in HMS *Britannia* on the Home Station (15 July 1883 to July 1885), *Triumphant* on the Pacific Station (1 August 1885 to 6 November 1888), *Excellent* for RN College (26 November 1889), *Leah* and *Pembroke* on manoeuvres (22 July to 28 August 1890), *Volage* on training (25 April 1891 to 30 June 1892), *Ringarooma* on the Australia Station (15 August 1892 to 8 May 1894), *Ringarooma* again in Australia (9 May 1894 to 2 September 1895), *Imperieuse* on the Pacific Station (5 March 1896), *Medea* on the Home Station (2 October 1899 to 22 January 1900), and *Pique* on the Home Station (15 February 1900 to 11 August 1903). Others listed are illegible.

In 1903, WM, then serving in the RN on HMS *Pique,* presented a Chinese bell to the city of Victoria. He took it from a ruined temple near Shanhaiguan during the Boxer Rebellion in 1900. It was a fine example of Ming iron casting in 1627 formed in the shape of eight-petal lobes, each embossed with plum blossoms, bamboo, lotus, peony, jasmine, and chrysanthemum flowers, and it weighed about 2,000 lbs. Inscribed with the names of 360 Chinese citizens who paid for it, it had originally hung in a White Robe Buddhist convent. Upon receiving it in 1903, the city of Victoria put it under a small shelter in Beacon Hill Park, but the weather and vandals were slowly destroying it. In 1989, the city moved it into the Art Gallery of Greater Victoria and Barry Till, curator of Asian Art, wrote a short article about it for a local newspaper.

WM's file preserved in the British National Archives affords a closer-than-usual scrutiny of his record over the years. Sprinkled through it is much approval: "zealous," "attention to his duty," "much zeal" and "judgment and tact," etc. As a young man, however, a lark brought the authorities down on him. Under "Special Reports or Service" is a mass of tiny partly illegible handwriting, for example, "21 June 1890 grand displeasure expressed at disreputable conduct in (along with Ret'd (?) Sub-Lieut. Barkley) introducing two women of immoral character into the RN College: to be deprived of two month's seniority, and conduct to be reported on every three months while under instruction at Portsmouth." By September, however, there were more reports of excellent results: "conduct of above officer satisfactory [several more such]; ... granted leave to Switzerland 6-24 October 1903; permission to accept and wear the Swedish Order of the Crown; private permission to wear Order of the Crown of Prussia"; and in March 1909, "Appreciation expressed of manner in which he discharged duties in charge of a party of Russian Officers who were visiting in London on the occasion of a visit of the Russian Squadron. Recommended by Admiral Fanshawe (Adal)" and on to

"Noted for Command of *Niobe* when handed over to Canadian government. Most valuable in social work, very energetic, able and tactful; Nov. 1911 recommended for promotion by Rear-Admiral Kingswell; 17/18 November 1911 tried by Court Martial for stranding *Niobe* but acquitted. Held deserving of high recommendation for navigation the ship to Clarke's Harbour after she was disabled.—May 1912 recommended by the director of naval service Canada, as deserving of promotion." On 19 February 1918, he returned to England, and he retired on 1 June 1920 with the rank of captain. After a long retirement, he died, aged on 20 July 1937, leaving his wife Isabel Capel *née* Mier, daughter of Colonel Capel Miers of the Cameron Highlanders.
Sources: *British National Archives* (PRO) (London), ADM 196/43, page 121; *Who was Who*, 1929-1940, p. 852; *London Gazette* 11 August 1917; 22 April 1919; *Colonist*, 5 August 1937, p. 3; 7 August 1937, p. 6 (photo), obit.

McDONALD, Sergeant Major Edward Henry "Pop" (c. 1875-1954). Born in England, he joined the Royal Scots Fusiliers in 1894 (aged nineteen) and a year later served on the North-West Frontier of India under General Anderson. He fought at Tirah and Chitral against tribesmen and was shot and wounded by tribesmen in the Khyber Pass, then in the South African War with the Union Fusiliers, which relieved Ladysmith, a town that had been under fire from 15 October to 28 February. He was in battles at Kimberly, Vryburg, Mafeking, and Tugela Heights. Fever ended his service in that war, and he was then posted to Singapore in 1902 in the Royal Garrison Artillery. After five years there, he was discharged in 1907 but joined the British Expeditionary Force in 1914, understating his age by four years to do so. He served at Mons and in the trenches.
    After the Great War, he went to Canada, took up industrial first aid, and joined the Canadian Corps of Commissionaires in which he became a sergeant major. He left his guard duty at a Victoria shipyard to join the army in 1942, this time taking seventeen years of his age to do so. After three and a half years, he received the Queen's Coronation Medal. In June 1949, he was seventy-four years old and living at 226 Ontario St, James Bay, Victoria. He died, aged seventy-eight, on 1 January 1954 in Saanich of complications from a broken hip incurred while pushing his small electric car into its garage. He was survived by his wife at home, a son John in Australia, a brother and sister in Edmonton, and two brothers in England.
Sources: NAC, CEF papers, Box 6718-18, regimental number 414858; *Colonist*, 5 June 1949, Magazine Section, p. 4; 3 January 1954, p. 12, obit.

MacFARLANE, Major James F. Lennox (1845-1940). Born into an Anglo-Irish family on 7 April 1845 at "Huntsdown House," County Dublin, he attended the Royal School, Dungannon, and Trinity College, Dublin, where his BA was dated 1866, and he took an LLB at Dublin University. He joined the Third Prince of Wales Dragoon Guards the next year, became a captain in 1870, and in the early 1880s was appointed major of the Third Brigade SI Division, Royal Artillery. After serving for several years in India at Ahmadnagar, Bombay District, and elsewhere, he retired from the army in 1887 and became a Justice of the Peace in County Dublin, busy hunting, fishing, and breeding horses—hunters and steeplechaser—there and in Scotland. A famous horseman, he won many steeplechases on horses which he trained and rode himself. He and his wife Amy had several sons born at Dublin, for instance, two who identified themselves by enlisting in the CEF during the Great War: Arthur Francis MacFarlane born on 19 November 1889 who had been in a towing business and a member of the Fifth Regiment CGA when he enlisted on 21 January 1916 in Victoria, naming his mother Amy MacFarlane of Cobble Hill as his next of kin and George Alex, born on 25 February 1897, who was an "Engineer Assistant" when he joined up on 26 August 1915. In 1898, as he recorded later, he lost a great deal of money to a dishonest lawyer in Ireland and so emigrated with his wife to Alberta, where he bought 440 acres and began to farm. "However," he wrote later, "I could not feel at home there. Americans were coming in all around, with whom I had no ideas in common."

He therefore sold up after five years and went out to the Island, where he and his wife arrived on 8 May 1903. In Sidney, he learned of an old army friend, *Livingston Thompson, once in the Eleventh Hussars but by then a land surveyor, whom he discovered in Victoria, and they were soon drinking Irish whiskey at the Union Club with four more Anglo-Irish friends: *Charlie and Forbes Vernon, *Richard McBride, and a Captain Taplow. In India in 1867, JM had read in *The Field*—"my favorite paper"—about a voyage up the pristine east coast of Vancouver Island, and the memory of it now prompted him to buy a hundred acres at Mill Bay near Cobble Hill through a real-estate agent named *Arthur St George Flint. There being no road to Mill Bay, he bought in Victoria "a Columbia River sloop" with a centre board and sailed up to his new property. Then he explored the coast as far as Qualicum, where he found no people and no buildings. He discovered the estuaries of the Chemainus and Comox rivers which he had read about in India thirty-six years earlier.

One of his first activities at Mill Bay was to agitate in favour of a provincial road from Victoria. Government officials told him that surveyors had given up trying to find a suitable way over the mountains of the Malahat and were cynical about his declared intention to find one. In one of several consistent accounts of what followed, the *Daily Colonist* printed JM's story on 1 September 1938 (p. 4): "Sir—In a very excellent article by Mr Frank Giolma in your Sunday's issue, the writer . . . makes a grave mistake in his reference to the Malahat Drive. He states, 'This was built by the Provincial Government in 1914 to replace the Old Summit Road.' There are two mistakes in this: First there never was an 'Old Summit Road'; second, the present road was finished and opened for traffic a week before Christmas, 1911. I had the honor to be the first to drive over it and 'hanseled' it with a bottle of Burke's whiskey to the road gang. Shortly after I had come to B.C. and taken up land at Mill Bay, I inquired at the Department of Works why it was that there was no road going north from the Capital City. The reply I got was that the Government had sent out surveyors and engineers for forty years at intervals and that they had invariably returned and reported that it was impossible to find a line. I asked for a map and told them I would find a line and mark it on the map. I did so but it took me many weary months. Everyone seemed to think it nonsensical for me to say a thing could be done when Government official said it was impossible! H. B. Thomson, M.P.P. for Victoria gave me a helping hand by employing Frank Verdier, a noted timber cruiser, to go over my line and report on it. So Frank went over and blazed the line, reporting it quite feasible. The present road was then built."

In 1936 and 1937 by which time JM was living near Victoria at 416 Craigflower Road, he tried to interest capitalists in a modified version of a project which his friend, Captain Livingston Thompson, had mooted thirty years earlier. This was to smelt iron ore found near Mill Bay with the coal being mined at Nanaimo. Thompson's idea had been to build a railway from Cobble Hill to Port Renfrew on the Island's west coast in order to facilitate the exporting of coal and iron ore. Thompson had interested in some American businessmen in the project but on his way to see them in Seattle had drowned on 9 January 1904 in SS *Clallam* when she sank in a storm. "Captain Livingston Thompson's body reposes in Ross Bay Cemetery," JM wrote, "where in his full dress uniform of the 11th Hussars we buried him with full military honours, the band of the fifth regiment giving their services free, the 5th Regiment also supplying the firing party." JM's project in the 1930s was to revive Thompson's plan by using the coal to smelt the iron and export it, but there was no enthusiasm for this in the depressed years before the Second World War.

JM had more success in his efforts to defend trout fishing in Gold Stream, which flowed into Mill Bay through his property. "I am a fly-fisherman, and have fished the Mill Creek for twenty-eight years," he wrote in June 1931. "During that period I never once met a fisheries officer in the vicinity of the Creek, or was ever asked as to the size or number of my catch. Of late years the number of fish over eight inches has sadly diminished, one out of every dozen being fit to put in my basket." He went on to complain that people were taking the little ones in great numbers and nobody cared, inspected, or intervened, and that another enemy of river trout, merganzers, were a protected species on the Island, though there was a bounty on them in England. He also tried to promote cider as a healthy drink and a way of using the huge quantities of apples which he thought were being wasted on the Island. He gave a lecture to two Farmers' Institutes on cider-making and recommended that a cooperative cider factory be founded. When prohibition was being implemented, he went to ask Premier John Oliver to make an exception of cider, but he afterwards remarked, Oliver "did not see it from my point of view."

JM lived at Mill Bay for many years but on his ninety-first birthday was living at 614 Craigflower Road and on his ninety-fourth birthday at 1353 Pandora Avenue in Victoria. He was proud of his six sons, a grandson, and a nephew, who served in the Great War, most of them in Imperial forces. His ninety-fifth birthday was celebrated at the Jubilee Hospital, Victoria, on 7 April 1939, just before the outbreak of the Second World War, and he died, aged ninety-six, on 2 June 1940, leaving four sons—Arthur on Richmond Road and Captain Fred on Quamichan Road, Captain George on Island Highway, and Walter in Australia—and three daughters including Mrs Colonel Selby in Ireland. His wife had died some years before and a daughter quite recently.

Sources: *Colonist*, 15 March 1929, p. 4; 10 June 1931, p. 4; 24 June 1931, p. 4; 4 May 1933, p. 4; 18 June 1933, p. 4; 7 April 1936, p. 2; 20 December 1936, Sunday p. 20, "Our Island Past and Present"; 15 April 1937, p. 4; 1 September 1938, p. 4; 30 May 1939, p. 4, Letters to the Editor, the first urging that the fishing season should begin in April, as 1 March was much too soon; 7 April 1939, p. 3; 7 April 1940, p. 9; 1 October 1940, p. 3, obit.; NAC, CEF files, box 6817-40 and 48; Adelaide Ellis, *Along the Mill Bay Road* (Cobble Hill, 1990).

MACKENZIE-GRIEVE, Lieutenant Commander Kenneth (1880-1942). He was born on 7 March 1880 at Ryde, northeast of Sandown on the Isle of Wight, son of Commander Frederick John Mackenzie-Grieve, a Yorkshireman, and his Scottish wife Charlotte Jane. KM's paternal grandmother, Louisa Jane Grieve *née* Salmond, was born on 16 August 1811 at Fort Marlborough, Bencoolen, on the north-west coast of Sumatra (now Bengkulu, Indonesia), daughter of Captain Francis and Ann Salmond, friends of the famous governor Raffles. Widowed in the 1850s, she took her two daughters and three sons to England, where KM's father, aged thirteen, was found by the 1861 census at the Royal Naval Academy at Alverstoke, near Gosport. By 1871, he was a lieutenant in the RN and his elder brother Robert James, KM's uncle, was away in South America. KM's father retired to Droxford, northwest of Southampton, where the 1901 census recorded him, aged fifty-three, living with his wife, KM's mother, Charlotte Jane, aged forty-seven, from Scotland. KM was a sub-lieutenant in the RN posted at Portsmouth, having been a midshipman since 15 September 1896, and was to be promoted to lieutenant (26 June 1902) and lieutenant commander (26 June 1910). He had qualified as a assistant surveyor, fourth class, on 19 July 1902 and received a master's certificate from the Board of Trade on 16 May 1912.

An attempt to make the first non-stop flight across the Atlantic Ocean made KM internationally famous. On 18-19 May 1919, he and an Australian pilot, Harry George Hawker (1889-1921), set off from Glendenning's Farm at St John's, Newfoundland, in a Sopwith aircraft with a Roll Royce "Eagle" engine capable of flying at 100mph for about thirty hours. KM was chosen to navigate because of his experience as second in command of HMS *Campania*, a seaplane carrier. After five hours, however, their engine overheated and they managed to fall into the sea near a Danish freighter, which put them ashore in Europe a few days later. They had gone some 1,200 miles of the 1,880 miles from Newfoundland to Ireland, but the *Daily Mail*, which had offered a £10,000 prize for the first trans-Atlantic flight, gave them £5,000 each. It was less than a month later, on 14 June 1919, that a pair of ex-RAF flyers, John Alcock and Arthur Whitten-Brown, made their famous flight, the first across the Atlantic, beating several other rivals including a U.S. naval team.

KM retired on 7 March 1920 as a commander with decorations from the Royal Human Society and the AFC conferred at Buckingham Palace on 28 May 1919 "in recognition of his attempted flight across the North Atlantic as navigator for H. Hawker." On 14 June 1923 at Dibden, Hampshire, he married Janet Clinton Baddeley and took her to Victoria, where they lived for some twelve years at 644

Island Road, Oak Bay. There he died, aged sixty-two, on 26 September 1942 and was buried at Royal Oak, leaving his wife and a daughter.

Sources: *British National Archives* (PRO), ADM 196/45, page 223; AVIA 2/2820, Code No. 23/1 5,150 (1919); *The Times* (London), 6 October 1942, p. 6; *Colonist*, 11 July 1930, p. 6; 27 September 1942, pp. 18 and 22, obit.; Howard Clayton, *Atlantic Bridgehead: The Story of Transatlantic Communications* (Garnstone Press, 1968), pp. 160-8; William Courtenay, *Airman Friday* (Hutchinson & Co., 1936), pp. 350-1; census 1881, England, RG 11/1183, p. 30; census 1901, RG 13/999, p. 6; 984, p. 3; and for the father: census 1861, RG 9/648, p. 28; census 1871, RG 10/4817, p. 30; census 1881, RG 11/5641, p. 99; census, 1901, RG 13/1090, p. 1.

MACKIE, Sergeant Major Alexander Gowans (1870-1947). Born at Aldershot, Hampshire, he was appointed at the age of fourteen as bugler to Major General Frederick Roberts (later Earl Roberts, 1832-1914) and served in India, Egypt, and South Africa. In the Great War, he fought in the Fifth Western Cavalry of the CEF and then retired with the rank of regimental sergeant major and fourteen medals, including the DCM. When he came to Canada, he founded the Prince Edward Branch No. 91 of the Royal Canadian Legion and served as its president for ten years. From 1919 to 1946, he was the postmaster at Langford near Victoria. The king noticed this soldier's huge row of medals including Egyptian campaign medals during a royal inspection tour at Victoria on 31 May 1939 and spoke to him. When he died, aged seventy-seven, on 7 February 1947, he and his wife Alice were living on Belmont Road, Colwood. He also left two nephews in Victoria and three sisters and a brother in Wales.

Sources: Dorothy Stranix, *Notes and Quotes: A Brief Historical Record of Colwood, Langford, Metchosin, Happy Valley, Glen Lake, on Southern Vancouver Island* (Victoria [?], Joint Centennial Committee, 1967), pp. 78-9; *Colonist* 3 June 1939, p. 18; 8 February 1947, pp. 11 and 18, photo and obit.

MACKIE, Lieutenant Colonel Ernest Ford (1873-1938). He was born on 2 June 1873 at Dover, Kent, son of James B. Mackie, a Trinity pilot born at Deal, Kent, and Rebecca Mackie, a Londoner. He had three brothers and two sisters. In the early 1890s, he went to Canada and was working as a telegraph clerk with the Grand Trunk Railway. He soon joined the militia in Winnipeg and became a very active recruiting officer. Before 1900, he had reached the rank of major and was adjutant of Strathcona's Horse when that famous regiment left for the South African War. He fought through that war and so declared his "trade or calling" to be "soldier" in the permanent force of Canada when he joined the CEF at Winnipeg on 5 October 1914. His next of kin was his wife, Una Lisle Mackie, c/o J. G. Waugh, Winnipeg. He remained in the regiment until about 1921, when he took a property near Cowichan Station and busied himself in his garden and in local activities. "He loved to share his simple pleasures with his friends," one of his neighbours wrote, "and we shall long remember the kindly personality of the 'old Colonel,' the cheery hand-wave inviting us to come and see his latest success with daffodil or peony, or perhaps to share his pride in the first bearing of some lusty young seedling which he had watched with tender care for several years. His interests were broad, his friends were many." This was at the news of his death, aged sixty-four, on 12 June 1938 at Cowichan Station. Buried at St Peter's Quamichan with Rev. T. M. Hughes officiating, he had among his pallbearers Colonel Homer-Dixon, *Mr Joseph Reade, *Mr Collings Wallich, Major W. R. Russell, Captain A. W. Barton, and Messrs H. Leney, W. H. Cresswell, L. C. Knocker (brother of *Major A. G. Knocker) and A. Kennington.

Sources: NAC, CEF files, box 6946-24; *Cowichan Leader,* 16 June 1938, p. 5, obit.; *Colonist,* 14 June 1938, p. 5, obit.; census 1881, England, RG11 1000/23 page. 40 (IGI).

McLAUGHLIN, Lieutenant Colonel Harry Dalzell (1878-1940). He was born on 10 April 1878 at Cannamore (or Cawnpore), India, to an Anglo-Irish father and a Scottish mother. They were part of a large Imperial family. His maternal grandfather and great-uncle were P. Dalzell, Bombay Uncovenanted Civil Service, and A. Dalzell, Bombay Forest Service, and a maternal great-uncle by marriage was A. Rogers, ICS, member of Council in the government of Bombay. There was also a second cousin, Captain W. Dalzell, in the IMS. On his father's side, Lieutenant Colonel W. P. McLaughlin, RSC, 107th Pioneers, died of wounds in the Great War and his father's half-brother, Lieutenant Colonel K. J. Gabbet, served as assistant director of Ordinance at Army HQ, Simla. Among his first cousins were Brigadier W. C. Walter, 104th Bombay Rifles, and H. Walter, Burma Police, and there were second cousins including Lieutenant Colonel A. Stewart, IMS, Colonel (or Brigadier) Davison, Bengal Cavalry, and Captain W. Walter, 2nd Gurkha Regiment. His stepfather and uncle, Colonel J. Gabbett, CB, served in the Madras Army and his stepbrother and first cousin, Lieutenant Colonel P. C. Gabbett, in the IMS. The next generation of Indian officers and civil servants was even more numerous. According to his Imperial service record, HM married Violet Charlotte Ada Little on 1 October 1912 at Bombay Cathedral, Rev. W. A. Sawtell, Anglican minister, and they had four surviving children: Peter Michael Dalziell Harry born on 11 March 1914, Anthony Patrick born on 17 February 1916, Harry Neil William born on 22 April 1917, and Sheilah Violette Barbara McLaughlin born on 10 January 1919, all of them born at Indore, Central India. The latter's second husband, Orrok William Roberts (1903-1989), was related to Sir James Reid Roberts who married Margaret Harriet Warburton, "Afghan princess."

HM learned soldiering as a cadet at Sandhurst from 28 January 1894 to 26 June 1898. On 20 July 1898, he was commissioned as an unattached second lieutenant "without purchase" and on 30 September landed at Bombay whence he was sent to Quetta next day. There he stayed until 1 February 1900 and next 20 October was appointed to the Malwa Bhil Corps as lieutenant until 20 July 1907 when he was promoted to captain in the 2/6 Gurkha Rifles. His promotion to major came on 1 September 1915 and to lieutenant colonel on 20 July 1924.

About 1928, he retired to a small farm in the Cowichan Valley on Norcross Road off Lake's Road near the Hadwen's Holly Farm, where he served for two years as president of the Cowichan Agricultural Society, for several years as chairman of its finance committee, and for several years also as a member of the Duncan Consolidated School Board. At the second annual Turkey Breeders's show in Duncan in November 1931, he and his wife won most of the prizes. He died, aged sixty-two, on Tuesday, 9 July in the King's Daughters Hospital, having been in ill health for some time. He was survived by his wife, a daughter Sheilah at home in Somenos, and two sons in the Indian Army: Lieutenant Peter Michael McLaughlin of the Sixth Gurkha Rifles, stationed on the North-West Frontier, and Lieutenant Anthony Patrick McLaughlin of the Tenth Baluch Regiment, serving in the Punjab. A third son, Larry, had been accidentally shot on an army range at an English agricultural college during rifle practice before the war. The pallbearers at his funeral at St Peter's Quamichan were such Imperial colleagues as only the Cowichan Valley could be expected to turn out: *Major J. H. G. Palmer, *Major General Sir Ernest Walker, *Captain J. D. Groves, John Gibb, W. Spencer, and N. R. Craig. The honorary pallbearers were *Admiral Rowland Nugent, *Colonel M. E. Dopping-Hepenstal, *Captain R. E. Barkley, Dr G. W. Bissett, J. Y. Copeman, and H. Leckie-Ewing.

Dr Dorothy Gilliam Thompson, a young neighbour who remembers the family after the Colonel's death, writes, "His widow and daughter had recently returned from India where, I believe, they had spent the War. The old Colonel had retired . . . and gone into turkey farming on that property, and had died before the war; his wife Violette had kept the enterprise going until just before the war. His two sons had also gone into the army and that is what took his widow and daughter back to India (and then the younger woman married there AND got divorced, so when she returned to Somenos with her mother in about 1948 or 1949 she was a fascinating and romantic figure). Her horse had been boarded in the field next to our place, so I connected her return with the departure of the horse; the McLaughlin place was more than a quarter of a mile from ours. The Colonel's daughter, Sheilah, has remained my friend for life; indeed, I believe she is still alive in a nursing home in Port Perry Ontario (I phone from time to time). She did NOT like 'The Jewel in the Crown', though some of us thought her experience was reflected in that story. It was a great event, in my childhood, when the widow McLaughlin invited us to tea: one had to be very much on one's best behaviour for tea and toast among the tiger skins and instruments of colonial war."

Sources: Family papers, courtesy of Ian Roberts, Shirley Road, Port Perry, Ontario, 16 November 2001; notes courtesy of Dr Dorothy Thompson, Department of History, University of New Brunswick, December 2001; notes courtesy of John Palmer, 19 August 2001; *Cowichan Leader*, 11 July 1940, obit.; *London Gazette*, 19 July 1898; *Gazette of India*, 1907, p. 658; *Gazette of India*, 7 April 1917, p. 499; *Gazette of India*, 8 August 1924, no. 969; *Colonist*, 21 November 1931, p. 18; John B. Hayward, ed., *Officers Died in the Great War 1914-1919* (New ed., Polstead, Suffolk, J. B. Hayward & Son, 1988) in 4_, p. 279.

McLAUGHLIN, Major Peter Michael Harry Dalzell (1914-1971), son of the above. Born on 11 March 1914 at Indore, Central India, he attended RMC, Kingston, Ontario, in 1931 and in 1936 accepted a commission in the Indian Army. At first, he served with the Northamptonshire Regiment on the North-West Frontier but in November 1937 was appointed to the First Battalion, Sixth Gurkha Rifles in which, for a time, he was supervising officer with the Kalibahadur Regiment lent by the king of Nepal to the British government for the duration of the Great War. In 1942, he attended the Staff College in Quetta and went with HQ Second Indian Division to Iraq, Palestine, and Egypt, returning to India in summer 1943. In 1944, as second in command of the 2/7th Gurkha Rifles, he served in Italy and Greece. In May 1945, he returned to India as brigade major of 115 Indian Infantry Brigade. After the war, he served in various staff appointments in India until India received its Independence, whereupon he retired and took employment with the BC government.

Before long, however, in 1951, he was commissioned in the Canadian Army with the rank of captain and served in various staff positions in Canada and Korea. He was twice mentioned in despatches, once with the Indian Army in Iraq and once with the Canadian Army in Korea. He retired from the Canadian Army in 1961 and took teacher's training at the University of Victoria. He then taught at Royal Oak Junior Secondary School. He was a member of the Masonic Order and of the Canadian Legion, Britannia Branch, Victoria. When he died there, aged fifty-seven, on 24 October 1971, he was survived by his wife Denys, two sons—Kevin and Shawn—and two married daughters. His funeral was at St Michael and All Angels Anglican Church, West Saanich Road.

Sources: *As You Were! Ex-Cadets Remember*, ed., R. Guy C. Smith, No. 1877 (Ottawa; The RMC Club of Canada, 1884-1984, 1984), vol. I, 1876-1918, p. 318; notes courtesy of Dorothy Thompson, History Dept, UNB, Fredericton, New Brunswick, 4 September 2001; *Colonist*, 26 October 1971, p. 25, obit.

McMULLIN, Lieutenant Colonel John Hugh (1868-1943). He was born on 5 October 1868 at Madras, India, son of Colonel John McMullin, late of the Indian Army, and Isabel Constance McMullin (née Beaumont), and educated at Haileybury School. After taking a university degree in history at an English university, he served with the Third Hussars in India until 1893, when he moved to the Okanagan Valley, BC. There he farmed until 1899, when he enlisted in Lord Strathcona's Horse, served in the South African War from January 1900 to May 1901, and fought in Cape Colony, Orange Free State, Natal, and the Transvaal. He returned to BC with the Queen's Medal and four clasps and in October 1901 took employment with the provincial civil service. In 1906-1909, he was government agent for BC at Fernie, in 1909-1910 inspector of police for BC, and in 1910 was appointed government agent at Prince Rupert and superintendent of recruiting in the northern part of BC. From 1911, he was inspector of police at Victoria with supervision over Vancouver Island and later lieutenant and captain in the Kootenay Rifles, major in the Canadian Militia, Sixty-eighth Regiment, and in March 1923 sworn in as superintendent of provincial police.

JM had accepted this post on two conditions: that he would meet no political interference and that the force would be reorganized immediately, as outlined in the New Police and Prisons Regulation Act. A number of urgent difficulties faced him immediately. Since 1919, the RCMP had been working in BC with

the BC Provincial Police and the Vancouver City Police, especially in trying
to control the drug trade in Vancouver. There were racial tensions, labour
conflicts, and federal concern over the spread of Communism. The Doukhobour
problem in the interior of the province also concerned both the federal and
provincial authorities. Conflicts between the three levels of government over
policing reached a point early in 1924 at which nearly all of the RCMP were
withdrawn. In all this, JM's work was satisfactory to the attorneys general, at
least, for when R. H. Pooley succeeded Manson as attorney general in 1928, he
asked JM to continue as superintendent. Among his other accomplishments
was a *B.C. Provincial Police Constable's Manual* of about fifty pages, which a
predecessor had begun and he finished. He began the practice of presenting
a comprehensive annual report to the legislature, summarizing administrative
statistics, operations, and equipment. He planned and established Douglas
House, a BC Provincial Police training school in Victoria, which began teaching
in 1930. He revived a small mounted squad of ten men based at Oakalla Prison
Farm. On his recommendation, the BC Game Department was separated from
the Provincial Police.

He retired in April 1939 and went to England for three months while his
successor, T. W. S. Parsons, took over the post. On returning near the end of July,
JM reported that although there were preparations for war (air-raid shelters, etc.)
"the question of war simply is not a current topic of conversation and anyone who
broaches the subject gets only an apathetic response." His wife, Ellie Mary Pelly,
whom he had married in 1902, daughter of R. S. Pelly of Armstrong, BC, had died
in Victoria on 8 March 1932 and their daughter and two sons had grown up. JM
went to stay with his sister, Miss C. M. McMullin at 37 Beach Drive. He remained
active in various local organizations, such as the Men's Canadian Club, which had
elected him to its committee on 14 March 1933. He died, aged seventy-four, on
11 May 1943 in Oak Bay, a few months after the death of his son, Flight Sergeant
Francis Hugh McMullin, RCAF, aged thirty-four, whose plane crashed into the sea
near Redcar, Yorkshire, on 17 March 1942.

Sources: *Who's Who in B.C.* 1933-1934, p. 123; *Colonist,* 15 March 1933, p. 6; 1 April
1939, p. 1; 16 April 1939, p. 5 (with photo); 22 July 1939, p. 2; 12 May 1943, p. 4;
15 May 1943, p. 16, with photo; Stonier-Newman, Lynne, *Policing a Pioneer Province:
The B.C. Provincial Police,* 1858-1950 (Madeira Park, BC, Harbour Publishing, 1991),
pp. 84, 94, 145-169, 170-198.

McPHILLIPS, Captain Albert Edward (1861-1938), KC, MPP. He was born
on 21 March 1861 at Richmond Hill, Ontario, into an ancient family of Irish
Roman Catholics, son of George McPhillips and Margaret *née* Lavin. Schooled at
St Boniface College, Manitoba, and Manitoba College, he became a barrister in
1882 and began practising law in Manitoba. In 1891, he was called to the Bar in
BC and practised at Victoria, specializing in corporate law, and in 1898-1899, he
was president of the BC Bar Association. He worked as solicitor for the Imperial
Bank, the BC Electric Railway Company, and other large concerns and became
president of the Vancouver Power Company. In 1900, he became a king's counsel,

in 1911 he served as a member of the Royal Commission on taxation in BC, and in 1913 was appointed to the Appeal Court of BC in which he remained for twenty-five years and served as attorney general during Premier Turner's term of office. He was elected to represent Victoria in the provincial legislature in the government of Premier McBride (1899-1903). As a youth, he liked riding, hunting, steeplechasing, and other sports. His soldiering began when he took a certificate at the Toronto School of Infantry and in 1885 became a lieutenant in the Ninetieth Battalion Winnipeg Rifles during the Riel Rebellion, serving at Fish Creek and Batoche.

In Victoria, he was one of the few Roman Catholics of his time in governing circles. While in Manitoba, he was active in supporting the campaign of 1896 in favour of publicly funded Catholic schools. He wrote pamphlets and newspaper articles on the subject. A strong member of St Andrew's Roman Catholic Cathedral, in 1896 he married Sophie Emily Davie, daughter of Hon. A. E. B. Davie, premier and attorney general of BC, who converted from the Anglican to the Catholic Church. They and their two sons and a daughter lived at "Clonmore House," Rockland Avenue. AM joined the Union Club, the Quadra Club, and the Men's Canadian Club, which elected him president in 1909. In 1910, he joined the British Campaigners' Association. He died, aged seventy-six, on 24 January 1938 in Victoria.

Sources: *Colonist*, 25 January 1938, pp. 1, 4 and 7, obit.; *BC Archives, "Minutes of the British Campaigners' Association,* 1908-1935"; Morgan, *Canadian Men and Women*, p. 790.

MacQUEEN, Major Dr Loudun Hope (c. 1873-1961). Born in Glasgow, he was schooled there, attended Glasgow University, qualified as a veterinary surgeon, and became a member of the Royal College of Surgeons. The English census of 1901 found him, aged twenty-eight, with a practice as veterinary surgeon and living with his English wife, Ada L. MacQueen, at 12 Bruce Grove, Tottenham, Middlesex (London), where their one servant was a groom from Alphington, Devon. In the Great War, LM joined the British Army on 13 February 1915 and served in the Veterinary Corps and the Royal Artillery in the Gallipoli campaign during which he was present at the landing in the Dardanelles. After the evacuation, he was sent to Egypt and Macedonia, served through the Salonika Campaign, and then went on to Southern Russia, the Black Sea, and Turkey. He was twice mentioned in despatches and named to the OBE. He retired to Canada in January 1920 though he was listed in the British *Medical Register* with a Scottish address, 108A Union Avenue, Glasgow, in 1944. For many years, he and his wife, whom he had married in London on 25 July 1900, lived at Tofield, Alberta. We know this because it was there he corresponded with Ottawa when Canadian authorities refused him an Imperial War Gratuity because "he was never on the strength of the Canadian Expeditionary Force, and at any rate he has not had any service in England with the Canadians." He claimed to have gone overseas on SS *Missinabi*, leaving Halifax on 22 February 1915 and returning to Canada from Liverpool on 27 December 1919 aboard SS *Metagama*. In 1920, during this correspondence, he and his wife were living at Tofield, Alberta.

About 1918, they moved to a place on the West Saanich Road near Brentwood Bay; in March 1922, their address was at Keating, Vancouver Island. There he kept a horse farm and riding stable. He used to take riding parties on trails around Saanich Mountain, Prospect Lake, Mount Newton, and elsewhere. In reply to someone who in 1929 argued in favour of the side-saddle for women, he said, "There is no doubt that the side-saddle gives a much more secure seat than the cross-saddle. At the same time, if I were a woman I should ride astride, and if I were a horse I should vote for prohibition of side-saddle entirely. As far as the appearance is concerned, it is of course a matter of taste, but very few women ride really well on a side-saddle, and the horse is the sufferer." Like most officers, he joined one or more veteran's organizations, notably the Army, Navy, and Air Force Veterans'Association, and on 25 April 1937, he was one of twenty-five English, Australian, and New Zealand veterans of the Gallipoli Campaign who met in Victoria at Speedie's Café to commemorate the first landing at Gallipoli on 25 April 1915. The meeting re-elected him to their committee along with Colonel H. H. B. Cunningham and Brigadier General J. G. Austin. They sang old songs and paid silent tribute for three Gallipoli veterans buried during the past year: W. Dennis, D. G. Hughes, and W. Barber.

As early as February 1931, LM and his wife became active members of the local Conservative Association, together with a Major Thorburn and others. In 1940, they worked at Royal Oak village hall as volunteers helping with the national registration of all citizens. Five years later, in September 1945, the Saanich Provincial Progressive Conservative Association chose LM to stand as an Independent PC candidate in the provincial general election. However, the North Saanich Conservative Association headed by Major A. D. Macdonald accused him and his supporters of splitting the Conservative vote and tried to persuade him to withdraw. Another group of Conservatives meeting at the Legion Hall on Mills Road also opposed LM's candidature but because they wanted to lend the party's support to the existing coalition government as a bulwark against the CCF, "who would welcome back the Japanese, give them back their fishing boats, and give them the vote." Among the delegates which that meeting elected to attend the nominations meeting at Royal Oak on 25 September were Major A. D. MacDonald, Frank Butler, and Lieutenant Colonel H. Lee-Wright.

LM was not elected, and some years later, on 11 June 1961, he died, aged eighty-eight, at the Veteran's Hospital in Saanich. They had been living for some time at Royal Oak at 4761 West Saanich Road.

Sources: NAC, RG9 series II-F-10, *Imperial War Gratuities*, vol. 187, file 12557-L-3; Daily *Colonist*, 28 April 1929, Sunday, p. 8; 27 April 1937, p. 3; 28 July 1938, p. 8; 21 August 1940, p. 2; 13 September 1945, p. 1; 19 September 1945, p. 5; 21 September 1945, p. 1; 11 November 1945, p. 9; 13 June 1961, p. 22: obit; Times 15/9/1945, p. 1; 17/9/1945, p. 1; 19/9/1945, p. 10; 21/9/1945, p. 3; *The Medical Register* (London), 1944, p. 1102; census 1901, England, RG 13/1249, p. 12.

MAGILL, Major Cecil K. (c. 1881-1935). Born in County Tyrone, Ireland, and educated at Irish universities, he went to Egypt as a commissioned officer in the Imperial Army. In Cairo, he met Miss Nora Drummond of Vancouver and they married. He served in South Africa in 1899-1902, then retired with his wife to Vancouver, where in 1906 he won the north-west amateur golf championship. In 1907, he moved to Seattle, where he managed the Seattle Golf Club and later went to India for the American Hawaian Steamship Co. He served in the Great War with the U.S. Army and after the war passed two years with the U.S. Shipping Board in London. His movements are hard to follow, but it was said that he later went to Java as a shipping executive and then to India with the Texas Co., returning to Victoria on 26 January 1925 aboard the *Empress of Asia*. For the last twenty-five years of his life, he had a summer home at Shawnigan Lake, and when he died in Seattle, aged fifty-four, he left a widow and a son at Shawnigan Lake.

Sources: NAC, RG76, *Immigration series* C-1-h, 1925 volume 1, page 9; *Colonist*, 27 January 1925, p. 17; 25 January 1935, p. 2, obit.

MAINGUY, ADMIRAL EDMOND ROLLO (1901-1979).

I. Family Background

He was born on 11 May 1901 in Victoria, son of Daniel Wishart Mainguy (1842-1906) and Mary Elizabeth *née* Fry (1856-1943), who had married in Victoria on 30 January 1884. The 1851 census found D. W. Mainguy, aged eight, born in England but living with his family at the Rectory of St Mary de Castel (Ste Marie du Castel) in Câtel Parish on the north-west side of the island of Guernsey, facing the coast of Devon and Cornwall across the English Channel. EM's paternal grandfather Rev. James Maingy [*sic*], aged forty-seven, was "[Anglican] Rector of St Mary de Castel in Câtel Parish" [originally Ste Marie du Castel], one of the island's two main churches, but born to a family of merchants and mariners at St Peter Port. His wife, EM's grandmother, Charlotte Maingy [*sic*], was Irish. D. W. Mainguy was the fourth son of six, and there were seven daughters. There were five servants: "nursery governess," cook, nurse, housemaid, and "outdoor servant." The first nine children, of whom EM was the ninth, were all born in England, but the last four were born locally at Câstel. EM's mother, Mary Elizabeth Fry (1856-1943), was born in "Canada West" [Ontario], second daughter of Henry and Jane Fry of Barnstaple, Devon, who had their son in London but had lived long enough in Ontario to have two daughters there. The 1861 census found EM's mother, aged four, living with her family in Bartholomew Street, St Olave Parish, Exeter, where her father was a grocer.

D. W. Mainguy went early to England, whence he sailed on 11 January 1863 aboard the bark *Strathallan* across the Atlantic and around Cape Horn to Victoria, a voyage of eighteen weeks. He built a cabin near Chemainus and then a house on a small island nearby, still called Mainguy Island, where he took EM's mother in 1884 after travelling back to the British Isles in 1876-1878. While he farmed, took odd jobs, and worked occasionally as a constable at Chemainus, they had five children of whom four survived and EM was the youngest. The eldest, Harold Wishart (1884-1964), married Alice Mignunette Martin on 28 March 1915 at Ashcroft and lived mainly in the Cariboo district near Williams Lake and Kamloops; Richard Cecil (1886-1946) trained as a land surveyor and on 3 June 1913 at Chemainus married Aileen Anketell-Jones, daughter of *Patrick Willoughby Anketell-Jones; and Barbara (1887-1946) married *Francis Barber-Starkey on 28 November 1911 at Westholme, when EM was about ten years old.

II. Education and Career

In 1911-1915, EM attended the little Quamichan Lake School kept by *Percy Truscott Skrimshire, who inspired him and others to rise to great heights doing their duty in Imperial forces during the Great War. In 1915-1917, EM attended the Royal Naval College of Canada in Halifax, Nova Scotia, and was at sea from February 1918 in HMS *Canada* as a midshipman; HMS *Barham* (March 1919) as second lieutenant; HMCS *Aurora* (September 1921), HMCS *Patriot* (September 1922), and HMS *Victory* (for a long signals course, September 1923); HMCS *Naden* (May 1925) as signals officer and supervising officer western division of the RCNVR; HMS *Frobisher* (September 1928) as flag lieutenant to vice admiral commanding the first cruiser squadron; HMS *London* (October 1928) at Vancouver Island as executive officer; HMCS *Vancouver* (May 1930) with the RN for special signal duty on American and West Indies Station; HMCS *Naden* (March 1931); HMS *President* (April 1931); HMS *Despatch* (May 1931); HMS *Delhi* (May 1931); Naval Service HQ (July 1932); HMCS *Stadacona* (September 1934); on HMCS *Saguenay* (December 1934) as commander; HMCS *Vancouver* (May 1936) in command; Naval Service HQ (January 1937) as director of naval reserves; at RN Staff College, Greenwich (January 1939); the destroyer HMCS *Assiniboine* in command (October 1939); HMCS *Ottawa* (April 1940) in command; HMCS *Sambro* (August 1941); HMCS *Avalon* (November 1941) at Halifax, promoted to captain (1941); Newfoundland as captain (1941); at National HQ as chief of naval personnel and third member of the naval board (1942); in command of HMCS *Uganda* (August 1944), taking part in the bombardment of Sakashima and of the Japanese-held base at Truk; flag officer Pacific Coast with rank of commodore (March 1947); and flag officer Atlantic Coast with rank of rear-admiral (September 1948). In 1949, he was appointed chairman of a commission investigating several mutinies in the fleet and in the resulting "Mainguy Report" recommended improvements in the handling of lower-deck grievances and some changes in naval traditions inherited from the RN. There followed command of HMCS *Niobe* (August 1950); HMCS *Magnificent* (September 1950); HMCS *Stadacona* (November 1950); and HMCS *Bytown* (December 1951) with the rank of vice admiral. He ended an outstanding career as a vice admiral, chief of the Canadian naval staff (1951-1956), and retired from the navy on 1 January 1956.

III. Family Life and Retirement

On 4 January 1927, EM married Maraquita Frances Cynthia Nichol (1906-1981), daughter of Walter Cameron Nichol, and they had three children: Daniel Nicholas Mainguy, who followed his father into the RCN and rose to the rank of admiral, Christopher David, and Quita Elizabeth. Their elder son recalls living as a child near Duncan at the corner of Herd Road and Crofton Road in a farm they called "Heavitree Farm" after the Fry family's old home in Devonshire. "We moved there to live in 1940 and mother took on running the farm as her war project. Most of the people we knew and with whom I went to school (Glenlyon and Brentwood College) were basically English who had left various parts of Asia because of the developing war. People I remember from the area included *Lieut.-Colonel Philip and Mrs Aileen Sealy, who had come from India. She was the sub-mistress of the Quamichan cub pack. *Lieut.-Colonel Dopping Hepenstal, a Gurkha officer and great Scouting movement enthusiast. I think I met *Mr P. T. Skrimshire once. He was the man who had been brought from England to start a school for boys, which produced a good many of the early naval officers in the RCN (including my father) as well as a bunch of other prominent citizens." In 1956, EM retired only from the RCN, and he established a home at 44 Lonsdale Road, Toronto, and an office at 11½ Spadina Road, where he worked as president of Great Lakes Waterways Development Association (1956-1965) and executive director of the Canadian Mental Health Association, Ontario Division. His full retirement, in 1965, left him free for the fishing, shooting, golf, tennis, and squash he listed as his recreations, and for these, he and his wife returned to the Island, where they settled at Qualicum Beach. There he died, aged seventy-seven, on 29 April 1979.

Sources: Notes courtesy of Admiral Dan Mainguy (a son), Ottawa, 11 February 2001; *MacFarlane*, p. 42; *The Canadian Who's Who*, (Toronto, Trans-Canada Press, 1960), vol. VIII (1958-1960), p. 707; Edward Mallandaine, *First Victoria Directory*, fourth issue (Victoria, 1871), p. 58; Marc Milner, "Mainguy, Edmond Rollo, naval officer," *Canadian Encyclopedia*, Internet; census 1851, Guernsey, HO 107/2531, fol. 263; census 1861, Guernsey, RG 9/1398, p. 4 (Mary E. Fry); D. M. Ogier, *Reformation and Society in Guernsey* (Woodbridge, Suffolk, The Boydell Press, 1996), map p. xv; *A People of the Sea:The Maritime History of the Channel Islands*, ed., A. G. Jamieson (Methuen, 1986), maps pp. xxxi, 21 and the Maingy [sic] family, pp. 176, 182, 212-13; (L. S. Butler, "Vice-Admiral Edmond Rollo Mainguy, OBE, CD, R.C.N.," in Canadian Department of National Defence, http://www.cadets.net/pac/100sea; members of the Mainguy family, "Overview of Some of the descendants of Daniel Wishart Mainguy," in http://www.mainguy.ca.

MAITLAND-DOUGALL, Corporal Hamish Kinear (1897-1917) and William McKinstry (1895-1918), were born at Duncan, VI, sons of Frederick St Leger Heriot Maitland-Dougall (c. 1854-1916), a "developer" there (descendant of Admiral Frederick Sears Maitland, the commander of the *Bellerophon*, which took Napoleon captive after Waterloo), and his wife Bessie Hopkins, daughter of a wealthy Georgia cotton broker. Soon after arriving in the Cowichan Valley in 1886, the father started a local chapter of the Order of the King's Daughters and Sons—the first in Canada. They were the group that inspired and promoted the King's Daughters' Hospital in Duncan, which opened in 1911. Meanwhile, F. S. H. Maitland-Dougall's cousin, Lieutenant Commander J. R. Boothby (c. 1884-1915), a veteran of the South African War and service in India, spent two years at his place in Duncan and played polo in the Koksilah Polo Club, golf, and tennis, before rejoining his regiment. He was killed, aged thirty-one, in battle on 3 May 1915 at Sari Bair (Dardanelles). The two Maitland-Dougall sons attended *Percy Truscott Skrimshire's Quamichan Lake School and were members of the Cowichan Cricket Club. Both of them joined up in the Great War, even though they were under age. William McKinstry Maitland-Dougall trained as a naval cadet in the first class at the Royal Naval College of Canada, enrolled in the submarine service of the RN, and died on 12 March 1918 "in the tragic attack of the French Airship A.T.O. when his submarine was destroyed in error in the North Sea. This was the only R.N. submarine to have been sunk by aerial bombs in World War One." Hamish Kinnear Maitland-Dougall was killed at Vimy Ridge serving in the 103rd Battalion. Their father, Frederick St. Leger Heriot Maitland-Dougall, died, aged sixty-two, on 21 October 1916 in Duncan.

Sources: *Colonist,* 15 May 1917, p. 5, a photo of the two Maitland-Dougall boys serving, Cpl. Hamish K. (1897-1917) now wounded in the 103rd Battalion; and Lieutenant William McK. (1895-1918); Tom Henry, *Small City in a Big Valley: The Story of Duncan* (in 4_, Madeira Park, BC, Harbour Publishing, 1999), pp. 61-2, 81-7; *MacFarlane*, p. 42; R. E. Gosnell, *A History of British Columbia* (The Hill Binding Co., 1906), pp. 433-4, and photo.

MALLANDAINE, Edward (1827-1905). He was born on 6 August 1827 in Singapore, the son of John Mallandaine of the East India Company and Mary Mallandaine *née* Smith. After being at school in Dinan, Brittany, he had some training as an architect at Camberwell, London, and worked in London at the architectural offices of J. C. Robinson and later of W. Tress of the IE Railway. But he did not do well and went off to spend in 1852-1854 at Australian gold fields, partly as a draftsman. Returning to London, he took up architectural drafting and married on 5 May 1855. When his wife, his first daughter, and his father all died, he left for California, whence he headed for the gold fields of British Columbia and arrived in Victoria on 12 October 1858. He was no more successful at gold mining in BC than in Australia and settled uneasily in Victoria, with visits to the United States, an unsatisfactory stay on Salt Spring Island, and a series of disparate activities. He taught French, worked for the Victoria District Road Commission and then as collector of taxes for the Esquimalt Commission, and went on to take the office of school-tax collector in Victoria and paymaster of Military District No.11 (April 1874 to July 1879) with the honorary rank of captain. In 1871, 1877, and 1882, he worked with survey parties employed by the railway intended to link Canada with the Pacific. He tried to establish himself on Yates Street as an architect but built few buildings other than St Luke's Anglican Church on Cedar Hill Cross Road in South Saanich. What he is remembered for, however, is the illustrated *First Victoria Directory* he published in 1860 and reprinted at least five times. It affords the best array of details about the city, its inhabitants and surroundings in that early period, as well as notes on the San Francisco businesses that were part of the same Pacific coast economic sphere. I have used the "Fourth Issue," dated 1871.

Meanwhile, on 1 September 1866, he married Louisa Townsend, who had arrived in Victoria from England on one of the famous "bride ships," the *Tynemouth.* They had two daughters and three sons.

Sources: R. Windsor Liscombe, "Mallandaine, Edward, architect, artist, surveyor, and publisher," *Dictionary of Canadian Biography* Online; Martin Segger and Douglas Franklin, *Victoria, A Primer for Regional History in Architecture* (New York, *A Pilgrim Guide to Historic Architecture,* 1979), p. 342; Lugrin, *Pioneer Women,* pp. 147-155; Edward Mallandaine, *First Victoria Directory,* Fourth Issue (Victoria, E. Mallandaine, 1871), 96 pp. and many unnumbered end-pages of advertisements;

Patricia Gregson, "Victoria's first directory," *Daily Colonist*, 26 Sept. 1971; J. K. Nesbitt, "Old homes and families," *Daily Colonist*, 17 May 1953. Margaret Sharcott, "Frustrated architect," *Daily Colonist*, 29 March 1964.

MANTLE, William Edward (c. 1895-1980). He was born at Littlehampton, Sussex, and appears, aged six, in the 1901 census records, living with his family at 4 Church Street, Littlehampton. His father, William E. Mantle, aged thirty-five, was a dairyman born at Gravesend, Kent, and his mother, Lily Mantle, aged thirty-six, was born at Arundel, Sussex. He had a younger brother and two younger sisters, all born at Littlehampton, and they had a fifteen-year-old servant girl. During the Great War, he served in the British Army at Gallipoli and in Palestine and later on the North-West Frontier of India.

After the war, he retired to a farm in the Comox Valley and was active enough in the affairs of the Island that in August 1941, the provincial Liberal Party chose him as their candidate for the Comox Riding in the election for the provincial legislative assembly. He died, aged eighty-five, on 10 May 1980 in Comox. His wife Irene Mabel Mantle had died there, aged sixty-four, on 22 February 1975.
Sources: *Colonist*. 9 August 1941, p. 3; census 1901, England, RG 13/962, p. 38.

MANUEL, Stewart Menelaws (1857-1943). Born in Edinburgh on 9 October 1857, son of John and Mary Manuel (*née* Taylor), he joined the Imperial Army and served in many parts of the empire, mainly as an armourer warrant officer first class in the Middlesex Regiment. The 1891 census found him, aged thirty-two, living at Franklin Place, Chichester, West Sussex, as a "Military Sergeant," together with his wife, Margaret Donaldson Manuel, aged thirty-two, also born in Scotland, both lodging in the house of a Chichester laundress. He retired in 1900 and settled in Victoria, where he was a prominent Freemason. Mrs Manuel died in Victoria, aged eighty-five, on 17 June 1942 and he, aged eighty-six, on 20 March 1943, both buried at Ross Bay. He was survived by two brothers in England.
Sources: *Colonist*, 23 March 1943, p. 14, obit.; census 1891, England, RG 12/846, p. 4.

MARTIN, George Bohun [Bohn?] (1841-1933). For several years, he worked for the Hudson's Bay Company near Kamloops in mainland BC (having walked there from Yale), but in 1882, he entered politics and sat for sixteen years for Yale in the BC legislature. There followed an appointment as chief commissioner of lands and works and another in the provincial Department of Agriculture. He retired in 1918 and settled at 426 Laurence Street, Victoria, with the lady he had married on 20 January 1914: Catherine Hallanin Chapman, a daughter of Hallanin Chapman of the Indian Army. When celebrated his ninetieth birthday in December 1931, a *Daily Colonist* reporter visited his house and the splendid garden he tended overlooking the Inner Harbour. He died, aged ninety-one, on 29 August 1933, leaving his widow, two sons, two daughters, twenty-four grandchildren, and a nephew, Lawrence Ashburnham, at Cowichan Lake. As a Roman Catholic, he had a funeral at St Andrew's Cathedral before being buried at Ross Bay.

He was born on 25 December 1841 in Nottinghamshire at Newton near East Bridgford, second son of Flag Captain G. Bohun Martin and grandson of Sir Thomas Briggs, admiral of Portsmouth. The family had a long tradition of service in the army and the navy. The 1851 census found GM, aged nine, living with his family at East Bridgford, his father born in London and his mother, Isabella H Martin, in Gloucester, both aged thirty-eight. Besides his elder brother Harry, aged ten, he had seven sisters ranging from fourteen to seven months. Schooled at Cheltenham and on HMS *Victory*, GM joined the Royal Navy in 1855 as a midshipman under Sir Charles Napier (admiral of the fleet) and celebrated his fourteenth birthday aboard HMS *Russel* in the Baltic Sea during the Crimean War. In 1860, he left the RN, entered the civil service of the East India Company under his uncle, General Willoughby Briggs, and was stationed at Poona in the Bombay Presidency. He suffered so much from the climate that he returned to England and, early in 1862, sailed for BC, which he reached in April via the West Indies, the Panama Canal, and San Franciso, whence he took the side-wheel steamer, *Jonathan,* to Victoria.
Sources: census 1851, England, HO 107/2139, fol. 39 (?); *Who's Who in B.C.* 1933-1934, p. 201; *Colonist,* 25 December 1931, p. 5; 30 August 1933, p. 5, obit., with photo.

MASON, William Robert (c. 1864-1940). Born in India at Waltair, a suburb of Vizagapatam, on the road between Calcutta and Madras, he was living in 1881, aged fifteen, with his family at "Whitley House," Hornsey, Highgate (London). His father was Charles Crawford Mason, then aged fifty-six, born at Lutterworth, Leicestershire, and a retired Major General of the Madras Staff Corps, Indian Army, who had retired in 1876. His mother Lucy Elizabeth Mason, aged forty-two, was born at Kilrea, Ireland. In the household were WM's three sisters: Charlotte E. Mason, aged fourteen, born at Brighton, Sussex, Ethel Mason, nine, and Sybil Mason, eight, both born at Quilon in India on the west coast of Travancore State. There too lived Harriet M. Robertson, "mother," aged sixty-eight, "widow of a writer to the Signet" born at Kilrea, Ireland, and her three children all born in Edinburgh: Janet M. Robertson, aged nineteen, Marion H. Robertson, eighteen, and Patrick Robertson, fifteen. With them were five domestic servants. Ten years later, in 1891, the census-taker found the same family living at "Lawn Villa," Compton Gifford, Devon, and with three other changes. Charles Crawford Mason, now aged sixty-six, gave his birthplace as Atherstand, Northampton; there was a new son, Francis J. H. Mason, aged eight, born at Highgate in London; and there were now only three servants.
At sometime in the early twentieth century, WM emigrated to the Island and lived for many years, first at Salt Spring Island, then at Duncan, and finally at 1505 Beach Drive in Victoria, where he died, aged seventy-six, on 17 November 1940. The *Daily Colonist* reported that he was born in India at Madras, had been a member of the Reformed Episcopal Church, and a was British Israelite. He left a brother, two sisters, and his wife Elizabeth, who died there, aged eighty, on 27 December 1961.
Sources: *Whitaker's,* p. 354; census, England, 1881, RG 11/1379, p. 52; census, 1891, RG 12/1723, p. 33; *Colonist,* 19 November 1940, p. 3, obit.

MASON-HURLEY, Frederick Charles (1877-1940). Born at Buckhurst Hill near London, he was educated there at private schools, joined the British Army, and served through the South African War and then in India, winning three medals and seven clasps. From India, he went to Hong Kong, where he entered into partnership with the trading firm of Hughes & Hough, was active in the Masonic Order, and remained until 1921. He and his wife then retired to Victoria but in 1926 moved to Shawnigan Lake, where they bought the DeSalis place on the west side of the Lake and called it "Glenduff" after the family seat in Ireland. To gain lake access, they also bought the *Neville Armstrong house on the shore, a lovely place where friends came from China and camped on the beach. They and others wanted to stay, and before long, FM was putting them up in the Armstrong house, which they began to keep open each summer as the Forest Inn. It became well known for good service and pleasant surroundings. Guests were charmed by the valuable collection of Chinese porcelains and art FM had gathered during his years in the Orient. It included much pottery of the various dynasties and was rich in rare old pieces, chiefly of the Ming and Kung-Hi periods. Collectors and artists from all over the country went to see it, and FM was always willing to talk about the history and legend that accompanied each piece. He was also a great Conan Doylist and a believer in spiritualism. FM died, aged sixty-three, on 1 January 1940 at Shawnigan, leaving his widow, two sons, and a daughter, and Annie Mason-Hurley died, aged eighty-four, on 21 May 1951 in Duncan.

The Forest Inn, which in 1939 they renamed the Shawnigan Beach Hotel, was taken over in 1945 by their son, Dennis Mason-Hurley (born c. 1910—died in Victoria 17 October 1986), and he developed it further as a "family hotel," adding more outdoor games and evening entertainment. He had come from China with his parents on the *Empress of Russia* about 1920, when he was about ten years old. One reason the family went to Shawnigan Lake was to make it easier for their two sons to attend Shawnigan Lake Boys' School, directed by *C. W. Lonsdale (1886-1952). For some reason, they quarrelled with Londsdale or disapproved of his school, so the boys were sent to St Aidan's School in Victoria and came home on weekends by train. But in 1922, one of Lonsdale's own masters, Odo Barry, set up a rival school, Leinster Preparatory School, in a big rambling house on top of a steep hill at the intersection of the Shawnigan and Cobble Hill roads. It opened with fourteen pupils, including *Colonel F. T. Oldham's children, Stuart and Frankie. Uniforms were sent out from England. Odo Barry had a wooden leg, and his mother came out from Ireland to help him. It was there that DM's brother, who became a professor at MIT, had his first schooling. This was the school, too, where Frances Oldham began the education which was to lead her to win the Congressional Medal of Honour for warning the U.S. authorities against thalidomide. But she soon moved to Strathcona Lodge for Girls, founded about that time by Miss Gildea and later named the Frances Oldham Kelsey School in the presence of the lady herself, who came back from Washington DC, aged seventy-nine, for the sod-turning.

In 1939, DM married *Joan Honor Austen-Leigh, who wrote plays and novels under her maiden name and was a descendant of Jane Austen's brother

James Austen. Annie Mason-Hurley died, aged eighty-four, on 21 June 1951 in Duncan.

Sources: *Colonist*, 9 February 1917, p. 5; 8 July 1934, p. 11; 3 January 1940, p. 4: obit.; *Times-Colonist*, Sunday, 3 June 2001, p. D9; 13 October 2001; Joan Mason-Hurley, "Twenty-four Colonels on the West Arm Road"; *Raincoast Chronicles*, vol. pp. 52-61.; Hughes, *Shawnigan Lake*, 1887-1967, p. 71; May Brown, "Joan Austen-Leigh," *Times-Colonist*, Sunday, 3 June 2001, p. D9.

MASSEY, Captain Herbert Henry (c. 1881-1942). He was born at Allerthorpe, Yorkshire, second son of Elizabeth Massey from Warwickshire and John Massey, a farmer of Allerthorpe, where the 1891 census found them at 17 Model Cottage when HM was ten. Early in the century, they migrated to Lethbridge, Alberta, but about 1931, HM and his wife Jessie, *née* Painter, settled near Victoria on Burnside Road near her mother, Mrs J. E. Painter of 874 Devonshire Road, Esquimalt. Though I find no details, HM doubtless spent time in the Orient because they were among the founding members of the China-Japan Society in 1931, and he was a pallbearer at the funeral in Victoria of *Sir Charles Delmé-Radcliffe. HM died, aged sixty-one, on 27 October 1942 in Saanich and was buried at Colwood Park. His wife died, aged seventy-eight, on 12 May 1956 in Victoria.

Sources: census England, 1891, RG12/3900, p. 3; *Colonist*, 19 December 1929, p. 7; 29 October 1942, p. 5: obit.

MATHIESON, Captain Thomas Barnes (1890-1966). He was born on 2 July 1890 at Hendon, London, third son of Gerard John Mathieson, a wholesale stationer born in Clapton, London, and his wife, Frances S. Mathieson. The 1891 census found them living with two servants at Annandale, Golders Hill, Hendon, Middlesex. TM attended Denham School and Wye College, and spent two years at an Officer's Training College in Aldershot. In 1911, he went to out to farm at Kelowna. There he lived until 1915, and when he enlisted at Vernon as a private in the Fifty-fourth Battalion on 25 October 1915, he gave his occupation as "Ass't Manager of a Packing House," and his next of kin as Mrs Mathieson, 10 Addison Mansions, Kensington, London. He was then 5' 9" tall with a fair complexion, an Anglican with blue eyes and brown hair. He went overseas on SS *Saxonia* with the Fifty-fourth Battalion, CEF, regimental number 445571, arriving in England on 2 December 1915. But in January 1916, he transferred to the East Riding Yeomanry and was on the Egyptian-Palestine Front as a staff officer; his colourful career in the Imperial forces is, as usual, not mentioned in the files at Ottawa. He resigned in 1920 and returned to Kelowna, where in 1921 he married Catharine Henrietta Dundas, daughter of Robert Napier Dundas of Inchgarire, Kelowna, and Mrs Katharine Elizabeth Dundas of Victoria. In 1930, he went back to England as director of a crêpe paper manufacturing company.

Three years later, however, they went to Victoria, and he became a partner in Oliver Stewart Clark & Co. Ltd. He was a fellow of the Royal Horticultural Society and a member of the Agricola Club. When he died, aged seventy-five, on 17 May 1966, they were living in Victoria at 1214 Fairfield Road.

Sources: *Who's Who in B.C.* 1933-1934, p. 108; NAC, CEF papers, RG150, Box 6037-55; census 1891, England, RG 12/1050, p. 15.

MATSON, John Samuel Henry (1867-1931). He was the editor of the *Colonist* and a distinguished and well-known figure in Victoria for many years. He was born at Perth, Ontario, on 21 April 1867, married Ada Teresa Galley (1868-1957) in Victoria on 29 April 1899, and died at Esquimalt on 1 November 1931, leaving several children, notably John Robert Meredith Matson, born 24 January 1899, and Hubert T. B. Matson, born 15 February 1901. The former attended St Michael's School, University School, Harrow, and Cambridge University (where he read law) and, after presiding over the *Colonist* for some years, died on 30 November 1934.

Sources: *Colonist*, 1 December 1934, p. 1, photo and obit.; Canadian census, 1901, Victoria.

MATTSON, Arthur Lewis (1882-1940). He was born in Leicester, second of the four sons of Eliza Mattson and Arthur Matteson, a fruit salesman born at Loddington, Northamptonshire. In 1891, they were living at 45 Bond Gate (?), St Leonard, Leicester. AM fought in the South African War with the Leicester Regiment and in the Great War with the Forty-fourth Regiment. In 1918, he went to live in Victoria, latterly on Burnside Road, and he died, aged fifty-eight, on 3 November 1940 in Victoria and was survived by a brother in England and another in Australia.

Sources: *Colonist*, 6 November 1940, p. 14, obit.; census 1891, England, RG 12/2541, p. 4.

MAUDE, Commander Eustace Downman (1848-1930). He was born on 31 August 1848 the second son of Lieutenant Colonel Sir George Ashley Maude (c. 1817-?), RA, KCB (1887), and his wife Katherine Katinka Beauclerck. Sir George was in the Royal Household as an equerry and secretary to the Master of the Horse, lived at the Stud House, Hampton Court, and at the Royal Mews in the winter. EM went into the navy in 1861, served on HMS *Scout*, and was promoted to lieutenant in 1871 for service in HMS *Rinaldo* against Malay pirates in which he was wounded. In 1876, he was appointed to the royal yacht *Victoria and Albert*, served for two years, and was then promoted to commander. In 1882, aboard HMS *Temeraire*, armour clad, with eight guns, under Captain Henry F. Nicholson, he was present at the attack on Alexandria (11-12 July) and landed with the naval brigade. He won the Egyptian Medal, the Khedive Star, Osmanli, third class, and retired from the navy in 1885 after twenty-one years of service. In the Great War, he offered his services at Vancouver and was employed during 4-31 August 1914 by the Royal Canadian Volunteer Naval Reserve at Esquimalt as acting commander at the rate of $4 *per diem*. He answered the appeal the Royal Engineers made in 1917 on the Pacific coast for volunteers for the Inland Water Transport Service and sailed overseas from Montreal about 22 May 1917 aboard the SS *Unnamed* (he recalled that the name was painted out). From then until 16 April 1919, when he sailed home from Southampton on SS *Olympic*, he held a commission in the Inland Water Transport Service and was promoted to lieutenant in it on 14 August 1917 at Richborough, Kent. He was demobilized on 30 April 1919. In claiming an Imperial gratuity after the war, he mentioned that an allowance of £2 a month had been paid to Valerie Maude, his dependent daughter in London, from 14 August 1917 to 27 April 1919, and there is evidence that his wife, too, had joined him in England during the war years.

Upon retiring from the RN in 1885, he had married Grace Henrietta Amy Williams, daughter of Oliver Willliams, on 15 July at St George's, Hanover Square, London, and soon took her out to a homestead near Silver Lake in Oregon. There they remained for nearly a decade and had three of their four children: Ruth Katinka (c. 1887-1914), Cyrene Marie Beauclerck (1888-?), and George (1889-1973). In 1895, they moved to the Island and kept a dry goods shop at Duncan, where they had their fourth child Valerie Beauclerck Maude on 23 November 1897. They moved again in 1900 to Miner's Bay on Mayne Island, where they carried on in the dry goods trade until about 1901. When the Point Comfort Hotel went up for sale, they bought it to be run as a summer hotel, but kept a small store and bar open all year. Point Comfort had been built in 1890 by the big-game hunter *Warburton Pike, and they lived there in the circle of expatriot British gentlefolk described by Winifred Grey (1871-1951) in her charming memoirs, *A Gentlewoman's Remembrance of Life in England and the Gulf Islands, 1871-1910* (1994), mentioning, for example, Ruth Katinka Maude's return from Beacon School at Rotherhithe, East Sussex, and subsequent marriage on 29 January 1907 to Harold Digby Payne, seventh son of Sir Salusberry G. Payne, Baronet of Bedfordshire.

In 1906, Maude Island, Nanoose harbour, was named after EM, and he became a JP for Mayne Island. About 1910, they gave up all business and lived at "Point Comfort" in retirement. In 1925 at the age of seventy-seven, he bought a twenty-two-foot ketch-rigged sailing boat, with an auxiliary engine, which he called *Half Moon*. After wide reading and careful preparations, he set out alone in her, intending to sail to England by way of the Panama Canal. During a violent storm off Eureka, California, he became exhausted and the boom hit him, leaving him injured; then *Half Moon* sprang a leak, and so he decided to return to Mayne Island, which he managed to do with the help of the U.S. coastguard. When he reached home, he had been at sea for ninety-seven days and travelled about five thousand miles, which must have been something of a record for a single-handed yachtsman at that time. *Major Lukin Johnston visited EM a short time later, then living "in a little shingled bungalow near the settlement . . . He stands well over six feet in his socks, and the brightness of his eye and keenness of his mind belie his silvery hair and beard. He is not through yet with the idea of sailing to England, and says he may try it again later." EM died, aged eighty-two, on 12 June 1930 and his wife, aged eighty-five, on 3 February 1946 at Lady Minto Hospital, Ganges. Long before then, in 1923, they had sold "Point Comfort" to Colonel and Lady *L. G. Fawkes, whom they befriended and whose expert watercolours of local scenery they acquired in large number. Their oldest daughter Cyrene Beauclerck Maude had married Captain Cecil Henry Hulton-Sams, RN, in 1899 and their youngest, Valerie Beauclerc Maude, had become Mrs Hopper, both apparently living in England. Their son settled at Fulford Harbour, Salt Spring Island, and spent many years as skipper of the *Cy Peck* ferry shuttling between Fulford and Swartz Bay in North Saanich. I travelled on her countless times in my childhood and knew *Cyrus Wesley Peck (and his family) for whom the ferry was named.

Sources: Notes courtesy of Miss Alison Maude (a granddaughter); *Colonist*, 1 February 1907, p. 11; 5 February 1946, p. 12, obit.; NAC, RG9, II-F-10, *Imperial Gratuities*, vol. 304, file 12013-E-2; *Whitaker's*, pp. 356 (Maude) and 459 (Hulton-Sams); Captain Eustace Maude, "A Lonely Log," *The Atlantic Monthly*, vol. 142, no. 3 (September 1928), pp. 379-387; Peter Murray, *Homesteads and Snug Harbours: The Gulf Islands* (Victoria, Horsdal & Shubert, 1991), pp. 24-5; Marie Elliott, *Mayne Island and the Outer Gulf Islands: A History* (Mayne Island, Gulf Islands Press, 1984), p. 52-3; Major Lukin Johnston (1888-1933), *Beyond the Rockies: Three Thousand Miles by Trail and Canoe with 52 illustrations and a map* (J. M. Dent, 1929), pp. 8-9; Walbran, *B.C. Coast Names*, pp. 325-6; *A Gulf Islands Patchwork: Some Early Events on the Islands of Galiano, Mayne, Saturna, North and South Pender* (1961) (9th printing, Gulf Islands Branch, BC Historical Federation, 1999), p. 167; Winifred Grey, *A Gentlewoman's Remembrance of Life in England and the Gulf Islands, 1871-1910*, ed., Marie Elliott (Gulf Islands Press, 1994), pp. 28, 170, 183, 192; Henderson's Directory for BC 1900-1901, p. 255; *Who's Who* in 1888, pp. 10 and 181; Captain Kettle (i.e., John H. Hamilton), *Western Shores: Narratives of the Pacific Coast* (Vancouver, Progress Publishing Co. Ltd., 1932), 218 pp.; Lieutenant Colonel G. A. Maude, RA [EM's father], Letters from Russia, 1856 ("For private circulation," n.p., n.d.), 78 pp.; census 1901, England, RG 13/897, p. 22 (? page number blurred, Ruth Maude at school).

MAUDE, Captain [Colonel?] Henry Horatio (c. 1832(?)-1888). Conflicting information from various sources leaves a blurred picture of this British officer. He seems to have been a captain in the Royal Navy who arrived on the Pacific Coast in the mid-nineteenth century with Captain [later Admiral Sir] Geoffrey Phipps Hornby (1825-1895) and took a thousand acres on Hornby Island, where he spent the rest of his life. He was one of that small island's first two settlers, the other being a certain Forde with whom he had political disagreements. At Tribune Bay, where HM built a large farmhouse, naval vessels found a convenient anchorage and liked to visit because, as Rona Murray, wrote, "Captain Maud kept horses and the men played polo on the beach, or the ship's company was lined up to do morning calisthenics." HM died, aged fifty-five, on 13 May 1888 in Victoria, had a funeral at Christ Church Cathedral, and left his island estate to a nephew, Douglas L. Herbert. Robert L. Hunt purchased it in 1927. HM may have been related to Commander Maude, who settled later on Mayne Island, but I could find no evidence of this.

Sources: Thomas K. Ovanin, *Island Heritage Buildings: A Selection of Heritage Buildings in the Islands Trust Area* (Victoria, Island Trust, 1984), p. 24; census, 1881, Vancouver Island; Rona Murray, "Hornby has a Lodge," *Colonist*, 15 May 1888, p. 4; 22 March

1959, *Sunday Magazine*, p. 15; Ben Hughes, *History of the Comox Valley*, 1862-1945 (Nanaimo, Evergreen Press, 1946?), p. 17.

MAY, Captain Arthur Douglas (1892-1941). He was born on 31 May 1892 in Hong Kong, where his father was master of Queen's College, but the 1901 census found him, eight years old, living in London at No. 21, Acacia Grove, Camberwell (West Dulwich), with his mother Mrs Mary Ellen May from Prestwich, Lancashire, and his seventeen-year-old brother, Ernest Alfred May. They had a servant.

In 1910, he joined the Royal Bank of Canada and worked for them as a bank clerk in Victoria for eighteen years, except for the years of the Great War. On 23 September 1914, he enlisted as a lieutenant at Valcartier, declaring his next of kin to be his mother, Mrs A. J. May, c/o Hong Kong-Shanghai Bank, London. He was then a member of a militia unit but had no previous military experience. He served overseas for four years in the Seventh Battalion and returned to the Royal Bank in Victoria until 1928, when he became manager of Branson-Brown, a stock and bond house in Vancouver. He made other career moves to S. P. Powell Co., then in 1931 to a firm in Chilliwack in 1931. From 1939 until his death, aged forty-nine, on 19 June 1941, he lived at Cultus Lake.

Sources: NAC, CEF files, box 6066-46; *Colonist*, 20 June 1941, p. 5, obit.; census 1901, England, RG 13/492, p. 31.

MAYNARD, Thomas Henry (c. 1865-1939). He emigrated to Victoria from India in 1912 with most of his seven children, Max, Theodore, Joyce, Lily, Harry, Norman, and Grace, having lost his wife, their mother, at some earlier time. On 20 July 1932 in Victoria, he married Margaret Emily Ann Ingram, born on 1 November 1885 at Ahmednagar, Maharashtra, India, daughter of John and Margaret Ingram, and christened on 28 November 1885. They settled at Cowichan Lake and lived there until his death, aged seventy-four, on 11 December 1939, leaving his widow and three sons. His funeral at Oaklands Gospel Hall is a mark of his identity as a former missionary in South India for about thirty years. Born at Croydon, Surrey, he was identified in the 1881 census as a fifteen-year-old pawnbroker's assistant living two miles from his parents near Tunbridge Wells (Kent). He joined the Salvation Army, which sent him to India as a missionary, and there in 1888, he met and married a fellow missionary, Eliza Anthony "Lily" Teague, who was born in Cornwall on 26 November 1867. Family lore has it that they met on the boat to India as Salvation Army missionaries. There followed periods of missionary work as Methodist field agents and with the mission of the Plymouth Brethren, which seems to have remained TM's faith for the rest of his life. The family made two visits to England, in 1894-1895 and in 1900-1901. The 1901 English census shows the entire family except TM, though at three different addresses, but they returned to India, where the youngest son Max was born in 1903.

A glimpse of the family, recorded by Sandra Djwa, shows them as members of the Plymouth Brethren meeting at Victoria Hall and Oak Bay Hall, where they met Roy Daniells, future professor of English at the University of British Columbia, who met TM's son Max in 1924. Daniells thought TM looked like an intelligent and emotional goat, with a narrow bony face and a high-bald forehead. Max had inherited TM's strong interest in literature. When TM died, aged seventy-four, on 11 December 1939, he left his widow and three sons. Margaret Emily Maynard died, aged sixty-one, on 9 November 1959 in Vancouver City.

Sources: census 1901, England, RG 11/913, p. 23; *The Daily Colonist*, 12 December 1939, p. 3, obit.; Sandra Djwa, *Professing England: A Life of Roy Daniells* (Toronto, University of Toronto Press, 2002), pp. 50-52; International Genealogical Index (Latter Day Saints) for the birth of Margaret Emily Ann Ingram in India.

MAYNE, Rear Admiral Sir Richard Charles (1835-1892). His first visit to the Island was in 1849 as a midshipman in HMS *Inconstant*, sent to Esquimalt for several weeks. "There was not a house to be seen on its shores; we used to fire shot and shell as we liked about the harbour . . ." (*Four Years*, p. 25). When he returned there in 1856, he saw "a row of respectable well-kept buildings on the south-east point of the harbour's mouth, with pleasant gardens in front of them," and a naval hospital that had been built in 1854 to receive the wounded from Petropaulovski, Siberia, in the Pacific sector of the Crimean War. He had just spent some time in the Sea of Azoff in HMS *Curlew* and in 1856 was beginning his four-year mission to the Island with a nautical survey being undertaken by HMS *Plumper* and HMS *Hecate*. His account of *Four Years in British Columbia and Vancouver Island* is a classic in the Island's history. He lived there through the gold rush of 1858, visited the goldfields of the BC continental interior, explored the coasts and certain parts of the interior of the Island, took a friendly and intelligent interest in the native tribes, and met everyone in the public life of Victoria during some busy social activity which he evidently enjoyed. It seemed to him that the town ought to have been built around the great harbour of Esquimalt rather than the cramped and awkward little harbour at Victoria, but he described the fort, foundry, boatyards, houses, streets, and other features of Victoria to show that it was already permanent and "capable, should the occasion ever arise, of springing into importance as Melbourne or San Francisco had done" (p. 31). Of course, much of his book is about the marine surveying, which was his main concern. There is also a long chapter about the missionary work at Metlakatla by *William Duncan, whom he quotes at length, and other chapters about routes to the Island from England and other matters of interest to prospective emigrants. Three of his appendices discuss the Island's natural horticulture and the official terms of land tenure.

RM was born in the west end of London, second son of Sir Richard Mayne, KCB. (1796-1868), whom the home secretary, Sir Robert Peel, had appointed commissioner of the London Metropolitan Police in 1929. This was at the very beginning of the new "Peelite" police force, and RM's father went on to serve for many years as its chief commissioner. Such was his importance that the *Oxford Dictionary of National Biography* devotes a biographical article to him in which RM has only an incidental paragraph. Sent to Eton and then into the navy at a young age, RM had a distinguished service record: in HMS *Inconstant*, the *Cumberland* on the North American Station, the *St Jean d'Acre* in the Baltic and the Black Sea during the war with Russia, in the *Curlew* in the Sea of Azoff, and then in the North-West Pacific in the *Plumper* and the *Hecate*. In 1860, he was promoted to commander and returned to England but soon sent to New Zealand in command of HMS *Eclipse* to fight in the Maori Wars. He was severely wounded in November 1863 at Rangiriri on the Waikato River, returned home, mentioned in despatches, promoted to captain, and (in 1867) made Companion of the Bath.

His next assignment was to command the steamer HMS *Nassau* on a mission to re-survey the Strait of Magellan (1866-1869). A naturalist was invited to join the expedition in order to study plants, animals, and native peoples but the main purpose was to gather information for more accurate charts to make the voyage through that desolate and stormy region safer for the increasing numbers of ships travelling to the west coast of the Americas. This purpose soon proved to be justified: On 22 December 1868, the *Nassau*'s survey party found an uncharted reef in the western entrance to the strait, outside the Bay of Mercy, and a month later, the *Santiago* (or *St Jago*) of the Pacific Mail Steamship Company, founded in 1848 by New York merchants, was wrecked on that very reef. The *Nassau* being fortunately near at hand was able to take its crew and motley gathering of passengers (nearly two hundred in all) to Monte Video. Establishing and charting this trade route was a considerable achievement. This incident shows how useful the Royal Navy's work was for the shipping of all nations. The Strait of Magellan was about 330 miles (530 km.) long, from 2½ to 15 miles (4-24 km.) wide, and ships were usually beset by fog, heavy rain, violent westerly winds, and sudden squalls. RM appears, aged thirty-five, in census records of 1871, with his wife Sabine *née* Dent—daughter of an East India and China merchant, Sir Thomas Dent (1796-1872)—a lady whom he had married in 1870 at St George's, Hanover Square (London). Living with them at 80 Chester Square in Knightsbridge were his mother, Georgiana Marianne Catherine *née* Carvick, a Londoner then aged fifty-nine, and his young brother Charles E. Mayne, fourteen and still at school. They had four servants. Ten years later, the 1881 census found them at 101 Queen's Gate in Chelsea, with nine servants and three children: Mabel Georgiana, aged eight, Norah Sabine, six, and Lancelot Richard, five. They were still there in 1891 with their nine servants and one more son, their last, Ronald Clinton Mayne, who followed his father into the navy in which he was promoted to lieutenant in 1902 and mentioned in despatches in July 1917. By 1901, the two sons had left home and Sabine, a widow aged fifty-eight, was still at 101 Queen's Gate with the two daughters and six servants.

Sources: RM, *Four Years in British Columbia and Vancouver Island, an Account of their Forests, Rivers, Coasts, Gold Fields, and Resources for Colonisation* (John Murray, 1862), 468 pp. and illustrations and an index; Clive Emsley, in Oxford DNB (one paragraph in an essay about his father); Admiral Sir George H. Richards, Obituary of RM in *Proceedings of the Royal Geographical Society and Monthly Record of Geography, New Monthly Series*, vol. 14, no 7 (July 1892), pp. 473-74; by Admiral Sir George H. Richards, KCB, FRS; Robert O. Cunningham, *Notes on the Natural History of the Strait of Magellan and West Coast of Patagonia made during the Voyage of H.M.S. Nassau, 1866-69* (Edinburgh, Edmonston & Douglas, 1871), pp. 462-64.

MAZE, Sir Frederick William (1874-1959). He was born on 2 July 1871 at 11 Abercorn Terrace, Belfast, youngest son of James Maze, linen merchant of Killultagh Cottage, Upper Ballinderry, and his wife Mary, one of two daughters of Henry Hart of Lisburn. More important for his career, his mother was a sister of Sir Robert Hart (1835-1911), inspector general of the Imperial Chinese Maritime Customs. FM was privately educated and attended Wesley College, Dublin. He entered the Chinese Maritime Customs as fourth assistant B in Chefoo in 1891, later in Sir Robert Hart's régime, and in 1899 was made acting audit secretary at the Inspectorate General in Peking. The next year, he went to Ichang as acting commissioner and in 1901 became deputy commissioner, first at Foochow and then, from 1902 to 1904, in Canton. He it was who opened the Custom House at Kongmoon, West River, in 1904, and in 1906-1908, he served as commissioner in Tengyueh on the Burma frontier. There followed a series of other commissions: at Canton (1911-1915), Tientsin (1915-1920), Hankow (1921-1925), and Shanghai (1925-1929). There were collateral appointments, of course, such as advisor to the Chinese National Board of Reconstruction, to which he was named in 1928, and membership of the Loans Sinking Fund from 1932. In 1928, the Chinese government appointed him deputy inspector general of Customs and in the troubled years 1929-1943, he was the inspector general. He continued to run the service in the Japanese occupation, which began in 1937, but after Pearl Harbour (7 December 1941), he was interned. Upon his release, he went to Chungking, where a temporary base for the Customs had been established, but he resigned only a few months later and returned to England, where he had been named a KCMG and a KBE.

What most sources do not say is that in 1948, he and his wife, Laura Gwendoline *née* Bullmore, retired to Victoria and lived in "Ravarnette Lodge," looking out to sea at 1121 Beach Drive, Oak Bay, next door to *Sir Robert Erskine Holland. Perhaps, they settled in Victoria to escape from the animosities FM had provoked during his career by sympathizing with Chinese nationalist forces. He was ostracized, asked to resign from the prestigious Shanghai Bowling Club, and accused by Warren Swire, the shipping magnate, of behaving "like a dirty dog in order to become I[inspector] G[eneral]." Even so, he seems to have retained his membership in at least some of his clubs, which had included the Athenæum, the Junior Carlton, the Royal Society, the Hong Kong, Shanghai, Shanghai Country, and in Victoria, they joined the Union Club and the Victoria Golf Club (just across Beach Drive from their house). In 1955, they were founding members of the English-speaking Union, Victoria branch. He died, aged eighty-four, on 25 March 1959 at the Jubilee Hospital, Victoria, and was buried at Royal Oak Cemetery on 28 March after a funeral at St Mary's Anglican Church, Oak Bay. An unfortunate circumstance, likewise not mentioned in most sources, is that employees of the Victoria newspapers were on strike at the time of his death, so no full obituary notice was published locally.

Sources: *Who was Who*, 1951-1960, p. 751; School of Oriental and African Studies (notes in the school's archives); Robert Sharp, Oxford DNB, vol. 37 (OUP 2004), pp. 628-9; Martyn Atkins, *Informal Empire in Crisis: British Diplomacy and the Chinese*

Customs Succession, 1927-29 (Ithaca, NY, 1995), 127 pp.; Nicholas R. Clifford, "Sir Frederick Maze and the Chinese Maritime Customs, 1937-1941," *Journal of Modern History,* vol. 37, no. 1 (March 1965), pp. 18-34; Robert Bickers, *Britain in China: Community, Culture and Colonialism* 1900-1949 (Manchester University Press, 1999), pp. 59, 103, 105, 121; *Colonist,* 27 March 1959, p. 3; 17 December 1972; *Victoria Times,* 28 March 1950; *The Times* (London), 30 March 1959.

MEADE, Robert Aubrey (1852-1912). At Cowichan Lake, he led a quiet, rustic life, and people in the district thought of him as a fine example of the "remittance man." He was born on 12 July 1852 at Grundisburgh, Suffolk, a son of Captain John Meade (1812-1886), who was a British army officer from the Isle of Madeira. His mother, *née* Elvira Ibbetson (c. 1820-1905), was born in Penang on the Malay Coast, and RM seems to have had property there. In 1864, the family inherited Earsham Hall, a splendid manor house near Bungay, three miles from Woodbridge, six miles from Ipswich, and not far from the Suffolk-Norfolk boundary. There, RM's father was a neighbour and friend of the writer H. Rider Haggard. But in RM's youth, the family seldom stayed at Earsham Hall. RM appears, aged eight, living with his parents and siblings in 1861 at 14 Adelaide Crescent, Hove, Sussex, and again with them ten years later, aged eighteen, at 3 Victoria Place, Bognor in Sussex, though his father was absent then. The large network of their relatives shows a distinguished family closely connected with the impecunious earls of Clanwilliam, whose family name was Meade, but securely anchored in the Imperial governing class. RM was, for instance, a second cousin of Sir Robert Henry Meade (1835-1898), permanent under-secretary at the Colonial Office and second cousin of Admiral Richard James Meade (1832-1907), RN. The family ramified in relationships with the Lascelles, Grenfell, and Brabazon families. As a young man, RM journeyed to the East Indies and worked in estates in Malaya, where his mother was born, but there was some kind of failure or disappointment. Family records on the subject are kept at the Norfolk County Record Office.

In 1889, he arrived on Vancouver Island and settled on a property at Cowichan Lake. There he kept what seems to have been a subsistence farm of the kind the British gentry used to call a "ranch" on which they did "mixed farming." He was recorded as a farmer in local directories and Canadian census records for 1891 and 1901. According to local memories, he had the only formal clothing in the neighbourhood and was occasionally called upon to meet distinguished visitors. Somewhat too solitary to be a classic example of the "remittance man," he nevertheless qualified as such by his manners and eccentricities: drinking champagne for preference and wandering off for drunken sprees occasionally, neglecting his livestock and returning to begin again. According to J. F. T. Saywell's *Kaatza: Tales of Cowichan Lake,* p. 183, Laura May Dunsmuir (1884-1959), daughter of the Island coal millionaire, happened to meet RM on 18 June 1904 while she was walking about near the Lakeside Hotel, a few days before her wedding to Admiral Arthur Bromley (1876-1961), RN. She had a long talk with him and remembered him as a tall, handsome man with greying hair, evidently a gentleman though wearing only a ragged jersey, and she understood that he had failed in an attempt to grow coffee in Ceylon. He died, aged fifty-five, on 23 March 1912 at Duncan, almost certainly in the King's Daughters' Hospital.

There followed a long bureaucratic process of settling his affairs, the sums involved being small. It was managed by the firm of J. Maude & J. E. Tunnicliffe on the Strand in London through their overseas agents, Sandilands, Buttery & Co. of Penang, and a Mr Rothwell on Vancouver Island. About three months after RM's death, a friend at Crofton, not many miles from Shawnigan Lake, wrote a letter to his elder brother's wife at Earsham Hall, a letter now preserved at the Norfolk Record Office. This was Florence Annie Barnes *née* Barkley (1859-1929), wife of *Lieutenant Colonel George Edward Barnes, who dated her letter 17 June 1912 and introduced herself by explaining that she and her husband had once been taken to visit Earsham Hall by her cousin Mabel Raikes: "I was asked by his mother many years ago in Thurston to be kind to him when I came out here to my brother for the first time. We used to meet & see him in Duncan & ask him to come & see us, but he never came." She went on to explain that RM had lived for many years about twenty-five miles from Duncan on a small ranch but, not long before he died, had paid $6,000 for another place at Cowichan Bay, on the sea facing Salt Spring Island. Sometime before he had said that, he intended to leave his money to two nephews whom he had never met and who were at Eton. RM had died two or three days after riding down from Cowichan Lake without a coat in a car and so contracting pneumonia. A Mr Lomas and other friends had buried him in the graveyard at St Peter's Quamichan Anglican Church near Duncan, and Rothwell had promptly written to his lawyers in England.

Sources: census 1861, England, RG 9/605, p. 5; census 1871, RG 10/1113, p. 7; Norfolk Record Office (Norwich), MEA 11/110 and 111, though the latter is closed, for some reason, until the year 2016; *Who was Who*, vol. I (1897-1916; John F. T. Saywell, *Kaatza: The Chronicles of Cowichan Lake* (Sidney, The Cowichan Lake District Centennial Committee, 1967), pp. 39, 43, 183; *A New Directory for BC*, 1910, p. 363; David Cannadine, *The Decline and Fall of the British Aristocracy* (1990; Vintage Books, 1999), p. 265.

MEARES, Colonel Cecil Henry (1877-1937). He was born on 14 February 1877 at Inistioge, County Kilkenny, Ireland, son of Major Meares, an army officer of Scottish origin who was serving in the Twenty-first RS Fusiliers at the Curragh. His mother, *née* Helen Townsend, died five days after his birth, and he lived at Inistioge until 1880, when he was taken to stay with his stepaunts at Hartley, Kent. By four years old, he had taught himself to read and at five, he was sent to a lady's school for a few weeks and then to Ayr Academy, on the banks of the River Ayr in Scotland, where he boarded with one of the masters. In 1883, his father and stepmother returned from India and he spent a few weeks with them at "Lendalfort," in the Lendalfoot Hills of South Ayrshire after which they returned to India. The father, then in the Bedfordshire Regiment at Thyatmyo, Burma, had a house there, which was burnt by *dacoits*, and everything was lost. At this time, Cecil was at the Lys School in Cambridge. In 1888 when he was at school in

Woking, his father returned to England and was attached to the Horse Guards in London. Soon after that, CM applied to the army but failed to pass the medical test, his chest measurements being too small. In 1894, he went to Bilbao, Spain, to study Spanish and in 1895 to Torrepellice, Italy, to study Italian. On this last expedition, he sailed for Genoa in a ship from Glasgow, which was wrecked at Ballywalter, County Down, Ireland.

In 1896, he sailed for India, where he engaged in coffee-planting at Quad Hutton but soon went off roving about, as he was to do for most of his life. In 1900, he went to Vladivostock and Peking. He fought in the South African War with the Scottish Horse and then resumed his travels in the Far East, venturing in 1903 to Kamchatka and Okotz. In 1904, he went to north-eastern Siberia and Manchuria where he traded in furs and was present at the battle of Mukden in the Russo-Japanese War. In 1906, he travelled in Burma, India, and Ceylon.

In March 1908, he and J. W. Brooke started off from Chentu to explore and map the unknown lands on the western Chinese frontier of Szechuan, known as "the country of the eighteen tribes." A mountainous region originally occupied by an aboriginal race called the Chang Ming, it was then held by tribes of eastern Tibet, which, with the collaboration of Chinese forces attacking on their side of the region, managed to win control. Meares and Brooke followed the Min River valley up to the Chinese village of Wenchuan, studying animals and plants along the way. They were then joined by Mr Fergusson of the British and Foreign Bible Society, and the three of them headed westward with Chinese porters to a Chinese trading post called Gakalas, not far from the castle of Colonel Gow, who knew Fergusson and entertained the party. Gow was one of five small chiefs who had been given the rank of colonel in the Chinese army, on the understanding that they would supply armed militia when requested. They left Gow and continued on northwest, past several lamaseries to the great castle of Damba. Then they followed the Kermer River to the Wassaland, the Wassau country, and spent much time trying to photograph an exotic animal, the *takin*, a beast resembling a musk-ox, and hunting with local tribesmen and their dogs. Late in December, J. W. Brooke having gone off with a party of porters into the Lolo country, he was first robbed and then besieged and killed by a large number of tribesmen on Christmas Day 1908. Meares was able to bring back his body as well as the accompanying Chinese.

In 1910, Meares went to Siberia, at Captain R. F. Scott's request, to buy sled dogs and ponies for Scott's Antarctic expedition, and later that year, he went on that expedition; he and Wilfred Bruce were in charge of the dogs. He managed well enough, though Scott complained that he persisted in the Russian practice of riding on the sled and wanted him to learn to run behind. Wilson found him to be "typically a man of action, a most entertaining mess-mate, and full of fun." The expedition continued into 1912, and early that year, he and four others on the expedition went home in the *Terra Nova*. His life on the expedition may be glimpsed in Captain R. F. Scott's, *Scott's Last Expedition*, ed., Leonard Huxley (New York, Dodd, Mead & Co., 1913), two vols., passim. And see photos of him, esp. p. 274.

In the Great War, he joined the Royal Flying Corps in which he rose to the rank of lieutenant colonel, and in 1921, he took part in a British Air Mission to Japan, which earned him the award of the Order of the Sacred Treasure, Third Class. After that, he went on travelling, ostensibly looking for a place in which to retire. On 13 May 1928, when CM was fifty-two years old, he arrived at Quebec City aboard the Cunard liner, *Ausonica*, and made his way across the country to Victoria, BC. Vancouver Island naturally interested him because he believed himself to be related to Captain John Meares (1756-1809), who sailed to the Island's Pacific coast with early British ships of war, established the settlement at Nootka, and built the first vessel constructed there. Meares Island and Meares Street were named after this relative. In Victoria, CM and his wife lived at 837 Burdette St and joined the China-Japan Society. In 1933-1934, they travelled in England, Germany, and Belgium. He had married Annie Christina Spengler, born at Sunninghill, Berkshire, on 29 December 1891, and they lived quietly in Victoria until he died on 12 May 1937. Local friends knew little about him and reported only that "he was a jolly reticent chap" with a good grasp of world affairs. He was buried in a private funeral. Mrs Meares was living at 1070 Joan Crescent when she died, aged ninety-five, on 6 September 1974.

Sources: *BC Archives*, MS-0455, Meares papers bequeathed by Mrs Meares; NAC, RG76, Immigration, series C-1-a, vol. 1928, vol. 4, p. 213; *Colonist*, 21 April 1931, p. 7; 29 April 1934, p. 6; 13 May 1937, p. 2; 14 May 1937, p. 14, obit.; Elspeth Huxley, *Scott of the Antarctic* (Weidenfeld and Nicolson, 1977), pp. 189, 217 and 178; Captain R. F. Scott, *Scott's Last Expedition*, ed., Leonard Huxley (New York, Dodd, Mead & Co., 1913), two vols., passim. And see photos of him, esp. p. 274; Cecil H. Meares, "Among the Unknown Tribes," *The Wide World Magazine*, vol. xxv (April 1910), pp. 82-91; (May 1910), pp. 111-116; (June 1910), pp. 241-246; J. W. Brooke, "Sport in Wassaland," *The Badminton Magazine*, NS, no. 159 (October 1908), pp. 437-449, p. 437; and "Hunting the Takin on the Borders of Tibet," *The Badminton Magazine*, NS, no 161 (December 1908), pp. 651-659; J. Richard Nokes, *Almost a Hero: The Voyages of John Meares, R.N., to China, Hawaii and the Northwest Coast* (Pullman, Washington, Washington State University Press, 1998), see index entries for "Meares, John" (c. 1756-1809).

MEDLEY, Lieutenant Colonel Ernest Jones (1859-?). At sometime after the South African War, he retired to Victoria, BC, where he joined the British Campaigners' Association on 19 November 1909 at the same time as *Major A. N. Heneage. On 9 October 1911 in Victoria, EM and his wife had a son John Medley, who served in the Shanghai Police Force from 1937 to 1943. EM moved on soon after that and died somewhere outside BC.

Born on 10 August 1859 at Lahore, India, he was recorded, aged eleven, in the 1871 census as living at 9 Lansdowne Square, Hove, Sussex, with his mother, [Adelaide] Charlotte Medley *née* Steel, aged forty-six, a "Landholder" born in London, her husband absent. With them were EM's brother, Alfred Medley, aged five, also born in India, and a sister, "infant," two weeks old, born in Brighton, Sussex. There was also a married visitor, Ada Medley, aged forty-eight, born at

Norwood, Sussex. EM was first commissioned on 11 May 1878 in the Suffolk Regiment. On 10 March 1882, he was appointed to the Staff Corps, Indian Army, in the Seventeenth Regiment of Bengal Cavalry (raised in 1858, disbanded in 1882, re-formed in 1885) and served in Burma in 1878-1879 and on 19 March 1886 arrived at Ferozapore from Meean Meer under orders to Loralai. From 11 May 1889, he was squadron commander. According to the Army List, he qualified for Army Staff, for instructor in army signalling, for a certificate from the Hythe, Fleetwood, or Indian Schools of Musketry—"Extra," for Persian (lower standard), and for Russian ("passed"). Among the squadron commanders, he was second in command from 12 April 1902 and had qualified for Army Staff. By that time, he was fighting the South African War.

Like all Indian Army officers he had long furloughs home in Britain. In April 1901, the census found him living in Kensington, London, (St John the Baptist Parish; Holland Ward), at #81 Glalam Rd with his mother, Adelaide Medley, then a widow aged fifty-nine, and his sister, Ethel Medley, aged twenty, born at Simla, India. He was recorded as Ernest Medley, age forty-one, "Major Indian Cavalry (Army Off.)" born at Lahore, India. With them was his mother's daughter-in-law (presumably Ernest's wife) Ethel [*sic*] Medley, aged thirty-six, born at Lahore.
Sources: India Office, *Indian Army List*, July 1891, p. 126, 278, 583, 595, 601, 613e; January 1905, pp. 88, 276, 652, 663, 694, 700, 712; census 1871, England, RG 10/1092. p. ?; census 1901, RG 13/22, p. 10; *BC Archives, "Minutes of the British Campaigners' Ass.,"* 19 November 1909; list of Shanghai Police, courtesy of Dr. Robert Bickers, Bristol University.

MELLIN, Captain Harry de Moleyns (1867-1961). He was born on 8 December 1867, eldest son of Ventry de Moleyns Mellin, Esq., of Crumpsall Old Hall, Lancashire, but the 1871 census found him, aged three, living at "Springfield," Wintfield [Winterfield?], Pilkington, Lancashire, with his parents. His father was a "buyer for export." His mother, Frances J. Mellin, then aged thirty-one, was born at Thornton, Yorkshire, and he had a younger brother and a sister also born in the north of England. There was also an eleven-year-old niece, Kelina M. Day, born at Frinsley, Surrey. The household had three female servants. Four years later, another son was born and this was Richard Guy Mellin (1875-1931), who also went out to live on the Island. HM was educated in Switzerland and in 1889-1892 served in the Second Norfolk Regiment as a captain.

About 1895, HM retired from the army and went out to farm in the Somenos and Quamichan districts of Vancouver Island. There he assisted in surveying the Malahat Road in 1907-1908 under Dennis Harris, CE, and in 1909 was appointed as inspector of construction until the road was finished late in 1910. The Survey Department of the Provincial Civil Service took him on to their permanent staff in 1911, but on 20 November 1914, he joined the British Army as a captain and served in France and Belgium in the Rifle Brigade until May 1918. Demobilized in 1919, he entered the BC Civil Service and worked as secretary to Lieutenant Governor Sir Frank Barnard during the first visit of the Prince of Wales and then in the BC Forest Branch. In 1892, before going to Canada, he had married Isabelle Edge (1872-1909), only child

of Rev. Andrew Edge of Cheshire, and they had a son, Andrew, born in England on 18 December 1894. Isabelle died, aged forty, on 19 March 1909 in Victoria, and two years later, HM married Anastasia Rose Musgrove (1864-1936), daughter of Edward Musgrove of Victoria and County Waterford, Ireland. HM also outlived his brother, Richard Guy Mellin (1875-1931), who lived nearby on the Island. But he died at last, aged ninety-three, on 23 November 1961.
Sources: *Who's Who in B.C.*, 1933-1934, pp. 108-9; census 1871, England, RG 10/3964.

MERSTON (alias Meyerstein), Major William Charles (1884-1962). He was born William Charles Meyerstein on 30 March 1884 in London, son of Charles James Lee Meyerstein (1854-?), a prosperous "general merchant" living at 51 Finchley Road and his wife Constance Polters Meyerstein. These parents were born in or near London, but WM's paternal grandparents, William and Henrietta Meyerstein, were immigrants, he from Hanover and she from Frankfurt. WM trained as a land surveyor and worked in BC as such from his arrival in 1908. When he joined the Canadian Army at Valcartier, Quebec, on 18 September 1914, he wrote his family name as "Meyerstein," but it was crossed out on the application form and Merston was printed in large letters above it. A German name being a handicap at that time, perhaps even a danger, the recruiting staff evidently made the sensible suggestion that he anglicize his name. He had already had two years in the Eighty-eighth Victoria Fusiliers (militia) and described his occupation as "surveyor (BCLS)." He was an Anglican, 5' 7" tall with a fair complexion, blue eyes, and brown hair. His service overseas with the Seventh Battalion was rewarded with the DCM and the MC.

After the war, he resumed his work as a land surveyor, married Helen Marcia Farrer on 7 October 1926 in Victoria, and a few months later built the Oak Bay Beach Hotel at 1187 Beach Drive. There they lived while he managed the hotel and had three children, Pamela, Ann, and James, but in 1946, they sold the place to Mrs Norma MacDonald from Seattle and moved down Beach Drive to No. 1159. Already a member of the Union Club, WM then became head of the Vancouver Island Corps of Commissionaires and president of Victoria Lawn Tennis Club. When he died on 16 May 1962, aged seventy-seven, his funeral was held at Christ Church Cathedral.
Sources: NAC, CEF files, box 8135-35; *Colonist*, 17 May 1962, p. 39, obit.; census 1871, England, RG 10/283, p. 7; census 1891, RG 12/105, p 3; census 1891, RG 12/114, p. 26; census 1901, RG 13/118, p. 3; Ron Baird, *Success Story: The History of Oak Bay* (Victoria, Daniel Heffernan and James Borsman, 1979), 192 pp., p. 104;

MESSITER, Lieutenant Colonel Charles Bayard (1871-1940). He was born at Offenburg, Germany, and christened at the British Chaplaincy in Baden-Baden. His father Charles Alston Messiter of "Barwick House," near Yeovil in Somerset, was "Magistrate for Somerset" born in London, son of Thomas Messiter, a barrister, CM's grandfather, who was in turn a son of George Messiter, a prosperous Yeovil glove manufacturer. CM's father and mother, Lucy Ashton Bayard of Philadelphia, had married on 30 September 1869 at St James Cathedral in Toronto, Canada. Besides CM, they had two daughters, his sisters, Evelyn Lucy Messiter and Helen Constance Messiter, born at Llannon, Carmarthenshire, South Wales. All this movement and what the father relates in his book, *Sport and Adventures among the North-American Indians* (1890), show a life of travel and adventure, but by 1881, the father had taken over "Barwick House" and was settled, aged thirty-nine, as a "Magistrate for Somerset" with six servants and a coachman with a family living nearby at Barwick Lodge. Meanwhile, after his schooling, CM became a "military cadet" and in 1891 was staying with a cousin at Odiham, Southampton. The next year, he obtained a commission in the Second Gloucestershire Regiment with which he served in India, Egypt, and South Africa for the next eighteen years. In 1893, he became a lieutenant and he was recorded in 1900 as Lieutenant Charles Bayard Messiter, Second Gloucester Regiment, stationed at the *Dépôt* in Bristol. In 1906, he was recorded as Captain Charles Bayard Messiter attached to the First Battalion Gloucesters as "Adjutant 1st West Jersey Militia."

On 12 January 1910, he retired to British Columbia with the rank of captain, the Queen's Medal and six clasps, and the King's with two clasps. He became a fruit grower at Waldo, South-east Kootenay, and on 11 March 1913, his wife having died, he married Olive Blanche Moore at Fernie. BC had become his home, but when the Great War began, CM went overseas on SS *Grampian* leaving Halifax on 26 December 1914, and on 7 January 1915, he joined the Ninth Royal North Lancashire Regiment in France as a captain, then a major, and finally (on 20 January 1917) as temporary lieutenant colonel in the Ninety-fourth Training Reserve later renamed the Fifty-second Royal Warwicks (at Lowestoft). His wife said later that he had sent her $45 a month throughout the war. He returned to Victoria in 1919 with the DSO and the OBE, sailing out of Liverpool on 12 April aboard SS *Grampian*. The five children he had by his first wife were growing up: John Charles Bayard Messiter, born in 1900, was apprenticed in an airplane works; Herbert Lindsell Messiter, aged seventeen, sheep-ranching in Australia; and Walter FitzRoy Messiter, fifteen, and Richard Moreton Messiter, fourteen, both at school at Victoria College, Jersey, where CM's two sisters were living.

CM and his second wife lived mainly in Victoria for the next twenty-one years, joined the Union Club, and donated large sums to various charities and institutions. In the provincial election on 1 June 1937, he ran as a Social Credit candidate for Victoria but was defeated with only 206 votes or the support of only 31 per cent of the electorate. He died in Victoria, aged sixty-nine, on 16 October 1940, leaving his wife and two sons, the elder an officer with the RAF in Egypt; his two sisters were still on the island of Jersey. His funeral was conducted by Rev. T. R. Lancaster, and the pallbearers were *Major R. G. H. Murray, *Colonel A. W. R. Wilby, *Major A. J. Piddington, *Major A. H. Jukes, H. J. Ketchen, G. H. Pethick, G. B. H. Stevens, and E. C. F. Allen.

Sources: NAC, RG9 series II-F-10, *Imperial War Gratuities*, vol. 189, file 12732-C-12; *Colonist*, 17 October 1940, p. 2, obit. and photo; 22 October 1940, p. 3; Charles

Alston Messiter wrote *Sport and Adventures among the North-American Indians* (R. H. Porter, 1890), 368 pp.; census 1861, England, RG 9/1639, p. 1; census 1881, RG 11/2389, p. 1; census 1891, RG 12/953, p. 7; census 1901, RG 13/2412, p. 4; *Whitaker's*, p. 362.

MICHELL, Captain John Berkeley (1832-1908). He was born on 6 November 1832 in Dublin, son of George Monk Berkeley Michell (1806-?) and Maria Stanley. He fought in the Crimean War, then emigrated to Australia, and later moved on to Canada, where he died, aged seventy-five, in Victoria on 6 April 1908. A sister, Cecilia Fancourt Michell (1840-1908), born in Dublin on 19 October 1840, died on 22 June 1908 in Duncan, VI. She had married Peter William Rolston (1831-1922), on 23 April 1863 and both of them were buried at St Peter's Anglican Church, Quamichan, near Duncan. Another sister, Maria Stanley Michell (1842-1912), was born in Dublin on 25 September 1842, married Valentine S. Spain on 10 July 1862, and died on 30 October 1912 in Victoria. A number of other Anglo-Irish relatives lived in India and Canada.
Sources: Family records compiled by Charles Anthony Lort.

MILESON, Philip Edward (c. 1881-1969). Born at Mile End Old Town, Middlesex (London), he was the youngest son of Edward A. Mileson, a "drawing instrument maker," and his wife Jane, both Londoners. The census of 1881 found them living at 11 Lyal Road, Mile End Old Town. In 1891, they were living at "Goforth Villa," Woodford, Essex, but otherwise much the same. He joined the British Army, served through the South African War, and then moved to Calgary, Alberta, where he eventually became chief accountant for natural resources for the CPR.

In 1952, he and his wife Rita moved to Cranmore Road, Victoria, where he joined the Kiwanis Club. He died, aged eighty-eight, on 30 November 1969 leaving his widow and five daughters of whom one, Doris, was then in the Dominican Republic.
Sources: census 1881, England, RG 11/484, p. 23; census 1891, RG 12/1359, p. 43; *Colonist*, 2 December 1969, p. 25, obit.

MILLETT, George (c. 1840-1927). He was born at Shorncliffe Barracks, Kent, where his father was in the Northumberland Fusiliers. Both parents served in the Crimean War, his mother as one of the nurses who served under Florence Nightingale. He too joined the Northumberlands and in time to fight in the Indian Mutiny. At age twelve, he served as a drummer boy when they landed, disarmed the Fifth Native Infantry, and then made a dash for Lucknow. They did a forced march of seventy miles in five days. After taking part in the Siege of Lucknow, the Northumberlands served near the city for a year, and Millett was severely wounded in the back of the neck by a splinter of shell, which made him deaf and paralysed the side of his face. As a bugler of the Northumberlands, he sounded the commence fire when two hundred mutineers were shot after being tried by court-martial. They were shot down by "C" battery of the RHA, and those who escaped that fire were picked off by the infantry with rifles. In a fight outside Lucknow, he was wounded by a lance when a rallying square was being formed against an attack by native lancers. The lancer who stabbed him was shot down by his chum. In another action, he was hit on the calf of the right leg and sent to hospital. He went home with his regiment and landed at Anglesey barracks. Of the Northumberland Fusiliers at that time, only five hundred of the original strength reached home. They had lost 1,150 men. During the Trent affair with the USA, they were on duty night and day. After sixteen years in the regiment in which GM was born, he retired on a pension.

He went out to Canada about 1887 and spent a year in Ontario before moving to Victoria. He was in the Point Ellice Bridge disaster in May 1896 and helped in the rescue. For several years, he was the gardener at Bishops Close for Bishop W. W. Perrin before working as gardener at the Jubilee Hospital, where he continued until forced by ill health to stop. He then became an inmate at the Jubilee. When he died, aged eighty-seven, on 6 January 1927 he left his widow at home at 225 Bowker Avenue, Oak Bay, and two daughters in the city. He was the oldest member of the Sons of England Benevolent Society here and also a member of the British Campaigners' Ass. Burial at St Mary's Oak Bay.
Sources: *Colonist*, 7 January 1927, p. 5, obit.; *BC Archives*, photo of British Campaigners, 1913.

MILNE, Sergeant John (c. 1864-1951). A British colour sergeant major in the Royal Marines, he fought for thirty-six years in campaigns in Egypt and the Sudan (1882-1885), Canada, Europe, and India. He retired at last to Victoria, where he lived to be one of the oldest Imperial veterans. As such, he took part in public gatherings of men who spoke about their careers around the empire in Spencer's dining room on 28 November 1936, at the annual dinner of the British Imperial Comrades Association in February 1940 and on other such occasions. When he died, aged eighty-six, on 15 November 1951 he was living at 3024 Jutland Road, Victoria.
Sources: *Colonist*, 22 November 1936, p. 3; 29 November 1936, p. 2; 11 February 1940, p. 17; 17 November 1951, p. 15, obit.

MITCHELL, Lieutenant Commander John Henry (1893-1925). He was born on 25 February 1893 at Cuttles, Atworth, Wiltshire, son of Arthur Charles Mitchell (1847-1917) and his wife Constance Lucy Elwes (c. 1857-1945) from Colebourne, Gloucestershire. The family was of the substantial upper-middle class with property and high-born relatives, such as Sir Michael Edward Hicks-Beach (1837-1916), who married one of JM's aunts, Caroline Elwes. The 1901 census recorded JM, aged eight, living with his family and nine servants at "Highgrove House" near Tetbury, Gloucestershire, which his father had bought in 1894 and where, much later, Prince Charles and Diana lived during their brief marriage. His father, a JP for Wiltshire and Gloucestershire, was a "fundholder, living on investments and interest," as did his father before him, JM's grandfather Francis H. Mitchell (c. 1794-?). For many years, the grandfather inhabited 12 Upper Wimpole Street,

Marylebone, London, attended by his eight servants, and with his children and grandchildren for long periods. In 1907, JM joined the Royal Navy. In 1910-1911, he served as a midshipman aboard the battleship HMS *Collingwood* and in July 1918 was a lieutenant on HMS *Westminster* under Lieutenant Commander Francis G. Glossop. He retired to the Island with the rank of lieutenant commander in 1920 and settled at French Creek near Parksville, where one of his sisters joined him, and there he died, aged only thirty-one, on 31 August 1925 and was buried at French Creek Anglican Church, leaving his sister at home and his mother and two brothers in England.

Sources: Navy List, 1911 (January-April) p. 294; *Nanaimo Daily Free Press*, 1 September 1925, p. 1, obit.; *Colonist*, 2 September 1925, p. 7, obit.; census 1901, England, RG 13/2445, p. 12; census 1881, RG 11/140, p. 19; census 1871, RG 10/157, p. 48.

MITCHELL, Captain William E. (1849-1934). Born in Dundee on Christmas Day 1849, at thirteen years of age, he joined the Dundee Highlanders, which was using muzzle-loading guns. In 1869, he went out to Ontario, where he joined the militia and served in the Second Riel Rebellion (1885). He moved to Victoria in September 1911 and joined the Fifth Regiment of the CGA, commanded at that time by *Arthur Currie. Later, he joined the Sixteenth Scottish and tried in vain to join up for service in the Great War. CM was a keen marksman from boyhood in the Dundee Regiment and in 1880 in Ontario won renown, a gold medal, and a prize of $100 by taking third place in the governor general's match. Later the same year, he won the Dominion Rifle Association badge, using an old Snider rifle, and in 1881, he was on the team which won the famous Kolapore Cup. In 1881, 1882, and 1887, he was a member of the Wimbledon and Bisley teams, and in 1882 he won the Prince of Wales prize at Wimbledon, which gave him $100 and a silver medal. When in 1887 at Wimbledon, he won second prize, "it being Jubilee Year the members of the Canadian team were presented to the Prince of Wales and Princess Alexandra, who were the guests of Lord and Lady Wantage. Lord Wantage was the secretary of the National Rifle Association. The Princess personally pinned the badge on the tunic of Captain Mitchell." In all, he gathered fourteen medals, a score of rifle badges, and many cups. He was living at 2560 Forbes Street when he died, aged eighty-five, on 8 September 1934.

Sources: *Report of the Proceedings of the Dominion of Canada Rifle Association, 1905* (Ottawa, R. J. Taylor, 1905, pp. 79, 81-2, 113, *Colonist*, 9 September 1934, p. 3: obit., and photo.

MOFFAT, Thomas Stuart (c. 1870-1938). Born at Riccarton, Ayrshire, son of John, a coal pit engineer, and his wife Jean, he was living at home in 1881 with his elder sister, a French polisher, and a brother, an unholsterer. TM worked for some years in engineering in Kilmarnock and Glasgowm and then had a long and colourful career at sea along the China Coast, around Cape Horn, and to the Far North in gold-rush days. For two years, he sailed in the *Jardine* of the Matheson Line on the China Coast. Early in the twentieth century, he migrated to Victoria, where he worked for eighteen months at Albion Iron Works. Then he found work on the old *Princess Joan*, plying between Victoria and Comox at that time. Before long, he joined the BC Coast Service as chief engineer of the *Otter*, and in 1910, he went to Scotland and brought out the *Princess Adelaide*. For many years, he sailed up and down the BC Coast but retired from the sea on 1 February 1920 and worked ashore for the company, becoming superintendent engineer in 1934. When he retired on 1 July 1936, he took his wife to live in Scotland for a year. He died, aged sixty-eight, on 12 July 1938 in Victoria with his wife and children around him.

Sources: *Colonist*, 14 July 1938, p. 5, obit.; census 1881, Scotland, cssct 1881_195, Riccarton, Ayrshire.

MONCKTON-CASE, Lieutenant John (1878-1917). Born on 30 October 1878 at Warwick, Warwickshire, son of Rev. Frederick Case, his mother died a year later giving birth to his sister Nora, born at Stratford-on-Avon, and the 1881 census found him, aged five, living with his sister and their father, then aged thirty-two, who was curate of St Michael, Highgate, London. They had two servants. JM became a civil engineer and appears in the 1901 census records boarding in Melcombe Regis, Dorset. He subsequently enlisted in the Royal Fusiliers and served for four years, mainly in the South African (Boer) War.

Like many others in that war, he then migrated to Victoria, where he was lived for some years, employed by the City Engineer's Department and becoming a member of the Canadian Society of Civil Engineers. On 4 December 1915, he enlisted in the 103rd Battalion, was commissioned as a lieutenant, transferred to the 2nd Tunnelling Corps, Royal Canadian Engineers, organized by Major Roach, and went overseas with them. In 1917, he transferred to the Inland Water and Dock Transport Service of the Royal Engineers (which recruited widely after the Kut-el-Amara disaster of 1916) and was expecting to leave soon for Mesopotamia, when he was overtaken by illness and died on 9 November 1917, leaving his wife Minnie, two sons, and a daughter. Well known in Victoria, he had been living on a "ranch" near Prospect Lake at the time he enlisted.

Sources: NAC, CEF files, box 6288-30; census 1881, England, RG 11/1379, p. 58; census 1901, RG 13/1993, p. 29; *Colonist*, 14 November 1917, p. 5, obit., and photo; Canadian Veterans' Affairs, Virtual War Museum (Internet).

MONEY, Captain Charles Francis Lethbridge (1869-1936). He was born in London on 26 September 1869, the seventh son of Rev. C. F. S. Money, vicar of Stirling, Kent, and Hon. Canon of Rochester. After attending Cheltenham and Corpus Christi, Cambridge, he ventured out to Western Ontario in 1892 to learn farming and went on to work in a merchant's office in Winnipeg. In 1892, he joined the North-West Mounted Police but purchased a discharge three years later and returned to England. In April 1896, he left for South Africa, where he served for a year or two at Salisbury in the Rhodesian Field Force during the Rebellion and so held the Rhodesian Medal for 1896 with a clasp for 1897. In the South African War (1899-1902), he served in the British South African Police and retired as a captain with two medals but went on to serve as a paymaster captain in the British South African Police in Rhodesia from 1 April 1903 until 1908. After serving the Matabele and South African campaigns, he retired on a pension on 1 December 1909, farmed in Rhodesia, was elected in January 1912 as president of the Rhodesian Gwelo Farmer's Association, and, on 19 August 1912, was appointed for a few months as land inspector to the British SA Company's Land Settlement Department. In 1914, he was back in Canada and re-enlisted in the RCMP but left again in 1917, this time in order to join the Canadian Army, which he did at Victoria on 14 June 1918. He was not sent overseas owing to a susceptibility to malaria. He applied to rejoin the Canadian Mounted Police after the war but was rejected as being too old. Settled by then at 1025 St Patrick Street, Oak Bay, with a wife, Lily Mary Money, he looked for local employment and in 1922 became secretary manager of the Army and Navy Veterans. He worked hard at expanding that organization, helped men to find employment and to obtain pensions, and was elected to the amalgamation committee devoted to creating a unified body (the future Canadian Legion) for war veterans. On 15 October 1925, the *Daily Colonist* printed a long letter he and Sergeant John Drummond wrote in support of that cause. He was a Freemason and very active in St Mary's Anglican Church, Oak Bay, where he read the lesson for almost twenty years. At the annual vestry meeting there, Canon Nunns much regretted his death on 23 December 1936. He left his widow and a daughter Eileen at 1557 Wilmot Place and one son in Vancouver, Charles Ernie Money, born in Surrey, who soon moved to 953 Transit Road, Victoria, and was shot accidentally in January 1940, aged thirty-six, while hunting near Langford.

Sources: NAC, CEF files, box 6291-2, regimental no. 2714175, attestation paper for the Canadian Overseas Expeditionary Force; NAC, RG18, series G, vol. 3397, file 2835; *Colonist*, 15 October 1925, p. 4; 24 December 1936, pp. 1 and 6; 27 January 1937, p. 3; 5 January 1940, p. 12; 6 January 1940, p. 2, obit.

MONEY, Brigadier General Noel Ernest (1867-1941), CMG, DSO, TD. He was born in Montreal on 17 March 1867, son of Captain Albert William Money (c. 1839-1933), who was born at Hernfield, Suffolk, and had joined the Royal Canadian Rifles. A. W. Money served *inter alia* under Lord Wolseley in the Red River Expedition. NM's mother was a Canadian lady who married his father in 1860 at London, Ontario. The 1871 English census found NM, aged four, living at Weybridge, a south-western suburb of London, with his parents and two Canadian-born sisters, all staying at a small lodging house on Montgomery Place. His father was then listed as "Captain Half Pay late Royal Canadian Rifles." NM was educated at Radley and Christ Church, Oxford, and went on to serve in the South African War 1900-1902 with the Shropshire Imperial Yeomanry and then the South African Constabulary. He returned home to England with wounds, several mentions in despatches, the DSO, the Queen's Medal with three clasps, and the King's Medal with two clasps. In 1913, he went on a fishing trip to northern Ontario and soon crossed Canada to Vancouver Island, where he fished in Shawnigan Lake on 17 July, spent ten days in August on Qualicum Beach and there bought six lots of land with a view to building a lodge or hotel. With this in mind, he returned to England and took his family out to Qualicum followed by the good wishes of the officers and men of his old regiment, the Shropshire Yeomanry, in which he had been a Major. In 1903, he had married Maud Boileau Wood, second daughter of Edward Wood of Culmington Manor, Shropshire, and they had a son and a daughter. They sailed to one of the Eastern Canadian ports aboard *The Empress of Britain* and arrived on Vancouver Island in February 1914. Once back at Qualicum Beach, NM became managing director of the Merchants Trust and Trading Company Ltd. and also of the Qualicum Water Company Ltd. The previous year, the latter had applied for (and received) licenses to bring water from Whiskey Creek and Grandon Creek to the hotel and its golf course. With his brother-in-law, Charles Wood, and others, NM owned the company by 1915, mainly as a device for evading the Trust Companies Act recently passed by the BC government.

In the meantime, the Great War broke out in August 1914 and about a month later, on 4 September, the Moneys returned to England from New York on SS *St Paul* and on 4 August 1915, NM rejoined the British Army. On 3 March 1916, he sailed for Alexandria and by the end of July had assumed command of the Royal West Kent Regiment at Railhead, Terry Port, in the desert, east of Ismailia, with the rank of colonel. On 26 March 1917, he was given command of the Gloucestershire Hussars as well as two companies of the Royal West Kent Regiment, and on 28 October, he was promoted to brigadier general in command of 159th Brigade, Welsh Division. In this command, he captured the Mount of Olives as part of General Edmund Allenby's liberation of Jerusalem. In Victoria, meanwhile, the *Daily Colonist* reported on 11 January 1917 (p. 4) that "Mrs Money, wife of Colonel Noel Money, D.S.O., of 'Homme House,' Qualicum Beach, who is in command of a Battalion of the Royal West Kent Regiment somewhere in Egypt, is working as inspector in a munitions factory in London, England, engaged on work for aeroplanes." She and the children lived during those years at the Tower of London, her father being Keeper of the Crown Jewels. They went back to Qualicum after the war, in the course of which NM had been wounded, mentioned in despatches, and awarded the CMG and a bar to his DSO with which he sailed from Liverpool on 30 May 1919 aboard SS *Tunisian*.

By July 1919, they were back in Qualicum. During the years of their absence, the hotel had been converted into a convalescent hospital for wounded officers and it was still so at their return. What exactly was their relationship to the hotel in these years is not clear, but at sometime in 1919 or 1923, they must have raised the funds to buy it and the golf course, possibly in collaboration with Mrs Money's brother, Charles Wood. At any rate, in 1923, NM was back, managing the establishment. When he wrote to Ottawa on 10 April 1923 to apply for a British War Gratuity, he used the letterhead of Qualicum Beach Golf Club ("Green Fees, Guests of Qualicum Beach Hotel, Day, 75 cents, Week, $3; All others, $1 a day"). Already he and his wife were beginning to entertain the first of many distinguished visitors. The king of Siam was followed by Edgar Rice Burroughs, Zane Grey, Bob Hope, Bing Crosby, Errol Flynn, Spencer Tracey, Shirley Temple, other movie stars, and every governor general of Canada in turn. At sometime in the 1930s, a small squadron of the Royal Navy on its way to Comox anchored briefly near Qualicum Beach while its commander, a nephew or cousin, came for a visit ashore. Among other activities, many of these visitors fished at his special fishing place on the Stamp River, which became known as the Money Pool. He had a cabin there, next to one owned by the John Jacob Astor family. He kept a membership in White's Club (London) and the Union Club (Victoria). Having served in Palestine under General Allenby, he was one of those who met the Allenbys when they visited Victoria in March 1926, and when Allenby died in May 1936, Money said, "Lord Allenby combined the qualities of soldier, statesman, sportsman, gentleman, and true patriot, which every Britisher admires." Later that month, the Moneys went to Cumberland, VI, on one of their frequent visits to their friends *Lieutenant Colonel C. W. Villiers, late of the Coldstream Guards, and his wife Lady Kathleen Mary Cole, daughter of the Fourth Earl of Enniskillen.

By no means, all of the family's contacts were famous outsiders. In the village of Qualicum Beach, the Moneys presided like the lord and lady of the manor, but in the best sense imaginable. They gave an annual party at New Year's to which everyone was invited. Although he always wore plus fours and bought a new Packard car each year with a license plate marked "1," he did not fail to stop and chat in a friendly way with workmen and others he met in the village. He was a convivial neighbour and employer, often taking employees fishing, teaching young men to play golf, gambling occasionally, and taking as much whiskey as his diabetic system allowed. Near the end of May 1933, he visited the Qualicum Beach High School to present a badge to the junior fire warden. He was known to the fishing fraternity as "the finest of western anglers" and "by all odds the finest and most experienced steelhead fly fisherman in B.C.," and *Roderick Haig-Brown dedicated a book to him for this reason. He was president of the Qualicum Board of Trade from November 1929 to November 1936 and was one of the delegates at the annual convention of the Associated Boards of Trade of VI held at Saanichton 5-7 July 1933.

For many years, they spent most winters in Victoria at the Empress Hotel, where they could be near the children, who attended St Christopher's School. One winter when the children were a little older, NM let them keep a wing of the Qualicum Beach Hotel open—it normally closed in winter, not being insulated—to try to make money, Mary Evelyn doing the cooking and cleaning and Gordon everything else. NM did not interfere when Mary Evelyn was fined $150 and costs for "driving to the common danger" and causing an accident at Somenos on 17 February 1933. Later that year, Gordon married Helen Eilbeck Wilson, daughter of a Victoria department-store family. In May 1937, the Conservative Association met at Courtnay, where *B. A. McKelvie, Conservative candidate in Victoria, vigorously denounced the government of the day, and the meeting unanimously named Gordon Money as their local candidate. Gordon came home from an army camp at Calgary, Alberta, as a lieutenant in the Seaforth Highlanders of Canada in time to see his father just before he died, aged seventy-four, on 30 May 1941. NM was buried at St Mark's Anglican Church at Qualicum and attended by

many veterans and a firing party from the Irish Fusiliers stationed at Nanaimo. Among the pallbearers were *H. T. Goward, Dr T. S. McPherson, Captain Nigel H. Kennedy, Captain J. S. Matterson, Captain R. Lee, and *Colonel James Lightbody. NM's wife, Maud Boileau Money, died of cancer, aged seventy-two, on 5 October 1939 and was remembered locally as a gentle, benevolent person. Their daughter Mary Evelyn Money (c. 1904-1966) was still at Qualicum but had married Arthur de Courcy M. Denny (c. 1899-1971) by whom she had two children (Gordon and Susan). A few days before NM's death, he appeared in a *Colonist* photo of a party in a Qualicum garden at the house of Mrs *Captain J. N. M. Hodgins, along with Viscountess Byng of Vimy, Captain Nigel Kennedy, and a few others. As for the Qualicum Beach Hotel, a neighbour, Major Lowery, bought it and the fifty-five acres that went with it for $5,000 and sold them a decade later for $60,000.
Sources: NAC, RG 9 series II-F-10 (British War Gratuities):Vol. 193, file no. 13008-N-5; Brad C. Wylie, *Qualicum Beach: A History of Vancouver Island's Best Kept Secrets* (Qualicum Beach Historical & Museum Society, 1992), chapter 7, pp. 45-55; *Colonist*, 11 January 1917, p. 4; 31 July 1921, p. 13; 2 March 1933, p. 9; 24 May 1933, p. 9; 7 July 1933, pp. 1 and 6; 12 January 1934, p. 7; 18 April 1934, p. 7; 15 May 1936, p. 5; 16 May 1936, p. 8; 5 May 1937, p. 3; 8 May 1937, p. 6; 27 May 1941, p. 8; 31 May 1941, p. 1; 4 June 1941, p. 2; *Who's Who in B.C.* 1933-1934, p. 111; 1940-1941, p. 168; *Who was Who*, 1941-1950, p. 806; Roderick Haig-Brown, *The Western Angler: An Account of Pacific Salmon & Western Trout in British Columbia* (New York, William Morrow & Co., 1939, 1947), Dedication and pp. 343-4.

MOODY, Colonel Richard Clement (1813-1887). He was born on 13 February 1813 at St Ann's Garrison, Barbados, West Indies, second son of Thomas Moody, RE, who served as private secretary to several officials. RM was schooled at the RMA, Woolwich, and the Ordnance Survey of Great Britain before joining the Royal Engineers in 1830. He spent several years in the Ordnance Survey of Ireland, in the West Indies, and as a professor of fortification at Woolwich. In 1841-1849, he was posted in the Falkland Islands as lieutenant governor and then governor. In 1852, he married Mary Susannah Hawks, daughter of Joseph Hawks, a banker and Justice of the Peace, and they had eleven children. After further service in Malta and Edinburgh and some promotions, he was chosen in 1858 by Sir Edward Bulwer-Lytton, secretary of state for the colonies, to command a detachment of about 165 Royal Engineers being sent to the new colony of British Columbia to make surveys, build roads and bridges, and keep order in the gold fields. He was also appointed lieutenant governor and chief commissioner of lands and works. RM arrived at Victoria on Christmas Day 1858, sailed over to the mainland, and journeyed up the Fraser River to Fort Langley and Yale, before returning to the coast to establish the new colonial capital at New Westminster. This was Queen Victoria's choice, but she later agreed to have the capital moved to Victoria, over on Vancouver Island. Meanwhile, RM bought more than three thousand acres near New Westminster for himself and turned it into a model farm called "Mayfield." His engineers soon turned to building the Cariboo wagon road from Yale, and when they were recalled home to England

in 1863, about 130 of them decided to retire from the service and remain in the colony. But RM returned to England, where he became a regimental colonel and in March 1864 was given command of the Royal Engineers in the Chatham District. On 25 January 1866, he retired on full pay and with the rank of major general. He lived for about twenty years at Lyme Regis and died on 31 March 1887 while on a visit to Bournemouth.
Sources: Margaret A. Ormsby, in the DCB, "Moody, Richard Clement, soldier, colonial administrator, and public servant"; Harbour Publishing (BC), Internet file; Beth Hill, *Sappers: The Royal Engineers in British Columbia* (Ganges, BC, Horsdal & Shubert, 1987), 182 pp.; Frances M. Woodward, "The Influence of the Royal Engineers on the Development of British Columbia," *B.C. Studies*, vol. 24 (1974-75), pp. 3-51.

MOORE, Captain John Joseph (1867-1966). Born on 21 November 1867 on the Isle of Man, one of several John Josephs there in his time, he ran away to sea at the age of thirteen and served in the South African War and again in the Great War, this time sailing out of Halifax, Nova Scotia. In the 1920s, he joined the Canadian Hydrographic Service, wherein he worked up to be master of the CGS *Lillooet* and then, from 1932, of the new surveying vessel, the *William J. Stewart*, a 1,295-ton ship built at Collingwood, Ontario, and named in honour of the first Canadian chief hydrographer, who served in the years 1904-1925. She carried a crew of fifty-five with seven officers. JM was in command of her when she struck Ripple Rock in Seymour Narrows on 11 June 1944 but managed to save her by beaching her at Plumper Bay three miles away. In 1945, he retired, did shore jobs until 1957, and died, aged ninety-seven, on 27 November 1966 in Saanich, leaving two sons—Edwin and Frank—and three married daughters.
Sources: *Colonist*, 19 November 1964, p. 15; Fred Rogers, *Shipwrecks of British Columbia* (Vancouver, J. J. Douglas, 1973), p. 33.

MORESBY, Admiral of the Fleet Sir Fairfax (1786-1877). Born in Calcutta, India, he joined the Royal Navy very young and spent much time in his career based at the Cape of Good Hope Station and fighting slave traders in which he was successful and praised by Lord Wilberforce. In 1850-1853, he was commander-in-chief, Pacific Station, based at Esquimalt in his flagship, HMS *Portland*, Captain H. Chads. He had two sons, both officers in the navy and lieutenants at Esquimalt while he was there. The elder, Fairfax, was flag lieutenant in the *Portland* and went down with HM brig *Sappho* in Bass Strait, off Australia, in 1858. The other son, John (1830-1922), had a career as an explorer and served *inter alia* as gunnery lieutenant on HMS *Thetis* for which Thetis Island was named. Moresby Island was named after FM in 1853 by Commander James Charles Prevost (1810-1891) of HMS *Virago*, who was a son-in-law and commander-in-chief at Esquimalt in 1857-1860. In 1861, FM and his wife Eliza Louisa *née* Williams (1796-1874), aged seventy-four and sixty-three, were living at Bronwylfe, Littleham, Devonshire, with his aged aunt Antonine Reston, born at Swansea, and three servants. FM was then vice admiral of the red, born at Calcutta, India, and his wife was a Londoner. The 1871 census found their household unchanged except that FM, now eighty-four, was "Admiral of the Fleet of Great Britain," and there were five servants.

Sources: J.K. Laughton and Andrew Lambert, in the Oxford DCB online (Fairfax Moresby); R.N. Rudmose Brown and R.O. Morris, in the Oxford DCB (John Moresby); Walbran, *B.C. Coast Names*, p. 342; census 1861, RG 9/1382, p. 16; census 1871, England, RG 10/2047, p. 32; Longstaff, *Esquimalt Naval Base*, pp. 114-15; *Fort Victoria Letters*, 1846-1851, ed., Hartwell Bowsfield, (Winnipeg, Hudson's Bay Record Society, 1979), see index entry, p. 268; John Moresby (a son), *Discoveries and Surveys in New Guinea and the D'Entrecasteaux Islands A Cruise in Polynesia and Visits to the Pearl-Shelling Stations in Torres Straits of H.M.S.* Basilisk, (London John Murray 1876), about his father's exploits.

MOREY, Captain Harold William (c. 1886-1960). Born in Devonshire, he spent most of his life in the Royal Navy. On 25 March 1911, he was serving as a lieutenant with a seniority of 30 July 1908 aboard HMS *Surprise* (home fleet). Promoted to lieutenant commander on 30 July 1916, he was in HMS *Antrim* from 14 August, but in January 1919 was aboard HMS *President* and in January 1927 in HMS *Frobisher* with the same rank. The Second World War brought his next promotion: He was acting captain of HMS *Saker* in October 1943.

At sometime in 1951, he retired to "Cypress Grove," Deep Cove, on Chalet Road (now Land's End Road) along the seafront, looking westward over Saanich Inlet. There he died, aged seventy-four, on 3 March 1960 and was buried as an Anglican, probably nearby at Holy Trinity, Patricia Bay, leaving a son Peter Morey and a granddaughter in Devonshire.

Sources: *Navy List* (London), April 1911, p. 52; 1917 (4) p. 68; January 1919, p. 132; January 1927, p. 42; October 1943, p. 117; *Colonist*, 4 March 1960, obit.

MORLEY, Henry Augustus Snow (1847-1936). He was born on 12 November 1847 in Sneinton, an eastern suburb of Nottingham, son of Henry August Morley and Mary Ann Morley. The 1861 census found him, aged thirteen, living at "55 Brid: Gate," St Peter's parish, Castle ward, Nottingham, with his father, then aged forty-two, a "Banker's Clerk" born in Nottingham. His mother was absent. Soon after that, HM took employment as a midshipman in the East India Company, making voyages to India and South America for several years.

In 1869, he went out to the Island and stayed at first with an uncle in the Cowichan Valley, John Morley (c. 1812-1883), who was the first magistrate there and the first reeve when North Cowichan was incorporated as a municipality and who also served as electoral returning officer and administrator of the estates of several intestate men of the district. HM pre-empted what became known as the Havermeyer property, at Somenos Lake, and became the first municipal clerk of the district. He also proved himself an excellent shot, a keen fisherman, and general outdoor sportsman, and before settling down, he went back to Nottingham for a while, joined the Robin Hood Rifles, a crack volunteer regiment of those days, and won prizes as a marksman.

On 14 July 1885, after his return, he married Jessie Thornton Fell (1857-1944), English-born daughter of *James Fell, who was elected mayor of Victoria in the same year. HM worked there as an accountant with the HBC and then transferred to the BC civil service. A Victoria city directory for 1900 and the 1901 census for Victoria found him living with his wife, two sons, and a daughter, at 198 View Street, employed as an auditor, "chief clerk, Treasury Department, Gov't Bldgs." The elder of their two sons, Henry Arnold Morley, born in Victoria on 17 June 1885, became a civil engineer and joined the CEF on 23 September 1914 after nearly seven years in the militia, the Fifth Canadian Garrison Artillery. He had been living at home with his parents, then at 1130 View Street. HM retired in 1922 after thirty-one years of service and died, aged eighty-nine, on 1 October 1936, leaving his widow, his sons, and a daughter, who buried him at Christ Church Cathedral and Ross Bay Cemetery.

Sources: *Colonist*, 3 October 1936, p. 3, obit., photo; census 1861, England, RG 9/2466, p. 14; census 1861, RG 9/2452, p. 1 (John Morley); Canadian census, 1881, Vancouver Island; Canadian census, 1901, *Victoria; B.C. Government Gazette*, vol. 10 (5 January to 30 December 1871); Hugh Armstrong, "People who Died Intestate, 1861-1883," Internet; NAC, CEF files, box 6378-4 (son).

MORRIS, Colonel Arthur Henry (1861-1939). He was born at Sale, Isle of Wight, son of Rev. Henry Morris and attended King's College Canterbury. After a brief spell in the Yorkshire Artillery Militia, he took a commission in the Royal Irish Regiment in 1833 and in 1891 was promoted to captain. Meanwhile, he served in the Sudan Expedition in 1884-1885 and in the Burmese War in 1885-1887, became transport officer for the Karen Field Force (mentioned in despatches), chief transport officer to the Chin Lushai Expedition (1889-1890), twice commanded expeditions against the tribes of the Northern Territories, and was inducted into the DSO with clasp, mentioned in despatches, and formally thanked by the government of India. He went on to serve in West Africa and during operations in Ashanti commanded a column that forced its way into Kumassi from the north, defended the place, and later commanded the column which cut its way out of Kumassi. In 1902, he commanded an expedition against the Tiansis and later was appointed chief commissioner of the Northern Territories of the Gold Coast. Next, he became commandant of the Mounted Infantry School of India (1906-1909) and was later in charge of the Duke of York's Royal Military College (1909-1913). He retired in 1913, decorated with the CMG, but was called up again in 1915 to command the internment camp for German prisoners at Amherst, Nova Scotia.

After the Great War, he retired and in 1927 moved to Victoria, where he lived quietly at 2100 Brighton Avenue, Oak Bay, but went off hunting, fishing, and shooting as often as possible. On 15 September 1929, the *Colonist* (p. 4) published a letter headed "The Racing Situation" in which AM defended the policy of the Colwood Parks Association of which he was a steward. On 11 August 1933, another of his letters entitled "In the Great War" contradicted a

Mr Martin of Oak Bay, who had said that Britishers did not even make up even 50 per cent of the First Canadian Division. AM found official figures showing that 42,195 soldiers in that division were British born in a total of 54,673. Only 12,418 were Canadian born. The percentages were 77 per cent British and 23 per cent Canadian. He referred, of course, only to the First Division. There were more than six hundred thousand officers and men in the CEF for whom files are still preserved at the NAC.

On 12 June 1934, AM published in the *Colonist* a letter revealing of his career and character in response to one of Gordon Sinclair's newspaper reports of his travels in West Africa:

> Sir—Having been five years the chief commissioner of the northern territories of the Gold Coast, a hinterland of nearly 100,000 square miles, I have some knowledge of West Africa, and would ask to be allowed to stoutly protest against the unmitigated nonsense talked by Mr Gordon Sinclair. Judging from his description of the Crown colonies of the Gold Coast and Nigeria, one would imagine that these colonies contained nobody except witch doctors and their victims, whereas a large proportion of the inhabitants are Mohammedans. Both colonies are most valuable possessions of the British Crown, and the following figures may be of interest, taken from *Affairs of West Africa* by Mr E. D. Morel: The total value of British produce and manufactures shipped to the British possessions in West Africa in the five years 1896-1900 amounted to nearly £10,000,000 while the total value of raw produce imported by Great Britain from British West Africa during the same period amounted to over £11,000,000. Since that time both exports and imports have increased enormously
>
> Does Mr Sinclair really suppose that people are going to believe that 200,000 persons die every year under the Voodoo curse in West Africa, as stated in *The Colonist* of June 9? Such a statement as this can exist in his own imagination only, or come from the lips of a drunken beach comber. He also does not appear to be aware that Lagos is the capital of British Nigeria, not French, as stated by him.

AM died, aged seventy-seven, at the Jubilee Hospital, Victoria, on 13 December 1939, leaving a widow, a son John Henry Morris at Nanaimo, and two brothers and three sisters all in England. Among the pallbearers at his funeral were *Lieutenant General Sir Percy Lake, *Major John Bayley Hardinge, and *Major Percival Theodore Stern.
Sources: *Who was Who*, vol. 3, pp. 969-700; *Colonist* 15 September 1929, p. 4; 11 August 1933, p. 4; 12 June 1934, p. 4; 15 December 1939, p. 5; 16 December 1939, p. 6 (photo); 17 December 1939, p. 3; General Sir James Willcocks, GCB, GCMG, KCSI, DSO, *The Romance of Soldiering and Sport* (Cassell & Co. Ltd., 1925), pp. 127, 136, 137, 153, 154, 155.

MORTON, Major Arthur William (1869-1945). Born at Bridge, Kent, he appears in the 1881 census, aged twelve, living in Croydon at "Surrey Villa" with his parents and six brothers and sisters. His father Robert Morton, aged fifty-six, was a retired artillery officer, and his mother Isabella, aged forty, was born in Burma. AM joined the British Army, served for five years in the Fifth Lancers, and then spent nineteen years in the Indian Army in which he served in India and Mesopotamia. On 8 May 1915, he took a commission in the Canadian Expeditionary Force at Sandling Camp, Kent, knocking three years off his age (as did many another soldier) by giving his birth date as 27 January 1872. He said that his trade or calling was "gentleman" and his next of kin was his daughter, Miss Clara Eileen Morton of "Oakleigh," Coolhurst Road, Crouch End, North London. AM was then a widower, 5' 9" tall, weighed 150 lbs and had a scar on his right cheek, and had grey eyes, and dark brown hair. His Certificate of Service records that he was in the CEF from 26 December 1914 to 14 August 1919 and was inducted as "an officer of the Military Division of the Order of the British Empire, L.G. #31370, date 30 May 1919." He had served in England and France with the Canadian Army Service Corps, Second Divisional Train, and HQ Canadian Corps. There is a detailed service record about his service in the Great War, all England and France, as lieutenant, then captain, and finally as major.

He retired after the war with various medals and moved out to British Columbia. Correspondence shows him living at 1654 Yale St, Oak Bay, Victoria, BC, but about 1920, he retired to Comox and tried to develop a chicken farm. After a few years, he gave up the farm, moved to Victoria, and was soon employed as secretary to the Royal Jubilee Hospital. About 1928, he moved to Vancouver city on the mainland and died there, aged seventy-six, on 5 May 1945.

Sources: Notes from his granddaughter, Diana Dakers, Ottawa, August 2000; census 1881, England, RG 11/819, p. 6; NAC, CEF files RG150, box 6426-46.

MOSS, Lieutenant Colonel Claude (1859-1930). He was born in Agra, India, fourth son of Thomas Moss of the East India Company and destined for the army from childhood, as were his brothers. He was educated at Cowley, Oxford, and St Peter's, York and then entered the Gloucestershire (Sixty-first) Regiment and served in India for eighteen years, acting as adjutant at Bombay in 1894-1898 and holding various staff appointments. He was a keen polo player and played no. 1 with the regimental team, which won the All-India Cup for infantry at Lucknow in 1892. He returned to England in 1899 as brigade major at Aldershot, but when the Second South African War began in December, he sailed for South Africa—where he took part with his regiment in the relief of Kimberley, Paardeberg, Dreifontein with the Sixth Division, and at Poplar Grove—marched with Lord Roberts into Bloemfontein, and served in the Transvaal. There followed two years of guerrilla warfare in which he held major staff appointments. When peace was declared in 1901, he was subsequently on the staff as deputy assistant adjutant general of the Orange River Colony for three years, at Bloemfontein on the staff of General Stephenson and later with General Broadwood. He was mentioned in despatches three times, decorated as brevet major with the Queen's Medal and four bars and the King's Medal with two bars. He had served in the Second Battalion, Gloucestershire Regiment, for a total of twenty-four years, eighteen of which were in India and six in South Africa. He then retired home to England under the age clause with the rank of major.

By that time, he had a wife, daughter of Maxwell Johnstone of Dumfrieshire, Scotland. She was christened Maggy, though often mistakenly called Margaret, and he married her on 24 December 1903 at the Presbyterian Church in Bloemfontein, Orange River Colony, Rev. James Craig. Like many brought up in Africa, she did not like living in England, and in 1908, they moved out to a place they called "Tempe" at Cowichan Station, Vancouver Island. In October 1914, he responded to the famous appeal by Earl Kitchener for the services of retired officers by volunteering to train and lead infantry in the Canadian Army. As he explained when applying for a British War Gratuity after the war, "On the outbreak of the Great War (1914) he offered his services to Canada but received no reply from Ottawa. Turning to England his services were accepted by Lord Kitchener and he was given the rank of Lieutenant-Colonel, and during the winter of 1914 commanded the 6th Service Battalion, South Lancashire Regiment at Tidworth." The War Office instructed him to report to Woolwich for duty with the Eleventh Battalion, Gloucestershire Regiment, which was about to be formed. He went overseas from Quebec to Liverpool on 12 November 1914 on SS *Scandinavian,* and his service began formally on 14 December. He commanded the Sixth Battalion of South Lancashire Regiment, and then too ill to lead his battalion to Gallipoli, he was transferred to the Fourteenth Battalion, Cheshire Regiment. In 1915, he went to France to study French warfare and returned to England to undertake intensive training duties with Kitchener's Army. In 1917, he was sent to Italy to command a reinforcement camp and an Austrian prison camp for six thousand prisoners at Arquata, where he served to the end of the war.

At the war's end, he left Liverpool on 5 May 1919 aboard SS *Scotian,* and his service ended on 19 May 1919 when he reached Cowichan Station. He was entitled to British War Gratuities and received a sum from Cox & Co., agents of the War Office, and other sums later. When he died on 20 January 1930, Maggy survived him, but his funeral at the local Anglican Church, St Andrew's was in the hands of the Cowichan Branch of the Canadian Legion. In his memory, the Health Centre at Cowichan, of which his wife was a leading member, "paid a silent tribute."
Sources: NAC, RG 9 series II-F-10 (British War Gratuities), vol. 309, file no. 13192-D-23; *Colonist,* 30 October 1914, p. 6; 22 January 1930, p. 5; 6 February 1930, p. 20, obit.; *Whitaker's,* p. 377.

MOSS, Mrs Claude (1871-1936). She was born in Scotland on 2 August 1871, fourth daughter of Maxwell Johnstone and his wife June Charteris of Gillrigg, Kirkmichael, Dumfrieshire. She was christened Maggy, and educated in Edinburgh. During the Second South African War (1899-1902), she was one of the women appointed by the Colonial Office to work among the Boer women and children in concentration camps at Bloemfontein, Orange River Colony, and was soon appointed to the staff of the Women's Training College there. In 1903, she married *Major Claude Moss of the Gloucestershire Regiment (later lieutenant colonel of the Fourteenth Cheshire Regiment) and in 1908 went out with him to a house on the Island they called "Tempe," at Cowichan Station, where she organized the Cowichan Branch of the Canadian Red Cross Society in 1914. A few months later, she joined her husband in England and supervised the Soldier's Home at Whitchurch, Shropshire, became a member of Queen Mary's Needlework Guild, and, upon the formation of a Women's Corps, took training at Crystal Palace Naval Depot and in February 1918 was gazetted "principal" of the Women's Royal Naval Service, Portsmouth Division. In November, she transferred to the Women's Royal Air Force and was gazetted assistant commandant on the staff of the major general commanding the South-east (London) Area of the RAF. She was then the senior WRAF officer on the staff of the South-eastern Area HQ of the Women's Royal Air Force in London, her command numbering eleven thousand women. In April 1919, she was decorated with the OBE (military division) by the King at Buckingham Palace.

After the war, Maggy Moss returned to "Tempe," Cowichan Station, and was soon immersed in public services. Deeply interested in public health and child welfare, she became president of the Cowichan Health Centre at its inception in 1920, was on the first Board of Directors of the Queen Alexandra Solarium at Mill Bay, became president of the South Cowichan Girl Guides, spent three years on the local Board of School Trustees, was honorary member in the Cowichan Branch of the Canadian Legion, and active in the IODE, the Women's Institute, the King's Daughters, the Mother's Union, and St Andrew's Women's Auxiliary, and became the local representative of the Society for Overseas Settlement of British Women, having served on its original board in London in 1919. On 3 May 1921, she was one of the speakers at the Duncan Opera House where a huge crowd assembled to denounce the provincial legislative assembly in Victoria for raising their own salaries. *Lionel Welby Huntington, who was in the chair, said the meeting should not hesitate to make a strong statement. He was born in Lancashire, where the public took the view that what Lancashire thinks today is what England will think tomorrow. Among the other speakers were *Mr Ruscombe Poole and *Lieutenant Colonel G. E. Barnes, CBE, who said that no Kaffir pow-wow would behave as disgracefully as the BC legislature.

After her husband died, she lived for two or three years in Victoria and then went home to Dumfries, Scotland. There she died on 20 August 1937, and her brother John J. Johnstone sent word of her death to friends in the Cowichan Valley, where she was widely remembered for her "great charm and personality, few people were better known or more widely esteemed on the Island." In all of her many public activities, she had been generous, progressive, and practical.

Sources: *Who's Who in B.C.* 1931, pp. 69-70; *Colonist*, 5 May 1921, p. 9; 11 September 1937, p. 3, obit.

MOYES, James (1870-1950). Of all the Tibetan adventurers who settled on Vancouver Island, the most exotic figure was not a soldier but a Christian missionary named James Moyes. On 3 April 1934, the *Victoria Daily Colonist* (p. 4) printed a letter he wrote to the editor, from his home at 115 Regina Avenue, Victoria, under the heading, "In Tibet":

> Sir—The picture of the Potala in Lhasa which you published last week, together with the news that it was soon to be lit up by an electric lighting system held a mixture of regret and thrill for me.
>
> As early as 1893 and 1894, while studying the Tibetan language, in Darjeeling, India, I had often seen a native hand-painting of the Dalai Lama's Palace in Tibet, and in those days we often dreamed of the time when we would see the great changes that would come to 'The Great Closed Land' through enlightenment and modern innovations, and my regret is that now Tibet is opening up, I am far removed from the scene of my early adventures there.
>
> But knowing the characteristics and extreme superstitious mentality of the Tibetan people, I can picture in my mind the awe and reverence and fear and excitement which the lighting up of the Potala by electricity will create in Lhasa among the Lamas and common people. I would so love to be there to hear and see the doings and exclamations of the multitude when the flash of electricity lights up the sky.
>
> But as one of the early pioneers in that little-known country, I have the satisfaction of knowing I had some share in bringing about the many changes that have taken place in public opinion in Tibet and in raising the mental attitude of its people to at least an improved understanding of the powers of nature around them.
>
> The [recently] reported discovery of a mountain peak higher than Mount Everest in Eastern Tibet is possible, but I think possibly it is that 22,000 foot peak in Lolo country on the China border of Tibet, which, because it stands alone, looks to be much higher than it is.
>
> We could see this peak from where I resided in Tachienlu City. I often thought it looked higher than Mount Everest because of its being more prominent and isolated.

JM first went to Tibet in 1893 as one of a dozen Anglican missionaries stirred by the reports of a Presbyterian missionary, Annie Taylor (1855-1918), who had almost managed to reach Lhasa before being turned back by Tibetan authorities. Most books about British relations with Tibet say nothing whatever about Moyes's mission to which the Imperial authorities were generally opposed. There is not a word about him in Perceval Landon's *The Opening of Tibet* (1905), *Sir Charles Bell's *Tibet Past and Present* (1924), Heinrich Harrer's *Seven Years in Tibet* (1953), Peter Fleming's *Bayonets to Lhasa* (1961), Han Suyin's *Lhasa, the Open City* (1977), Tsering Shakya's *The Dragon in the Land of the Snows: A History of Modern*

Tibet (1999), and Charles Allen's *Duel in the Snows* (2004). In Alvyn J. Austin's *Saving China: Canadian Missionaries in the Middle Kingdom* (1986), there are two lines about him on p. 68. The term "mission" has several meanings, and when diplomats, soldiers, or journalists use it, they are normally thinking of diplomatic or military missions. The "missions" they refer to were such as the Younghusband expedition in 1903-1904 met at Yatung by *Captain W. R. McDonnell Parr. For British authorities, relations with Tibet seemed complicated enough without the intrusion of Christian missionaries. In 1893, the government in India therefore refused to let JM and his colleagues enter Tibet from Darjeeling, where they had gone to learn the language and to meet wandering Tibetans. JM is not quite fair in accusing these authorities of fearing "that flirting with Tibetans for trade purposes would be upset if we entered the country" (*Colonist*, Sunday 3 October 1937, p. 3). In retrospect, it seems clear that the British purpose was principally strategic: to keep the Russians out by maintaining good relations with Tibet, which was in fact accomplished with great skill in later years by *Sir Charles Bell. It was "the Great Game," which moved the authorities of the empire in this instance.

Prevented from entering Tibet through India, JM & co. stayed in Darjeeling for another year and then decided to go down to the Indian Ocean in order to sail round to China by sea, up the Yangtse River, and into Tibet from the Chinese side. They succeeded in reaching the Tibetan frontier by that route, though not without risking assaults by the fierce Lolo tribes, the Boxers, the Big Sword Society, and other forces hostile to Europeans. With the help of Chinese groups that were sympathetic to Christians, however, JM & co. were able to reach that belt of territory, half Chinese and half Tibetan, which was the old disputed border between the two countries. China was still ruled, though not very firmly, by the Manchu dynasty, had been receiving Christian missionaries for a considerable time, and had not yet fallen prey to the chaos of warlords' regimes, which was to begin about 1911. Various British diplomatic agents in those parts, such as the consul general at Chengtu, Alex Hosie, were also helpful. After a number of narrow escapes, and dressed in Tibetan clothing, JM penetrated a short way into the country, retreated with others down the Yangtse to avoid death at the hands of the Boxers, and then settled for a time at Tachienlu [Ta-chien lu, and other spellings], the eastern gateway to Tibet.

When JM returned to Tachienlu in 1903, Sir Francis Younghusband was about to enter Tibet with British forces and, among other things, to arrange for a joint Frontier Commission for establishing clear boundaries between Tibet and the neighbouring principalities of Nepal, Sikkim, and Assam. But the most vital issue was whether Russia was establishing a foothold in Tibet, and JM wrote letters on this subject which were forwarded to India and to England by Alex Hosie (at Chengtu) and Walter Townley (at Peking). What he had to tell was the gist of reports from passing Tibetans about Englishmen and Russians said to be at Lhasa. JM wrote *inter alia*, "A few days ago Mr Ma, the owner of our house here, brought a Thibetan with him to see us. He said this Thibetan most likely knew more about Thibetan affairs than any other on this border. We took them into our sitting room, thinking we were now likely to get the latest Thibetan news, but we were soon disappointed: the man had other purposes and he told us only as much as he thought wise. After requesting secrecy, he began by telling us who he was and also some of his past history. He is well known here as one of the chief's headmen, and I had heard of him before in another connection, *viz* the stealing of his wife by the chief's brother. His name is Chang-si-t'ai. He seems to be a man of considerable ability . . . (He has heard details of a Russian initiative to interest the Dalai Lama *et al* in collaboration against the British and also about a gun factory at a monastery. Being angry at the stealing of his wife, this man is inclined to help the British.) As a missionary I would rather keep out of all such, but we were into it before we were aware." [signed James Moyes]

Surrounded by other people with interesting stories to tell, JM has remained obscure and his remarkable life may appropriately be summarized here as far as I have been able to trace his movements. He was born in 1870 at Cowdenbeath, Fifeshire, Scotland, and first went to Tibet as a young man in his twenties together with a dozen members of the first British Christian mission which set out to convert Tibetans in 1893. In November 1898, he was at Tachienlu when a Canadian medical missionary, Susanna Rijnhart *neé* Carson (1868-1908), came staggering, exhausted out of Tibet with a story about her husband having been murdered by Tibetans and she herself bullied and threatened with death. It appears that JM was the first person she met on reaching Tachienlu, and about seven years later, in 1905, they married.

Her story has been explained in some detail, first in a book she published at Chicago in 1901, *With the Tibetans in Tent and Temple: Narrative of Four Years' Residence on the Tibetan Border, and of a Journey into the Far Interior,* and later by various historians. Nowhere are there more than a few words about JM who, like Susanna Carson's first husband—a Dutch Canadian named Petrus Rijnhart—was denounced by her Christian sponsors, the China Inland Mission, as having too little education to make a satisfactory missionary; Rijnhart they even regarded as an imposter. According to Mr Alvyn Austin, JM "had to resign in order to marry Susie because of her past connection with Rijnhart." In 1903, however, Alex Hosie in Chengtu reported JM as a missionary for the China Inland Mission. In 1907, the Moyes couple returned to Canada and settled at Chatham, Ontario, her birthplace. There she died on 7 February 1908, leaving him with a two-month-old baby, which he in turn seems to have left with her relatives. At any rate, within the week, JM applied to the China Inland Mission and then to the Canadian Methodist mission in Sichuan, both of which refused to send him to Western China, and he eventually returned there in the employ of the American Bible Society, which he served for many years.

JM's first visit to Victoria seems to have been in 1911 when, on 31 July, he there married Elizabeth Tod, a Scottish lady born in Kirkcaldy, Fifeshire, in 1881. It appears that they married on their way to China by way of Vancouver and the Pacific route. Back in Western China, they had four sons: James Todd Moyes (1912), Horace Barry Moyes (1914), Eric Andrew Moyes (1915), and Kenneth Sturrock Moyes (1917). In 1919 or 1920, they returned to Britain, where for a time he kept a grocery store at Elie, a small coastal town, but five or six years later,

Mrs Moyes died and JM decided to move to Victoria. He and the two eldest sons, James aged thirteen and Horace aged eleven, arrived at St John, New Brunswick, on 4 April 1926, aboard the CPR liner, *Montcalm*, and went over to Vancouver Island, where they lived at times in Victoria and at other times on a piece of land he bought at Cobble Hill. The younger sons soon came out in the care of Ann Tod, their mother's sister. According to Eric Moyes—a son—in 1938 or 1939, his father, the retired missionary, married Nell Richardson, a widow from a pioneer Victoria family who lived next door.

From 1927 until his death in 1950, JM was semi-retired. He worked as a school custodian and was active in two Baptist churches in Victoria. His letters and articles in the *Daily Colonist* show that he had a lively interest in world affairs, particularly in China and the Orient generally. Impressed by accounts of his life as a missionary at Tachienlu, the *Colonist* published an article about it in two parts as well as several letters. He tended to stress the backward, primitive, violent aspects of Tibetan life, and was soon engaged in a debate with a critic, Mr H. Henderson, who had never been to Tibet but had read books by *Sir Charles Alfred Bell and claimed to have visited British friends in Darjeeling thirty years later than Moyes, "friends who knew possibly a little more of the lamas than Mr Moyes does." Henderson was probably charmed, like the public in general, by James Hilton's popular novel, *Lost Horizons* (1933), which had recently cast a fanciful, romantic light over Tibet. JM thought Henderson ought to go and see for himself how backward and corrupt Tibet was. "The monasteries are often monopoly pawnshops, the priests are real-estate agents, money lenders, mortgage manipulators, cruel and heartless oppressors, highway robbers, murderers, male prostitutes, and criminal bestiality of degrading kinds is common among them, with only an occasional pure-minded good-living lama as a rare exception."

"At times," he went on, "the monasteries become so oppressive by confiscating lands, homes, property, also taking people as slaves, for debt, that the people have revolted and attacked the monasteries, but always with the same results. The lamas are always victorious, because they are housed within high stone walls. They own all the wealth and can purchase modern weapons and ammunition and are organized to withstand a lengthy siege, whereas the common people are often underfed, poorly clad, with no sense of strategy, and armed with crude weapons . . . The large number of male children who are practically conscripted as lamas, together with the prevalent low birth rate, due to unnatural modes of living, is slowly depleting the Tibetan nation. The system of lamaism is the curse of the country and any efforts made to enlighten public opinion in Tibet I consider to be a service to humanity" (*Colonist*, 10 and 11 April 1934, p. 4). In another letter, "Trade with China," JM urged Canada to be more enterprising in trade and business investments in India and China: "I have travelled extensively in China, from Canton in the south to Tientsin in the north, and from Shanghai on the east to Tibet in the west, and everywhere with few exceptions the country is bare of standing timber. I have also been in charge of building operations and know of the slow hand-sawing process by which all timber for building must be treated. It is true labour is very cheap but primitive methods more than offset this advantage, and I am confident a vast trade in timber could be developed in China along certain lines."

"But most of the millions living in the interior of China do not know or have only a vague idea that there is a country called Canada. They know nothing of our sawmills or what they produce and yet they are building houses by the million every year. Their hand-made doors and windows are crude and often the workmanship is very poor . . . The Chinese mind is essentially conservative, and when you capture their trade and confidence they are very slow to change; but their inborn affability and politeness to strangers and trade commissioners may make you feel good, but when you analyse the results you will find nothing there" (*Colonist*, 19 June 1931, p. 4). He thought it would be worth running risks in order to show the Chinese what is possible with Canadian timber of which they had no idea.

Whether JM ever had occasion to meet the other Tibetan adventurers living on the Island is now uncertain, and I find no evidence of their ever having moved in the same circles. His name does not appear among those reported as joining the China-Japan Society or the India-Burma Society. Without further information, one can only speculate about relations among the Island's extraordinary veterans of Tibetan adventure.

JM died, aged seventy-nine, on 12 April 1950 at his home at 1029 Johnson Street, Victoria, leaving a widow, Nell Moyes, and four sons. He is also said to have left a brother, Nean Moyes, and a sister, Mrs D. Thomson, both of Victoria. He had served for twenty-six years as a missionary in China with the American Bible Society.

Sources: Information courtesy of Eric Moyes, a son, January 2001; *Colonist*, 5 January 1930, p. 4; 19 January 1930, p. 4; 5 March 1930, p. 11; 19 June 1931, p. 4; 11 April 1934, p. 4; 1 February 1935, p. 4; 19 May 1936, p. 8; 3 October 1937, Sunday, p. 3; 10 October 1937, Sunday, p. 5; 21 November 1937, p. 4; 19 January 1940, p. 4; 27 October 1940, p. 18; 14 April 1950, p. 21, obit.; *Victoria Daily Times*, 15 April 1950, p. 13; Alvyn J. Austin, "Carson, Susanna (Rijnhart; Moyes)," *Dictionary of Canadian Biography*, vol. XIII, pp. 175-176; Alvyn J. Austin, *Saving China: Canadian Missionaries in the Middle Kingdom, 1888-1959* (University of Toronto Press, 1986, p. 68; BNA (Kew), FO 17/1746, p. 72, Townley to Lansdowne, 13 May 1903; p. 298, Hosie to Townley, 1 August 1903 enclosing a letter from Moyes dated 18 July 1903; NAC, RG76-Immigration-series C-1-c, 1926, vol. 3, page 138; Peter Hopkirk, *Trespassers on the Roof of the World: The Race for Lhasa* (Oxford, Oxford University Press, 1982), chapter 9, "*The Nightmare of Susie Rijnhart*"; Patrick French, *Younghusband. The Last Great Imperial Adventurer* (Flamingo, 1995), p. 205; Peter Fleming, *Bayonets to Lhasa*, (Rupert Hart-Davis, 1961), p. 115.

MUMFORD, Newman (1862-1942). He was born at Hugh Town, Cornwall on St Mary's, the largest of the Scilly Isles, twenty-eight miles southwest of Land's End, and there the 1871 census found him, aged nine, living with his family in Church Street. His father, Clement W. Mumford, was a schoolmaster and registrar of births, marriages, and deaths and "clerk to justices." His mother, Annie F. Mumford, was a local woman. NM was apprenticed, aged fourteen, as a marine engineer at Newcastle-upon-Tyne, and at nineteen, in 1881, he was lodging in Tynmouth with a family of mariners and calling himself an engineer. After some years at sea with the P&O Line, he transferred to a shipping line running between New York and the West Indies and became a chief engineer at the age of twenty-three. A few years later, he left the sea and took work in a sugar mill at Singapore. There the shipping and engineering surveyor for Lloyd's Register of Shipping soon died; Mumford was hired to replace him and promptly married a Miss Janie Gibson Sherris (c. 1865-1942), who came from his home on the Scilly Isles. In 1895, she gave birth to a daughter, Joyce, at Singapore but soon went to live with her widowed mother at home on the Scilly Isles, where the 1901 census found her with Joyce and a son, Patrick Foster Mumford, born there four years earlier. NM had spent five years at Singapore after which Lloyd's moved him to Hong Kong as their shipping surveyor. While at Hong Kong, he supervised the building of the first steel ship to be built in Japan. In 1907, Lloyd's moved him to Constantinople, still as their shipping and engineering surveyor, and when Turkey entered the Great War in 1915 as a German ally, he and his wife escaped to Bulgaria at the last moment. Because of all this experience, he served as an adviser to the Royal Navy in the Dardanelles Campaign during the Great War. His last Lloyd's assignment before retiring to the Island was at Sulzer's Diesel engine works in Switzerland.

In retirement, he lived from 1927, and probably earlier, at "Lyonesse," Deep Cove in North Saanich. There he fished, sailed, and amused himself doing historical research on the battlefields of the Napoleonic wars and the U.S. civil war. He was a Freemason with a worldwide circle of friends and was visited early in July 1927 by Sir James Owen (1869-1939), a director of Reuters News Agency and of the British Press Association, owner of two large British provincial newspapers, the *Western Times* and the *Devon and Exeter Gazette*, who wrote a column that week for *The Sidney and Gulf Islands Review* (7 July 1927, p. 2). When NM died, aged eighty, on 28 June 1942, his address was given as 876 Leslie Drive in Saanich, and the *Daily Colonist* reported that he had worked as Lloyd's shipping surveyor in Victoria for twenty-two years, though the lists of marine surveyors in *Loyd's Register* do not seem to confirm this. His wife had died three months earlier on 18 March 1942, aged seventy-six, but he was survived by a son, Patrick Foster Mumford, in Victoria, and a sister, Mrs M. G. Gifford, at Bognor Regis. He was buried at Royal Oak as an Anglican. Patrick died, aged sixty-one, on 18 May 1958 in Sidney.
Sources: census 1871, England, RG 10/2347, p. 25; census 1881, RG 11/5080, p. 7; census 1901, RG 13/2259, p. 4; *British National Archives* (PRO), *Lloyd's Register of Shipping, List of Lloyd's Surveyors, 1896-1897*; *Sidney and Gulf Islands Review*, 7 July 1927, p. 2; 1 July 1942, p. 3, obit.; *Colonist*, 30 June 1942, p. 2, obit.; BC Directory 1927 (for Deep Cove); Cornwall Outline Census Project 1871 (Internet).

MUNRO [alias Munroe], Alexander (1824-1911). Born at Tain, Ross and Cromar in Ross-shire, Scotland, on 19 March 1824, he went out to Canada in 1857 and was employed by the Hudson's Bay Company as an accountant working under William Charles, head of the western department. He was living in Victoria by the time his daughter Elizabeth Jane Hannah married *R. P. Rithet, a leading Victoria businessman, on 27 October 1875. Another daughter married *Captain John Irving there on 12 June 1883, both men whom he had business dealings with.

When he died, aged eighty-seven, on 27 February 1911 in Victoria, he was living at 6 Michigan Street (near my great-uncle, *Captain William McCulloch) and was buried in the Presbyterian part of the Ross Bay Cemetery. Only a few weeks later, his son, Arbuthnot Dallas Munro (1861-1911), employed as a purser on the *Iroquois*, died when she was wrecked in a storm near Sidney on 10 April 1911. AM's Scottish widow, Jane Urquehart Munro (1825-1914), who had followed him to Victoria in 1858, outlived father and son by only a few years, but there were other grown children, such as Kenneth Munro (1871-1953), employed as a bank clerk.
Sources: Begg, *History of British Columbia*, pp. 442-4; John Adams, *Ross Bay Cemetery* (revised ed., Victoria, Sono Nono Press, Heritage Architectural Guides, Victoria, 1998), p. 17.

MURISON, Major General Charles Alexander Phipps (1894-1981). He was born on 7 October 1894 in Grenfell, Saskatchewan, son of Alice Lepel *née* Phipps and William Johnson Holt Murison (1866-?), a six-foot Anglican from Montreal who was manager of the Tryon Bank at Grenfell. "This was a private bank owned by Charles Tryon," wrote Mrs Ethel Box of the Grenfell Museum in June 2001, "and I read in the Anglican Church minute books that he [Murison *père*] was also treasurer of the church . . . of course the Murisons and Phipps were long gone . . . I had never heard the name [Murison] till the 100th Anniversary of our church in 1985 and the Murison name came up, then I saw it in old ads for the bank. The Phipps lived on a farm a few miles from me. I 'phoned Lance Lake [nephew of *Lieut.-General Sir Percy Lake] when I was out to the coast for Christmas and had a nice chat . . ." CM's mother died during his childhood; when his father enlisted in 1916, he was married to Blanche E. H. Murison (1881-1949), who became a prominent Vancouver club woman, social service worker, poet, and writer. Meanwhile, CM himself attended Trinity College School, Port Hope, Ontario, and McGill University, graduating in time to serve in the Great War. He joined the British Army, perhaps moved by the background of his mother's family, the Phipps, with its roots in England. His service took him to France (1915), Macedonia, and Turkey (1915-1919), and he was wounded, mentioned in despatches, and decorated with the MC. After the war, he remained in the British Army, went through the Military College of Science at Woolwich (1923) and the Staff College at Camberley (1929), and held various posts between the wars, including membership of the General Staff, RMC, Kingston, Ontario (1933-1934). In the Second World War, he held various appointments, including DA and QMG in the Canadian Corps in England and Deputy QMG to the Forces (1940-1941), a post in the War Office (1942-1945), and served as major general in charge of administration, Middle East land forces (1945-1948). He retired at last as a CBE (1940) and a CB (1944).

After the Second World War, he went out to the Pacific Coast, where on 13 April 1920 at Christ Church Cathedral, Vancouver, he married Mary Pope Shirley Clement, a Methodist born in Toronto, daughter of Hon. Mr Justice Clement, a Vancouver judge. They soon retired to the Cowichan Valley, where CM became a councillor in the North Cowichan Municipality (1952-1953), reeve there from 1954, a member of the BC Labour Relations Board (1953-1954), president of the Vancouver Island Municipal Union (1955-1956), a member of the Cowichan Branch

J.F. Bosher

of the Royal Canadian Legion, vice-president of the BC Division of the Canadian Cancer Society (1955-1958), and director of the BC Cancer Foundation from 1956. In 1959, he became a life member of the Union of BC Municipalities and in 1973 a Freeman of the Municipality of North Cowichan. Their home, "Anchorfield," RR 1, Duncan, made them parishioners of St Peter's Quamichan, where he became a staunch supporter and read the lesson at the Sunday services for many years "in a clear, strong voice." He was a widower when he died, aged eighty-seven, on 31 October 1981 in Vancouver and was survived by his daughter Allyn Janet Lepel Murison, a brother W. L. P. "Bobs" Murison, a sister Mrs Janet M. Cave, a sister-in-law Mrs P. D. V. "Aileen" Murison, and some nephews and nieces.

Sources: Letters and notes to the author kindly sent from Grenfell by Mrs Ethel Box, 18 June 2001; *The Canadian Who's Who*, vol. VIII (1958-1960), pp. 823-24; NAC, CEF files box 6502-38; UBC, Vancouver, Archives: Blanche E. Holt Murison collection: Blanche Murison fonds.-1921-[ca. 1965], 13 cm of textual records; A.I. Yule, *Grit and Growth, The Story of Grenfell* (Grenfell Historical Committee, 1980), pp. 90-98; *The Social Register*, vol. 2, p. 115; Williams, *The Story of St Peter's*, pp. 65 and 73; *Cowichan Leader*, 3 November 1961, obit.; North Cowichan Centennial Committee, "A Goodly Heritage," 1873-1973 (The Corporation of the District of North Cowichan, 1973), 38 pp., p. 15, photo (1967) of CM in North Cowichan, where he served as reeve, etc., in 1954-1959.

MURRAY, Major Robert George H. "Robin" (1888-1973). He was born on 11 November 1888 at Quetta, India, like his father before him, but the family had originally come from Scotland. After a schooling in England, he took a commission in the Ninth Gurkha Rifles dated 20 January 1909 and was soon serving in India as a "Double Company Officer." In 1912, however, he learned to fly. "I first flew in 1912 on Bleriot's channel-crossing monoplane, qualifying for Civilian Pilot's certificate number 320," he told the War Office in 1940 when applying to serve in the Second World War. In 1915, after a year in the trenches, he qualified for the Royal Flying Corps at Upavon and served in France for thirteen months with number 13 Squadron, doing principally artillery cooperation work, photography, and night-flying. "I commanded the London Home-Defence Squadron from March to July 1917 and commanded the RAF in India and Aden from August 1917 to April 1918, which was then in the process of being created from the choosing of landing-grounds upwards. In April 1918 I was transferred to Palestine, and commanded the Squadron doing liaison with General [Edmund] Allenby's cavalry during the 1918 victory. Subsequently, I officiated as Wing Commander in Kantara and Ismailia. After that I was on the sick-list for a year and finally in 1920 returned to the Indian Army, where my last few years of service were spent mostly officiating either as CO or as second in command of a Gurkha Battalion." His simple, factual summary does less than justice to his record of service in which he crashed five times and became known as "mad Murray" for his flying adventures and his "gallant conduct" at the Battle of Neuve Chapelle and on other occasions for which George V presented him with the IDSM, the DFC, and the MC at Windsor Castle.

In 1932, the economic depression of the time having raised financial difficulties, he took advantage of a special gratuity and retired to Victoria, where he and his wife opened a business known as the Island Weavers. This provided a much-needed supplement to his army pension, especially after sterling currency was devalued in a series of post-war steps. Mrs Murray, *née* Enid Gregory, was daughter of Charles Gregory, a civil engineer in India, and granddaughter of Micah Gregory, a medical doctor and inspector general of Indian hospitals. Like RM, she had a traditional Anglo-Indian childhood with years of schooling in Britain away from her parents. When they were married and had two children of their own, they decided they wanted their daughters to grow up near them, not go away and return as strangers. Their life was changed by a game of golf at Gumarg in Kashmir where RM met a Commander Fraser, RN, whose wife had started a woollen business in Kashmir. Fraser had been on loan to the Royal Canadian Navy at Esquimalt and had observed that there might be a good market on Vancouver Island for fine hand-woven tweeds. As Mrs Murray recalled later, "Robin came home and said, 'Enid, you know you are going to be a weaver'; I laughed. I had never heard of anything so silly." But on second thoughts, she liked the idea better and went off to study weaving in Scotland at Kilbachan, Radnorshire; Garvin, Ayrshire; the London School of Weaving; and the Woollen Technical College at Galashiels, Hawick near Edinburgh.

During their first few years in Victoria, they lived at "West Bay" on Dunsmuir Road in Esquimalt, where in May 1933, they gave a public display of Enid's beautiful hand-woven woollens. Nearly two hundred people came, among them a number of invited guests including *Colonel and Mrs C. B. Messiter, Captain and Mrs Moorhouse, Major and Mrs H. Norman, Mrs (Major) *A. G. Piddington, *Colonel and Mrs A. A. Sharland, and *Major and Mrs A. E. Jukes. Like RM, Major Jukes had held a commission in the Ninth Gurkha Rifles and served for several years in India. The Jukes were farming at "The Vines" out on the West Saanich Road between Mount Newton and Brentwood Bay, and before long, the Murrays were temporarily lodged next door at "Kildoone," Major Parr's lovely home while they built their own place, "Kernsary," nearby. The Murrays joined the India-Burma Society in Victoria. When RM died, aged eighty-four, in Victoria at the Veteran's Hospital on 12 August 1973, he was survived by his wife and two daughters, Dawn (Mrs Eoin Ruthven), who eventually moved into "Kernsary," and Rona (Mrs Walter Dexter) at Sooke, who later published her memories and reflections in *Journey Back to Peshawar* (1993). RM was buried in a funeral at St Stephen's Anglican Church, Mt Newton Crossroad near "Kernsary."

Sources: Family papers courtesy of his daughter the late Rona (Murray) Dexter; Rona Murray, *Journey Back to Peshawar*, (Victoria, Sono Nis Press, 1993), 304 pp., see p. 33; *Indian Army List*, October 1910, pp. 446 and 1530; Lieutenant Colonel Frederick Sinclair Poynder, *The 9th Gurkha Rifles*, 1817-1936 (The Royal United Service Institution, 1937), pp. 57, 73, 82, 86, 260; *Victoria Times*, 14 August 1973, p. 20; *Colonist*, 17 January 1933, p. 8; 20 May 1933, p. 8; 17 February 1943, p. 4; 17 February 1943, p. 4; *Colonist*, 6 May 1956, G. E. Mortimer, "*This Week's Profile*"; 14 August 1973, p. 18: obit.

MUSGRAVE, Sir Anthony (1828-1888). Born at St John's, Antigua, on 31 August 1828, he had a career in Imperial service leading to the governorship of Newfoundland (1864-1869), British Columbia (1869-1872), Natal (1872-1873), South Australia (1873-1877), Jamaica (1877-1883), and Queensland (1885-1888), where he died on 9 October 1888. His principal task in Victoria was to coax the reluctant colony of British Columbia to join the Canadian Confederation. This was accomplished with effect from 20 July 1871. AM wrote two serious books, and his three sons all served the empire in one way or another.
Sources: Kent M. Haworth, in the DCB, vol. XI, pp. 634-37 and online; Geoffrey Bolton, in the *Oxford DNB* online.

MUSGRAVE, Commander Phillip Cranstoun (1863-1920). He was born on 6 August 1863 at Shillington, Bedfordshire, son of Edgar Musgrave and Henrietta Maria Musgrave *née* Teschemaker, who had married in July 1860. The 1871 census found them living at "Cornwallis Grove," Clifton, Bristol, Gloucestershire, on "income from parents." The parents were recorded as born, he in London and she in Bath; an elder brother, Horace Musgrave, aged nine, was born at Exmouth, Devon, and a younger sister Ethel H. Musgrave, aged six, in Shillington. There were four servants: butler, nurse, and two housemaids. On 10 December 1871, PM became a naval cadet in the RN and served in HMS *Britannia* (15 January 1877 to 20 December 1878), in *Temeraire* as a midshipman (1 September 1879 to 2 May 1882), in *Lark* as lieutenant (1 October 1886 to 19 August 1887), and after several more such postings was in SS *Esquimalt* in June 1891 followed by a long series of ships in the 1890s, when he became a hydrographic surveyor. He resigned from the RN on 31 March 1896 and by 1914 was employed with HMCS *Naden* on the Pacific Coast Survey.

In 1916, the Overseas Club listed PM among its membership as "Musgrave, Lieut.-Colonel P.C., Hydrographic Survey, H.M.C. Dockyard, Esquimalt." When he died, aged fifty-four, on 17 February 1920 "of heart failure" in his room on Admiral's Road, Esquimalt, the *Daily Colonist* described him as "the head of the hydrographic survey work of the Naval Department on this coast" and went on to report, "After working in the Nfld. survey for some years, he spent over ten years charting the sea floor of the B.C. coast. For some years he headed the work here, on the *Lillouet* from the time she was built (by Marine Ways, Esquimalt) and commissioned in 1908. The only year he did not take the *Lillouet* out was in 1918. Captain F. H. Griffith has been Captain and pilot of the vessel since her commissioning. Musgrave has surveyed the Prince Rupert approaches, part of Hecate Strait, approaches to Victoria etc. Earlier he served in the Royal Navy. He leaves one son, Sub.-Lieut. A. Musgrave, with the Canadian Branch of the R.N. overseas."
Sources: PRO; ADM 196/20, page 478; *MacFarlane*, p. 47; census 1871, England, RG 10/2539, p. 13; *Over-Seas Club List of Members with Rules and some Notes and Notices* (Over-Seas Club, HQ at General Buildings, Aldwych, London, WC, 1916), p. 89; *Colonist*, 18 February 1920, p. 7, obit.; IGI (Latterday Saints).

MUSGRAVE, Sir Richard John (1850-1930). He was the Fifth Baronet of Tourin, and on 23 September 1891, he married Jessie Sophia Dunsmuir (1866-1946) at Christ Church Cathedral in Victoria, a splendid wedding with twenty-seven bridesmaids and flower girls. Jessie, who gave birth to two girls, was a daughter of the Island's coal baron, Robert Dunsmuir (1825-1889) and his wife Joan Olive *née* White (1828-1908), both from Ayrshire in Scotland. RM was the eldest son and heir of the fourth baronet, Sir Richard Musgrave (1820-1874), and his wife Lady Frances Mary *née* Yates (1824-1895) and at his father's death inherited some 8,282 acres in Waterford County, Ireland. He had been a pupil at Eton of Oscar Browning, who was then an undergraduate at Trinity College, but RM had the instincts of a sporting squire and loved fishing. He went out to the Island in the wake of his uncle, Edward Musgrave (1834-1911), who on 10 June 1858 had married Anastasia Lætitia Gee (1834-1902) and soon had taken her out to a farm on the west side of Salt Spring Island, facing across Satellite Channel to Maple Bay, at a place subsequently known as "Musgrave's Landing." It had been pioneered by the Pimbury brothers from a village near Minchinton, Gloucestershire. RM's uncle eventually sold it to *Edward Trench, and it was purchased after the Second World War by *Brigadier and Mrs Miles Smeeton. RM's first cousin, John Musgrave (1868-1942), from Buenos Aires, Argentina, also settled on the Island, married there, and died in Oak Bay, Victoria.

RM had other relatives on the Island, notably his first cousin Edward Christopher Musgrave (1872-1955), uncle Edward's son whose mother was a half-sister of *Air Marshal Sir Philip Clermont Livingston, and *Edward Cosby Trench and his mother Maria Musgrave (c. 1852-1938). Was Maria RM's sister? A careful distinction must be drawn between four different families of noble Irish Musgraves, who were only distantly related if at all. However that may be, RM soon took Jessie to live at Tourin, Cappoquin in Waterford, where they led a luxurious life in the aristocratic Anglo-Irish circles of Dublin, with frequent visits to Monte Carlo, to London, and to the Dunsmuir family on the Island. After RM's death on 4 March 1930, Jessie was joined by her sister, Henrietta Maud *née* Dunsmuir (1872-1960), and her sporting husband, Lieutenant Colonel Reginald Spencer Chaplin (1872-1940) of the Tenth Hussars, who were marooned on the Tourin estate by the Second World War and eventually died there. It was in Ireland, too, that Jessie died in 1946.

Sources: Terry Reksten, *The Dunsmuir Saga* (Vancouver, Douglas & McIntyre, 1991), pp. 128-31, 188, 202-03, 213-14; Howay and Gosnell, *British Columbia*, vol. IV, pp. 413-4; Kahn, *Salt Spring Island*, pp. 95, 113.

MUSKETT, Aubrey Dashwood (1877-1941). He went out to the Island in 1908 from Norfolk to join the Staff of Collegiate College, a boys' school at 1157 Rockland Avenue in Victoria, and served as its headmaster for about twenty-five years. His name appeared regularly in the school's advertisement in the *Victoria Daily Colonist*. In 1912, he was living at "The Laurels," 1249 Rockland Avenue. On 11 July 1917, he married Margery Adelaide Walker (1886-1968), born in Esquimalt to Mary Maberly Crease (1856-1915) and her husband, Frederick George Walker, who had married on 19 January 1886. Thus AM's mother-in-law was a sister of *Lindley Crease and of Josephine Crease (1864-1947), an artist in Victoria known for her watercolour landscapes, born in New Westminster but having studied art at King's College London (1889-1891). AM was moving in Victoria's higher social circles. He was a guest, for instance, on 9 May 1931 at a small luncheon party which Miss Josephine Crease held at Shawnigan Lake in the Forest Inn, another of the guests being Lady Constance Fawkes, wife of *Colonel Lionel Grimston Fawkes of Mayne Island. About 1935, AM moved to become senior master at Qualicum School in Qualicum Beach, north up the Island, and there he died, aged sixty-four, on 12 December 1941 and was buried. Among the honorary pallbearers were *Colonel Alan Playfair and *Captain James Ernest Courtney Cox.

AM was born at Clippesby, Norfolk, son of the local rector, Rev. Henry Joseph Muskett, and appears, aged three, in the 1881 census with his family. His father, "probably 60," was born in Norwich, and his mother Sophia A. Muskett, aged forty, was born at Bury St Edmunds in Suffolk. AM had three sisters and two brothers, all elder except Norah, aged one. There were four servants: cook, housemaid, nursemaid, and a "general servant." Clippesby was in the Norfolk Broads about nine miles NW of Yarmouth and had about 120 inhabitants during most of the nineteenth century. AM's father was heir to a prosperous agricultural and land agent who in 1808 had bought Clippesby manor and parish, and so he lived on the manor as "patron and incumbent of the living" of St Peter's Church. AM was brought up on the manor, but in 1891, he was boarding with four other pupils at a small school in Great Yarmouth, run at her home by a fifty-year-old maiden lady. Ten years later, he was assistant schoolmaster at another small school in Rye, Sussex, at 4 the Grove, where there were seven resident pupils. The schoolmaster, one Joseph Molyneaux Jenkins, lived next door with his wife and family.

Sources: *Colonist*, 8 January 1914, p. 8; 12 May 1931, p. 8; 18 December 1941, p. 23, obit.; John Burke, *A Genealogical & Heraldic History of the Commoners of Great Britain and Ireland* (London, Henry Colburn, 1835), vol. II, pp. 102-103; census 1871, RG 10/1792, p. 8; census 1881, RG 11/1917, p. 8; census 1891, RG 12/1500, p. 23; census 1901, RG 13/859, p. 22; *Henderson's Greater Victoria Directory* 1912; Canadian Census, 1901, Victoria.

MUTTER, Major James Mitchell (1845-1920). He was born on 8 April 1845 in Glasgow, eldest son of James Mutter, JP for Argyle County, and his wife Agnes, *née* Cruickshanks. At the age of eighteen, he went out to Australia to learn sheepfarming and returned years later to take up the family business on the Isle of Islay, where he married and his children were born. There he followed his father as JP for Argyleshire and as junior partner in the family firm of W. & J. Mutter, which owned the Bowmore Distillery as well as bonded warehouses in Glasgow. He also joined the Argyle and Bute Artillery in which he was promoted to major in 1891. That year, he sailed for Canada in October 1891 with his wife and family and settled on the Island in the Somenos District. He had married Isabella Allan Morrison, born at Kilmaun and Holy Loch, Scotland, daughter of Alexander Morrison. She was born at Kilmaun and Holy Loch, Scotland, daughter of Alexander Morrison.

At Somenos, they bought a large farm from James Kier and brought in pedigree Jersey cattle and South Down sheep. JM was a good judge of livestock, the farm did well, and he became a pillar of the Cowichan Valley Creamery. In July 1894, he entered the legislature by acclamation to represent Cowichan-Alberni. He later became superintendent of the provincial jail at Victoria. When the governor general, Lord Aberdeen, and his party went to "Duncan's Station" in November that year, it was JM who conducted them to the Agricultural Hall, where a large assortment of farm produce was on exhibition, and in his address mentioned Aberdeen's knowledge of farming and his sympathy with farming communities. In 1896, while their three sons and three daughters were growing up, a fellow Glaswegian, the future "Canadian" poet, Robert W. Service (1874-1958), lived and worked with them on the farm for six months before moving on to two other farms in the Cowichan Valley and then to Victoria, where he worked at the Canadian Bank of Commerce, which sent him up to White Horse, Yukon, and then to Dawson City. In 1917, JM became president of the North Cowichan Red Cross Society.

JM died, aged seventy-five, on 31 May 1920 at Somenos and his widow, aged eighty-four, at Duncan on 4 November 1933. They were buried as Anglican parishioners at St Peter's Quamichan. Many of their six children and eighteen grandchildren remained in the district. James Islay Mutter was mayor of Duncan (1924-1928) and died, aged seventy-five, on 15 September 1950 in Victoria. A grandson, Hamish Mutter (c. 1910-2004), married Daphne Hale, daughter of *Marris Hale of "Halewood" at Glenora near Duncan. Jean Mutter (c. 1883-1972) became a writer in Vancouver.

Sources: Notes courtesy of John Palmer; Williams, *The Story of St Peter's*, p. 55; James Mackay, *Robert Service: A Biography* (Edinburgh and London, Mainstream Publishing, 1995), pp. 115-16; Begg, *History of British Columbia*, pp. 536, 552-3; *Colonist*, 17 June 1917, p. 4; 2 June 1920, pp. 4 and 9, obit.; 4 November 1933, p. 1;

NAGLE, Captain Jeremiah (c. 1802-1882). Born in Ireland, he went to sea and sailed often to the Pacific Ocean, becoming a ship's captain in due time. He settled in New Zealand where, in March 1838, he and two partners, William Abercrombie and William Webster (1815-1897), bought an island on the Great Barrier Reef known to the Maoris as "Aotea." With an area of approximately twenty-six by ten miles, it offered more than seventy thousand acres and, much later in 1913, became a county of New Zealand. After the British-Maori Treaty of Waitangi (1840), JN's purchase was held to be invalid and an adjudication by the Land Claims Commissioners awarded him and his partners a crown grant of only 24,269 acres—scarcely more than a third of the island.

About 1857, JN migrated to Victoria, Vancouver Island, where he spent a year or two as captain of the steamer *Commodore* running regularly between Victoria and San Francisco. On 14 April 1858, he happened to attend a meeting of a Black community planning to escape from slavery in California by migrating in a mass to Panama, Sonora, or somewhere else and was able to attract them to Vancouver Island by answering questions about it and presenting a letter from an HBC officer inviting Black immigrants. When *Governor James Douglas welcomed a visiting

Black committee, some eight hundred Blacks soon moved to the Island, mainly to Victoria, Saanich, and Salt Spring Island. Their arrival was celebrated at Shady Creek in Central Saanich on 20 February 2000, when Heritage Canada presented a commemorative plaque to the United Church built there by the Alexander family, one of the first to settle. During the 1930s, my father often pointed out their house while driving to Victoria.

JN was employed for a while as port warden at Duncan but then became harbour master in Victoria where in November 1859, he placed a lantern at MacLaughlin Point, at the harbour's entrance, as a guide for shipping; acquired enough downtown lots in Victoria during the Fraser River gold rush to make himself a major landowner; bought Thetis Island in Esquimalt Harbour for £1 as a speculation; and was made a JP for the Island in 1859 and for Victoria on 17 May 1875. The 1881 census found him employed as a harbour pilot living in the James Bay district with his wife Catherine Nagle, *née* Abercrombie. Their daughter, Susan Abercrombie Nagle (c. 1841-1921), remained at Duncan, where she married an English clergyman, *Rev. David Holmes, and wrote songs and newspaper articles that encouraged young *Robert William Service while he worked on nearby farms. "A 'gentle soul with a great heart,' she was loved by the Indians and all who met her" (Glynn-Ward). Another of JN's daughters married *Major James Douglas Groves. JN died, aged eighty, on 5 January 1882 in Victoria.

Sources: Crawford Kilian, *Go Do Some Great Thing, The Black Pioneers of British Columbia* (Vancouver, Douglas & McIntyre, 1978), pp. 24-5, 34, 36; *Dictionary of New Zealand Biography*, [Internet], an article about William Webster (1815-97), trader, land speculator; *Canadian census 1881*, British Columbia; Barry Gough, *The Royal Navy and the North-West Coast of North America* 1810-1914 (Vancouver, UBC Press, 1971), p. 184-5; Donald Graham, *Keepers of the Light*, p. 8; Harry Gregson, *A History of Victoria*, 1842-1970 (Victoria, Victoria Observer Publishing Co., 1970), p. 23; *Colonist*, 2 February 1921, p. 7, "*Appreciation*" by H. Glynn-Ward; Elliott, *Memories of the Chemainus Valley*, pp. 97-101.

NANTON, Brigadier General Herbert Colbourne (1863-1935). He was born on 21 July 1863 at Cobourg, Ontario, youngest son of Augustus Nanton, barrister of Osgood Hall, and brother of the Sir Augustus Meredith Nanton of Winnipeg and Toronto. He attended Upper Canada College and RMC Kingston, where he qualified as an officer, and in 1885 fought during the Riel Rebellion in the Canadian Militia under General Sir Frederick Middleton. He spent a short time at Chatham, England, and then took permanent service with the Royal Engineers in India, where he served in the Chin Lushai Expedition (1888-1889) and the Chitral Relief Force (1895) and commanded armoured trains throughout the South African War (1899-1902). Promoted to captain (1894), major (1902), and lieutenant colonel (1910), in 1913, he became deputy director general of Military Works in India. In August 1914, he left India as colonel and chief engineer with the Indian Expeditionary Force under Sir James Willcocks and remained in France until 1918. The mining operation at Vimy Ridge was carried out under him. He was three times mentioned in despatches and decorated with the Queen's Medal for South Africa with three clasps, the King's Medal with two clasps, the CB (1915), and the Star of India (CIE) (1919).

Vancouver Island was well known to the Nanton family. HN's brother, Sir Augustus Nanton, had various investments in western Canada and stayed in Victoria in August 1917 with his wife and five children. Several months earlier, he had visited together with Thomas George, Lord Shaughnessy, who was on one of his customary trips of inspection of the CPR. They probably went on fishing expeditions in the Cowichan Valley with their friend F. L. Hutchinson, head of the CPR hotels, who appeared in Victoria at the same time. When HN went there in 1928, seven years after retiring from the army, his widowed sister, Lillian Caroline Nanton (Mrs John Davidson Clark), was already living in Victoria, and near Sidney, twenty miles away, lived a cousin, Gertrude Jarvis, and her husband *Lieutenant Colonel Arthur Murray Jarvis. HN may have arrived alone, without the wife he had married in 1891, Margaretta de Lotbinière, daughter of Sir Henry J. de Lotbinière. City directories show HN living in the early 1930s at 805 Gordon Street, which was the address of the Union Club. By 1934, he had moved to 629 Beach Drive in Oak Bay, but when he died on 2 May 1935, his wife was living in England. Nor did she attend his funeral at St Mary's Anglican Church, Oak Bay, or his burial at Royal Oak. He may have intended to return to England, as he had retained his membership in the Naval and Military Club in London.

Sources: *Who was Who*, 1929-1940; Lieutenant Colonel E. W. C. Sandes, *The Military Engineer in India* (2 vols.; Chatham, Royal Engineers Institution, 1933 and 1935), vol. II, p. 71; Brian A. Reid, *Our Little Army in the Field: The Canadians in South Africa*, 1899-1902 (St Catharines, Ont., Vanwell Publishing Ltd., 1996), p. 153; *Globe & Mail* (Toronto), 3 May 1935, obit.; *Colonist*, 7 August 1917, p. 8;, 17 April 1937, p. 2, obit.

NAPIER, George Paxton (1880-1953). He was born on 7 June 1880 in London, graduated as an engineer at the Royal India Engineering College, Cooper's Hill, England, and served through the South African War as a subaltern in the Manchester Regiment. He retired to Victoria where in 1909, he joined the Provincial Ministry of Railways as an engineer, and when he joined the Canadian Army on 17 January 1916, he was working as "Assistant Public Works Engineer of B.C." and living in Victoria at 418 Menzies Street with his wife, Hilda Napier. He spent the years of the Great War with the Royal Canadian Engineers in France and Belgium. When he returned after the war, his job was waiting for him and he rose through the ranks to become deputy minister of railways by the time he retired in April 1941 after thirty-two years of service. When he died on 16 February 1953 after a long illness, he and his wife were living out in North Saanich at Deep Cove. They had a daughter, Mrs H. V. Bartholomew, and the John Paxton Napier who had married Margaret Miriam Griffin in Victoria on 17 April 1933 and died, aged forty-two, on 4 January 1947 in Saanich, was probably their son.

Sources: NAC, CEF files, box 7233-12; *Colonist*, 29 April 1941, p. 5; 17 February 1953, p. 18, obit.

NAPPER, Lieutenant Colonel Henry George, MC (1871-1936). He was born at East Wittering, a suburb of Chichester, Sussex, on 3 March 1871, not 1873 as he told the Canadian Army when signing up for the CEF on 23 November 1915. (Many soldiers either forgot their birthdates or pretended to be younger or older than they were.) The English census of 1871 had found him, one month old, living at East Wittering at the "Oak Public House" with his family. His father, George Napper, then aged twenty-four, was a "Blacksmith & Inn Keeper" born at Portsmouth, Hampshire, and his mother, Mary Ann Napper, aged thirty-one, was born at Telford, Lincolnshire. There were two sisters: Florence A. T. Napper, aged four, born at Smithwick, Warwickshire, and Gertrude Napper, aged two, born at Yardley, Worcestershire. They employed a thirteen-year-old girl as a "general servant domestic." Ten years later, they were living on Sea Road, East Wittering, and HN had five sisters and a brother, but in 1891, when he was twenty, he was employed as a "Corn Merchant" lodging in Chichester at 1 West Polland Street.

At sometime early in the twentieth century, he went out to Canada, where he worked for the CPR from 1908 to 1931 (except for the war years), based mainly in Winnipeg. There he was a leading cricketer playing for Alberta and Manitoba in western tournaments and elected president of the Western Canadian Cricket Association in 1914. When, on 23 November 1915, he joined the Thirteenth Canadian Mounted Rifles at Medicine Hat, Alberta, as a lieutenant, he had been living with his wife at Macleod, Alberta, and was already a member of the Twenty-third Alberta Rangers. The Nappers were Anglicans, and he recorded his occupation as "C.P.R. Official." Once overseas, he soon transferred to the Fifty-fourth (Kootenay) Battalion in which he won the MC for conspicuous gallantry on the Somme. He was wounded, invalided out of the army, and discharged in England, whence he returned to Canada and took up working with militia units, particularly the Manitoba Rangers beginning in 1926. At the end of the year 1935, he and his wife retired to Victoria, where he died, aged sixty-five, on 23 July 1936 and was buried at Royal Oak, leaving his widow and three sons, two of them in Winnipeg.

Sources: NAC, CEF files, RG150, box 7234-6 , a lieutenant; *Colonist*, 24 July 1936, p. 3; 26 July 1936, p. 5, obit.; census 1871, England, RG 10/1111, p. 13; census 1881, RG 11/1122, p. 1; census 1891, RG 12/846, p. 5; census 1901, RG 13/4641, p. 14.

NATION, Major Harold Turtin (1876-1967). Born on 15 April 1876 at Dunedin, New Zealand, he went to Canada as a young man and joined the BC provincial civil service. In October 1907, he was in Victoria attending the banquet for Rudyard Kipling, then a visitor, and in 1908, he went to Manchuria at a time when no one knew who controlled the country and he was regarded as an expert on Manchuria. Whether he went as an adventurous tourist or for some other reason is not clear, but his civil-service work was in the mineralogical branch of the BC Department of Mines. On 8 November 1914, he joined the Eighty-eighth Victoria Fusiliers as a lieutenant, citing as his next of kin his sister, Miss Isabel Nation, of 1813 Burns St, Victoria. Nothing on file shows a family relationship with Frederick Nation of 1328 Rockland Avenue, Victoria, or the latter's two Canadian sons who enlisted about the same time in Victoria. On 23 February 1915, HN embarked on SS *Megantic* for the voyage overseas and arrived in England on 8 March. He spent December 1915 and May 1916 at CMS, Shorncliffe, for the Fourth Lewis Machine Gun Course and was promoted to captain on 11 February 1915. What came next is not clear, but he transferred on 4 January 1917 to the First Canadian Reserve Battalion, CEF, landed in France at the end of that month, but was in Victoria on 5 October 1917 when he retired from the army on 5 October 1917.

Meanwhile, he had married Audrey Oke Smith (she then aged thirty-one) at Crediton Parish Church on 2 May 1916; in 1917, her address was 1613 [1813?] Burns Street, Oak Bay, Victoria. Long after the war, on 29 February 1933, he gave a lecture to the Reveller's Club, Victoria, on the Manchurian situation, Japanese forces having recently invaded that country. He spoke at length with lantern slides about the economy, flora, fauna, and society of Manchuria and about the Trans-Siberian Railway. In October 1934, he was elected president of the BC Historical Association at its AGM, its second vice-president being a retired journalist, Bruce Alistair McKelvie (1889-1960), and three years later was elected to its council along with *Major George Sisman. In November 1939, HN was the convenor of that association's mining committee at the AGM of its Victoria Section held at the Empress Hotel. On 8 May 1941, he spoke to the BC Historical Association (Victoria Branch) about the Yukon and the NWT. When he died, aged ninety-one, on 21 April 1967, he was a widower but there were some children, notably his eldest son, Lieutenant Philip Nation, who in May 1941 had married Nancy Haultain in London.

Sources: NAC, RG 150 Box 7239-37; *Colonist*, 10 October 1907, p. 3; 26 February 1933, p. 3; 2 March 1933, p. 5; 20 October 1934, p. 2; 29 October 1937, p. 2; 16 November 1939, p. 11; 9 May 1941, p. 2; 13 May 1941, p. 8.

NEILL, George (c. 1880-1951). He was born in St Patrick's Ward, Toronto, son of a Scottish family which had migrated about 1873. Of his five elder brothers and sisters listed in the Canadian census of 1881, the first born in Ontario was Christina, aged eight; the rest were Scottish born. GN's father, Archibald Neill, then thirty-five, was an engineer and his eldest brother, also Archibald, aged thirteen, was a "factory hand" in Toronto. They were all Presbyterians like their mother Elizabeth Neill, aged thirty-five, and their father.

GN was living in Victoria as a printer when he enlisted, aged twenty-two, on 20 October 1899 in the RCR, Second Battalion, for service in the Second South African ("Boer") War. He cited his father, "Archie Neill" of Toronto, as his next of kin and claimed to have been a member of the Fifth Regiment, Canadian Artillery. After being sent home with "enteric fever," he was eventually pronounced fit by an army doctor and discharged from the army on 5 November 1900. He had the Queen's Medal with clasps for Paardeberg, Dreifontein, and Cape Colony. GN evidently regarded Victoria as home, joined veterans' organizations, found employment in the provincial government's printing bureau, and by 1940 was foreman of its pressroom. He died, aged seventy-one, on 8 September 1951 in Victoria.

Sources: *Colonist*, 28 February 1940, p. 3.; NAC, RG 38, A-1-a, vol. 79 (T-2081), regimental no. 7083; Canadian census, 1881, IGI no. 1375883, film C-13247, district 134, sub-district H, division 2, page 147, household no. 725.

NELLES, Admiral Percy Walker (1892-1951). He was born on 7 January 1892 at Brantford, Ontario, son of Brigadier General Charles M. Nelles (1865-1936), CMG, a distinguished Canadian soldier, and became a naval cadet in the RN on 1 August 1908. In 1909, he joined the Fishery Protection Service, which was intended to train men for a future Royal Canadian Navy, and so he soon joined HMCS *Niobe* as a midshipman. After service and training in the RN (1911-1917), he became flag lieutenant to the chief of staff of the RCN, *Admiral Sir Charles Kingsmill. PN spent more years with the RN in the British Isles, including courses at the Royal Naval College, but in December 1925 was appointed senior naval officer, Esquimalt, with the rank of commander. In March 1930, he took command of the cruiser HMS *Dragon*, so becoming the first RCN officer to command a capital ship. He achieved another "first" in 1933 by reaching the rank of captain in the RCN while in command of HMCS *Stadacona*; the next year, he was promoted to commodore and appointed chief of the naval staff; and in 1938, he became rear admiral. Promoted to full admiral in 1941, he had much to do with the development of the RCN before and during the Second World War and he was in command of it during the invasion of the European Continent in 1944. George VI appointed him CB in 1943, and in 1946, the U.S. government named him commander of the Legion of Merit.

By then, he had retired with his wife, Helen Schuyler Nelles, *née* Allen, to live in Victoria, where he died on 13 June 1951 and was buried at sea from HMCS *Sault Ste Marie*. He was survived by his wife and two sons, Charles M. Nelles of Victoria and Midshipman William A. Nelles.

Sources: CFB Esquimalt Naval and Military Museum; *MacFarlane*, p. 48; G. N. Tucker, *The Naval Service of Canada: Its Official History* (3 vols., Ottawa, King's Printer, 1952), vol. I, pp. 154-55, 354 (photo).

NEWBY, Captain John (1849-1926). He was born in Liverpool on 28 March 1849, third son of a "joiner," John Newby from Lindale, Cartmel, Lancashire, and his wife Jane from the Isle of Man. The census of 1851 found him, aged two, living with them at 2 Elgin Street, Liverpool, but by 1861, they were at 93 China Street, Everton, Liverpool, with a fourth son and three daughters. JN went to sea and rose to command various vessels, and after taking cargoes to Borneo, Batavia, on the Island of Java, passing through the South Sea Islands, and to Hong Kong and Shanghai, he left Liverpool in autumn 1880 in command of the barque, *Tiger*, owned by De Wolf & Sons of Liverpool, with a general cargo for the Pacific Northwest by way of Cape Horn. In the *Tiger* and other vessels, he often carried timber from lumber mills on Burrard Inlet, BC, the principal agents for the BC timber trade being Walsh, Richet & Co. The *Tiger*'s last trip across the Pacific Ocean was in the early part of 1883, leaving Shanghai with a cargo of clay as ballast carried aboard in baskets by Chinese coolies. En route they picked up a drifting, derelict Japanese ship in the China Sea and took off the crew, leaving them later in Victoria, whence the Japanese consul in San Francisco arranged for their return to Japan. The Emperor Mutushito awarded JN a medal for his trouble.

Having first reached Victoria in 1880, JN eventually settled there as a harbour pilot for which in 1901, he was paid $1,800 a year. His last employment was as senior pilot at the Ogden Point pilot station at the entrance to Victoria. In 1886, his wife and daughter, both named Melicent, joined him from Liverpool and they lived at 25 Rithet Street in the James Bay district. On 17 August 1910, their daughter (1880-1951) married Gilbert Goodwin Fraser (1885-1957), who had arrived from England in 1898 with his parents, Presbyterian shopkeepers from England. JN's wedding gift to them was a new house at 621 Simco Street. Much earlier, JN's sister Elizabeth Newby had married Edward George Kermode (1844-1918), a Liverpool shipwright who had joined the *Tiger* in 1880 at North Shields as ship's carpenter, and in 1885, they settled in Victoria with their son Francis Kermode (1874-1946). The latter was appointed assistant curator of the BC Provincial Museum in 1890 and became a distinguished student of natural history and a member of the American Ornithological Union, the American Museum Association, the Natural History Society of BC, the National Geographical Society, and the Cooper Ornithological Club (not to mention the Union Club and an order of Freemasons). Somebody sold him a small, naturally white bearskin, and about 1900, after much investigation, he discovered *Ursus Kermodei*, a famous white bear living in the region of the Skeena and Nass rivers. A specimen was captured and kept for many years in Victoria at Beacon Hill Park.

JN and his wife Melicent both died in Victoria, she aged fifty-nine on 4 August 1908 and he aged seventy-seven on 6 April 1926. Both lie in Ross Bay Cemetery.

Sources: Letter to the author from John Newby Fraser (son of JN's daughter) of 120 Fairview Rd, *Salt Spring Island*; J. N. Fraser, "Album" in *The Beaver*, vol. 84, no. 2 (April/May 2004), p. 60; census 1851, England, HO 107/2176, fol. 49; census 1861, RG 9/2712, p. 31; census 1891, RG 12/2956, p. 17; F. Kermode, "Arrival of First Japanese in Victoria," *Colonist*, 8 April 1926, p. 5, obit.; Sunday 20 November 1932; Canadian census, 1891, VI; Howay and Gosnell, *British Columbia*, vol. IV, pp. 486-9.

NEY, Major Frederick John James (1884-1973). He was a devoted professional Imperialist who spent most of his life promoting the empire in one way or another from Winnipeg, Manitoba, but died on the Island at Nanaimo, some of his brothers having established a home there earlier. He had often visited Victoria in the course of his career, as in 1929 when he organized a great conference there, in December 1947 when he spent most of that month staying at the Melbourne Club, and in autumn 1954 when he stayed at the Empress Hotel.

FN was born on 19 September 1884, second of the nine children of Edward Frederick Ney, a farmer who lived at Hawkinge, Kent, with his Spanish wife, Susannet Maria Vicenta Barra, whom the father had met near Bilbao. FN appears, aged six, in 1891 staying at 7 Bridge Place in Rye with his grandparents, James Ney, an elderly "grazier," and his wife Elizabeth and their children. The 1901 census shows him, still with his grandparents but now employed as a "Board School Teacher." Strange to relate, his mother had died and his father had remarried and was living next door in Rye at 8 Bridge Place with the rest of the family.

In 1909, FN migrated to Winnipeg, befriended Robert Fletcher, the provincial deputy minister of education in 1908-1939, and with his help arranged a tour of Britain in July 1910 for 165 Manitoba teachers. Later that year, Ney became secretary to Fletcher at the Department of Education and edited and financed a book, *Britishers in Britain*, about the tour and the ideas behind it. FN went on promoting exchanges with Britain and around the empire and in 1910 founded a scheme he called *Hands Across the Sea*, which by 1913 was patronized by the governments of Newfoundland, Canada, and all nine Canadian provinces except Ontario, and it became the Overseas Education League for arranging exchanges of teachers between Canada and other parts of the British Empire. In 1937, at the time of the coronation of George VI, FN established the Empire Youth Movement (later known as the Commonwealth Youth Movement) to encourage tours, meetings, an exchange of ideas, and so to strengthen the bonds of the Commonwealth.

FN joined the British Army in 1914 and became a captain in the RAMC, but transferred later to the South Wales Borderers and received the French *Croix de Guerre* with Palm and the Belgian *Croix de Guerre* and was twice mentioned in despatches. Promoted to major late in 1918, he returned to Manitoba after the war and joined an Ontarian and Manitoba group formed to improve Canadian education. He helped to found the National Council of Education and in March 1920 became its first organizing secretary at $4,000 a year. With headquarters in Winnipeg, the league cooperated with the British Overseas Education League and launched a "National Lectureship Scheme." He began to collaborate with Vincent Massey, future governor general of Canada, and Sir Michael Sadler of the University of Leeds in organizing tours and conferences. In 1923, FN persuaded Sir Henry Newbolt to make a tour of three months across Canada, lecturing everywhere he went and later the poet Alfred Noyes did much the same. In 1929, FN organized a great conference in Victoria and Vancouver that was attended by Winston Churchill, Leo Amery, Ernest Raymond, Sir Rabindranath Tagore—the Bengali reformer and Nobel Prize winner—and other notable figures, including several distinguished women.

Meanwhile, in 1922, FN made a rather unhappy marriage with Helen Aikins, one of the eight children of Mary Elizabeth Jane *née* Somerset and her husband Sir James Cox Aikins (1823-1904), a wealthy lawyer who became lieutenant governor of Manitoba. Helen eventually divorced FN, probably for neglect or desertion, but by then, her sister Elizabeth had married FN's brother, Reginald Osbourne "Ronnie" Ney (1900-1966) in Kenya, at Mombasa Cathedral on 20 June 1926, where this brother had been farming. The brother and family moved about 1940 to Nanaimo on the Island, putting their son Michael into English schools and then in Ashbury College in Ottawa, followed by the University of Toronto and training in the RCN at Esquimalt. Another brother, Frank Alfonso Ney (1884-1962), also moved to Nanaimo and that was where FN retired, late in life, and died, aged eighty-eight, on 7 March 1973.

Sources: James Sturgis and Margaret Bird, *Canada's Imperial Past: The Life of F. J. Ney, 1884-1973* (Edinburgh, University of Edinburgh Centre of Canadian Studies, 2000), 325 pp.; census 1891, England, RG 12/751/68, p. 15; *Education and Leisure:*

Addresses Delivered at the Fourth Triennial Conference on Education held at Victoria and Vancouver, Canada, April 1919, ed., S. E. Lang (J. M. Dent, 1930), pp. 15, 27, 29, 121, 170, 208, 210, 214, 223; *Pioneers and Early Citizens of Manitoba: A Dictionary of Manitoba Biography from the Earliest Times to 1920* (Winnipeg, Peguis Publishers, 1971), compiled by the Manitoba Library Association, p. 3 (Aikins); Ney, *Britishers in Britain* (The Times Book Club, 1911), 298 pp.; UK Incoming Passenger Lists 1878-1960 online, no. 160482 (1952); no. 143674 (1948); Ney, "The Empire in Africa and the Middle East," *Empire Club Speeches* (Toronto), 21 March 1946 (1945-1946), pp. 298-312; Ney, "The Commonwealth on Trial," *Empire Club Speeches* (Toronto), 9 December 1948 (1948-9), pp. 117-129; NAC, CEF files, box 7303-42 (Frank Alfonso Ney).

NICHOLLS, Herbert Fitzherbert (1869-1940). He was born at Newcastle-on-Tyne, Northumberland, son of Samuel J. Nicholls, a chief constable there for many years, who was from Shrewton, Wiltshire. His mother, Mary A. Nicholls, was born in a Somerset village. When HN was one year old, the 1871 census found him living with his parents and three brothers and sisters at 23 St Mary's Terrace, Jesmond, Newcastle-on-Tyne and ten years later, they were still in Newcastle but at 6 Park Terrace, St Andrew's parish. He went out to Alberta as a young man and was working as a "rancher" when on 6 February 1900, he joined Lord Strathcona's Horse at Calgary to fight in the Second South African War (1899-1902). He was nearly thirty-two, still unmarried, an Anglican, and cited his mother as his next of kin. At his return and discharge on 16 March 1901, he held the Queen's Medal with five clasps for Belfast, Orange Free State, Natal, and SA 1900 and SA 1901.

What his occupation was upon his return from the war is not clear, but he married and settled on Reynolds Road on the Saanich Peninsula and died there, aged seventy, on 18 November 1940. He was survived by his widow at home and two sisters in Northumberland.

Sources: NAC, Men enlisted in the South African War, RG 38 A-1-a, vol. 79; census 1871, England, RG 10/5108; census 1881, RG 11/5057; *Colonist*, 19 November 1940, p. 3: obit.

NIXON, Captain Charles Patrick "Pat" (1917-2008). Born at Kentville, Nova Scotia, on 21 August 1917, he once provoked a humourless Russian official at St Petersburg to laughter by adding, when asked for his birth-date, "I believe something else happened in that year." He was a son of *Commander E. A. E. Nixon and his wife Arabella Cicely Porteous from a distinguished Montreal family. Her sister married *Major A. G. Piddington, and the two families lived near one another on the Island. CN emerged as a baby from the Halifax explosion on 6 December 1916 with a small scar on his head and went to Victoria with his family as a result of the Officer's Training College being transferred to Esquimalt in 1918. He grew up there in the admiral's house at the naval station, and after the abolition of the Naval College in 1922 and his father's death in 1924, he lived at 4040 Wilkinson Road, South Saanich, in a large house they called "Hill Farm" of which he kept a colourful oil painting on his bedroom wall during his retired years in Ottawa at 54 Rideau Terrace. It was painted by William F. U. Copeman, a talented amateur artist who was Blytha Copeman's father and father-in-law of *General George Pearkes. CN was surrounded in his childhood by relatives and friends. He recalled trips with other boys on the yacht, *Discovery,* owned and commanded by *Ernest Godfrey Beaumont, and met Sir Ronald Storrs (1881-1955), a cousin of his mother's, who came for a visit and spoke to the Kiwanis and Canadian Clubs combined on 7 August 1934. This emerged when he wanted to lend me Storr's book, *Orientations* (1945), and urged me to read it. CN was remarkably well informed on many matters of modern history and enjoyed talking about them, having subscribed to the popular English journal, *History Today,* from its very beginning.

CN attended Shawnigan Lake Boys School and used to tell the story of how he met one of the school's governors, *Lord Colville of Kilross, when refuelling his destroyer during the Second World War on the Atlantic island of Horta, where Colville was then a British representative. That was late in CN's naval career, which had begun in 1935 when he joined the RCN as a cadet, becoming a midshipman on 1 September 1936 and then a young officer in training with the RN. Two years passed in a heavy cruiser, HMS *Exeter,* sailing from port to port around South America. During the Second World War, he was captain of HMCS *Chaudière* in the Atlantic and the English Channel, working mainly out of British ports. He sank a number of German submarines. On one occasion, as he told me, he was in a destroyer on the west coast of Ireland that happened to pick up survivors of a ship, *Arrandorra Starr,* to carry them to England; it was the monstrous overcrowding that was etched in his memory. Among his decorations were the DSC, MID, Chevalier of Niadh Nask (Ireland), GCLJ, KMLJ, and the Order of Karl I of Austria. The last of his decorations was the *Légion d'Honneur,* conferred by the French ambassador, who brought it to his flat with a bottle of champagne on a summer day in 2006, the French government having decided that he ought to be decorated for saving some French soldiers at St Valéry-en-Caux at the time of Dunkirk in 1940. CN had been sent as captain of his ship to pick up a British unit, but they were not there so he took as many French soldiers as he could back to England. In describing the ambassador's visit, he was visibly pleased but wondered with amusement why it had taken Paris sixty-six years to decide upon it.

In the post-war years, before his retirement, CN commanded a ship at Esquimalt in which, he told me, he took several dignitaries up the Pacific Coast to Prince Rupert and beyond. He had particularly favourable memories of Lord Alexander, the last British governor general of Canada. On one voyage northwards calling at various ports, he recalled spending twenty-four hours at Naden, a remote and neglected whaling station at the north-west corner of the Queen Charlotte Island, where there was only one resident. That one man paddled out to them in a dugout canoe, when they had anchored, and asked them for some bread, which they gave him. He wanted them to visit him ashore, so Pat and his second, who was also a friend (and Pat added, in telling the story, "I was on the phone to him today"), duly went ashore and in his shack found a table set for four. The poor fellow explained that he set it for his dogs, they being his only companions.

In retirement in Ottawa, CN had over his mantelpiece a painting done c. 1836 of HMS *Bellerophon*, the vessel that took Napoleon off the Ile d'Aix in 1815 and which an ancestor commanded at one time. CN was for many years a faithful member of the charitable Order of St Lazarus. In Ottawa, he belonged for several decades to the Royal Golf Club near Aylmer, Quebec, where he often entertained his many friends among whom my wife and I were proud to be counted. We lunched with him weekly for many years, as did his Ottawa friends Alfred Pick and Bill Wood, but in small private groups. He was widely missed when he died in Ottawa on 16 August 2008 and was buried in a funeral held at St Bartholomew's Anglican Church on what would have been his ninety-first birthday.

Sources: Conversations with CN; Robert W. White, *The Ancestors and Naval Service of Captain Charles Patrick Nixon*, D.S.C., C.D. (North Vancouver, Privately Printed, 2007), 182 pp., and appendices (in consultation with CN,); *MacFarlane*, p. 48; *Colonist*, 5 August 1934, p. 5.

NIXON, Commander Edward Atcherley Eckersall (1878-1924). An Anglo-Irish officer of the RN, he retired with the rank of lieutenant on 6 December 1910 at Halifax, Nova Scotia, in order to accept a post there as commander-in-charge of the new Royal Naval College of Canada. He was confirmed in that post on 1 August 1915. At Halifax, he met and married Arabella Cicely Porteous (1888-1964) from a distinguished old family that had moved from Scotland to Quebec in the 1760s at the British conquest of Canada and had prospered at Montreal. One of her sisters married *Major Arthur Grosvenor Piddington. In 1916, EN and his wife had a son, *Captain Charles Patrick "Pat" Nixon. Later that year, on 6 December, the truly terrible explosion of a munitions cargo on a merchant ship in the Halifax harbour wounded both EN and his baby son and destroyed the Naval College as well as most of the city. Mrs Nixon and their first son, Eckersall Nixon (1916-1976), had been less affected by the explosion. While EN was recovering, he was promoted to commander on 1 January 1918 and moved temporarily to Kingston, Ontario, with his family and the Naval College. Later that year, Ottawa decided to transfer the college to Esquimalt, BC, where it reopened on 21 September 1918, at first in HMCS *Rainbow* and later on the Dunsmuir estate in Esquimalt, which became known as Royal Roads. EN remained in command until the Liberal government in Ottawa closed the college in June 1922, having announced on 16 May 1921 that the RCN was to be reduced to one destroyer on each coast. This event came as a terrible shock and disappointment to EN. Some 150 students had passed through the college by then and forty-three were still on the roll.

At Esquimalt in 1918, EN was "Senior Naval Officer, Coast of B.C." As such, he lived with his family in the admiral's house. (During the years 2000-2008, when I came to know Pat Nixon, who remembered living in the admiral's house, he was emphatic on this point and anxious to correct F. V. Longstaff, who had mistakenly written the contrary in his *Esquimalt Naval Base: A History of its Work and its Defences* (Victoria, 1941). Four years later, having been forcibly retired, EN contracted pneumonia after attending a game at Shawnigan Lake Boys' School and died, aged forty-six, on 10 November 1924 at "Hill Farm," his home in Saanich to which the family had moved by then. EN's widow later married Edward Boydell (1887-1949) and had a second family.

EN was remembered by cadets as capable and devoted to the college but in Admiral F. L. Houghton's words, "a strict disciplinarian, a physical fitness fanatic, and a strong believer in naval tradition." To Rear Admiral H. F. Pullen, "he seemed of another world, barely mortal," and Captain B. D. L. Johnson recalled that he "could look one in the eyes and tell if one's shoes were properly polished" (quoted by Hines). Such severe authority was, of course, not entirely personal but imposed by other authorities: His son, *Captain Charles Patrick Nixon, remembered seeing a letter on EN's desk at Esquimalt from the Anglican bishop after the Great War (about 1921) saying that he hoped none of the Naval Cadets at Royal Roads Naval College was dancing on Sunday. The bishop had heard that this was happening.

Born on 12 July 1878 at Athy, King's County, Ireland, EN was a descendant of the Nixons of Fermanagh and Cavan, southern Irish Protestants, not from Ulster but part of the same society as the Parnell, Sheridan, and Yeats families. The Nixons, like the Armstrongs and other families, had moved to Ireland earlier from the Scottish borderlands and among ENs relatives were descendants of a baronet Armstrong, who lived in Ireland at "Gallen Priory" near Birr, Offaly County (formerly King's County). One of EN's cousins was this baronet's youngest son, *Charles Frederick Nesbitt Armstrong, who married Nellie Melba, the famous soprano. EN entered the RN on 15 January 1892 as a cadet in HM training ship *Britannia* and then in HM cruiser *Narcissus* in the Channel Squadron. Promoted to midshipman on 15 March 1894, he served in HM battleship *Centurion*, flagship of the China Station. Promoted to sub-lieutenant on 15 September 1897, he served in HM screw vessel *Columbine* (tender to the battleship *Renown*) engaged on the Newfoundland Fisheries Patrol. He then qualified as a navigator and was promoted to lieutenant on 1 April 1900. In 1904, he was in HM Cruiser *Juno* in the Home Fleet and in 1908 in HM battleship *Swiftsure* in the Mediterranean Sea until 1910, when he retired from the RN on 6 December at Halifax. He then accepted a post as commander-in-charge of the Royal Naval College of Canada at Halifax, Nova Scotia, and was listed as in HM Training Ship *Niobe*. Under him the director of studies at that time was *Instructor Commander Basil S. Hartley, from the RN like the entire staff of the college. It was established, like the RCN itself, as a result of the Imperial Conference on Naval and Military Defence held in London in 1909. Wilfrid Laurier's government provided for the college in a Naval Service Act, which received royal assent on 4 May 1910. Boys aged fourteen to sixteen were to have a two-year course in naval science, tactics, and strategy followed by a year in an RN training squadron. On Trafalgar Day 1910, the college took six cadets, including *P. W. Nelles and *V. G. Brodeur, and another thirty-four were soon added.

Sources: Interviews and conversations with *Captain C. P. Nixon, a son, in Ottawa (e.g., formally on 18 March 2002); notes courtesy of Morgan Scott-Ostler, Helen Piddington, and others; NAC, R2461-0-3-E (formerly MG 30-E218), personal papers; Robert W. White, *The Ancestors and Naval Service of Captain Charles Patrick Nixon*, D.S.C., C.D. (North Vancouver, Privately Printed, 2007), 182 pp., and appendices; P. Willet Brock, "Cmdr. E. A. E. Nixon and the Royal Naval College of Canada 1910-22," in

James A. Boutilier, ed., *The R.C.N. in Retrospect, 1910-1968* (Vancouver, UBC Press, 1982), pp. 33-43; *MacFarlane*, pp. 48-9; G. William Hines, "The Royal Naval College of Canada, 1911-22," in Adrian Preston and Peter Dennis, eds., *Swords and Covenants: Essays in Honour of the Centennial of the Royal Military College of Canada, 1876-1976* (Croom Helm; Rowman & Littlefield, 1976), pp. 167-189; Dr A. G. Bricknell, "The Royal Naval College of Canada, 1911-1922," in *As You Were! Ex-Cadets Remember*, ed., R. Guy C. Smith, No. 1877 (Ottawa; The R.M.C. Club of Canada, 1884-1984, 1984), vol. I, 1876-1918, pp. 209-218; Jennifer Nell Barr, *Saanich Heritage Structures: An Inventory* (Victoria, 1991), p. 33; *Colonist*, 11 November 1924, p. 1, obit.; 4 May 1976, p. 34, obit.; Longstaff, *Esquimalt Naval Base*, p. 82; *Whitaker's*, p. 388; Barry Porteous, *The Porteous Story: A Scottish Border Family from 1439 A.D.* (Westmount, Quebec, privately published, 1980, NLC, AMICUS No. 2769744), 368 pp.; John Griffith Armstrong, *The Halifax Explosion and the Royal Canadian Navy: Inquiry and Intrigue* (Vancouver, UBC Press, 2002), 248 pp.

NUGENT, Admiral Rowland [*alias* Roland] (1861-1948). Born on 22 December 1861 in Stirling, Scotland, fifth of seven sons and three daughters of Major General Charles L. W. Nugent, of Southsea, Sussex, and his wife Charlotte *née* Pitt, he was descended from the Anglo-Norman family of Savage, their ancestor being one of de Courcey's knights who invaded Ireland from England in 1177. RN's grandfather, Andrew Savage of Portaferry House, County Down, had assumed the name of Nugent in 1814. RN entered the RN as a cadet in 1875 and the 1881 census found him, aged nineteen, a midshipman aboard HMS *Agincourt*. He served in many parts of the world, spending some years on the Pacific Coast in old sealing days, and took part at Suakin in the Sudan Campaign (1884-1886). By 1900, he was a commander and was serving aboard HMS *Magnificent*. During the Great War, he served in the North Sea and the Mediterranean, commanding (among others) the battleship HMS *Illustrious*.

Soon after retiring in 1925, he and his wife settled in the Cowichan Valley at "Fosswell," Norcross Road, Somenos Lake, where they raised sheep on land they cleared and he became president of the Vancouver Island Flockmasters' Association. He was also active in public affairs, such as efforts to improve Somenos Lake drainage. He owned many objects of historic interest, for instance, a gold watch presented to him by President Woodrow Wilson for heroically rescuing some American merchant seamen, and other things he presented to the Royal Canadian Naval College at Royal Roads. Monica Oldham, daughter of *Lieutenant Colonel F. T. Oldham, recalls RN as a loveable old neighbour who used to sing, accompanied on the piano by his Scottish wife. As an occasional babysitter, he used to amuse her and her sister with stories about how he ran away to sea as a boy and joined the RN because he was beaten at his grammar school, became involved somehow in the Russo-Japanese War, and eventually married and retired to Quamichan Lake. In September 1947, the Nugents sold "Fosswell" and moved to Victoria, intending to return to England the next spring, but they both became ill and he died on 24 March 1948 at the Jubilee Hospital, leaving his wife at St Mary's Priory and a brother, Admiral Raymond Andrew Nugent, in retirement at Southsea, Sussex. When he was buried in the churchyard at

St Peter's Quamichan, his coffin draped in the White Ensign and Rev. T. M. Hughes officiating, the active pallbearers were *Captain C. D. Donald, RCN, *Commander G. S. Windeyer, RCN, Messrs H. E. Donald and *E. M. Anketell-Jones, the estate agent *R. W. Whittome, and the editor of the *Cowichan Leader* Hugh Savage (who was probably a relative). *Colonel M. E. Dopping-Hepenstal and *Lieutenant Colonel F. T. Oldham were honorary pallbearers. Also present were men from the Canadian Legion, which RN had joined twenty-one years earlier. Mrs Jean Sharp Nugent died, aged seventy-three, on 23 August 1962 in Duncan and was buried beside her husband at St Peter's Quamichan.

Sources: *Whitaker's*, p. 391; census 1881, England, RG 11/5635, p. 3; *Cowichan Leader*, 1 April 1948, p. 5, obit.; *Colonist*, 26 March 1948, p. 13, obit; notes courtesy of Monica Oldham (511 Victoria St, Victoria); Williams, *The Story of St Peter's*, p. 73; *Victoria City and Vancouver Island Directory*, 1952, p. 853.

NUNN, Robert Henry (c. 1856-1937). Born at Twybaston, Bury St Edmunds, Suffolk, he joined the British Marines as a young man and served in Egypt (1882-1884), at the battle of El Teb (29 February 1884), and was with the Witu Expedition (17-27 October 1890) about 230 miles north of Zanzibar on the African east coast, where ships of the Royal Navy were sent after several Europeans were murdered. On 5 April 1891, the English census recorded RN's presence as an unmarried gunner in the Royal Marine Artillery aboard HMS *Reindeer*, Commander Hon. Edward Thomas Needham, somewhere on the coast of Devonshire. In 1894, he was drafted to Esquimalt for service with the Royal Marine Artillery at Work Point Barracks and remained until he retired after twenty-one years of service. He was living at 825 Nelson Street, Victoria, when he died, aged eighty-one, on 13 May 1937. His wife was in England, and he had two sons: Robert William Nunn, an employee of the British Columbia Electric Railway, and Alfred H. Nunn, employed by the BC Forest Service, both in Victoria. There were also two daughters—one in Australia and the other in Victoria—nine grandchildren, two great-grandchildren and other relatives in England. He was buried in a family plot at Ross Bay Cemetery.

Sources: census 1891, England, RG 12/1743, p. 2; *Colonist*, 14 May 1937, p. 14, obit.

O'DONOGHUE, Edward (c. 1879-1931). Born on 5 April 1879 in Wallasey at the mouth of the River Mersey, he served for nearly eight years in the Corps of Hussars in India and retired to Canada about 1911. On 22 June 1918, he joined the Canadian Army at Regina, giving his occupation as a professional soldier, naming his wife Florence as his next of kin, and stating that he was Roman Catholic. His war service was as a lieutenant in the Royal Canadian Ordnance Corps and on the headquarters staff in Ottawa. After the war, at sometime in 1920, he moved to 1749 Lillian Road, Victoria, BC, and died on 20 November 1931, leaving his wife, three daughters, and a son, all in Victoria.

Sources: NAC, CEF files, RG 150, box 7424-4; *Colonist*, 22 November 1931, p. 5, obit:

OGILVIE, Lieutenant Colonel Alexander Thomas (1867-1935). Born in Montreal on 17 April 1867, he was the eldest son of John Ogilvie and Margaret *née* Watson. He joined the Ninetieth Regiment and was gazetted second lieutenant in 1889 and lieutenant (1890) and transferred to the Third Regiment (1891), captain (1892), second lieutenant in the Third Field Battery (1896), captain again (1897), lieutenant in the RCA (1898), captain yet again (1902), and major (1905). In the meantime, he had been serving in the South African War (1899-1902) and returned with the Queen's medal and three clasps. He then became an officer in the Active Militia, and the *Canadian Almanach* listed him as such in the years before the Great War. He had married Gladys Gwendolen in November 1899, just before leaving for South Africa, but she died in January 1911.

In 1912, he was serving at Halifax, Nova Scotia, and by 1914 was posted at Work Point Barracks, Esquimalt, where he was ordered on 20 July 1914 to lead fifty gunners and NCOs of the RCA on board HMCS *Rainbow* to act as marines in meeting trouble in the harbour at Vancouver City. A Japanese passenger vessel, *Gomagata Maru*, Captain Yamamoto, had been chartered at Calcutta by one Gurdit Singhe to carry several hundred East Indians to Vancouver. There, the immigration authorities held them up for quarantine and refused immigrant status to some 352 of them. They became defiant and violent but faced with determined opposition; the ship and its passengers soon left for the voyage back to India. Two years later, when AO joined the CEF on 5 July 1916 at Victoria, he had spent eighteen years in the RCA and ten years in the Canadian Active Militia. He and his second wife Alice *née* Campbell, whom he married on 26 May 1916 in Oak Bay, lived at 1046 Belmont Ave., Victoria, and attended the Anglican Church. But they moved eventually to England, where he died, aged sixty-eight, on 25 May 1935.
Sources: NAC, CEF files, RG 150, box 7428-52; *Canadian Almanach*, 1902, p. 149; 1909, p. 162; Longstaff, *Esquimalt Naval Base*, pp. 71-3; Morgan, *Canadian Men and Women*, p. 864; *Victoria Daily Times*, 27 May 1935, p. 15.

OLDFIELD, Lieutenant Kenneth John (1893-1970). He was born on 24 July 1893 at Scoulton, Norfolk, youngest son of George and Sarah Oldfield, small landholders whom the 1901 census found aged fifty-two and forty-six, living at Bedingfield, Suffolk, when KO was seven years old. Two of his sisters were then schoolmistresses and their father had been recorded as "gentleman," but the census-taker had crossed this out in favour of "living on own means." The father and four eldest children were born at Ashill, Norfolk, where in 1851 KO's grandfather Henry Oldfield (c. 1804-?) had been farming eleven hundred acres, employing forty labourers, eleven boys, and five women, at a time when George, aged two, was the youngest of six children. In 1851, the household also employed a "family governess," a dairymaid, a housemaid, and a nursemaid. By 1871, Henry had died and George was managing the farm for his widowed mother and three elder sisters, but there were only 418 acres employing eighteen men, three boys, and two women. By 1881, George was still in Ashill but managing "Church Farm" with a wife Sarah from London, three small children, and two servants. The 1891 census found them, aged forty-two and thirty-six, with four children at "Hall Farm," Scoulton, where KO was born two years later.

He emigrated to Esquimalt, where he was working as a carpenter when he joined the Eighty-eighth Fusiliers and enlisted in the CEF on 16 June 1915 by which time his father lived in "Church Cottage" at Fleet near Aldershot. KO arrived in England on 5 September aboard SS *Scandinavian* and was sent to Salonika (1916), to a series of posts in Malta, then to Aldershot (1917), embarked at Southampton (14 October 1917), and landed at Alexandria (3 November). By 17 November, when "taken on strength" at Aboukir and sent to Heliopolis, he was ready for duty in the Royal Flying Corps. There followed a period of service in the desert in the air support for T. E. Lawrence as one of the "Arabian knights of the air" (Lowell Thomas) together with lieutenants Divers, Junor, Makins, Sefi, and others with bouts in hospital at Salonika and Salford. KO was discharged from the RAF with the DFC. Soon after returning to the Island, he married Elsa Schrattenholz on 16 December 1922, and when interviewed by Barry McKinley for the *Daily Colonist*, he was living at 1106 Wychbury Avenue, Victoria. He died, aged seventy-six, on 23 November 1970 in Saanich, and Elsa died, aged ninety, on 28 August 1983 in Victoria.

Sources: NAC, RG150, box 7443-27; Barry McKinley, "Victoria Man Knew Lawrence of Arabia," *Daily Colonist*, 10 April 1949, *Sunday Magazine*, p. 4; Lowell Thomas, *With Lawrence of Arabia* (Hutchinson, 1924), p. 251; *London Gazette*, 18 April 1918; census 1851, England, HO 107/1831, folios 7, 8; census 1861. RG 9/1263, pp. 27-8; census 1871, RG 10/1871, pp. 8-9; census 1881, RG 11/2009, p. 9; census 1891, RG 12/1550, p. 12; census 1901, RG 13/1767, p. 11.

Lt.—Col. F.T. Oldham

OLDHAM, Lieutenant Colonel Frank Trevor (1869-1960). Born in October 1869 in Melbourne, Australia, he journeyed to England as a child with his parents on SS *Melbourne* and was sent to Clifton College and the Royal Military Academy at Woolwich. He joined the RFA in 1889 and served with the British Army in India, on and off, for almost twenty-two years. His service also took him to China in 1900 to face the Boxer Rebellion as a gunner in the RFA. He was promoted to major in 1904 and retired in 1910. While on holiday in Japan, he had met Katherine "Kitty" Booth Stewart of Edinburgh and married her on 14 July 1911 at Murrayfield Established [Presbyterian?] Church, Abinger Gardens, Edinburgh, with Rev. Robert Johnstone officiating.

They went immediately to Canada in order to live as cheaply as possible on his pension and bought thirty acres on Old Victoria Road, Cobble Hill, Vancouver Island, near Mill Bay in one direction and Shawnigan Lake in another. They cleared enough land for a house, a garden, and a cow and called the place "Balgonie." There they lived for the rest of their lives, except for his service in the Great War, and they had two sons before that war and two daughters after it. (Between the wars, too, FO took his oldest son Stuart to England and put him into his old school, Clifton College.) On 9 September 1914, he set out to rejoin his Imperial regiment and sailed from Halifax on 27 September on SS *Prætorian*. Promoted to lieutenant colonel the following year, he served and returned to Canada on SS *Adriatic*, sailing from Liverpool on 18 September 1918. On 18 December 1919, he applied for the regular British War Gratuity, and Cox & Co. of London, agents of the War Office, sent him $801.77, having already paid him something earlier.

From the time of his return in 1919, the Oldhams were active in the public affairs of their district. He became a Justice of the Peace, chairman of the Boy Scout Association at Mill Bay, and introduced Shawnigan Lake to the game of badminton, which he had played during his time in India. When the Cobble Hill Board of Trade met on 17 January 1923, he chaired the meeting. At the Cobble Hill Fair in most years, his garden produce won prizes: on 7 September 1929 first prize for his six red onions, first prize for his greengage plums, and various others and in September 1931 first prize for his pickling onions and second prize for his "Jules Guyot Pears." In January 1933, he was the president of the Shawnigan Farmers' Institute and was re-elected at its AGM on that occasion. He represented the Duncan Chamber of Commerce at a meeting at Shawnigan Lake late in May 1933. He presided over the twenty-sixth annual Cobble Hill Fair when it opened on 6 September 1934, and Mrs Oldham and the St John's Anglican Women's Auxiliary had charge of the ice cream. FO nevertheless won prizes for his six red onions, "parsley, one plant," pickling onions, and "a collection of vegetables." Meanwhile, the Spring Flower Show at Shawnigan Lake was for many years under the auspices of the Farmers' Institute and arranged by the same five members under FO's chairmanship.

FO was particularly busy with veteran's affairs. In November 1934, the thirteenth annual veterans' reunion at Shawnigan Lake was attended by eighty-two veterans and guests including some from Duncan and Victoria. As a member of the managing committee, FO announced that future arrangements for the dinner were to be made by the Canadian Legion. Later, he proposed the "toast to the King" and *Captain Arthur Lane the toast "to fallen comrades." Captain Lane, *Major [later Lieutenant Colonel] Walter Bapty and a Major Henderson sang songs. There was community singing with a regimental song by Canadian Scottish officers. A Major Warner's sleight-of-hand tricks were much appreciated. FO was in the chair when the Malahat Branch of the Canadian Legion met at Bamberton on 5 March 1940. A special executive meeting of the Malahat Branch of the Canadian Legion met the next June at his house, he being its president, and it was decided to form a volunteer defence unit among veterans in this district. FO appointed a committee to interview all veterans in the area: V. E. Zellinsky (for Bamberton), D. B. Kier (for Mill Bay), C. A. Whittle (for Cobble Hill), T. G. Stokes (for Bench), and A. J. Dyson (for Shawnigan). In November 1940, local veterans held their annual dinner at Shawnigan Lake, where guests were piped in by two pipers. FO presided as branch president and proposed the toast to the King. J. C. Rathbone proposed the toast to "Fallen Comrades," a bugler played "Last Post," and a piper followed with "The Flowers of the Forest." Among three recitations, one by *Major George S. Ap'John Yardley was particularly appreciated. FO chaired the meeting of the Malahat Branch of the Canadian Legion on 3 December 1940 and was elected this time to the committee, glad to relinquish the presidency to Rev. E. M. Willis.

The Oldhams contributed a great deal to the local Anglican community and to the Red Cross of which they became strong supporters. FO chaired a public meeting at Cobble Hill on 4 December 1939 to form a unit of the Canadian Red Cross, and Mrs Oldham was immediately elected to its committee. At Shawnigan Lake in January 1940, a meeting of All Saints Anglican Church elected FO as auditor. Meanwhile, he retained a membership in the Junior United Services Club (London) and the British Public Schools Club (Victoria). His long military experience around the world had left him with a firm belief in the British Empire's benefits. He thought, for example, that if it had not been for British-educated political agitators in India, where he had lived for more than twenty years and travelled widely, India would have remained a peaceful and contented part of the empire. G. E. Mortimer, who interviewed him for the *Daily Colonist* in July 1959, wrote that "his guiding principle seems to be a warm, if ironic, respect for the rights and feelings of others . . . He is one of the last specimens of a nearly extinct kind of gentleman."

After his wife, Katherine Booth Oldham *née* Stewart, died aged sixty-eight on 12 August 1950 and was buried in the Anglican churchyard at Cobble Hill, FO lived alone, attended by a housekeeper and visited faithfully from Victoria each weekend by his youngest daughter, Monica. She was a newspaper reporter who became an occupational therapist. The two Oldham sons were living, Stuart Trevor at Vernon, BC, where he owned a sash-and-door factory, and John Moncrieff in Vancouver, where he was an engineer. The elder daughter, Frances Oldham, born at Cobble Hill on 24 July 1914, had a remarkable career in medicine. After taking a BSc at McGill University, she went on in 1935 to an MSc in pharmacology and her professor helped her to find a post in the Pharmacology Department of Chicago University under E. M. K. Geiling, MD. In 1950, she graduated as MD at Chicago and began to review articles for the *Journal of the American Medical Association* and to teach at the University of South Dakota. In 1960, the Federal Drug Administration hired her and she went to Washington DC, where under her married name of Dr Frances Kelsey—her husband was Fremont Ellis Kelsey—she discovered the evil effects of the drug thalidomide. When she stubbornly refused to approve thalidomide, the story appeared on the front page of the *Washington Post* on 15 July 1962. For averting in the United States what was a major tragedy in other countries, she was decorated by President Kennedy on 17 August 1962 and awarded various other honours. She became a kind of national heroine, and the procedures for approving pharmaceuticals were changed to make them safer and less vulnerable to the pressure of drug companies.

Some knowledge of her triumph may have reached FO before he died, aged nearly ninety-one, on 23 November 1960 in Saanich, probably at Resthaven Hospital.

Sources: Conversations with Monica Oldham in Victoria; RG 9 series II-F-10 (British War Gratuities), Vol. 204, file no. 13904-F-23; *Colonist,* 14 September 1921, p. 9; 21 January 1923, p. 13; 10 September 1929, p. 15; 12 September 1931, p. 18; 27 January 1933, p. 15; 24 May 1933, p. 15; 8 September 1934; 20 November 1934, p. 9; 8 December 1939, p. 11; 17 January 1940, p. 6; 9 March 1940, p. 8; 25 June 1940, p. 5: 20 November 1940, p. 16; 6 December 1940, p. 17; 18 December 1940, p. 6; G. E. Mortimer, "*An Old Soldier Recalls Adventure in Asia,*" *Colonist,* 5 July 1959, *Sunday Magazine,* pp. 12-13; *Who's Who in B.C.* 1933-1934, p. 131; *Who's Who in B.C.* 1942-1943, p. 243; Hughes, *Shawnigan Lake,* 1887-1967, pp. 45. 49. 51; *Who's Who in America,* 37th edn. (1972-1973), vol. I, p. 1684; *U.S. Food and Drug Administration, FDA Consumer Magazine,* March-April 2001, Linda Bren, "*Frances Oldham Kelsey: FDA Medical Reviewer Leaves Her Mark on History,*" 7 pp.; Trent Stephens and Rock Brynner, Dark Remedy: *The Impact of Thalidomide and its Revival as a Vital Medicine* (NY, Perseus, 2001), 228 pp.

OLIVER, Brigadier Henry Herbert Montague (1897-1984). Born in Dharwad, Maharastra, India, on 22 April 1897, son of the deputy conservator of forests, Indian Forestry Service, he was sent home to England as a baby with his sister Frances (aged three) to be installed at a kindergarten boarding school run by two Miss Leweses. Then he attended Dover College, and he and his sister spent their holidays with Anglo-Irish relatives at Oughtrad, Galway. There the groundsman taught them to fish and to ride a donkey, which spent most of its time avoiding being caught. Oliver did not see his parents again until he was sixteen, when they finally retired to England. He resented their absence in his early life, and their relationship never recovered. It had been decided that he would enter the army, and he passed fourth, out of more than a hundred, into the Royal Military College at Woolwich (which he called "the shop"). He also recalled being harangued by the sergeant teaching them to ride "arms and stirrups crossed," who shouted, "If Jesus Christ rode his donkey the way you're riding that ruddy horse, it's no wonder they crucified him." HO went from Woolwich to the Great War, at first as an observer in a two-seater airplane with a pilot who was usually drunk, to report on enemy positions, but after three crashes, he transferred to "the comparative safety" of the trenches and served as a communications officer. He was awarded the Military Cross for "conspicuous gallantry and devotion to duty in maintaining communications. As a forward observation officer under heavy shellfire on six occasions he went out himself under heavy fire and mended telephone wire. He also brought in four wounded men who were lying out exposed to fire."

After the war, he served in Ireland during the Troubles—1920-1921—where he deplored the use of the infamous Black and Tans and had some sympathy for the Irish people, though not for the terrorists of the Irish Republican Army. In 1922 or 1923, he was posted to India. His daughter has pictures of him in 1924-1926 with an Indian hockey team and with artillery in mountain passes. Next, he was posted to Hong Kong, where he met his Canadian wife, Elizabeth Jones (1895-1971), she having been sent to stay with her elder sister, wife of a naval officer stationed there. By the time they married, HO was posted to Aden and his bride set out from Victoria by steamer, arriving in the heat and the dirt, and was married on 23 March 1928 at the Garrison Church, Aden, "attended by all the troops and their dogs and followed by a reception feast of liver and onions. Their wedding night was spent under the stars at the end of a row of fellow officers' cots, whose legs were standing in tins of kerosene to keep off the bugs." HO arrived in Victoria alone on 2 April 1930 aboard the *Protesilaus*, one of two unrelated passengers, the ship having sailed from Hong Kong on 6 March 1930.

By the time their daughter Elizabeth Oliver [now Mrs Conlon, the source of these notes] was born in December 1932, the Olivers had returned to England, where they lived at Portsmouth until 1936, when they were posted again to Hong Kong, much to their delight. "Hong Kong was a wonderful place to be a soldier. Soldiering meant going to the office in the morning, lunch at the Club or the Peninsula Hotel, race meetings at Fanling or Macao in the afternoon and dinner parties at night. We had a Chinese cook, two house boys, a 'fah wong' (gardener), an 'amah' and a Portuguese nanny—all on a Major's pay! My father kept two race horses, *Double Chance*, a little grey China pony, and *Sea Urchin*, an Australian mare. They won the Governor's Cup twice, much to his delight. He rode himself as a 'bumper' or gentleman jockey, being too tall—6' 1"—and heavy for anything else. They also ran a 'drag hunt,' using a bag of scent rather than murdering foxes, and we raised two foxhound puppies every year for the hunt."

All this came to an end in 1939. While they were on six months' leave in Victoria, Vancouver Island, visiting HO's father-in-law, they were recalled to Hong Kong, where they remained for another year. Fortunately, HO's posting elapsed and they made the six weeks troopship journey back to England during the "phoney war" (1939), crossing from Marseille to Cherbourg. By this time, HO wore an acting brigadier's red tabs, and his regiment was scattered over England from Shropshire to Pembroke Dock in Wales. In late summer 1941, they were recalled and posted by steamship around South Africa to India, where HO spent the rest of the war in the Burma fighting the Japanese in alien jungle conditions, in an appalling climate. He suffered from recurring bouts of malaria for the rest of his life. He was also permanently haunted by the nightmare of having to round up frightened and confused Burmese deserters for punishment, sometimes even execution. To improve his pension, he stayed on after the war in command of a territorial regiment in Cumberland. In 1947, after thirty-six years of service, including the two world wars, he retired as a brigadier to Victoria with a pension of $90 a month, though he was pleased and amazed at being pensioned at all for what he regarded as doing nothing. He declined the only job offered in Victoria, which was watering the boulevards at 4:00 a.m. in the summer, and he never adjusted to living in Canada, where people in general struck him as "uncouth Colonials." His own family he never saw again, except his sister once briefly after his marriage in 1928. In Victoria, he took little trouble to make friends or develop a life and spent his time gardening and recalling the happy days in Hong Kong of the 1920s and 1930s. After his wife died, aged seventy-five, on 8 October 1971, he lived a reclusive life, his best friends being his neighbours' dogs, whom he dearly loved and indulged. He died, aged eighty-six, on 8 February 1984.

Sources: Notes and family papers kindly sent to the author on 7 November 2000, by a daughter, Elizabeth (Oliver) Conlon, 1630 Rockland Avenue, Victoria; Canadian Passenger Lists, 1865-1935, T-14895.

ORCHARD, Major Albert John (1881-1963). He was born on 5 May 1881 in Burma, son of Colonel Albert F. Orchard, an Indian army officer born in India, and his wife, Cornelia C. Orchard, born in Bath, Somerset. In April 1891, the Orchards and two servants were living in Kensington, London, at 22 Neville Gardens, the father recorded as "Colonel, Infantry (Retired)." AO, aged ten, had a brother and two sisters, all born in India except the youngest sister, aged seven, born at Cambridge. A year or two later, AO was sent to school at Trinity College, Stratford-on-Avon, and followed his father into the British Army by way of the Permanent Militia and (from 1901) the First Battalion Cheshires. He fought in South Africa from 5 January 1901 to 16 May 1902 and was awarded the Queen's Medal with clasps for Cape Colony, Orange Free State, and Transvaal and the King's Medal with clasps. In 1903, he passed a course in musketry. From 17 May 1902 to 20 October 1904, he served in the East Indies and from 14 April 1906 in West Africa. The War Office then recorded him as being 6' 6¾" tall and with a good knowledge of military Hindustani. His widowed mother was living at Badsey, near Evesham, Worcestershire.

In 1914, he was stationed at Jubbulpore as a captain in the Eighth Rajputs when he took leave to marry Miss Edith Mary Idiens (c. 1886-1981), born where his mother was living at Evesham, Worcestershire, second daughter of Alice and John Idiens (a merchant) who had migrated from Evesham to 2625 Roseberry Avenue, Victoria, BC, not many years before. The wedding was at Christ Church Cathedral on 4 July 1914, and the couple left that day, on the three o'clock boat, for England, where they were to stay for three weeks and then proceed back to India. Two of her brothers, one a bank clerk and the other a dyslexic "solisitor" who had served two years in the "yemonary," both born at Evesham and fought in the Canadian Army during the Great War. At sometime in 1920, after the Great War, the Orchards settled in Victoria, where they had two sons and a daughter and

lived mainly at 3329 Linwood Avenue. It was there that he died, aged eighty-one, on 13 June 1963, leaving his wife and their daughter Alice at home. Mrs Orchard lived to be ninety-five and died on 26 December 1981.
Sources: PRO, WO 76/217, page 52; census 1891, England, RG 12/26, p. 35; census 1891, RG 12/2335, p. 3; *Colonist*, 5 July 1914, p. 3; 15 June 1963, p. 20, obit.; NAC, CEF files, boxes 4683-2 and 3.

OSBORN, Danvers (1864-1929). He was born on 14 November 1864 at Burdwan, India, son of Lieutenant Danvers Henry Osborn (1827-1898), lieutenant colonel in the ICS and Indian Army. His mother was Annette Wilson, daughter of Thomas Watkins Wilson, MD, surgeon major, Indian Medical Service at Calcutta, and he had an elder brother, Arthur Osborn (1863-1934). He descended from a well-known family in English history that, as *Burke's Peerage* specifies, must be distinguished from the Osborne family with its different coat of arms and its own history. "The third baronet, Sir Danvers Osborn," the *Colonist* reported at OD's death, "was on this continent with the Hon. Edward Cornwallis and it was Sir Danvers who named Halifax after his father-in-law the Earl of Halifax, son of 'The Trimmer.'" In April 1881, aged sixteen, OD was "Studying Telegraphy" as a boarder at a telegraph station at Porthcurnow, Penzance, Cornwall, with many other young British subjects, including John Retallack from Toronto, Philip Jackson from the Philippine Islands, Frederick George from Cairo, Egypt, and William Miller from "Nyrcetal," India. They were probably working under the ægis of the Eastern Telegraph Company with which he claimed to have learned about submarine cables. DO was first stationed at Suez. Next, he went to Pennsylvania and after a short period with the U.S. Marines was employed in cable work at Panama and then at Canso, Nova Scotia. It was mainly there that he worked with Sir Sandford Fleming for several years assembling all the data needed to defend the Imperial Pacific Cable project against the Eastern and Extension Company and other opponents, who thought a Pacific submarine cable was merely an impracticable vision. At Halifax, Nova Scotia, on 23 October 1899, aged thirty-five, DO joined the Canadian Special Force for the South African War and served in the Royal Canadian Regiment, Nineteenth Brigade, under Sir William Otter. By 31 July 1900, when he was invalided to England (apparently with "sciatica"), he had the Queen's Medal with four clasps for Paardeberg, Dreifontein, Johannesburg, and Cape Town.

In 1904, he joined the Pacific Cable Board at Bamfield on the west coast of Vancouver Island. There he wrote a lot for the press, for instance, "Byng and his Sisters," published in the *Victoria Daily Colonist*; "Writers I have Known" and "Asiatic Immigration and B.C.," published in *The Empire Review*, which aroused much comment. From 1902, he campaigned for a West Coast road. In 1910, he served on the executive committee of the Victoria and Esquimalt branch of the Navy League. In 1925, he was a member of the Author's Association of Victoria and was one of those writing "in the cause of Imperial unity," along with John R. Rathom, *Sir Clive Phillipps-Wolley, and others. On 14 January 1906, he married Inez Smith, second daughter of Henry Smith of Victoria, and they had two children, George and Dorothy. When he died, aged sixty-four, on 20 May

1929, they were living in Oak Bay and his funeral was held there at St Mary's Anglican Church.

Sources: *Colonist*, 3 March 1925, p. 12; 21 May 1929, p. 5, obit., and photo; NAC, RG 38, A-1-a, vol. 81, reel T-2082, soldiers of the South African War; *Burke's Peerage*, 106th edn. (1999), vol. 2, p. 2174; census 1881, England, RG 11/2351, p. 8.

OXENHAM, Amyas Kenneth N. (1884-1927). Born at Poona, India, only son of Constance and Robert G. Oxenham from Devonshire, he spent his childhood at a series of schools in England while his parents remained in India in the employ of the Bombay Civil Service. The 1891 census found him, aged eight, living at "Pen Craig," Enderby, Leicestershire, with his great-aunt Sarah Brook, a fifty-four-year-old maiden lady born at Leytonstone, Essex, and her friend a middle-aged maiden lady from St John's Wood described as "governess." The rest of the household consisted of cook, housemaid, and kitchenmaid. Ten years later, he was a resident student at Malvern College, Worcestershire. By then, his parents had retired from India to 3 Baring Crescent, Exeter, but AO had grown to be somehow very different and had a quarrel with them, as he told his daughter in later years. Her memory of his account was that he was sent to Eton, but the 1901 census found him at Malvern. In any event, his parents and his life in childhood filled him with such resentment that he went to Vancouver Island to get away from it all. There in Victoria, he married Kathleen Faith R. Ashton on 4 April 1918 and taught at St Michael's School, but they moved later to Ganges, Salt Spring Island, where he played the organ at the Anglican Church, and they ran a school of their own called Formby House School. She may have been the Kathleen F. R. Ashton whom the 1901 English census found employed as a governess in the home of a cotton manufacturer in Cheshire, though that Miss Ashton was six years older than AO. He died, aged forty-three, on 2 February 1927, leaving his wife and a daughter. Much accurate information is lacking.

Sources: Notes courtesy of Miss Allison Maude, *Salt Spring Island, Christmas 2001*; census 1891, England, RG 12/2500, p. 31; census 1901, RG 13/2784, p. 31; census 1901, RG 13/2033, p. 2; inscription on AO's tombstone in St Mark's graveyard, Ganges, Salt Spring Island.

PADDON, Lieutenant Colonel Sir Stanley Somerset Wreford (1881-1963). He was born at Reigate, Surrey, son of Samuel W. Paddon, born at Okehampton, Devon, who was "living on income from lands and houses," and his wife, Rebecca P. Paddon, born at Milton, Wiltshire. SP attended Wellington College, was commissioned on 15 August 1900 and made lieutenant on 10 February 1901 while attached to the Royal Scots (Lothian Regiment). In the South African War (1899-1902), he served with the Third Dragoon Guards, then went to India where he was at Kamptee on 22 February 1903 and on 13 February 1904 transferred to the Indian Cavalry (Thirty-sixth Jacob's Horse). He was recorded in the *Indian Army List* for January 1905 as "Officer app'ted as supernumerary to British regiments serving in India for admission to the Indian Army when qualified." During the Great War, he served on the Imperial General Staff, was mentioned in despatches, and decorated with two

Brevets, the Russian Order of Ste Anne and the CIE. In 1923-1940, he was director general of the India Stores Department and served later as governor of the School of Oriental Languages. He was a Freeman of the city of London and a Companion of the Institution of Mechanical Engineers and was knighted in 1932.

SP married Nora Howell in 1911 and when she died in 1943 he then married the widowed Mrs Lilian Emily Burns *née* Holden in Victoria, BC, on 21 October 1944. She was the daughter of Dr and Mrs D. B. Holden of Victoria, but the marriage took place at 812 Newport Avenue, Oak Bay, home of Mr and Mrs Hugh Peters, who gave her away. SP had been in Victoria for more than a year and in other parts of Canada for several years previously. It was their intention to settle in Victoria after a honeymoon up Island. How long they remained on the Island is not clear, but when he died on 5 December 1963, his address was c/o Bank of America, Redlands, California.

Sources: BL, India Office, *Indian Army List,* January 1905, pp. 150, 201; *Who was Who*, vol. VI (1961-70); *Colonist*, 22 October 1944, p. 6; census 1881, England, RG 11/797, p. 26.

PADDON, William Francis L. (c. 1844-1922). He was born at Chipping Wycombe, Oxfordshire, where his father, Rev. Thomas Paddon, was vicar of Wycombe but born at Farnham, Hampshire. His mother Anne was born at Rowde, Wiltshire, and he had a younger brother and sister born locally. In 1861, when he was sixteen, there was also a governess, a cook, and a housemaid. What WP did in life I could not discover, but late in life, he settled on Mayne Island in the Strait of Georgia. In March 1917, he wrote to the *Colonist* about whether it was correct to spell "Baghdad or Bagdad." "It is many years since—living in Syria—I learned to speak and write Arabic, but I can well remember the almost insuperable difficulty which most Europeans found in pronouncing the deeply guttural letter which we represent by gh ('ghain'). Since in the Arabic alphabet there is no other letter answering to our g (but only this guttural), it is clear that Bagdad is a mistaken pronunciation arising no doubt from this very difficulty." When he died, aged seventy-eight, on 28 August 1922, he had been living at Ganges, Salt Spring Island, perhaps at the hospital there.

Sources: *Colonist*, 22 March 1917, p. 4; census 1861, England, RG 9/856, p. 3.

PALMER, Charles George (1847-1940). He was born on 15 October 1847, at Jullundur, India, son of General Henry Palmer of the Indian Army (1807-1892) and his wife, *née* Susan Wiltshire. His father was born at Mussoorie, India, on 11 June 1807 and died there on 23 August 1892. CP's mother died in 1856, and his father married Mary Fraser, a widow, on 2 October 1863. In 1847, when CP was a ten-year-old ensign in the Royal Navy but staying with his family at Lucknow, the notorious Indian Mutiny broke out in certain regiments. Mutineers besieged Lucknow, and CP was employed carrying ammunition and messages. During one attack, a cannon ball crashed through a wall of the family house and killed one of his sisters standing near him. He was decorated later with the medal for the Indian Mutiny with a clasp "Defence of Lucknow" for duty on a battery as a boy.

At Duncan, Vancouver Island, long after his retirement there, he lived to be the last survivor of the Siege of Lucknow, when in June 1939 another survivor died in England. After the siege, CP was sent home to England, where he attended King Edward VI School at Sherborne and then returned to Thomasen's Civil Engineering College, Rurkee, India. In 1868, he joined the Indian Public Works Department in which he spent many years building canals and laying out the agricultural irrigation systems of India for the British government—something Indians seemed incapable of doing for themselves—and directing famine relief. For his work in the two terrible famines of 1896 and 1897, CP was decorated with the CIE (Commander of the Order of the Indian Empire). By 1895, he had risen to be superintending engineer, and in 1900-1902, he was chief engineer of the Irrigation Branch and Secretary to the Government of the North-West Province.

During one of his furloughs, CP visited Australia and in 1880, he married Annie Isabella Porter, daughter of T. S. Porter of Australia, a family he had known during his visit. In 1902, they retired to England and eight years later, in 1910, "on the recommendation of a friend in India," they went to live at Cowichan on a farm not far from Duncan, where for thirty years, they were staunch supporters of St Peter's Church at Quamichan on the Maple Bay Road near Duncan. For many years, he was director of the Cowichan Creamery and in 1917, served as president of the United Farmers of BC. In 1914-1918, he was a councillor for the North Cowichan Municipality and in 1915-1924 a police commissioner. Like so many other Imperials on the Island, he took part in many community activities. He took charge, for instance, of the bingo games at a Women's Auxiliary garden party held on 7 July 1933 in the rectory grounds. From time to time, he used to recall for his friends and neighbours the thrilling story of the Indian Mutiny and the Siege of Lucknow. In 1933, when CP was eighty-six years old, the *Daily Colonist* printed a brief summary of his career and did the same again in June 1939, when he was ninety-two. Mrs Palmer died, aged sixty-seven, on 1 May 1927, and CP, aged ninety-three, on 13 August 1940. They were survived by two sons—Major C. H. Palmer, RE (1882-1893) retired in England and France, and *Major J. H. G. Palmer, Indian Army, retired at Quamichan Lake—and by three daughters, one at home in Quamichan and two married and living in England.

One of these latter, Dorothy Isobel Palmer, married Colonel Arthur Orr Sutherland (c. 1880-?) of the Twenty-second Punjabi Regiment on 29 April 1914 at St John's Church, Calcutta, where he had been born the second son of parents both born in India. Sutherland fought in the South African War and then sent with his regiment to Mesopotamia during the Great War, was taken prisoner in 1915, and held by the Turks for three years. He earned the DSO for keeping up the morale of his battalion, half-starved and bullied on the long, murderous march as prisoners from Kut-el-Amara to Kastamun in Turkey. On being released, he returned to India for further service on the North-West Frontier with his regiment, the Twenty-second Punjabis, and won the Frontier Medal with two clasps for Waziristan (1919-1921) and Waziristan (1921-1924). Upon his retirement in 1925, the Sutherlands visited CP at Quamichan Lake and again in 1935 when they rented Dr R. N. Stoker's house at Cowichan Lake, but they never moved permanently to the Island. They settled in Bedford at "Asia Holm" *alia* "The Homestead" and there he served as an ARP Warden during the Second World War.

Sources: Notes, family records, and photographs lent to the author, courtesy of John Palmer, a grandson in Victoria; *Colonist*, 8 July 1933, p. 8; 26 September 1933, p. 3; 15 June 1939, p. 10; 14 August 1940, p. 5; 15 August 1940, p. 5: obit.; *Who's Who in B.C.*, 1933-1934, p. 132; 1940-1941, obituary p. III; Williams, *The Story of St Peter's*, p. 55; census 1891, England, RG 12/1248, p. 13 (Sutherland); census 1901, England, RG 13/1488, p. 9 (Sutherland); Ronald Millar, *Death of an Army: The Siege of Kut*, 1915-1916 (Boston, Houghton Mifflin Company, 1970), p. 294 (Sutherland); S. W. Jackman, *Portraits of the Premiers: An Informal History of British Columbia* (Sidney, Gray's Publishing Ltd., 1969), p. 111.

PALMER, Major General Henry Spencer (1838-1893). Not evidently related to the Palmers cited above and below, he was born on 30 April 1838 in Bangalore (India), third and youngest son of John Freke Palmer, colonel of the Madras Staff Corps, and Jane James, sister of Sir Henry James. He entered the RMA, Woolwich, by passing an examination with first place in mathematics, was commissioned in the Royal Engineers, and had a distinguished career around the empire, notably in British Columbia and Japan. Appointed ADC to Colonel Moody, who in 1858-1863 commanded the detachment of REs sent to British Columbia, HP was sent there again three years later as assistant commissioner in the Parliamentary Boundaries Commission under Benjamin Disraeli's Reform Act. He made a series of admirable surveys, wrote outstanding reports, lectured at Cambridge, and contributed papers on the colony to the Royal Geographical Society of London. And he linked himself forever with BC on 7 October 1863 by marrying Mary Jane Pearson Wright (1848-1934) at Holy Trinity, New Westminster. She was born on Cephalonia, one of the Ionian Islands in the Mediterranean Sea, and arrived in BC in 1859 when her father, Rev. Henry Wright (1816-1892), took a clerical post as archdeacon. Her brother Frederick Wright became the first Anglican rector in Saanich. At her wedding to HP, the bishop, *George Hills, offered them either the land on which the city of Vancouver now stands or an oil painting—they chose the painting, as she later related with amusement! Scarcely less interesting and exotic was HP's Sinai expedition with Sir Charles Wilson, which enabled him to publish a book on Sinai for the SPCK. He also spent twelve years in the Ordnance Survey of Kent and Sussex, sailed to New Zealand to make observations on the transit of the planet Venus, and was ADC to the governor of the Windward Island. HP and his wife lived in Japan for several years while he constructed waterworks at Tokio and a harbour for Yokohama, the port chosen by the Japanese government for western shipping, and in 1879 HP was sent to Hong Kong, where he was ADC and private secretary to Sir John Pope Hennessy and drew up plans for a British observatory and physical laboratory. The occasional letters from "Our Correspondent in Japan" printed in *The Times* were HP's. Late in his career, while on a posting to Manchester, the Japanese government asked for his services again, and in 1887, he retired from the Royal Engineers with the rank of major general in order to take up a civil practice in Yokohama. He was widely admired in Japan and had warm friendships there, in particular with a Japanese lady, Uta Saito, by whom he had a daughter. He was making plans for his wife and family to join him when he died suddenly on 10 February 1893. Mrs Palmer eventually went back to Victoria and died there, aged eighty-six, on 10 January 1934, leaving two daughters, Mrs John Rogers of 745 Yates Street, Victoria, and Mrs E. M. Bennet of Northam, North Devon.

Sources: Frances M. Woodward, "Palmer, Henry Spencer," in the *DCB* online; *The Times*, London, 15 March 1893, p. 5, obit.; *Colonist*, 11 January 1934, pp. 1 and 15, obit., for his widow, Mary (Wright) Palmer; PABC, C/AB/30.6, .6J/1; GR 1372, F 1302. PRO, CO 60/1û16; WO 25/3913û15. *Japan Weekly Mail* (Yokohama), 31 May 1890, 11-18 Feb. 1893. *Royal Engineers Journal* (Chatham, Eng.), 23 (1893): 110-12. DNB. F. M. Woodward, "The influence of the Royal Engineers on the development of British Columbia," in *BC Studies*, no. 24 (winter 1974-75): 3-51; Henry Spencer Palmer, *Ancient History from the Monuments; Sinai from the Fourth Egyptian Dynasty to the Present* (SPCK, 1878, repr. 1892), 224 pp.; A collection of Palmer's letters from Japan to *The Times* (London) was issued shortly after his death as *Letters from the Land of the Rising Sun . . . between the years 1886 and 1892 . . .* (Yokohama, 1894); a Japanese translation, *Reimeiki no Nihon kara no tegami*, prepared and edited by his grandson Jiro Higuchi, appeared there in 1982; Pritchard, *Letters of Edmund Hope Verney*, pp. 267 note, 278 n.10.

PALMER, Major John Harald [*sic*] Gore (1884-1967). He was born on 11 July 1884 at Adelaide, South Australia, son of *Charles George Palmer, who was there during two years' leave from India with his Australian wife, Annie Isabella *née* Porter. JP was sent home to England for schooling, according to custom, and the 1901 census found him, aged sixteen, boarding at 50 Marboro Hill, Marylebone, London, the dwelling of Rev. Arthur Stokes and his wife Ellen E. Stokes. Their son, Claude B. Stokes, aged twenty-five, already a lieutenant in the Bengal Cavalry and born in India, lived in the house, as did other boarders such as Charles P. C. Beresford, aged eighteen, also India-born. JP joined the Indian Army and had a career mainly with the Twenty-first Punjabis. He served *inter alia* as brigade major to Brigadier General Sir Percy Lake in Mesopotamia (1917).

During his long service in India, JP married Susan Emily Sime (1887-1974) on 26 July 1914 at All Saints Church, Srinagar. She was a daughter of Dr John Sime (c. 1843-1911), director of public instruction for the Punjab, who had Rudyard Kipling's father on his Education Department staff in the Punjab at a time when Kipling senior printed Sime's textbooks at a print shop in Lahore. The Palmers' son John recalls his mother repeating what the senior Kipling used to say about his young son, "I don't know what to make of Rudyard; he doesn't seem to be interested in anything." At sometime in the middle of the twentieth century, Humphrey Davey of the Victoria Kipling Society told JP that Rudyard Kipling probably took C. G. Palmer as his model for an engineer in a short story about a woman who would have nothing to do with men until this particular engineer came along. One of John Sime's daughters, Catherine Mary Sime (1875-1945), who eventually died at

Duncan, was a lifelong friend of Rudyard Kipling and received a letter from him shortly before his death in 1936.

The family migrated to the Cowichan Valley after JP went out on a hunting expedition in 1910. He found the Island captivating, as he explained in an article, "Life in Vancouver Island," which appeared at Alahabad in *The Pioneer* (pp. 3-4) on 6 January 1913 and another printed therein on 8 October 1913 (pp. 7-8) under the title, "A Baltistan Holiday." *The Pioneer* was the most prestigious of several newspapers published at Allahabad, capital of the United Provinces of Agra and Oudh, India. For well over half a century, the family were active in the community life of the Cowichan Valley and staunch parishioner of St Peter's Church at Quamichan near their house on the Maple Bay Road. Several relatives joined them later. JP was the official bell-ringer for more than thirty years. Notwithstanding his military background, he was a gentle person with a mischievous sense of fun. If there were children sitting behind him in church, he would sometimes wiggle his ears and when they tittered or laughed would frown at them in mock disapproval. On one occasion when a boy with long hair was to be confirmed, JP marched him into the vestry and cut it short. JP died, aged eighty-two, on 16 June 1967 in Saanich and was survived by his wife, who died, aged eighty-seven, on 27 January 1974 in Central Saanich, and their children.

Sources: Notes and family records, courtesy of J. H. Palmer, a son; tombstones in the graveyard at St Peter's Quamichan; PRO, *Indian Army List,* January 1923, p. 504, war service of British officers of the Indian Army, "The War of 1914-21 [sic]—Operation in Persia and Persian Gulf from 29 October 1916 to 27 April 1919"; despatches reported in the *London Gazette,* 15 August 1919 and 17 and 3 February 1920; census England, 1901, RG 13/118, pp. 17-18; microfilmed copies of *The Pioneer of Alahabad,* India, at the India Office Library, British Library; *The Times* (London), 7 March 1911, p. 11, Sime obit.; Williams, *The Story of St Peter's,* p. 73; *A Handbook for Travellers in India, Burma and Ceylon* (11th edn., John Murray, 1924), 728 pp., p. 46.

PARKER, Arthur Henry (1874-?). He was an artist painting in water colours who lived with his wife, Alice Elizabeth *née* Foster, in the Cedar Hill district of Victoria for some years. Passenger records show them arriving at Halifax, Nova Scotia, on 7 April 1912, and they were in Toronto at one time. According to his entry in *Who's Who in B.C.,* he had studied painting under well-known masters at various schools in England and exhibited paintings, widely admired, in London, Birmingham, Manchester, Bolton, Stoke-on-Trent, Toronto, and on the European continent. He belonged to several clubs of artists, enjoyed tennis, golf, and bowling, and attended the Church of England. His wife, whom he had married at Stoke-on-Trent in 1904, was a writer and poet "of considerable note." The same source cites AP's date of birth as 15 August 1878, but other sources confirm his Attestation Paper in the CEF files, which records a birthdate of 15 August 1874. When he enlisted in Victoria on 1 March 1916, his next of kin was Alice Elizabeth Parker living at Mount Tolmie (close to Cedal Hill), and he was an "artist" who had already spent three years in the North Staffordshire Territorials. The Parkers left the Island at sometime after 1939.

AP is clearly identified in three sets of English census records growing up in a family of Staffordshire potters. He appears in 1871, aged two, born in Staffordshire at Newcastle-under-Lyme and living in that town at 14 Leech Street with his parents as well as four sisters and a brother. Their father, Henry Parker, was a potter aged thirty-eight, their mother Ellen *née* Espley aged thirty-six. With them was her brother Richard, a bookbinder, and a young nephew. A decade later, AP, aged twelve, was still at school, but his father, aged fifty, was a "Potter, Hollowware Presser," his brother Richard, aged fifteen, was a "Solicitor's General Clerk," and two of his sisters had become dressmakers, and his bookbinder uncle was still with them. The 1901 census shows that the father had died, and the widowed mother was living with the rest of the family at her bookbinder brother's house, 17 West Crescent, Newcastle-under-Lyme. AP, now aged twenty-nine, was recorded as a "Potter Finished Earth Warehouse Wrapper." Alice appears meanwhile, aged six, in the 1891 census living in Stoke-on-Trent as the second daughter of a grocer, Samuel Foster, aged thirty, born in Crewe, Cheshire, and his wife Elizabeth, born in Staffordshire. Perhaps, three years in the North Staffs Territorials left AP with a desire to launch out as an artist and to emigrate. The Island was a favorite destination for people wanting a fresh start in life for one reason or another.
Sources: NAC, CEF files box 7582-38; *Who's Who in BC*, 1937-1939, p. 117; census 1871, England, RG 10/2832, p. 26; census 1881, RG 11/2698, p. 24; census 1901, RG 13/2578/47, p. 3; census 1891, RG 12/2177/103, p. 21 (Alice Foster); Canadian Passenger Lists, 1865-1935, T-4692, arriving April 1912 at Boston in *Scotian*; T-4743, arriving 7 April 1912 at Halifax from Liverpool in *Megantic*, AP aged thirty-eight, Alice aged twenty-seven; Alice Elizabeth Foster Parker, *Bonds in a Family* (Toronto, CVI Press, 1933), 212 pp.

PARKER, Major Richard Gilbert Lewes (1898-1961). Born on 11 May 1898 at Stockton, Warwickshire, he was recorded, aged three, living there at "The Rectory" with his widowed mother Mary E. C. Parker, aged thirty-one, born at Colwall, Herefordshire, and two brothers, Michael E. L. and Frederick H. L. Parker, aged six and six months. Also, there was his uncle Major John Lewes Parker (c. 1862-?), Royal Artillery, with a wife and son. There were four servants. Presumably, RP's father was an Anglican minister (he himself was Anglican) and must have been one of the major's four brothers: Charles L. E. Parker, Gilbert Parker, Edward Parker, or Wilfred Parker, who in 1871 and 1881 were living with their parents, RP's grandparents. The latter were Caroline Parker and Charles Parker, an Irish-born solicitor, established in 1871 at 95 Gloucester Terrace, Paddington, and in 1881 at Harrow in the High Street.

RP's widowed mother apparently remarried a Mr Nichol and migrated with him and RP to Parksville, VI, before the Great War. RP cited "Mrs Nichol," as his next of kin, when he enlisted at Victoria on 18 March 1915, adding two years to his age in order to join the Forty-eighth Victoria Battalion. Once overseas, he transferred to the Twenty-ninth Vancouver Battalion. Wounded at Ypres and twice more elsewhere, he recovered in England and was posted to the officer's training wing of the RAF at Hastings and gazetted second lieutenant. After the war, he took employment in 1926 as a master at the Grammar School on Gibbins Road in Duncan, and John Palmer, who grew up at Duncan, writes, "I knew him from 1928-1936 as the Sports Master, and as our teacher in Latin, French and English, and from 1937-1938 as the Officer Commanding "A" Company of the Canadian Scottish Regiment in Duncan, my first Reserve Army Unit . . . I remember his having at least two medals from WW I." RP did, indeed, carry on with military service and in 1930 was promoted to major and CO of "A" Company, Second Battalion, Canadian Scottish. In July 1939, he was promoted to lieutenant colonel to replace Lieutenant Colonel Walter Bapty as CO of the Second Battalion. During the Second World War, RP commanded the First Battalion Canadian Scottish Regiment (Princess Mary's) and was a popular officer but was too old for front-line service and in 1943 returned to Canada to command the third infantry training battalion at Debert, NS. In 1945, he taught at Duncan again briefly but became senior master of Athlone Private School in Vancouver, where he lived with his wife Helen. When he died, aged sixty-two, on 9 February 1961 in Burnaby, a suburb of Vancouver, he also left several half-brothers and half-sisters, children his mother had with her second husband. Among them was Jack Nichol, at Courtenay. Pallbearers were old colleagues from Scottish Regiments in Vancouver.

Sources: NAC, CEF files, box 7593-7, regimental no. 430569; census 1901, England, RG 13/2949, p. 14; census 1881, RG 11/1357, pp. 39-40; census 1871, RG 10/24, p. 68; *Colonist*, 30 July 1939, p. 22; *Cowichan Leader*, 16 February 1961, obit.; notes courtesy of John Palmer, 20 Dec. 2001 and 15 January 2002.

Maj. W.R. McDonnell Parr in Tibet

Maj. W.R. McDonnell Parr buried in Saanich

PARR, Major William Randall McDonnell (1865-1938). Born on 7 May 1865 in Ulster, he was hired in 1887 for the Chinese Maritime Customs Service by its inspector general, Sir Robert Hart (1835-1911), whose London agent had recommended him as "a smart, intelligent, well set up and go-ahead young fellow." WP was posted at various Chinese cities but took leave from time to time for other activities. He assisted in the defence of the Foreign Settlement at Wuhu during the Yangtze Riots in 1891, was on special service with the Chinese forces during the China-Japan War 1894, commanded a Service Company of the Third Royal Irish Rifles, and in 1900-1902 was with the Eleventh Battalion of Mounted Infantry in the South African War. During those years, he became a field officer with the rank of captain, later major, and in 1903 was appointed Chinese joint commissioner with the Tibet Frontier Commission. Among his decorations for these services were Civil Rank of the Third Class, China; ICA of the Double Dragoons Second Division; the Queen's Medal for South Africa and four clasps; and the Tibet Frontier Commission Medal.

WP was posted in Tibet at Yatung, not far from Sikkim, in time to receive Colonel Francis Younghusband and his expedition in 1903-04 and to play a part in their relations with Tibetan and Chinese authorities on the road to Gyantse and later to Lhasa. He appears in at least seven of the photos taken on the expedition by Younghusband's photographer, Frederick Marshman Bailey, and John MacGregor describes him as an "enigmatic expatriate, who found himself in the difficult position of having to satisfy his Chinese employer without appearing disloyal to his own countrymen." He reported to Hart, who kept his London agent informed, for instance, in a wire on 5 May 1904: "A long telegram of 10th from Parr yesterday; they're in a tight place at Gyantse and the Tibetan blood is up; if they don't get some reinforcements and also ammunition and provisions speedily, it is quite on the cards we may have a terrible disaster. Four of his own servants were hacked to pieces while he was absent with the other wing; had he been there, he'd have received the same treatment or worse." And on 14 June, "If the Dalai Lama disappears, Younghusband will be in a dilemma! Parr must be having a wonderful time: adventure and danger and trickery all around."

Early in 1902, before leaving England, WP married Mollie, daughter of Rev. Canon Whitebell of Doone, County Limerick, and in 1903 at Yatung, she bore him a son, Randal Robert McDonnell Parr, the first British subject born in Tibet, according to Sir Robert Hart, who agreed to stand as his godfather. After another quarter of a century of service—and retirement, probably in Ulster—and three more children, the Parrs settled on the Saanich Peninsula near St Stephen's Anglican Church between Mount Newton and Brentwood Bay. WP visited alone at first in the early 1920s and then arrived at Halifax, Nova Scotia, with the family on 13 March 1927 aboard the White Star Dominion liner, *Regina*, and they made their way across the continent. They built a house they called "Kildoone," joined the Union Club in Victoria, and took part in community events, such as the Women's Auxiliary's garden fete for St Stephen's and St Mary's churches. In 1933, their daughter Sheelagh became engaged to Martin H. Ellis, eldest son of Rev. and Mrs H. M. Ellis of Comox. When WP died on 4 August 1938, he was buried in St Stephen's churchyard in a coffin draped with the Union Jack. Among the pallbearers was his Yatung-born son, who returned for the occasion from Shanghai, where he worked for Manufacturers Life Insurance Co. WP's will revealed assets, in addition to whatever came his way from the British Army and the Chinese Customs Service, of 132,441.00 Shanghai dollars invested mainly in rubber plantations and other Anglo-Dutch enterprise in Java, Malaya, and elsewhere in the East.

Sources: PRO; FO 917/ 3794 and 4026, WP's will and the probate process over it, details kindly sent by Dr Richard A. Smith, Curatorial Officer, Historical MSS Commission, Quality Court, Chancery Lane; *Colonist,* 28 March 1933, p. 9; 14 June 1934, p. 8; School of Oriental and African Studies (London), Rare Book Room, *Archives of China's Imperial Maritime Customs Confidential Correspondence Between Robert Hart and James Duncan Campbell 1874-1907,* (4 vols., Beijing, Foreign Languages Press, 1990), passim; Army List, 1906, October, part 2, pp. 87 and 1646; October 1907, part 2, p. 2221; Hart's Annual Army List, 1911, p. 1181; *Saanich Peninsula and Gulf Islands Review,* August 1938, p. 3; *Who's Who in B.C.* 1931, pp. 83-4; Charles Allen, *Duel in the Snows: The True Story of the Younghusband Mission to Lhasa* (John Murray, 2004), pp. 62-5, 166, 320; Peter Fleming, *Baynets to Lhasa: The First Full Account of the British Invasion of Tibet in 1904* (Rupert Hart-Davis, 1961, pp. 114-115, 162, 187; John MacGregor, Tibet: A Chronicle of Exploration (Routledge, 1970), pp. 303 and 325; Patrick French, *Younghusband: The Last Great Imperial Adventurer* (Flamingo, 1995), pp. 184-5, 189, 205, 237; Alastair Lamb, *Britain and Chinese Central Asia: The Road to Lhasa, 1767 to 1905* (Routledge and Kegan Paul, 1960), pp. 264-6, 268-9, 293; NAC, RG76-immigration, series C-1-b, 1927, vol. 3, p. 74, reel T-14808; Perceval Landon, *Lhasa, An Account of the Country and People of Central Tibet and the Progress of the Mission Sent There by the English Government in 1903-04* (2 vols., 1959); *Colonist,* 2 August 1938, p. 8; John MacGregor, *Tibet: A Chronicle of Exploration (Routledge, 1970), pp. 303 and 325; Perceval Landon, The Opening of Tibet: An Account of Lhasa and the Country and People of Central Tibet and of the Progress of the Mission Sent there by the English Government in the Year 1903-4* (New York, Doubleday, Page & Co., 1905), pp. 87, 413; Alastair Lamb, *The McMahon Line: A Study in the Relations Between India, China and Tibet,* 1904-1914 (2 vols.; Routledge and Kegan Paul, 1966), pp. 39-40; British Library, India Office Library, in the Younghusband Collection of Photographs, filed under Ms Eur F 157/457, there are six photos taken in Tibet, mainly by F. M. Bailey, with Younghusband's expedition, three or four of them with General Ma, etc., and mainly in 1904. They are numbers (66), (93), (189), (190), (191), (192), and (193).

PARSONS, Commissioner Thomas William S. (c. 1883-1960). Born at Old Charlton, Kent, he was eighteen in April 1901 and working as an "Auctioneer's Clerk," while living at 11 Rockbourne Road with his parents. His father, Thomas Parsons, a butcher, was born at Ramsgate and his mother, Lydia F. Parsons, at New Cross. They had a servant and a bookkeeper as a boarder. TP was already enrolled in the City of London Artillery, but went on to serve in the First Bedfordshire Regiment in 1899-1904 and the South African Constabulary in 1904-1909. He went to BC in 1912 and joined the BC Provincial Police. Stationed by degrees all over the province, he was a police superintendent by 1938 and police commissioner by 1939 living in Victoria. It was said that few men knew the province better than he. After thirty-five years of service, he retired to his home at 977 Foul Bay Road with his wife, Lucille, and took up volunteer work for young people. He worked as provincial commissioner of the Boy Scout Association and administrator of the Queen Alexandria Solarium. When he died, aged seventy-seven, on 13 July 1960, his funeral was held at an Anglican Church. He was survived by his wife and a son Richard (in New York).

Sources: *Colonist,* 14 July 1960, pp. 4 and 16, editorial and obit.; Lynne Stonier-Newman, *Policing a Pioneer Province: The B.C. Provincial Police,* 1858-1950 (Madeira Park, BC, Harbour Publishing, 1991), pp. 92, 118, 127, 182-3, 200-242; *Colonist,* 14 July 1960, pp. 4 and 16, editorial and obit.; census 1901, England, RG 13/560, p. 32.

PAYNE, Harold Digby (1871-1954). Born on 22 September 1871 in Bedford at "Blunham House," The Park, Blunham, a household of no fewer than twenty-one people, family and servants, he was the seventh son of Sir Salusberry Gillies Payne (1829-93), baronet and JP for Bedfordshire, and his wife Catherine Ann Chadwick (1837-1902), born at Prestwich, Lancashire. In 1887 HP left England, aged 16, for Australia on the wool-clipper, *Rodney,* and after two voyages transferred to the *Tamar,* where he was a shipmate of *George Bradley-Dyne, later to become his brother-in-law. In 1891, HP visited Saturna Island in the Gulf of Georgia, and he returned in 1894 to settle there at Saturna Beach, where he kept a store and post office. After several years there, he bought land at Winter Cove on Mayne Island and built a house. In 1896, he went with Warburton Pike and *Clive Phillipps-Wolley to start a trading post at Telegraph Creek, which had become a gold-mining centre. They carried their freight on a stern-wheeler across Queen Charlotte Sound and up the Stikine River and on from there by mules, which they had bought in Portland, Oregon. In 1900, HP returned to England in order to enlist in the Warwickshire Yeomanry and fight in the South African War. A few years after the war, he married Ruth Katinka Maude, eldest daughter of *Eustace Maude, late commander in the RN and Mrs Maude of Point Comfort, Mayne Island, and granddaughter of the late Sir George Maude, Crown Equerry. The marriage was conducted on 29 January 1907 at the tiny church of St Mary, Mayne Island, by HP's twin brother, Rev. Hubert St John Payne (1871-1963), rector of Esquimalt. When HP's wife died, aged twenty-eight, on 27 September 1914, he moved to North Saanich to be near his sister Katherine Janet "Polly" (1868-1954), who had married George Bradley-Dyne, an old friend from England who had bought a farm in Saanich from Dr J. S. Helmcken in 1906 and two years later acquired Pike's Saturna property. In 1918, HP moved to Victoria and from there to Sidney, where he died, aged eighty-two, on 22 July 1954.

Sources: PRO, CD version of the 1881 English census, RG/11, 1627, folio 62, page 19, for the Payne family at "Blunham House," The Park, Blunham, Bedford; *Colonist,* 1 February 1907, p. 11; Peter Murray, *Homesteads and Snug Harbours: The*

Gulf Islands (Victoria, Horsdal & Shubert, 1991), p. 50; *(A) Gulf Islands Patchwork: Some Early Events on the Islands of Galiano, Mayne, Saturna, North and South Pender* (1961) (9th printing, Gulf Islands Branch, BC Historical Federation, 1999), pp. 57-8; Dod's Peerage, *Baronetage and Knightage of Great Britain and Ireland for 1894* (fifty-fourth year), (1894), p. 618; *Colonist*, 1 February 1907, p. 11; a Payne family site online.

PEARKES, Major General George Randolph (1888-1984). He was born on 26 February 1888 at Watford, Hertforshire, where his father was a partner in a family department store, and he attended Berkhamsted School nearby. Like so many in his generation, a boyhood reading of such things as *The Boys Own Annual*, Rudyard Kipling's stories, and the historical novels of G. A. Henry had a strong effect on his outlook. Unable to find the funds for higher education in England, he followed the advice of his headmaster, who had at one time owned a farm near Red Deer, Alberta, and emigrated to Canada in 1906 aboard the SS *Hungarian*. He farmed in Alberta as a homesteader for awhile, then worked on a Dominion Land Survey Crew, and in 1913 joined the RCNWM Police from which he purchased a discharge in 1915 in order to go overseas in the army. His unit was the Second Canadian Mounted Rifles in which he remained for the next thirty years, rising in 1918 to the rank of lieutenant colonel and general officer, Pacific Command. He won the DSO, the MC, and for conspicuous bravery near Passchendaele, Belgium, on 30 October 1917, the Victoria Cross. In short, he had a brilliantly successful military career. When the Canadian government forced him to retire on 16 February 1946, it was because there seemed to be no job for an officer of his rank. He had already taken up a political career for which his experience and abilities were great assets on the Island at that time. In February 1945, he was elected Conservative MP for the Nanaimo riding, which at that time included the Saanich Peninsula as well as the Gulf Islands. Saanich was soon transferred to a riding called Esquimalt-Saanich, and GP was re-elected there in 1953, 1957, and 1958. On 12 October 1960, he was named lieutenant governor of BC, the first to be appointed from Saanich, and his term of office was twice extended.

He had strong connections with North Saanich. During the Great War, while he was overseas, his mother and his sister Hilda bought a dairy farm on Mills Road they called "Fairways" and lived there for many years. They attended Holy Trinity Anglican Church, only a short walk away, and it was there that GP met his wife, Blytha Copeman, whose parents had lived near the northern end of the peninsula since 1908. The marriage took place on 26 August 1925 at Esquimalt, while he was still in the army, but they were often in Saanich, where they both had many friends and he many political supporters. My mother, for instance, *née* Grace Simister (1903-1999), had known Blytha ever since they were in the same Anglican confirmation class together, and my parents admired and voted for GP along with other staunch supporters of church, monarchy, and empire.

In 1929, for a typical instance of the Pearkes family and their supporters, Mrs Pearkes was president of the Women's Auxiliary of St Andrew's (Sidney) and Holy Trinity (Patricia Bay) and read the WA's report at the annual vestry meeting held in January at St Augustine's Hall, Deep Cove. *Brigadier General R. J. Gwynne was re-elected rector's warden and delegate to the Synod along with such other veterans as Guy Frank Pownall (c. 1867-1939), a Londoner, and Alan Calvert (c. 1884-1964), a Freemason from Leeds; *Major A. H. Buck was appointed auditor and in the chair was the rector, *Rev. T. M. Hughes (who baptized me later that year), and some of the above were on the Church Committee together with Mrs Pearkes, Mrs General Gwynne and Miss Evelyn Gwynne, Mrs Lieutenant Colonel W. P. Belson (sister of Sirs Percy and Richard Lake), Mrs Pownall (sister-in-law of Rev. T. M. Hughes), and others. If I am not mistaken, they all came from the British Isles except J. J. White, who read the cemetery report. At the February meeting, Mrs Pearkes read her monthly report and the literary secretary, Mrs General Gwynne, "gave an interesting talk on India." When GP was appointed lieutenant-governor of the province he typically chose Captain Patricius Chaworth-Musters (1925-2010), who was born at Rawalpindi, India, as an A.D.C. Did Pearkes know that he had chosen a relative of *General Sir Arthur Currie's wife, Lady Lucy Sophia née Chaworth-Musters (1875-1969), a second cousin twice removed, who was born near Comox to an emigrant couple who had sailed out to escape family hostility?

GP's political career kept him away in Ottawa for long periods, sometimes with his wife, though their two children kept her near home. In March 1945, they bought a house on Tattersall Drive, Victoria, but having rented it while away in Ottawa were unable to evict the tenants upon their return and so bought another near Brentwood Bay. This was when the Diefenbaker Conservative government came to power in June 1957, and GP was serving as minister of national defence (21 June 1957 to 10 October 1960). It was at Brentwood that Mrs Pearkes lived while he was away on ministerial duty, though she was never far from her parents who managed a real-estate firm in Saanich and then at 1529 Fort Street, Victoria. In 1968, a hybrid tea rose was named "Madame Blytha Pearkes" in her honour. When GP died in 1984, he was buried in the churchyard at Holy Trinity, Patricia Bay.
Sources: R. H. Roy, *For Most Conspicuous Bravery: A Biography of Major-General George R. Pearkes, V.C., Through Two World Wars* (Vancouver, University of British Columbia Press, 1977), especially pp. 94-5, 242-4; *The Canadian Directory of Parliament, 1867-1967*, ed., J. K. Johnson (Ottawa, Public Archives of Canada, 1968), p. 458, where there is a brief summary of Pearkes's career to about 1967; Raymond Rodmond, "Heroes of British Columbia: Lieut.-Colonel Pearkes, V.C., D.S.O., M.C."; *Colonist*, 17 July 1940, p. 3; *The Sidney & Gulf Islands Review*, 28 February 1929, p. 1; Raymond Rodmond, "Heroes of British Columbia: Lieut.-Colonel Pearkes, V.C., D.S.O., M.C." in *Colonist*, 25 December 1921, p. 5; *Colonist*, 12 January 1929, p. 18.

PEASLAND, Lieutenant Albert George (c. 1890-1940). Born in Hong Kong, he was sent home to be schooled in England and Scotland and in 1912 joined the staff of the Hong Kong & Shanghai Banking Corporation in London. He fought in the Great War with the famous Territorial Regiment, the London Scottish, and on 15 September 1914, he was the first territorial soldier to set foot in France. He was wounded in the charge at Messines Bridge on 1 November 1914 but rejoined his regiment later and was promoted to lieutenant. He then joined the Twenty-first Squadron of the RAF and served in it to the end of the war. In 1920, he transferred to the Bank of Montreal and worked for it at various places in Canada. In the late 1930s, he was sent to Victoria, where he was well known as a member of the "Old Contemptibles" and lived with his wife, Williamina Christina Peasland, at 2644 Cavendish Avenue. There he died, aged fifty, on 3 November 1940, leaving her and a son and daughter. Mrs Peasland died, aged ninety, on 12 August 1981.

Sources: *Colonist*, 5 November 1940, p. 6, obit.

Lt.—Col. Cyrus Wesley Peck

PECK, Lieutenant Colonel Cyrus Wesley (1871-1956). He was born on 26 April 1871 at Hopewell Hill, New Brunswick, descendant of a family that had emigrated from England to Massachusetts in 1638 and moved to Nova Scotia as Loyalist "planters" in 1761, just as British forces were securing the entire territory of what had been New France. In 1887, he was one of five children who moved with their parents from New Brunswick to New Westminster, BC, where their father, Wesley Peck, was employed as a shipbuilder. CP worked with him at first, then travelled to the United States, worked on a farm in Kansas, took some business training, and went to England to enlist in the British Army fighting in the South African War (1902-1905). He was rejected for some reason and on returning to Canada went north to the Klondike and then pioneered in business in the Port Simpson and Prince Rupert areas of the Pacific Coast. He is listed twice at Prince Rupert in *Henderson's British Columbia Gazeteer* for 1910: "Peck, Cyrus W. of Peck, Moore & Co. and Secretary of the Georgetown Saw Mill Co. Ltd." and "Peck, Moore & Co., General Brokers, Real Estate and Insurance." Not long after that, in 1903, he and his cousin Donald M. Moore, together with four other shareholders, acquired the Cassiar Cannery on the north arm of the Skeena River's mouth. To this, they later added the Georgetown Sawmill, a towboat company, and an insurance brokerage at Prince Rupert. He was also active there in Freemasonry, the Board of Trade, and the militia.

It was through the militia that CP went to France in the Great War as a captain in the Sixteenth Battalion of the Canadian Scottish and served in the trenches for three and a half years, rising to lieutenant colonel, commanding officer, in 1916. A courageous and active leader, he was loved by his men and won the Victoria Cross on 2 September 1918 at the second battle of Arras "for most conspicuous bravery and skillful leading when in an attack under intense fire." In addition, at the battle of Vimy Ridge and others, he twice won the DSO and was mentioned in dispatches five times. In January 1923, he was elected president of the British Campaigners Association in Victoria, where it met at the Forester's Hall, Broad Street, and the *Daily Colonist* published a photo of him with a longish report.

About five years earlier, in 1917, while still overseas, CP had been elected a Union MP for Prince Rupert and Skeena, but had been defeated in the federal election of 1921. In 1924, however, he was elected to the Legislative Assembly of BC for "The Islands," which included Sidney. He was re-elected in 1928 but did not stand for election in 1933. He had strong backing in Sidney, where the annual meeting of the Liberal-Conservative Party in April 1925 gave him a vociferous vote of confidence and elected a supporting executive committee that included such prominent local people as John and Samuel Brethour and my great-grandfather, James Treadwell Readings, of the Bazan Bay Brickyard. It was Readings, indeed, who nominated CP again in July 1928 for an election in which he ran—and won—against the Liberal candidate, Alex McDonald. CP used to visit his constituents on the Gulf Islands in a small clinker-built boat with an outboard motor. On Mayne Island, he gave "an excellent address on the political situation" in mid-July 1928. At the beginning of 1931, he resigned from his seat in the Legislature in order to accept an appointment as western judge on the Federal Pensions Board. In 1936, he went to the Canadian Pension Commission, then served as ADC to two governors general of Canada, Lord Byng and Lord Tweedsmuir.

CP moved to Victoria in 1922 and thence to Sidney, where he worked with a local carpenter to build a house at the end of All Bay Road on what we knew as Peck's Point. There he and his wife, *née* Kate Elizabeth Chapman (1885-1988) [*sic*]—born at Canora to the publisher of a local newspaper who moved with his family to Prince Rupert, where she met and married CP on 11 March 1914—brought up three sons, Horace (born 1915), Edward (born 1924), and Douglas (born 1926). Better known locally as Joe, Ed, and Doug, the two youngest were at school in Sidney when I was there, though they were a few years older. In 1942-1945, CP, then a famous, gruff, old campaigner, was in command of the Pacific Coast Militia Rangers in which I practiced shooting and bushcraft with other local Boys Scouts under Freeman King and with local veterans, on a rifle range we built ourselves out near Horth's Cross Road, later known as Barrow's Range after *Francis John Barrow, our range officer. Some years later, CP died at Resthaven Hospital on 27 September 1956, aged eighty-five. He and his wife, who died aged 103 in 1988, had been active for more than thirty years in the parish of St Andrew's Anglican Church of which she was a member and in various ways in the Sidney district. CP and Sam Matson of the *Daily Colonist* helped to form the Gulf Islands Ferry Co. and the first ferry was named *Cy Peck* in his honour.

Under his gruff, taciturn exterior, CP was a thoughtful and generous person, public-spirited, fond of the Scottish pipes and pipers in the war, and known to the local Salish Indians as someone they could count on for help in hard times. Ed recalls that he learned to speak their language with some fluency and resorted to it at a military event in his Scottish regiment where others were speaking Gaelic; it was said that no one noticed the difference! On 4 May 1925, CP chaired a meeting of the North Saanich Women's Institute held to discuss plans for a war memorial to be built in the Memorial Park. Later, he had much to do with building the Sidney Post Office in 1936 and with making the marine park at the north end of Sidney Island and the lookout park on East Saanich Road near the Experimental Farm. He was fair-minded and empirical in his opinions. For example, on retiring from the BC Legislature, he said in his speech, "Some people sneer at politicians and hint at them being 'grafters'. Well, all I can say is that I have never seen it during my experience in any party. The political science is the most difficult and abstruse of all sciences and demands the best that is in a man." In a speech he gave on Mayne Island on 9 April 1929 (Vimy Day), he spoke out vigorously against the efforts of an organized group of people who were then trying to remove the history of the Great War from the public school curriculum. He was familiar with Keats, Shelley, Dickens, Thackeray, and other great writers. Ed remembers his father reading Dickens to his children and explaining, on other occasions, why he thought Napoleon and Oliver Cromwell were the world's greatest generals. Ed also has, as he said—"vivid memories of my father, of boating, camping and fishing among the Gulf Islands, of felling large trees, sawing logs and of tending to his many roses."

Sources: Notes, drafts, and conversations, courtesy of Edward Peck (a son); *The Sidney Review,* 12 and 19 June 1924 passim; 30 April 1925, p. 1; 22 July 1926, p. 1; 5 July 1928, p. 1; 12 July 1928, p. 1; 19 July 1928, p. 1; 21 February 1929, p. 2; *Colonist,* 26 September 1920, p. 15; 24 January 1923, p. 6; 17 April 1929, p. 9; 4 January 1931, pp. 1-2; H. M. Urquhart, *History of the 16th Battalion, Canadian Scottish,* passim; *The Canadian Directory of Parliament,* 1867-1967, ed., J. K. Johnson (Ottawa, Public Archives of Canada, 1968), p. 459; *Who's Who in B.C.,* 1942-1943, p. 251; Gladys Young Blyth, *Salmon Canneries, British Columbia North Coast* (Lantzville, BC, Oolichan Books, 1991), p. 130.

PEERS, Sapper Harry (1873-1952). He was born on 5 January 1873 at Pensnett near Kings Winford, Staffordshire, son of Hannah Marie Peers from London and William Peers, a "Park Ranger" born at Wolverhampton. The 1881 census found him, aged ten, living with his parents, two brothers, and three sisters at Sutton Park Lodge, Sutton Coldfield, Warwickshire (north-east of Birmingham). Ten years later, he was working as a "sawyer," still living with his family in Back Lane, King's Winford, where his father was now a "timber dealer," but by April 1901, he was a "foreman at timber yard," with a wife Elizabeth and with a four-year-old daughter, Guinevere Peers. He soon went to fight in the South African War in the South Staffordshire Volunteers and remained with them for eleven years, then in the South African Constabulary (two years), and finally the Staffordshire Imperial Yeomanry (four years). His South African medals had five bars.

Before 1915, they migrated to the Island, where HP was working as a carpenter when he enlisted in the Forty-seventh Battalion of the CEF at New Westminster on 21 April 1915, leaving Elizabeth on the Island at Cape Scott. For six months, he had been in the Canadian militia and his medical examination now was at Work Point, Esquimalt. Once overseas, he transferred to the First Canadian Pioneers and then to the Ninth Canadian Railway Troops. On 6 April 1918, he was sent home from the battle front and reached home late that month, as the *Cowichan Leader* reported; "home" was now at Cowichan Bay, but when he died, much later, aged eighty, on 29 March 1952, it was at Courtenay. There Elizabeth Peers had died, aged seventy-three, on 5 August 1947.

Sources: NAC, CEF files, box 7700-6; census 1881, England, RG 11/3050, pp. 48-9; census 1891, RG 12/2307, p. 10; census 1901, RG 13/2758, p. 19; *Cowichan Leader,* 30 May 1918.

PEMBERTON, Joseph Despard (1821-1893). Appointed colonial engineer and surveyor of Vancouver Island, he arrived in June 1851 and by January 1852, he and his assistant, Benjamin William Pearse (1832-1902), had surveyed the Victoria region, setting prices at £10 for city plots, £15 for suburban lots, and £1 per acre for land in the country. In spring 1854, he went home to England, renewed his HBC appointment for three years, and was back on the Island in time to lead expeditions to the wild west coast in 1856. He had induced his uncle, Augustus Frederick Pemberton (1809-1881) to emigrate, and this uncle was soon appointed commissioner of police for Victoria. Both men were born to a prominent Protestant family in Dublin, and between them, they laid the foundation for the leading Victoria family in the real-estate business and much else. In 1870, JP and one of his sons formed the firm of Pemberton & Son. Meanwhile, on 15 August 1861, the uncle had married Jane Augusta Brew, sister of the Island's chief of police, *Chartres Brew, children of an Anglo-Irish magistrate, Tomkins Brew. In 1864, JP married Theresa Jane Despard Grautoff (1843-1916), born in England to a German father. A total of at least nine children were born to these families, and they intermarried with other leading families.

Two examples—JP's daughter Sophia Theresa Pemberton (1869-1959), a well-known Victoria artist, was married on 11 September 1905 to *Rev. Canon Arthur John Beanlands, rector of Christ Church Cathedral, and after his death, she was married again on 7 January 1920, this time to Horace Deane-Drummond (1854-1930), an English coffee and rubber grower in Ceylon and later India. In the next generation, JP's granddaughter, Philippa Despard Pemberton (1897-?) was married on 12 October 1917 to *Major Henry Cuthbert Holmes, born at Bellary, India, who soon joined the family business, which then became the prominent firm of Pemberton-Holmes Real Estate.

Sources: Richard Mackie, JP in the *DCB*, vol. XII, pp.832-34; *Colonist*, 4 June 1921, p. 8; 11 June 1921, p. 8; *Fort Victoria Letters*, 1846-1851, ed., Hartwell Bowsfield (Winnipeg, Hudson's Bay Record Society, 1979), see index entry, pp. 270.

PENROSE, Frank Philip (1864-1943). Born at Kinsale, County Cork, Ireland, son of Rev. and Mrs Samuel Penrose-Westead, he was in Malaya for many years working as a civil engineer for the British government. After travelling widely, he migrated to Pittsburg, then Winnipeg, settling finally at St Mary's Lake, Salt Spring Island, where he lived for thirty years. He married in 1936 (Miss Florence Eagle of Victoria), and died, aged seventy-nine, on 14 November 1943.

Sources: *Colonist*, 18 November 1943, p. 3, obit.

PERCIVAL [Perceval?], Spencer (1864-1945). There is another problem in research on SP, beside the spelling of his name: When he died, aged eighty-one, on 19 August 1945 at Ganges, Salt Spring Island, the recording clerks in Victoria thought there had been a mistake and reversed his names, calling him "Perceval Spencer"! They knew of David Spencer's department store on Douglas Street but had apparently never heard of a Percival/Perceval family. SP may have been related to the only British prime minister ever to be assassinated, Spencer Perceval (1762-11 May 1812), son of the Second Earl of Egmont, but he only claimed to be a grandnephew of Rev. Peter Percival of Ceylon, an oriental scholar who translated the Bible into the Tamil language and old Tamil proverbs into English, and through him to Ascelin de Percival, a companion-in-arms of William the Conqueror, including in their pedigree the Emperor Charlemagne. SP was born in Manchester, and the 1871 census found him, aged six, living at 12 Cleveland Road, Crumpsall, Lancashire, with his father, Samuel Percival, a Manchester woollens merchant. His mother Medosa [Medora?] was born in Liverpool, and listed with them were SP's three brothers and three sisters.

There were no servants. The family was not destitute, however, for in 1900, SP married Annie Mary Lowe, a daughter of Henry Lowe of "The Moat House," Leek, and "Rauceby Old Hall," both in Lincolnshire, and also a niece of Dr John Lowe, physician extraordinary to HM, the late King Edward. They emigrated to Baldur, Manitoba, one of the prairie settlements to which immigrants were directed from Winnipeg.

Driven by the same instincts as many other British people, SP and his wife soon went out to Pender Island in the Gulf of Georgia and, in 1902, bought 160 acres at Port Washington from a Mr Washington Grimmer, including a house built in 1892, which they called "Sunny Side Ranch." There SP planted an orchard, grew fruits, and bred poultry, notably White Wyandottes of which he became a noted breeder, and was able to sell his stock as far away as Japan and Australia. About 1910, he built a general store close to the wharf at Port Washington and two years later became postmaster, carrying on until 1921, when he sold out to J. B. Bridge. Two years later, his niece, Florence Percival, married a Mr Bridge, and they kept the store until 1956, when they sold it to Mr W. Cunliffe. Long before that, SP had become active in community life, helped to build the community hall in 1912, and donated an acre of land for St Peter's Anglican Church. In the middle 1920s, *Major Lukin Johnston called on SP and found him painting a boat. "Every poultryman in British Columbia is familiar with his name," Johnston wrote, "for he made a reputation as a White Wyandotte man and, furthermore, as a fruit-grower on a small scale. Twenty-four years he has been on Pender Island, and his house, surrounded by fruit trees in full blossom, was a sight to gladden wearied eyes. 'The finest pears in the world are grown here, sir—without exception'—these were Spencer Percival's last words to me." SP went on farming well enough to win first prize in September 1931 for his Golden Russett and delicious apples and prizes for his grapes, at the thirty-fourth annual exhibition of the Island's Agricultural and Fruit Growers' Association held at Ganges, Salt Spring Island (a short ferry ride away). His sister, Medora Ann (Percival) Wiley, who had been on Pender Island for thirty years, died on 26 January 1930, leaving her husband, a brother, and three daughters. In 1939, he sold "Sunny Side Ranch" to a Mr William Brown from Calgary and retired to another property he called "Sunny Nook," where he laid out another lovely garden and an orchard.

An educated man, SP had time enough to follow world affairs and wrote frequent letters to the *Victoria Daily Colonist*, which reveal an Imperial cast of mind, hostility to pacifists ("human ostriches!"), a dislike of the Labour government in England, and strong views on many subjects. Most references listed below in the **Sources** are to his letters to the editor. From 1899, he had Percival relatives living in the foothills of the Rocky Mountains at "Two Dot Ranch" in the Nanton district of Alberta, the tenth and eleventh earls of Egmont, as described in the *National Post* in December 2001, long after SP had died in 1945 and his wife, aged seventy-three, on 20 September 1934 at Port Washington.

Sources: census 1871, England, RG 10/4063, pp. 24-25; *Who's Who in B.C.*, 1933-1934, p. 137; *the Daily Colonist*, 1 February 1933, p. 5; *A Gulf Islands Patchwork*, pp. 100-101; *Colonist*, 27 July 1917, p. 4; 13 November 1929, p. 4; 12 September

1931, p. 18; 31 January 1934, p. 4; 21 September 1934, p. 16: obit.; 8 October 1940, p. 4; Major Lukin Johnston (1888-1933), *Beyond the Rockies: Three Thousand Miles by Trail and Canoe with 52 illustrations and a map* (J. M. Dent, 1929), p. 12; *Colonist,* 21 November 1940, p. 4; 19 January 1941, p. 4; 11 May 1941, p. 4; *National Post* (Ottawa), 12 December 2001, p. A9, with photo.

PETCH, Alfred (1860-1923). Here is an enterprising watchmaker from Wales whose life illustrates the Island's place in the social progress of a family of domestic servants. He lived with his wife and family in Victoria as a watchmaker/jeweller for about thirteen years early in the twentieth century, returned to Wales at least once, but died in Victoria on 1 June 1923. Five of his seven sons, born variously in Wales and Derbyshire, served in the CEF during the Great War and most of them settled on or near the Island and died there. Robert Alfred Petch settled at Turgoose on the Saanich Peninsula.

AP's father, Robert Petch, born at Culford, Suffolk, about 1821 was a domestic coachman who appears, aged thirty-one, in census records for 1851 as a "helper" in the stables of the Second Earl of Eldon at Shirley House, Croydon, near Greenwich and just west of Blackheath. As such, Robert Petch was the lowest of three servants of Eldon's "Coachman Dwelling at the Stables" and the coachman's family: Thus above AP's father was a groom and a coachman—coachman to the earl's coachman! Their names were all listed after the earl, his family, and their fourteen domestic servants living in Shirley House. Incidentally, the earl, John Scott, Second Earl of Eldon (1805-1854), MP for Truro, had married Hon. Louisa Duncombe, who gave birth to six daughters before producing the son needed to inherit the earldom, and the census-taker found them all at home in 1851. When, two years later, the earl went mad and soon died, Robert Petch found employment as coachman to Archdeacon Hugh Chambers Jones (c. 1783-1869), who was living with his sister in North Wales at Brynsteddfod, Llansantffraid, Glan Conwy, Denbighshire, with nine domestic servants and a coachman, Robert Petch, who lived at the lodge with his family. AP appears in the 1861 census, aged eleven months, recently born in that place, with a sister and two elder brothers. The sister, Marie, was born at Watford, Hertfordshire, while her mother (AP's mother also) *née* Mary Ann Dolamore was visiting her parents there. Ten years later, the archdeacon having died, his sister was "Landed Proprietor" of the Brynsteddfod estate, Robert Petch was still coachman there, one son had become a "joiner," and AP was a schoolboy aged ten. But in 1881, AP appears, aged twenty, as an unmarried watchmaker boarding with several other tradesmen in Church Street at Festiniog, Merionethshire, and in 1891, he was a married "watch & clock maker" established at 33 Castle Street, Conway, Carnarvonshire.

He had married Annie on 1 December 1880 in Salford, Lancashire, near her home in Liverpool, which is only a few miles east of AP's birthplace at the base of the Llandudno peninsula in North Wales. In 1891, they already had five sons, two of whom born at Tibshelf, Derbyshire, where the family had evidently spent two or three years, and in 1901, there were seven sons at home, which was now at 25 Iron Square in Bangor, Carnarvonshire. A year or two later, the family migrated to

the Island, where AP went into business as a watchmaker. When he and Annie and their two youngest children made a voyage home to Wales, landing at Liverpool on 14 December 1912 on a White Star Liner, the *Celtic*, and returning to Quebec on 18 July 1913, he declared that they had lived in Canada for thirteen years. Only a year later, the Great War engaged five of the Petch sons in the Canadian Army. Two of them, Robert Alfred Petch and George Meredith Petch, returned from overseas aboard the *Olympic*, reaching Halifax, Nova Scotia, on 8 July 1919, about four years before AP's death. Thereafter, the sons settled on the Island or in Vancouver City. They had, at last, a sister Violet Petch, born in 1906.
Sources: Census 1851, 107 / 1601 / 526 /2 at Croydon; census 1861, RG 9 /4358 / 189, p. 81; census 1871, RG 10 / 5738, p. 12; census 1881, RG 11 / 5551 / 51, p. 95; census 1891, RG 12 / 4670 / 6, p. 5; CEF files, box 7755-16 (George Meredith Petch); box 7755-19 (Robert Alfred Petch).

PETTER, James Henry Branscombe (1871-1943). Born at Yeovil, Somerset, on 8 June 1871, he was the elder of two brothers who went out to the Pacific Northwest to promote the Petter diesel engine, which they had developed with a third brother, Percy W. Petter, who remained at the firm's headquarters in England. They appear among the eight children of James Branscombe Petter (c. 1846-?), an "Ironmonger (Master)" from Barnstaple, Devon, recorded in the 1871 and 1881 censuses, living at 15 High Street, Yeovil, with their wife and mother, Charlotte, born in Bristol. Sometimes, they lived at "The Park," near Yeovil. In due time, their no-nonsense father apprenticed them to the iron business, wherein they grew into informal mechanical engineers. Perhaps the leader of the three—certainly the most successful—was Sir Ernest Willoughby Petter (1873-1954), a member of the Institute of Mechanical Engineers who, in 1894, with his twin brother, Percy Willoughby Petter, built the Petter Horseless Carriage, claiming it to be the first British car with an internal combustion engine (a diesel). Petter Engineering also built two electric cars and in 1915 the first British seaplane to take part in a naval battle, the Battle of Jutland (31 May 1916), when it was attached to the battleship *Lion*. Sir Ernest was politically and vocally active in the Conservative cause and wrote many letters to *The Times*. In 1925, George V knighted Sir Ernest Willoughby Petter, who retired the next year and, shortly before the Second World War, went out to make his home on the Island. He bought McCutcheon's Point near Comox, where in 1938, he built a great stone-trimmed manor house he called "The Fort" overlooking the waterfront. Of a benevolent patriotic disposition, he soon welcomed fourteen children who had been sent out to avoid the London blitz and employed seven servants and an English nanny to care for them and the house. He also bought and sold real estate and built several houses in Comox.

Meanwhile, JP went over to assist him, having been in Vancouver City since 1920 in connection with the business of Petter Engineering. There are signs of uneasy relations between them but in any event, JP soon established a home, a few miles south in the Cowichan Valley on the corner of Lakes Road and Townend Road. SP had founded the Vancouver branch of the British-Israel Federation (Canada) Inc., and the Cowichan branch elected him president soon after his arrival. He died there, aged seventy-one, on 8 January 1943 after only a few years of residence, leaving his wife and four daughters by an earlier marriage, all themselves married and living at various places on the coast, except for one who died in an aircraft crash somewhere in the BC interior. After a funeral in Vancouver, JP was buried in Capilano Cemetery. His brother Sir Ernest returned to England after the war and died on 18 July 1954 at his home at New Milton, Hampshire.

Sources: *Colonist*, 25 June 1939, p. 3; *Cowichan Leader*, 14 January 1943, obit.; 18 February 1943, p. 6; 15 June 1945, p. 8; census, 1881, England, RG 11/2392, p. 3; census, 1891, RG 12/1898, p. 30; census, 1901, RG 13/1243, p. 3; *Who was Who*, IV (1951-1960), p. 869; *The Times* (London), 19 July 1954, page 10, obit.; *Land of Plenty: A History of the Comox District*, ed., D. E. Isenor, W. N. McInnis, E. G. Stephens, D. E. Watson (Campbell River, Ptarmigan Press, 1987), pp. 162-3.

PHETHEAN, Mrs Evelyn (1886-1964). She was born at East Sheen, Surrey, fourth daughter of Sir Montagu Frederick Ommanney, GCMG, KCB, ISO (1842-1925), permanent under-secretary of state for the colonies in 1900-1907, who had her educated at Bournemouth and Folkstone. During the years 1899-1908, she lived in London, then until 1913 in Finchamstead, Berkshire. The Ommanneys were a considerable family of officials, public figures, professionals, and engineers. For some reason yet to be discovered, however, EP migrated to Winnipeg and in 1915 married John Phethean, a rancher. Were they among the romantic refugees on the Island, like Alfred Denis Faber and his lady, or the Chaworth Musters family, whose daughter married *Sir Arthur Currie? In 1920, the Phetheans retired from Manitoba to Victoria, where they lived in Oak Bay at 1258 St David Street. EP was public-spirited, like so many of her kind, and soon became a member of the Senior Women's Auxiliary to the Royal Jubilee Hospital, its convenor of collections in 1929, and in 1933 was elected president. Meanwhile, she was active in the IODE and the St John's Guild, playing tennis as a recreation and attending the Anglican Church. Her husband died, aged seventy-one, on 18 October 1955, and she, aged seventy-seven, on 29 October 1964, both in Oak Bay.

Sources: *Who's Who in B.C.*, 1933-1934, p. 139; census 1881, England, RG 11/847; census, 1901, RG 13/19, p. 5; Pritchard, *Letters of Edmund Hope Verney*, p. 271 n.3; John A. Whittaker, ed., *Early Land Surveyors of British Columbia* (P.L.S. Group) (Victoria, Corporation of B.C. Land Surveyors, 1990), pp. 50-52 (Faber's story).

PHILLIPPS-WOLLEY, Captain Sir [Edward] Clive Oldnall Long (1853-1918). He was born on 3 April 1853 at Wimborne, Dorset, son of Richard Augustus Long Phillipps, who was born in India, and grandson of a soldier who died fighting in India. CP's father was master of the public school at Wimborne and before moving there with his wife Anne (*née* Redfern) had been headmaster at the Grammar School in Rotherham, Yorkshire. CP attended Rossall School in Lancashire, where he was good at boxing, and was appointed, aged twenty, as vice consul at the British legation in Kerch [Kertch], on the Crimean Peninsula of southern Russia. This posting was probably arranged by his father, who had influential friends and had become a member of the Royal Geographical Society. In 1877, CP succeeded to the two-hundred-acre estate of a family of vintners, the Wolleys, and added their name to his own. He also dropped his first name, Edward, and began to use his second name, Clive. Resigning from the consular service, he may have spent some time in the house on the estate, "Woodall," in Hanwood near Shrewsbury, and in 1879, he married Janie, born on 31 August 1865 at Clifton, Gloucestershire, daughter of Rear Admiral William Henry Fenwick (c. 1827-?) of Woodborough, Nottinghamshire, and his wife Jane. [Fenwick served in retirement, while living in Kensington, as "Inspector of Prisons."] However, the 1881 census found CP and his wife established at "Morgan Hall," Fairford, Gloucestershire, where a decade later the artist Sargent painted as a guest of some friends from the United States. CP was recorded as a "Landowner Student Barrister," and they had a daughter, Janie A. M. Phillipps-Wolley, aged eight months, and five servants: nurse, housemaid, parlourmaid, groom, and cook. He is said to have joined the fourth battalion of the South Wales Borderers, taught musketry, and risen to the rank of captain. Several books he published in the 1880s show much time writing about his stay in the Crimea, the Caucasus, and elsewhere in southern Russia.

In 1882, he spent two months, hunting in British Columbia, and wrote of it in *Trottings of a Tenderfoot: A Visit to the Columbian Fiords, and Spitzbergen* (1884). In this book, he wrote, "I came across no place in America in which I would be so content to stay as in Victoria." During autumn 1887, he took his wife Janie with him on another visit, stopping at various places in Canada and lingering in Victoria. The book, which followed in 1888, *A Sportsman's Eden*, was in the form of twenty letters home, and the seventeenth, ostensibly written by Janie, is full of praise for Victoria. She concludes (p. 190), "If only my husband would give up the world and all its pomps and vanities, I would be only too glad to live out the rest of my life in this land of sunshine and sea-breeze, doing all I could to tempt my friends at home to come and share my happy lot." As Canadian census records show, they and their children arrived to settle permanently in 1891 and had *William Ridgeway Wilson build them a house in Oak Bay on Clive Drive, which may have been named in CP's memory. They called this house "Woodall," and CP went on writing when he was there. But he was a restless man, travelled about a good deal, and spent enough time in the mainland interior of the province to buy the *Nelson Miner* and write for it, too. On 14 October 1901, he bought Piers Island, between Salt Spring Island and the north end of the Saanich Peninsula, moved into a handsome estate he built on it, but sold the island again on 24 September 1909 to *Lieutenant Colonel J. S. Harvey. After another spell in Victoria, they went up to Somenos in the Cowichan Valley, where they lived at "The Grange," not far from Duncan.

These property transactions and CP's industrious writing smack of a gentleman anxious to supplement his income, but he certainly had other motives as well. Observing the growing menace of imperial Germany, he took up the cause of naval defence, particularly for the Pacific coast, became a local leader of the Navy League, which had been founded in Toronto in 1895, and toured Ontario in 1909 or 1910 to promote support for a Canadian navy. His loyalty, however, was with the Royal Navy which, to his great regret, turned Esquimalt over to

Canada about that time. In November 1910, back in Victoria, he sent the text of the speeches he had made on his Ontario tour to Toronto for publication at his own expense, and they show his strong Christian and Imperial loyalties. What may seem to some like the splutterings of a "blimp" expressed well the realism of his kind: "Human beings are still predatory. Only the strong can command peace." He went into politics apparently with the intention of supporting the Imperial cause, criticized W. E. Gladstone and other liberals for their anti-Imperial views, and was elected third vice-president of the Cowichan Conservative Association on 17 April 1914. His verse in books and journals was intensely patriotic and expressed the feeling of Imperial loyalty which impelled him to work for the Navy League and for which he was knighted in 1914. In *Is Canada Loyal?* for instance, he wrote such lines as,

> Have we seemed to forget? Here where our furthermost fleet
> Rides on the selfsame wave that rolls to the Russian's fleet,
> Named in the name of the Queen is the town where our Parliaments meet.

> God! how we love you still! Do you think in the hours of gloom
> There comes no whisper of home? Look where our dead find room!
> Are those *native* flowers you find, heather and rose and broom?
> War? We would rather peace; but, mother, if fight you must,
> There be none of your sons on whom you can lean with a surer trust;
> Bone of your bone are we, and in death would be dust of your dust.

In the *Colonist*, he wrote an intensely patriotic response to an article in the *London Chronicle*, "Essau's Dream of Home," in which Harold Begbie (1871-1929), a fellow versifier in England, told of the loyalty to Edward VII he had witnessed during a visit to Victoria in summer 1907. When CP's son was killed in the Great War, he published a second edition of his *Songs of an English Esau* with some of his later poems first printed in the *Spectator*, the *Navy*, and—"my old friend *The Week* and other local papers to which I tender my thanks . . ." It was dedicated to the memory of his son, Lieutenant Commander Clive Phillipps-Wolley, RN, "and those others from Canada, who like him have given their lives for their country in this war, this volume is humbly dedicated by one who when the war came was found to be too old and too crippled to be of any use in the only place where a man should be."

One of his purposes was to attract English people of his own kind to the Island. He wrote continuously—articles, essays, pamphlets, and books—to encourage emigration, including a series of pieces in the London *Mining Journal.* When, in 1893, he returned from a visit home to England, he felt he had convinced at least fifty people to emigrate. Probably a case in point is the emigration of John Speir Robinson (1877-1959), who married his daughter, Judith Gladys Phillipps-Wolley, at Cowichan on 1 October 1910. Born on the handsome "Lynhales" estate at Lyonshall, Herefordshire [now an old-age home], where his father Stephen Robinson was "J.P. & G.L. for County of Hereford," Robinson was still in England in April 1901 visiting Edward Dubois Phillips, a retired "Naval Staff Commander, R.N.," and his son Bertram. When Robinson later settled at Cobble Hill as CP's son-in-law, Bertram Dubois Phillips (c. 1876-1934), established himself in Vancouver in the marine insurance business and ultimately died there. Both were attracted by CP, though perhaps leaving England was all the easier for Bertram because he was born in Jamaica during his father's naval service there. And was another of CP's emigrants Joseph Reade (c. 1862-1938), a barrister born at Shipton-under-Wychwood, Oxfordshire, who married CP's daughter Janie A. Phillipps-Wolley (1880-1941) on 29 August 1903 in Victoria, and who died at Duncan on 12 August 1938? He was no relation of *Frederick Murray Reade or any other of the several Reades on the Island, mostly descendants of the famous Victorian novelist Charles Reade (1814-1884).

When CP died, aged sixty-seven, on 8 July 1918 at Somenos, he was of course buried at St Peter's Quamichan, where his pallbearers included *J. H. Whittamore, L. A. Coles *Dr H. T. Rutherford, C. F. Walter, S. M. Land, and a Bradley-Dyne. CP's wife Janie died, aged fifty-eight, on 29 April 1921 in Victoria, and their daughter Janie A. M. Reade died, aged sixty-one, on 8 November 1941 in Duncan, recorded as "Maude Reade."

Sources: census 1881, England, RG 11/2557; census 1881, RG 11/2920, p. 15; census 1891, RG 12/2077, p. 3; census 1901, RG 13/3446, p. 2; Canadian census, Victoria; *Colonist*, 23 March 1893, p. 3; 19 April 1914, p. 3; *Colonist*, 10 June 1917, p. 19; 11 July 1918, p. 8; Peter Murray, *Home from the Hill* (Victoria, Horsdal & Schubert, 1994), pp. 78-133; Harold A. Skolrood, *Piers Island: A Brief History of the Island and its People*, 1886-1993 (Lethbridge, Alta, Author, 1995), pp. 7, 11-13; Ron Baird *Success Story: The History of Oak Bay* (Victoria, Daniel Heffernan & James Borsman, 1979), p. 164; T. W. Paterson, "Welcome Mat's Out for Heritage Buffs," *Cowichan Valley Citizen* 7 May 2003, p. 18; Clive Phillipps-Wolley, *Sport in the Crimea and Caucasus* (1881); CP, *Savage Swanetia* (2 vols., 1883), about a remote corner of southern Georgia, not far from Kertch; CP, *Trottings of a Tenderfoot: A Visit to the Columbian Fiords, and Spitzbergen* (1884); CP, *A Sportsman's Eden* (Richard Bentley & Son, 1888), 261 pp.; CP, *Songs of an English Esau* (Toronto, George N. Morang & Co. Ltd., 1902), 133 pp. in 12_, printed by Spottiswoode & Co. Ltd., New-Street Square, London; CP, *Songs from a Young Man's Land* (Toronto, Thomas Allen, 1917), 160 pp. in 12_; CP, *The Canadian Naval Question: Addresses Delivered by Clive Phillipps-Wolley, F.R.G.S., Vice-President Navy League* (Toronto, William Briggs, 1911), 70 pp., see pp. 26 and 32; census England, 1861, RG 9/4503, p. 123 (Fenwick); census 1881, RG 11/49, p. 26 (Fenwick); census 1891, RG 12/33, p. 40 (Fenwick); census 1901, England, RG 13/19, p. 12 (Fenwick).

PHILLIPS, George (1868-1941). Born in London on 21 (23?) March 1868, son of Captain and Mrs John Phillips, he joined the Admiralty Works Department at eighteen and was sent in 1894 to represent the Admiralty at Esquimalt. There he began as second officer in the Department of Architectural and Engineering Works. The 1901 Victoria census found him living in Esquimalt as "Government Clerk." There, on 16 December 1903, he married Laura Ashton Devlin and continued his work, was promoted to Admiralty agent in 1905 upon the departure of C. H.

S. Harris, and managed the dockyard for the Admiralty until 9 November 1910. It was then turned over to the new Naval Service of Canada, which invited him to stay on in their employ as dockyard superintendent. As Admiralty agent, he had moved into the big square brick house (built in 1885) in the dockyard until it was taken over by the Dominion authorities in 1910. When he transferred to the Dominion Service and stayed on as civil manager of the dockyard, he remained in the house with his family until 1917, when they went temporarily to Halifax. He was needed to train new staff as well as to run the dockyard, and in an age when there was no such thing as Canadian nationality, he had only to stay on. No political pressure in Ottawa of the kind that had interfered with the lighthouse service was allowed to displace GP or interrupt his work. In an equivalent process, various RN officers, such as *Walter Hose, stayed on to direct and train the Canadian Navy. It was therefore little more than a formality when Commander Gerald W. Vivian, RN, commanding the sloop-of-war *Shearwater*, whose title was "Commander-in-charge for Station Duties on the West Coast of America," transferred the dockyard to Deputy Minister S. J. Desbarats, who had come from Ottawa for the purpose. Early in the Great War, GP had much to do with arranging for Richard McBride's government at Victoria to purchase two submarines from Seattle and to fit out the hospital ship, *Prince Rupert*, based on Esquimalt. He also helped to fit out the Stefansson expedition to the Arctic in 1918, and Stefansson named Phillips Strait after him. By serving as the civil admiralty officer in the establishment at Esquimalt from 1894 to 1917, he became the longest-serving officer in that post, longer than J. H. Innes (20 January 1873 to 16 July 1894), W. H. Lobb (16 July 1894 to 16 July 1900), H. S. Simmins (16 July 1900 to 25 July 1901), or C. H. S. Harris (25 July 1901 to 1905). In 1918, GP transferred to Halifax, spent five years there and in Ottawa, but returned to Esquimalt in 1923 and retired in 1933.

GP was also active in Victoria's musical life, having been a member of the Royal Choral Society of London in his youth, and he was a charter member (and president for years) of the Victoria's Arion Male Voice Choir and one of the founders (and the secretary-treasurer) of the Victoria Choral and Orchestral Union. He took part in many musical and theatrical events locally and in Halifax. A life member of the Engineering Institute of Canada, he became secretary of the Naval Veterans' Branch of the Canadian Legion after his retirement in 1933. A genial and notable raconteur, he worked to have the Victoria Choral and Orchestral Union's annual performance of Handel's *Messiah* freely open to the public and this was decided shortly before he died, aged seventy-three, on 4 November 1941 and was buried four days later at the Naval Cemetery at Esquimalt. He was survived by his widow, Laura, and two daughters at home, 430 St Patrick Street, and also by a sister in England. It was one of his daughters, "Betty Greenhouse, 430 St Patrick Street," who signed his death certificate. She had married *Major F. S. Greenhouse in August 1938 at the Garrison Church, Esquimalt, at a time when GP and his family lived in Oak Bay. These daughters, Ruth Elizabeth "Betty" and Joy Phillips, had both been christened at St Paul's Naval and Garrison Church, Esquimalt, and grown up in the maritime community of Esquimalt; they later recalled how their mother's hospitality had made the house almost like an informal naval club for lonely young officers and men: "Captain House of H.M.C.S. *Rainbow* was like a second father to us." Occasionally, the two girls accompanied their parents to Comox, where the navy had rifle and artillery ranges, and during the Great War, Joy Phillips worked at the dockyard on the signal bridge and later as coder and decoder.

Sources: BC Vital Statistics, Death Certificate; *Colonist*, 5 November 1941, p. 11, obit.; Miss Joy Phillips, "'We had the Run of the Dockyard,'" in Duffus, *Beyond the Blue Bridge*, pp. 82-5; Longstaff, *Esquimalt Naval Base*, pp. 69-71, 82, note 7.

PHILLIPS, Leonard Legge (1885-1956). A Londoner who farmed and tried various occupations in Calgary, at San Francisco, and on the Island, he eventually ran the Ben Bow Inn at Qualicum Beach for the rest of his life. He was born at Enfield, London, on 5 July 1885, a son of John Samuel Phillips and his wife Mary Adelaide. The father and paternal grandfather were both "law stationers" in the St Pancras quarter of London, later in Hampstead, both named John, as appears in census records from 1851 to 1891. In 1851, for instance, aged twenty-one and fifty-two, they were "law stationers . . . employing twenty men." LP attended Frampton Court Preparatory School and Dulwich College, but then migrated in 1906 to Calgary, Alberta, and tried farming. In 1911-1916, he worked there in the insurance and real-estate firm of Lott & Co. but moved to the Island in 1906.

Still unsettled in his employment, he tried poultry farming near Victoria and escaped from that by going overseas with the Canadian Expeditionary Force in August 1917. After the war, he worked for about three years in San Francisco for the accounting division of the Owl Drug Company, but then returned to the Island and in 1937 bought the Ben Bow Inn at Qualicum Beach, where he played golf and gardened with his wife. He had married her on 16 February 1911 at Immanuel Church, Streatham Common (London), during a visit home. She was Margery Grace Walker (1888-1956), daughter of Henry Bird Walker (1848-?), and was said to be a great-granddaughter of the Duke of Wellington, though this relationship might be difficult to trace. One wonders about LP's relations with *General Noel Money and his wife Maud, who kept the much-grander Qualicum Beach Hotel at Qualicum. LP claimed to be a Freeman of the city of London, a Freemason, and in Victoria a member of the Public Schools Club and the United No. 12 Army & Navy Veterans' Club. They both died in 1956, she, aged seventy-eight, on 4 August and he, aged seventy, on 8 November.

Sources: CEF files, box 7799-13, regimental no. 525369; census 1851, England, HO 107/14988/48-49; census 1861, RG 9/91, p. 36; census 1871, RG 10/190/ 65, p. 1; census 1881, RG 11/168/80, p. 8; census 1891, RG 12/107/154, p. 17; census 1891, RG 12/614, p. 14 (Walker); *Who's Who in B.C.*, 1942-43, p. 255.

PHILP, Captain Francis Edward Lamb (c. 1877-1949). Born at Salperton Park, Gloucester, he was living at "Pondogget House" at Timsbury near Clutton, Gloucestershire, in 1881 when he was three years old and his sister Gertrude M. Philp was five. They were apparently alone with four servants: a nurse, cook, housemaid, and coachman, and no sign of parents. In due time, FP attended Emmanuel College, Cambridge, and then joined the British Army. He served in the South African War

and was promoted to captain on 7 July 1917 during the Great War. At sometime in 1924, he retired to Victoria. There he lived at 1422 Newport Avenue, Oak Bay, with his wife Faith, and they attended St Mary's Anglican Church. After twenty-five years, he died at home, aged seventy-two, on 30 September 1949.
Sources: Army List; *Colonist*, 2 October 1949, p. 23, obit.; census 1881, England, RG 11/2427, p. 9.

PHILPOT, Lieutenant Frederick William (1866-1931). He was born on 3 March 1866, probably in Hampshire somewhere near Bishop Waltham, birthplace of his mother Catherine A. Philpot, or at Woolston or Barleston, where three of his sisters were born. The 1881 census found the family living at 6 Maple Park Road, Folkestone, where his father, Frederick Philpot, aged forty-seven, born at Peckham, Surrey, was a "Captain of Orderlies Army Hospital Corps (Active)," but registered by later censuses as "Army Major ret'd." There were two servants. FP and his elder brother were away at school or otherwise busy in the world. FP attended Cranbrook and St John's College, Cambridge, and went on to five years of medical training in London hospitals. This he either detested or failed at—or perhaps ran out of funds—as he went abroad in search of adventure without finishing his medical course. In the years that followed, he went to Canada, New Zealand, Australia, South Africa, and India, whence he sailed to Cape Colony when the South African War began and served in the Cape Police, the Matabele Relief Force, and Beeton's Mounted Infantry and later joined the SA Light Horse under Colonel (later General) Lord Byng. He then gained a commission in the Imperial Yeomanry. "He took part in many of the principal engagements," the *Colonist* reported at his death, "and one of his most prized possessions was the S.A. medal with five bars." After the war, FP worked in the Transvaal in the Mines Department and, in 1903, married Miss Ella Rose Campbell-McEwan of "Bellewan," Pietermaritzburg, Natal. They had three children in South Africa and a fourth later in Canada.

The family migrated to Canada in 1908 and settled at Stony Plain, west of Edmonton, where they farmed until 1917 and then moved to New Zealand, where they lived near Aukland for four years. This suited them even less and so they returned to Alberta, homesteaded north of Edmonton, near the Athabaska River on the Edmonton-Whitecourt line, but in 1926 moved to the Cowichan Valley. There they lived at Somenos but moved later to Duncan and settled probably on the Maple Bay Road. "A true patriot and Empire builder was Mr Frederick William Philpot," the *Cowichan Leader* remarked at his death later. "[His] military figure was very familiar in Duncan and Somenos during the closing years of his life." On 23 May 1931, the *Daily Colonist* printed a long letter to the editor about Britain in India: "As an old soldier and student of war, the question which interests me mostly is, can Britain evacuate India without fighting a big war . . . ? Two centuries of warfare in the East have taught us that it is far easier to advance than to retreat; that it is easier to get into a country than to get out of it . . . Meanwhile, lying tongues in the bazaars are doing their work effectively, and daily the prestige of the white man is seeping away, 'til the end is armed rebellion." When he died, aged sixty-five, on 31 October 1931, he was buried at

St Peter's Quamichan, a Union Jack on the casket, and among the pallbearers were *Colonel Sheridan Rice, *Colonel B. A. Rice, *Major H. A. H. Rice, and Mr Harrison Piele representing the Canadian Legion to which FP had belonged. He left his wife, a daughter Jean, and three sons at home: Fred, Roy, and Guy. His three sisters were still living in Folkestone.

Sources: *Cowichan Leader,* 5 November 1931, p. 5, obit.; *Colonist,* 23 May 1931, p. 4; census 1881, England, RG11/1010; census 1891, RG 12/771, p. 11; census 1901, RG 13/871, p. 10.

PHIPPS, Major Charles Edmund (1844-1906). Born on 11 June 1844 in London at St George's Hanover Square, he was a son of Margaret A. Phipps (*née* Bathurst) and Sir Charles B. Phipps, KCB (Keeper of the Privy Purse and Treasurer to the Prince Consort) and grandson of the First Earl of Mulgrave. At seven years of age, he became a page of honour to Queen Victoria and this until he joined the Scots Guards at sixteen, but in the meantime, he had attended Wellington College. When his father died, he exchanged into the Twenty-ninth Foot, then stationed at Hamilton, Ontario, where he married, in June 1865, Susan Stewart Geddes, second daughter of the Very Reverend J. G. Geddes, dean of Niagara. Returning to England in October 1865, he was attached to the Eighth Depot Battalion as instructor of musketry. The 1871 census found him living as a "Captain 29th Regiment" on the London Road at Reigate, Surrey, with his wife and a daughter, Alice Phipps, aged six months, born at Southsea, Hampshire. Later that year, CP transferred as captain instructor to the School of Musketry at Hythe, where he remained until promoted in autumn 1872 to deputy assistant adjutant general at Edinburgh under Sir John Douglas and General Ramsay Stewart. In 1878, he exchanged again with the rank of major and was obliged to join his regiment, the Eighteenth Royal Irish, then stationed in Ireland. In 1879, he retired on half pay, and in 1881, the census found him and his wife staying as visitors at "The Hooke," Chailey, East Sussex, home of Major General Henry P. Hepburn, aged fifty-nine, "Major General (unemployed)-Farms about two hundred acres, employs eight men and two boys." There were two other military visitors: Lieutenant General Frederick Stephenson, CB, aged fifty-nine, born at Hammersmith, Middlesex, and Colonel Frederick W. Walker, aged thirty-six, "Colonel C.B. Scots Guards" born at St George's Hanover, London. There was a crowd of other visitors, domestic servants, etc. In addition to his military duties, CP was in Queen Victoria's household, first as an usher, then as groom-in-waiting, but in 1882 he resigned to move to Canada.

In 1888, he was made Dominion lands agent at Cannington Manor, Assiniboia, but resigned there in 1898 and went in 1899 to Victoria, where he and Mrs Phipps lived at 228 Yates Street and later on at Carbury Gardens, a short street rising steeply from Oak Bay Avenue. He was one of the officers leading the contingent of veterans that paraded before Lord Minto, the governor general of Canada, in Victoria on 1 September 1900. CP declared to the BC census of 1901 that he earned $1,200 a year, could read and write French, and attended St Barnabas Anglican Church. He died, aged sixty-two, on 29 November 1906, leaving his wife, three daughters, and four sons, who held his funeral at St Barnabas, where Mrs Phipps, too, was buried when she died, aged eighty-seven, on 8 September 1930.

Sources: *Victoria Daily Times*, 1 September 1900, "*The Island Veterans; List of Ex-Fighting Men Who Parade To-Night Before Lord Minto*"; Canadian census, Victoria, 1901; *Colonist*, 30 November 1906, pp. 5 and 6, obit; 1 December 1906, p. 5, obit.; 9 September 1930, p. 20, obit.

PICKLES, Sydney (1894-1975). Born on 17 June 1894 in Sydney, Australia, he went to England early in 1912 to learn to fly and passed the tests for an English FAI, Certificate No. 263. As early as May 1912, he attracted public notice at Flower Down near Winchester by exhibitions of flying. The *Hampshire Chronicle* (Winchester) reported on 10 May 1912 that he chatted with the mayor and mayoress, Councillor and Mrs Howard Elkington, and after some false starts and delays, landed on the Downs early one morning: "His arrival . . . was witnessed by about twenty-five persons who expressed their great admiration at the splendid manner in which the aviator approached the end of the Down and then, after a bank to the left and a short dive, recovered his balance a few feet from the turf. He ran up the course amid resounding cheers. These he acknowledged by a wave of the hand just before the machine had pulled up. On getting out, there were loud shouts of 'Bravo Pickles.'" In 1913, he passed more official tests for Superior Certificate No. 8 and, when the Great War broke out in 1914, joined the Royal Naval Air Service. His duties included submarine patrols over the North Sea, raids over the continent, and training other pilots for the service. After a year, he resigned his commission and returned to civilian life as a test pilot for the Admiralty. In 1919, he received Air Ministry License No. 9 and soon returned to Australia, taking with him his own plane, an American Curtiss "Jenny," with which he established many "firsts." For instance, in November of 1919, he made the first east-west crossing of New South Wales, flying from Richmond through Broken Hill to the South Australian town of Cockburn and back. He battled high winds, oppressive heat, overheating radiators, and a hailstorm, which punched three hundred holes in his aircraft's fabric.

In 1925, he moved to the Island by way of Quebec City, where he arrived on 18 October aboard the *Ausonia* (Cunard). In Victoria, he designed a large house at 380 Newport Avenue, Oak Bay, well back from the road but with a clear view across the golf links to the Strait of Juan de Fuca, and had it built in 1926 for $7,000. He joined the Royal Victoria Yacht Club at sometime in the 1920s and devoted much time and care to its management, which provoked the hostility of less scrupulous club members and feuds with some of them. Before the Second World War, he bought a farm on the mountain side of Mount Newton Crossroad and raised sheep and crops on it. It is alleged that he also started the first commercial strawberry production on the Saanich Peninsula, later known for its huge berry crops (in which we local children earned money as berry pickers.) In time, SP became involved in local politics, and after working for some years to promote the incorporation of Central Saanich, he was elected reeve for four years and attended the municipal council's first meeting on 16 January 1951. Part of his land he donated to John Dean Park, thus adding to the park, which already included the top of Mount Newton, and in 1960, he sold the rest of his farm and moved back to Oak Bay with his family. Meanwhile, he had also organized the Victoria Aero Club and was its chief instructor until one of the members smashed the aircraft in an accident, which ended this phase of SP's career as he could not afford to buy another plane. He turned to the philanthropic activity of lending appliances of various kinds, without cost, to handicapped people and became president of The Handicapped Equipment Loan Association, devoted to helping victims of arthritis. Much of the equipment he made himself, helped by friendly machine shops, and he lent it out freely on condition that it be returned when not needed. For this, he was elected Good Citizen of the Year in 1968 and earned an award. After living on the Island for half a century, he died, aged eighty, on 23 November 1975, leaving his wife, Adelaide, and their two sons both living in the United States: Norman at Ceres, California, and Arthur at Puyallop in Washington State.

Sources: Stuart Stark, *Oak Bay's Heritage Buildings: More than Just Bricks and Boards* (Victoria, Corporation of Oak Bay, 1986), p. 71; *Hampshire Chronicle* (Winchester, England), 10 May 1912; *Colonist*, 25 November 1975, pp. 19 and 25, obit. and photo; Terry Reksten, *A Century of Sailing, 1892-1992: A History of the Oldest Yacht Club on Canada's Pacific Coast* (Victoria, Orca Book Publishing, 1992), pp. 107, 112; John MacFarlane and Robbie Hughes, *Canada's Naval Aviators* (new ed., Shearwater, Nova Scotia, Shearwater Aviation Museum Foundation, 1997), p. 254; *NAC, RG76-immigration series C-1-a.* 1925 vol. 15, page 134, reel T-14720; Jarrett Thomas Teague, *Blessings in Plenty from John Dean: A Life and Park History* (Sidney, BC, privately published by the author, 1998), 59 pp., and sixty-one unnumbered pages of photographs, ISBN 0-9684453-0-6, p. 5 from the back (photo); http://www.early aviators. com/epickles.htm; http://www.crwflags.com/fotw/ flags/ ca-bccsa.html. (no spaces).

PIDDINGTON, Major Arthur Grosvenor (1878-1960). He was born on 8 October 1878 at Beauport, Quebec, son of Thomas Angelo Piddington (c. 1844-1906) from Jersey in the Channel Islands but established at 83 St Louis Street, Quebec. AP was educated at Quebec High School, Morrin College, and RMC, Kingston, Ontario, where he did so well that he could choose his regiment and in 1900 took a commission in the RFA. He was on parade for Queen Victoria's funeral in 1901 and in 1905 was promoted to major and posted to X Battery, Royal Horse Artillery. When his father died, he resigned his commission in 1907 and returned to Canada. In 1910, he married Helen Mary Porteous, second daughter of C. E. L. Porteous of "Les Groesardière," Isle d'Orléans, descended from a family that had been there almost since the Conquest (1759-1763), and they had four sons and five daughters. In 1914, he rejoined his regiment and served throughout the Great War in command of C/116 Brigade and B/99 Brigade, RFA, in the Salonika campaign and elsewhere. He was twice mentioned in despatches and awarded the MC. After the war, his address was 491 Mt Pleasant Avenue, Westmount, PQ but changed after 31 March 1920 to "The Pines," Abbotsford, PQ, where he took up fruit orchards. When this property was destroyed by fire in autumn 1924, he took his family out to BC. One of their reasons for leaving Quebec, to which they were attached, was to help Mrs Piddington's twin sister, Arabella, whose husband, *Commander E. A. E. Nixon, commandant of the Royal Canadian Naval College in Halifax, had miraculously survived the explosion on 6 December 1917 and been despatched with the college to Esquimalt. There Nixon died in 1924, leaving his wife with four children in a house in Saanich.

Investments AP made in a sheep ranch and other BC companies were lost in the depression years, and he then took a job running the Wychbury Riding School in Esquimalt, where they lived in a splendid old house, "Wychbury," at 441 Lampson Street. Later, they moved out into Saanich. The family was much given to sports, and AP listed among his recreations riding, skating, boating, swimming, dancing, tennis, golf, and polo; he revived polo in Esquimalt, where it had lapsed for some years. Among his clubs were Toner Bay Country Club, Gorge Vale Golf Club, British Public Schools Club, the Union Club, and the United Service Institution. The *Daily Colonist* (12 November 1933, p. 10) printed a photo of the family on horseback, except Michael and the youngest daughter, Helen, who was a baby. Their family and the Nixons had a happy life and an interesting one. They were visited early in August 1934 by Mrs Piddington's cousin, Sir Ronald Storrs (1881-1955), who had served as governor of Jerusalem and who spoke in Victoria to the assembled Kiwanis and Canadian Clubs. The saddest event was the death of their son, Peter G. Piddington, who joined the RCN as a midshipman and was lost, aged twenty, with the *Royal Oak* in October 1939. AP died, aged eighty-one, on 19 March 1960 in Saanich,

Sources: Notes kindly sent by Helen (Piddington) Campbell; RG 9 series II-F-10 (British War Gratuities):Vol. 214, file no. 14531-A-88; *Who's Who in B.C.*, 1933-1934, pp. 139-140; *Colonist*, 12 November 1933, p. 10; 5 August 1934, p. 5; 17 October 1939, p. 6; 19 December 1939, p. 12; Helen Piddington, *The Inlet: Memoir of a Modern Pioneer* (Madeira Park, BC, Harbour Publishing, 2001, p. 47.

PIERCY, George (c. 1856-1941). He was born in Canton, China, son of the Rev. George Piercy, the first Methodist missionary in South China and his wife. On 1 April 1879 at St John's Cathedral, Hong Kong, he married Jane Smailes, born c. 1857 at Chatteris, Cambridgeshire. For nearly forty years, he was headmaster of the Diocesan Boys' School in Hong Kong, and Mrs Piercy was the matron there for thirty years. However, the 1901 census found her living in Selby, Yorkshire at "The May," Meiklegate, with their son, George Harold Piercy, aged three, and daughter, Mary Frances Piercy, aged one, both born at Hong Kong. Another son, James Edward Piercy, born at Hong Kong on 19 October 1887, was probably away at school somewhere in England.

This son was already living on the Island at Willows [Training] Camp, Oak Bay, when GP and his wife retired to Victoria in 1918 and on 17 March 1917 had taken a commission as lieutenant in the CEF. He (the son) had already served as a gunner in the Hong Kong Volunteer Artillery and had been living on the Island as a married civil engineer, his wife living at Maywood, BC. He declared himself an Anglican, though GP and his wife in Victoria were soon regularly attending Fairfield United Church. When GP died, aged eighty-five, on 3 October 1941, this son was "Major James E. Piercy" based on York Island, BC. GP was also survived by his widow, a daughter, and three other sons of whom Arthur Piercy was in Shanghai and George Harold Piercy in Hong Kong. Mrs Jane Piercy died, aged eighty-nine, on 21 January 1947 in Vancouver. I could find no connection with the Piercys of Denman Island.

Sources: *Colonist*, 4 October 1941, p. 13, obit.; census 1901, England, RG/4428, p. 14; NAC, CEF files, box 7680-52.

PIERS, Captain Sir Charles Pigott (1870-1945), ninth baronet. Friend and sporting companion of *General Sir Arthur Currie, he was born on 27 June 1870 in Hartford, Cheshire, son of Sir Eustace Fitzmaurice Piers (1840-1913), descended from an Irish baronetcy conferred in 1660 and who in 1869 had married Rose Saunders, daughter of Charles Saunders, a London-born JP and a "Brazil merchant," living in Liverpool at Fulwood Park, Toxteth Park. There the 1871 census found her and CP, aged eight months, staying with her parents but in 1881, when he was ten, he was living with his parents. His mother, then thirty-eight, was born at West Derby, Lancashire, and his father, aged forty-one, was a "J.P. Civil Engineer" born in Clapham, Surrey. There were nine servants: governess, two nurses, two housemaids, cook, kitchenmaid, footman, and gardener; and the neighbour on one side was a farmer of 315 acres. CP was sent to Eton and then Trinity Hall, Cambridge. The 1891 census recorded him as an "Undergraduate," aged twenty, staying with an uncle, Alfred Castellain, a retired merchant born at Liverpool but settled at Defferhaugh, Hosne, Suffolk, not very far from Cambridge. With them, there was another uncle, Charles Castellain, a "retired cotton broker," and there were seven servants. In April 1891, about the time the census was taken, CP's father was declared bankrupt. "It appears that from 1868 to 1887," *The Times* reported, "[Sir Eustace Fitzmaurice Piers] carried on business as an engineer and millwright at the St George's Works, Manchester, under the style of Ormerod, Grierson & Co., [which in 1887] was converted into a limited company . . ." and eventually fell into the hands of a receiver for debt. Sir Eustace retreated to Tristernagh Abbey, Westmeath, where he died in May 1913, and in 1895, CP obtained a commission in the Fourth Sherwood Foresters with whom he remained for twenty-one years, including campaigns in the South African War.

He moved to British Columbia with his wife, Hester Brewis, daughter of Samuel Brewis of Ibstone, Buckinghamshire, whom he married in 1902, and their son Charles Robin Fitzmaurice Piers (1903-1996) was born the next year. When CP joined the CEF on 12 November 1914 in Vancouver, he had been employed there as a "timber broker" and cited his son, aged eleven, as his next of kin living (probably with his mother, CP's wife Hester) at Trestanagh Checham Bois, Buckinghamshire. After the war, CP settled on the Island, where his son and daughter-in-law were also soon established, in Victoria and then at Cowichan, and he joined the Union Club. In 1923, he published *Sport and Life in British Columbia* (Heath Cranton Ltd., 159 pp., not the worst of its kind). His sporting companion, *General Arthur Currie, wrote a preface for it. CP's wife died in 1936. He resided for some years at the Union Club and died, aged seventy-five, on 27 June 1945. His son and heir was then a lieutenant commander in the RCNVR "at present attached to the Royal Navy" but died at Cowichan in 1996, his wife having died there, aged sixty-three on 16 December 1975.

Sources: NAC, CEF files, box 7820-26; census 1871, England, RG 10/3804, p. 19; census 1881, RG 11/1418, p. 21; census 1891, RG 12/1460, p. 2; *Times* (London), 27 April 1891, p. 4; 14 May 1913, p. 9, obit.; *Who was Who*, 1941-1950, p. 914; *Colonist*, 28 June 1945, pp. 8 and 12, obit.

PIRRIE, Noble Washington (1878-1961). Born 10 January 1878 in Bombay, India, son of John Sinclair Pirrie, he was educated at Chatham House (Ramsgate) and the Royal College of Science (South Kensington). In 1899-1901, he served in the South African War and then went into metallurgical work in Australia, Nevada, California, Mexico, and British Columbia, where he settled. In 1911-1915, he owned and operated "Vancouver Assay Office." Mining entailed working with explosives, and NP did research on ammonium nitrate explosives, as a result of which he accompanied Lord Rhonda's mission in June 1915 to England, Canada, and USA. In 1915-1919, he served as director of explosives in Canada and in March 1919 was appointed managing director of Sabulite Explosives Ltd. From October 1924 to 1942, he was employed in Victoria in the Boorman Investment Co. Ltd. He and his wife lived at "Byculla," 241 Island Highway, View Royal, Victoria. She was Fanny Mabel Corbett, daughter of Brigadier Surgeon John Corbett of the Rifle Brigade, who was born in Kamptee, India, and went to British Columbia about 1896. They had married on 16 October 1913 in Vancouver. After she died, aged sixty-three, on 20 January 1936 in Victoria, he married Muriel Evelyn Young, daughter of *Colonel T. F. Young. She and NP were Anglican, fond of gardening and golf. He died, aged eighty-three, on 17 December 1961 in Saanich, but Muriel lived until 20 April 1988, when she died aged 102.

Sources: *Who's Who in B.C.*, 1942-1943, p. 256; 1947-48, p. 174; *Colonist*, 21 January 1936, p. 5; Bradley Family History Website, bradfamhisto@aol.com.

PITTS, Sidney John (1850-1942). A prominent Island merchant and wholesale commission agent in Victoria, he was born in London on 14 March 1850, son of John Henry Pitts (1817-1887), who was born in a well-known county family at West Teignmouth, Devon, and was christened there on 15 January 1818. The father worked in London for sixteen years as an East India merchant with a branch house in Calcutta and married Marian Hopkins on 11 July 1843 in Islington. He appears with his wife and six children, including SP, in the 1861 census, living at 106 Conell Street.

A few years later, in 1864, perhaps affected by the Indian Mutiny (1857-1858) or the Cariboo gold rush of 1858, but probably soon after the death of the mother, Marian Pitts, the family emigrated to Victoria, where SP was in business as a wholesale commission agent and eventually became a member of the Victoria Board of Trade. His father died, aged seventy, on 23 December 1887 at SP's home in Victoria at 9 St Charles Street. SP invested in real estate, paid for new buildings in the town, and about 1882 married Margerite (1856-1900), who gave birth to several

J.F. Bosher

children and died in Victoria on 31 July 1900. The Canadian census of 1901 shows SP at home with several young children. He was prosperous enough to take two of his daughters on a visit home to England, whence they arrived back at St John, New Brunswick, on 25 November 1911 aboard the *Empress of Britain*. After the Second World War, he made another trip to England, arriving on 7 June 1925 at Liverpool on the White Star liner, *Megantic*, with his spinster daughter, Marian Hopkins Pitts (1884-1961), the one who remained at home to care for her father. Two other daughters had made good marriages: Ethel Margaret Pitts (1882-?) married the land surveyor *Thomas Blanshard Pemberton on 11 September 1919, thus linking the family with the Island's great Pemberton real-estate clan. On 19 April 1922, another daughter, Gladys Irene Jennie Pitts (1890-1947), married Captain Henry Charles Victor MacDowall (1891-1947), born in Winnipeg, Manitoba, on 2 May 1891, who had recently returned from service overseas during the Great War in a Canadian Scottish Regiment, having earlier joined the seventh battalion of the Eighty-eighth Fusiliers of Victoria in which her brother, Clarence Harold Pitts (1888-1967) was also enrolled. Born in Victoria on 2 May 1891, son of a retired Scottish MP for Saskatchewan who had retired to the Island, MacDowall died there on 26 March 1947 after living with his family at 9170 Ardmore Drive, North Saanich, as a close neighbour of *General R. J. Gwynne. His wife Gladys (Pitts) MacDowall outlived him by twenty years, dying, aged seventy-five, on 23 April 1966 in Victoria. It was the following year that her husband's friend, SP's son Captain Clarence Harold Pitts died in Victoria on 15 August 1967.

SP had died meanwhile, aged ninety-two, on 1 August 1942 in Victoria, survived by several of his children.

Sources: *Colonist*, 24 December 1887, p. 4, obit.; census 1861, England, RG/2383, page 4; census 1891, RG 12/749, p. 57 (Pemberton); NAC, CEF files, box 7713-4 (MacDowall); box 7856-23 (Pitts); R. E. Gosnell, *A History of British Columbia*, 1906, pp. 646-7; notes courtesy of Katharine Richmond; Burke's *Landed Gentry of Great Britain*, 1495 pp., see pp. 884-85; Canadian Passenger Lists, 1865-1935, T-4825 (1911); UK Incoming Passengers, no. 127981 (1925); *The Canadian Directory of Parliament* 1867-1967, ed., J. K. Johnson (Ottawa, Public Archives of Canada, 1968), p. 497 (MacDowall).

PLAYFAIR, Lieutenant Colonel Alan (1868-1952). He was born on 15 January 1868 in the British consulate at Algiers, where his father, Sir Robert Lambert Playfair, was the British consul general. Sir Robert (1828-1899) was born into an old Scottish family, had a distinguished diplomatic career, and published *A History of Arabia Felix or Yemen from . . . including an account of the British settlement of Aden* (Bombay, Government Printer, 1859), 193 pp.; *The Fishes of Zanzibar* (1866, with Gunther); *Travels in the Footsteps of Bruce in Algeria and Tunis,* (1877); and *The Scourge of Christendom. Annals of British Relations with Algiers prior to the French Conquest (Smith, Elder, 1884), 327 pp.; and several bibliographies of The Barbary States, Algeria, Cyrenaica and Morocco* (John Murray, 1882-1892). He sent AP to be educated in England, Germany, and Italy and to attend RMC at Sandhurst. AP then took a commission in the Royal Irish Rifles and served on the Nile in Sudan as a second lieutenant. He went on to India in the Fifteenth Madras Regiment of the Indian Army and after some years left the army to join the ICS as a military member. He was appointed assistant commissioner in Assam, later deputy British commissioner of Eastern Bengal and Assam. There he not only fought in various engagements and carried out other official duties, but also learned enough about the languages and culture people of the Lushai Hills, southeast of Manipur, to write an anthropological treatise he called *The Garos* (1909) to which Sir J. Bampfylde Fuller, KCSI, CIE, wrote an introduction. In 1917, the British Army commissioned him to go into the bush and recruit two thousand natives, which he did. He formed them into the Twenty-seventh British Army Labour Corps and went with them to France to carry out demolition work. After a year in command of the Sixty-second Labour Group near Arras, comprising six thousand mixed Lushai, Nagos, and Pathan tribesmen along with some Chinese, he returned to India, where he was involved in controlling the Moplah Riots in which Mahatma Gandhi took part. AP was awarded the MBE.

In 1921, he retired to Qualicum Beach, Vancouver Island, though he had never been there before. Possibly, the Island was brought to his attention by his wife's father, Dr George W. Noad, who was born at Sydney, Cape Breton Island, about 1828, though the latter's medical training was at St Andrew's University, and the 1881 census found him in general practice in Broad Street, Wokingham, Berkshire, where his daughter, Caroline G. Hilda Noad, was born c. 1875. She attended a girls' boarding school in London and married AP late in the century. After some quiet years at Qualicum Beach, they bought the Sunset Inn and managed it from 1927 to 1937. The Playfairs were soon playing vigorous parts in the public affairs of the district. In particular, AP became secretary of the Canadian Club and invited and formally thanked speakers, such as an American who addressed the club in May 1936 on the subject of Maya civilization. AP became a devoted worker for the Anglican churches of the district, St Mary's at Qualicum and St Mark's at French Creek nearby. In February 1933, he went as delegate of St Mark's to the Diocesan Synod for the Diocese of Columbia, and in 1937, he was the people's warden at St Mary's. The Playfairs, like the Moneys, attended countless baptisms, weddings, funerals, and weekly services at these churches. AP joined the Qualicum Beach Legion and was elected to its sick and relief committee in January 1941. That year, Mrs Playfair, who played an active part like her husband, was elected vice-president of the Qualicum Beach Girl Guides Association and held its AGM at her house. Meanwhile, they had a busy family life with their two sons. Early in September 1930, the *Qualicum Beach News* reported, "Colonel and Mrs Playfair with their two sons, Geoffrey and Anthony, left on a hiking trip on Monday, going by motor to Great Central Lake, then by boat twenty-five miles up the lake. They will take the trail nine miles to Della Lake at the southern part of Strathcona Park."

Deeply committed, like all of their kind, to schooling in leadership for their children, they put the boys in Brentwood College at Brentwood Bay, some fifteen miles north of Victoria. Both of them joined the forces in the Second World War, and the younger, Pilot Officer Anthony Richard Playfair (c. 1912-1939), was the

first Canadian casualty of the 1939-1945 war being killed on 9 September 1939 in
the RAF, when his plane was shot down over England. Buried in the churchyard
of Holy Trinity and St Oswalds, Finningley, Nottinghamshire, he was survived
by his wife Joan. The elder son, Geoffrey Playfair, was living in St Patrick Street,
Victoria, when AP died, aged eighty-three, on 30 September 1952 in Victoria and
was buried at Christ Church Cathedral on 3 October, scarcely a year after moving
from Qualicum to 753 Sea Drive, Brentwood Bay. His widow died, aged eighty-three,
on 14 November 1959 in Oak Bay.

Geoffrey Playfair's widow, remarried and widowed again as Mrs White, kindly
received me at her house at Brentwood Bay with her daughter Judith on 10 May
2001 and produced a copy of AP's book, *Garos*, and other things inherited from
AP: a large ornamental Indian brass tray, other pieces of Indian brassware, and a
Georgian silver teapot in which they served tea. She recalled that Geoffrey Playfair
had been born in India about 1904 and sent to a boarding school in England and
then to Brentwood College, where he had arrived in time to take part in building
the chapel. It survived the fire, which later destroyed the college some years ago,
and is now used as a parish church. She believed that Mrs Caroline Playfair wrote
memoirs, which have since disappeared.

Sources: Notes from an interview at Brentwood Bay on 10 May 2001 with Joan
Playfair, widow of Geoffrey Playfair, a son, and her daughter, Judy White; Rev.
A. G. Playfair, *The Playfair Book*, or *Notes on The Scottish Family of Playfair* (n.p.,
n.d., 1932?), 80 pp.; *Colonist*, 5 September 1930, p. 7; 15 February 1933, p. 6; 29
October 1933, p. 2; 3 May 1936, p. 14; 7 January 1937, p. 16; 23 January 1941, p.
2; 10 April 1941, p. 8; 1 October 1952, p. 14, obit.; 2 October 1952, p. 22, obit.;
Letter from Hugh Playfair, Blackford House, Blackford near Yeovil, Somerset
BA22 7EE, England, 7 July 2001; census 1881, England, RG 11/1310, pp. 2-3;
census 1891, RG 12/146, p. 19; Wemyss Reid, *Memoir and Correspondence of Lyon
Playfair, First Lord Playfair of St Andrew, P.C., G.C.B., L.L.D., F.R.S. etc.* (Cassell &
Co., 1900), 287 pp.; Riddick, *Who in British India*, p. 292 (father); C.E. Buckland,
A Dictionary of Indian Biography (Swan, Sonenschein & Co., 1906); (repr. Westport,
Conn., Greenwood Press, 1969), p. 338 (father); Major A[lan] Playfair, IA, deputy
commissioner eastern Bengal and Assam, *The Garos* (David Nutt, 57, 59 Long
Acre, 1909), 172 pp., with index, a map, and an Introduction by Sir J. Bampfylde
Fuller, KCSI, CIE.

POCOCK, Richard Lawrence (1874-1943). Born in London on 9 January
1874 to a prosperous professional family, he was the son of an engineer, William
Archbutt Pocock (c. 1842-1901) of London's west end, and grandson of William
Willmer Pocock, an architect and surveyor born c. 1813 in Knightsbridge. He
was educated at Somersetshire College, Bath College, and Pembroke College
Oxford (classics) and went out to BC in 1897. There he spent time prospecting
and mining around Nelson; then he went into industrial work and business for
some years and went to China to mine mercury for the Anglo-French Quicksilver
Co. at Kweichow. He returned to BC and joined the staff of the *Colonist* in Victoria
on 10 May 1907. He did nearly everything at the paper from being sports editor

(for twelve years) to a feature columnist. He had been crewman of the Pembroke College, rowing eight, at Oxford, and played on the cricket eleven. In Victoria, he took up fishing, shooting, and golf. On 1 May 1907, just before joining the *Colonist,* he married Emma George at Christ Church Cathedral, and on that occasion, she was the first bride to drive to the Cathedral in a motor car. They had a daughter and four grandchildren and were living at 1145 View Street when he died, aged sixty-nine, on 25 October 1943.

Sources: *Colonist,* 26 October 1943, pp. 1 and 2, obit.; census 1861, England, RG 9/55, p. 17; Oxford Men, *Alumni Oxiensis,* 1880-1892, p. 482.

POCOCK, Roger (1865-1941). Author and adventurer, he passed through Victoria once briefly in 1888 on his way north to Port Essington with an expedition sent to support police who were investigating crimes and unrest in tribal communities there. He was one of the eleven men at the officer's mess of "C" Battery photographed on that occasion. One of the few figures in this book who only visited the Island, he qualifies for inclusion as the founder of the worldwide Legion of Frontiersmen, which had an active unit in Victoria. His aggressively Imperial story helps to explain the lives of *George Gray-Donald, *Norman Penrose Hocking, *Frederick Victor Longstaff, and other active Frontiersmen. He was born at Tenby, Pembrokeshire, a small port in Wales, the second son of a commander in the Royal Navy, Charles Ashwell Boteler Pocock (1829-1899), and his wife, Sarah Margaret Stevens. When RP was seventeen, the family moved out to Canada and settled at Brockville, Ontario, and in 1882, RP enrolled at the Agricultural College in Guelph. For some reason that is not clear (lack of funds?), he left the next year to become a surveyor and was hired to work in the building of the Canadian Pacific Railway, which had reached the north shore of Lake Superior. In 1884, he joined the RCNWM Police at Fort Osborne, Winnipeg (regimental number 1107) and was posted at Regina when the Riel Rebellion broke out in 1885. His feet were badly frozen during a journey to Prince Albert in a detachment of ninety men, and he was discharged from the force when the toes of one foot had to be amputated. In 1887, he established a trading post at Kamloops and while there wrote his first book. After being dangerously kicked by a horse, he became a seaman on the *Adele* on a winter's voyage to the Behring Sea and then gathered much information about the life of the West Coast Indian tribes. He drifted to California in 1888, prospected, wrote several novels, and generally pioneered until returning to Canada in 1897, when he rode Boundary Patrol with the RCNWM Police, did some range riding for cattle ranchers in Alberta and some gold mining in BC. In 1889, he went on a famous long ride of thirty-six hundred miles from Fort McLeod, Alberta, to Mexico City. While running a pack horse train north from Ashcroft, BC, in 1898, he was engaged as a guide by Sir Arthur Colin Curtis (1858-1898), who disappeared and was frozen to death in the BC interior. Foul play was suspected, but RP was eventually cleared of suspicions of murder.

Hearing about the South African War, he returned to England and went on to serve with British forces in South Africa and then in the Great War. It was in the

South African War that he was impressed with the benefits of the British Empire and the dangers that seemed to beset it in those years. He began to think that British Military Intelligence might benefit if men were organized and scattered throughout the world to observe and report. So it was that on Christmas Eve in 1904, he held a meeting of some prominent men in London who were sympathetic with his ideas. The Legion of Frontiersmen was founded as a result. In the founding process, he was much assisted by his younger sister Lena, a well-known London actress known as Lena Ashwell (1872-1957), born in Durham, South Shields. She had been in Ontario with the family and had spent some time at Bishop Strachan's School in Toronto. She eventually married Sir Henry Simpson (1842-1900), the royal family's obstetrician, who drowned mysteriously on his estate at Datchet, Buckinghamshire, in August 1900. In 1901, she and another sister, Ethel Pocock, were living in London at 23 Clareville Grove in South Kensington with RP, who was identified as "novelist, journalist, author." It has to be added that he quarrelled with others in the Legion of Frontiersmen and ceased to be its leader, but it spread all over the empire and beyond as a kind of men's version of the Boy Scouts. RP died, aged seventy-six, on 12 November 1941 at Weston-super-Mare.

RP's publications are as follows:

Tales of Western Life: Lake Superior and the Canadian Prairie (Ottawa, C. W. Mitchell, 1888), 164 pp.

The Rules of the Game (Tower Publishing Ltd., 1895), 320 pp.

Rottenness A Study of America and England (Neville Beeman, 1896), 208 pp.

The Dragon-Slayer (Chapman & Hall, 1896), 402 and xi pp., reissued in 1909 as *Sword and Dragon* (Hodder & Stoughton, 1909), 311 pp.

The Blackguard (New Vanguard Library, vol. 4, 1896), 175 pp.

The Arctic Night (Chapman & Hall, 1896), 176 pp.

Following the Frontier: Horseback Adventures on the Infamous Outlaw Trail (New York, McClure, Phillips, 1903), 338 pp. [repr. Long Rider's Press, 2001]

A Frontiersman [Autobiographical narrative] (Methuen, 1903), 307 pp.

Curley: A Tale of the Arizona Desert (Gay & Bird, 1904), 312 pp. [Boston, Little, Brown & Co., 1905), 320 pp.

The Frontiersman's Pocket-Book, Compiled and Edited by R. Pocock on Behalf of the Council . . . (John Murray, 1909), 463 pp. and xx pp.

The Chariot of the Sun: A Fantasy (Chapman & Hall, 1910), 305 and xi pp.

"Canada's Fighting Troops" in *The Rally of the Empire: Our Fighting Forces* [32 pp., one of 3 parts]

Jesse of Cariboo (John Murray, 1911), 285 pp.

A Man in the Open (Indianapolis, Bobbs-Merrill, 1912), 352 pp.

Captains of Adventure (Indianapolis, Bobbs-Merrill, 1913), 376 pp.

The Splendid Blackguard (London John Murray, 1915), 331 pp.

Horses . . . *With an Introduction by Professor J. C. Ewart* (John Murray, 1917), 252 pp.

The Wolf Trail. A Novel (Oxford, Basil Blackwell, 1923), 309 pp.

Reflections from Shakespeare, by Lena Ashwell, ed., Roger Pocock (s. l., 1926) 238 pp.

Chorus to Adventurers (John Lane, 1931), 304 pp.

Sources: NAC, RG18, Series A-1, vol. 371, RCNWM Police Records (Pocock letters and papers); census England 1891, RG 12/11, p. 46; census 1901, RG 13/35, p. 12; *Colonist,* 21 October 1941, p. 8 (photo 1888 of eleven men, including RP); Sir Henry Seton-Karr (1853-1914), L to E, "The Legion of Frontiersmen," in *The Times* (London), 15 May 1909, p. 10; Geoffrey A. Pocock, *Outrider of Empire: The Life and Adventures of Roger Pocock* (Edmonton, University of Alberta Press, 2007), 382 pp.; *Chorus to Adventurers, Being the later Life of Roger Pocock,* (John Lane The Bodley Head Ltd., 1931), 304 pp.; *The Times* (London), 31 January 1899, p. 15, col. A, Lady Sarah Jessie Curtis and her lost husband, who had married on 26 October 1880; *The Times* (London), 30 December 1922, p. 10, col. F; 15 March 1957, p. 13, col. A, obit.; Margaret Leask, "Lena Ashwell (1869-1957), Actress, Patriot, Pioneer," PhD thesis, Department of English, University of Sydney, NSW, Australia, June 2000, 478 pp.; *New York Times,* 18 August 1900, p. 7 (Simpson's drowning); David Trotter, *The English Novel in History,* 1895-1920 (Routledge, 1993), pp. 178-9; T. C. Bridges and H. Hessell Tiltman, *Heroes of Modern Adventure* (George G. Harrap & Co. Ltd., 1927), chapter XV, "Roger Pocock's Record Ride."

POMEROY, Samuel James (1868-1936). Born on 21 October 1868 in London, he joined the Fiftieth Queen's Own Royal West Kent Regiment and served for seven years, notably on the Nile in the middle 1880s. He retired to Esquimalt, where he joined the British Campaigners' Association on 17 July 1908, was soon active with *H. A. Treen on its Sick Committee delegated to visit sick members, and in 1912 "gave us a stirring account of his experiences through the cataracts and across the desert with General Sir Gerald Graham to the Relief of General Gordon," according to the association's minutes of 19 December 1912. When he enlisted in the Canadian Army on 17 February 1916, he was living at 471 Admiral's Road, Esquimalt, working as a tailor, and cited his wife Winifred as his next of kin. Being over forty-eight years old (and only 5' 4" tall), he was not sent overseas and remained active in the British Campaigners' Association, which reported on 17 May 1917 that he had planted an English oak tree "in front of the New High School, Fernwood Road & Grant Street, in memory of the late Lord Kitchener, under whom he served in the Egyptian Campaign, 1884-5." The Pomeroys were Anglican and buried as such when they died in Victoria, she aged seventy-four, on 22 December 1932 and he, aged seventy-eight, on 11 November 1936.

Sources: NAC, CEF files RG 150, box 7893-67, regimental number 826115; *BC Archives, "Minutes of the British Campaigners' Ass.,"* 19 December 1912; 17 May 1917 and passim.

POOK, Frederick George (1874-1945). He was born on 24 November 1874 at "Mill Leat," Dulverton, Devonshire, son of a farm labourer and his wife Emily, both born in Devon villages. FP enlisted in the Second Manchester Regiment and served for seventeen years as a corporal in India, Egypt, and the South African War. In 1911, he settled in Victoria, where he was living near Mount Tolmie, Saanich, when he enlisted in the Canadian Army on 8 May 1916. He served overseas in the Sixty-second Battery and after the war joined the Victoria Police Force on 22 April 1918. From February 1932, he was the Beacon Hill Park officer, and children there became fond of him. He was superannuated on 31 May 1939 and died on 21 February 1945 at the Jubilee Hospital, leaving his wife Mary at home at 1407 Chambers Street and a nephew and niece. Mrs Pook died, aged eighty-eight, on 8 April 1957 in Victoria.

Sources: NAC, CEF files, box 7896-35; census 1881, England, RG 11/2358, p. 5; *Colonist*, 22 February 1945, p. 11, obit.

POOLE, Lieutenant General Gerald Robert (1868-1937). He was born on 17 January 1868 at Clifton, near Bristol, son of Rev. Canon Robert Burton Poole, MA, DD, who was a schoolmaster at Clifton College and later at Bedford School. The bare facts of his military career may be summarized as follows: He became a probationary lieutenant in the Royal Marine Artillery on 1 September 1885 and was promoted to lieutenant (1 September 1885), captain (19 June 1896), brevet major (1 September 1906), major (1 July 1908), brevet lieutenant colonel (1 September 1915), lieutenant colonel (9 February 1915), colonel second commandant (2 July 1920), colonel commandant (3 October 1921), major general (11 September 1922), and lieutenant general (9 July 1924). He served meanwhile in the South African War (1900-1902) in Canada employed by the Canadian government (1906-1812), "appointed with local rank of Major and a favourable report from Chief of Canadian Staff on returning to the Corps"; in the Great War (1914-1917), he commanded an RMA Howitzer Brigade in France (1915-1916) and commanded the Twenty-sixth Heavy Artillery Reserve Group of the First Army (4 April 1916 to 24 February 1919). Among the ships on which he served were HMS *Black Prince* (1889), *Audacious* (1891-1893) at Hull, *Ramillies, Royal Arthur,* and *Imperious* in the Mediterranean and for duty at Vancouver Island (1894-1899), SS *German* (1901-1902); and HMS *Irresistible* (1902-1904) in the Mediterranean again; HMS *Victory* for duty at Scapa Flow commanding special service forces at manoeuvres (1912); and *Inflexible* in the Mediterranean once more (1912-1914). He had meanwhile qualified himself in horsemanship (1900), as a gunnery instructor with a high commendation and a First Class Certificate (1893), and had been appointed to a committee to consider arrangements for the defence of Scapa Flow during naval manoeuvres (1912). He had had additional appointments as superintendent of the RN School of Music (1914-1915) and ADC to King George V (1921-1922).

Among his medals and decorations were the CMG (1917), the DSO (1918), the CB (1922), a 1914 Star, British War Medal, Victory Medal, and South African Medal, and he was three times mentioned in despatches of the commander-in-chief of the British Expeditionary Force in France. Among the commendations contributing to his promotion was a confidential report on his service while serving with Canadian militia forces from 1 September 1906 to

29 March 1912: "Major Poole is an excellent officer in all respects. He is most energetic, efficient, hard-working, and reliable. His judgement and common-sense are excellent and much above the average. His duties throughout his service have been of an instructional nature. He has commanded No. 3 (Heavy) Battery of the R.C.A. of the Permanent Force throughout his Canadian Service. He has the most marked instructional ability. He arranged for Active Militia Heavy Artillery training at Petawawa, 1911, and acted as Chief Umpire throughout the gun-practice, showing remarkable ability throughout, not only in the general supervision of the work and the power of imparting instruction to others, but also in his method of dealing with Active Militia. He is a keen sportsman, excellent in the woods and one of the best big-game hunters in the country. [signed] H. Buntoff (spellling?), lieut.-colonel commanding R.C. Artillery." To this was appended a note in another hand, "Major Poole has rendered excellent service. He has gained the esteem and liking of the Military and civilians to an unusual degree, while his quick manner and good professional knowledge have enhanced the value of his instructional work, [signed] Colin Mackenzie, M.G., C.G.S." His service afloat and abroad totalled twenty years, seven months, and he had served ashore for nineteen years, eight months; the total was therefore forty years and five months.

On 3 September 1924, GP married Gertrude Katherine Dunne (1902-?), daughter of C. W. Dunne of Crofton, north of Duncan, VI, and after returning from their honeymoon voyage, landing at Victoria on 24 March 1925 aboard SS *Loch Goil*, a Royal Mail Steam Packet, he was entered on the retired list on 11 December 1925. They made their way up the Island to a wooded seaside property near her parents at Crofton. As their granddaughter writes, "When he was stationed at Esquimalt, he enjoyed the surrounding area for its hunting and fishing. While stationed at Esquimalt, he became good friends with a Colonel Barnes who accompanied him on various hunting trips on Vancouver Island. Colonel Barnes introduced my grandmother to my grandfather and they later married in 1924. After retiring in 1925 he returned to Crofton to raise a family and to continue his friendship with Colonel Barnes." He and *Colonel G. E. Barnes used to take trips to the north of BC to hunt big game and bring the heads as trophies to mount on the wall, as hunters do (or did!). His property being rather wild, he also used to spend much time clearing it of brush and trees and planting fruit trees. The house he built was still there when I photographed it in 1900 and was kindly received there by a son, Charles Poole. From time to time, as in early May 1931, they made visits to Victoria but otherwise lived quietly in retirement until his death, aged sixty-nine, on 20 October 1937 at the Duncan hospital, leaving a son Charles and a daughter.

Sources: PRO (London), ADM 196/ 62 /5, page 131; *Who was Who*, vol. 3, p. 1090; Longstaff, *Esquimalt Naval Base*, p. 60, note 23; notes of 31 December 2000 from a daughter, Sylvia Dunn, a son Charles, and nephew, Mike Dunn; NAC, Immigration 1925-1935; NAC, Election rolls for 1935, reel T4760; *Colonist*, 8 May 1931, p. 8; 21 October 1937, p. 3, obit.

POOLE, Henry Joseph Ruscombe (1861-?). He arrived at Quebec on 26 August 1914, coming from Liverpool, as a passenger on the *Andania*. Then aged sixty-three, he declared that he had no occupation and his destination was Vancouver, probably meaning the Island, where he was soon living in the Cowichan Valley. He was elected one of the directors of the Cowichan Agricultural Society on 20 November 1919, the society having just gained $1,100 from the local Fall Fair. On 3 May 1921, he was one of the speakers at a Cowichan district meeting of indignant citizens held at the Duncan Opera House to criticize the provincial legislature's recent vote to increase the salaries of its members. MLA's salaries were always a hot topic. Under the chairmanship of *Lionel Welby Huntington, the meeting also heard remarks by *Mrs Colonel Claude "Maggy" Moss, OBE, *Lieutenant Colonel G. E. Barnes, and Mr H. P. Tooker. At sometime in the 1920s, HP seems to have left the Island.

Born at Weston-super-Mare, Somerset, he appears, aged nine, in the 1871 census, living at "The Grange" in Cannington, Somerset, youngest child in the family of Joseph Ruscombe Poole, then aged fifty-two and born nearby at the village of Rodney Stokes. HP's father was an "attorney & farmer of ninety-three acres employing three men and two boys," and his mother, Charlotte A. Poole, aged fifty-three, came from Madeley in Shropshire. He had four elder sisters, all named Mary—Mary P, aged twenty-four, Mary R, twenty, Mary Rose, twelve, and Mary N, eleven—born variously at Cannington and Weston-super-Mare. There were six servants: lady's maid, housemaid, cook, kitchenmaid, parlourmaid, and schoolroom maid. Ten years later, the family were still in Somerset but living at "Eastern House" in Weston-super-Mare, where HP, aged nineteen, was a "solicitor's articled clerk." At home now in 1881 was an elder brother, Walter Joseph Ruscombe Poole, aged twenty-seven, born at Cannington and already a solicitor, clearly in the firm of J. R. Poole & Son said to have continued in that district up to the 1960s. There were two sisters still at home and five servants. By 1891, HP was a solicitor away from home, and in 1901, he appears, aged thirty-nine, as a "retired solicitor," living at Minehead, Somerset, with a wife Mary from Weston and a two-year-old son, Joseph Ruscombe Poole, born at Colchester.

Brief references hint at other aspects of the family's life. In Bombay, India, on 7 October 1882, HP's sister Mary Rose married Lieutenant William Jane Richard Wickham of the Sixtieth Rifles. In 1888, HP appears in England as the co-respondent in a suit for divorce brought by Roderick Gwynne Lewis against his wife, Constance Ada Lewis. But I could not discover where HP went when he left the Cowichan Valley.

Sources: *Cowichan Leader*, 20 November 1919; census 1871, RG 10/2379, p. 12; census 1881, RG 11/2421/146, p. 41; census 1891, RG 12/1922/47, p. 13; census 1901, RG 13/2260, p. 40; BNA, J77/411/2504 (1888), Divorce Court File 2504; Canadian Passenger Lists, 1865-1935, T-4812, arriving 26 August 1914.

POPE, Thomas Archdale (c. 1859-1940). Born in Hull, Yorkshire [not in Manchester as reported in some sources], he joined the Survey of India on 17 July 1880, became second assistant superintendent in September 1881, assistant superintendent, Survey of India, in October 1886, deputy superintendent in March 1891, this again and also assistant surveyor general in October 1899, and finally, in February 1907, was appointed superintendent of the Forest Survey. In 1890, the surveyor general of India, his superior, was *Colonel H. R. Thuillier, RE. Lengthy furloughs were usual, and in 1901, the English census found TP living as "Assistant Surveyor-General Survey of India (on furlough)" at 37 High Street, Great Berkhamsted, Hertfordshire, with his wife and two sons. She was Mary Laird Pope, aged forty-seven, born in Scotland, and the sons were Christopher L. Pope, aged nine, born in Kensington, and Kenneth M. Pope, aged four, born in India. They had a third son, Hugh Lethbridge Pope, who was born in India and registered in 1901 as a "gentleman cadet" at RMA, Woolwich, aged sixteen, on the same census page as *Charles Hedley Palmer, also born in India, a son of *C. G. Palmer. In Berkhamsted, TP and family were living near relatives at Tring, Hertfordshire: Rev. Arthur Frederick Pope, vicar of Tring, and his wife, Catherine J. E. Pope, born in "East Indies, British Subject," who in 1891 had four sons and a daughter.

In February 1912, TP retired and was recorded in *Thacker's Indian Directory* for that year as being on leave. Nearly twenty years later, he and his wife, Margaret, retired to Victoria, but we may suppose that she was his second wife because in 1901, he was husband of Mary Laird Pope. In Victoria they lived at 2259 Central Avenue, Oak Bay, and attended meetings of the India-Burma Society. After a residence of nine years, he died, aged eighty-one, at St Joseph's Hospital on 11 April 1940, leaving his wife and two sons, Major Hugh L. Pope in Surrey, England, and Kenneth M. Pope in Vancouver. He also had a brother-in-law and sister-in-law, *Colonel and Mrs G. A. Phillips, who lived nearby in the Uplands district of Oak Bay. The funeral was at St Matthias Anglican Church, and TP was buried at Royal Oak. Among the pallbearers was *Colonel W. R. Wilby.
Sources: India Office List, 1910, p. 617, "*Record of Service*"; *Colonist*, 17 January 1933, p. 8; 12 April 1940, p. 16; 14 April 1940, p. 3, obit.; census 1901, England, RG 13/1329, p. 5; census 1891, England, RG 12/1127, pp. 19-20; census 1891, RG 12/2825, p. 24; census 1901, RG 13/569.

POPHAM, Captain Home Courtney Vyvyan (1884-1944). Born on 10 June 1884 at Sevenoaks, Kent, he was found by the 1891 census, aged six, living at 124 High Street, Hythe, Kent, with his parents: Vyvyan Popham, aged forty-four, "resident Bank Clerk," born at Sithwy, Cornwall, and his wife, Ada E. Popham, aged thirty, born at Winchester, Hampshire. They employed a cook. HP attended a grammar school at Faversham Within, Kent, under Rev. Frederick Crapper, headmaster, and was sent next to Dover College, and finally to RMC, Sandhurst. He served briefly as a commissioned officer in the Duke of Cornwall's Light Infantry.

In 1907, he went to the Cowichan district, where he stayed for a year at Somenos with *Major J. A. Mutter and later farmed "at different places" in that district. When the Great War broke out, he returned to England and enlisted with the Seventeenth Royal Fusiliers but later obtained a commission in his old regiment, the Duke of Cornwall's Light Infantry, and was promoted to captain while serving in France. From November 1915 to June 1916, he served at Salonika but was then discharged

for reasons of health and sent back to Canada. Restored to health by July 1917, he joined Lord Strathcona's Horse, went overseas, and was attached to the Labour Corps in France from September 1918 to April 1919. After the war, HP returned again to Canada and lived for some years at Parksville, where he married Evelyn Ethel M. Willcocks on 30 September 1925 and they had two daughters. When Mrs Popham died (when and where?), HP lived for some years at Maple Bay with one of his daughters, but they all returned later to England, where they stayed with his widowed mother in Hove, Sussex at 37 Denmark Villas. In the Second World War, he again offered his services, but ill health forced him to retire and he died in England of a heart attack in July 1944 and was buried as an Anglican.
Sources: NAC, CEF files, RG 150, box 7903-30, regt. no. 2293439; *Cowichan Leader*, 10 August 1944, obit.; census 1901, England, RG 13/805; census 1891, RG 12/753, p. 6.

PORCHER, Captain Edwin Augustus (c. 1826-June 1878). He was at Esquimalt and the North-West Pacific Coast in general for nearly three years, from 28 October 1865 to 31 August 1868, as captain of HMS *Sparrowhawk*. Apparently an educated and sociable man, he met everyone in the governing elite in Victoria and district and many others besides. Innumerable British naval officers did the same, but EP is distinguished by having written a detailed diary and painted clear, almost photographic, landscapes and buildings in watercolours wherever he went. His diary and paintings during this voyage of the *Sparrowhawk*, now kept at Yale University, have been reproduced in a splendid scholarly volume by the University of Alaska. There are several views of Esquimalt, including St Paul's Naval and Garrison Church, a picture of the skyline of Victoria and another of Christ Church Cathedral before it burnt down in 1869, and scenes at Nanaimo and Quamichan, not to speak of Honolulu, the Falkland Islands, and Patagonia, where the *Sparrowhawk* stopped during its long voyages around Cape Horn. This book has one flaw, disastrous from an editorial point of view but unimportant for the scholarly reader: Porcher is consistently named "Edmund Augustus" instead of Edwin Augustus, which all documents and many books show to have been his name. I could find no other errors in the Porcher family tree as related by the editor, though he did not carry it very far.

EP was born in Berkshire at Mitchum, a southern suburb of Reading, second son of Rev. George Porcher (c. 1791-1861) and his wife Frances Amelia Porcher (c. 1792-1870), who were both born in Madras, India, and moved about in England from parish to parish, as clergymen usually did, but with more servants than most could afford. In 1841, they lived at 4 Lower Berkeley Street, Marylebone (London), with nine servants; in 1851 at Redgrave House in Suffolk with ten; and in 1861 at 45 Bryanstone Square, Marylebone, with seven, but by then their children had all left home. Rev. Porcher died later that year. EP's elder brother George Du Pré Porcher (1823-1876) became a barrister in the Home Counties and their sister, Charlotte Amelia Porcher (1825-1846), married into the famous family of bankers and East India merchants, the Baring Brothers, whom EP's parents must have been acquainted with in India. This acquaintanceship is clear enough through an uncle, Thomas Du Pré Porcher, whose tomb at North Park Street Burial Ground in Calcutta, where he died in 1812, bears a long inscription of his "eminent virtues and endowments" as a factor in the HEIC. And EP's grandfather, Josias Du Pré Porcher (1761[?]-1820), was a mayor of Madras, India, and a successful merchant in the East India trade who served as an MP (1802-1818) for Bodmin, Cornwall, Dundalk (County Louth, Ireland), Bletchingly (Surrey), and Old Sarum (Wiltshire). His paternal uncle Henry Porcher (1795-1857) was MP for Clitheroe (Lancs. 1822-1826), and his paternal grandmother was the daughter of an admiral who was also a baron. Through his own sister, EP was related by marriage to Francis Thornhill Baring (1796-1866), who had been a cabinet minister and first lord of the Admiralty in 1849-1852. Such family connections smoothed EP's path in Victoria and wherever he went in the empire.

Sources: E. A. Porcher, *A Tour of Duty in the Pacific Northwest: E. A. Porcher and H.M.S. Sparrowhawk, 1865-1868*, ed., Dwight L. Smith (Fairbanks, Alaska, University of Alaska Press, 2000), 172 pp. in 4o; census 1841, England, HO 107/680/7/30; census 1851, HO/107/28/1; census 1851, HO 107/1795/289/28; census 1861, RG 9/77, p. 24; census 1861, RG 9/2222, pp. 20-21; census 1861, RG 9/4440, p. 2; census 1871, RG 10/166, p. 4; Holmes & Co., *The Bengal Obituary, or A Record etc.* (Calcutta and London, W. Thacker & Co., 1851), p. 187; David Steele, "*Baring, Francis Thornhill, first Baron Northbrook* (1796-1866), politician," Oxford DNB online.

PORTEOUS, Major Donald Valpy (1873-1959). PORTEOUS, Major Donald Valpy (1873-1959). He was born on 8 June 1873 at Rajahmundary, South India, son of Major Charles Arckcol Porteous of the Madras Staff Corps and his wife Catherine Sophia Porteous. The 1881 English census shows her and the children living in Hampstead, London, at 83 Fellows Road, the father mentioned but absent. DP, then aged 7, had four brothers: Charles McLeod Porteous, aged 15, born in India; Herbert Llewellyn Porteous, 10, born at Reading, Berks.; Percy Gwynedd Porteous, 9, born in India; and Ernest Rowland Porteous, 2, born in south Hampstead; and they had four sisters. There were four servants. DP joined the 3rd Middlesex Regiment, aged 20, in 1893, and two years later he became a trooper in the 1st Royal Dragoons. He was promoted to the rank of acting sergeant, then to captain and major during the South African War, in which he won the Military Cross, the Queens medal with five clasps and the King's medal with two. He had served in the dragoons for eight years. After that war he was chief constable and crown prosecutor in the South African Constabulary for six years.

DP married on 26 August 1914 and took his wife (not named in my sources) to Victoria, where they were living at 1422 Newport Avenue, Oak Bay, when on 18 August 1915 he joined the Eighty-eighth Fusiliers. He was recorded as an Anglican, six feet tall, with a fresh complexion, blue eyes, and dark hair. He spent the war in the Forty eighth Battalion, CEF, Third Canadian Pioneers. One of those soldiers who was restless in the post-war years, he joined the Canadian Legion but moved about from Cowichan, Sooke, and Sayward to Victoria again with his wife and three daughters. In July 1933, he was appointed fire warden for the district of

J.F. Bosher

Sooke and he and his family spent the summer of 1936 there at Saseenos. But he had been living for six years at 241 Beechwood Avenue, Victoria, when he died, aged eighty-six, on 28 September 1959 in Saanich, leaving a son, three daughters, a sister in England, and nine grandchildren.
Sources: Census 1881, England, RG 11 / 174, pp. 2-3; NAC, RG150, box 7906-19; *Colonist* 11 January 1917, p. 5; 7 July 1933, p. 7; 20 May 1936, p. 8; 30 September 1959, pp. 5 and 14, obit.

PORTER, Douglas Goodman (1885-1959). He was born on 25 March 1885 at Aldershot, son of William Goodman Porter and his wife Jane, who in 1881 were living at 1 Arthur Street, Aldershot, where the father was "Manager Aerated Water Co[mpan]y" employing eight men. The mother was born at Hastings, Sussex, the father at Liverpool, where thirty years earlier he was reported by the 1851 census to be living, aged nine, in the family of his father, DP's grandfather, who described himself as a "Gentleman" and was born likewise in Liverpool. In 1916, DP was working in Nanaimo as a clerk at the Windsor Hotel when he enlisted in the CEF at Victoria on 22 April 1916. He had already served for four years in the Third Middlesex Voluntary Artillery, possibly in the South African War (1899-1902). He cited his father as his next of kin, then living in Hertfordshire at Woodlands Gun Road, Knebworth. DP returned after the war to Victoria and died there, aged seventy-seven, on 25 January 1959.
Sources: NAC, CEF files, box 7909-11, regtal. No. 532685; census 1881, England, RG 11/781, p. 49; census 1851, HO 107/2506, fol. 311.

PORTER, Mrs Mildred Alice (1887-1937). She and her husband Edmund Phillip Porter lived for most of her twelve years (1925-1927) in Victoria at "Kelvin Lodge," Kisbet Street, Mount Tolmie, and this entry is about who she was rather than anything she did. Born at Peshawar on the North-West Frontier of India, she was a daughter of Colonel James William Abbot Michell retired from the Bengal Indian Staff Corps, himself born in India on 22 November 1840, and his wife Edith E. Michell (c. 1856-?) from Islington, London. The colonel had been commissioned on 4 April 1858 and promoted to lieutenant on 25 January 1861 and to colonel on 4 April 1884. He served in "Bhootan" [Bhutan] (1864-1866), in "Duffla" (1874-1875), and in Sikkim (1888), all on the North-East Frontier of India. The 1891 English census showed him and his family living in London at 4, Cloysters, Gordon Square, St Pancras, with three children: Henry H. Michell, aged six, Ella C. Michell, five, and Mildred Alice Michell (MP), aged three, all born in India. They had a governess, a cook, and a housemaid. In 1901, they were much as before but living in Hampstead, London, at 19 Canfield Gardens and with a new young sister, Beatrice W. H. Michell, aged six. The father, now aged sixty, was a pensioned "Colonel H.M. Staff Corps Army" born in India.
MP's husband, Edmund Philip Porter (1880-1972), whom she seems to have married in England, was born in Hampstead, London, son of a "Director of Wholesale Drapery" and his mother was a Londoner. They appear in the 1881 census, living at Springfield, Bickley Park, Bromley, London, with four servants,

when Edmund was aged one and had a brother and sister both older. In 1891, Edmund, aged eleven, was boarding at Hill House School, Bradfield, Berkshire. As a married couple in Victoria after the Great War, MP and Edmund had two children and took them on a voyage to England on the Royal Mail Steam Packet SS *Lochmona*, arriving at Liverpool on 2 November 1926, having boarded in Vancouver or Victoria. Edmund described himself as a "farmer" and she as a "housewife," and the children were Robinson Michell Porter, aged ten, and Audrey Kate Porter, aged three. In 1931, MP, aged forty-three, travelled alone to England, arriving at Liverpool on 9 July and giving her forwarding address as c/o W. Lefroy, 3 Tregmater Road, The Boltons, London SW. She died in Victoria, aged forty-nine, in February 1937, leaving her husband, a son, and three daughters, and Edmund died, aged ninety-two, on 11 August 1972 in Saanich.

Sources: *Colonist,* 17 February 1937, p. 3, obit.; 18 February 1937, p. 18, obit.; census 1881, England, RG 11/854, pp. 7-8; census 1891, RG 12/987, p. 15; census 1891, RG 12/119, p. 4; census 1901, RG 13/123, p. 14; *Monthly Army List,* May 1891, p. 729; *Bulletins and Other State Intelligence for the Year 1867, Part II—July to December,* by T. L. Behan, Superintendent (Gazette Office, 1870), p. 897; *Whitaker's,* p. 363; *Indian Army Quarterly List* for 1 January 1912, p. 77; UK Incoming Passenger Lists, 1878-1960, no. 147677 (arriving at Liverpool 2 November 1926); no. 160482 (arriving at Liverpool 9 July 1931).

POTTINGER, Lieutenant General Brabazon Henry (1840-1913). He was born on 18 September 1840 in India, the eldest son of Major General John Pottinger, CB (?-1877), of Mount Pottinger, County Down, descendant of a distinguished Imperial family established in Belfast for three centuries. His father was the half-brother of Eldred Pottinger (1811-1843), the soldier and diplomat famous for his defence of Herat against a Persian army in 1837, and also the nephew of Sir Henry Pottinger (1789-1856), who concluded a peace with China in 1842 and was the first British governor of Hong Kong. BP was commissioned in the Royal Artillery in 1857 and took part in the Abyssinian expedition of 1867-1868 during which he was mentioned in dispatches. He married Rosa Stewart Southey (c. 1846-?), daughter of Lieutenant Colonel William Southey, in 1866 and had a family of three sons and five daughters. She was born ca. 1846 at Bellary, India, but the 1881 census found her living at 19 Orchard Gardens, West Teignmouth, Devon, with her daughters—Nora Pottinger, aged fourteen, born in Karrachi, East Indies (future wife of *Colonel E. A. P. Hobday; Mary Pottinger, aged nine, born in Mhow, India; Edith M. Pottinger, aged eight, born at Port Stewart, Ireland; Rose B. Pottinger, aged two, born at Teignmouth—and her sons: Robert S. Pottinger, aged eleven, and Brabazon W. A. Pottinger, aged three, both born at Poonah, India. With them were a governess and three other servants. BP was evidently away on duty. In 1891, he was promoted to lieutenant general, the youngest in the British Army.

BP retired in 1902 and at sometime before his death a decade later, he bought land in the Cowichan Valley. When in September 1917 the Supreme Court in Victoria assessed it at $7,300, the *Daily Colonist* described its late owner as "formerly of Bombay, India, and Duncan." It reported *inter alia* that he had died at Portrush, Ireland, on 21 September 1913, though *Who was Who* gave his address as Thornpark, Coombe Road, Teignmouth. Less than six months after his death, a Major E. Pottinger spoke to Victoria audiences on military matters on 13 and 28 February 1914. The first was given in the boardroom of the Belmont Block on "General Intelligence Work" to men interested in forming a local squadron of the Legion of Frontiersmen. Pottinger illustrated his talk "by experiences drawn from his own service in China, Burma and India." In the second, addressed to the YMCA, he focussed on his experiences of China and the Chinese, "gained far in the interior, when he was engaged on a survey of the Yangtze River with a view to ascertaining its navigability. He was there a year before the Boxer Rebellion, which he said expressed a hatred of foreigners and not a religious feeling. Missionaries were then attacked as foreigners, not as missionaries. He showed some marvellous photos to illustrate his lecture." The Pottingers would repay more careful study.

Sources: *Who was Who*, 1897-1916, p. 572; *The Times*, London, 23 September 1913, page 9, obit.; *British National Archives*, National MSS Commission, National Register of Archives: NRA 12712; census 1881, England, RG 11/2156, p. 21; *Colonist*, 14 February 1914, p. 6; 12 February 1914, p. 7; 26 February 1914, p. 7; 1 March 1914, p. 6; 9 September 1917, p. 24; Riddick, *Who in British India*, p. 294 (Eldred and Sir Henry); Buckland, *Dict. of Indian Biography*, p. 341 (Eldred and Sir Henry); Frank Welsh, *A History of Hong Kong* (rev. ed., HarperCollins, 1997), see full index entry, p. 645 (Sir Henry at Hong Kong).

POTTS, Dr George Gerald (1835-1915). Born on 14 May 1835 in Ireland at "Moher House," County Cavan, he was the fourth son of Alexander Potts and Jane, *née* Lovitt, and a grandson of Major John Potts, who had served in Egypt with General Sir Ralph Abercrombie. Taken out to Canada in 1847, GP attended Belleville Grammar School, Victoria University, Cobourg, Ontario, and became a member of the Ontario College of Physicians and Surgeons. He began a career as an army surgeon in the Second Battalion of the Prince Edward County Militia, but in the early 1850s, he went to Australia and thence to England. In 1857, he was appointed surgeon to HM Consulate in Bangkok, Siam, and was ordered to serve in India during the early stages of the Mutiny. He arrived at Calcutta on 12 June 1857. After carrying out special assignments there, he was dispatched to China, where he was in Beijing during the Anglo-French "opium war" with China and witnessed French forces looting the Summer Palace. When that war ended, he was ordered to Hong Kong but there resigned from the service and returned to Canada in 1861. A few months later, he applied to Hammond, surgeon general of the United States and was admitted to the posts of surgeon major, then colonel, in the Twenty-third Regiment of U.S. Infantry to which President Abraham Lincoln appointed him in Washington DC on 12 March 1863. He was admitted to the Royal College of Surgeons (Edinburgh) in 1867, and after joining the Canadian Medical Association (1868) and the Ontario Medical Association, he obtained licenses to practice in Illinois (1885), Missouri (1885), and Florida (1888) and qualified in Ontario as coroner in the united counties of Victoria, Northumberland and Durham, and of Peterborough. He began to publish in the *Lancet* (London) and other medical journals and in 1872-1874 was employed as editor of the Toronto *Daily Leader*.

At sometime in the 1890s, GP and his wife moved to Victoria, BC, where the 1901 census found him, aged sixty-six, living at 316 Yates Street with the wife he had married in 1868: Agnes S. Potts (1843-1911), *née* fourth daughter of Alexander Stewart of Stirling, Ontario. They were members of the Church of England, and he served occasionally as a lay reader. He soon became a JP, and he was also a practicing Freemason, an enthusiastic Conservative, and a founding member of the British Campaigners' Association of Vancouver Island. Even before that body was formally organized, he read two papers to meetings of fellow veterans in 1900 and 1902 at Pioneer Hall, Broad Street, Victoria: "The Chinese War of 1859-60" and "The Outbreak and Final Collapse of the Indian Mutiny." He based them partly on his personal experience and partly on historical study. Mrs Potts died on 5 July 1911 in Portland, Oregon, and GP himself died, aged eighty-three, at Clinton, Ontario, in April 1915 and was buried in Toronto. Their children remained in Ontario except for a daughter, Georgena [*sic*] Barbara Potts, who was born in Ontario on 25 June 1872 and married *Charles Edward Clarke on 7 August 1906 in Victoria.

Sources: Canadian census, Victoria, 1901; *BC Archives* 74-A-79; Add MSS 381: *The Veterans' Association of Vancouver Island, Scrap Book*, July 1900-December 1901; Morgan, *Canadian Men and Women*, p. 912.

POWELL, Commander Alfred David Steadman (1858-1939). Difficult to know, he is included here as one of the retired employees of Sir Robert Hart's Chinese Maritime Customs in Victoria, like *Captain Alfred Torrible and *Admiral Antony Hubert Gleadow Storrs. AP was born at Stranton, Durham, and appears, aged three, in the 1861 census as the eldest of the three children of Alfred Powell, twenty-five, a "Railway Accountant Clerk" from Salhouse, Norfolk, and his wife Sarah, twenty-seven, from Whicham, Durham. They had a railway clerk boarding with them and a servant girl. AP may have joined the Royal Navy, but I could find his name in no official Navy List, perhaps because only commissioned officers were listed. He certainly sailed on the China Coast as a commander in the Chinese Maritime Customs. Looking no doubt for a place to retire, he visited Victoria in 1920 and the next year arrived from Shanghai on 12 January 1921 aboard the *Fushimi Maru*, one of the many trans-Pacific liners owned by Japanese shipping companies. In Victoria, he was a member of the China-Japan Society in 1931, probably earlier. In 1933, he returned to England and died, aged eighty-one, at Portslade, Sussex, in September 1939, leaving his widow there and a son in Victoria, Alfred S. Powell, who married Joyce H. Holt Newell on 15 May 1932 and then moved away.

Sources: *Victoria Daily Times*, 23 September 1939, p. 11, obit.; *Colonist*, 17 October 1931, p. 8; 23 September 1939, p. 6, obit.; census 1861, England, RG 9/3704, p. 12; Canadian Passenger Lists, 1865-1935, T-14877.

POWELL, Lieutenant Colonel Israel Wood (1836-1915). Born on 27 April 1836 into a United Empire Loyalist family of Norfolk County, Ontario, originally from Wales, he was an Anglican and firmly loyal to the empire. He attended McGill University, qualified as a medical doctor, and went to Victoria where he arrived on 13 May 1862. Dr Helmcken persuaded him to stay and at first he worked as a physician. But on 7 October 1872, IP was appointed to the Federal Indian Affairs Department and soon promoted to superintendent with a salary of $3,000. He played various parts in public affairs, and the town of Powell River, BC, was named after him. He was a member of the Church of England, active as a Freemason, founded the Grand Lodge of BC in association with the Grand Lodge of Scotland, and became provincial grand master of the Freemasons of BC. St Andrew's Presbyterian Church saluted him as such when its foundation stone was laid on 20 August 1868. In addition, he married Jane "Jennie" Powell, née Branks, born 28 Sep 1849 in New Zealand, daughter of Scottish parents who had moved to California during the gold rush of 1849. She was active in the musical and theatrical life of Victoria. He consented to stand for election in Victoria because his own father had been an MP for twenty-five years, and he became a staunch advocate of Confederation. He was the first chairman of the Board of Education set up by the Public School Act and the first chairman of the BC Medical Board. He died on 25 February 1915. His rank seems to have come from the local militia.
Sources: *Civil Service List of Canada, 1883-1884* (Ottawa, Queen's Printer, 1884), pp. 104-5; B. A. McKelvie, "Lieut.—Colonel Israel Wood Powell, M.D., C.M.," in *British Columbia Historical Quarterly*, vol. XL, no. 1 (1947), pp. 33-54; Begg, *History of British Columbia*, p. 494; Lugrin, *Pioneer Women*, pp. 233-8; Canadian census, 1901, Victoria.

POWELL, Lieutenant Robert Branks (1881-1917). He was born on 2 April 1879 in Victoria, youngest son of *Dr I. W. Powell and Jane "Jennie" Powell, née Branks (1849-?), born 28 September 1849 in New Zealand. He was schooled locally, became an outstanding athlete, and was famous worldwide as a tennis player. Champion of BC for many years and until 1904, in that year, he founded the North Pacific Lawn Tennis Association. In 1905, he won the championship of Scotland and in 1908 represented Canada in the Olympic Games. In England, he was generally recognized as one of the best six or seven players of the time and won the singles championship of Cumberland in 1910 and the championship of Sussex the next year. He served in 1900-1904 as private secretary to Sir Henri Joli de Lotbiniere, then lieutenant governor of BC, and then went to the Fiji Islands, where he entered the British Colonial Service. In 1905-1906, he was a member of the lieutenant governor's staff on the Western Pacific High Commission. Meanwhile, he was studying law and was admitted to the Bar in London, while on a visit there in 1910. Still in England when the Great War began, he enlisted in the Forty-eighth Battalion, CEF, at Lydd, Kent, on 18 August 1915, had a medical exam at Shorncliffe, and was commissioned immediately having already become a lieutenant in the Fiftieth Regiment of Gordon Highlanders of Canada on 1 September 1914. He died in action on 24 April 1917 serving in the Canadian

Infantry (Manitoba Regiment), Sixteenth Battalion, and was buried as an Anglican leaving his widowed mother, three brothers, and four sisters.
Sources: NAC, CEF files, box 7942-46; *Colonist*, 4 May 1917, p. 5, obit.; Canadian census, 1901, Victoria.

PRENTICE, Commander James Douglas (1899-1979). He was born on 26 April 1899 in Victoria, son of Hon. James Douglas Prentice, who was born on 3 February 1861 in Scotland, and migrated to BC in 1882. In 1897, the father was representing East Lillooet in the BC Legislature, and on 6 September 1897, he married Mabel Clare Galpin (1868-?) in Victoria. By 1901, the father employed there as provincial secretary and he died there ten years later, aged fifty, on 27 October 1911. Meanwhile, JP attended St Michael's School and in due time entered the Royal Canadian Naval College. In 1939, he was called for service, with seniority from 15 June 1927, and appointed as staff officer to the naval officer at Sydney, Nova Scotia. He became a temporary commander (1 January 1942) in command of HMCS *Chambly*, then of *Stadacona* at Halifax (1942) and temporary captain in Ottawa (1942) and in command of *Qu'Appelle* (1944). He was credited with the first Canadian sinking of an enemy U-boat in the Second World War and won the DSC and the DSO. A younger colleague, *Captain C. P. Nixon, told me with humorous admiration that JP wore a monocle unsupported.

In 1946, JP and three other former students of St Michael's School were decorated at Government House, Victoria, in the presence of Lieutenant General H. D. G. Crerar and their former headmaster, *Kyrle Charles Symons, who remembered the occasion with particular delight. In March 1947, Kyrle visited JP and his wife at "Arbutus," a house they had recently purchased on the seafront at Gordon Head, where they spoke of offering him a cottage there as a retirement home. In January 1952, while they were still in that district, JP was elected to the church committee of St Luke's Anglican Church at Cedar Hill. Later, they went to live at Curtis Point in North Saanich and there JP died, aged seventy-nine, on 14 March 1979 at Saanich Peninsula Hospital, leaving his wife Patricia *née* O'Carrol-Derby, a son, James D. Prentice, and a daughter, Heather Hilliard Prentice.
Sources: *MacFarlane*, p. 52; notes from Captain C. P. Nixon, 3 August 2003; *Colonist*, 30 January 1952, p. 7; 16 March 1979, p. 52, obit.; Canadian census, 1901, Victoria; Kyrle C. Symons, *That Amazing Institution: The Story of St Michael's School, Victoria, B.C., from 1910-1948* (Victoria, Privately Printed, 1948?), pp. 161, 168-9.

PRESSEY, Lieutenant Colonel Arthur (1860-1923). He was born in Blackheath, Kent, third son of Rebecca and Arthur Pressey, who in 1861 declared himself to be a forty-six-year-old colonial merchant born in Chelsea. At the age of seventeen, AP joined one of the Kentish volunteer rifle corps, transferred three years later to the Seventh Royal Lancashire Militia, but in January 1882 passed from the militia into the regulars and was gazetted to the Royal Irish Regiment. Soon after that, he exchanged into the West Kents and served with them in the Egyptian campaign of 1882, being present at several engagements. He received the Egyptian medal and the Khedive's bronze star. At the end of that campaign, he exchanged into the Suffolks, at that time serving in India, and stayed with them until June 1885, when he was transferred to the Bengal Staff Corps and appointed to the Fourth Rajputs. With this regiment, he saw service in the Hazara expedition in 1891 (N-W Frontier medal and clasp) and commissioned as an officer in 1893. He was serving in the same regiment when, in 1895, he was put in command of the escort to the Sikkim-Tibetan Boundary Commission. In 1900, he was a captain wing commander in the Fourth Bengal Infantry and was serving in the Indian Staff Corps. On being promoted to lieutenant colonel in June 1907, he left the Fourth Rajputs to take command of the Tenth Jats and remained so until his retirement in January 1911.

In May 1911, AP went with his wife and some of their children to Vancouver Island. He had married Thekla Roddy twenty-six years earlier in May 1885. She was one of the three daughters of Colonel Patrick Roddy, VC (1827-1895), an Anglo-Irish soldier who also had six sons. The Presseys bought "the old Lloyd house in Westholme," a property on Somenos Lake near Duncan in the Cowichan Valley, where they farmed and were still there when AP died, aged sixty-three, on 28 August 1923. He was survived by his widow, two sons, and five daughters. His elder son, Major H. A. S. Pressey, MC, RE, was serving in India, and his younger son, Lieutenant Arthur Roddy Pressey, RCN, in Esquimalt in command of HMCS *Thiepval.* Two unmarried daughters, Thekla and Margaret, were at home and three were married, notably Erica, born on 18 February 1892, who married Stephen Harvey Yvon Birley, RN, on 3 November 1914. He was born on 23 October 1883 in Pendleton, Manchester, took a BSc at Manchester University, served in the Great War with the RN and the RCN, and settled at Duncan. AP was buried at St Peter's Quamichan on 30 August. The pallbearers were *J. H. Whittome, I. W. Sherman, R. H. Bannister, E. R. Hamilton, I. Birley, and W. T. Mason, the three last named being sons-in-law.

Sources: *Cowichan Leader,* 30 August and 6 September 1923, p. 5, obit.; VI Directory, 1922, p. 189ff.; notes courtesy of John Palmer; census 1861, England, RG 9/154, p. 27; notes on the Roddy family courtesy of Margaret Denton; *Whitaker's,* p. 424; Joe Garner, *Never Forget the Good Times: A Story of Life in British Columbia* (Nanaimo, Cinnebar Press, 1995), p. 103; *MacFarlane,* p. 52.

PREVOST, Admiral James Charles (1810-1891). He visited Esquimalt/Victoria at least three times in his naval career: in 1850 in command of HMS *Portland,* flagship of his father-in-law, Rear Admiral Fairfax Moresby (1786-1877); in 1857-1860 as captain of HMS *Satellite;* and in 1878-1879, mainly to visit the Metlakatla mission to tribes in the north near Alaska, whose founder, *William Duncan, he had taken over from England on his voyage to the Island in 1857. It was JP, indeed, who urged the Church Missionary Society of which he was a firm supporter, to recruit such a missionary in the first place. While visiting Fort Simpson, a northern HBC post, he had been impressed by the character and condition of the Tsimshian tribe and thought the CMS might be as successful in a mission to them as it had been in missions to the Maoris in New Zealand. His Christian enthusiasm is hardly surprising when we take account of his family's refugee Huguenot origins. JP's grandfather, Major General Augustin Prevost (1723-1786), was born in a Huguenot refugee family in Geneva and served as an officer in the British Army fighting in the Imperial cause during the American Revolution. Of course, JP's duties took him elsewhere than to the Pacific Ocean: In 1864-1869, for instance, he was in command of the RN Station at Gibraltar. He died at last in the west end of London, at 113 Ebury Street, on 28 January 1891. But the Island was much on his mind, and when in 1872 Kaiser Wilhelm I of Germany was appointed to arbitrate in the dispute over the San Juan Islands, JP appeared as one of the witnesses. Further evidence of his interest in the Island is the migration of his son, James Charles Prevost (1846-1920), who settled in Victoria about 1863, found employment as a civil servant, married and had nine children, and died on 15 May 1920 among a community of other Imperials near Duncan, forty miles north of Victoria. Nearly all of the many senior naval officers who visited or were posted at Esquimalt came to love the Island, but only a fraction of their number settled or left descendants there. *Lieutenant Commander Hon. Horace Douglas Lascelles, who lies buried at Esquimalt, is the best-remembered but JP is no less interesting.

"No man is an island" and JP's family circles, to whom he doubtless talked about the North-West Pacific Coast, ramified in southern England and Wales. When he married at Newton Ferrars, that pretty, rocky coastal village in Devon, the service was conducted by Rev. Sir George Prevost, second baronet (1804-1893), a first cousin, born in the West Indies on the island of Dominica. But there were further connections with the Island. His wife, Ellen Mary Moresby (born c. 1820 in Wales), daughter of Admiral Fairfax Moresby (1786-1877), had a younger brother, Rear Admiral John Moresby (1830-1922), who had at least six children. Of these, the eldest daughter, Elizabeth Louisa Moresby (c. 1862-1931), a most elusive and mysterious person, wrote many novels of exotic fantasy under several pseudonyms: Elizabeth Louisa Beck, Eliza Louisa Moresby Beck, Lily Moresby Adams, E. Barrington, and *Lily Adams Beck. After living for long periods in the Orient and taking up the cult of "theosophy," she spent most of the 1920s in Oak Bay, Victoria, where she is remembered at the Maltwood Gallery; a full collection of her writing is kept there. She arrived shortly after the death of JP's emigrant son, her first cousin, who had lived there for most of his life. It would be interesting to know whether she was in touch with any of his nine children during the 1920s. This seems quite possible as one of them, Harold Fairfax Prevost (1878-1941), for example, was a public figure in the Cowichan Valley who became mayor of Duncan. In 1873, JP's emigrant son married Anna Jane Fry (1853-1923), whose sister Mary Elizabeth Fry (1856-1843) married Daniel Wishart Mainguy (1842-1906) in 1884. From the Channel Islands, Mainguy's family had a maritime bent and his third son, *Edmond Rollo Mainguy (1901-1979), became an admiral in the Royal Canadian Navy, as did his son Dan (Mainguy's grandson), but in answer to questions about the family's past, Dan has no memory of the above except of course his own grandparents. The two Fry wives were daughters of Henry Fry (1825-1892), a merchant's son born in Barnstaple, Devon, who led a restless, roving life until 1864, when he went into business in Victoria, and then settled on a farm in Cowichan and joined the Episcopal Church. In 1887, the Cowichan district elected Fry to the Legislative Assembly of the Province. In these ways, JP's early favourable impression of the Island had permanent social effects.

Sources: Prevost Papers, Archives of the University of Victoria; Dorothy Blakey Smith, "*The Journal of Arthur Thomas Bushby*," 1858-1859, *BCHQ* 21, (1957-1958): 191-192. VI 23.1; *The Times*, 31 January 1891, p. 1; Barry M. Gough, *The Royal Navy and the Northwest Coast of North America*, 1810-1914: A Study of British Maritime Ascendancy (Vancouver, University of British Columbia Press, 1971), pp. 133-34, 139, 154-55, 160, 187-88; Jean Usher, *William Duncan of Metlakatla: A Victorian Missionary in British Columbia* (Ottawa, National Museum of Man, 1974), pp. 26-29; Walbran, *B.C. Coast Names*, pp. 400-01; Longstaff, *Esquimalt Naval Base*, p. 20.

PRIMROSE-WELLS, Dr Albert (1854-1948), MA (Cantab.), LRCS, LRCP, LM (Edin.). He and his wife moved about 1919 to "Pinner Wood" near Duncan in the Cowichan Valley, where he served the district as a medical doctor for nearly forty years. They had emigrated from England to Creston in the Kootenay Valley in mainland BC in 1911 and cleared land for an apple orchard but soon took up a medical practice. They moved to the Island following the loss of a son, James Bowen Primrose-Wells (1887-1918), who had joined the Canadian Army in November 1914, transferred to the Fourth Battalion of the Bedfordshire Regiment of the British Army, and died in action, aged thirty, in the Somme campaign in France on 4 April 1918. AP thought of himself as a specialist in medical treatment by "Light, Electricity, and Vibration" and had spent some time as an "Electrical Physician" at St Luke's Hospital in the west end of London. In England, as a young man he had played football and cricket, and on the Island, he took up hunting, shooting, and gardening. Like so many Imperials, he joined St Peter's Anglican Church at Quamichan, near Duncan. A friend who grew up in that parish recalled AP in his later years reading one of the two lessons during Sunday services:

> He was stone deaf and after reading the First Lesson in church he would depart from church, warm up the motor of his old Essex car, and to make sure it was going he would press down the accelerator as far as possible and control the speed of the car by the clutch. The poor fellow who read the Second Lesson had to compete with that motor noise. Of course all ears in the congregation were on Dr. P-W's car rather than the lesson. That was in the days when the road was open all the way and not blocked off as it is now. So we heard him from three directions.

He was undoubtedly one of the Imperial personalities described in general terms by *Conrad Swan, son of the other principal physician in Duncan at the time, though Swan was careful not to mention him by name.

AP was born north east of London in an Essex village, variously cited in census records as "Little Wrentham" (1861), "Chelmsford" (1891), "Broomfield" (1901), and "near Chelmsford" (1933-1934). His father was plain Joseph Wells (c. 1813-1893), born at Braintree, Essex, and variously cited as a "farmer," "farmer maltster," and "landowner" living in 1861 on 476 acres at "Wood House" in or near Little Waltham, Essex. His wife, AP's mother, was Maria *née* Primrose, born at Wrentham, Suffolk, daughter of a surgeon, John Thomas Primrose, and this family appears in 1851 living in Ipswich at St Margaret's Green. Maria, already married, was recorded as Maria Wells, aged thirty-two, staying with her parents, John Thomas Primrose, seventy-two, a retired surgeon, and Phebe [*sic*], sixty-six, along with Maria's younger unmarried sister, Sarah Jane Primrose, twenty-nine. These four were all born at Wrentham, Suffolk, but with them was Maria's daughter by AP, Jessie Wells, aged six, born at Broomfield, Essex, and one servant girl. Joseph Wells had married somewhat above his own station in life, as men often did—so often that this sometimes appears to be almost customary—which is why AP adopted his hyphenated name, though there may also have been a property inheritance contingent on this change of name. John Thomas Primrose, his wife Phoebe *née* Crisp, and their six daughters, including Maria, were all buried in due time in a family grave at St Nicholas Parish Church in Wrentham, the married daughters with their married names.

After an education at Repton School and Cambridge University, AP became assistant house physician and assistant medical registrar at Addrubrookes's Hospital, Cambridge, and St George's Hospital, London, and qualified in medicine at Edinburgh in 1882. On 10 January 1883 at Weston-super-Mare, he married Grace Woosnam (1857-1938), born in India a daughter of Major General James Bowen Woosnam (1812-1877) and his wife *née* Agnes Bell. AP had married into a devoted Imperial family. Woosnam rose in the Indian Army to be inspector general of ordnance, Bombay Artillery, after serving in the Afghan Campaign in 1839, retired with his wife to Wales, and died at Aberhafesp Hall, Newtown, Montgomeryshire. His brother (her uncle), Dr Richard Woosnam (1815-1888), was appointed in 1841 to be surgeon to Sir Henry Pottinger, HM plenipotentiary to China (1842-1845), acting secretary and assistant secretary to Pottinger's mission, and deputy colonial secretary of Hong Kong. Then, in 1846-1848, he was secretary to Sir Henry Pottinger as high commissioner to the Cape of Good Hope and Kaffraria and private secretary to Pottinger in 1848-1854 during his government of Madras. Grace also had two older brothers, one a civil engineer who had a career in India, notably in Assam, and the other a distinguished Anglican clergyman. Soon after their marriage, AP was appointed surgeon to the household of the lieutenant governor of the Isle of Man, and so the first three of their children were born there in Douglas. Four years there were followed by sixteen years in general practise at Beckenham, Kent, and then some years specializing in light, electricity, and vibration treatments in the west end of London, where he had an appointment as electrical physician at St Luke's Hospital.

It was from there that he took the family out to Creston, BC, then back to England during the Great War (1914-1918), where Grace served at St Dunston's Home for the blind, and AP did some work in relation to the war. On returning to BC, they settled on the Island and moved to Duncan in 1921. There Grace died, aged eighty, on 11 June 1938 and AP, aged ninety-four, on 5 December 1948, leaving two sons in England and three daughters. In 1921, one of these,

J.F. Bosher

Mona Kathleen Primrose-Wells (1893-1982), had married Leonard Fordham Solly (1885-1978) of "Lakeview Farm" at Westholme in the Cowichan Valley. Born and educated in Victoria, he was a son of L. H. Solly, who had emigrated from Wales and found employment on the Island as Land Commissioner to the Esquimalt & Nanaimo Railway Company. Young Solly had spent two years with the Canadian Bank of Commerce but in 1907 bought 150 acres near Duncan and took up poultry and dairy farming. It was perhaps as a member of the Duncan Hospital Board, a church warden at All Saints, Westholme, and a member of various agricultural associations that he befriended AP and family.

Sources: Notes from John Palmer, 1 September 2002; *Colonist*, 14 September 1918, p. 7, photo and obit. (Captain J. Bowen Primrose-Wells); 14 June 1938, p. 5, obit.; *Who's Who in B.C.* 1933-1934, p. 180; 1942-1943, pp. 285-86 (Solly); NAC, CEF files, box 10222-22, regimental no. 77820; *Collections Historical & Archaeological relating to Montgomeryshire and its Borders*, vol. 19 (Powys Land Club, 1886), pp. 185-198; census 1861, England, RG 9/1081/77, p. 3; census 1891, RG 12/625, p. 30; census 1901, RG 13/687, p. 14.

PRIOR, Lieutenant Colonel Edward Gawlor (1853-1920). Born at Dallowgill, Yorkshire, on 21 May 1853, son of Henry Prior and Hannah Mouncey (*née* Kendell) Prior, he appears, aged seven, living with his family in 1861 at "The Parsonage," Laverdon, near Dallowgill. His father, aged forty-nine, was "Perpetual Curate & Incumbent" born in Plymouth, Devon, and his mother, aged forty-three, was born at Leeds, Yorkshire. He had five sisters and there were two domestic servants. EP attended Leeds Grammar School, studied engineering at Wakefield, and then emigrated to Vancouver Island in 1873 as a mining engineer and surveyor for the Vancouver Coal Mining and Land Co. He kept in touch with his Yorkshire home, however, as may be inferred from the marriage of his youngest daughter, Jessie Burton Prior, at Newcastle-on-Tyne on 5 December 1914 to Captain James Watson, Second Northumbrian RFA, of Hendon Hall, Yorkshire. EP had a remarkable career in Victoria. From August 1887 to May 1880, he worked as a government inspector of mines. Then he became an iron and hardware merchant at Victoria with a shop at the corner of Government and Johnson streets. The business grew and established a branch in Vancouver, and he rose to be president of E. G. Prior & Co. Ltd. From the 1890s to the 1920s, the *Daily Colonist* and newspapers all over the province carried large advertisements of his wagons, carriages, firearms, and ironmongery. Meanwhile, he became a lieutenant colonel commanding the Fifth Regiment, Canadian Artillery.

In 1886, EP was elected to the BC Legislature for Victoria City, resigned on 23 January 1888, was elected to the House of Commons for Victoria on 23 January 1888, and re-elected in 1891 in another by-election. Re-elected more than once in both provincial and federal ridings, he served as BC minister of mines from 26 February to 21 November 1902 and as premier and minister of Mines from 21 November 1902 to 1 June 1903, was defeated in 1904, became a member of the Privy Council on 17 December 1895 and controller of Inland Revenue from 17 December 1895 to 10 July 1896. Shortly before the Great War, he and his second wife, Genevieve Boucher *née* Wright (1863-1955), returned from England on the

Megantic, arriving at Quebec on 4 May 1914 with their daughter Jessie, aged twenty. EP had a strong popular following and was appointed lieutenant governor of BC on 9 December 1919, died in office on 12 December 1920, and was buried in the Anglican part of the Ross Bay Cemetery in a grand funeral procession. It is true that he was obliged to retire because of a conflict of interest. He was survived by his second wife, Genevieve Boucher Wright, whom he had married on 4 February 1899, the first Mrs Prior, *née* Suzette Work (married on 30 January 1878), having died, aged forty-two, on 9 December 1897. During her long widowhood of thirty-five years, the second Mrs Prior was befriended by my kind old aunt, Mabel Constance Ferguson (1899-1964), who had been a housemaid at Government House and with whom I lived for a year in 1947-1948 in Beechwood Avenue, Victoria. Mrs Prior gave my aunt a signed photograph of Prime Minister John A. Macdonald, who had presented it to EP as a token of friendship, a photo now in my possession. After retiring in Ottawa, I scanned it and took a copy to the British High Commission established in John A. Macdonald's house, which did not have this photo.

Sources: J. K. Johnson, ed., *The Canadian Directory of Parliament, 1867-1967* (Ottawa, Public Archives, 1968), p. 476; census 1861, England, RG 9/3198/39, p. 1; census 1871, RG 10/4571, p. 10; S. W. Jackman, *Portraits of the Premiers: An Informal History of British Columbia* (Sidney, BC, Gray's Publishing, 1969), pp. 146-152; *Colonist,* 22 March 1893, p. 8; 10 September 1921, p. 11.

PUNNETT, Captain Harold Rodd (1874-?). Born in England, he attended King Edward's School at Bromsgrove, Worcester, where the 1891 census found him, aged seventeen, without recording his place of birth. This may mean that he was a brother of *Raymond Bellinger Punnett, who was born in India and moved to the Island in 1889. Perhaps, too, he was a brother of Second Lieutenant Percival Rodd Punnett, RGA, who served in the Siege Train Corps in South Africa (1899-1900), aged about twenty years, and who is equally elusive in the records. HP went out to BC in 1891 but returned to England to serve in a British unit as a scout in Matabeleland (1896), as a lieutenant in Bechuanaland, and as a captain in the second South African ("Boer") War. He stayed on to serve on the Royal Commission on Compensation at the Cape in 1903. In 1915-1918 and 1939-1941, he was with the Canadian Department of National Defence. In the years 1910-1939, he kept his home in Duncan, having married Kathleen Jessie Francis on 5 May 1911 in Victoria, and where he played golf and was active in hospital and public library work. Later, he moved to 1853 Nelson Street, Vancouver, but they moved away before their deaths.

Sources: *Who's Who in B.C.,* 1942-1943, p. 259; census 1891, England, RG 12/2344, p. 22; *Whitaker's,* p. 428.

PUNNETT, Raymond Bellinger (1871-1943). He was born on 29 April 1871 in India, attended Highgate School in London and Oxford University, and migrated in 1889 to Victoria. There on 30 April 1892, he married Sylvia Gertrude Jenns, daughter of Emma and Rev. Percival Jenns, an Anglican minister from England, where the older Jenns's children were born. RP was employed in 1901 as a twenty-nine-year-old clerk in the Land Registry Office at $640 a year and living on Whittier Avenue. By then, they had joined the Reformed Episcopal Church. He became a successful real-estate agent, joined the Union Club and the Conservative Party, and moved to 1044 McClure Street. He was one of those rare citizens who, in 1901, claimed to be able to read and write French, though in fact many British officers could. The Punnetts had a daughter, Susan V. Punnett, who served at one time in the British Embassy in Tokio and was in England at the time of RP's death. One of RP's five sons, Schuyler Lionel Punnett (1895-1979), served overseas with Canadian forces during the Great War. RP died, aged eighty-four, on 23 May 1979 in Victoria, and his widow died there, aged ninety-eight, on 3 January 1964. **Sources:** Canadian census 1901 Victoria; *Colonist*, 5 March 1943, p. 5, obit.; NAC, CEF files, box 8021-8.

PURVER, William Harrington (1879-1965). He was born on 17 December 1879 at Nettlebed, five miles down the river from Henley-on-Thames, son of Thomas and Esther Purver and, after joining the militia volunteers at 15, enlisted in the Royal Artillery in 1897, which soon sent him to Bermuda. Posted in 1903 to Esquimalt, he married Dorothy Elva Parke there on 15 September 1906 and transferred to the Royal Canadian Garrison Artillery at about the time they took command of the Esquimalt base at Work Point. The RCGA kept him at Work Point Barracks for a few years before sending him to Halifax and then Quebec. Promoted in 1911 to sergeant major and staff superintending clerk, he went overseas with the Canadian Field Artillery in 1915, served for a year in France, and returning to Canada in 1919 was stationed successively at Halifax, Quebec, Kingston, and Ottawa. His wife having died before the war and his father on 14 July 1915, he retired to Duncan in July 1924 as a warrant officer with the rank of hon. lieutenant and took his children to live with his mother, near sisters, and a brother and sister-in-law. His son, Gordon M. Purver, attended the state school in Duncan and his daughter Margaret Elva Purver (whom he had cited as his next of kin in 1915) was at school in Portland, Maine, where she lived at 705 Stevens Avenue. At Duncan he remained, except for two years in England on the staff of the Canadian Government Exhibition Commission, and for several years he was the Duncan city clerk charged with policing the town. He was one of the founders and the first secretary of the Cowichan Branch, Royal Canadian Legion, and during the Second World War, he served in the Duncan unit of the Pacific Coast Militia Rangers. He was a Royal Arch Mason and a member of St John's Anglican Church. When he died in Duncan hospital, aged eighty-five, on 27 February 1965, he left a second wife, Jessie, a prominent church woman, an accomplished needlewoman, and a tireless worker for the Red Cross and the Legion's women's auxiliary. His son Gordon was in Vancouver and his daughter Margaret was still in South Portland, Maine, as Mrs K. B. Dow. Representatives from the Legion attended his burial in St Mary's Cemetery at Somenos, near Duncan. **Sources:** *Cowichan Leader*, 4 June 1925; 3 March 1965; letter of 28 June 2002 from John Palmer, who remembered WP and his wife Jessie; NAC, CEF files, box 8028-27, regimental no. 87351.

RANSOM, Captain Alan Adair (c. 1893-1968). He was born at Sydney, Australia, as was his mother, Mary. His father, Alfred George Ransom, was a Trinity sea pilot born at Dover, Kent, and there the census of 1901 found them all three, with a servant, living at 23 Priory Hill, next door to a hotel porter. AR's paternal grandfather, William Ransom, was also a Trinity pilot at Dover, though born at Ramsgate, and there may have been a family connection with *Shearman Ransom, who joined the Bengal Pilot Service in India, where he was born. This seems all the more probable because both families moved to Vancouver Island and spent time in the Cowichan Valley. AR and his father (though not his mother) were there well before AR joined the Twenty-seventh Anti-Aircraft Battery in Victoria during the Second World War and went on to serve in the British Army. His father died, aged eighty-two, in Victoria on 19 November 1942, and AR went on to become CO of the anti-aircraft unit at Tofino on the Island's west coast. He and his wife Irene had a son and five daughters, one of whom, Vivian Ransom, on 29 October 1940, married Lieutenant James Sutherland Chisholm Fraser, RCA, son of J. S. C. Fraser's widow, then at Shanghai, China. AR and his wife were living at 4985 Cordova Bay Road, Victoria, when he died, aged seventy-five, on 7 March 1968 and was buried there at St David's-by-the-Sea.
Sources: *Colonist*, 8 October 1940, p. 8; 9 March 1968, p. 24, obit.; census 1861, England, RG 9/549, p. 29; census 1901, RG 13/838, p. 3.

RANSOM, Shearman (1840-1936). He was born on 2 December 1840 at Calcutta, India, to an English-born father and a French mother. He became a ship's pilot and served in the Hooghli (Bengal) Pilot Service on the river leading up to Calcutta. At sometime in the early 1870s, he married Amelia Ann Guichet, born on 5 February 1845 in Ryde, Hampshire, daughter of William Guichet, "Professor & Schoolmaster" born c. 1795 in Paris. RS and his wife had two sons who were sent to be schooled in London, where the 1881 census found them, young Shearman Ranson, aged nine, and Richard seven, living in Brixton at a small school kept by a middle-aged widow, Susanna Ellaby, with her daughter and two sons, one a railway clerk and the other a printer's clerk. Ten years later, the Ransom brothers were farming together in the Cowichan Valley, aged eighteen and nineteen, while their parents were still in India.

RS and his wife went to Canada in 1899 and in 1901 were living on Trunk Road, Somenos, in the Cowichan district with their son Richard, born on 18 August 1873 in India. SR recorded in the 1901 census on the Island that he had no profession, but the son, Richard, was a farmer and there was a daughter, Dorothy Olive Ransom, born on 15 August 1876 in England, who married Patrick Beswick Johnston at Chemainus on 3 September 1904 and died in due time, aged ninety-three, on 17 March 1970 at Langley. With RS in 1901, too, was Mrs Amelia Ransom's mother, Mary Jane Guichet, born on 7 June 1814 in London, who had likewise gone to Canada in 1899. The family had a Japanese cook aged twenty-four. Young Shearman Ranson, Richard's brother, had already gone to live at Langley Prairie in the Fraser Valley on the mainland, where he died, aged eighty-one, on 21 April 1953 (leaving a son of the same name, who in due course died there, aged seventy-one, on 27 February 1979). RS's mother-in-law Mary Jane Guichet died, aged ninety-two, on 7 January 1907; Amelia Ann Ransom died, aged ninety, on 12 August 1935; and SR died, aged ninety-five, on 7 April 1936 at Duncan Hospital and was buried at St Peter's Quamichan.

Sources: *Colonist*, 9 April 1936, p. 18, obit.; *Cowichan Leader*, 9 April 1936, p. 5, obit.; census 1861, England, RG 9/657, p. 3 (Guichet); census 1881, RG 11/618; Canadian census 1891, VI, 1891; Canadian census, 1891, VI, 1891.

RASMUSSEN, Albert Henry (1883-1972). He was born on 2 October 1883 at Skien, South Norway, and went to sea, aged fourteen, sailing the oceans of the world until he was twenty-two. Then he went ashore and settled in China, where from about 1905, he found employment with the British-run Chinese Maritime Customs service. From that, he went on to work for European firms with branches in China, such as the Asiatic Petroleum Company at Kongmoon, in the province of Kwangtung, and was with Arnhold, Karberg and Company when the Great War broke out. "My firm was registered in Berlin," he wrote later, "and the outbreak of the First World War made it necessary for the partners to declare themselves. Two of the German partners left for Berlin, but the two Arnhold brothers, who had been brought up in Britain and were British citizens, liquidated the firm of Arnhold, Karberg and started their own firm of Arnhold Bros., registered in Hong Kong as a British firm. They were sons of the founder and held most of the shares, so the whole China business was taken over by them. The firm had wide ramifications with important branches and large staffs in Hong Kong, Canton, Tsingtau, Tientsin, Peking, Hankow and Chungking. Chinkiang [where he spent ten years] was the newest and smallest of the branches. After receiving the registration certificate from Hongkong, I registered the firm at the British Consulate and business went on as usual . . ."

"In 1923 I left for Vancouver Island, where I bought a small ranch. We were expecting another child by then and I wanted it to be born in a white man's country . . . In March 1923 Elizabeth Rosemary was born on the ranch at Mt Newton outside Victoria, but the year we spent in that wonderful island is another story." At their small farm on the West Saanich Road, they had fruit trees, White Wyandot hens, and a quiet life with retired Imperial officers as neighbours. Late in 1923, however, the Arnhold brothers offered him a post as manager in Tientsin, and early the next year, they sailed from Victoria to Yokohama on the *Empress of Asia*. AR attempted at one time to cross the Atlantic alone in a small boat, and perhaps he was attracted by the Orient for the adventures it offered. In May 1925, the *Victoria Daily Colonist* reported that he and his wife had been seized by bandits while travelling in a motor boat on the West River. In 1937, when the Japanese invasion came too close, they made preparations to leave China. During World War II, he worked as a naval correspondent for the BBC, became a war historian to the Royal Navy, and then turned to writing. He published several books: *Sea Fever* (Constable, 1952, repr. 1960), an autobiographical volume entitled *China Trader* (Constable, 1954), *Return to the Sea* (Constable, 1956), *The House of Contentment* (Faber, 1961), and with Commander R. F. P. Halliday (1894-1973), RN, a book of

songs, *Blow Boys Blow, Sea Songs, Shanties & Sail-Talk.* After the Second World War, he settled in Norway and died there on 6 December 1872.
Sources: *Colonist,* 27 May 1925, p. 13; A. H. Rasmussen, *China Trader* (Constable, 1954), pp. 159, 163, 171ff.

RATTRAY, Major Laurence Chapman (1877-1961). Born in Edinburgh, member of a well-known Perthshire family, he attended Sedbergh School in Yorkshire's West Riding, where the census of 1891 found him, aged thirteen, and later he went into the Colonial Service. Fort Jameson in Northern Rhodesia was the centre of his work for several years. He had a great deal to do with African tribes and their chiefs, as he negotiated the moving of herds of cattle and saw to other Imperial tasks. A keen student of African affairs, he always spoke with respect about chiefs who became his friends and who impressed him with their wisdom. He served during the South African War as a trooper in the Thorneycroft Horse Regiment, named for Lieutenant Colonel Alexander W. Thorneycroft, a special services officer whom General Wolseley sent out before the war in command of a regiment of five hundred irregulars, mounted infantry, mainly Uitlander refugees operating in Natal, where they had worked as scouts accompanied by a group of Zulu guides, paid for out of Thorneycroft's own pocket. After that war, LR retired to a quiet life as a married farmer at home in Scotland, but the Great War drew him back into Imperial service as a captain in the Sixth Battalion of the King's Royal Rifles. In July 1915, he was ADC to General T. D. Pilcher, GOC, Seventeenth Division. He then retired with the rank of major, the military cross, having already been twice mentioned in despatches.

LR seems to have intended to migrate to Victoria even before the Great War. For two years, he owned a house built in 1913 at 2400 Dalhousie Street, but does not seem to have lived there. He gave his address at that time as c/o F. Landsberg, Empire Realty Company, Victoria. After the war, however, he settled at Duncan and was soon active in the life of the Cowichan Valley. Like many others of his kind, he loved fishing with a fly in lakes and rivers. He soon came to be regarded as an expert on the stream fishery of the region. He worked actively with the Duncan Board of Trade and later the Chamber of Commerce, in the interests of a biological survey of the Cowichan watershed, and in the 1930s, he argued strongly for such a development. At a Board of Trade luncheon in April 1925, he spoke about the unique ten-month fishing season in streams in the region. On 1 May 1929, he served as the representative of Duncan Board of Trade at a meeting of the Island's Associated Boards of Trade held at Duncan. Near four years later, he wrote to the Duncan Chamber of Commerce, "asking that a special meeting of the Associated Boards of Trade of V.I. be called to discuss and urge the inflation of currency and the remonetization of silver and a national bank to lend money to farmers at 2 percent interest. The matter was filed." On the voter's list in 1935 for what was then called the Vimy district, he was listed without title as a married farmer, and the listing in 1958 was for "Mr and Mrs Laurence C. Rattray, Quamichan, Park Road, Duncan, V.I." A historian of the local Anglican Church, St Peter's Quamichan, which he attended, recalled him as "A tall man of fearsome visage. He invariably carried a shepherd's crook longer than he was tall when walking about the streets of Duncan. Once, in his automobile, he collided with a train; he survived but his car did not. When asked whether he had seen the train, he replied imperiously, 'Of course, I honked at it.'" On his property beside the Cowichan River at Sahtlam, he gardened energetically and well, and when it became too much for him, he moved to a property at Quamichan Lake. There his widow, Catrin, survived him when he died, aged eighty-four, on 15 July 1961.

Sources: PRO, WO 339/17919; census 1891, England, RG 12/3489, p. 30; *Colonist*, 10 April 1925, p. 16; 3 February 1933, p. 17; *Cowichan Leader*, 19 July 1961, p. 3, obit.; Williams, *The Story of St Peter's*, p. 73; NAC, Election rolls for 1935, reel T4760; *The Social Register of Canada* (at the Ottawa Public Library), 1st ed., Montreal, 1959; Thomas Pakenham, *The Boer War* (New York, Random House, 1979), pp. 298-9; Stuart Stark, *Oak Bay's Heritage Buildings: More than Just Bricks and Boards* (Victoria, Corporation of Oak Bay, 1986), p. 18.

RAVENHILL, Alice (1859-1954) and Horatio Thomas (1862-1941). Sister and brother, they went out to the Island in 1910 with their younger sister, Edith, and HR's only son and settled on rural wooded property at Shawnigan Lake. AR kept house for the men while they cleared the land but soon found time to do what she had long done in England. She lectured on issues of public health, hygiene, and childcare, travelling more and more widely to address audiences all over North America. In April 1931, for instance, she spoke on "The Five Ks" at the twelfth annual meeting of the BC Teacher's Federation of which Ira Dilworth was president. Local people sometimes resented her gratuitous advice "about how they ought to air their beds etc." A daughter of *Colonel F. T. Oldham recalls her mother making a mischievous call on the Ravenhills and pretending to offer them similar help and advice, a little of their own medicine. As AR became known, she was able to "entertain a succession of Bishops" and such distinguished public figures as Dr D. Jenness, chief of the Anthropological Section of the National Museum in Ottawa and an expert on Indian cultures who involved her more and more in promoting the arts and crafts of tribes on the Pacific Coast. In 1948, the University of British Columbia conferred on her an honorary degree in recognition of her public-spirited activities. She passed her life in the footsteps of Florence Nightingale the social reformer.

Having attended Marlborough College, the famous public school in Wiltshire, HR was given to other causes but was no less public-spirited. He devoted himself to the Boy Scout movement and became a scout commissioner and a leader in the province. In May 1925, he went home to England for four months to visit Boy Scout troops and leaders, staying with a sister in Winchester. At home in England, he had been a prominent amateur tennis player and had also played nationally and internationally for the Marlborough Nomads Football Club. He became well known on the Island as an expert cyclist and spent three months in 1935, crossing Canada on his bicycle, avoiding the cities as much as he could. Like his sister, he sympathized with a number of causes: For instance, he became a member of the Island Council of Social Hygiene and accompanied Mrs Emmeline Pankhurst when she spoke to an audience in Sidney late in September 1921. He served as a guide and counsellor for Toc H for fifteen years. He was a founding member of the Social Service League, which amalgamated with the Friendly Help Association as the Friendly Help Welfare Association, and he assisted in forming a Council of Social Agencies. He joined the Navy League of Canada, the British Public Schools Club of Victoria, and the Overseas League of which he was vice-president in 1925. He also played the organ at a local church in the settlement at Shawnigan Lake, patronized the Diocesan Church Embroidery Guild, and was generally active, like his sister. They suffered much when his son, Horace Leslie Ravenhill (1889-1915), who enlisted on 17 April 1914, died in battle near Ypres on 24 April 1915.

Census records show that AR was born at Leyton, Essex, and HR at Walthamstow, their father, John Richard Ravenhill (15 April 1824-28 December 1894) born at Battersea, London, and their mother Fanny at Heytesbury in Wiltshire. There were several brothers and sisters by 1861, when the family was living at Delaford, Iver, in Buckinghamshire, with six domestic servants, including a coachman. A variety of birthplaces show that the family moved a good deal. In 1861, the father was a marine engineer. In 1871, he was a "marine engineer employing 500 men" somewhere near Walthamstow, and there were now nine servants. But in 1891, he was a "soils engineer chairman of public companies" and lived at Delaford, Iver, in Buckinghamshire, but the mother and children were elsewhere. HR married Eleanor Frances Cunningham in 1887 at Hatfield, Hertfordshire, and declared that he was "a wire rope manufacturer" on the baptismal certificate of his son, Horace Leslie Cunningham Ravenhill, dated 18 January 1889 at St Stephen's Church in Kensington. But in 1901, he was employed as a "brewer's cashier" and living with Eleanor alone. She was born about 1866 in Paddington, daughter of a wine merchant, and in 1881 was living with her family at Hove, Sussex, with seven domestic servants. Why HR and his son moved to the Island in 1910 with his sisters, an only son, and no wife can only be a matter of conjecture but a tragic death in childbirth is a strong possibility.

HR died, aged seventy-nine, on 18 October 1941 in Victoria and AR died, aged ninety-four, on 27 May 1954, both in Victoria.

Sources: Alice Ravenhill, *The Memoirs of an Educational Pioneer* (Toronto, J. M. Dent, 1951), pp. 181, 204 and passim; *Colonist*, 30 September 1921, p. 9; 7 February 1925, p. 6; 8 May 1925, p. 9; 2 April 1931, p. 5, photo of Alice; 19 October 1941, pp. 20 and 24, obit.; census 1861, England, RG 9/1060, p. 83; census 1871, RG 10/1626; census 1881, RG 11/1095/72, pp. 19-20 (Cunningham); census 1891, RG 12/1133, p. 19; census 1901, RG 13/1218/13/p. 17; Monica Oldham, daughter of *Colonel F. T. Oldham of Cobble Hill, interviewed in Oak Bay ca. 2003; NAC, CEF files, box 8108-42, regimental no. 16812; Civil Engineer obituaries, Internet site by B. A. Curran; Baptismal register of St Stephen's Anglican Church, Kensington, entry for 18 January 1890.

RAWSON, Phillip Warrick (1883-1974). He was born in October 1883 at Bradford, Yorkshire, son of Joyce Rawson and her husband, Philip Stansfeld Rawson, who in 1891 was a Yorkshire "stuff salesman." They came from what Burke's

Colonial Gentry describes as "a very ancient family for many generations settled in Yorkshire," and indeed PR's father appears, aged two, in the 1861 census living with his father (PR's grandfather), Jeremiah Stansfeld Rawson (1817-1891), a "land agent farming twelve acres" at Rawdon in Yorkshire, and his mother, Jeremiah's second wife. In 1891, PR was sent to be schooled at Bradford Grammar School. In 1899, he joined the Royal Horse Artillery and went to India.

In 1906, he returned and went out to Canada, where he served in the RCNWM Police until 1916. That year, he retired and joined the Alberta Provincial Police, but in 1924 retired again and went to Victoria, where he started an insurance adjusting agency at 625 Fort Street. It must have prospered as he was able to live near the Oak Bay waterfront at 495 Beach Drive with his wife, Florence Gertrude Jackson of London, whom he had married in 1912 and by whom he had a son and two daughters. The 1901 census recorded her, aged eight, at a school in Bradley, London, with an elder sister. PR died, age ninety, on 18 February 1974, a Freemason and an Anglican, and Mrs Jackson died, aged ninety, on 13 February 1979 in Saanich.

Sources: *Who's Who in B.C.*, 1933-1934, p. 144; census 1861, England, RG 9/3215/40, p. 3; census, 1891, RG 12/3625, p. 18; census, 1901, RG 13/1652; Wrigley's Greater Victoria Directory, 1933-4, pp. 347-8; Sir Bernard Burke, *A Genealogical and Heraldic History of the Colonial Gentry* (1891), pp. 425-30.

READE, Frederick Murray (1848-1933). He was born at Ipsden, near Henley-on-Thames in Oxfordshire, one of the younger sons of William Barrington Reade (1803-1881) and his Scottish wife, Elizabeth Murray. He was also a nephew of the famous Victorian author and dramatist, Charles Reade (1814-1884), who wrote of FR's father, "My dear lamented brother William Barrington Reade was first a sailor, then a soldier, then a country squire, and had from his youth an eye for character and live facts worth noting by sea or land. He furnished me from his experiences several tidbits that figure in my printed works . . . In 1849 my brother inherited the Ipsden estates, and a year or two afterward occupied an old house of his near Scott's Common . . ." Before this inheritance, FR's father had served in India in a cavalry regiment of the East India Company. In April 1871, by which time FR had left home, census records give interesting details of his family. They were living at 11 St Mary Abbott's Terrace, Kensington, where the father, William Barrington Reade, aged sixty-eight, declared himself to be a "Magistrate Landowner" born at Ipsden. Besides his wife, then aged sixty, two unmarried daughters (FR's sisters), aged twenty-four and twenty, born one at Birkenhead, Cheshire, and the other at Henley-on-Thames, Oxfordshire, were each recorded as "Landowner." FR's elder brother, William Barrington Reade (junior), aged thirty-two, declared himself to be an "African Explorer Author" born at Crieff, Scotland. Investigation shows that before he died prematurely in 1875, the latter published several books and many letters to *The Times* under the name "Winwood Reade," but occasionally wrote as "William Winwood Reade." There was a housemaid and a cook, and their neighbours were a retired wine merchant and an assistant secretary of a

Foundling Hospital. Another brother, absent like FR, was away in the Royal Navy and by 1881 had became Commander Charles Edward Reade, aged thirty-nine, born at Reading, Berkshire, but by then was at home with the family, which had moved to 8 Clarendon Villas in Margate. There were two "Trained Nurses" as well as the cook and the housemaid.

FR married Marianne Cecilia Coleman at Turtle Mountain near Toronto, Ontario, on 18 July 1882, and they had a daughter in London who was christened Edith Madeleine Reade at St Barnabas Church in Kensington on 26 September 1884. She grew up and on 25 December 1909 became the second wife of *G. W. V. Cuppage, a civil servant in Victoria. Not being in Victoria when the Canadian census of 1901 was taken, this Reade family evidently arrived at sometime between 1901 and 1909. In 1911, they built the neoclassical Mount Edwards Apartment House, with thirty private suites. Whether FR did anything else on the Island did not emerge in my research but when he died, aged eighty-four, on 11 August 1933 in Victoria, he had been living there for many years. Buried as an Anglican, he was survived by his widow and their married daughter, Mrs Cuppage. Marianne Cecilia (Coleman) Reade, lived until 11 May 1950, when she died, aged ninety-one, in Oak Bay.

It is worth noting that FR may have been a distant relation of the Reade baronets of Shipton Court, Shipton-under-Wychwood, Oxfordshire, usually identified as "the Reade Baronets, of Barton (1661)" to distinguish them from other Reades. The short-lived third baronet in that line, Sir Winwood Reade (1682-1692), may have been the person whom FR's explorer brother had in mind when he adopted "Winwood Reade" as his *nom-de-plume*. But FR was certainly no blood relation of the barrister Joseph Reade, who married Janie, daughter of *Sir Clive Phillipps-Wolley and lived on Vancouver Island. According to a plausible account explained at length in the *Washington Post*, that Joseph Reade was a son of Joseph Wakefield (1815-1893), a footman in the household at Shipton Court who witnessed the seventh baronet killing his butler in a fit of rage and contrived to acquire the estate by blackmail. He then pretended to belong to the family by changing his name to Joseph Reade by royal license upon the death of the seventh baronet in January 1868. Genealogists who watch over these matters were not deceived by these manoeuvres and everywhere omitted his name from tables of the dynastic line. They knew that the only legitimate heirs, by blood, to the baronetcy were the seventh baronet's imbecile daughter Emily (1820-1871) and his grandnephew Chandos Stanhope Hoskyns Reade (1851-1890), legitimately the eighth baronet, followed by his nephew George Compton Reade (1845-1908), ninth baronet, who was living in Michigan and unable to challenge the succession to the estate until too late. Details of Joseph Wakefield's usurpation circulated widely at the level of popular gossip, but I could find no report in *The Times* of London. Was it Victorian discretion combined with a fear of libel laws which kept these events out of the public record in England, leaving them for American newspapers? In any case, it is easy to be muddled about these families for lack of official records. Internet files following different paths come up with different relationships, and this paragraph will not be the last word on the subject.

Sources: *Colonist* 13 August 1933, p. 20, obit.; census 1851, England, HO 107/1732/162/1; census 1861, RG 9/492, p. 24; census 1861, RG 9/909, p. 8; census 1871, RG 10/35; census 1871, RG 10/1455, p. 18; census, 1881, RG 11/986, p. 31; census 1881, RG 11/1518, p. 10; Washington Post (USA), Monday 29 November 1909, p. 6 signed "Marquise de Fontenot"; Fort Wayne Sentinel (Indiana), 1 October 1903, p. 6; Charles Reade (1814-1884), "Rus" [short story]; Ruvigny and Raineval, *The Plantagenet Roll of the Royal Blood* (1905), p. 114; *Kelly's Handbook to the Titled, Landed and Official Classes* (1882), pp. 696-97; *The Gentleman's Magazine*, vol. 224 (January to May 1868), p. 388; Felix Driver, "Becoming and Explorer: The Martyrdom of Winwood Reade," in *Geography Militant: Cultures of Exploration and Empire* (Oxford, 2001); Felix Driver, "Distance and Disturbance: Travel, Exploration and Knowledge in the 19th Century," in *Transactions of the Royal Historical Society*, 6th series, vol. xiv (2004), pp. 73-92.

REDDIE, Arthur Campbell (1849-1922). Born in Bengal, India, on 2 September 1849, he served for a time in the Hong Kong Artillery and Rifles and may well have been related to T. Reddie whom the *India List* recorded in January 1884 as a master in the Bengal Pilot Service. AR moved to Canada in 1885 and a year or two later settled in Victoria, where he joined the provincial civil service during the premiership of John Robson. A very reserved man, apparently unmarried, he became engrossed in departmental work, had a great knowledge of public affairs, and rose in 1919 to become deputy provincial secretary. He lived at 1495 Fernwood Road, died as an Anglican in December 1922, and was buried at Ross Bay Cemetery.
Sources: PRO, India List, January 1884, p. 82; *Colonist*, 16 December 1922, p. 13, obit.; Canadian census, 1901, Victoria; *Victoria Daily Times*, 1 September 1900, "*The Island Veterans; List of Ex-Fighting Men Who Parade To-Night Before Lord Minto.*"

REDDING, Joseph Thomas (1863-1943). Born a lawyer's son at Berkhampstead, Hertfordshire, on 14 January 1859, he went to Quebec in 1882 and joined the RCA, but in 1885 became a member of the North-West Field Force and fought in the Riel Rebellion with the Gatling Gun Detachment at Fish Creek and Batoch. In 1887, he went to Victoria with "C" Battery of the Artillery and the next year took part in the Skeena Expedition sent to pacify native tribes. In 1893 at Christ Church Cathedral, he married Kathleen Hope Gabriel, an English girl born on 30 April 1875, who survived him when he died, aged seventy-nine, on 27 December 1943 at Port Alberni, leaving five children, ten grandchildren, and two great-grandchildren. In 1901, JR and his wife were living on Catherine Street and the corner of Craigflower Road, where he kept a grocery shop.
Sources: *Colonist*, 29 December 1943, p. 3, obit.; census 1871, England, RG 10/1299/105, p. 85; Canadian census, 1901, Victoria.

REECE, Rev. Archdeacon William Sheldon (1830-1904). He served on the Island as an Anglican minister for about ten years, first in Victoria and then in the Cowichan Valley, where he and his wife, Maria Louisa Reece, were established by 28 March 1867 in St Peter's Rectory at Quamichan Lake. The same age as he, Maria was born at Tring, Hertfordshire. AR had a reading room in St Peter's, Quamichan, and was the moving force in founding the Cowichan and Salt Spring Island Agricultural Society and the Lending Library and Literary Institute. Born in the Madras Residency, India, he attended Emmanuel College, Cambridge (BA, 1853; MA, 1857); he was ordained in 1855 and had a series of appointments in England before going out to the Island as a missionary clergyman. He contributed to a serious controversy in Victoria by promoting high Anglican rituals and so antagonizing *Edward Cridge, dean of Christ Church Cathedral. Posted back in England, he died on 4 October 1904 at Salisbury, Wiltshire.

Sources: *Memories Never Lost: Stories of the Pioneer Women of the Cowichan Valley and a Brief History of the Valley, 1850-1920*, ed., Jan Gould (Altona, Manitoba, Compiled by the Pioneer Researchers, 1986), pp. 18, 22, 30, 52, 54, 58; Pritchard, Letters of Edmund Hope Verney, p. 272 note 3; census, 1861, England, RG 9/753; census 1881, RG 11/1661; census 1891, RG 12/1616, p. 1; census 1901, RG 13/1951, p. 13.

REVELY, Captain Frederick (1839-1901). He was baptized on 17 August 1839 at St Nicholas, Newcastle-upon-Tyne, son of William and Catherine Revely. After many years at sea, he went to Victoria in the 1870s and there married an American woman, Catherine E. Gowen, on 15 May 1876 and in 1879 succeeded James Cooper as marine and fisheries agent for British Columbia. The BC census of 1881 found them living in the Johnson Street Ward with their two sons, aged four and two. He died, aged sixty-two, on 17 April 1901 in Vancouver City on the mainland.

Sources: Canadian census, 1881, VI; IGI record; Walbran, *B.C. Coast Names*, p. 111; Thomas E. Appleton, *Usque ad Mare: A History of the Canadian Coast Guard and Marine Services* (Ottawa, Department of Transport, 1968), p. 233.

RHODES, Brigadier General Sir Godfrey Dean (1886-1971), Kt (cr. 1934), CB (1943), CBE (1919), DSO (1917). He was born on 18 July 1886 in Victoria, British Columbia, son of Harry and Marion Rhodes, who sent him to Trinity College School, Port Hope, and then to RMC, Kingston, Ontario, where he was battalion sergeant major in 1906-1907 and won the college's Sword of Honour. In June 1907, he was commissioned in the Royal Engineers, won the Haynes Medal at the British School of Military Engineering, and was posted in 1910 to the North-Western Railway of India as an assistant engineer. He had reached the rank of captain when the Great War began in 1914 and was immediately appointed adjutant with the Railway Construction Troops in France. In 1915-1916, he was attached to the Railway Construction Company at Salonika. Made a temporary major in 1916 and then temporary lieutenant colonel, he became assistant director of railways in Salonika in 1917 and from 1918 to 1920 was director of railways in the Army of the Black Sea at Constantinople, with the temporary rank of brigadier general. Among his honours in that war were four mentions in despatches, nomination to the Distinguished Service Order and as a commander of the Order of the British Empire and to the Order of Redeemer (Greece), the Order of White

Eagle (Serbia), and the Legion of Honour (France). In November 1920, he was serving as a major in the Royal Engineers when he was seconded from the Indian Railways to the Uganda Railway. In 1925, he was acting general manager and in the 1920s was quoted again and again from his reports, notes, and opinions as one of the few who truly understood the issues concerning the railway. When Sir Christian Felling died, Rhodes took his place as general manager of railways and harbours in Kenya and Uganda. On 28 September 1928, the Prince of Wales and the Duke of Gloucester landed there and were transported in a special train as far as Murchison Falls on the Nile and in boats across the lake Victoria Nyanza. Rhodes's speech introduced the railway's budget to the Legislative Council in November 1930, mainly about projected surveys and extensions. On 1 October 1942, GR was seconded to the army and appointed director of transportation in Iran with the rank of brigadier and the task of organizing a supply route to Russia. He resigned the post of general manager from 10 June 1942 after twenty years service with the Uganda railway, eight years as chief engineer, and twelve years as general manager. He had faced the often-unpleasant task of directing the railway through the years of depression and had done it well.

As director of military transport in Iran during the Second World War, he organized the Trans-Iranian Rail Service, which helped to save Stalingrad by carrying over five million tons of supplies 850 miles from the Persian Gulf through Teheran to the Caspian Sea. Successful once again, GR was rewarded in September 1943 with the CB (Companion of the Bath). He turned once again to Africa after the war and in 1947-1948 and was employed as chief representative of Sir Alexander Gibb and Partners, consulting engineers in East Africa. This was a result of his earlier collaboration with Gibb in Iran, where that company had been the biggest supplier of technical expertise after the Second World War. In 1944, the Iranian Ministry of Agriculture signed an agreement with Gibb for the survey of a large irrigation and hydroelectric project on the River Lar. There were delays in that project, but it brought other contracts to Gibb, of which the biggest in the years 1946-1956 was to provide a modern water supply for Tehran. As Davenport-Hines and Jones relate, "Gibb was the only British firm to continue working through the period of crisis when the oil industry was nationalised and diplomatic relations between Britain and Iran were broken off." And their services continued, for instance, in building the Esfahan power station, even after the Iranian government began to turn to U.S. firms.

In 1945, GR became regional port director at Calcutta under the government of India and he spent the years 1948-1951 as special commissioner for works and chief engineer for the government of Kenya. While in that colony, he was chief commissioner of Boy Scouts and also colony commander of the St John's Ambulance Brigade, while maintaining his membership in the Engineers Institute of Canada, the Institute of Transport, and the South African Society of Civil Engineers (London). It was there in Kenya, with his family, that he spent the last period of his life. In 1915 in London, he had married Marian Jessie Topping, daughter of W. Topping, and they had three children whom they brought up as Anglicans: Godfrey H. Rhodes, John H. Rhodes, and Jill M. K. Rhodes. His general address for long periods was c/o Lloyd's Bank Ltd., 6 Pall Mall, London SW 1, but in 1958, he used PO Box 5077, Nairobi, Kenya. There he died on 21 February 1971. His obituary in *The Times* was very short and few, if any, obituaries appeared in Canada.

Sources: *Who was Who,* 1971-1980, p. 664; *Canadian Who's Who,* vol. VIII (1958-1960), p. 935; M. F. Hill, *Permanent Way: The Story of the Kenya and Uganda Railway: Being the Official History of the Development of the Transport System in Kenya and Uganda* (Nairobi, East African Railways & Harbours, 1949), pp. 97, 109, 110, 406-7, 416-417, 455, 458-61, 475-6, 479, 501-3, 515-517, 523-4, 553-4, 559; R. A. Preston, *Canada's R.M.C.,* p. 392; R. P. T. Davenport-Hines and Geoffrey Jones, eds., *British Business in Asia since 1860* (Cambridge University Press, 1989), pp. 54-5, 64; R. Guy C. Smith, ed., *As You Were!: Ex-Cadets Remember,* vol. I, 1876-1918 (Toronto, RMC Club of Canada, 1884-1984, 1983), pp. 149-152; *The Times* (London), 22 February 1922, p. 12, column G.

RICE Family

RICE, Major General Harry [Henry?] Chippendale [Chippindall?] Plunkett (1837-1922). He was born on 2 November 1837 at or near Calcutta, India, and baptized on 8 January 1841 at Bareilly, Archdeanery of Calcutta, son of James George Allerton Rice (lieutenant and adjutant, Sixth Native Infantry) and Mary Charlotte Rice. They sent him to Cheltenham College, where he studied classics and mathematics; while there, he was cited as son of a major in the company service with an uncle living at 66 Oxford Terrace, Hyde Park, London. This was because the East India Company had already granted him a cadetship on the nomination of Russell Ellice, Esq., director of the company, with a supporting recommendation by Lieutenant General Robert James Latter of 66 Oxford Terrace. HR sailed from Southampton to India on the ship *Colombo* on 20 December 1853, bearing a certificate from Addiscombe House signed a fortnight earlier by the professors of mathematics, classics, fortification, and French. He arrived at Fort William on 30 January 1954 and was posted six months later to the 73 N.I. G.O where he learnt some Hindustani. There followed a series of postings in rapid succession partly driven by the Indian Mutiny of 1857-1858. On 6 May 1856, he was sent as adjutant to the Ninth Regiment of Oude, Irregular Infantry, GO, and three weeks later as adjutant to a wing of his corps on detached duty at Baraitch. On 30 January 1857, he joined the Second Infantry, Punjab irregular force GO, and on 5 March with 4 Coy, Punjab irregular force, and became adjutant to his corps and station staff at Ismail post GO on 5 March 1857. He was capable, devoted, and efficient and his postings led to promotions and at last on 22 November 1883, he became a colonel in the Seventy-third Regiment NI Cadre of Officers, 1 Sikh Infantry at Dera Ismail Khan. Behind the dry list of official notices is a record of service on the North-West Frontier of India in the Sikkim Expedition (1861), the Dour Valley Expedition (1872), the Jowaki Expedition (1877-1878) in which he was mentioned in despatches and dangerously wounded, in the Zaimukht Expedition to Afghanistan (1879), and the Mahsud Waziri Expedition (1881). By 1 February 1886, he was on the Retired List as a major general with many medals and other decorations.

"He came of a younger branch of the Dynavor family," according to family records and on 7 December 1865 married Maria Knowles Marshall, daughter of Rev. W. Ross Marshall, a Presbyterian Military Chaplain. They had three sons—Harington, Sheridan, and Brinsley—all officers in the Indian Army, and a daughter, Mia Lilian Holmes Rice, born on 18 November 1869 and baptised on 26 December 1869 at Dera Ismail Khan. A fifth child, Maud, died in infancy. In due time, the sons married and had children. During the unbearable hot summer, these families usually met at Thandiani, a remote and relatively primitive hill station about 30 km east of Abbottabad and north of Murree and 2,691 metres above sea level, higher than Abbottabad (1,222 metres) or Murree (2,413 metres). As late as 1924, it was reached by unpaved tracks not suitable for wheeled traffic. Even in the 1990s, it was said by travellers to have no electricity or telephone or running water. One of HR's granddaughters recalled later that "it was during one of these summer leaves that the family decided to emigrate to British Columbia. 'Life in India,' they said 'is not what it was in our young days, and there is no future in soldiering.' (This must have been in about 1910). There must, they thought, be some place in the world where they could own their own land and farm it, live a gentleman's existence on their retired pay and enjoy their shooting and fishing without too many restrictions. I must have been nine or ten at the time but I can well remember these discussions. The three brothers were fully agreed and wrote a united letter to their parents saying what they wanted to do and suggesting that the parents should join them." In 1913, they decided to emigrate to one of the settled white colonies and tossed a coin to see whether it was to be Australia or Canada. Gradually, according to careers and circumstances, they all arrived at Maple Bay, Vancouver Island, where they took land and tried to farm. HR felt unable to afford to put his sons into British regiments and thought they would have better opportunities in Canada. The first to arrive, being retired the earliest, HR and his wife built a large wooden house at a remote part of Maple Bay that was scarcely accessible except by boat and they named the place "Kelston" after a house by that name at Bracknell, Berkshire, where they had once lived. On 14 September 1914, not many months after the house was built and while it was occupied by one of the sons and his family, recently arrived from India, HR and his wife being absent, "Kelston" caught fire and burnt to the ground. There was insurance on the house itself, which was valued at $7,000, but not on the contents, notably Indian curios and valuable pictures, one of which was said to have been worth $10,000. The family set to, however, and rebuilt the house.

HR was remembered by a granddaughter as "a small man with snow white hair and beard, a grave gentle face and very fine skin. He served all his life in a Sikh regiment until he retired as a Major General, and until he died he held himself straight like the soldier he was, although his years of studying had given him more the aspect of a scholar. He was a clear and erudite speaker and preacher." At Cheltenham, he had been listed as a member of the established church but was in fact brought up in his family as a strict and committed member of the Plymouth Brethren. What this meant may be seen in the life of HR's sister Mary, who never married but "was one of the first people to recognise the plight of prisoners who when they were released from Gaol found themselves unemployable and with no means of maintaining life except by returning to a life of crime. She was deeply concerned about this and founded in Dublin the first branch of the Prison Gate Mission . . . She was still running her Mission when we went to see her in Dublin."

Happily surrounded by children and grandchildren, HR died at Maple Bay, aged eighty-four, on 25 February 1922, and Mrs Rice nine months later, aged eighty-one, on 25 November. They were both buried at sea near Maple Bay, according to their wills.

Sources: British Library, India Office Collection, Reference (courtesy of David Waymouth); *Memoirs of Mrs G. L. Waymouth* (courtesy of David Waymouth); Rice Family Documents, from Harington "Harry" Rice, Ottawa; notes and documents from Miss M. G. Rice, Victoria; notes from Mrs Harington Molesworth Anthony "Tony" Rice (1900-1970); undated newspaper obituary, probably from the *Cowichan Leader*, India List, January 1890, p. 370; *War Services of British Officers of the Indian Army*, (HMSO (?), p. 963; *Colonist*, 17 September 1914 p. 3.

RICE, Lieutenant Colonel Brinsley Alexander McHenry (1876-1940). Born on 7 February 1876 and baptized on 2 April at Kohat, on the North-West Frontier of India, he was a son of *Major General H. C. P. Rice of the Indian Staff Corps and his wife Maria. Consequently, he grew up mainly in India, though he probably attended school in England, as most children of such parents did. On 5 September 1896, he was commissioned in a British regiment and on 26 April 1898 appointed to the 1-6 Gurkha Rifles, Indian Army, as lieutenant. He was seconded for duty in Africa and appointed on 1 April 1900 as assistant resident in Nigeria, ranked as a "Double Company Officer." This was under Sir Frederick (later Lord) Lugard, whose brother was a family friend, and he liked big-game hunting and adventure in a new continent. He had already qualified for employment in the supply and transport corps and, like two of his brothers, passed exams in Pushtu and Parvatia (Khaskura). During the Great War, BR was sent with his regiment to Mesopotamia. There he fought in the Second Battalion at the battle of Ramadi (27-9 September 1917) and then commanded the First Battalion until about halfway through its epic march, 260 miles to Kangayar and another 589 miles on to Enzeli in north-western Persia, that is, from 18 September 1918 (starting at Ruz) to 6 October, when he returned to India. This march was over mountainous territory and with poor equipment and inadequate supplies. BR resumed command as the battalion made its way back to India, and the family has Persian items he brought back with him. By September 1920, when he retired, he had been mentioned in despatches many times and decorated with the DSO (1918 for service in Mesopotamia) and other medals including one for India with a Punjab Frontier 1897-1898 clasp, Edward VII Africa with a Northern Nigeria 1906 clasp, Great War medals, and King George V India with an Afghanistan NW Frontier clasp.

He had married Miss Wilbraham Taylor on 17 March 1900 at Lahore, India, and they had two daughters, Gweneth Lillian and Olive Lenora. When these were just starting school, their mother left them with a nanny and went out to Africa with BR to Bida in Nigeria and then to Kano. There they received a wire on 14 February 1906 telling of a rising in Sokoto "with the Mahadi" at its head, and Mrs Colonel Rice was taken for safety to Government House, probably then at Kaduna, where she was entertained by Sir Frederick Lugard who, "came out and welcomed me very kindly and showed me my bedroom . . . a charming room nicely furnished and looking *most* comfortable after the bare Rest Houses. Then a little girl from Slaves Home came to wait on me and was most useful." From there, she was taken to a port called Lokojo [Lokodjo], where she boarded the Mail Boat *Sarota* for England. When BR's Nigeria appointment ended, he took his family with him to Abbottabad, India, headquarters of the First and Second Gurkha Rifles. Gweneth being six and Olive four, they remembered the hot and dusty journey to the North-West Frontier, some of it in horse-drawn vehicles with overnight stops at Dak bungalows. They lived in a bungalow with high ceilings, a garden, and a lounge with BR's big-game trophies on display and where other officers would come for dinner. "In the curious way of those days," Olive recalled many years later, "my sister and I were sometimes taken into the dining room during desert, though we must have been half asleep . . . First names weren't bandied about as they are now and my father called them all by their surnames only, which we also did behind their backs." When she grew up, Olive took up missionary work in Nepal and remembered life at the little hill station of Thandiani, where the Rice families went during the hot summer: "Travelling up by a one horse cart called an ekka . . . an inferior vehicle to a tonga. As usual we had a fair retinue of servants bringing up the rear. Father joined us for short periods, returning to the regiment in Abbottabad for duty . . . Towards the end of our four-year stay in India, before my father's next long leave, letters passed between my grandparents and my uncles and father that changed the course of our lives. Indeed, these letters crossed, so there was no original collusion and this was taken to be a sign of Divine guidance. My grandfather's suggestion that we should all settle in Canada no doubt stemmed from the fact that Uncle Gerald had become increasingly difficult . . . This left Aunt Lilian with the care of her two boys and two girls, and with the optimism born of ignorance it was thought that the boys could learn to farm and they would all start a new life in the brave new world. The families in India would join them in due course. At the same time the three brothers must have had a longing for the land and the great open spaces, little caring that half a lifetime in the army did not equip them to follow the plough and harrow or wrestle with the problems of cattle and the rotation of crops. So to Canada we would go. It was probably about this time that Tony gave me what I will call my first challenge on Spiritual things. He said something like, 'Are you saved?' In the late 1960s when I stayed with Tony and his wife Lorna in Ottawa, I told him about this as he drove me to the airport. Not surprisingly, he had forgotten the incident, but he was touched and impressed . . . He died about a year later."

After some travelling back and forth between England and British Columbia, GR and his family settled on fifty acres of rocky, wooded hillside at Maple Bay near his parents' place. The girls had happy memories of life there, even though their grandfather, the brigadier general, used to hold religious services for the settlers round about. The house they had built had walls of V-joint boards: "ready to take my father's trophies which were on their way from India. So were the Kashmire carvings and quantities of Indian rugs made in the jails and lasting a lifetime." They played badminton, did much boating, and listened to tales of their famous ancestor, the playwright Richard Brinsley Sheridan, after whom their father and an uncle were named.

Many years later, they returned to England, where BR died, aged sixty-four, on 27 July 1940 and was buried in plot no. 641, next to his brother *Sheridan Rice, at Headley All Saints' Churchyard, Headley-by-the-Wey, Bordon, Hampshire, and his wife after him.

Sources: *Indian Army List,* January 1905, pp. 125, 441, 678, 689, 705; notes and family records, courtesy of Miss Marguerite Gretta Rice, a niece, and David C. R. Waymouth, a grandson; Miss O. L. Rice (a daughter), "*Look Back with Joy,*" unpublished in family records; Major D. G. J. Ryan, Major G. C. Strahan and Captain J. K. Jones, *Historical Record of the 6th Gurkha Rifles,* vol. I, 1817-1919, pp. 156-182, 212-213, 222-231; *Who's Who in B.C.* 1933-1934, p. 146; records of gravestone inscriptions at Headley All Saints' Churchyard, Headley-by-the-Wey, Bordon, Hampshire; for the West African context, see Margery Perham, *Lugard: The Years of Authority, 1898-1945: The Second*

Part of the Life of Frederick Dealtry Lugard, Later Lord Luagrd of Abinger, P.C., G.C.M.G., C.B., D.S.O. (Collins, 1960), part I.

RICE, Major Harry Arthur Harington (1868-1956). He was born on 13 August 1868 and baptised at Abbottabad on 5 September. Educated privately in Ireland, he attended Trinity College Dublin, was commissioned on 3 April 1886 as a lieutenant in the militia, served for a time in the First Suffolk Regiment, and then followed the family tradition by entering the Indian Army. He obtained a commission in the Fifty-fourth Sikhs on 4 February 1891, served through the Waziristan (1894-1895), Chitral (1895), Darwesh Khel (1902) and Zakka Khel (1908) campaigns, received his brevet majority in 1908, was twice mentioned in despatches, and recommended for the DSO. He was staff officer to the Malakand movable column in 1907 and staff officer in Peshawar to 1908 and brigade major until in 1914, he retired for reasons of ill health. He had learnt to speak Hindustani, Punjabi, and Pushtu with the fluency of a native.

In July 1914, he went out to Duncan with his wife, Eveline, *née* Molesworth, born in Ceylon c. 1869, daughter of Lieutenant Colonel Anthony O. Molesworth of the Royal Artillery and his Scottish wife, Anne, and brought up partly in Ceylon and partly in villages near Weymouth, Dorset, and Bristol, Gloucestershire. They took along their son, Harington Molesworth Anthony Rice, who was born at Weymouth, England, on 7 September 1900 but spent most of his childhood on the Indian North-West Frontier, and their daughter, Helen Rice, who in due time married a Protestant minister, Malcolm C. Martin (c. 1894-1961) of Maple Bay. From 1914, the family lived between Maple Bay and Duncan in a house they called "Listlaw." It was possible to live on an officer's pension at that time by fishing, hunting, and gardening, which HR enjoyed, but there were problems. In August 1917, the North Cowichan Council objected to his using "5,000 gallons of water a day . . . for domestic purposes." The value of sterling currency declined between the twentieth-century wars, making life harder for British pensioners. In 1925, HR and his two younger brothers, Colonel Sheridan Rice and Colonel Brinsley Rice, bought Acme Motors in Nanaimo and in 1927 established a branch in Duncan under S. H. Saunders. The Duncan branch was sold in 1930 to E. H. Plaskett, who renamed it Napier Motors, and in 1938, HR sold the Nanaimo branch, too, and retired from the business. Through all those years, the Rice brothers had the Chrysler and Plymouth dealership, north of the Malahat. HR was a deeply pious Christian, interested in foreign missions and Sunday School work and ready to sponsor summer outings at Maple Bay for children of the neighbourhood. He even wrote a short essay, "Faith and Fear," published in the *Colonist* just before Christmas 1936. Mrs Rice died, aged seventy-one, on 8 December 1939 at St Joseph's Hospital, Victoria, but HR carried on and during the Second World War served as a musketry instructor in the Cowichan company of the Pacific Coast Militia Rangers. He died, aged eighty-eight, on 8 October 1956 and was buried at sea off Maple Bay, as his parents had been. The son, Harington Molesworth Anthony Rice (1900-1970), attended Victoria High School, graduated in mining engineering at the University of British Columbia and Cal. Tech, and had a career as a mining engineer at first in BC and then, from 1934, with the Geological Survey of Canada. His descendants live in Ottawa.

Sources: Obituary in the *Cowichan Leader, Colonist,* 12 August 1917, p. 18; 19 December 1936, p. 4; 9 December 1939, p. 5; *Canadian Who's Who,* vol. VIII (1958-1960), p. 936; census 1881, England, RG 11/2103, p. 4; census 1891, RG 12/1988, p. 14; *Proceedings of the Royal Society of Canada,* series IV, vol. X (1972), pp. 88-91; *War Services of British Officers of the Indian Army,* p. 963.

RICE, Colonel Sheridan Knowles Brownlow (1872-1936). Born on 29 July 1872 at Shakebadine [Sheikhbeddin], Dersfot (?), in North-Western India, son of *Major General H. C. P. Rice, he attended Magee College in Belfast, Ireland, and Sandhurst Military College before obtaining a commission in the Bedford Regiment on 3 September 1892. He was appointed to the Indian Army, Thirty-fifth Sikh Regiment, on 26 December 1893 but served with the Fifty-fourth Sikh Frontier Force for many years. In one regiment or the other, he served in the Sudan on the Dongola Expedition (1896l) and in the campaigns at Suakim from 1 June to 4 December 1896 under Major General Sir H. Kitchener, in the relief of Malakand and Chakdara from 1 August 1895 under Major General Sir Bindon Blood, in the Mahmund [Mohmund] country and the campaign against the Utman Khels on the North-West Frontier in 1897-1898, in Waziristan from 23 November 1901 to 15 February 1902 as adjutant to Major General C. E. Egerton, in Tibet in 1903-1904 on the march to Lhasa in the Nineteenth Punjabis with Brigadier General J. R. Macdonald, in France with the Forty-seventh Sikhs from 10 May to 15 December 1915, and with them in Mesopotamia from 8 January to 1 July 1916. Promotion to major came on 3 September 1910 and to lieutenant colonel in the 1/35th Sikhs on 14 March 1918. Invalided to India, he raised and commanded a new Indian regiment at Jhansi. Next he was given command of his own regiment, the Thirty-fifth Sikhs, and was severely wounded and lost an arm in the expedition against Afghanistan in 1919. After eighteen months in hospital, he was invalided out of the army with many medals and other honours.

One of the family's pioneers in the Vancouver Island venture, he was out exploring Maple Bay probably as early as 1910 and moved to Maple Bay from Somerset with others in the family in 1912. On 17 September that year, he married Annie Buchan Dobbie, born in India, daughter of *Colonel Herbert Hugh Dobbie. The British census of 1901 had found her, aged ten, living at "Simcoe House," Budleigh Salterton, Devon, with her Glaswegian grandmother, Jessie Gordon, her two younger brothers, John and William, likewise born in the "East Indies," and a governess. They had two children, David Rice and Margaretta Gretta Rice, who grew up at Maple Bay and in the Cowichan Valley generally. SR liked the Island and wrote several articles about it for the *Times* of India soon after arriving. Like most in the district, he gardened assiduously and was elected in 1935 to represent Cowichan at the AGM of the Vancouver Island Horticultural Society held at the Victoria City Hall early in June. He was an all-round sportsman, an expert shot with shotgun and rifle. In India and elsewhere, he had gathered many trophies. He played back for his regiment at polo, won the rackets championship of North

India, and was proficient at tennis and other games. On the Island, he was active in the Duncan Badminton Club for many years and one of its strongest supporters. He and his wife played in a badminton tournament in Victoria early in February 1930. Like others in his family, he was an active Christian and a tower of strength at the Gospel Hall the family founded and led.

SR died in England on 25 May 1936 while on a visit and lies in grave no. 640, next to his brother *Brinsley Rice and Brinsley's wife Olive, at Headley All Saints Churchyard, Headley-by-the-Wey, Borden, Hampshire. His wife and daughter then moved to 4112 Cedar Hill Road, Victoria, where Mrs Rice lived to be 101 and was buried at Royal Oak, Victoria Section K, VGS-ROBP-MRK, when she died in 1992.

Sources: Notes courtesy of Miss Marguerite Gretta Rice (a daughter), Victoria, and James Harington Rice, Ottawa; census 1901, England, RG 13/2026, page 11; *Cowichan Leader*, 28 May 1936, obit.; *Colonist*, 5 February 1930, p. 7; 3 June 1933, p. 2; *War Services of British Officers of the Indian Army*, p. 963; records of gravestone inscriptions at Headley All Saints' Churchyard, Headley-by-the-Wey, Bordon, Hampshire.

RICHARDS, Admiral Sir George Henry (1819-1900). One of the outstanding naval officers sent to survey the waters around the Island, he was the greatest of Captain George Vancouver's successors. He was christened on 27 February 1819 at Antony, Cornwall, eldest of three sons of Captain George Spencer Richards, RN, and Emma Jane, *née* Harvey, and followed his father into the RN in 1832. He fought in the first Opium War with China (1839-1842) and in a conflict with Argentina (1847-1851) and in 1852-1854 was second in command on Belcher's ship *Assistance* dispatched to search for Sir John Franklin, whose Arctic expedition had been missing since 1845; but he spent most of his career on surveying duty around the empire: the West Indies, the Falkland Islands, New Zealand, and most of all the coast of British Columbia. Arriving at Esquimalt on 9 November 1857 as captain of the steam sloop, *Plumper*, and then transferred to the paddle sloop, *Hecate*, he made the first surveys of much of the coast waters, including boundaries with the United States, before returning to England in 1863. Appointed hydrographer the next year, he worked until retirement in 1874, winning such credit by his accomplishments that he was rewarded with the highest decorations and ranks by the time of his death in 1900. He had married Mary Young (24 July 1847)—daughter of an officer in the Royal Engineers, by whom he had four sons and four daughters—and Alice Mary Tabor (1882). He needs to be carefully distinguished from another capable officer posted at Esquimalt, Sir Frederick William Richards (1833-1912)—apparently no relation—who served as a lieutenant in HMS *Ganges* on the Pacific Station in 1859-1860 under Rear Admiral R. L. Baynes and grew to be one of the lords of the Admiralty and a leading administrator of the RN.

Sources: G. S. Ritchie and Elizabeth Baigent, in *Oxford DNB* online; Helen B. Akrigg in *DCB*, vol. xii, online, using unpublished private papers; Barry M. Gough, *Gunboat Frontier: British Maritime Authority and Northwest Coast Indians 1846-1890* (Vancouver, University of British Columbia Press, 1984), pp. 9-10, 78, 51-2, 107,

109, 146, 153-4, 179-80, 192; V. W. Baddeley and Andrew Lambert, "Sir Frederick William Richards," in Oxford DNB online.

RICHARDS, Lieutenant Robert William (1875-1940). He was born on 24 December 1874 in Birmingham, son of William Richards, a shoemaker, and the census of 1881 found him, aged five, living with his widowed father and several brothers and sisters in Solihull. He joined the British Army very young and spent eighteen years in infantry units. After fighting in the South African War, he retired to Lasquetti Island off the east coast of Vancouver Island, where he lived as a "rancher" with his wife Elizabeth. He joined the Eighty-eighth Victoria Fusiliers and then on 11 January 1916, the CEF in which he soon became a lieutenant. By 1918, his wife had moved to Luxton in Happy Valley, Vancouver Island, and after the war, that was where he returned. He died there, aged sixty-four, in October 1940, and was buried at Colwood as an Anglican, survived by his widow, two sons, two sisters, and a brother on Valdez Island.
Sources: NAC, CEF files, box 8237-33; *Colonist*, 11 October 1940, p. 16: obit.; census 1881, England, RG 11/3082, p. 20.

RICHARDSON, Captain Malcott [Mallcott] Sydney (1844-1904). He was born on 22 September 1844 at Blackheath, Kent, and secured a commission in the British Army when young. Possibly, the James Malcott Richardson who was a bookseller at 23 Cornhill, London, in the years 1808-1853 was a relative. In any event, the 1871 census found MR aged twenty-six, a lieutenant in the Thirty-fifth Regiment, living at 2 Middle Street, Altham, Kent, with his wife, Catherine Richardson, *née* McCane, aged twenty-eight and born on 27 June 1842 in Madras, India. They had a seven-year-old daughter Muriel born on 13 August 1870 at Fleetwood, Lancashire. After twelve years of service, MR retired and was recorded in 1881 as "late Captain 35th Reg't, Stock Brkr," living with his family at 10 Victoria Road, Eltham, Kent, now with an unmarried son, Lawford Moray Richardson, aged twenty-six, born on 13 Nov 1874 at Eltham, Kent. Along with a cook and a housemaid, they had living with them Mrs Richardson's brother, William M. McCane, aged nineteen, born at "Poona, East Indies," employed as a "Clerk & Stockbroker." In 1891, MR was "late Captain 35th Royal Sussex Regiment, Member of the Stock Exchange," still with his family in Eltham but living at 9 Victoria Road.
    In 1893, he took his family out to Duncan, Vancouver Island, and bought what was known locally as the Theodore Davie property. It seems probable that Edward Mallcott Richardson (1839-1874), an English artist who visited the Island in the early 1860s and painted an aquarelle of Victoria seen from the sea, was a relative drawn to British Columbia in the gold rush. At sometime in 1896, MR moved his family to Victoria, where he became secretary to Lieutenant Governor Dewdney and then secretary to the minister of mines, which he still was at his death. The voter's list for 1898 shows Malcott Sydney Richardson still living at "The Knoll," Quamichan, Cowichan, as a farmer. But in 1901, the census in Victoria found them living on Oak Bay Avenue, the son employed as a bank accountant. MR died, aged fifty-nine, on 10 May 1904 and was buried in a service at Christ Church Cathedral.

Almost two years later, on 14 February 1906, the son married Emma Wharton S. Hanington in Victoria.

Sources: *Victoria Daily Times* November 1903 (?), obit.; census 1871, England, RG 10/5121, p. 29; census 1881, RG 11/0728/92, page 52; census 1891, RG 12/516, p. 6; *BC Archives*, the voter's list for 1898; NAC, pictures, etc., R 9266-342.

RICKARD, Dr Thomas Arthur (1864-1953). He emigrated to the United States in 1885 to work in mining and geology and became an American citizen in 1925, but in 1932, he moved to Victoria and soon became Canadian—"under the old flag... a subject of Great Britain," as he put it. His parents were Cornish, but he was born at Pertusola, Italy, on 29 August 1864, son of Thomas Rickard, a mining engineer from Illogan, Cornwall, and his wife, Octavia Tachel Forbes (1837-1879), who was born on 2 May 1837 in Moraston House, Bridstow, Herefordshire, and died, aged forty-two, in Wandsworth, Surrey. The birthplaces of AR's brothers and sisters show the family's peregrinations: Winifred Grace Florence Rickard, born in Vertusela, Italy (1864); Forbes Rickard, born at Andeer, Grisons, Switzerland (1867); Herbert Edward Rickard, born in Hyde Park, London (1870), and christened on 10 June 1870 at St James, Paddington; Florence Marcia Rickard, born at Andeer, Grisons, Switzerland (16 April 1870); Alfred Rickard, born in Russia (1874); and Maria Alexandria Mania [Maria?] Rickard born in Russia (1876). TR attended the Royal School of Mines in South Kensington and came to know H. G. Wells, one of his contemporaries there.

With such a family life, it was perhaps natural that TR should travel even more widely. In July 1885, he emigrated to the United States and then back and forth several times before establishing a permanent residence at 250 Tunnel Road, Berkeley, California, where he had several relatives who were also employed in the mining business. He first arrived in Victoria in 1897 as geologist for the state of Colorado on his way to Australia and made a sensation by being followed about by a picturesque Indian servant in uniform. After living continuously at Berkeley in 1915-1925, as an editor in the field of mining, he applied for citizenship to the U.S. District Court of Northern California at San Francisco, which issued a passport on 25 February 1925. There followed journeys to several European countries, but he remembered the Island and retreated to it in 1932 with his wife, Marguerite Lydia. Thirteen years younger than he, she was born in Algeria at Ain Barbar. For some twenty years, TR was a prominent citizen, active in various ways, notably as an author of books in the mining field. He also wrote a rambling study, *Historic Backgrounds of British Columbia* (Vancouver, The Wrigley Printing Co. Ltd., 1948), 358 pp. He died, aged eighty-nine, on 15 August 1953 in Oak Bay, Victoria, and Marguerite Lydia Rickard died, aged seventy-seven, on 24 April 1955.

Sources: *Colonist*, 29 August 1951, p. 11, notes by J. K. Nesbitt; 18 August 1953, p. 13, obit. and photo; U.S. Application for a passport, ending with an Oath of Allegiance dated 24 February 1925; "*Mining and Scientific Press*," published by the Dewey Publishing Company, San Francisco, Calif., vol. 102, no. 13, page 483 dated 1 April 1911; *Berkeley Gazette*, 29 February-March, pp. 3,9,11,12; April 21; May 12, 1896; Winnipeg Free Press, 27 August 1953, p. 1, obit.; *Oakland Tribune* (Calif.), 25

March 1911, p. 1; Thomas Arthur Rickard (1864-1937), *Historic Backgrounds of British Columbia* (Vancouver, The Wrigley Printing Company Ltd., 1948), 358 pp.; New York Passenger Lists—6 of them: (1) arriving at NY on 10 May 1913 from Southampton on the Amerika, (2) on 23 January 1915 from Liverpool on the Lusitania, (3) on 16 March 1915 from Liverpool on the *Orduna,* (4) on 10 November 1926 from Southampton on the *Olympic,* (5) on 17 June 1929 from London on the *Minnetonka,* and (6) on 9 April 1930 from Liverpool on the *Cedric.*

RIDGEWAY-WILSON, Lieutenant Colonel William (1862-1957). He was born a British merchant's son at Hankow, China, on 24 July 1862, lived for some years in England, and emigrated in 1887 to the Island, where he lived in Victoria for some seventy years as a successful architect. He first appears, aged eight, in English census records for 1871, living with his family at "Ferse Thornton Dale" in Wimbledon (London). His father, Craven Wilson, aged forty-five, was an "East India Merchant" born in London; his mother Margaret, aged forty-six, was born in Huddersfield, Yorkshire, but his elder brother, James C. Ridgeway-Wilson, aged thirteen, was born in China at Shanghai, as was one of their sisters, Agnes M., aged ten. Their other sister, Margaret E., aged seventeen, was born at Birkenhead, Cheshire. There were three servants: nurse, cook, and housemaid. Ten years later, WR had another sister, Eva, aged thirteen, born in Wimbledon, their brother James, now twenty-three, was a "Mechanical Draughtsman," their father was described as a "shipping agent," and WR himself, now eighteen, was an "apprentice (architect)." By 1891 by which time brother James was working as a "mechanical engineer draughtsman" in a village on the coast of Lancashire, WR had finished a four-year term as apprentice with Bromitan Cheers, an architect in Liverpool, a period of employment with Sir Horace Jones in London, and another there with Searles and Hayes and gone out to join Elmer H. Fisher in a partnership in Victoria. In 1899, he joined the local militia, which may have improved his delicate health. When he enlisted in the Artillery, Military District No. 11, in December 1913 and served until 30 November 1919, the medical officer described him as 6' 1" tall, 166 lbs. with a fair complexion, grey hair, blue eyes, and a double inguinal hernia—which the army then repaired by a surgical operation. He rose to the rank of colonel and spent most of the Great War in command of a camp for prisoners of war at Vernon in the Okanagan Valley.

For most of his active career, until 1940, he had an architectural practice of his own, though there was a short spell as partner of T. C. Sorby. He built (or provided the plans for) many private houses and other buildings, including the Bay Street Armouries, the Wilkinson Road Mental Home, the Five Sisters Block, the opera house at Nanaimo, and the Colquitz Jail in Saanich. He also built St John's Church to replace the old iron church, the second Anglican Church in Victoria, sent out with the first Anglican bishop, *Rev. George Hills, by his patron, the philanthropic Lady Angela Burdett-Coutts. It stood on Douglas Street where the Hudson's Bay Company later built the department store where my father bought new boots each fall for my brother and me in the 1930s. Curiously enough, on 24 April 1889, WR married a daughter of the first rector of the old iron church, Rev. Percival Jenns (1834-1915), "an ardent student of botany and astronomy" who had emigrated from England in 1868 with his family. Mrs WR was Flora Alexandra Jenns (1866-1939), born near Westminster Bridge in the Surrey part of London, whence she had gone to the Island, aged two, with her family. They had five children: Basil, Guy, Percy, Hebden, and Daisy. When one of Flora's sisters married *Raymond B. Punnett in 1892, WR became a brother-in-law of this India-born British officer, and a third sister brought James Gourlay Lang into the family circle by a marriage in 1903.

WR became a member of the British Empire Club, with its office at the rooftop of the Royal Trust (Union) Building in Victoria, and remained staunchly loyal to the empire. He wrote to the *Daily Colonist* in January 1930 under the head, "The Flag Question":

> Sir: Why should Canada or any Dominion need a distinctive flag? There are, I venture to say, only a very few noisy individuals in any of those countries who have ever raised the question. The large majority say nothing because they are more than content to rest under the folds of the good old Union Jack which has sheltered those who fought for them in their youth and under which they have fought in their manhood . . . [Still . . .] I suggest that as each colony has gradually sprung from the heart of the Empire, so a plain white star might spring from the heart of the Union Jack, having four large points denoting Canada, Australia, Africa, India, and four smaller points for smaller colonies; and on this could be engraved something symbolical of each colony to form its particular flag—beaver for Canada, kangaroo for Australia etc. Then a ship at a distance would first see the unmistakable union Jack and therefore British; and later, if necessary, which particular Dominion it hailed from.

He died, aged ninety-four, in 1957 and was buried from St John's Anglican Church, which he had designed. His wife had died on 27 June 1939 and been similarly buried.

Sources: NAC, CEF files, RG150, box 8270-44; census 1861, England, RG 9/2607, page 5; census 1871, RG 10/856, p. 18; census 1881, RG 11/3695, p. 22(?); census 1891, RG 12/4195, p. 27; Martin Segger and Douglas Franklin, Victoria, *A Primer for Regional History in Architecture* (New York, A Pilgrim Guide to Historic Architecture, 1979), pp. 236-9, 270-1, 322-3, 349-350; Notes courtesy of Rosemary James Cross in Victoria; *Colonist*, 23 January 1915, p. 7, obit. (Rev. Jenns); 15 January 1930, p. 4, Letter to the Editor by W. Ridgeway Wilson, "*The Flag Question*"; 23 February 1957, p. 18, obit.

RIGBY, Major Gerard Christopher, (1868 ?). He was born at Torquay, Devonshire, son of Matilda Rigby and her husband Major General Christopher Palmer Rigby (1820-1885) of the Indian Staff Corps, who was born at Yately, Hampshire, who had been posted at Zanzibar as British consul in 1858-1861, and who died when GR was seventeen. Earlier, the 1881 census found GR, aged twelve, at school at Elm Lodge, Streatham Common, whence he moved to Marlborough College, then to RMC, Sandhurst, and joined the Duke of Edinburgh's Wiltshire Regiment (formerly sixty-second foot) on 22 August 1888. With this regiment, he arrived in India on 7 October 1895 and at Rawalpindi on 27 October 1904, under Colonel J. H. Dunne. Appointed superintendent of army signalling on the Mohmund Expedition (1897) and divisional signalling officer, Second Division Tirah Field Force (1897-1898), he was mentioned in despatches (*London Gazette* 7 June 1898). He went on to serve as superintendent of army signalling with the China Expeditionary Force in the Boxer Rebellion (1900) and at the Relief of Peking, taking part in actions at Pietsang and Yangtsun and being mentioned in despatches (*London Gazette* 14 May 1901). These were matters of pride for his sister and widowed mother, whom the census of 1901 recorded as living at 14 Portland Place, Marylebone, London, with five female servants, all Londoners. Meanwhile, GR had passed exams for the rank of major, for the cavalry pioneer class, for a Musketry Certificate, as an instructor in army signalling, and had qualified for the Supply and Transport Corps. In languages, he had passed examination in Persian (lower standard), Pushtu (higher standard), and Urdu (higher standard). In the South African War, he took part in the operations in the Transvaal and held the Queen's Medal with three clasps. After retiring in 1908, he served during the Great War as censor-in-charge of Cable Offices in Cornwall (1914-1917).

GR's personal life was affected by his sister Lilian M. Rigby (c. 1876-1949), who in 1909 married Charles E. B. Russell with whom she wrote books of an improving kind. Together they wrote *Working Lads' Clubs* (Macmillan, 1913), and Russell became famous for his work with boys' clubs and writing about them. She became a follower, devotee, assistant, and translator for Albert Schweitzer and spent long periods in Africa in connection with Schweitzer's work, and her translations and other works were variously published under her married or her maiden name. She translated, for instance, Schweitzer, *Indian Thought and Its Development* (NY, Beacon Press, 1957).

In 1908, GR married Ella Manbelow, daughter of Captain H. Manbelow, and they had a son, C. P. Rigby, named after his grandfather, and a daughter E. C. Rigby. GR and his wife decided to move to Vancouver Island, arrived at Quebec on 26 April 1925 aboard the CPR vessel, *Montcalm*, and after an unsettled period moved into a house at Maple Bay in 1933. I discovered little or nothing about their life there, but after nine years, they moved away in 1934 and were not heard of on the Island again.

Sources: BL, India Office, *Indian Army List,* January 1905, pp. 242, 694, 701; *Hart's Army List,* 1893, p. 308; 1915, p. 1582; *Army List* October 1905, p. 242; General Christopher Palmer Rigby (1820-1885), *Zanzibar and the Slave Trade, with Journals, Dispatches,* etc., ed., Mrs Charles E. B. Russell (his daughter Lilian) (Allen & Unwin, 1935), p. 312; Riddick, *Who in British India,* p. 307 (father); p. 312; census 1871, England, RG 10/1198; census 1881, RG 11/0140/56, p. 20; census 1881, RG 11/667; census 1901, RG 13/104, page 16; *Who's Who in B.C.* 1933-1934, p. 147;

NAC, RG76, immigration, series C-1-a, 1925, vol. 1, p. 50, reel T-14714; Reginald Coupland, *East Africa and its Invaders from the Earliest Times to the Death of Seyyid Said in 1856* (Oxford, Clarendon, 1938), pp. 302, 316, 318, 319, 322, 325, 326, 339, 340, 426, 433, 434, 484, 550, 554, and chapter xiv: "The French at Zanzibar."

RIORDAN, Michael (c. 1863-1930). Born in Cork, Ireland, he served for twenty-one years in the Second Royal West Regiment and twelve years, nine months in the Royal Canadian Garrison Artillery. He was posted at Esquimalt about 1908 and remained until his death, some twenty-two years later. He died, aged sixty-seven, still at Esquimalt, early in September 1930. "The cortege, with the casket mounted upon a gun carriage and escorted by a firing party, left Sands Funeral Chapel at eight forty and proceeded to St Mary's Church, Victoria West, where Rev. Father A. B. Wood celebrated Mass. Interment was in Ross Bay Cemetery, a volley being fired at the graveside, while Comrade S. Cowsey, bugler of the Army & Navy Veterans, sounded the Last Post."
Sources: *Colonist*, 3 September 1930, p. 5, obit.; 4 September 1930, p. 5.

RITCHIE, Captain Thomas Kerr (1888-?). Born on 21 June 1888 at 114 Berkeley Street, Glasgow, son of Duncan Ritchie, a fisherman, and his wife Lillian Kerr, he attended public school there and Allan Glen's School (whose headmaster gave him a warm recommendation), and he was farming in Argyleshire when in December 1915, he applied for a commission as a second lieutenant in the 3/9th ATS Highlanders, 3/9th Battalion. On the form, he gave his surname as Kerr Ritchie and his Christian name as Thomas. He had earlier been a lance corporal in the 3/8th A&SH and had served in France (BEF) from 1 May to 3 July 1915, this in the 152nd Brigade Guards Company. Wounded in the thigh on 15-16 June 1915, he had been sent home from St Omer and Boulogne. On a "minute sheet" is a note of 9 February 1918: "He is now under orders for a Garrison Battalion in India." The reason seemed to be that his health required a warm climate, perhaps because he already had TB or was in danger of catching it.
His service record on the file, dated 3 April 1936, is as follows:

Attested 9 September 1914

Embodied for service (Argyle & Sutherland
Highlanders, Territorial force 22 September 1914
Discharged on appointment to commission 20 January 1916
Appointed to a commission as 2nd lieutenant,
Argyle & Sutherland etc 21 January 1916
Attached to the Royal Flying Corps from 8 February to 22 May 1917
Promoted to lieutenant 27 July 1917
Relinquished commission on account of ill-health contracted on Active
    Service and granted honorary rank of lieutenant 31 October 1918
    (*London Gazette*, 30 October 1918)

After the war, he moved to Victoria and was living at 1077 Davie Street in 1931 when he began to write letters to the editor of the *Daily Colonist*, referring occasionally to his own career. Under the heading, "The Imperial Heritage," he baited a pacifist critic by defending his own wartime service with the Fifty-first Highland Division and the Royal Flying Corps, in France, Flanders, Egypt, and India: "Personally I was wounded twice, missing once, and officially reported killed another time. Some of us have a beggarly pension; most of us have none at all. We ask for work and are set to dig ditches at seven dollars per week—when we have no beggarly pension. But I venture to affirm that we who won the war and lost our earthly possessions yet have some guts and will storm the very gates of Hell for the preservation of our Imperial heritage so hardly won. *Non amittuntur sed praemiftuntur.*" He published a short article in the *Colonist* on 22 November 1931, Sunday, p. 5, "Shadows of India," which shows that he served there on the North-West Frontier. In February 1933, he broadened the scope of his comments: "Over a year ago I pointed out in your columns that the only sane method to promote prosperity in this country and vitalize British Imperial trade was to abandon the gold standard and inflate the currency. Instead, we keep on gallantly piling more debt on the shoulders of future generations, and bravely continue destroying the noble heritage bequeathed by British pioneers, who had more gumption in each of their individual trigger fingers than is possessed by the whole race of present-day weak-kneed demagogues living on hot air. Sitting out in 'No Man's Land' dreaming of democracy, technocracy, plutocracy, or other things crazy is not the way to take trenches. It may engender an attack of the `flu and calls for aristocracy. Carry on!" In a letter of 1 June 1933, he mentioned that he had been present at the Battle of Festubert, 9-15 May 1915.

He returned to Scotland before the Second World War and applied in August 1939 from an Edinburgh address for some sort of wartime post. The War Office replied that they could offer him nothing. A note of 17 August 1939 on the file explains, "It does not appear to be desirable to employ this officer as, apart from the fact that he has a 100 percent award for T.B. you are confidentially informed that a warning was received last year from the British Consulate at Nantes that he had been the cause of considerable trouble in France and had fled to England leaving heavy debts to tradesmen and others." There was no further sign of him on the Island.

Sources: BNA (PRO, Kew), WO 374/57778; *London Gazette*, 30 October 1918; *Colonist*, 19 November 1931, p. 4; 3 February 1933, p. 4, L to E; 1 June 1933, p. 4.

RITHET, Robert Paterson (1844-1919). One of the biggest pioneer businessmen and politicians in Victoria, he was born on 22 April 1844 at Cleuchhead, near Applegarth, Scotland, the fourth son of a Presbyterian farmer. After schooling in the classics, he was apprenticed to a Liverpool merchant firm and then ventured out to British Columbia in 1862. After some prospecting and work in road building, he was hired in Victoria by Gilbert Malcolm Sproat, who in 1865 left him in charge of the commission and shipping business he managed for the London commission and shipping firm, Anderson and Company. From this beginning, RR built up a many-sided business of his own, sometimes alone and sometimes in partnership with others like himself, spending time in San Francisco as well as Victoria before Vancouver existed. Prominent among his partners were Englishmen such as William Curtis Ward (c. 1842-1922), manager of the [London] Bank of British Columbia, but more particularly Scots such as Andrew Welch, J Robertson Stewart, Robert Dunsmuir, and Alexander Ewen. RR had a strong hand in forming the Albion Iron Works (1861) and the Canadian Pacific Navigation Company (1883), which merged two steamship lines operating between Vancouver Island and the mainland, was president of the Victoria [salmon] Canning Co., and came to own canneries on the coast and flour mills in Enderby and Vernon in the Okanagan Valley. On 27 October 1875 in Victoria, he married Elizabeth Jane Hannah Munro (1854-1952), daughter of a leading HBC employee, and about 1888 bought some fifteen thousand acres on Vancouver Island at the rate of a cent an acre. He owned large farms on the Island and the mainland and was a big shareholder in the BC Cattle Company. With firm connections in San Francisco, Liverpool, and London, he was a leading figure in the economy of the Island in the period when it was a British colony and before it became enmeshed in Canadian business centred on Vancouver, Winnipeg, Toronto, and Montreal. For several years, he was president of the Board of Trade in Victoria and consul for Hawaii there. When he died, aged seventy-five, on 19 March 1919 at his home "Hollybank" in Victoria, the world he had known was already beginning to crumble.

Sources: Daniel Clayton, in the DCB online; Valerie Green, *Above Stairs: Social Life in Upper-Class Victoria, 1843-1918* (Victoria, Sono Nis Press, 1995), pp. 92-101; Morgan, *Canadian Men and Women*, p. 945; Begg, *History of British Columbia*, pp. 552-3, 563-4; *Colonist*, 20 March 1919, pp. 1, 4 and 7, obit.

RIVETT-CARNAC, Charles Edward (1901-1980). Born in August 1901 at Eastbourne, Sussex, son of a deputy inspector general of police in India, he was the nephew of *Colonel P. T. Rivett-Carnac, who died at Duncan. For generations, the family had been in the service of the church, the British and Indian armies, the civil services, and other pillars of the empire. His ancestors were particularly active in India even in the time of the East India Company, and because his parents were serving in India, he lived as a boy in England with an uncle who was a retired Indian Army colonel. He attended St Cyprian's Preparatory School and Eastbourne College, and when he was just over sixteen years of age, he joined an ambulance unit attached to the French army and served in the Great War for about eighteen months. Then he went to India for three and a half years, running elephant camps on the Borelli River in the Himalayan foothills and gathering cottonwood timber to be milled and turned into tea boxes on the Brahmaputra River. When he was twenty-one, he was transferred to Bisra in Central India, where he became manager of a lime factory. Later, he worked as private and social secretary for one of the partners in Bird & Co., a large industrial firm with headquarters at Calcutta, handling everything from jute to timber.

Dissatisfied with this life, he thought of joining the French Foreign Legion, returned to England with almost no money, then sailed to Canada in 1923 with the intention of joining the RCMP. He was soon posted in the north at a lonely detachment on the Mackenzie River, where he policed the country with skis and a dog-sled. After three and a half years, he went to BC in 1927 for a year, then to Regina as division orderly with the rank of corporal, then to the Yukon for three years. Eventually, he was appointed inspector at Regina in charge of a training depot, and there in 1932, he married Mary Dillon-Ware, daughter of Colonel F. B. Ware, DSO, of London, Ontario. At first, they went to live in the Western Arctic in a small frame building; their first child was born at Aklavik. His name appears in histories of the RCMP telling of policing and hardships in the north. He was posted in due time from the Western Arctic to RCMP headquarters in Ottawa, where he was put in charge of intelligence. In 1947, he became assistant commissioner in command of Saskatchewan and in March 1951 was sent to command "E" Division in BC, the largest division in the force. He served as commissioner of the RCMP from 1 April 1959 to 31 March 1960. Meanwhile, their first daughter trained as a nurse in Victoria at the Royal Jubilee Hospital. It was to Victoria that CR retired and lived until his death, aged seventy-eight, on 18 July 1980 in Victoria. His wife, Mary Dillon Rivett-Carnac, died there, aged sixty, on 13 July 1970.

Sources: *Colonist*, 16 December 1951, Sunday, p. 6, G. E. Mortimore, "Charles E. Rivett-Carnac: Guardian of Law and Order"; 14 July 1970, p. 21; Rivett-Carnac, *Pursuit in the Wilderness* [memoirs] (Boston, Little, Brown, 1965; London, Jarrolds, 1967), 341 pp.; Major Harwood Steele, *Policing the Arctic: The Story of the Conquest of the Arctic by the Royal Canadian* (formerly North-West) *Mounted Police* (Toronto, Ryerson Press, 1935?), 390 pp., pp. 306-307, 344, 351, 355; Riddick, *Who in British India*, p. 308 (father).

RIVETT-CARNAC, Colonel Percy Temple (1852-1932). Like so many other Rivett-Carnacs, PR was born in India, in his case on 12 January 1852 at Rawalpindi, fourth child of William John Rivett-Carnac, who was then in the Bengal civil service. (The father was born on 19 April 1822 and married in September 1846 Mary Anstruther Wilkinson, daughter of Rev. Percival Spearman Wilkinson. He died on 9 July 1874, having had four children and served in the Honourable East India Company.) PR was educated in England, going from Durham Grammar School to Harrow and then returning to India, where he was posted to the Forty-third Light Infantry stationed at Cannanore, Madras. Later, he was in Burma and then again in the Madras Presidency, where he won the shield given by the South India Rifle Association. In 1879, he was stationed at Bangalore, Mysore, and until 1882 was private secretary to the resident commissioner. He was then posted to the First Battalion, Duke of Wellington's West Riding Regiment (formerly the Thirty-third foot). He served with this regiment in England, Egypt, Aden, Halifax, NS, and Barbadoes. He was at the latter station for two years (1887-1889), then sent to St Helena and later to Cape Town. After serving with his battalion in Cape Colony, he was seconded to the HQ staff in the second Matabele War, serving in Mashonaland (1896-1897) as chief staff officer to Sir Richard Martin. He was present on 4 November 1897 at the opening of the Bulawayo Railway. Shortly afterwards, he was appointed deputy commissioner and commandant general for Rhodesia. Whilst there, he became a personal friend of Cecil Rhodes and Dr Jameson and at Salisbury met Earl Grey, who had been his friend when they were at Harrow together. He had left South Africa and was stationed at Dover when the war began in 1899 but returned. One of his many services was helping to organize Brabant's Horse, but he was present at the action at Paardeburg and the relief of Kimberley as a lieutenant colonel commanding the First Battalion of the West Riding Regiment.

About this time, he met Miss Alice Mary Herbert, second daughter of Major Philip Sydney Herbert of Pietermartizburg, Natal, and they were married at Umtali on 1 January 1898. Their daughter Alice Mary Rivett-Carnac was born at Dover on 28 March 1899 and their son, Percival "Val" Sydney Rivett-Carnac, in Yorkshire on 4 November 1904. When PR retired from his regiment, they went to live at Brighton, but two or three years before the Great War (probably in 1912), they migrated to the Island on the advice of a Mr Broadbent and built a house at Chemainus, where they lived for almost twenty years. He gardened and was active in local affairs, like most British officers. He served in 1920-1926 as a member of the North Cowichan Council and became a Justice of the Peace. When he died, aged eighty, at his home in Chemainus on 5 November 1932, the editor of the *Cowichan Leader*, well qualified to judge such matters, thought he was "one of the most distinguished and one of the oldest of the many soldiers who have made their homes here. Of his long life of eighty years, thirty-two were spent in the army. He served with the West Riding Regiment in three campaigns, the first being as long ago as Egypt, 1884-86, for which he held the Queen's Medal and the Khedive's star. He was a captain then." His funeral was at St Michael's and All Angels Church, with a cast of local pallbearers, and at the Chemainus cemetery, a bugler played last post and the coffin was covered with the Union Jack. Among the wreaths were one from the Cowichan branch of the Canadian Legion and another from the Old Harrovian Society, Victoria, "in which were real cornflowers grown from seed sent from Harrow." His wife had died, aged fifty-six, nearly five years earlier on 23 March 1928. His daughter, then Mrs Captain N. B. Scott, was living at Salmon Arm. His son Percival "Val" was then in Kowloon, Hong Kong, where he stayed on for twenty years working as an electrician for a cement manufacturing company. In 1941, this son joined the Hong Kong Defence Corps, resisted the enemy for some time at Kowloon, but was taken prisoner and held until the end of the war. There were many other relatives in the offing, such as a nephew, Inspector Charles Edward Rivett-Carnac of the RCMP at Regina, who eventually moved to Victoria.

Sources: *Burke's Peerage*, 106th edn. (2 vols., Switzerland, 1999), vol. II, pp. 2417-2419; *Cowichan Leader*, 10 November 1932, obit.; 17 November 1932; Lieutenant Colonel Herbert Plumer, *With an Irregular Corps in Matabeleland* (Kegan Paul, Trench & Tübner & Co. Ltd., 1897), p. 120; Who's Who, 1920; Elliott, *Memories of the Chemainus Valley*, p. 277.

ROBERTS, Major Cecil Morton (1866-1961). He was born on 30 January 1866 in London, son of Dr Colin R. Roberts (from Newark, Nottinghamshire), and the 1871 census recorded him, aged five, living at Elleslater House Ladies' College,

---

of which Emily Roberts (his sister?) was the principal. His father, head of the household, was listed as "P. Secretary" and his mother Jane Roberts was there. He attended private schools and Henley Grammar School, joined the Royal Navy, and was soon employed as an engineer aboard HMS *Marlborough* at Portsmouth. In 1888, when he had evidently left the navy, he went out to Victoria and worked for two years with the Dominion Public Works Department. In 1898-1899, he went to the Yukon but had joined the Fifth BC, CGA, in 1889 and so went to serve in South Africa as a gunner for the years of the South African War. Soon after returning to Victoria, in 1902, he married Georgina Penelope Storey, daughter of Thomas Storey of Victoria. He took employment in the Surveyor General's Department and then went as chief draughtsman to the BC Provincial Government until 1911, when he resigned in order to practise as a BC land surveyor. He had the soldierly instincts of his generation and in 1904 was commissioned as lieutenant in Fifth Regiment, CA. He was promoted to captain (1905), joined the Corps Reserve (1907-1913), and in 1913 was a captain in the Fiftieth Gordon Highlanders. All that was essentially militia work, and when he enlisted in the CEF on 8 November 1914, he gave his occupation as "B.C. Land Surveyor." He soon had the rank of major, sailed overseas with the battalion in February 1915, transferred to CFA in May 1915, and went to France on 17 December that year. From 27 February to 15 June 1916, he was in England but on 17 June was appointed ADC to General Sir Arthur Currie in France with the First Canadian Division. Before long, he developed serious neuritis in his right shoulder, had spells in hospital, and returned to Canada in December 1918. Appointed OC of the Dispersal Station T, Vancouver, in 1919, he was himself demobilized on 5 September 1919 with decorations: SA Medal and 5 bars, 1914-1915 Star, Service and Victory Medal, and the Long Service Medal. When he died, aged ninety-five, on 10 April 1961, he was living at 913 Burdett Ave, Victoria. He was survived by his son, Cecil Monteith Roberts (c. 1911-1971).
Sources: NAC, CEF papers, Box 8327-50; *Who's Who in B.C.* 1933-1934, p. 148; census 1871, England, RG 10/766.

ROBERTSON, Major Alistair [Alastair] Irvine (1870-1934). Born on 24 March 1870 at Blair Atholl, near Perth, Scotland, son of John Robertson, he always signed his name "Alistair," but too many records cite him as "Alastair." About 1892, he migrated to British Columbia, where he found employment "ranching & packing" at Fort Steele, East Kootenay. On 25 December 1899, he wrote to Superintendent Cuthbert of the North-West Mounted Police at Macleod, "I see by the papers that the government is sending another contingent to South Africa, and I beg to offer myself for service with the Mounted Rifles. I have been seven years in B.C. and can ride and shoot above the average; am 5 ft. 8 ins. in height and of 39 in. chest measurement." Scarcely a week later, on 1 January 1900, he signed on at Macleod, NWT as a private in the Canadian Mounted Rifles, declaring himself to be single and Episcopalian (though he recorded "Church of Scotland, Protestant" on joining the army in 1916). He served for about a year and was discharged on 14 January 1901 with the Queen's Medal and four clasps for Johannesburg,

Diamond Hill, Cape Colony, and Orange Free State. Medical reports recorded him as having flaxen hair, blue eyes, a sanguine temperament, and being "inured to hard work."

Soon after returning to BC, he married Maud Violet Jeffrey (c. 1880-1931) on 21 October 1907 in Victoria and became a BC land surveyor, particularly active on the Island's west coast. When he joined the Eighty-eighth Battalion of the CEF as a captain on 5 June 1916, he was living with his wife at 1606 Belmont Avenue, Victoria, and already a member of the Eighty-eighth Victoria Fusiliers. He returned from the Great War, took up his surveying work, and joined the Army and Navy Club and the British Public Schools Club in Victoria. In 1933, he was vice-president of the latter and presided over a meeting on 4 February which defeated a motion to have the club's name change to "The Empire Club." His wife had died, aged fifty-one, on 28 May 1931, and he dropped dead, aged sixty, on 22 June 1934 at the home of a friend, *Captain M. D. Harbord, 554 Niagara Street. What brought them together was their experiences in South Africa, where Harbord had spent enough time to acquire a knowledge of several African languages. AR was survived by a son.

Sources: NAC, CEF files, box 8349-23; *NAC, South African War* files RG 38, A-1-a, vol. 90; *Colonist*, 5 February 1933, p. 2; 23 June 1934, p. 4: obit.

ROBERTSON, Frederick William Rountree (1876-1960). He was born in India in December 1876, son of W. R. Robertson of the ICS. Educated at St John's College, Cambridge, he entered the ICS in 1900 and served as assistant collector and sub-collector in various districts of Madras Presidency. In 1913, he was appointed Trustee of the Maharajah of Vizianagram's estates; in 1920-1925, he was collector and district magistrate of Guntur, Salem, and Nellore districts; and in 1925, he retired and settled in Victoria the next year. He married Agnes Graham Johnston, daughter of Captain and Mrs J. McD. Johnston of Liverpool, and in 1933, they were living in Oak Bay near Willows Beach at 2633 Estevan Avenue. They belonged to the Church of England and the British Public Schools Club. Near the end of their lives, they must have moved to Vancouver because he died there, aged eighty-three, on 26 December 1960 and she, aged sixty-six, on 25 April 1962.

Sources: Notes courtesy of John Palmer, Victoria; *Who's Who in B.C.*, 1933-1934, p. 149.

ROBERTSON, Captain Horatio John "Race" (1834-1903). Born at Foochow, China, son of Horatio Robertson, he became a tea clipper seaman, a pilot on the Yangtze River and a merchant at Foochow. His grandfather had been a signals officer under Admiral Horatio Nelson. HR married Agnes, the daughter of a wealthy British trader in China, and they had three daughters and eight sons. The family left China partly because of the climate and partly because Robertson wanted to set up a tea importing business in Canada. He was also, for a short while, in the shipping and whaling industries in BC.

In 1888, he bought Moresby Island and designed and built a house consisting of two octagonal towers joined by a hundred-foot-long verandah, which he later glassed in. The towers were three storeys high and built of ten-inch timbers, coated on the outside with plaster. One of the towers was for the boys and the other for the parents and their three girls, and there were a dining room and kitchen as well. From Foochow, they brought with them a Chinese couple, who made and served their meals. Robertson brought sixty acres under cultivation but farming was not a success, partly because the boys refused to take part in the work and rebelled, some running off to sea, others going to schools in Europe. When he tried to bring Chinese labourers in, he became embroiled in a dispute with the Canadian government officials over the "head tax." When he tried to employ local Indians, they failed to show up for work and he set fire to their village and was ordered to pay compensation. He gained a local reputation for behaving in BC as he had as an overseer in China. "Victorians were bemused to see him on occasion being pulled in a rickshaw along city streets by one of his coolies. Robertson was constantly launching lawsuits which he invariably lost." Things came to a crisis when his Chinese couple attempted to escape on a small raft and were found two days later drifting in cold and almost unconscious off Cadboro Bay. When the *Daily Colonist* published front-page stories of his cruelty to this Chinese couple, Robertson brought a lawsuit for slander and a long court case ensued. The judge, Henry Crease, settled the trouble with a moderate decision of compromise, but Robertson had had enough. He moved to Victoria and tried to get into politics and wrote cranky letters to the editors of the local newspapers. But he had made his way back to the Island by 17 January 1903 when he died, aged sixty-nine, leaving the family to squabble over the estate. The island was purchased in 1906 by Thomas W. Paterson who, three years later, was named lieutenant governor of BC.

The family, as recorded by the census in 1901, consisted of nine members: HR himself, aged sixty-six, born on 16 May 1834 in England, came to BC in 1887; his wife, Wilhelmina A. Robertson, aged forty-nine, born on 18 December 1851 in Scotland, arrived here in 1888; and seven children all born in China except the youngest, H. W. Moresby Robertson, aged eleven, born on 23 May 1889 in BC. The others were Horatio L., aged twenty-nine, born 30 August 1871; Bertie L., aged twenty-five, born 14 December 1875; Agnes L., his twin; Darwin C., aged eighteen, born 14 January 1883; Manlius C., aged fourteen, born 6 March 1886; and Hypatia L., thirteen, born 17 January 1888.

Sources: Peter Murray, *Homesteads and Snug Harbours: The Gulf Islands* (Victoria, Horsdal & Shubert, 1991), pp. 80-2; Canadian census, 1901 online, lists nine members of HR's family on Moresby Island.

ROBINSON, Brinkley (1835-1918). Born at Billingborough, Lincolnshire, on 15 July 1835, he was living there with his parents, according to English census records for 1841: his father Michael Robinson, aged forty, "agr. laborer," and his mother Sarah, thirty-five, "charwoman." He had an elder brother, John, aged seven, and a younger sister Elizabeth, aged two. In the 1851 census, BR was the only child, recorded, aged thirteen, as "agr. laborer," but his parents were as before, both born in nearby Lincolnshire villages. BR enlisted in the old Eighty-second Regiment called the "Billygoats" and in the Twenty-third Foot Regiment saw service in the Crimean War, took part in the siege of Sebastopol, and was then sent under the command of General Sir Colin Campbell and General Sir Henry Havelock to face the Indian Mutiny (1857-1858) at Cawnpore, Lucknow, and other centres.

After ten years of service, he retired to Ontario in 1870 but moved in 1891 to Victoria. There in 1901, he was living at 34 Humboldt Street with his wife Elizabeth, born in England on 19 December 1848, and two daughters: Amy Robinson, born 22 May 1877 in Ontario, employed as a "shirt maker," and Elizabeth Robinson, born 27 December 1879 in Ontario, working as a "waitress." BR was one of the founding members of the British Campaigners' Association when it began in 1908. In 1913, he appeared in an association photo of its oldest Imperial veterans. Another photo was printed in the *Daily Colonist* at his death, aged eighty-three, on 1 December 1918. He had worked for the city at one time and, during the Great War, had helped in military training at the Willows Camp near his house. The young men there called him "Old Dad" and listened to his tales of the Mutiny and life in the Imperial army in the 1850s. He caught cold while taking part in the peace celebrations and died at the Jubilee Hospital of pneumonia. He was famous at the British Campaigners' Association for his last words, "I fought for Britain when she was one of many nations. I did my little to strengthen her in my youth; I thank God that I have lived to see the days when she triumphs over all who would withstand her; and I die content to know that the peace of the world rests in the hands of my country and so is sure for all time." They buried him at Ross Bay with a firing squad, an escort headed by *Major General R. G. E. Leckie, and full military honours. He was survived by a son William, then at Vantwort, Ohio, and his two daughters who had married in Victoria, Mrs Sarah Elizabeth Armason of Higgins St, and Mrs Amy Demers of Orillia St.

Sources: *Colonist*, 3 December 1918, p. 7, obit., and photo; Canadian census 1901 for Victoria; census 1841, England, HO 107/613/11/13; census 1851, HO 107/2095/239/50.

ROBINSON, Colonel Charles Wilson (1877-1964). Born on 8 February 1877 at Loftus, Yorkshire, son of Richard Robinson, he emigrated to Regina, NWT, with his parents and there joined the Canadian Mounted Rifles on 2 January 1900 for service in South Africa, where he remained for two years. He received the Queen's Medal with clasps for Johannesburg, Diamond Hill, Cape Colony, and Orange Free State. When he joined the CEF on 26 September 1924 at Valcartier, he was living as a married farmer. After the Great War in which he was decorated with the OBE, he lived for some time at Munson, Alberta, but moved to Victoria about 1942 and died there, aged eighty-seven, on 15 May 1964, a resident of 2104 Quimper Street. He left two sons, Richard (Victoria) and Arthur (Penticton), a daughter Edith (Drumheller, Alberta), a brother, Luke Robinson, at Munson, Alberta, and a sister in Los Angeles.

Sources: *Colonist*, 17 May 1964, p. 22, obit.; NAC, CEF files, box 8379-51; NAC, RG 38, A-1-a, vol. 91, T-2094, regimental number 267.

ROBINSON, Lieutenant Colonel Sir Heaton Forbes (1873-1946), CMG (1930), M. Inst. CE, ACGI. He arrived in Victoria about 1938 with Lady Robinson and settled at Colwood in a place they called "Fircones," where he took an interest in public affairs and painted in oils. He was born in Singapore, son of Major General Wellesley G. W. Robinson, CB, a Scot whom the 1871 census found, aged thirty-two, at 5 Dollmere Street, Paddington, Marylebone, with his wife Annie, *née* Smith, aged thirty, born in Ireland, and one son, HR's elder brother, aged four. HR, born two years later, appears in the 1881 census, aged seven, living with his mother (the father away at the wars) and two younger brothers: J. F. D. Robinson, aged five, also born in Singapore, and A. C. Robinson, aged one, born in London. They had four servants: cook, nursery maid, parlourmaid, and nurse. Ten years later, the family was living at 15 St John's Park, Greenwich, the father being recorded as "Colonel Army Service Corps," the mother as before, and four sons listed as Wellesley H. Robinson, aged twenty, and Charles L. Robinson, aged nineteen, both bank clerks born in London; Heaton F. Robinson, aged seventeen, "Student Engineering"; and Annesley C. Robinson, aged eleven, born in London. Besides the cook, housemaid, and parlourmaid, the father had two relatives there: his mother-in-law, Elizabeth Smith, aged eighty-two, and the father's aunt, Harriet Morris, aged seventy-four, both born in Ireland.

HR was schooled at United Services College Westward Ho! in Germany and at the City and Guilds School of Engineering in South Kensington. Attached as a civil engineer to the staff of Sir John Wolfe Barry and Partners, who built the London Tower Bridge, he began in 1900 by working on the construction of the Natal South Coast Railway and spent altogether twelve years in South Africa, making bridges, waterways and surveys. Then he went to South America where he built the Buenos Aires dock extension. There was also a project in the Near East. When the Great War began, he went to France in September 1914 in charge of docks and railways and served in the RASC in France from August 1914 to 1919. He rose to major (1915), commandant of Outreau Depôt and camp commandant (1916), lieutenant colonel (1917), CO of No. 3 Base Supply Depôt (1917-1919), deputy director of works, Imperial War Graves Commission (1920-1925), and director of works (1926-1938) establishing and caring for cemeteries. Eventually, over eight hundred thousand headstones were placed in cemeteries tended by five hundred gardeners. After eighteen years as administrative head of the Imperial War Graves Commission, he was knighted for his work.

Early in June 1939, soon after retiring in 1938, HR arrived in Victoria with Lady Robinson and settled at Colwood. *Colonel H. T. Goodland, who for thirteen years had been in charge of war-cemetery work in France and Flanders, had something to do with HR's choice of Victoria. It was Goodland who introduced him when he spoke about his work and travels to the Rotary Club at the Empress Hotel at noon on 11 April 1940. Later next November, he lectured to the Island Arts and Crafts Society on "Portraiture" and showed *inter alia* two portraits he had painted, both copies of masters. Typically of such occasions at that time, Mrs *T. A. Rickard sang three solos "Bens of Jura," "My Laddie," and "When We Go." He was in demand as a speaker and also for his portraits. On 10 April 1941, he spoke to the Overseas League on "The

Native Problem in South Africa," a part of the world he knew well. The native problem he saw was a dramatic increase in the black population south of the Zambesi, then some thirteen million, owing to British methods of preventive medicine. A fortnight later, he attended the St George's Society's annual St George's Day banquet at the Douglas Hotel, where he gave the reply to the toast, "The Land of our Adoption." One of the first things, he painted was a portrait of *Lieutenant General Sir Percy Lake, shortly after his death, from memory and photographs, a picture which he presented to the Lake family. The Victoria Arts and Crafts Society showed it in their annual exhibition at the Crystal Gardens, which was opened on 28 April 1941 by Lady Byng, then staying in Victoria. It was on the study wall at the home of Lake's nephew, Lancelot Lake, in North Saanich when Lance and Valerie Lake kindly admitted me in January 2001. HR died, aged seventy-three, on 13 July 1946.

Sources: *Who was Who*, vol. 4, p. 989; census 1871, England, RG 10/14; census 1881, RG 11/7, p. 43; census 1891, RG 12/512, p. 43; *Colonist*, 7 June 1939, p. 4; 12 April 1940, p. 2; 21 November 1940, p. 2; 11 April 1941, p. 16; 27 April 1941.

ROBINSON, Lieutenant Henry King (1878-1929). He was born in Abbotabad, Punjab, North-West Province of India, where his father died when he was a child and his mother, Clara L. Robinson, took him back to England. In 1891, they were living at "Methven," Clevedon, Somerset, beside a boarding school. He was then twelve, and she was a widow aged forty, born at Topsham, Devon, and "living on her own means." He attended Clifton College and the Royal Indian Engineering College at Cooper's Hill and worked in 1901-1911 as a forestry engineer in the Indian Imperial Forestry Service.

HR went out to Victoria in 1912 and joined the BC Forestry Service on 1 April as one of the four men hired when that service was first established. In October 1915, he went overseas with the Fifth Regiment of the Canadian Garrison Artillery and served in France until he was wounded and transferred to the Canadian Forestry Corps in England as a lieutenant. Demobilized on 4 July 1919 in Victoria, he soon became assistant forester managing the Forestry Branch, but he resigned in October 1921 to return to India. "I look on Victoria," he declared to the *Colonist*, "as being my home and hope to come back again. It is the nicest town I have ever seen." Off he went to India, where he spent much time at Rawalpindi but in October 1929, on his way to England on leave, he died in the wreck of the flying boat, *City of Rome*, which crashed in the Gulf of Genoa on 26 October that year. He had intended to retire to Victoria three years later, when his superannuation was due. His wife and two children were living in England at the time, and his sister was visiting him in India.

Sources: *Colonist*, 12 October 1921, p. 14; 15 November 1929, p. 5, with photo, obit.; census 1891, England, RG 12/1954, p. 55.

RODNEY, Captain George Brydges Harley Guest, Eighth Baron Rodney (1891-1973). In 1919, two years after their marriage, he and his wife, Hon. Marjorie Lowther (1895-1968), daughter of the Sixth Earl of Lonsdale, took "Cottismore Farm" at Fort Saskatchewan north-east of Edmonton, Alberta, where they farmed for about forty years and became local leaders of the Boy Scout and Girl Guide movements. But GR was a special scoutmaster in that he had attended the founding Boy Scout camp, held on Brownsea Island in Poole Harbour on the south coast of England during the first week in August 1907. Some claim that he was the very first of Lord Baden-Powell's recruits. In 1963, the Rodneys retired to a country place on the Island at Colwood near Esquimalt and eventually died there, she on 29 July 1968 and he five years later on 18 December 1973. They were both buried at St Mary's Anglican Church at Metchosin, where they are commemorated by a bronze plaque in the churchyard.

Born in London, GR was the eldest of the four sons of George Brydges Harley Bennet, Seventh Baron of Rodney Stoke (1857-1909), an officer in the Life Guards, the Shropshire Yeomanry, and the Sixteenth Middlesex Regiment, and his wife, Hon. Corisande Evelyn Vere Guest (1870-1943), who sent him to Eton and Oriel College, Oxford. GR became a captain in the Second Brigade of Dragoons, Royal Scots Greys, and served in the First World War. He and his wife, Marjorie Lowther, daughter of the sixth earl of Lonsdale, had two daughters and three sons, the eldest of whom was killed in the Second World War. The title passed therefore to their second son, Hon. John Francis Rodney (1920-1992), who became the Ninth Baron Rodney. It had been created in 1782 for Admiral George Brydges Rodney, First Baron Rodney (1718-1792), in recognition of his success in battles at sea. The family seat for several generations was at Berrington Hall near Leominster.
Sources: *The Times* (London), 21 December 1973, p. 17 (mistakenly naming GR as the seventh baron.); *The Leader*, August/September 2007, p. 9; *Kelly's Handbook to the Titled, Landed and Official Classes* (8th edn., Kelley & Co., 1882), p. 712; several websites, e.g., Grant Menzies, http://newsgroup. derkeiler. com/Archive/ Alt/ alt. talk.royalty/2006-07/mag00076.htm

RODOCANACHI, Admiral John (1930-2002). He was born on 10 June 1930 in Darsham, Suffolk, England, to a wealthy sheep farmer, who descended from a family which had fled from the Greek island of Chios when an anti-Turkish rebellion resulted in a massacre of Chian Christians in 1822. He attended Rugby School and went into the Royal Navy. He was assigned to Halifax as part of the Sixth Submarine Squadron and, years later, transferred to the RCN submarine programme. After the Cuban missile crisis in 1962, he was sent to Seattle where he developed a Pacific Coast shipping plan with the U.S. Navy, and in 1964, he was made commanding officer of *Grilse*, a twenty-one-year-old submarine purchased from the United States and based at Esquimalt. She was once deployed to follow a Soviet warship that was hovering around the West Coast. In 1978, he became director of intelligence and security for the Canadian forces. When he retired in 1995, he settled in Victoria with his wife Dorothy and two children, both born in Vancouver. When he died on 27 April 2002, he left two sisters in England and a brother in New York.
Sources: *Globe & Mail* (Toronto), 2 August 2002, p. R5, obit.

ROGERS, Colonel Henry Cassady (1839-1914). Born at Grafton, Ontario, son of Lieutenant Colonel James G. R. Rogers and his wife Maria *née* Burnham, daughter of a Canadian senator, he was descended from Lieutenant Colonel

James R. Rogers of the Queen's Rangers, who in 1784 brought the first party of United Empire Loyalists to the Bay of Quinte. He attended the Toronto Model and Kingston Grammar schools and went into business at Peterboro under an uncle, Lieutenant Colonel R. D. Rogers. He then took up a lumbering, mining, and general mercantile business in partnership with a brother-in-law, Harry Strickland. In the years 1871-1879, he was postmaster at Peterboro. Meanwhile, from the age of sixteen, he was active in the volunteer militia and during the Fenian raids in 1866 commanded the Peterboro Rifles. He was later commissioned as a major in the Fifty-seventh Regiment but went on to organize an independent troop of cavalry which in 1872 became "C" Squadron of the Third Regiment of the Prince of Wales Canadian Dragoons. On 3 May 1877, he was promoted to lieutenant colonel and took command of the regiment on 9 February 1895. After retiring in 1899, he was recalled in 1901 to command a cavalry brigade. In 1896, he was elected president of the Peterboro History Society and was also active in the Ontario History Society. At sometime early in the twentieth century, he moved to the Island, settled at Shawnigan Lake, and there he died, aged seventy-five, on 7 August 1914.
Sources: *Colonist*, 9 August 1914, p. 5, obit., and photo; Morgan, *Canadian Men and Women*, p. 963.

ROLSTON, Dr Peter Williams (1831-1922). He was born on 7 December 1831 at Devonport, Devonshire, third son of George and Ellen Rolston. His father was a medical doctor there, and his mother was daughter of Captain Peter Williams, RN. After medical training at Guy's Hospital, London, and Edinburgh University, he joined the RN as assistant surgeon and was first appointed to HMS *Nile* (98), the flagship of the squadron sent to the Baltic during the Russian War in 1854-1855. After that war, he was aboard HMS *Agamemnon* and was helping to lay Atlantic cable at Woolwich. His next appointment was as surgeon to HMS *Falcon* (sloop of war), which was on the Australian Station for five years and took part in the Maori War in New Zealand (1866-1867). In 1869, he was appointed port health officer at the naval station at Port Royal, Jamaica, where he contracted yellow fever during an epidemic but recovered without apparent ill effects. His next appointment was at Devonport, where he served as fleet surgeon posted aboard HMS *Impregnable* and where his son, *Colonel J. M. Rolston was born in 1881. After later appointments at Aboukir and elsewhere, he retired, having had twenty-two years of service, and took up a private practice at Saltash, near Plymouth. The census found him there in 1881, aged forty-nine, living with his family at 86 Fore Street, listed as "General Practitioner, M.R.C.S. (Head surgeon, R.M.)." His wife Cecilia Fancomb Michell Rolston (*née* Michell), whom he had married in 1863, was a forty-year-old Dubliner, eldest daughter of George Berkeley Michell, and there were five sons whose births are clues to the family's movements. William George, aged sixteen, and Cecil Michell, aged eleven, were born at Plumstead, Kent; George Halstain, aged ten, was born in Jamaica; Orde Michell, aged six, was born at East Stonehouse, Devon, and John Michell, aged three, there at Saltash. The births of the three daughters were all at one or another of the same places. The family had three Cornish serving women (cook, housemaid, and "monthly nurse.")

In 1882, they decided to go to Canada, attracted by the land boom in Manitoba, and arrived at Winnipeg in July that year. PR volunteered to serve during the Riel Rebellion in 1885 and was surgeon to Major Boulton's Scouts, a body of mounted infantry raised near his home. In 1899, they left the prairies and went out to BC, where PR became medical officer to the Indians near Duncan. He took no part in public affairs, was known for his strong religious convictions, but seems to have been tolerant of disagreement. When his wife died in June 1908, he gave up his private practice to his son, Dr Cecil Michell R Rolston, who was established at Antigua but took a long leave at Maple Bay. PR had been living with this son at Maple Bay for some time when he died, aged ninety, on 13 June 1922. Surviving him were his daughters, Grace Williams Rolston, who had married *Percy Truscott Skrimshire on 10 August 1907 and lived at Quamichan, and Cecilia Marion F. Rolston, who married Ross Anthony Lort (c. 1890-1968) in Victoria on 22 July 1913. He also left two sons in addition to Cecil: W. G. M. Rolston of Victoria, and Colonel J. M. Rolston (1881-1950), DSO, CE, *Chevalier de la Légion d'Honneur*, honoured for services with the Railway Construction Corps during the Great War.

Sources: *Cowichan Leader*, 15 June 1922, obit.; notes courtesy of Charles Anthony Lort; census England, 1881, RG11, 2282/96; Major Charles Arkoll Boulton, *Reminiscences of the North-West Rebellions, with A Record of the Raising of Her Majesty's 100th Regiment in Canada and a Chapter on Canadian Social & Political Life* (Toronto, Grip Printing & Publishing Co., 1886), 531 pp., passim; *Colonist*, 22 July 1917, p. 4.

ROOME, Lieutenant Colonel Henry Napier (1864-1938). He was born on 2 July 1864 at Poona, India, son of General Frederick Roome, CB (1829-1907), who was himself born in India and had a long and distinguished career in the Bombay Army of the East India Company, the Osmanil Irregular Cavalry (Hazhi Bazouka) (1853-1856), in command of the Bassoda Field Force during the Mutiny, in the Political and Intelligence Department during the Abyssinian Campaign (1867-1868), and in the second Afghan War (1879-1880), when he took part in General Sir Robert Phayre's march to Kandahar. This father sent HR to be schooled at Hastings, Hurst Court College Oxford, and RMA, Sandhurst. He was then gazetted as a lieutenant to the King's Own Yorkshire Light Infantry on 23 May 1885, transferred on 2 June 1887 to the Thirty-seventh Lancers, Baluch Horse, an Indian Cavalry regiment, and appointed to command it on 3 September 1910 with the rank of lieutenant colonel. Most of his service was on the North-West Frontier of India, where he served with distinction in the campaigns against the Zakha (Zakka) Khel (1908) and others. He held various staff appointments during the Great War, mainly in Mesopotamia and the Far East, until he was invalided out of the service in 1918.

He retired in 1919, went to Canada, and settled on Lake's Road, Somenos Lake, with his wife, Hilda Mary [May] Roome (c. 1870-1952), daughter of Colonel Charles Peter Newport of the Indian Army. HR enjoyed fishing, golfing, and motoring, kept a yacht near Duncan, and was remembered locally for his fine etchings, this being one of his hobbies. The rock for the First World War memorial at Duncan came from his property. In 1929, however, he and Mrs Roome returned to England and

settled at Crowborough, Sussex, where he died, aged seventy-four, on 9 January 1938. He was survived by his widow, a daughter, Mrs L. H. Phinney, Winnipeg, and four sons: V. H. Roome, New York; Ian Roome in England; Leslie and Ronald Roome at Duncan. He also leaves a brother, *Colonel R. E. Roome, at Quamichan Lake.
Sources: Interviews with a son, John Roome of Cowichan, a nephew Barry Roome of Cobble Hill, and their cousin Bevan Gore-Langton of Saanichton; PRO, Kew, *Indian Army List,* January 1923, p. 527; *Who's Who in B.C.* 1933-1934, p. 150; *Colonist,* 13 January 1938; *Cowichan Leader,* etc.; census 1891, England, RG 12/32, p. 66; census 1881, RG 11/1124, pp. 41-2; census 1901, RG 13/3331, p. 37; a family collection of newspaper cuttings, all undated [why do people do that?].

ROOME, Colonel Reginald Eckford (1866-1946). Born on 12 July 1866 at Carisbrook, Isle of Wight, he was a son of General Frederick Roome (1829-1907), CB, of India, and a brother of *Colonel Henry Napier Roome. His army career began in the Guernsey Militia, which he joined with the rank of ensign. Then on passing out of Sandhurst, he was awarded the "Queen's Sword" and, on receiving a commission in 1887, joined the Royal Scots Fusiliers and served with them in Burma for several years. In 1892, he transferred to the Indian Staff Corps and, on being posted to the Thirty-sixth Jacob's Horse, served with that regiment on the North-West Frontier of India and throughout the Waziristan Campaign (1901-1902). Later he was seconded to the Zhob Levy Corps, which he commanded for several years, with headquarters at Fort Sandeman, Baluchistan, until early in 1907. He then returned to the Thirty-sixth Jacob's Horse and assumed command of that regiment in 1912. When the Great War began, he took them from the Punjab directly to the front in France, arriving in November 1914. His regiment, after engaging in several successful cavalry campaigns, was dismounted and served as infantry in the trenches. At one time, they remained in front-line trenches for a continuous period of ten weeks. Early in 1915, after moving up in relief of the Canadians at the time of the first German gas attack, he was severely gassed. After convalescing in England, he returned later that year to India as inspector general of re-mounts, with the acting rank of brigadier. He served in the Afghanistan Campaign of 1919 and was wounded. In 1920, after thirty-three years of active service, he retired with a notable collection of medals, including Waziristan (1901-1902), the Mons Star, and the Afghanistan Medal (1919).

In 1921, he moved with his family to Duncan. His wife, whom he had married on 26 March 1898 at Kamatha, Samil, India, was Isobel Margaret Barry (born 6 April 1876), daughter of Colonel A. Barry, Indian Army. He cruised about in his pleasure launch, *Falcon,* became well known among yachtsman on the BC coast, and was a leader in forming the Maple Bay Yacht Club. After serving as commodore of it for many years, he was elected an honorary member, but he also belonged to the Cowichan Bay Yacht Club and Royal Victoria Yacht Club. During the Second World War, he helped to organise the flotilla of power boats formed to supplement local naval forces in the event of a need to evacuate women and children to the mainland. He died, aged seventy-nine, on 17 April 1946, leaving his wife and a daughter, Elspeth, at Duncan, two sons, Frederick Roome

(Victoria) and Reginald Roome (Trail), and two grandsons, Barry and Roderick. But according to the Victoria city directory, Mrs R. E. Roome was living at 1505 Beach Drive, Oak Bay, in 1944.
Sources: BNA, *Indian Army List,* January 1923, p. 527; *Vancouver Daily Province*, 23 April 1946, p. 22, obit.; *Cowichan Leader*, 25 April 1946; *Colonist*, 23 April 1946, p. 5, obit.; *Victoria Times*, 23/4/1946, p. 7, obit.

ROSCOE, Francis James (1830-1878). One of two members of Parliament for Victoria, he sat in 1874-1878 as an Independent Liberal in the House of Commons, Ottawa, where he joined the Rideau Club, and when he died, John A. Macdonald (1815-1891) was elected to fill the vacant seat and held it in 1878-1882. It was twenty years earlier, in 1862, that FR emigrated to Victoria from Liverpool, where he was born, and became a dealer in iron and hardware as a partner in the firm of Fellowes & Roscoe. Later, he was also a commissioner of the Savings Bank of British Columbia and captain of No. 1 Company of Victoria's Volunteer Rifles. Meanwhile, he returned home to England long enough to marry, on 22 November 1864 at Lyme Regis, one Anna Lætitia Le Breton (1833-?), daughter of a barrister of the Inner Temple, Philip Hemery Le Breton (born 1806 in Jersey, Channel Islands), and his wife Anna Lætitia *née* Aitkin of London, who lived in Hampstead. This latter lady edited a volume of correspondence about religion and politics between Lucy Aitkin and William Ellery Channing, DD, published in Boston (1874). As for FR and his wife, they lived in the Ross Bay quarter of Victoria in what has been preserved as an example of a pre-confederation colonial house. Better known than FR was his elder brother, William Caldwell Roscoe (1823-1859), a poet and essayist remembered for two tragedies entitled *Eliduc* (1846) and *Violenzia* (1851) and for contributions to the *National Review* when Walter Bagehot was also writing for it. Their father, William Stanley Roscoe (1782-1843), was educated at Peterhouse, Cambridge, and was employed first as a partner in his father's (FR's grandfather's) bank and later as serjeant-at-mace at the Court of Passage, which tried civil cases concerning imports and exports passing through Liverpool. With a good knowledge of Italian literature, this father published a volume of poems when FR was fourteen, a biography of Lorenzo de Medici, and several other books including a biography of his own father (FR's grandfather), William Roscoe (1753-1831), who is remembered as a historian, a collector, and a patron of the arts, as well as a Liverpool banker. FR's grandfather was also a Unitarian opponent of the slave trade and a founder of the Liverpool Royal Institution and Athenæum, who developed an interest in botany and published studies of ginger (monandrian plants). FR himself was a younger son (like so many on the Island) and the only emigrant in a family of interesting people. They all descended from FR's great-grandfather, who as a young man was a butler at Allerton Hall near Liverpool but later kept an inn at Old Bowling Green.

At sometime in the 1870s, FR took over to the Island from England two batches of what were at first called meadowlarks, but as the only meadowlarks (*Sturnella magna*) are native to North America and as the English skylark (*Alauda arvensis*) nests in meadow grass, they were probably skylarks. Though FR released them in or near Victoria, it is not clear whether they survived because in 1903, the Victoria Natural History Society imported another hundred pairs of skylarks in a further attempt to establish them in the wild. This society was financially assisted by the government, and in 1913, they took over yet another fifty pairs. Already in June 1907, an English resident of Oak Bay, who noticed some soaring and singing near the Jubilee Hospital, said they reminded him of Gloucestershire meadows. Members of the society took as good care of them as they could, for instance, asking the councils of Victoria and Oak Bay to authorize the destruction of crows: "As we have evidence of their rapacity and cruelty to both robins (native and imported) as well as skylarks, three nests of which in one field that we know of were ruthlessly destroyed last summer by the crows." In February 1914, the Natural History Society asked the Oak Bay Municipal Council to kill off the crows. There was much correspondence on this subject in local newspapers that spring; for example, *Captain (later Sir) Clive Phillipps-Wolley wrote perversely in defence of crows, and even the Victoria Natural History Society was divided on the question. One member, *Colonel Marshall Aubrey Kent, quoted *inter alia* in his letter:

> The stately homes of Oak Bay
> How silently they stand,
> For the crows have killed or hunted
> Every song-bird from the land.

But when the authorities then decided to put a bounty on crows, it was only to stop them from attacking ducks and other domestic birds in Beacon Hill Park. Again in 1934, the superintendent of city parks declared war on crows on Beacon Hill but only because they preyed on new-born ducks and pheasants. Songbirds were unimportant to him as to most of the Canadian-born public, who rarely noticed that crows were the bandits of the bird-world, though only a few weeks earlier the Victoria Branch of the SPCA was sensitive enough to report that marauding cats were destroying the skylarks. A vigorous member of the SPCA who loved English songbirds on the Island was that extraordinary lady, *Dora Frances Eales Kitto. Skylarks were one of the features of life in North Saanich that cheered many local residents, including my parents, who were perennially homesick for rural England.

When FR died in Victoria on 20 December 1878, his wife, Anna Lætitia (Le Breton) Roscoe, took the children back to England, where the 1881 census recorded them living in Hampstead at 5 Willow Road with a servant; but the 1891 census found them in Birmingham at 15 York Road, Edgbaston, with a cook and a housemaid. The widowed Mrs Roscoe was aged forty-six in 1881 and fifty-six in 1891 and born in the Strand, London. There were four children, all born on the Island in Victoria: Katharine Roscoe, aged thirteen and twenty-three; Francis Aikin Roscoe, eleven and twenty-one, a "merchant apprentice"; Millicent Roscoe, eight and eighteen; and Thomas Le Breton Roscoe, two and twelve. The *BC Archives* has a photograph of FR as a balding gentleman in jacket and waistcoat, with a watch-chain and a huge Victorian beard.

Sources: Ross Bay Villa: *A Colonial Cottage* 1865-2000, ed., J. N. Barr, M. E. D. Jones and H. Edwards, (2nd ed.; Victoria, Hallmark Society, 1998), p. 27; G. D. Sprot (Cobble Hill), "Notes on the introduced skylark in the Victoria district of Vancouver Island," *The Condor*, vol. XXXIX (January 1937), pp. 24-31; *Colonist*, 2 June 1907, *Sunday supplement*, p. 17; 14 February 1914, p. 5; 18 February 1914, p. 3; 24 March 1914, p. 7; 4 March 1914, p. 5; *Colonist*, 30 March 1926, p. 4; 1 March 1934, p. 12; 24 February 1934, p. 14; census 1851, HO 107/1603/6/45 (Le Breton); census 1881, RG 11/168/p. 38 (FR's widow and family); census 1891, RG 12/2358, p. 36 (FR's widow and family); *The Canadian Directory of Parliament*, 1867-1967, ed., J. K. Johnson (Ottawa, Public Archives, 1968), p. 505; *The Canadian Parliamentary Companion and Annual Register*, 1877, ed., Charles Herbert Macintosh (Ottawa, Citizen Printing & Publishing, 1877), p. 186; William Roscoe (1753-1831), *The Wrongs of Africa, A Poem* (R. Faulder, 1787-1788) against the slave trade; *Correspondence of William Ellery Channing, D.D., and Lucy Aitkin from 1826 to 1842*, ed., Anna Lætitia Le Breton née Aikin (Boston, Roberts Brothers, 1874), 426 pp.; *The Record of Old Westminsters to 1927*, vol. 2, p. 562 (Philip Hemery Le Breton).

ROSS, Brigadier Edward Johnson "Teddy" (1884-1943). Born on 2 March 1884 into an old Scottish border family, he became a cadet at RMC, Sandhurst, but got off to a bad start. He was chosen to play rugby for Scotland in the Calcutta Cup, the annual rugby international match between Scotland and England, a great honour for a nineteen-year-old, and so he ignored an order not to attend the game and went to Edinburgh anyway. Upon his return, he was arrested, tried, and sentenced to lose six months' seniority. Upon graduating, he joined the Second Gurkha Regiment in which he did well and went on to be promoted on 9 April 1906 to lieutenant in the Eighth Gurkha Rifles. In 1911-1917, he was engaged in operations in the Abor country. During the Great War, he won the DSO and the MC and after the war became an Indian army staff officer. By the early 1930s, he was at army headquarters in charge of the war plans and the mobilization section of the adjutant general's branch. The writer of ER's obituary notice in the *Cowichan Leader*, one "K.A.W.," evidently an Indian army officer himself, wrote, "Ross was a first-class staff officer, good brain, keen, hard-working, and a good mixer. I owe him a great deal personally, as I was at that time [early 1930s] engaged on a similar job in my own line, and it was from him that I got the sound advice and criticism that I needed so badly." After a while, ER was promoted and given the appointment he wanted—command of a brigade on the North-West Frontier of India, "which meant real soldiering in peace time, with Afghans slipping over the border to raid his area, or the local Pathans putting up a minor battle along the only road. Ross dealt very adequately with this situation, with an occasional day off to shoot hill partridges or catch a few fish, always with an armed escort and the chance of a scrap."

ER retired when he reached the age limit, and in 1940, he and his wife went out to settle in the Cowichan Valley on the Maple Bay Road. As KAW recalled, ER was "very happy catching steelhead in the Cowichan River or salmon down in the bay, and training and working his dogs over ducks and pheasant. He was a skilled shot, a fine fisherman, a man who loved dogs. When this war started, Ross tried every possible means to get re-employed in Canada but—very foolishly, I think—he met with a flat refusal. Eventually he was accepted as an unpaid volunteer at Pacific Command Headquarters on his own job, war plans and mobilization. For over a year, day in and day out, six days a week, he drove to Victoria and back working on this problem for the bare cost of his gasoline. When and if the Japs ever decide to land in B.C. they will curse the brains and military knowledge of Teddy Ross . . . Essentially a man's man, he did his job as he saw it for the Empire right up to the end. May God rest his soul in peace." [by KAW]

He died, aged fifty-nine, on 22 June 1943 of a heart attack while packing household effects to move to Mr Eric Powell's house at Maple Bay, where he and his wife intended to move the following week. Besides his wife, he was survived by two sons: Surgeon Lieutenant W. L. Ross, RNVR, and a younger son at school in England. He also had three daughters: Mrs M. H. Wace, a sergeant with the WAC in India; Miss J. E. Ross, who trained as a nurse in London at University College Hospital; and Lieutenant Corporal Dorothy M. Ross, CWAC, who had just returned to the east coast after two weeks' furlough at home with her parents. He was buried at St Peter's Quamichan.

Sources: *British Library/India Office/Indian Army List*, October 1910, p. 153; January 1923, p. 527; *Cowichan Leader*, 24 June 1943, p. 8; 19 July 1943, p. 8; 1 July 1943; *Colonist*, 25 June 1943, p. 3, obit.; *London Gazette*, 15 August 1918; and 17 and 21 February 1919.

ROW, Captain Herbert Newton Edward "George" (1884-?). He was born at Long Melford, Suffolk, where he was living, aged six, at "The Laurels," St Mary Street, with his family in 1891. According to the 1891 census, his father, Charles J. N. Row, aged forty-eight, was a "Manure, Cake Coal, Hay and Straw Merchant-Superintendent of Resident Insurance Funds-Resident Life and Fire Agent-Secretary for Gas and Coal Company-Farmer" [*sic*]. HR's mother, Rosetta Row, aged forty-five, was born at Diss, Norfolk, and he had an elder brother, Charles J. H. Row, aged seventeen, who worked as a "Merchant's Clerk." Living with them was his mother's sister, Ellen Welham, aged fifty, born at Diss, Norfolk, and there were two servants—a cook and a housemaid. One neighbour was a shoemaker. HR joined a territorial unit of the British Army very young, but in 1908, he was out in the Okanagan Valley working. He returned to England in 1909, where he married and took up the family insurance business. In 1914, he rejoined his territorial unit in the Army Service Corps and was fighting in France the following year. In 1916, he transferred to the Royal Flying Corps and flew Sopwith Camels at the Italian front. As a friend of William George Barker, a Canadian ace, and also of P. B. Joubert (who became air chief marshal in the RAF later), he was gazetted out of the RAF as a captain in 1919. In 1925, he left home, after trying insurance again, and settled finally at Thetis Island, in the Chemainus district, where he joined the newly formed Canadian Legion. Many years later, on 28 November 1972, an acquaintance wrote to the *Colonist* with the news that Row, a retired RN officer now aged eighty-eight, was returning to England,

where he was to live with his son, also a retired RN officer, at Bures, Suffolk, eight miles from his birthplace, Long Melford.
Sources: census 1891, England, RG 12/1443, p. 1; Elliott, *Memories of the Chemainus Valley*, pp. 339-341.

RUDLIN, Captain George (1836-1903). Born on 10 March 1836 somewhere in Essex, he went to sea aged twelve in the fishing vessel *Colchester* and served on the transport *Victoria* in the Russian (Crimean) War (1854-1856). He went through the great gale at Balaklava when, on 14 November 1854, many vessels and lives were lost. He arrived on the Pacific coast in 1856 and took a series of jobs there to do with sea traffic. In 1862-1863, he and a partner had a logging establishment on Discovery Island, east of Victoria, and built and named their schooner *Discovery* after that island when they had her built in Victoria and launched on 8 April 1863. Rudlin then commanded her in the coasting trade until he took charge of another, the well-known schooner, *Black Diamond*, busy in the coal trade between Nanaimo and Victoria. Like many at that time, GR learnt to manage steam vessels beginning with the *Emma*, followed among others by the *Grappler* and the historic *Beaver*. He and Henry Saunders, a grocer, together with five other Victoria citizens, bought the old *Beaver* on 10 October 1874 for $415,700 and transferred her registration from London to Victoria on 15 October 1874. He then captained her for three years. In 1883, he joined the Canadian Pacific Navigation Company and so remained until the company was purchased in 1901 by the Canadian Pacific Railway Company in which service he continued until his death. Among the ships he commanded was the *Enterprise* when she was competing with the *Princess Louise* under my great uncle William McCulloch, then employed by the People's Navigation Company Ltd. GR was skipper of the *Enterprise* when on 28 July 1885 she collided with the *R.P. Rithet* under Captain Asbury Insley, who was judged guilty in the affair. GR commanded the *Islander* on 30 December 1888 on her first trip on the Vancouver run when she had just arrived from Scotland and was much admired, and he was the usual captain of the *Islander* on the Victoria-Vancouver run, though she went on northern voyages under Captain John Irving. GR was the first captain of the *Princess Victoria*, and she was also his last command. By 1901, when he told the census-taker that he earned $150 a month, was married, and an Anglican, he was widely known on the Victoria-Vancouver run as a picturesque old veteran with big side whiskers. He died suddenly, aged sixty-eight, on 23 September 1903 at Vancouver during one of his short voyages there and was buried at Ross Bay. Rudlin Bay on Discovery Island was named after him.
Sources: Canadian census, Victoria, 1901; city of Victoria records; Walbran, *B.C. Coast Names*, p. 433; *Colonist*, 22 April and 7 May 1863; 29 December 1868.; 24 September 1903; Norman R. Hacking and W. Kaye Lamb, *The Princess Story: A Century and a Half of West Coast Shipping* (2nd ed., Vancouver, Mitchell Press, 1976), pp. 64, 69, 77, 106, 109, 110, 120, 122, 123, 127*, 131, 134, 198.

RUSSELL, Arthur A. (c. 1862-1936). Born in England, he joined the British Army and, as Island newspapers were always glad to repeat, was in the British expedition

which responded to the Dervish uprising in the Sudan by marching to the relief of Khartoum in 1898. He then retired to farm at Nanoose Bay near Nanaimo, where he and his wife had two daughters. He served as captain of the Church Lads Brigade of St Paul's Anglican Church, Nanaimo, which Canon Cooper had organized. At the time of his death, aged seventy-four, on 5 July 1936, he was said to be one of the six known survivors of the march on Khartoum. His wife had died earlier. His funeral was at French Creek Church, and he was buried in Parksville Cemetery.
Sources: *Colonist,* 7 July 1936, p. 5, obit.; *Nanaimo Daily Free Press,* 6 July 1936, p.1.

RUTHERFORD, Colin Henry (1877-1973). He retired to Victoria about 1928 after many years at Shanghai, China. He and his wife were active members of the China-Japan Society in Victoria until their deaths. Born at Waltham Holy Cross near London, he appears, aged three, fifth of five children born to Emily, aged thirty-four, born there, and her husband Peter Rutherford, forty-six, "Iron & Brass Founder" from Dundee, Scotland. They lived at Cheshunt, Hertfordshire, in "Rutland Cottage" with one servant girl, aged eighteen. Ten years later, when he was thirteen, his father was "Foreman, R.S.F. Factory," and his brother Andrew, eighteen, was an "Engineer Apprentice." In 1900, CR went to China, where he worked as a merchant for Collins & Company for twenty-eight years and retired as its managing director. He was a thirty-second-degree Freemason and had served as company commander in the Shanghai Scottish, a unit affiliated with "his old regiment, the London Scottish," though I could find no record of his service in the latter. He had also married and divorced (in 1916) Elsie Eleanor Agnes Rutherford and remarried at Shanghai, Cicely Rose Emily, who was born at Shanghai to a British family there about 1884.

When they retired to Victoria in 1928, arriving at Vancouver from the Orient on 30 June aboard the *Empress of Canada,* this was by no means their first visit to the Pacific coast. They had passed through in 1920, when sailing from Liverpool on the *Prinz Friedrich Wilhelm,* arriving at Quebec on 18 August *en route* to China, and in 1927, they landed at Victoria on 19 June on the *Empress of Canada* with their son Peter Colin Rutherford, aged six, born at Shanghai. They lived at 1227 Beach Drive, which faces the Strait of Georgia looking east across Oak Bay, in which there were many other British immigrants from various parts of the empire. CR served as chairman of the Oak Bay School Board and joined the Victoria Golf Club that had been pioneered by *Captain Harvey Walter Henry Combe. Cicely was elected secretary-treasurer of the China-Japan Society on 15 October 1931 and its president in 1937 at the eighth annual meeting held on 1 October at the Oak Bay Beach Hotel. Also present at these meeting were a couple of dozen other members, such as *Captain James Urquhart Gordon, *Herbert Percy King, *Captain Vernon-Jackson, and Captain and Mrs *Alfred David Steadman Powell. Cicely died, aged sixty-three, on 28 August 1947, and five years later, in 1952, CR, then aged seventy-four, went on a cruise out of New York on the *Oslofjord* with his third wife, Amy Julia Rutherford, then aged sixty-six, a cruise that was perhaps a kind of honeymoon. When CR died, aged ninety-five, on 8 November 1973, he left his son, Colin Peter Rutherford, then living nearby at 2570 Nottingham Road, and his own wife, whom local reporters called Dora, but seems in fact to have been Amy Julia Rutherford, who died five years later, aged ninety-three, on 2 July 1978. **Sources:** *Colonist*, 17 October 1931, p. 8; 6 October 1937, p. 3; 10 November 1973, p. 30, obit.; census 1881, England, RG 11/1397/10, p. 13; census 1891, RG 12/1091/16, p. 25; BNA (Kew), J77/1243/7855: Divorce Court File 7855 (1916); Canadian Passenger Lines 1865-1935, T-14708 (arriving 18 August 1920 at Quebec from Liverpool); T-14908 (arriving 19 June 1927 at Victoria from Hong Kong); T-14892 (arriving 30 June 1928 at Vancouver from Manila); New York Passenger Lines, 1820-1957, T715_8125, p. 406 (arriving 2 April 1952).

ST JOHN, Lieutenant Colonel Frederick Oliver (1886-1977). He was born on 13 October 1886 at the British Legation in Caracas, Venezuela, eldest son of Sir Frederick Robert St John, KCMG (1821-1923), a diplomat then serving as consul. He was educated at Ascham School in Bournemouth and on 9 October 1912 was commissioned in the Royal Signals, becoming then a second lieutenant in the Royal Scots. He was promoted to captain (1915), to major (1923), and to lieutenant colonel (1932). In the Great War of 1914-1918, he was mentioned in despatches and in 1917 won the MC and was named to the DSO. After the war, he was attached to the staff, Eastern Command in India, where he commanded the Third Indian Divisional Signals at Meerut and in 1932, the Army Signals School of India, in 1933, the Second Indian Divisional Signals, and then the Depot Battalion Royal Signals. By the time he retired in 1937, he had spent twenty-five years in India with the Royal Scottish Regiment and was a member of the Royal Geographical Society. He was a traveller and explorer, enjoyed big-game shooting, and contributed occasionally to *Blue Peter* and other journals.

At sometime in the late 1930s, he arrived in Victoria, stayed for a few years, and then moved to Peachland, BC, where his second wife, Elizabeth Pierce, whom he married in 1931, had been a resident as the daughter of Edward Horace Pierce (c. 1863-1959). In Victoria, FS was much in demand as a speaker on aspects of India, then much in the forefront of Imperial affairs. On 26 July 1938, for instance, he addressed the Kiwanis Club at the Empress Hotel, telling of the huge diversity of languages, religions, and conditions of life. When asked why the British were in India, he said that he thought the Indians must want them there and said at length that before the British came, India was a prey to invasions, such as that of the Moslems who were most bloodthirsty. British administration assured justice for all, security, and a measure of peace the country would not otherwise enjoy. On 2 October 1939, he was again at the Empress Hotel, where *Sir Robert Erskine Holland introduced him to a meeting of the Overseas League and he described the fauna and flora of the Himalayas. On 27 December 1939, he was the guest speaker at a Kipling Society dinner in Spencer's dining room, introduced by the president, A. E. G. Cornwell, and thanked by *Colonel H. T. Goodland. He spoke about British rule in India, where he had served for twenty-five years: "He defended British rule, pointed out the nature and vast extent of the difficulties of government, and declared that the administration is being carried out in a most marvellous way . . . there is no truth beyond Port Saïd," he said. "This is the main difference between these people and us. Truth is simply not applied—they don't believe in it and they don't live it . . . we are no further ahead than we were a hundred years ago." He quoted Rudyard Kipling several times and recommended *Kim* to all interested in India.

On 27 June 1940, he was once more at the Empress Hotel, where he spoke to the Rotary Club on "India in Relation to the Empire." Drawing on his considerable knowledge of the subject, he declared that since the British had been governing India there had been less bloodshed than ever before. On Gandhi, he said, "With over 365,000,000 people in the country, and less than 10 per cent of those educated, and a still smaller percentage of that educated group Gandhi followers, we have no need to give him a second thought." On 6 August 1940, he spoke to the Kiwanis Club at a lunch at the Empress Hotel about British efforts to reduce suffering and prevent famine. He had been to Tibet, knew a good deal about the country, and so was able to address the Canadian Anti-Vivisection Society at the Royal Bank Building on "The Road to Tibet" to raise money for the care of animals in devastated parts of Britain. He was introduced on that occasion as "the well-known explorer and traveller." Again on 6 February 1941, he spoke about Tibet to the same society for the same purpose. "He mentioned," *The Colonist* reported the next day, "that nowhere in the Himalayas was it safe for one to go without a rifle. 'Anyone who does will certainly be eaten by something,' he said." On 3 April 1941, he spoke again and to a large audience, at a meeting of the Anti-Vivisection Society on "Britain and India," recounting many of his own experiences on the North-West Frontier of India. On 28 September 1943, he spoke to the Canadian Club at the Empress Hotel in defence of the British government in India. Only that government has had success in preventing the constant tribal and religious warfare and in struggling to end the slave trade in the Indian Ocean.

After the Second World War, he and his family settled in the Okanagan Valley and lived a peaceful rural life in a British community there until September 1954. It was reported then that he was heir apparent to the Earl of Orkney and other titles and might become the eighth earl if the seventh, a cousin in his thirties, should die first. The *Daily Colonist* in the post-war years had an ambiguous, self-consciously Canadian attitude to such people and wrote about him now as a curiosity. His grandfather was born in Rome, his father in Florence, and he in Venezuela more than sixty years ago. The title came through his mother, a Fitz Maurice and a descendant of Malcolm II of Scotland. "It is one of the three titles in the British Empire that can be passed on to a female." He was now in Victoria on his way to Britain and did not intend to return to the Okanagan. He had a Canadian passport, a son [Oliver] Peter born in Victoria to his second wife, having divorced the first wife, Dotie Bierney, in 1929, and the son might become Lord Kirkwall. He and his family then left Victoria. He died at last, aged 90, on 10 February 1977.

Sources: *Who's Who*, 1943, p. 2731; *Indian Army List*, October 1927, pp. 37, 524, 529; *Colonist*, 27 July 1938, p. 2; 4 October 1939, p. 6; 28 June 1940, p. 18; 29 January 1941, p. 6; 7 February 1941, p. 2; 4 April 1941, p. 2; 28 September 1943, p. 11; 27 March 1940, p. 6; 11 September 1954, p. 13.

SALIS, Major Charles Frederick de Fargus [Fergue] de (1875-?). He was born on 30 October 1875 at Aldershot, Hampshire, son of Edward John de Salis (1853-1929), a soldier born at Grahamstown, South Africa, who was recorded in 1881 as "Deputy Assistant Commissary, General of Ordnance, Ordnance Active List," in 1891 as "Major and Assistant Com Gen." and in 1901 as a lieutenant colonel serving in the Admiralty Naval Ordnance Department at HM Gun Wharf, Chatham. CS's mother Margaret E. Augusta Lafarque (1853-1932) was born at New Romsey or Littlestown, Hampshire, and in 1891 he had three brothers: Edward A. A. de Salis, aged sixteen, born at Aldershot; Henry W. de B. de Salis, aged thirteen, born at St Leonard's, Sussex; and Herbert J. N. de Salis, aged twelve, born in Yorkshire. Later that year, another brother, Frank Robert Lawson de Salis (1891-1916), was born at Portsmouth. A sister, Adeline A. de Salis, born about 1877 at Pembroke, Bermuda, was not there, perhaps at school. In 1881, the family lived at Carlton Terrace, York, and in 1891 at 4 The Terrace, Royal Dockyard, Woolwich, London. They had two servants. As a young man, CS joined the Corg and Mysore Volunteer Rifles in India as a private soldier but in 1901 was commissioned as second lieutenant in the Third (Militia) Battalion of the Essex Regiment and went with them to the South African War, where he duly received the Queen's Medal and was promoted to lieutenant.

He stayed in South Africa until 1907, continued to serve in England, but in 1911 went to Vancouver Island, where he resigned his commission to command a company in the Eighty-eighth Victoria Fusiliers when it was formed in autumn 1912. He was rector's warden at St Mary's Church, Oak Bay, when it was dedicated in 1911 and either he or one of his brothers lived at Shawnigan Lake for a time. In July 1914, he was sent to Nanaimo with the Civil Aid Force intended to watch rebellious coalminers. On 8 November 1914, he took a commission as a major in the CEF, declaring his occupation to be "Gentleman" and listing his wife as Frances Mildred de Salis, resident at 10 Magdalen Road, Hastings, England. He was recorded as an Anglican with a fair complexion, blue eyes, and light hair. A few months later, his younger brother, Frank R. L. de Salis, working in Victoria as an accountant, joined the CEF on 26 July 1915, left his wife Eileen Lissie de Salis on a property near Victoria, and was killed in Belgium on 2 June 1916. Another brother, Herbert J. N. de Salis (c. 1880-1956), was listed in *Henderson's Greater Victoria Directory* for 1912 as Captain H. J. N. de Salis living at "Insovenajh," 31 Pleasant Ave, Victoria, having served with the Royal Engineers in the South African War, but when he returned to England to rejoin his unit as a major in the Great War, had moved to the Cowichan Valley. H. J. N. de Salis survived, returned, and died, aged seventy-six, on 25 March 1956 in Sidney. CS, too, may have returned but I found no further sign of him on the Island.

Sources: census 1881, England, RG 11/4721, p. 41; census 1891, RG 12/529, p. 37; NAC, reel T6958, "Active militia with Service before World War 1," notes in a ledger; NAC, CEF files, box 2458-65; *Colonist*, 12 April 1914, p. 14; 28 July 1914, p. 11; Ron Baird, *Success Story: The History of Oak Bay* (Victoria, Daniel Heffernan & James Borsman, 1979), p. 131; *Henderson's Greater Victoria Directory* 1912; [*Cowichan Leader*, 17 August 1916, "Cowichan Roll of Service."

SANDYS-WUNSCH, Colonel Theodore Vincent (1892-1966). He was born on 9 January 1892 at Knutsford, Cheshire, son of Mrs Mary Wunsch, born at Trenton, Cheshire, second wife of Edward Wunsch (c. 1847-?), a Scottish cotton merchant with several employees. The 1901 census found TS, aged nine, living at Brook House, 2 Brook Street, Knutsford, with his parents and three elder brothers and a younger sister. It was TS's widowed mother who added the name "Sandys" to make Sandys-Wunsch before the Great War when a German-sounding name was an embarrassment. TS's grandfather, Edward A. Wunsch (c. 1822-?), was born in Germany and in 1871 was staying in Ilkley, Yorkshire, as a visiting merchant at "Ben Thudding," apparently kept as a hotel by a Scottish physician with a wife born in India.

In 1910, aged eighteen, TS went out to Winnipeg and drove a team for W. Gorman of Birds Hill. The next year, he joined the RCNWM Police as a trumpeter, but at the beginning of the Great War, he bought his way out of the police, sailed for England, and tried to enlist in the British Army. He was rejected because nearly blind in one eye—astonishing in view of his later accomplishments as a marksman—and he must have thought so, too, as he promptly went to Brussels, where he joined the Belgian Cavalry, Third Lancers, as a volunteer. Apparently, he managed perfectly with one good eye. He fought through the retreat to Ypres, was wounded at Nieuport, and decorated with the Yser Cross by King Albert for capturing seven prisoners on 21 October 1914 and saving the regimental flag. The British Army then approached him in hospital and commissioned him as a temporary captain in the Royal Scots on 14 April 1915, and his service went on until 30 April 1919, when the British Army rewarded him with a permanent captaincy. Meanwhile, they had posted him to Libya, Egypt, and Palestine, where he served from 15 September 1915 to June 1918. At first, he took an officers' general and musketry course at the Imperial School of Instruction at Zeitoun, Egypt. On 14 January 1916, he was promoted to second lieutenant and on 14 July 1917 to lieutenant. From 4 April 1916 to 15 February 1917, he served as an instructor at that school, but at sometime in 1917, he took a staff course at Mena, Egypt. Then from 4 May 1917 to 7 January 1918, he was in Palestine serving on the L of C defences as GSO 3 and from then until 13 May 1918 much the same. From 8 June 1918 until 14 April 1919, he was GSO 3 at Forth Garrison. He had served in the Senussi Campaign out there in the Middle East. Colonel Harry Wright, AQMG, GHQ, testified that Captain Sandys-Wunsch had served under him well for four months while he was in command of L of C defences. Lieutenant Colonel H. M. Biddulph, Rifle Brigade, testified that in his staff course at Mena House Staff School of which Biddulph was commandant, "he worked very hard and I placed him as a result of his work in the first half dozen out of a class of thirty officers. He has considerable administrative ability." In the same period while on General Edmund Allenby's staff, TS also served on the staff of the Fourth Command, met Lawrence of Arabia and General Wavell, and made a patrol with the Camel Corps to the Dead Sea before the attack on Jerusalem. As reward or recognition, he was then offered a permanent commission but resigned in 1919 and went back to Canada.

Soon taken on strength of the RCMP as a sergeant, he was promoted to inspector on 15 July 1919. For four years, he taught musketry at the Regina depot. In summer 1923, he was granted two months' leave to shoot at Bisley, Surrey, and while there was granted permission to take a two-week cavalry training session. In 1924 while posted in or near Vancouver, he inaugurated the BC Police Revolver Association and acted as its range officer until 1930, when sixteen BC police officers signed a letter of warm appreciation for his service there in revolver shooting. He was promoted to superintendent in 1935 and assistant commissioner in 1941 when he went to Winnipeg as head of "D" Division. Shortly before retiring, he became the third-ranking senior officer in the entire force, stationed at Winnipeg. As such, he was in charge of escorts for the Duke of Windsor (then Prince of Wales), the King of Siam, and President Roosevelt on their visits to Canada.

TS had one of those rigorous, adventurous careers for which the NWM Police became famous. For instance, he was dispatched from Vancouver in 1914 in response to a report of a killing by a murderous group of Indians from a tribe called the Loots. Choosing Constables Neville and Martin from among his colleagues, he set off on 14 June by boat to Wrangel, Alaska, ascended the Stikine River to Telegraph Creek, and on by canoe and on foot to Dease Lake, where they arrived on 19 July. After eleven days of questioning and much investigation, they learnt exactly what had happened, pursued and captured the Loot Indian perpetrators of the murder, and brought them back to Vancouver, having travelled 2,540 miles. TS set a record never equalled since by travelling seventy-five miles alone on foot in twenty-seven hours in the Liard River district of northern BC—difficult country, as I know from having spent a summer there with a surveying party in 1948. In 1937, he was shot in the head by an insane trapper after an attempted arrest but recovered and got his man.

There were many such events in his career, but more unusual was his extraordinary record as a marksman. On 20 January 1922, in the Birks Medal Competition at Regina, according to Colt's Patent Fire Arms Mfg. Co., Hartford, Connecticut, *Three New World's Records made with Colts*, p. 2, TS established a world's record—which stood for many years—by firing nineteen consecutive hits in a one-inch bull's eye with a .45 Colt service revolver. This broke the previous world's revolver record for twenty shots at twenty yards 191 × 200 made by S. F. Sears of St Louis, Missouri, on 4 March 1904. TS did this, as reports the Colt pamphlet, "by the phenomenal [*sic*] score of 198 out of the possible 200 points, running, by a singular coincidence, also nineteen straight 'tens.' This score is all the more remarkable when it is considered that *Inspector Sandys-Wunsch used his regulation Caliber .45 'New Service' Colt*, with full service charge cartridges, standard fixed sights and a trigger pull of 5½ lbs." He had already won the Dominion Championship Gold Medal Match in 1921, the Saskatchewan Gold Medal, and the first bronze medal awarded by the Canadian Rifle Association. It is no surprise that he was a member of the Bisley rifle team in 1923 and its adjutant in 1928.

As soon as the Second World War began, Sandys-Wunsch inquired in London about the chances of his rejoining his old regiment, the Royal Scots Guards. The replies were discouraging until suddenly, on 29 May 1940, he and the Canadian

Department of National Defence received cablegrams: "Major T.V. Sandys-Wunsch, R.C.M.P., has applied to serve with British Army. Stop. If you can spare and he is medically fit he may be despatched to United Kingdom for service with the Royal Scots forthwith." On 29 May 1940, he himself wrote from Dawson, Yukon Territory, to the commissioners to ask for permission to take up this command:

> I sincerely trust that you will allow me to go to pension and join my Regiment. I was given a permanent commission as a reward and specially allowed to resign to return to this Force when I was told that we were taking over all Canada and needed all ex-members. I trust you will believe that I came back to this Force through a sense of duty, and wish to leave it for the same reason. It is hard to leave my wife and child but I have no hesitation in my decision. I think I shall be of more value fighting than here.

Commissioner S. T. Wood supported his request, but Ottawa refused to let him go. He would have lost his police pension had he insisted.

When TS retired on a pension in March 1947, after thirty-five years of service and a year's leave, it was to a place they called "Dogwoods," then at 2205 Maple Bay Road near Duncan, where another side of his character emerged, though no doubt his intimates had always known. He settled into family life with his wife, Jean Eleanor Rossiter, whom he had married on 8 July 1935 at a chapel in Sault Ste Marie, Ontario, and their ten-year-old son John. He wrote on 29 March 1947 to Commissioner Wood, "We are getting settled down, and like the place more each day. It is strange to think of the East and the Prairies when our grounds are a mass of daffodils and other Spring flowers." Like many other British officers, he took up fishing, gardened with a passion, growing begonias, gloxinias, and many other things, and was president of the local Boy Scouts' Association for several years. He was a Freemason, a member of Temple Lodge, No. 33, AF and AM, and a serving brother in the Order of St John. On 4 October 1946, he presented a sterling silver rose bowl to Cst. E. L. Hammer of the BC Provincial Police. Known as the Sandys-Wunsch trophy, it was to be awarded annually for the best score in revolver shooting by recruits of the force on Vancouver Island. He had just been elected honorary member of the BC Police Revolver Club, and the Canada Gazette of 6 July 1946 listed him as receiving the OBE from the Crown. On 17 August, the Calgary Herald printed an article about him: "Take a chapter from Kipling, another from Robert Service, season them with a dash of pulp-magazine fiction and you'll have the career of Ass't Commissioner T. V. Sandys-Wunsch of the R.C.M.P., a story-book hero if there ever was one. He has ridden with the Camel Corps in the Middle East, fought with the Belgian cavalry in Flanders, holds a world's revolver record, has been shot in the head by a crazy trapper, and makes his own fishing flies out of polar bear hairs."

Many years earlier in the lonely North, with its endless winters, he had taken up a couple of hobbies for which he was sometimes criticized in his superiors' reports and sometimes mocked in the press. He took up making Indian coloured bead work, sent some of his creations to art competitions in Montreal, and won several prizes. He also began to carve in ivory. The *School Arts* magazine, vol. 43, no. 8 (April 1944) published monthly at Worcester, Massachusetts, pp. 272-3, printed a double-page spread with six black-and-white photos of his work, under the title, "Royal Canadian Mounted Police Creates with Ivory, Wood and Beads." He signed this, with the permission of Commissioner S. T. Wood. In it, he said that carving in prehistoric mastodon ivory was better than in green walrus tusk, because the latter tended to split. Some two years later, on 31 December 1946, H. Crowell, director of Handicrafts at MacDonald College, McGill University, wrote to Sandys-Wunsch, "We are most anxious to have a pamphlet written on 'Ivory Carving' for our handicraft series. Would it be possible for you to write a pamphlet on this subject?" There was to be a fee of $50 on publication. TS applied to Commissioner Wood for permission and duly wrote this pamphlet, a copy of which is in the National Library, Ottawa.

Eventually, he suffered three heart attacks and died, aged seventy-four, on 25 July 1966. His wife died many years later on 9 April 1991. Their son, Rev. John Sandys-Wunsch, was an Anglican minister on the Island for many years and had two sons of his own. At the time TS died, he also left a sister in Abersoch, North Wales, and his elder brother Donald in New Plymouth, New Zealand.

Sources: Notes and photos kindly sent by Rev. John Sandys-Wunsch (a son); 1901 census returns for Knutsford, Cheshire, courtesy of Mr J. D. Heaton, Librarian; census 1871, England, RG 10/3658, p. 13; census 1881, RG 11/3917; census 1891, RG 12/2828, p. 28; *Cowichan Leader*, 25 July 1966, obit.; Major Harwood Steele, *Policing the Arctic: The Story of the Conquest of the Arctic by the Royal Canadian* (formerly North-West) *Mounted Police* (Toronto, Ryerson Press, 1935?), pp. 249-50, 259, 272, 275, 284, 302, 314, 341; *Colt's Patent Fire Arms Mfg. Co., Hartford, Conn., Three New World's Records made with Colts*, p. 2; NAC, RG18, vol. 7207, access code 32; officer 195 5185; notes kindly sent by John Palmer, 20 December 2001; *Montreal Star*, 17 April 1915, "How Man Below Standard Won a Crack Command"; *Toronto Saturday Night*, 14 August 1928, with photo; *Ottawa Morning Journal* 26 July 1939; *Regina Leader Post*, 26 July 1939; Joe Garner, *Never Forget the Good Times: A Story of Life in British Columbia* (Nanaimo, Cinnebar Press, 1995), pp. 156-8, 161-2, 164-5, 175; T. V. Sandys-Wunsch, *Ivory, Bone and Horn Cutting* (Toronto, Macmillan, 1945), 16 pp. 18 cm.; *The School Arts magazine*, vol. 43, no. 8 (April 1944) pp. 272-3; TS's birth certificate, at the Knutsford District, Cheshire East KNU/26/35, may be obtained from Macclesfield Register Office, Park Green, Macclesfield, SK11 6TW, for £6.50 [2002].

SAVAGE, Hugh George Egioke (1883-1957). He was born on 5 June 1883 in Stratford-on-Avon, Warwickshire, where the 1891 census found him, aged seven, living at 59 West Street, with his family. His father, Richard Savage, a Shakespearian scholar then aged forty-four, was a "Secretary and Librarian" born at Merston, Warwickshire, and his mother, Mary Savage, aged forty-one, was born at Stratford, as were his two brothers and six sisters. One brother, Richard W. Savage, aged sixteen, was a "merchant's clerk." HS's maternal grandmother lived with them: Mary Mills (Hills?), aged seventy-nine, born at Stratford. There were no servants and the neighbours were a steam engine fitter and a pump maker. HS joined the

Second Volunteer Battalion of the Royal Warwickshire Regiment in 1900 and fought in the South African War with the 103rd Company of Imperial Yeomanry, winning the Queen's Medal and five clasps. In 1902, right after the war, he tried the flour-milling business, but soon left England to work his way around the world. He visited the United States, Canada, Australia, New Zealand, and South Africa and returned home in 1908. In 1909, after helping his father in Shakespearian research for a while, he went to Northern Ontario and in 1910 moved on to Northern Alberta. He found while working for the *Vancouver Daily Province* that newspaper work suited him and became a freelance reporter in the Peace River region of BC until finding steadier employment as editor of the *Daily News* and then *The British Columbian* of New Westminster.

In 1914, HS settled down at Duncan, Vancouver Island, on Craig Street as editor of the *Cowichan Leader* (after *Major E. H. Lukin Johnston) and worked at this job for forty-three years. It put him at the centre of life in the Cowichan Valley and he served at various times as president of the Duncan Board of Trade, of the Associated Boards of Trade of VI, of the Cowichan Newspaper Association, and of the *Canadian Weekly Union* in Victoria (where he belonged to the Union Club). He joined the local Country Club and the Rotary Club. At various times, he was a Sunday School supervisor at St John's Anglican Church, Duncan, honorary chairman of the Salvation Army's annual campaign, a Boy Scout leader, and a member of the Canadian Legion. In 1933-1937, he was a member of the BC Legislature for Cowichan-Newcastle (on Oxford Group Platform). He was a Freemason, an Anglican lay reader, an advocate of the Oxford Group, and was not afraid to support other causes as they appeared. He was fiercely patriotic but in a way that needs to be carefully explained; that is, he favoured a distinctive national flag for Canada, which he thought of as a permanent part of the British Empire, like Scotland and Wales which had their own flags. In November 1914, he spoke at a meeting called by the British Campaigners' Association and the Volunteer Guard to discuss the subject of a national reserve army based on an official register of all men fit to fight. He explained how the National Reserve had been established in England after a long struggle with the War Office and how he had come to have the honour of being the first to start the movement in BC "There are on Vancouver Island," he said, "412 old servicemen already enrolled in the ranks of the Imperial Veterans' Association, practically all of whom will join the National Reserve." Several soloists and sometimes the assembled company sang rousing songs, and George Milne recited the nineteen verses of Robert Lowell's, "The Relief of Lucknow (1857)," of which campaign Milne was said to be a veteran.

> And the pipers' ribbons and tartan streamed,
> Marching round and round our line;
> And our joyful cheers were broken with tears,
> As the pipes played "Auld Lang Syne."

In that year (1914), HS and a few others used to gather in the evening at the Exhibition Grounds at Duncan to drill under the city clerk, Mr James Greig, an experienced soldier in retirement who in 1936 was to serve as mayor of Duncan. In 1914 they used to be visited by William Keating Walker (1888-1961), a young man of twenty-six from Cleator Moor, Cumberland, who later became a lieutenant colonel and was still in touch when he joined Elliott's Horse and went overseas early in the Great War.

On 16 July 1913 at New Westminster, BC, HS married Margaret E. Bicknell, daughter of Mrs Bicknell of Westminster, England, and had a son and a daughter. He died, aged seventy-four, on 7 February 1957 at Cobble Hill and Mrs Savage, aged eighty-one, on 20 June 1966.

Sources: census 1891, England, RG 12/2477, p. 25; *Canadian Who's Who*, 1958-59, p. 988; *Who's Who in B.C.*, 1940-41, pp. 204-5; 1942-3, p. 273; 1947-48, p. 187; *Cowichan Leader*, 14 February 1957, pp. 1 and 4, obit.; *Colonist*, 21 November 1914, p. 11; 8 November 1936, Sunday p. 3; Tom Henry, *Small City in a Big Valley: The Story of Duncan* (in 4o, Madeira Park, BC, Harbour Publishing, 1999), p. 46.

SCOONES, Alexander Edward (c. 1877-1952). He was born at Langley Marish, Buckinghamshire, where his father, Rev. William Dalton Scoones, born at Tonbridge, Kent, was the vicar of the parish, as his father Rev. William Scoones (AS's grandfather) had been before him. The census-taker found AS in 1881, aged four, the youngest of six children living with their parents at the vicarage in Langley Marish, but the eldest child, Offley Scoones (1865-1899), was not listed, being then a boarder at Westminster School, and he went on to study painting at the Slade School of Art in London. Ten years later, AS was a naval cadet in HM. *Worcester* and found by the census-taker in London visiting a large family at 40 England's Lane in Hampstead.

Having served in the Royal Navy as a midshipman, AS landed at Victoria in 1897 and was attracted by reports of life on Galiano Island, where he bought 5.8 acres at Mary Ann Point. While he was there, Offley arrived via Japan stricken with tuberculosis and died there, aged thirty-five, on 9 December 1899, having advised AS to return home to finish the engineering course he had given up when he went to sea. Offley's death was doubly sad, as only two years earlier, at Axbridge, Somerset, on 10 February 1897, he had married Isobel Frank Fenella Salmond, only daughter of Lieutenant Colonel Francis Mackenzie Salmond of the Twenty-first Scots Fusiliers. Records of British citizens returning to England show that AS took Offley's advice and sailed from St John, New Brunswick, to Liverpool on SS *Germanic* in February 1900. He is said to have spent some years as a civil engineer in Brazil, designing and building bridges and learning to speak Portuguese, but he then returned to England and built Martello Towers at various places on the east coast. It was while at Newcastle-on-Tyne that he met his future wife, Edith Isabel Olliff from Northumberland, and after the Great War, he returned to Galiano Island and married her at Revelstoke in mainland BC on 14 May 1920. She had a trained soprano voice, and he, too, was fond of singing; together, they did much to encourage music in the Gulf Islands. Settling immediately on his island property, they soon had children and by October 1923, when they sailed from Quebec to

Liverpool on SS *Montlauric*, there were two small daughters, Mary Isobel and Anne Elisabeth, aged two and one. With them on that voyage was his elder sister, Diana Jane Scoones, then aged fifty-seven and unmarried, who must have joined them on Galiano Island earlier. AS was recorded as an engineer aged forty-seven and his wife then aged thirty-two. He had reason for further voyages to Buenos Aires, England, and back to Canada, where he landed at Halifax, NS, on 24 May 1925 from Liverpool on SS *Baltic*.

A few years later, Lukin Johnson, ex-editor of the *Cowichan Leader*, travelled through the islands in the Gulf of Georgia and met AS, a tall "energetic and public-spirited citizen" who had been farming on Galiano Island for seven years. With him was his brother Paul Scoones (c. 1875-1961), two years older than AS, who had gone out to join them after seventeen years as a mathematics master at Eton, sailing from Liverpool on SS *Megantic* and arriving at Quebec city on 3 June 1919. He bought a sixty-acre property near AS, but including Lion Island, and called the place "Lyons" after the ancient Scoones property near Tonbridge Wells in Kent, birthplace of their father. Paul was in working overalls, with a bushy beard, when Johnston met him and spoke of having been employed until nine years earlier teaching mathematics at Eton, not far from his birthplace in Buckinghamshire. Paul became a school trustee, a JP, secretary of the local branch of the Canadian Legion, organizer of the Galiano Club, and was widely known for holding popular musical evening on the island, using his great record collection. AS took his family in 1924 to England for the year 1924, with visits to La Lavandou near Hières in France, and in 1926, he chartered a bus to take the family and a piano from Newcastle to Liverpool, where they embarked on SS *Baltic* and arrived at Halifax, NS, on 24 May. Back on Galiano Island, as their daughter Elisabeth (Mrs Gerald Steward) explained, AS and Paul exchanged properties—something to do with convenience for schooling—but she recalled how large, rambling, and cold both houses were. AS died at last, aged seventy-five, on 23 June 1952, still on his island farm. Six years later, Paul retired to a residential hotel in Victoria, where he died, aged eighty-six, on 14 November 1961. The last of the English generation to die was Edith Isobel Scoones, who was in Vancouver city when she passed away, aged seventy-two, on 17 September 1963. But we visited the Gulf Islands often throughout my childhood and believed that their communities remained fond of the old British connections.

Sources: census 1871, England RG 10/1399, p. 9; census 1881, RG 11/117, p. 8; census 1871, RG 12/108, p. 2; census 1881, RG 11/1457, p. 37; *Oxford University Alumni*, 1715-1886, p. 1263 (son and father); *Old Westminsters to 1927*, vol. 2, p. 825; *Crockford's Clerical Directory, 1868*, p. 585 (William Dalton Scoones); *Kelly's Directory for 1911*, p. 93 (Paul Scoones); UK Incoming Passengers, no. 93725, arriving 12 February 1900; no. 144402, arriving 12 October 1923; no #, arriving 26 January 1924; Canadian Passenger Lists 1865-1935, T-14805, arriving 24 May 1926; Mrs Gerald Steward, (née Elizabeth Scoones), "Pioneers and Old-Timers on Galiano Island," in *(A) Gulf Islands Patchwork: Some Early Events on the Islands of Galiano, Mayne, Saturna, North and South Pender* (1961) (9th printing, Gulf Islands Branch,

BC Historical Federation, 1999), pp. 85-7; Lukin Johnston, *Beyond the Rockies: Three Thousand Miles by Trail and Canoe Through Little-Known British Columbia* (J. M. Dent & Sons Ltd., 1929), pp. 3, 10; A. Elizabeth Steward (née Scoones), "The Scoones Family," in Gulf Islands Branch, BC Historical Federation, *More Tales from the Outer Gulf Islands: An Anthology of Memories and Anecdotes* (Pender Island, 1993), pp. 223-8, two photos.

Col. Gerald Bassett Scott

Col. Gerald Bassett Scott—North West Frontier of India

SCOTT, Colonel Gerald Bassett (1875-1964), CB, DSO. He was born in 1875 in Lucan County, Dublin, Ireland, son of Lieutenant Colonel Hopton Bassett Scott, KCB, grandson of General Sir Hopton Stratford Scott, KCB, who entered the Madras East India Company in 1793, served in the Mysore Campaign (1799), was present at the Battle of Malavilly and at the siege and capture of Seringapatan, and after joining the Hyderabad force (1800) served through the campaign in the Deccan against the Confederated Mahrattas, up to the year 1805. His career went on year after year with brilliant success, and on 20 May 1818, he commanded and led in person a storming party at the capture of Chanda. GS's father, too, served well in the Indian Army and so it seemed natural that GS himself, after attending the United Service College, Westward Ho! and RMC, Sandhurst, should follow their example soon after graduating in 1895. GS was promoted to captain (1905), major (1914), lieutenant colonel (1921), and colonel (1926). First commissioned in January 1896, he was posted on the North-West Frontier of India with the Twenty-seventh Punjabis in 1901-1902 and fought in Waziristan as "Double Company Officer" in a campaign which was at its most intense from 23 November 1901 to 10 March 1902. In 1903-1904, his regiment was dispatched to Somaliland in North Africa, where the "Mad Mullah" was leading a tribal revolt, and the fighting reached a climax in an action at Jidbali on 10 January 1904. Medals and clasps for these two campaigns were to be found in GS's collection.

At sometime in the next few years, perhaps in 1911, he transferred to the Wano Militia and then, in April 1913, to the North Waziristan Militia, with a view to his taking command whenever Major Charles Smith (both CO and political agent) should go on leave. This occurred in September 1913, when GS became commanding officer and the new political agent (PA) was one A. O. Fitzpatrick. GS explains in one of his autobiographical MSS that a PA was appointed to each Agency in the North-West Frontier province and supported by a highly trained native Militia Force, without which he could neither make himself obeyed nor even survive himself. Each Militia Force was organized in companies, platoons, and sections under British Officers "who are specially selected from the Indian Army for this work." According to Trench, *Frontier Scouts* (p. 291), Scott served thus in the Frontier Corps in 1911-1919 as captain, then major, and finally colonel. In 1915, he was still CO of the North Waziristan Militia when it was deployed in the Tochi Valley Expedition during fighting there in January 1915. After the death of Captain Eustace Jothan of the North Waziristan Militia and his party in an ambush on 7 January, GS led that Militia in an assault on ten thousand armed Khostwal tribesmen advancing on Miranshah and drove them back across the Durand Line with heavy casualties. They were quiet for the next four years. It was mainly for this that he was inducted into the DSO on 29 October that year.

In the years of the Great War, GS served as inspecting officer and secretary to the chief commissioner, Frontier Corps, on the North-West Frontier, essentially aide-de-camp to Field Marshall Lord Kitchener. He was still ranging around the frontier province in 1917 and in the week of 19-26 January was with Colonel G. V. Kemball driving around in a Nash car, and occasionally a Fiat, to where GS was proposing to set up a "signalling block to link up the Upper Tochi posts with the H.Q. at Miranshah" and on other such expeditions. He also rode about in two airplanes which appeared in January that year and which must have been new to that province because he comments on the astonishment of Indians at seeing them. He went hunting frequently and casually between bloody engagements with Mahsuds and other tribesmen. In 1918-1925, GS was mentioned as CO of the Third Battalion of the Fifteenth Punjab Regiment; on 1 September 1926, he was appointed—or reappointed—as secretary to the chief commissioner and inspecting officer, Frontier Corps; and his unpublished journal for 1928 shows him still moving about in the region of Ambeyla Pass, Parachinar, Miranshah, Peshawar, Kohat, etc., on horseback and in cars. On 4 February 1928, he played golf and had evidently been playing for many years. He rode to hounds often that year, especially in February and March, and on 9 March 1928, he reported in his journal, "We had two conferences this morning . . . In the afternoon we shot snipe. Farwell, Joyce and I shot at Ahmedzai and got 45 . . ." He was still flying around now and then in airplanes, as for instance on 30 April 1928. Above all, the primary task of maintaining law and order preoccupied him until the end of his career. In 1930, as inspecting officer of the Frontier Corps and one of four officers responsible to protect Peshawar, he commanded a mixed group of Frontier Scouts—mainly Kurram Militia and South Waziristan Scouts—sent to stop bands of Afridis and Mamunds from assaulting that centre. As B. D. Bromhead, a PA, recalled, GS succeeded admirably in this task. When Bromhead went in search of him—"We found the HQ with old Colonel Scott sprawled in the hot sun on a slab of rock. It would have baked the hide off a lesser man, but he was unconcerned and seemed to enjoy the heat" (Trench, *Frontier Scouts*, p. 132). According to one of his reports dated 18 and 19 June 1930, he led two hundred South Waziristan Scouts and two hundred Kurram Militia against Utmah (Utman?) Khels near Palli and he reported on the incident from "Barachinar, Kurram Valley, N.W.F. Province." It was for such long and efficient service in that dangerous part of the empire that he was decorated on 1 January 1930 with the CB. He retired in 1931.

GS and his family went out to the Island almost immediately and settled on Wilkinson Road, South Saanich, on twelve acres which they called "Scottsville." They had arrived at Quebec on 16 May 1931 aboard the CPR vessel, *Duchess of Richmond*. Mrs Scott, *née* Brigid Mary Lyons, daughter of Taomas Lyons, was his second wife and the mother of a son Terence and three daughters, Morgan, Grace, and Shelagh. The first Mrs Scott, Blanche de Caen, daughter of G. F. de Caen, also had a daughter, Mareen. At first, GS spent much time in business as a partner in Victoria Homes and Gardens Ltd., played golf, and collected antiques. His investments in Malayan rubber gave him a substantial income until the Japanese invasion during the Second World War. Suddenly pressed to make money, he planted four acres of his farm with commercial quantities of flower bulbs, founded the Saanich Bulb Growers' Association, and visited the Dominion Agricultural Station in Saanichton, where two bulb inspectors, William Foster and J. E. Bosher, offered advice and the results of their research into bulb diseases. Bulb-growing was profitable then because the Dutch industry had been crushed by the German invasion of the Netherlands in 1940. Public-spirited like most British officers, GS remained a director of the Saanich Bulb Growers' Association and became an Air Raid Precaution (ARP) warden. At a meeting of wardens on 18 February 1941, he proposed the toast to the king (the toast to the army was by Colonel Frederick William Louis Moore (1866-1949), to the air force by P. J. Sinnott, and to the navy and merchant marine by Colonel Harry Tetlow Hardinge (1879-1955). Much concerned, like so many others, with the effects of the depression in the 1930s, GS took up the study of social credit as worked out by Major Clifford Hugh Douglas (1879-1952), and with his friend, *Major A. E. Jukes, founded the Social Credit Movement on the Island. Occasionally, he explained his views in letters to the *Daily Colonist*, as on 3 October 1937, when he criticized the Australian Royal Commission for a heartless analysis of economic life without concern for popular welfare. When he died, aged eighty-eight, on 1 September 1964, he was living at 4581 Pipeline Road, Royal Oak, a northern suburb of Victoria. He was survived by his wife, four daughters, a son, and two sisters in England.

Sources: MSS among GS's papers and notes courtesy of Mrs Morgan Scott-Ostler; *Who's Who in B.C.* 1933-1934, pp. 156-7; *The Quarterly List of Civil Officers serving in the North West Frontier Province*, corrected up to July 1930 (Calcutta, The Government of India, Central Publication Branch, 1930), pp. 2, 22, 134, 137; NAC, RG76-immigration, series C-1-a, 1931 vol. 3, p. 22, reel T-14771; *Colonist*, 3 October 1937, p. 4; 14 January 1941, p. 5; 20 February 1941, p. 11; 2 September 1964, p. 18, obit.; Charles Chenevix Trench, *The Frontier Scouts* (Jonathan Cape, 1985), pp. 28, 130-2, 291; *Who was Who*, vol. VI, p. 1013.

SCOTT-MONCRIEFF, Lieutenant Colonel William Emsley (1871-1945), MD, FRCS. Born 4 March 1871 at Dalkeith, Scotland, son of Robert Scott-Moncrieff, he attended George Watson's College, Edinburgh, and the University of Edinburgh and became a physician. Among his relatives was Sir Colin Campbell Scott-Moncrieff, KCSI (1903), KCMG (cr 1887), born in Scotland on 8 August 1836, who became second lieutenant in the Bengal Engineers in 1856 and retired as a colonel in 1883; this relative then joined the Irrigation Department in the North-West Province of India and later became chief engineer in Burmah; then under-secretary of state public works at Cairo, 1883-1892; under-secretary for Scotland, 1892-1902; and president of the Indian Irrigation Commission 1901-1903, and died on 6 April 1916. It therefore seemed natural for WS to take a commission in the Indian Army (28 July 1894), be promoted to captain (28 July 1897), and go on to join the Indian Medical Service (Bengal) on 25 November 1903. Employed in Rajputana in 1904, he passed a "higher standard" examination in the Pushtu language. His duties took him to the North-West Frontier of India, where he served with the Chitral Relief Force and in 1900 accompanied the China Expeditionary Force dispatched to face the Boxer Rebellion.

After several more years in India, WS retired and moved to Victoria in 1912. He built up a medical practice there as an ear, eye, nose, and throat specialist and lived first at 1535 Richardson Street and then at 745 Newport Avenue, Oak Bay, with his wife, Margaret Vera *née* Irving, daughter of Colonel L. A. Irving, RAMC.

They had two sons. When on 1 February 1919 WS signed an enlistment form for the Canadian Army Medical Corps at Esquimalt Military Hospital, he was described as 6' 6¼" tall with a fair complexion, blue eyes, fair hair, and tattoo marks on both forearms. He had had a "moveable kidney" since 1912, also had haemorrhoids and wore glasses. He joined the India-Burma Society and the Union Club. When he died, aged seventy-four, on 22 June 1945, leaving a son, R. Scott-Moncrieff serving with the army, his funeral was held at Christ Church Cathedral. His wife died, aged seventy-five, on 7 November 1954 in Victoria.
Sources: BL, India Office, *Indian Army List*, January 1905, pp. 465, 604, 701; *Who's Who in B.C.*, 1933-1934, pp. 157-8; 1937-39, pp. 157-8; NAC, RG 150, (CEF papers), box 8741-53; *Colonist*, 17 January 1933, p. 8; 23 June 1945, pp. 5 and 12, obit.

SEALY, Lieutenant Colonel Philip Temple (c. 1889-1972). He was born at Boston, Lincolnshire, second son of Rev. William Bellett Sealy and his wife Catherine, who sent him to Lawrence College, Ramsgate, and Cambridge University. He was gazetted in 1912 as second lieutenant, Army Service Corps, and went to France in 1914 with the British Expeditionary Force. Mentioned in General Douglas Haig's despatches while serving in battle, in the King's Birthday Honours List of 1919 he was gazetted OBE. He left France in 1920 but remained in the army and in 1927 spent four months in Hong Kong. The rest of his career was in the Indian Army Service Corps.

In 1939, PS and his family migrated to Duncan, where they lived on the Maple Bay Road, and were public-spirited, like most of their kind. Mrs Eileen Egerton Sealy served as Wolf Cub mistress of the Quamichan Cub Pack. PS's pension was reduced by devaluation of sterling currency, which affected all British pensioners. The Sealy family thought seriously of returning to England but in 1955 moved to Victoria, where PS soon took over Westerham School, which became Malvern House School in 1963. He ran it successfully for several years. When he died, aged eighty-three, on 14 November 1972 he was survived by his wife and an adopted son, Robin Sealy. His funeral was at St Mary's, Oak Bay, followed by burial at Royal Oak.
Sources: Recollections of Admiral Daniel Mainguy and Mr John Palmer; *Colonist*, 16 November 1972, p. 64, obit.

SEBRIGHT-GREEN, William Saunders (1830-1906). See GREEN, William Saunders Sebright.

SELFE, Captain Hugh Ronald (1880-1917). He was born on 2 June 1880 in London at Brixton, a place invariably given as South Norwood, Surrey, in this family's census records. His father rose from bank clerk to bank manager in the first twenty years of HS's life. He grew up with an elder brother and sister and a younger brother, and when he joined the Canadian Army on 28 September 1914, he cited his only sister, Miss Violet E. Selfe of North Carry, Somerset, as his next of kin. He had already served some years in units of the British and Canadian armies and in the former had fought through the South African War. Like so many British soldiers, he joined the Canadian Army in the Great War but later

transferred to a British unit, the North Staffordshire Regiment in his case. He
was killed fighting in that regiment, part of the Eighth Battalion, on 9 July 1917.
Canadian records give his age as thirty-two, but he was in fact thirty-seven years
old. The *Daily Colonist*, learning that his next of kin was a sister in Somerset or
Cornwall, gave his birthplace as Cornwall, but there can be no doubt that this is
another error. He had gone to British Columbia about 1907 as an employee of the
Bank of British North America at Dawson and three years later moved to Victoria
to work for the firm of Shallcross & Macaulay. He became a Boy Scout leader at the
very beginning of the movement in Victoria, was widely known in the movement,
and was for some time scoutmaster of the Third Victoria troop. He also joined
the Fifth Regiment of the CGA as a signals officer and became lieutenant in the
District Signal Company at Work Point. He volunteered for service overseas, and
when he was killed, there was no one in Canada who knew him well enough to
report the facts of his life correctly.
Sources: NAC, CEF files, box 8770-36; NAC, Virtual Cemetery online, Dep't of
Veteran's Affairs; census 1881, England, RG 11 /1091; census 1891, RG 12/1032,
p. 3; census 1901, RG 13/1196, p. 8?; *Colonist*, 15 August 1917, p. 5, obit.

SERVICE, Robert William (1874-1958). A "Canadian" poet born in Preston,
Lancashire, and brought up in Scotland, he worked in a Glasgow bank until
May 1896, when he sailed, aged twenty-two, from Glasgow on the *Siberian* to
Montreal and travelled on to the Island. For six months, he worked at Somenos
in the Cowichan Valley on the farm of *Major James Mutter, uncle of a friend in
Glasgow. Then he went up the valley to stay with a Welsh farmer, Harry Evans. In
spring and summer 1897, he worked for George Treffry Corfield, a Cornishman,
on a four-hundred-acre dairy farm near Duncan called "Eureka." After wandering
about the western United States for a couple of years, RS returned to Cowichan
in 1898 and settled in again with the Corfields, at first in charge of a herd of fifty
cows and twenty calves and then for four years as a store-keeper, caring also for the
tennis court. He read a lot at the local library, tutored the Corfields' seven sons,
became a good horseman, a good shot, and a good swimmer, and it was then that
he became locally famous for public recitations of verse by Henry Newbolt and
Rudyard Kipling. Journals in Glasgow had occasionally published his poems and
now *The Victoria Daily Colonist* published a poem by RS about the South African War
entitled "The Christmas Card." In May 1903, he left George Corfield's employ and
went to live in Victoria to work and to pass examinations that might qualify him
to teach school. This proved to be too difficult, for several reasons, and he went
to work from 10 October 1903, then aged twenty-nine, in the Canadian Bank of
Commerce at its branch on the corner of Fort and Government streets. Like the
other bank clerks, he slept on the premises. Less than a year later, he was sent to
work at the Kamloops branch in the BC continental interior, beginning on 9 July
1904. In March 1907, he published his first slim volume of poems and before the
end of the year sailed for Skagway on the CPR steamer, *Princess Beatrice*.
    Thus began a more famous phase of his life. It was when the bank transferred
him to White Horse in the north that RS gained the experience reflected in his

Songs of a Sourdough and other verse. But life on the Island left a permanent mark on him. His mother was staying at "The Chalet" at Deep Cove at the end of the Saanich Peninsula in August 1931. Visiting Victoria with his wife and child *en route* to California late in 1940, RS said on 17 December that he intended to return in May to make his home there permanently. He said he was looking forward to showing his family the old store on the Koksilah River, where he had worked as a clerk and his old branch of the Bank of Commerce in Victoria. As things turned out, he visited only for a few days in May 1941 and then moved on. He was of two minds about the Island and could sometimes be sharply critical of what he called its "mid-Victorian atmosphere." As things turned out, he married Germaine Bourgoin, daughter of Constant Bourgoin, who owned a distillery near Paris, and with the considerable profits from his writing, RS spent his later life in France and Monaco. UK Incoming Passenger Lists show him, his wife, and daughter Iris, landing at Liverpool on 11 September 1948 *en route* to their home in Monte Carlo at 64 boulevard d'Italia.
Sources: *Colonist*, 19 December 1940, p. 3; 7 August 1931, p. 8; census 1881, Scotland, roll cssct1881_191, line 17; Canadian Passenger Lists, 1865-1935, C-4541, arriving 4 May 1896; UK Incoming Passenger Lists, 1878-1960, no. 160631, arriving 11 September 1948; New York Passenger Lists, 1820-1935, T-715_7622, p. 62, arriving 29 June 1948; James Mackay, *Robert Service: A Biography* (Edinburgh & London, Mainstream Publishing, 1995), pp. 22-24, 115ff.; C. F. Klinck and Angus Calder, in Oxford DNB online; Robert Service, *Ploughmen of the Moon: An Adventure into Memory* (New York, Dodd, Mead, 1945), p. 152-53; Peter Murray, *Home from the Hill: Three Gentleman Adventurers* (Victoria, BC, Horsdal & Shubert, 1994), p. 120.

SEYMOUR-BIGGS, Captain Henry (1876-1952). He was born on 27 August 1876 in Bombay, India, and enrolled at St Mary's (Catholic) High School there on 3 April 1888. Sent next as a Roman Catholic to St Vincent's School at Poona, he ran away to sea in March 1891 and joined the cadet training ship *Conway* maintained by the shipowners of the merchant navy in England. In the next many years, he served on the sailing ship *Bankhall* for one shilling, eight pence a day, sailed nine times around the Horn, and eventually became the *Bankhall's* second mate. He qualified for his Extra Master's Square-rigged Certificate in 1908, transferred later to steamships, and became third officer on the *Lake Manitoba*, the biggest ship of the Beaver Line, which was bought out by the CPR. During the South African War (1899-1902), he fought at the Battle of Majuba Hill as a midshipman together with a group of sailors and a gunnery officer and survived a burst of gunfire that killed the gunnery officer and others. During the Great War (1914-1918), he was commissioned to HMS *Dwarf* and sent to the Cameroons, where he acquired a pet parrot, which he kept for many years. After missions to the coast of Africa, he returned to the UK and was in charge of minesweepers off the coast of Ireland. His ship was sunk in the battle of Jutland and he then became an intelligence officer in the Shetland Islands until 1918.

In 1923, HS retired from the Royal Navy to Vancouver Island, where he arrived with his wife and a daughter Molly. At first, he rented a small farm at Saltair, near

Ladysmith. Then they moved to Cowichan; but he decided he was not a farmer and soon settled at Lake Hill, Victoria, where he was hired by a fish packer. By 1928 or 1929, he had saved enough money to buy a house near the sea on the edge of the Uplands district at 2697 Lincoln Road in north-eastern Victoria. There he bought a boat, which he called *Fairwind* after the ship that had picked him out of the water when his ship sank in the battle of Jutland (1916). Then he found a job as a lighthouse keeper at Carmana on the west coast of the Island, where he was alone but in touch with Bamfield by radio. His daughter Molly, who was boarding at school in Duncan, remembers visiting him at the lighthouse and being bored there. During the late 1930s, he was living at the house in Victoria, where he joined the Thermopylae Club on 9 October 1935.

One day in 1937, a young man, Andy Southall, came with his father to repair the furnace. It turned out that his hope was to fly, and HS encouraged him to travel to England and to join the RAF. Thus began HS's remarkable scheme for assisting Canadian boys under twenty-one years of age to do the same, and he did this voluntarily without payment. He selected the boys, found passage for them overseas, gave them directions and letters of introduction, and most were received into the RAF or some other military service in England. Many who travelled from outside Victoria stayed for a time at HS's house. In this way, he sent 719 boys, a few at a time, to join the RAF. Now and then, the *Daily Colonist* gave reports of them, usually with photographs. HS also sent several groups of young women to serve in British forces: for example, Miss Joyce M. Strachan, who applied to the RAF secret service, and Miss Mary D. Litster, who wanted to join the Army Transport as a chauffeur.

At sometime early in the war, in fact not long before Pearl Harbour (7 December 1941), HS decided to do something useful himself and went to serve as staff captain on the *Empress of Japan* on her last voyage before Pearl Harbour. At about that time, he bought another house in Victoria, on Feltham Road, Mount Douglas, rented a field that went with it to a Chinese vegetable gardener, left his wife there, took the train to Montreal, dyed his hair brown, and joined the merchant marine as third officer on a ship sailing to Britain. "I just want one more crack at the Germans," he said. "I am going to sign off and get a job in the British navy. That's where I want to be." He seems to have remained with merchant ships, however, and to have survived the sinking of two vessels and then retired once again to his house and garden in Victoria. Meanwhile, in 1937, his daughter Molly had married Mr Stanley Jackson, an RCMP officer, and they were stationed at Nakusp, BC, in 1942. In May 1953, the HS and his wife decided to move to the BC interior, where a dry climate might relieve his asthma. With their daughter and son-in-law, they bought a place at Kamloops, and there he died, aged seventy-seven, of pneumonia on 19 December 1953. Having married his wife in an Anglican church, he had been excommunicated by the Catholic Church many years earlier and had also become a Freemason. His funeral was held in Victoria by Rev. Canon Frederick Pike followed by burial at Royal Oak. Friends and neighbours remembered HS as forthright, courageous, generous, kind, patriotic, and extraordinarily vigorous.

Sources: Notes, newspaper cuttings, and personal letters kindly sent from Australia by Molly (Seymour-Biggs) Jackson, a daughter, and from Victoria by Ken Stofer;

Ken Stofer, *The Biggs' Boys: The Story of Young Canadians Who Paid their Way to England to Join the Royal Air Force during World War Two* (Victoria, Kenlyb Pub, 1995), pp. 5-6; *Colonist*, 8 January 1939, p. 20; 18 January 1939, p. 14; 21 January 1939, p. 3; 5 February 1939, p. 17; 9 April 1939, p. 21; 23 June 1940, p. 11; 3 August 1941, p. 28; Sunday 17 June 1951; *Kamloops Sentinel*, December 1953; Ursula Jupp, *Home Port Victoria* (Victoria, privately printed by Morriss Printing Co. Ltd., for 2254 Arbutus Road, 1967), p. 159.

SHARE, George Greenwood (1877-1959). Born in November 1877 in London, son of George Wade Share, he worked in a publishing firm 1894-1898; then he joined the British South African Police and served through the South African War. In 1908, he went out to Alberta and farmed until 1918, when he moved to Duncan, VI. There in 1921, he took up growing asparagus on a ten-acre farm on the delta land of the Cowichan flats and become widely known across Canada for his produce. He married Edith, daughter of *Frederick Maitland-Dougall and Bessie Hopkins, daughter of a wealthy cotton broker of Savannah, Georgia. Edith Share was therefore a granddaughter of Admiral William Heriot Maitland-Dougall of Scotland. He became a member of the British Public Schools Club and the Cowichan Golf Club. In the late 1930s, they lived on Tzouhalem Road, Duncan, VI, where he died, aged eighty-two, on 1 December 1959.
Sources: *Who's Who in B.C.*, 1937-1939, p. 133; 1947-1948, p. 190.

SHARLAND, Lieutenant Colonel Alan Abbott (c. 1884-?). He was born in Catford, Kent, but the 1891 census recorded him, aged seven, living at 31 Wickham Road, Sevenoaks, Kent, with his family. His father was Charles Sharland, aged thirty-seven, a "Colonial Merchant," born at New Plymouth, New Zealand, and his mother, Annie Amelia Sharland, aged thirty-two, was born at St James, London. He had two sisters, Edith Grace Sharland, aged five, born at Auckland, New Zealand, and Ellen May Sharland, aged three, born at Beckenham, Kent, and one brother, Charles Norman Sharland, aged one, born at Beckenham. They had a nurse, a cook, and a housemaid, and next door, at #33 Wickham Road, lived a "silk merchant" and his family. He obtained a commission as a second lieutenant in the Indian Army and arrived at Sitapur, India, from Singapore on 17 December 1904 under Major General W. O. Barnard. During the Great War, AS was attached to the First Battalion of the Sixteenth Canadian Scottish Regiment. Upon his return home to England from India in 1908, AS introduced his niece, Edith Grace Sharland, to Lieutenant Colonel Arthur Rowland Greenwood, RAMC, and these two were married a year later. It was perhaps through members of the Greenwood family, including his only son, Lieutenant Colonel Kemble Greenwood born in 1919, that AS became aware of Vancouver Island.

In any event, he went out to settle there in 1929, arriving at the port of Victoria on 6 July with his wife, Eleanora (aged thirty-nine), and their three children. They lived on several acres of land they purchased out of the 207 acres of a property named "Queenswood" between Arbutus Road and the sea, stretching from Haro Road to

Telegraph Bay Road. The whole property had been known locally as "Janes" Woods because the Janes family had bought it in 1872 from J. M. McKay, the original owner. Mr Janes built a snake fence all the way from Haro Road to Telegraph Bay Road, and he sold cordwood for a living until 1914. After that, the Janes family moved away and the land was not used until 1929, when the Queenswood Land Company bought it in order to divide it into homesites. It was shortly before the terrible financial crash of 1929 that AS bought his part of the property. There he built a large, beautiful house surrounded by lovely gardens with a game farm stocked with deer and pheasant out on the south side of the place. He called it "Queenswood House," naturally enough, and one year, their garden was one of forty-one opened to the public on 18-23 April for the VI Horticultural Association's annual spring flower festival. "Queenswood" stood for twenty years until fire gutted it one night, and even then the original gate posts were still standing in the 1980s at the entrance to the sisters of St Anne's Queenswood House of Studies at what had become 2494 Arbutus Road.

That was long after the Sharlands' time. By 1931, they also had a cottage at Shawnigan Lake, where they often went for weekends. Mrs Sharland's sister and her husband, Major Edwards, came from England to stay with them one summer. AS and his wife were generous and public-spirited, gave $250 to the Solarium in December 1931, and were always willing to assume leadership. In June 1931, AS was appointed to the board of governors of Brentwood College and spoke at the school's eighth annual speech day. He also became president of the United Service Institution, which met at the Armories in Victoria on 15 June 1933, with Major H. Cuthbert Holmes in the chair, to bid the Sharlands farewell. They had decided to return to live somewhere in the south of England, which turned out to be Tenterden, Kent. In June 1936, they were back in Victoria, where they stayed at the Glenshiel Hotel until 22 August, and then continued on a round-the-world tour. The main purpose of this visit was to see their daughter, Vera Sharland, who was staying with her uncle and aunt, Dr and Mrs H. R. Nelson of Sylvan Lane, Victoria. AS and his wife talked vaguely of returning to live in Victoria at sometime, but had left their two sons in England, one at school, the other at university. However, they kept in touch with Victoria: in April 1940, the *Daily Colonist* printed a letter to the editor by AS who gave his address as Canadian Legion, War Service Inc., Cockspur Street, London SW 1. Under the heading, "In the British Isles," he described life in wartime London. (Food is plentiful; gasoline is in short supply; but we are OK, etc.)

Sources: BL, India Office, *Indian Army List,* January 1905, p. 242a; census 1891, England, PRO, RG 12/625, page 3; *Colonist,* 7 June 1931, p. 8; 21 June 1931, p. 2; 16 June 1933, p. 6; 11 April 1936, p. 6; 6 June 1936, p. 2; 13 April 1940, p. 4; letter to the author from *Major A. A. Greenwood, 28 February 2003; Ursula Jupp, *Cadboro: A Ship, A Bay, A Sea-Monster,* 1842-1958 (Victoria, Jay Editions, 1988), p. 56.

SHEARING, William John (1845-1916). Born in England at Eltham, Kent, on 21 June 1845, he is recorded in 1851, aged six, as the oldest of the four sons of Harriett and her husband, William Shearing, a wheelwright living at Lee Green, Kent. WS left for India in January 1859, stayed there some eighteen months, went on to China for a similar period, and arrived in Victoria on 31 July 1862. It is possible, as T. W. Paterson writes in the local *Cowichan Valley Citizen* (17 June 2001), that WS had served as a boy in the Indian Army. At all events, in autumn 1862, he took land on Cowichan Bench [*sic*] as a pre-emption and it became his family home. For five years, he was foreman of Sayward's sawmill, an old water-power mill at Mill Bay; then for nine years, he worked in a sawmill for the Dunsmuir interests at Nanaimo. He left that in 1884 and lived at home as a farmer at Cowichan for fifty-four years, according to his death certificate. The identity and fate of his wife seems uncertain in the records. He died on his birthday, 21 June 1916, and was buried at St John's Anglican Church. His pallbearers were Messrs E. H. Forrest, W. and R. Manley, R. Bazett, T. Colvin, and P. Frumento. He was survived by three sons and two daughters: William, Edward, and Herbert Shearing; Mrs Robert Miller (Duncan) and Mrs J. Humphreys (Vancouver).

Sources: *Cowichan Leader*, 29 June 1916, obit.; T. W. Paterson, in the local *Cowichan Valley Citizen*, 17 June 2001; census 1851, England, H.O. 107 / 1591 / 3; census records for Vancouver Island 1881 and 1891; Vital Statistics, death registration GR 2951, vol. 034, 16-09-034788.

SHERMAN, Victor (c. 1883-1960). From 1936, when he retired from India to 2901 Seaview Road in Saanich, he lived on the Island as a humanist, founder of the Humanist League of Canada, with his wife, *née* Marion Noel Bostock, daughter of a BC senator, a medical lady doctor who worked in the field of mental hygiene for the Canadian Council of Women. He was born in London, where 1891 census records show him, aged eight, and his brother Hugh, aged seven, living as boarders at 30 Cornwall Road, the dwelling of Charles L. Brown, a commercial traveller, and his wife Agnes Brown, both aged twenty-seven and born in India, who appear to have been relatives. As an adult, VS was a banker employed in India for more than twenty years in the Bank of Bengal until it became the Imperial Bank of India. They had a married daughter and two grandchildren who survived them when they died in Victoria, VS aged seventy-seven on 17 December 1960, and his wife, aged eighty-three, on 18 August 1975.

Sources: *Colonist*, 20 December 1960, p. 24, obit.; census 1891, England, RG 12/11, p. 10; Jennifer Nell Barr, *Saanich Heritage Structures: An Inventory* (Victoria, 1991), p. 18.

SHRAPNEL, Colonel Edward Scrope (1845-1920). He was born on 12 January 1845 on Stoke Road, Alverstoke (near Southampton), second son of Louisa Sarah Shrapnel *née* Jonsiffe (?) and her husband, Captain Henry Needham Scrope Shrapnel (1812-1896), an officer in the Second Regiment of Somerset Militia. The 1851 census for the Parish of Alverstoke, Hampshire, shows ES aged six living on Stoke Road with two brothers and a sister in a household headed by their mother, Louisa S. Shrapnel, a wife aged thirty, born in Middlesex, their father being absent. This father being the eldest son of General Henry Shrapnel (1761-1842), celebrated inventor of the exploding artillery shell, it was natural for him to join the Royal Artillery, as he did on 9 July 1779. He spent much time and effort, as had his father, ES's grandfather, making technical improvements: to howitzers, for example, and to the accuracy of cannon by inventing the "tangent slide," the "hollow shoe," and the "spherical case shot." Like the great General Henry Shrapnel, too, ES's father spent his own money on his inventions and struggled to have them accepted, used, acknowledged, and rewarded. As a second preoccupation, ES's father went to law, apparently without success, to win a clear title to Midway Manor House, near Bradford, Wiltshire, inherited from his father the general, and to recover some £16,360 owing to his father in payment for inventions. In short, the family was anxious about money and property, which was reason enough to emigrate. ES's father was used to living abroad, having served in Newfoundland (1780-1784), at Gibraltar (1787-1790), in Holland under General Sir William Congreve, at Capetown, at various colonies in the Caribbean, and in various parts of eastern Canada. About 1870, after ES had spent several years at school in Ireland, his father gave up the struggle and took the family to live out in Ontario, where they settled at last in a house on Borland Street in Orillia, on Lake Simcoe north of Toronto, whence ES and other young members of the family eventually made their way out to Victoria.

Following the family tradition, ES obtained a commission in the army and served in the Victoria Rifles of Quebec *inter alia* during a six-month campaign against the Fenian Irish attacking Canada from the United States. Much later, in its Sunday Magazine of 5 April 1908, the *Daily Colonist* devoted a full page to his "Reminiscences of the Fenian Raid." Making accurate, detailed drawings was part of an officer's training in the British Army, and ES was one of those who took full advantage of this training to became an artist.

It is not clear when ES and his wife, Edith Mary Shrapnel, arrived in Victoria, but a turning point in their life was in November 1890 when he sold the family house on the north side of Borland Street, Orillia, Simcoe County, Ontario, to one William M. Moore of Orillia. According to Alexander Begg's *History of British Columbia* (1894), "The B.C. Art Association, with Mr E. S. Shrapnel [misspelled as Sharpnel] as president, was founded in 1890." ES was among the "principal artists" belonging to the Canadian Academy and Ontario Society of Artists along with W. Wilson, a landscape artist living at Cowichan who had exhibited work in Glasgow and Edinburgh, T. Bamford of Victoria, a landscape and portrait painter from Liverpool, and O. L. Barff, another English landscape painter who had recently been in China. The 1901 census found ES describing himself as an artist and living on Oak Bay Avenue, Victoria, with his wife Edith M. Shrapnel and their four Ontario-born children of whom the eldest, Edith (born 22 November 1877), described herself as a teacher and had won a prize for her painting in 1894. Their son Alfred Scrope Shrapnel (1873-1942) gave his occupation as "gold miner." ES joined the British Campaigners' Association and in 1920 presented them with a picture of his famous grandfather. Living in Victoria at 1703 Denman Street was a relative, Helena Scrope Barter, *née* Shrapnel, whose son, Private John Shrapnel Barter of Victoria, was killed fighting overseas in May 1917. Yet another relative, Captain Alfred Shrapnel (1853-1927), born on 2 June 1853 in England, had gone to Canada in 1888 and was living in 1901 on Cadboro Bay Road, Oak Bay, as a self-employed ship's captain. These were all Anglican, like ES and his family. ES died, aged seventy-five, on 25 September 1920 in Oak Bay and his wife, aged eighty-four, on 18 August 1930.

Sources: NAC, MG24. F 113 Shrapnel papers from the family house in Orillia, Ontario; Timothy Dubé, NAC finding aid no. 1777, *Henry Shrapnel and Family*, Ottawa, 1989 and 1994, passim; *Colonist*, 5 April 1908, Sunday, p. 9, "Reminiscences of the Fenian Raid"; 23 May 1917, pp. 5 and 7, obit.; 26 September 1920, p. 7, obit.; 27 January 1927, p. 5, obit.; Family Record Centre, London: birth certificate BXBZ 690565 for Edward Scrope Shrapnel, born on 12 January 1845; PRO, ADM 160/159, "A Statement of the Contents or Particulars of the Petition of Henry Needham Scrope Shrapnel, Esquire, of Midway Manor House, near Bradford, in the County of Wilts, now residing at Elm Lodge, Gosport, in the County of Hants [Hampshire], a Captain in the second regiment of Somerset Militia, now before The Honourable the House of Commons, 1847"; Begg, *History of British Columbia*, pp. 474 and 565.

SIME, Miss Catherine Mary (1875-1945). Born in India in 1875, daughter of Dr John Sime, CIE, LLD, LitD, of the Indian Educational Service and of Inchture, Perthshire, Scotland, she spent her youth in the Punjab and Scotland, graduated as a nursing sister at Guy's Hospital, London, and then joined the Queen Alexandra's Military Nursing Service of India. In 1916-1918, she was on active service in Mesopotamia and on hospital ships in the Persian Gulf, and then she became nursing sister in charge of the hospital at the Lawrence Royal Military School, Simla Hills, India.

Moving out to Canada in 1926, she was for a short time on the staff of the Solarium, a nursing home at Mill Bay for patients with tuberculosis. A resident of Maple Bay Road for about eighteen years, she was an active churchwoman, "ever ready to help anyone in distress," and long remembered by her many friends and neighbours after she died in Duncan at King's Daughters' Hospital on Friday, 20 April. Her three brothers had all died in service overseas before the Great War: Captain C. G. Sime, Royal Inniskillin Fusiliers; Captain F. W. Sime, Indian Medical Service; and Captain H. St J. Sime, Fourth Gurkha Rifles. But she was survived by her sisters, Mrs Crawford (New Delhi, India) and Mrs J. H. G. Palmer in Duncan. She was buried at St Peter's Quamichan, Canon T. M. Hughes officiating. *Major J. H. G. Palmer was one of the pallbearers.

She was a sister of John Palmer's maternal grandmother, Mrs J. H. G. Palmer, *née* Sime (John's mother was born a Sime), and John says that she was a friend of Rudyard Kipling, corresponded with him and received a letter from him only shortly before he died in 1936, a letter which the family no longer has. Some twenty-three Simes died in BC, according to Vital Statistics Records, including Matilda (died 16 October 1918, aged eighty-five, at Chemainus), Catherine Mary (the above lady, Palmer's aunt, died 20 April 1945, aged seventy, in Duncan), Harry Ross Sime (died 27 May 1956, aged sixty-nine, at Ganges), Alice (died 23 October 1961, aged seventy-four, in Victoria), Isabella Mathiesson Sime (died 29 September 1964, aged seventy-three, in Victoria), and William Sime (died 1

June 1966, aged eighty-five, in Saanich). The rest died in Vancouver or Nelson or elsewhere in BC. But were they all members of the same family?

Sources: Notes, courtesy of John Palmer, from family papers and personal acquaintance; *Cowichan Leader*, 26 April 1945, obit.; J. F. Bosher, "Vancouver Island and the Kiplings," *Kipling Journal* (London), vol. 83, no. 332 (June 2009), pp. 12-14.

SIMMONDS, Lieutenant Frederick Hedderley (1879-1950). He was born on 18 September 1879 at "Cashar, S. Syblet, India," and lived in Assam for a number of years. At sometime before the Great War, he migrated to Victoria. From a letter he addressed to the editor of the *Daily Colonist* in 1914, one might infer that he had grown up and worked as a tea planter. He explained how the tea growers lived and worked and that the words "blighty" and "blighter" have nothing to do with one another. "Blighty," he wrote, is the Hindustani word for England and has passed into the language from soldiers posted in India. When FS took a commission as a lieutenant in the 103rd Battalion at Victoria on 18 November 1915, he had been working as a clerk and living with his wife, Maude Isabelle Simmonds, at 1439 Mitchell Street, Oak Bay. In earlier years, he had spent twelve years in the Sixteenth Lancers, five years in the Royal Garrison Artillery, and was now a member of the BC Horse. He wrote with a sophisticated hand. He died, aged seventy, on 10 August 1950 in Vancouver City, and his wife died there, aged seventy-six, on 16 March 1958. They were buried as Anglicans.

Sources: NAC, CEF files, Box 8912-20; *Colonist*, on 30 June 1914, p. 4; 28 November 1914, p. 12.

SISMAN, Major George (1876-1968). He was born on 27 August 1876 at Sherborne, Dorset, one of the seven children of William Sisman, a coachman born in Essex, and his wife Elizabeth. At sixteen, he was already employed as a footman among seven servants at a house in Kensington, London, but in 1894 he enlisted in the Royal Artillery. He was stationed in Bermuda (1898), then Halifax, Nova Scotia, and in 1903 at Work Point Barracks, Esquimalt. In 1906, he transferred to the Royal Canadian Garrison Artillery, rose to be a captain, and was living at 1974 Munro Street, Esquimalt, with his wife, Caroline Louise Sisman, when he signed a belated attestation form for the CEF on 7 January 1919. In 1922, he retired, served on the Esquimalt School Board, as secretary of the Macaulay Point Golf Club, as a Freemason, and as people's warden at St Paul's Naval and Garrison Church for a total of twenty-seven years. In 1937, he was a member of the BC Historical Association. Helen Piddington recalls that her family knew the Sismans in Esquimalt. Mrs Sisman died, aged seventy-seven, on 15 December 1950 and GS died, aged ninety-three, on 28 November 1968 while resident at 1626 Wilmot Place, leaving a daughter, Frances W. Price of Victoria, as well as nephews and nieces in England. They were buried as Anglicans.

Sources: NAC, RG150, box 8952-37; 30 November 1968, p. 24, obit.; census 1881, England, RG 11/2117, p. 51; census 1891, RG 12/30, p. 23.

SKRIMSHIRE, Percy Truscott (c. 1878-1954). An influential schoolmaster in and near the Cowichan Valley for many years, he was born in Birmingham, Warwickshire, the second son of Canon Ernest Skrimshire (born at Holt, Norfolk), clergyman at Llandaff, Wales, and showed exceptional ability during his years at the Cathedral School and Highgate School. He was musical, had a lovely voice, and might have followed his father and uncles into the church but instead he took up teaching and tutoring. In 1902, after several teaching posts in England, he went out to BC, where he tried working in the bush and taught at Brenton's School in Vancouver, the Collegiate School in Victoria and at a church school in Nanaimo. Applying to the BC Department of Education, PS was appointed to a small school at Quamichan, near St Peter's Church, where there were boys whose British fathers wanted to have them educated along the lines of their own schooling. Finding PS's methods with boys entirely to their satisfaction, they asked him about 1905 to take charge of a small private school for which they formed a company and built a useful building on Maple Bay Road, on property later owned by Mr and Mrs W. Hornby. Known as Quamichan Lake School for Boys, it produced excellent results, and PS inspired many Cowichan boys to become distinguished naval and army officers. Several went from his school to Royal Naval College, Halifax: for example, *Captain Barkley Barnes, *Dr Eric Elkington, *Group Captain Joseph S. T. Fall, *Sir Philip Livingston, *Admiral E. R. Mainguy, and *Lieutenant William McKinstry Maitland-Dougall. On 10 August 1907, he married a daughter of *P.W. Rolston, Grace Williams Rolston (c. 1877-1957), with whom he lived near Cobble Hill in an old schoolhouse, where they were hospitable to the boys and Mrs Skrimshire sometimes offered them plum cake and hot scones before a fire in the sitting room.

This was recalled by the boys at PS's next school, where he went after about twenty years. This was Shawnigan Lake School for Boys to which he was invited in 1925 by *C. W. Lonsdale. There he became known for his ability as a mathematics master. He was choirmaster at St Peter's Quamichan for some years. He was also interested, like so many of his kind, in fly-fishing, boating, swimming, soccer, and sketching, and was a keen naturalist. As senior master for years, he occasionally directed the school as acting headmaster. He retired in June 1951 and his health rapidly declined. He had been a heavy smoker for most of his life. When he died on 2 October 1954, aged seventy-six, of a stroke in a nursing home in Vancouver City, he left his wife Grace, two daughters, two sons, John Truscott Skrimshire (field engineer with the BC Electric) and Peter Mitchell Skrimshire, an architect, both of Vancouver, and a brother, Major C. V. S. Skrimshire, RA, in England, as well as his stepmother, Mrs Ernest Skrimshire, then living in England at Worthing. The funeral was at St Peter's Quamichan. Mrs Skrimshire died, aged seventy-nine, on 12 June 1957 at their home near Cobble Hill.

His pupils, who called him "Skrimmy," remembered him as a scholarly teacher, short, stout, with a small grey mustache, well-dressed in a three-piece suit, puffing on a cigarette as he walked about energetically. They viewed him with affection and respect because he taught clearly and with a minimum of fuss.

Sources: *Cowichan Leader,* 7 October 1954, obit.; R. H. Milne and Lucille Kocurek, eds., *Shawnigan and the War* (Duncan, BC, Solitaire Press Ltd., 1990), p. 125; *Cowichan Leader,* 15 June 1922, obit. (*P. W. Rolston); Philip Livingston, *Fringe of the Clouds, passim.*

SLATER, Colonel Alfred Frank M. (1882-1944). Born on 26 September 1882 at Fategarh, India, he was a son of Alfred W. Slater of the Indian Public Works Department and Florence Slater *née* Wiltshire, who sent him to be educated at Bedford College, the public school in Bedfordshire. He was commissioned in the Sherwood Foresters when he was seventeen, served with them in the South African War, and then transferred to the Indian Army. In the Great War, he was with the Indian Army, Tenth JATS, on the North-West Frontier and later transferred to the Indian Police in Burma as deputy inspector and retired as assistant inspector general. In 1909, he married Gwladys Bainbridge, India-born daughter of Major General Frederick T. Bainbridge, a Norfolk soldier with a wife from Nova Scotia who had retired to Cheltenham from the Indian Army Staff Corps. AS and his wife had two sons and a daughter all born in India.

Their first contacts with Vancouver Island were when they sent their elder son and daughter to schools there, and in 1930, they retired to the Island, moved to Cowichan in 1931 and remained there for the rest of their lives except for the three years 1936-1939, which they spent in Victoria. AS joined the British Israelites, was a keen golfer, acted as president of the Cowichan Golf Club, and was interested enough in gardening to serve as vice-president of the Cowichan Crop Growers' Protective Association. He presided at one of its meetings attended by fifty irate farmers who wanted the depredations of deer, pheasants, and quail stopped. AS and *Major L. C. Rattray had already had a meeting about this matter with the standing committee on Agriculture of the Legislative Assembly. They thought the permit system too slow and petitioned the Game Commission in Victoria to instruct wardens to issue licenses to their members to shoot farmers' pests. The main obstacle was the resistance of hunters, "sportsmen," who wanted game protected for shooting in season. AS became a close friend of *Captain V. C. Best on Salt Spring Island and visited the Bests from time to time, sometimes with his sons. They may have had political interests in common, as they all met early in August 1931 for a "basket picnic" with the Salt Spring Island branch of the Canadian Legion attended by Captain MacIntosh, MPP.

AS sent his eldest son, Eric Murray "Mike" Slater, to St Aidan's School and Shawnigan Lake School and the boy then joined the Shanghai International Police force. Three years later, he was killed in Shanghai on New Year's Eve 1936 in a gun battle with bandits who had just carried out a robbery. One of them shot him from above when he challenged them at the foot of a stairway. He was twenty-four years old and known as a rugby player and a cricketer. Their second son, Sub-Lieutenant A. H. M. "Tony" Slater, also attended Shawnigan Lake School but joined the Royal Canadian Naval Reserve and served through the Second World War. Their daughter Aileen Murray "Betty" Slater became a registered nurse and on 24 June 1940 in Halifax, Nova Scotia, married Lieutenant Commander S. T. T.

"Terence" Parsons, RNVR, son of Mr and Mrs O. S. Parsons, of the ICS, who had retired to 89 Holland Park, London.

AS died, aged sixty-one, on 29 January 1944 of double pneumonia, while recovering from a throat operation in Duncan and was buried at St Peter's Quamichan by Rev. Canon T. M. Hughes, with the choir of Shawnigan Lake School attending in gratitude for his interest in the school. Both of his sons had attended it. The choir sang "Fight the Good Fight," and the coffin bearing his sword, medals, and the Union Jack was carried by friends and relatives as pallbearers: Edwin Jackson, M. C. Koechlin, *Captain J. D. Groves, *Major J. H. G. Palmer, *Colonel P. T. Sealy, and P. Sweatman. AS was a first cousin of Major Palmer's father, their mother's being sisters. Besides his widow and two remaining children, AS left one sister in India and another, Mrs Maude Florence Barclay, widow of *Captain Thomas Barclay, an officer who had retired from the Indian Army to Duncan and died there.

Sources: *Colonist*, 3 March 1931, p. 7; 2 August 1931, p. 7; 1 January 1937, p. 2; 27 June 1940, p. 7:; 4 April 1943, p. 2; 1 February 1944, p. 11, obit.; *Cowichan Leader*, 3 February 1944, p. 10, obit.; C. G. Palmer, Duncan, "*The Book of the Palmers*," p. 95, family collection courtesy of John Palmer; census 1891, England, RG 12/2047, p. 13 (Bainbridge); census 1901, RG 13/2466, p. 22 (Bainbridge); census 1891, RG 12/1954, p. 27 (Barclay); census 1901, RG 13/2368, p. 11 (Barclay at Clifton).

SLEE, Major Arthur Boyson (1886-1940). He was born in London, son of Arthur Charles Slee, a timber importer born at Lee, Kent, and Mary M. Slee *née* Boyson born at Wandsworth, Surrey. In 1891, the census found them living in London at 35 Earle's Court Square, AS being five years old, his sister Grace M. B. Slee, aged two, and his mother's sister, Margaret A. S. Boyson, aged twelve. There were four female servants. AS attended Clifton College, Bristol, and from 1905, he became a tea planter in Ceylon and then went into rubber. He planted rubber in Malaya and at various times was manager of Carnivon Rubber Co., chairman of the Katozany Rubber Co., chairman of the Bradbune Co. Brokers, and director of the Vimy Rubber Co. In 1915, he joined the RFA, spent several years in France, and became major of "O" Anti-Aircraft Battery. He won the MC and was mentioned in despatches. After the war, he returned to British Malaya until 1930, when he went out to British Columbia, arriving at Vancouver on 26 April 1930 aboard the CPR vessel, *Empress of Russia*. No doubt this was because in 1922 he had married Monica Clare Green, daughter of L. O. Green of Vancouver.

They settled on the Island in Herd Road near Duncan, on a property they called "Kelston House," and he was soon active in the Cowichan Cricket and Sports Club, serving as hon. secretary of sports. He was also a member of the Cowichan Fish and Game Association. From about 1935, he commanded the Sixty-second Field Battery in Duncan, which became his main occupation, and he trained it to a pitch of efficiency that drew praise from inspecting officers. When it was sent to eastern Canada in September 1940, he was transferred to the Gordon Head Militia Training Centre as an instructor, and two months later, he died there, aged fifty-four, leaving his wife and a son Richard at home. He was buried at St Peter's

Quamichan, Rev. T. M. Hughes officiating, with many Imperial officers and other friends attending, notably *Major A. G. Dobbie, Captain W. D. Hewlett, and Mr N. Fish of Brentwood Bay representing the district of Malaya, who was one of his associates for many years. Among the honorary pallbearers were Major A. E. Bell-Irving (in charge), Major Wilfred Arthur Roy Hadley (1889-1981), Major A. W. Puttick, Captain J. Mehan, Lieutenant J. P. C. Attwood, MC, Lieutenant J. D. O'Toole, MM, Lieutenant R. F. Haig, MC, Lieutenant Herbert Mottershead, DMC, and *Lieutenant R. L. C. Nyblett. Among them, too, were company sergeant majors Crozier and Muir, company quartermaster sergeants Builder, Buxton, and Tough, and sergeant Robertson and Armour. A firing party from his own company gave a salute of three volleys, a bugler sounded last post, and members of the Canadian Legion dropped poppies into the grave.

Sources: *Who's Who in B.C.* 1933-1934, p. 160; census 1891, England, RG 12/33, p. 40; census 1901, RG 13/2368, p. 30; NAC, RG76, immigration, series C-1-i, 1930, vol. 3, p. 75, reel T-14896; *Colonist*, 1 November 1940, p. 2: obit.; *Cowichan Leader*, 7 November 1940, p. 1, obit.

SLINGSBY, Commander Charles Henry Reynard (1874-1941). He was born in Yorkshire, eldest son of Susan Ann, youngest daughter of Charles Reynard of Beverley, Yorkshire, and her husband Rev. Charles Slingsby, MA, JP, of Scriven Park, formerly rector of Harswell and of Kirby Sigston, both places in Yorkshire. The Slingsby family of Scriven Park was a well-known old Yorkshire family, one Henry Slingsby of Scriven having been created a baronet of Nova Scotia in 1640 by King Charles I, and during his retirement on the Island, CS was said to be lord of the manor of Scotton, Yorkshire. Slingsby Channel in Bramham Island, Queen Charlotte Sound, was named after one of his ancestors. As a youth, CS entered the Royal Navy at first as a cadet on HMS *Britannia* and was later stationed at Bermuda and Hong Kong.

He went out to Victoria before the Great War and was immediately active in several local organizations, but in 1914, the navy recalled him to Britain to command a mine flotilla in the Channel. He was promoted to commander in 1917. When the war ended, he returned to Victoria, where he and his wife lived at 2187 Oak Bay Avenue. He had married Dorothy Morgan Warner, daughter of James Mann Warner of the USA in 1900, and in 1910, they had a son, Charles Eugene Edward Slingsby. CS founded and organized the local Naval Veterans Branch of the Canadian Legion and was on its executive until he died. Active in the Rainbow Sea Cadets, he was also the vice-president for several years of the Victoria and Island Division of the Navy League of Canada, which sponsored the Sea Cadet Corps. On 14 May 1934, he spoke to the Gyro Club at the Empress Hotel about the Canadian Navy League, predicting a showdown between the world's navies in the years to come. In March 1910, he started the Sixth Victoria Boy Scout Troop. He loved horses, presided for many years over the Victoria Riding Club and the Victoria Polo Club, and on 14 December 1934, the *Daily Colonist* printed a photo of him on horseback. All the while, he was a member of the Junior Naval and Military Club (London), the United Service Club (London), the Public Schools

Club (Victoria), and Uplands Golf Club (Victoria). Mrs Slingsby died, aged sixty-five, on 16 January 1925 and after many years CS himself died on 29 March 1941. Their funerals were held at St Mary's Anglican Church, Oak Bay. CS left his son Edward at home and a brother, Major Thomas Slingsby, and a sister, Mrs M. A. Williamson, both in England.
Sources: *Colonist*, 15 May 1934, p. 18; 14 December 1934, p. 3; 1 April 1941, p. 10, obit.; *Who's Who in B.C.* 1933-1934, pp. 160-1; Walbran, *B.C. Coast Names*, p. 460.

SMEETON, Brigadier Miles (1906-1988). He was born on 5 March 1906, together with his twin sister, at home near Hovingham, North Yorkshire, son of Dr Charles Smeeton. He was schooled at Wellington College in Berkshire, took up riding and boxing, and on 3 September 1925 was commissioned in the Second Battalion of the Green Howards and posted to Jamaica, then to Gibraltar and later to Egypt, Shanghai, and Poona, India (1931-1934). There he hunted foxes to hounds and, with the Poona Tent Club, hunted wild boar on horseback with spears. In 1936, he volunteered for the Indian cavalry, served with Hodson's Horse, and in 1940 attended the Staff College at Quetta, Baluchistan. He was pleased at the memory of having had dinner with Rudyard Kipling on one occasion. During the Second World War, a brigadier by then, he served with General Bernard Montgomery in the Western Desert and then commanded an armoured brigade, Probyn's Horse, in Burma and won the DSO. While in India, he met his friend Tom Peddie's wife, Beryl *née* Boxer (1905-1979), sister of C. R. Boxer (1904-2000), an army officer turned historian who had retired to take the chair of Portuguese Civilisation at King's College London. She and MS shared a love of mountain-climbing and wild, sometimes risky, adventure. They became very close, travelled home to England together in spring 1934, stopping off to visit Baghdad, Persia, and other places, and eventually after more adventures and some tricky arrangements became man and wife in 1938.

He retired from the army when Burma became independent after the Second World War, and they bought a farm on Salt Spring Island in 1947 through someone Beryl met in India. It turned out to be a remote place at Musgrave's Landing on the west side of the island more or less opposite Maple Bay and Cowichan Bay. There they had a daughter, Clio Smeeton, and made a hard-working game of renovating and maintaining the farm, but farming is usually too difficult for people not brought up to it and like other British pensioners, they suffered financially when the British government devalued the pound sterling in 1949. MS joined a Canadian reserve artillery unit in Duncan, across the Trincomalee Strait, accepting the rank of major to do so. He went as second in command of Exercise Sweetbriar on the Donjek River in the Yukon Territory, but that only whetted his appetite for more adventure. In 1968, they sold the farm, returned home to England, and bought a sea-going yacht, a forty-six-foot ketch called *Tzu Hang* in which they spent nearly twenty years, sailing about the seas of the world. To help with expenses, MS wrote books about their travels as well as two autobiographical volumes: *A Taste of the Hills* (1961) and *A Change of Jungles* (1962). In 1951, 1955, and 1965, they visited Victoria in *Tzu Hang*, and friends recorded their presence on a brass plate, which is still fixed to the wall surrounding Victoria harbour almost opposite the Empress Hotel.

When they tired of life at sea, particularly the cramped quarters aboard a yacht, they bought a tract of land near Calgary, Alberta, in the foothills of the Rockies. That was in 1968 and, with their daughter Clio and their son-in-law, set up the Wild Life Reserve of Western Canada, a charity devoted to the care of endangered species, and Clio's house on Vancouver Island became part of that reserve. There Beryl Smeeton died of cancer on 14 November 1979 at Cochrane, Alberta. MS kept an interest in the preservation of endangered species of foxes and other animals, visited his twin sister in Yorkshire, took up flying and also ice-yachting, a few miles west of Cochrane, Alberta. He died on 23 September 1988 in the Foothills Hospital in Calgary.

Sources: Miles Clark, *High Endeavours: The Extraordinary Life and Adventures of Miles and Beryl Smeeton* (Vancouver, Douglas & McIntyre, 1991), 447 pp.; *The Times* (London), 30 September 1988, p. 16, obit.; *Vancouver Province*, 20 February 1950, p. 7; *Colonist*, 26 October 1955, p. 1, photo; Charles Chenevix Trench, *The Indian Army and the King's Enemies*, 1900-1947 (Thames & Hudson, 1988), pp. 176, 185-6, 188, 281-3, 285-6, 289; *Louis Allen, *Burma, The Longest War*, 1941-1945 (Phoenix Press, 1984), 686 pp., pp. 426-8, 463-4, 505, 537, 539, 540, 566, 613-6; Miles Smeeton, *A Taste of the Hills* (Rupert Hart-Davis, 1961), 207 pp.; and *A Change of Jungles* (Rupert Hart-Davis, 1961), 192 pp.

SMITH, George Edwin (1836-1925). Born on 2 January 1836 in London, he was sent to Greenwich Naval College in 1845 and six years later enlisted in the Royal Navy. When the Crimean War with Russia began in 1854, he was serving in HMS *Tribune*, which patrolled the Black Sea until driven out by a plague of cholera. He always remembered watching the battle of Alma on 20 September 1854 from the crosstrees and seeing the enemy driven back to Sevastopol. He was still aboard the *Tribune* when she bombarded and destroyed Fort Constantine. He later joined the brig *Camelia*, which went to hunt down pirates in the seas around China and to keep order in China and Formosa. It was out there that his service time expired; he signed off at Chefoo and worked his way home on the crew of a merchant ship.

He first arrived at Esquimalt on 2 April 1861 aboard HMS *Tartar*, having rejoined the navy in 1859. In 1864, the ships at Esquimalt were ordered to Yokahama, where on 5 September, Vice Admiral Sir Augustus L. Kuper's squadron of nine British, four Dutch, three French, and one American vessels forced open the Inland Sea of Japan to the shipping of the world by bombarding and dismantling Japanese batteries, which had been in the habit of firing on any western shipping entering the Shimonoseki Straits. GS took part in the battle aboard the *Tartar*, commanded by Captain J. M. Hayes. The Japanese surrendered. In 1867, GS was again in Chinese waters and fell out of the rigging, breaking a leg. This led to his retirement with a pension, but he signed up again and went out again to Esquimalt on HMS *Chameleon*. Two years later, he took his discharge there and settled in Victoria.

For a long time, he ran the water boat supplying the navy for Williams and Arthur, but later tended the bar at *The King's Head*, a naval rendezvous on Johnson Street, which he eventually came to own. In 1871, he joined the volunteer fire brigade. "When the Prince of Wales visited Victoria in 1919 he made a personal call on Mr Smith one morning before the old sailor was out of bed." His medals include Baltic 1854; Crimean Medal and Sebastopol Bar 1854, 1855, 1856; Turkish Medal (ditto); China Medal 1857, 1858; card of thanks from Her Majesty 1874. He was a senior member of the British Campaigners' Association, the Naval Veterans Association, and an order of Freemasonry.

In 1871, he married Miss Elizabeth Farrell (1848-1928), who had come from England around the Horn, though this marriage is not recorded in the BC Vital Statistics. The Victoria census of 1901 found them living with their two daughters, he recorded as a grocer on the corner of Government and John streets. He died, aged eighty-nine, on 18 January 1925, after living in Victoria for fifty-six years, and she died, aged eighty, on 20 April 1928.

Sources: *Colonist*, 4 April 1914, p. 10; 7 April 1914, p. 3; 20 January 1925, p. 5, obit., with photo; despatches from Vice Admiral Sir Augustus L. Kuper, in *London Gazette*, 18 November 1864, reprinted in *The Times* (London), 19 November 1864.

SMITH, Major Joseph Gordon (1874-1951). Born on 16 August 1874 in Edinburgh, he attended British private and public schools and started a newspaper career in Montreal in 1895 with the *Montreal Herald*, part of the time with J. W. Dafoe. At twenty-one, he went to Victoria and took a job sculpturing cornice stones for the Parliament Buildings then being built; he had studied sculpture and painting. In May 1896, however, he rushed to wire to the *New York Herald* the news of the Victoria streetcar, which had just fallen through the Point Ellice Bridge killing fifty-five people. The *Victoria Daily Times* then hired him, but he soon moved to the *Colonist*. "Victoria was then a big news centre," the *Colonist* wrote at his death. "Ships called here first from the Orient, Oceana and Alaska. Smith built up a string of outside newspapers and his income from correspondence exceeded his salary. He scooped the world with news of the arrival of the steamer S.S. *Portland* from the Klondike [1898] with a load of gold and new millionaires. Other newsmen including fourteen top men from the *San Francisco Examiner* under Hearst's news editor 'Long Green' Lawrence had the telegraph line sewn up. Smith and Harry Davy, veteran *Colonist* telegraph operator, went to Metchosin, cut in on the west coast wire, and intercepted Lawrence's story. They then chartered a tug to Port Angeles and wired the story on. The *Colonist* and the *San Francisco Call* were the first with the news."

Alfred Harmsworth, later Lord Northcliffe, appointed Major Smith correspondent of the *Daily Mail* in the Russo-Japanese War (1904-1905), but in Japan, he resigned over a disagreement about his salary and immediately went to work for the *London Morning Post*, then run by Sir Algernon Borthwick, First Baron Glenesk (1830-1908). A series of energetic successes followed. JS evaded Japanese censors and sent the first news of the battle of Nanshan Hill (25-6 May 1904), which he learned during a drinking bout with the son of Japan's war minister. He ran through Russian rifle fire to fetch help for the hard-pressed Japanese Major General Oshima [there were several generals called Oshima], for which Prince Nashimoto Morimasa (1874-1951) gave him the Order of the Rising Sun and two bottles of champagne. He rode for twenty-three hours through dangerous country so that his newspaper would be the first to print news of the immense battle of Liaoyang in Manchuria (26-30 August 1904) and so beat all other newspapers again. Throughout the war, JS was one of the most successful newspaper correspondents and the *London Morning Post* offered him a ten-year contract.

JS refused this offer and return to the *Colonist* in order to be at home at 111 Medina Street, Victoria, with his wife, Emily Mabel *née* Gale (1876-1940), whom he had married there on 5 July 1899. Born in the city of London, she was the daughter of a "gas fitter" from Exeter and a dressmaker from Wisbech in Cambridgeshire. Restless as ever, he reported activities on the waterfront for A. P. Reuters and the French news agency Havas, as well as the *Colonist,* and joined the Fifth Regiment of the Canadian Garrison Artillery. After publishing some short stories, which drew favourable comments from Jack London, he became magazine editor at the *Colonist.* In 1912, he went to work for the BC government, and when he joined the 143rd Battalion of the CEF as a lieutenant on 13 March 1916, he described himself as a "Statistician, Department of Lands, B.C." He went overseas as company commander of the 143rd Battalion, but to get into the fighting in France, he dropped a rank and joined the Seventy-second Battalion. After fourteen months in the trenches, he was appointed to a special section of the British Intelligence Corps and when the war ended commanded the Depot Battalion of the Canadian Scottish Regiment in Victoria until 1930, when he was appointed director—later commissioner—of publicity and information in the provincial government. That marked the pinnacle of his thirty-year career in the BC government. Mrs Smith died, aged sixty-three, on 10 February 1940. About 1946, JS retired from the travel bureau and went to live in Sidney on Admiral's Road near what was then called All Bay. He played at Ardmore Golf Club for many years and belonged to their "hole-in-one club." When he died, aged seventy-six, on 28 September 1951, two weeks after winning the Pacific Club's open golf tournament, he was buried at Ross Bay and was survived by a brother David Smith in Victoria and three married sisters in interior BC towns.

Sources: NAC, CEF files, box 9080-43; *Who's Who in B.C.* 1931, p. 103; 1933-1934, p. 161; 1937-1939, pp. 137-8; 1942-1943, pp. 284-5; census 1881, England, RG 11/370/33, p. 5; *Colonist,* 29 September 1951, p. 16, obit., and photo. Various histories of the Russo-Japanese War (1904-1905).

SMYLY, Colonel Frederick Philip (1856-1945). He was born on 15 June 1856 in Dublin, younger son of Major General P. A. Smyly and Mrs Smyly of Monkstown, Dublin, Ireland. He was registered by the 1861 census, aged four, living at 4 Spring Green Villas, Cheltenham, with his family. His father, Phillip A. Smyly, aged fifty, was a "Major General Infantry" born in Dublin and his mother, Agusta [*sic*] Smyly, aged thirty-six, was born in Australia. His eldest brother, John George Smyly, aged ten, was also born in Australia, as was his next eldest brother William Smyly, aged eight. He had a younger sister, Agusta [sic], aged three, born like him in Dublin. There were four servants: governess, parlourmaid, cook, and nurse. The nearest neighbour at 3 Spring Green Villas was Phillpotts W. Taylor, aged forty-five, "Army Colonel retired" born in Jamaica, and on the other side was a "fundholder." FS passed through Hythe Musketry School—first class extra—and on 12 July 1875 became a sub-lieutenant in the Antrim Militia. He was promoted to lieutenant on 22 September 1876 and transferred to the Twenty-fourth Foot (South Welsh Borderers) on 12 April 1879. In these units, he was employed in the East Indies from 28 February 1877 to 5 June 1879, in South Africa from 6 June 1879 to 12 January 1880, in the Mediterranean from 13 January 1880 to 11 August 1880, and in the East Indies from 12 August 1880. He served in the Zulu War in 1879 and qualified as a musketry instructor on 19 April 1880. He had a medal and clasp from the SA Campaign of 1877-1879 and was inducted into the OBE.

FS married Charlotte Mary Emily Price, eldest daughter of Sir Frederick Price, KCSI and of Lady Price, of Exmouth, England, in St George's Cathedral at Madras on 17 October 1885, the marriage performed by J. F. Brown, DD, archdeacon of Madras. After his retirement, they went to live in Victoria at 601 Transit Road and in 1933 were members of the India-Burma Society. On 6 October 1934, their second son, Philip Smyly, late of the Second Dorset Regiment, died in London, where he had been living at 12 Lawrie Park Crescent, Sydenham. When Mrs Smyly died on 15 August 1943, they were living at 644 Beach Drive, Oak Bay, and her funeral was held at St Mary's Anglican Church, Oak Bay. PS himself died, aged eighty-eight, on 11 June 1945 at 644 Beach Drive. One of his nearest relatives was a nephew, Philip Austin Smyly, born on 14 December 1890 in London, a son of his Australia-born brother Rev. William Smyly, and working as a bank clerk when he enlisted in the CEF in Alberta during the Great War.

Sources: *British National Archives* (PRO), WO76/233, page 20 [or 75?]; *Colonist*, 17 January 1933, p. 8; 9 October 1934, p. 14, obit.; 17 August 1943, p. 14; 13 June 1945, p. 10, obit.; census England 1871, RG 10/775, p. 82; Donald R. Morris, *The Washing of the Spears: A History of the Rise of the Zulu Nation under Shaka and its Fall in the Zulu War of 1879* (New York, Sim & Schuster, 1965), pp. 264, 272, 295, 316, 320, 387, 459, 507, 508, 620; CEF files, box 9129-65.

SMYTH, General Sir Edward Selby (1819-1896). He was the first GOC, Canadian Militia, sent out from England to Ottawa in 1874 on the Duke of Cambridge's recommendation that he was a suitable British officer for the task. He was a colonel in the Seventy-second Foot Regiment. In 1875, he went to BC on an inspection tour and made recommendations for fortifying Esquimalt and Victoria and places in the Kootenay Valley. At the same time, another British officer, Colonel G. F. Blair, late Royal Artillery, was sent to BC to survey the sites for possible defensive works at Victoria and Esquimalt. Blair wrote a military intelligence report about the province's defences for the federal authorities. Both men recommended artillery for Victoria and Esquimalt. ES had served with distinction in India, South Africa, and Mauritius. It was during his tour of duty that RMC was founded in Kingston, Ontario.

ES was born at Belfast on 31 March 1819. In 1891, the census-taker found him, aged seventy-three, living at Darby House, Sunbury, Middlesex (parish of St Mary), and identified as a "General in the Army, J.P. for Middlesex." With him there was his wife, Lucy J. Smyth, aged sixty-one, born in Armagh; their son, Edward G. S. Smyth, aged thirty-nine, born in Ireland at Black Rock, "Major in the Army, Royal Irish Rifles"; a daughter Geraldine L. J. Haggard, aged twenty-nine, born in Ireland at Stellargar (?) and married on 1 July 1882 to Charles Haggard (1852-1919); and a grandson, Christopher Haggard, aged five, born at Sunbury, Middlesex, as well as eight domestic servants.

EC died in 1896, still in service.

Sources: R. H. Roy, "The Early Militia and Defence of British Columbia, 1871-1885," *British Columbia Historical Quarterly*, vol. XVIII, nos. 1 and 2 (Jan.-Apr. 1954), pp. 10-12; Richard Arthur Preston, *Canada and "Imperial Defense": A Study of the Origins of the British Commonwealth's Defense Organization, 1867-1919* (Durham, NC, Duke University, 1967), pp. 75-9, 81, 120, 122-4, 127, 135, 139, 141, 155, 165, 169; census 1891, England, RG 12/1015, p. 36.

SNOW, Lieutenant Colonel Arthur Baring (1866-1949). Born on 23 April 1866 at Simla, India, he became a professional soldier and spent four years in the Dorset Militia as a lieutenant and twenty years in the Mounted Police in Africa, emerging with four medals and six clasps. He went through the Matabele War, Landberg, the South African War, and then the Great War. In 1889, he was commissioned as major in the Bechuanaland and Border Police, and won a medal for the first Matabele War (1893-1894) and another for the Landberg Campaign of 1897. Upon the annexation of Bechuanaland, he joined the Cape Mounted Rifles in 1899 and was on patrol duty on the Free State border, with headquarters at Fourteen Streams outside Kimberley, until the outbreak of the South African War. On the relief of Kimberley, he commanded Lord Roberts's escort on its way to Paardeberg after which he was on the staff of Major General Charles C. W. Cavendish, Third Lord Chesham (1850-1907), who led the Imperial Yeomanry in the Orange Free State, and then AS transferred to Sir Charles Warren's staff. From Campbell a column was detached to make its way into Griquatown, and AS was appointed to command all the mounted scouts, while Colonel Sam Hughes (later Canadian minister of militia) acted as chief of intelligence. The column succeeded and did its job in twenty-four hours. AS later praised the way in which Hughes, with only twenty men, succeeded in capturing a force of 480 Boers between Krooman and Daniel's Kraal. AS was then appointed commandant of Griquatown, where he remained for nine months and afterwards served at Barkley West and Freibourg. In August 1900, he married Amelia Millicent Stewart Pringle (1881-1922), daughter of a Scottish family settled at Glen Thorn, Cape Province, and had six children: Agnes Gertrude Snow, born 1901; Millicent Jane Snow, born 1901, died in infancy; Thomas Eric Snow, born 1904, who married Jean Matthews and rose in the Canadian Army to be a brigadier general; Thelma O'Daley Snow, born 1908 and still living in 2001; Arthur James Snow, born 1913, who married Hazel Buxten, was living at Powell River, BC, in 2001, and who generously responded to my questions; and Flora Hope Snow, born in 1920 but died in 1932.

A few years after the South African War, the Snows went to live in Fredericton, New Brunswick, where Mrs Snow and their four remaining children stayed while AS went in search of employment. The sequence of events is hard to establish. As an officer in the Corps of Guides, AS was appointed in 1912 to organize and inspect the British Columbia Cadet Corps. In February 1914, he was ordered to do the same in the Sixth Divisional Area, which comprised New Brunswick, Nova Scotia, and Prince Edward Island, and when AS attended a farewell parade of the Esquimalt schools cadets on 25 February 1914, his own little son was among the cadets. There is a photograph of AS on this occasion (*Colonist* on 27 February 1914, p. 3), but Mrs Snow seems never to have gone farther west than New Brunswick. In any event, on 25 September 1914, AS accepted a commission as a major in the CEF at Valcartier, Quebec. At that time, he was 6' 1" tall with a forty-two-inch chest, weighed 187 lbs., and declared his birthdate to be 23 April 1866. At first, he was appointed acting assistant provost marshal (24 February 1915), then sent to France on "an instructional tour" in 7-23 March 1917 and seconded for duty with the War Office (Inland Waterways, Dock Section, RE) from 30 October 1917 to 23 February 1919, and early in his service in Britain, he was promoted to lieutenant colonel (30 November 1915). Finally, when the war was over, he embarked on the *Corsican* for New Brunswick, Canada, on 14 April 1919 and found to his wife's dismay that he was entitled only to a major's gratuities and pension. Mrs Snow found that she and her four remaining children could hardly live on this income. On 8 December 1919, she wrote an anxious letter to the Paymaster in Ottawa arguing that AS deserved the pay of a lieutenant colonel: "I lived in Africa all my life until I came to Canada and two of our children were born there, so I can assure you we feel the cold very much. We have four children—our eldest boy is at college here, we have absolutely *no* private means and all my friends and relations are in South Africa, so I have no one to appeal to for help in this crisis. I have economised in every way, I have no maid, but do all my own work, and we have taken a small cottage in the country as house rent is so high in St John and we go nowhere, as we cannot afford to entertain . . . it is terrible to have to do without coal when the weather is below zero . . ." The file seems to show that her entreaties brought no change [NAC, RG9 Series II-F-10, vol. 343, file 17001-A-8]. Meanwhile, AS travelled west to Salt Spring Island in hope of an independent life in a mild climate, but before he was able to arrange for the family to join him, his wife died on 29 January 1922.

At sometime in the early 1930s, AS settled on Salt Spring Island whence he visited Victoria occasionally and became the Cub master to the Wolf Cub Pack of Ganges, assisted by other officers on Salt Spring Island, notably *Major F. C. Turner, president of the Wolf Cub organization, and *Captain C. V. Best, who gave the Cubs boxing lessons. AS joined the Gulf Island branch of the Canadian Legion and attended its annual dinner held at Mayne Island on 9 April 1936. By then and probably since 1934, he was scoutmaster of the Salt Spring Island Scout Troop; they attended an armistice memorial service and dedicated a Union Jack flag presented to them by the Ganges Chapter of the IODE. On 13 November 1936, AS was one of forty guests of Mr and Mrs N. Wilson at "Barnsbury Grange" in Ganges, assembled to meet Mr and Mrs A. C. McNabb of the ICS, who were about to sail to India. At a garden party organized in 1939 at Rainbow Beach by the Layard family, AS presented trophies to the Cubs, and in June that year, he wrote a public letter, giving his address as Vesuvius Lodge, Salt Spring Island, complaining that children could not see the royal family during their parade in Victoria. AS died, aged eighty-four, on 2 August 1949 at Ganges and was survived notably by his sons Arthur James Snow and Brigadier General Thomas Eric Snow, who had served through the Second World War and had been an instructor for four and a half years at RMC, Kingston.

Sources: Eric, Mark E., and John A. Pringle, *Pringles of the Valleys, Their History and Genealogy* (Adelaide, Cape Province, South Africa, Eric Pringle of Glen Thorn, 1957), 242 pp., privately printed in a limited edition of 1,000 copies, courtesy of Arthur James Snow, whose mother was Amelia Millicent Stewart Pringle; *Cape Times Week-end Magazine*, 8 April 1961; NAC, RG9 Series II-F-10, vol. 343, file 17001-A-8; NAC, RG150, acc. 1992-93/166, Box 9140-11; *Colonist*, 24 January 1934, p. 15; 16 December 1934, p. 23; 15 April 1936, p. 4; 10 November 1936, p. 4; 20 December 1936, p. 20; 10 June 1939, p. 4; 15 August 1939, p. 7; 1 April 1943, p. 11.

SOLLY, Leonard Hollis (1853-1929). A Welsh emigrant to Victoria born at Port Madoc, Carnarvonshire, he arrived in 1884 with his wife, Mary Rebecca, and found employment as land commissioner for the Esquimalt and Nanaimo Railway. He was born on 16 September 1853, his wife on 9 June 1854, and they had married in 1884 at Fareham, Hampshire, just before emigrating. They settled in Victoria in Phoenix Place, and the son they had there, Leonard Fordham Solley (1885-1978), attended Victoria Public School and Mr Bolton's Private School, later called University School, and spent two years with the Canadian Bank of Commerce. In 1907, this son bought 150 acres at Westholme near Duncan, which he called "Lakeview Farm," and took up poultry and dairy farming. By 1940 there were seventy-five buildings producing seventy thousand chicks a year. L.F. Solly served as a member of the Duncan Hospital Board, as church warden at All Saints, Westholme, and as member of various agricultural associations. In 1921, he married Mona, daughter of *Dr Primrose Well and they had two daughters (granddaughters of LS). L.F. Solly died, aged ninety-three, on 20 April 1978 at Duncan and his wife, aged eighty-nine, on 23 January 1982, leaving several grown-up children.

LS was born into a substantial family. His father, Nathaniel Neal Solly (1811-1895), was born in Clapton, London, on 16 June 1811 and became an iron master and a JP at Bushbury, Staffordshire. In 1844 at Royston, a market town on the Hertfordshire-Cambridgeshire border, he married LS's mother, Martha *née* Fordham (1811-?), second daughter of Sarah Nash (LS's grandmother) and her husband, John George Fordham (1784-1875), who had married on 13 May 1802 at Guilden Morden, Cambridgeshire. Fordham began life as a corn merchant but then became a banker. The 1861 census shows LS, aged seven, and his nine-year-old sister Marion and their mother, Martha Solly, aged forty-nine, staying with Fordham, Martha's widowed father (the children's grandfather), at "The Priory" in Royston, with a governess and four servants. During LS's childhood, the family lived normally at Odsey House, Guilden Morden in Cambridgshire. LS's grandmother, Sarah Nash, was the daughter of a solicitor at Royston, William Nash (1745-1829) and his wife, Hester Wedd (died 1810), who had married on 22 March 1774 at Fowlmere and were both buried there in due time near the Nash family home. The researches of Dennis Hitch reveal a widespread network of relatives in Cambridgeshire.

LS died, aged seventy-six, on 17 August 1929 and his wife, aged seventy-eight, on 23 March 1933, both in Victoria.

Sources: *Who's Who in B.C.*, 1940-1941, pp. 213-4; census 1861, England, RG 9/813/80, p. 21; census 1871, RG 10/2923/30, p. 7; census 1881, RG 11/1093/88, p. 35; Dennis Hitch, "*The Nash Family of Fowlmere*," www.geocities.com/ weddfamily/ documents.html [no spaces].

SOUPER, Noel Beaumont (1877-1916). He was born on 20 December 1877 at Eastbourne, Sussex, where the 1881 census found him, aged three, living with his family at a school taught by his father, Rev. Francis Souper, aged thirty-seven, a "Schoolmaster Clerk in Holy Orders without cure of souls," born in Bedfordshire. His mother, Fanny Souper, aged thirty-two, was born at Highgate. His brothers and sisters were Oriana F. Souper, aged six, and James F. T. Souper, aged four, both born at Bradfield, Berkshire, and Constance Souper, aged two, born at Eastbourne, along with several other masters and pupils. Ten years later, the census recorded NS, aged thirteen, as a visitor in the large family of Colonel Adophus Vallings at South Hill, Paignton, Devon. The colonel, aged fifty-two, was an officer in the Bengal Staff Corps but born in St Pancras, London, though his wife, Blanche Vallings, aged forty-three, was born in India, as was their daughter Blanche Vallings, aged seventeen. Their younger children were born in Wimbledon, and they had two servants. He served in the South African War in the Cambridge University Rifle Voluntiers and the Suffolk Regiment.

By 1910, NS was living on the Island at Esquimalt, where on 7 April, he married Rosalie Frances Norie, born 20 December 1872 at Elgin, Morayshire, Scotland, daughter of Alexander Dickson Norie and his wife Louise Ulrica *née* Nash. They went to live as Anglicans in the Cowichan Valley, and there NS joined the Fiftieth Gordon Highlanders. The *Cowichan Leader* listed him with other men in uniform on their Roll of Honour when he joined the CEF on 23 September 1914 at Valcartier, Quebec, leaving Rosalie at home on the Island. Less than two years later, he died, aged forty, on 1 July 1916, fighting in the Royal Berkshire Regiment, Sixth Battalion, to which he had transferred overseas. The Canadian Department of Veterans' Affairs recorded him as a son of Rev. F. A. Souper of Grantchester Meadows, Cambridge, and husband of Rosalie F. Souper of 54 Fitz James Avenue, London W 14. His name is inscribed on the Thiepval Memorial, Somme, France, and on the Lynch Gate, West of Fonstanton, four miles southwest of St Ives in Huntingdonshire.

Sources: NAC, CEF files, box 9160-49; census 1881, England, RG 11/1038, p. 9; census 1891, RG 12/1707, p. 2; *Cowichan Leader*, 17 August 1916, Roll of Honour; Dept. of Veterans' Affairs; IGI of the Latter Day Saints.

SOUTHGATE, Captain James Johnson (c. 1821-1894). Signing invariably as "J. J. Southgate," he was a retired English sea captain, born in Tottenham, London. He arrived on the Island in 1858 from San Francisco, where he had been working as a commission merchant and ship-handler. He had a letter of introduction to Governor James Douglas and soon prospered in a variety of business activities as J. J. Southgate & Company. He gained a contract to provision ships of the Royal Navy lying nearby in Esquimalt harbour and, with the financial support of Commander H. D. Lascelles, RN, built a brick store (still standing) in Victoria, where he dealt in real estate. He was a staunch supporter of the HBC and took the lead at a meeting on 12 July 1858 upstairs in his new store to establish the Ancient Order of F. and A. Masons by petition to England. As a result Masonic Lodge No. 1085 ER was founded on 20 August 1860, JS being elected and re-elected as its first worshipful master. He was elected to the BC legislature at various times for Esquimalt, Salt Spring Island, and Nanaimo and was active from June 1861 to July 1865. In a list of men who died intestate in 1883, JS is twice listed as managing the estates of such men, namely, William Salmon and (in Liverpool) James L. Southey. In the *British Colonist* for 13 March 1867, it was reported that "a deputation, composed of the Hons. Southgate, Helmcken, De Cosmos and Pemberton, waited upon His Excellency the Governor to suggest the propriety for telegraphing to the Government as follows: 'That provision be made in the Confederation bill now before the Imperial Government for the admission of British Columbia into the Confederacy on such fair and equitable terms as may be agreed upon thereafter.' His Excellency received the deputation courteously, and at once acceded to their request. The despatch will be sent at once." The request was politically premature but as a result of such activities Southgate Street in Victoria, Southgate River in Bute Inlet, and the Southgate group of the Queen Charlotte Islands were all named in JS's honour.

In 1865, the Lowe brothers bought JS's business and he retired to England, where he was identified in census records as a retired merchant living in "Esquimalt Villa", Chiswick (or Ealing), Greater London, with his wife Elizabeth, and their daughter Annie. Elizabeth was about JS's age, born in a Cambridgeshire village, and they had married in 1843 in Poplar, London, and had their daughter Annie in the early 1850s in San Francisco, California. In 1871 JS's mother, Martha, aged 83, from Stoke Lyne, Oxfordshire, was living with them in London, JS's father Joseph (or Josiah) from Battersea having died. By 1891 Annie had married a Mr. Yates and had an eight-year-old son, Joseph S. Yates, born in London. Mr. Yates must surely be one of the Yates family of Victoria but the relationship is not obvious. In 1891 JS was described as "Retired Merchant & Shipowner" and they all still lived at "Esquimalt Villa" in Chiswick (or Ealing) with a cook and a housemaid. JS died in 1894 and the 1901 census showed Elizabeth as a widow, aged 80, Annie Yates still there, aged 47, and her son Joseph Yates aged 19. JS is easily confused with James J. Southgate, a "gunmaker" born c. 1854 to Robert Southgate in Newington, London, and married to Clara Fewtrell (from Lambeth, London) in St James, Westminster.

Sources: census 1871, England, RG 10/1320, p. 43; census 1881, England, RG 11/1352, p. 42; census 1891, England, RG 12/1034, p. 45; census 1901,

England, 13/1199, p. 39; J. M. S. Careless, "The Business Community in the Early Development of Victoria, British Columbia," in *Canadian Business History: Selected Studies* 1497-1971, ed., David S. Macmillan (Toronto, McClelland & Stewart, 1972), pp. 104-124, see p. 110; John T. Marshall, ed., *History of Grand Lodge of British Columbia* (1871-1970) (Victoria, Grand Lodge of British Columbia, AF and AM, 1971), pp. 18, 19, 20, 22, 23; W. George Shelton, ed., *British Columbia & Confederation* (Victoria, University of Victoria, 1967), p. 78; records of Freemasonry, Victoria; *BC Archives*, Records of BC Legislature; Walbran, *B.C. Coast Names*, p. 466; Derek Pethick, *Victoria: The Fort* (Vancouver, Mitchell Press Ltd., 1968), pp. 207 and 227 note 63; J. K. Nesbitt, in the *Colonist* for 11 December 1949; *Colonist*, 2 February 1865; *Victoria Gazette*, 10 July 1858; Edgar Fawcett, *Some Reminiscences* (1912) , p. 62; IGI of the Latter Day Saints.

SOWERBY, Charles William (c. 1865-1940). He was born in Southgate, Middlesex, son of William Sowerby, secretary of the Royal Botanical Gardens at Regent's Park and grandson of John de Carle Sowerby, a famous botanist. The 1871 census found him, aged five, living at Botanical Gardens Villas, Marylebone, London, with his family. His father was recorded as born at Lambeth, Hampshire, and his mother, Charlotte F. Sowerby (*née* Bryant) born at Stockwell, Hampshire. Living with them was CS's maternal grandfather, James Bryant, aged seventy-three, a "Retired East India merchant" born in Hackney, and also CS's three elder brothers and sisters, all born in Camdentown. They had one domestic servant. CS was schooled at Christ's Hospital and travelled widely in North and South America. In 1901, however, the census recorded him, aged thirty-five, as a "visitor" at 18 Ickford Street, Clerkenwell, London, together with his elder brother, James Sowerby, aged forty-two, who was a "Secretary Scientific Society." They were living in the home of the latter's father-in-law, Edward Scargill, who subsisted on a "Salary of Ickford Bank Account," and the household seems to have been organized around the Ickford Bank. The immediate neighbours were "Book Keeper," "Accountant," etc., probably also employed at the bank.

At sometime around the end of the nineteenth century, CS migrated to British Columbia, where he enlisted at Victoria in the 143rd Overseas Battalion of the CEF on 14 February 1916, giving his occupation as "prospector" and his brother, J. Bryant Sowerby of Weir Cottage, Chertsey, England, as his next of kin. CS then lived at 1017 Fisguard Street, and except for the war years, he stayed there on and off for the rest of his life and died, aged seventy-five, on 23 October 1940, an unmarried Freemason and an Anglican.

Sources: *Colonist*, 25 October 1940, p. 3, obit.; census 1871, England, RG 10/177; census 1881, RG 11/379, p. 25; census 1901, RG 13/250, p. 17.

SPARKS, Francis Ashley (1882-1942). He arrived from England sometime in 1905-1907 and taught at Corrig School and University School until 1914, when he opened St Aidans' School in the Victoria suburb of Royal Oak as owner and headmaster. His own venture, it was an Anglican preparatory school known, until 1916, as Victoria Prep. School. In 1926, the school moved to the suburb of Langford and *Colonel Gerald Bassett Scott bought its old Victoria building to use as a private house. Meanwhile, FS engaged the architect H. J. R. Cullen to design a house for him at 1073 Monterey Avenue. Prominent in sporting circles, FS played rugby and was an outstanding captain of the local Incogs Cricket team, which was founded in 1912. On 10 July 1920, he married Margaret Frances Hewett in Oak Bay, and they had two daughters and a son, John Ashley Sparks, who fought in the Second World War in the Twenty-seventh Anti-aircraft Battery. In Royal Oak, the family attended the Anglican Church of St Michael and All Angels.

FS was born in England at Potter's Bar, near London, second to the youngest son of John Ashley Sparks and his wife, Amy Francis, who had him christened at North Mimms, Hertfordshire, on 27 August 1882. His family appears in the 1881 census, shortly before his birth, living at "Heath House," North Mimms, where the father was a "Commission Merchant," aged thirty-seven, born at North Wenfleet, Essex, and the mother, aged twenty-nine, born at Watford, Hertfordshire. They had five children; FS's elder brothers and sisters: Beatrice Amy, aged seven, born at Abbott Langley, Hertfordshire; Alice F., five, born in St Pancras, London; Thomas Ashley, four, also in St Pancras; John C., two, and William J., three months, both born at North Mimms. They employed a general servant and a nursemaid, both teenaged girls. The father appears, aged seven, in the 1851 census, living with his family at "Bradfields," Northwenfleet, Essex, where his father, John Sparks (FS's grandfather), aged thirty-four, born locally, was a "farmer of 750 acres [employing] 17 labourers" and his mother (FS's grandmother), Eleanor, aged thirty, was born not far away at West Thurrachy (?).

FS's elder brother, Thomas Ashley Sparks, born on 23 March 1877, grew up to become, in 1917, the resident director of the Cunard Steamship Company in New York and in 1918-1919 was director general of the British Ministry of Shipping in the USA. He was knighted in 1919 and made KCMG in 1941. In 1900, he had married Mina Jane Roberts of New York, with whom he had two daughters, and lived in a mansion at Seyosset, Long Island, where he died, aged eighty-seven, on 21 May 1964, and Lady Sparks on 28 March 1958. He and FS had a younger brother, Vernon Ashley Sparks, who in 1917 became a second lieutenant in the Yeomanry Territorial Force. FS himself died in Victoria, aged sixty, on 29 October 1942, when his brothers William and Thomas were both living in the USA. His wife died, aged eighty-two, on 28 July 1984.

Sources: *Colonist*, 31 October 1942, pp. 2 and 16, obit.; notes courtesy of Mrs Morgan Scott Ostler; Jean Barman, *Growing up British in British Columbia: Boys in Private School* (Vancouver, UBC Press, 1984), pp. 35, 190; photos 11, 12 at p. 72; St Michael's University School, *School Ties*, (Victoria, 2001), 35 pp., see p. 22: http://www.smus.bc.ca/ publications/ smus_sch_ties_s . . . [no spaces]; census 1851, England, HO 107/1774, p. 1; census 1881, RG 11/1427/49, p. 23; census 1891, RG 12/794, p. 8; *The Times* (London), 12 April 1958, p. 8, col. E, obit.; 22 May 1964, p. 17, col. C, obit.; U.S. Landmarks Preservation Commission, September 19, 1995; Designation List 266, LP-1928, see footnote 4, p. 27 (Cunard and Sir Thomas Ashley Sparks).

SPARKS, Major James Richard (1868-1934). Born in London on 16 December 1868, he became a soldier and served two years in the Imperial Army before coming to Canada in 1889. The next year, he joined the Canadian Mounted Rifles and served in the South African War. On returning, he was appointed cavalry instructor for the northwest and stationed at Medicine Hat and Vernon. In 1914, he transferred to Lord Strathcona's Horse and served overseas until wounded in May 1915. When on 25 October 1915 in Vernon, BC, he signed the "attestation" form required for the CEF, perhaps for the second time, he was married and had spent twenty years and four months with Lord Strathcona's Horse, Permanent Force, and seven years with the First Volunteers, Kele (?), EDRA and J. Invalided home, he was attached to Regina HQ as instructor in the Canadian Signals Corps, but rejoined Strathcona's Horse in 1918. JS was stationed at Calgary as adjutant, listed on 1 April 1920 as a captain, and retired in 1924 after thirty-five years of service. A medical report dated at Calgary 24 April 1924, preliminary to his retirement, identified him as a captain living in Calgary at 1811, 12th Avenue West, and his wife as Sarah Pearl Sparks, who appears to have been born in Sarnia, Ontario.

They retired to Deep Cove, North Saanich, about twenty miles north of Victoria. When he died there, aged sixty-five, on 17 August 1934, the pallbearers were Major G. D. Edwards, Major Squire Baxandall, Colonel J. L. Potter, *Colonel W. H. Belson, W. R. Steer, and D. G. Bristowe. He left his wife, who died on 22 May 1953, a daughter in Calgary and two sons at home, as well as a brother Frederick and two sisters, Maria and Marion, in London.

Sources: NAC, RG150, CEF files, box 9171-46; *Sidney and Gulf Islands Review*, 22 August 1934, p. 1; *Colonist*, 19 August 1934, p. 5; 22 August 1934, p. 3, obit.

SPINKS, John Charlton (c. 1845-1936). He and his wife, *née* Emma Birch, moved to Calgary, Alberta, in 1911 and in 1913 settled in Victoria as a retired couple. He had been a police inspector. They lived at 1936 Quamichan Avenue and were active parishioners of St Mary's Anglican Church. Born in County Cavan, Ireland, JS married Emma on 7 April 1875 at Manchester Cathedral, she born at Cheetham, Lancashire. Before emigrating, they lived for twenty-three years at various places in Lancashire and Cheshire and thirteen years in Dublin. Emma died in Victoria, aged seventy-seven, on 31 May 1929. When JS died, aged ninety-one, on 5 February 1936, he was a member of the British Israelite sect. It was while they were in Cheshire that they had their two sons, William H. Spinks and Charleton Watson Spinks. The family appears in the 1881 census, living at 17 New Road, Latchford, JS, a police inspector aged thirty-four, Emma aged twenty-nine, William H. Spinks aged five, born at Warrington, Lancashire, and Charleton W. Spinks, aged three, born there at Latchford and christened on 2 December 1877.

In due time, this three-year-old boy became Major General Charlton Watson Spinks (1877-1959), DSO, OBE, inspector general of the Egyptian Army. He was first commissioned in the Royal Artillery and sent to subdue warlike tribes in northern Nigeria, (1903-1904). He was a captain when in 1912 he was engaged in operations against tribes in the Sudan. Promoted to major in 1914 shortly after the outbreak of the Great War, he served in Gallipoli and Egypt and in 1916 with the Hediaz-Arab forces. By the end of the war, he had been decorated with the OBE, the DSO, the Grand Cross of Leopold II of Belgium, and the Grand Cordon of the Order of the Nile. After the war, the [British] Egyptian government appointed him inspector general of troops in Egypt. In 1924, he took leave to spend several weeks visiting his parents in Victoria. In 1927, he was promoted KBE and retired with the rank of major general. In his sixties in 1939, JS proved to be useful because of his long experience in the Middle East. He worked in 1940-1941 as a travelling commissioner for the British Red Cross Society and the order of St John of Jerusalem and a year later was appointed director for the Egyptian Auxiliary Defence Service. In 1915, he married Marguerite Stuart, daughter of R. H. Coleman of Toronto, and they had three daughters.

Sources: Census 1881, England, RG11 3799/39, page 18; *Colonist*, 8 April 1925, p. 8; 6 February 1936, p. 2, obit.; *Times* (London), 26 October 1959, p. 12, obit.

SPRATT, Joseph (c. 1834-88). Born in England, he trained there as a marine engineer and, after gaining experience at San Francisco, went to Victoria at sometime between 1858 and 1862. The BC census of 1881 recorded him as a Presbyterian "ship's construction engineer" aged forty-eight living with his wife Emma, also from England and aged fifty-nine. In Victoria JS established the Albion Iron Works, a foundry and marine machinery workshop, which played a considerable part in the Island's early shipping life. In 1877, for instance, the famous *Beaver* was refitted there. In 1882, Joseph Spratt bought property at 343 Bay Street and set up a foundry and shipyard he called Victoria Machinery Depot (VMD), which was still building ships during the Second World War. In time, JS ventured into shipbuilding, salmon-canning, and whaling. He also organized the East Coast Mail Line with three ships plying the waters of the straits between the Island and the mainland: the *Maude* (named after a daughter of Captain Delacombe of the British garrison at San Juan Island), the *Cariboo & Fly*, and a side-wheel steamer called the *Wilson G. Hunt*. In 1883, he sold this company to the Canadian Pacific Navigation Co., which then had a monopoly of BC coast steamships. It was in the same year that JS built what became known as "Spratt's Ark," an immense steam-powered scow that worked for canneries, quarries, and enterprises, hauled coal for the *Empress of India* (1891), and was used as a salvage ship. When JS died in 1888, his son Charles managed the business until 1941 when his wife took over as managing director. In 1907, they added a three-thousand-ton marine railway and, after a devastating waterfront fire in 1908, rebuilt and refitted the plant for service during the Great War and produced munitions. The son also built and equipped two 8,800-ton steel freighters: *The Canadian Winner* and *The Canadian Traveller*. In 1940, the Victoria Machinery Depot (VMD) won a contract to build five corvettes for the Canadian Navy.

A considerable expansion followed for which VMD bought seventeen acres of land around the Outer Wharf at 33 Dallas Road, renovated the old Rithet piers, and built two launching ways capable of handling 100,000-ton cargo vessels. All this grew out of the early industry of JS, who died, aged fifty-five, on 12 January 1888 at San José, California.

Sources: Canadian census, 1881, VI; *Camas Chronicles of James Bay, Victoria, British Columbia* (Victoria, Camas Historical Group, 1978), pp. 15-16; J. M. S. Careless, "The Business Community in the Early Development of Victoria, British Columbia," in *Canadian Business History: Selected Studies, 1497-1971*, ed., David S. Macmillan (Toronto, McClelland and Stewart Ltd., 1972), pp. 115, 117; Norman R. Hacking and W. Kaye Lamb, *The Princess Story: A Century and a Half of West Coast Shipping* (Second ed., Vancouver, Mitchell Press, 1976), pp. 64, 77, 98-103, 338;

SPROAT, Gilbert Malcolm (1834-1913). He was born on 19 April 1834 at Brighouse Farm, on the Solway Firth, in the County of Kirkcudbright in southern Scotland, son of Alexander S. Sproat, a farmer with a large family. He attended Borgue Grammar School, Haddon Hall in Dumfries, and King's College, London. Although his intention was to train for the ICS, he went to Vancouver Island in 1860 in the service of James Anderson & Co., a London firm of shipowners and ship-brokers whose agent at Victoria, *Captain Edward Stamp, had advised them to build a sawmill on the Island for exporting ship-spars and other timber. GS took with him the necessary equipment on two armed vessels, the *Woodpecker* and the *Meg Merrilies*, which reached Victoria in April 1860. When Stamp resigned in 1862, GS took his place as local manager for Anderson & Co. and later that year, on 23 December, married Catherine Anne Wigham. He established an importing, commission, and insurance business in Victoria and employed, among others, *R. P. Rithet. In the years 1860-1866, GS was active in public affairs and succeeded Stamp as a JP and a magistrate for the West Coast district, and on a visit to England in 1865, he organized a "London Committee for watching the affairs of British Columbia," which had the support of *Captain G. H. Richards, RN. Among the committee members were *Donald Fraser and *A. T. Dallas, who agreed with GS in trying to defend Vancouver Island and its free port of Victoria against the damaging effects of joining it with the unstable and much less developed colony of British Columbia. Although the Island was attached to BC in 1866, this committee did much to establish the new provincial capital at Victoria and a permanent agent general in London. In 1871, GS became the first agent general, though as chairman of the London Committee since 1865, he simply went on doing the same work under a new name. His task was to advertise the province, attract suitable settlers, encourage British investments, and generally promote BC's interests in the British Isles. He was a cultivated man, did his best to assist the Pacific Coast tribes, and wrote anthropological studies of them, including *Scenes and studies of savage life* (1868), translated some of Horace's *Odes*, wrote a book about *The Education of the Rural Poor in England*, gathered material for another book, *The Rise of British Dominion in the North Pacific*, and in 1875-1877 was the Victoria correspondent of *The Times* (London). When he died on 4 June 1913, he was living in the James Bay District near the Methodist Church. Sproat Lake, near the head of Alberni Inlet, was named after him.

Sources: Hamar Foster, "Sproat, Gilbert Malcolm, businessman, government agent," *DCB* online; T. A. Rickard, "Gilbert Malcolm Sproat," *British Colonial History Quarterly*, (January 1937), pp. 21-32; J. M. S. Careless, "The Business Community in the Early Development of Victoria, British Columbia," in *Canadian Business History: Selected Studies*, 1497-1971, ed., David S. Macmillan (Toronto, McClelland & Stewart, 1972), pp. 104-123, see pp. 110-111.

SPURGIN, Major Karl Branwhite (1877-1936). He was born on 17 April 1877 in Maryport, Cumberland, son of Emma Spurgin, from York, and her husband Dr William H. Spurgin, who was a practicing physician born in Northampton. The 1881 census found them living at 20 Curzon Street, Crosscanonby near Maryport. KS, then aged three, had a younger brother, Basil Edward Spurgin, aged two, and a sister Ruby Spurgin aged one, and there were two domestic servants. A decade later, the census recorded KS as a scholar aged thirteen at Grosvenor House, a school on Warwick Square, Rickergate, Carlisle, Cumberland, headed by a forty-three-year-old Anglo-Irish schoolmaster, Robert J. Baillie. KS became an architect but soon joined the Northumberland Yeomanry and served through the South African War and, on returning, published *On Active Service with the Northumberland and Durham Yeomanry, under Lord Methuen, South Africa 1900-1901 . . . with an Introduction by Major Savile Clayton* (Walter Scott Publishing Co., 1902, 323 pp.). In 1911, he went out to Victoria and joined H. S. Griffiths in an architectural practice, but also joined a militia unit. On 1 July 1914, the *Daily Colonist* showed a photograph of him on horseback. During the Great War, he went overseas in 1916 as second in command of the 103rd Battalion CEF ("Timber Wolves") but, like many others, transferred to Imperial Forces soon after arriving in England. When the war ended, he was in the army of occupation and did not return to Victoria until 1919.

Resuming then his practice in an office at 1848 Fern Street, he joined the BC Institute of Architects and designed many large buildings in and near Victoria: the drill hall and office building for the Dominion Naval Department at Esquimalt, the Prince of Wales Fairbridge Farm School near Duncan, Brentwood College at Brentwood Bay north of Victoria, St Margaret's Girls School in Duncan, and Margaret Jenkins School in the Gonzales District of Victoria. He was associate architect for a new wing of the Jubilee Hospital and for Oak Bay High School. In June 1921, he took part in an inspection of cadets at St Michael's School, along with *General Noel Money and Captain St Clair; in July 1922, he was again at the school supervising the drill competition and giving out prizes. In 1930 he made a professional inspection of the school building and (as a grateful but alarmed headmaster put it)—"decided that the School itself was falling down and must have new bearers underneath. Apparently we had dry rot under the school." During the hard years of the depression in the early 1930s, KS was member of a deputation to the provincial government to ask that any public building being planned ought to be shared among the architects and building trades in general. Meanwhile, he was active in war veterans' circles, joined the United Service Institution of VI, and served a term as president of the 103rd Battalion Association. Among his friends were *Major and Mrs A. R. Layard of Rainbow Beach, Salt Spring Island, whom he and his wife visited occasionally. On 14 June 1934, he presided over a reunion of some fifty veterans of the 103rd "Timber Wolves" Battalion from the Great War at which the speaker was *Major B. H. T. Drake. KS had been present at the relief of

Mafeking and, on 28 February 1936, told some of his reminiscences to the British Campaigners' Association in Victoria at their annual banquet in Speedie's Café to commemorate the battle of Paardeberg (18-27 February 1900). He was also active at St Matthias Anglican Church on Foul Bay Road not far from his home at 3455 Richmond Road, joined in the Oxford Group Movement of the time, and in 1936 went to Western Ontario in that cause. He was an expert horseman and associated with the Victoria Riding Academy.

His first wife, Janet Coote Spurgin (c. 1880-1927), died in Victoria on 1 March 1927 and almost two years later, on 27 December 1928, he married Ann Isobel Paterson (c. 1893-1980). She lived for many years after his death, aged fifty-nine, on 27 November 1936, as did his two sons and a daughter. He was also survived by his mother, two brothers, and a sister in England. At his funeral at St Matthias Church, a piper played "The Flowers of the Forest" and the pallbearers included *Major B. H. Tyrwhitt-Drake, *Captain F. G. Dexter, *Lieutenant Charles Napier Milligan and members of the Oxford Group. KS was buried at Royal Oak and on 20 November 1937, some sixty surviving members of the 103rd Battalion paid tribute to his memory as the second in command who had led them overseas in 1916. In 1937, too, his daughter Joan Spurgin, who had been employed as a secretary at St Margaret's School, which she had attended as a girl, married Dr E. C. Curran in England. They lived at Oak Gates in Shropshire until Curran died of a heart attack in April 1941, leaving her with a small son. Her brother, KS's son Eric Spurgin, had married Margaret D. Hervey, daughter of Brigadier General C. L. Hervey, on 27 December 1934 in Toronto and settled at Noranda, Quebec.
Sources: *Colonist*, 1 July 1914, p. 9; 8 July 1934, p. 5; 14 July 1934, p. 3; 15 July 1934, p. 5; 8 August 1934, p. 4; 12 August 1934, p. 10; 28 December 1934, p. 8; 1 March 1936, p. 5; 28 November 1936, pp. 1 and 8; 1 December 1936, p. 3; 21 November 1937, p. 3; 27 April 1941, p. 3; census 1861, England, RG 9/803, p. 22; census 1881, RG 11/5180, p. 32; census 1891, RG 12/4289, p. 36; K. B. Spurgin, *On Active Service with the Northumberland and Durham Yeomanry, under Lord Methuen, South Africa* 1900-1901 . . . with an Introduction by Major Savile Clayton (Walter Scott Publ. Co., 1902, 323 pp.; Kyrle C. Symons, *That Amazing Institution: The Story of St Michael's School, Victoria, B.C., from 1910-1948* (Victoria, Privately Printed, 1948?), p. 54.

STAMP, Captain Edward (1814-1872). He was born on 5 November 1814 at Alnwick, Northumberland, went to sea as a young man, and qualified as a ship's captain in 1851. His first visit to the north-west Pacific Coast in 1857 was to pick up timber for Australia, and he returned later to buy shipbuilding materials for the London firms of Thomas Bilbe & Co. and James Thomson & Co. In 1858, as the first gold rush in BC was beginning, he set up a commission and importing business in Victoria and bought land on the Island. One of the Island's early entrepreneurs, he was always ready for a new venture, tried and failed to win a contract for a shipping service between Victoria and San Francisco, but succeeded in interesting James Thomson & Co. (which soon became Anderson, Anderson & Co.) in establishing a lumber mill on the Island. Governor James Douglas arranged for a grant of two thousand acres on Alberni Inlet (then called Alberni Canal), where the mill was duly built in May 1861. It was not a great success, but by the time this became apparent, ES had moved on to mining and prospecting and then, while in England in 1865, formed a new timber company: the British Columbia and Vancouver Island Spar, Lumber, and Saw Mill Company, which brought in machinery from Glasgow to cut and mill timber on Burrard Inlet where Vancouver City now stands. ES had trouble with this enterprise also and in the 1860s established a ship-chandlery in Victoria and put up an office building there. In 1867-1868, he sat in the Legislative Council of BC for the Lillooet District but was most interested in his various business ventures, which came to include fish packing. While in England seeking support for a salmon canning business, he died in November 1871. Surviving him were his wife, Maria, four sons, and a daughter. Stamp Falls Provincial Park, the Stamp River, and Stamp Harbour on Alberni Inlet were named after him.

Sources: W. Kaye Lamb, "Stamp, Edward," in the DCB, online; Walbran, *B.C. Coast Names*, p. 469.

STEER, Lieutenant Charles Pearson (1882-1917). He was born on 26 January 1882 in Hampstead, London, where the 1891 census recorded him, aged nine, at 27 Fairfax Road with his family. His father, Charles Steer, was a builder and decorator, aged fifty-three, born in Hampstead and his mother, Sarah Elizabeth Steer, aged forty-three, was born at Cromer, Hertfordshire. He had three sisters and a brother. There were no servants. CS enlisted in the Thirty-fourth Middlesex, Yeomanry, and gave twelve years of service, including two or three years in the South African War in which he was wounded. He then went to Canada, where he spent one and a half years in the North-West Mounted Police. When on 16 November 1914 he took a commission as a lieutenant in the Second Canadian Mounted Rifles, he had become a land surveyor on Vancouver Island and joined a militia unit. Still unmarried, he cited as his next of kin his mother, Mrs Steer, 16 Cortleigh Road, West Hampstead, London. He went overseas with his unit early in 1915 and was killed in France, aged thirty-four, on 22 May 1917.

Sources: NAC, CEF files, box 9261-41; census 1891, England, RG 12/113, p. 13; *Colonist*, 22 June 1917, p. 5, obit.

STEPHENS, Surgeon Commander Harold Frederick Dale (1861-1936). He was born on 11 May 1861 at Dunsford, Devonshire, elder son of Dr E. B. Stephens, attended Sherborne School, and qualified as a medical doctor at the universities of Edinburgh and Cambridge. He then served in the Royal Navy for twenty-three years, including several years in charge of HM hospital ship *Maine* presented by American sympathizers. He was aboard HMS *Camperdown* at the time of its tragic collision with HMS *Victoria*.

In 1889, HS married Miss Agnes Grace Cripps, daughter of General L. M. Cripps of the Bengal Staff Corps, India, and when he retired in 1907, they went to the Island, where they settled on a farm in Glenora, a district in the Cowichan

Valley. There he was soon named to the board of directors of the King's Daughters' Hospital at Duncan and became a Justice of the Peace. Seven years later, the Great War broke out and HS joined the RCN, which stationed him at Halifax, Nova Scotia. While he was away, Mrs Stephens died, aged fifty-nine, on 3 February 1917 and HS gave up farming in the post-war years. By 1930, when on 6 March their daughter Grace Mary "Bobbie" Stephens (1893-1930) died at Los Angeles, he was living at 2431 Currie Road, Oak Bay, Victoria. His son Harold Godfrey Stephens died, aged twenty-seven, on 2 March 1927 in Vancouver. HS himself was bedridden for eleven years following a paralytic stroke and died in Duncan, aged seventy-five, on 25 October 1936. Friends and neighbours held his funeral at St Peter's Quamichan. He was survived by his brother, Dr Cecil Stephens of Cheltenham, and his son Rupert Stephens.

Before his death, HS lived for five years with Rupert, who had attended Duncan's first high school, taken over the farm at the age of sixteen, and spent the years of the Great War with the 48th and 129th Battalions, from which he had retired as a lieutenant. For some years after the war, Rupert worked on the farm with his brother Godfrey Stephens, and later on a farm at Little River, Comox. In 1938, Rupert found that using sawdust as a mulch made farming easier, and this idea attracted attention in *The B.C. Farmer.* He then went on to grow a special species of strawberries, which he named Goldstream, and sold successfully. Then he began to write and produce musical shows in Duncan, and in 1953 his song, *The Jacaranda Tree* had some success on Canadian radio as sung by Pat Berry of Victoria. H. E. Bates, author of the novel, *The Jacaranda Tree,* liked it. Having written some seventy-five songs by 1956, Rupert was planning to give up farming and try his hand at making a living writing songs, with the assistance of his wife Gwen as a pianist and envoy. She had made several trips to Hollywood and had sold *The Lord Looks after His Own* to London Records in England.
Sources: *Cowichan Leader,* 29 October 1936, obit.; *Colonist,* 7 March 1930, p. 18, obit.; 16 December 1956, *Sunday Magazine,* p. 3; *Whitaker's,* p. 491.

STEPHENSON, David (1858-1937). Born in England on 8 December 1858, he spent much of his childhood in Missouri, USA, but returned to London, where he served for a time in the Metropolitan Police Force before migrating to the Island and joining the Provincial Police Force. He became chief of police in Nanaimo and served for many years and in some notorious cases until his retirement in 1918. He had married Mary Randall of Nanaimo on 12 August 1880 and they had three children. Well known because of his work and his entertaining lectures on it, he died at last, aged seventy-eight, on 3 February 1937 in a Vancouver hospital and his wife, aged seventy-eight, on 15 November that year at their home at Departure Bay near Nanaimo.

DS seems to have been either the son of David, a west-end London tailor, and his wife Jane, or of Solomon, a modest Lincolnshire landowner, and his wife Mary.
Sources: Howay and Gosnell, *British Columbia,* vol. III, pp. 912-915 and photo; *Colonist,* 4 February 1937, p. 6, obit.; *Nanaimo Free Press,* 3 Feb 1937.

STERN, Major Percival Theodore (1880-1945). He was born on 19 September 1880 in Liverpool, son of Lizette Stern, a Londoner, and her husband David Stern, a Liverpool "Commission Agent." The 1881 census found him there, aged seven months, at 50 Huskisson Street, with his parents as well as a brother Hyam Stern aged three, a young sister Dove M. Stern, and a visitor, Abraham Marks, aged forty-one, born in Russia. There were two servants. Ten years later, they were much the same but living at 15 Linnet Lane, Toxteth Park, Liverpool; the father was a "General Merchant" and there were four sons—Sidney, Albert, Hyam, and Percy—and three servants. PS joined the Imperial Army and fought in South Africa (1899-1901) and in the Zulu Rebellion (1906).

Two years later he went out to Victoria. There he married Bessie Keene (c. 1895-1945) on 29 July 1913 and joined the Fifth Regiment. When he joined the CEF on 21 December 1914, he had had soldiering experience in five units, but cited no dates: the West Middlesex Rifles, the Royal Fusiliers, the Imperial Yeomanry, the Transvaal Light Infantry, and the Natal Rangers. There are two enlistment forms on file, one naming his wife as Mrs Bessie Stern, living at Cobble Hill, BC, the other putting her at an address in Montreal. On the first, he calls himself a farmer and on the second a civil engineer. He was an Anglican, 5' 8" tall, with a dark complexion, brown eyes, and black hair. Upon returning from overseas in the Great War, he began farming near Duncan. Several years later, he opened the Wilmot Place Hotel at Cobble Hill. This seems to have failed or perhaps he sold it, but he returned to Victoria, where he was appointed secretary of the Canadian Manufacturers' Association and so remained until his death. He joined the Union Club and the Pacific Club. In the Second World War, he volunteered and served with the Fifth BC Coast Reserve until 1941, when he was forced by ill health to retire. He died, aged sixty-four, on 19 January 1945 in Victoria, leaving a sister and two brothers in London. Mrs Stern died, aged forty-nine, three months later on 26 April.
Sources: *Colonist*, 20 January 1945, pp. 13 and 24, obit.; *Cowichan Leader*, 17 August 1916, Honour Role; census 1881, England, RG 11/3626, p. 55; census 1891, RG 12/2940, p. 33; NAC, RG 150, CEF files, box 9280-56.

STOKER, Lieutenant Colonel Dr Richard Nugent (1851-1931). Born on 31 October 1851 in Dublin, one of the six children of Abraham Stoker, who was employed in the Chief Secretary's Office at Dublin Castle, RS attended Trinity College, Dublin, qualified as a physician, joined the Indian Medical Service, and took part in the second Afghan War (1878-1881), the Sikkim Expedition (1888), and the Chitral Relief Force (1895). In 1893, he and his wife Susan (1850-1936) passed through Duncan and Cowichan on their way home to England on leave, and the memory of these places made them return to Canada in 1898 when he retired from the army. The 1901 census for the Cowichan Valley recorded him there as a "Surgeon" with a Chinese servant and a Chinese labourer. Like so many British officers, he had used his time and opportunities well and become a knowledgeable amateur zoologist as well as a botanist.

Much of his time had been spent with Gurkha Regiments in the Himalayas, where he had made a hobby of collecting botanical specimens. Now he explored the wild country at the head of Lake Cowichan and brought back plant specimens which his wife added to the remarkable garden they developed near Duncan. They painted pictures of it in watercolours and it became famous, attracting visiting botanists from various parts of the world. As well as Chinese labourers, they employed young people, such as Bruce Hutchison (1901-1992), known later as a journalist and writer who worked for the Stokers in 1916. Most years, RS and his wife spent only the summer months at Cowichan Lake and retreated each winter to their house in Quamichan. He died, aged seventy-eight, on June 1931 nearby at the King's Daughters' Hospital in Duncan, survived for another five years by his wife, who kept up the garden until her death, aged eighty-four, on 13 June 1936. They were both buried at St Peter's Quamichan. The praise their deaths provoked among their neighbours was not merely perfunctory: "Dr Stoker possessed among his other loving qualities that unusual gift of not making one feel overwhelmed by his unvarying thoughtfulness, in fact almost reversing things, as if it were you yourself who were conferring the favor by the receiving of his care. Childless, but at the same time a great child lover, many of the younger generation can testify to never leaving without succulent fare from the house or garden, or having been personally shown his wonderful collection of obsolete Tibetan firearms or his numerous trophies shot on the highest and most inaccessible Himalayan peaks, where he used to wander in search of the rarest flowers for his wife, who is known as a great authority both on Himalayan and B.C. wild flowers."

RS was also known as a younger brother of Bram Stoker (1847-1912), an Anglo-Irish civil servant and London writer who published eighteen books but won fame as the author of *Dracula* (1897). At least three of their brothers, notably Sir Willliam Thornley Stoker (born 1845) and Dr George Stoker (born 1955), became successful physicians practicing in Dublin and London.

Sources: The *Colonist*, 16 June 1931, p. 18, obit; 17 June 1931, p. 20; 18 June 1931, p. 6; 14 June 1936, p. 14; Lynne Bowen, *Those Lake People: Stories of Cowichan Lake* (Vancouver, Douglas & McIntyre, 1995, pp. 171-3; Paul Murray, *From the Shadow of `Dracula': A Life of Bram Stoker* (Cape, 2004), 340 pp., *passim.*

STOKER, Sergeant William D (?-1917). He was born at Cork, eldest son of Dan Sallford Stoker of Ardmore Cottage, Passage, Wick. He went, aged sixteen, to California to learn fruit growing but returned home after a couple of years and enlisted for military service in South Africa. After fighting through the South African ("Boer") War, he went out to India, where he was in the British Army for about three years. Next, his health failing, he went to Manitoba and settled at Virden, where he bought a farm in 1908 but sold it after a few years in order to go west to Kelowna and then, about 1913, to Courtenay on the Island. When the Great War began, he immediately went to enlist in his former regiment, the Royal Horse Artillery, and was killed in France on 9 March 1917, reportedly in "B" Battery, 312th Brigade, RFA. He was survived by his wife, Inez (Winter) Stoker, whom he had married in 1909,

and their two small children. "Mr Stoker was a generous, whole-souled fellow, and an enthusiastic sportsman. He was a member of the Orange Order."
Sources: *Colonist*, 20 April 1917, p. 4, obit.; NAC, Department of Veterans' Affairs, RFA, reg. no. 786387.

STOKES, William Henry (c. 1875-1937). Born in Simla, India, he was a son of Dr Whitely Stokes (1830-1909), an Irish scholar and barrister who went to Madras in 1862, joined the Bar there, and rose through the magistrature by a series of official appointments under Sir Arthur (later Lord) Hobhouse, this during Lord Lytton's administration. Whitely Stokes became president of the Indian Law Commission and chief adviser to the viceroy. After a distinguished career in India, Whitely Stokes retired to Cowes, Isle of Wight, where the census found him in 1901 living on the Esplanade with his wife, Elizabeth, a Londoner aged sixty-three, and four servants. There he died, aged seventy-nine, on 13 April 1909.

Meanwhile, WS and his brother Frank emigrated to Alberta and moved on to Victoria about 1900. WS was hired in 1905 as a draftsman in the Forestry Branch of the provincial government. He and his wife lived at 438 Dallas Road, Victoria. When he died, aged sixty-two, on 16 February 1937, he left a son, John A. Stokes living in England, and a daughter, Mrs C. H. Coull in Victoria. He also had brothers and sisters "overseas."
Sources: *Colonist*, 18 February 1937, p. 5, obit., and photo; *The Times* (London), 14 April 1909, p. 8, obit.; census 1901, England, RG 13/1018, p. 14.

STONE, Colonel William R. (1896-1970). Born in Toronto, son of Mr and Mrs W. T. Stone, he attended St Andrew's College, Toronto, and RMC, Kingston, Ontario, and served in the Great War with the Royal Canadian Horse Artillery and then the Royal Flying Corps (RFC). In the Second World War, he joined the Canadian Artillery and in 1945 retired to Victoria, where he lived for many years at the Union Club. He died, aged seventy-four, on 11 March 1970 in Saanich, leaving a wife Hilda in Halifax and "a wide circle of friends in Victoria and elsewhere."
Sources: *Colonist*, 12 March 1970, p. 44, obit.

STORRS, Admiral Antony Hubert Gleadow (1907-2002). He was born on 1 April 1907 at Overton, Wales, son of a doctor and his wife who took him as a baby with them to Rhodesia, where his father went to study the tse-tse fly, and AS's first language was Swahili. His mother died when he was five and his father when he was fourteen, and he was offered a choice by his guardian of articling for a bank in London or enrolling in a naval college. He returned to England to go to Weymouth College, then trained with the merchant navy in the training ship, HMS *Worcester*, sponsored by P&O, and left as chief cadet captain with two first-class extra certificates. He signed indentures with John Stewart & Co. to serve in the *William Mitchell* and sailed around the world on voyages, the longest of which lasted 150 days, while the crew did not see another ship for weeks. They amused themselves, when becalmed, by trying to capture albatrosses and other such games. The *William Mitchell* was one of the last British—owned sailing freighters to frequent the route between between America and Australia and one of the last three-masted sailing ships in the British commercial fleet. She was retired in 1927. In Australia, AS found a qualified examiner to pass him as a master mariner in sail, though he afterwards remembered hearing the advice, "Never command a sailing ship." When the *William Mitchell* was sold, AS rejoined P&O and served in various ships until the onset of the depression in the early 1930s. Then, in 1932, he joined the Chinese Maritime Customs and worked for them for eight years, in command of revenue cutters patrolling Chinese waters to catch smugglers of opium and other contraband. He was stationed at Foo Chow when the Japanese invaded.

AS and his wife Joy, whom he married in 1940 at Shanghai, set off on foot from Foo Chow. After a long walk, they reached a sampan, slept in a junk for several nights, and succeeded in finding a blockade runner to take them to Shanghai, whence another ship took them across the Pacific Ocean to Victoria, British Columbia, where they arrived in November 1940. There AS joined the Royal Canadian Naval Reserve and began by taking command of the trawler, *Armentières,* at Esquimalt. He was next appointed to the destroyer, *Gatineau,* and after the USA went to war with Japan, he commanded the corvette, HMCS *Dawson,* which proceeded to Dutch Harbour, Alaska, as part of an operation with the U.S. Navy on convoy duty between Dutch Harbour and Adak in the Aleutians. This tour of duty lasted for twenty harrowing months. In September 1943, he was moved to the Atlantic Coast and appointed commanding officer of HMCS *Drumheller,* assigned to protect convoys at a critical stage of the Battle of the Atlantic. He began sweeping the English Channel in HMCS *Caraquet* and was affectionately remembered by Frank Curry, who served under him. They faced repeated U-boat attacks for long periods, and AS subsequently led a crucial minesweeping operation, as leader of the Thirty-first Mine Sweeping Flotilla, a Canadian naval unit, in advance of the allied invasion at Omaha Beach in Normandy on 6 June 1944. He told his son Andrew later that he had not expected to survive but, as Andrew recalled, "He was willing to take risks but he always weighed the odds carefully, and whatever he did, he researched it very well. He always made sure he was well prepared." British authorities awarded him the Distinguished Service Cross and he also received the Legion of Merit (USA), and the Légion d'Honneur and the *Croix de Guerre avec palmes* (France).

At the end of the war, AS took command of the frigate, *Antigonish,* then the *Nootka,* and was next given shore jobs, ending up at naval headquarters as director of naval plans and operations. In 1954, his career took a new direction when he was appointed commanding officer of the air station at Dartmouth, Nova Scotia, where he was soon offered the command of the aircraft carrier, HMCS *Magnificent,* the biggest ship in the RCN. He had begun to take flying lessons in a Gypsy Moth while in Shanghai and now began again in a Piper Cub fitted with floats. He commanded the naval air station at Clearwater, Nova Scotia. But Naval Headquarters in Ottawa refused to authorise him to be trained, like other Canadian flyers, by the U.S. Navy. His last naval appointment was as commandant of the National Defence College at Kingston, Ontario, and he was the first naval reserve officer to reach admiral's rank in the RCN. After retiring from the navy in 1962, he became director of marine operations for the Department of Transport, established the Coast Guard School in Sydney, Nova Scotia, and directed the Canadian Coast Guard. He it was who began using hovercraft as Coast Guard vessels in Vancouver. In the late 1960s, as director of the Canadian Coast Guard, he escorted the American icebreaking oil tanker *Manhattan* through a controversial voyage across the Canadian Arctic. On an official trip to Russia, he inspected the Soviet fleet of icebreakers, including a prized nuclear-powered icebreaker, the *Lenin*. After he retired from government service in 1972, he was hired by P. S. Ross & Co., an Ottawa firm, to head a team of thirty-five officers to work as consultants in setting up a Coast Guard service for the government of Iran. He travelled regularly between Ottawa and Teheran for some time, but the project was scrapped shortly before the revolution in which the Shah fell from power in 1979. AS spent his retirement mainly on the Saanich Peninsula at a house with a big garden on five acres of land near Heal's Range and Butchart's Gardens, a few miles north of Victoria. He spent much time clearing out bush and improving the garden and was busy with photography, a hobby he had taken up in China, whence he had sent hundreds of photos by mail back to England in a large packet, which disappeared and was never found. A friend from the Chinese Maritime Customs, George Hall, who retired to the Island with AS, recalled seeing Storrs on the bridge of a ship photographing the Japanese as they were strafing the town with machine guns by airplane; everyone else was taking shelter. AS had not been long on the Island before he was on the board of the Maritime Museum in Victoria, the board of governors of the British Columbia Corps of Commissionaires, and active in the Naval Officers' Association of Canada and other organizations. The Storrs had been friends of *Sir Frederick Maze (1874-1959) and his wife, who had signed their marriage register in Shanghai, but they cannot have spent much time together in Victoria, where Maze retired in 1948 and died in 1959. When AS himself died, aged ninety-five, on 9 August 2002, a naval vessel scattered his ashes out at sea. He was survived by his wife Joy and two sons, Andrew in Ottawa and Robin in Milan. He also left a stepbrother, Adrian Storrs, in England.

Sources: Interview and notes courtesy of Andrew Storrs, a son; telephone conversation and letter courtesy of Mrs Joy Storrs; interview with Captain C. P. Nixon; *Daily Telegraph* (London), 19 September 2002, obit.; *Colonist*, 25 February 1945, p. 3; *Globe & Mail* (Toronto), 24 September 2002, obit; the Halifax Herald, 19 March 1945, p. 3; Frank Curry, *War at Sea: A Canadian Seaman on the North Atlantic* (Toronto, Lugus Productions, 1990), 147 pp., *passim*.

STORY, Rear Admiral William Oswald (1859-1938). Born on 10 April 1859 at Bingfield, County Cavan, Ireland, he entered the Navy in January 1872 by way of the training ship *Britannia* before he was thirteen. As a midshipman of the *Modeste*, he took part in operations in the Malay Peninsula during the Perak Expedition (1875-1876) and was awarded the Perak medal and clasp. In the Egyptian War of 1882, he was sub-lieutenant of the screw gunboat *Mosquito* and was specially promoted to lieutenant for gallantry on that occasion. Then he was put aboard the sloop *Dryad* as a lieutenant during campaigns of 1884 in the Eastern Sudan, and for this, he added the Suakin clasp to the Egyptian medal he had won two years earlier. He was promoted to commander in 1896 and to captain in 1902, commanded various ships, including the battleships *London* and *Canopus*, and in April 1909 was appointed to command the Eastern Coastgoard District, which extended from Dover to St Abb's Head on the Berwickshire coast. He had commanded *inter alia* HMS *Hearty, Narcisus, Grafton, Cumberland, Canopus,* and *London*.

WS retired to Guelph, Ontario, in October 1911 with the rank of rear admiral and various decorations, including the French Legion of Honour and the Spanish Order of Merit, but he remained a loyal son of the empire and, when the Great War broke out, offered his services. On 29 October 1914, Ottawa appointed him admiral superintendent at Esquimalt and senior naval officer on the Pacific Coast. In January 1918, he was transferred to Halifax Dockyard as admiral superintendent and served there until the establishment was demobilized in May 1919. His services during the war brought him the CBE and the Japanese Order of the Rising Sun, second class. He was promoted to vice admiral in April 1917 and full admiral on the retired list in October 1918. As might be expected, his interest in the navy did not stop at retirement and he joined the executive committee of the Navy League of Canada, Ontario division. He died, aged sixty-nine, on 14 January 1938 in Montreal.

Sources: *The Times* (London), 15 January 1938, p. 12, obit.; *MacFarlane*, p. 59; Roger Sarty, *The Maritime Defence of Canada* (Toronto, Canadian Institute of Strategic Studies, 1998), p. 65; *Colonist*, 8 May 1917, p. 11.

STREET, Lieutenant Frederick (c. 1865-1912). Born at Monemein, Burma, he was sent home to England and in 1871, aged six, was living in Long Street, Williton, Somerset, with an elderly solicitor and his family. Ten years later, aged sixteen, he was boarding at "Edgeborough," a small school in Stoke, Guildford, kept by John H. Robson, an Anglican clergyman "without cure of souls," and his family. FS took a commission in the Queen's Own Royal West Kent Regiment and served around the empire. What he did, or where, from the time he left the army is not clear, but he became well known as a landscape gardener and a fellow of the Royal Horticultural Society. Arriving in Victoria about 1909 or 1910, he was put in charge of landscaping the Uplands development, north of Oak Bay. When he died, aged fifty-eight, on 9 November 1912 in Victoria, he left a wife and two daughters. *Colonel E. A. P. Hobday and his two sons were prominent pallbearers at the funeral.

Sources: Notes of Leona Taylor, Victoria; census 1871, England, RG 10/2352, p. 29; census 1881, RG 11/777, p. 23; *Colonist,* 10 November 1912; *Army List,* May 1891, p. 462.

SUTHERLAND, Colonel Arthur Orr (1879-?). His long visits to relatives in 1926 and 1935 illustrate an aspect of Imperial life on the Island. Born in India at Calcutta on 21 December 1879, he was a son of Arthur B. Sutherland (born in Burma c. 1846) and Louisa F. Sutherland, *née* Orr (born at Lucknow, India, c. 1851), and in 1891, the census-taker found him, aged eleven, living with his family in Bedford at "Asia Holm" or "The Homestead" in the parish of St Peter.

The youngest of his three brothers, Herbert Orr Sutherland, aged eleven months, was born there but Robert Orr Sutherland, aged nine, and Douglas G. Sutherland, aged thirteen, were born in Calcutta, as were their sisters, Marion Orr Sutherland, seven, and Louisa Orr Sutherland, five. They had four domestic servants. This household was much the same in 1901, except that there were five servants and Douglas, aged twenty-three, was employed as an "Insurance Agent." AS was at the RMC at Sandhurst when the Second South African War broke out in 1898, was sent to fight as an ensign, and was awarded bars to his Queen's and King's medals for Transvaal, Orange Free State, and Cape Colony. He joined the Indian Army and was commissioned in the Twenty-second Punjabis on 20 January 1900, promoted to captain on 20 January 1909, and held a prisoner for three years by Turkish forces after serving in Mesopotamia in 1915. He was decorated later with the DSO for keeping up the morale of his battalion on the terrible death-march of prisoners from Kut-al-Amara to Kastamun in Turkey. On being released, he returned to India for service on the North-West Frontier with his regiment, the Twenty-second Punjabis, and won the Frontier Medal with clasps for Waziristan, 1919-1921, and Waziristan, 1921-1924.

Shortly before the war, on 29 April 1914 at St John's Church in Calcutta, he had married Dorothy Isobel Palmer, daughter of *C. G. Palmer, who retired with his family to the Island, where they settled in the Cowichan Valley at "Stoneypatch." Dorothy was born in India but recorded in 1901, aged fourteen, boarding at Ashleigh College, Mortlake, Surrey. AS and Dorothy planned to retire to his parents' place in Bedford, and while on leave there in 1924, they had a daughter, Isobel Mary. Back in India, two years later, this little family sailed from Hong Kong on the "Empress" passenger liner, *Empress of Australia*, arriving in Victoria harbour on 5 May 1926. They spent the summer at "Stoneypatch," Palmer's house, and reached Liverpool on 24 September aboard the CPR liner *Montrose*, giving their destination as 2 Oaklands Road, Bedford. In 1935, they made a similar visit to "Stoneypatch," this time renting *Dr R. N. Stoker's house in Duncan, the Stokers spending their usual summer at Cowichan Lake. AS never resided permanently on the Island, and during the Second World War, he served as an ARP Warden in Bedford. aboard HMCS *Caraquet*. His long visits to relatives in 1926 and 1935 illustrate an aspect of Imperial life on the Island.

Sources: Letter and documents courtesy of John Palmer, son of *J. H. G. Palmer; census 1891, England, RG 12/1248, p. 13; census 1901, RG 13/1488, p. 9; census 1901, RG 13/678, p. 2 (Dorothy Isobel Palmer); *Indian Army List*, 1/1/1912, p. 133; Ronald Millar, *Death of an Army: The Siege of Kut*, 1915-1916 (Boston, Houghton Mifflin Company, 1970), p. 294; Canadian Passenger Lists, 1865-1935, T-14884; UK Incoming Passenger Lists, 1878-1900, no. 145919.

SUTHERLAND, Captain John Angus (c. 1875-1936. Born at Lossiemouth, Scotland, he joined the Royal Engineers as a young man and served in Egypt and Mesopotamia. When he retired, he moved to Victoria about 1913 and was for many years the chief engineer of the Pacific Coast lighthouse tender, CGS *Estevan*, a Canadian Marine and Fisheries vessel. While living in Aberdeen at

5 Urquhart Street in 1903, he had married Helen Buchan (1874-?) on 14 July. She was a spinster living there at 21 Roslin Terrace with her mother, widow of John Sutherland, a journeyman; they married at the Cromby Hotel, parish of St Nicholas, Aberdeen, in the Presbyterian Church. When he enlisted in Victoria on 16 February 1917, leaving his wife there at 16 Mount Douglas Apartments, he was apparently responding to an appeal for qualified boatmen to serve in the Imperial Water Transport section of the Royal Engineers. He was sent to Cairo, Egypt, and then in September 1918 posted to a camp in Winchester, promoted to captain, and kept busy until demobilized at last on 25 February 1920. Almost as soon as he rejoined Helen, he applied for a British War Gratuity, giving his address as c/o Marine and Fisheries Dep't, Victoria, BC. In Victoria, he was a member of the United Church, a Freemason, and a member of the Canadian Legion. When he died, aged sixty-one, on 3 December 1936, he left his wife at home, then at October Mansions, Cook Street, Victoria, with instructions to send his ashes to be buried in Scotland. It seems probable that she complied and eventually died in Scotland herself.

Sources: NAC, RG 9 series II-F-10 (British War Gratuities): Vol. 253, file no. 17666-J-140; *Colonist*, 5 December 1936, p. 5, obit.

SUTTON, Major-General Francis A "One-Arm" (1884-1944). He was born on 14 February 1884 at Widford, Essex, son of Francis Richard Sutton and his wife Edith L. Sutton, and the census of 1891 found him, aged seven, living with them, two sisters, and an elder brother at "The Cannons," Brandon Road, Thetford in north-west Suffolk. There were seven servants—governess, cook, lady's maid, nurse, parlourmaid, kitchenmaid, and housemaid—and the immediate neighbours, apparently attached to the estate, were a gardener and his family on one side and a "warrener" and family on the other. FS's father was a brewer, born at "Wiseton Hall," Nottinghamshire, second son of Robert Sutton, landowner and "clergyman of the Church of England without cure of souls," and his mother was born at Wandsworth, Surrey. The 1871 census found the landowning clerical grandfather living with his wife Charlotte, three sons (including FS's father, aged eighteen), four daughters, and ten servants at "The Hall" Scanby, Lincolnshire, and as his wife Charlotte was the only Lincoln-born member of the family, perhaps the estate came from her side of the family. Whether funds were supplied by these grandparents or by his brewer father, FS was sent to Eton and University College, London, where he became a railway engineer.

In 1904-1909, he was in Argentina engaged in railway construction and contracting; in 1909-1910, he was in Mexico working for the Mexican Eagle Oil Company recently launched by Weetman D. Pearson, a public-works contractor recently created Viscount Cowdray (1856-1927); in 1910-1914, FS was himself a contracting engineer in railway and bridge work in Argentina. He fought as an officer in the Royal Engineers throughout the Great War and lost an arm at Gallipoli. In 1917, while he was recovering and learning to manage with one arm, the British government sent him to the United States to supervise and instruct in the use of Stokes trench mortars and other weapons on which he became an expert.

Released from the army in 1919, FS went to Siberia to transport and erect the first modern gold dredge in the remote Amur Province. Then he moved to Szchwen on the Upper Yangtze River to construct an arsenal for General Yang-sen (1921-1922), but spent the next five years assisting a northern Chinese warlord, Marshal Chang-tso-lin [alias Zhang Zuolin] (1875-1928), at Mukden, Manchuria. Warlords had been struggling to win control of China since the collapse of the Qing dynasty in 1911. Chang-tso-lin, known abroad as "the Christian general," made FS director general of the arsenal at Mukden, where he reorganized the artillery and supervised the manufacture and use of the Stokes trench mortar. This portable weapon, ideal at that time for guerrilla warfare, was invented in 1915 by Sir Frederick Wilfrid Scott Stokes (1860-1927), KBE, an engineer and inventor from Liverpool who had become the managing director of a mechanical engineering firm, Ransome & Rapier of Ipswich. FS describes in his memoirs, *One-Arm Sutton*, how he went abroad and procured this weapon in quantity for Chang-tso-lin's army. Gavan McCormack (p. 121ff) gives details of how FS employed Japanese, Swedish, Danish, German, and Russian technicians, purchased materials from Denmark, Japan, the United States, Germany, and Italy, and, to keep the smuggling of arms secret, organized a smuggling service "via ports in Shantung, transport from there being arranged in a fleet of five-masted trading junks." In these and other ways, FS assisted in the occupation of Pekin and the defeat of Wu-pei-fu (1874-1939), a rival and the dominant warlord of north-central China during the early 1920s. FS remained with Chang-tso-lin [alias Zhang Zuolin] for eight years at $75,000 a year. He was one of only three Englishmen who held the rank of general in Chinese armies, the other two being the celebrated Charles George "Chinese" Gordon of Khartoum (1833-1885) and Morris Abraham Cohen (alias "Two-Gun Cohen") (1889-1970), a Jewish soldier from a Polish refugee family in Stepney, London, employed by Sun-yat Sen and Chiang Kai-shek.

In 1927, FS suddenly turned up in the city of Vancouver, apparently disposing of almost unlimited funds of his own and Chang-tso-lin's, and created a sensation by making a series of investments and talking of even greater things to follow. He was reputed to have paid $1,200,000 for a big Vancouver office block, $80,000 for a house in Point Grey, spent another $15,000 on alterations, and "as side issues," local newspapers reported, "he has acquired interests in fur farms, a bond investment house, a contracting company, and is said to be negotiating for part ownership of a newspaper." The *Daily Colonist* announced on 8 October that he had just bought Portland Island, near the Saanich Peninsula, from Thomas E. Westerton for $40,000 cash, though it turned out later that he had taken over Westerton's mortgage held by the Clovelly Company Ltd. of Victoria. On the 480 acres of Portland Island, of which 160 had been cleared, there was an eleven-room house "fitted with every convenience, including electric lights, radio and a modern water plant." He planted plum and apple trees, built barns, stables for racing horses, and pens for raising pheasants, and took parties of visitors from Victoria and Vancouver there for weekends. His recreations were shooting, fishing, and golf; he was a member of the Peking Club (Peking) and the Tientsin Club (Tientsin); and he was proposing to spend Christmas with his mother at the ancestral home in

Lincolnshire. Where his wife, Carina Descou Chester of Bedford, was at this time is not clear. They married in 1910 and had two daughters, as shown in a photo in his memoirs, *One Arm Sutton* (Toronto, 1933, p. 7).

Like most people, FS had troubles. Soon after buying a thirty-eight-foot yacht, *Tulameen*, for use at his Portland Island estate, he wrecked her on a rock at the entrance to his cove and sold her to Brownie and Nellie Horth "for a penny." Nellie was a friend of my mother and well known in Sidney as the local telephone operator. She and her husband spent summer weekends in 1930-1931 making *Tulameen* seaworthy. Meanwhile, having bought an aircraft originally intended for Major Pedro Zanni, the Argentinian aviator whose round-the-world flight in 1924 ended with a crash in South America, and having learnt about the Americans and other foreigners settling in the Peace River region, FS declared that the British empire needed to take command of the Peace River and spent $50,000 (according to reports) airing this problem in public. In October 1927, he went to see the Peace River for himself, travelling by car, railway, canoe, motorboat, and pack-train, was reported lost and then found in the woods somewhere near Hudson Hope. He eventually decided to take over and extend the Pacific Great Eastern Railway (PGE), which then ran from Squamish, near Vancouver, to Quesnel in the Cariboo country (from nowhere to nowhere, we used to say). Unfortunately, nobody would invest the $45 millions he reckoned would be needed, owing to the opposition of Sir Donald Mann of Sir William Mackenzie's group in Canadian railway construction. Resourceful as ever, FS went to England with a staff of railway and immigration experts and lectured and wrote on the subject of Canada's Last Great West, this to such purpose that a group of British businessmen became interested developing the Peace River region.

What all this might have led to will never be known because FS's great fortune collapsed shortly after the death of his warlord patron, Chang-tso-lin, who died on 3 June 1928, when Japanese forces blew up a train in which he was returning to Mukden. The financial crash in 1929 finished off FS as a Pacific Coast capitalist, and he was last seen sailing out of Vancouver harbour late in November 1932 with two cargoes of coffins to sell to the Chinese government. He was intending to take up mining there again and did, indeed, take up mining in Korea in 1933-1938. Meanwhile, in January 1934, the Clovelly Company secured legal consent to begin foreclosing the mortgage on Portland Island, on which FS owed something over $15,000, and on 1 September, a court in Victoria ordered the island to be sold in order to satisfy Clovelly's investors. Efforts to reach FS had resulted only in telegrams from Korea and rumours of his activities in the Orient. News eventually emerged that Japanese forces invading Korea and China captured him and interned him in a prison camp at Hong Kong, where he was reported to have been tortured and to have died on 22 October 1944.

Sources: Charles Drage, *General of Fortune: The Biography of One-Arm Sutton* (Heinemann, 1963; repr. White Lion Publishing, 1973), 265 pp.; Graham Hutchings, *Modern China: A Companion to a Rising Power* (Penguin, 2001), pp. 136, 248, 279, 317, 319, 460; Gavan McCormack, *Chang Tso-lin [died 3 June 1928] in Northeast China, 1911-1928* (Stanford UP, 1977), using inter alia Chinese sources, pp. 107ff., 122; Robert Bickers, *Britain in China: Community, Culture and Colonialism*, 1900-49 (Manchester UP, 1999), pp. 118, 121, 151; *Colonist*, 2 October 1925, p. 3; 8 October 1927, p. 1; 16 October 1927, p. 1; 4 December 1927, p. 27; 30 August 1931, p. 7; 10 January 1934; 2 September, 1934, p. 3; *Victoria Daily Times*, 15 October 1927, p. 1; *Vancouver Province*, 16 October 1927, p. 1; *Vancouver Province*, 20 November 1932, p. 1; *British National Archives* (PRO, Kew), census, 1891, England, RG 12/1577, p. 17; census, 1901, England, RG 13/1342, p. 36; census 1871, England, RG 10/3427, p. 1; Nellie Horth, *North Saanich, Memories and Pioneers* (Sidney, Porthole Press Ltd., 1988), pp. 56-7; Major General F. A. Sutton, *One-Arm Sutton* (Toronto, Macmillan, 1933), 277 pp.

SWAN, Sir Conrad Marshall John Fosher (1924-?), [CVO, 1986]. He was born on 13 May 1924, younger son of the late Dr Henry Peter Swan, who served during the Great War as a major in the RAMC and RCAMC of BC. CS himself joined the Indian Army in 1943 and became a captain in the Madras Regiment. In 1957, he married Lady Hilda Swan, *née* Mary Northcote (died 1995), She was the great-granddaughter of Sir Stafford Northcote, Eighth Baronet and First Earl of Iddlesleigh who, as governor of the Hudson's Bay Company, arranged for the transfer of Rupert's Land (which was still over 50 percent of the Canadian land mass) to the then-new Dominion government in 1870. When I met CS in London at the British Library in 2005, he was living at a farm in Suffolk, which he called Boxford House, Suffolk, CO10 5JT (Telephone: (01797) 210208. Then in retirement, he was tending a huge, splendid *curriculum vitæ*. He took me to lunch at a neighbouring pizza parlour and talked affably for an hour without answering my questions about the Cowichan Valley, perhaps because he was then writing his autobiography about his early life there.

By deed poll dated 20 December 1919, CS's father, Henry Peter Swan (1892-1963), changed his name to Swan from the Polish-Lithuanian Święciki. The father was born in Vancouver son of Paul Constantine Święciki (1850-1929), whose mother, Isabella Paulina Besierkierska (1848-1895), widow of Julian Constantine Andrew wi ciki, had taken her five sons and two daughters and fled from Pasusvys (Lithuania) to British Columbia in 1884 with enough money in gold roubles from the family estate "to buy a farm for each of the sons and a dowry for the two daughters" (Swan, p. 62). They were escaping from Russian tyranny and settled near New Westminster, then the principal town in continental BC, and there Paul Constantine (CS's grandfather) married "Sylveria of the distinguished and historic Lithuanian family of Dowgia_" (Swan, p. 63). Their son, Henry Peter Swan (1892-1963), CS's father, was born in Vancouver City only a few years after it was founded in 1886, became a medical doctor, and set up his practice on the Island at Duncan. He joined the army in the Great War, using the name "Swancesky," went overseas, and at Folkestone married Edna Hanson Magdelen Green (1899-1988) on 8 September 1917. She was daughter of what the 1901 census describes as a "tailor & outfitter, shopkeeper" at Tring, Hertfordshire, not far from Harrow School, and granddaughter of John Green, a humble "plait maker," all of whom CS explains candidly in his autobiography.

CS went to school first at Queen Margaret's in Duncan, then at the Duncan Grammar School for the gentry of the Cowichan Valley run by Mr R. E. Honour, an English schoolmaster from Tring, Hertfordshire, where CS's mother's family had lived for at least two generations. Honour was assisted by *R. G. L. Parker and other Englishmen. In 1937, CS was taken by his parents to visit his mother's relatives in England and sent to school there at St George's College, Woburn Park, Weybridge in Surrey, a Roman Catholic school not far from Windsor Castle and run by the Congregation of St Joseph. It was through a connection with the recruiting office of the Indian Army in London that CS enlisted in November 1943 in the Queen's Royal Regiment and then, with thirty-one other recruits, took a course in Urdu and other suitable subjects in London at SOAS by arrangement with the India Office. On 29 March 1944, they were dispatched to India on SS *Otranto* of the Orient Line and a month later reached Bombay, whence he was sent to Bangalore. Being Roman Catholic, CS was continually in the company of other Catholics, mostly English recusants, wherever he went in the empire. In November 1944, he was promoted to second lieutenant in the Madras Regiment and trained at Saugor as an instructor in small arms.

The Indian Army Recruiting Board in London "naturally had questions to ask, and these led to my telling them of the good number of retired Indian Army Officers and members of the I.C.S. in Cowichan, along with the lumbering community of Sikhs . . . all of which much interested them" (Swan, p. 104). After the Second World War, he read philosophy at Assumption College, University of Windsor, Ontario (BA, 1949; MA, 1951) and in time was able to obtain employment in the College of Arms and finally as Garter Principal King of Arms, by Letters Patent dated 10 December 1962, an office originally established in 1485 by Henry VII. The College of Arms studies, checks, and validates noble genealogies and coats of arms in an office block on Queen Victoria Street in the city of London. This post offered CS an ideal environment in which to compile his own family's history, which he duly did. He wrote a scholarly autobiography, a model of its kind, with wit and learning. It and he will inevitably appear to many as supremely vain and snobbish, but it must be admitted that he has worked out the Imperial context of his early life in the Cowichan Valley and written an interesting explanation of it. **Sources:** University of Windsor (Ontario) website; Conrad Swan, *A King from Canada* (Stanhope, Weardale, County Durham, The Memoir Club, 2005), 334 pp., passim; census 1881, England, RG 11/1448, p. 24 (Green); census 1891, RG 12/1127, p. 8 (Green); census 1901, RG 13/1209, p. 32 (Green); NAC, CEF files, box 9452-62 (Swancesky).

SWETTENHAM, Lady Mary Emily (1875-1953). Wife of Sir James Alexander Swettenham (1846-1933), she shared his life as governor of Jamaica in 1905-1933 and after his death in 1833 went to Victoria, where she stayed for months at the Empress Hotel before moving to a place in Colwood. On 20 April 1943, she spoke about the history of Jamaica at the home of Colonel and Mrs J. K. Cornwell in aid of the Oak Bay Unit of the Red Cross Society. The chairman of the occasion was *Sir Robert Holland, and it was *Lieutenant Colonel R. S. Worsley who made a formal thanks. Typical of her kind, she was immensely public-spirited and on 29 August 1943 acted as formal hostess at a picnic to welcome men from French and French-Canadian forces, for whom she made frequent charitable efforts, being also an active member of the French Canadian Club. She died, aged seventy-seven, on 27 January 1953 in Victoria, and her valuable collection of papers and other records was eventually presented by the BC Provincial Archives to the Commonwealth Library at Cambridge University.

Born Mary Emily Copeland at Oulton near Stone in Staffordshire, she was a granddaughter of William Taylor Copeland (1797-1868), lord mayor of London, and a daughter of Richard Pirie Copeland (1841-1913), and of his wife Emily Henrietta Wood. In the 1871 census, she appears, aged five, living at Kibbleston Hall, Oulton, with her young sister, Harriette Fairfax Copeland, aged one, and six domestic servants, their parents being absent. The relevant page in the 1891 census being badly smudged, the first and last satisfactory census of the family, in 1901, shows her, aged twenty-five, with her father, "Manufacturer of China," aged fifty-nine, born at Leighton, Essex, and her mother, aged fifty-three, born a British subject in Germany. The family had a partnership with the Spode family in bone chinaware. She had two brothers then, William F. M. Copeland, aged twenty-nine and already in the China business with his father, and Alfred C. Copeland, aged eleven. They had eight domestic servants, including a "hospital nurse," and next door on the estate lived a coachman and family. On 26 August 1905, MS married Sir James Alexander Swettenham (1846-1933), who had already been receiver general in Cyprus, colonial secretary in Ceylon, governor of British Guiana (1901-1904). He is much less famous than his younger brother, Sir Frank Athelstane Swettenham (1850-1946), author of books on travel and an influential governor of the Straits Settlements. Sir James also suffered from the misfortune or misjudgement of a famous quarrel with a visiting American officer in 1907 and resigned the governorship of Jamaica in consequence. But he and MS had done much good in Jamaica and had survived an earthquake that destroyed Government House at Kingston early in the century.

Sources: *Colonist*, 6 April 1907, p. 7; 11 April 1943, p. 7; 21 April 1943, p. 8; 8 June 1943, p. 6; 26 August 1943, p. 6, with photo; census 1851, England, HO 107/2144/1 (Swettenham); census 1871, RG 10/2823, p. 12 (Edward Capper Copeland); census 1891, RG 12/2143, pp. 7-8 (Richard Pirrie Copeland); census 1901, RG 13/2575, p. 13; Thomas Norris Ince (1799-1860), parish records of Wirksworth, Derbyshire, transcribed by John Palmer of Wirksworth; *Wikipedia online encyclopedia*, (Richard Ronald John Copeland); Cambridge University Library: Royal Commonwealth Society Library, Lady Swettenham Collection (Malaya and Jamaica) presented by the BC Provincial Archives, Victoria; http://janus. Lib.cam.ac.uk/ db/node. xsp?search=swettenham (no spaces).

SYKES, Edward Ernest (c. 1877-1950). He was born at Haselor, Warwickshire, son of Rev. John Heath Sykes, a parson from Devon who in April 1881 was a widower, rector of Billesley, and vicar of Haselor, with nine children. ES was educated at Malvern and Warwick. He went into shipping and marine insurance, lived in Malaya

for nearly ten years, and travelled extensively in India and Burma. He served in the South African War 1900-1901 (Queen's Medal and four clasps) and then became a director of Dale & Co. Ltd., Marine Underwriters, but retired in May 1945 and settled at Ganges on Salt Spring Island. In 1910, he had married Rosalind Edith Clements, daughter of Engineer Commander Clements, RN, and they had a son and a daughter. Declaring himself a Protestant, he was a member of the Capilano Golf & Country Club and enjoyed fishing, shooting, and golf. Residence: Ganges, Salt Spring Island. Mrs Sykes died, aged sixty-nine, on 5 November 1949, and he died six months later, aged seventy-three, on 3 May 1950 in Ganges.
Sources: *Who's Who in B.C.*, 7th ed. (1947-1948), p. 204; census 1881, England, RG 11/3106, p. 2.

SYMONS, Kyrle Charles (c. 1882-1965). Born at Saidpore [Sarpors?], Bengal, he lived in India until 1885, when his father died, and his mother Margaret took him and his sister home to England. There he appears, aged nine, in 1891 with his sister and their mother in a lodging house kept by a Walter Newman at 23 Beacondale Road, St Mary, Lambeth, London. Mrs Symons was a "teacher of music" born in India at Agra. In 1901, the census-taker found KS, aged nineteen, boarding as an "undergraduate student" at 3 Abernathy Villas, Synton, North-West Devon. He had been attending Dulwich College in south-east London, a school founded in 1619 as Alleyns's College and renewed as Dulwich College by special act of Parliament in 1857. KS married Edith Annie Lovelock at Hungerford in 1908, and they immediately emigrated to Victoria, where he spent a year or two teaching school on Salt Spring Island.

In 1910, they moved to 2176 Windsor Road, Oak Bay, Victoria, and he founded St Michael's School for Boys, which had a good deal of support in the city. He became a member of the Kipling Society, founded in Victoria in September 1933, and served for several years as president of the Royal Society of St George. But their life turned largely around the school, which he supervised and directed until 1946, as his privately published history of it shows. When he died, aged eighty-three, on 19 November 1965, the pallbearers at his funeral held at St Mary's Anglican Church in Oak Bay were Hamish Bridgman, whose father, Montague Bridgman, was the first pupil at the school; *Captain J. B. Prentice; Kenneth Barnes; J. W. M. Barber-Starkey; Dr A. E. Gillespie; and John Nation. Mrs Symons had died in Oak Bay, aged sixty-one, on 29 November 1942. They were survived by two sons. The school began to admit girls in 1977 and eventually amalgamated with University College School in the Shelbourne Street district.
Sources: *Colonist*, 20 November 1965, p. 26; 24 November 1965, p. 9, obit.; census 1891, England, RG 12/419, p. 38; census 1901, RG 13/2146, p. 26; St Michael's School website; Kyrle C. Symons, *That Amazing Institution: The Story of St Michael's School, Victoria, B.C., from 1910-1948* (Victoria, Privately Printed, 1948?), p. 165 and passim; Jan Piggott, *Dulwich College: A History, 1616-2008* (Dulwich College, 2009), 305 pp.; ttp://www.gov.saanich.bc.ca/visitor/pdfs/ Heritage %20Register/ Shelbourne.pdf (no spaces).

Lt.—Col. John Talbot

TALBOT, Lieutenant Colonel John (1868-1932). He retired from the Indian Army, about 1920, to Vancouver Island, where he and his family settled at "Halewood" in Glenora, southwest of Duncan, a property of about 160 acres, which they bought from an English settler, Marris Hale. There must have been trips home to England; immigration authorities recorded the arrival at the port of Victoria on 17 December 1934 of Dorothy Talbot, aged forty-nine, together with her two daughters, Althea, aged twenty-four, and Vivien, aged twenty-one. JT kept a cow, tried to farm in a small way, and joined the Cowichan Country Club as well as the Union Club of Victoria. Having been an enthusiastic polo player in India, he first arrived with a string of polo ponies and kept horses almost until his death. There is evidence of exemplary kindness and Christian duty on JT's part in discreetly caring for the daughter of parents who, while waving to her as she sailed for Victoria from Japan, died in an earthquake as she watched from the ship. He may have learnt of her predicament at Queen Margaret's Girls School in Duncan, which she attended as did JT's own daughters. JT died, aged sixty-four, on 13 April 1932 and was buried at St Peter's Quamichan, his coffin carried by pallbearers including *Colonel R. E. Roome, *Commander Hon. E. A. Gore-Langton, *Lieutenant Colonel C. E. Collard, and *Major G. C. Rigby. He was survived by his widow, Dorothy (Humphries) Talbot, who died on 16 July 1970, leaving two daughters, Mrs C. H. (Vivian) Marshall, and Lady Hugh Yates (Althea) Aylmer, wife of the Twelfth Baron Aylmer (1907-1982), Baron of Balrath, an Irish peer. Lady Althea Aylmer died, aged about ninety-two, in Victoria on 14 April 2002.

JT was born on 4 February 1868 in Singapore, son of a colonel in the Royal Horse Artillery, but the 1881 census recorded him, aged thirteen, living at 13 Ashburnham Road, Bedford, with two sisters, Ada Talbot, aged twenty-three, born in Kilbeggan, Ireland, and Ethel Talbot, aged seven, born in Bermuda. Other census data shows that his mother, Henrietta S. Talbot, born in Ireland c. 1837, was already in 1881 the widow of a British officer. Somehow, the family had means to send JT to the Royal Military College at Sandhurst as a Queens Cadet from 1 September 1886 to 15 July 1887. On 14 September 1887, he was commissioned as a second lieutenant in the Second Battalion of the Royal Munster Fusiliers, reached India on 3 January 1888, was appointed to the Indian Army with effect from 24 February 1890, and rose to become a captain in the Seventh Bombay Lancers and, on 14 September 1905, a major in the Thirty-seventh Lancers. Most of his service was in India or Upper Burma, but there were campaigns abroad and long furloughs in England: at Aden as Fourth Squadron Commander with the Seventh Bombay Lancers from 1 April to 18 November 1900 and from 1 December 1900 to 8 February 1901; in Arabia as Third Squadron Commander with the Thirty-seventh Lancers and on other errands; at Rajkot [Rajkol?] for several tours of duty; and home on leave from 15 October 1894 to 6 October 1895, from 3 December 1898 to 28 January 1900, from 14 May to 10 November 1904, from 7 July to 17 October 1907, and from 13 May 1909 to 13 February 1910.

His service by then totalled twenty-one years and 110 days and he had qualified meanwhile in Hindustani and Pushtu; his French was "good"; and he had passed his riding certificate at Sandhurst on 15 July 1887 and a cavalry certificate at Mhow

on 16 July 1890. He had also built up a considerable record of special service as
first-class cantonment magistrate at Jacobad (Upper Sind) from 18 August to
12 October 1898; CO of troops in Aden from 23 March to 10 December 1900;
commandant escort to HM the Sultan of Lahej during operations against Soubaihee
Arabs in the Aden Hinterland from 19 to 30 November 1900; commander of a
composite Regiment of Gwalior Indian Service Lancers for the Delhi Manoeuvres
and Durbar in 1902-1903; inspecting officer, Kathiawar Imperial Service Cavalry in
1902; and duty with Indian Troops during visit of the Prince and Princess of Wales
to Bombay. At one time, JT was seconded for service as military secretary to Sir
A. Hunter, GOC, the Southern Army in India. In 1912, he assumed command of
the Sixth Bengal Cavalry, went with them to France in the Indian Expeditionary
Force, and served continuously throughout the Great War, being mentioned in
despatches. He retired at last after thirty-two years of service.

On 6 November 1908, he had married Dorothy Humphries, and their first
daughter, Althea Talbot, was born on 6 December 1909 and baptized in Sussex at
Bexhill-on-Sea. Their second daughter, Vivian, was born in India, but Mrs Talbot's
address in England was sometimes given as c/o Henry S. King, 9 Pall Mall, London,
and JT was also in touch with a sister, Mrs Evan Cameron, and other relatives living
at Stroud, near Painswick in Gloucestershire. Whatever their attachments in the
British Isles, they did not deter JT and his family from retiring to the Island, as
explained above.

Sources: Private family collection, "Record of Officers' Services, Indian Army,"
for Major John Talbot, Thirty-seventh Lancers; notes courtesy of a daughter,
Lady Aylmer, and a granddaughter, Ann Miller, July 2001; census 1881, England,
RG 11/1623, p. 1; census 1881, RG 11/3892, p. 31; census 1891, RG 12/1049, p.
14; *London Gazette*, 14 September 1887, 19 March 1889, 28 May 1918; *Cowichan
Leader*, 21 April 1932, p. 5; *Colonist*, 14 April 1932, p. 15; 17 July 1970, p. 31, obit.;
Toronto Globe & Mail, 20 April 2002, p. S9; *Burke's Peerage & Baronetage*, 106th edn.
(1999), vol. I, p. 152.

TATLOW, Captain Robert Garnet (1855-1910). He was born at Scarva, Northern
Ireland, on 6 September 1855, attended Cheltenham College in Gloucestershire
and, still in his teens, went out to Montreal, where he was employed by the Montreal
Ocean Steamship Company. He moved later to a brokerage office but soon joined
the militia and in the First (Prince of Wales's) Regiment of Volunteer Rifles and rose
to become a captain attached to "B" Battery of the Garrison Artillery in 1878-1879.
On 13 August 1879, he arrived in Victoria on an inspection of coastal defences
and, deciding to stay there, transferred to the post of instructor to the local militia
and custodian of artillery stores. He fitted well into Victoria's Anglo-Irish élite
and in April 1880 became private secretary to the lieutenant governor. Six years
later, he moved to Vancouver during its early mushroom growth and went into
finance, mines, and railways, played a part in building Stanley Park, and in 1900
was elected to represent Vancouver in the provincial legislature.

On 4 June 1903, he was appointed minister of finance in a Conservative
government. This took him back to Victoria with his second wife, Elizabeth Cambie,

whom he had married in 1893, daughter of J. H. Cambie, a CPR engineer. During his six years as finance minister, RT succeeded in turning a provincial debt of $12 million into a surplus of $8 million, mainly by selling crown lands and forest rights and imposing a license fee on commercial travellers and agents who were not resident in British Columbia. He was minister of agriculture for a time during which he arranged with the Salvation Army to bring in one or two thousand British unskilled labourers and domestics to reduce the need for Asian workers to whom he was firmly opposed. Until his accidental death, aged fifty-four, on 11 April 1910 in Victoria, he was one of the successful Anglo-Irish Protestants among the many British capitalists in British Columbia before the Great War. He left an estate assessed at $125,000.

Sources: J. S. Lutz, "Tatlow, Robert Garnett, businessman, militia officer, office holder, and politician," in *DCB* online; R. E. Gosnell, *A History of British Columbia* (The Hill Binding Co., 1906), 783 pp. in 4o, pp. 365-6.

TAYLER [*sic*], Major William Fothergill Cooke (1868-1962). Born on 1 March 1868 in India, he was commissioned on 30 January 1889 in the East Surrey Regiment and appointed to the Indian Army on 24 July 1890. From 15 June 1897, he served in the Cantonment Magistrate's Department and in 1900 was listed with the Indian Staff Corps as a lieutenant in the First Punjab Cavalry, and a cantonment magistrate at Peshawar. By 1905, he was in Peshawar with the Twenty-first Cavalry and had passed an examination in Pushtu.

Having retired by 1910, he went out to the Island in that year and soon settled in a house at Brentwood Bay, a few miles north of Victoria. He kept a boat on Saanich Inlet and on fine days in the 1920s and 1930s often took parties of Boy Scouts and Brentwood College boys for cruises. *Captain C. P. Nixon recalled many such events during his boyhood and WT's kindness and generous meals, provided by a housekeeper, Mrs Evans, WT being a widower. He used to speak about the indigo business in India, in which he was active at one time, and about the sport of pig-sticking, of which he had fond memories. He wore a steel brace on one leg—result of a wound—which clicked when he stood up. Captain Nixon also recalled meeting him at the Piddington's house in Esquimalt. When WT died, aged ninety-three, on 19 January 1962 in Victoria, he left a daughter, Mrs Violet M. Knox, and a nephew, Colonel A. Grimley, who was visiting him in Victoria at the time. Archdeacon Nunns took his funeral in Victoria. Was WT a relative of William Tayler (1808-1892), an employee of the HEIC in an earlier generation?

Sources: Interview with Captain C. P. Nixon, Ottawa, 18 March 2002; NAC, CEF files, RG150, box 9511-29; BL, India Office, *Indian Army List,* January 1905, pp. 6, 13, 109, 701; *Whitaker's,* p. 507; *Colonist,* 21 January 1962, p. 22, obit.

TEAGUE, John (1833-1902). Born in June 1833 in Cornwall, England, he became a mining engineer either by formal education or practical experience and set out on 19 May 1856 to join an uncle in Costa Rica. Fighting in Central America induced him to join in the goldrush to California instead, and in 1858-1859, he left San Francisco for the Cariboo gold fields of British Columbia. Like many others, however, he was soon looking for opportunities in Victoria. He began with contracting and construction work for the Royal Navy at Esquimalt and in the middle 1860s was working as both architect and contractor out of an office in Trounce Alley, Victoria.

A Presbyterian and a Freemason, he may have had religious sympathies, which in 1874 brought him one of his first commissions: to build the Church of Our Lord for the rebellious Anglican *Dean Edward Cridge (also a Freemason) and his Reformed Episcopal congregation. JT soon became one of the town's leading architects and (writes Martin Segger), "set the tone for the city's commercial architecture from the late 1870s to the early 1890s." Among his buildings were the Turner, Beeton and Company warehouse (1882), St Ann's Academy (1886), Victoria City Hall (1878), the Masonic Temple (1878), the city's two main hospitals, and several hotels including the Oriental (1883-1888), the Driard (1892), the New England (1892), and the Burnes House (1899). He also designed many private houses, notably Hatley Park (1892) for the Dunsmuir family.

JT eventually became a storekeeper for the Royal Navy and the house he built for the Admiralty in Esquimalt (1885) at a cost of $12,000 became the admiral's house, later occupied by such figures as George Phillips, a British naval architect stationed there from 1905 to 1917, and *Commander Edward Atcherley Eckersall Nixon, ex-RN, while he was CO of the naval college in Esquimalt. In 1894-1895, JT served as mayor of Victoria. He had four children by his two wives, Emily Abington and, secondly, Eliza Lazenby, twin sister of Emma Lazenby, who married David Spencer after working as head of the Millinery Department in his well-known department store. JT died, aged sixty-seven, on 25 October 1902 in Victoria, leaving prominent descendants. Captain Frank William Teague (1883-1945) headed a company of the Boys' Brigade in Victoria at the time it was inspected by Governor General Lord Aberdeen and served overseas with Canadian forces during the Great War. In 1928, Dorothea Ursula Teague married *Major Police Commissioner F. W. Gerrard of the Indian and Shanghai Police forces.

Sources: Martin Segger, "John Teague, Contractor and Architect," *DCB*, vol. XIII, online; Martin Segger and Douglas Franklin, *Victoria, A Primer for Regional History in Architecture* (New York, A Pilgrim Guide to Historic Architecture, 1979), pp. 31, 40, 41, 59, 60, 67, 95, 185, 201, 206, 207-9, 223, esp. 347-8; Dana Humphreys, *Building Victoria, Men, Myths, and Mortar* (Surrey, BC, Heritage House, 2004), pp. 14, 30, 36, 56, 59, 61-2, 66, 68-9, 103; Robin Ward, *Victoria and Its Remarkable Buildings* (Madeira Park, BC, Harbour Publishing, 1996), pp. 33, 36-7, 108, 159, 186, 189, 197, 207-8, 289, 315, 335; S. W. Jackman, *Portraits of the Premiers: An Informal History of British Columbia* (Sidney, Gray's Publishing Ltd., 1969), p. 59; Harry Gregson, *A History of Victoria, 1842-1970* (Victoria, Victoria Observer Publishing Co., 1970), p. 151; NAC, RG 150, accession 1992-1993/166 box 9557-51; John Adams, *Ross Bay Cemetery* (revised ed., Victoria, Sono Nono Press, Heritage Architectural Guides, Victoria, 1998), p. 16; Betty Bell, *The Fair Land, Saanich* (Victoria, Sono Nono Press, 1982), p. 39 n. 19; Begg, *History of British Columbia*, p. 539.

TELFORD, Major Edward Miller (1871-1935). Born on 21 May 1871 in Ireland, he first joined the RNWM Police in Calgary in 1891, went to the Yukon Territory in 1895 with "B" Division, and served there for thirty-two years. On 1 October 1910, he was appointed inspector at a salary of $1,000, and from 1923 to 1927 served as officer commanding the division with the rank of major. Superannuated in 1927, he moved to Victoria, where he was active as a Freemason and lived with his wife, a daughter, and a son. When he died, aged sixty-three, on 22 January 1935, they were living at 953 Hampshire Road. *Colonel G. S. Worsley, president of the Victoria Division of the RNWM Police Veterans' Association, attended the service with Major G. B. Moffat, *Captain C. F. L. Money, *P. W. Rawson, and other veterans of the NWM Police.

Sources: *Civil Service List of Canada, 1911*, (Ottawa, 1911), p. 50; *Colonist*, 23 January 1935, p. 6, obit.; 26 January 1935, p. 6.

TEN BROEKE, Lieutenant Colonel Melville Rysdale (1891-1963). Born in July 1891 at Simla, Punjab, India, son of James Arnold Ten Broeke of the ICS, he attended Bishop Cotton School, Simla, and Bedford Modern School in England. Their ancestors had been Dutch. CT went out to Canada in 1910 to work as a surveyor and lived for many years mainly at Winnipeg. In 1914, he enlisted in the Twenty-third Battalion as a private, transferred to the PPCLI on 1 March 1915, and was commissioned on 18 June 1916. Promoted in 1918 to captain, then major, he commanded and inspired No. 2 Company, which captured four German officers and fourteen other ranks at Vimy Ridge. He was awarded the Military Cross. Still commanding No. 2 Company at Passchendaele and at Jigsaw Wood, he "fought his command forward with great skill" and won a bar to his Military Cross. He became Colonel Stewart's second in command and was invited to attend the marriage of HRH Princess Patricia on 27 February 1919 at Westminster, where he was in charge of a Royal Guard of Honour consisting of three officers and a hundred men. "The choice of Major Ten Broeke to command the Guard," writes a military historian, "was a particularly happy one. He had seen long service with the Regiment as an enlisted man; and as an officer he fought and led his company with conspicuous gallantry in every important action from the attack on Courcelette to the capture of Jigsaw Wood." Later, he became second in command of the PPCLI in the Permanent Force and served in 1927-1932 as lieutenant colonel in command of the regiment.

In 1931, he retired to 1143 Munro Street, Victoria, where joined the Union Club and enjoyed football, tennis, badminton, and squash. In 1920, he had married Marjorie Ellen Haslock Cook, daughter of W. H. Cook of Hertford, Hertfordshire. She died, aged forty-one, on 11 March 1936 and was buried at St Paul's Naval and Garrison Church in Esquimalt, leaving MT and her son by a previous marriage, Barrington Simeon Haslock. When MT died, aged seventy-one, on 3 May 1963 in Saanich, he had been living at 1510 Oakcrest Drive. He was survived by his stepson, a brother in Las Vegas, and a brother and sister in England.

Sources: *Who's Who in B.C.* 1933-1934, pp. 168-9; *Colonist*, 12 March 1936, p. 18; 14 May 1939, Sunday section, photo; 5 May 1963, p. 27, obit; The *Social Register of Canada* (1st ed., Montreal, 1958); Ralph Hodder-Williams, *Princess Patricia's*

Canadian Light Infantry, 1914-1919 (2 vols., London and Toronto, Hodder and Stoughton, 1923), vol. I, pp. 216, 221, 226, 242.

THACKER, Major General Herbert Cyril (1870-1953). He was born on 16 September 1879 in Poona, India, son of a Colonel John Thacker, Bombay Staff Corps, and his wife Emily, also born in India. When HT was only a few months old, she took him and his two brothers and four sisters "home" to England, where the 1871 census recorded them living in Cheltenham at 7 York Terrace, with a nurse and one servant. The father eventually retired as a major general and took the family out to settle in Canada. There HT was sent to Upper Canada College and, in 1887, to RMC, Kingston, Ontario, where he became company sergeant major in 1890 and graduated with a diploma in 1891. At first, he joined the Canadian Militia and did survey work for the CPR. Promoted to captain, he was one of the three gunner officers dispatched in 1898 to join the Yukon Field Force with a RCA detachment of forty-six gunners. In 1903, the RCA gave him a commission, and in 1899-1900, he served in the South African War in which he earned the Queen's Medal and three clasps. About 1904, he graduated from the British Army Gunnery Course at Shoeburyness and was attached in 1904-1905 to the Japanese army (billeted with the army of General Oku) with other foreign observers during the Russo-Japanese War, probably the last war to which foreign governments sent observers. The decision to send such a junior officer was made by Major General Lord Dundonald, then general officer commanding the Canadian Militia. HT witnessed the fighting in Manchuria, received the Japanese war medal and the Japanese Order of the Sacred Treasure, and returned to Ottawa via Victoria, where he arrived on 4 January 1905 aboard the *Empress of Japan*. His reports from that war were full, expert, and unique, but scarcely appreciated in Canada. They would have been simply filed away if *Lieutenant General Sir Percy Lake, then chief of the Canadian General Staff, had not insisted that HT be invited to speak about his experiences, which he did on 6 April 1907 to a mainly military audience at St George's Hall in Ottawa and again at RMC, Kingston, two days later. Half a century afterwards, Ottawa recognized its mistake and Colonel C. P. Stacey's Directorate of History prepared a report on the matter dated 8 September 1967. On returning in 1907 from Japan, HT had been appointed director of artillery in Ottawa and during the Great War, he served in France and Belgium as brigadier general with the First Canadian Division. He was mentioned seven times in despatches and decorated with the CB, CMG, and DSO. After the war, he was appointed DOC in Military District No. 6, at Halifax, NS, and in 1927 chief of the Canadian General Staff.

HT retired in 1929 and lived quietly in Victoria, where he died, aged eighty-two, on 2 June 1953, a resident of Lansdowne Avenue. He was buried at Royal Oak after a funeral at Christ Church Cathedral. He had kept up his membership of the East India Club and the Sports Club in London, where he occasionally made long visits, as, for instance, in the winter of 1933-1934.

Sources: *Who was Who*, 1951-1960, p. 1075; NAC, CEF files, box 9580-37; *As You Were! Ex-Cadets Remember*, ed., R. Guy C. Smith, No. 1877 (Ottawa; The RMC Club of Canada, 1884-1984, 1984), vol. I, 1876-1918, pp. 125-131; census 1871, England,

RG 10/2673, p. 40; NAC, reel T 6958, "Active Militia" etc., "*Officers with Service Prior to World War I*"; Directorate of History, Canadian Forces Headquarters, Report No. 14, 8 September 1967, 15 pp.; J. G. Armstrong, in *Canadian Defence Quarterly*, spring 1983; *Colonist*, 5 January 1905, p. 8; 15 November 1933, p. 8; 3 June 1953, p. 11, obit.

THACKER, Major General Percival Edward (1873-1945). Younger brother of *Herbert Cyril Thacker, he was born on 28 October 1873 at Bangor, Wales, son of Major General John Thacker, Bombay Staff Corps, and his wife Emily and spent his childhood partly in Canada. He was schooled at Upper Canada College and RMC, Kingston, Ontario, and joined the Canadian Permanent Force. His file in Ottawa offers an unusually full record of a military career, which is worth summarizing for its detail as an example: He became a lieutenant, RO (27 June 1894), lieutenant, Thirty-sixth Regiment (12 January 1895), lieutenant, Royal Canadian, RI (1 April 1895), brevet captain (1 April 1895), adjutant in the Yukon Field Force (1898-1900), and Second Regiment CMR in South Africa (1900-1902); operations in the Transvaal (30 November 1900 to 31 May 1902); operations in Cape Colony (30 November 1900 to 31 May 1902); transferred as captain, RCMR (1 October 1904); Fortress of Halifax (1906); entered staff college, Camberley (1907); graduated Staff College, Camberley (1908); major in Royal Canadian Mounted Rifles (5 March 1907); major, Lord Strathcona's Horse (1 October 1909); assistant adjutant general, Militia HQ in Ottawa (1 January 1909 to 1910); director of military training (1 January 1911 to 1912); lieutenant colonel (1 April 1912); attached central section, Imperial General Staff, War Office, London (1 April 1912 to 1914); appointed assistant adjutant and quartermaster general, Second Canadian Division (4 March 1915); signed the CEF "Attestation" form at Shorncliffe, England, on 28 June 1915; proceeded to France with the Second Canadian Division (14 September 1915); to be temporary colonel (17 September 1915); colonel, Canadian Militia (24 May 1916); transferred to England (12 December 1916); to be adjutant general, from assistant adjutant and quartermaster general and to be temporary brigadier general (5 December 1916); granted temporary substantive rank of brigadier general in OMF of C (5 December 1916); ceased to be adjutant general, Canadian forces in British Isles on appointment to adjutant general OMF of C (18 May 1918); to be adjutant general, overseas military forces of Canada (18 May 1918); to be temporary major general (31 July 1918); sailed for Canada (16 August 1919); SOS, OMF of C (30 September 1919); transferred to reserve of officers, at the rank of major general (1 August 1919); named Companion of the Most Distinguished Order of St Michael and St George (3 June 1916); mentioned in despatches (15 June 1916); appointed to the Most Honourable Order of the Bath (1 June 1917); adjutant general, Canadian Overseas Forces (1917-1919), struck off strength as adjutant general in the general demobilization (30 September 1919).

PT married (1) in 1912, Gladys Howland, whose address in June 1915 was c/o Cox & Co., Charing Cross Road, London SW; she died in 1919; (2) in 1920, Mabel Louise Gye (maid of honour to Queen Mary, 1911-1920), second daughter of Captain Herbert F. Gye, MVO, RN, and Hon. Mrs Gye of 5 Westbourne Gardens,

722   J.F. Bosher

Folkstone. The couple retired to Victoria, where they were living quietly in Oak
Bay when he died, aged seventy-two, on 3 July 1945. He, like his brother, had
kept up membership in London clubs. Mrs Thacker died, aged eighty-three, on
4 January 1966, still in Oak Bay.
Sources: *Who was Who*, 1941-1950:, p. 1141; NAC, RG150, box 9580-41; *London
Gazette* no. 29608, 3 June 1916; no. 30207, 27 July 1917; no. 29623, 15 June
1916.

THOMAS, Hugh Basil (1877-1958). He was born in Southgate (Middlesex),
London, one of the twelve children of a "mining engineer & share dealer," Alfred
Thomas, born c. 1845 in Clapham, London. The 1881 census recorded HT as a
boarder, aged three, together with two brothers and a sister (the youngest aged
one) in the household of one Louisa Carroll, an elderly widowed "annuitant" at
Upper Stranraer, Holdenhurst near Bournemouth. Ten years later, these three
children and a younger brother, Aubrey Thomas, were all "scholars" boarding at
a school in Cliftonville, Margate, Kent, kept in "Surrey House" by one Percival
Boger and his wife. Meanwhile, the other eight children (four sons and four
daughters) were all living with their widowed father at "Camden House,"
Chase Road, Edmonton, Southgate, Middlesex, where the 1891 census found
them. HT eventually joined the Seventy-second Company of Rough Riders and
served through the South African War, being taken prisoner three times and
having other adventures. After the war, he settled on a homestead near North
Battleford, Saskatchewan, and on 22 June 1906 married Gwendolyn Evelyn Davis
on her arrival from England. They were active in St Paul's Naval and Garrison
Church, and in 1917-1919, he served as mayor of North Battleford. Two of his
younger brothers, and perhaps other members of the family, were also living
at North Battleford, where they married and where one of them, Noel Gordon
Thomas (1884-1973), joined the 232nd Battery "C" on 10 June 1916. A year or
so later, this brother moved out to Royston on Vancouver Island and another
brother, Edwin Felix Thomas (1886-1952), also moved to the Island and settled
at Courtenay.
     Much later, in June 1936, HT and his wife, together with a son and daughter,
followed them out to the Island, where they took a house in Comox on Beaufort
Avenue on the old Robb Estate, which overlooks the Bay. Fond of fishing and
gardening and active in community work and as a lay leader at St Peter's Anglican
Church and community work, HT eventually died, aged eighty-one, on 28 July
1958 and was buried in Sandwick Municipal Cemetery. He was survived by his
wife, a brother at Royston, three brothers and two sisters in England, another
sister in Tasmania, a son Laurence Basil Thomas at Qualicum, and a daughter
Mrs Margaret J. Harrison in Ottawa.
Sources: *Comox District Free Press*, Wednesday July 30, 1958, p. 10; *Colonist*, 7 June
1936, p. 6; NAC, CEF files, box 9612-2 and 9604-17; census 1881, England, RG
11/1195, pp. 32-3; census 1891, RG 12/729, pp. 36-7; census 1891, RG 12/1084,
p. 13; census 1901, RG 13/1681, p. 22.

THOMSON, Alan Stuart "Spike" (1887-1984). He was born in Bristol, England, on 9 September 1887, third son and fourth child of William Thomson of Brook House, Water Lane, Brislington, Bristol. The census-taker found him, aged thirteen, at 338 Church Road, St George Parish, Bristol, living with his family. His father, then aged fifty-five, was a Scottish chemical engineer and his mother, Mary Ann, aged forty-six, was born at Spittal, Northumberland. His brothers and sisters, all born in Bristol, were George Thomson, twenty-three, "clerk commercial," Edith Thomson, twenty-two, and a brother Evelyn Thomson, sixteen. There were no servants. The neighbours were engineers, manufacturers, medical practitioners, etc.

In 1909, AT went out to Vancouver City, where he worked at first for Canada Westinghouse, but in 1911, he spent the summer on Moresby Island and then took a job on the Queen Charlotte Islands, surveying gold leases and the Shannon Timber limits for Frank D. Rice, a BC land surveyor. The east coast of Graham Island in the Queen Charlottes reminded him of England—sandy beaches, cattle grazing on the shoreline—and he was interested in Haida Indians there. After that, a temporary post with the BC Department of Lands (Survey Branch) occupied him for thirty-four years, and he spent the rest of his life so employed except for service overseas during the Great War and a few years of private practice in the 1920s. During the Great War, AT joined the Canadian Royal Engineers but was employed, in fact, by the Inland Waterways and Docks of the Royal Engineers. Army doctors reported that he was 5' 6" tall, with blue eyes, "slightly flat feet, and a deviated septum." He was discharged at Vancouver on 24 June 1918, listed as a surveyor's assistant, and intended to reside at 1740—34th Avenue East in South Vancouver. Apart from his service years, AT worked in 1913-1921 on the BC—Alberta Boundary Survey with *A. O. Wheeler, and much later when he heard in 1962 of a colleague being sent on a government survey party to Roger's Pass, AT lent him A. O. Wheeler's book about the Selkirk Range.

AT was a good friend of my own family. He met my mother, Grace Simister (1903-1999), at Banff or elsewhere in the Rocky Mountains during the 1920s, while she was employed as a stenographer by *A. O. Wheeler, president of the Alpine Club of Canada. AT married my mother's school friend in Sidney, Gladys May Bowcott, on 30 June 1928, a few weeks after my parents were married there on 13 April. When I was a child in Sidney during the 1930s, the Thomsons lived in a brown wooden house near the United Church on Fifth Street, less than half a mile from our place on Third Street, and had a son, Alan Stuart Thomson (junior), almost exactly my age. Mothers and sons, we visited back and forth almost daily but we saw less of the Thomsons when they moved to Cook Street in Victoria. Later, in spring 1948, after a year at Victoria College, BC, I needed a summer job and my mother suggested that I go to see whether her old friend, Spike Thomson, still employed at the Parliament Buildings in Victoria, might offer any advice. Mr Thomson, a quiet, dignified person, suggested that I apply to work as a surveyor's helper, which I did and was hired to assist a Mr Pollard on the Alaska Highway. We flew to Fort St John, took a pickup truck, and drove up to Muncho Lake and then to the Liard River, across from the hot springs (then entirely wild and isolated) where Mr Pollard was to survey the three-hundred-feet road bed of the Alaska Highway. This we did for the entire summer with a group of seven or eight other young men and a cook. There were wolves and bears in plenty, and the fishing was extraordinary. In nearby streams, a piece of coloured shirt tail on a hook would catch edible trout in minutes.

G. S. Andrews, surveyor general of BC in 1951-1968, wrote in his official report for 1952, "Noteworthy at this time is the retirement on superannuation of two staff members of long distinguished service . . . Alan S. Thomson, chief draughtsman, topographical division, retired after some seventeen years of official service, but with almost an equal length of prior service as a so-called temporary employee . . . Many topographical manuscript maps in the original hand of Spike Thomson bear permanent witness to his superlative skill in both the field and cartographic phases of topographic mapping." At the age of seventy-three, however, AT was brought out of retirement to do draughting for the BC—Yukon border survey. During his last many years, he spent much time reading books about BC's mountains, seas, and rivers. Colleagues remembered him, as we did, as a friendly, bright, happy individual. He died, aged ninety-six, on 22 May 1984 in Victoria. In June 1984, the Canadian Permanent Committee for Geographic Names officially commemorated him by naming "Thomson Lake," a small tarn in the Akanina Creed—Waterton Lakes National Park area of the Southern Rockies.

Sources: NAC, RG150, box 9621-47, regimental number 2024378; John A. Whittaker, *Early Land Surveyors of British Columbia* (P.L.S. Group) (Victoria, BC, The Corporation of Land Surveyors of the Province of BC, 1990), pp. 148, 152-53; John A. Whittaker, "Spike Thomson. He surveyed B.C.'s Borders," *The Islander/ Victoria Times-Colonist*, 9 September 1984, pp. 6-7; Margaret S. Belford, "Spike Thomson Remembers," *The Islander, Colonist*, 8 February 1970, pp. 4-5.

THOMPSON, John Lee (1914-2002). Born on 1 August 1914, son of an engineer, he attended Dover College in Kent and at seventeen became a playwright and a stage actor with the Nottingham Repertory Company, playing a part, for instance, in "Midshipman Easy," and having his play *Murder Happens?* performed in Croydon and another, "Double Error," briefly shown in the West End of London. He also took up boxing as a bantam weight. He found employment at Elstree Studios in London as editorial assistant and for five years wrote screenplays as a staff writer for Associated British Pictures. In 1939, he was dialogue coach for Alfred Hitchcock's film *Jamaica Inn*. JT served through the Second World War in the RAF as a tailgunner in a B-29 Superfortress. About 1950, he began to direct films and for the next forty years directed some fifty movies in England and the United States, the first being *Murder without Crime* (1950) and the last *Kinjinte* (1989). One of his best films was *North West Frontier* (1959), called *Flame over India* in the United States, showing a British officer of the Indian Army (Kenneth More) being cheerfully patient with a rude American woman (Lauren Bacall) he is busy saving from Muslim assaults. But his best-known film was *The Guns of Navarone* (1961), which made him famous, and it was then that he moved to the United States.

Having retired in 1989 from the film business, JT soon moved to Sooke on Vancouver Island, where he gardened and continued to write but wintered in Los Angeles. He died, aged eighty-eight, on 30 August 2000, leaving his third wife, Penney, and a daughter, Lesley, from his wartime marriage to Florence Bailey. His son, Peter Lee Thompson, who had worked as an editor on his father's films, had died earlier.
Sources: Steve Chibnall, *J. Lee Thompson* (Manchester University Press, 2000), 380 pp.; Tom Hawthorn, "Shot to Fame with Guns of Navarone," *Globe & Mail* (Toronto), 9 September 2002, p. R5, obit., with photo.

THOMPSON, Captain Livingston William Norman (1851-1904). He was born on 19 June 1851 at Kilquade House, County Wicklow, Ireland, attended the RMC at Sandhurst, and became an officer in the Eleventh Prince Albert's Own Hussars, rising to captain and adjutant. His brother was an officer in the same corps before him. LT served in India in 1873-1875, where at Umballa he met and married (in Simla in 1874) Edith Mary Gillies Tytler, born in Marylebone, London, on 27 June 1854, daughter of Harriet Christina Earle and her husband Colonel Robert Christopher Tytler (1817-1872) of the East India Company's Bengal Army.

About 1898, they retired to Victoria, where he became a land surveyor with an office in the McGregor Block, surveyed many local mining properties and timber limits, and worked for long periods up the Island at Clayoquot and elsewhere. He and Captain John Martin Sly (1880-?), a surveyor from Salisbury, England, surveyed the townsite of Crofton. In Victoria, LT was convivial and active in town life, became a member of the Loyal Orange Lodge, and took the part of the British consul, Sir Harry Preston, in a production of the play *Nan Toy* directed by Mrs H. D. Helmcken. In 1903, an old friend and army colleague, *Major J. F. Lennox Macfarlane arrived on the Island with his wife and settled on a large property at Mill Bay. LT managed to interest a group of American businessmen in building a railway from Port Renfrew across the mountains to Mill Bay to take iron ore out to their smelters in the USA, and they arranged to establish their depot at Mill Bay on Macfarlane's place. Construction was to begin in 1904 and to make final arrangements, LT set out on 8 January that year aboard SS *Clallam* for Port Townsend in Washington State to meet his business partners. She was owned by the Puget Sound Steamship Company, was not built for the open sea, and as the *Daily Colonist* reported next day, was "last seen scudding before the gale under jib towards San Juan." A lifeboat that was launched full of women and children immediately foundered, as did the vessel itself off Smith's Island. Captain Roberts and the first officer survived, were pulled out of the sea, and confirmed the surmise of the company's Victoria agent, E. E. Blackwood, that the engine had broken down, though it was widely believed that the *Clallam* was too top-heavy to remain upright in such a gale. Mrs Thompson identified and claimed LT's body but his funeral was managed by the Loyal Orange Order. He was buried in the Ross Bay Cemetery, "where in his full dress uniform of the 11th Hussars," Macfarlane recalled thirty years later, "we buried him with full military honours, the band of the fifth regiment giving their services free, the 5th Regiment also supplying the firing party." It may be that the Lieutenant Livingston

William Norman Thompson (c. 1879-?), an Irish officer retired from the Royal
Horse Artillery who married Annetta Matheson in Vancouver on 8 September
1909, was LT's son, though he was not mentioned at the time of LT's death, perhaps
because he was abroad at that time.
Sources: *Colonist*, 9 January 1904, p. 3; 10 January 1904, p. 1: "*Fifty-six Find Watery
Grave*"; 12 January 1904, p. 6; 15 April 1937, p. 4: Letter to the Editor by Major
J. Lenox *MacFarlane*, 416 Craigflower Road, "Iron Ore Deposits"; census 1871,
England, RG 10 /1296; census 1901, England, RG 13/613, p. 10; *Who's Who in
B.C.*, 1940-1941, p. 212; 1842-43 (Sly); Harriet Tytler. *An Englishwoman in India:
The Memoirs of Harriet Tytler* (1828-1858), ed., Anthony Sattin, Introd. by Philip
Mason (Oxford UP, 1986), p. 182.

   THORPE-DOUBBLE, Captain Thomas Leslie (1871-1942). Born on 4 April
1871 at Sevenoaks, Kent, sixth of the eleven children of Alfred Doubble, a
"Companies Agent," and his wife Emily living at "Stoneville Lands" in Sevenoaks,
but he and the rest of the family were living in 1881 at "Lingfield House," Longridge
Road, South Kensington with four servants. They were still there ten years later
by which time TT had become a midshipman in the Royal Navy (February 1887)
and had just passed out of the training ship *Britannia* as acting sub-lieutenant.
One of his younger brothers was then an engineering student. In March 1893,
TT was a lieutenant serving in East Africa and in 1900 he was in HMS *Black Prince*
at Queenstown. By 1901, his father had died and the family were living with
their widowed mother at Arnison Road, East Molesay, near Epsom in Surrey. On
25 October that year, TT was appointed to HMS *Amphion* as the first lieutenant
when she was commissioned at Devonport and dispatched to the Pacific Station
under Captain J. Casement, with Lieutenant J. D. D. Stewart (later to command
the *Rainbow*) as the navigating officer.
   TT had already visited the Pacific coast in July 1889 aboard HMS *Dreadnought*.
On arriving at Esquimalt in 1901, he was expected to assist in carrying out a
recruiting campaign all over Western Canada for building up the permanent
naval force and at the same time to secure the support of prominent men and
organizations in arousing public interest in the training of a Pacific Naval Force for
the defence of trade routes. While in Victoria, TT married Blanche B. Foster on 23
May 1903 at Christ Church Cathedral, and so the seed for an eventual retirement
on the Island was planted. In the intervening years, he served on the usual long
series of vessels, including HMS *Britannia, Superb, Sultan, Dreadnought*, and others,
a total of some thirty ships. He had moved about from station to station, was at
Malta in 1909, and was at one time invalided for diabetes, though he recovered
somewhat. His service record shows that he was judged to be "zealous" but "not
robust." He retired at last on 5 June 1920 with the rank of captain.
   TT and his wife settled in Oak Bay, Victoria, at 1712 Monteith Street in the
early 1920s and were soon active in the town's life, particularly its naval activities.
He joined with other Imperial officers in presenting a teak relic of HMS *Ganges* to
the Ganges chapter of the IODE on 17 June 1931 at Ganges, Salt Spring Island,
that town having been named after the ship. On 21 October 1931, he was one

of the speakers at the Trafalgar Day services and celebrations sponsored by the IODE, the Navy League, and the veterans' associations. In May 1937, he wrote to the *Daily Colonist* to protest at length about servicemen's pensions being unfairly taxed. Though he did not say so, his own naval pension at his retirement was £65; he recalled, "When I came out here to settle in 1922, there was appearing in the Old Country papers statements that Indian and Imperial pensions did not pay provincial income tax in B.C. This was observed until, I think, 1928 when the then-government went back on its word and made such pensions liable. Retired naval and military officers, and presumably all others enjoying such pensions, now pay Imperial income tax on their pensions and on all British investments at the rate of 5 shillings on the pound or 25 per cent." Federal income tax was levied on all foreign investments not liable to imperial taxation. "And what do we get for it? Now what do we get? The Provincial Government does practically nothing for Imperial defence for which the retired officers are taxed a large proportion of a quarter of their incomes, and the roads, Ye Gods! The roads!" TT thought highly of Victoria, however, and did not regret moving there. He took a practical and helpful interest in local theatricals. "It is no use arguing that Victoria is just a 'hick' town and can't appreciate what is good," he wrote to the *Colonist* on 9 June 1937, "for there is probably no place in the British Empire or outside of it that, for the size of its population, contains so many people of such wide and varied experiences as those on the south end of Vancouver Island." Closer to his heart, perhaps, were issues of regional and national defence. Like so many other Imperials, he was alert to the dangers of a Japanese invasion and appalled at the ignorant indifference of the Canadian government. *Major F. V. Longstaff relied on him for assistance in writing his history of the Esquimalt naval base and had much respect for him. TT died, aged seventy-one, on 5 March 1942 and his wife died more than twenty years later, aged eighty-seven, on 21 July 1962.

Sources: *National Archives* (PRO), London, ADM 196/43, p. 198; *Colonist*, 20 June 1931, p. 18; 21 October 1931, pp. 2-3; 9 May 1937, p. 4; 9 June 1937, p. 4; ADM 196/43, page 198; *Whitaker's*, p. 158; Longstaff, *Esquimalt Naval Base*, p. 67; census 1871, England, RG 10/922, p. 27; census 1881, RG 11/50, p. 27; census 1891, RG 12/34, p. 16; census 1891, RG 12/865, p. 23; census 1901, RG 13/670, p. 38.

THUILLIER, Lieutenant Colonel Henry Shakespear (1895-1982). He was born on 10 September 1895 at Murree, Punjab, founded during the 1850s in the foothills of the Himalayas to be the summer capital of the British Indian Army's Northern Command. He was a son of Major General Sir Henry Fleetwood Thuillier (1868-1953), KCB, CMG, and a grandson of Sir Henry Ravenshaw Thuillier (1838-1922), KCIE (1895), both also born in India. His great-grandfather, Sir Henry Edward Landor Thuillier (1813-1906), Kt. cr. (1879), CSI (1872), FRS, General Royal Artillery, was born on 10 July 1813 at Bath, Somerset, son of John Pierre Thuillier, Baron de Malapert, who had fled from France, attended the East India Company College at Addiscombe (1831-1832) and risen in the Survey of India from 1836 until he became surveyor general of India (1861-1878) and joint-author of a *Manual of Survey* for India. John Henry Rivett-Carnac (1839-1923) remembered meeting this surveyor general of India at Calcutta in 1858 and quoted his views on the cheating ways of Indian servants. HT's grandfather Sir Henry Ravenshaw Thuillier attended Wimbledon School and the Company College at Addiscombe and became a colonel in the Bengal Engineers (1857). In 1859, he too entered the Survey of India Department and served as surveyor general of India in 1886-1895. In 1867, he married Emmeline, third daughter of Fleetwood Williams of the ICS and they had two sons and two daughters. One of these sons, Henry Fleetwood Thuillier, appears in the 1901 census records as a captain in the Royal Engineers living at 2 Clarence Villas, Dovercourt, Essex, with his wife Helen (*née* Shakespear), whom he had married in India in 1894, and their two sons of whom the eldest was HT, then aged five. They were all born in India. There were three servants.

As a result of early life in India, HT spoke fluent Urdu, the language of the Indian Army at that time, and in England he attended the Dragon School, Dover College, and the Royal Military Academy at Woolwich, and was commissioned in the Royal Artillery in 1915. Promoted to captain (1917), major (1935), acting lieutenant colonel (1940), and lieutenant colonel (1942), he served during the Great War at Gallipoli (1915), which he remembered as "an operation bold in its conception but inadequate in its preparation and execution, where courageous but poorly trained raw troops were pitted against superior numbers of veteran Turkish troops fighting in their homeland." Returning to Egypt in December 1915, he was posted to the Twenty-sixth Jacobs Mountain Battery (Commander Major K. G. Campbell, DSO), camped at El Shatt on the east bank of the Suez Canal opposite Suez. In 1916, his unit was ordered to Mesopotamia, disembarked at Basra, and early in May marched through the desert to occupy Nasiriyah. There they built embankments to create two bridgeheads connected by a pontoon bridge over the Euphrates. Before long, however, they were moved to the Baghdad area, then eastwards up the Diyala River to Baqubah and Khanaqin, towards the Persian mountains. "The object," he wrote later, "was to join up with the Russian Czarist column [under General Barstov] which had advanced as far as the Pai Tak pass on the Kermanshah road and to guard against harassment by Kurdish tribesmen in the north." HT was then promoted to the rank of acting major to command a six-inch Howitzer horse-drawn battery taking part in the final operations on the Tigris, south of Mosul, the ancient Ninevah. The purpose by then, in autumn 1918, was to do as much damage as possible to the retreating Turkish forces. After the local armistice in October 1918, HT was sent back to Baghdad to raise a new Indian Mountain Battery needed for operations against the Kurdish tribesmen under Sheik Mahmud in the region of Sulamaniyah, east of Kirkuk. This became critical when the British political officer was imprisoned at Sulamaniyah in summer 1919. In the event, a troop of Indian Cavalry galloped to Sulamaniyah, surprised the guards, and rescued the political officer. "During the battle," HT wrote later, "a Gurkha soldier found a wounded Kurd by the roadside and was about to dispatch him when our C.O., Colonel Climo, seeing he was obviously a chief, stopped the Gurkha and took the Kurd to headquarters. Here it was discovered that he was the redoubtable Sheik Mahmud."

Early in 1920, HT was sent back to the base at Basra *en route* to England via Bombay. Near the end of 1922, he was ordered to return to India to serve as the first instructor in gunnery at the new artillery school at Kakul, near Abbottabad. On this assignment, he remained in India for four years, instructing at camps near Quetta, Lahore, Benares, and Bangalore and practicing firing six-inch Howitzers at Razmak Camp in Waziristan tribal territory. Among his papers are photographs of these events. In the years 1931-1934, he was adjutant of the Fourteenth Field Brigade, Royal Engineers, at Bangalore. When late in 1934 the army called for volunteers to help in raising and training a new Indian Field Artillery Brigade, he became one of the officers on that assignment. "I had long been convinced," he wrote later, "that the need to prepare the Indian nation for the granting of independence implied in the Proclamation by Queen Victoria when taking over from the East India Company in 1858, was urgent. I often spoke of my conviction that independence would be granted much sooner than most people realised . . ." During the Second World War, he served in France with the British Expeditionary Force (1939-1940), retreated with his unit across the Channel at Dunkirk on 2 June 1940, then served in the North African campaign in 1942-1943, and finally in the Italian Campaign in 1943-1945. In 1950, he was commissioned in the RCA as lieutenant colonel.

By the time he retired to Victoria in 1955, HT had been mentioned in despatches at least twice and named to the Distinguished Service Order. He had married Beatrice Winifred Walter, daughter of *Captain F. H. Walter, RN, who had settled at Ganges, Salt Spring Island, and they had two sons. In 1980 and no doubt earlier, his address was 2424 Beach Drive, Victoria, BC, a small house on the landward side of the street, but in the few years before his death, he lived at Apt. 403, then Apt. 404, 685 Niagara Street. He had a good friend in *Brigadier H. H. M. Oliver with whom he had gone through the Military College at Woolwich and who retired to Victoria at about the same time. There they lived permanently, except for the years of the Second World War in which HT joined the RCA and served through the war, as related above. He died, aged, on 25 March 1982.

Sources: Notes by Lieutenant Colonel H. S. Thuillier, 1970-1971, kindly sent by Mrs Elizabeth Conlon; *Who's Who*, 1982, p. 2206; *Who was Who*, 1897-1916, p. 708; *Who was Who* 1981-1990, p. 757; Riddick, *Who in British India*, p. 362 (forebears); census 1901, England, RG 13/1698, p. 29; census 1881, RG 11/843, p. 21; *National Archives* (PRO) GB/NNAF/P28432 and P28433, Thuillier papers; Riddick, *Who in British India*, p. 362 (forebears); John Henry Rivett-Carnac, (1839-1923), *Many Memories of Life in India, at Home and Abroad* (William Blackwood & Sons, 1910), 448 pp., pp. 30-2.

THURBURN, Thory Vincent (1860-1946). Born in March 1860 at Lucknow, Oude, India, he was a banker when he moved to Victoria about 1890, soon after the birth of his son, August Edward Charles Sedgwick Thurburn, on 12 February 1890 at Norwood, Surrey. In 1871, the census-taker found TT, aged eleven, living at "Linkwood," Croydon, England, with his family. He was the second son of Felix

Augustus Victor Thurburn, then aged forty-seven, born in Egypt, a lieutenant colonel retired from the Bengal Staff Corps, Indian Army, and his mother, Kezia Thurburn, aged thirty-seven, was born in Louth, Lincolnshire. TT had two sisters: Marion C. Thurburn, aged eight, born in Sussex, and Augusta M. Thurburn, aged five, born at Kensington Park, Middlesex. They had a cook, a housemaid, and a general servant. Next door lived the widow of a General Dunlop. In 1911, TT was living as a "banker" in the Mount Tolmie district of south Saanich, at 970 Heywood Avenue, with his wife, Mary, aged fifty, born in the United States of an Irish family, and they had a daughter Eileen, aged fourteen, and a son Hector, aged twelve, both born on the Island. They attended St Luke's Anglican Church on Cedar Hill Cross Road.

Their elder son, August Edward Charles Thurburn, became a land surveyor in BC and enlisted in the Canadian Expeditionary Force at Valcartier on 23 September 1914 as a single man, transferred to the Essex Regiment in which he was commissioned as a captain, and was killed in battle on 28 May 1917. His brother Hector Maclaine Thurburn, born 28 January 1899 in BC, enlisted in Victoria on 17 April 1918 when he was still a student, and lived to survive his parents. Both sons cited TT as their next of kin living at Mt Tolmie in Victoria. Mary Thurburn died, aged sixty-one, on 28 November 1920 and TT on 21 May 1946 [his name misspelled in the record]. They were also survived by their daughter Eileen, who had married J. U. Byrne.

Sources: *Colonist*, 22 May 1946, p. 10, obit.; census 1871, England, RG 10/819, p. 6; Canadian census, 1911, Canada, NAC, RG 31, Statistics Canada, Saanich, Ward 1, Ward 6; NAC, CEF files, box 9685-4 and box 9685-6; *Whitaker's*, p. 516; J. B. Hayward & Son, *Officers Died in the Great War*, 1914-1919 (New Enlarged Ed., Polstead, Suffolk, J. B. Hayward & Son, 1988), p. 132.

TISDALL, Captain Ernest Patrick (1906-1965). Born at Newchwang, North China, on 29 October 1906, he became a naval cadet at the Royal Naval College of Canada in 1921 and served from 1924 on a series of Royal Navy vessels (here listed) but was in the RCN during the Second World War, rising to captain on 1 January 1948, to director of weapons and tactics at NHQ in 1949, ADC, to the governor general in 1953, senior Canadian officer afloat in 1955, etc., and vice-chief of naval staff in 1958. He was a member of the twelfth and final term of the RNCC, qualified in RN gunnery long course on HMS *Excellent* in 1932, and commanded the Royal Guard at Victoria for the presentation of the King's Colours to the RCN, by George VI, in May 1937. He retired on 1 June 1961 and died at Victoria, aged fifty-eight, on 19 March 1965.

Sources: *MacFarlane*, p. 61.

TORRIBLE, Captain Alfred (c. 1869-1965). Born at Port Stewart, Northern Ireland, he became an apprentice on the sailing ship *Parthia* in 1883 at the age of fifteen. He made several voyages on sailing ships around Cape Horn, up to the west coast of North America, and as far south as Australia. In 1893, he obtained a master's certificate in sail and the next year transferred to steam vessels and joined the Knight shipping line. In 1900, he was in the wreck of the *Knight Companion* off the Japanese coast in which many drowned, but was among those rescued by some Japanese fishermen. He eventually made his way to Shanghai, where he joined the firm of Butterfield & Swire. He served with them for thirty years along the China coast and the Yangtze River. On 7 April 1906, he married Christina at Kirkwall, Orkney Islands, where she was born; she had teacher's credentials from Edinburgh Ladies' College and Edinburgh University.

After an adventurous career in the Far East, AT and Mrs Torrible retired to BC, where they landed at the port of Victoria on 23 March 1930 from the *Empress of Asia*. They settled five years later at Brentwood Bay, where they were among the founding members of Brentwood United Church and where he owned a boat for many years and was often in fishing derbies. When the men who had been running the Mill Bay Ferry went to the Second World War, AT ran the ferry for three years. He was a charming man with many tales about the Oriental curios and mementoes in his Brentwood house. They spent their last years in Sidney at "Shoreacres" east of Third Street. When AT died at Resthaven Hospital, aged ninety-six, on 28 July 1965, they had been living for four years in Sidney at "Shoreacres." He was survived by his wife, who died, aged eighty-nine, on 16 December 1967, a son Alfred W. Torrible, 4360 Summit Drive, La Mesa, California, and a daughter Margaret, who was Mrs John Burbank, living in Hove, Sussex. At his funeral, the pallbearers were C. LeBas (French consul general of Canada, from Vancouver), A. Vickers, Captain D. H. McKay [who was he?], G. V. Card, T. Parkins, and R. E. Hindley. Canon F. C. Vaughan-Birch took the service at Royal Oak Crematorium.

Sources: NAC, Immigration records, 1925-1935; *Colonist*, 29 July 1965, p. 31, obit.; 19 December 1967, p. 23, wife's obit.; *The Sidney and Gulf Islands Review*, 4 August 1965, pp. 1 and 4; Graham R. Torrible, *Yangtze Reminiscences: some notes and recollections of service with the China Navigation Company Ltd. 1925-1939* (Hong Kong, Swire & Sons, 1975 and 1990), 104 pp. (makes no mention of AT).

TOWNEND, George Harold (1876-1968). At sometime early in the twentieth century, he bought seventeen acres on Somenos Lake in the Cowichan Valley, and when he enlisted in the Canadian Expeditionary Force at Victoria on 15 December 1915 (regimental no. 180146), he registered as a married farmer at Duncan. By 1919, he was a neighbour of *Colonel Arthur Pressy, *Captain Harry de Moleyn Mellin, *Hugh George Egioke Savage, and the rest of the twenty-five landowners living around that lake. As recently as 1901, he had been living as a stockbroker's agent at "Heath Lodge," Fleet, Hampshire, with his wife, Annie L. Townend—two years older than he and born in India—and a servant girl. GT was himself born at Southborough, Kent, on 7 July 1976, third son and fifth child of Edward Townend, who was "a China merchant" born at Streatham, Surrey. Edward's brothers (GT's uncles) were similarly employed: Montague S. Townend as an "East India merchant," Alexander Townend as a "colonial broker" (1871) or "East India merchant" (1881), and Herbert Townend as a "tea broker" (1871). The 1881 census shows GT's three eldest siblings, aged ten, eleven, and twelve, as born in Hankow, China, whereas the next child, aged nine, was born at Brighton, father and children then living in Kent at Springhead, Sandhurst Road, Tunbridge Wells. They had a governess, a cook, a housemaid, and a schoolroom maid. Their mother was absent, nowhere mentioned, and the father appears in 1891 and 1901 as a widower. By 1891, one of GT's brothers, Edward W. Townend, aged twenty-one, was employed as a "Colonial Broker's Clerk." GT himself was then boarding at a grammar school in Sevenoaks, where he appears in 1891 under a headmaster, Daniel Maule Biskett.

GT died, aged ninety-three, on 24 October 1968 at Shawnigan Lake, and his wife Annie Lorna Townend died, aged ninety-eight, on 28 March 1970, nearby at North Cowichan.

Sources: NAC, CEF files, box 9749-24; *Cowichan Leader*, 14 August 1919, p. 2; census 1841, England, HO 107/1068/4, no. 24; census, 1861, RG 9/413, pp. 17-18; census 1871, RG 10/775, p. 23; census 1871, RG 10/763, pp. 4-5; census 1881, RG 11/864, p. 9; census 1881, RG 11/916, pp. 25-6; census 1891, RG 12/528, p. 6; census 1891, RG 12/673, p. 1; census 1891, RG 12/582, p. 34; census 1901, RG 13/1101, p. 14; census 1901, RG 13/1691, p. 3.

TREEN, Captain Horatio Alfred (1842-1918). Born in Stockton-on-Tees, Durham, he claimed to be a descendant of Admiral Lord Nelson through his mother's family. He appears, aged seven, in census records for 1851, living at the schoolhouse in the village of Somerleyton, Suffolk, where his father, William Treen, aged forty-one and born in Coventry, was a "British Schoolmaster," as the census-taker wrote. His wife Naomi, aged forty, was a "British Schoolmistress" born at Neatishead, Norfolk. Their seven children of whom HT was the fifth were born variously at Coventry, London, Durham, and Somerleyton, and a visitor in the house, Mordecai C. Cooke, aged twenty-six, was a "Pedagogue" born at Horning, Norfolk. In 1866, HT went to Canada to work for the Grand Trunk Railway and immediately joined the Victoria Rifles in Montreal. He took part in the Fenian Raids Campaign and worked for thirty-five years for the Grand Trunk Railway and the CPR.

In 1901, he went to Victoria to manage the agency of the Victoria-Mexican Steamship Company. In 1912, he went into the real-estate business on the Island together with W. M. Wilson and then worked as bookkeeper for the Crown Realty Company. He was an active member of the British Imperial Campaigners' Association and president of the local Imperial Service Club. Twice married, he died a widower, aged seventy-six, on 11 October 1918 in Victoria.

Sources: *Colonist*, 12 October 1918, pp. 12 and 14, obit.; *BC Archives*, "Minutes of the British Imperial Campaigners' Ass., 1908-1935"; census 1851, England, HO 107/1805/452/32.

TRENCH, Edward Cosby (1881-1961). In 1910, he and his brother, Clive Newcombe Trench (1884-1964), bought a house and its surrounding farm of some seven thousand acres near Musgrave's Landing on the wild west side of Salt Spring Island, across Satellite Channel from Maple Bay. They bought it from their relative, *Edward Musgrave, who had owned it for a quarter of a century, raised sheep there, and somehow given his name to the place. But Musgrave had bought it in 1885 from the Pimbury brothers, emigrants from a village near Minchinton, Gloucestershire, who were the original pioneers of English settlement at Musgrave's Landing. ET had taken with him his bride, Evelyn de Courcy Daniell (c. 1894-1965), daughter of Colonel Daniell of the Royal Artillery. ET had served in 1905-1909 as honorary attaché in the diplomatic service, and during the Great War, he served in the Naval Intelligence Division in (1915-1918) and then returned to Musgrave's Landing. In 1929, they moved across Satellite Channel, through Maple Bay, to Duncan, where they settled at "Lanagour" on Herd Road. He sometimes played the organ at St Peter's Quamichan and joined the Cowichan Country Club and the Union Club in Victoria, both full of Imperials like himself. ET loved shooting and tennis (Cowichan Bay was the second oldest tennis court in the empire).

ET was the fourth son of an Anglo-Irish gentleman, Captain Hon. Cosby Godolphin Trench (1844-1925) of the First Royal Dragoons and his wife, Maria Musgrave (c. 1852-1938), daughter of Sir Richard Musgrave, fourth baronet in the Tourin line, who served in 1874 as lord lieutenant of Waterford. ET was brought up at Sopwith Hall in Tipperary—in the Church of Ireland (Anglican) like so many others on the Island. Eventually, ET and Evelyn moved to Oak Bay in Victoria, where ET died, aged seventy-nine, on 21 October 1961 and Evelyn on 22 November 1965. Clive Newcombe Trench had evidently moved back to England, where he died on 24 February 1964.

Sources: *Who's Who in B.C.*, 1933-34, p. 171; Kahn, *Salt Spring Island*, pp. 113-14.

TRUTCH, Sir Joseph William (1826-1904), KCMG. Born on 18 January 1826 at Ashcott near Bath, Somerset, he was schooled in Exeter, apprenticed to Sir John Rennie, a prominent British engineer, and worked on the Great Northern and Great Western railways. It was as a civil engineer that he emigrated to San Francisco in 1849 and ten years later moved to Victoria, BC, where he worked as an engineer and contractor and became a member of the Vancouver Island House of Assembly, later surveyor general and chief commissioner of Lands and Works (1864-1870), governor of BC (1871-1876), and agent for the Dominion of Canada (1876-1889). He was an enthusiastic supporter of Confederation and, in 1871-1876, served as the first lieutenant governor of BC after it joined Canada. He also had a term as resident agent of the Dominion government in British Columbia.

His brother John Trutch, born in Jamaica, was a civil engineer and surveyor who was engaged in the construction of roads in the interior of British Columbia and, in 1889, was appointed land commissioner for the Esquimalt and Nanaimo Railway. JT also joined and encouraged a syndicate of British capitalists who invested in the Silver King Mines in the West Kootenay district. He married Julia Elizabeth Hyde in Oregon City, Oregon, on 8 January 1855, but had no children. He retired eventually to "Willett House" at Elworthy near Bath, Somerset, where the 1901 census found him, a widower aged seventy-five, living with his widowed brother John Trutch (1829-1907), born in Kingston, Jamaica, aged seventy-two, and their two nieces, Josephine Emily Pender, aged twenty-three, born at Victoria, and Charlotte Emily Caroline Trutch, aged nineteen, born at Yale, BC. There were

six servants including two grooms. JT died, aged seventy-eight, on 4 March 1904 in
Taunton, Somerset. His mother and his wife had both died earlier in Victoria, the
former, Charlotte Hannah Trutch, aged seventy-seven, on 7 November 1876 and
the latter, Julia Elizabeth Trutch (*née* Hyde), aged sixty-eight, on 16 July 1895.
Sources: Robin Fisher, "Trutch, Sir Joseph William," *DCB*, vol XIII, pp. 1034-1037;
Lugrin, *Pioneer Women*, pp. 271-5; census 1901, England, RG 13/2265, p. 15; *Who
was Who*, 1897-1916, p. 717; *Colonist*, 6 February 1907, p. 12 (John Trutch).

   TRYON, Charles Robert (1857-1916). There is more to be discovered about
this interesting but elusive figure. Some of the following is open to doubt, but
it seems certain that he died on the Island at French Creek near Parksville on 1
October 1916, aged fifty-nine, having been there since about 1911. He was born at
Leamington, Warwickshire, eldest son of Admiral Robert Tryon (1810-1890) and
his third wife, Lelia [Lilias?] Sophia Skipwith from Hampton Lacy, in Warwickshire,
who had married on 3 June 1855. The admiral himself was the eldest son of Thomas
Tryon (CT's grandfather) and Harriet Brereton of Bulwick Hall, Northamptonshire,
where this branch of the Tryon family had lived for more than one generation, but
the admiral settled with his wife at Heathfield House near Titchfield, Hampshire.
There is a general belief that the first of the family in England had arrived from the
Netherlands, perhaps as Huguenot refugees. The admiral's brother, Major General
Samuel Tryon (CT's uncle), married a woman at Halifax, Nova Scotia, and some of
their children were born there, others in New Brunswick, before moving back to
England. CT himself first went to Canada to make his way at Grenfell, in that part of
the NWT, which was to become Saskatchewan in 1905. He and another Englishman
took over Routh's general store at Grenfell in the 1890s and advertised themselves
locally as "Importers and General Merchants." His partner, Ralph H. Skrine, had
been living not far away at a settlement called Ceylon, which his family may have
founded, the Skrines having arrived from Colombo, Ceylon (now Sri Lanka). About
1894, CT had a new building constructed at Grenfell as a private bank, which he
managed until 1901, when it was absorbed into the Dominion Bank of Toronto.
It is uncertain whether CT's bank was connected with the big Tryon Bank in the
USA and uncertain what CT did after he sold it.
   On 9 May 1905 in Southwark, London, he married Esther Bromley (c.
1882-1958), daughter of Adele Augusta Richards and her husband, Sir Henry
Bromley (1849-1905), who lived at Stoke Hall in Nottinghamshire. Esther's brother,
Admiral Sir Arthur C. B. Bromley (1876-1961) was forever linked with Vancouver
Island when on 24 June 1904 in Victoria he married Laura Mary [May?] Dunsmuir
(1884-1959), daughter of James Dunsmuir (1851-1920), who served a term later
as lieutenant governor of BC. James was born at Fort Vancouver on the Columbia
River, son of the Island's Scottish coal baron, Robert Dunsmuir (1825-1889),
before the family took charge of the coal mines at Nanaimo. Admiral Bromley
took his bride to live in England, but it may have been this family connection
that prompted CT and his wife to settle on the Island. However, all except the
youngest of the six children born to CT and Esther were born in England in the
years 1906-1914. Thomas Charles Tryon was the exception, being born at or near

Parksville on 1 October 1916, the very day of his father's death, or so the sources indicate. Passenger records show Esther taking the children home to England with astonishing frequency, sometimes going to Dallam Tower or Parkside at Milnthorpe or Kendal in Westmorland and at other times to the Manor House at Haslemere in Surrey. Most of the children stayed in BC, however, and Esther is reported to have died, aged seventy-six, on 22 July 1958 in Nanaimo. On her last few voyages to England, she had travelled alone.

Sources: Letter to the author courtesy of Mrs Ethel Box, Grenfell Museum, Saskatchewan, 18 June 2001; A. I. Yule, *Grit and Growth: The Story of Grenfell, Saskatchewan* (Grenfell, Grenfell Historical Committee, 1980), pp. 71, 78, 91-2; BNA, census 1871, England, RG 10/1965, pp. 13-14; census 1881, RG 11/1167, p. 2 (parents); census 1881, RG 11/1212/15, p. 23 (brother); *Kelly's Handbook to the Titled, Landed, and Official Classes* (1882), p. 833; UK Incoming Passenger Lists, 1878-1960, online, for instance no. 145908, arriving 9 June 1923; no 142717, arr. 9 September 1927, no 140579, arr. 11 May 1930, 160505, arr. 4 June 1988 (Esther and children); *The Times* (London), 24 July 1958, p. 1, col. A, obit. (Esther); Rear Admiral C. C. Penrose Fitzgerald, *Life of Vice-Admiral Sir George Tryon, K.C.B.* (Edinburgh, Blackwood & Son, 1897).

TURLEY, Frank (1876-1952). He was born in 1876 at Hartlebury, Worcestershire, son of Joseph Turley, "farmer of 14 acres," and the 1881 census recorded them living there in Summerfield Lane. Frank was five years old, his father thirty-four, his mother Elizabeth aged forty, and an elder brother Arthur Turley aged seven, all except FT born at Stone, Worcestershire. He joined British forces fighting in the South African War for which he had the Queen's Medal and six clasps. At some stage, he became a mining engineer, educated in Philadelphia he later claimed, and spent a number of years in China, three of them in the Chinese Maritime Customs, five years as an engineer on the Panama Canal, and some time in Australia and on the Gold Coast in West Africa. It was in 1912 while he was on his way to Alaska that he passed along the BC coast and decided to stay in Canada. There he worked for the Imperial Oil Company, mainly at Edmonton, until 1937 and then retired. He had been living in Victoria since 1933 with the wife he had married in 1912, Margaret Mahon, daughter of J. Mahon, and they had a son. They lived at 318 Newport Avenue, Oak Bay, where he joined the Victoria Golf Club, served as president of the Rotary Club in 1942-1943, and as an Oak Bay councillor in 1941-1944. His wife may have been the Margaret Hayburn Turley who died, aged fifty-five, on 28 January 1936 in Harrison Hot Springs, but in any event, FT himself died, aged seventy-five, on 3 November 1952 in Victoria.

Sources: *Who's Who in B.C.*, edn. 7 (1947-1948), p. 213; *Colonist*, 4 November 1952, p. 6, obit.; census England, 1881, RG 11/2935, p. 13; census 1901, RG 13/768, p. 7.

TURNER, Major Frank Cecil (1868-1953). Born on 16 September 1868 at Peebles, Scotland, son of William Doering Turner, he fought through the South African War in the Cheshire Regiment in which he won the DSO. He then moved out to the interior of British Columbia, where he soon joined "D" squadron of the Thirty-first Regiment of BC Horse as a major and was later remembered by a more senior officer as "one of the most popular militia officers in the whole of the Upper Country. Major Turner had made a name for himself while serving with the Cheshire Regiment in South Africa, and the knowledge gained in that far-off theatre of military operations stood "D" squadron in good stead on many an occasion." When he joined Lord Strathcona's Horse of the CEF on 2 October 1914 aboard SS *Bermudan* at sea, he listed his father as living at Fife Lodge, Staines, Middlesex. He had already had two years in the Thirty-first Regiment of the BC Horse and six years before that in the Fourth Battalion of the Cheshire Regiment through the Great War in the Fifth BC Light Horse, winning the DSO. He gave his occupation as a rancher in the BC interior. He was 5' 8" tall, with a fair complexion, grey green eyes, and dark hair, and belonged to the C of E. He had a mole under his right arm and a scald on his buttocks and "webb toes on both feet."

He served in England and France with Lord Strathcona's Horse, then attached to HQ Cavalry Corps, Canadian Cavalry Regimental Depot. In France in 1915, he was granted leave to England; this was extended, and he rejoined his unit on 19 August 1915. A medical report of 5 October 1916 says, "This Officer went sick on Sept. 21st 1916 while in the Somme. Had abdominal apis, diarrhoea, slight headache and slight fever. Sent to No. 2 Red Cross Hospital, Rouen, for about a week. Admitted to 3rd Southern General Hospital, Oxford, on 1st October 1916. He has improved. There is considerable debility, and he will require a rest to regain his strength." There are several other medical reports. One of them says, for example, "Enteric & dysentery in South Africa—infection—1901." A medical report of September 1917 reads, "On July 23rd entered No. 6 Stationary, frevent, with scabies. Ten days later while there very severe lumbago came on, lasting two weeks. On Sept. 23rd entered Prince of Wales Hospl. He states he now feels weak only—but has no pain . . . Is Perspiring profusely . . . He looks weak." He was, in general, suffering from "Infection and exposure." In hospital in Oxford and Shorncliffe in autumn 1916, he was given provost duties in the HQ Cavalry Corps in 1917. He was ill and in England late that year—and seems to have been shunted around England for the rest of the war—and sailed to Canada on 10 March 1919. He was struck off strength on 27 March 1919 by reason of general demobilization.

With his wife, Elizabeth Susan Turner, FT had two children then, Norah Cecilia Turner aged 6½ and Francis William Scott Turner, aged 4½, and their British address was Brathay, Cookham, Berks. At one time, she was living at Nicola, BC, and his address was Merritt, BC. There are no details concerning the awarding of his DSO. About 11 August 1929, he attended the AGM of the Islands Conservative Association along with a group from Sidney including *Colonel Cy Peck, Alan Calvert, *Freeman King, and W. C. Clarke, and on 18 May 1933, he was present at a meeting of the Salt Spring Island Conservative Association at A. J. Eaton's Tearooms and proposed a resolution, seconded by *Captain V. C. Best, in support of Captain M. F. MacIntosh as an Independent Conservative in the Islands riding. FT also attended an Armistice Day Dinner at Harbour House, Ganges, on 11

November 1929 and as chairman read out a greeting from the Prince of Wales. In April 1936, he attended the annual dinner of the Gulf Islands Branch of the Canadian Legion on Mayne Island, along with *Colonel A. B. Snow and others. In a lighter vein, FT and Captain V. C. Best took part in a play put on by the Salt Spring Island Players in Ganges in May 1931. This was a farce in three acts called *Tons of Money*. Early the next July, however, he left for Bruce Mountain to take up summer employment as fire lookout. FT was public-spirited, like many officers, and served as president of the island's Wolf Cub organization. "He paid a well-deserved tribute to the Cub master, Colonel A.B. Snow, for the state of efficiency of the pack." And he hoped somebody would come forward to lead a Boy Scout troop. An Anglican, he attended a vestry meeting at St Paul's Ganges in January 1937 and was elected to the church committee. He had been president of the Salt Spring Island Choral Society for four years when it met at "Barnsbury" in May 1940 and then retired but was elected secretary-treasurer. This entailed weekly practices there at "Barnsbury." In 1941, he was its vice-president. FT died, aged eighty-four, on 4 September 1953 at Ganges and was buried nearby in St Mark's churchyard.

His son, Francis W. S. ("Roscoe" or "Peter") Turner, was born at Merrit, BC, on 11 April 1914, attended Ganges Preparatory School and the Vancouver Technical College, and joined the RAF in 1935. In September 1939, Francis married Rosemary Josephine de Clairmont-Travers of Shoreham, Sussex. After a ten-month spell of bombing Germany, he was sent to Canada in January 1941 as a flying instructor under the terms of the British Commonwealth Air Training Plan.

Sources: NAC, CEF files, RG150 Box 9834-31; *Colonist*, 13 August 1929, pp. 7 and 12; 16 November 1929, p. 20; 21 May 1931, p. 8; 24 May 1933, p. 15; 15 April 1936, p. 4; 5 January 1941, p. 11; 8 January 1941, p. 2 (photo); Lieutenant Colonel C. L. Flick, *A Short History of the 31st British Columbia Horse* [with portraits] (Victoria, BC, J. Parker Buckle, 1922), p. 15.

TURNER, Lieutenant Colonel Hon. John Henry (1834-1923). He was born on 7 May 1834 at Claydon near Ipswich, son of John and Martha Turner, and emigrated to Halifax, NS, in 1856. Two years later, he moved to PEI and went into business in Charlottetown. He was successful enough to return to England and marry Elizabeth Eilbeck of Whitehaven, Cumberland, in 1860. One way or another, he became a leading citizen. In search of adventure and further fortune, he followed the gold rush to Victoria in July 1862 on the steamer *Oregon* and soon decided that mining would be less profitable than supplying mines and miners. Together with Jacob Hunter Todd, the future salmon-canning magnate, he went into the Victoria Produce Market and prospered. In 1859, he had joined the Volunteer Militia in PEI and he now joined the VI Volunteers. A keen interest in military affairs lasted throughout his life, and by 1882, when he retired, he was a lieutenant colonel. In 1872, he was made a JP and became a warden at St John's Church and in 1876-1878 served as an alderman. He was elected mayor of Victoria and served in 1879-1881. He played a big part in raising funds to build the Jubilee Hospital. After a spell purely in business, and

J.F. Bosher

with a trip back to England, he was elected to the provincial legislature and sat until 1901 during which he was minister of finance and agriculture (1887-1898; 1999-1901) and premier (March 1895-1898). He often went to England to raise money for the province. He was eventually hustled out of office with suspicion of rashness and irregularities in his administration. When Dunsmuir became premier, he again offered the ministry of finance to Turner, who carried on as before. In September 1901, he went to London again, this time as agent general of BC and he was good at "selling" BC to investors and emigrants in Britain. In 1915, he retired with a pension of $6,000 a year. In Victoria, he was a member of the Union Club and in London of the Colonial Club and the United Empire Club. When his wife died, he went to live with his only son and daughter-in-law in Surrey and soon died there.

Sources: Valerie Green, *No Ordinary People: Victoria's Mayors Since 1862* (Victoria, Beach Holme, 1992), pp. 76-80; S. W. Jackman, *Portraits of the Premiers: An Informal History of British Columbia* (Sidney, Gray's Publishing Ltd., 1969), pp. 99-108; Morgan, *Canadian Men and Women*, p. 1118; David Farrell, "*Keeping the Local Economy Afloat: Canadian Pacific Navigation and Shipowning in Victoria, 1883-1901,*" *The Northern Mariner*, vol. VI, no. 1 (January 1996), p. 37; *Colonist*, 7 May 1914, p. 3; 11 December 1923; Begg, *History of British Columbia*, pp. 552-3; Canadian census, 1891, BC.

TWIGG, Captain Harold Despard (1876-1946). He was born on 5 April 1876 at Dungamon, County Tyrone, Ireland, son of Dr William Twigg of Dungamon and of Clogher in the same county. The Twigg family had gone to Ireland from England in 1600 and become big landowners, though HT used to say that the land was now all gone. He was educated privately and in public schools and spent some time in India before going in 1899 to British Columbia. There he studied law, articled to the firm of Messrs McPhillips and Williams of Vancouver, and in 1901 went over to Victoria, where he was called to the BC Bar in 1904 and entered the firm of Messrs Eberts & Taylor. On 1 January 1916, he enlisted in Victoria in the Eighty-eighth Battalion, CEF, and went overseas to England and France, where he reached the rank of captain and on returning to Victoria in April 1919 practised law until June 1921, when he took up the insurance business with the Great West Life Insurance Co. He also worked for volunteer veterans' groups, joined the Army and Navy Veterans Association, was one of the speakers at the formal opening of their new premises on 12 April 1924, and was soon elected as the association's Dominion director. The Island's many veterans were impressed by his presentation of their arguments about pensions to the Ralston Commission. The movement to amalgamate the many veterans' organizations attracted him, and when the Canadian Legion was at last formed, he was the first commandant in Victoria, while another Victorian, *Lieutenant General Sir Percy Lake, was serving as the first national president elected at the founding meeting in Winnipeg. These activities led HT into political life, and in 1924, he was elected to the sixteenth provincial legislature. Speaking to the Kiwanis Club on 2 December 1924, he expressed a qualified belief in democracy, arguing that it was often tainted by corruption and anarchy: "The voice of the people is not the voice of God." In the federal constitutional crisis of 1926, he spoke out against corruption in certain provincial political circles. A tall, handsome Anglo-Irish lawyer and a bright and clever speaker, he appeared often in public and was successful in public life. He wisely chose to be one of the people, however, when he ceased to be active in the exclusive clubs of Victoria and told the *Daily Colonist* in November 1924 that he could not afford clubs in those hard times and kept only his membership in the Canadian Legion and the Victoria Golf Club.

H. Despard Twigg, as he called himself, sat in the legislature for two terms, a total of nine years during which he was a Conservative in politics, BC organizer for the Conservative party in 1932-1933, an Anglican, and a staunch supporter of the British Empire. At the fifth annual reunion dinner of the Eighty-eighth Battalion on 23 May 1931, he replied to the toast to the empire, asking the 125 veterans present to stand by the empire in peacetime as they had done during the war. He was to do much the same again and again, as on 24 May 1940. In June 1934, he was joining two distinguished and loyal Canadian officers, the *Jukes brothers, when he became managing director of the firm A. E. Jukes & Company, a bond brokerage and insurance business. Three years later in a further change, he was appointed Vancouver Island manager for the National Life Insurance Company of Canada, a Toronto firm with its Victoria offices at 215-216 Central Building. Dealing with Toronto and Vancouver, however, seems to have disgusted HT, as it did many others on the Island. At sometime in the middle 1930s, HT appealed to some Conservatives by becoming an outspoken supporter of the movement to make Vancouver Island a separate province. This was a current of feeling that had simmered under the surface ever since the Island had joined BC in 1866 and become part of Canada in 1871. On 27 September 1936, the *Daily Colonist* published a letter from HT under the heading "A Separate Province," arguing that this could be done by amending the BNA Act of 1871. It was at about this time that he became secretary organizer of the Vancouver Island Provincial Association and began to speak publicly in its favour. On 7 January 1937, he told a meeting of the Active Club at the Dominion Hotel that capitalists would be attracted to the Island if it seceded from British Columbia because the original union had been unfair to the Island, and a speech along those lines to the Chamber of Commerce later that month led them to set up a committee to examine the question.

HT was also a family man. On 6 September 1911, he married Marguerite Jean Little, eldest daughter of Mr and Mrs Francis Dean Little of Rockland Avenue, Victoria, by whom he had two children, a boy and girl. The daughter, Barbara Mary Frances Twigg, had as grand a wedding as Victoria could offer at Christ Church Cathedral in March 1937. The *Daily Colonist* printed photographs of the event showing Princess Chickmatoff and Brigadier General J. G. Austin (in a top hat) on the cathedral steps. It was Austin who proposed the toast to the bride. The groom was Henry Meredith Bumpus, son of Henry F. Bumpus (c. 1858-c. 1903), a well-known London bookseller, but was established at Brandan, Sumatra, where he was planning to take his bride to live after a honeymoon in England, Norway, and Roumania. Reports of the marriage gave no details of Bumpus's business, but Anglo-Dutch firms had been investing in rubber, tea, and oil on the island of Sumatra, which the Dutch government ruled indirectly through the wealthy Sultan of Langkat. Late in August 1940, Mrs Bumpus, the Twiggs' daughter, turned up in Victoria with a baby daughter (Barbara)—Japanese forces having begun sporadic assaults on the Dutch East Indies—and her husband was expected to follow early the following summer. Her brother, the Twiggs' son died on 7 October 1942 while in action as a wing commander in the air force. HT died, aged seventy, on 12 November 1946 in Victoria and, more than twenty years later, Mrs Twigg died, aged eighty, on 5 October 1969 also in Victoria.

Sources: NAC, RG150, Box 9856-25; *Colonist,* 8 February 1917, p. 5 (photo); 26 November 1924, p. 5; 3 December 1924, p. 18; 17 July 1930, p. 3 (photo); 24 May 1931, p. 6; 22 May 1934, p. 3 (photo); 15 June 1934, p. 18 (photo); 27 September 1936, p. 4; 9 January 1937, p. 18; 26 January 1937, p. 3; 11 March 1937, p. 7; 25 June 1937, p. 7; 5 May 1940, Sunday Section, pp. 1 and 3; 15 May 1940, p. 5; 1 September 1940, p. 7; Russell R. Walker, *Politicians of a Pioneering Province* (Vancouver, Mitchell Press, 1969), pp. 159ff.; Kyrle C. Symons, *That Amazing Institution*, p. 143; Martin Robin, *The Rush for Spoils* (Toronto, McClelland & Stewart, 1972), pp. 221-2.

TYRWHITT-DRAKE, Hon. Montague William (1830-1908). He was born on 20 January 1830 at Kings Walden, Hertfordshire, son of Rev. George Tyrwhitt-Drake, "a representative of an old county family of Shardeloes, Buckinghamshire, but descended originally from a brother of Sir Francis Drake." According to John Bateman, a Thomas Tyrwhitt-Drake of Shardeloes, Amersham, born 1817 and married 1843, owned 8,402 acres in Lincolnshire, 5,767 acres in Buckinghamshire, 3,834 acres in Cheshire, and 360 acres in Oxfordshire, totalling 18,463 acres and worth £24,686 in the mid-nineteenth century. Schooled at Charterhouse, MT was admitted as a solicitor in England in 1851.

Eight years later, he went out to Victoria by way of the Panama Canal and, after mining for a while in the Cariboo, began to practice law in Victoria. From 1868 to 1870, he represented the city on the Legislative Council and in 1872 became a member of the Board of Education. In 1873, he was called to the BC Bar and ten years later became a Queen's Council. In 1883-1886, he again represented Victoria in the BC Legislative Assembly, and in 1883-1884, he was president of the executive council. He tried some important cases and in 1889 was raised to the Supreme Court of BC. He seems to have owned land in North Saanich, which was later held by William Towner. In 1904, he retired. In 1862, he had married Joanna Tolmie, daughter of James Tolmie of Ardersir, Scotland, and at the time she died in 1901, they had four daughters and a son. One daughter, Helen Louise Tyrwhitt-Drake married Arthur Douglas Crease (1872-1967) on 16 April 1903 in Victoria. MT died, aged seventy-eight, on 19 April 1908 and was buried as an Anglican, honoured as a pioneer and leading citizen.

Sources: Howay and Gosnell, *British Columbia*, vol. IV, pp. 288-291, photo; Gosnell, *The Year Book*, p. 45; Bateman, *The Great Landowners*, p. 138; Canadian census, 1901, Victoria.

Maj. E.B. Underwood

UNDERWOOD, Major Ernest Brownlow (1873-1959). He first reached the Island in 1922, when posted to "B" Coy R.C. machine-gun brigade at Esquimalt near Victoria. The years 1922-1923, he spent at the Canadian Small Arms School, as adjutant quartermaster, then as adjutant, attached to "B" Company, Princess Patricia's Canadian Light Infantry. In 1923-1924, he served as district weapon training officer. In 1925-1932, he was general staff officer grade 3, MD XI (Weapon Training), at Esquimalt with periods as adjutant quartermaster in the Canadian Small Arms Camp School at Sarsa near Calgary and, in 1926, at the infantry machine-gun school at Edmonton. On two occasions, he was sent to command troops in Vancouver and detailed to keep watch on industrial strikes in that rowdy city. At last in December 1932 after a total of forty-four years of military service, he retired with the rank of major.

EU and his wife Alice had settled by 1923 on the Island, where she lived for the next thirty-four years and he for thirty-six. In retirement, they lived on the Gorge Road and then the West Saanich Road, where their place was recognizable by a row of whitewashed stones in front and a flagpole whereon a flag flew on Sundays and holidays, sometimes the Union Jack and sometimes the Canadian red ensign, always lowered at sunset. They kept a few ducks and geese, a pair of guinea fowl, and a thirty-year-old parrot, and for a time they had a monkey. Like most retired Imperials, they hung their walls and filled their shelves with a variety of army mementoes—EU's old shako or hat from the Highland Light Infantry, his bearskin from the Guards, his regimental badges, swords, photographs, and scrapbooks. He was a practising Freemason and for some time, he took charge of officers' messes in Chilliwack and at Work Point. A *Daily Colonist* reporter saw him as "a short, cheerful man with a white mustache. His manner is friendly and devoid of military stiffness." He tried to join up in the Second World War, passed the physical examinations, but was turned away because he was sixty-six years old. Many in Victoria looked upon him as a leading authority on military matters. Soldiers and ex-soldiers—some of fairly high rank—called on him for advice on questions of dress, colours, battle honours, and military etiquette.

In later years, they moved to 2181 Haultain Street, Victoria, where he died, aged eighty-six, on 20 July 1959 leaving four sons: Arthur Victor George Underwood, Leslie Harold Underwood, Ernest Albert Underwood, and Ghazi Kenal Underwood, all living in Victoria. Another son, Reginald Cyril Underwood, had died in 1937. EU was also survived by three daughters: Mrs Arthur (Lillian) Songhurst of Victoria, Mrs Fred (Muriel) Burch of Vancouver, and Mrs R. T. (Mena) Miller of Ottawa. There were two sisters still alive in England, as well as twelve grandchildren. One of his brothers, Sergeant R. C. Underwood, was drowned in 1906 in a tributary of the Ganges River; his eldest brother, Trumpeter Leslie H. Underwood, was killed at the Battle of Abu Klea in the Sudan War of 1884-1885; and another brother, F. S. G. Underwood, served in the First World War and retired in the early 1950s as a barrister in London. EU left an entry in his diary, discovered at his death: "I want no funeral services, no praying over my grave and no parson ... Cover my body with the Union Jack; I have had a good innings under it, and assisted in a small way to plant it, and keep it flying in various quarters of the globe. Thus, the British Empire still is: but without the British soldier it would never have been. Oliver Cromwell made the British soldier and his work was taken over by a succession of great men."

He was born on 1 March 1873 in St Paul's, Deptford, London, eldest son of George G. Underwood, a "draper's assistant" born at Luton, Bedfordshire, and his wife Lucy Anne *née* Frazer, a "dressmaker" from Bedfont, Middlesex. In 1881, the census recorded EU as eight years old and living with his parents, a younger brother Philip, aged six, and two sisters, Ada and Ethel, aged three and one. His mother's brother, Philip Frazer, a "pawnbroker's assistant," was staying with them, and they employed a thirteen-year-old servant girl. Their address was 8 Clyde Street near Deptford railway station in the Kentish part of London, south of the Thames, though a decade earlier their address was 36 Strickland St, and by 1891, they had moved to a place in New Road, Bedfont. In 1888, when EU was fifteen years old, he joined the Coldstream Guards as a drummer boy, transferred after a few months to the Fourth Battalion of the Middlesex Battalion and again in 1891 to the First Battalion of the Highland Light Infantry. He seems to have been escaping from a life in his parents' drapery business but in later years told a reporter of the *Victoria Daily Colonist* that he had enlisted "following an incident in which he refused to apologize to a vicar's daughter after he told her to mind her own business when she remarked that he sang too loud." This incident occurred at the Anglican Church at Bedfont, Middlesex, where one of his uncles was the organist. Thereafter, he served around the empire as follows:

1891-1892 With the First Bn. Highland Light Infantry at Dover

1892-1895 Moved to Aldershot in the First Brigade under Major General Gregory, CB. The Aldershot command was at that time under Lieutenant General Sir E. Wood, VC, afterwards HRH lieutenant general, the Duke of Connaught, KC.

1895-1898 Moved to Malta in February and was stationed at Verdala (?), Barracks; Fort Monoch; Pembroke; and St Elms. In the Malta Regatta, he won the 1897 sculling championship with his boat, the *Benbow*. Also visited Sicily and Italy. He took mounted infantry and signalling courses and received a series of promotions, which raised him to the rank of lance sergeant. In 1898, he was promoted to full sergeant in Malta.

1898 The regiment went to Crete in August 1898 and fought there on 6 September. He defended Assangalo Bastion for two days with fifteen members of the Highland Light Infantry under a sergeant and forty men of the Turkish regular army. He was wounded and mentioned in despatches (*London Gazette* 24 January 1899)

1899 Moved to Devonport and took part in manoeuvres on Salisbury Plain

1899 EU and two of his brothers went in October to fight in the South African War and formed part of the Third Highland Brigade under Major General A. G. Wauchope, CB (killed leading the Brigade at

Majersfontein). Reached Cape Town on 28 Oct and moved to DeAr Junction Orange River Bridge on the day the Battle of Belmont was fought. Crossed the river and was in the advance to Kimberley, the Battle of Modder River (28 November 1899), Magersfontein (11 December 1899), Koodesberg Drift (8 February 1900).

1900   Took part in Lord Robert's advance across the Free State. Relief of Kimberley. Was at Klip Drift, Paardeberg, and the advance on Bloemfontein.

1900-1902 Present in the advance to Pretoria, the capture of Lindly [Lindby?], Wimberg Venterberg, Battle of Witport, Capture of Heilbron, Bethelhum, Harrismith Relief Work, the Battle of Willabergen, operations around Weptner (?), the Commissie Drift, Great Reinet, Queenstown, Dordrecht, the line at Stormberg, Odendankstroom and Alieval Morte. At the war's end, he was awarded the Queen's and King's medals with clasps. He and one of his brothers served as NCOs in same battalion throughout the whole war.

1902 EU   moved to Port Elizabeth.
Moved to Cairo, Egypt (Kass-el-nil Barracks)

1903   Moved to Khartoum, Soudan (British Barracks South of Khartoum).

1903-1904 Presented at Khartoum with the King's SA Medal by Sir R. Wingate, KCB, the Sirdar of the Egyptian Army. Was attached to the Staff of HRH, The Princes Bessrier (?), and Princess Enid of Battenberg during their visit to Khartoum and took part in the Desert Patrol to El Fasher (?) Went with Captain Walker to Bahr-el-Ghazal. From Egypt, EU and his brothers went to serve in India where one of the brothers drowned in the Ganges River, and he himself was promoted to quartermaster sergeant.

1904-1908 Moved to Meerut, India, and from there to Chakrata, Dinajpor, Darjeeling, Patnia, and a number of other stations in India. In 1908, he moved to Lucknow. At a garrison parade in Lucknow in 1909, Kitchener awarded E. B. Underwood and others long service and good conduct medals and he was promoted to quartermaster sergeant and took a three-month course with the First Royal Dragoons. He was present in 1909-1910 at the Delhi Durbar, the Delhi manoeuvres, and the visit of the Emir of Afghanistan.

1908-1910 At Lucknow, Agra, Delhi, Lahore, Rawalpindi, Murree, Srinagar, Kashmir, Peshawar, Kohat, Dera Ismal Khan (Landi Kotal to Lanid Khasa via Jumrud Khyber Pass), and Bannu-Rasmak

1910-   To England

He had served in the Coldstream Guards for nineteen years and, for shorter periods, in the Highland Light Infantry and the Royal Grenadiers. In Crete, he had taken part in the notorious violent affair of 6 September 1898. His service in South Africa in 1899-1902 had led him to fight at Modder River, Willeburger, and many other engagements. He and his two brothers (who called him "the Sheik" because of his interest in the Muslim religion and people) had all served at Magersfontein, the relief of Kimberly, Klip Drift, Paardeberg, the advance to Bloemfontein, the advance to Pretoria, the battle of Westpoort, and other engagements. They received the King's and Queen's medals with clasps.

On 21 February 1899 at Antony, near Devonport, during a short visit home to England, EU had married Alice May Hogben, daughter of the regimental bandmaster. A decade later, after service in South Africa, he took a discharge in 1910, and a few months later, they emigrated to Toronto, where he worked for a time with the Home Bank of Canada, but also joined the Tenth Royal Grenadiers of Toronto and was in the Duke of Connaught's guard of honour. A year later, he went to Winnipeg to join the One-hundredth Winnipeg Grenadiers. He then organized a veteran's company of the 106th Winnipeg Light Infantry from among the Imperials who had seen war service. The company presented him with a fine brass clock for his services when he returned to the Grenadiers. The regiment was ordered in 1911 to form a company of the Twenty-seventh (city of Winnipeg) Battalion, Canadian Expeditionary Force. He was appointed company sergeant major and promoted to regimental quartermaster sergeant. As such, he complained about the poor quality of boots being issued to Canadian troops and was called to give evidence in Ottawa, and better boots were then issued. When war was declared in 1914, he was employed as a "bank messenger" in Winnipeg and living there with Alice. Then aged 41½, he was 5' 6" tall, with fair complexion, grey eyes, fair hair, a scar on his left cheek, and another on his forehead. He enlisted on 28 October in the CSM C Company of the Twenty-seventh Battalion (city of Winnipeg), and on arriving in England in May 1915, he had training at Shorncliffe, reached France with the Second Canadian Division in September 1915, was promoted to regimental sergeant major, and served in France and Germany in 1915-1919. He took part in actions at Mount Sorel, Somme (1916-1918,) Flens-Couscolette, Thiepval, Amore Heights, Arras (1917-1918), Vimy (1917), Arleux, Saarpes[?] (1917-1918), Hill 70, Ypres (1917), Passchendaile, Amiens, Drocourt-Queant, the Hindenburg Line, Canal du Nord, Cambrai (1918), Mons, and Flanders (1915-1918). Although wounded on 5 May 1917, he was almost continuously in France, Belgium, and Germany from 16 September 1915 to 12 April 1919 and emerged with the Distinguished Conduct Medal (14 November 1916) and the Military Cross (19 November 1917) as well as the long service and good conduct medals, and others. He had earlier received a Star from the Amir of Afghanistan, awarded at Calcutta.

Perhaps more satisfying for EU was his commission as captain on 3 May 1918. For many years in his early career, he had been employed around officers' messes and in regimental bands; indeed, his wife was a bandmaster's daughter. "He was a full corporal in Aldershot," a reporter in Victoria learnt from him later, "when Winston Churchill came there as a new lieutenant." For a man with his background, almost without formal education, a commission in the British Army was most improbable, but the Canadian Army did not scruple to promote so experienced a soldier, though he was almost illiterate, as his journals and other papers show. Scrawled in an atrocious hand, almost without punctuation or capital letters, his journal often calls for patient guesswork—but remains a fascinating document for the historian.

The most interesting aspect of EU's career is that although he declared himself to be an Anglican when enlisting in 1914, he seems to have become a Muslim. This did not emerge clearly until after he had retired to Victoria, but he was then quite firm about it and explained it as the result of a harrowing experience on the island of Crete. During "the weekend war," an insurrection in which he said, "he was detailed to a hanging fatigue charged with the execution of Muslim Bashi-Bazouk ringleaders who were said to have murdered Christians." He thought they were not guilty at all—and "this turned me against Christianity." Four years later, while stationed in Egypt in 1902, EU formally renounced Christianity and became a Muslim, which he remained until his death. On the North-West Frontier of India, "he made himself a blood brother to an Afridi—a ceremony which a number of soldiers went through." He changed his middle name from Brownlow to Basheer and exchanged blood with a member of the Muslim faith. He also called one of his sons by the Muslim name of Ghazi Kenal. It was by that name, as it happens, that I was able to distinguish his family from all the other Underwoods in Victoria and contact a grandson through whose courtesy I had access to some of EU's papers.

After the war, EU sailed for Canada on 14 May 1919, was demobilized in Toronto, and was sent to serve with the forces in the general strike, forming a machine-gun battery at Minto Barracks. Later, he was ordered to organize several militia units and a cadet machine-gun unit. He returned to Winnipeg and was appointed in 1920-1921 to Permanent Force, Royal Canadian Machine-Gun Brigade with orders to organize the Non-Permanent AM—First Machine Gun Squadron—Tenth Machine Gun Battalion—Second Moto Machine Gun—Tenth Machine Gun Cadets—all to full strength. A comparison of EU with *Major William Richard Wingfield-Digby shows that with such startlingly different backgrounds, they had only two things in common: their retirement on the Island and their soldierly loyalty to the empire to which it might be added that EU admired Oliver Cromwell, who had bombarded the Wingfield-Digby family castle in the seventeenth century.

Sources: Family papers, courtesy of Les Underwood, a grandson; Major E. B. Underwood's journal and service record; NAC, RG150, CEF files, box 9870-19; G. E. Mortimore, "This Week's Profile," *Daily Colonist* (*The Islander*), Sunday, 8 November 1953, pp. 1 and 12; *Colonist*, 8 September 1937, p. 18, obit.; 22 July 1959, pp. 5 and 19, obit.; census 1871, England, RG 10/748 (or 743?), p. 34; census 1881, RG 11/705, p. 29; census 1891, RG 12/1916, p. 8.

VERNEY, Captain Edmund Hope (1838-1910). He commanded HMS *Grappler* at the Esquimalt naval station in 1862-1865 and commented on the Island and the people he met in letters to his father, who was Sir Harry Verney, second baronet (1801-1894). The latter attended a meeting at the Mansion House in London on 30 November 1860 as a patron of the British Columbia Mission, together with Chichester Fortescue (under-secretary of state for the Colonies) and W. E. Gladstone. While in Victoria, EV was a member of the local committee of the

Columbia Immigration Society chaired by the lord bishop of Columbia and acted as commissioner and secretary of the Colonial Lighthouse Board and as JP as well as one of the founders in 1864 of the Mechanic's Institute in Victoria. His name was on the list of contributors to the building fund for a female infirmary. He left on 3 June 1865 for England by way of San Francisco, and the naval surveyor, Captain Daniel Pender, RN, gave his name to Verney Passage and Verney Cone on Cunningham Island.

EV had fought earlier in Indian Mutiny campaigns, ranging around India from HMS *Shannon*, which was at Calcutta from August 1857 to 15 January 1858. His book about his unit's adventures there was signed on 16 November 1861 at Claydon House, Winslow, Buckinghamshire, where he was born on 6 April 1838 and died in due time. The family name was Calvert until EV's father inherited Claydon House, in its beautiful country park, from a cousin and changed his name to Verney by royal licence dated 23 March 1827. The Verneys had been there for four hundred years but, in the eighteenth century, Lord Verney had speculated unwisely in the HEIC and (wrote Professor Lucy Sutherland (1903-1980), "by his extravagance . . . in electioneering and his building operations at Claydon, he entirely failed to check his expenditure . . . dying hopelessly insolvent." EV and his younger brother Frederick (1846-1913), a barrister, JP, and MP for Buckinghamshire, married sisters, the daughters of Sir John Hay Williams (1794-1859) and his wife Sarah Amherst (1801-1876), and both couples had children. In June 1858, while EV was still in India, his father made a second marriage with Frances Parthenope Nightingale (1819-1890), a writer and the sister of Florence Nightingale (1820-1910), who was "Aunt Florence" to EV's children, a close friend of his wife Margaret *née* Williams (1844-1930), and godmother to his daughter Ruth. "Aunt Florence" did her best to smooth over the wider family's hostility to EV when he was convicted in May 1891 of "conspiring to procure a minor—a nineteen-year-old woman—for immoral purposes," forced to resign as MP and councillor, and sent to prison for a year. EV was one of her allies in her campaigns for public health in India and the British Isles. Shortly before his death, on 3 May 1910, and hers on 13 August that year, he sent Florence Nightingale a photograph of the cypresses at Claydon, "grown from cones which she had brought back with her from Scutari" during the Crimean War.

Sources: Pritchard, *Letters of Edmund Hope Verney*, see index; Mark Bostridge, *Florence Nightingale: The Woman and Her Legend* (Penguin Viking, 2008), pp. 348-51, 488, 511-12, 516-17, 539; M. M. Verney and H. C. G. Matthew, "Verney [formerly Calvert], Sir Harry, second baronet (1801-1894), in *Oxford DNB; Colonist*, 31 January 1861, p. 2; 9 June 1862, p. 3; 18 September 1862, p. 3; 3 December 1862, p. 3; 26 November 1864, p. 2; and 10 July 1865, p. 4; William Loney, RN—Album, http://www.pdavis.nl/Verney.php; Walbran, *B.C. Coast Names*, p. 511; Edmund Hope Verney, *The Shannon's Brigade in India, Being Some Account of Sir William Peel's Naval Brigade in the Indian Campaign of 1857-1858* (Saunders, Otley & Co., 1862), 153 pp.; *Kelly's Directory, Buckinghamshire*, 1928, p. 89; Lucy Sutherland, *Politics and Finance in the Eighteenth Century*, ed., Aubrey Newman (The Hambledon Press, 1984), p. 330.

VERNON-JACKSON, Captain Percy "Tony" (c. 1881-1958). This elusive figure seems to have spent much of his life as a young man in China at Canton, Hong Kong, and Shanghai employed by Jardine, Matheson & Co. and by the Chinese Maritime Customs Service under Sir Robert Hart and his successors. We know that he served as an officer in the British Army during the Great War and that he sailed from Liverpool to Philadelphia in the *Haverford*, arriving on 3 April 1920 *en route* to Shanghai, China. He married Frances Raymond Hardinge, who was born a British subject in Germany and was found in 1901 by the census, living aged fifteen at St Mary's Hall, a girls' school in Brighton, headmistress Edith Louisa Potter. At sometime in the late 1920s, PV and his wife settled on the Island in Oak Bay at 1580 Beach Drive. On 27 September 1931, *The Daily Colonist* (p. 4) printed a letter he wrote to the editor on "Trade with China":

Sir—One often reads in the daily press about the great possibilities for Canadian trade with China. Various provincial and federal officials have spoken at meetings and over the radio on the same subject, but none has advanced a practical way to bring this about The same vague phrases are repeated. Immense possibilities; China's millions; now is the opportunity etc. Nothing else. The fact is, owing to lack of experience with China and Chinese business methods, none of them knows.

In your issue of Saturday, under the caption of "Transpacific Hop Planned," it is stated in part, "If the Chinese were told they could bridge the Whang Ho River with steel bridges and pay for them on time, there would be 120 bridges in no time." The writer has had many years experience in China, speaks Chinese and has some knowledge of business conditions prevailing there. The fact is the Chinese know full well that the large established European firms in Shanghai and Tientsin are quite prepared to build bridges and undertake other similar work on a large scale on time payments. These firms, however, find it difficult to obtain the necessary guarantees and security for repayment of principal and interest. These safeguards can only be successfully negotiated by businessmen of long experience with China and Chinese commercial methods. This also applies in other lines of business.

In London there is a Chinese association composed mainly of businessmen and retired officials from China, and the Foreign Office in the past has received and acted on valuable suggestions from them on affairs connected with China.

Here in Victoria there exists a society called the China-Japan Society, many of whose members have spent a lifetime in China and Japan, speak the languages and thoroughly understand business methods of the Orient. Valuable commercial information might be obtained from this source, which would be of great benefit in promoting Canadian trade with China.

The Victoria China-Japan Society had only recently been founded, with members retired from various British activities in the Orient, and its meetings over the years were reported in the *Daily Colonist*.

A dozen years after the Second World War, PV died, aged seventy-seven, on 5 August 1958 in Oak Bay, leaving a son Hugh, then in Nigeria, where he later served as first secretary (development) at the Canadian High Commission and wrote two books about African problems. PV's widow, Mrs Frances Raymond (Hardinge) Vernon-Jackson, then moved home to England, where she lived at Pitney House, Pitney, Langport, Somerset. In August 1963, *The Times* (London) posted two notices about the family within a few days of each other: (1) "In Memoriam"—in loving memory of Percy Vernon-Jackson, dear husband of Frances and father of Hugh; (2) "Vernon-Jackson—On 2nd August 1963, suddenly at Pitney House, Pitney, Langport, Somerset, Frances Raymond Vernon-Jackson, *née* Hardinge, widow of Percy Vernon-Jackson of Oak Bay, British Columbia."
Sources: Interview with Monica Oldham, Shoal Bay, Victoria; *Colonist*, 27 September 1931, p. 4; 6 August 1958, p. 16, obit.; 13 August 1963, p. 18, obit.; census 1901, England, RG 13/927, p. 8; Philadelphia Passenger Lists, 1800-1945, T-840_135; British Army WW I Medal Rolls, Index Cards, 1914-1920; *The Times* (London), 5 August 1963, p. 1, col. A, *In Memoriam*; 8 August 1963, p. 1, col. A, obit.

VIGGERS, Francis Henry (1879-1930). He was born on 11 March 1879 at Banbury, Oxfordshire, and enlisted in the Imperial Army at seventeen years of age. While stationed with the First Battalion of the King's Royal Rifles in India, where he served for many years, he was sent with the battalion to the South African War and was caught in the siege of Ladysmith. After the famous Relief of Ladysmith, he was sent to Ceylon, where his battalion guarded Boer prisoners at an internment camp. He went to Victoria after the South African War and in 1911 began working for the city of Victoria. He joined the CEF, Canadian Army Medical Corps, early in the Great War, giving his occupation as "Sanitary Inspector," his military experience as "50th C.G.H. K.R.R. 8 years Corporal," and his address as 1540 Burton Avenue. He served overseas as a sergeant but, after the war, rejoined his wife Edith and his work for the city of Victoria. When he died, aged fifty-one, on 11 July 1930, he was an assistant sanitary inspector, still at 1540 Burton Avenue, and was survived by his widow, a daughter, and a son.
Sources: CEF files, box 9948-55, rank SPR, reg'tal no. 524607; *Colonist*, 12 July 1930, p. 5, obit.

VILLERS, Major Walter S (1892-1987). He was born in Birmingham, son of Beatrice Villers and her husband Walter Villers, a "manufacturer's clerk" in 1891 and a "manager" by 1901. He was grandson of Jane Villers and her husband Joseph Villers, a silversmith, who had brought up WV's father in Aston, Birmingham. The 1901 census found WV, aged eight, living at 37 Dora Road, Aston (St Oswald's Parish), with a sister Doris, seven, and two brothers, Leslie, six, and Cecil E., three. There was one servant girl, aged twenty-one. WV served in the British Army in the Great War and then moved with his wife to the Island, where they brought

up their children in an upright stone house in Sidney on Marine Drive [now
Resthaven Drive], corner of Amelia Avenue. WV was employed in the Sidney post
office, built on Beacon Avenue in 1936, and he delivered the rural mail in an old
Wyllis car. While working at the post office during the Christmas rush in the early
1940s, I came to know him a little, but of course never asked him about his military
service. Cultivated, cheerful, generous, and reliable, he took an interest in public
affairs. In February 1931, the *Daily Colonist* printed a letter he wrote entitled "High
Finance," an intelligent and indignant reply to a letter by G. H. Walton opposing
the government's policy of employment in the lumber mills. My mother noted
in her diary that one of his daughters, Marjorie (Villers) Antonelli, brought him
around to "Arbourfield" on 7 August 1985. He was deaf and blind by then, and
he died, aged ninety-four, on 2 January 1987.
Sources: census 1901, England, RG 13/2866, p. 22; census 1891, RG 12/2411, p.
16; census 1871, RG 10/3140, p. 11; *Colonist*, 21 February 1931, p. 2.

VILLIERS, Lieutenant Colonel Charles Walter (1873-1938). He was born on
23 September 1873 at "Closeburn Hall," Closeburn Village, County of Dumfries
in Scotland, a son of "Frederick Earnest Villiers, Gentleman" and of Jane Isabella
Villiers *née* Baird, twelve years younger than her husband. Signing the birth
certificate as witness was George Francis Worrell, butler at Closeburn Hall. The
parents had married on 20 July 1869 at St Peter's, Eaton Square, London, but the
father and his sister, Viscountess Cole, owned 13,573 acres in Dumfries, which the
family had held at least since Henry VII's reign (1485-1509). The father, born in
1840 at Kenilworth, Warwickshire, had served as a captain in HM Bodyguard of
Scottish Archers and was a member of Brooks's Club in London. The 1881 census
recorded him as "Landed proprietor, J.P." living at 4 St George's Place, Westminster,
with CV (aged seven), the rest of the family, and four servants. Ten years later, they
were all living in Chelsea at 18 Cadogan Square. As a child, CV survived enteric
fever, malarial fever, and the removal of his appendix. After schooling at Eton,
he became an officer of the Third Battalion, Royal Scots Fusiliers. Shortly after
that, he became a lieutenant colonel in the Coldstream Guards Reserve and one
of HM Bodyguards for Scotland and fought in both the Matabele War (1896)
and the South African War (1899-1902). A few months after that war ended, he
married Lady Kathleen Mary Cole, born c. 1873, daughter of the Fourth Earl of
Enniskillen; in time, they had a son and two daughters. And he began a business
career in the Rand gold fields of South Africa, which he had just helped to defend
from the Boers and the Matabele tribesmen. He kept his hand in that business for
the next twenty years though business was interrupted by the Great War.

On 16 August 1915, CV applied for a commission in the territorial force and
was instructed to report for duty at Windsor on 25 August 1915 as lieutenant in the
Coldstream Guards but moved on 5 October to the Irish Guards and three days
later was appointed APM vice-lieutenant to Viscount Powerscourt, MVO. Before the
end of 1915, he was sent to Salonika as APM at HQ, temporary major. Promoted
to lieutenant colonel on 15 May 1916 while acting as provost marshal of an army,
he was named to the DSO on 3 June 1916 (*London Gazette* No 29834), mentioned

in Major General Sir C. Munro's despatch for "distinguished and gallant services rendered during the period he was in command of the M.E.F." (*London Gazette*, 13 July 1916 no. 29664), mentioned in Lieutenant General G. F. Milne's despatch of 5 December 1916 as deserving of special mention, and on 1 October 1917 went on leave from Salonika to England via the Santa Quaranda Route. This leave must have been very brief as he was mentioned on 28 November 1917 in a despatch of Lieutenant General G. F. Miles. On 10 October 1918, he was awarded the Order of the Redeemer, Third Class, by "H.M. the King of the Hellenes." Altogether, he was decorated with the DSO (1916), the OBE (1918), the CBE (1919), the Greek Order of Redeemer, the French *Croix de Guerre* with Palm, and the Siberian Order of White Eagle with swords. He relinquished his appointment on 23 May 1919, retired with the rank of temporary lieutenant colonel, and returned to his business in South Africa as "Director of Co[mpan]y" on 18 August 1919. His permanent address was still "The Rand Club, Johannesburg, Cape Town," and on 10 May 1920, the War Office informed someone that he "has been demobilized and left for Johannesburg in August last."

For some reason that is not explained in my sources, CV and his family moved out to the Island in 1923. He may have simply been attracted by the offer of employment as general manager of the Canadian Collieries (Dunsmuir Ltd.) with its mines in Nanaimo and the village of Cumberland. He took the post upon the death of the previous manager, J. M. Savage. CV and his family settled near Cumberland and remained there for the rest of his life, though they travelled a great deal, had the philanthropic and public-spirited interests usual in such families, and moved in the Island's highest social circles. In May 1929, CV and his family went to England. In 1932, Lady Kathleen Villiers sailed to England to spend a few months with her parental family and returned in the *Empress of Britain* early in August 1931. King George V had raised CV to the rank of commander of the Order of St John of Jerusalem, and CV took that as a serious responsibility. He remained active in the work of the St Johns Ambulance Association and in 1934 was made a member of the chapter at Ottawa. From 1928 to 1930, he was honorary president of the Nanaimo and Cumberland centres and remained a member of the BC Executive Council of the St John's Ambulance Association until his death. He donated the "Villiers Cup" for an annual competition in first aid at Nanaimo and in 1931 donated another Villiers Cup to be awarded for lawn bowling, which was and remained popular in Nanaimo. He patronized the Ladysmith—South Wellington Band and became its honorary president in 1934. In September 1929, he was appointed president of the BC Mining Association.

At Christmas 1930, CV and his wife and their daughter Helen were guests of the lieutenant governor at Government House, Victoria, for a few days. CV became a member of the Union Club in Victoria and kept his membership in White's Club (London). On the Island, he played golf and enjoyed sailing in the protected waters of the Gulf of Georgia. They soon made friends such as *General Noel Money, resident proprietor of the Qualicum Beach Hotel, who visited them in Cumberland from time to time. In August 1938, CV complained of back pains and his physician, Dr H. E. Ridewood, describing his condition as "quite serious," sent him in a special railway carriage to the Jubilee Hospital, Victoria. There he died, aged sixty-five, on 3 September 1938, leaving his wife and their three children: Berkeley Villiers in London, Miss Helen Villiers at home, and Mrs Charles Kerr, wife of Lieutenant Colonel Charles I. Kerr. *Major Paul Frederick Villiers, sometime resident of Victoria, was one of his first cousins. A funeral was held in Victoria, but CV was cremated and his ashes sent to be buried at home "in the Old Country." Locally, he was greatly missed: Major V. B. Harrison said, "He was a most kindly gentleman and just, and it was only three weeks ago last Friday that the Colonel and I discussed the idea of arranging for waterfront land for city park purposes. His death is a great loss to the whole Island." H. N. Freeman, currently president of the Vancouver Island Chamber of Mines, said that the coal mining industry of the province had just lost a leader of sterling character who tried to bring labour and capital together and was a valued member of the Vancouver Island Chamber of Mines.

Sources: *National Archives* (PRO), London, WO 339/37393; *Nanaimo Daily Free Press*, Saturday, 3 September 1938, page 1; census 1881, England, RG 11/98, p. 21; census 1891, RG 12/62, p. 28; *Colonist*, 24 May 1929, p. 8; 26 September 1929, p. 5; 28 December 1930, p. 7; 9 August 1931, p. 8; 27 January 1934, p. 17; 16 May 1936, p. 8; 4 September 1938, pp. 1, 6 and 16, obit.; notes courtesy of Jonathan Berry, Nanaimo; *Who's Who in B.C.* 1933-1934, p. 174; *Who Was Who*, 1929-1940, p. 1391; Bateman, *The Great Landowners*, p. 458.

VILLIERS, Major Paul Frederick (1884-?). He was born on 8 July 1884 in Belgravia, London, a son of Charlotte Emily Louisa Villiers, *née* Cadogan, and Rev. Henry Montague Villiers, "clerk in Holy Orders," who christened him on 6 August at his own church, St Paul's, Wilton Place. His father was Anglican, but PV declared himself a Presbyterian when he joined the Canadian Army on 23 September 1914. He was schooled at Harrow (September 1898 to Easter 1902) and Henley House, France (?), Summer Term 1902. On 30 March 1903, he applied for admission to the Royal Military College, Sandhurst, when his address was still St Paul's Vicarage, Wilton Place, London SW. His choice was to join the infantry, rather than the cavalry, foot guards, Indian staff corps, or King's royal rifle corps, etc. During the seven years he spent in the Fourteenth King's Hussars, he became a second lieutenant on 16 August 1905, lieutenant therein on 6 September 1906, and captain on 17 November 1911. His record of service shows him "at home," from August to September 1906, in India from September 1906 to December 1908, in Somaliland with the Sixth King's African Rifles from October 1909 to April 1910, in Nyasaland with the First King's African Rifles from May 1910 to 4 September 1911, and "in British East Africa" from 5 September 1911 to May 1912. When he applied for permission to resign his commission on 23 September 1912, he had the African General Service Medal with a clasp for Somaliland, 1908-1910, and was still single. His resignation of his captain's commission was approved and was to appear in the *London Gazette* on or after 24 September 1912. He wrote, "I have completed thirty months of service in the King's African Rifles and am therefore entitled to six months' leave—which is due to end on 23 September [1912]," and wanted his resignation to take effect that day.

He soon moved out to Canada, where he had spent a year in the Eighty-eighth Fusiliers by the time he joined the CEF in Victoria on 23 September 1914 and signed papers at Valcartier on 9 February 1915. He was married by then to Evelyn Anne Villiers, 7 Queen's Garden, Lancaster Gate, London. He was then 5' 8½" tall, with fair complexion, brown eyes, and black hair, weighing 160 lbs. Sent overseas, he became brigade major on 26 May 1915, staff captain on 31 August 1915, general staff officer on 20 January 1916, and brigade major on 11 October 1916. At the front, he was severely gassed on 21 September 1917, "suffered a severe bronchitis and conjunctivitis," and was treated in the Liverpool Hospital at Étaples. Whatever the action in which this occurred, he was highly regarded and awarded the DSO on 19 February 1917 after being mentioned in despatches on 30 November 1916. On 12 April 1914, the *Daily Colonist* cited him as having served until 1912 in Somaliland, Nyasaland, and Zanzibar with the Sixth Battalion of the King's African Rifles and about to join the Eighty-eighth Battalion of Hussars. It printed a photo of him on 21 January 1917 as a former resident of Victoria and adjutant of the Eighty-eighth Fusiliers who had transferred to the Fiftieth Gordon Highlanders on 7 June 1914. He embarked for Canada on 24 June 1919 and was demobilized on 8 July 1919 with the declared intention of settling in Victoria. Meanwhile, his wife had been receiving her allowance c/o Colonial Trust Co., Victoria. They moved away at sometime between the wars and I could trace them no further.
Sources: *National Archives*, London (PRO), WO339/6294, a very thin file; NAC, RG150, acc. 1992-1993/166, Box 9952-27; *Colonist*, 12 April 1914, p. 14; 21 January 1917, p. 5.

WACE, Dr Cyril (1870-1966). He was born at Camberwell, Surrey, son of Henry Wace, a clergyman born at Islington, Middlesex, and his wife Elizabeth, born at Westminster, Middlesex. The 1871 census recorded him, eight months old, living with his parents and two older brothers born at Marylebone, London: Henry C. Wace aged three and Robert Wace aged two. There were two uncles (their father's brothers) living with them, both students born at Goring, Oxfordshire: Herbert Wace aged nineteen and Arthur Wace aged twenty-two, a "Cambridge Student." The household had four servants: nurse, housemaid, cook, and a fifteen-year-old girl described as a "machinist." Ten years later, CW and his brothers were at a school at 146 High Street, Ramsgate, under Charles Hesledon Rose, "M.A. Cambridge," and in 1901, CW was a "Doctor in Practice" living with his wife Clara M. Wace, from Cheltenham, at 11 St Thomas, Winchester. They had three servants: cook, housemaid, and boy. They migrated to the Cowichan Valley and there the *Cowichan Leader* reported after the Great War that CW had been sent to England for three months, at the request of the executive of the Canadian Red Cross Society, to examine and report on British arrangements for the care and employment of disabled war veterans. His efforts resulted in the establishment of a Red Cross Workshop in Victoria, employing twenty men, the first such institution in Canada. CW died, aged ninety-five, on 3 April 1966 in Saanich.
Sources: census 1901, England, RG 13/1081, p. 37; census 1881, RG 11/987, p. 16; census 1871, RG 10/723, p. 30; *Cowichan Leader*, September 1921?

WADMORE, Colonel Robinson Lyndhurst (1855-1915). Born on 5 January 1855 in Hackney (or "Upper Clapton"), London, he was the eldest son of Anne Elizabeth Wadmore *née* Holt and her husband, James Foster Wadmore (1822-1903), a London architect who worked in partnership with W. R. Mallett in offices at 35 Great St Helens [*sic*]. The 1861 census found RW aged six living with his family at 2 Sheldon Villas, Hackney; he had three sisters and there were three servants. Ten years later, they were living at Day Hill, Tonbridge, and RW, now sixteen, was attending Tonbridge School. He had four sisters, two younger brothers, and there were still three servants. A younger brother, Clyde Wadmore, went to work in a tea-merchant's office and by 1891, aged twenty-seven, was employed as a "Tea Planter in Ceylon." RW had meanwhile trained as an architect but been commissioned as a lieutenant in the London Rifle Volunteers. He then migrated to Ottawa, where he worked for a time in the Canadian civil service and married Annie Knight Skead, aged thirty-six, eldest daughter of Senator James Skead and his wife Rosina, *née* Mackey, on 18 April 1882 at Nepean, south of Ottawa. The next year, he joined the permanent force in Canada and was promoted to captain (1888), major (1889), lieutenant colonel (1905), and colonel (1910) in command of a regiment. His first military service was as a lieutenant in the campaign against the North-West Rebellion of Louis Riel, and he was present at the relief of Battleford, at Cut Knife Hill, and in the last operation against Big Bear's band. At the opening of the Imperial Institute, London, in 1893, he was present in Queen Victoria's escort; in 1897, he took a three-month course at RMC in Kingston, Ontario; and in 1909, he commanded the troops sent to Cape Breton during a miners' strike there. He then served as CO at various places in Canada: St John's, Quebec [*sic*], Fredericton, NB, and Victoria.

RW arrived in Victoria on 1 September 1910 with his wife to take command of Military District No. 11, and they settled at 380 Moss Street. He was reputed to be a soldier with a deep interest in public affairs and soon became vice-president of the local Imperial Campaigners' Association. Their children had already grown up by then. In 1911, their daughter Leila Ione Wadmore married *Lieutenant Colonel Alexander Ernest Harris, and her sister Rose Blanche L. Wadmore married *Colonel Horace Westmorland. When RW retired, he and his wife remained in Victoria, and there he died, aged sixty, on 2 April 1915. He had fallen ill with jaundice and been cared for by *Major Walter Bapty and Dr Leeder. His widow died, aged sixty-eight, on 20 November 1929 in Victoria.

Sources: Robert Collier Fetherstonhaugh, *The Royal Canadian Regiment*, 1883-1933 (Fredericton, Centennial Print & Litho Ltd., 1981), pp. 7, 12, 26, 31, 40, 43, 48, 51, 53, 158, 167, 172-186, chapter 13, and a photo opposite page 54; *Colonist*, 4 April 1914, p. 4; 3 April 1915, pp. 2-3, photo and obit.; 8 October 1933, p. 22; Vital Statistics for Carleton County, Ontario, 1882 no. 001747-1882; census 1861, England, RG 9/153, pp. 32-3; census 1871, RG 10/931, p. 34; census 1881, RG 11/918, p. 22; census 1891, RG 12/681, pp. 42-3.

WAKE, Captain Baldwin Arden (1813-1880). He was born in January 1813 in Northamptonshire, son of Baldwin Wake, MD, and nephew of Sir William Wake of Courteen Hall, Northamptonshire. BW joined the Royal Navy in 1827 as a volunteer on HMS *Espoir* and was posted for some time at the Cape of Good Hope. Then he joined HMS *Falcon* on the West India Station, where he also served on the *Forester*, the *San Josef*, and the *Racehorse*. In 1837, he was promoted to lieutenant and joined HMS *Melville*, flagship of Sir Peter Halkett, commander-in-chief of the North America and West India squadron. BW was promoted to commander in 1849 and appeared as captain on the retired list in 1866. The Royal Humane Society and the Royal Shipwreck Institution recorded several occasions on which he saved lives at sea.

BW married Adelaide Maria Wake (1830-1894), and they had four children. When he retired from the RN in 1866, he and his family lived in Esquimalt and in 1876 also pre-empted land at the northern end of Valdez Island, where they raised sheep, cattle, and vegetables. For a couple of years, BW taught at the Gabriola Island School, rowing over to it daily, but he was dismissed in June 1878 as a result of objections to his methods. On 16 January 1880, he left Nanaimo Harbour for Valdez Island in his small sloop but never arrived. His son, George Wake, offered a reward for clues about his father's disappearance, but the body was never found. Reports of BW's disappearance and the discovery of his damaged sloop appeared in the *Colonist* and in the *Nanaimo Free Press*, 17, 21, and 31 January 1880. During his long retirement on and around Vancouver Island, BW had become well known, and his mysterious death was therefore widely discussed. His younger son, Baldwin Hough Wake, stayed on Valdez for the rest of his life, working as the telegrapher at the first telegraph station there, though in 1884 he went to England and returned with a bride from Yorkshire named Amelia. This son died accidentally in 1904, and his widow died in 1946 at Nanaimo. BW's widow lived on at Esquimalt until her death, aged sixty-three, on 20 November 1894. In June 1881, their daughter Amy Rosamund Wake married her first cousin, Gervais Wake, at St Paul's Naval and Garrison Church, Esquimalt, and thirty-three years later, in 1914, this family left Esquimalt to live at Crompton Hill, Herefordshire, England. In June 1886, BW's younger daughter, Florence Myrna Wake, married Henry Cobourne Maunoir Ridley at St Paul's Naval and Garrison Church, Esquimalt, and they settled at Ridley's home in Kamloops, BC.

Sources: Notes courtesy of Barrie Humphrey, Gabriola Island; census 1861, England, RG 9/1566, p. 17; *Colonist*, 7 April 1880, p. 3, obit.; 9 April 1880, p. 2; 16 April 1880, p. 1; 30 April, p. 1; 2 June 1880, p. 1; 3 June 1880, p. 1; 21 July 1880, p. 1; 24 July 1880, p. 1; 5 August 1880, p. 1; 10 June 1881, p. 3; 22 November 1894, p. 8, obit. (Mrs Wake); Internet files maintained by descendants, based on *Colonist* entries and other sources; *The Times* (London), 19 February 1880, p. 8, obit.

WALBRAN, Captain John Thomas (1848-1913). Born at Ripon, Yorkshire, on 23 March 1848, he was sent to a local grammar school, which may have been the one on the High Street, Agnesgate, Ripon, where he lived with his maternal grandfather, Thomas Horsfall, born c. 1800, and his grandmother, Caroline Helen Horsfall, listed as "clergyman's wife." This grandfather was recorded in 1861 as "Schoolmaster, grammar school, Chaplain of House of Correction" Also resident with these grandparents were JW's eleven-year-old brother, Christopher

John Walbran, and their widowed mother, Sarah Walbran *née* Horsfall. JW
went on to serve as a cadet on HM School Frigate, *Conway*. In 1888, he joined
the Canadian Pacific Navigation Co. as first officer on the *Islander* and then as
captain of SS *Danube*. He next joined the Canadian marine and fisheries service
and commanded SS *Quadra* in the years 1891-1898. After retiring, JW and his
wife lived in Victoria at 306 Dallas Road at the corner of Menzies Street until
her death, aged fifty-eight, on 9 September 1907 and his death, aged sixty-four,
on 31 March 1913. Their house was still standing in 1960. "Like many another
British Columbian," Professor Phillip Akrigg writes, "Walbran had a little difficulty
in recognizing Ottawa as the centre of things." Evidence of this is found in an
unconsciously amusing letter he wrote in 1894 to the Hydrographer of the Navy
in London:

> I had been so used, for I may say years, to send all my marine information
> to you direct that I was not aware when becoming an officer in the
> Dominion Service it should have gone through the Department at
> Ottawa.
>
> The Dominion Government are my employers and I do not wish
> to offend them in any way by breaking through any rules, and am very
> sure you will agree with me that in so doing so I am only acting rightly. I
> shall always be pleased to correspond with you as a friend, and shall also
> be pleased to give any information I can to the officers of His Majesty's
> ships serving in these waters.

In 1909, JW published his remarkable reference book, *British Columbia Coast
Names 1592-1906*, based on what he had been able to gather from a great variety
of sources.

He had married his wife Anne Mary (1849-1907) in England and had two
daughters at Bootle, Lancashire, before going out to the Island. Before they
went to join him in 1893, wife and daughters lived at 17 Langland Way, Lescart,
Chester, where the census found them in 1891. One daughter, Florence Horsfall
Walbran, born on 18 March 1873, married Thomas Hugh Worthington on 14
Sep 1916 in Victoria and died there on 14 November 1950. The other, Ethel
Margaret Elizabeth Walbran, born on 6 Jan 1875, married Francis Napier Denison
(1866-1946) on 21 July 1904, in Victoria. Denison was a Torontonian who became
the first meteorologist in Victoria and the first director of the Gonzales Hill
Observatory. In 1912, the *Daily Colonist* published a series of his articles under the
title "Observations in Science." JW and his wife lived and died as Anglicans.
Sources: census 1861, England, RG 9/3196, p. 16; census 1891, RG 12/2895, p. 27;
Hydrographic Department, Royal Navy (Taunton, Somerset), File BC (A); George
Nicholson, *Vancouver Island's West Coast* (Victoria, Privately Printed, 1965), p. 176;
Canadian census, 1901, Victoria; Phillip Akrigg, introduction to a late edition
of Captain John T. Walbran, British Columbia Coast Names 1592-1906 (1909),
(Vancouver, J. J. Douglas, 1973), 546 pp., p. vii; J. R. Mathieson, entry on Francis
Napier Denison in *The Canadian Encyclopedia*.

WALKER, Major General Sir Ernest Alexander (1880-1944). He was born on 20 October 1880 at Rescoble Angus, Scotland, son of Rev. Alexander Walker, senior chaplain in the Church of Scotland, and his wife Mary Mowbray Esdaile. After attending Forfar Academy and the University of Edinburgh, he entered the Indian Medical Service in 1902, was appointed to the Peshawar Division on 2 October 1904, and passed a higher-standard examination in Pushtu. The only interruption in his IMS career was the Great War in which he served (1914-1921) mainly in Mesopotamia, was taken prisoner in the disastrous defeat of British forces at Kut-al-Amara, and survived two and a half years during 1916-1918 in one of the barbarous Turkish prison camps. He was twice mentioned in despatches and decorated with the 1914-1915 star and two medals. Upon his release, he became deputy assistant director of the Army Medical Service (1920-1921). Rejoining the IMS, he was named deputy director, director (1929-1932), and finally deputy director of the medical service in the Eastern Command (1932-1933). Meanwhile, in 1930 he was appointed honorary surgeon to the viceroy of India and, in the years 1932-1937, honorary surgeon to the king. At some stage, he was made an officer of the Order of St John of Jerusalem, in 1934 named CB, later MB, ChB, and FRCSE, and in 1938 knighted as KCLE. He retired in 1937.

In 1906, EW had married Juanita Mary Power, born in Melbourne, Australia, daughter of Brigade Surgeon Richard Power of the IMS, and she migrated to the Island with him in April 1938. Their only son David Walker was then a journalist in London on the staff of the *Daily Mirror*, known for his column, "Talking Shop." They had been receiving the *Cowichan Leader* for the previous two years, and it was this local weekly's general impression of the Cowichan Valley that had attracted them to the Island. For their first few days, they stayed in Victoria with *Lieutenant Colonel and Mrs A. F. M. Slater, sometime residents of Cowichan, but then they went to stay near Maple Bay for a fortnight with the *Dopping-Hepenstals. Towards the end of May, after a few days with a Miss L. Harden and about four months in a place owned by the Hogan family of Duncan (who went to spend four months in Leicestershire with a daughter, Mrs S. A. N. Watney *née* Hogan), they bought J. H. Pritchard's property on Stamps Road at the north end of Quamichan Lake and began to develop it as a country estate in the familiar English manner, with a driveway leading to a house surrounded by shrubbery, flower borders, a variety of gardens, and a view over the lake. There EW enjoyed the excellent shooting and fishing for which the district was famous and took part in community affairs; for a time, he was president of Cowichan Branch, Canadian Red Cross Society, and vice-chairman of Cowichan War Activities Committee.

He also watched world events with increasing anxiety as the Second World War approached and began to express his views in the local newspapers. By 1940, he was evidently exasperated by Canadian authorities and the public which had elected them. In June 1940, he wrote to the *Daily Colonist* under the head, "The Tragedy of Canada":

I am not a politician, thank God. I am merely an old soldier who had forty years' service, first in the ranks and then as an officer. I came to this delightful country two years ago as the best place I knew in the Empire to pass my remaining days. What is my reaction now, in June 1940? It is one of black, bitter, and burning shame. Did any Canadian who listened to Premier Reynaud's final appeal to the United States tonight for help in France's hour of agony think what we might have done and have left undone. Did he think how many French and British boys would have been saved from a brutal death if the Government in Ottawa had not refused two years ago to join the Empire air training scheme? They lacked the protection from the air which this scheme would have given them and they just died. They were not politicians; they had no interest in contracts.

Did any Canadian think what the situation might and should have been in the North of France tonight if we had a fraction even of the troops we should have over there? Does he think that 23,000 men from a population of 11,000,000 is a fair share in this life and death struggle for freedom and everything that makes life worth living for us and for our sons? This country's foreign policy in the past was—and still is, apparently—a reliance on the Royal Navy to which it has never contributed a penny, and on the Monroe Doctrine, which amounts to cowering behind the tall feathers of the American eagle.

I do not believe that this represents the feelings of the majority of Canadians. We have a great and rich country, with a grand lot of men and women living in it, many of whom feel just as I do. They know just as well as I that there is a price to be paid for freedom and for liberty, and that in the past we have not attempted to pay the price. The instalments on our insurance policy are woefully overdue. We lack leadership and we cannot, as individuals, escape the liability for that lack. After the outbreak of war we returned by an overwhelming majority a Government which, to me, appears to combine all the worst attributes of Ramsay MacDonald and Chamberlain in his days of appeasement. Let us make it clear in Ottawa that we, the people, want to get on with the job. I pray with all my heart that it is not too late.

EW had evidently not yet understood the basis of the Liberal Party's political obsession with placating Quebec and its stubborn delays while waiting for contrary public pressures. In March 1941, he wrote another letter headed "Dr Goebbels Scores Again": "One of the minor horrors of this war is undoubtedly the Canadian Broadcasting Corporation," which he thought was reporting German propaganda as though it were news. He went on to say, in a letter to the *Cowichan Leader* in October 1941, that none "of the three parties [in Canada] have the slightest appreciation of the world situation today. They all offer various baits or bribes to the electors, which may or may not be fulfilled . . . [but] I am proud to be a member of the Canadian Legion. At their annual conference they have passed unanimously a motion in favour of conscription. THIS is the biggest question in any election in Canada today and all our candidates refuse to face the issue." On one of the most troublesome issues in BC, he wrote in February 1944 under the head, *Japanese Atrocities,* "I was a prisoner . . . in the last war for over 2½ years and have a very deep and personal interest in this question . . . Are we to permit some 30,000 fanatically loyal subjects of the Rising Sun to live on this vital coast to spy out the land, to displace Canadians in logging camps, in the fishing industry, and the truck farms of the Fraser Valley? I feel very strongly on the subject, and I have spent the greater part of my life in the Orient. We must formulate our postwar policy as regards the Japanese in Canada now to be ready for the peace to come." It was his opinion that only those Japanese who were Canadian citizens should be allowed to remain after the war.

EW died suddenly, aged sixty-three, on 5 September 1944 at their home and, being a Roman Catholic, was buried at St Ann's graveyard in Tzouhalem after a service at St Edward's Church. He had been a president of that church's Holy Name Society, and some of its members were the active pallbearers at the funeral: *Major F. A. Considine and Messrs Hector Marsh, R. O. Tait, Jules Weicker, A. X. Rey, and Joseph Drennan. The honorary pallbearers, few of them Catholic, were *Colonel M. E. Dopping-Hepenstal, *Lieutenant Colonel R. B. Longridge, *Captain J. D. Groves, Captain Struan Robertson, and Messrs W. Waldon Jr, J. Y. Copeman, and *Marcel Charles Koechlin. He had learnt to love the Cowichan District in which he found great enjoyment in his favourite hobby, angling, and he interested many others in its beauties.

Sources: *Who was Who*, vol. 3 (1941-1950), pp. 1191-2; BL, India Office, *Indian Army List*, January 1905, pp. 477, 701; *Cowichan Leader*, 21 April 1938; 26 May 1938; 9 October 1941, p. 7; 6 September 1944, p. 8, obit.; *Colonist*, 4 May 1940, p. 4; 15 June 1940, p. 4; 13 March 1941, p. 4; 10 April 1943, p. 4; 1 February 1944, p. 4; *Who's Who in B.C.*, 1942-1943, p. 311.

WALKER, Rev. Reginald Edmund (1866-1945). In summer 1912, he resigned his clerical living as rector of Frant, Sussex, where he had been installed since 1901, and retired with his wife to Victoria, where they settled at 649 Admiral's Road. This move may have been prompted by the death of a son that year. RW's father was Sir James Walker, second baronet (1829-1899) of Sand Hutton, Yorkshire, MP for Beverley, Yorkshire, and his mother was Lady Louisa Susan Marlborough Heron-Maxwell (1840-1920), a Scottish lady. Born at Foston Hall, Yorkshire, on 27 June 1866, RW was sent in due time to Harrow and Christ Church, Oxford, where he matriculated on 16 October 1885 (BA, 1889; MA, 1898) and became an Anglican clergyman. Various vicarages in the north of England followed, as well as a chaplaincy to the bishop of Ripon, Dr Boyd Carpenter. RW was the second son and therefore inherited neither the baronetcy nor the family estates, which in the 1880s comprised 5,819 acres in Yorkshire, 795 acres in Buckinghamshire, 241 acres in Lancashire, and 51 acres in Derbyshire, totalling 6, 906 acres, then worth £13,982.

However, on 19 September 1895, RW married into an old noble family at Alcester, Warwickshire, with even great estates: 10,281 acres in Warwick, 217 acres in Worcestershire, 998 acres in County Antrim, and 793 acres in County Down, totalling 12,289 acres, then worth £18,392. The lady was Emily Mary Seymour (1873-1948), born at Arrow, Warwickshire, second daughter of Lord Hugh de Gray Seymour, Sixth Marquess of Hertford (1843-1912), of Ragley Hall, and his wife, a granddaughter of the Fifth Marquess, Lord Francis George Hugh Seymour (1812-1884). RW and his wife had five children before leaving England, but five years after their arrival, a second son was killed accidentally while flying with the

Royal Flying Corps. Lady Walker, undaunted, set herself to found a Farmers' Institute in East Sooke, which she accomplished in December 1921, and served as its secretary until 1948. After RW died, aged seventy-nine, on 23 August 1945, she took an even more active interest in women's affairs on the Island and was also life honorary vice-president of the naval veterans of Victoria. In spring 1948, she flew to England for the wedding of her niece, Lady Margaret Seymour (1918-1975), lady-in-waiting to HRH Princess Elizabeth, and returned in October in time to help with the poppy-selling campaign for Armistice Day that year. It was all too much for her and she died, aged seventy-five, on 6 November 1948. Surviving them were two of her sisters in England, a third son, Rupert Alexander Walker of Nanaimo, and a daughter, Mrs Margaret Edith Mary Derbyshire (1901-1975), who in 1941 had married William Derbyshire (c. 1907-1968), a couple with two children living on the Island in East Sooke.

Sources: *Crockford's Clerical Directory*, 1898, p. 1405; *Colonist*, 7 November 1948, obit., and photo; 9 November 1948, p. 15, obit.; *Oxford University Alumni, 1500-1886*, vol. IV, p. 1486; Oxford Men, 1880-1892, p. 627; Bateman, *The Great Landowners*, pp. 219 and 462; *Who's Who in B.C.*, 1942-43, p. 312.

WALLICH, Collings (1865-1954). He was born in London in March 1865, son of Surgeon Major George C. Wallich, who was born in Bengal and had a career in the Indian Army. His mother, Caroline E. Wallich, was born at Lowestoft, Suffolk. The 1871 census shows CW aged six, living at 2 Warwick Gardens, Kensington, with his parents, three brothers and four sisters. The two eldest, Charles A. H. Wallich, aged seventeen, and Alice M. Wallich, fourteen, were born in Bengal. Beatrice H. Wallich, eleven, was born on the island of Guernsey; Edith Wallich, nine, was born in Devonshire; and Elinor Wallich, eight, was born in London. The two youngest were born in London: Marmaduke G. Wallich, three, and Horace Wallich, eighteen months. There were four domestic servants. Ten years later, CW was still at home but his mother was absent, and his father was recorded as "Doctor of Medicine of University of Edinburgh practising as physician surgeon." With them was a patient, Mary A. S. Sibbald, a widow aged seventy-six born in Bengal, and a boarder aged twenty-four, Koomar Gogendra Marayam, born at Kooch Behar in Bengal. With this background, it is hardly surprising that CW became a tea planter in Darjeeling. He was in the Dooars district from 1884 to 1897, becoming manager of Queenalooka in the old Selim Company in 1886, and in November 1887, he opened the Chalouni Garden and remained there until 1897. Then he returned home to England and tried farming in Gloucestershire. When this proved to be unprofitable, he returned to India in 1904 for three years until an old friend, Colonel Tom Moss, persuaded him to emigrate to the Cowichan Valley, where he arrived in 1911. There they built a house named "Cotswald" on a hill overlooking the Cowichan Bay Road—then part of the Island Highway—near the Hillbank Cross Road, then called Wallich Road.

There CW went into the real-estate and insurance business at Cowichan Station. He became known locally as a supporter of good causes and a worthy advocate of better school facilities for rural children. On one occasion during the First

World War, he visited the Department of Education in Victoria to protest against a $50 levy on Cowichan Station—children attending Duncan High School. He was successful and children then began to attend that school. He took a keen interest in other matters of taxation and was fond of sports. He annually attended the tournaments at South Cowichan Lawn Tennis Club. When he fell and broke his hip, he never really recovered from the shock of it. But he never lost his interest in the tea-growing industry with which, for so many years, he was actively connected. As late as March 1948, *The Planters Journal and Agriculturist*, published in Calcutta, printed a letter he wrote to the Tea Planters Association of India. In it, he told something of his career (as above) and also of his efforts to improve the lot of the labour force in the industry. Conditions in the Dooars were appalling, and the lives of many planters and their labourers were unnecessarily lost because of malaria and other ailments resulting from defective hygiene and sanitation. Wallich's efforts did not go unnoticed, and an extract from the minutes of the Planters' Association, 28 October 1907, commended his work in trying to combat and control conditions leading to malaria and blackwater fever. A number of other testimonials were pressed upon him when he retired from the firm Duncan Brothers & Co. after fourteen years of service.

In 1890, CW had married a cousin, Mary Leonora Wallich (1867-1938) from Norfolk, daughter of Rev. L. C. Wallich and his wife *née* Fanny Wilkinson, and they had several children. For many years, Mrs Wallich played the organ at St Andrew's Anglican Church at Cowichan Station, and like many other British women, she painted watercolours of local scenery that were much admired. When CW died, aged eighty-eight, on 30 January 1954 at Duncan, he left a son in Vancouver, Maurice Wallich, a daughter at Cowichan Bay, Mrs E. C. Springett, and several grandchildren. His funeral was at St Peter's Anglican Church at Quamichan Lake, where the pallbearers included *Percy Jaynes, J. H. Moore, and Magnus Colvin, with *Air Marshal Sir Philip Livingston and *Major J. H. G. Palmer as honorary pallbearers. **Sources:** *Cowichan Leader*, 4 February 1954, obit.; census 1871, England, RG 19 32, pp. 17-18; census 1881, RG11 0626/17, p. 27; census 1901, RG 13/2428, p. 2; *Memories Never Lost: Stories of the Pioneer Women of the Cowichan Valley and a Brief History of the Valley, 1850-1920*, ed., Jan Gould (Altona, Manitoba, Compiled by the Pioneer Researchers, 1986), pp. 299-300, 303-4;

WALTER, Captain Frederick Henry (1872-1949). He was born on 18 August 1872 at Aldershot, Berkshire, son of Major Frederick Edward Walter (1848-1931), who had attended Eton College, entered the Royal Artillery, and served as commanding officer of the Corps of Commissionaires in London for thirty years. FW's grandfather John Walter III (1818-1894) was owner of *The Times*, member of Parliament, and landowner at Newland, Hurst, Berkshire. The father and grandfather appear, with members of the family, in the census records for 1861 and the father again in 1901, but FW may have been abroad with his family in 1881 and was certainly away on the training ship HMS *Britannia* from 15 January 1886 to December 1887. He went on to serve on HMS *Imperieuse* on the China Station (March 1888-1891), HMS *Volage* (1892), HMS *Champion* in the Pacific

(1893), and the flagship *Royal Arthur* as lieutenant (1893). About 1897, he was assigned to surveying ships, beginning with HMS *Egeria* in BC waters until 1903, when he joined HMS *Penguin* in Australia, and then commanded HMS *Goldfinch*, surveying from 24 July 1906 to 24 October 1908 and was promoted to commander. There followed command of HMS *Merlin* in China, HMS *Odin* in the Persian Gulf (1910), and HMS *Shearwater* (1912-1914) as senior naval officer on the west coast of North America, command of HMS *Caribbean* and *Victorian* (1914-1918) as captain, and an appointment to the Naval Staff of the Admiralty (1919-1921). According to his record, in October 1912, he received an "appreciation of Government of India for services in the Persian Gulf," but later among the remarks is "Friction with Acting Vice-Consul at Guaymas, Mexico, informed that he went beyond his powers in advising the Vice-Consul to resign ALM 10 October 1913." He was "to remain in *Shearwater* to complete three year as L.C.W., 5 March 1914" but gave up his command of that ship on 20 January 1914 and arrived home on 17 August. He was at various times judged zealous, efficient, etc., and very good at gunnery, but had health problems and was placed on the retired list on 12 September 1921 as "Unfit for service. Damaged lungs after pleurisy (twice)."

While stationed at Esquimalt and surveying in Pacific coast waters, FW established himself on Salt Spring Island by marrying, on 8 November 1898, Winnifred Lois Wilson (c. 1877-1931), born at Collingwood, Ontario, to *Rev. E. F. Wilson, who served as vicar of Salt Spring Island for eighteen years. FW and his wife lived for some years in Victoria and near Ganges, Salt Spring Island, but she accompanied him later to Australia, New Zealand, and then to England, where the RN took him during the Great War and where they remained until sometime in 1927. Returning then to settle permanently at Ganges, they built a family house they called "Winfrith" where they could receive their two daughters, her many Wilson relatives, and other friends. One daughter married *Lieutenant Colonel H. S. Thuillier and the other married A. O. Buchanan. When Mrs Walter died, aged fifty-eight, on 4 November 1931, she also left four sisters, and the pallbearers at her funeral included three of her five brothers as well as Colonel F. B. Wilson of Toronto.

FW carried on in the retired life they had meanwhile established in the social circles of Victoria and both islands in general. Known familiarly to his brothers-in-law and other familiars, for no obvious reason, as "Fritz Walter", he was a member of the Overseas Club and the Salt Spring Island Golf Club. On 23 February 1934, he gave a lecture to the BC Historical Association on his "Ten Years on the Pacific Naval Station," which he said had begun in April 1898 with a marine survey at Qualicum but led to adventures in the Sandwich Islands and elsewhere. The meeting was chaired by *Major F. V. Longstaff. He wrote occasionally to the *Daily Colonist*, as for example, a rambling letter in February 1934 about two remembered mysteries: "Beri-Beri and the Chinese . . . who are a peculiar people . . . I well remember, in March 1910, picking up three Chinese in a small boat. They were without oars, sail, food or water; in fact there was nothing in the boat and they were one hundred miles from land. We fed them, and as soon as we could, passed them over to a native junk. But they appeared to be profoundly indifferent to the whole proceeding, and I never heard any more of them again."

His experience of beriberi occurred in January 1911 while surveying the mouth of the Euphrates River. His ship and others, though well supplied with fresh food by steamers from Bombay, lost men to what looked like beriberi, which puzzled British and Turkish doctors. FW's own death is another mystery, as British sources give the date as 29 July 1949 but report neither the place nor the circumstances. **Sources:** *National Archives* (PRO), London, ADM 196/43, page 307; Navy List, 1899 (July-October), p. 64; *Who's Who in B.C.* 1933-1934, p. 176; *The Times*, London, 13 July 1928, "Eton 70 Years Ago, [his father's] Memories of Hawtreys"; *Colonist*, 1 February 1934, p. 4; 24 February 1934, p. 2; 19 August 1934, Sunday, p. 1; F. M. Kelley, "Saltspring Calling"; 5 November 1931, p. 5, obit.; 12 November 1931, p. 7; Kahn, *Salt Spring Island*, pp. 128-131, 136; census 1861, England, RG 9/752, p. 16 (father); census 1871, RG 10/1239, p. 15 (grandfather); census 1881, RG 11/94, p. 5 (grandfather); census 1901, England, RG 13/1188, p. 12 (father).

WARD, Arthur (1870-1920). A West-Country gentleman born at "Yatton Court" near Aymestrey, Herefordshire, his mother's birthplace, he was a son of John George Rodney Ward, a landowner and Justice of the Peace from Somerset, and his mother was *née* Agnes Woodhouse Snow (1839-1886), born there at Aymestrey. AW was recorded as a baby of eight months in the 1871 census, the youngest of four children living at "Yatton Court" with their father, aged forty, and their mother, aged thirty-one. There were then five domestic servants: nurse, nursery maid, cook, housemaid, and general servant. In 1881, AW was boarding at a small school, Hillside, at Mathon, Worcestershire, and ten years later was recorded as a student of botany at Kew.

He reached Vancouver Island at sometime in the 1890s, arrived on Salt Spring Island with his wife about 1903, and bought the Tolson's property near Ganges. According to descendants, notably AW's only daughter Katherine Valdez Ward, born on Vancouver Island at Westholme on 12 July 1901 and living at Aymestrey a century later, they were self-supporting on Salt Spring Island with goats, sheep, cattle, apple orchard, and chickens and they hired Chinese apple-pickers in the fall of the year. The house was large, wooden, and had running water and a proper bathroom. The mother was a capable shot with a rifle, and the family believed that AW had proposed to her because of this. Katherine was still living at the family place in Shropshire, when I reached them by telephone from London early in the twenty-first century. AW's wife, *née* Grace Elizabeth Elkington (1871-1960), was a daughter of Hyla Elkington (1839-1901), partner in a well-known family of merchant silversmiths, who had settled his family in Cheltenham by the time Grace married AW. Much later, on 24 June 1848, she made a second marriage with E. A. Crofton, both of them having been widowed, and they returned home to settle at the village of Sellack, near Ross-on-Wye in Herefordshire. There they eventually died, she in 1960 and he the next year. Reporting the death of his "beloved wife" in *The Times*, he described himself as "Ernest Crofton of Salt Spring Island, B.C." where they had first met while both were married to others. According to Ward's daughter Valdez Katherine Ward (1901-2005) and his granddaughter, Alexis Gardiner, AW had owned a paddle-wheel steam launch, which hit a rock and sank

off Salt Spring Island. Then, at sometime in 1920, he disappeared mysteriously
one day while out fishing in a rowboat. The family returned sometime later to
the English West Country.
Sources: census England, RG 9/1833, p. 8 (AW's mother as a girl at home); census
1871, RG 10/2718, p. 8; census 1881, RG 11/2607, p. 1; census 1881, RG 11/2582,
p. 7; census 1891, RG 12/622, p. 21; *The Times* (London), 1 April 1960, p. 1, col.
A, obit.; 28 December 1961, p. 1, col. A, obit. Information kindly offered by a
daughter of the Ward family born on *Salt Spring Island*, Katherine Valdez Ward
(1901-2005) and a granddaughter, Alexis, both living near the family estate in
Herefordshire, telephone no. 0208 997 4174.

WARD, Robert (1848-1925). A younger brother of *William Curtis Ward (but
no relation of *Arthur Ward above), RW was born in Hampshire at Winton,
near Winchester, youngest son of William Ward, living lately at Cranborne,
Hampshire, and seems to have been the only other member of the family
active in Victoria. There he married Mary Pauline King (1861-?) at Christ
Church Cathedral on 12 October 1876—Rt. Rev. Bishop Hills officiating—in
a wedding with six bridesmaids and a large congregation. The bride was the
eldest daughter of the late *Captain Edward Hammond King, but was given away
by her stepfather, a Londoner named Thomas Lett Stahlschmidt (1833-1888),
who accompanied the bridegroom "Per steamer *Cariboo-Fly* this morning," the
British Colonist reported on 20 October, "to pass the honeymoon on the East
Coast of the Island." Stahlschmidt had been in Victoria from the early 1960s
holding official posts, such as administrator of trade licenses, and he was active
in a wide range of businesses, particularly a firm of commission agents, Lowe,
Stahlschmidt & Co. The governor, Joseph Trutch, appointed Stahlschmidt
agent general for BC in 1876, and he therefore moved home to London with
his family, selling some of his business interest to RW with whom he had been
in business for some years.

RW sat on the city council, became a magistrate and held official posts, became
a pilotage commissioner and consul for Sweden and Norway, and invested widely
in sealing and salmon canning, insurance, especially importing and exporting, and
he represented the English wholesale firm of Hendersen & Burnaby. He was also in
the real-estate business and had close relations with his brother *W. C. Ward. When
the latter arrived at New York on 17 September 1915, coming from Liverpool, he
named RW as his nearest relative, living then at "Oak Lawn," Leatherhead, Surrey.
RW prospered enough to have the architect Thomas Sorby build him an imposing
house in Victoria, at 1249 Rockland Avenue, which he called "The Laurels." But
the 1901 census recorded him living at 4 Holland Villas in Kensington with Mary
Pauline and four of their children, all born in Victoria. Robert Oscar Cyril Ward,
born on 5 May 1881, served in the Great War as an officer in the East Kent Regiment
("the Buffs") and then the tank corps, meeting his death in battle on 20 November
1917. Constance Irene Ward was born on 23 December 1885. Gladys Heatley Ward
was born on 17 July 1889, and Hilda Douglas Ward was born on 26 April 1891. In
1901, RW kept a governess and four domestic servants.

There is evidence that he crossed the Atlantic from time to time. He went out to Victoria and put up at the Oak Bay Hotel not long before his brother died and stayed to take care of family business. At sometime later, he moved from London onto a country estate near Wycombe, Buckinghamshire, where he died early in 1925. Meanwhile, his house in Victoria, "the Laurels," was used as the Collegiate School for Boys and later as St George's School for Girls. Among the students, there was a daughter of Lieutenant Colonel O. T. Oldham, who as Dr Frances Kelsey was the FDA physician famously warned the U.S. government about the dangers of thalidomide.

Sources: census 1901, England, RG 13/22, p. 25; British *Colonist*, 20 October 1876, p. 1, marriage; *Colonist*, 14 February 1922, pp. 4 and 6; DCB, vol. xiii, "Ewen, Alexander," by Keith Ralston,; Martin Segger and Douglas Franklin, Victoria, *A Primer for Regional History in Architecture* (New York, *A Pilgrim Guide to Historic Architecture*, 1979), pp. 266-69; *Clifton College Register and the University War List*, Cambridge University Alumni—online.

WARD, William Curtis (c. 1842-1922). Born at Winchester, Hampshire, he was found by the census-taker in 1851, aged nine, living with his family at 10 County Prison Cottages, Winchester. His father, William Ward, aged thirty-seven, was "Warden of Hants. County Prison," born at Ringwood, Hampshire. His mother, Ann Smith, aged forty, was born at Ryde, Isle of Wight. He had two older sisters and four younger brothers: Amilia Ward, twelve, Mary A. Ward, ten, George Ward, seven, Leonard Ward, four, Robert Ward, two, and Thomas Ward, six months old. With them was their maternal grandmother, Ann Smith, a nurse aged sixty-four born at Poole, Dorset. Their immediate neighbour at 11 County Prison Cottages was another prison warden and his family. In 1861, WW was recorded as a "banker's apprentice" at Portsea, Portsmouth, Hampshire, boarding in the family of a "tailor and outfitter" at 145 Queen Street. He was in fact articled to the National Provincial Bank. With this preparation, he emigrated to Victoria in 1862 or 1863 as a clerk employed by the Bank of British Columbia, which was managed in London. Twenty years later, the Canadian census for 1881 showed him as a "banker" living in the James Bay quarter of Victoria with his English wife Lydia, aged thirty-three, *née* Lydia Sothcott, elder daughter of a prosperous tailor at Portsea with relatives employed as mariners. They had married in 1864 at Portsea. In 1881 in Victoria, WW and Lydia had eight children: Alice Lydia, aged fifteen, William Coltron, thirteen, Mary Eleanor, eleven, Cecil Walford, nine, Edith Laetitia, seven, Francis Bulkley, five, George Desborough, three, and Florence Anne, born on 7 August 1880. They had a Chinese servant. The only other child recorded with these parents was Violet Eileen Ward (born in Victoria on 17 March 1890), who was aged eleven when staying with them at St Ermin's Hotel near Winchester, a niece, cousin, or perhaps a grandchild.

WW was a capable banker, became manager in Victoria and, in 1893, superintendent of the bank's branches in BC. It was entirely a British bank, not Canadian at all, and its only serious competitor was another British bank, the Bank of British North America, which was different in that it had branches all over Canada.

In time, the Bank of British Columbia founded branches all over the province and in San Francisco as well as other towns in the north-western USA, but nowhere else in Canada. In 1897, the bank moved WW home to London as superintendent there with a seat *ex officio* in the bank's Court of Directors, replacing him in Victoria by Frederick Townsend and then George Gillespie. In the course of his time on the Island, WW had formed close relations with *R. P. Rithet, whose wife was a daughter of Alexander Munro, manager of the Hudson's Bay Company's lands in the province, and had also done business with his own younger brother, *Robert Ward. WW bought land in various parts of the province, notably a considerable acreage just east of the Nicola Valley, where he went into cattle ranching in anticipation of railways passing nearby. His Douglas Lake Ranch soon became the largest cattle ranch in the province, perhaps even in Canada, with its one hundred thousand acres of land and thousands of Hereford and Shorthorn cattle. Two of his sons, Cecil Walford Ward and George Desborough Ward, ran the ranch with him and became well-known polo players in BC and Alberta. As the *Colonist* wrote at his death, "his heart has always been here although during recent years much of his time was spent in England. In the financial life of the province he has been an active figure . . . keenly interested in the development of the province . . . in every sense a pioneer." A faithful member of Christ Church Cathedral in Victoria and a close friend of *Bishop George Hills, he helped to organize the Synod. He and Lydia were living in Shasta Avenue when she died, aged seventy-three, on 1 January 1920, and he then moved out to 1377 David Street in Oak Bay. Two years later, he went to California, hoping to recover from an illness, but he died there at Paso Robles, aged eighty, on 12 February 1922. His remains were returned to Victoria, where he was buried at Ross Bay Cemetery on 17 February.

WW was very much a family man. His youngest son George Desborough Ward (1876-1913), born in Victoria on 15 December 1876, had trained for the Royal Navy as a teenager aboard the training ship *Britannia*, married a daughter of Mr and Mrs W. Burnyeat, a JP at Millgrove, Moresby, and died at sea in September 1913 at a time when WW and Lydia were living at Harbourne, High Halden, Kent, and WW was London chairman of the Canadian Bank of Commerce, which had absorbed or amalgamated with the Bank of British Columbia. At his death, WW left three sons: (1) Francis Bulkley Ward (1875-1953), who was then in the Cariboo but had taken the Two Dot Ranch near High River, Alberta, until 1908, when he sold out and became manager of the Douglas Lake Ranch. This son had married Ethel Kennedy of Fort Macleod, Alberta, daughter of George Kennedy, a surgeon in the North-West Mounted Police. Francis ("Frank" they called him) was born on 26 February 1875 and died, aged seventy-seven, on 27 April 1953 in Saanich. (2) William Coltron Ward settled in Vancouver. (3) As for Cecil Walford Ward, he became a barrister and in 1899, when WW and Lydia were living in London at 73 Elm Park Gardens, he married Ida Marcia Augusta Shrubb, youngest daughter of John Lane Shrubb, a Verderer of the New Forest, and of Mrs Lane Shrubb, who lived in Hampshire at Boldre Grange, Lymington. Cecil and his wife settled in England and were still there at WW's death. Of WW's daughters, Alice Lydia Ward married Captain Mortimer Percy George Douglas Drummond (1860-1936) and they too settled in England; Edith Letitia Ward married Lieutenant Aylmer Herbert Garnons Williams, RN, on 17 March 1894, who also settled in England; and Mary Eleanor Ward married William Edgar Oliver (1867-1920), a Scottish barrister, who settled on the Island, where he died at Cowichan Lake on 9 August 1920 and, much later, she died on 17 February 1959 in Victoria. WW's younger brother, Robert Ward, had recently come out from England to see the family and stayed at the Oak Bay Hotel during his visit.

Sources: census England, HO 107/1658/39 (Lydia Sothcott); census 1851, HO 107/1674, p. 352; 1861, census 1861, RG 9/637, p. 8; census 1861, RG9/652, p. 20 (Lydia Sothcott); census 1891, RG 12/1710, p. 17; census 1901, RG 13/96, p. 1; *Colonist*, 25 September 1913, p. 1; 14 February 1922, pp. 4 and 6, obit.; BMD (UK), Lydia Sothcott married in 1864 on Portsea Island, Hampshire; *Government Gazette* (BC), vol. 10. 1871, entries for 18 March and 23 December 1871; NY Passenger Lists, 17 September 1915; Tony Rees, Polo, *The Galloping Game: An Illustrated History of Polo in the Canadian West* (Cochrane, Alberta, Western Heritage Centre Society, 2000), pp. 78-9, 255-8; Victor Ross, "The Bank of British Columbia," in *The History of the Canadian Bank of Commerce* (Toronto, Oxford University Press, 1920), pp. 251-350. pp. 318-20, 329, 349, 470-2; *Whitaker's*, p. 543; thanks to Colin M. Bower for his Internet site about the Shrubb family.

WARDEN, Lieutenant Colonel John Weightman (1871-?). Born on 8 November 1871 to a Baptist family in King's County, New Brunswick, he enlisted in the Canadian contingent raised for the Second South African War (1899-1902), and exchanged later into the South African Constabulary. He returned to Canada in March 1906 and migrated to Vancouver, where he went into business as a general broker and real-estate dealer but also joined the Sixth (DCOR) Regiment and took a commission in it in May 1911. On the very day in August 1914 when Austria declared war on Serbia, he volunteered for service and was perhaps the very first in Canada to join the CEF. Sent to France with the First Contingent as a captain in the Seventh Battalion, he was seriously wounded at Ypres on 24 April 1915, invalided to England, then for convalescence to Canada, and commissioned on 3 November 1915 as lieutenant colonel to raise the new 102nd (Comox-Atlin) Overseas Infantry Battalion. He immediately began to travel around BC to organize recruiting among the fishermen, miners, and loggers of the province and proved to be immensely successful as the unit's leader. Battalion headquarters were established in Victoria, near the HQ of Military District No. 11 at Work Point, along with quartermaster's stores on Bastion Street; but the mobilization camp was set up at Goose Spit, near the little port of Comox on the Island's east coast, about 150 miles north of Victoria but only three miles beyond the northern end of the E&N Railway. In colonial times, the Royal Navy had established artillery and rifle ranges on Goose Spit. Among the many officers recruited for the battalion were Major L. M. Hagar (in Victoria), *Major C. B. Worsnop (as second in command, q.v.), Captain H. B. Scharschmidt (as adjutant and a battle-hardened officer), Lieutenant R. D. Forrester (as assistant adjutant), Lieutenant T. P. O'Kelly (as transport officer), and W. H. Long (an ex-Hussar with a long Indian Service record, as regimental sergeant major).

The winter of 1915-1916 happened to be unusually severe so that training and setting up the camp became arduous tasks, but JW was a source of vital encouragement during his visits between recruiting journeys. When the camp's water supply failed in the summer, the 102nd Battalion was due to be quartered in Sidney but suddenly ordered overseas, a sign of successful training. In 1917, JW and *Major C. B. Worsnop were named to the DSO.

Sources: *Colonist,* 5 July 1917, p. 5, photo; NAC, CEF files, box 10091-1; NAC, RG9, *Militia and Defence, War Diary,* series III-D-3, vol. 4944, chapter 1, "Early Experiences in Canada—The Spit, Comox, B.C., The First of Many Moves."

WARDER, Major Albert Alfred (c. 1878-1965). He was born at Dunmow, Essex, son of John M. Warder, a "Farm Bailiff" born nearby at High Easter; his mother, Emily Warder, was born at Chelmsford. He had two elder brothers who became farm labourers and three sisters, all older except for Jessie, aged three months, and all born nearby in Essex. In 1881, they lived at "Mount Marshall's Farm" in Bruham, Essex, but ten years later, AW, aged thirteen, was living in Cottage Hall Road, Tolleshunt Major, Essex. By then, he had a new young brother born locally at Bocking. AW joined the British Army, and the 1901 census recorded him as a "Soldier gunner, Royal Garrison Artillery" aged twenty-two and stationed at Shoeburyness Barracks, South Shoeburyness, Essex, near an artillery range. His mates were mixed, but there were several from Essex, some from Ireland, one from Canada (John Gurnett, aged twenty-nine), and one from India.

After the South African War, AW migrated about 1905 to Victoria and on 3 May 1906 married Mary Annie Crocker (c. 1883-?), daughter of a carpenter from Staverton, Devon, who had emigrated with his wife and children in the early 1880s. AW immediately joined the Canadian Army, rose to the rank of major during the Great War, and was then stationed for many years at Work Point Barracks, Esquimalt. There they lived at 1117 Esquimalt Road for more than half a century. Public-spirited like so many of his kind, he became almost a permanent chairman of the Esquimalt Board of School Trustees, being elected in 1931, again in January 1933 and 1934; re-elected late in January 1936 and again in January 1937; still in that office in December 1939; and re-elected on 23 January 1941 for what was said to be a ninth consecutive term. He was also one of the founders of the Uplands and Gorge Vale Golf Clubs. When he died, aged eighty-seven, on 10 September 1965 he left two sons, A. Thomas Warder and W. Donald Warder, and three grandchildren. He was buried as an Anglican after a funeral at St Paul's Naval and Garrison Church, Esquimalt.

Sources: NAC, RG150, box 10091-18; *Colonist,* 27 January 1933, p. 2; 26 January 1934 (with photo); 2 February 1936, p. 24; 29 January 1937, p. 2; 9 December 1939, p. 3; 27 January 1940, p. 3, photo; 24 January 1941, p. 2; 12 September 1965, p. 26, obit.; census 1881, England, RG 11/1765, p. 18; census, 1881 RG 11/2177, p. 7; census 1891, RG 12/1399, p. 1; census 1901, RG 13/1686, p. 6; Canadian census, 1901, Victoria, BC.

WARDROPER, Wilfrid Henry Strickland (1874-1942). He was born at Burford, Oxfordshire, on 24 March 1874, second son of Rev. Henry Timins Wardroper (1842-1912), who was born on 2 January 1842. The latter, WW's father, was the only son of Charles Wardroper and Laura Matilda Montagu Wardroper and on 20 June 1871 married Margaret Strickland (WW's mother), daughter of Carrol Strickland; after her death in 1878, he married Alice Andrews on 22 October 1884, she being the daughter of Lieutenant Colonel Mottram Andrews of the Twenty-eighth Gloucestershire Regiment and his wife Julia Barbara Andrews. Schooled at Uppingham and with an MA from St Mary's College, Oxford, H. T Wardroper became a clergyman in the Church of England but converted to Roman Catholicism in 1878 and settled at Ladye Park, Linkeard, Cornwall. He died at Worcester on 4 May 1912 and was buried there at Astwood Cemetery, leaving four children (including WW) by his first wife, Margaret, and four by his second, Alice. To pass the essentials in review, WW's elder brother was William Strickland Wardroper (1872-1903), who married Christina McDonald and spent the rest of his life in London, Ontario. Their sister Hilda Margaret Strickland Wardroper was born on 11 February 1876, and there was another sister who died in infancy. When WW's mother Margaret died, WW's father married Alice Andrews. They had a daughter Mary Clarice Wardroper, born 21 July 1885 and died unmarried on 27 August 1911 at Ladye Park, Liskeard, Cornwall, and buried in the parish churchyard there. They also had a son, John Baptist Francis Wardroper, born on 1 December 1886 and educated at Downside School, near Bath, Somerset. He joined the staff of the Local Government Board's District Auditor of the Northumberland Audit District in January 1905. He compiled a family tree, kept in family records, and married Rose Marie Bailer in December 1910.

As he told one of his sons, WW reacted to family trouble in his youth by going off to become a merchant seaman and in time earned a mate's certificate. Sailing sometimes to China, he heard about the official Chinese contract with Sir Robert Hart to run the Maritime Customs Service as a British operation. In 1894, he went to Canada, crossed over to Victoria, and sailed on to Shanghai, where he found employment in the Customs Service and was posted to Tientsin near Peking. Still there during the Boxer Rebellion (1900), he joined the international force and was wounded and decorated in the campaign to raise the siege of Peking by attacking forts at Taku. He eventually saw opportunities in trade with the outside world in tea, china, and other commodities and so started an import-export business at Peking. In this, he was successful, soon had a house and a go-down warehouse, and was able to take trips back to Britain. His route took him on the CPR Empress passenger liners to BC, and about 1913, he stopped off at Victoria and bought a quarter-section of land (160 acres) between Duncan and Cowichan Station. His intention was to develop it as an estate, and he soon rented his establishment at Peking and moved to his Cowichan property, which he called *Avonlea, Edenlea,* or *Glen Eden* or some such name (Ken Wardroper, my correspondent, could not remember exactly). WW then visited England on holiday, went back to China to wind up his business, returned to England in 1914, and joined the Inns of Court Officers' Training Corps. Being fluent in Chinese, he was commissioned in 1917 as a lieutenant in the Chinese Labour Corps and served in France behind the lines, building railways and army camps, moving supplies, etc., this until December 1919, reaching the rank of acting captain.

After demobilization in 1919, he returned to Vancouver Island, where he bought property on Mountain Road at Cowichan Station and, at St Andrew's Anglican Church there on 1 January 1921, married Miss Maud Lythall, whom he had met during the war. They remained there for the rest of their lives. They had two sons, John Edmund and Wilfrid Kenneth (my correspondent), who served with the Canadian forces before joining the Canadian Department of External Affairs. WW had rented his establishment at Peking to another Englishman and the Wardropers lived mainly on the rental of that property, but in the course of the warlord disorders in China, that tenant lost his property and the rent stopped. Then WW lost more invested money in the financial crash of 1929. Having to make their own way, his two sons attended Duncan High School (where Ken went to school with John Palmer, grandson of *Charles George Palmer) and in the late 1930s went to pick pears in the Okanagan, with a view to earning enough to attend the University of BC. This was where Ken Wardroper was when the Second World War broke out. He joined a regiment there, went overseas with the Canadian Scottish, was active in the D-Day invasion, and was twice wounded. After the war, Ken went into the Canadian Department of External Affairs and had a career as a diplomat, which he recounted in a book privately printed in Victoria: *Some Recollections of an Envoy Plenipotentiary*. He was Canadian ambassador to Norway at one time.

Meanwhile, early in the Second World War, his father WW died, aged sixty-seven, on 30 May 1942 at St Joseph's Hospital in Victoria. Besides his wife and two sons, WW left a half-brother John in England; and at Cowichan Lake he had a more-distant relative whom he had seen little if at all. This was Mrs Edith March, *née* Wardroper, a cousin of his father, the late Reverend Henry Timins Wardroper. She had married a Captain Henry March in Victoria on 19 January 1893, having met him when he commanded a ship, laying cable across the Pacific Ocean from the Bamfield cable station. Once he had seen life on the Island, Henry March decided to settle there and walked from Bamfield through the wilderness to Cowichan Lake in order to pre-empt land there. Edith died, aged eighty-two, on 25 April 1843 at Lake Cowichan and Henry March, aged eighty-three, on 21 January 1950 at Duncan. In local histories by Bowen and Saywell, listed below, further details of Wardroper relatives in the Cowichan district call for further investigation.

"Of a retiring disposition," the *Cowichan Leader* wrote of WW at his death, "Mr Wardroper took no active part in district affairs, but was well known to many here, particularly in the Cowichan Station area." At his funeral, the pallbearers were all from Victoria: A. Wardman, *Charles Victor Embleton, A. S. Lock and *George Meredith Petch, as well as Lieutenant Kenneth Wardroper, who went to the funeral on special leave. Ken kept no letters or other records of his father's life, but he did have two magnificent photograph albums containing photos his father took in China. At one time, Ken had lent them to Arthur Menzies, a colleague in external affairs, and at the time of my inquiry, they were kept by Ken's son, Lawrence Wardroper, a librarian in a federal science agency in Ottawa, who generously brought them on his bicycle to 280 Chapel Street, where I was able to scan some of the photographs. There was one of WW sitting in a courtyard in China, with a hat and mustache. According to Ken's memory, his father did not like Christian missionaries in China because they seemed to be corrupting the normal Chinese culture and basically causing trouble, though he thought well of the medical missionaries. WW had told him that in Tientsin, there was a polo club, mainly British, which formed a cavalry unit and went overseas to fight in France in 1915.

Sources: Wardroper family papers; notes courtesy of Ken Wardroper, Apt. 306-1370 Beach Drive, Victoria, BC; notes courtesy of Bill Rodney (Victoria); *Cowichan Leader*, 4 June 1942, obit.; *Colonist*, 31 May 1942, obit.; Lynne Bowen, *Those Lake People: Stories of Cowichan Lake* (Vancouver, Douglas & McIntyre, 1995), pp. 5-6; John F. T. Saywell, *Kaatza: The Chronicles of Cowichan Lake* (Sidney, The Cowichan Lake Centennial Committee, 1967), pp. 40-1; Kenneth Wardroper, *Some Recollections of an Envoy Plenipotentiary* (Victoria, privately printed).

WATKIN, Sir Edward (1819-1901). When he arrived on the BC coast in 1886, almost as soon as the CPR reached the Pacific Ocean, this imaginative capitalist, described by a recent biographer as "the second railway king," was disappointed to find that the railway was not going to have its terminus on the Island. He did not linger long in Victoria but admired it as "an English town, with better paved streets, better electric lighting, and better in many other ways . . . than many bigger American and English towns I know of." He met *Sir J. W. Truch, minister of lands and works, later lieutenant governor of the province, as well as Sir Matthew Begbie, the chief justice there, and Robert Dunsmuir (1825-1889), the Island's coal-mining millionaire. Citing notes by Edward Wragge, a civil engineer from Toronto, EW gave more attention to coal mines in Nanaimo and the little railway that connected them with the naval station at Esquimalt.

Somewhat disorderly but written in an intimate, sometimes passionate spirit, EW's book could only have encouraged British people to migrate to the Island. His views were Imperial and he hated what he called "little Englandism." He had travelled to India and inspected railways there. His first visit to Canada was in 1861 at the request of George Carr Glyn (1797-1873) and Thomas Baring (1799-1873), a brother-in-law of *Captain Edwin Augustus Porcher. Devoted to the memory of the Duke of Newcastle, as early as 1852 EW shared the Duke's vision of "one country extending from the Atlantic to the Pacific," long before it was widely held in Canada. Like the consortium of British bankers who had invested in the CPR, he was deeply interested in what the new railway might do for the empire.

Sources: David Hodgkins, *The Second Railway King: The Life and Times of Sir Edward Watkin, 1819-1901* (Cardiff, Merton Priory Press, 2002), 713 pp.; Sir Edward Watkin, *Canada and the States: Recollections 1851 to 1886* (Ward, Lock & Co., 1887), pp. 6-7, 11, 59, 66, ch. 6; C. W. Sutton and Philip S. Bagwell, "Watkin, Sir Edward William, first baronet (1819-1901)", in the *Oxford DNB*.

WEBBER, Captain Frederick William (1871-1940). Born on 19 January 1871 at Henfield, Sussex, son of John Webber, a gardener born at Tiverton, Devonshire, and Jane Webber, from Bath, he was recorded in the 1871 census, aged three months, living with them at No. 2, Rascals, Shipley, together with three older brothers and a sister. Ten years later, they had moved to 18 Summerfield Road, Lee, West Kent, and in 1891, FW, aged nineteen, was a private soldier stationed in Lancashire at the barracks in Broughton near Preston. Letters to him from relatives, dated 20 April 1884 at North Saanich, 21 December 1888 at Hayward, Assa (?), and 12 January 1892 at Cowichan Post Office, show that he reached the rank of captain and migrated to Ontario but was contemplating a further move to the Island. When he enlisted in the CEF on 29 July 1916, he was staying in Victoria at the Brunswick Hotel with his wife, Eliza Jane Webber, and described himself as a farmer aged forty-five. He had already spent twelve years and four months in the Royal Sussex Regiment. He died in Victoria, aged seventy-one, on 29 March 1940 and was buried as an Anglican.

Sources: NAC, MG24. F 113, three volumes, which consist of two boxes and some large folders, rescued from the Shrapnel family house in Orillia, Ontario, as it was being dismantled; NAC, CEF files, box 10185-54, reg't. no. 826190; census 1871, England, RG 10/1096; census 1881, RG 11/732; census 1891, RG 12/3448.

WELSH, Alfred Peter (c. 1858-1949). Born at Somerton, Somerset, son of Edward Welsh, a draper from Shipham, Somerset, and Susan M. Welsh from Halifax, Yorkshire, he was recorded, aged two, in the 1861 census, living with his family in Broad Street, Somerton. He had three brothers and three sisters, all older except one, and there were five servants of whom three were [shop?] "Assistants." He attended a Quaker school at Winscombe, Somerset called Sidcot, founded in 1699 (and still there in 1999). In 1881 when he was twenty-two, he was again living at home and employed as a clerk, probably at his father's workshop. Edward Welsh was then described as "Linen Shirt Collar Manufacturer employing eighty-one women, thirty-four girls, nine men and seventeen boys." AW soon went out to settle as a pioneer at Millarville, Alberta, where he married, and fought in the Riel Rebellion (1885). After the Great War, they moved to the Cowichan Valley, where they had a son and three daughters, and lived quietly until he died on 5 October 1949 and was buried at St Peter's Anglican Church, Quamichan, near Duncan, where he had lived for thirty years.

Sources: census 1861, England, RG 9/1628, p. 3; census 1871, RG 10/2464, p. 11; census 1881, RG 11/2379, p. 14; Colonist, 7 October 1949, p. 19, obit.

WELSTEAD, Captain Arthur Douglas (c. 1872-1936). He was born in Cheltenham, son of Gertrude A. Welstead, a Londoner, and her husband Arthur H. Welstead, whom the 1871 census recorded as a fifty-five-year-old "Land Agent & Annuitant" from Fenstanton, Huntingdonshire. These parents had evidently moved frequently, as AW's elder brothers and sisters (he appeared a few months later) were born in Hampshire (Fascombe), Leicestershire, and Hertfordshire. In 1881, AW, aged eight, was living with his widowed mother and the other children at 31 Longton Grove, London.

After a career in the British Army, he moved to the Island about 1924 and settled at Mill Bay. He died twelve years later, aged sixty-four, on 13 October 1936 at the Jubilee Hospital in Victoria, leaving two sisters at Mill Bay and a brother, Francis A. S. Welstead at Oliver, BC, as well as a brother and a sister in England. The pallbearers at his burial at Royal Oak show English connections, such as George Alfred M. Cheeke (c. 1871-1950) and his wife, who were Cheltenham friends settled at Shawnigan Lake; Trevor Keene (c. 1861-1937), who died the following year at Mill Bay, a public-spirited English emigrant employed as an auctioneer and appraiser; and the rector, Rev. William Evans Cockshott (c. 1863-1946), who was a Cambridge man. AW's brother Francis came down from Oliver.

Sources: *Cowichan Leader*, 22 October 1936, obit.; *Colonist*, 15 October 1936, p. 20, obit.; census 1881, England, RG 11/736, pp. 10-11; census 1871, RG 10/2664, p. 16.

WEST, Major Dr Christopher Harfield (1860-1935). He was born on 29 September 1860 in Plymouth, son of Lieutenant Colonel William Henry H. West, who was thirty-one—and still a captain—and his wife Ann M. S. West, aged thirty-two. The 1861 census found them living at 8 Barkley Place, Plymouth. CW was then six months old and had two older sisters born at Teddington, Middlesex, and Princestead, Hampshire. Ten years later, they were still in Plymouth but at 29 Whyndam Place; with them were another seven-year-old sister and four cousins (the father's nieces) born in Melbourne, Australia, as well as two servants. In 1881, CW, aged twenty, was a medical student at St George's Hospital and was living with his parents, one sister, and a servant at "Royal Marine Barracks, Chatham." Later, he was attached to Guy's Hospital in London.

CW was evidently recruited in England by the Royal Canadian North-West Mounted Police, as a letter of 26 April 1888 by Frederick White, comptroller of that force at the headquarters in Ottawa, announced that he was proceeding to Canada aboard SS *Sarmation* in order to enlist in the force. His engagement document dated 10 May 1888 recorded him as a medical student, an Anglican 5" 7½" tall, 140 lbs, with black hair, grey eyes, and fair complexion. He took an oath of allegiance to Queen Victoria for a five-year engagement. On 15 October 1889, he was promoted to staff sergeant at $1.25 a day. On his file are letters of support from Frederick White and from Captain C. E. A. Patterson of Montreal, whose daughter, Isabel Alice Sinclair Patterson, he married in 1888 at Prince Albert, Saskatchewan, notwithstanding a general objection to marriage in the service. CW re-engaged several times, always on 10 May, in 1888, 1893, and 1896 and was discharged at Maple Creek on 9 May 1899. But he re-enlisted and was commissioned as inspector on 1 August 1900 at a salary of $1,350. In 1907, he was doctor to Indians at Lesser Slave Lake, apparently working for the Indian Department as well as the Police. In 1912, he went to England and recruited about forty men for the NWM Police, many of whom served out full careers. After his return, he was posted in various parts of the Canadian west and north and also acted as a doctor for the Indian Department.

Rising to be superintendent of the Prince Albert Division in Saskatchewan on 1 April 1913 by Order-in-Council, CW retired in August 1922 to become the resident physician on Mayne Island in the Gulf of Georgia. There he and his wife lived in a mixed community with several officers like himself and other emigrants from the British Isles. Lukin Johnston, once editor of the *Cowichan Leader*, visited him there in the late 1920s and recalled that his "stories of thirty-four years in the force, chiefly in the north, kept me enthralled for a whole evening." After twelve years on Mayne Island, CW died, aged seventy-four, on 12 January 1935 in his room at the home of a friend in Vancouver, Colonel L. F. Field, of 1011 West 45th Avenue, Vancouver. He had been on his way home to England. He left his wife, two sisters (one at Weymouth), a nephew, and five sons, four of whom—Edward, Thomas, Phillip, and Henry—were among the pallbearers at his funeral. He was remembered locally with such gratitude and respect that on 25 August 1940 the bishop, Harold Eustace Sexton (1888-1972), arrived at Mayne Island to dedicate a brass plaque to his memory in the Anglican Church. It was *Captain E. G. Beaumont in his yacht *Discovery Isle* who brought Sexton for this occasion.

Sources: *Civil Service List of Canada, 1908*, (Ottawa, King's Printer, 1908), p. 24; NAC, RG 18, series G, vol. 3443, file O-118, access code 90, parts 1, 2, and 3; census 1861, England, RG 9/1439, p. 56; census 1871, RG 10/2117, pp. 43-4; census 1881, RG 11/896, p. ?; *Colonist*, 25 January 1935, p. 9; 30 August 1940, p. 16; *Vancouver Province*, 14 January 1935, p. 8; Lukin Johnston, *Beyond the Rockies: Three Thousand Miles by Trail and Canoe Through Little-Known British Columbia* (J. M. Dent & Sons Ltd., 1929), p. 3.

WESTMORLAND, Colonel Horace "Rusty" (1886-1984). He was born on 24 April 1886 at Penrith, Northumberland, son of a "Farmer & Currier of Hides," Thomas Westmorland of Milburn, Westmorland, and his wife Emma of Watermillock, Cumberland. The 1891 census found him, aged four, living with them and one servant at 33 Old London Road, Penrith. They were still there in 1901, along with a sister Alice, two year older than HW. He went out to the Island in 1911 and married Rose Blanche Lyndhurst Wadmore at St Paul's Naval and Garrison Church, Esquimalt, on 25 June 1913, just before enlisting in the Fifth Regiment. He joined the Canadian Army Medical Corps in Halifax, NS, on 22 August 1915, and was soon transferred to the Canadian Army Service Corps as a lieutenant. His wife was a daughter of *Colonel Robinson Lyndhurst Wadmore and bore a son on 7 February 1914, who in due time joined the Fourteenth Punjab (Pathan) Regiment of the Indian Army and fought during the Second World War in Libya and elsewhere as Captain H. Lyndhurst Westmorland (1914-1994).

Meanwhile, HW had become a devoted climber in the Rocky Mountains as well as at home near his birthplace, where his father had "inoculated his son with the climbing bug early on," writes Colin Wells. As a teenager, HW had climbed Pillar Rock, as his Aunt Mary had done in 1873, and joined two cousins climbing with ropes. They made the first ascent of Chock Gully on Tarn Crag, Helvellyn Range, and "Westmorland's Route" was named after him. It was in 1911 that he joined a group of pioneering surveyors mapping the Alberta-British Columbia border, so moving his hobby of adventuring in the wild to BC and making his home on the Island.

Sources: NAC, CEF files, box 10249-18; census 1891, England, RG 12/4275, p. 13; census 1901, RG 13/4854, p. 19; Colin Wells, *Who's Who in British Climbing. A Brief History of British Mountaineering* (Mountain Heritage Trust, 2007), pp. 514-15.

WHEELER, Arthur Oliver (1860-1945). He was born on 1 May 1860 into a distinguished Anglo-Irish family living in Dublin, Ireland, where his father Edward Wheeler, an army captain, moved in official circles and then retreated to his own father's estate. A gradual impoverishment induced the family to emigrate to Canada, where they landed on 14 May 1876 and Wheeler senior eventually found a modest post as harbour master at Collingwood on Georgian Bay, Ontario, where they lived in a house they called "The Birches." AW had just spent two years at Dulwich College, London, and after travelling to the northwest, he eventually qualified as a land surveyor. This career entailed much travelling in wild country, and he explored many parts of the Canadian west and north, as well as doing some of the surveying attendant on the flood of settlers moving west in the 1880s. In 1882, he was appointed assistant land commissioner for the new CPR and soon moved to Ottawa as "third class clerk" in the Department of the Interior and thence to the office of the surveyor general of Canada. During the Riel Rebellion (1885), he served in the Dominion Land Surveyors' Intelligence Corps of fifty men in which he was promoted to captain. His career developed with appointments to explore and survey, notably for irrigation systems on the prairies and for the boundary between British Columbia and the new province of Alberta. No one played a bigger part than AW in the fundamental laying out of the Canadian west.

On 6 June 1888 at St Andrew's Presbyterian Church, Ottawa, he married Clara Macoun, daughter of Professor John Macoun (1831-1920), an Anglo-Irish explorer and naturalist who had a long career in the service of the Dominion of Canada. Soon after the birth of their only son, Edward Oliver Wheeler (usually called "Oliver"), on 18 April 1890, the family moved out west, where AW obtained various surveying and other contracts and eventually became an authority on the Rocky Mountains. After much debate and consultation, he founded the Alpine Club of Canada in 1906 at Winnipeg in collaboration with Mrs Elizabeth Parker and J. W. Dafoe, editor of the *Manitoba Free Press*. AW served for many years as its president, leader, and guiding spirit and soon established its headquarters at Banff, Alberta. But this was to be only one of its—and their—homes. In 1908, the Macouns moved out to Sidney, on the Island, and remained there until John Macoun's death. In 1912, when the Dominion government decided not to support the Alpine Club and forced AW to choose between it and his career as a civil servant, he resigned at considerable cost to himself and began to devote himself entirely to the club. Partly in order to manage on the slender salary the club could pay and partly because Clara wanted to live near her parents, they joined them in Sidney, where in 1910 they had already begun to build a house near St Andrew's Church on Third Street. There AW set up the club's office. In addition, he owned property nearby at All Bay "adjoining Marine Drive," which he was trying to rent as pastureland in February 1928. But he was immensely public-spirited on the Island in various ways. He was an early enthusiast for the Overseas League, and as early as September 1910, he started the first Boy Scout troop in Sidney, counted as the eighth Victoria troop, less than a year after *Captain H. H. Woolison had founded the first Victoria troop in November 1909.

Clara Wheeler died on 24 August 1923, and the next year on 8 October 1924 at St John's Church, Salmon Arm, AW married the hostess/secretary of the Alpine Club at Banff, Emmeline Savatard. She was a daughter of Rev. Louis Savatard of Sutton Coldfield, Lancashire, and it was she whom we knew in Sidney, though my grandparents, the Simisters, must have known the first Mrs Wheeler in her time. In 1925-1926, and probably earlier, my mother, Grace Simister (1903-1999), was a secretary or stenographer in the club's office, working with AW and Alan Stewart "Spike" Thomson (1887-1984), whose wife, Gladys Bowcott, was a school friend of my mother's. When I was a child in the 1930s we knew, often met, and occasionally visited both the Thomsons and the Wheelers in Sidney, then a very small village. For many years, the Wheelers were reported in the *Sidney Review* as travelling to Banff early each summer and returning in the fall. Photographs in my parents' collection show that in 1926, and probably in other years too, my mother spent the summer in Banff with them.

For twenty years, AW led the Alpine Club of Canada, of which he had been the principal founder, and was immensely active raising funds for it. These were remarkable accomplishments, but he went on to fight a second battle, this one for the preservation and protection of Canadian wilderness by the establishment of national parks. Using the Alpine Club to gather support and lobby governments, he waged a long struggle with logging and hydroelectric interests, the CPR, and Ottawa's chief bureaucrat in the West, an Ontarian from Elgin County named William Pearce (1848-1930), who consistently resisted attempts to protect large tracts of territory from exploitation for profit. For some years in the 1920s, AW was secretary of the Canadian Parks Association, and in April 1926, he retired as director of the Alpine Club in order to devote himself to the cause of national parks by writing and giving lectures illustrated with lantern slides to public audiences. Examples are two lectures he gave in Sidney, one in May 1926 about the National Parks of Canada and the other in January 1927 on the Canadian Rockies to a gathering organized by the local Parent Teacher's Association. On 8 January 1929, he spoke in Victoria on "Mapping Mountains" at the AGM of the BC land surveyors. This went on until 1943 when he moved to his house in Banff, and it was there that he died on 20 March 1945, leaving his wife and a son by his first wife, *Sir Edward Oliver Wheeler.

Sources: Notes and conversations, courtesy of John Wheeler (a grandson); *Sidney and Gulf Islands Review*, 7 December 1922, p. 6; 16 October 1924, p. 2; 15 April 1926, p. 1; 6 May 1926, p. 2; 13 May 1926, p. 1; 6 January 1927, p. 1; 10 February 1927, p. 1; 9 February 1928, p. 3; 23 May 1929, p. 1; *Colonist*, 15 March 1914, Sunday Section, p. 1; 25 January 1923, p. 9; 2 January 1929, p. 6; John A. Whittaker, *Early Land Surveyors of British Columbia* (P.L.S. Group) (Victoria, BC, The Corporation of Land Surveyors of the Province of BC, 1990), pp. 145-153; Esther Fraser,

Wheeler (Banff, Alberta, A Summerthought Publication, 1978), 164 pp.; Leslie Bella, *Parks for Profit* (Montreal, Harvest House, 1987), pp. 40-6, 48, 50-4, 57-8, 62, 68, 70; AW, *The Selkirk Mountains: A Guide for Mountain Pilgrims and Climbers* (Winnipeg, privately published, 1912), 191 pp.; James G. MacGregor, *Vision of an Ordered Land: The Story of the Dominion Land Survey* (Saskatoon, Western Producer Prairie Books, 1981), pp. 98-9, 116, 127-33, 155, 158; D. W. Thompson, *Men and Meridians: The History of Surveying and Mapping in Canada* (2 vols., Ottawa, Queen's Printer, 1966-1969), passim.

WHEELER, Brigadier Sir Edward Oliver (1890-1962). Born on 18 April 1890 in Ottawa, son of *A. O. Wheeler and Clara (Macoun) Wheeler, he attended Ottawa Collegiate (later Lisgar Collegiate), Trinity College School, Port Hope, Ontario, where he became head boy, and RMC, Kingston, Ontario, where he was at the top of his class throughout and BSM (head cadet) in his final year. At RMC he also won the governor general's gold medal and the Sword of Honour. In June 1910, he was commissioned in the Royal Engineers as a second lieutenant and then spent two years at the Royal Engineers Training Centre in Chatham, England. There he won the Haines Memorial Medal for Military Engineering and in 1912 was posted to India, where he was to remain throughout his career, until 1946. In 1914-1915, early in the Great War, he was with the First KGO Sappers and Miners in France; in 1916-1918, he was in Mesopotamia and India, and thereafter on the general staff, as brigade major. In a letter home in 1918, he described a flight over the countryside in airplanes which he thought were vastly improved over the 1916 models. He was mentioned in despatches seven times and won the MC and the *Légion d'Honneur* fifth class. Demobilized in 1919, he joined the Survey of India in 1919 and nearly twenty years later was appointed director of the Survey of India, which led on to the post of surveyor general of India in the years 1941-1946. He was a member of the first Mount Everest Expedition in 1921, and it was he who made the first topographical map of the mountain and discovered the best route to the North Col (23,000 ft). He reached it on 21 September 1921 with George Mallory and Guy Bullock. On 23 February 1943, he was knighted and in 1947 he retired.

There was a personal side to EW's life, which included visits to see his parents on the Island and at Banff, where he had his first lessons in mountaineering with his father. Mountaineering and surveying were the principal activities of his life, private as well as professional, and he climbed with his father's friends in the Alpine Club of Canada during furloughs at home. Among his closest friends were the Longstaff family, and before the Great War, he went on climbing expeditions with Tom and Kate Longstaff, whose brother *Frederick Victor Longstaff eventually settled in Victoria. In 1920, EW was at the home of Kate Longstaff, by then the widowed Mrs Wedgwood, whose husband had died fighting, and there he met his wife, Dorothea Sophie Danielson, of Edgcbaston, Birmingham. They became engaged in five days, just before he returned to India. In January 1921, they went to visit to his parents in Victoria, where the *Daily Colonist* reported that "Lieut.-Colonel and Mrs Wheeler are among the guests at the James Bay Hotel," though they were married in fact the following March, just before he left for six months on the Everest Expedition, leaving her with other expedition wives in Darjeeling. He had been chosen by Sir Francis Younghusband, president of the Royal Geographical Society, as one of two surveyors to accompany the Mount Everest Expedition, as determined by the government of India. During the trek into the Himalayas, EW suffered from kidney stones but felt better once they arrived at a base where he was able to cook for himself (in 1925 he had the kidney stones removed in London). Early in November 1922, his parents reported to an interested Island public the substance of a long letter from him dated 19 July at Tingi Tzong, Tibet.

A couple of years later, on 19 December 1924 at Mussoorie, India, EW and his wife had a son, John Oliver Wheeler, and in December 1925, they all spent a two-month furlough with his parents in Sidney, travelling from Darjeeling, where he was then stationed. Much later, in 1933, they went again in order to put him, then aged eight, into Shawnigan Lake School but returned to Quetta on the North-West Frontier, where EW was stationed at the time, and the next time John saw his parents was during their long furlough in 1937-1938. John spent holidays with his grandparents in Sidney, where I recall meeting him on various occasion in the 1930s. Upon leaving school, John entered the University of British Columbia and graduated in geological engineering in 1947, which led to a career with the Canadian Geological Survey.

The various stages of EW's career were reported, often in detail, by his proud parents and relayed in the *Victoria Daily Colonist* to an admiring public throughout the Island and beyond. He spoke to many audiences in many places and contributed articles to the *Canadian Alpine Journal*. During his visits home, he was in demand as a lecturer, and as early as 23 January 1923, he gave an illustrated lecture about India and Tibet to raise money for a charitable fund. In mid-January 1933, he was the guest speaker at the North Saanich Horticultural Society, where he showed slides of the 1921 Mount Everest Expedition as well as his father's slides of the Rocky Mountains. It was Dr William Newton, director of the Dominion Plant Pathology Station in Saanich, who formally expressed the delight of the audience. On 3 April 1933, he spoke for five minutes at the Alpine Club banquet at the Empress Hotel in Victoria, where he was still on furlough from Quetta, India. Still on the Island in mid-May, he lectured the Woman's Auxiliary at Deep Cove, with slides, about a tour he made of South Africa, England, California, and Canada. When he came again in June 1937, he had just had a long journey from Calcutta through the Dutch East Indies, Australia, New Zealand, and points between. On retiring, he returned to BC, settled at Vernon in the Okanagan Valley, closer to his beloved mountains than the Island, and served in 1950-1954 as president of the Alpine Club of Canada. He died at Vernon, aged seventy-one, on 19 March 1962.

Sources: Notes, interviews, and photocopies courtesy of John Wheeler (a son); *Who was Who*, 1961-1970, pp. 1190-1; *The Canadian Who's Who*, 1997, p. 1304; The *Canadian Alpine Journal*, vol. XXVII (1940), no. 2, pp. 205-212; vol. XXIX, no. 1 (1944-1945), pp. 140-6; F. C. Bell, "In Memoriam: Brigadier Sir Edward Oliver Wheeler, K.B., M.C., Leg. Hon., R.E., 1890-1962," in The *Canadian Alpine Journal*, vol. XLV (May 1962), pp. 160-3; *Colonist*, 5 October 1918, p. 14; 6 October 1918, p. 7, photo; 12 January 1921, p. 8; 9 March 1921, p. 7; 10 December 1925, p. 9; 11 January 1933, p. 15; 4 April 1933, p. 5; 13 May 1933, p. 8; 20 June 1937, p. 6; 16 January 1943, p. 5, photo; Riddick, *Who in British India*, p. 385; Tom Holzel & Audrey Salkeld, *First on Everest: The Myster of Mallory and Irvine* (NY, Henry Holt, 1986), pp. 66, 71, 80.

WHITTOME, James Henry (1871-1936). Born in London in January 1871, he appears, three months old, in 1871 census records, living with his family at 25 Chenies Street, "The Goat," Finsbury (St Giles), London. His father, James Whittome, aged forty-five, was a "Licensed Victualler" born at Hiljay, Norfolk; his mother Elizabeth, aged thirty-nine, was born at Hierless Hill, Kent, and he had two sisters, Mary A. E. Whittome, aged four, born at Alexandria, Egypt, and Elizabeth Whittome, aged three, born at Walworth, Surrey. He had a brother, Arthur C. Whittome, aged one, born like him in London. They had four servants: cook, nurse, and two men.

In 1892, aged twenty-one, he migrated to the Cowichan Valley, settled at Duncan, and on 26 November 1894 married Miss Clara Florence Jaynes (c. 1873-1968), eldest daughter of *William Penn Jaynes, which brought him into a substantial Gloucestershire family circle, including the *Tyrwhitt-Drake family. A decade later, on 2 September 1903 in North Cowichan, her sister, Miss Alberta Louisa Jaynes (1879-1946), married Edward Howe Hicks-Beach (1875-1967), son of William Hicks-Beach, JP of Cranham Lodge, Gloucestershire, and grandson of the cabinet minister Sir Michael Edward Hicks-Beach (1837-1916). Meanwhile in Duncan, JW opened a real-estate and insurance office known as J. H. Whittome & Co., one of the biggest such businesses in the district. Together with Clermont Livingston, father of *Air Marshal Sir Philip Livingston, he acquired a building on the north side of Station Street, where he moved in along with the Tyee Copper Company's office. In 1906, he and his family, then with two children, moved to South Africa, but they were back two years later, when JW acquired Livingston's interest in the building and established a home on the Maple Bay Road, which they named "Dogwoods." The mature dogwood trees flowered copiously each spring, and JW spent much time gardening, fishing, and shooting. He was active in the Cowichan Agricultural Society and became a Freemason in Temple Lodge no. 33, AF and AM. When he died of a heart attack in May 1936, he had an Anglican funeral at St Peter's Quamichan and was buried there in the churchyard. The editor of the *Cowichan Leader* wrote,

> A figure in the whole growth of the district, attaching to whom was an importance not generally realized nor perhaps easily recognized, Mr. Whittome possessed capabilities of unusual merit. He was for many years assessor for the Municipality of North Cowichan, and had exceptional knowledge of land and timber values with a reputation in this respect unequalled on the Island. He was interested in early mining ventures in Cowichan, and to his grasp of conditions a number of local enterprises owe their existence.

In an unobtrusive way, JW had done a great deal to populate the Cowichan Valley with middle-class families from the south and west of England. He was survived by his widow, one son, Robert William Whittome, a daughter (Mrs H. F. B. Stamer), and five grandchildren.

Sources: *Cowichan Leader*, 14 May 1936, obit.; *Victoria Daily Times* 4 September 1903, p. 5; census 1871, England, RG 13/348, p. 13.

WILBY, Colonel Arthur William Roger (1875-1942). He was born on 27 March 1875 at Curragh, County Kildare in Ireland, eldest son of Lieutenant A. E. Wilby, Sixty-first Regiment, and Mrs Wilby, of Knebworth, Hertfordshire, who took him as a small boy to live in Alberta, and in due time, he attended RMC, Kingston, Ontario. When he enlisted in Strathcona's Horse at Calgary on 6 February 1900, prompted by news of the South African War, he recorded himself as a "Rancher," Anglican, and with his mother as his next of kin living at Southsea in England. He returned to Canada on 8 March 1901 and was discharged with the Queen's Medal and three clasps for Belfast, Orange Free State, and Natal. He had been promoted to squadron quartermaster sergeant. Army doctors had found his temperament to be "sanguine," his complexion medium, hair light brown, and eyes blue. He moved to Victoria and was employed there as a married civil engineer when he joined the CEF on 23 October 1915, giving the Colonial Trust Company as the address of his wife, Marie Elise Wilby *née* Gaudin, born in Jersey, Channel Islands, daughter of Agnes Gaudin and her husband James, a master mariner and shipowner who took his family out to the Island in 1881. AW went overseas with the Sixty-second Battalion and was attached to Canadian General HQ in France. He was mentioned in despatches and named CBE. When he returned to Victoria in 1920, he succeeded Captain G. E. L. Robertson as agent of the Marine Department and served therein until the department was reorganized, and he was put in charge of the lighthouse service and all marine work on the coast as agent of the Department of Transport. He took an intense interest in the youth of Victoria, was president of the Boy Scout's Association, and was at one time president of the Navy League of Canada, which sponsored the Rainbow Sea Cadets. He was also active in the Seamen's Institute and the United Service Institution and the Canadian Club, all this at the director's level. Among his friends were *Major A. G. Piddington and his family; AW duly became godfather to Helen Piddington, who became a well-known artist in BC. In 1940, he acted as a pallbearer at the funeral of another friend, *Lieutenant Colonel Charles Bayard Messiter. AW died, aged sixty-seven, on 2 April 1942 in Victoria, leaving his wife and three sons, Nicholas, Gerald, and Derek. Among the pallbearers were *Major H. C. Holmes, *Major A. H. Jukes, *Norman Yarrow, and *Major A. G. Piddington.

Sources: *Colonist*, 5 April 1942, p. 9, photo and obit.; *Who was Who*, 1941-1950, pp. 1234-5; NAC, RG 38, A-1-a, vol. 112, T-2089, South African War, *Lord Strathcona's Horse*; NAC, CEF files, box 10349-24; census 1881, England, RG 11/5617, p. 5; Canadian census, 1901, Victoria (Gaudin).

WILLIAMS, Ernest Alfred Mountford (1879-1955), FSAA (Eng.), AICA (Eng.). After twenty years in Hong Kong (1903-1922), he retired to Victoria with his wife, Lilian Lizzie Dillon, daughter of Alfred Dillon Smith of Shrewsbury, headmaster of its Trinity School. Three of their children were born at Hong Kong. The family sailed from Liverpool on the *Empress of France*, arriving at St John, New Brunswick, on 23 December 1920, and were recorded as Ernest Alfred M. Williams, accountant aged forty-one; Lilian Mountford Williams, housewife aged thirty-seven; Francis Dillon M., nine; Kathleen Lilian, six; and Edwin Mountford, three. At first, they lived at 311 Foul Bay Road but later at 1946 Ferndale Road.

EW was born in Shropshire, as were his father and mother, as well as his wife. His father, Alfred Williams, was born at Ludlow but employed as a "draper & outfitter" in Shrewsbury, where EW's mother, Emily, was born. The family appears in census records for 1891 when EW was eleven and his parents both thirty-eight. There were three other children: Nellie, aged ten, Kathleen, aged eight, Edith, aged four, and Harry R., aged three months, and one domestic servant, all living at "Severn Bank, Hawthorn Villa, Sunnyside." Ten years later, EW was living in London with two other young men at a boarding house at 34 Ryland Road, Islington, kept by a widow, Fanny Muir, aged fifty-nine, and her younger unmarried sister, Hannah Collins. EW had been educated privately and at Shrewsbury College, an old public school, and was now articled to a London firm of chartered accountants, Lowe, Bingham & Matthews. Two years later, they sent him to Hong Kong, where he would soon have learnt about the Island as a place of retreat or retirement. Throughout his life in both colonies, he kept up membership in the Thatch House Club (London) and the Shanghai Club (Hong Kong), and in Victoria they joined the Uplands Golf Club.

EW died, aged seventy-five, on 26 November 1955 in Saanich (probably at Rest Haven Sanitorium) and Mrs Williams, aged eighty-four, on 14 February 1969 in Victoria.

Sources: *Colonist*, 29 November 1955, p. 20, obit.; *Who's Who in B.C.* 1933-1934, p. 184; census 1891, England, RG 12/2109, p. 30; census 1891, RG 12/2111/28, p. 15 (Smith); census 1901, RG 13/196, p. 12; Canadian Passenger Lists, 1865-1935, T-14841 (Internet).

WILLIAMS, John (c. 1832-1915). Celebrated in 1913 by the British Campaigners' Association as one of their oldest members, he had a career in the Royal Navy proudly described by the *Victoria Daily Colonist* at his death, aged eighty-one, on 4 December 1915, when he lived at 2275 Cadboro Bay Road. He was born at Devonport, England, and went to sea as a boy, employed at first as a civil servant but during the Crimean War as a "first-class Boy" and "a powder-monkey," serving during the battle in the Baltic in company with *Dr Peter Williams Rolston, later fleet surgeon. In the Crimean War, JW was in HMS *Nile* at first but transferred a year later to HMS *Duke of Wellington*, a two-decker with ninety-one guns. After the war, he was posted for three and a half years to the Cape of Good Hope. Not accepted for service in the Indian Mutiny, he was sent in HMS *Jason* to the West Indies Station, then to Bermuda, Falmouth, and China in HMS *Rodney*.

There followed fifteen years at the China Station during which he was sent up the Yangtse-Kiang in the China War to the siege of the walled city of Swatow. He then resigned and went to Australia, where he worked at pearl fishing. After three years on the pearl grounds of the South Pacific and the Indian Ocean in a sealing lugger with a Malay crew, he was hired as mate under a Captain Cadie. He shipped next on the bark *Glengowan*, bound for Portland, Oregon, with a cargo of grain and then on to the Old Country, but she foundered in heavy seas off Cape Flattery and the shipwrecked crew rowed to Barkley Sound on the Island's exposed west coast, where they spent Christmas on an island.

Arriving at Victoria, JW decided to stay there and worked at Albion Iron Works, then for twelve years at the Dominion Government Fish Hatchery at "Lakelse" [Elk Lake?]. He retired at last to the Old Men's Home in Oak Bay, joined the Pioneer's Branch of Native Sons, and in due time became the oldest member of the British Campaigners' Association, which managed his funeral when he died on 4 December 1915. A large party carried his body on a gun carriage, covered with the Union Jack, to Ross Bay Cemetery on Dallas Road, facing the Strait of Juan de Fuca.

Sources: *Colonist*, 5 December 1915, p. 3, obit.; *BC Archives*, MS-0372, "British Campaigners' Association, Minute book (1908-1935)," and correspondence concerning the dissolution of the association (1951-1952).

WILLIAMS-FREEMAN, Major Francis Clavering Peere (1876-?). One of the Imperials who lived briefly in the Cowichan Valley, he married Dorothy Edith F. Dunne there at Westholme on 19 October 1922 and was a pallbearer at the funeral of *Colonel James Sweet Hodding at St Edwards Roman Catholic Church in March 1930. Dorothy was born at Westholme on 25 June 1897, daughter of *Charles Walter Dunne and sister of Katherine Mildred Dunne, who married *Lieutenant General Gerald Robert Poole. FW's younger brother, Harry Peere Williams-Freeman (1880-1918), bought nine acres on Lake Somenos in the Cowichan Valley before the Great War but died during that war on 9 August 1918, fighting in France in the Royal Warwickshire to which he had transferred from the CEF. Neither FW nor his wife died on the Island.

FW was born at Lymington, Hampshire, eldest son of Captain Francis M. Williams-Freeman and his wife Ada. He appears, aged five, with his family, then living in Marine House near the castle in Dover, Kent, where they were lodgers, the father aged thirty-nine, born in Oxfordshire at Henley-on-Thames and the mother, thirty-nine, born at Lymington. FW had three sisters and a brother, Harry Peere Williams-Freeman, aged eleven months, born in Dover, who also turned up on the Island later. There were three servants. The hyphenated name had been adopted on 25 November 1821 by their ancestor, Admiral-of-the-Fleet William Peere Williams, who thereby inherited much property from the Freeman and Clavering families. The admiral was born in the Episcopal palace at Peterborough on 6 January 1741/42 while his mother was staying with her father, the bishop of Peterborough, and, after a distinguished career in the RN, died on 11 February

1832 at Hoddesdon, Hertfordshire. As these forebears show, FW and his brother descended from a prominent family of public men.

Sources: *Cowichan Leader*, 18 March 1930, p. 10; 14 August 1919, p. 2; *Whitaker's*, p. 198; Army List, 1911, pp. 568, 571a; census 1881, England, RG 11/1001/30, p. 5; NAC, CEF, box 10410-56; *Gentleman's Magazine*, vol. 102, part I (1832), pp. 864-66.

WILLIAMSON, Robert John (1882-1975). He was born at Gateshead, a southern suburb of Newcastle-upon-Tyne, Durham, elder son of John T. Williamson, a consulting engineer, and his wife Eleanor F. Williamson from Sunderland nearby. The census of 1891 found him, aged twelve, living at "Taymont," Camberwell, London, with his parents, five sisters, and a brother. He apprenticed as a ship's engineer with Hawthorn Leslie in Newcastle and then worked on various passenger steamers; in 1901, for instance, he was an engineer on the crew of the *Crown Prince*. In 1913, he was appointed second engineer under Captain Robert Abram Bartlett, a Newfoundlander who commanded the *Kartuk*, one of the vessels which sailed north from Esquimalt on the well-known western arctic expedition led by Vilhjalmur Stefansson, an explorer born in Manitoba to an Icelandic family. When the *Karluk* was crushed by ice near Wrangle Island in January 1914, Williamson was one of the fifteen survivors who walked to Wrangel Island and were rescued in September that year. Six of his companions on the *Kartuk*'s crew and five of the scientific staff died, and six left the ships and were not seen again. The expedition was plagued by various animosities, especially between Stefansson and the others. In 1915, RW joined the Royal Navy and served on HMS *Woodnut* and *Sunhill* before returning to Canada in 1919. He then joined the Royal Canadian Navy and spent much of the next twenty years (1921-1941) in HMCS *Malaspina*. In 1939, he was listed with the Royal Canadian Naval Reserve, but ill health obliged him to retire two years later and he settled in Victoria with his wife, Florence Lisette MacKay, whom he had married on 11 January 1922 in Oak Bay. He died, aged ninety-six, on 9 February 1975 in Saanich.

Sources: NAC, reference numbers: new: R1633-0-1-E former: MG30-B44, Robert J. Williamson fonds; census 1891, England, RG 12/471, p. 1; census 1901, RG 13/3382, p. 21.

WILLEMAR, Rev. Jules Xavier (1841-1936). Son of a wealthy landowner of Luxeul in north-eastern France, he wanted to be a soldier but his father had him educated as a Roman Catholic priest. Church authorities sent him to the Island to serve with the congregation of Oblates of Mary Immaculate, and he taught in Victoria at the Catholic College of St Lowes. After a few years, he took an independent step, applying to the bishop of [British] Columbia to join the Church of England and was added to the Missionary Board of the diocese, which posted him to Alberni on the Island's west coast. Then he was sent with a colleague to serve at Comox, where they arrived by sea on 3 October 1871, and built a raft to carry their effects up the Courtenay River to Sandwick, and by 1877, the parish had built a log church and a primitive parsonage. JW had the happy idea of taking the church bell from the wreck of an Australian sailing vessel, the *Lady Blackwood*. It was in that parish that Sophie Chaworth-Musters, future wife of *General Sir Arthur Currie, was born in 1878. The parish work there entailed much travelling in dugout canoes paddled by local tribesmen, and JW recalled the life with pleasure in later years.

On 1 July 1879 during a visit to Victoria, JW married Mary Isabel Munro and they had at least five children in the years 1881-1893, several of whom married and had families. He served at Comox for forty-two years and died there at last on 30 July 1936. Mrs Willemar died, aged eighty-six, on 6 March 1942 at North Vancouver.
Sources: Ben Hughes, *History of the Comox Valley* 1862-1945 (Nanaimo, Evergreen Press, 1946?), pp. 18-20, 37-8; *Canadian Almanach*, 1902, p. 272; 1909, p. 343; Anglican Journal, *Diocesan Post*, vol. 41, no. 2 (February 2007), p. 15.

WILLIS, Rev. Eric Mackay (1885-1982). Born in May 1885 at Cheltenham, Gloucestershire, he was a younger son of Captain Horace George Willis (c. 1840-1911), a JP living in 1891 with his wife, Emily Rachel (EW's mother) at "The Glenfells," Cheltenham, with five domestic servants and a governess "teacher of foreign languages." The father was born a British subject in Italy and served with the Royal Artillery in India; the mother was born at Upton Grey in Hampshire, and EW's siblings were variously born in Switzerland, France, Devon, and Gloucestershire. He attended Eastbourne College, studied at Stratford-on-Avon, Keble College Oxford, and Lincoln, and was ordained an Anglican minister in 1916.

He went to Victoria in 1911 and taught at the Union School until 1914, when he went overseas to serve as a chaplain in France with the Ninth Battalion of the British Army. In 1919, he returned to the Island, where he joined the Union Club in Victoria and was appointed successively as Anglican rector at St Luke's, St Saviour's, and St John's Cobble Hill and finally as chaplain at Shawnigan Lake Boys' School and University Boys' School. He resigned in 1933 and settled at Mill Bay near Cobble Hill. He was living at Comox when he died, aged ninety-seven, on 11 October 1982. I could find no sign of a wife.
Sources: census 1901, England, RG 13/ 2938, p. 1; census 1901, RG 13/2458, p. 14; census 1891, RG 12/2041, p. 2; *Who's Who in B.C.* 1933-1934, p. 184; *Times-Colonist*, 13 October 1982, p. C-12, obit.; Keble College Oxford, Alumni Directory online.

WILSON, Major Charles C (c. 1879-1954). Born in the Murree Hills, India, son of a British officer and his wife, Frances Wilson, he appears with his mother and a servant in the 1901 census records, described as an "Articled Clerk" aged twenty-one, living at 13 Fairfax Road, Chiswick, London. His mother, a widow aged sixty, was born at Preston, Lancashire, and recorded as "living on own means." Ten years earlier, she had been living at 3 Bickness Place, Beach Road, at St Saviour on the island of Jersey, with two daughters, Florence M. aged eighteen, born at Gosport, and Frances B. aged fifteen, born like their brother in the "East Indies." However that may be, CW had a career of thirty years in the Indian Forestry Service, rising to chief forester at Madras, fought in a British unit in the Great War, and then retired to Victoria. On 25 March 1941, the Kipling Society of Victoria heard him speak about his years in the Indian Forest Service, showing slides of elephants, the cutting of teakwood, and as a climax to the evening, "a colour film of the fight to the death between a mongoose and the deadly hooded cobra." On 26 June that year, he spoke to the Kinsmen's Club at their luncheon on "Capturing and Training Wild Animals in India." He was a Companion of the Order of the Indian Empire and also had a VD (Voluntary Decoration.). He died, aged seventy-six, on 26 October 1954 at Haney, BC.

Sources: *Colonist*, 26 March 1941, p. 2; 22 June 1941, p. 17; census 1891, England, RG 12/4697, p. 15; census, 1901, RG 13/1199, p. 32.

WILSON, Rev. Edward Francis (1844-1915). From 1894, when he retired to St Mark's parish on Salt Spring Island, he and his family were widely known and influential there. EW went out to Canada with his wife in 1868, to Algoma, Ontario, to work among Indians first for the Church Missionary Society and then for the Colonial and Continental Church Society. He founded homes for Indian boys and girls and another home later at Elkhorn, Manitoba, where his eldest son was the principal at the time of EW's death. In 1886, during this missionary phase of his life, he published an interesting book about his work among the Ojibway tribes. Let us here only add details to David A. Nock's competent biographical essay in the *Dictionary of Canadian Biography*. The devotion of his family to evangelical missionary work overseas may have been due to the influence of Huguenot refugees, Calvinists, employed by his great grandfather, who had been a silk manufacturer in the Spitalfields district of London. In any event, one of the sons, EW's grandfather Daniel Wilson (1778-1858), acquired the advowson for St Mary's Parish in Islington and lived there as vicar in the years 1824-1832 before going out to India as bishop of Calcutta, leaving his son, EW's father Daniel (1805-1886), as the vicar of Islington living at the vicarage in Barnsbury Park. It was there that EW was born and grew up, but at sixteen he was living in Wingham, Kent, as the pupil of a veteran "land agent and valuer." It was only after emigrating to Ontario that EW decided to enter the church as a missionary. He had before him the famous career of his grandfather Daniel, a friend of the Clapham Sect of evangelical anti-slavery reformers—one of EW's brother was christened Wilberforce—who as bishop of Calcutta in 1832-1858 raised a storm of trouble in India and indirectly in London while trying to improve the lives of Untouchables (Dalits) by working against the evil Hindu caste system. Once persuaded to work as an evangelical Anglican missionary, EW never looked back, except perhaps in his retirement on Salt Spring Island, where he called his vicarage "Barnsbury." There the family's influence was considerable.

In 1868 in a Gloucestershire village, he had married Elizabeth Frances Spooner (1840-1926), daughter of the vicar of Inglesham, Wiltshire. She bore eleven children, five of whom married Imperials or people from middle-class British families either in Victoria or at Ganges on Salt Spring Island. Two other sons married women born in the USA, both with English backgrounds.

The Wilson Children's Marriages in Victoria or on Salt Spring Island			
Wilson	Marriage	Spouse	Spouse's Birthplace
Evelyn Grace (1)	15/9/1895	Charles Wm. Tolson	Fazeley (Staffs)
Kathleen Manorie	12/2/1898	Frank Louis ScottLieutenant, CEF, WW I	Bradford (York.)
Winifred Lois	8/11/1898	*Capt. Frederick Henry Walter, RN (1872-1949)	Aldershot (Berks)
Frances Nona	17/9/1903	Alfred Gerald Crofton	Southern Ireland (Anglican)
Florence Muriel	1524	Ernest George BorradaileSA Constabulary; WW II	Stroud (Kent)
Evelyn Grace (2)	2071	William Scott Ritchie	Stirlingshire (Scot.)
Daniel Keith	2165	Kate Constance King	Portland, Oregon, USA
Norman Wolfe	14/8/1909	Ethel Crowe	USA
Sources: NAC, Canadian censuses 1901, 1911; CEF files, WW I; St Mark's Anglican Church, Ganges; Salt Spring Island Historical Society; BNA, censuses 1841-1901.			

On retiring, EW went to Santa Monica, California, for his health, but returned to spend his last days in Victoria. He wrote a number of works on religion and missionary work, also a dictionary of an Indian language published by the SPCK. EW died, aged seventy-one, on 11 May 1915 in Victoria, where his wife died, aged eighty-five, on 17 June 1926, both much missed on Salt Spring Island.

Sources: *Colonist*, 12 May 1915, p. 7, obit.; BNA, census 1861, England, RG 9/541, p. 4; *Canadian Almanach*, 1902, p. 272; 1909, p. 343; David A. Nock, in the *DCB*, vol. XIV, pp. 1070-1071; Josiah Bateman, *The Life of the Right Rev. Daniel Wilson, Late Lord Bishop of Calcutta and Metropolitan India,* with extracts from his journals and correspondence (2 vols.; John Murray, 1860), vol. I, pp. 8, 20, 29-31, 92 (grandfather's marriage), 230, 280-86, 323-25; BNA, British History Online, Churches in London; from: 'Islington: Churches', *A History of the County of Middlesex:* Vol. 8: Islington and Stoke Newington parishes (1985), pp. 88-99. URL: http://www. british-history.ac.uk/report. aspx?compid=2310; E. F. Wilson, *Missionary*

Work among the Ojibway Indians (SPCK, 1886), 255 pp; Kahn, *Salt Spring Island,* pp. 133-6; Andrew Porter, "Wilson, Daniel (1778-1858), bishop of Calcutta," Oxford DNB online.

WILSON, Major John (c. 1828-1914). Born in England, he enlisted in 1844 as a private in the First Royal Highlanders, Black Watch Regiment, and saw service in the Crimean War, in Turkey, and in the Indian Mutiny; he was decorated with the Turkish Order of Medije. He won his first commission after ten years' service; a year later, he became a lieutenant and, in 1858, a captain. In 1872, he reached the rank of brevet major. He served in the Forty-second Highlanders for twenty-eight years, witnessed the charges of the Heavy Brigade and the Light Brigade, and took part in the storming of the Heights of Alma, "in the mists at Inkerman, and on the ridges of Balaclava; he was in it at the capture of Kertsch and Yenikale and in the trenches before Sebastopol; then ordered to China [Singapore] to be sent back to Calcutta." He marched with Sir Colin Campbell's force to the relief of Cawnpore and Lucknow and remained in India after the Mutiny, for ten years in all. While there, he made three long trips into Tibet, the first of them in 1860, and had many adventures. In 1873, he retired from the service and went to Kansas, where he spent six years in cattle ranching, followed by mining at Leadville, Colorado, and in 1883 went into business at San Francisco as a commission merchant.

In 1885, he went out to Victoria and, after ten years as a commission agent, joined the BC Civil Service in which he was attached for the last ten years to the provincial Secretary's Department. He was one of the founders of the British Campaigners' Association of Victoria in 1907 and joined it formally on 18 December 1908. From January 1909 until his death, he presided over it and the members were evidently fond of him. He was living at 1147 Fairfield Road when he died, aged eighty-six years and three months, on 27 September 1914. The British campaigners took charge of the funeral arrangements, and the pallbearers were taken from among them. The funeral was held at Christ Church Cathedral (Archdeacon Scriven) of which he was a parishioner. "His funeral took place on Wed. 30 September with full military honours," the British campaigners recorded in their minutes. "The 50th Highlanders formed the firing party under Captain (local Major) Roberts. The four-horse gun carriage kindly lent by the 5th Regiment, Lieut.—Colonel W. N. Winsby, also the full band of the 5th Regiment, the Pipers of the Highlanders. The bearers were Messrs Beaumont Boggs; Major W. Bapty, B.C.H.; E.C.B. Bagshawe; W. C. Winkel; Mr J. A. Andrew; Major de Salis, 88th Regiment, whilst the parade was marshalled by Mr W. J. Edwards, the service at the graveside was taken by Rev. Andrew Chaplain to forces and the British Columbia Horse." "Among the old soldiers present" local newspapers reported, "were the following Crimean veterans who saw service with Major Wilson: Captain Curtis; R. N. Brinkley Robinson; P. C. Fernie; and Messrs Smith and Gordon. Mr Williams, an Indian Mutiny veteran who also saw service with him was there. Attending were Clive Phillipps-Wolley; Fleet Surgeon Home; George Jay; [and] A. D. McDoull." In an editorial, the *Victoria Times* (29 September 1914, p. 4) wrote, "The late Major Wilson, like the true British soldier, never could be induced to talk of his career in the army."

Sources: *Victoria Daily Times*, 28 September 1914, p. 13, obit.; 29 September 1914, p. 4; 1 October 1914, p. 5; *Colonist*, 29 September 1914, pp. 1-2 and 7, obit, photo; *BC Archives*, "*Minutes of the British Campaigners' Association*" (1908-1935), 21 October 1914 and photo.

WILSON-HAFFENDEN, Colonel Eric Lawrence (1898-1986). Born on 19 October 1898 in the west end of London, he spent his early years with his family in country towns. In 1901, the census-taker found him, aged two, living in Bisley Road, Stroud, Gloucestershire, with his father, Lawrence A. W. Haffenden, then aged twenty-seven, a Baptist minister born in Kent at Teverdon and his mother Mary, aged thirty-eight, born at Myland, Essex. With him were two brothers, Clive C. W. Wilson-Haffenden, aged four, born in London, and David J. N. Wilson-Haffenden, aged four months, born at Uplands, Gloucestershire. They had one general servant. Ten years earlier, the father Lawrence A. W. Haffenden was a seventeen-year-old hospital clerk staying in London with his brother James, a commercial traveller, at 7 Bernard Street, St George's Bloomsbury Square. According to his own account, EW, aged 17½, followed his brother Donald James Haffenden out to India and became a cadet there at Wellington College. This brother rose in the Indian Army, eventually becoming a major general. Meanwhile, in 1916, EW was commissioned in the Thirty-second Sikh Pioneers and went as a volunteer to join the Sixth King Edward's Own Cavalry in which he soon fought in the battle of Cambrai. Sent next to Palestine, he fought with General Allenby in the encirclement of the Turkish forces. "From the high reaches of the Musmus Pass he watched the very last cavalry charge to take place in modern warfare . . ." This was in General Edmund Allenby's famous bluff to mislead the enemy. EW's division rode sixty-one miles in that operation. So rapid and unexpected was this Allied advance that the German general, Liman von Sanders, had to escape in his pyjamas. The Cavalry of Arabia arrived, each body of troops from opposite sides of the city. After that, Haffenden was posted to the 155th Pioneers with whom he served in Asia Minor, working on the Taurus Tunnels destroyed earlier by the Turks. During service in the Middle East, EW caught malaria and ended up convalescing in Alexandria. He then had five months' leave in England. Rejoining the Sikhs, he stayed with them until they were disbanded about 1932. In the meantime, he had taken part in the Razmak Campaign (1928-1929) and in restoring lost or demolished outposts resulting from the Afghan War. He was next attached to the Sappers and sent to the military academy at Dehra Dun ("the Indian Sandhurst") as an instructor.

As the Second World War approached, he had a period of duty with the Second Battalion of the Nineteenth Hyderabad Sikh Regiment and then sent to Malaya to command his own battalion, with the rank of lieutenant colonel. As a musician, EW was called upon to organize and train a Sikh military band for the regiment. Wounded in the futile defence of Singapore against invading Japanese forces, he was evacuated twenty-four hours before the capitulation of February 1942. Shortly after that, the Japanese entered Singapore and killed all the wounded in the hospital. Aboard a hospital ship, EW was fitted with a "walking iron" and taken to Java, then to Karachi. His convalescence was long, and in 1942, he badgered the army to send him to GHQ at Simla. After months of sick leave and convalescence, he got his wish and, after some time in Simla, was sent to the Tactical School at Poona as senior instructor in the senior wing. Granted more sick leave, he proposed to spend it in Australia, but his ship was torpedoed and he spent eleven days in an open lifeboat in the Indian Ocean with thirty-seven other survivors. They were eventually rescued by the Royal Navy in a Canadian-built frigate, HMS *Lossie*, on its way to Ceylon, and EW disembarked there at Colombo. There he had a brother-in-law who was a squadron leader in the RAF. Relaxing in the officers' mess one evening, playing the piano for a singsong, W-H was asked by a senior RAF officer why he was in Colombo and arrangements were made to fly him to Australia, where his wife was born. By the end of 1944, he was second in command of a training brigade at Mysore, and in 1946, he was in command of the regimental centre with eighteen thousand men under him. Finally, in 1947, he was sent to Agra, India, as colonel in charge of administration at Ambala, a large district northwest of Delhi. When India was declared independent on 15 August that year, he retired home to England on a pension.

Like so many Indian army officers before him, however, he had already decided to emigrate to the Island and so arrived at Victoria with his wife and children on 12 September 1947. He soon went up the Island to Comox, where he found a house on the beach and then went looking for a job. He tried working as an "inspector" on the Hope-Princeton Highway and spent four months as assistant instrument man on a survey. Discouraged in those early months, he nearly went back to England but friends persuaded him to stay. He went to Victoria Normal School and became a schoolteacher and, from 1949 to 1962, taught classes at Comox Elementary School and then, as vice-principal, at Robb Road School. He was instrumental in having music and drama made part of the curriculum of School District 71 and introduced French into his classroom. He was active in the community: He served on the School Board from 1968-1970; he was active in the Horticultural Society, the Comox Valley Exhibition Association, the Canadian Club, the Overture Concert Association, and the original Courtenay Drama Club, serving as president of those groups from time to time. For many years, he also served as the organist for St Peter's Anglican Church. He was an ardent gardener and won many prizes locally for his flowers. He joined Comox Branch 160 of the Royal Canadian Legion, and he served it for several years as vice-president and member of the executive council and was in charge of the Colour Party and Queen's Honour Guard when Queen Elizabeth visited the Comox Valley. One of his friends in that branch of the Legion was Douglas "Duke" Warren whom he first met at a luncheon on 19 August 1970 to commemorate Canadians lost at Dieppe. They discovered that they had both flown at the Battle of Dieppe in 1942 and remained close friends.

EW had four wives. His first, from Australia, was in Singapore with him during the disastrous invasion of 1942 but escaped, as he did, eventually and emigrated to the Island with him and their children, but died an alcoholic. He met his second wife, Dorothy Cousins (c. 1920-1956), who was a teacher at the Victoria Normal School, Victoria, but died of cancer at Comox on 4 March 1986. EW then lived alone for a while, but during a visit to a brother in England, he met and married his brother's housekeeper when she followed him to Comox. Two weeks later, she returned to England, and EW told Warren that marrying her had been the stupidest thing he had ever done. His fourth wife, Genevieve Martina, was the widow of an American technical representative who had met EH earlier while her husband was stationed at Comox. They met while EW was visiting his son Michael, who was married and living in Vancouver. There followed a happy phase of EW's life, still in Comox, which ended with his death there on 4 March 1986 at St Joseph's Hospital, survived by Genevieve, his son John Michael and his wife Patricia, and their daughters, Cara and Gilliam, all in Vancouver. In England, he still had his sister Joyce and their brother Major General Donald James Wilson-Haffenden, who had long been active in the post-war years as a supporter of Billy Graham's evangelistic campaign in England. When EW made a will on 8 September 1975, he was living at 1820 Buena Vista, Comox, BC, but when he made his last will, on 17 February 1981, he was living at Pad 27, Trailerland, R. R. #1, Comox. EW's son John Michael Wilson-Haffenden, of 7977 Birch Street, Vancouver, later gave the court some information about his birth. EW's estate at his death contained no property, but bonds, and amounted to c. $92,000. His wife, Genevieve Martina Wilson-Haffenden, of 27-1240 Wilkinson Road, Comox, applied for executorship and trusteeship of the estate. She is said to have remained in Comox until her death, but I find no sign of this in public records.

Sources: Vivienne Chadwick, "The Colonel is a Character," *Colonist*, 25 November 1962, Sunday pp. 5 and 15; copious notes courtesy of Douglas "Duke" Warren, Comox, BC, 1 August 2003; notes from the *Comox District Free Press*, 12 March 1986, p. A9, courtesy of Barbara Page; *BC Archives* GR-2994, Records of the BC Supreme Court (Courtenay) 1949-1986: microfilm reel B09123, file 868044; courtesy of Barrie Humphrey, Gabriola Island; census 1901, England, RG 13/2438, p. 1; census 1891, England, RG 12/209, p. 16; information from the Billy Graham Archives, Wheaton, USA, Collection 141, Box 14, Folder 33, courtesy of Robert Shuster; Donald James Wilson-Haffenden, *Red Men of Nigeria* (Fulani) (1930), and *Operation Exodus* (1957).

WILSON-JONES, Captain Harold (c. 1876-1931). He was born at Roby near Huyton, a suburb of Liverpool, son of Anne E. Jones, from Silverdale, Lancashire, and John Jones, a "Publisher & Printer employing twenty-five men," as the 1881 census recorded. HW was four years old and living in Tarbock Road, Roby, with his parents and several brothers and sister. There was a resident aunt and a visitor but no domestic servants. They were still there in 1891 but had two servants. As a young man, he joined the Royal Horse and RFA and served in France during the Great War, but transferred at some point to the Fifteenth Light Horse, Canadian Militia, in which he obtained a commission. He was one of those who volunteered for service in Siberia in 1918-1920, and had the medal of St Stanaelaus and St Anne of Russia as well as the Mons Star 1914, and General Service and Victory Medals.

About 1921, he settled in Victoria and became known not only as a distinguished military officer, but also as a zoologist representing the Royal Zoological Society and in search of a specimen of white bear of which there was only one in captivity, *Ursus Kermodeii*, which was kept at Beacon Hill Park. He made several trips to the north of the province and on the west coast of the Island. It was while engaged in these activities that he decided to settle permanently. He soon found accommodation at 1466 Mitchell Street and joined the Army and Navy Veterans Association and the British Public Schools Club. Like the overwhelming majority of officers, he belonged to the Church of England and was buried in it when he died, aged fifty-five, on 30 November 1931, as a result of a serious injury while using an axe.

Sources: *Colonist*, 2 December 1931, p. 5, obit.; census 1881, England, RG 11/3722, pp. 4-5; census 1891, RG 12/182, p. 41.

WINDEYER, Commander Guy Stanley (1910-1984). He was born in 1910 at Pymble, near Sydney, Australia, and when he was twelve years old, he joined the Royal Navy training establishment at Osborne, Isle of Wight, and then attended Dartmouth Naval College. He was appointed a midshipman in 1916, served in the Great War, for some time on the China Station, at Malta, and in the Admiralty, and then spent three years in Japan, where he learnt the language and obtained a black belt in judo. He had also been trained as a submariner. Retiring from the RN in 1937, he settled on a farm at Somenos in the Cowichan Valley, where he and his wife Noelle, an industrious Irish woman from Lismore, kept fifteen dairy cows, and had a milk route in the district. In 1939, GW volunteered his services, joined the RCN at *Naden* in Esquimalt, served on the staff of the commanding officer Pacific Coast as intelligence officer, and then sailed a new ship around to Halifax, where he was assigned to command convoys in the Atlantic. After several harrowing experiences at sea and distinguished services for which he won the DSC, he suffered a nervous collapse while defending a convoy against a German submarine and was obliged to leave the command of the ship to his second in command, Commander F. C. Frewer. The author of a book dedicated to GW in admiration for the ship's actions that day was an officer on a merchant ship in the convoy and unaware of the incident. In any event, GW was relieved of sea duty and assigned to direct the Commando Training Centre in Courtenay, VI. His appointment ended on 14 June 1945, when he returned to the farm with the rank of commander (retired) and resumed the milk business. However, his wife had changed the herd to beef cattle during the war, and they soon concentrated on raising Black Angus cattle and keeping a market garden; Mrs Windeyer ran a roadside produce stand by Somenos Lake. There he died on 27 November 1984.

Sources: Henry Revely, *The Convoy that Nearly Died: The Story of ONS 154* (William Kimber, 1979), 222 pp. passim, conversations with Commander Frederick Charsley Frewer (1920-2004), RCN; notes from a daughter, Katherine, courtesy of John Palmer (3 September 2002); *MacFarlane*, p. 64; Tom Henry, *Small City in a Big Valley: The Story of Duncan* (in 4o, Madeira Park, BC, Harbour Publishing, 1999), p. 61.

WINDLE, Harry Watson (1868-1932). He was born on 21 March 1868 in India, and the 1881 census found him, aged thirteen, living in suburban Surrey at 13 Acadia Grove, Camberwell, with his widowed mother, Anne M. Windle, a "Pensioner Indian" born in Ireland. He had siblings: Charles H. Windle, aged fourteen, Mary Windle, eleven, and Whetfield Windle, six, all born in India. Their two-year-old sister Ethel Windle was born in London, and living with them were their late father's sister, Henriette E. Windle, aged twenty-eight and unmarried, born in India; an English boarder born in France; and a servant girl. In 1890, he migrated to Victoria, where he found employment as a bank clerk at a salary of $1,200 a year. He lived with his wife at 53 Vancouver Street, declared himself an Anglican, and retired in due time to Comox, where he died, on 17 May 1932. **Sources:** census 1881, England, RG 11/0669/108, p. 15; India Office List, 1930, p. 905: "*Record of Service*"; Canadian census, 1891, VI; Canadian census, 1901, Victoria; Herbert Feldman, *Karachi Through a Hundred Years: The Centenary History of the Karachi Chamber of Commerce and Industry* 1860-1960 (Karachi, Oxford University Press, 1960), photograph between pp. 236-7.

WINGFIELD-DIGBY, Major William Richard (1869-1944). He was born on 8 April 1869 at Bournemouth, Hampshire, fourth son of John Digby Wingfield-Digby of Sherborne Castle, Dorset, and Coleshill Park, Warwickshire. There he appears, aged two, in census records for 1871 with his family and thirteen servants—governess, cook, ladies' maid, three nursemaids, laundrymaid, housemaid, kitchenmaid, schoolroom maid, butler, valet, hall boy, and next door in the village a lot of labourers and their families. In due time, he became an uncle of the Colonel Frederick James Bosworth Wingfield-Digby (1885-1952) whom James Lees-Milne visited at the castle early in 1944 for the National Trust and denounced, along with his wife Gwendolen Marjory *née* Fletcher, as offensive "blimpish owners." The family of Digby had acquired Sherborne Castle under Elizabeth I, and it was much later, about 1800, that WW's great-grandmother, Lady Charlotte Digby, inherited Sherborne Castle and married William Wingfield, making the composite name of Wingfield-Digby. The castle had once been bombarded by Oliver Cromwell. Walter Raleigh built the first part of the present manor house and dammed the river to make a lake. Capability Brown designed the grounds. WW's father, the youngest son in a family of four or five boys and eight girls, sent WW to Harrow and RMA at Sandhurst. In April 1893, WW joined the Rifle Brigade, an infantry regiment of British regulars, and served during the South African War as a captain in a special reserve unit and was awarded the Queen's Medal with five clasps.

After further service in Malta, Calcutta, and Hong Kong, he retired in 1908 and went to the Island about 1912 during a land boom in which he bought about twenty acres on Parksville Bay and farmed in a small subsistence way, with chickens and a large garden. His son Ronald, who graciously received me in a small house off Cook Street, Victoria, said that throughout his career as a professional soldier, WW was unhappy with the social side of the British Army, especially all the drinking. In 1914, however, he rejoined the Rifle Brigade, served until 1919, and then returned to the Island, where on 6 October 1920 he married Maggie, daughter of W. N. Werry of Ulverston, Lancashire. They remained on the Parksville property but gradually sold most of the land in the expansive years that swelled Parksville's population from some four hundred to more than nine thousand. For many years, they kept the house and he was a member of 49 branch of the Legion, Mt Arrowsmith, and he kept up memberships in the Army and Navy Club (London), the Bath Club (London), and the Pacific Club (Victoria). Nearby was a neighbour, *Captain Courtney Cox, RN, with whom the family used to have afternoon tea in a living room overlooking the bay. About 1941, they moved to 1279 Hewlett Place, Victoria, and there he died, aged seventy-five, on 20 October 1944 and was buried as an Anglican, leaving his wife and their only son, Ronald, then serving in the Canadian Dental Corps engaged in the Second World War. When I visited him at Hewlett Place many years later, Ronald courteously and modestly told me a few facts about his family. Sherborne Castle had been ceded to the National Trust at some time in the 1980s.

Sources: Conversation and correspondence with Ronald Wingfield-Digby (a son), 12 May 2001; *Who's Who in B.C.*, 1933-1934, pp. 50-51; *Colonist*, 21 October 1944, p. 12, obit.; census 1871, England, RG 10/3168 [or 5168], p. 2; census 1881, RG 11/3077, p. 2; census 1891, RG 12/2440, p. 6; James Lees-Milne, *Some Country Houses and their Owners* (1975; Penguin, 2009), pp. 58-61.

WINKEL, William Charles (1878-1959). Born in London on 1 February 1878, he was the second son of Frederick George Winkel (1857-1948) and his wife Lydia (1858-1945), who had several other children. In 1880, the family moved out to Manitoba, where two more daughters were born, and then migrated west to Victoria, where the 1901 census recorded them living at 32 Niagara Street in the James Bay district. There the father worked as caretaker of the James Bay Methodist Church of which they were members. WW worked as a logger or lumberman until 10 February 1900, when he joined Lord Strathcona's Horse, regimental number 502. He was twenty-three years old, 5' 8½" tall, with fair complexion, brown hair and eyes, and a "sanguine" temperament. Sent to South Africa with his unit, he served there in actions at Orange Free State, Natal, and Belfast (SA), for which he was awarded the Queen's Medal and three clasps, and discharged in Ottawa on 16 March 1901. On 8 December 1903, he married Ethel Jessie Prescott, daughter of C. A. Prescott of Victoria and they planned to live at Nicola.

He joined the Canadian Militia and had served in it for six years when, on 17 August 1915, he enlisted in the First Canadian Pioneers, regimental number 154042, and was soon sent overseas. Promoted to sergeant on 20 October 1915, he arrived in England on 30 November and embarked for France on 9 March 1916. He was granted a commission as a temporary lieutenant but wounded in the shoulder by shrapnel and contracted lumbago from "working in water in trenches" and spent some time recovering at the Fishmongers Hall Hospital, London Bridge, and Perkin Bull Hospital at Putney. Treatment included "hot baths and massage." He was granted leave to Canada from 14 July to 14 October 1916 and on returning for duty was appointed an instructor in 1918. He was transferred to the Second Canadian Engineers' Reserve Battalion and sent to the Canadian School of Military Engineering. Struck off strength on 6 January 1919 by reason of the general demobilization, he returned to Victoria and became an active member of the British Campaigners' Association. He turned out for its parades and attended its meetings until he died, aged seventy-seven, on 4 May 1959, by which time they were living at 218 Simcoe Street.

Sources: NAC, RG150, box 10495-27; RG 38, A-1-a, vol. 114; T-2090; Canadian census, 1901, Victoria; BC Archives, records of the British Campaigner's Association.

WINSBY, Lieutenant Colonel William Norman (1874-1957). He was born on 28 October 1874, son of William Prest Winsby (1947-1921) and Annie Winsby *née* Theakston (1848-1920) in Yorkshire at Leyburn, where the Winsby family had proliferated. His grandparents were Thomas Winsby (1811-1890) and Ann Prest (1807-1889). At sometime in the 1880s, the family (but not the grandparents) emigrated to Victoria, where the 1901 census found them living at 22 Stanley Avenue. The father was working as a city tax collector, later a customs appraiser, and WW was teaching at Central School, which he had attended as a teenager, and was living at home with several brothers and sisters. One brother in particular, Walter Winsby (1876-1943), is often confused with him but had a different career. In 1898, Walter joined the Dominion Finance Department and was posted to Ottawa, Calgary, Winnipeg, and Regina. When the Dominion Savings Bank was taken over by the Bank of Canada in 1935, Walter went to manage the Vancouver branch, but retired in 1941 and died two years later. Meanwhile, WW became a provincial school inspector, joined the Fifth Canadian Garrison Artillery, No. 2 Company, in Victoria and rose to the rank of major. In 1913, he and *Captain H. H. Woolison won a gun contest at Fort Macaulay, for which a banquet was held at the James Bay Hotel late in January 1914. He was about to assume command of the No. 2 Company and signed the CEF "Officers' Declaration Paper" as lieutenant colonel on 6 November 1915 at New Westminster, by which time he had had twenty-one years of service in that militia unit. By then, too, he had married Edythe Mary Winsby and settled at 1054 Southgate Street, Victoria, still a school inspector. He was sent overseas at the head of the Forty-seventh Battalion and served for four years, three of them in France. After the Great War, he joined the Victoria branch of the Great War Veterans' Association and served at least two terms as its president. In 1921, he was employed as principal of the Victoria West, South Park, and Boys' Central Schools and was also appointed to the provincial Liquor Control Board, and in 1937, he was elected president of the Victoria and District Teacher's Association. When he died, aged eighty-four, on 17 April 1957, he was in Vancouver, with relatives scattered about the province.

Sources: NAC, CEF files, box 10497-29; Canadian census, 1901, Victoria; *Colonist*, 1 February 1914, p. 5; 14 April 1921, p. 4; 3 August 1921, p. 7; 19 June 1937, p. 3.

WISE, Major James (c. 1887-1955). He was born at Blairgowrie, Scotland, migrated to Canada in 1910, and settled in Victoria the next year. Early in the Great War, he joined the Sixteenth Scottish Regiment and went overseas but soon transferred to the Gordon Highlanders in the British Army. After the war, he came back and devoted himself to the Boy Scout movement, acting for many years as district commissioner. He used to take Scouts on trips in his big open car. A bachelor, he lived at the Union Club, was a governor of University School from 1911 to 1945, and was employed in real estate and insurance. Occasionally, as in the winter of 1924-1925, he took trips back to Scotland, where he had relatives such as B. W. Wise of Blairgowrie House, Blairgowrie. When he died, aged sixty-eight, on 19 January 1955, still a bachelor and leaving a brother in East Africa, he was buried at Christ Church Cathedral, Victoria. He is easily confused with several other men in BC of the same name.

Sources: NAC, RG76 immigration series C-1-C 1925, vol. I, p. 26, reel T-14845; *Colonist*, 20 January 1955, p. 13, obit and photo;

WOLFENDEN, Lieutenant Colonel Richard (1836-1911). He was born on 20 March 1836 at Rathwell, Yorkshire, third son of Robert Wolfenden, who sent him to school at Arkholme and Kirkby Lonsdale, Westmoreland. His parents moved to Kirkly Lonsdale when he was a small child and there he was apprenticed at age fourteen to a printer, John Foster. He wanted to be a surveyor and eventually articled to his elder brother, George, who was a land surveyor there. In 1855, he decided to join the Royal Engineers for the surveying experience but was sent to the School of Musketry in Hythe, then to Woolwich, where he became such a good shot that he was appointed instructor of musketry (1856-1858) using the old Lancaster rifle. In 1858, he volunteered for service in British Columbia under Colonel R. C. Moody, RE, sailed with others around Cape Horn in October 1858 on the *Thames City*, and was posted at New Westminster, where he was employed as an accountant in the Lands and Works Department until 1862. In 1860, he established the government printing office in Victoria and was appointed, in 1863, superintendent of printing, which post he continued to hold for many years, having retired from the Royal Engineers when they left BC in 1862.

In 1863, he was appointed superintendent of printing for the BC government and after the union of the Island and BC in 1866, he had to move to Victoria, the provincial capital, where he and his family soon settled on Simcoe Street, near Beacon Hill. Having joined the militia on arrival, he was promoted in the Victoria Rifles to ensign (1874), lieutenant (1876), captain (1878), major (1885), and lieutenant colonel (1886) and retired with that rank in 1888, the first militia officer in BC to reach this rank. In 1874, he was on the Canadian Wimbledon team, and over the years, he won several trophies. He had many friends in Victoria, such as Edgar Fawcett, and became a member of the Victoria Board of School Trustees, president of the Victoria Rifle Association, a member of the Victoria Club, and a practicing Anglican. He had married Kate Corby in 1865, daughter of George Corby of Canterbury, and after her death married Felicitée Bayley, daughter of John Bayley of Victoria, in 1879. By the first marriage, he had a son, Arthur Richard Wolfenden (c. 1872-1935), and by the second, a daughter Madge. In 1903, he was made a Companion of the Imperial Service Order, and in 1908, he and his wife, Madge's mother, took six months' leave and visited England. RW died, aged seventy-five, on 5 October 1911 and was buried three days later as an

Anglican and with military honours. His son, A. R. Wolfenden, who eventually died, aged sixty-three, on 23 October 1935 in Victoria, had a daughter Beatrice (RW's granddaughter), who married *Commander J. R. Beech. A grandson, Richard Wolfenden (1912-1992), became a naval cadet in 1919 and attended the Royal Naval College of Canada in 1919. He transferred to the RCNR, wherein he became a lieutenant, transferred again to the RNR, and was mobilized for service in the Second World War, serving on a number of RN vessels. After the war, he went into the merchant service with Canadian Pacific, and later, he served with the Chinese Maritime Customs Service. He died on 8 July 1992 at Kuala Lumpur, Malaysia. **Sources:** J. B. Kerr, *Biographical Dictionary of Well-Known British Columbians,* pp. 323-4; Goldwin Terry and Madge Hamilton, "*1st Queen's Printer a Sharpshooter,*" *Time-Colonist,* 6 August 1988; Edgar Fawcett, *Some Reminiscences of Old Victoria* (Toronto, William Briggs, 1912), pp. 203-5, with photo; Madge Wolfenden, paper to the BC Historical Association 27 April 1934 in *BC Archives,* MS-0677 (Longstaff Papers), vol. 406, file 355; *MacFarlane,* p. 65;

WOLLEY-DOD, Lieutenant Colonel Arthur George (1860-1936). He was born on 4 May 1860, not at Chester but at Eton, Buckinghamshire, where his many brothers and sisters were also born and where their father, Rev. Charles Wolley-Dod (1826-1904), was employed as "M.A. Classical Ass't Master at Eton College & Clergyman without Cure of Souls." The latter was also a landowner, and the confusion over the children's birthplaces arises no doubt because he established a home in Cheshire at "Edge Hall," Maspas, where he lived as a squire and, in 1868, added the name "Dod" to "Wolley," probably as a condition of an inheritance. In Lord Curzon's opinion, he had serious deficiencies as a schoolmaster, but as a father he taught his children to love woods, gardens, and what was then called "natural history." AW's brother Lieutenant Colonel Anthony Hurt W-D (1861-1948) became a respected amateur botanist, an authority on wild roses, and wrote several books. In 1891, however, the census identified him as a "Military Adviser . . . Projectile Maker" living at Elmhurst, Shooters Hill, Plumstead, London, with his wife Agnes W-D born in Gibraltar. Life at "Edge Hall" was grand, with a dozen domestic servants, and Eton, where most of the boys were schooled, was devoted to games and the classics, but this family grew up with practical interests and an inclination towards Imperial service that was common in their social class: Francis W-D (1855-?) became a civil engineer at the Royal Indian Engineering College in Windsor Great Park and had a career in the Public Works Department of [British] India. The 1891 census recorded Frederick Hove W-D, aged nineteen, as a "Student in Land Agency" and Thomas Crew W-D, twenty-two, as a "Student in Electricity." The 1901 census found Owen Cadogan W-D (1862-?) living at the District Chatham Barracks, Kent, as an infantry captain.

By then, AW had returned home to "Edge Hall" as a "farmer" after some months in Minnesota and a dozen years in Alberta, where he and his India-born wife Annie Frances W-D *née* Brown (c. 1865-1945) had had five children on their ranch at Pincher Creek. For some unspecified reason, he soon took his family back to Alberta, bought eight hundred acres in the Pine Creek district, was elected a fellow of the Royal Colonial Institute in December 1912, joined the Canadian Mounted Rifles (Fifteenth Light Horse), and was living in Calgary at 616-30th Avenue when he was commissioned in the CEF as a major in the Thirty-first Battalion on 15 September 1915, describing his occupation as "gent." He was six feet tall with a ruddy complexion, blue-grey eyes, and grey hair. He served as second in command of reinforcement camps on the Somme and the Colinrequart and commanded one of the wings in an action at Epson (France). After the Armistice, he was appointed to assist in the repatriation of prisoners of war at Ripon. Returning to Alberta with the rank of lieutenant colonel, he remained with his wife and near their children, helped to found the polo club at Calgary, and was active in St Paul's Anglican Church at Midnapore and in the Calgary Horticultural Society.

True to his family's special bent, he had a deep interest in nature and horticultural life and spent much time at Victoria, where he and his wife visited for long periods from c. 1924, as the *Daily Colonist* reported, "being attracted by the natural beauty and the many woodland walks to which he was devoted." He wrote to the *Colonist* in April 1929 urging the city and the province to protect wild flowers, especially dogwood, lady slippers, and dog tooth violets, which he called by their Latin names and accused the public of ruthlessly destroying all over the Island. On 8 February 1931, another of his letters, written at "Roccabella," a favorite guest house in Victoria, was in protest against a rule to have dogs always on the leash. He died, aged seventy-six, in 1936, leaving his widow and grown-up children. One of them, Charles Frederick W-D (1892-1937), born on 25 August 1892, seems to have been farming at Somenos when the Great War began and served in the Royal Flying Corps. In the post-war years 1919-1920, he worked as a pilot for Vickers and as a flying instructor for Spanish pilots ferrying Dh-4, Dh-9, and Dh-6 planes bought by the Spanish Air Force. In 1928, after some years as a pilot on the airmail line Seville-Larache and for Instone Air Line and Imperial Airways, he became director of Imperial Airways for Oriente Medio and North Africa and in 1932 for Europe. On 16 March 1937, he died in a crash near Cologne, Germany, in a Havilland Dh-86 of Airways G-ACVZ in which he was travelling as a passenger.

Sources: *Colonist*, 20 November 1936, p. 5, obit; 28 January 1917, p. 20, (Somenos news); NAC, CEF files, box 10520-49, regimental no. 623; Alberta pioneers website; Canadian census, 1901, Alberta website; census 1871, England, RG 10/1091, p. 27; census 1891, RG 12/2126, p. 3; census 1901, RG 13/654, p. 3; census 1901, RG 13/732, p. 1; *Canada, An Illustrated Weekly Journal* (London), vol. XXVIII, no 362 (14 December 1912), p. 409; *The Times*, 23 June 1948, p. 7, obit.; Kenneth Rose, *Superior Person: A Portrait of Curzon and His Circle in Late Victorian England* (Wiedenfeld & Nicolas, 1968; Phoenix Press, 2001), 475 pp., pp. 28-30, 35-37, 39, 41, 215.

WOOD, Walter (1866-1940). Born at Barking, Essex, third of the five sons of William and Sarah Wood, he was five years old in 1871 and living with his family in Maypole, Barking, an eastern suburb of London. His father, aged forty, was an "Ag[ricultural] Lab[ourer]" and born nearby in Barkingside, like his mother, aged thirty, and his four brothers. Ten years later, WW was serving, aged fifteen, as a "Boy 2nd cl[ass]" aboard HMS *Impregnable* with several dozen others like him, including several from his part of Essex. After twenty-five years in the Royal Navy, he returned to Victoria, which he had seen during his peregrinations in the fleet, and lived there in retirement for thirty years, mainly at 1007 McCaskill Street. When he died, aged seventy-five, on 25 September 1940, he left a brother and a sister in England. **Sources:** *National Archives* (PRO), ADM 188/198; *Colonist*, 26 September 1940, p. 5, obit.; census 1871, England, RG 10/1627, p. 28; census 1881, RG 11/2210, p. 28.

WOOLISON, Major Harry Howlett (1870-1936). Born on 9 April 1870 in Warwick, son of Henry Woolison, a house painter from Leamington, Warwickshire, employing three men, and Mrs Mary W. Woolison, he appears in the 1881 census records, aged ten, living at 34 Brook Street, Warwick, with his parents and a brother Thomas, born there about 1880. In the middle 1890s, HW married his wife Jane, a native of Birkenhead, who bore their first child, James Glover Woolison, at Seacombe near Liverpool on 12 May 1897 and the next year they moved out to Victoria. There they had another son, Harry L. Woolison, on 27 October 1899 while they were living in the Mt Tolmie district of Victoria at Pt. sec. 64, Saanich Road. By 1916, when on 13 April their elder son, J. G. Woolison, enlisted in the Canadian Field Artillery, they had moved to 940 Keywood Avenue, Victoria. The son had been working as a clerk in "Gents furnishings" and cited his mother as his next of kin. Meanwhile, HW must have been serving in the British Army as he is not recorded in Canadian Army records but retired with the rank of major. At a banquet at the James Bay Hotel in January 1914, he and *Major W. N. Winsby received a prize for winning the 1913 six-inch gun contest at Fort Macaulay. But HW served for many years with the old Fifth Regiment in Victoria and retired as second in command of it. Meanwhile, from about 1916, he was agent in BC for a number of British chinaware and pottery manufacturers. An active member of Christ Church Cathedral, at one time a churchwarden, he was also a pioneering scoutmaster of the First Victoria Scout Troop. He died, aged sixty-six, on 28 May 1936, and was buried as an Anglican, leaving his widow, four sons, a daughter, a brother in Buffalo, and relatives in England. His widow lived on at Victoria until 8 October 1949, when she died, aged eighty, leaving her four sons. Among her pallbearers were two Canadian officers, Colonel Edwin Richard Tooley (1872-1964) and Colonel Theodore Benning Monk (1884-1959). **Sources:** census 1881, England, RG 11/3088, p. 13; Canadian census, 1901, Victoria, Harry Howlett Woolison [misspelled "Wollisson"]; NAC, CEF files, box 2153-31; box 9734-4; box 6293-50; *Colonist*, 1 February 1914, p. 5; 29 May 1936, p. 1; 2 June 1936, p. 5; 9 October 1949, p. 23, obit.

WOOTTON, Captain Henry (c. 1826-1875). Born in England, he joined the service of the British East India Company as a mariner and was commissioned in 1858 to assist in taking a new HBC steamer, the *Labouchère*, out to Victoria, a voyage around Cape Horn, which took nearly a year. His wife Eliza Yardley (c. 1827-1918), born at Stoke Newington, whom he had married two years before, made the voyage by way of the Isthmus of Panama and arrived on the Island at almost the same time. They remained for the next fifty-six years at 852 Courtney Street, corner of Quadra Street, Victoria, in a house he built of California redwood cedar. He served for a time as clerk of the Writs in the Supreme Court, and in October 1861, Governor James Douglas appointed him the first postmaster general for the colony; for many years, he was also the harbour master in the port and occasionally the customs officer. Regular mail service to Esquimalt and Saanich began in March 1863. Edgar Fawcett remembered the long queue that used to form for the fortnightly mail arriving from England and being sorted by HW and his two assistants. He also recalled that as a choir boy he used to see Mrs Wootton at Christ Church, which became Christ Church Cathedral. Of their three sons, Stephen Y. Wootton became the registrar general of titles at the Land Registry Office, and Edward E. Wootton became a barrister. A daughter Anne Wootton married Elliott Hammond King, who started a newspaper, the *Victoria Gazette*, which had a troubled history, and their sons, Henry and Ted King, founded the King Brothers Shipbrokers and helped to fit out the famous thirty-foot dugout vessel, the *Tillicum*, which Captain John Voss sailed around the world. HW died, aged forty-nine, on 25 December 1875 and his wife, aged ninety-one, on 23 September 1918.

Sources: *Colonist*, 25 September 1918, p. 7, obit.; Edgard Fawcett, in the *Colonist*, 26 September 1918, p. 4; Harry Gregson, *A History of Victoria*, 1842-1970 (Vancouver, J. J. Douglas, 1970), pp. 51-2; Alfred Stanley Deaville, *The Colonial Postal Systems and Postage Stamps of Vancouver Island and British Columbia*, 1849-1871 (Victoria, C. F. Banfield, King's Printer, 1928), pp. 77, 95, and *passim*; Lugrin, *Pioneer Women*, p. 202; Gosnell, *The Year Book*, p. 44.

WORSLEY, Lieutenant George Norman (1887-1972). Born on 13 May 1887 at Birkdale, Southport, Lancashire, he was the elder brother of *James Harrison Worsley and *Ralph Stanley Worsley, sons of a Lancashire cotton merchant, Ralph S. Worsley, and his wife, Susan. GW was recorded there, aged three, in 1891 living with his parents, four siblings, and three servants at 20 Oxford Road. The neighbours were a chartered accountant and an "African Merchant" (born at Old Trafford, Lancashire). Ten years later, he was at a "Private Boarding School" in Birkdale, headmaster Henry Matheson. GW and his brothers emigrated together a few years later to the Okanagan Valley, British Columbia, but when he enlisted on 6 December 1914 in the Second Canadian Mounted Rifles, CEF, he was working in Victoria as a land surveyor. He had spent three years in the Sixth DCOR and was soon commissioned as a lieutenant. He returned to BC after the war partly because he loved riding, exploring, and camping in the great outdoors. In 1920, he qualified as a BC land surveyor, but after the Great War, there was hardly any demand for surveyors; he and his family eked out a livelihood on a small farm at Armstrong, BC. He moved with his family to Victoria in 1927 by which time he was crippled by arthritis and unable to do field work. During much of the 1930s, he was in and out of hospital, including the veterans' hospital in Vancouver. He worked then with the BC Electric Company in their mapping and records division. In the late 1930s and during the Second World War, he was a volunteer secretary

for the local Red Cross Society. "He was not quite a Kiplingesque imperialist," his son writes, "but kept very close ties to England and everything English; that is, until 1954 when he went back 'home' for a visit. That cured him; after that he accepted being a Canadian. On the other hand his brother [James] Harrison came to Canada in 1920 to be a Canadian and was always very proud of it." GW finally retired to Crofton, where he lived next door to *James Harrison Worsley. He had two sons, one who died and another, Norman Worsley Jr, who was living in Victoria at 4067 Haro Street when he kindly replied to my inquiry. GW died, aged eighty-five, on 16 January 1872 at Crofton.
Sources: Letter to the author courtesy of Norman Worsley (a son), 21 January 2001; Brentonian, Fall 1998-Spring 1999, Special Edition, *Reunion: Old Brentonians 1923-1948*; seventy-fifth anniversary of the founding of the school, p. 36; census 1891, England, RG 12/3033, pp. 24-5; census 1901, RG 13/3533, p. 20.

WORSLEY, George Stanley (1865-1945). Born 20 June 1865 at Saint-Hyacinthe, Québec, he was a son of Colonel Pennyman White Worsley and of his wife Albina Sicotte, who lived at one time in Halifax, whence they wrote letters of support for him. In later life, he met *G. N. Worsley in Victoria and discovered that they had sixteenth-century ancestors in common. He was schooled at Trinity College School, Port Hope, and RMC, Kingston, where he graduated in June 1885 and took a commission in the Royal Artillery on 30 June. After ten years in India and two more in Gibraltar and Malta, GW retired with the rank of captain and was on the reserve list of officers until 1910. In the meantime, he went to the North, and in Edmonton about 1899, he wrote a letter to a friend of his father's, Fred White (1847-1918), comptroller in Ottawa of the North-West Mounted Police, saying, "I have just come back from two years stay in the North, in the Peace River trading with the Indians and waiting to see if gold would not be found in the Peace River." He wanted to join the NWMP and had the support of his father, who wrote to tell Fred White that GW was 6' ¼" tall, 172 lbs weight, "a most temperate man, never touches liquor of any sort." GW became an inspector on 1 April 1901 and a superintendent on 1 October 1914. Late in the Great War, he commanded the RCMP squadron that served with the Canadian forces in Siberia from October 1918 to July 1919, and he was awarded the Order of the Rising Sun, fourth class, Japan. Next came an appointment on 1 April 1923 as assistant commissioner in Ottawa, and in 1928, he was in command of the whole force in Saskatchewan. *Charles Rivett-Carnac writes in his memoirs of being posted to the training division of the RCMP in Regina and being led to "the Officers' Mess, a large, massive building which stood next to Assistant Commissioner G. S. Worsley's house at one corner of the square. I got out, filled with trepidation . . . he was a big man, tall and heavy, a gentleman of the old school with a white pointed moustache." When GW retired in 1931, a newspaper wrote, "Tall, a typical British soldier in bearing, with keen grey eyes and hair turning to grey, for all his years Colonel Worsley looks like a man in the prime of life." He retired to Victoria with his sister and lived at Gordon Head. Rather late in life, he married Evelyn Marriott, who survived him along with their two sons, living then in Ontario, when he died, aged eighty, on 20 December 1945 in Victoria. The funeral was at Christ Church Cathedral.

Sources: NAC, RG18, series G, vol. 3444, file O-123, access code 90, parts 1, 2; *As You Were! Ex-Cadets Remember*, ed., R. Guy C. Smith, No. 1877 (Ottawa; The RMC Club of Canada, 1884-1984, 1984), vol. I, 1876-1918, p. 341; Charles Rivett-Carnac, *Pursuit in the Wilderness* (Boston & Toronto, Little, Brown & Co., 1965, p. 239; *Colonist*, 21 November 1945, p. 12; 22 November 1945, p. 14, obit.

WORSLEY, Captain James Harrison "Binks" (1890-1975). Born in Birkdale, Lancashire in 1890, he lived around Aughton near Ormskirk and worked in Liverpool on the Cotton Exchange. In 1914, he joined the Seventeenth (S) King's Liverpool Regiment, served overseas, and won the Military Cross. Although the war horrified him by its death and destruction, he saw it as a heroic time and made friends. What he did between 1918 and 1922 is not clear, but he then went to join his two brothers in the Okanagan Valley. In 1924, he married a girl he had met in Ireland, where he had lived briefly after being wounded in France, and they settled on a farm in the Hillbank Valley, Cowichan district, in which he bought a half-ownership. There and later at Crofton, he was active in the Church of England and other community organizations. After his first wife died tragically of cancer in 1947, he married an English cousin of Mrs *Eric (Kathleen) Long. Nearby lived a friend, Francis Augustus "Frank" Considine, who with his brother St John Considine, had married sisters and emigrated to Maple Bay, near Duncan, where they kept a farm, raising chickens and foxes. As it happened, my father knew JW and Frank Considine during the 1930s and 1940s in the Sixteenth Battalion of the Canadian Scottish Reserve Regiment, and I have a wartime photograph of them together with a fourth soldier, one Vaughan Pritchard. During visits to the *Eric Longs after the war, my parents used to meet JW and the Considines at the same time and were evidently fond of all three families. JW died, aged eighty-four, on 22 December 1975 at Chemainus.

Sources: Notes from my parents and from the late Phyllis "Biddy" Worsley, of 5418 Gore-Langton Road, Duncan; census 1901, England, RG 13/3530, p. 3; census 1891, England, RG 12/3033, pp. 24-5.

WORSLEY, Lieutenant Colonel Ralph Stanley (1885-1963). He was born on 2 January 1885 at Birkdale, Lancashire, one of the four sons of Ralph Leigh Worsley, a doctor and surgeon, and his wife Jessie, both born Protestants in Ireland. The census found him, aged six, in 1891 at 20 Oxford Road, Birkdale, with his parents, a sister, and three brothers: Charles L., nine, Alice D., eight, George N., three, James H., five months, and three servants. Ten years later, he and his brother George N. were boarding at a private school at 33 York Road in Birkdale—headmaster Henry Matheson. In 1908, he emigrated to Vancouver and stayed with family friends named Jackson while he qualified as a BC land surveyor. About 1911, he signed articles as a student land surveyor with a Mr Frank Tupper, BCLS, but after a year or so transferred his articles to Mr G. S. Pelly, another land surveyor, grandson of Sir John Henry Pelly, governor of the Hudson's Bay Company. Mr Pelly practised out of Armstrong, BC, in the Okanagan Valley and Worsley was attracted to that raw new country, where travelling was perforce on horseback, which he loved. By 11 August 1914 when he enlisted in the Second Canadian Mounted Rifles, he had spent three years in the Canadian Militia (BC Horse) but mounted rifle regiments being pretty well obsolete by then, he transferred to the Royal Canadian Engineers on 7 January 1915 and was sent to the Canadian Engineers Training Depot, Seventh Field Company, CE, Temp. Att. HQ Third Canadian Division Engineers, First Army Troops Company. His service was in Canada from 11 August 1914 to 11 June 1915, much of this time in Victoria. While in Armstrong, he had become engaged to Leena Pelly and they married at Christ Church Cathedral, Victoria, in 1915, just before he was posted overseas. He was in England from 11 June 1915 to 21 September 1915, when he embarked for France and landed at Boulogne on 22 September 1915, spent some time at a Canadian Concentration Camp at Rhyl, and remained in France until 21 November 1918, except for a short period of leave from 4 November 1916 and a few days beginning 11 November 1918 when his files show that he "proceeded to Tennis Tournament, Paris." He had been wounded on the side of his head in December 1915 and had a long medical history form: the war left him debilitated; "any exercise tires him"; "he feels exhausted at times"; "can do very little without sitting down." Mrs Worsley had followed him to England and stayed with his relatives in Aughton throughout the war. He was struck off strength on 17 October 1919 in the general demobilization and awarded the Military Cross.

He returned to Canada on 3 October 1919 from Liverpool on the *Minnedosa*, a lieutenant colonel by then, and proposed to live at Armstrong, BC. There he passed examinations and became a qualified BC land surveyor, but the land boom of 1900-1914 was over and opportunities were few. In the 1920s, he became seriously debilitated with arthritis. For both medical and financial reasons, in 1927, he took his wife and three children to the Island and settled first in Victoria and later at Mill Bay. He was public-spirited, like so many Imperials, and took up volunteer work for the Canadian Red Cross Society, Victoria and district branch, in which he was active as a leader. From 1938, he served for many years as honorary secretary and, for instance, gave a resumé of Red Cross activities at a meeting of the Overseas League held at the Empress Hotel on 2 October 1939. On 4 June 1941, he opened a garden party for the Guild of Friendship to raise money for the "bombed-out kits" that were being sent to England. In April 1943, he spoke the formal thanks of the Red Cross Society for a lecture by *Lady Swettenham, who was introduced by *Captain F. G. Dexter, all this at a meeting held in the house of *Colonel and Mrs J. K. Cornwall. RW died, aged seventy-seven, on 4 July 1963 at Cobble Hill near Mill Bay.

Sources: Notes dated 4 January 2001 kindly sent to me by Norman Worsley (a nephew); NAC, RG150, box 10583-8; *Colonist*, 4 October 1939, p. 6; 5 June 1941, p. 7; 21 April 1943, p. 8; *BC Archives*, MS-0677 (Longstaff papers), vol. 407, file 373; *London Gazette*, No. 29713, 19 August 1916.

WORSNOP, Lieutenant Colonel Charles Arthur (1858-1921). Born on 18 October 1858 in Manchester, he was noted by the 1861 census, aged two, living at 1 Stedman Street, Newark, with his family. His father, Charles Barnett Worsnop, aged thirty-six, was "Clerk, Science & Art Department," born in Leeds, and his mother, Martha A. Worsnop (née, Bellhouse), aged twenty-eight, was born in Manchester. He had one sister aged four. Ten years later, they were living in Fulham, London, and there were then five children, a visitor, and one servant. The father had become "Assis't Keeper, South Kensington Museum." His parents died: the father, aged fifty-nine, in 1883 and the mother, aged fifty-five, in 1888. CW's education was somehow connected with the museum of science and art, which qualified him to journey to Philadelphia in 1876 in charge of an exhibition at the Centennial Exposition. He stayed there until October 1881 and then went to Winnipeg, where he took up the real-estate business and joined the Winnipeg Field Battery of Artillery. In November 1883, he became a lieutenant in the Ninetieth Winnipeg Rifles and so went to fight in the Riel Rebellion campaign (1885) in command of No. 4 Company. In 1887, he went out to Vancouver, one of the town's earliest settlers, and worked as city editor of the *Daily News and Advertizer* but entered the Vancouver Customs House on 1 October 1889. By 1906, he had become surveyor of customs in Vancouver. There he became lieutenant colonel in the Second Battalion, Fifth Regiment of Garrison Artillery on 28 May 1897.

On 22 October 1878, he had married Mary Benson, daughter of Colonel Benson of Peterborough, Ontario; they had two sons of whom Charles Benson Worsnop, born 5 August 1879, grew to be 6' 3½" tall and to weigh 225 lbs. He became a captain in the Duke of Connaught's Own Rifles and by January 1917 was a major and second in command of the 102nd Battalion of the Sixth Regiment DCOR under *Lieutenant Colonel J. W. Warden. He won the DSO. Soon after the Great War, CW died, aged sixty-three, on 30 December 1921 in Vancouver, where his widow, Mrs Priscilla Worsnop, subsequently died, aged sixty-two, on 12 January 1951

Sources: R. E. Gosnell, *A History of British Columbia*, 1906, pp. 576-7; census 1861, England, RG 9/2489, p. 1; census 1871, RG 10/70, p. 20; Major Charles Arkoll Boulton (1841-99), *Reminiscences of the North-West Rebellions, with A Record of the Raising of Her Majesty's 100th Regiment in Canada and a Chapter on Canadian Social & Political Life* (Toronto, Grip Printing & Publishing Co., 1886), p. 505; *Colonist*, 21 January 1917, p. 5; 13 January 1917, p. 5.

WRAGG, James Chesterfield (1893-1974). Born at Derby, son of Thomas Benjamin W. Wragg, a "turf agent" of Derby, and his wife, Ellen M. Wragg from Ripley, Derbyshire, he was recorded, aged seven, in the 1901 census, living with his parents, two brothers, and a servant at 113 Upper Dale Road, Derby. He attended Derby Training College and St Chads School and then spent twenty years as a bakery proprietor. During the Great War, he served for four years and two months as a sergeant in the RFA, was twice wounded, and was mentioned in despatches (Ypres, 1917).

After the war, he married Ella Elizabeth Lundmark on 22 November 1921 in Vancouver, and they settled on the Island at Duncan. There he built several of the town's main buildings, served as an alderman, a school trustee, and a hospital director, and was elected mayor in 1947. His office was then in the Wragg Block and his residence at 940 Island Highway. During the Second World War, he served as regional director in the Aircraft Detection Corps and district warden in the Air Raid Precaution service. His daughter spent four years in the war with the Canadian Women's Air Corps, partly in Holland and Belgium. JW was a Rotarian, an Anglican, and enjoyed "anything in sport." In retirement, the Wraggs moved to Oak Bay and there he died, aged eighty, on 7 February 1974 and she, aged eighty-one, on 25 March 1978.
Sources: *Who's Who in B.C.*, 1947-1948, p. 230; census 1901, England, RG 13/3223, p. 18.

WRIGHT, Sir Charles Seymour "Silas" (1887-1975). Born in Toronto on 7 April 1887, he was educated at Upper Canada College and at Gonville and Caius College, Cambridge (1908-1910), working meanwhile at the famous Cavendish Laboratory. CW joined Captain R. F. Scott's expedition to the Antarctic in 1910 at the age of twenty-three. He was one of the scientists on the expedition but the only Canadian. Scott found him athletic, strong, keen, capable, and good hearted. In November 1912, he was the navigator to the party who spotted the top of the tent in which Scott and his companions died. Scott remarked in his diary, referring to the then-young Wright, "Nothing ever seems to worry him and I can't imagine he ever complained of anything in his life." The part he played is explained in some of the many historical accounts of Scott's famous expedition. He was one of the survivors and in 1914 joined the Royal Engineers as a second lieutenant. He was sent to France, but soon served as a wireless officer, rising to be a general staff officer in wireless intelligence. He was awarded the MC, the OBE, and the *Légion d'Honneur* for his services. From 1919 until 1947, he was on the scientific staff of the Admiralty and became the director of scientific research and then the first head of the Royal Naval Scientific Service at Teddington. He played an important part in the early development of radar and detection of magnetic mines and torpedoes.

The Royal Geographical Society had welcomed him as a Fellow. In 1946, he was knighted as KCB and in the following year made his first visit to Salt Spring Island, BC, though he went on to act as a consultant to the Pacific Naval Laboratory at Esquimalt and to do research from 1951 as director of the Marine Physical Lab of the Scripps Institute of Oceanography at La Jolla, California. A member of the British Joint Services Mission to Washington DC, he went on to join the staff of the Pacific Naval Laboratory at Esquimalt in 1955. In 1960 and 1965, he revisited the Antarctic as a guest of the U.S. Antarctic Research Programme's Scott Base in McMurdo Sound. In 1967, he joined the Institute of Earth Sciences at the University of British Columbia in Vancouver City. In 1969, he retired to Salt Spring Island and died in Victoria on 1 November 1975, leaving a son and two daughters. On 13 November 1975, the Royal Canadian Navy consigned his ashes to the sea from the deck of HMCS *Restigouche* off Esquimalt.

At Tewkesbury, Gloucestershire, in 1914, CW had married Edith Mary Priestley (1892-1968), sister of his colleague and friend Sir Raymond Edward Priestley (1886-1974) and one of the eight children of Joseph Edward Priestley, headmaster of Tewkesbury Grammar School. Another daughter of that family, Doris Marjorie Priestly, married another colleague, the Australian geologist Thomas Griffith Taylor (1889-1963). J. E. Wright's wife, CW's mother-in-law, was *née* Henrietta Rice, and the members of this Priestley family were all born at Tewkesbury.

Sources: census 1891, England RG 12/2049, p. 16; census 1901, RG 13/2467, p. 2; *The Geographical Journal*, vol. 142, no 1 (March 1976), pp. 193-94; Scott Polar Research Institute, Archives, Internet notes; Adrian Raeside (CW's grandson), *Return to Antarctica: The Amazing Adventures of Sir Charles Wright on Robert Scott's Journey to the South Pole* (Toronto, John Wiley & Sons Canada Ltd., 2009), 324 pp.; Elspeth Huxley, *Scott of the Antarctic* (Weidenfeld & Nicolson, 1977), p. 283; Diana Preston, *A First-Rate Tragedy: Captain Scott's Antarctic Expeditions* (Constable, 1997), pp. 235-36; Joseph G. Frey, "The Remarkable Wright," *The Legion Magazine*, 1 September 2005.

WRIGHT, Captain Frederick Robert (1869-1936). He was born on 22 July 1869 at South Molton, Devonshire, where the 1871 census found him, aged two, living at "Ash Moor," Rose Ash, with his grandfather, William Wright, an agricultural labourer. Twenty years later, he had become a sapper in the Royal Engineers and was living in Brompton Barracks at Gillingham, Kent. The 1901 census recorded him as a "Corporal, Royal Engineers," aged thirty-two, living at 66 Mill Road, Gillingham, with his wife Kate Wright, aged twenty-two, born at Plymouth, Devon.

After serving in the South African War, he retired to the Island, where he lived at 1467 Esquimalt Road with his wife, Kathleen Mary Wright, and worked as a carpenter and builder. When he enlisted in the CEF at Victoria on 1 October 1918, he listed his previous military experience as "Royal Engineers, Imperial Army, eighteen years, 184 days. Royal Canadian Engineers, twelve years, forty days." He was soon commissioned as a lieutenant. He retired in 1924 with the rank of captain and became a pillar of the United Church of Canada and his wife active in the IODE. They lived at 1640 Gladstone Avenue, and when he died, aged sixty-six, on 10 March 1936, he left two sons and a daughter as well as his wife. Brigadier James Secretan Dunbar was an old friend.

Sources: NAC, CEF files, box 10599-9; census 1871, England, RG 10/2177, p. 6; census 1891, RG 12/666; census 1901, RG 13/734, p. 42; *Colonist*, 11 March 1936, p. 6; 14 March 1936, p. 2, obit.

WURTELE, Lieutenant Commander Alfred Charles (1897-2000). Born at Kingston, Ontario, on 17 August 1897, he became a naval cadet on 1 August 1913, a midshipman on 1 August 1916, posted on IIMS *Leviathan* in 1916, on HMS *Renown* later than a year for a short gunnery course, at Shearwater in 1917, on HMS *Swift* in command, and as flotilla leader in the Dover Patrol in 1918. He was promoted to lieutenant on 1 May 1920 when he was on HMS *Oriana, Oracle,* and *Cleopatra* successively, on the latter for service in the Baltic Sea. His career continued in the RN until 1931 when he was sent to Naval Service Head Quarters as assistant naval staff officer and in 1932 to RCN barracks, Esquimalt, for duty as new entry training officer, etc., until 1942 when he was captain-in-command at RCN barracks, Halifax, and finally at *Naden* in 1944. He was a member of the fourth term of the Royal Naval College of Canada, present in HMS *Swift* at the surrender of the German Fleet in November 1918, and commanded the RCN personnel lining the streets of Victoria for the presentation of the King's Colours in 1939.

He retired on 8 March 1945 to a place in Esquimalt and lived with his wife, Anne Sherwood, whom he had married in April 1937 in Victoria. Public-spirited like so many officers, he served in 1946 as a councillor of Esquimalt municipality, in 1952-1965 as reeve of the Municipality of Esquimalt, and was made a freeman of Esquimalt in 1987. In addition, he was for many years the treasurer of the Monarchist League, Victoria branch, during Molly Ingram's time as chairman. He loved the outdoors and took daily walks until his death in the year 2000.

His older brother, Colonel William Godfrey Wurtele (1895-1979), attended RMC at Kingston, Ontario, where he was born, and had a career rising to command of the governor general's footguards and aid-de-camp to governor generals Lord Tweedsmuir and the Earl of Athlone. Later, he was employed in Ottawa in the Department of Veterans' Affairs.

Sources: *Colonist,* 18 April 1937, p. 7; *Canadian Monarchist News* (Victoria), vol. 5, no. 3-4 (Fall-Winter 2000), p. 26, obit.; *MacFarlane,* pp. 66-7; Martha Edmond, *Rockcliffe Park: A History of the Village* (Ottawa, The Friends of the Village, 2005), p. 71; NAC, CEF files, box 10615-42.

WYATT, Horace Graham (1879-1971). He was born in Chichester, son of Margaret H. B. Wyatt (*née* Bucknell) and her husband, Oliver N. Wyatt, an "Auctioneer & Valuer" of the town. The censuses of 1881 and 1891 found him there with his parents, several brothers and sisters, a governess, two nurses, a cook, and a housemaid. In 1901, he was recorded as an "Undergraduate at Oxford," living with his family in Chichester at 10 West Pallant. One of his brothers, Cecil. E. Wyatt, aged twenty-five, was then a "Stockbroker's Clerk" and another, Herbert G. B. Wyatt, an "Auctioneer & Surveyor." HW joined the Indian Educational Service (IES) in 1905 and was also recorded on 1 November 1906 as a "supernumerary" in the First Punjab Volunteer Rifles. He had various teaching appointments, serving in 1918 as principal of the Central Training College of Secondary Teachers in Lahore, and in 1923 published a book about the teaching of English in India. At the end of his life, authorities in Victoria recorded him as an "educator" in the Punjab from 1905 to 1924.

During that time, on 22 November 1913, almost certainly in India, he married Mary Aimée Strickland, seventh child of Robert Strickland (1848-1925) and his wife Mary Katharine *née* Sharpe (died 1938) and had the usual periods of leave at home in England. They arranged educational voyages to North America that were also exploratory. For instance, they sailed from Southampton to New York, arriving on 24 March 1921 aboard the *Finland*—she aged thirty-seven and he listed as a "tutor" aged forty-two. He recorded their last permanent address as Lahore, India, citing his father as O. N. Wyatt of West Pallant, Chichester. Their movements later are not entirely clear, but after retiring in 1924 from the IES in the Punjab, they reached New York, a second time on 11 November 1924, aboard the *Olympic* from Southampton *en route* to the west coast. After some time at Stanford University, California, they retired in 1935 to Saanich, a few miles north of Victoria. There they had two sons, Laurence Reginald Wyatt (1921-1992) and Gerard Robert Wyatt (born in 1925), who survived them when they died in Saanich, she aged eighty-six on 17 April 1970, and he, aged ninety-two, on 31 July 1971.

Sources: *Colonist*, 5 August 1971, p. 42, obit.; census 1881, England, RG 11/1129, p. 11; census 1891, RG 12/846, p. 8; census 1901, RG 13/970, p. 12; *BC Archives* (Victoria), MS 0013; *Indian Army Quarterly List*, dated 1 January 1912, p. 559a; New York Passenger Lists; Horace G. Wyatt, *The Teaching of English in India* (Humphrey-Milford and Oxford University Press, 1923), 174 pp.; Richard C. Smith, *Teaching English as a Foreign Language, 1912-1936: Pioneers of ELT* (vol. I, Wren and Wyatt), various editions, see p. xliv (notes on HW).

WYLLYS, Captain Gerard Alfred Edward (1873-1950). He was born on 27 November 1873 at Great Yarmouth, Norfolk, where the 1881 census found him, aged seven, living with his family at 25 King Street. His father was a "Surgeon (Col. Surgeon Edinburgh)," then aged thirty-six and born in Stanton Drew, Somerset. His mother was Anne Wyllys, aged thirty-four, born at Southtown, Suffolk. He had an elder brother, Henry Ian Maclean Wyllys, aged eight, and a younger one, George Harvey Wyllys, aged five, both born at Great Yarmouth. There were three servants—cook, housemaid, and nursemaid—and the neighbours were a county court usher and a medical doctor. GW joined the Royal Navy on 15 July 1891 and on 27 February 1892 was appointed clerk to the flag officer on HMS *Imperieuse* 14, a twin screw cruiser on the China Station. In 1899, he was serving as assistant paymaster on HMS *Terror*, his seniority at that rank being recorded as 27 November 1894.

After rising to the rank of paymaster captain, GW retired to North Saanich with his wife Janet Nita Wyllys, and they lived for many years at a place they called "Quails," which was north of Point Colville on a tiny cove, where they had a pleasant house, a small wharf, and boathouse facing west onto Saanich Inlet, a sheltered coast where arbutus trees grew in profusion. There they became great friends of *Major A.E. Jukes and his family, who were almost neighbours. GW died, aged seventy-six, on 15 May 1950 and was buried in the churchyard at St Stephen's Anglican on the West Saanich Road. *Captain C. P. Nixon remembered him as a pleasant, convivial man. His wife died, aged eighty, on 29 November 1971 in Victoria.

Sources: census 1881, England, RG 11/1909, p. 2; *Navy List*, July and October 1899, p. 67; records of St Stephen's Church, Central Saanich; *Colonist*, 17 May 1950, p. 17, obit.; interview with Captain C. P. Nixon, Ottawa, 18 March 2002; notes from Mrs Rachel (Jukes) Mackenzie; *The Navy List*, Corrected to The 20th December 1892 (HMSO, 1892), pp. 64, 228; *Whitaker's*, p. 617.

WYNNE-EYTON, Lieutenant Robert Mainwaring (1886-?). He was born on 12 January 1886 at Whitchurch [or Marbury?], Cheshire, son of Lieutenant Colonel Charles Edward Wynne-Eyton of Mold, Flintshire, North Wales, and his wife Aline M. Wynne-Eyton. The 1891 census found him, aged five, living with them at "Plas Matlin Hall," Northop near Mold in Flintshire, North Wales. His father, born on 17 August 1857 at Mold, was recorded as a "Gentleman" and his mother, aged twenty-nine, as a Londoner. Three sisters and a brother lived with them, along with five servants. They were descended from an old Flintshire family of gentry, and RW's grandfather, Thomas Wynne-Eyton, had been a "Treasurer of the County," born at Leeswood, Flintshire.

At sometime before the Great War, RW migrated to the Cowichan Valley, where he was living as an unmarried "rancher" at Cowichan Station, an Anglican and active in the Cowichan Polo Club, when he enlisted in the CEF, Second Regiment of the Canadian Mounted Rifles, on 16 November 1914. His only military experience had been three months in the Royal North-West Mounted Police. Once overseas, he was posted to Egypt with an armoured car squadron, and by June 1917, he had transferred to the Royal Flying Corps. I could trace him no further, but his father was said to have made a second marriage on 7 August 1907 with Dorothy Katharine Nevill, whose death occurred on 11 August 1923.

Sources: *Colonist*, 17 June 1917, p. 16; NAC, CEF files, box 10624-31; census 1891, England, RG 12/4697, p. 10; census 1861, RG 9/4275, p. 1; census 1871, RG 10/5349, p. 33; Flintshire Record Office, Leeswood MSS, GB 0208 D/LE.

YARROW, Norman Alfred (1891-1955). He was born on 10 July 1891 in London, son of Sir Alfred Fernandez Yarrow (1842-1932), Bart., FRS, LLD, head of the great firm that bore his name and which he had founded at Poplar in 1866. NY was apprenticed on 19 August 1911 to engineering with D. Napier & Sons, London, but in 1912-1913 moved, still an apprentice, to W. H. Allen Sons & Co. Ltd., Bedford. After a time, he went to work for Yarrow & Co, Ltd., Glasgow. In 1914, the company acquired the small Ship Repair Yard of the BC Marine Railways Co. Ltd on the Island at Esquimalt, and he went out, assisted by *Edward Whitaker Izard, to direct it under the name of Yarrows Ltd., in association with Yarrow & Co. Ltd. of Glasgow. Under his direction, the firm built, in 1914, HMS *Miranda*, a destroyer for the fleet 260 ft long and with a speed of thirty-five knots, and went on to build many ships through the Great War, between the wars, and during the Second World War, many of them for service in remote parts of the empire. In 1925, his father, then about eighty-five years old, travelled out to visit his son and inspect the Esquimalt branch of the Yarrows firm. In 1946, NY retired and sold his interest in the firm to Burrard Dry Dock Company Ltd. of Vancouver.

NY had married Ada Hope Leeder, daughter of Dr Forrest Leeder, MRCS (Eng.), LRCP (London), on 9 November 1915, and they had two daughters and a son. The latter attended Shawnigan Lake School. They lived mainly at 925 Foul Bay Road, Victoria, but NY also built a grand place in Saanich and later assigned the address 5720 Patricia Bay Highway, which he named "Orchard Gate." He became a director of the BC Power Corporation, member of the advisory board of the Royal Trust Corporation (Victoria branch), honorary vice-president of the Canadian Red Cross Society and the Boy Scouts Association, and a member of the Institute of Naval Architects, London, of the Engineering Institute of Canada, Montreal, of the BC Association of Professional Engineers, of the Victoria Chamber of Commerce, of the Union Club, of the Vancouver Club, of the Church of England, of the Automobile Club of BC, and of the Royal Victoria Yacht Club. Among his hobbies were tennis, motor-boating, fishing, and photography. He died outside BC, probably in England, on 25 June 1955.

Sources: *Who's Who in B.C.* (1944-1946; 1947-1948, p. 232; *Canadian Who's Who*, vol. viii (1958-1960), p. 1195; *Colonist*, 3 July 1914, p. 10; 11 April 1925, p. 1; *Burke's Peerage*, 1999, p. 3086; Captain C. P. Nixon, interview in Ottawa, 18 March 2002; NAC, Immigration 1925-1935; T. C. Bridges and H. Hessell Tiltman, *Kings of Commerce* (George G. Harrap & Co. Ltd., 1928), ch. xxv, pp. 273-88, "Building the Fastest Boats on Record, The Romance of Sir Alfred Yarrow."

YOUNG, Bertram Frederick "Bert" (1883-1961). Born on 18 May 1883 in Suffolk, England, he went out to Manitoba as a young man and served in the Sixty-fifth Battalion of Saskatoon during the Great War. In 1919, he moved to Victoria and in 1921 to Duncan, where he lived for forty years. He was president of the Cowichan Creamery for three years and director of it for six, and president of the Cowichan Agricultural Society and the Horse Breeder's Association. For seven years, he acted as chairman of the local administrators of the Veteran's Land Act. In 1952, the farmers of the district presented him with a scroll "for twenty-five years of unselfish devotion to the cause of agriculture, towards the betterment of field crops, for his encouragement of better methods and his invaluable co-operative marketing of farm produce throughout the years." The ceremony took place in the Cowichan Valley at the Illustration Station, Koksilah, where he had his first farm, some thirty acres. Later, he farmed 134 acres, maintained a rotation system of grain seeding, and kept thirty head of cattle, twenty-five pigs, and about sixty chickens. During the Second World War, he grew mangle, beet, and cabbage seeds at his Koksila station for the British government. He was modest about the numerous trophies and ribbons he won for field crops, both on the Island and at Toronto exhibitions. His wife Esther died in 1931 and he on 18 July 1961 at Koksilah, leaving a daughter, Mrs B. D. (Rose) Roberts of Cowichan Station, and eight grandchildren. He was buried at the family plot in the Mountain View Cemetery, Somenos.

Sources: *Cowichan Leader*, 19 July 1961, obit.

YOUNG, Colonel Dr Thomas Frederick (1852-1943). He was born to an Anglo-Irish family in Dublin on 21 April 1852, became a physician (1868) at the medical school in Liverpool, and had a practice nearby for many years. The censuses of 1881 and 1891 recorded him, aged thirty and forty, a medical practitioner living in Bootle, at 12 Merton Road, with his wife, Mary Ellen *née*

Baker, from Leeds, whom he had married on 24 April 1878 at the parish church at Woodside, Wharfdale in Yorkshire. She was a daughter of Henry Granville Baker, "gent," and his wife. The Youngs had three children in 1881 and five in 1891. He was a Freemason and for thirty-eight years was attached to the Fourth West Lancashire (Howitzer) Brigade, RFA (TF), and decorated with the VD. The family was musical in the manner of that age: TY played the cello, one daughter played the violin, and another the piano, and they enjoyed Gilbert and Sullivan Operas, as did so many British families.

In 1900, he visited Victoria and in 1910 moved with his family to Somenos in the Cowichan Valley, north of Duncan, where they settled on a farm they called "Inchegeelagh." In 1914, they moved home to England for the duration of the Great War, and after the war, they returned, about 1920, to 2130 Central Avenue, Victoria, where TY built a house. But he also built houses nearby at 2108 and 2118 Central Avenue for his daughters. Mrs Young died, aged eighty, on 13 March 1927 in Oak Bay, and TY died, aged ninety-three, on 5 May 1943, leaving a son and two daughters, one of whom was Mrs *N. W. Pirrie of View Royal, who lived to be 102.

Sources: census 1881, England, RG 11/3693, p. 5; census 1891, RG 12/2973, p. 38; census 1901, RG 13/3325, p. 46; *Colonist*, 7 May 1943, p. 2, obit.; 5; Bradley Family History website, bradfamhisto@aol.com. (No spaces).

Sir Richard McBride
The Last Spike Deep Cove, North Saanich, terminus of the Interurban
Railway Line

APPENDIX
A Mixed Bag of Books before the Great War

Chronological List

Note: published in London unless otherwise marked

1848—James Edward Fitzgerald (1818-1896), *Vancouver's Island, The New Colony* (Simmonds & Co., 1848), 16 pp.

1849—James Edward Fitzgerald (1818-1896), *An Examination of the Charter and Proceedings of the Hudson's Bay Company with Reference to Vancouver's Island* (Trelawney Sanders, 1849), 293 pp.

1849—Robert Montgomery Martin (1802[?]-1868), *Hudson's Bay Territories and Vancouver's Island with an Exposition of the Chartered Rights, Conduct and Policy of the Honorable Hudson's Bay Corporation* (T. & W. Boone, 1849), 293 pp., and folding map.

1858—Kinahan Cornwallis (1839-1917), *The New El Dorado, or, British Columbia* (T. C. Newby, 1858), 405 pp., and map and illustrations.

1858—R. M. Ballantyne, (1825-1894), *Handbook to the New Gold Fields, and a Full Account of the Richness and Extent of the Fraser and Thompson River Gold Mines; with a geographical and physical account of the country & its inhabitants* (Edinburgh, A. Strahan, 1858), 124 pp.

1858—William Parker Snow (1817-1895), *British Columbia: Emigration and Our Colonies Considered Practically, Socially, and Politically* (Piper, Stephenson & Spence, 1858), xii and 108 pp.

1858—William Carew Hazlitt (1834-1913), *British Columbia and Vancouver Island* (Routledge & Co., 1858; repr. Wakefield, England, SR Publishers, Johnson Reprint, 1966), 247 pp.

1859—Paul Kane (1808-1871), *Wanderings of an Artist among the Indians of North America from Canada to Vancouver's Island and Oregon through the Hudson's Bay Company's Territory and back again* (Longman, Brown, Green, Longmans & Roberts, 1859), 455 pp.

1859—Henry DeGroot (1815-1893), *British Columbia: Its Conditions and Prospects, Soil, Climate and Mineral Resources, Considered* (San Francisco, Alta California, 1859), 24 pp.

1860—Joseph Despard Pemberton (1821-1893), *Facts and Figures Relating to Vancouver's Island and British Columbia* (Longmans, Green, 1860), 171 pp.

1862—Commander [later Rear Admiral] Richard Charles Mayne (1835-1892), *Four Years in British Columbia and Vancouver Island* (John Murray, 1862; facsimile repr. Toronto, Clark, Irwin, 1969), 468 pp.

1862—Captain Charles Edward Barrett-Lennard (1835-1874), *Travels in British Columbia, with the Narrative of a Yacht Voyage round Vancouver's Island* (Hurst & Blackett, successors to Henry Colburn, 13 Great Marlborough Street, 1862), 307 pp.

1862—Alexander Rattray, *Vancouver Island and British Columbia* (Smith Elder, 1862), 182 pp.

1862—Duncan George Forbes Macdonald (c. 1837-1884), *British Columbia and Vancouver's Island, Comprising a Description of these Dependencies* . . . (Longman Green, 1862), 524 pp.

1862—Alfred John Langley (1820-1896), *A Glance at British Columbia and Vancouver Island in 1861* (R. Hardwicke, 1862), 44 pp.

1862—Charles Forbes, (c. 1820-1886), *Vancouver Island; Its Resources and Capabilities as a Colony; Prize Essay* (Victoria, published by the Colonial Government, 1862), 62 and 19 pp. Forbes also read a paper to the Royal Geographical Society, "Notes on the Physical Geography of Vancouver Island," in *Journal of the R.G.S.*, vol. 34 (1864), pp. 154-170.

1863—Rev. R. C. Lundin Brown, MA (1831-1876), *British Columbia. An Essay* (New Westminster, Royal Engineer Press, 1863), 64 pp.

1865—Rev. Matthew Macfie, *Vancouver Island and British Columbia: Their History and Prospects* (Longman Green, 1865; facsimile edition, Toronto, Coles Publishing Company, 1972), 574 pp.

1865—John Emmerson, *British Columbia and Vancouver Island, Voyages, Travels and Adventures* (Durham, William Ainsley, 1865), 154 pp.

1865—William Fitzwilliam, Viscount Milton (1839-1877) and Dr Walter Butler Cheadle (1835-1910), *The North-West Passage by Land. Being the narrative of an expedition from the Atlantic to the Pacific with the view of exploring a route across the continent to British Columbia through British territory, by one of the northern passes in the Rocky Mountains* (London, Cassell, Petter, and Galpin, June 1865), 397 pp., with two maps and twenty-three engraved pictures.

1865—Thomas Rawlings, *The Confederation of the British North American Provinces; Their Past History and Future Prospects, including also British Columbia & Hudson's Bay Territory; with a map, suggestions in reference to the true and only practicable route from the Atlantic to the Pacific Ocean* (Sampson, Low, Son, and Marston, 1865), 244 pp.

1866—J. D. Churchill and J. Cooper, *British Columbia and Vancouver Island Considered as a Field for Commercial Enterprise* (1866), 20 pp.

1866—John Keast Lord, FJS (1818-1872), *The Naturalist in Vancouver Island and British Columbia* (Bentley, 1866), 375 pp.

1870—Edward Graham Alston (1832-1872), *A Hand-book to British Columbia and Vancouver Island* (F. Algar, 1870), 18 pp.

1871—William Fraser Rae (1835-1905), *Westward by Rail: The New Route to the East* (Longmans, Green, 1879), 391 pp., and map

1871—Charles Marshall, *The Canadian Dominion* (Longmans, Green, 1871), 331 pp.

1872—Alexander Caulfield Anderson (1814-1884), *The Dominion at the West: A Brief Description of the Province of British Columbia* (Victoria, Richard Wolfenden, 1872; Victoria, R. T. Wiliams, 1883), 33 pp.

1872—Richard Byron Johnson (c. 1868-1958), *Very Far West Indeed, A Few Rough Experiences of the North-West Pacific Coast* (Sampson Low, Marston, Low & Searle, 1872), 280 pp.

1872—*Colonization Circular, no. 31* (Groombridge, 1872), 194 pp.

1873—*Our Journal in the Pacific by the Officers of H.M.S. Zealous*, ed., Lieutenant S. Eardley-Wilmot (Longmans, Green and Co., 1873), 333 pp., and appendix

1873—Mary Stannard, *Memoirs of a Professional Lady Nurse* (Simpkin, Marshall & Co., 1873), chapters 20-22.

1873—Rev. George Monro Grant (1835-1902), *Ocean to Ocean: Sandford Fleming's Expedition through Canada in 1872, being a diary kept during a journey from Atlantic to Pacific with the expedition of the engineer-in-chief of the Canadian Pacific and Intercolonial Railways* (Toronto, James Campbell, 1873; London, Sampson Low, Marston, Low & Searle, 1873; enlarged and revised edition, repr. M. G. Hurtig, 1967; 306 pp., with a folding map; no index; Toronto, Coles Facsimile edition, 1979), 371 pp.

1874—Charles Horetzky (1838-1900), *Canada on the Pacific: Being an Account of a Journey from Edmonton to the Pacific by the Peace River Valley and of a Winter Voyage along the Western Coast of the Dominion, with Remarks on the Physical Features of the Pacific Railway Route and Notices of the Indian Tribes of British Columbia* (Montreal, Dawson Brothers Publishers, 1874), 244 pp.

1874—*John Whetham Boddam-Whetham (1843-1918), *Western Wanderings: Record of Travel in the Evening Land* (R. Bentley, 1874), 364 pp., and 12 pp.

1876[?]—Donald Fraser (1826-1897), *Canada as I Remember it, and as It Is* (1876[?]), 33 pp.

1876—Molyneux St John (1838-1904), *The Sea of Mountains: An Account of Lord Dufferin's Tour through British Columbia in 1876* (Hurst & Blackett, 1877), 2 vols. in one.

1886—Molyneux [Molyneaux] St John (1838-1904), *The Province of British Columbia: Its Resources, Commercial Position and Climate, and Description of the New Field Opened up by the Canadian Pacific Railway, with information for Intending Settlers Based on the Personal Investigations of the Writer, and upon the Reports of Scientific Explorers and Government Surveyors* (Montreal, The CPR, 1886[?]), 56 pp.

1880—Rev. Daniel M. Gordon, *Mountain and prairie; a journey from Victoria to Winnipeg, via Peace River pass* (Montreal, Dawson Brothers, 1880), 310 pp.

1882—Newton Henry Chittenden (1840-1925), *Settlers, Prospectors, and Tourists Guide, or Travels Through British Columbia* (Victoria, 1882; repr. Vancouver, G. Soules, 1984), 86 pp.

1884—William Henry Barneby (1843-1914), *Life and Labour in the Far, Far West, Being Notes of a Tour in the Western States, British Columbia, Manitoba, and the North-West Territory* (Cassell, 1884), 432 pp.

1884—Sandford Fleming (1827-1915), *England and Canada: A Summer Tour between Old and New Westminster* (Montreal, Dawson Brothers, 1884), 449 pp.

1887—Henry Tanner (1851-1915), *British Columbia, Its Agricultural & Commercial Capabilities and the Advantages it Offers for Emigration Purposes* (London, George Kenning, Freemason Printing Works, 1887; Montreal, Dawson Brothers, 1887), 50 pp., and maps.

1887—Stuart Cumberland (c. 1857-1922), *The Queen's Highway from Ocean to Ocean* (London, Sampson Low, Marston, Searle & Rivington, repr. 1888), 431 pp., and folding maps

1887—Sir Edward Watkin, *Canada and the States: Recollections 1851 to 1886* (Ward, Lock & Co., 1887), 524 pp.

1887[?]—Charles Elliott Elliott, *A Trip to Canada and the Far North-West* (W. Kent, 1887[?]), 93 pp., and folding map

1889—William Henry Barneby, *The New Far West and the Old Far East: Being Notes of a Tour in North America, Japan, Ceylon etc.* (E. Stanford, 1889), 316 pp.

1890—Susan Margaret MacKinnon St Maur, Duchess of Somerset (c. 1852-1936), *Impressions of a Tenderfoot During a Journey in Search of Sport in the Far West* (John Murray, 1890), 344 pp.

1890—Henry Theophilus Finck (1854-1926), *The Pacific coast scenic tour, from southern California to Alaska, the Canadian Pacific railway, Yellowstone Park and the Grand Cañon* (New York, Henry T. Finck, Publisher; Scribner, 1890), xiv, 309 pp., and map.

1891—Edward Roper (1833-1909), *By Track and Trail: A Journey Through Canada* (W. H. Allen & Co., 1891), 455 pp.

1891—Harriet, Marchioness of Dufferin and Ava, *My Canadian Journal 1872-8* (London, John Murray, 1891), 422 pp., (chs. 15 and 16). She visited the Island with her husband in August-October 1876.

1891—Rev. Canon Arthur John Beanlands (1857-1917), *British Columbia as a Field for Emigration and Investment* (Victoria, R. Wolfenden, 1891), 60 pp.

1892—Julian Ralph (1853-1903), *On Canada's Frontier: Sketches of History, Sport, and Adventure and of the Indians, Missionaries, Fur-Traders, and Newer Settlers of Western Canada* (New York, Harper, 1892; London, J. R. Osgood, 1892), 337 pp.

1893—Ishbel Maria Marjoribanks, Countess of Aberdeen (1857-1939), *Through Canada with a Kodak*, ed., Marjory Harper (Edinburgh, W. H. White & Co., 1893; Toronto, University of Toronto, 1994), 285 pp.

1893—Ernest Ingersoll, *The Canadian Guide-Book*, Part II: *Western Canada* (New York, D. Appleton and Co., 1893), 262 pp.

1893—Oliver Hezekiah Cogswell (1806-1888), *History of British Columbia Adapted for the Use of Schools* (Victoria, BC, *Colonist* Press, 1893), 101 pp.

1894—Alexander Begg (1825-1905), *History of British Columbia from its Earliest Discovery to the Present Time* (Toronto, William Briggs, 1894; facsimile edition, Toronto, McGraw-Hill-Ryerson, 1972), 568 pp.

1895—E. W. Wright, *Lewis & Dryden's marine history of the Pacific Northwest an illustrated review of the growth and development of the maritime industry, from the advent of the earliest navigators to the present time, with sketches and portraits of a number of well known marine men* (Portland, Oregon, Lewis & Dryden Printing Company, 1895; repr. NY, Antiquarian Press, 1961; repr. Seattle, Washington, Superior Publishing Company, 1967) 494 pp.

1895—Sir George Robert Parkin (1846-1922), *The Great Dominion: Studies of Canada* (Macmillan, 1895), 251 pp., and 3 maps

1898—Frances MacNab, [said to be a pen name for Miss Agnes Fraser, born 1859], *British Columbia for Settlers, its Mines, Trade, and Agriculture* (Chapman & Hall, 1898), 369 pp., and 3 folding maps

1898—Edward Jerome Dyer, *The Gold Fields of Canada and How to Reach Them, Being an Account of the Routes and Mineral Resources of North-Western Canada* (London & Liverpool, G. Philip & Nephew, 1898), 268 pp.

1900—J. W. C. Haldane, *3800 Miles Across Canada* (Simpkin, Marshall, Hamilton, Kent & Co., 1900), 344 pp., and map.

1900—William Saunders Sebright Green (1830-1906), "British Columbia," in *British America* (Kegan Paul, Trench, Trübner & Co., 1900), pp. 153-171.

1900—William Adolf Baillie-Grohman (1851-1921), *Fifteen Years' Sport and Life in the Hunting Grounds of Western America and British Columbia* (Horace Cox, 1900; repr. 1907), 403 pp.

1900—Edward Bolland Osborn (1867-1938), *Greater Canada: The Past, Present, and Future of the Canadian North-West* (Chatto & Windus, 1900) 243 pp.

1902—Bernard McEvoy (1842-1932), *From the Great Lakes to the Wide West: Impressions of a Tour between Toronto and the Pacific,* (Toronto, Wm Briggs, 1902), 288 pp.

1903—A. G. Bradley, *Canada in the Twentieth Century* (Westminster, Archibald Constable & Co. Ltd., 1903), 428 pp.

1903—James Lumsden, *Through Canada in Harvest Time: A Study of Life and Labour in the Golden West* (T. Fisher Unwin, 1903), 363 pp.

1904—Frances Elizabeth Herring (1851-1916), *In the Pathless West with Soldiers, Pioneers, Miners, and Savages* (T. Fisher Unwin, 1904), 240 pp.

1905—[Sir] John Foster Fraser (1868-1936), *Canada as It Is* (Cassell & Co. Ltd., 1905), 303 pp.

1905—Arthur Lincoln Haydon (1872-1954), *Canada: Britain's Largest Colony* (Cassell, 1905), 206 pp.

1906—John Atkinson Hobson (1858-1940), *Canada To-day* (T. Fisher Unwin, 1906), 143 pp.

1906-1907—Karl Baedeker, *Baedeker's Canada: The Dominion of Canada with Newfoundland and an Excursion to Alaska, Handbook for Travellers* (3rd revised ed.; Leipzig: Karl Baedeker Publishers, 1907), 331 pp.

1906—Henry "Harry" Richard Whates (c. 1865-1923), *Canada, the New Nation: A Book for the Settler, the Emigrant, and the Politician* (J. M. Dent, 1906), 284 pp.

1906—Richard Edward Gosnell (1860-1921), *A History of British Columbia* (Chicago, Hill Binding Co., 1906), 783 pp.

1907—Howard Angus Kennedy (1861-1938), *New Canada and the New Canadians* (Horace Marshall & Sons, 1907; Toronto, Musson Book Co., 1907; repr. Kessinger Publishing, 2007), 264 pp., and map.

1907—Rev. Lewis Norman Tucker (1852-1934), *Western Canada* (series *Handbooks of English Church Expansion,* Toronto, Musson Book Company, 1907), 164 pp., and map.

1908—Basil Stewart (1880-?), *The Land of the Maple Leaf, or Canada as I Saw it* (Routledge, 1908), 216 pp.

1908—Henry Ernest Harry Brittain [*alias* Sir Harry Brittain] (1873-1974), *Canada, There and Back* (Bodley Head, 1908), 157 pp.

1909—Moses Bruines Cotsworth (1859-1943), *British Columbia's Supreme Advantages in Climate, Resources, Beauty and Life* (Victoria, BC, R. Wolfenden, 1909), 77 pp.

1909—Robert Shields, *My Travels: Visits to Lands Far and Near, European, British, American, and Canadian, Illustrated by Pen and Pencil* (Toronto, William Briggs, 1909), 339 pp.

1910—Mrs George Cran [*née* Marion Dudley (1875-1942)], *A Woman in Canada* (John Milne, 1910; Philadelphia, J. B. Lippincott, 1910; Toronto, Musson, nd. (1910[?]); W. J. Ham-Smith, 1911), 283 pp.

1910—Ernest Way Elkington (1872-1935), *Canada, the Land of Hope* (Adam & Charles Black, 1910), 239 pp.

1910—Thomas Miller Maguire, *The Gates of Our Empire: I. British Columbia* (Anglo-British Columbian Agency, 1910), 76 pp.

1911—Robert Ernest Vernede (1875-1917), *The Fair Dominion: A Record of Canadian Impressions* (Kegan Paul, Trench, Trubner & Co., 1911; New York, James Pott & Co., 1911; Toronto, William Briggs, 1911), 296 pp.

1911—Arthur Edward Copping (1865-1941), *The Golden Land: The True Story and Experiences of British Settlers in Canada* (London, Hodder & Stoughton, 1911), 263 pp.

1911—Frank Carrel (1870-1940), *Canada's West and Farther West* (Quebec [City], The Telegraph Printing Company, 1911), 258 pp.

1911—Frederick Arthur Ambrose Talbot, *The New Garden of Canada: By Packhorse and Canoe Through Undeveloped British Columbia* (London, Cassell & Co., 1911), 308 pp.

1912—Norman Noel, *Blanket-Stiff; or, A Wanderer in Canada, 1911* (London, St Catherine Press, 1912), 190 pp.

1912—Ella Constance Sykes (1864-1939), *A Home-Help in Canada* (1912; 2nd ed., Smith, Elder & Co., 1915), 304 pp.

1912—B[essie] Pullen-Burry (1858-1937), *From Halifax to Vancouver* (Mills and Boon Ltd., 1912), 352 pp.

1912—Henry J. Boam, *British Columbia: Its History, People, Commerce, Industries and Resources*, ed., Ashley G. Brown (Sellers Ltd., 1912), 495 pp.

1912—Joseph Adams, *Ten Thousand Miles Through Canada: The Natural Resources, Commercial Industries, Fish and Game, Sports and Pastimes of the Great Dominion* (Methuen, 1912), 310 pp.

1912—Sir John Godfrey Rogers (1850-1922), *Sport in Vancouver [Island] and Newfoundland* (Chapman & Hall Ltd., 1912), 275 pp.

1913—John Bensley Thornhill (1875-?), *British Columbia in the Making* (Constable & Co., 1913), 175 pp.

1913—Frank Yeigh (1861-1935), *Through the Heart of Canada* (Toronto, S. B. Gundy, 1913), 319 pp.

1913—E. O. S. Scholefield (1875-1919), *A History of British Columbia*, vol. I (Vancouver, The S. J. Clarke Publishing Co.; and Vancouver, Historical Ass., 1913), 688 pp. (large size)

1914—F. W. Howay (1867-1943), *British Columbia from the Earliest Times to the Present*, vol. II (Vancouver, The S. J. Clarke Publishing Co., 1914), 727 pp. (large size)

1914—E. Alexander Powell, *The End of the Trail: The Far West from New Mexico to British Columbia* (New York, Charles Scribner's Sons, 1914), 463 pp.

1914—Adam Shortt and Arthur T. Doughty, eds., *Canada and its Provinces* (Edinburgh, T. & A. Constable; Toronto, The Publisher's Association of Canada Ltd., 1914), vol. XXII, 660 pp.

1914—Ford Fairford, *British Columbia* (Sir Isaac Pitman & Sons Ltd., 1914), 137 pp.

INDEX

J

K

L

LaVergne, TN USA
30 March 2011
222227LV00003B/90/P